W9-CLL-431

ANNUAL REVIEW OF PSYCHOLOGY

ANNUAL REVIEW OF PSYCHOLOGY

VOLUME 35, 1984

MARK R. ROSENZWEIG, *Editor*

University of California, Berkeley

LYMAN W. PORTER, *Editor*

University of California, Irvine

ANNUAL REVIEWS INC.   4139 EL CAMINO WAY   PALO ALTO, CALIFORNIA 94306 USA

ANNUAL REVIEWS INC.
Palo Alto, California, USA

International Standard Serial Number: 0066-4309
International Standard Book Number: 0–8243-0235–4
Library of Congress Catalog Card Number: 50-13143

Annual Review and publication titles are registered trademarks of Annual Reviews Inc.

Annual Reviews Inc. and the Editors of its publications assume no responsibility for the statements expressed by the contributors to this *Review*.

Typesetting by Kachina Typesetting Inc., Tempe, Arizona; John Olson, President Typesetting coordinator, Dennis Phillips

PREFACE

It has been the custom for recent volumes of this *Review* to contain one or two "special topic" chapters that are commissioned on subjects not regularly covered among the areas comprising our Master Plan. Two such chapters, which are usually prepared under a shorter deadline, are included again this year. One reviews the many and diverse developments of the broad field of psychology in Mexico and is authored by Rogelio Diaz-Guerrero. The other special topic chapter describes and evaluates the rapidly emerging area of "Sport Psychology." Its authors are Margaret A. Browne and Michael J. Mahoney. We believe our readers will find both of these chapters to be of unusual interest.

The prefatory chapter, again a feature of recent volumes of this *Review,* is this year authored by the distinguished French psychologist, Paul Fraisse, and is on "Perception and Estimation of Time."

As regular readers of the *Annual Review of Psychology* are aware, in some years (including the present one), we have presented chapters on developments in psychology in countries other than the United States. Frequently these chapters have been coordinated with the meeting of the International Congress of Psychology. This volume's chapter on Mexico, for example, coincides with the 23rd Congress that will take place this year. At its most recent meeting, the Editorial Committee decided to schedule chapters on psychology in countries other than the United States on a regular basis, with chapters commissioned to appear on host countries of meetings of both the International Congress and the International Association of Applied Psychology. Thus, the next such country scheduled to be covered will be Israel (where the IAAP will meet) in Volume 37 (1986). Thereafter, these chapters ordinarily would appear in every odd-numbered volume of *ARP.*

We remind readers once again that it is possible to learn which topics are regularly reviewed under the current Master Plan by referring to the list of recent chapter titles that is contained in the back of this volume. This list indicates the broad categories of coverage as well as the specific coverages within those categories as they have appeared in the most recent five-year time span. We also would note that interested readers can refer to the Preface for Volume 32 (1981) if they wish to know the kinds of instructions provided to authors with regard to the intent and scope of chapters for this *Review.*

With great regret, we bid farewell to Richard L. Solomon, who completes his five-year term on the Editorial Committee with the publication of the present volume. The Editors and the Committee have greatly valued his sagacity and his extensive knowledge of psychological research and researchers. We extend our greetings to the newly appointed member of the Committee, Allan R. Wagner.

L.W.P.
M.R.R.

Annual Review of Psychology
Volume 35, 1984

CONTENTS

(*continued*)   vii

SOME ARTICLES IN OTHER *ANNUAL REVIEWS* OF INTEREST TO PSYCHOLOGISTS

From the *Annual Review of Anthropology,* Volume 12 (1983)

A Decade of Morphology and Word Formation, *Mark Aronoff*
Schemata in Cognitive Anthropology, *Ronald W. Casson*
Contemporary Hunter-Gatherers: Current Theoretical Issues in Ecology and Social Organization, *Alan Barnard*
Biomedical Practice and Anthropological Theory: Frameworks and Directions, *Robert A. Hahn and Arthur Kleinman*

From the *Annual Review of Sociology,* Volume 9 (1983)

Resource Mobilization Theory and the Study of Social Movements, *J. Craig Jenkins*
Distributive Justice, Equity, and Equality, *Karen S. Cook and Karen A. Hegtvedt*
Individual and Collective Behaviors within Gatherings, Demonstrations, and Riots, *Clark McPhail and Ronald T. Wohlstein*
Changing Family and Household: Contemporary Lessons from Historical Research, *Andrew Cherlin*
Toward Integration in the Social Psychology of Emotions, *Thomas J. Scheff*
Sociological Aspects of Attribution, *Kathleen S. Crittenden*
Psychoanalysis and Sociology, *Jerome Rabow*
Social Indicators, *Kenneth C. Land*
The Sociology of Values, *James L. Spates*
The Sociology of Scientific Knowledge: Studies of Contemporary Science, *H. M. Collins*
The Sociology of Knowledge: Retrospect and Prospect, *Henrika Kuklick*

From the *Annual Review of Medicine,* Volume 35 (1984)

Epidemiology of Alcoholism and Prospects for Treatment, *Edgar P. Nace*

From the *Annual Review of Neuroscience,* Volume 7 (1984)

Downward Causation?, *János Szentágothai*
Central Neural Integration for the Control of Autonomic Responses Associated with Emotion, *Orville A. Smith and June DeVito*
The Neural Basis of Language, *Antonio R. Damasio and Norman Geschwind*
Endogenous Pain Control Systems: Brainstem Spinal Pathways and Endorphin Circuitry, *Allan I. Basbaum and Howard L. Fields*

From the *Annual Review of Public Health*, Volume 5 (1984)

Modifying and Developing Health Behavior, *Lawrence W. Green*
Type A Behavior: Epidemiologic Foundations and Public Health Implications, *Judith M. Siegel*
Stress and Health, *Stanislav V. Kasl*
Alcohol Control and Public Health, *Robin Room*

From the *Annual Review of Pharmacology and Toxicology*, Volume 24 (1984)

Neurobehavioral Techniques to Assess the Effects of Chemicals on the Nervous System, *Hugh A. Tilson and Clifford L. Mitchell*

Coming for 1985 . . .

CHAPTERS PLANNED FOR THE NEXT
ANNUAL REVIEW OF PSYCHOLOGY, VOLUME 36

Prefatory Chapter, *Harriet Rheingold*
Brain Functions, *Daniel Alkon*
Genetics and Behavior, *Richard Wimer*
Auditory Physiology, *John Brugge*
Speech Perception, *David Pisoni*
Cognitive Science, *Allan Collins and Al Stevens*
Animal Learning and Memory, *Alan Kamil*
Social-Behavioral Motivation, *Susan Mineka*
Cognitive Development, *Kurt Fischer*
Personality, *Lawrence Pervin*
Psychopathology: Social Approaches, *Richard Price*
Individual Psychotherapy and Behavior Change, *Morris Parloff, Irene Waskow, and Perry London*
Social Cognition, *Nancy Cantor*
Intergroup Relations, *Marilynn Brewer*
Organizational Behavior, *Benjamin Schneider*
Engineering Psychology, *Christopher Wickens and Arthur Kramer*
The School as a Social Situation, *Seymour Sarason and Michael Klaber*
Measurement and Psychometrics, *Ross Traub*
Hypnosis, *John Kihlstrom*
Sex Roles, *Kay Deaux*
Health Psychology, *David Krantz, Neil Grunberg, and Andrew Baum*

Ann. Rev. Psychol. 1984. 35:1–36

PERCEPTION AND ESTIMATION OF TIME

Paul Fraisse

Laboratoire de Psychologie Expérimentale, Université René Descartes, 28, rue Serpente, 75006 Paris, France

CONTENTS

INTRODUCTION

The opportunity to prepare a prefatory chapter has provided me with a welcome occasion to survey the field of perception and estimation of time with greater historical depth than is usual in *Annual Review* chapters. Some of the topics to

1

be considered here—and even some of the data—were known to pioneer psychologists such as Wilhelm Wundt, Pierre Janet, and William James. My own research in this area began more than 30 years ago. But although this field has deep roots in psychological research, it has flourished especially in the last two decades as the cognitive approach encouraged the reexamination of many aspects of human experience, including that of time. This has led to an outpouring of research, to new and revised theoretical formulations, and to important clarifications of concepts and methods. Although no revolution has appeared in this field, the knowledge obtained and the conceptual insights that have been achieved recently appear to set the stage for important new advances.

There is no single way to approach this extremely intricate subject. Time is a highly complex notion; the clearest way to begin is by an analysis of the notion of time commonly held by the adult. The adult lives in an ever-changing world. Even before becoming conscious of his own evolution over time he is witness to constant changes where he himself is the point of reference. The concept of time is first of all associated with world time; however, I can also conceive of changes in my thoughts and have a notion of personal time which is not fundamentally different from world time.

The term *notion* is used in connection with time because it is a more general and complex term than *concept;* despite this difference, the two are often erroneously substituted for each other. The term *concept* applies to a defined class of objects or experiences having a set of common characteristics which distinguishes them from all others. The notion of time applies to two different concepts which may be clearly recognized from our personal experience of change: (*a*) the concept of succession, which corresponds to the fact that two or more events can be perceived as different and organized sequentially; it is based on our experience of the continuous changing through which the present becomes the past; (*b*) the concept of duration, which applies to the interval between two successive events. Duration has no existence in and of itself but is the intrinsic characteristic of that which endures. As Gibson (1975) so aptly put it, "Events are perceivable but time is not."

These two concepts are related to specific characteristics of change and should be defined precisely, yet the scientific and philosophical literature is replete with examples of the indiscriminate use of "idea," "notion," and "concept" when referring either to succession or duration. There is, of course, no duration without succession. It is quite possible that personal experience can provide the basis for abstract representations having a wide application. The concepts we possess are thus dependent upon changes conceived or perceived by each of us.

These concepts may be extrapolated from the changes that occur beyond the range of our own experience. A slightly anthropomorphic view lets us speak of animals' perception of time: classical conditioning reveals that animals are equipped with a form of perception of succession, and operant conditioning, or more simply choosing between two durations, shows that they adapt to duration as well.

Our notion of time involves two concepts that apply to perceptible physical changes and allow us to measure time by referring to a regular sequence of succession. It also characterizes our own personal time. However, it bears no relationship to macrophysical time, as is apparent in the relativity of time and space.

The concepts of succession and duration which specify our notion of time are quite naturally empirical in their origins. This does not necessarily imply that their development is empirical. Research in this field shows that perception of both duration and succession are present very early in life, but that their joint functioning is not acquired until age 7 or 8, when the child first becomes capable of logical thinking. An abstract notion of time is gradually elaborated from that age forward (Friedman 1982). The objective sought in presenting these generalities has been to provide a framework for the present review of contemporary research in the field of the psychology of time, rather than to end the philosophical debate on the notion of time, outlined in the introduction to the *Psychology of Time* (Fraisse 1963), which in any case will never find a satisfactory conclusion.

The present article will be limited to what the human being is able to know about time as manifested through perception and estimation of duration. The distinction will be made between perception and estimation on the basis of phenomenological and experimental data. Animal research has been voluntarily excluded from this study because it provides little insight into our own knowledge of time. Also excluded is research on conditioning that focuses on the role of the time factor as one of the elements influencing our environment but in other ways than succession and duration. Finally, no mention will be made of the large body of research on temporal perspectives to be described elsewhere (Fraisse 1983).

In a review of this type, any attempt at summarizing is difficult given the rapid increase in the amount of literature on the subject. The deliberately restricted inventory of Eisler et al (1980) shows that the number of studies reported annually since 1970 has attained 150, whereas between 1900 and 1960 the annual average was about 15. One explanation lies in the growing number of research psychologists, but the underlying reason is the change in orientation in the sixties from behaviorist to cognitive approaches. Behavioral research was hard put to include time as a variable, in that it is closely linked to the phenomenal aspects of our experience of time and is not a physiological factor. Cognitive approaches were, however, not limited by this restriction. The "new look" in the field of perception was thus also extended to studies on time.

To what extent does the perception of time depend on the conditions under which the perception itself takes place and on the expectations of the knowledgeable subject? At first glance, research on perception and estimation appears to replicate experiments conducted prior to the advent of behaviorism, but in fact new emphasis has been placed on context, motivations, and the subject's own resources. In the area of time research, the role of the subject is even more obvious than in physiological studies, because stimuli which are durations have no specific sensory impact, but are relativized by the perceiving subject. On this point, current confirmations of past research findings will be identified distinctly from new discoveries in contemporary research.

A recent bibliography on time, comprising 1652 entries from 1839 to 1979, may be found in Eisler et al (1980); additional references may be found in Fraisse (1967), Doob (1971), and Zelkind & Spring (1974). The latter work alone provides 1172 references.

THRESHOLDS OF SUCCESSION AND DURATION

When does the perception of time, that is to say the perception of succession and duration, begin? These two aspects of the question will be treated in that order, thus respecting the necessity to handle each one on its own ground. Succession may be distinguished from simultaneous occurence, and duration distinguished from instantaneous. The concern here is with phenomenal particularities of our perceptions, and in no way may they be considered as physical data in which a continuum separates the end of one stimulation and the beginning of the next, each stimulation having its own duration as well. Since the advent of experimental psychology, it has been established that perceived simultaneity does not conform to physical simultaneity. The steadily increasing quantity of research on this point is aimed at providing more accurate means for measuring these phenomena as well as attempting to explain and interpret them. Contemporary technology has rendered possible more accurate definitions of the stimuli as well as the comparison of physical data to those of psychophysics. From this contemporary standpoint, the threshold figures that we established in 1963, while within the same general range, were slightly higher. Over the past few years, as a matter of fact, scientific research in this field has been less concerned with sharpening the accuracy of threshold figures than with the construction of models capable of explaining their duration and scatter.

From Simultaneousness to Succession

The distinction between succession and simultaneity may appear elementary at first sight; however, operational evidence for it may be obtained in many different ways, none of which are either neutral or equivalent from the perceptive point of view. To begin with, succession must be distinguished from discontinuity, which is most evident perceptually when two or more stimuli excite the same peripheral sense organs. For auditory sensations, a crackling sound is identified at a separation of about 1 ms between very brief stimuli, while a discontinuity requires 10 ms.

In the tactile area, the same holds true for the sensation of vibration. As for vision, the comparable phenomenon is flicker. In addition, when two retinal receptors, A and B, are excited by two stimuli, a so-called apparent movement of A toward B is perceived before the succession. The Gestaltists consider the optimum interval for this movement to be about 60 ms. However, recent findings by Westheimer & McKie (1977) show that this movement can be perceived for an interval as short as 3 ms provided the stimuli both strike the fovea.

However, the transition from simultaneity to succession properly speaking may be studied by presenting two pulses of more or less variable duration of intensity (cf Oostenbrug et al 1978, Mills & Rollman 1980), or through focusing on the onset of two durable stimuli (cf Allan 1975), or again, by focusing on the offset of two durable stimuli (cf Allan & Kristofferson 1974), or yet again, through the relationship between the offset of one stimulus and the onset of another (Efron 1970a, Allan 1976). Other authors have compared two pairs of stimuli, the S being asked to determine in which pair simultaneity or succession had occurred. Stimuli may be visual, and presented in monocular, binocular, or dichoptic vision (Rutschmann 1973); auditory stimuli may be presented in monoaural, binaural, or dichotic contexts; tactile of motor stimuli may be used as well. Here again, these experiments concern stimulations of one sensory system and introduce variations in distance or intensity. However, many other studies have focused conjointly on more than one system (visual-auditory, visual-motor, auditory-motor, etc). The stimulations may be simple or complex, and more than two may be presented (Carmon & Nachshon 1971). They may consist of shapes (Lichtenstein 1961), syllables (Fraisse 1978), or strings of letters (Hylan 1903). Furthermore, methods in psychophysics differ from one study to another: the constant method, the method of limits, and signal detection are among several commonly used. Finally, the criteria that the Ss are required to apply may not always be identical. Asking the subject to respond to a discontinuity, a succession, or to an order of events while measuring his degree of confidence in his answers does not set out equivalent tests for the subject. Consecutive to conclusions drawn from observations of Ss performances, authors have in general given up trying to establish averages and now present individual scores, which they almost unanimously recognize as being extremely divergent, sometimes to the extent of representing opposing tendencies. Allan (1976) for example found that out of three subjects tested, only two were homogeneous. Efron (1974) trained six subjects but retained only two for the final experiment. It is difficult to compare naive subjects to trained or overtrained ones, as was the case in Hirsh & Sherrig (1961). This list of experimental situations, while incomplete, provides a sufficient explanation for the fact that in the area of the psychology of time, where no specialized sensory receptor is available, final judgments are subject to all sorts of stimulation bias as well as to the type of task. This would not be an important point had the authors of explanatory models not formulated their theories on the basis of one single situation while disregarding all others.

One event in particular has been responsible for initiating numerous studies over the last 15 years. Hirsh & Sherrig (1961) showed that regardless of sensory modality, the succession order threshold was constant: approximately 20 ms. Their results were obtained after long training sessions. The stimulus pair was presented as often as the S requested before giving his response, which was always a forced choice, since the interval range was very limited. These results were the object of wide controversy. Hirsh & Fraisse (1964) showed, furthermore, that the thresholds for naive subjects were much higher when measured between an acoustical click and a brief flash of light, requiring either a judgment on simultaneity vs nonsimultaneity, or a judgment requiring a forced choice on the order of the two stimuli. The thresholds were the same in all three tasks (simultaneity, succession, and order). It was approximately 60 ms when the sound preceded the light, and from 90 to 120 ms when light preceded sound. This dyssymmetry has not always been taken into account in previous research. Allan (1975) identified this dyssymmetry but focused primarily on the fact that judgments of succession and order are given at the same stimulus values. However, this dyssymmetry emphasizes the importance of latencies in auditory and visual stimulation. Differences in latencies have often been used to explain discrepancies between successions of stimuli and successions of perceptions. It certainly plays a role, for example between louder and softer sound, brighter and dimmer light, and a lateral vs a central visual stimulation (Oostenbrug et al 1978).

It has been shown that reaction time to an auditory stimulation is approximately 40 ms less than for a visual stimulation, which gives a general idea of the size of respective latencies, although the values obtained in a reaction time task are not directly related to the succession threshold (Gibbon & Rutschmann 1969). To confirm the role of latencies, Fraisse's (1980) experiment may be mentioned. Synchronization, i.e. in this case simultaneity between hand tapping and the sound of a simple repetitive auditory rhythm, has been found easy to achieve. Data show that on the average, hand tapping (as a tactile measure) anticipates the sound by about 30 ms. This anticipation is approximately 20 ms longer when made by the foot. It is difficult not to attribute these anticipations to the fact that the tactile stimulus must precede the sound in order to be perceived as simultaneous by the brain. In fact, if a subject is asked to tap simultaneously with his hand and with his foot, at his own spontaneous rhythm, the foot tap also precedes the hand tap by about 20 ms. Finally, these are median values, with very high individual differences, even to the point of reversing the direction of the results. This variability can be explained by the subject's attitude, criteria for simultaneity, etc.

If the latency problem is left aside and only the succession or order thresholds of two identical stimuli are taken into consideration, once again there must be a notable disparity between the two stimuli if there is to be perception of succession and order. This is the case, for example, in Hirsh's (1959) experiment on two acoustic stimuli, or Mills & Rollman's (1980) experiment on dichotic perception. Ignoring for the moment the asymmetry between the two ears, results show a threshold of about 32 to 35 ms by the limits method and 55 to 60 ms by the constant method. In all these studies, there is true perception of an order in the succession of two distinct stimuli, and not a more or less total fusion.

A perception threshold equal to or greater than 20 ms thus cannot simply be attributed to disparity between the arrival of two impulses on the brain. A decision mechanism having its own duration must be postulated. A very complex model that incorporates the largest amount of data and hypotheses has been proposed by Sternberg & Knoll (1973). A value of Δt possessing its own variability must be added to the possible differences in arrival of impulses from the different stimulations. This decision function can be explained by a variety of mechanisms. Kristofferson (1967) as well as Kristofferson & Allan (1973) thought that decision time was related to the attention-switching hypothesis: in other words, that the time involved was nothing more than the length of time necessary to focus attention on each of the stimuli successively. However, there would also be a time quantum involved that would impose a minimum duration for this operation. The role assigned to attention corresponds in particular to all the studies showing the influence of attention directed voluntarily to one or the other stimulus. In the case of selective attention, as was well documented by Wundt, the stimulus receiving attention is perceived more rapidly than the other, which may modify the threshhold or even the order of succession. This attention factor, or the subject's attitude, which he may not always be aware of, can doubtless be explained in terms of numerous individual or interindividual differences. This decision mechanism is also compatible with a hypothesis proposed by Stroud (1955) called the "discrete moment" hypothesis, which has had considerable impact among researchers. It postulates that the perception of time is not continuous but intermittent and discrete. Elements of information are integrated at distinct moments. Their order is distinguished only if each one is treated at a different moment from the other. Within a given moment, order is not discriminated. Allport (1968) provides another version of the same hypothesis. The perceptive moment corresponds to a "window" which is in continuous movement. The attractiveness of these hypotheses does not permit construction of predictions other than those included in the models already mentioned. Baron (1971) made an attempt but did not succeed. Furthermore, no physiological process corresponding to this time quantum has yet been identified.

Finally, it should be noted that the succession threshold, which varies considerably for simple stimuli, greatly increases when these become more complex. Indeed, Stroud (1955) estimated that the moment duration could vary between 50 and 200 ms. Hylan (1903) had already shown that six letters forming a word, when presented successively and in any order, were perceived as simultaneous, provided that the total duration did not exceed 90 ms.

If four dots corresponding to the apexes of a diamond are lighted successively, they are perceived as being simultaneous if the separation between the first and the last does not exceed 125 ms (Lichtenstein 1961). Within the range of 100–150 ms, if two identical superimposed triangles are projected, they are perceived as an hexagon (Fraisse 1966). Eriksen & Collins (1967) superimposed two cards by means of a tachistoscope, each card having a random set of dots such that when grouped together they formed a meaningless syllable. Integration was possible within a duration range of 75–100 msec.

Although the parameters which determine succession threshold (or on the other hand, determine simultaneous integration) are numerous and their relative importance difficult to assess, it appears nonetheless that localization of decision in the left temporal lobe can be clearly asserted. This assertion is based both on neurological studies of well-identified lesions in the left as well as right hemispheres and on studies using double stimulation of each hemisphere (Efron 1963). In Ss with lesions of the left hemisphere, the succession threshold can attain 300–400 ms. This result was confirmed with normal subjects as well. Mills & Rollman (1980) studied the succession threshold of two clicks when each was presented to a different ear. The results showed that the threshold of temporal order was lower when the right ear click preceded the left ear click as compared to the opposite order of presentation. The difference was slight : 5,7 ms with the limits method, and 3,2 ms using the method of constant stimuli. The authors attribute these differences in thresholds to the differences in the time necessary for transfer from one lobe to the other according to direction. The values given are averages and the differences in thresholds vary from 2 to 16 ms among Ss. It may be noted, however, that these results do not affect decision time since the average threshold is approximately 60 ms using the limits method and 35 ms with the method of constant stimuli, as stated previously.

Differences emphasizing the role of the temporal lobe have also been found in dichoptic vision (Efron 1963, Oostenbrug et al 1978) as well as in tactile stimulation (Efron 1963). When the right lobe is stimulated first, this stimulation must be transferred to the left lobe, thus accounting for the delay in the junction of the two stimuli. In this type of dichotic or dichoptic experiment, explanations based on peripheral processes prove to be insufficient.

Instantaneous and Durable Events

Considerably less research has been carried out in this area. Early experiments, which indicated that up to a certain threshold apparent duration varied with the intensity of the stimulus, will not be discussed. The problem will therefore be dealt with only in terms of apparent constant intensity. When very brief stimuli are used, perception of instantanteity can be obtained; in more concrete terms, the *on* moment cannot be distinguished from the *off* moment. This problem has been studied in recent years by Efron (1970b, 1974) through comparison of measured apparent perceived duration to measured stimulus duration. He found a minimal duration of 130 ms for apparent perceived duration, a result which Allan (1976), however, was unable to confirm. The most reliable results have been obtained by Servière, Miceli & Galifret (1977a,b). These authors established a preliminary instantaneity threshold based on several psychophysical measurement methods and obtained a value of 60 ms with a range of uncertainty from 30 to 130 ms. Here again it was found that untrained subjects produce higher thresholds. Using evoked potential recording techniques, these same authors found that beyond 140 ms, the *on* and *off* constituents were clearly differentiated. On the other hand below 125 ms, the *on* and *off* components were increasingly interactive up to the point of coincidence. However, a closer examination of the *on* and *off* response values in relation to stimulation durations indicates the presence of a zone of uncertainty more or less equivalent to that obtained by means of the psychophysical measures. Experiments on pigeons in the same papers confirmed this relationship and support the hypothesis that the perception of instantaneity corresponds to the nonseparation of the *on* and *off* components of evoked potentials.

PERCEPTION OF DURATION

The following section will be entitled "Estimation of Duration." The distinction between that section and this one refers to two specific types of procedures for the evaluation of duration. Estimation of duration takes place when memory is used either to associate a moment in the past with a moment in the present or to link two past events, whereas perception of duration involves the psychological present.

The Psychological Present

Perception of duration refers to the ability to apprehend successive events as perceptively more or less simultaneous, within the framework of the psychological present first identified by William James (1890) under the name of "specious present," reexamined by Fraisse (1963), and later examined extensively by Michon (1978). Such a present has no fixed duration. It is based on what is perceived and refers to our capacity to apprehend sets of objects. Different schools of thought have called this ability "capacity of apprehension," "short-term memory," or "very short-term memory." More concretely, it applies to the perception of a telephone number, for example, or of a sentence simple enough to be repeated, or of a rhythmic pattern identified as a rhythm provided that its elements are perceived as being linked to each other in such a way as to form a unified group.

The psychological present corresponds to the duration of a experiential process and not to a given period of duration. However, it has an upper limit which hardly exceeds 5 sec, and has an average value of 2 to 3 sec. Within these limits one can speak of the perception of duration, which thereby becomes a quantity whose beginning has not yet been stored in memory.

Through ignorance of this distinction, psychologists studying time have compared durations associated with differing psychological processes. Such was the case for those studies using stimuli ranging from a duration of under one second to that of several dozen seconds or even to several minutes. The resulting confusion led to the formulation of a large number of misconstrued issues which continue to maintain ambiguities in an already sufficiently complex area. The present author's discussion of duration perception is to be found elsewhere (Fraisse 1978) and will not be repeated here. Poppel (1978) and Allan (1979) have discussed those recent studies presenting the most interesting findings.

Methodological Problems

As in previous sections, methodological problems will receive preferential attention over other issues; this should not surprise the reader since time is not a specific sensation.

Measurement methods play an essential role and have been greatly refined since the pioneering work of Bindra & Waksberg (1956). In addition to methods of estimation, of production, and of reproduction which yield continuous measures, there is a growing trend toward methods that tend to reduce responses to binary or trinary choices. This is the case for the forced choice method used to compare differing durations, also called the *single stimuli* method, which stipulates that one single duration must be judged by a binary choice as longer or shorter than a learned criterion (or criteria). The *magnitude estimation* or *category rating* method—a simplified version of numerical classification—is less frequently used; in this the S is asked to assess a stimulus duration in terms of several classes.

This variety of methods is a positive outcome of the development of contemporary research; however, the immediate caveat is that results are neither comparable nor homogeneous across methodologies, nor are the explanations suggested by the construction of theoretical models generated from these results.

Methods of comparison (scaling or discrimination) have renewed prime interest in the *time order error*, and numerous recent studies have dealt with it. Allan (1977) presents an overview showing that no definitive results have emerged to date. Time order error is considered as either positive or negative, depending on the authors, durations, and methods. The debate is set between those like Hellstrom (1977) who claim that the time order error is essentially perceptual, based on adaptation processes and differential weighting of sensation magnitude, and those who believe along with Allan (1977) that the time order error depends on the particular mode of responding and thus on a decision process which creates a response bias in function of the task. This would explain the variety of results ranging from null to positive or negative values.

Methods of comparison drew attention to the problem of masking. It was connected with the identification of a precategorical stage of stimulus perception having a non-negligible duration of about 250 ms. Any event intervening in this process has an effect upon it. For example, studies were conducted to determine whether during a brief stimulus (in general less than 100 ms) the occurrence of another stimulus would have an effect on the perception of the original stimulus. Massaro & Idson (1976, 1978), in the field of auditory stimulation, as well as Cantor & Thomas (1976) in the field of vision, showed the effects of masking on duration. In the latter experiment, a second stimulus (the mask) followed the first or target stimulus, which had one of two possible values (50 ms and 90 ms for example), after an interval (ITI) that could vary from 0 to 250 ms. The results showed that the target stimulus had a longer apparent duration when the ITI was longer, as though the perception of the target could be prolonged. Furthermore, the perceived duration of the mask adds something to the final duration judgment. There appears to be an integration of mask duration to target duration. These findings extend to identical sounds and also to the case where the mask frequency is different from the target frequency (Massaro & Idson 1978). The conclusion is that duration, like other stimuli, is dependent on the amount of available processing time. Durations must be close to precategorical duration values if they are to be perceived with a certain amount of precision and to be clearly distinguished (Fraisse 1974).

Along the same lines, studies were carried out on the possible presence of aftereffects in duration perception. Huppert & Singer (1967) reported aftereffects in the perception of a two-second duration. This was reproduced with 18% diminution when it was preceded by another two-second duration with an optimal interval of 3 to 7 sec. This diminution did not occur when the two-second sound was presented alone. One aftereffect which lends itself to interpretation as a time order effect has been demonstrated best by Walker et al

(1981), who in a series of experiments showed the presence of an aftereffect for lights and sounds: the duration of a test stimulus (600 ms) was displaced in a direction away from the duration of a repeated inspecting stimulus (200 to 800 ms). They also showed that if a pair of unequal lights or sounds ranging from 200 to 800 ms are presented repeatedly, and are followed by a pair of equal sounds (600 ms), the duration of the first of the two stimuli is perceived as longer than that of the second. This is called the contingency effect because it involves the relationship between two stimuli and not the absolute value of one.

The time order effects, whose similarity to aftereffects and masking effects (in the case of very brief durations) must be taken into consideration, and which appear in many types of sensations, further complicate the laws of duration perception by functioning as additional variables.

The Psychophysical Law

The relationship between the intensity of a sensation and the force of the physical stimulus has been studied since Fechner. The problem was restated by Stevens (1967), who attempted to show that the relationship between input and sensation was governed by a power law. However, Stevens himself admitted that the duration exponent was equal to 1, i.e. that the perceived time was in a direct relation with physical time. Since that time, numerous studies have attempted to prove or disprove this theory by varying methods of measurement and experimental situations. As could be expected, exponents varied widely from one experiment to another. Eisler (1976) recognized that reality but thought nevertheless that the power law was valid for an average exponent of 0.9. Studies have been conducted to reduce methodologically linked differences. Eisler (1975) claims to have demonstrated the power law but only found a correlation of .14 between exponents estimated from reproduction data and from half-setting data. The present author tends to agree with Allan (1979) that a linear relationship between duration of the physical stimulus and the perceived duration is linear only for methods that do not use ratio setting temporal data (for example producing a double stimulus or half the stimulus presented). This finding was not disproved by Bobko, Thompson & Schiffman (1977), who reported exponents varying from .90 to .99 using four methods for durations ranging from 0.5 to 5 seconds. Furthermore, they conclude that the exponent is approximately 1 and that consequently there is a linear relationship between judged duration and physical duration. This finding is particularly interesting in that it was obtained with brief durations, whereas studies such as those by Eisler take durations up to 30 sec into consideration.

While accepting the notion of a psychophysical power law, Eisler has continued to perfect his own model (1981a,b) which basically postulates that when two durations are compared, the two are stocked in different sensory registers which work along with a comparator between the total recorded duration in the first sensory register and the variable duration stocked in the second sensory register. When the difference between the two durations is equal to the standard duration, the response is given. Eisler has constructed mathematical models which have become more and more complex to accomodate his experimental data along with Allan's (1977) and Kristofferson's (1977). Space does not permit a presentation of his model. However, it suffices to say that its basic principles are extremely questionable: posing the existence of two sensory registers functioning together, when it is well-known that below 200–400 ms it is difficult to switch from one perception to another, leaves little to be said for sensory registers whose durations can attain 30 ms.

The Nature of Stimulations

The nature of stimulations has always received a great deal of attention from researchers. A review of the question was provided by the present author (Fraisse 1963). New developments in recent years have been in the area of experiments on brief durations, under 100 ms.

Modern equipment capable of producing and controlling stimulations on the order of 1 ms are partially responsible for these findings. They are certainly interesting, but what has previously been said on succession and duration thresholds can still be applied here. The findings can be expressed in terms of perception of duration, but in fact what is perceived are not durations but qualitative changes in the stimulation which allows the Ss to respond in terms of longer-shorter in discrimination task paradigms or to quantify perceived differences along a set 0,1,2, scale. Time order errors or masking effects should also be taken into consideration when comparative judgments on successive brief durations are solicited.

These reserves are justified. Divenyi & Danner (1977) report that for durations of 80 ms and over, duration marker effects are no longer present, as is the case for shorter durations. Efron (1970a) shows that although the perceptual onset latency is independent of the stimulus duration, the perceptual offset latency was longer for brief duration than for stimuli that exceeded a critical duration of about 130 ms. This is true for vision as well as for audition, and Efron concludes that durations under 130 ms have a fixed duration which exceeds the stimulus duration.

EMPTY INTERVALS–FILLED INTERVALS   Thomas & Brown (1974) report that filled intervals are always reproduced as longer durations than empty intervals. This finding was also reported for vision by Long & Beaton (1980), although in another framework.

STIMULUS INTENSITY   More intense sounds and lights are judged longer than less intense auditory and visual durations, and this effect is greater for vision (Goldstone et al 1978).

ROLE OF EMPTY INTERVAL MARKERS   Divenyi and Danner (1977) and Divenyi & Sachs (1978) varied the type of stimulus marking the beginning and the end of empty intervals. When the two sound burst markers are very similar, the perceived duration follows the regular psychophysical law, but if there is an important difference between the two markers in terms of intensity, spectrum, pitch, or duration of sounds, the results show nonmonotonic relationships which can be explained above all by the fact that 25 ms intervals are poorly distinguished when the intensity of one of the markers is very weak or when the two markers are too disparate. However, these authors are not primarily interested in duration, but rather in the nonmonotonicity that may be observed for voice onset time discrimination functions.

VISUAL AND AUDITORY TEMPORAL JUDGMENTS   An auditory stimulation seems longer than a visual one. This relatively old finding has been confirmed by more recent studies and in more varied situations. Longer durations of about 1 sec, however, are involved here. Sound seems longer than light, even when the two are presented simultaneously. This is equally the case for gaps in auditory or luminous visual stimuli (Walker & Scott 1981). However, the weight of this finding should not be overemphasized. Furukawa (1979) has stressed that the stimulus conditions and the orientation of attention in this study render the results shaky.

THE KAPPA EFFECT   The effect of distance on time is usually measured by comparing time intervals between two luminous stimuli placed horizontally, defining two points in space. If a sound corresponding to each point is introduced, estimation of time is greater as the space lengthens between the points. Previous results had shown the opposite effect, called the Tau effect, in which, under the same conditions, differences in duration had a direct effect on spatial estimation. The Japanese, as well as certain researchers elsewhere, remain interested in the question (see Matsuda & Matsuda 1981 for a bibliography of their own work; see also Ono 1976).

A very complete discussion of this issue is to be found in Jones & Huang (1982). The Kappa effect is highly stable, and although studies have been conducted primarily on adults, the results are even more pronounced in 7–10 year olds (Matsuda & Matsuda 1979). The explanation of this effect provided by these authors, who have also studied the effects of velocity, lies in what they call "cue selection sets," if the S can choose as an estimation cue either one of the two dimensions, that is, velocity or distance (or, time or velocity). It is important to note that the Kappa effect is not systematically found for durations under 160 ms (Collyer 1977). Collyer points out in addition that the Kappa effect is related to the S's tendency to perceive apparent movement in constant velocity. This hypothesis was further treated by Huang & Jones (1982).

Content of Stimulations

This topic was dealt with in depth by the present author in 1978. Few new developments which modify previous data have appeared since then. However, they have provided important details particularly in terms of models used.

Important developments concern the context effects, i.e. the background used during presentation of the stimulus to be evaluated. Previous research had shown that a divided interval (within certain limits) appears longer than an empty interval. However, Adams (1977) has shown that this "illusion" decreases if the auditory pulses originate from a source other than that of the duration markers, for example from the other ear, or if they appear as part of an ongoing sequence of background pulses.

If in a pulse task the S has to compare the duration of two brief increments in an ongoing sinusoid, performance is independent of the changes in context (noise alone, noise plus continuous sinusoids, or noise plus continuous sinusoids chosen to induce a pitch segregation effect). However, if the S is asked to compare the duration of two brief interruptions during a gap task in an ongoing sinusoid, the S experiences great difficulty in comparing the two gaps when the stimulus ensemble induces the pitch discrimination effect (lasting 40 ms) (Woods et al 1979).

The results of these experiments on audition may be compared to those obtained in visual presentations of brief durations (under 100 ms) where the apparent duration is in direct relation with stimulus size. (Thomas & Cantor 1975, 1976). When the frequencies of stimulus duration (short vs long) and stimulus area (small vs large) are varied, perceived size and duration are directly related to the frequency of the lower attribute value (short or small). It is assumed that perceived size and perceived duration grow together over the course of time spent sampling size information and that attribute frequency affects the rate of sampling and/or the point at which sampling stops.

Information Processing

The present author (1978, p. 234) discussed studies showing that perception duration was dependent upon the content of the stimulus to be identified for durations under 100 ms. Thomas & Cantor (1975, 1978) attempted to define more precisely the relationship between temporal (f) and nontemporal (g) information processing which was presented by Thomas & Weaver (1975).

The task consists of estimating stimulation duration of a luminous zone on a two- or four-point scale, and on a two-point scale the presence or absence of a specific target presented on the luminous zone and inserted in a letter array. Two conditions are used. In the pure duration condition, the S judged the duration of the array, and in a detection condition the S judged whether or not the array contained the target letters. The results of these two conditions were compared with two mixed conditions where the S performed both detection and duration tasks; in one case the duration task was emphasized, and in the other the detection task was emphasized. Decrements in duration accuracy were observed in going from pure to mixed conditions, but not in the detection task.

It is argued that in the pure duration condition, judgments are based partly on a timer that starts shortly after stimulus onset and stops shortly after stimulus offset, or as soon as a critical duration is reached, whichever occurs first. When the duration task is emphasized in a mixed condition, duration and detection judgments are done simultaneously but with a decrement in each. When the detection task is emphasized, priority is given to this task and the duration judgment is derived mainly from the outcome of processing in the detection task (Thomas & Cantor 1955, p. 43). This asymmetry can be explained by the fact that the two types of stimulation are treated simultaneously but that attention is spontaneously directed to information provided by the stimulus and not to its duration. There are limits in the ability to process information

Other studies have dealt with this problem by using longer durations of about 1 second. Berg (1979) used an estimation-reproduction task for durations ranging from .58 to 3 sec. The durations were accompanied by a film showing two triangles and a circle in motion. Each film showed each object moving along a randomly chosen path. The task was presented to the S in two conditions: first, to describe the movement of the objects, and second, to imagine that the figures are representing people doing different things, and to describe the social interaction portrayed. In the second situation, the S is expected to form an organizing scheme which reduces the perceived duration of the film. The results are congruent with this hypothesis but only for durations superior to 1.6 sec. Counterbalancing the two situations did not produce significantly different scores in the two situations. Fraisse (1979) studied the relationship between temporal judgment in a duration production task and that of an information processing task. It was hypothesized that the easier the processing, the more overestimated the duration would be, since the S would be more attentive to the duration itself. The production of one duration was compared in tasks of naming four different colors or reading the names of four colors. It is well established that naming is longer and in consequence more difficult than reading. As expected, the Ss, after being trained to produce responses (reading letters) at the rate of one per second, responded with average durations of 814 ms for reading and 932 ms for naming.

The model elaborated by Thomas & Weaver (1975) postulates that attention is divided between the two processes: estimation of duration and information processing. In the study of Fraisse (1979), the easier the task is, the more attention the S is able to give to the duration, which results in an overestimation of the duration and thereby the production of a shorter duration. This finding confirms the thesis of the interaction of the two processes beyond the limits of the very brief durations studied by Thomas & Weaver (1975).

Long & Beaton (1980a,b, 1981) worked on a different aspect of the question, attempting to explain several of the effects observed with brief durations (40 and 70 ms) by retinal persistence, instead of by information processing; they thus follow Efron (1970), Efron & Lee (1971), and Kristofferson (1977). The findings of these latest experimental studies are not in contradiction with those found by Avant et al (1975). An effort was made to demonstrate that it is more parsimonious to interpret the results by sensory persistence. Efron, Lee, and Kristofferson thus showed that target size, target luminosity, target contrast, and spatial frequency of the target influence the duration of the perception "in a manner predictable from the consideration of the retinal effects of such manipulations." Likewise, Mo (1971, 1975) found that the number of dots on a given surface would lengthen the perceived duration. In this case they thought that the number of dots simply increases the contrast to the surface. However, if at the same time, the surface area is increased, the effect is weaker. The effect is also diminished if these stimuli are perceived through peripheral vision. It is yet again diminished when the background lighting and the lighting of the stimulus surface are equalized.

The proofs advanced for retinal persistence as a function of the different variables are based on rather wide considerations. The fact that persistence plays a role does not invalidate the other models, and is not applicable to auditory stimuli. It is difficult indeed to reach a decision between these two approaches to the question, but the present author points out that Long and Beaton themselves admit that their hypothesis applies only to very brief stimuli where Bloch's Law comes into play. In the case of all these experiments concerning very brief durations, the present author is of the opinion that when the Ss are asked to evaluate the durations, they make use of the qualitative differences apprehended during the preliminary experiments in which they learn a binary or ternary code, but that comparable results would be obtained if they were asked to apply another criterion of judgment such as intensity. The cognitive model has a wider range of application than the model which accords a prominent place to retinal persistence; nonetheless, the latter is not to be neglected.

Individual Differences

Within the area of perceived duration, few studies have explored the role of individual differences. Ever since the research carried out in the nineteenth century (of Fraisse 1963), it has been established that expectations and attention play an important role in the perception of durations, generally by producing an overestimation of the perceived duration. The present author has already alluded to this fact above. This single variable by itself can explain differences in results since the S's attention depends not only on instructions but also on the quality of one stimulus in relation to another.

The absence of notable differences between normal Ss and the mentally ill (Banks et al 1966, Chattajea et al 1978) in the case of perception of a duration lasting about one second explains why hardly any research has been oriented toward personality variables. However, this last remark is too general. Mentally ill Ss, even those displaying trouble in temporal orientation but excluding neurological cases, obtain more variable results than normal groups. A few differences, particularly with schizophrenics, are found when more sophisticated methods of judgment are employed. Lhamon & Goldstone (1956), using their method in which Ss are asked to compare various durations to their own idea of a one-second duration, thus found that schizophrenics overestimate a one-second duration. However, Crain et al (1975) suspect that such differences might be traced to organic differences between the Ss. By the method of absolute judgments in which the S is required to associate with 3, 5, or 9 stimuli varying from 0.10 to 1.9 sec, numbers whose quantity is equal to that of the stimuli, it is possible to measure in bits the capacity of the canal, which for normal Ss reaches 2.07 bits whereas for schizophrenics only 1.62. One understands immediately that this treatment brings into play more than just perception of duration, strictly speaking. Mo & Kersey (1982) have for several years been seeking to define the role of a preparatory period on the duration of perception cards containing one or several dots. Nothing clear has come out of several studies. The present author adopts the following conclusion: "weakness and instability of time expectancy as characteristics of schizophrenia were demonstrated." In other words, the foreperiod produces a lesser systematic effect in the case of schizophrenics than in that of the control groups which in the experiments of Mo and Kersey were generally composed of alcoholics.

Cerebral Localizations

This is a knotty issue. It can be studied on animals only through learning techniques which can succeed only with durations extending beyond the present. In addition, although it is suspected that the right and left hemispheres in humans have different roles, this specialization is not the same in animals. Such studies on humans have been limited to Ss suffering brain damage. However, even with these Ss, greater interest has been accorded to temporal disorientation problems than to the perception *stricto sensu* of duration. In those cases where this variable has been taken into consideration, the brain-damaged Ss provide results very inferior to normal ones (Marchman 1969), and even inferior to those of schizophrenics in their capacity to transmit information (Locke 1974, Crain et al 1975).

A few research studies have nevertheless attempted to identify the roles of the two cerebral hemispheres in perception of duration on groups of adults said to be normal. Vroon et al (1977) found asymmetrical results according to whether the stimulations first reached the right or the left hemisphere. These results varied to a lesser extent when the left hemisphere was brought directly into play. This hemisphere was also more accurate in predicting events in time. On the basis of complex research, Polzella et al (1977) came to the conclusion that following Thomas and Weaver's model, the left hemisphere "relies on a timer to estimate duration while the right hemisphere relies on a visual information processor to estimate duration," p. 1187. These results need to be confirmed.

ESTIMATION OF DURATION

The research area now considered requires the S to judge durations that cannot be perceived and in which memory intervenes in the making of a global judgment about the duration. Many authors do not draw this distinction. They merely speak of the experience of time or of the judgment of time, and in the time scales they study, they sometimes use durations inferior to one second, which requires a different process. However, this is not of very great importance since there is clearly a certain continuity in the results as between perception and estimation of time, the S being able to mobilize the processes of both at the same time. It will nonetheless be seen that in the case of durations which go beyond perception, new problems arise. It may be pointed out immediately that time order error also plays a role in estimation of duration. In order to avoid this inconvenience, many authors take recourse either in the production method or in estimation of a duration in traditional units or in category scales, or by absolute judgments. Those research works based on comparison and above all on reproduction need careful interpretation. Finally, it may be added that for practical reasons, the durations studied in such research rarely exceed one minute.

The Psychophysical Law

Researchers continue to preoccupy themselves with this law, but through greater and greater variations in the content of durations. They seek to know whether one and the same psychophysical law always applies.

The first problem consists in knowing whether the law applies to estimation of durations. The results published by Eisler (1975) showed that the average exponent was 1 following the power law, but he pointed to a slight change in the curve that could take place between the perceived durations and the estimated durations. This result has not been challenged in the most recent research works, but it may vary as a function of the method employed and the task required. Bobko et al (1977) thus wonders whether the central tendency effect of judgment, often found in psychophysics, might not also characterize durations. If a duration of 25 sec is the lowest value in a series of durations, or the central value in a series of durations, or finally the longest in a third, then using an estimation method does not yield this effect, and the power law with an exponent close to 1 applies to the three series (Schiffman, Bobko & Thompson 1977). However, when the reproduction method was used, Bobko et al (1977) found a central tendency effect with overestimation of short intervals and underestimation of long intervals, especially after numerous trials, which is quite normal.

Other variables also modify estimation of duration. Repetition of estimations diminishes their size, but this does not hold true when the S is allowed to count. In this case a truncation of the psychophysical function occurs (Hicks & Allen 1979a). These same authors (1979b), using the reproduction method, found that the psychophysical function increases with repetitions between the reproductions whether the interval lasts 5 min or even several days. However, estimation decreases from day to day when the verbal quantification method is employed.

Content of Duration

By varying the number and the familiarity of visual stimuli presented in a series of slides, Schiffman & Bobko (1977) found an effect concerning the number of stimuli but not their familiarity. The present author is of the opinion that the latter variable was inadequately operationalized (estimation of duration method).

Block & Reed (1978) and Block (1978), like the preceding authors, critically tested Ornstein's (1969) hypothesis which accords an essential role to the duration of storage size in memory. This variable, which is difficult to measure, is inferred from the number, the familiarity, and the complexity of a series of stimuli, as well as from their treatment. Block's experiments can hardly help advance the inquiry since he undoubtably employed inadequately different stimuli. We tend to accept his conclusion. To explain his results, he proposes a contextual change hypothesis that, incidentally, he finds similar to the present author's (Fraisse 1963) hypothesis, namely that the duration depends on the number of perceived changes. According to the present author, Ornstein has adopted the same hypothesis, but has better spelled out the nature of the changes. In fact, it may be that the S in certain cases takes into account the objective number of changes in the situation, for example, the number of slides projected, but that in other cases it would be the number of changes memorized in an individualized manner that he takes into account. Thus are explained, in particular, the results obtained in prolonged research work in which the S lives at his personal rhythm outside of any cosmic or social influence. In a 6-month longitudinal study on a subject living in a cave 70 meters deep, the present author ran several temporal experiments (Fraisse 1973). For example, the S was to estimate the duration between waking up and lunch. For 64 days, his average estimation was 4 h 40 min, but the clocked duration was 10 h 26 min.

His errors were proportionally similar for the production and reproduction of shorter durations (between 30 and 120 sec). In this case there was a repetition effect but the author thinks that such gross errors were attributable to the fact that in that life of seclusion, which reminds one somewhat of perceptual deprivation situations, few changes took place in the life of the S, and for that reason he greatly underestimated the real durations.

The nature of material and task are fundamental factors, which explains the variety of results described so well by Kowal (1981). In the same way, we can explain the same author's (1976) results in which he found no effects on estimation of duration using material endowed with greater or lesser significance: reading stories of highly cultural salience to Ss of widely varying cultural backgrounds (American and Indian students).

It is thus possible to agree with Hogan's (1978) hypothesis, when he expresses concern with authors such as Ornstein who claim that the more a duration is filled with complex stimuli the longer it seems, whereas others find that an empty duration seems longer than one filled with complex stimulations. For him, it all depends on the degree of complexity. According to Hogan, the apparent duration diminishes from very simple to optimum complexity, whereas on the contrary the apparent duration increases from optimum to excessive complexity, since it is no longer possible to stock poorly perceived events. As one goes from an absence of complexity to an excessive complexity, the established curve would be U-shaped at optimum. Having presented the thesis (1963) that apparent duration depends on the number of perceived changes, the present author adheres to this conceptualization of the problem, since when stimulus complexity is too great, individualized changes are not perceived. Unfortunately, the present author has knowledge of no experimental results confirming Hogan's hypothesis, undoubtedly because it is difficult to experiment with a range of situations going from zero complexity to a degree of complexity where events are poorly identified and can no longer be stocked.

This difficulty is not present in research where the duration to be estimated is filled in with a specific activity by the S, and where the information treated by the S is no longer a hypothetical variable introduced by the experimenter through a difference in material. The subjects of Hicks et al (1976) had to classify 104 playing cards into a single stack (0 bit), into 2 stacks, namely the 2 colors (1 bit), and into 4 stacks by suit (2 bits). They were stopped at the end of 42 sec and requested to evaluate the duration of their activity in seconds. However, one group had been advised ahead of time about this question (prospective judgment) while the other had not (retrospective judgment). For the prospective judgments, the estimated duration decreased very greatly in linear fashion with the uncertainty. Of course, an interpretation based on the number of cards processed could be attempted, since it varies from 75 to 34 in going from 0 to 2 bits. However, such reasoning cannot be accurate since this proportionality is not found in the retrospective judgments which vary neither with the information processed nor with the number of cards manipulated. The authors conclude, rightly it would seem, that when the task is difficult, the Ss are not able to pay attention to the duration and that in reality they are making a retrospective estimation. In another study, Miller et al (1978) found that in tasks of learning a list of words, the prospective judgments were longer than the retrospective judgments, which tends to make one think that in the case of prospective tasks, the Ss divide their attention between the task and the duration to be evaluated. Here again, the present author's position coincides with Thomas & Weaver's (1975) hypothesis on perceived durations. Mulligan & Schiffman (1979) reran the study of the relationship between memory organization and perceived duration along Ornstein's lines. The Ss were supposed to perceive ambiguous stimuli within durations around 60 sec. The organization was manipulated by employing or not employing a code which simplified the stimulus. Facilitating memory organization by presenting the code before or after the stimulus interval shortened apparent duration compared to the no-code condition.

Learning Estimation of Duration

Estimations of duration—above all verbal—can be modified by numerous parameters, but they differ in general very notably from physical duration. Is learning possible here? If so, under what conditions, and is it transferable?

By the method of production and reproduction, Fraisse (1971) evaluated the effect of immediate correction on a duration of 30 sec. To prevent the S from counting, he constantly had to produce the syllable "top" during the estimation of the duration. With correction, learning is very rapid and the effect of correction persists when it is stopped. The "tops", however, do not furnish landmarks for the S. It is as if the cadence of the productions of the "tops" corresponded to the S's personal tempo. However, counting at a learned cadence diminishes the variance in relation to the estimation of a time interval (Getty 1976). Learning the estimation of duration is also possible with 6- to 10-year-old children in the reproduction of a 30 sec duration (Fraisse & Orsini 1958). Friedman (1977) found the same type of result with preschool children for the production of a 15 sec duration, which makes him propose that there really is an inner clock.

It is also possible to create a time conditioning in humans in relation to a duration of, for example, 8 sec. If the alpha rhythm of the EEG is recorded during this interval, it is observed that the alpha arrest precedes by about 1 sec the S's response, as if the alpha stop and the S's response depended on one and the same alert process at the end of the duration (Fraisse & Voillaume 1969).

Is such learning transferable? From one direction to the other it undoubtedly is with the same durations (Warm et al 1975), but from one duration to another the results are not as clear. According to Hicks & Miller (1976) there is some transfer from long durations (40–80 sec) to short ones (5–10 sec) which are presented alternatively with error corrections. The transfer, however, takes place better from long to short durations than the reverse.

The Brain's Role

The role of the brain from a physiological angle remains to be considered in the estimation of duration. The respective roles of the two cerebral hemispheres have been studied less concerning estimations than for perceived durations. Vroon et al (1977) found that durations from 20 to 60 sec were equally well estimated by visual and auditory stimuli terminating on either of the two hemispheres (reproduction method that makes a negative time order error appear). The found a difference only when they calculated the variances of each S in each situation. The differences are greater when the stimuli first terminate on the right hemisphere than on the left hemisphere, which would therefore imply a predominance, but they are less marked than in the perception of durations. Hicks & Brundige (1974) attempted to demonstrate the respective roles of the two hemispheres by carrying out a recognition experiment with lists of 300 items of which 50 were present twice. The items consisted either of abstract nouns or of photographs of faces. This difference in roles of the two hemispheres was to be tested by using right-handed and left-handed Ss. The results were negative, but also the hypotheses were weak. Does a recognition task not always involve the dominant hemisphere?

By considering large groups of Ss having brain lesions in widely differing areas, and by subjecting them to a test battery (involving manipulation of temporal concepts estimating time periods, sequence of events, judging and producing short and long intervals singly and in pairs), Bruyer & Bontemps-Devogel (1979) found that by comparison with a control group, the Ss with lesions showed a lower level of performance. The group with frontal lesions showed a marked disability. A final point to indicate, and it is merely a confirmation, is that there is no relationship between the alpha rhythm and temporal estimations (Adam et al 1971). However, Coffin & Ganz (1977) found in the estimation of a 5 sec task a high correlation between the estimations and the weighted mean frequency of the EEG close to the alpha frequency.

Expectation and Attention

The study of these variables is not a recent phenomenon. Expectation raises the apparent duration (cf Fraisse 1963). "A watched pot never boils," goes the familiar saying. Lordahl & Berkowitz (1975) attempted to show that there was no expectancy effect, properly speaking, but merely the effect of a comparison of this type of experience with that of intervals occupied by varying events.

Cahoon & Edmonds (1980) state that this expectancy effect is transfered to the estimation of another duration. Block et al (1980) carried out an important research on this topic using a situation close to the reality expressed in the quoted aphorism. One group of Ss is to watch for the moment when a vessel of water starts to boil and they know ahead of time (prospective situation) that they will have to evaluate the duration between turning on the heat and the boiling point. Another group is simply asked to watch over the water in a similar beaker to the other group's, and at the end they are then asked to estimate the past duration (retrospective situation). However, the heat is regulated in such a manner that in one case the water starts boiling after about 240 sec, which is shorter than the anticipated duration (270 sec), or else it does not boil at all.

The subjects make a double estimation, reproducing the duration and verbally estimating it. In the condition where the water does not boil, and in a prospective attitude, the reproduced duration is longer (278 vs 209 sec). When estimating verbally, the result takes the same direction but is less pronounced. On the other hand, in the condition where the water boils, reproduction results are reversed (240 vs 260 sec) and the same goes for verbal estimation; with retrospection there is practically no difference.

This result has been verified in several experiments using different variables. The present author underlines the fact that an expectation seems long when it is nothing more than expectation, but once the expectation has reached its goal, the overestimation of the duration of the expectation disappears rapidly. Also the fact that the verbal estimation is always followed by the reproduction renders the results less reliable. What is being estimated? Is it the duration of the expectation or that of the reproduction? If it concerns the expectation, then there is a 4 min interval between the observation of the water and the response.

Again in the area of expectations, Edmonds et al (1981) persuaded their Ss that their expectation would be followed by a pleasant, unpleasant, or subjective neutral experience. Results indicate that the positive expectancy group overestimate the actual interval time (time passed relatively slowly) whereas there is an underestimation in the other groups. Evidently the expectation itself of an agreeable event leads to paying more attention to the passing of time.

It is possible to make attention vary in different ways. In general, it has been found that the duration seems shorter when the estimation concerns the duration of a task than when the S is simply asked to pay attention to the passing of time (Curton & Lordahl 1974).

Listening for a minute to a selection of more or less interesting prose passages has shown that the interesting passages are judged shorter than the others (Hawkins & Tedford 1976). A more original experiment was carried out by Thayer & Schiff (1975), who used a face-to-face eye contact situation between two Ss of the same or opposite sex. This eye contact is established with contemporaries who are either smiling-friendly or scowling-angry. The time is overestimated in eye contact with unpleasant faces in relationship to the case of pleasing faces.

Results reported by Underwood (1975) are more surprising. The Ss encoded nonsense syllables, unrelated words, or related words for 50 sec and then recalled for 50 sec. The Ss judged that they had taken more time on retrieval than on encoding, and this difference increased as the meaningfulness of the material decreased. Should it then be concluded that retrieval requires more attention than encoding and that greater attention then corresponds to a longer time? But is not 50 sec too long a duration for retrieval, carrying as a consequence the possibility to pay more attention to time, given that in any case the Ss have only a limited number of elements to recall?

Individual Differences

Given the wide variability of duration estimations, one might well suppose that it would be difficult to demonstrate interindividual differences that are not pathological. However, taking into account what has been said above about the roles of expectation and attention, it is not very surprising that very anxious Ss such as those detected by the Test Anxiety Scale, for example, give a longer estimation of waiting, and even of an intellectual task, than the less anxious (Sarason & Stoops 1978). Along the dimension of field dependence and independence, i.e. cognitive style, the results are not very enlightening. In several situations, Davidson & House (1978) found that cognitive style had very little importance on the estimation of the durations. Using another situation, Phillips (1977) came to the same conclusion.

As for the variable *Introversion-Extroversion* such as can be estimated by Eysenck's tests, Wudel (1979) found, after Ss spent 100 sec in relaxation or in arithmetical operations, the extroverts gave shorter estimations and had greater confidence in their responses. However, Gray et al (1975), working with a larger group but limited to extreme populations on the introversion-extroversion axis, did not find any difference between the groups when estimating 3 min readings of dull or interesting texts. Both groups estimated the intervals to be shorter when the reading was interesting.

Still on results concerning normal Ss, if the S is asked to use mental images as cues in estimating a given interval, it is observed that, as a function of individual differences in the vividness of visual images, children in the strong image group were more accurate than those in the weak group. In adults, there was no difference between groups (Orihara 1980).

Populations that are more readily identifiable by an easily recognizable trait can also be studied. Estimation of time by the *overweight* has particularly attracted attention since the 1960s. It would seem that it was Witkin (1965) who first spoke of the overweight as being more field dependent. The study of the effect of the content of the duration on the estimation of the latter by overweight subjects began across the field dependency dimension. Hughs & Reuder (1968) tested this hypothesis concerning the duration of reading either sensitive or neutral word lists. Absolute errors indicating a variability were greater for the overweight than for the control group, and more pronounced with the sensitive list than with the neutral list.

The same hypothesis has been employed in many various forms, all of which suppose that the overweight are more sensitive to external than to internal stimulations. Stutz et al (1974), using a reproduction method, found that overweight Ss made larger errors than those in a control group. This result was confirmed by Rodin (1975) on a population of men but rejected by Nail et al (1981), who found no such effect with men but did find such an effect in women. These latter authors wisely conclude, "In general, results offer little support for the existence of a generalized insensitivity to interval cues on the part of the overweight" (p. 139).

Schizophrenia has also captured the attention of numerous researchers. The most significant results seem to be as follows: schizophrenics overstimate brief durations, whether in estimation at various moments of an interview-testing session or in operational estimation. In this method the S was required to indicate when a specified number of seconds had passed (Wahl & Sieg 1980). This overestimation of brief durations must have been brought out by the well-known characteristic of chronic schizophrenics. For them, "time stood still," and when they are age-disoriented they underestimate past durations (birth date, length of stay at the hospital, and current year) (Crow & Stevens 1978). However, with schizophrenics disorientation is not as pronounced as with brain-damaged patients (Josly & Hutzell 1979).

Doob (1971) reviewed research as to estimations of duration by Ss under *hypnosis,* and showed that these estimations are above all dependent on suggestions. Two groups of volunteer Ss were given the Stanford Hypnotic Susceptibility Scale, Form C, either with a hypnosis condition or without that induction. Prior to the termination of the scale, Ss were asked to recall the activities they had performed and the time that had elapsed since they began the scale. The 10 hypnotized Ss were significantly less sequential in their recall of activities and less accurate in their estimation of the passage of time than were the 10 nonhypnotized Ss (Schwartz 1978).

The author concludes that the hypnotized Ss were less sensitive to the context that the world provided for their activities than the nonhypnotized Ss. Bowers (1979) comes to the same conclusion. Although the Ss in these groups, for the most part, underestimated the duration during which they had been hypnotized, there were also some who overestimated it. Those who underestimated it were those who were the most hypnotizable.

Estimation of Duration in Retrospect

Having studied up to now the estimation of time between the present moment and the beginning of an event that has just terminated, i.e. according to some, the estimation of time in passing, it is time to study the estimation of a duration which ran over a period of past time, i.e. between two past events. The role of long-term memory is going to be vital here whereas the durations studied previously often called upon the intervention of short-term memory.

All sorts of transitions are certainly possible between the two situations. It is thus possible to compare the reproduction of a duration right at the end of the interval or after a period of 20 sec (Guay & Bourgeois 1981). Whether during this period the S is simply at rest or occupied with an activity (counting backwards by threes) it simply has the effect of raising the variability of the reproduction responses for intervals 4, 8, 16, and 32 sec.

The dominant hypothesis on the role of memory in these estimations is obviously Ornstein's (1969), which has already been mentioned. The estimated duration at a given moment is proportional to the storage size. It constitutes a hypothetical variable which would depend on the number of events stored and retrieved as well as on the complexity of the coding of the events. Block (1974) tried to test this hypothesis with three durations to be compared: the first is a piece of music for 240 sec, the second a duration of 180 sec occupied with the audition of either 30 words at 6 sec intervals or 60 words at 3 sec intervals; this duration is followed by another interval of music lasting 120 sec. The Ss are not advised ahead of time about what will be asked of them, but they do know that they will be questioned. At the end of the presentation they are required to evaluate the last two durations by lengths proportional to a line 50 cm long representing the duration of the first musical interval. Finally they are asked to write all the words they have retained and to evaluate the number of words presented. The duration occupied with 60 words is judged relatively longer than that with 30 words, but nonetheless the number of words recalled is approximately the same in each of the two situations. What really changes is the evaluation of the number of words presented. In another experiment of the same type, Block varied the organization of the stimuli rather than their number (80 words presented in groups of 4, either belonging to the same semantic category or in disorder). The group that perceived the stimuli by semantic groupings recalled more of them and judged the duration of the presentation to be longer, whereas both groups of Ss gave identical estimates of the number of words presented.

These experiments have been described at some length because by their contrast they illustrate the two possible interpretations of Ornstein's hypothesis. In certain cases, it is not the events taken individually, but rather their numerical quality that is stocked in memory. In other cases, the criterion retained is the number of stimuli stocked in memory; this explains the different roles assigned to codes in Ornstein's experiments according to whether they increase the number of stimuli identified (which is the case in Block's second experiment) or whether they diminish the number of stimuli by integrating the complex elements into smaller sets. This double face in the role of storage size was a development of the present author's hypothesis published in 1963, namely that the estimated duration was proportional to the perceived changes. It must be pointed out that for the present author, what is involved here is either the number of events that take place in the outside world and that are perceived, or else the number of events that are identified at the perceptive level and then memorized.

A special modality for the estimation of a duration distant in time consists of classifying in order or of dating one or several events. Squire et al (1975) had Ss classify highly familiar television broadcast programs two by two. In the case of programs dating from 2 to 4 years the Ss were able to distinguish them from programs older than 5 years. However, beyond that (from 5 to 17 years) the discrimination was very weak. Linton (1975) every day for 20 months noted a personal event on file cards with the date on the back. She used a method for discrimination of order and of dating. The discrimination depends both on the time interval between two events, for example, and on how long ago they took place. Thus in the case of an interval of 17 to 32 days, there was no error on events up to 2 months past, and 20% error after 8 months. As concerns dating, the error rate was null for events of 2 to 8 days past, but the estimated error attained 10–12 days in the case of events occuring 4 to 18 months previously. Lieury et al (1979, 1980) attempted to determine more precisely not only the size of the error, but its sign as well. By requesting Ss to date numerous public events having occurred 4 to 17 years previously, and of which the Ss were well aware, he found an underestimation of the durations the farthest in the past and an overestimation concerning the most recent events. He also attempted to demonstrate the processes involved in dating; he found three; either an event which serves as a reference point, or the use of a personal calendar consisting of a series of well-dated events, or finally direct contact with the specific time period. The preceding emphasizes rather well that we do not remember long durations situated in the distant past. We can only situate past events on the basis of remembrances that are not temporal: for example, recalling the date of an event (Today is my 20th wedding anniversary); or, *knowledge about* a duration (That trip lasted a month); etc . . .

Thus, in cases of the estimation of a period of time in the distant past, subjective time is spoken of rather than estimation of a duration. Subjective time, i.e. the relative estimation of a period of time, decreases, for example, as the S advances in age. Paul Janet (1877) had maintained that this fact was due to the relationship between the subjective duration of a year and the S's chronological age. The S would establish a proportion between a given duration and his remaining life expectancy. One year at the age of 10 amounts to 10% of one's lifetime, whereas at the age of 60 it only amounts to 1.6%; life expectancy constantly grows shorter, and thus life passes more rapidly. Paul Janet used the term illusion in discussing this. More recent authors have sought to quantify this acceleration of time as a function of age. The operationalization involved is intricate. Lemlich (1975) asked Ss to evaluate at their present age the duration of a year by comparing it to the middle or to a quarter of a lifetime. The subjective relationship was evaluated as 2 for a quarter and as 1.6 for half of a lifetime. The author suggested that subjective duration varies inversely with the square root of chronological age, which equally represents subjective time at the moment of the response. Walker (1977) handled the same problem by asking that the present year be evaluated as 10, and then that the duration of a year at the middle point of lifetime and at a quarter of lifetime be evaluated in relationship to the established value given to the present year. He did not find exactly the same values as did Lemlich, nor his arithmetical formulation, but nonetheless his values were not all that different: 1.4 times longer at the half-way point, 1.6 times longer at the quarter point of life span. The present author points out that in both of these studies, there was a high variability between Ss as well and that not all of the responses were in the same direction. Thus, in Walker's research, 74% agreed that time passes faster as one grows older, but on the contrary, 18% judged the opposite, so it is difficult to formulate an abstract estimation of the passing of time. The present author, however, relates this subjective phenomenon to the fact that with advancing age, there are less novel events in life that are worthy of being stored in memory.

CONCLUSION

Having reached the end of this chapter, the evidence obliges one to concede that no revolution has taken place over the past few years in the field of perception and estimation of durations. Psychologists, however, are becoming more and more interested in the problem of time. This issue corresponds to a phenomenological order of knowledge that is placed in relationship to physical time. Such knowledge is no longer proscribed by the behaviorists' taboo. From that point of view, one is led to identify three orders of duration on the physical continuum, orders which do not hold the same status, epistemologically speaking. These orders are the following: (a) less than 100 ms, at which the perception is of instantaneity; (b) 100 ms–5 sec, perception of duration in the perceived present; and (c) above 5 sec, estimation of duration involving memory.

Durations shorter than about 100 ms are not perceived as such. The perception of a succession appears beyond the level of 20 ms. In fact, successions are the raw material of the physical world. This latter is nothing but successions, or if one prefers, changes that can engrave their date on physical objects. It is thus possible to date prehistoric fragments by means of carbon 14. A tree's age is recorded by means of the concentric circles produced as the trunk develops. However, duration is a construct of the human mind. Human eyes perceive succession at first, but duration is linked to the identification of on and off effects, to use the language of physiology. Nevertheless, much recent research has been devoted to brief durations; differences, qualitative in the present author's opinion, allow the comparison of two durations by a relative criterion: longer-shorter, for example.

The perception of duration, *stricto sensu,* is situated at a level above 100 ms and within the limits of the psychological present as described by W. James (1890). It includes a unity among perceptive events as is revealed, for example, by the perception of rhythmic patterns. On the other hand, the perception of rhythm disintegrates if the stimuli are spaced too far apart; there then are nothing more than more or less regular successions. The duration of the presentifiable can hardly extend beyond 5 sec. The choice of methods for its apprehension is therefore fundamental. Although estimation and production theoretically correlate negatively, each one of the methods for reproduction, for comparison, and for absolute evaluation on a small scale produces differing results. In the absence of systematic research on the comparison of methods and their interaction with the content of durations and expectations, it is difficult to separate differences arising from the method from those attributable to individual and/or interindividual variability. Within the limits of the perception of durations, the effects of time order and error, and, for the shortest durations, those of masking, are of utmost importance.

Beyond the limits of the perceived present, duration can only be estimated by the S's construct which brings to bear short- and long-term memory. The problem of methods remains even though the choice of pertinent ones has been reduced. What could possibly be learned from experiments in which one is required to produce or reproduce empty durations of 60 sec without the use of instruments of measure? In all those cases where measures are employed, a new process intervenes. A comparison between two types of contemporaneous successions can be made, whether by the differences in the movements of two runners using a clock, or by the creation of an internal clock, as for example by counting. This necessity has led numerous authors to imagine, in those cases where voluntary measurement is impossible to employ, the existence of a physiological clock and of a time counter even though that audacious hypothesis has never been confirmed directly.

In estimating durations, variability becomes a more and more difficult obstacle to overcome on the path toward accurate laws. Thus the *sources* of variability have been accorded greater and greater importance on account of attitudes, according to whether the estimation is prospective or retrospective with a very high interval effect between the experienced duration and the moment when it is estimated.

However, the most characteristic aspect of recent research has been the importance accorded to the content of the experienced duration under a passive aspect (complexity) or an active aspect (duration of an activity) within the three duration registers that have been identified. With the growing importance accorded generally to information processing, authors have sought to analyze the underlying processes of perception and of time estimation. Several models have been proposed, but it is the present author's opinion that they would be difficult to generalize in application to results obtained with other methods. One can limit oneself to general models (Fraisse 1981). Among the other models, the most potential seems to lie in the generalization of Thomas & Weaver's (1975). Within a given task, there is a compromise between temporal and nontemporal information. Temporal information is all the more taken into consideration when it is emphasized in the task (prospective judgments) and/or the nontemporal task leaves the S greater liberty to pay attention to the temporal aspect of his activity. The more one pays attention to time, the longer it seems, with the extreme being expectancy which is nothing but expectancy of a desired or feared event. Reciprocally, duration seems short when the task is difficult and/or interesting.

These are strategies proper to adults. Space has not allowed the inclusion here of research on the development of the notion of time in children. A child perceives rhythms from the age of two months (Demany et al 1977), adapts gradually to durations, and learns to speak of them (through adverbs of time and verb tenses). This omission in this chapter is happily compensated for by the recent publication (Friedman 1982) of a work in which many authors, including the present one (Fraisse 1982), presented their themes. The stages in the development of the notion of time permit a better understanding of the treatment of temporal information by adults.

In tomorrow's psychology, progress will probably be conditional on not subrepticiously mixing together sizes of durations studied and above all on clarifying the results that can be obtained by using the different methods. In other words, choose among tasks those which appear to be most revealing, and apply them over the entire choice of methods. At a time when the variation of the content of durations is being carried out, our knowledge about the construction of duration cannot progress unless the methodological mortgage is paid off, which will shed light on the way we treat temporal information as well.

32   FRAISSE

Literature Cited

Adam, N., Rosner, B. S., Hosick, E. C., Clark, D. L. 1971. Effect of anesthetic drugs on time production and alpha rhythm. *Percept. Psychophys.* 10:133–36

Adams, R. D. 1977. Intervening stimulus effects on category judgments of duration. *Percept. Psychophys.* 21:523–34

Allan, L. G. 1975. Temporal order psychometric functions based on confidence rating data. *Percept. Psychophys.* 18:369–72

Allan, L. G. 1976. Is there a constant minimum under light and dark adaptation? *Q. J. Exp. Psychol.* 28:71–76

Allan, L. G. 1977. The time order error in judgments of duration. *Can. J. Psychol.* 31:24–31

Allan, L. G. 1979. The perception of time. *Percept. Psychophys.* 26:340–54

Allan, L. G., Kristofferson, A. G. 1974. Successiveness discrimination: two models. *Percept. Psychophys.* 15:37–46

Allport, D. A. 1968. Phenomenal simultaneity and the perceptual moment. *Br. J. Psychol.* 59:395–406

Avant, L. L., Lyman, P. J., Antes, J. R. 1975. Effects of stimulus familiarity on judged visual duration. *Percept. Psychophys.* 17:253–62

Banks, R., Cappon, D., Hagen, R. 1966. Time estimation by psychiatric patients. *Percept. Mot. Skills* 23:1294

Baron, J. V. 1971. The threshold for successiveness. *Percept. Psychophys.* 10:201–7

Berg, M. 1979. Temporal duration as a function of information processing. *Percept. Mot. Skills* 49:988–90

Bindra, D., Waksberg, H. 1956. Methods and terminology in studies of time estimation. *Psychol. Bull.* 53:55–59

Block, R. A. 1974. Memory and the experience of duration in retrospect. *Mem. Cognit.* 2:153–60

Block, R. A. 1978. Remembered duration: Effects of event and sequence complexity. *Mem. Cognit.* 6:320–26

Block, R. A., George, E. J., Reed, M. A. 1980. A watched pot sometimes boils. A study of duration experience. *Acta Psychol.* 46:81–94

Block, R. A., Reed, M. A. 1978. Remembered duration: Evidence for a contextual change hypothesis. *J. Exp. Psychol: Hum. Learn. Mem.* 4:656–65

Bobko, D. J., Schiffman, H. R., Casteno, R. J., Chiapetta, W. 1977. Contextual effects in duration experience. *Am. J. Psychol.* 90:577–86

Bobko, D. J., Thompson, J. G., Schiffman, H. R. 1977. The perception of brief temporal intervals: Power functions for auditory and visual stimulus intervals. *Perception* 6:703–9

Bowers, K. S. 1979. Time distortion and hypnotizability: Understanding the duration of hypnosis. *J. Abnorm. Psychol.* 88:435–39

Bruyer, R., Bontemps-Devogel, N. 1979. Lésions du cortex cérébral et perception de la durée: approche neuro-physiologique de la "chronognosie". *J. Psychol. Norm. Pathol.* 79:279–97

Cahoon, D., Edmonds, E. M. 1980. The watched pot still won't boil: Expectancy as a variable in estimating the passage of time. *Bull. Psychon. Soc.* 16:115–16

Cantor, N. E., Thomas, E. A. 1976. Visual masking effects on duration, size and form discrimination. *Percept. Psychophys.* 19: 321–27

Carmon, A., Nachshon, I. 1971. Effect of unilateral brain damage on perception of temporal order. *Cortex* 7:410–18

Chattajea, R. G., Chatterjee, P. K., Bhattacharyya, A. K. 1978. Time estimation in psychotics and neurotics. An experimental study. *Psychologia* 21:237–40

Coffin, S., Ganz, L. 1977. Perceptual correlates of variability in the duration of the cortical excitability cycle. *Neuropsychologia* 15:231–41

Collyer, C. E. 1977. Discrimination of spatial and temporal intervals defined by three light flashes: Effects of spacing on temporal judgments and on timing on spatial judgments. *Percept. Psychophys.* 21:357–64

Crain, P., Goldstone, S., Lhamon, W. I. 1975. Temporal information processing and psychopathology. *Percept. Mot. Skills* 41: 219–24

Crow, T. J., Stevens, M. 1978. Age disorientation in chronic schizophrenia. The nature of the cognitive deficit. *Br. J. Psychol.* 133:137–42

Curton, E. D., Lordahl, D. S. 1974. Effects of attentional focus and arousal on time expectation. *J. Exp. Psychol.* 103:861–67

Davidson, W. B., House, W. J. 1978. Influence of reflection impulsivity and cognitive style on time estimation under different ambient conditions. *Percept. Mot. Skills* 46:1083–91

Demany, L., McKenzie, B., Vurpillot, E. 1977. Rhythm perception in early infancy. *Nature* 266:719–19

Divenyi, P. L., Danner, W. F. 1977. Discrimination of time intervals marked by brief acoustical pulses of various intensities and spectra. *Percept. Psychophys.* 21:125–42

Divenyi, P. L., Sachs, R. M. 1978. Discrimination of tone intervals bounded by tone bursts. *Percept. Psychophys.* 24:429–36

Doob, L. W. 1971. *Patterning of Time.* New Haven: Yale Univ. Press. 472 pp.

Edmonds, E. M., Cahoon, D., Bridges, B. A. 1981. The estimation of time as a function of positive, neutral or negative expectancies. *Bull. Psychon. Soc.* 17:259–60

Efron, R. 1963. Temporal perception aphasia and déjà vu. *Brain* 86:403–24

Efron, R. 1970a. The effect of stimulus duration on perceptual onset and offset latencies. *Percept. Psychophys.* 8:231–34

Efron, R. 1970b. The relationship between the duration of a stimulus and the duration of a perception. *Neuropsychologia* 18:37–55

Efron, R. 1974. An invariant characteristic of perceptual systems in the time domain. In *Attention and Performance*, ed. S. Kornblum, 4:713–36. New York: Academic

Efron, R., Lee, D. N. 1971. The visual persistence of a moving stroboscopically illuminated object. *Am. J. Psychol.* 84:365–76

Eisler, H. 1975. Subjective duration and psychophysics. *Psychol. Rev.* 82:429–50

Eisler, H. 1976. Experiments on subjective duration 1968–1975: a collection of power functions exponents. *Psychol. Bull.* 83: 1154–71

Eisler, H. 1981a. Applicability of the parallel-clock model to duration discrimination. *Percept. Psychophys.* 29:225–33

Eisler, H. 1981b. The parallel-clock model: reply and note. *Percept. Psychophys.* 29:516–20

Eisler, H., Linde, L., Troeng, G., Lazar, R., Eisler, B. M., et al. 1980. *A Complementary Bibliography of the Psychology of Time*. Am. Psychol. Assoc. J.S.A.S. Catalog Sel. Doc. Psychol. No. 2101. 151 pp.

Eriksen, C. W., Collins, J. F. 1967. Some temporal characteristics of visual pattern perception. *J. Exp. Psychol.* 74:476–84

Fraisse, P. 1963. *Psychology of Time.* New York: Harper & Row. 343 pp.

Fraisse, P. 1966. Visual perceptive simultaneity and masking of letters successively presented. *Percept. Psychophys.* 1:285–87

Fraisse, P. 1967. *Psychologie du temps.* Paris: P.U.F. 2nd ed.

Fraisse, P. 1971. L'apprentissage de l'estimation de la durée et ses repères. *Année. Psychol.* 71:371–79

Fraisse, P. 1973. Temporal isolation, activity rhythms and time isolation. In *Man in Isolation and Confinement*, ed. J. L. Rasmussen, pp. 85–98. Chicago: Aldine. 330 pp.

Fraisse, P. 1974. *La Psychologie du Rythme.* Paris: P.U.F. 244 pp.

Fraisse, P. 1978. Time and rhythm perception. In *Handbook of Perception*, ed. E. C. Carterette, M. P. Friedman, 8:203–47. New York: Academic

Fraisse, P. 1979. Influence de la durée du traitement de l'information sur l'estimation du'une durée d'une seconde. *Année Psychol.* 79:495–504

Fraisse, P. 1980. Les synchronisations sensori motrices au rythme. In *Anticipation et Comportement,* ed. J. Requin, pp. 233–57. Paris: C.N.R.S.

Fraisse, P. 1981. Cognition of time in human activity. In *Cognition in Motivation and Learning*, ed. G. d'Ydewalle, W. Lens, pp. 233–58. Hillsdale, NJ: Erlbaum

Fraisse, P. 1982. The adaptation of the child to time. See W. J. Friedman 1982, pp. 113–40

Fraisse, P. 1983. Le futur dans les perspectives temporelles. *Int. J. Psychol.* In press

Fraisse, P., Orsini, F. 1958. Etude expérimentale de conduites temporelles III. Etude génétique de l'estimation de la durée. *Année Psychol.* 58:1–6

Fraisse, P., Voillaume, Cl. 1969. Conditionnement temporel du rythme alpha et estimation du temps. *Année Psychol.* 69:7–15

Friedman, E. R. 1977. Judgments of time intervals by young children. *Percept. Mot. Skills* 45:715–20

Friedman, W. J., ed. 1982. *The Developmental Psychology of Time.* New York: Academic. 286 pp.

Furukawa, M. 1979. A study on the difference in visual and auditory temporal judgment II. *Tohoku Psychol. Folia* 38:18–28

Getty, D. J. 1976. Counting processes in human timing. *Percept. Psychophys.* 20:191–97

Gibbon, J., Rutschmann, R. 1969. Temporal order judgment and reaction time. *Science* 165:413–15

Gibson, J. J. 1975. Events are perceivable but time is not. In *The Study of Time*, Vol. 2, ed. J. T. Fraser, N. Lawrence. Berlin: Springer

Goldstone, S., Lhamon, W. I., Sechzer, J. 1978. Light intensity and judged duration. *Bull. Psychon. Soc.* 12:83–84

Gray, C. T., Gray, C. R., Loehlin, J. C. 1975. Time perception: effects of intraversion/extraversion and task interest. *Percept. Mot. Skills* 41:703–8

Guay, M., Bourgeois, J. 1981. Short-term retention of temporal information. *Percept. Mot. Skills* 52:719–26

Hawkins, M. F., Tedford, W. H. 1976. Effects of interest and relatedness on estimated duration of verbal material. *Bull. Psychon. Soc.* 8:301–2

Hellstrom, A. 1977. Time errors are perceptual. *Psychol. Res.* 39:345–88

Hicks, R. E., Allen, D. A. 1979a. Counting eliminates the repetition effects in judgments of temporal duration. *Acta Psychol.* 43:361–66

Hicks, R. E., Allen, D. A. 1979b. The repetition effect in judgments of temporal duration across minutes, days, and months. *Am. J. Psychol.* 92:323–33

Hicks, R. E., Brundige, R. M. 1974. Judgments of temporal duration while processing verbal and physiognomic stimuli. *Acta Psychol.* 38:447–53

Hicks, R. E., Miller, G. W. 1976. Transfers of time judgments as a function of feedback. *Am. J. Psychol.* 69:303–10

Hicks, R. E., Miller, G. W., Kinzbourne, M. 1976. Prospective and retrospective judgments of time as a function of amount of information processed. *Am. J. Psychol.* 89:719–30

Hirsh, I. J. 1959. Auditory perception of temporal order. *J. Acoust. Soc. Am.* 31:759–67

Hirsh, I. J., Fraisse, P. 1964. Simultanéité et succession de stimuli hétérogènes. *Année. Psychol.* 64:1–19

Hirsh, I. J., Sherrig, C. E. 1961. Perceived order in different sense modalities. *J. Exp. Psychol.* 62:423–32

Hogan, H. W. 1978. A theoretical reconciliation of competing views of time perception. *Am. J. Psychol.* 91:417–28

Huang, Y. L., Jones, B. 1982. On the interdependence of temporal and spatial judgments. *Percept. Psychophys.* 32:7–14

Hughes, R., Reuder, M. E. 1968. Estimates of psychological time among obese and nonobese women. *J. Psychol.* 70:213–19

Huppert, F., Singer, G. 1967. An aftereffect in judgment of auditory duration. *Percept. Psychophys.* 2:544–46

Hylan, J. P. 1903. The distribution of attention. *Psychol. Rev.* 10:373–403

James, W. 1890. *The Principles of Psychology.* New York: Holt. 2 vols.

Janet, P. 1877. Une illusion d'optique interne. *Rev. Philos.* 1:497–502

Jones, B., Huang, Y. L. 1982. Spacetime dependency in psychophysical judgment of extent and duration: Algebraic models of the tau and kappa effects. *Psychol. Bull.* 91:128–42

Josly, D., Hutzell, R. R. 1979. Temporal disorientation in schizophrenic and brain damaged patients. *Am. J. Psychiatry* 136:1220–22

Kowal, K. H. 1976. Apparent duration of long meaningful events and meaningless intervals. *Mem. Cognit.* 4:215–20

Kowal, K. H. 1981. Growth of apparent duration: effect of melodic and not melodic tonal variation. *Percept. Mot. Skills* 52:803–17

Kristofferson, A. B. 1967. Successiveness discrimination as a two state, quantal process. *Science* 158:1137–39

Kristofferson, A. B. 1977. A real-time criterion theory of duration discrimination. *Percept. Psychophys.* 21:105–17

Kristofferson, A. B., Allan, L. G. 1973. Successiveness and duration discrimination. In *Attention and Performance,* ed. S. Kornblum, 4:738–50. New York: Academic

Lemlich, R. 1975. Subjective acceleration of time with aging. *Percept. Mot. Skills* 41:235–38

Lhamon, W. I., Goldstone, S. 1956. The time sense: Estimation of one second durations by schizophrenic patients. *Arch. Neurol. Psychiatry* 76:625–29

Lichtenstein, M. 1961. Phenomenal simultaneity with irregular timing of components of the visual stimuli. *Percept. Mot. Skills* 12:47–60

Lieury, A., Aiello, B., Lepreux, D., Mellet, M. 1980. Le rôle des repères dans la récupération et la datation des souvenirs anciens. *Année Psychol.* 80:149–67

Lieury, A., Caplain, P., Jacquet, A., Jolivet, C. 1979. La contraction du temps dans les souvenirs anciens. *Année Psychol.* 79:7–21

Linton, M. 1975. Memory for real-world events. In *Explorations in Cognition,* ed. D. A. Norman, D. E. Rumelhart. San Francisco: Freeman

Locke, S. A. 1974. Temporal discrimination of brief auditory stimuli by schizophrenics, neurologically impaired and normals. *Percept. Mot. Skills* 39:1111–20

Long, G. L., Beaton, R. J. 1980a. The effects of spatial frequency and target type on perceived duration. *Percept. Psychophys.* 28:413–21

Long, G. L., Beaton, R. J. 1980b. The contribution of visual persistence to the perceived duration of brief targets. *Percept. Psychophys.* 28:422–30

Long, G. L., Beaton, R. J. 1981. The effects of stimulus numerosity, retinal location, and rod contrast on perceived duration of brief visual stimuli. *Percept. Psychophys.* 29:389–94

Lordahl, D. S., Berkowitz, S. 1975. The watched pot does not boil: A case of a wrong control group. *Bull. Psychon. Soc.* 5:45–46

Marchman, J. N. 1969. Discrimination of brief temporal relations. *Psychol. Rec.* 19:83–92

Massaro, D. W., Idson, W. L. 1976. Temporal course of perceived auditory duration. *Percept. Psychophys.* 20:351–52

Massaro, D. W., Idson, W. L. 1978. Target-mask similarity in backward recognition masking of perceived tone duration. *Percept. Psychophys.* 24:223–36

Matsuda, F., Matsuda, M. 1979. Effects of spatial separation as a cue of time estimation in children and adults. *Jpn. Psychol. Res.* 21:132–38

Matsuda, F., Matsuda, M. 1981. The anti-kappa effect in successively presented stimuli: a developmental study. Jpn. Psychol. Res. 23:9–17

Michon, J. A. 1978. The making of the present. In *Attention and Performance,* ed. J. Requin, 7:90–111. Hillsdale, NJ: Erlbaum. 730 pp.

Miller, G. W., Hicks, R., Willette, M. V. 1978. Effects on concurrent verbal rehearsal and temporal set upon judgments of temporal duration. *Acta Psychol.* 42:173–79

Mills, L., Rollman, G. B. 1980. Hemispheric asymmetry for auditory perception of temporal order. *Neuropsychologia* 18:41–47

Mo, S. S. 1971. Judgment of temporal duration as a function of numerosity. *Psychon. Sci.* 24:71–72

Mo, S. S. 1975. Temporal reproduction of duration as a function of numerosity. *Bull. Psychon. Soc.* 5:165–67

Mo, S. S., Kersey, R. 1982. On ego regression and prior time information effect in schizophrenia. *J. Clin. Psychol.* 38:34–38

Mulligan, R. M., Schiffman, H. R. 1979. Temporal experience as a function of organization in memory. *Bull. Psychon. Soc.* 14:417–20

Nail, P., Levy, L., Russin, R., Crandal, R. 1981. Time estimation and obesity. *Pers. Soc. Psychol. Bull.* 7:139–46

Ono, A. V. 1976. A study of the literature on the interrelations between subjective time, distance and speed. *Tohoku Psychol. Folia* 35:1–11

Oostenbrug, M. W. M., Horst, J. W., Kuiper, J. W. 1978. Discrimination of visually perceived intervals of time. *Percept. Psychophys.* 24:21–34

Orihara, S. 1980. The effects of mental image in time estimation. *J. Child Dev.* 16:13–20

Ornstein, R. E. 1969. *On the Experience of Time.* Harmondsworth, England: Penguin

Phillips, J. R. 1977. Relationship of field dependence-independence to posture and judgment of time duration. *Percept. Mot. Skills* 44:931–40

Polzella, D. F., DaPolito, F., Huisman, M. C., Dayton, C. V. 1977. Cerebral asymmetry in time perception. *Percept. Psychophys.* 21:1187–92

Poppel, E. 1978. Time perception. In *Handbook of Sensory Physiology,* ed. R. Held, H. W. Leibowitz, H. L. Teuber, 8:713–29. Berlin/Heidelberg: Springer

Rodin, J. 1975. Causes and consequences of time perception differences in overweight and normal weight. *J. Pers. Soc. Psychol.* 31:898–904

Rutschmann, R. 1973. Visual perception of temporal order. In *Attention and Performance,* ed. S. Kornblum, 4:687–711. New York: Academic

Sarason, I. G., Stoops, R. 1978. Test anxiety and the passage of time. *J. Consult. Clin. Psychol.* 46:102–9

Schiffman, H. R., Bobko, D. J. 1977. The role of number and familiarity of stimuli in the perception of brief temporal intervals. *Am. J. Psychol.* 90:85–93

Schiffman, H. R., Bobko, D. J., Thompson, J. G. 1977. The role of stimulus context on apparent duration. *Bull. Psychon. Soc.* 10:484–86

Schwartz, W. 1978. Time and context during

hypnotic involvement. *Int. J. Clin. Exp. Hypn.* 26:307–16

Serviere, J., Miceli, C., Galifret, Y. 1977a. A psychophysical study of the visual perception of "instantaneous" and "durable". *Vision Res.* 17:57–63

Serviere, J., Miceli, D., Galifret, Y. 1977b. Electrophysiological correlates of the visual perception of "instantaneous" and "durable". *Vision Res.* 17:65–69

Squire, L. R., Chase, P. M., Slater, P. C. 1975. Assessment of memory for remote events. *Psychol. Rep.* 37:223–34

Sternberg, S., Knoll, R. L. 1973. The perception of temporal order: fundamental issues and a general model. In *Attention and Performance,* ed. S. Kornblum, 4:629–85. New York: Academic

Stevens, S. S. 1967. Intensity functions in sensory systems. *Int. J. Neurol.* 6:202–9

Stroud, J. M. 1955. The fine structure of psychological time. In *Information Theory in Psychology,* ed. H. Quastler, pp. 174–205. Glencoe, Ill: Free Press

Stutz, R. M., Warm, J. S., Woods, W. 1974. Temporal perception in obese and normal weight subjects. A test of the stimulus binding hypothesis. *Bull. Psychon. Soc.* 3:23–24

Thayer, S., Schiff, W. 1975. Eye contacts, facial expression, and the experience of time. *J. Soc. Psychol.* 95:117–24

Thomas, E. A., Brown, I. 1974. Time perception and the filled-duration illusion. *Percept. Psychophys.* 16:449–58

Thomas, E. A., Cantor, N. E. 1975. On the duality of simultaneous time and size perception. *Percept. Psychophys.* 18:44–48

Thomas, E. A., Cantor, N. E. 1976. Simultaneous time and size perception. *Percept. Psychophys.* 19:353–60

Thomas, E. A., Cantor, N. E. 1978. Interdependence between the processing of temporal and non-temporal information. In *Attention and Performance,* ed. J. Requin, 7:43–62. Hillsdale, NJ: Erlbaum

Thomas, E. A., Weaver, W. B. 1975. Cognitive processing and time perception. *Percept. Psychophys.* 17:363–67

Underwood, G. 1975. Attention and the perception of duration during encoding and retrieval. *Perception* 4:291–98

Vroon, P. A., Timmers, H., Tempelaars. 1977. On the hemispheric representation of time. In *Attention and Performance,* ed. S. Dornic. Hillsdale, NJ: Erlbaum

Wahl, O., Sieg, D. 1980. Time estimation among schizophrenics. *Percept. Mot. Skills* 50:535–41

Walker, J. T. 1977. Time estimation and total subjective time. *Percept. Mot. Skills* 44:527–32

Walker, J. T., Irion, A. L., Gordon, D. G. 1981. Simple and contingent after effects of perceived duration in vision and audition. *Percept. Psychophys.* 29:475–86

Walker, J. T., Scott, K. J. 1981. Auditory-visual conflicts in the perceived duration of lights, tones and gaps. *J. Exp. Psychol: Hum. Percept. Perform.* 7:1327–39

Warm, J. S., Stutz, R. M., Vassolo, P. A. 1975. Intermodal transfer in temporal discrimination. *Percept. Psychophys.* 18:281–86

Westheimer, G., Mckee, S. P. 1977. Perception of temporal order in adjacent visual stimuli. *Vision Res.* 17:887–92

Witkin, H. V. 1965. Psychological differentiation and forms of pathology. *J. Abnorm. Psychol.* 70:317–36

Woods, D. D., Sorkin, R. D., Boggs, G. J. 1979. Stimulus context and duration discrimination. *Percept. Psychophys.* 26:127–32

Wudel, P. 1979. Time estimation and personality dimensions. *Percept. Mot. Skills* 48:1320

Zelkind, I., Spring, J. 1974. *Time Research, 1172 Studies.* Metuchen, NJ: Scarecrow Press. 248 pp.

Ann. Rev. Psychol. 1984. 35:37–53

QUANTITATIVE METHODS FOR LITERATURE REVIEWS

Bert F. Green

Department of Psychology, Johns Hopkins University, Baltimore, Maryland 21218

Judith A. Hall

Department of Psychology and Social Relations, Harvard University, Cambridge, Massachusetts 02138

CONTENTS

INTRODUCTION

In reviewing the general field of experimental design and data analysis, we have chosen to focus on a novel, rapidly growing application of statistical methods that is especially appropriate to the *Annual Reviews:* the use of quantitative methods to summarize and analyze research literature. This enterprise has been given several names. It is most often called meta-analysis (Glass 1976), but it is also called research integration (Walberg & Haertel 1980) and quantitative assessment of research domains (Rosenthal 1980). For clarity

37

0066-4308/84/0201-0037$02.00

and brevity we use the term "quantitative review" to describe this kind of literature review, which treats the study as the unit of analysis and is entirely based on quantitatively expressed study attributes and outcomes. Though reviewers have long employed quantification to a limited extent, systematic efforts to develop and to assess the strengths and weaknesses of quantification are new in the past decade.

Statistical methods have proved remarkably useful in analyzing all kinds of data in the social and behavioral sciences, so their application to collections of studies should not be surprising. A single study is never definitive no matter how memorable and newsworthy it may be. Many convergent findings are needed to establish a scientific fact, and statistical methods can discern important facts in a group of individually unimpressive studies.

This chapter describes the basic methods used in quantitative reviews of the literature, some illustrative applications, and some virtues and problems that seem inherent in such an approach. Our goal is to present an overview of the quantitative review and an introduction for professionals who are not experienced in doing or interpreting such reviews. More advanced knowledge can be gained by reading other sources, in particular, *Meta-analysis in Social Research* (Glass et al 1981) and "Quantitative Assessment of Research Domains" (Rosenthal 1980). We do not describe all the statistical procedures that have been proposed for quantitative reviewing, but only those that seem to have wide applicability. Nor do we list or evaluate all the quantitative reviews that have appeared, since these probably number in the hundreds. For numerous references to quantitative reviews, as well as additional statistical procedures, the reader should see Rosenthal (1980), Walberg & Haertel (1980), Glass et al (1981), and the *Psychological Bulletin* starting in 1978. Other useful balanced discussions of quantitative reviews are given by Light & Smith (1971), Cook & Leviton (1980), Hunter et al (1982), Strube & Hartmann (1982), Rosenthal (1983), and Wortman (1983).

Although most quantitative reviews published thus far have been in educational and social-personality psychology, in principle any research topic for which there are multiple studies can be reviewed in this way. The only requirements are that the studies to be reviewed address a common hypothesis, broadly defined, and that study results can be stated in common quantitative form—usually in terms of effect size or statistical significance, both of which will be discussed below.

How broadly or narrowly the research hypothesis in question is defined is a matter of choice, but most quantitative reviewers have opted for a broad definition and have made it an empirical matter whether there are differences between subsets of the literature—for example, subsets defined by major methodological variations. Thus, in one of the best-known quantitative reviews, on the benefits of psychotherapy, Smith and her colleagues (1980) chose to define "psychotherapy" broadly but were careful to categorize subsets of the literature according to the type of psychotherapy and the type of dependent measures used (e.g. fear and anxiety versus achievement). In almost all cases, a quantitative reviewer includes classifying variables, their nature depending on the particular literature at hand.

The variety and potential usefulness of quantitative reviewing can be seen in a few examples. Some quantitative reviews are extremely complex and cannot be given justice in these brief sketches. Smith et al (1980), in the psychotherapy review mentioned, concluded that psychotherapy works surprisingly well, considerably better than placebo treatments (though these work too). Shapiro & Shapiro (1982), in a quantitative review of the same question but one which was practically nonoverlapping in the literature covered, reached a similar conclusion. Each of these reviews analyzed over 1500 results.

Rosenthal & Rubin (1978) reviewed 345 studies of interpersonal and inter-species expectancy effects and concluded that the phenomenon of self-fulfilling prophecy is well supported, being present, though with widely varying magnitudes, in over eight different research areas involving both animals and humans.

Sex differences are now commonly reviewed using quantitative analysis. Hall (1978), for example, reversed the conclusions of some previous writers by showing that men and women do differ, though not dramatically, in their ability to understand nonverbal expression of emotion. Eagly & Carli (1981) demonstrated that women are more subject to persuasion and pressure to conform than men, but not by much on the average, and that the extent varies with the influence setting; conformity experiments in which subjects believe the group is witnessing their responses produce the largest sex differences.

Eagly and Carli also discovered that the sex of the original authors was significantly related to the magnitude of reported sex differences, not only in influenceability but also in nonverbal decoding skill (in a reanalysis of Hall's literature mentioned above). Male authors have tended to find women more influenceable, but less nonverbally sensitive, relative to men, than female authors. Eagly and Carli speculated that authors succeed, via unknown mechanisms related to the reporting or execution of experiments, in making their own sex look good.

Finally, White (1982) examined the socioeconomic status-achievement relationship and concluded that SES does predict achievement, though not strongly when the individual person is the unit of analysis in the original studies, and especially not when IQ is partialled out. In this field, authors had apparently believed the SES-achievement relationship to be stronger than it actually is. Of course, these are but examples of the many quantitative reviews that are available.

ADVANTAGES OF THE QUANTITATIVE REVIEW

The traditional "verbal" literature review has been eloquently criticized by other authors (e.g. Glass et al 1981), not for its heuristic value but for its weaknesses as a means of arriving at a firm understanding of a research tradition. Here we list several important advantages of the quantitative review over a review that is entirely verbal or only minimally quantified.

The quantitative review is an efficient way to summarize large literatures. Beyond a certain point, the traditional reviewer cannot describe or even grasp all the study designs and results. Though the quantitative reviewer spends considerable time coding attributes of study outcomes, once this is done, 500 studies can be analyzed as easily as 10.

The quantitative review is likely to be more objective than the traditional review. The quantitative reviewer is more likely to find and include all relevant studies and is less likely to give undeserved weight to studies that are consistent with his or her prejudices. This is not to say there is no room for bias in quantitative reviewing. Many decisions are made in the process of quantification, and one's prejudices could enter in. Further, the quantitative reviewer has, like any author of a complex research report, considerable discretion as to which of the results of the quantitative analyses to emphasize. Debate has indeed arisen over whether authors of quantitative reviews may sometimes oversimplify the results by focusing on overall effects and downplaying factors that seem to moderate the outcomes of studies.

Statistical analysis can find relationships and trends too subtle to be seen otherwise. Just as no primary investigator would attempt to understand multivariate data without recourse to statistics, so does the quantitative reviewer use statistics to discover what factors, substantive or methodological, are associated with various study outcomes. One of the greatest advantages of the quantitative review is its ability to ask not simply whether there is overall support for a hypothesis, but also whether the extent of support varies with attributes of the studies. In other words, the quantitative reviewer can investigate interactions and not just main effects.

The ability to look for interactions in the data means that the quantitative reviewer can test hypotheses that were never tested in individual studies. Eagly & Carli's (1981) analysis of the impact of author sex on the outcomes of sex differences studies, described above, is an example. Author sex can only be a between-studies variable and therefore only an aggregate analysis can detect its effects. In permitting tests of new hypotheses, quantitative analysis should, to some extent at least, reduce the need for new research.

Finally, quantitative analysis, because of the more confident conclusions it permits (a point to be discussed more below), highlights gaps in the literature and is therefore a better source of insight into appropriate new directions for research. The "more research is needed" slogan can be phrased more precisely after a quantitative analysis, and on some topics the quantitative reviewer can even announce, "No more research is needed!"

METHODOLOGY

Many of the standard methods of statistical analysis are useful in quantitative · reviews. New procedures have also been developed specifically for quantitative reviews (e.g. Kraemer & Andrews 1982, Rosenthal & Rubin 1982). Opportunities sometimes arise for special Bayesian methods (Rubin 1980). In most cases the major problem, as in any statistical analysis, is to choose the appropriate dependent and independent variables; the needed statistical analysis is then usually obvious.

Dependent Variables

The most common form of quantification, often used in traditional literature reviews, is the "box score," which consists of counting the number of significant results favoring a hypothesis, the number of significant disconfirming results, and the number of nonsignificant results. This approach, also called "vote-counting," is weak because it ignores the magnitude of effects across all available studies. The box score thus utilizes only a fraction of the data (Hedges & Olkin 1980). Further, box score analysts seem often to forget how many significant results to expect under the null hypothesis. If "only" 30% of all studies show significant results, a traditional reviewer might be skeptical that a given hypothesis is supported. In fact, that 30% is far in excess of the 5% that would be expected under the null hypothesis, and if the direction of the results is fairly consistent, a strong conclusion is warranted. Figures of around 30% have been found in several quantitative analyses that obtained good support for the hypothesis in question on the basis of total data analysis (Hall 1978, Rosenthal & Rubin 1978, Eagly & Carli 1981).

A variant of the box-score method is available when two groups are being compared, as men vs women, blacks vs whites, external vs internal locus-of-control, etc. Here a tally can be made of the direction of the effect. Taylor & Hall (1982), for example, in assessing the associations between masculinity and femininity scales and measures of psychological health, tallied how many studies showed positive versus negative correlations between the masculinity (and femininity) scales and such measures. Of course, there will be some studies for which the report of the data is too meager to permit determining the direction of the difference.

Additional information can be obtained from a study by using not just the achievement of a certain level of significance or the direction of a difference, but the actual probability (p) of the chance occurrence of the null hypothesis.

The p-values can be analyzed in many ways. They can be tallied for comparison with expectations based on the null hypothesis (as in Eagly & Carli 1981), or they can be combined in some other fashion (Rosenthal & Rubin 1979). A relatively simple and effective way of combining ps is to transform them to the equivalent zs through the normal distribution. That is, z is the point on the normal curve above which p percent of the distribution will be found. When the zs are added and the sum divided by the square root of the number of zs, the result is approximately a z value, which can be referred to a standard normal distribution (Mosteller & Bush 1954). Rosenthal (1978) discusses this and several other methods that have been proposed for combining probabilities.

Counts and probabilities are mainly useful in establishing the statistical significance of a particular effect across studies; they say nothing about the size of the effect. Most quantitative reviews use some index of the size of the effects, which not only helps to establish the statistical significance of the results, but also describes their magnitude. Generally, size of effect is measured by d, a statistic popularized by Cohen (1977) as a way of determining the statistical power of a two-group comparison. Cohen's d, as it is known, is simply the mean difference between the two groups, divided by the pooled within-group standard deviation. When one group is clearly a control group and when within-group variances may differ, some authors divide the mean difference by the standard deviation of the control group (e.g. Smith et al 1980). When the group standard deviations differ, and neither group is obviously the control group, then one group can be designated arbitrarily. The choice may depend on the circumstances of the review.

Other measures are available, such as point-biserial correlation and Hays's omega-squared (Hays 1977), but the simple interpretation of d is attractive: d is the standardized mean difference between two groups (conditions, etc); that is, it is the mean difference in standard deviation units. The index d is called delta by Glass et al (1981), and psychophysicists will immediately recognize it as the d' so prominent in signal detection theory (Green & Swets 1966).

The index d is often interpreted in terms of overlap of distributions of the two groups being compared. If these distributions are normal with a common variance, then the amount of overlap is a function only of d. When $d = 1.0$, the median value in the distribution with the greater mean exceeds 84% of the values in the other distribution, or if a symmetric statement is wanted, 69% of the values in the distribution with the higher mean exceed 69% of the values in the other distribution (Cohen 1977).

If d is viewed as a sample estimate of a population standardized difference, Hedges (1981) has shown that the estimate is biased, being slightly too large. Hedges (1982) presents a simple correction factor. For purely descriptive work, the factor is too near unity to make much difference, being above .96 for n's above 10.

When an analysis of variance has been done, the size of an effect can be measured by its relative variance component—i.e. the variance component of the effect divided by the error variance component. Glass et al (1981) advocates reconstructing error variances by pooling terms "beneath" the effect of interest. Although this seems wise in repeated measure designs, we question pooling error variances as a general rule because identifiable variance is being treated as error. The matter needs more study.

When the outcome measure is dichotomous, such as the proportion of students who have drivers' licenses, the proportion scale itself is not a suitable metric. Glass et al (1981) propose using a probit transform; the proportions are transformed to z-scores through the assumption of an underlying normal distribution. Cohen (1977) offers a variety of effect size estimates for different situations, for example differences between proportions, between a proportion and .50, and between correlation coefficients.

Outcomes of correlational studies are usually reported as correlations, which can be used directly. Since the size of the correlation depends on the heterogeneity of the cases, correlation is not an ideal index, but alternatives are not readily available. In validity studies, for example, the group has usually been selected from a more heterogeneous group of applicants. Corrections for selection are helpful, but are often not easy to apply. Thorough discussions of the treatment of correlations in the context of validity studies can be found in Schmidt & Hunter (1977) and Pearlman et al (1980); an example is given by Linn et al (1981), who examined the validity of the Law School Admission Test.

Selection will affect d measures as well, but the direction of the effect will depend on the nature of the selection and the within-group regressions of the criterial variable on the selection variable. For example, the standardized mean weight difference between men and women is probably smaller for police officers than for the entire adult population. Methods are needed for adjusting such differences.

Measures of effect size, although relatively natural in social psychology and personality research, are more problematic in cognitive psychology and biopsychology. In these areas, the effect size can often be manipulated dramatically by experimental design. The size of the effect of list length on learning time depends on which list lengths are used in the experiment. The effect is essentially linear, and will seem larger if the list lengths are 8 and 16 than if they are 4 and 8. Some other measure of effect may be more revealing in such situations; rate of learning is the important parameter in list learning. Of course, that may not have been the parameter of interest to the author of the original study, so the values may be as difficult to determine as d is in other studies.

The point is to find a way of comparing studies that will be meaningful and revealing. Level of significance is almost never very revealing. Effect size is widely applicable and often meaningful. When effect size seems clearly dependent on the choice of levels of the independent variable, then some other measure should be sought. Alternatively, one could use d but include the strength of the experimental manipulation as an independent variable in the quantitative analysis.

When outcome measures are clearly identifiable and comparable across studies, these values can be used directly rather than resorting to an index like d. Thus, a review of studies of intelligence can use the Stanford-Binet IQ as the standard; other IQ measures can be transformed to that scale. Studies of SAT score decline (College Board 1977) or SAT coaching (Messick & Jungeblut 1981) have used the SAT scale directly. Because the SAT is well equated, this metric is meaningful. However, if several different tests were involved, with no common metric and no way of equating scores, the d-metric would be preferable.

Independent Variables

The most frequent criticism of quantitative reviews is that findings cannot be combined uncritically. Eysenck (1978), who characterized meta-analysis as an exercise in mega-silliness, and many other critics, point out that the quality of the study, the type of analysis done, the nature of the sample, even the age of the study, must all be weighed. This is no criticism at all, but rather a prescription for analyses to be made of study outcomes. All of these character- istics can be treated as independent variables, which can be coded for each study and their effects determined by statistical analysis rather than by subjec- tive impression. Certainly the quantitative review should do more than estab- lish the overall existence and size of an effect, as mentioned earlier. If there are enough studies, many aspects of the studies can be examined.

The quality of the study is always a major concern. One aspect of quality is the study's source—e.g. a refereed journal, an unrefereed journal, an edited book, a dissertation. Conceivably the discipline of the journal might be worth checking since disciplines may be differentially critical of certain methods or hypotheses. Many quantitative reviewers have coded source as an independent variable (e.g. Smith 1980, Smith et al 1980, Johnson et al 1981, White 1982). Glass et al (1981) summarize, quantitatively of course, a set of quantitative reviews in which study outcomes were calculated separately for different sources.

Another possible aspect of quality is the research design. The number of cases may be an issue. A within-subjects design will be more sensitive than a between-subjects design. Procedures for controlling other relevant factors may be critical. Some studies will hold particular factors constant, others will measure the factor and use it as a covariate, others will ignore the factor and trust to randomization. Quantitative reviewers have coded such design quality variables as degree of experimenter blindness, degree of randomization, sample size, and controls for cheating and recording errors (e.g. Hall 1978, Rosenthal & Rubin 1978, Smith et al 1980). There may be so many aspects to the research design that the best way to analyze design quality is to make a subjective overall rating, as in Smith (1980). Glass et al (1981) summarize a number of quantitative reviews that assessed the impact of internal validity on study outcomes.

The effect size may vary with a number of methodological variables. Correlations will be low if the range of the variables is restricted or if the variables are less reliable. The unit of analysis is likely to matter; a relation may seem smaller if students are the units of analysis than if the units are class-rooms, schools, or school districts, as in White (1982). The effect may get larger as better methods of measurement are devised, or it may decrease as better controls are instituted on other variables. Early ESP experiments found dramatic effects that shrank and finally disappeared as more and better controls were used in the experiments (Boring 1962). Glass et al (1981) summarize a set of quantitative reviews in which date of publication was related to effect size.

Characteristics of the sample may also be related to effect size. Ethnicity, age, sex, socioeconomic status, and educational level may all affect some outcome measures. The type of dependent variables may also be relevant. A validity study is likely to get different results if the criterion measure is self-reported GPA rather than actual GPA; retrospective self-reports are especially tenuous.

Characteristics of the author may be relevant. The ubiquitous expectancy effect (Rosenthal & Rubin 1978) cannot be ignored. Thus, the sex of the author may be related to the size and direction of sex effects, as described earlier. The location of the laboratory may make a difference. Subjects in memory experiments in the midwest are rumored to remember more than subjects on the east and west coasts. Of course, something else is at work here, and the reviewer should look further, but the effect should not be ignored.

Finally, independent variables of major theoretical importance may be developed for particular literatures. Eagly & Carli (1981), in reviewing sex differences in influenceability, tested an often-stated hypothesis about the origins of such sex differences: that the topics used are sex-typed in the masculine direction, leading to a predictable but perhaps not generalizable tendency for women to be more influenceable due to their relative ignorance of the subject matter. Eagly and Carli determined the sex-typing of topics by having men and women rate each of the 83 topics that had been used in earlier work. The relationships between the mean ratings and the outcomes of the studies revealed that the more masculine topics did tend to be associated with greater female persuasibility, but there was in fact no preponderance of masculine topics among the studies as a whole. So the sex differences cannot be attributed to an oversupply of masculine topics.

Given one or more dependent measures, and whatever independent variables seem relevant, the statistical analysis is generally straightforward. Descriptive summaries are required, such as average ds, ps, or rs, or proportions of positive findings. The data will frequently permit t-tests, chi-square tests, and other simple statistics. Correlation and regression, even covariance analysis may be useful. In general, the usual panoply of statistical techniques is available for analyses in which the study is the unit of analysis. Rosenthal & Rubin (1982) have proposed some new methods for comparing effect sizes.

Hunter et al (1982) warn strongly of the danger of overanalyzing the data. They advocate comparing the overall variance of effect sizes—ds, rs, or whatever—with the variability to be expected by sampling considerations. Analysis is warranted, in their opinion, only when the observed variance is larger than the expected sampling variance. We believe that this strict view is overly restrictive, and see no reason not to look for correlates of effect sizes. However, caution is certainly needed when many potential sources of variance are being examined. With enough chances, something is sure to turn up.

PROBLEMS WITH THE TARGET LITERATURE

Finding It

Finding the literature, though a mundane and often tedious effort, is of utmost importance for the quantitative review. Though some quantitative analyses are deliberately limited to the same set of studies previously analyzed by traditional methods, in order to compare conclusions (e.g. Hyde 1981), most quantitative reviewers would ideally want to find every study that fits their definition of the research area to be analyzed. Estimates of effect size and even of overall direction can be off if a biased portion of the literature is retrieved. Further, statistical analysis are made more convincing if based on the largest possible Ns.

No single method of locating literature is perfect. Most quantitative reviewers probably use a combination of methods. The major methods that have been used, in order of increasing adequacy, are existing bibliographies, computer searches and abstracting services, and source-by-source search, that is, identifying all or most of the appropriate sources, such as particular journals, and examining their contents exhaustively. Few investigators have the patience for this last procedure, yet it is guaranteed to retrieve the highest proportion of nonsignificant and incidental results in published studies.

Publication Bias

Psychologists have long been concerned about Type I error publication bias. Some quantitative reviewers make a special effort to include unpublished sources as a control for this possibility. Lane & Dunlap (1978) have argued that average ds from published studies are likely to be overestimates, since studies with small ds did not pass editorial scrutiny. Glass et al (1981) provide empirical support for this argument in their summary of quantitative reviews that compared published to unpublished sources.

To address the problem of the "file-drawer"—unpublished and unretrievable null results stored away by unknown investigators—quantitative reviewers often use a simple calculation developed by Rosenthal (1979). This formula enables one to calculate how many such null results would have to exist in order for the combined probability of the entire set, retrieved and unretrieved together, to exceed .05 or any other desired level. Application of this formula reveals that if the available data are reasonably consistent in direction and are fairly numerous, the number of null results stuffed into "file drawers" is implausibly large. Rosenthal & Rubin (1978), for example, estimated that it would take 65,000 null results to cancel out the overall statistical significance of their data set of 345 studies of expectancy effects. If one's data set is small and/or not very consistent, however, relatively few null results would be needed to cancel out a significant overall p. In these cases a reviewer is wise to be concerned about publication bias.

Inadequate Reporting

A quantitative reviewer often finds that the data are reported inadequately. Although this is especially true when results are incidental to the main goal of a research report, it is often a problem even for major results. Reviewers would be greatly helped if authors reported effect sizes, standard deviations along with means, actual test statistics rather than vague phrases such as "no difference," standard normal deviates or exact ps (e.g. .032 rather than $<.05$), mean squares within cells, or all of these. Inadequate reporting is partly the fault of journal editorial policies that encourage brevity, but author and editor alike should realize that quantitative information is extremely important to future reviewers.

COMPARISONS

Since 1978 many quantitative literature reviews have been published. They differ from traditional reviews in their methods, of course, but in other ways too. They tend to include many more studies than traditional reviews. The traditional reviewer may reject more studies for poor or marginal quality, and tends to review only published articles.

The validity of quantitative reviews can best be evaluated by comparison with other reviews. Smith et al (1980) reported that on average, psychotherapy was beneficial, with a d of about .6 in comparison with untreated controls, but they found very little evidence indicating that one method of psychotherapy was better than another. This finding drew the expected criticisms, mainly for including too many questionable studies. Shapiro & Shapiro (1982) replicated the quantitative review in spirit, but with more stringent criteria for inclusion and with attention focused on behavioral therapies. Because many new studies had been published, only about 15% of their studies were included in the earlier work of Smith et al. Shapiro and Shapiro concluded, as did Smith et al, that psychotherapy is beneficial. They found some weak indications that behavioral therapies worked better than more subjective procedures, but the differential effect was small.

An interesting series of studies followed Maccoby & Jacklin's (1974) monumental survey of sex differences. One important aspect of sex differences is the frequently proposed hypothesis that women are more easily influenced than men. Maccoby and Jacklin, and later Eagly (1978), in traditional reviews, found very little evidence, over a wide range of situations, that men and women differed in influenceability; too small a proportion of the available studies yielded significant differences. Cooper's (1979) quantitative review of the same studies used by Maccoby and Jacklin did find significant differences in some types of experiments. Eagly & Carli (1981) suspected that Cooper's equivocal results were due partly to inadequate retrieval of experiments. Using Eagly's (1978) collection of studies, which was much larger than the set found by Maccoby and Jacklin, they found that men were less influenceable than women in persuasion studies, group conformity studies, and other types of conformity studies as well. The effect sizes were uniformly modest, but definitely non-zero.

Cook & Leviton (1980) compared traditional and quantitative reviewing methods, with particular reference to studies of self-serving attribution of success or failure. Arkin et al (1980) had used a quantitative analysis to argue that people tend to attribute success to their own actions and failure to the situation or to the action of others. Zuckerman (1979), in a traditional review, had argued that this happens only when people are motivated to maintain self-esteem. The argument turned out to rest largely on the sample of studies used. The quantitative review used more, and according to Cook and Leviton, a traditional review of the larger set would have led to the same conclusions as the quantitative review.

Cook and Leviton concluded that quantitative reviews, like any statistical analysis, can be very useful when used wisely. They pointed out that quantitative reviewing is dangerous mainly when the available studies are few in number and are so heterogeneous that they cannot reasonably be taken as a sample of anything. They also noted that when a faulty method becomes the common procedure in some field of study, then aggregating many faulty studies can be dangerous in seeming to certify a flawed result by consensus.

Finally, Cooper & Rosenthal (1980) performed an experiment in which graduate students and professors were assigned randomly to "traditional" and "quantitative" review conditions and given the same set of seven studies to review. In the quantitative condition, subjects were given instructions on combining ps. Stronger conclusions were reached by subjects in the quantitative condition, favoring the hypothesis that was, in fact, supported in the studies. Subjects in the traditional condition drew conservative conclusions, with more than half of them saying "probably no" when asked whether the literature supported an overall effect.

It appears, then, that the quantitative reviewer is likely to reach stronger conclusions not only because more studies are typically analyzed, but also because the statistical procedures used bring real effects into sharper focus. A string of weak or apparently conflicting results, whether in terms of d or p, could easily be discounted by a traditional reviewer but would add up to a credible pattern for the quantitative reviewer.

DANGERS IN THE QUANTITATIVE REVIEW

Although potential problems and criticisms of quantitative reviewing have been mentioned throughout this chapter, some of which pertain to traditional as well as quantitative reviews, here we focus on several that seem unique to the quantitative review.

Though any reviewer can err in stating a study's results, the quantitative reviewer has many more opportunities to be wrong. Because so few research reports give effect sizes, standard normal deviates, or exact p-values, the quantitative reviewer must calculate almost all indices of study outcome, as well as code study attributes, which can be very numerous. Little of this calculation is automatic because results are presented in a bewildering variety of forms and are often obscure. Effect sizes can sometimes be recovered. The value of d can be recovered from a between-groups t if the ns are known, but not from a t on paired observations. Although quantitative reviewers differ in how much recalculation they are willing to do, some do extensive reanalysis (recalculating an analysis of variance, for example). Errors, or at least differences in judgment, are inevitable. Some quantitative reviews report reliability checks on coding of study attributes and outcomes. Shapiro & Shapiro (1982) reported that "at least 80% agreement" was obtained between two coders on the variables coded in their psychotherapy review. Strock et al (1982) found that coder reliability was generally above r = .90, but was poorer in some categories. Though acceptable by usual standards, such lack of perfect agreement demonstrates our point.

Next, quantitative reviewers probably focus on main effects in coding results of studies. In principle, interaction results can also be coded and entered into quantitative analysis, but in practice they may be left out because too few studies have interactions involving the same or comparable factors. To illustrate, in Hall's (1978) review of sex differences in nonverbal decoding skill, the handful of studies that tested the sex of expressor X sex of decoding subject interaction was left out of the quantitative review. However, by coding sex of expressor as a between-studies variable (possible because some studies had only male expressors and some only female), Hall did test for this interaction on an aggregate basis. It is fortunate in this example that the between-studies interaction result (that is, correlation between sex of expressors and study outcomes) could be corroborated by comparison with the analogous within-studies results. Unfortunately, most within-studies interaction effects will not find an analog in between-studies comparisons and therefore may be lost to scrutiny. If quantitative reviewers are not alert to this problem, theoretical progress may be retarded. The charge that a quantitative reviewer oversimplified a research domain by coding chiefly main effects has in fact been made (Cotton & Cook 1982).

To ignore within-study interactions is a different matter from deemphasizing between-study interactions in favor of the main effects obtained in the quantitative review, for example the mean d over all studies (Eysenck 1978, Cotton & Cook 1982, McGlynn 1982). To underplay between-studies interactions seems to us to be less serious than ignoring within-studies interactions, as long as the between-studies interactions are reported somewhere in the quantitative review. It is definitely an error for a reviewer to oversimplify in his or her final summary, but at least the evidence for moderating factors is available to readers. Ignoring within-studies interactions is more dangerous because the reader does not even know they exist.

Another danger, akin to ignoring within-study interactions, is that of ignoring entire studies because they do not fit neatly into the conceptual and methodological framework established by the quantitative reviewer. Faced with unusual methods or ways of defining variables or subject populations, the quantitative reviewer may set some studies aside, producing a paradoxical situation in which the most conventional, often merely replicative, studies are summarized but more innovative and possibly more important studies are forgotten. The solution to this is for reviewers to develop coding categories capable of accommodating the largest possible proportion of the literature and to remember to deal nonstatistically with any remaining studies that seem worthy of discussion.

Finally, quantitative reviewers are often faced with a data set with considerable nonindependence. White (1982), for example, analyzed 636 correlations between SES and achievement, but these came from only 101 independent studies. Quantitative reviewers seem split on whether they ensure independence by entering only one result per sample in each analysis or whether they include all that are available (for example, results for several similar dependent variables measured on the same group of subjects). When nonindependence is frequent, significance testing and estimation both become problematic (see Glass et al 1981).

These, then, are legitimate problems faced by the quantitative reviewer. Other criticisms have been made which have been more than adequately answered elsewhere, either in explicit rebuttals or simply in the practice of quantitative reviewers. The two most common such criticisms are summarized here.

Many have claimed that quantitative reviewers compare "apples and oranges"—that is, they lump together studies that differ in major ways such as the definition of independent variables. In defense, Glass et al (1981) argue that such comparision is what quantitative reviewers do and *should* do, but they code apples as apples and oranges as oranges; they do not just throw all the fruit in the basket.

Quantitative reviewers have also been criticized for ignoring study quality and giving as much weight to the worst research as they give to the best. But by coding quality and source, as described earlier, quantitative reviewers are able to see if quality and source actually make a difference. In this way knowledge clearly advances and at the same time the potentially biasing effect of excluding "poor" studies is avoided. Such exclusions are potentially biasing because judgments of study quality may be somewhat subjective, and since a reviewer would rarely be blind to the results of a study when deciding whether to exclude it, he or she may exclude studies more because the results are not pleasing than because the methodology is in fact flawed to the point where the results are not credible.

SUMMARY

The many problems encountered by quantitative reviewers indicate that new methods and imaginative solutions will be needed, but the advantages of the technique are manifest. The opportunity to discover between-study interactions has already been noted. In general, the quantitative review offers the possibility for more objective amalgamation of results and weighing of disparate outcomes. Perhaps the main advantage is that the reviewer takes an active approach to the literature—asking how the literature shall be organized and put together, and looking for ways in which different studies can reinforce each other, or counteract each other, if consensus is not evident.

There is, of course, no single best way of doing anything as complex as a literature review. In some areas, where results are few and very selective, the traditional review will often be best. But in many areas statistical analysis can help, and in some areas it seems definitely necessary.

The main job of the quantitative reviewer is to establish the consensus. An equally useful outcome is to identify the outliers. In an ordinary statistical analysis an outlier may not be very interesting, and may be dismissed as an uncooperative subject. But in a quantitative review, an unusual study cannot be dismissed so lightly. All such results deserve special attention. Perhaps the reasons for the aberrant results are not clear, but they deserve thorough examination.

Statistical methods, to be useful, must be used thoughtfully. Data analysis is an aid to thought, not a substitute. No mechanistic formula will work. But careful quantitative reviews are likely to play a larger role in further advances in psychology.

Literature Cited

Arkin, R., Cooper, H., Kolditz, T. 1980. A statistical review of the literature concerning the self-serving attribution bias in interpersonal influence situations. *J. Pers.* 48:435–48

Boring, E. G. 1962. Parascience. *Contemp. Psychol.* 7:356–57

Cohen, J. 1977. *Statistical Power Analysis for the Behavioral Sciences.* New York: Academic. Rev. ed.

College Entrance Examination Board. 1977. *On Further Examination.* New York: Coll. Entrance Exam. Bd.

Cook, T. D., Leviton, L. C. 1980. Reviewing the literature: a comparison of traditional methods with meta-analysis. *J. Pers.* 48:449–72

Cooper, H. M. 1979. Statistically combining independent studies: meta-analysis of sex differences in conformity research. *J. Pers. Soc. Psychol.* 37:131–46

Cooper, H. M., Rosenthal, R. 1980. Statistical versus traditional procedures for summarizing research findings. *Psychol. Bull.* 87:442–49

Cotton, J. L., Cook, M. S. 1982. Meta-analysis and the effects of various rewards systems: some different conclusions from Johnson et al. *Psychol. Bull.* 92:176–83

Eagly, A. H. 1978. Sex differences in influenceability. *Psychol. Bull.* 85:86–116

Eagly, A. H., Carli, L. L. 1981. Sex of researchers and sex-typical communications as determinants of sex differences in influenceability: a meta-analysis of social influence studies. *Psychol. Bull.* 90:1–20

Eysenck, H. 1978. An exercise in megasilliness. *Am. Psychol.* 33:517

Glass, G. V. 1976. Primary, secondary, and meta-analysis of research. *Educ. Res.* 5:3–8

Glass, G. V., McGaw, B., Smith, M. L. 1981. *Meta-analysis in Social Research.* Beverly Hills, Calif: Sage

Green, D. M., Swets, J. A. 1966. *Signal Detection Theory and Psychophysics.* New York: Wiley

Hall, J. A. 1978. Gender effects in decoding nonverbal cues. *Psychol. Bull.* 85:845–57

Hays, W. 1977. *Statistics for Psychologists.* New York: Holt, Rinehart & Winston

Hedges, L. V. 1981. Distribution theory for Glass's estimation of effect size and related estimators. *J. Educ. Stat.* 6:107–28

Hedges, L. V. 1982. Estimation of effect size from a series of independent experiments. *Psychol. Bull.* 92:490–99

Hedges, L. V., Olkin, I. 1980. Vote-counting methods in research synthesis. *Psychol. Bull.* 88:359–69

Hunter, J. E., Schmidt, F. L., Jackson, G. B. 1982. *Meta-Analysis: Cumulating Findings Across Studies.* Beverly Hills, Calif: Sage

Hyde, J. S. 1981. How large are cognitive gender differences? A meta-analysis using w-squared and d. *Am. Psychol.* 36:892–901

Johnson, D. W., Maruyama, G., Johnson, R., Nelson, D., Skow, L. 1981. Effects of cooperative, competitive, and individualistic goal structures on achievement: a meta-analysis. *Psychol. Bull.* 87:47–62

Kraemer, H. C., Andrews, G. 1982. A nonparametric technique for meta-analysis effect size calculation. *Psychol. Bull.* 91:401–12

Lane, D. M., Dunlap, W. P. 1978. Estimating effect size: Bias resulting from the significance criterion in editorial decisions. *Br. J. Math. Stat. Psychol.* 31:107–12

Light, R. J., Smith, P. V. 1971. Accumulating evidence: procedures for resolving contradictions among different research studies. *Harvard Educ. Rev.* 41:429–71

Linn, R. L., Harrisch, D. L., Dunbar, S. B. 1981. Validity generalization and situation specificity: An analysis of the prediction of first-year grades in law school. *Appl. Psychol. Meas.* 5:281–89

Maccoby, E. E., Jacklin, C. N. 1974. *The Psychology of Sex Differences.* Stanford, Calif.: Stanford Univ. Press

McGlynn, R. P. 1982. A comment on the meta-analysis of goal structures. *Psychol. Bull.* 92:184–85

Messick, S., Jungeblut, A. 1981. Time and method in coaching the SAT. *Psychol. Bull.* 89:191–216

Mosteller, F. M., Bush, R. R. 1954. Selected quantitative techniques. In *Handbook of Social Psychology*, Vol. I, ed. G. Lindzey. Cambridge, Mass.: Addison–Wesley

Pearlman, K., Schmidt, F. L., Hunter, J. E. 1980. Validity generalization results for tests used to predict job proficiency and training success in clerical occupations. *J. Appl. Psychol.* 65:373–406

Rosenthal, R. 1978. Combining results of independent studies. *Psychol. Bull.* 85:185–93

Rosenthal, R. 1979. The "file drawer problem" and tolerance for null results. *Psychol. Bull.* 86:638–14

Rosenthal, R., ed. 1980. Quantitative assessment of research domains. *New Directions for Methodology of Social and Behavioral Science*, No. 5. San Francisco: Jossey-Bass

Rosenthal, R. 1983. Assessing the statistical and social importance of the effects of psychotherapy. *J. Consult. Clin. Psychol.* 51:4–13

Rosenthal, R., Rubin, D. B. 1978. Interpersonal expectancy effects: the first 345 studies. *Brain Behav. Sci.* 3:377–86

Rosenthal, R., Rubin, D. B. 1979. Comparing significance levels of independent studies. *Psychol. Bull.* 86:1165–68

Rosenthal, R., Rubin, D. B. 1982. Comparing effect sizes of independent studies. *Psychol. Bull.* 92:500–4

Rubin, D. B. 1980. Using empirical Bayes techniques in the law school validity studies. *J. Am. Stat. Assoc.* 75:801–16

Schmidt, F. L., Hunter, J. E. 1977. Development of a general solution to the problem of validity generalization. *J. Appl. Psychol.* 62:529–40

Shapiro, D. A., Shapiro, D. 1982. Meta-analysis of comparative therapy outcomes studies: a replication and refinement. *Psychol. Bull.* 92:581–604

Smith, M. L. 1980. Sex bias in counseling and psychotherapy. *Psychol. Bull.* 87:392–407

Smith, M. L., Glass, G. V., Miller, T. I. 1980. *The Benefits of Psychotherapy.* Baltimore: Johns Hopkins Univ. Press

Strock, W. A., Okun, M. A., Haring, M. J., Miller, W., Kinney, C. 1982. Rigor in data synthesis: a case study of reliability in meta-analysis. *Educ. Res.* 11 (6):10–14

Strube, M. J., Hartmann, D. P. 1982. A critical appraisal of meta-analysis. *Br. J. Clin. Psychol.* 21:129–39

Taylor, M. C., Hall, J. A. 1982. Psychological androgyny: theories, methods and conclusions. *Psychol. Bull.* 92:347–66

Walberg, H. J., Haertel, E. H., eds. 1980. Research integration: the state of the art. Special issue of *Evaluation in Education: An International Review Service*, 4:1–135

White, K. R. 1982. The relation between socioeconomic status and academic achievement. *Psychol. Bull.* 91:461–81

Wortman, P. M. 1983. Evaluation research: A methodological perspective. *Ann. Rev. Psychol.* 34:223–60

Zuckerman, M. 1979. Attribution of success and failure revisited, or: the motivational bias is alive and well in attribution theory. *J. Pers.* 47:245–87

Ann. Rev. Psychol. 1984. 35:55–81

SCALING

Forrest W. Young

Psychometrics Laboratory, University of North Carolina, Chapel Hill, North Carolina 27514

CONTENTS

INTRODUCTION

The purpose of scaling is to quantify qualitative data. Scaling procedures attempt to do this by using rules that assign numbers to qualities of things or events. A quality of a thing or event is an attribute (characteristic) of the thing or event observed in circumstances assumed by the observer to be qualitative. Scaling replaces qualitative observations about the attribute of the thing or event with numeric measures of the attribute of the thing or event.

    This is my definition of scaling: Scaling is the process that uses rules to assign numbers to attributes of things or events observed in circumstances

55

0066-4308/84/0201-0055$02.00

assumed by the observer to be qualitative. Scaling produces measurements, and these measurements are called scale values.

My definition of measuring is only very slightly different: Measuring is the process that uses rules to assign numbers to attributes of things or events observed in circumstances assumed by the observer to be quantitative. Measuring produces measurements.

Note that scaling and measuring both produce measurements by applying rules to assign numbers to observed attributes of things or events. The difference is that scaling derives measurements from qualities, whereas measuring derives measurements from quantities. How do we know if the observation circumstances are quantitative or qualitative? We don't know. Rather, we must assume one or the other. In fact, the distinction does not reside in the observation circumstances, but is in the mind of the observer.

My review concentrates on developments which fall within the definition of scaling just given. Specifically, the review focuses on rule-based processes to attach numbers to data which are at least in part qualitative. Contributions are reviewed which involve: (*a*) models (rules) used in scaling; (*b*) algorithms (rule-based processes) for applying models to qualitative data; and (*c*) applications of scaling to empirical situations. No attempt has been made to provide complete coverage. Rather, I have covered what I believe to be the most important developments in scaling during the review period. However, because of the vast application of some developments, applications have been slighted in this review.

My review specifically omits certain models and algorithms: factor analysis and regression analysis are covered only when the developments apply to qualitative data. Latent trait theory, test theory, and cluster analysis are completely excluded from the review, even though these developments often apply to qualitative data. These topics are periodically reviewed elsewhere.

DATA THEORY

Scaling techniques may be structured into two very broad categories according to the kind of data being scaled: The data may be *multivariate* data or *dissimilarity* data. Multivariate data have observations that are (qualitative or quantitative) values on one or more variables (thus including univariate data as well). Dissimilarity data have observations that are (qualitative or quantitative) dissimilarities (or similarities) between pairs of things.

This structure may also be seen according to the model being used to scale the data: scaling techniques for quantifying multivariate data use *linear* models (including bilinear and multilinear). Principal components and multiple regression are examples. Scaling techniques for quantifying qualitative dissimilarity data use *distance* models. Multidimensional scaling and unfolding are examples.

The two-level structure just given forms the broad outline of this review. The next section of the review is on scaling dissimilarity data via distance models, and then comes a section on scaling multivariate data via linear models. The remainder of the present section of the review briefly introduces and defines some data theory terms used in the rest of the review. The terms are from a data theory that I first discussed in a manuscript circulated in the scaling community in 1975, which will appear in Young & Hamer (1984). Condensations of this data theory have appeared in Young & Lewyckyj (1979), Young et al (1980), Young (1981), Schiffman et al (1981), and Young (1983a). The theory rests on the following basic assumptions:

1. *Data are always categorical:* Data are obtained by a classification process that assures we can decide whether two observations are empirically equivalent. Equivalent observations form an observation category. This assumption underlies the measurement aspects of the data theory.
2. *Data are always designed:* Data are always obtained in an empirical situation that has an objective design. This assumption underlies the empirical aspects of the data theory.
3. *Data are always modeled:* Data are always obtained in the context of a specific model of the empirical situation. This assumption underlies the model aspects of the data theory.

Measurement Aspects

The categorical assumption that underlies data theory provides a very nice organizing principle for three important measurement concepts: measurement process, which concerns the relationships among all of the observations within a single data category; measurement level, which concerns the relationships among all of the observations between different data categories; and measurement conditionality, which concerns the relationships within sets of observation categories.

There are two types of measurement processes: discrete and continuous. The discrete process implies that we believe that all of the observations in a category should be represented by a single number after they have been scaled. Alternatively, the continuous process implies that we believe that all observations in a category should be represented by a bounded interval of real numbers after they have been scaled. Notice that the measurement process assumption concerns what happens within a single observation category.

The familiar measurement level notions correspond to assumptions about what happens between observation categories. Levels of measurement differ from each other in the ways that restrictions are imposed on the numbers that can be assigned to different observation categories. There are a variety of restraints which could be discussed, but only three are needed to satisfy the characteristics of the four familiar measurement levels.[1]

For the nominal level, there are no measurement level restraints. The characteristics of this level are completely specified by the within-category restrictions implied by the chosen measurement process. For the ordinal level we require, in addition to the process restraints, that the real numbers assigned to observations in different categories reflect the order of the empirical observations. For the numeric (quantitative) levels of measurement (which include interval and ratio, among others) we require, in addition to the process constraints, that the real numbers assigned to observations in different categories be related to each other by some form of numeric function.

The final type of restraints placed on the numers used to scale the observation categories concerns relationships among sets of categories. It may be, for a particular set of data, that one measurement level and process apply to all of the data. Such data are called unconditional. On the other hand, it may be that different levels and processes apply to different portions of the data. These data are called conditional.

Empirical Aspects

One important aspect of the data theory is the shape of the data: data may be either square or rectangular. Square data are in matrices whose rows and columns refer to the same set of things. Usually (perhaps always), square data are "relational" data: data which indicate the degree of relation between the rows and columns of the matrix. Such data include distances, dissimilarities, similarities, etc. Square data can be symmetric or asymmetric. Rectangular data are in matrices whose rows and columns refer to two different sets of things. Thus, the matrix is rectangular in shape. These data are usually called "multivariate" data because the (multiple) columns often refer to variables.

The shape of a set of data can be reexpressed in terms of the number of ways and the number of modes of a set of data. The number of ways of any data matrix is always two (its rows and columns). The shape of the matrix actually refers to whether the two ways are distinct. The number of distinct ways is the number of modes. Thus, a square matrix is one-mode and a rectangular matrix is two-mode. Whereas a *data matrix* is always two-way, *data* may be more than two-way. Multi-way data are organized into several matrices and may be called three-way data, four-way data, etc.

---

[1]To be faithful to my distinction between scaling and measuring (made in the opening paragraphs) I should refer to nominal and ordinal as levels of "scaling," and interval and ratio as levels of "measuring." However, the phrase "levels of measurement," which is always used to refer to all four levels, is in such common use that I will use it instead of the other more precise terms.

My classification of recent developments in scaling involves the distinction between multivariate data and dissimilarity data. Multivariate data are rectangular data which consist of repeatedly observed values on many variables. The two ways of the data are the repeated observations (oftentimes people) and the variables. Dissimilarity data are usually square, but may also be rectangular. When square, the two ways are usually some type of stimuli. When rectangular, the two ways are usually people and variables (as with multivariate data). Usually, multivariate or rectangular dissimilarity data are two-way and row or column conditional, whereas square dissimilarity data are usually three-way and matrix-conditional.

The fundamental difference between multivariate and dissimilarity data is in the nature of the individual datum. For multivariate data the basic datum is the amount of each variable for each observation. For dissimilarity data the basic datum is the distance (or proximity) between the row-thing and the column-thing. [I use "dissimilarity" generically to include proximity (similarity) data as well as distance (or difference) data.]

Model Aspects

It may seem a bit strange to include the nature of models as one of the three major organizing principles of a data theory. After all, doesn't data theory concern data and not models? Actually, the answer is no; data theory concerns both the data and the model of the data. In particular, it is my view that data in themselves do not possess measurement characteristics. Rather, the measurement characteristics which appear to be possessed by a particular set of data are actually dependent on the interaction of that data with the model chosen to describe the data.

When a set of data are analyzed by some model, the analysis necessarily assumes that the data have certain specific measurement characteristics. As suggested by Takane et al (1977), empirical information about the most appropriate measurement assumptions can be obtained by repeatedly analyzing the data several times, each time changing only the measurement assumptions. But as they point out, the measurement assumptions which appear to be most appropriate necessarily appear this way in a context created by the data analysis model. When a different model is used it can appear that different measurement assumptions are most appropriate. The apparent measurement characteristics of a set of data interact with the chosen data analysis model.

Although many different models are used in data analysis, I confine my review to three broad model classes: the linear, bilinear, and distance models. I confine my review to these three model classes because they are the ones which have been used in most recent developments in scaling. The next two sections cover these three model classes.

SCALING DISSIMILARITY DATA
VIA DISTANCE MODELS

This section reviews recent developments in multidimensional scaling and unfolding: scaling methods which use distance to model dissimilarity data. The distinction between multidimensional scaling (MDS) and multidimensional unfolding (MDU) is in the data analyzed. MDS is always based on square dissimilarity data, whereas MDU is always based on rectangular dissimilarity data. However, they both share in common the use of distance models.

For example, the simplest form of MDS involves Euclidean distances between all the members of one set of points:

$$d_{ij} = \{(x_i - x_j)(x_i - x_j)'\}^{1/2},$$

where the x_i and x_j (the parameters of the model) are row vectors each having r elements that specify the location of points i and j in an r-dimensional Euclidean space. The x_i and x_j are the ith and jth rows of the stimulus coordinates matrix X, an n points by r dimensions matrix. Notice that the one set of points (X) is used to model the one mode of the square data. Similarly, the simplest type of MDU involves Euclidean distances from each member of one set of points to each member of another set:

$$d_{ij} = \{(y_i - x_j)(y_i - x_j)'\}^{1/2},$$

where x_j is the jth row of a coordinates matrix X, and y_i is the ith row of a second coordinates matrix Y. Notice that the two sets of points (X and Y) model the two modes of the rectangular data.

There are four major streams of development in MDS during the review period. These are: 1. the continued generalization of MDS models; 2. the introduction of confirmatory (constrained) MDS models and algorithms; 3. the introduction of maximum likelihood MDS models and algorithms; and 4. the improvement of least squares MDS algorithms. Each of these developments is discussed in the following sections, as is multidimensional unfolding.

Generalized Multidimensional Scaling

One research trend during the review period was a continuation of interest in generalizing the very popular weighted Euclidean model discussed by Bloxom (1968), Horan (1969), and Carroll & Chang (1970). (The model is usually known as the INDSCAL model.) Much of this work has continued the early (and unpublished) generalizations of the weights proposed by Harshman (1972) and by Carroll & Chang (1972). During the review period, no work has generalized the Euclidean aspect of the model. Also, there was no work that continued the earlier extension of MDS to Minkowski models.

The first work published during the review period was by Bloxom (1978), who proposed what he called the generalized Euclidean model (GEM):

$$d_{ijk} = \{(x_i - x_j) W_k (x_i - x_j)'\}^{1/2},$$

where the three subscripts on d_{ijk} refer to the three ways of the data, i and j for the one mode of the basic square matrix (usually stimuli) and k for the third mode (usually subjects). In Bloxom's paper, W_k is positive semidefinite, with the rank of W_k controlled by the user just as he/she controls the dimensionality of X. Bloxom proposes decomposing W_k into

$$W_k = V_k V_k',$$

where V_k and V_k are the upper and lower triangular gram factors of the weights for subject k.

The GEM was also proposed, independently, at about the same time by Young & Lewyckyj (1979) but was not published until recently (Young 1984). The name Principal Directions Scaling (PRINDSCAL) reflected our choice to decompose W_k into its principal components. Note that for either decomposition, V_k can then be applied to the group's stimulus space X to obtain an individual's space X_k by the formula

$$X_k = X V_k.$$

The space X_k is a subspace of the overall space X, and its dimensions constitute the subject's principal dimensions. When oriented in a principal components orientation, as in PRINDSCAL, each successive dimension accounts for as much variance in the subject's data as possible. The space X_k is the subject's principal subspace in the maximum variance sense.

Interesting applications of GEM appear in Bloxom (1978), Young (1984), Jones & MacCallum (1984), Forsyth (1984), Dunn & Harshman (1982), and Easterling (1984). The model is discussed by Young (1982), Ramsay (1982b), and by Lingoes & Borg (1978b). Several authors propose the model in the context of constrained MDS (see below).

Despite great interest in this model, two problems emerge: (a) all of the algorithms that have been proposed are still essentially experimental in nature, none having been fully investigated; (b) very few applications have appeared, and it may be that the model is too complex to be of much use to those who are not experts on MDS models. The ultimate usefulness of this line of development remains to be seen.

Lingoes & Borg (1978b) proposed an interesting extension of the weighted Euclidean model which they call the perspective model. The model posits that a subject has a unique perspective on the stimulus space X which translates it to a new origin and then dilates the space around the new origin. Algebraically, this is done by adding a constant vector a_k (having r elements, one for each dimension) to X and then premultiplying the translated space by a diagonal weight matrix U_k (an n by n matrix having a row and column for each stimulus). Thus the individual's perspective on the common space is defined as:

$$X_k = U_k(X - 1A_k),$$

where 1 is an n-element column vector of 1s. The Euclidean distances for the subject are calculated in the usual way.

This model can be very useful in, for example, the cognitive geography situation in which people judge the perceived distance between geographic locations. It should be useful here because it is well known that people subjectively expand geographic space around a point with which they are familiar. Unfortunately, no convincing applications are presented by Lingoes & Borg (1978b), and their algorithm is very cumbersome and does not appear to be one that will be very useful. Thus, the final reviews are not in on this development either.

Finally, two somewhat eclectic and very interesting developments should be mentioned. One of these (Holman 1978) is a "completely nonmetric" multidimensional scaling method. By this Holman means that the method is one which (a) only uses the order of the dissimilarities and (b) does not posit a specific distance metric in which to construct a stimulus space. The first characteristic is common, of course. It is the second characteristic that is eclectic. The notion that replaces a distance metric is "betweeness": stimulus j should be located between stimuli i and k on every dimension if i and k are the farthest apart of the three stimuli. Holman presents numerous convincing examples of his method.

The other somewhat eclectic development (Takane 1980a) is a novel way to scale a particular type of dissimilarity data called sorting data. These data are obtained when subjects are asked to sort a set of stimuli into as many groups as they wish, where the groups consist of "similar" stimuli, and "dissimilar" stimuli are placed in different groups. As mentioned by the author, this type of similarity data is particularly appealing in many common situations. The method is very similar to correspondence analysis, and has the advantages of (a) being nonmetric and (b) constructing a joint space having both stimulus points and group centroids for each subject. Thus, the model is an individual differences model. Takane presents two interesting examples which show that for this type of data his method is quite useful.

Constrained Multidimensional Scaling

Another major trend in the MDS literature is the introduction of constraints on the parameters of the model. As mentioned in the previous section, the simplest form of MDS occurs when we have two-way, square dissimilarities from just one subject. The analysis invokes the Euclidean model to define distances between all points in a set of points. The parameters of the model are the coordinates x_i and x_j that give the location of points i and j in the Euclidean space. The points have a configuration represented by the complete matrix of coordinates X.

As pointed out by de Leeuw & Heiser (1980) in their lucid review of the use of constraints in MDS, when the data are three-way the most straightforward generalization of the preceding analysis is to apply it to each dissimilarity matrix separately. When this is done we obtain completely independent configuration matrices X_k for each subject k. Each configuration X_k is totally unconstrained by any possible relationship to other X_ks.

A much more interesting way of analyzing such data is via constraints of the form $X_k = XW_k$ where X is now a common stimulus configuration presumed to underlie every subject's judgments, and where W_k is a diagonal matrix of weights for each subject. This is, of course, the INDSCAL model discussed above but discussed from the viewpoint of constraints on X_k. Furthermore, W_k can be generalized to other forms, introducing different constraints on the X_k.

The form $X_k = XV_k$, where V_k are the factors (of one type or another) of a positive, semidefinite, nondiagonal W_k, is one of the generalizations mentioned in the previous section. This model has been discussed from an explicitly constrained MDS viewpoint by Bloxom (1978), Young & Lewyckyj (1979), de Leeuw & Heiser (1980), Carroll et al (1980), and by Young, et al (1983). In these developments, the matrix X is assumed to be a known matrix of experimental design coefficients or other a priori information about the stimuli, and what is desired is to constrain the analysis of the dissimilarities according to the design or other information. Here V_k can be looked on as the coefficients which constrain the X_k to be linear combinations of the information in X.

Young, et al (1983) present the linear constraints $X_k = X\dot{V}_k$ as an analog of multiple regression in which X is the independent information on multiple measurements for each observation (just as in multiple regression) and the dependent information is dissimilarities between the observations instead of a single value for an observation. Two very interesting applications of this notion are found in Forsyth (1984) and in Jones & MacCallum (1984).

Bentler & Weeks (1978, Weeks & Bentler 1982) develop a different class of constraints. In their work the coordinate x_{ia} can be fixed to an a priori value $(x_{ia} = c_{ia})$, can be proportional to the value of another coordinate $(x_{ia} = c_{ia}x_{jb})$, or can be free to take on an unconstrained value. They discuss the interesting special cases of coordinates being set to zero or being proportional to externally provided information, and the case of stimuli having unique dimensions. These types of constraints appear in more primitive form in several generally distributed algorithms and in the published work of de Leeuw & Heiser (1980), Takane (1978a, 1981), Takane & Carroll (1981), and Bloxom (1978). Superb applications appear in the work of Takane, especially in 1981. Circular constraints are the focus of work by Lee & Bentler (1980), and ordinal constraints are discussed by Noma & Johnson (1977). These last two notions are also discussed briefly by de Leeuw & Heiser (1980).

Maximum Likelihood Multidimensional Scaling

A major trend during the review period is the development of maximum likelihood multidimensional scaling. There are two major lines of development, one by Ramsay and collaborators (1977, 1978a,b, 1980a,b; Winsberg & Ramsay 1981), the other by Takane and collaborators (1978a,b, 1980b, 1981, 1982a,b, Takane & Carroll 1981, Takane & Sergent 1983). Zinnes & MacKay (1983) have also worked on the topic.

These lines of development are similar but not the same. The work of Ramsay and his collaborators is fundamentally metric since they assume that the error process introduces erroneous dissimilarity values. The work of Zinnes and MacKay is similar in this regard. On the other hand, the work of Takane and his collaborators is fundamentally nonmetric since they assume that the error process introduces violations of monotonicity.

Ramsay discusses a variety of transformations of the data, especially power transformations and monotone splines. The splines permit monotonic transformations of the dissimilarities, but the data are still fundamentally at the interval or ratio levels of measurement. The data must be matrix conditional and may be asymmetric. Takane discusses optional constraints on the data transformations which allow him to deal with data at the ordinal, interval, or ratio levels of measurement. He also discusses asymmetry and a wide variety of conditionality situations. It does not appear that Zinnes and MacKay permit any transformation of the data in their work; thus they apparently assume that the data are ratio (and perhaps interval). Their data may be unconditional or matrix conditional and may be asymmetric.

Ramsay extends his developments to a very wide range of distance models, including GEM. He explicitly discusses (1982b) the simple and replicated Euclidean models, the INDSCAL-type model, and the full and reduced rank GEM models. The developments provided by Takane and by Zinnes and MacKay are restricted to the simple and replicated Euclidean models.

The motivation for developing maximum likelihood MDS is clearly presented by Ramsay in his first paper (1977). It is his view that in almost all data analysis there is some curiosity about the way the observed data vary around the fitted values. He asserts that "a maturing of a data analysis technology usually brings a desire for . . . an explication of the error model involved in the fitting process."

Maximum likelihood satisfies this desire in a way which many feel has one major advantage: the approach changes multidimensional scaling from a descriptive tool into an inferential tool. Associated with this change is the introduction of significance tests. In particular, if we feel comfortable adopting certain assumptions, then maximum likelihood multidimensional scaling allows significance tests to determine the appropriate dimensionality, the appropriate MDS model, and the appropriate error model. Also, this approach provides confidence regions for the stimuli and, with weighted models, for subjects.

The crucial assumption that we must accept in order to believe the conclusions suggested by the significance test is the specific nature of the error model posited by the chosen maximum likelihood MDS method. If the model is an appropriate mirror of the actual error processes active in the empirical situation, then the significance tests may be meaningful. If it is not, then they are not. This aspect is particularly important since the three teams of researchers working on MLMDS have proposed five error models, Ramsay and Takane two each and Zinnes and MacKay another.

Throughout their work, Ramsay and Takane actually posit the same pair of error models, but they differ in their assumptions about how these models influence the data. They both argue that error is normally distributed and is either added to or multiplied times the true distance. Thus, their procedures are alike in providing the user with the choice of assuming that the dissimilarity judgments are normally (additive model) or log-normally (multiplicative model) distributed about the true distance. However, the two procedures differ in the implied effect of the two assumptions: Ramsay's implies that the data are erroneous dissimilarity *values*. Takane's implies that the data are erroneous dissimilarity *orders*.

In contrast, Zinnes and MacKay make the fundamentally different assumption that the *stimuli* (not their distances) are normally perturbed during the subject's judgment process. This implies that the dissimilarities have noncentral chi-square distribution around the true distance. Like Ramsay, Zinnes and MacKay then proceed to assume that the data are erroneous dissimilarity values (not orders).

Although the mathematical virtuosity of the preceding developments is truly impressive, I question just what has been gained. From the viewpoint of the user, what seems to have been gained is that the user no longer has to decide on the "proper" distance model (dimensionality and weighting scheme) because the significance tests automate the decision. Furthermore, with two of the algorithms the program even indicates which error model is best. But this state of affairs may lead the unsophisticated user into a false state of confidence.

Of particular concern are those users who do not know that selecting a specific computer program implies selecting a specific choice of error models. What such a user knows is that the chosen program provides guidelines, via a series of significance tests, to choose the "proper" error and distance models. But what this user does not know is that what appears to be the "proper" error and distance models depends on the program doing the analysis. This occurs because (*a*) no two programs incorporate the same error models, and (*b*) the results of the significance tests for selecting the distance and error models will differ between programs because of the different error models. Unfortunately, there is no way to use internal consistency as a guideline because none of the approaches provide such a test. Consequently, these methods and their associated significance tests and confidence regions may induce a false sense of confidence in the results.

Furthermore, there are several technical problems with the significance tests. One technical problem is the assumption made by Ramsay and by Zinnes and MacKay that the dissimilarity judgments are independent. Their likelihood functions are critically dependent on this assumption. If this assumption is violated, then the significance levels are wrong. This problem has been addressed directly by Takane (1978a). He has proposed several different likelihood functions, each one specifically designed for the dependencies induced into the dissimilarity judgments by a specific experimental design, so his work is not subject to this criticism.

There is also the question, in the work of all three researchers, of whether the samples are large enough to justify the inferential claims. The question arises from the fact that hypothesis testing is only justified for very large sample sizes because the tests are based on asymptotic characteristics of maximum likelihood estimation. In many cases the sample size (number of subjects usually) is small, thus suggesting that the tests are not asymptotic.

As pointed out by Ramsay (1980b), the sample size problem is exacerbated for those models which have parameters for subjects, as in the very popular INDSCAL model. Clearly, for these models a large sample size can never imply asymptotic estimates of the parameters because the number of parameters increases without bound as the number of subjects increases. For these models the inferential aspects will never be completely appropriate. The importance of this problem is unknown, although Ramsay (1980b) suggests it is minor. Note that this is not a problem for the simplest model discussed by Ramsay, nor for any of the work of Takane and of Zinnes and MacKay, because in these cases there are no parameters for subjects.

Finally, it is unclear to me just exactly what the confidence regions mean. Do they mean that for other samples of subjects the recovered stimulus locations will be in the region 95% of the time? I am not sure. Furthermore, there are several complicated technical issues which affect the presentation of these regions. By comparing the various papers discussed in this section, you will see that the developers of these techniques do not agree on the presentation method.

Fundamentally, what the user usually needs from MDS is not inferences but a picture. Most often the probabilistic (statistical) notion is irrelevant to the application, and what is needed is an exploratory (descriptive) graphical technique. In these cases MDS does just fine without the excess baggage introduced by inferential notions based on questionable and potentially misleading error models. True, in some cases the theoretical understanding of the phenomenon being studied is sufficiently advanced (perhaps through previous use of descriptive MDS) that the error processes are well understood. Here the maximum likelihood MDS may prove particularly useful as a confirmatory analysis following earlier exploratory MDS analyses. However, during the earlier stages of scientific development the significance tests of these new procedures should be used with care.

Multidimensional Scaling Algorithms

During the review period there was much effort focused on developing new multidimensional scaling algorithms. This effort has resulted in "third-generation" algorithms which are faster, easier to use, more general, and more accessible than previous algorithms. Because of this, the application of multidimensional scaling techniques has increased markedly.

ALSCAL is the program which is certainly the most widely distributed and is among the most general and easiest to use (Takane et al 1977, Young & Lewyckyj 1979, 1983, Verhelst 1981, Young 1982). It is incorporated into SAS, a major statistical system (SAS Institute 1982), further increasing its availability and usefulness. It performs metric or nonmetric analyses of two- or three-way square or rectangular data with unweighted, diagonal, or general Euclidean models. The algorithm is convergent, optimizing the fit of squared (weighted) Euclidean distances to transformations of the data. This is currently the program of choice because of its availability and generality. However, more efficient algorithms exist, and ALSCAL fits squared Euclidean distances, which is not as desirable as fitting the distances themselves.

SMACOF is another very general program. It is based on a very simple, fast and elegant algorithm (de Leeuw & Heiser 1980, Stoop & de Leeuw 1982). While not widely distributed, this algorithm is certainly the most efficient general algorithm currently available. It performs metric and nonmetric analyses of two- or three-way data, but is currently limited to the unweighted Euclidean model. It is a convergent least squares program, optimizing the fit of the Euclidean distances to transformations of the data. If this algorithm, which is still under development, is extended to a wider selection of models and is made available in a major statistical system, it will be the program of choice, at least among the least squares programs.

MULTISCALE is another very general and easy to use program (Ramsay 1977, 1978a,b, 1982a). It performs metric analyses of two- or three-way square data with unweighted, diagonal, or general Euclidean models. Arrangements are being made to incorporate this program into a major statistical system. There are two MULTISCALE algorithms, both of which are maximum likelihood algorithms that maximize the fit of log (weighted) Euclidean distances to tranformations of the data. Generally, maximum likelihood estimation takes more computer resources (time and memory) than least squares estimation, and that seems to be true for both MULTISCALE algorithms when compared to ALSCAL or SMACOF. MULTISCALE-I suffers from certain convergence problems and inefficiencies and has been replaced with MULTISCALE-II. This newer algorithm is certainly the most completely developed and tested general maximum likelihood algorithm. However, it is still a fairly new algorithm and should be used with some caution until it has received further study. Also, please note the recommendations given at the end of the previous section.

A number of other algorithms have been proposed, but the programs based on them are either not as easily available or not yet fully mature. The most important of these are the many algorithms proposed by Takane (see references above, plus Takane 1981, 1984); however, they still seem to be maturing. The PROSCAL program by MacKay & Zinnes (1982) is another promising maximum likelihood algorithm, but only very recently proposed. Saito (1978, 1982) is developing a new approach to constructing least squares procedures, as are Null & Sarle (1982). The SUMSCAL algorithm (de Leeuw & Pruzansky 1978), a very efficient way of optimizing the function used by the INDSCAL program, has not received the attention it deserves. The DISTREG procedure (Young et al 1983) is an interesting new development in constrained multidimensional scaling. The books by Schiffman, Reynolds & Young (1981) and by Coxon (1982) evaluate a number of the older algorithms and some of the newer ones.

There has been some work during the period to investigate the robustness of various multidimensional scaling procedures. The main work has been that of Sibson (1978, 1979), Sibson et al (1981), and MacCallum (1978, 1981). Weeks & Bentler (1979) have compared nonmetric and metric approaches. Mardia (1978) and Takane (1977) have investigated the mathematical characteristics of several algorithms. Best et al (1979) defined an index of the potential robustness of a stimulus space.

Multidimensional Unfolding

There continues to be some work attempting to resolve the algorithmic problems associated with multidimensional unfolding (MDU), still with only mixed results. The most advanced and encouraging work is that of Heiser, who proposed and evaluated many improved unfolding algorithms appropriate to rectangular preference data (Heiser 1981, Heiser & Meulman 1983) and pairwise preferences (Heiser & de Leeuw 1981). He and his co-workers, investigate the relationship of unfolding to MDS, Principal Components, and Correspondence Analysis, and have proposed algorithms based on notions in those areas. Other work on unfolding appears in papers by Winsberg & Ramsay (1981), DeSarbo & Carroll (1980), Ramsay (1980a), Young (1982), and Rodgers & Young (1981).

Books and Reviews

The last article on scaling (Carroll & Arabie 1980) in the *Annual Review of Psychology* provided extensive coverage of the developments in multi-dimensional scaling up to 1978. Since that review appeared there have been many review articles. Certainly the one to reach the widest general scientific audience was the review of models and applications of multidimensional scaling and cluster analysis published in *Science* by Shepard (1980).

There have been a number of reviews tailored for various kinds of specific scientific audiences. Reviews of the models and algorithmic methods used in multidimensional scaling have been written for statisticians (Wish & Carroll 1981), computer scientists (Kruskal 1977), psychologists (Carroll 1980), e-thologists (Spence 1978), and in numerous other fields. At least three encyclopedia entries have been written (Carroll & Kruskal 1978, Jones 1983, Young 1983a). Two extensive mongraphs have been written, one on unidimensional scaling (McIver & Carmines 1981) and the other on multidimensional scaling (Kruskal & Wish 1978).

The first introductory textbook on the theory, application, and methods of multidimensional scaling was written during the review period and has received uniformly very positive reviews (Schiffman et al 1981). Books have also been written on multidimensional scaling in German (Borg 1981b) and in Japanese (Takane 1980c). Collections of previously published papers have been edited by Lingoes et al (1979), Lingoes (1977), and by Davies & Coxon (1982). Collections of new papers written by invited contributors appear in Young & Hamer (1984) and in Law et al (1984). Conference proceedings have been edited by Golledge & Raynor (1982) and by Lantermann & Feger (1980). A system of unified scaling programs is documented in Coxon (1982), and an interesting treatise on multidimensional scaling was written by Borg (1981a).

SCALING MULTIVARIATE DATA VIA LINEAR AND BILINEAR MODELS

This section reviews recent developments in scaling methods which use either a linear or bilinear model of qualitative multivariate data. The distinction between the two types of models can be understood from the following equation:

$Y = XA + E$,

where Y is an (n by r) matrix; X is (n by p); A is (p by r); and E is (n by r). This one equation can be either a linear or a bilinear equation, depending on the specific nature of its matrices.

1. Linear model:
   1. Y is observations from n sources (subjects) on r variables.
   2. X is observations from the same n sources on p different variables.
   3. A contains r coefficients of p linear equations that are the parameters of the linear model. These are estimated to optimize some fit criterion.
   4. E is a matrix of residual error from perfect fit.
2. Bilinear model:
   1. Y is still observations from n sources (subjects) on r variables.
   2. X is now no longer observed, but represents estimates of scores of the n sources on p latent (unobserved, hypothetical) variables.
   3. A is still r coefficients of p linear equations that are the parameters of the bilinear model. These are estimated to optimize fit, as before.
   4. E is still a matrix of residual error from perfect fit.

Note that the crucial difference in these models is that X is observed in the linear model but is unobserved in the bilinear model. Both models have observed multivariate data in Y, and both models posit a set of linear equations to model this multivariate data. Since both models use linearity as the basic idea, they both have the word "linear" in their name. The "bi" aspect of the bilinear model refers to the fact that it requires the estimation of *two* matrices (X and A).

There are four major streams of development in scaling with linear and bilinear models during the review period. The first two of these, conjoint analysis and multiple (or canonical) regression, use the linear model. The second two, principal components and correspondence analysis, use the bilinear model.

Conjoint Analysis

Conjoint analysis, in its simple form, is nothing more than main effects ANOVA performed on ordinal data. Stated in the usual ANOVA fashion, the simplest conjoint model is

$$y^*_{ik} = a_i + b_j,$$

where y^*_{ij} is the model's prediction of y_{ij}, the ordinal level observation in the experimental condition produced when level i of factor A is empirically combined with level j of factor B. The prediction represents the simple additive combination of a_i, the effect of the ith level of factor A and b_j, the effect of the jth level of factor B.

Naturally, the simple additive model underlying conjoint analysis is a special case of the general linear model formula given in matrix form above. The matrix X is a design matrix specifying a main effects ANOVA design (one column for each experimental variable), and where Y is univariate (has only one column) and is at the ordinal level of measurement. (Some researchers refer to ANOVA on interval level data as conjoint analysis, but this only confuses the discussion because such an analysis is simply ANOVA. Since these developments do not fall into my definition of scaling I do not review them.)

During the review period, de Leeuw et al (1976) proposed ADDALS, an efficient least squares algorithm for conjoint analysis. Their approach is notable for its great flexibility with regards to the measurement characteristics of the data (Y). These data may be at the binary, nominal, ordinal, or interval levels of measurement (or may be mixtures of each); may be generated by a discrete or continuous process; may have known degrees of imprecision; may be balanced or unbalanced; and may have any arbitrary type of conditionality. (The last characterisitc permits the data to be partitioned into any number of arbitrary subsets, each with its own separately stated measurement characteristics.)

In addition to the flexibility in the observed data, the experimental variables (i.e. X) may have order or linear constraints placed on them, thus also permitting them to be measured at the binary, nominal, ordinal, or interval levels of measurement. The main limitation of ADDALS is in the model: it must be the univariate main effects model specified above. That is, there can only be one Y variable, and X can represent only main effects. Perreault & Young (1980) present an overview of this approach to conjoint analysis.

As you would expect, more complicated ANOVA models have been discussed in the context of conjoint analysis. The WADDALS algorithm (Takane et al 1980) extends ADDALS to the weighted additive model:

$$y^*_{ijk} = w_{ka}a_i + w_{kb}b_j,$$

where a_i and b_j are the same as before, and where the subscript k on y^*_{ijk} indicates that the prediction is for the kth individual. Note that the weights w_{ka} and w_{kb} are specific to indivdual k, and that there is one weight for each way of the experimental design. The general linear model matrix formula has a column in the observed data Y for each subject k. Thus, Y is now multivariate. The model posits that each subject (column in Y) has a weight for each way of the experimental design (column in X). This is the nonmetric main effects multivariate analysis of variance model.

The %CONJOINT algorithm, a SAS macro written in the MATRIX language by me and my students (Young 1983b), extends ADDALS in a different direction. It permits generalized (optional interaction terms) univariate conjoint analysis. This is a full-fledged nonmetric ANOVA program. MANOVALS, a program developed by de Leeuw (personal communication), is a complete nonmetric MANOVA program that incorporates both the multivariate and generalized (interaction term) notions.

A very promising new direction has been taken by Takane (1982a) in his work on MAXADD, a maximum likelihood program for conjoint analysis. This work covers the univariate, main-effects, weighted or unweighted additive model. MAXADD can analyze nominal data or certain types of ordinal data. Takane (1984) compares MAXADD to ADDALS and WADDALS. Falmagne (1978) has developed a procedure similar to MAXADD, though it is more limited.

Takane (1982a) assumes that nominal and ordinal data represent incomplete information about interval data. In particular, a metric (interval) process is assumed to underlie the nonmetric (nominal or ordinal) data, with the metric information getting lost in the observation process, leaving only nonmetric information. Takane then proposes specific models linking the unobserved metric process with the observed nonmetric data. A different model is proposed for categorical data, paired comparison data, and directional rankings data. In each case the model is Thurstonian, but with the normal error model replaced with a (univariate or multivariate) logistic error model. In the case of paired comparison data the model is equivalent to the BTL model discussed by Bradley & Terry (1952) and by Luce (1959).

The main advantage of MAXADD is that it allows various statistical inferences not possible with the least squares procedures discussed above. The assumptions underlying the significance tests are essentially the same as in Takane's maximum likelihood MDS developments, and the comments made above about those developments apply here. In particular, the lack of empirical independence seems to be very well handled by his developments. However, small samples violate an assumption required by the asymptotic significance tests and may adversely affect the significance levels they generate.

Nonmetric Regression Analysis

Nonmetric regression refers to a very general class of situations in which multiple or canonical regression is applied to multivariate data having at least one ordinal variable. The work of Young et al (1976) is a simple extension of their conjoint analysis work. They propose CORALS, a least squares algorithm that extends canonical regression so that the variables may be measured at the binary, nominal, ordinal, or interval levels of measurement; may be discrete or continuous; and may have any type of conditionality. There is no restriction on the mixture of measurement characteristics. Of greatest importance is the fact that each variable has its own separately defined measurement characteristics.

Since the canonical regression model includes all other linear models as special cases, all of the least squares conjoint analysis developments discussed in the previous section are subsumed under CORALS.

The article by Young and co-workers on CORALS proposes an algorithm limited to obtaining the first pair of canonical variates. This limitation was eliminated by de Leeuw (personal communication) in later developments. My students and I (Young 1983b) have written %CORALS (a SAS macro in the MATRIX language) which also removes this limitation as well as providing nonmetric maximum redundancy analysis for the first time. Tenenhaus (1979) presents an interesting mathematical comparison of ADDALS, MORALS (the multiple regression version of CORALS), and Kruskal's MONANOVA (1981). Cunningham (1982) has discussed four monotone multiple regression models, two of which are special cases of MORALS and two of which are not cases of the general linear model.

Breiman & Friedman (1982) have independently developed a nonmetric multiple regression procedure named ACE that is also very flexible with regard to the measurement characteristics of the variables. Like MORALS, ACE extends multiple regression to ordinal variables. However, the two approaches differ in the way these variables are transformed. Whereas the MORALS approach transforms ordinal variables according to Kruskal's least square monotonic transformation, the ACE approach transforms ordinal variables according to Tukey's smoothing transformations. This implies that the overall behavior of the ACE algorithm is not quite as "nice" as MORALS (since smoothing is not least squares), but that ACE obtains "nicer" transformations of the ordinal variables (since least squares monotonic transformations are step functions which are not smooth).

CORALS extends the descriptive (but not the inferential) power of the canonical model to data that include ordered variables. This is an important development because for many decades canonical analysis has been possible on data with categorical (nominal) and continuous (interval) variables but not on data with ordinal variables. There is some work that also extends the inferential power of the canonical model to ordered variables. This work is by Winsberg & Ramsay (1980), who propose a maximum likelihood procedure for nonmetric multiple regression with nominal, ordinal, or interval level variables. The proposal uses B-splines to transform ordinal variables monotonically so that the likelihood function is maximized. This follows on previous work by Ramsay (1977) which permitted a limited class of monotonic transformations of the dependent variable.

As an apporach to defining monotonic transformations, B-splines are attractive alternatives to either least squares monotonic transformations or Tukey-type smoother transformations. B-splines provide flexibly shaped but smooth monotonic transformations, and they have relatively small number of easily identified parameters. So from this viewpoint, B-splines are a valuable tool for constructing monotone transformations.

While this approach extends the inferential power of multiple regression to ordinal variables, I question the robustness of the inferential process to violations of the assumptions about independence and sample size. Furthermore, it is the monotonically transformed variables that must have a known (and tractable) probability density function, implying that the residuals of the transformed variables from the model are, for example, normally distributed. I would feel more comfortable with the statistical inferences if the framework taken by Takane in MAXADD were extended to the canonical situation, since Takane's inferential framework seems to be more in keeping with the basic nature of ordinal data.

Nonmetric Principal Components Analysis

Principal components analysis is a well-known data analysis technique that uses the bilinear model to analyze multivariate data whose variables are all quantitative (at the interval level of measurement). There are several developments during the review period concerning nonmetric PCA, also called nonlinear PCA. These developments apply the same bilinear model to multivariate data that have at least one variable which is qualitative (ordinal or nominal).

The paper by Young et al (1978) proposed PRINCIPALS, a nonmetric PCA algorithm (each variable can be binary, nominal, ordinal, or interval, and can be discrete or continous). The algorithm is in the tradition of metric PCA because it maximizes the variance accounted for by the first several components. It transforms the variables to maximize the variance accounted for by a stated number of components, with the added proviso that each variable's transformation must strictly satisfy the restrictions implied by the variable's stated measurement characteristics. Unlike metric PCA, the user must specify the desired number of components as well as the measurement characteristics of each variable.

Tenenhaus (1977) independently and simultaneously proposed PRINQUAL, an algorithm that is identical to PRINCIPALS with two exceptions. The two differences are (a) PRINQUAL has a superior initialization approach for nominal variables, and (b) it does not handle ordinal variables at all. A SAS macro named %PRINQUAL has been written by me and my students (Young 1983b) in the MATRIX language. %PRINQUAL adds the superior Tenehaus initialization to the PRINCIPALS algorithm. Tenenhaus (1982) has thoroughly studied the mathematical properties of the resulting algorithm, and he and I (Tenenhaus & Young 1983) have compared it to Correspondence Analysis. The PRINCIPALS notion has been extended to three-way, three-mode data (i.e. many matrices of multivariate data) by Sands & Young (1980) and Kroonenberg & de Leeuw (1980) in independent but closely related developments. An algorithm that fits the common-factor model to mixed measurement level data was proposed by Takane et al (1979).

While the %PRINQUAL approach has the desirable feature of maximizing the variance accounted for by an algorithm that is very stable and is convergent, it has the undesirable feature of obtaining transformations of qualitative variables which are discontinuous step functions. Two similar but separate developments have appeared that use splines to obtain transformations of the qualitative variables which are smooth but which do not strictly maximize the variance accounted for by the stated number of components.

de Leeuw and co-workers (1982) use the least squares framework and linear combinations of B-splines to transform the variables. Such transformations are not necessarily monotone, implying that the variables are nominal. They investigate the mathematical relationship of their approach to the %PRINQUAL approach and to Correspondence Analysis.

Ramsay & Winsberg (1984) employ maximum likelihood estimation and use non-negative combinations of monotone splines (M-splines) to obtain the transformations of the variables. Since the resulting transformations are monotonic, the implication is that all variables are thought of as being ordinal. They proceed to develop significance tests on the foundation of their maximum likelihood algorithm. While I have reservations about significance tests in this context, I do think that M-splines are a very nice way of obtaining smooth monotonic transformations. Perhaps it would be desirable to develop an algorithm which permits B-splines for nominal variables and M-splines for ordinal variables.

Correspondence Analysis

As pointed out by Nishisato (1980a, 1982), the basic idea underlying correspondence analysis has existed for at least 50 years. However, the technique has suffered from being independently invented and named by a large number of people during those years. Some common names for this type of analysis are: method of reciprocal averages, appropriate scoring, additive scoring, Hayashi's theory of quantification, principal components of qualitative data, Guttman scaling, optimal scaling, dual scaling, biplot, and nonlinear multivariate analysis.

As can be imagined, there are nearly as many ways to describe the analysis as there are inventors and names. Yet they all have in common the fact that the data are fundamentally categorical (nominal or binary), although such data can be presented easily as frequencies or as contingencies. The analysis can be described alternatively as submitting such data to (*a*) a singular-value decomposition; (*b*) a principal components analysis; (*c*) a simple additive (conjoint) analysis; or (*d*) a canonical analysis. To add to the confusion, the method has been studied extensively in several countries, including the USA, Canada,

Britain, Austrialia, South Africa, France, Japan, and the Netherlands. Naturally, papers have been written in several languages (English, French, and
Japanese, predominately).

During the review period, work has continued on the topic, with emphasis on
a synthesis of the many different developments. I do not presume to review all,
or even most, of the literature, but simply to make reference to those whose
work I know the best. Nishisato has published extensively on "Dual Scaling"
both in English (1979a,b, 1980a,b) and in Japanese (1982). Some portions of
this work appear to represent new directions, while other portions are histories
or syntheses. Tenenhaus (1981) and Tenenhaus & Young (1983) present
syntheses covering the French and English literature (in English). Gifi (1981)
and Meulman (1982) are representative of the work in The Netherlands (in
English). Heiser (1981) relates unfolding to correspondence analysis. All of
these workers have developed computer programs that perform correspondence
analysis of one type or another.

Books and Reviews

There are not very many books and reviews focusing on linear scaling methods
for multivariate data. This is an accurate reflection of the state of the art: linear
scaling methods have not yet matured to the level where such books and
reviews would be appropriate. The main exception to this is the area of
correspondence analysis, where most work seems to be synthesizing information from various sources. Here there is one introductory book and at least two
advanced reviews.

Nishisato (1980a) has written a very readable, current, and accurate introductory book on correspondence analysis that is appropriate for courses taught
at the graduate level. Gifi (1981) (a pseudonym for de Leeuw and his co-
workers) presents a very comprehensive treatment of non-linear multivariate
analysis, including major chapters on correspondence analysis, multidimensional scaling, and many innovative scaling methods based on the linear
and bilinear (and multilinear) models. Tenenhaus (1982) presents a very
advanced and general mathematical treatment of scaling based on the linear and
bilinear models (in French). The last two books are excellent for the researcher
interested in detailed information.

POSTSCRIPT

Comparing this review with the two previous ones on scaling in the *Annual
Review of Psychology* (Cliff 1973, Carroll & Arabie 1980) reveals that the
predominate trend during the last decade is an explosive growth in MDS
methods that peaked somewhere around 1980 and has begun to subside. In fact,
this trend is reflected in the titles of these three reviews ("Scaling," "Multi-

dimensional Scaling," and "Scaling," respectively). While the major portion of the present review has been on MDS developments, I see the developments as ones which consolidate earlier gains (improved algorithms, generalized models) or strengthen earlier foundations (constrained and maximum likelihood MDS).

I do not mean to belittle these developments. They are critical developmental stages of a maturing methodology, but they may also be the final significant methodological developments. Kruskal, who wrote his foreword to the Schiffman, Reynolds & Young book on MDS in 1980, stated that "at the age of 20-odd, multidimensional scaling should be in the full vigor of youth—and I am happy to report that it is just graduating from college and doing very well."

In the 4 or 5 years since that was written, MDS has become a vigorous 30-year-old. It has, as Kruskal hoped, begun to develop further the "self-critical tools of assesment and diagnosis," as can be seen in the development of maximum likelihood methods, certainly the single most important trend during the review period (no matter how harshly I criticized them). And I expect that MDS will continue a healthy adulthood for the next several decades in essentially its current form.

As an individual in the family of scaling methods, MDS appears to be reaching full maturity, while the family continues to expand and grow. Perhaps Conjoint Analysis is now the budding teenager, soon to reach maturity. And many new linear scaling models have been born recently, with their futures yet to unfold. I expect that we will hear much more from Conjoint Analysis in the near future, and from its younger sisters and brothers after that.

If I were to venture a guess as to the identity of the next member of the family, I would say that it will be methods for graphically displaying the results of scaling analyses rather than new scaling methods as such. I can see that taking full advantage of the current revolution in high-resolution color graphics technology will greatly enhance the appeal of scaling methods. Three-dimensional color graphics displays that can be interacted with in real time, that are based on quantitative analyses of qualitative data (scaling), and that are based on sound psychological and perceptual principles, should be very useful and attractive to a wide audience, Thus, I think they will become the next member of the scaling family.

Literature Cited[1]

Bentler, P. M., Weeks, D. G. 1978. Restricted multidimensional scaling models. *J. Math. Psychol.* 17:138–51

Best, A. M., Young, F. W., Hall, R. G. 1979. On the precision of a Euclidean structure. *Psychometrika* 44:395–408

Bloxom, B. 1968. Individual differences in multidimensional scaling. *Educ. Test. Serv. Res. Bull.* 68–45

Bloxom, B. 1978. Constrained multidimensional scaling in N spaces. *Psychometrika* 35:283–319

Borg, I. 1981a. *Multidimensional Data Representations: When and Why.* Ann Arbor: Mathesis

Borg, I. 1981b. Anwendungsorientierte Multidimensionale Skalierung. Berlin: Springer (In German)

Borg, I., Lingoes, J. C. 1980. A model and algorithm for multidimensional scaling with external constraints on the distances. *Psychometrika* 45:25–38

Bradley, R. A., Terry, M. E. 1952. The rank analysis of incomplete block designs. I. The method of paired comparisons. *Biometrika* 39:324–45

Breiman, L., Friedman, J. H. 1982. Estimating optimal transformations for multiple regression and correlation. *Dep. Stat. Orion 010.* Stanford Univ.

Carroll, J. D. 1980. Models and methods for multidimensional analysis of preferential choice (or other dominance) data. See Lantermann & Ferger 1980

Carroll, J. D., Arabie, P. 1980. Multidimensional scaling. *Ann. Rev. Psychol.* 31:607–49

Carroll, J. D., Chang, J. J. 1970. Analysis of individual differences in multidimensional scaling via an *n*-way generalization of "Eckart-Young" decomposition. *Psychometrika* 35:283–319

Carroll, J. D., Chang, J. J. 1972. *IDIOSCAL (individual differences in orientation scaling): A generalization of INDSCAL allowing idiosyncratic reference systems.* Presented at Psychom. Soc. Meet., Princeton, N.J.

Carroll, J. D., Kruskal, J. B. 1978. Multidimensional scaling. In *International Encyclopedia of Statistics,* ed. W. H. Kruskal, J. M. Tanur, pp. 892–907. New York: Free Press

Carroll, J. D., Pruzansky, S., Kruskal, J. B. 1980. Candelinc: A general approach to multidimensional analysis of many-way arrays with linear constraints on parameters. *Psychometrika* 45:3–24

Cliff, N. 1973. Scaling. *Ann. Rev. Psychol.* 24:473–506

Coxon, A. P. M. 1982. *The User's Guide to Multidimensional Scaling.* Exeter, NH: Heinemann

Cunningham, J. P. 1982. Multiple monotone regression. *Psychol. Bull.* 92:791–800

Davies, P. M., Coxon, A. P. M., eds. 1982. *Key Texts in Multidimensional Scaling.* Exeter, NH: Heineman

de Leeuw, J., Heiser, W. 1980. Multidimensional scaling with restrictions on the configuration. In *Multivariate Analysis,* ed. P. R. Krishnaiah, 5:501–22. Amsterdam: North-Holland

de Leeuw, J., Pruzansky, S. 1978. A new computational method to fit the weighted Euclidean model. *Psychometrika* 43:479–90

de Leeuw, J., van Rijckevorsel, J., van der Wouden, H. 1982. Non linear principal components analysis with B-splines. *Methods Oper. Res.* 43:379–94

de Leeuw, J., Young, F. W., Takane, Y. 1976. Additive structure in qualitative data: An alternating least squares method with optimal scaling features. *Psychometrika* 41:471–503

DeSarbo, W. S., Carroll, J. D. 1980. Three-way metric unfolding. In *Marketing Measurement and Analysis,* ed. J. W. Keon, pp. 157–83. Providence, RI: TIMS Coll. Marketing

Dunn, T. R., Harshman, R. A. 1982. A multidimensional scaling model for the size-weight illusion. *Psychometrika* 47:25–44

Easterling, D. V. 1984. Ideological shifts in the US Senate between 1971 and 1978: Principal directions scaling. See Young & Hamer 1984

Falmagne, J.-C. 1978. Probabilistic choice behavior theory: Axioms as constraints in optimization. In *Cognitive Theory,* Vol. 3, ed. J. N. Castellan Jr., F. Restle. New York: Erlbaum

Forsyth, B. 1984. The subjective attributes of cups and bowls: A principal directions analysis. See Young & Hamer 1984

Gifi, A. 1981. *Non-Linear Multivariate Analysis.* Leiden, The Netherlands: Dep. Data Theory, Univ. Leiden

Golledge, R. G., Raynor, J. N., eds. 1982. *Proximity and Preference: Problems in the Multidimensional Analysis of Large Data Sets.* Minneapolis: Univ. Minn. Press

Harshman, R. A. 1972. Foundations of the PARAFAC procedure: Models and condi-

---

[1] A key-word indexed bibliography of about 250 papers published during the review period is available upon request. This bibliography includes all the papers reviewed here, plus many not reviewed. It also includes a section on other bibliographies.

tions for an "explanatory" multi-modal factor analysis. *UCLA Work. Pap. Phonetics 16*

Heiser, W. J. 1981. *Unfolding Analysis of Proximity Data*. Leiden, The Netherlands: Univ. Leiden Dep. Datatheorie Press

Heiser, W. J., de Leeuw, J. 1981. Multidimensional mapping of preference data. *Math. Sci. Hum.* 19:39–96

Heiser, W. J., Meulman, J. 1983. Analyzing rectangular tables by joint and constrained multidimensional scaling. *Ann. Appl. Econometrics*. In press

Holman, E. W. 1978. Completely nonmetric multidimensional scaling. *J. Math. Psychol.* 20:1–15

Horan, C. B. 1969. Multidimensional scaling combining observations when individuals have different perceptual spaces. *Psychometrika* 34:139–65

Jones, L. V. 1983. Psychological scaling. In *Encyclopedia of Statistical Sciences*, Vol. 5, ed. S. Kotz, N. L. Johnson. New York: Wiley

Jones, M. R., MacCallum, R. C. 1984. An application of principal directions scaling to auditory pattern perception. See Young and Hamer 1984

Kroonenberg, P. M., de Leeuw, J. 1980. Principal component analysis of three-way data by means of alternating least squares algorithms. *Psychometrika* 45:69–98

Kruskal, J. B. 1977. Multidimensional scaling and other methods for discovering structure. In *Statistical Methods for Digital Computers*, ed. K. Enslein, H. S. Ralston, H. S. Wilf, 3:296–339. New York: Wiley

Kruskal, J. B. 1981. Multilinear models for data analysis. *Behaviormetrika* 10:1–20

Kruskal, J. B., Wish, M. 1978. *Multidimensional Scaling*. Beverly Hills, Calif: Sage

Lantermann, E. D., Feger, H., eds. 1980. *Similarity and Choice: Papers in Honour of Clyde Coombs*. Bern, Switzerland: Huber

Law, H. G., Snyder, C. W., MacDonald, R. P., Hattie, J., eds. 1984. *Three-Mode Models for Data Analysis*. New York: Praeger. In press

Lee, S.-Y., Bentler, P. M. 1980. Functional relations in multidimensional scaling. *Br. J. Math. Stat. Psychol.* 33:142–50

Lingoes, J. C. 1977. *Geometric Representations of Relational Data*. Ann Arbor: Mathesis

Lingoes, J. C., Borg, I. 1978. A direct approach to individual differences scaling using increasingly complex transformations. *Psychometrika* 43:491–519

Lingoes, J. C., Borg, I. 1983. A quasi-statistical model for choosing between alternative configuations derived from ordinarily constrained data. *Br. J. Math. Stat. Psychol.* 36: In press

Lingoes, J. C., Roskam, E., Borg, I., eds. 1979. *Geometric Representations of Relational Data*. Ann Arbor: Mathesis. 2nd ed.

Luce, R. D. 1959. *Individual Choice Behavior*. New York: Wiley

MacCallum, R. C. 1978. Recovery of structure in incomplete data by ALSCAL. *Psychometrika* 44:69–74

MacCallum, R. C. 1981. Evaluating goodness of fit in nonmetric multidimensional scaling by ALSCAL. *Appl. Psychol. Meas.* 5:377–82

MacKay, D. B., Zinnes, J. L. 1982. PROSCAL: A program for probabilistic scaling. *Discussion Paper 218,* Grad. Sch. Bus., Indiana Univ., Bloomington

Mardia, K. V. 1978. Some properties of classical multi-dimensional scaling. *Commun. Stat.* 7:1233–41

McIver, J. P., Carmines, E. G. 1981. *Unidimensional Scaling*. Beverly Hills, Calif: Sage

Meulman, J. 1982. *Homogeneity Analysis of Incomplete Data*. Leiden, The Netherlands: Univ. Leiden DSWO Press

Nishisato, S. 1979a. Dual scaling and its history. *Math. Sci.* 190:76–83

Nishisato, S. 1979b. Dual scaling and its variants. In *Analysis of Test Data (New Directions for Testing and Measurement)*, ed. R. E. Traub, pp. 1–12. San Francisco: Jossey-Bass

Nishisato, S. 1980a. *Analysis of Categorical Data: Dual Scaling and its Applications*. Toronto: Univ. Toronto Press. 276 pp.

Nishisato, S. 1980b. Dual scaling of successive categories data. *Jpn. Psychol. Res.* 22:134–43

Nishisato, S. 1982. *Quantifying Qualtitive Data: Dual Scaling and its Applications*. Tokyo: Asakura Shoten. 241 pp. (In Japanese)

Noma, E., Johnson, J. 1977. Constraining nonmetric multidimensional scaling configurations. *Tech. Rep. 60*. Ann Arbor: Hum. Perform. Cent., Univ. Mich.

Null, C. H., Sarle, W. S. 1982. *Robust multidimensional scaling*. Presented at Spring Psychom. Soc. Meet., Montreal

Perreault, W. D. Jr., Young, F. W. 1980. Alternating least squares optimal scaling: Analysis of nonmetric data in marketing research. *J. Mark. Res.* 17:1–13

Ramsay, J. O. 1977. Maximum likelihood estimation in multidimensional scaling. *Psychometrika* 42:241–66

Ramsay, J. O. 1978a. Confidence regions for multidimensional scaling analysis. *Psychometrika* 43:145–60

Ramsay, J. O. 1978b. Multiscale: Four programs for multidimensional scaling by the method of maximum likelihood. Chicago: Natl. Educ. Resources

Ramsay, J. O. 1980a. The joint analysis of

direct ratings, pairwise preferences and dissimilarities. *Psychometrika* 45:149–65

Ramsay, J. O. 1980b. Some small sample results for maximum likelihood estimation in multidimensional scaling. *Psychometrika* 45:139–44

Ramsay, J. O. 1982a. *Multiscale II Manual.* Montreal: Dep. Psychol., McGill Univ.

Ramsay, J. O. 1982b. Some statistical approaches to multidimensional scaling data. *J. R. Stat. Soc. Ser. B* 145:285–312

Ramsay, J. O., Winsberg, S. 1984. Monotone spline transformations for dimension reduction. *Psychometrika* 49: In press

Rodgers, J. L., Young F. W. 1981. Successive unfolding of family preferences. *Appl. Psychol. Meas.* 5:51–62

Saito, T. 1978. The problem of the additive constant and eigenvalues in metric multidimensional scaling. *Psychometrika* 43: 193–201

Saito, T. 1982. Contributions to e_{ij}-type quantification and development of a new method of multidimensional scaling. *Behaviormetrika* 12:63–83

Sands, R., Young, F. W., 1980. Component models for three-way data: An alternating least squares algorithm with optimal scaling features. *Psychometrika* 45:39–67

SAS Institute. 1982. *SAS User's Guide: Basics, 1982 Edition.* Cary, NC: SAS Inst.

Schiffman, S. S., Reynolds, M. L., Young, F. W. 1981. *Introduction to Multidimensional Scaling: Theory, Methods and Applications.* New York: Academic

Shepard, R. N. 1980. Multidimensional scaling, tree-fitting, and clustering. *Science* 210:390–98

Sibson, R. 1978. Studies in the robustness of multidimensional scaling: Procrustes statistics. *J. R. Stat. Soc. Ser. B* 40:234–38

Sibson, R. 1979. Studies in the robustness of multidimensional scaling: Perturbational analysis of classical scaling. *J. R. Stat. Soc. Ser. B* 41:217–29

Sibson, R., Bowyer, A., Osmond, C. 1981. Studies in the robustness of multidimensional scaling: Euclidean models and simulation studies. *J. Stat. Comput. Simul.* 13:273–96

Spence, I. 1978. Multidimensional scaling. In *Quantitative Ethology,* ed. P. W. Colgan, New York: Wiley

Stoop, I., de Leeuw, J. 1982. *How to Use SMACOF-IB.* Dep. Datatheorie, Univ. Leiden, The Netherlands

Takane, Y. 1977. On the relations among four methods of multidimensional scaling. *Behaviormetrika* 4:29–43

Takane, Y. 1978a. A maximum likelihood method for nonmetric multidimensional scaling: I. The case in which all empirical pairwise orderings are independent—theory. *Jpn. Psychol. Res.* 20:7–17

Takane, Y. 1978b. A maximum likelihood method for nonmetric multidimensional scaling: I. The case in which all empirical pairwise orderings are independent—evaluations. *Jpn. Psychol. Res.* 20:105–14

Takane, Y. 1980a. Analysis of categorizing behavior by a quantification method. *Behaviormetrika* 8:75–86

Takane, Y. 1980b. Maximum likelihood estimation in the generalized case of Thurstone's model of comparative judgment. *Jpn. Psychol. Res.* 22:188–96

Takane, Y. 1980c. *Tajigen Shakudoho* (Multidimensional Scaling). Tokyo: Univ. Tokyo Press (In Japanese)

Takane, Y. 1981. Multidimensional successive categories scaling: A maximum likelihood method. *Psychometrika* 46:9–28

Takane, Y. 1982a. Maximum likelihood additivity analysis. *Psychometrika* 17:225–41

Takane, Y. 1982b. The method of triadic combinations: A new treatment and its application. *Behaviormetrika* 11:37–48

Takant, Y. 1984. The weighted additive model. See Law et al 1984

Takane, Y., Carroll, J. D. 1981. Nonmetric maximum likelihood multidimensional scaling from directional rankings of similarities. *Psychometrika* 46:389–405

Takane, Y., Sergent, J. 1983. Multidimensional scaling models for reaction times and same-different judgments. *Psychometrika.* In press

Takane, Y., Young, F. W., de Leeuw, J. 1977. Nonmetric individual differences multidimensional scaling: An alternating least squares method with optimal scaling features. *Psychometrika* 42:7–67

Takane, Y., Young, F. W., de Leeuw, J. 1979. Nonmetric common factor analysis: An alternating least squares method with optimal scaling feature. *Behaviormetrika* 6:45–56

Takane, Y., Young, F. W., de Leeuw, J. 1980. An individual differences additive model: An alternating lease squares method with optimal scaling features. *Psychometrika* 45:183–209

Tenenhaus, M. 1977. Analyse en composantes principales d'un ensemble de variables nominales ou numeriques. *Rev. Stat. Appl.* 25:39–56 (In French)

Tenenhaus, M. 1979. La regression qualitative. *Rev. Stat. Appl.* 27:5–21 (In French)

Tenenhaus, M. 1981. Multiple correspondence analysis and duality schema: A synthesis of different approaches. *Cah. Rech. CESA No. 693,* Jouy-en-Josas, France

Tenenhaus, M. 1982. Analyse canonique generalisee de p cones polyedriques convexes: Application a l'analyse en composantes principales qualitative. *Cah. Rech. CESA,* Jouy-en-Josas, France (In French)

Tenenhaus, M., Young, F. W. 1983. Multiple correspondence analysis and the principal components of qualitative data. *Psychom. Lab. Rep. 169.* Univ. NC, Chapel Hill

Verhelst, N. D. 1981. A note on ALSCAL: The estimation of the additive constant. *Psychometrika* 46:465–68

Weeks, D. G., Bentler, P. M. 1979. A comparison of linear and monotone multidimensional scaling models. *Psychol. Bull.* 86:349–54

Weeks, D. G., Bentler, P. M. 1982. Restricted multidimensional scaling models for asymmetric proximities. *Psychometrika* 47:201–8

Winsberg, S., Ramsay, J. O. 1980. Monotonic transformations to additivity using splines. *Biometrika* 67:669–74

Winsberg, S., Ramsay, J. O. 1981. Analysis of pairwise preference data using integrated B-splines. *Psychometrika* 46:171–86

Wish, M., Carroll, J. D. 1981. Multidimensional scaling and its applications. In *Handbook of Statistics, Volume 2: Classification, Pattern Recognition, and Reduction of Dimension,* ed. P. R. Krishnaiah. Amsterdam: North-Holland

Young, F. W. 1981. Quantitative analysis of qualitative data. *Psychometrika* 46:357–87

Young, F. W. 1982. Enhancements in ALSCAL-82. SUGI Proc.

Young, F. W. 1983a. Multidimensional scaling. In *Encyclopedia of Statistical Sciences,* Vol. 5. New York: Wiley

Young, F. W. 1983b. SAS %MACRO's for conjoint analysis, principal components of qualitative data, and canonical analysis of qualitative data. *SAS Tech. Rep.* Cary, NC: SAS Inst.

Young, F. W. 1984. The general Euclidean model. See Law et al 1984

Young, F. W., de Leeuw, J., Takane, Y. 1976. Regression with qualitative and quantitative variables: An alternating least squares method with optimal scaling features. *Psychometrika* 41:505–29

Young, F. W., de Leeuw, J., Takane, Y. 1980. Quantifying qualitative data. See Lantermann & Ferger 1980

Young, F. W., Hamer, R. M. 1984. *Multidimensional Scaling: Theory and Applications.* Hillsdale, NJ: Erlbaum

Young, F. W., Lewyckyj, R. 1979. *Principal directions scaling: A new individual differences model.* Presented at Ann. Psychom. Soc. Meet., Monterey, Calif.

Young, F. W., Lewyckyj, R. 1983. ALSCAL: A procedure for multidimensional scaling. In *SAS Supplemental Users Guide.* Cary, NC: SAS Inst

Young, F. W., Null, C. H., Hamer, R. M. 1983. DISTREG: A procedure for distance regression. In *SAS Supplemental Users Guide, 1982 Edition.* Cary, NC: SAS Inst.

Young, F. W. Takane, Y., de Leeuw, J. 1978. The principal components of mixed measurement level multivariate data: An alternating least squares method with optimal scaling features. *Psychometrika* 43:279–81

Zinnes, J. L., MacKay, D. B. 1983. Probabilistic multidimensional scaling: Complete and incomplete data. *Psychometrika* 48:27–48

Ann. Rev. Psychol. 1984. 35:83–112

CONTEMPORARY
PSYCHOLOGY IN MEXICO

Rogelio Diaz-Guerrero

Facultad de Psicologia, Universidad Nacional Autonoma de Mexico,
Mexico City,D. F.

CONTENTS

INTRODUCTION

The mushrooming development of psychology in Mexico is—even to this author—a continuing source of surprise. How could the three men and three women formally registered in the career of psychology in 1940 ever forecast

83

0066-4308/84/0201-0083$02.00

that by 1978, 42,090 individuals would have been enlisted to become psychologists at the National University of Mexico alone! Of course, the original 50/50 distribution of the sexes was never to be repeated again. While soon, in 1943, it was to become 83% women of the 23 students, it was to reach a new low of 60% women from 1973 to 1975, of the 9,000 total students enrolled in those three years. The overall ratio of females to males from 1940 to 1978 was 65:35.

But it is not merely numbers that is striking. After all—as will be seen later—desertion has been high and the percent obtaining final degrees low. The variety of psychological movements also is impressive. While—as is the case in many other Latin American countries—empirical psychology in Mexico was originally promoted by physicians, educators, and philosophers, and the Wundtian roots remained strong until the late 1930s, mental testing, which started in the twenties, and Gestalt, phychoanalysis, behaviorism, and humanistic psychologies, in that order, entered with force in Mexico. Beginning with the late fifties, modern, eclectic, and expansionistic psychological theory and practice was making its appearance. Subsequent to the partial disillusionment with psychoanalysis and Skinnerianism, psychology in Mexico, outside weakening political and ideological thrusts, is becoming a more mature and, interestingly, an original discipline, not only progressively more conscious of its own history and making critical analysis of its own development, but offering new, more interdisciplinary and socially conscious facets and a brand of theoretical-applied insistence in its research, that can contribute to the worldwide development of the discipline.

There have been several papers and even theses dealing with historical aspects of psychology in Mexico (see section on *History of Psychology*). In this article, I shall make incursions into the distant past only when required by present developments. In this fashion, I shall try to do justice fundamentally to what has been happening in the last 15 to 20 years.

TRAINING

The formal antecedent for the teaching of psychology in Mexico is to be found in the project for a renewed University of Mexico that Justo Sierra, a Mexican educator, writer, lawyer, historian, politician, and philosopher, presented to the Congress of the Republic in 1881. "Teaching will be encyclopedic and rigorously elementary (for the preparatory schools), grounded, just as the teaching in the professional schools, on the scientific method. Fundamental studies here will begin with mathematics and will ascend to cosmography and geography, physics, chemistry, biology, psychology and will terminate with sociology and general history" (Hernandez Luna 1948, p. 44). While the entire project for a renewed, and now labeled National University of Mexico, did not pass until 1910, Ezequiel Chavez, lawyer, educator and self-educated psychologist, inaugurated a course in psychology at the "preparatorias" in 1893 (Robles 1952). Chavez was strongly influenced by Herbert Spencer, Théodule Ribot, William James, Edward B. Titchener, William J. McDougall, Mark Baldwin, and Pierre Janet.

Educational Systems

Let me describe here the structure of the Mexican educational system and compare it to others. The best source for the latter endeavor is a book on international opportunities in psychology published in 1966 by the American Psychological Association.

The Mexican system has not changed significantly since the beginning of the century. Also, from the book cited above and from Ardila's (1978), it is clear that the structure of education including psychological training is about the same in all Latin American countries. There are from 11 to 12 years of education, about 6 in primary elementary schools and about 6 in secondary and preparatory schools, before students can enter training for a career in psychology. Also, in most of Latin America as in Mexico, there is a course in the tenth to twelveth grades covering an introduction to general psychology. Finally, a professional degree of psychology is granted after 4 to 5 years of university training. This degree is labeled Licenciate in Psychology or simply psychologist degree.

Although there are some variations, training in Mexico and Latin America includes theoretical courses in general, experimental, and the best established branches of psychology: physiological, educational, clinical, social, industrial, etc and practice courses. Also, by the last semesters a degree of specialization in one area is encouraged and the student must prepare at least a bibliographical, but preferably an actual research project with numerous subjects to be presented as a thesis.

When compared with the structure of education in Germany, the United Kingdom, and *mutatis mutandis* with France, as represented in the APA *International Opportunities* publication (1966), it is clear that the European and Latin American systems coincide and are clearly different from the North American.

The German Diploma is almost the same as the psychologist degree from Mexico if type and years of training are taken into account. The United Kingdom ordinary or general honor's degree is again quite similar. The "licencé en psychologie" from France, while having more courses outside psychological subjects, also completes his studies in 3 or 4 years but does not need to present a dissertation. A research thesis is not required in Germany or the U.K. either. However, there are comprehensive examinations in all three countries after 1 or 2 years of the psychological career. The similarities between the European scheme and the Latin American are increased because in all cases after 11–13 years of primary and secondary-preparatory education, the student enters a psychological program that permits him to exercise a profession. A clear and interesting difference is that psychology is not taught in Europe, as it is in Latin America, at the secondary level. All of these systems contrast with the U.S. Liberal Arts College education. While here again 12 years of primary and high school education are required to enter a university, the 4-year undergraduate program leads to a bachelor's degree, which is intended to instruct, at greater depth, what the secondary-preparatory education is supposed to do in the rest of the world. At most the U.S. student may have a major in psychology in the B.A. degree, and this implies no more than 2 years of training in psychology and related subjects. To become a professional psychologist in the U.S. usually requires obtaining the PhD or equivalent higher degree, and this normally entails at least 4 years of postgraduate studies and a thesis.

Because the training is for practice and to some extent for research, I strongly believe that a good Latin American student with a licenciate or psychologist degree is comparable in training and ability with a good U.S. master's degree in psychology. Interestingly enough, the usual PhD from a good university in the U.S. is far better trained to do good research than, up to now, the average Doctor in Psychology from Latin American faculties.

Programs and Degrees

Guzman (1981) describes the vicissitudes of a career of psychology from its inauguration in 1938 to 1960. On April 7, 1960, the University Council of the National University of Mexico (U.N.A.M) approved formally three levels for its psychological program: (*a*) a professional level to be completed in about 3 years and include theoretical and methodological subjects, practical training, and a dissertation; (*b*) a Master's level designed for the teaching of psychology including theoretical subjects, practical training, seminars, and a dissertation to be completed in about 1 year; and (*c*) a Doctor of psychology level to be completed in about 2 years including courses and seminars and a dissertation. The objectives of the doctoral degree are to train specialists in clinical, industrial, educational, criminological, counseling, or social psychology and to enable the graduate to do research in his field (Curiel 1962).

By 1966, however, it had become clear that these courses lacked updating, a pragmatic orientation, and emphasis on technologies and scientific methodologies. These omissions were perceived by several groups of students and young teachers who by this time had visited, for intensive seminars and calls to specialized agencies, the departments of psychology of The University of Texas (Holtzman et al 1964, Holtzman 1970). By 1964, a group of young psychologists from The University of Mexico inaugurated a program of psychology at the University of Veracruz in Jalapa. Here the experimental analysis of behavior and behavioral technology was the basis of the program. A commission at U.N.A.M. formed by H. Cappello, A. Cuevas, G. Davila, R. Diaz-Guerrero, F. Garcia, L. Lara Tapia, J. Llanes, J. McGregor, S. Ramirez, and G. Vazquez devised a new curriculum for the professional degree to be completed in about 5 years. It included courses in how to make educational, personality, vocational, industrial, attitudinal, and intelligence tests and inventories. It was heavily loaded with statistics, measurement, and experimental design credits. This new curriculum turned out, however, to be too ambitious (see details in Guzman 1981). After student protests, it was changed to what fundamentally has been the curriculum since 1971. The fundamental difference, besides less measurement and statistics, is in dedicating the first six semesters to philosophy of science, mathematics, theories and systems, statistics and the fundamental contents of psychological science plus its practicums; the following four semesters are open for elective and specialization subjects. These were originally in the areas of clinical, educational, industrial, and social psychology and later also in general experimental and physiological psychology. First at least 5 and later 9 courses were required for the specialization from more than a dozen possibilities in each field (Facultad de Psicologia 1976).

The laboratories and practicums initiated with great difficulties have undergone a continuous evolution (Lopez Rodriguez 1978). Medina-Liberty, the present coordinator of this curriculum, has provided the environment for improvements. I have been particularly impressed by a recently published volume for the "Fourth level of practices" (Garcia et al 1982). Utilized in the fifth semester of the program, it prepares the students to deal with the full sociophychological reality they will face and provides a clear presentation of theoretical approaches, including Latin American, North American, European, and international, typical problems dealt by them, an abstract of a paper illustrating how the problems were dealt with and a section on instruments that can be utilized and methods that can be followed. While it is still incomplete, I believe this is a contribution to the teaching of a social, almost interdisciplinary, scientific psychology.

Another important development, besides a 23,000 volume library, is the Open University Division. It was organized after the Department (Colegio) of Psychology became in 1973 an independent faculty, which is now lodged in three buildings. The Division was created fundamentally to serve students of psychology unable to follow rigid calendar and class hours. The program to be completed is the same but has been developed in modules for self-instruction (Alvarado Tenorio & Nieto Sotelo 1976, Facultad de Psicologia 1979). Finally, all professional students of psychology must complete 6 months of social service and a thesis before their final examination by three jurors.

The reader may be asking by now if the present Faculty of Psychology is the only institution granting degrees in Mexico. It certainly is not. It is, however, the oldest by far and continues to be the most important model.

The Ibero-American University, with its Department of Psychology incorporated into the National University, and also located in Mexico City, recently celebrated its twenty-fifth anniversary (Meneses 1976). This university, besides the professional degree, grants a doctorate, and three or four other institutions award or are in the process of conferring masters degrees. The National University, on the other hand, has been offering both degrees in an increasing number of fields and for by far the longest time.

While presently registration at the professional level often requires no more than graduation from high school, to be admitted to a Master's or Doctoral degree demands entrance examinations, ability to translate from two modern languages, and participation in a selection competition. On the other hand, adequate applicants with "licenciaturas" other than psychology (in anthropology or sociology, for example) may be admitted to graduate studies or specializations.

Graduate studies at the National University include those for the degrees of Master, Doctor, and Specialist. The first two prepare mostly for academic and research activity; the last furthers professional specialization. The Master's degree is obtained after four semesters of study and a research dissertation in clinical, social, or educational psychology and in psychobiology, general experimental and experimental analysis of behavior. A Doctor's degree is granted only in the last two areas or in clinical and social psychology. It requires another 2 years of studies and a research dissertation.

There are two areas in which the specialist degree may be obtained: child development and group psychotherapy in institutions. The requirements for entrance are similar to the Master's degree. After four semesters of study and without a thesis, a certificate of specialization is granted to a successful student. Full details regarding graduate studies can be found in Facultad de Psicologia, Organizacion Academica (1979).

There is little doubt that the level of organization and sophistication reached by the program at the Faculty of Psychology of U.N.A.M. is very high. It would be excellent training if it was not for the population explosion that at one time reached over 5000 students at the professional level. Other schools in the Republic, while generally having the advantage of a far smaller number of students may lose it because of a lower quantity or quality of teaching personnel, although at one time or another provincial schools like those in Jalapa, Veracruz, and Merida, Yucatan, have reached high standards in their training.

There has occurred, however, an unruly growth of private schools and the granting of graduate level degrees at some state schools that threaten a lowering of the professional and scientific standards of the Mexican psychologist (Lafarga 1977a).

The Consejo Nacional para la Enseñanza e Investigacion en Psicologia (CNEIP), which includes over 25 schools of psychology, is fully aware of the presence of over a dozen such inadequate schools and, beyond certain internal turmoil of its own, is searching for lawful ways to curb this growth (i.e. CNEIP 1977). At the bottom of the problem is the lack of sufficient psychologists with a Master's or a Doctor's degree. Even in many schools of the CNEIP there is an abundance of teachers with no more than the Licenciate degree. Actually, outside the U.N.A.M., where several dozen teachers hold Doctorates, particularly at the graduate level, it is the exception to find them in other institutions. The upgrading of teachers is a continuous concern at U.N.A.M. and other institutions (Alcaraz 1977, Ribes 1977, Lafarga 1977b, Barocio 1978).

Accomplishments and Issues

Numbers now become necessary. Those published belong to U.N.A.M. (Guzman 1981). The number of students registered at the professional level was 6 in 1940, 196 in 1950, 623 in 1960, 1705 in 1970, and 4650 in 1978. Fortunately, teachers also increased from 145 in 1973 to 406 in 1978. In 1978 about 30% of these teachers were either half or full time. The remaining 70% consists either of capable professionals who teach only one subject or partial (less than half) time instructors and teaching assistants. Close to 50% of the teaching personnel is female, and 85% are psychologists. About 25% of the psychologists hold a PhD or an MA.

According to Guzman (1981), only one-fourth of those who embark on studies for the professional degree obtain it, with a total of 1437 degrees granted between 1947 and 1978. On the other hand, between 1958 and 1976, 3139 completed all credits for the professional degree but did not present a thesis and take the final exam. It is probable that only 40% of those who finish the program obtain a degree. Those without it are called "pasantes" and often practice or teach psychology.

In his index of failure to complete, Guzman shows an irregular histogram through the years (1981, p. 170), for how many of those that started the program completed it. With an incompletion rate over 80% in the 1958–1961 program, he shows an irregular decrease through the years to a 39% incompletion in the 1971–1975 cycle. He is also careful to compare this efficacy of the psychology program to an overall higher education efficacy reported by Castrejon Diez (1976). Between 1967 and 1976 the psychology program of U.N.A.M. had 41% incompletion compared to 49% for all the universities and polytechnics in the Republic combined. The failure to complete is as high as 54% for the state universities in Mexico.

While the data for number of graduates of masters and doctors programs are less certain, it appears that between 1963 and 1978, 174 graduate degrees were granted; 58% of these were to women and 42% to men. It appears that at U.N.A.M., 74% of those enrolled in the PhD program obtained the degree.

CNEIP published detailed data for 1979 on the structure, functions, number of teachers and students, etc from most of its 27 member schools of psychology. From the data reported one can estimate that there were at the time 17,000 individuals studying for the professional degree of psychology in these 27 institutions. At the Iberoamerican University there were 25 registered for an M.A. and 21 for the PhD (Lafarga 1979). At U.N.A.M., 218 were registered for the M.A. and 17 for the PhD. The orginal thought when the Faculty of Psychology was established at U.N.A.M. was to be very selective for degrees higher than the professional, in order to create a cadre of excellent graduates. At the Universidad de las Americas in Cholula, Puebla, 15 are registered for the M.A.

Mouret Polo & Ribes Iñesta (1977), besides canvassing 15 state schools and 15 private schools, identified 10 other private schools. Since 1977 no one knows how many more small private schools have opened to offer training in psychology. I personally know of one that opened in 1982 in Ensenada, Baja California. To further show this expansive development—in 1960 you could count the schools with the fingers on one hand—B. M. Alvarez (1977) cites 18 teacher training institutions of a higher level, both state and private, which offer programs in educational psychology. Thus, conservatively, there are 59 organizations concerned with the training of psychologists in Mexico but relatively few that offer Masters and PhD degrees. It is important that state and private schools are made aware of the extreme importance of hiring capable teachers with graduate degrees.

Mouret Polo & Ribes Iñesta (1977) calculate 35 students per teacher in the state schools (33 per teacher at U.N.A.M.) and 55 per teacher at the private schools canvassed. Besides these authors, Lafarga (1976a, 1977b and Mercado et al (1979) wrote critical essays concerning programs of training and the proliferation of schools, and they offer recommendations.

THE PROFESSION

Areas of Interest

What in the U.S. is known as industrial psychology and recently in Mexico has been labeled "Psicologia del Trabajo" or Psychology of Labor has received more critical professional attention than other areas of psychology. It may not be accidental that the present Director of the Facultad de Psicologia of the National University, Darvelio Castaño, is an industrial psychologist. While there are probably others, one early statement about this field was written by Garza Garcia (1953); see also the perceptive statement concerning the use of psychometric instrumentation in private and state organizations by Gomez Robleda (1959). Lively descriptions of what the industrial psychologist actually did in his work in the years prior to 1967 were published by Aranda Lopez (1974) and Huerta-Ibarra (1974). A more sophisticated characterization of the Psychology of Labor in Mexico up to 1976 was provided by Castaño & Sanchez (1978).

Testing in Mexico, while displaying one of the longest histories (Ortega & Lopez 1953) and probably representing the technique most used by all professional psychologists, has not produced a single thorough book on testing. The number of papers published and theses dedicated to different tests, including standardizations for local populations, is so great that only a whole review dedicated to this topic alone might come close to doing it justice. It is important, however, at least to enumerate in order of the amount of psychometric work done in Mexico the following workers: Reyes-Lagunes, Lara-Tapia, Morales, Choynowski, Ferreira, Velazquez-Medina, Witzke, Fernandez, Re, Moreau, Chao, and Laosa.

Clinical psychology has been and probably continues to be—under its several guises of diagnosis, counseling, guidance, psychotherapy, and community psychology and its psychodynamic, behavioral, cognitive, and cognitive behavioral and humanistic approaches—the most common form in which to practice psychology. There are, however, few critical or descriptive papers about it. There are early local statements by Nuñez (1962) and Villalpando Nava (1953), but more often the portrayal appears in international publications (e.g. David 1964, Iscoe 1972, Appelbaum 1975). Professional clinical psychology has had great teachers in Mexico such as Erich Fromm, Guillermo Davila, Santiago Ramirez, Abraham Fortes, and Raymundo Macias.

There was an early interest in special education (Solis Quiroga 1953), and the effort was maintained against difficult odds (Gonzalez Cipres 1968) until behavior modification revitalized this field (Ribes 1972). Finally, school psychology as practiced in Mexico was originally discussed by Fernandez in 1967 (Fernandez 1974).

Surveys of the Profession

The first survey of the profession was carried out in 1964 (Diaz-Guerrero 1974) on 108 psychologists.[1] At that time 70% of the psychologists had more than one employment. One position might be in clinical and the other in educational, industrial, or in teaching or research in psychology. For their main job, 40% were in counseling, 25% in clinical, 12% in teaching, 9% in research, and 7% in industrial psychology. Covarrubias de Levy (1970) found that in the Federal District (fundamentally Mexico City), 31% of the schools and 18% of the

---

[1] A current informal estimate would be that there are about 3000 to 4000 psychologists working in psychology-related activities in Mexico.

industries employed psychologists, and 36% of schools and 25% of industries consulted them. She found also that psychologists' work in the schools was 81% counseling and 13% teaching, while in industries 75% implied selection of personnel and 25% general consulting services.

Velasco Hernandez (1978) found in a survey of schools across the Republic that 68% adopted eclectic teaching, 16% psychodynamic, 12% behavioral, and 4% humanistic. From 34 schools canvassed, he found that 22 offered the professional degree in clinical, 19 in educational, 16 in social, 15 in industrial, and 1 in developmental psychology.

Macotela & Espinosa (1979) were interested in the image of the psychologist held by the public. Their survey covered 697 individuals from different sections of Mexico City representing diverse socioeconomic levels and occupations. Fundamentally the public perceives the psychologist in a clinical role and generally ignores his other capabilities and talents. The lower the socioeconomic status the less the knowledge about the psychologist and his functions. From unpublished data obtained for the Atlas of Meanings (Osgood et al 1975, Diaz-Guerrero & Salas 1975), it was found that the subjective-affective meaning of the concept of psychology for Mexican male adolescents in the ninth grade of schooling was quite neutral in evaluation, potency, and activity, as it was in the average for 30 language localities around the world. Also, among 27 philosophical concepts such as Justice, Knowledge, Eternity, Infinity, Love, etc it appeared in the average rank of 15.7 for evaluation, 16.7 in potency, and 15.6 in activity, definitively below the concept of philosophy in evaluation and potency but slightly above in activity and exactly the same 17.6 in familiarity! The subjective meaning of psychology for Mexicans is closest to Afghanistan Dari and Hong Kong Chinese subjects, the three Third World communities geographically close to the U.S., Soviet Russia, and Communist China, respectively! It is interesting that among the 27 philosophical concepts the synonyms in affective meaning to psychology were Pleasure, Mind, Free Will, and Luck, and the antonyms were the Universe, Pain, Fatalism, and Sin. There is a positive connotation for psychology among these adolescents that may be at the root of its relatively large election as a profession.

Mercado et al (1979) surveyed 310 psychologists working for the Mexican government: 69% were women and 31% males, 68% were between 21 and 30 years of age, and 78% obtained their first jobs as psychologists after 1970. Their income was not different from that reported earlier by Diaz-Guerrero (1974) and Covarrubias de Levy (1970). The profession provides for a low to upper middle class income, but the higher incomes in the three studies can be traced to the fact that most psychologists have two or more jobs—69% in the results of Mercado et al. Congruent to training inquiries, 67% of those holding jobs in the government were "pasantes," and only 33% had completed a degree. More women than men (37% to 29%) had graduated. When asked the number of years it took to complete the professional courses, 92% indicated it took them from 4 to 6 years; 62% said 5 years.

Mercado et al (1979) asked the main type of activities carried out by these psychologists: 28% recorded, measured, and evaluated behavior; 24% engaged in the planning and development of human resources; and 11% each assessed and guided or were involved in adminstration. Only about 7% each engaged in teaching, research, or therapy. Of those recording, measuring, and evaluating, 40% utilize standarized instruments; of those developing human resources, 40% use practice and training techniques; and of those in guidance, 44% utilize clinical assessments. Finally, 48% confessed that they developed most of their knowledge and abilities in their jobs. Only 32% felt that such was obtained during their professional training and 12% in workshops or conferences attended beyond their schooling. Of those reporting, 76% felt that they had sufficient knowledge to exercise their duties.

Judging from the fact that most psychologists have developed two or more employment activities, there appears to be a defined need for psychologists' skills. It probably also signifies ignorance of and scarcity of utilization of the many talents of psychologists.

RESEARCH AND APPLICATION

In this section we will survey the main areas of research, taking them up in alphabetical order. It is hoped that the citations of many specific studies will help psychologists outside of Mexico to find Mexican research in their areas of interest and perhaps also to make contact with investigators in Mexico.

Clinical Psychology

Research in clinical psychology has been abundant but not systematic. This is partially due to the many theories utilized in practice. The research often takes the form of a dissertation that can be criticized methodologically and that has not been followed by additional studies. Nuñez (1968), with the help of Hathaway, introduced the MMPI to Mexico. Several theses and dissertations were inspired by this effort. However, Navarro and co-workers (1971, 1973, 1976a,b, 1979) have investigated most extensively and published utilizing the MMPI. In one study (Navarro et al 1976a,b), 1203 government workers of both sexes, two age levels, four levels of employment, four levels of schooling, and three levels of intelligence completed the MMPI. Because men and women differed greatly in both level of employment and education, analyses of variance were carried out separately for men and women. While there were age differences (young-old) for men, the most notable differences appeared with employment level, schooling, and intelligence. Generally older age and lower level of employment, schooling, and intelligence were associated with greater problems of social and personal adjustment. With women the results were similar except that level of employment did not differentiate as well for women, who had a significantly lower level of education in comparison to the males. Later, Navarro (1979) applied the MMPI to 12,377 students entering the Ibero-American University. A needed standarization resulted since the U.S. norms gave very psychopathological profiles to the average Mexican. No notable differences were found between male and female students, but there were numerous and intriguing differences by vocational inclinations. Men and women in the social sciences, including psychology, show higher scores in the Hysteria and M. F. scales, greater preference for artistic activities, are less tied to religious dogma, less competitive, show lower preoccupation with achievement and higher hypochondriasis scores than individuals in other vocations.

Lara Tapia has been an active investigator in the realms of local psychopathology and psychopharmacology. It is unfortunate that he has published relatively little (i.e. Lara Tapia & Ramirez 1975, Lara Tapia & Velez 1975). Three of his students, Escoto, Ruiz, and Vazquez (1982), recently completed a most comprehensive study of hysteria in Mexico. The experimental design permitted them to compare 30 female and 30 male normals with 30 female hysterics and 30 male drug addicts. They used TAT plates and developed original content analyses of responses to determine a high interjudge reliability quantitative measure of coping style. There are a number of intriguing differences across the design, but in these fantasy protocols, hysterics were characterized by the highest score in both active coping and active defense among the four groups, and the drug addicts had the highest scores in passive coping and equally as high in passive defense as hysterics, with both groups significantly above normals in this trait. Mexican hysterics, as psychiatrically and psychologically diagnosed (with the help of the MMPI), could be excellent writers of soap operas! They constitute a group almost opposite psychodynamically to drug addicts.

Centering on the needs of psychiatric and psychological clients, an organized interdisciplinary team has been working at the Instituto Mexicano de Psiquiatria (Calzada Xochimilco 101, Mexico, D.F. C.P. 14370). The result is realistic research on biomedical, drug addiction and alcoholism, mental health, psychopharmacological, treatment and epidemiological topics, some of which will appear in other sections. Recently the team held its first meeting on research and training (*I Reunion sobre Investigacion y Enseñanza* 1982).

Emmite (1977) made an enthusiastic attempt to apply Diaz-Guerrero's historic bio-psycho-socio-cultural premise as a macrosystem where many subsystems, particularly the self premises system and the coping style systems of three cultural groups—black and white Anglos and Mexican-Americans—could be compared on their contribution to student achievement. The historic bio-psycho-self system of each student is seen as the repository of all other aspects of the ecology. Emmite feels that multiple regression on achievement criteria permits one to order the importance of cultural premises, self premises, coping premises, etc in regard to achievement. Since the informational, cybernetic, actuarial and even psychodynamic approaches can so easily be handled by the premises system which includes historic, genetic, biological, social, and cultural components, Emmite feels this is a useful explanatory macrosystem for clinical and other theoretical and applied branches of psychology.

Lichtszajn (1979) explores the attitudes toward death in Mexican adolescents and their correlates. Two hundred 15-year-old high school subjects equally divided by sex and social class were the subjects. They all completed a protocol including a demographic questionnarie, two inventories of Mexican sociocultural premises, a trait anxiety scale, semantic differentials for the concept of Death and 19 other clinically critical concepts such as insanity, pain, old age, life, sadness, divorce, crime, fear, separation, etc, and finally Spielberger's Anxiety State Scale. On the semantic differential, these adolescents find death very bad, quite potent, and neutral in activity. No differences were found by social class, but women feel that death is more potent, with amount of familiarity with the concept being equal across all groups. The concept of death appears independent from the sociocultural premises except for the scales of "Machismo" and Fear of Authority. High scores of Machismo go with lower potency (threat) of the death concept, and the more it is thought that children fear their parents, the more active death appears. Clinical concepts most highly and positively correlated to death were cancer followed by funeral, drunkeness, and sadness. The most negatively correlated concept among the 20 was I MYSELF.

Diaz-Guerrero, who practiced psycotherapy for 20 years (1959a,b, 1963), showed in collaboration with Lichtszajn & Reyes-Lagunes (1979) that the subjective meaning of the "insult to the mother," as measured by the Semantic Differential Technique, was clearly associated with almost all of 20 clinically critical concepts. It was argued that clinical understanding in Mexico could be derived from how the individual scored on evaluation, potency, activity, and familiarity with the Insult to the Mother. Later Diaz-Guerrero (1982a) illustrates how an economical correlational method can discover the sources of anxiety for given populations in given sociocultures. In Mexico the sources of anxiety—as measured by Spielberger's Spanish STAI—for Mexico City high school adolescents vary greatly according to sex and social class. The threat of sadness looms large in this population as well as a low evaluation of the self.

Nieto-Cardoso, also very interested in psychotherapy, has tried to measure the effects of group training on Carkhull's Helping Discrimination Scale (1977), the relationships between self-disclosure, anxiety, and therapeutic efficiency (1979), and learning through a human mediator (1981).

Cueli & Biro (1975) have developed a psychoanalytic model of community psychology, and Cueli with his students (Cueli 1976, Lartigue 1976, and Michaca 1977) have made interesting efforts to apply and research it.

Cognitive Psychology

A good stimulus to theoretical and some research papers in this topic was a reaction to the impact in Mexico of behaviorism, particularly in its Skinnerian version. The names of Serafin Mercado, Jesus Figueroa, and Araceli Otero come immediately to mind.

Mercado, whose present interest is more on the theory and methodology of science and in ecological psychology, started early with a paper on cognitive control (1963) and his interesting studies on the Müller-Lyer and other illusions which he felt were due to adjustments of the constancy effect (Mercado et al 1967, Maldonado & Mercado 1974).

Figueroa, who went to teach in Great Britain for several years and published in European journals (i.e. 1974), has been back in Mexico for several years. Creative and restless, he has recently explored reconstruction in memory (Figueroa et al 1976, 1982a,b,c,d).

Otero studied in Geneva under Piaget and Inhelder. Engaged in teaching at U.N.A.M. and program development for the government schools in Mexico (1982), she had time for research on conservation (i.e. Delgado & Otero 1978).

Gustavo Fernandez is difficult to pigeonhole. He has been productive in several fields. He exemplifies well one more characteristic of research in Mexico. Often done for love rather than money, it displays a unique friendly and selfless feature. The researcher is often surrounded by a group of eager students. He offers free consultation for thesis research to many. Some become voluntary assistants. The researcher, and Fernandez is a good example, is frequently a friend of the collaborator and/or gives secondary authorship and not infrequently leading authorship in the publication of the results. Fernandez has published in psychometrics (Fernandez et al 1970, M. Fernandez & G. Fernandez 1974, Fernandez et al 1974), has been a behaviorist (Brahan & G. Fernandez 1974, Fernandez et al 1971) and commonly with Dolores Mercado, his colleague, an open-minded cognitivist (Carredano, Mercado & Fernandez 1974; Mercado & Fernandez 1974; Mercado, Gonzalez & Fernandez 1974 a,b).

Fevreiski (1982), who is presently with the Department of Psychology of the University of Toronto, recently did an experimental study of primary and secondary reviewing and its relation to long-term memory.

Luis Castro is another kaleidoscopic researcher. He was early doing research on communication (Castro 1974). He has done work on predicting mortality in a hospital (Witzke et al 1969), psychophysiological studies (Castro et al 1974,

Castro & Carrillo 1976) and on cognition (Castro & Rodriguez 1975, Lopez et al 1978).

Educational Psychology

As is the case with research on psychometric tools, the amount of work done in this field is beyond this paper to review. Indirectly, in other sections, some research pertinent to the field will be described. The best source, particularly for the teaching of psychology, is the journal *Enseñanza e Investigacion en Psicologia*. Here the names of Javier Aguilar, Victor Alcaraz, Victor Arredondo, Luis Castro, Guillermo Delahanty, Jose Gomez del Campo, Cirilo Garcia, Juan Lafarga, Maria Teresa Lartigue, Jorge Martinez, Jorge Molina, Lourdes Quintanilla, and Emilio Ribes appear, in some cases repeatedly, as contributors.

Environmental Psychology and Ecopsychology

Given the environmental conditions of Mexico City with its close to 15,000,000 inhabitants, it is welcome that an enthusiastic group has been formed around Javier Urbina and Serafin Mercado and has began to carry on with serious research in environmental psychology. In interdisciplinary association with architects and others, they prepared the publication of an influential monograph on the problems of the city (La Ciudad 1982), with a large section dedicated to psychology and the environment. A number of psychologists participated. Among them, Urbina & Ortega (1982) wrote about the general conceptual and research scheme of environmental psychology, Alvarez et al (1982) reported on Mexican children's perceptions of the city, and Mercado (1982) and Santoyo (1982) operationalize noise and crowding, respectively. Ortega & Urbina (1982a,b) contribute to the Seventh International Conference on Man and His Environment in Barcelona, Spain, with research papers on the effects of crowding on workers' productivity and other behavior and the effects of environmental organization on academic and social activities of school children.

Eduardo Almeida, social psychologist, and Maria Eugenia Sanchez de Almeida, sociologist, form an extremely active research team. Almeida (1978), following in the footsteps of Bronfenbrenner, has worked on the effect of parental involvement with teachers and children on the achievement and development of the latter. Sanchez de Almeida, in collaboration with Almeida (1978), has formed an interesting interdisciplinary team which has broadened the concepts of ecopsychology. At the time of this writing, their team included 12 members with 8 social science specialties. The team is doing action research to help in the development of a community in the mountains of Puebla, a state of Mexico.

History of Psychology

The first known article on the history of psychology in Mexico was written by Robles (1952). He endeavored to cover the development of psychology from around 1554 to 1951 and considered the Mexican tradition in psychology as modest but comparable to the most advanced Latin American republics.

Great was the stimulus provided by the International Union of Psychological Science (I U Psy S) and the American Psychological Association (APA) in organizing the "La Napoule Conference" in southern France in 1962. As a result, Diaz-Guerrero (1966) wrote on psychology in Mexico. This in turn led to several brief accounts (Alvarez & Ramirez 1979, Cevallos 1953, Colotla & Gallegos 1978, Diaz-Guerrero 1974, 1976b, 1979a, 1981a, Gallegos 1980, Ribes 1968, 1975, Rodriguez de Arizmendi 1971–1972).

In the last decade enthusiastic colleagues have formed at least two groups interested in the history of psychology, one led by Nieto (1979a,b) and another by Alvarez and Molina, who have recently organized, among other events, a seminar on the history of psychology in Mexico. Some publications of this group are Alvarez & Molina (1981) and Alvarez (1982).

Human Development

In 1949 Diaz-Guerrero (1952) carried out a survey to try to determine the degree of mental health of the Mexican in Mexico City. Ten items in the survey were intended to measure the degree of flexibility-rigidity with which sociocultural norms were held. One conclusion was the following: "It is interesting that the scale shows such high degree of rigidity (70% mean across items agreement). The result could have been foreseen. The Mexican defends such concepts as irrevocable; these sociocultural norms are probably among the most rigidly implanted in Mexico. Mexicans frequently consider such values as primordial, almost natural characteristics, 'constitutional' of the Mexican nationality" (1952, p. 38). Later these items were referred as historic-sociocultural premises (HSCPs). The reason for the label was that the fundamentally logical and paralogical nature of man's thinking and behavior, whether constructive or destructive, was beginning to be apparent. The "irrationality" of man refers to irrational, often egocentric or ethnocentric premises, not to his logical and paralogical processes.

Diaz-Guerrero (1972) felt that the psychology of personality and human development (Holtzman et al 1975, Diaz-Guerrero 1976a, 1979c) cannot be understood except in terms of the beliefs embraced by, not the elites, but the masses of the people in each nation or culture. Diaz-Guerrero (1976a, 1977a) extracted 13 factorial dimensions of HSCPs from the Mexican culture. There are two forms for the factorial scales which operationally define these dimensions.

The HSCPs of the Mexican family are statements such as: "The place for women is in the home" or "Men are, by nature, superior to women." These items could be checked for agreement or left blank or could be followed by a scale of 5 equally appearing intervals. The 9 factors derived in this form are: Machismo, with items such as "Docile women are best", Affilative Obedience with: "A son should always obey his parents"; Virginity with: "A woman should be a virgin until she marries"; Abnegation with: "Life is much harder for a woman than for a man"; Fear of Authority with: "Many children fear their parents"; Family Status Quo with: "A good wife should always be faithful to her husband"; Respect over Love with: "It is more important to respect than to love a parent"; Family Honor with: "A married woman should not dance with a man who is not her husband"; and Cultural Rigidity with: "The stricter the parents the better the child".

The "Filosofia de Vida" has four factor scales of which only the first two have shown promise in research. It was built upon the realization (Diaz-Guerrero 1967a,b) that there were HSCPs that commanded the way or style of coping with problems. Comparing the U.S. and Mexican cultures (Diaz-Guerrero 1972, 1982c, Holtzman et al 1975), two styles of coping were postulated: a passive self-modifying and an active environment and other modifyer style. The Filosofia de Vida in its early form contained 60 items and according to a pancultural analysis of the results from 3200 14-year-olds in 8 national samples provided 22 dimensions (Diaz-Guerrero 1973). Items in this early form and in the 28-item 4-factor form derived for Mexican children (Diaz-Guerrero 1976a, 1977b) are presented in a forced choice format for selection of one of a pair of alternatives. The two useful factors are Passive Affiliative Obedience vs Active Self-Assertion and Passive External Control vs Active Internal Control. Examples of items for the former are these:

(*a*) The orders of the teacher should always be obeyed, vs
(*b*) If the orders of the teacher are not reasonable, one should feel free to doubt them.

(*a*) One should never doubt the word of the mother, vs
(*b*) All mothers can make mistakes, one should feel free to doubt their word when it appears mistaken.

Examples of items for the second factor are these:

(*a*) The world is the way it is and man can do little to change it, vs
(*b*) Man can change the world to satisfy his needs.

(*a*) When I do well in a school exam, it is almost always because I studied for it, vs
(*b*) When I do well in a school exam, it is almost always because the exam was easy.

The fundamental interest of these old vs new belief scales is that besides fulfilling the aim to extricate dimensions from a culture, they implement the culture-counterculture dialectic. It has been theorized and provisionally substantiated (Diaz-Guerrero 1979c, 1980, 1982c, Diaz-Guerrero & Castillo Vales 1981) that human and social system development are best understood in terms of a culture-counterculture dialectic that includes all of the following: ecosystematic dimensions (Bronfenbrenner 1977, 1979), a cultural ecosystem with biopsychological variables, like adherence or rebellion to traditional values, passive vs active coping styles, and at least economic and information variables.

What makes the HSCPs scales pertinent to human development, besides the underlying theorizing, are the empirically determined significant correlations with cognitive perceptual, cognitive, and personality, developmental and other behavioral science variables (Diaz-Guerrero, 1976a, 1977b,c, 1980, Diaz-Guerrero & Castillo Vales 1981, Reyes Lagunes 1982) which recently have been found to yield up to moderate correlations in the .40s and .50s with Witkin's Field Dependence-Independence construct and Rotter's Internality-Externality measures (Diaz-Guerrero 1982c,d, Reyes Lagunes 1982).

The Division for the Study of Development of UNESCO (Paris) through the initiative of W. Schwendler has organized conferences successively on "Trends in Social Science Research on Children" in Austin, Texas, 1979, with the collaboration of the Hogg Foundation for Mental Health, "Studies on Development and on the Reduction of Inequalities in Different Socio-Cultural Contexts, specially with regards to Children and Family Life-Styles" *(Childhood Inequalities and Development* 1982) in Doha, Qatar, 1981, with the collaboration of the University of Qatar and "The Changing Family in a Changing World" in Munich, West Germany, 1982, in collaboration with the German Commission of UNESCO in Bonn and the University of Munich. Diaz-Guerrero has been an invited contributor to all three (1979b, 1981b, 1982b).

Learning

There has been some pure and extensive applied research in learning; mainly this has been in the experimental analysis of behavior together with theoretical and review papers. Several behaviorists from North America, notably Sidney Bijou, have been helpful in local developments. The names of E. Ribes, E. Rayek, A. Bouzas, P. Speller, J. Molina, L. Castro, V. Arredondo, F. Lopez, S. Macotela, C. Garcia, N. Perez Vyeites, F. Cabreu, B. Dominguez, C. Fernandez, J. Peralta, and several others appear commonly in publications. Much of the research is actually clinical with the retarded and other client populations but also with instructional problems. The following are publications that can easily be obtained: Bijou & Ribes (1972), Sociedad Mexicana de Analisis de la Conducta (1977), and Speller (1978).

Neuropsychology

"Raul Hernandez Peon died on April 16th, 1968, in the City of Mexico as a result of injuries sustained in an automobile accident . . . at the time of his death

[he] . . . was generally recognized as the foremost investigator in the neurological sciences in Mexico and one of the leading world investigators in the field of neurophysiological mechanisms of sleep" (Morgane 1970, p. 379). I had the honor to pronounce the funeral oration at his grave.

Hernandez Peon's research with more than 100 papers published spanned many areas: attention, orientation reactions, arousal, and habituation, particularly as they related to sleep and dreaming. Perhaps even more important than his personal research contribution was the number of researchers in neuropsychology that were fundamentally formed under him. Several of them have in turn encouraged new researchers. Neuropsychology, with its aura of real science and its many allied disciplines, variously called biomedicine (I Reunion sobre Investigacion y Enseñanza 1982), psychopharmacology, physiological psychology, psychobiology, etc, is one of the most, if not *the* most active field in Mexico. Again, at least one full article would be needed to do it justice. In order not to make the *Literature Cited* interminable, I shall only list first the most productive students and colleagues of Hernandez Peon: A. Fernandez-Guardiola, H. Brust Carmona, R. Drucker-Colin, G. Chavez Ibarra, C. Guzman Flores, J. Peñaloza Rojas, and J. A. Rojas Ramirez.

Some of the very long list of younger researchers in these fields include V. Alcaraz, V. Colotla, L. Castro, A. Escobar, A. Nava, and H. Lara Tapia. There are groups doing research in different areas in several institutions. Thus, biofeedback has recently been investigated at the Unidad de Investigaciones Cerebrales del Instituto Nacional de Neurologia y Neuro-Cirugia (Insurgentes Sur 3877, Mexico 22, D. F.), and also at U.N.A.M., Behavioral Psychopharmacology and Toxicology at U.N.A.M., at Universidad Anahuac, and in several areas of neuropsychology at the Instituto Mexicano de Psiquiatria, and at U.N.A.M.

Psychology of Labor

Fernando Arias Galicia is perhaps the most persistent researcher in this area. We can mention here only one of his first papers and two of his later studies (1964, 1982; Arias Galicia & Fernandez, 1982). Gutierrez has stimulated research on the bases of Moscovici's social representation theory (Bustos & Gutierrez 1982), and in Naldes and Lawler's theory of expectation (Reyes & Gutierrez 1982). Cardenas Ojeda (1963) early published a volume on an extensive study based on an original modification of Jung's Association Test. The approach, created by Jose Gomez Robleda, labeled the Test of Double Association, requires an individual to write the first 30 words that come to his mind and when finished he is asked to write again the same words and finally relate fully his thinking in the moment each word came to his mind. Cardenas subjected 844 individuals to the technique and reported fully on the intricate relationships between the first and second lists. Thus, there is a relationship between age and the proportion of words in the first list that appear in the second list. This proportion is largest at 25, equal at 10 and 40 years of age, and lowest in older ages. The test was used as a projective method in a battery for use in industrial and also in other areas of applied psychology. I have no information regarding the present use of this test, but it is an example of many local creations.

Others involved in research in this area are D. Castaño, C. Gomez-Robledo, G. Herrera, G. Sanchez Bedolla, and A. Shore.

Social Psychology and Personality

There is extensive interest in research in social psychology. Much of it is applied. Pick de Weiss has explored family planning in Mexico (1978, 1980) and recently presented a paper on the present state of social psychology in Mexico (1982). Morales did several studies, also with a sociopsychological approach, in family planning (Morales 1977; Diaz-Guerrero & Morales 1976, 1977).

Dominguez has stimulated work on criminological psychology and captive communities (1974; Dominguez & Garcia 1979, Gomez et al 1982).

Cappello (1975), presently absorbed by administrative duties, did some research on attitudes toward the medical services and in world interaction simulation. Reidl de Aguilar (1981) has worked on interpersonal attraction. G. Rodriguez de Arizmendi, presently engaged in the psychology of health, has done cross-cultural comparative work across developed and Third World nations on women's sex role behavior and its correlates (1980).

Diaz-Loving has recently opened two systematic avenues to research in social psychology and personality. His main interest is in empathy and prosocial behavior (Archer et al 1981) as it is related to values (Earle et al 1984) and self-disclosure in Mexican culture (Diaz-Loving & Nina Estrella, (1984). He has also psychometrically adapted to Mexico Spence & Helmreich's Personal Attributes Questionnaire, introducing the MEPAQ (1981). In a study with the MEPAQ and Diaz-Guerrero's HSCPs, he is trying to predict family planning attitudes and behavioral intentions.

Gomez Perez-Mitre (1981), utilizing a complex multivariate design, finds that in Mexico external conditions affect more change in subjects with low self-esteem than self changes when carrying on with a task. Also, that high self-esteem subjects anticipate success and low self-esteem subjects failure on a group solving task.

W. H. Holtzman, Jr. (1980), using the Toreane Tests of Creative Thinking with bilinguals and monolinguals in Spanish and English, finds that Spanish monolinguals do better than Anglo monolinguals and bilinguals of the same social level on creative artistic ability, and bilinguals better than all others on the verbal section of the test. Hernandez Holtzman & Holtzman (1983) have completed a psychometric study to adapt to Mexico the Attitudes Towards

Women Scale of Spence and Helmreich. Hernandez-Holtzman (1984) investigated working Mexican-American couples. Life satisfaction scores for the males were highest when they felt backed by their wives and social millieu. For the wives, highest scores have a negative correlation with role conflict followed by a positive correlation with educational level. Reciprocal support was indispensable for the maintenance of the dual working couple.

M. Choynowski, a Polish psychologist living in Mexico, deserves special mention. His work on aggression in Mexican adolescents has led to a factorial instrument for its measurement and further research (Choynowski 1977, 1978). Presently, in spite of difficulties, he is working at the Universidad Pedagogica Nacional on an ambitious program to try to determine individual and environmental factors important in personality development.

Applied Interdisciplinary Research

Reyes-Lagunes (1982) studied attitudes, cognitive style, and personality characteristics of 583 primary teachers in a national sample. The complex factorial design considered sex, years of study, years of teaching, and type of school (urbanization). Measurement instruments included attitudes toward teaching and teaching innovations, semantic differentials about the teacher as an expert, authority, instructor, model, and person, Diaz-Guerrero's HSCPs, Witkin's Hidden Figures Test and an extensive demographic inventory. Among the many interesting findings, some of which should be easy to apply, there were these: 1. The strong field dependence of teachers which decreased with years of study, urbanization, and the male sex. 2. The high degree of dependence on the traditional cultural beliefs and the prevalence of the self-modifying coping style. Although high, this was lower than that of parents in the same social class.

Almeida, Diaz-Guerrero & Sanchez (1980) piloted a program to detect public opinion about national problems and to explore the reasons for low electoral participation. Among the salient results of the pilot but representative sample in Mexico City were those: (a) 93% of the citizens interviewed disagreed with the statement that most Mexicans have adequate living quarters. (b) Those that vote have a higher self-evaluation, and consider themselves more active (in semantic differentials), and the study strongly suggested that if voting was made easier, almost 20% more citizens would vote. (c) Citizens with a self-assertive coping style were significantly more dissatisfied than the passive-obedient with their personal and Mexico's development from 1976 to 1980 (before the drastic devaluation) and not optimistic about this development from 1980–1984.

Ayala and co-workers (1981, 1982) have stimulated research on mental health, dealing with the rehabilitation of chronic mental patients and drug addicts. Ayala has also worked on evaluative studies.

Reyes-Lagunes, Almeida, Diaz-Guerrero, Ferreira, Velazquez-Medina, Morales, Emmite, and Bauer have participated in much applied and basic research, at times interdisciplinary, at the Instituto Nacional de Ciencias del Comportamiento y de la Actitud Publica (INCCAPAC) (see Almeida & Diaz-Guerrero (1979).

Other Investigators

Other workers should be cited: O. Loredo, J. J. Sanchez Sosa, and V. M. Castillo Vales. They work in areas that we are not dealing with in this article or that are difficult to classify. Loredo (1982; Loredo & Diaz-Guerrero 1971, 1972) has probed vocational and occupational interests. Sanchez Sosa (1976, 1980; Sanchez Sosa et al 1978), while also involved in administrative matters, has investigated complex academic processes in higher education. Castillo Vales, in faraway Yucatan, has participated in many research activities (Castillo Vales, Hansen & Strodtbeck 1966a, Castillo Vales, Steffere, & Morley 1966b, Castillo Vales 1971, Diaz-Guerrero & Castillo Vales 1981).

A Quantitative Study of Psychological Research in Mexico

In September 1982, and with the attendance of Raul Bejar Navarro, Academic Secretary of U.N.A.M., Darvelio Castaño, Director of the Faculty of Psychology, officially instituted the Programa de Apoyo a la Investigacion. A committee formed by Urbina, Mercado, Colotla, Sanchez Bedolla, & Aguilar (1982) assumed the task of preparing a quantitative analysis of research at the Faculty between 1977 and 1980. Of the 703 studies found, 309 were classified as applied research and 204 as basic, 171 were reviews and 7 technological. Of the total, 83 had been published and 199 manuscripts had been completed.

While psychological research in Mexico is teeming, outside of three or four areas it is seldom systematic. It is still generally overly exposed to whoever grants the money or the opportunity or to very personal interests. While the research personnel is becoming increasingly sophisticated, only a few researchers feel sufficiently secure to stay in one area or even a specific field. Colleagues from the industrial nations, whether capitalist or socialist, will find enthusiastic response from younger local researchers to proposals for collaborative work, as long as their local interests are taken into account. Personal contact is far more effective than correspondence.

SOCIETIES, CONGRESSES, MEETINGS, PUBLICATIONS

At present there are at least five psychological societies in Mexico. The oldest is the Sociedad Mexicana de Psicologia, A.C., which is a member of the International Union of Psychological Science. There are societies of clinical, behavioral, and industrial psychology and one of psychologists who work for the government. Recently some state societies have been formed. The Consejo

Nacional para la Enseñanza e Investigacion en Psicologia, founded by L. Lara and E. Ribes, has delegates from about 25 departments and/or schools of psychology around the Republic. With psychiatrists and other physicians and psychologists as members, there are the Asociacion Psicoanalitica Mexicana, the Sociedad Psicoanalitica Mexicana, and the Sociedad Mexicana de Neurologia, Psiquiatria and Neurocirugia. There is also a Sociedad Mexicana de Salud Mental.

Congresses have been held by local and the Interamerican Societies. The Sociedad Mexicana de Psicologia has held three national congresses. At the second, held in 1979 with attendance of 3000, Mexican psychologists had the opportunity to hear formal invited addresses by most members of the Executive Committee of the International Union of Psychological Science, and smaller interested groups participated in at least 2-hour-long informal seminars with them.

The Sociedad Mexicana de Psicologia Clinica and the Sociedad Mexicana de Analisis de la Conducta have organized several well attended national congresses and conferences.

Actually, hardly three months pass before a meeting called by psychologists and related professionals takes place. Many schools of psychology now celebrate annually what they call "Semanas de Psicologia." Here during a week they have meetings, papers, and invited addresses by figures in different fields of psychology. The Interamerican Society of Psychology has held 4 of its 19 congresses in Mexico City, where the Society was founded in 1951.

There have been many journals of psychology. They have often depended for their existence on the dedication and often on the economic resources of their main editors. Presently edited in Mexico are *Enseñanza e Investigacion en Psicologia, Revista Mexicana de Analisis de la Conducta, Acta Psicologica Mexicana, Salud Mental,* and the *Revista de la Asociacion Latinoamericana de Psicologia Social.* Since M. Cicero became President 4 years ago, the *Boletin of the Sociedad Mexicana de Psicologia* has appeared regularly.

Editorial Trillas in Mexico has translated many classic textbooks and published a number of originals by Mexican and Latin American authors, maintaining its intent to produce at the lowest possible price in the Spanish language combined with the highest possible quality. Up to the present, between the *Biblioteca Tecnica de Psicologia* and other publications, it has distributed more than 250 titles in the field. Modern psychology has sometimes reached the student and the professional through programmed texts.

EPILOGUE

In spite of the many pages and around 200 references in this article, we are concerned that about 10% of all of those who should appear in these pages have not been mentioned. Those omitted probably include particularly colleagues in professional work—friends and competitors alike. This is true in spite of the notice that I distributed requesting information. It is clear from the article that a small Mexican annual review of psychology is becoming necessary to keep Mexican psychologists and others abreast of developments.

Literature Cited

Alcaraz, V. M. 1977. Programas academicos formales y adscripcion a proyectos de investigacion bajo tutoria individual, en la formacion de investigadores. *Enseñanza Invest. Psicol.* 3(2):65–69

Almeida, E. 1978. Effects of parental involvement in teacher training. *Int. J. Psychol.* 13(3):221–36

Almeida, E., Diaz-Guerrero, R. 1979. The National Institute for the Behavioral Sciences and public opinion. *Int. Rev. Appl. Psychol.* 28(1):49–56

Almeida, E., Diaz-Guerrero, R., Sanchez, M. E. 1980. *Un sistema para analizar la opinion publica acerca de la coyuntura nacional.* Mexico: INCCAPAC (Mimeo)

Alvarado Tenorio, R., Nieto Sotelo, J. 1976. Universidad Abierta en la facultad de psicologia. *Enseñanza Invest. Psicol.* 1 (2): 35–46

Alvarez, B. M. 1977. Educational psychology in Mexico. In *Psychology in the Schools in International Perspective*, ed. C. D. Catterall. Columbus, Ohio: Catterall

Alvarez, G. 1982. *Breve Panorama Evolutivo de la Psicologia Mexicana.* Mexico (Mimeo)

Alvarez, G. Molina, J. 1981. *Psicologia e Historia.* Mexico: Univ. Nac. Auton. Mexico

Alvarez, G., Ramirez, A. M. 1979. En busca del tiempo perdido. *Enseñanza Invest. Psicol.* 5(1):386–91

Alvarez, G., Russo, S., Ramirez, A. M. 1982. De Como Perciben los Niños la Ciudad. *Comunidad CONACYT* 8(136–137):84–86

American Psychological Association. 1976. *International Opportunities for Advanced Training and Research in Psychology.* Washington DC: Am. Psychol. Assoc.

Appelbaum, S. A. 1975. Psychotherapy in the Americas. *Interam. J. Psychol.* (Special issue) 9:1–2

Aranda Lopez, J. 1974. El panorama actual de la psicologia industrial en Mexico. In *Memorias del Primer Congreso Mexicano de Psicologia,* ed. L. Lara Tapia, pp. 285–88. Mexico: Imprenta Univ. U.N.A.M.

Archer, R. L., Diaz-Loving, R., Gollwitzer, P. M., Davis, M. H., Foushee, H. C. 1981. The role of dispositional empathy and social evaluation in the empathic mediation of helping. *J. Pers. Soc. Psychol.* 40:786–96

Ardila, R. 1978. *La Profesion del Psicologo.* Mexico: Trillas

Arias Galicia, F. 1964. Una encuesta sobre

intereses laborales en algunos grupos de trabajadores de Mexico, D.F. *Rev. Inst. Tec. Adm. Trab.* 22:7–69

Arias Galicia, F. 1982. Un instrumento para medir factores organizacionales. *Tercer Congreso Mexicano de Psicologia, Resumenes de Sesiones Tematicas,* p. 8. Mexico: Soc. Mex. Psicol. A.C.

Arias Galicia, F., Fernandez, A. 1982. Actitudes laborales, estres y relaciones familares entre obreros y obreras. *Tercer Congreso Mexicano de Psicologia, Resumenes de Sesiones Tematicas,* p. 8. Mexico: Soc. Mex. Psicol., A.C.

Ayala, H. E., Chism, S. K., Cardenas, G., Rodriguez, M., Cervantes, L., Caballero, P. 1982. Una alternativa al tratamiento y rehabilitacion de enfermos mentales cronicos. *Salud Mental* 5(1): 87–93

Ayala, H. E., Quiroga, A. H., Mata, M. A., Chism, S. K. 1981. La familia enseñante: Evaluacion del modelo en Mexico, en terminos de reincidencia en su aplicacion a una muestra de niños inhaladores de solventes industriales. *Salud Mental* 4(1):11–15

Barocio, R. 1978. Consideraciones sobre el desarrollo de programas de capacitacion docente. *Enseñanza Invest. Psicol.* 4(2):3–26

Bijou, S. W., Ribes, E. 1972. *Modificacion de la Conducta, Problemas y Extensiones.* Mexico: Trillas

Brahan, J., Fernandez, G. 1974. Un analisis conductual de la adquisicion del concepto de conservacion. *Proc. 15th Interam. Congr. Psychol.* Bogota, Colombia, p. 301

Bronfenbrenner, U. 1977. Toward an experimental ecology of human development. *Am. Psychol.* 32(7):513–31

Bronfenbrenner, U. 1979. *American Research on the Development of Children in their Environment.* Reports/Studies, ChR2, Div. Study Dev. Paris: UNESCO

Bustos, J. M., Gutierrez, R. E. 1982. Productividad y representacion social en un grupo de obreros. *Tercer Congreso Mexicano de Psicologia, Resumenes de Sesiones Tematicas.* Mexico: Soc. Mex. Psicol. A.C. 82

Cappello, H. M. 1975. Tension internacional como una funcion de la reduccion en comunicacion. In *La Psicologia Social en Latinoamerica,* ed. G. Marin. Mexico: Trillas

Cardenas Ojeda, M. 1963. *La Prueba de Doble Asociacion.* Mexico: Ojeda

Carredano, J., Mercado, D., Fernandez, G. 1974. Un estudio sobre la formacion esquematica de conceptos en funcion del nivel de redundancia y del tipo de estimulos. *Proc. 15th Interam. Congr. Psychol.* Bogota, Columbia, pp. 281–82

Castaño, D. A., Sanchez, G. 1978. Problemas de la importacion tecnologica psicolaboral en los paises en desarrollo. *Rev. Latinoam. Psicol.* 10(1):71–82

Castillo Vales, V. M. 1971. Cross-cultural similarities in the development of the concept of kindness. In *Comparative Perspectives on Social Psychology*, ed. W. Lambert, R. Weisbrod. Boston: Little, Brown

Castillo Vales, V. M., Hansen, A. T., Strodtbeck, F. L. 1966a. Vision panoramica de las actividades del Instituto Interuniversitario para Investigaciones en Ciencias Sociales de Yucatan. *Proc. 10th Interam. Congr. Psychol.*, Lima, Peru, pp. 111–19

Castillo Vales, V. M., Steffere, V., Morley, L. 1966b. Language and cognition in Yucatan: A cross-cultural replication. *J. Pers. Soc. Psychol.* 4:111–15

Castrejon Diez, J. 1976. *La Educacion Superior en Mexico.* Mexico: Secr. Educ. Publica

Castro, L. 1974. Un modelo de comunicacion en psicologia. See Aranda Lopez 1974, pp. 55–67

Castro, L. Carrillo, J. 1976. Ritmos circadianos y control comportamental. *Rev. Latinoam. Psicol.* 8(3):459–566

Castro, L., Moller, J., Morell, D. 1974. Ritmo circadiano de un organismo bajo un programa de reforzamiento IV, 2. *Proc. 15th Interam. Congr. Psychol.* Bogota, Colombia, p. 279

Castro, L., Rodriguez, M. 1975. Control de los componentes de primacia y recencia en la memoria de corto termino. *Rev. Latinoam. Psicol.* 7(1):7–18

Cevallos, M. A. 1953. La psicologia en Mexico en los ultimos 50 años. In *Memoria del Congreso Cientifico Mexicano, Ciencias de la Educacion, Psicologia-Filosofia*, ed. Univ. Nac. Auton. Mexico, 15:563–69. Mexico: U.N.A.M.

Childhood Inequalities and Development. 1982. University of Qatar in collaboration with UNESCO. Paris: UNESCO

Choynowski, M. 1977. Estudio de la agresividad en los adolescentes Mexicanos. *Enseñanza Invest. Psicol.* 3(6):87–103

Choynowski, M. 1978. Estudio de la agresividad en los adolescentes Mexicanos II. *Enseñanza Invest. Psicol.* 4(7):73–96

CNEIP. 1977. Acuerdos tomados en la XXI asamblea. *Enseñanza Invest. Psicol.* 3(2):21–24, 129–30

CNEIP. 1979. Datos basicos sobre instituciones de enseñanza de la psicologia en Mexico. *Enseñanza Invest. Psicol.* 5(1):522–26

Colotla, V. A., Gallegos, X. 1978. La psicologia en Mexico. In *La Profesion del Psicologo*, ed. R. Ardila, ch. 5. Mexico: Trillas

Covarrubias de Levy, A. C. 1970. La realidad del psicologo mexicano. Estudio del mercado de trabajo de la psicologia en la industria y en escuelas del Distrito Federal. *J. Psicol.* 4: 3–8

Cueli, J. 1976. Psicocomunidad. *Enseñanza Invest. Psicol.* 2(2):78–86

Cueli, J., Biro, C. 1975. *Psicocomunidad.* Mexico: Prentice-Hall

Curiel, J. L. 1962. *El Psicologo. Vocacion y Formacion Universitaria.* Mexico: Porrua

David, H. P. 1964. *International Resources in Clinical Psychology.* New York: McGraw-Hill

Delgado, G., Otero, A. 1978. "Conservacion del Volumen," en alumnos de sexto ano de primaria. *Enseñanza Invest. Psicol.* 4(2):292–302

Diaz-Guerrero, R. 1952. Teoria y resultados preliminares de un ensayo de determinacion del grado de salud mental, personal y social del mexicano de la ciudad. *Psiquis* 2(1–2):31–56

Diaz-Guerrero, R. 1959a. *Tres Contribuciones a la Psicoterapia.* Mexico Dir. Gen. Publ., Univ. Nac. Auton. Mexico

Diaz-Guerrero, R. 1959b. Socratic therapy. In *Critical Incidents in Psychotherapy*, ed. S. W. Standal, R. J. Corsini. Englewood Cliffs, NJ: Prentice Hall

Diaz-Guerrero, R. 1963. *Estudios de Psicologia Dinamica.* Mexico: Trillas

Diaz-Guerrero, R. 1966. Mexico. In *International Opportunities for Advanced Training and Research in Psychology*, ed. S. Ross, I. Alexander, H. Basowitz, M. Werber, P. O. Nicholas, pp. 203–9. Washington DC: Am. Psychol. Assoc.

Diaz-Guerrero, R. 1967a. Sociocultural premises, attitudes and crosscultural research. *Int. J. Psychol.* 2:79–81

Diaz-Guerrero, R. 1967b. The active and the passive syndromes. *Rev. Interam. Psicol.* 1(4):263–72

Diaz-Guerrero, R. 1972. *Hacia una Teoria Historico-Bio-Psico-Socio-Cultural del Comportamiento Humano.* Mexico: Trillas

Diaz-Guerrero, R. 1973. Interpreting coping styles across nations from sex and social class differences. *Int. J. Psychol.* 8(3):193–203

Diaz-Guerrero, R. 1974. El psicologo mexicano ayer, hoy y mañana. See Aranda Lopez 1974, pp. 11–17

Diaz-Guerrero, R. 1976a. *Hacia una Psicologia Social del Tercer Mundo.* Cuadernos de Humanidades No. 5. Mexico: Univ. Nac. Auto. Mexico, Difusion Cult.

Diaz-Guerrero, R. 1976b. Mexico. In *Psychology Around the World*, ed. V. S. Sexton, H.

Misiak, pp. 280–92. Monterey, Calif: Brooks/Cole

Diaz-Guerrero, R. 1977a. *Sociocultura, Personalidad en Accion y la Ciencia de la Psicologia.* Mexico: INCCAPAC

Diaz-Guerrero, R. 1977b. A Mexican psychology. *Am. Psychol.* 32(11):934–44

Diaz-Guerrero, R. 1977c. Culture and personality revisited. *Ann. NY Acad. Sci.* 285:119–30

Diaz-Guerrero, R. 1979a. Mexico. In *International Directory of Psychology,* ed. B. B. Wolman. New York/London: Plenum

Diaz-Guerrero, R. 1979b. *Social Science Research on Children in Mexico and Hispanic America.* Reports/Studies, ChR12, Div. Study Dev. Paris: UNESCO

Diaz-Guerrero, R. 1979c. Origines de la personnalité humaine et des systemes sociaux. *Rev. Psychol. Appl.* 29(2):139–52

Diaz-Guerrero, R. 1980. The culture-counterculture theoretical approach to human and social system development. The case of mothers in four Mexican subcultures. *Proc. 22nd Int. Congr. Psychol.,* Leipzig, GDR, pp. 56–60

Diaz-Guerrero, R. 1981a. Momentos culminantes de la historia de la psicologia en Mexico. *Rev. Hist. Psicol.* (Spain) 2(2):125–42

Diaz-Guerrero, R. 1981b. *Sociocultural Premises and Child Development.* Reports/Studies, ChR16, Div. Study Dev. Paris: UNESCO

Diaz-Guerrero, R. 1982a. Fuentes de ansiedad en la cultura Mexicana. *Enseñanza Invest. Psicol.* 8(1):65–75

Diaz-Guerrero, R. 1982b. Child and family in Mexico. Presented at *Conference on The Changing Family in a Changing World,* Munich

Diaz-Guerrero, R. 1982c. *Psicologia del Mexicano.* Mexico: Trillas

Diaz-Guerrero, R. 1982d. The psychology of the historic-sociocultural premises. *Spanish Lang. Psychol.* 2:383–410

Diaz-Guerrero, R., Castillo Vales, V. M. 1981. El enfoque cultura-contracultura y el desarrollo cognitivo y de la personalidad en escolares yucatecos. *Enseñanza Invest. Psicol.* 7(1):5–26

Diaz-Guerrero, R., Lichtszajn, J. L., Reyes-Lagunes, I. 1979. Alienacion de la madre, psicopatologia y la practica clinica en Mexico. *Hispanic J. Behav. Sci.* 1(2):117–33

Diaz-Guerrero, R., Morales, M. L. 1976. La paternidad responsable y las actitudes hacia la procreacion. *Neurol. Neurocir. Psiquiatr.* 17(2):103–14

Diaz-Guerrero, R., Morales, M. L. 1977. *La Contribucion de INCCAPAC respecto al Problema de la Planeacion Familiar.* Mexico: Ediciones INCCAPAC

Diaz-Guerrero, R., Salas, M. 1975. *El Di-ferencial Semantico del Idioma Español.* Mexico: Trillas

Diaz-Loving, R., Diaz-Guerrero, R., Helmreich, R. L., Spence, J. T. 1981. Comparacion transcultural y analisis psicometrico de una medida de rasgos masculinos (instrumentales) y femeninos (expresivos). *Rev. Asoc. Latinoam. Psicol. Soc.* 1(1):3–38

Diaz-Loving, R., Nina Estrella, R. 1983. Factores que influyen la reciprocidad de autodivulgacion. *Rev. Asco. Latinoam. Psicol. Soc.* 1(2):In press

Dominguez, B. 1974. Contingencias aplicables al control de grupos institucionalizados. In *El Analisis Experimental del Comportamiento. La Contribucion Latinoamericana,* ed. R. Ardila, pp. 430–50. Mexico: Trillas

Dominguez, B., Garcia, V. M. 1979. Ambientes educativos en instituciones de custodia. *Enseñanza Invest. Psicol.* 5(1):424–36

Earle, W., Diaz-Loving, R., Archer, R. L. 1984. Empathy and moral values as determinants of helping behavior. *Pers. Soc. Psychol. Bull.* Submitted for publication

Emmite, P. L. 1977. *La Medicion del Estres y los Patrones de Confrontacion en Tres Grupos Culturales: Negro, Anglo y Mexicano-Norteamericano. Una Aplicacion de la Teoria de Premisas Historico-Bio-Psico-Socio-Culturales.* PhD thesis. Univ. Nac. Auton. Mexico

Escoto, N. E., Ruiz, M. R., Vazquez, M. L. 1982. *El Modelo de Confrontacion Activo-Pasiva del Estres a Traves del TAT en Dos Grupos Psicopatologicos.* Thesis to obtain the Psychologist Degree. Univ. Nac. Auton. Mexico

Facultad de Psicologia, Organizacion Academica. 1976. Mexico: Univ. Nac. Auton. Mexico, Sec. Rectoria

Facultqd de Psicologia, Organizacion Academica. 1979–1980. Mexico: Univ. Nac. Auton. Mexico, Sec. Rectoria

Fernandez, G. 1974. La funcion del psicologo en las instituciones de ensenanza. See Aranda Lopez 1974, pp. 293–98

Fernandez, G., Lara Tapia, L., Hereford, C. F. 1970. Replica de factores en el inventario de intereses profesionales de Hereford. *Rev. Interam. Psicol.* 1:51–57

Fernandez, G., Lopez, J., Tejada, R., Montejano, A. M., Fernandez, M. E. 1974. La prueba modificada Alfa 9. Estandarizacion y primer estudio de confiabilidad. See Aranda Lopez 1974, pp. 201–6

Fernandez, G., Natalicio, L. F., eds. 1972. *La Ciencia de la Conducta.* Mexico: Trillas

Fernandez, G., Natalicio, L. F., Natalicio, D. S. 1971. El condicionamiento de fonemas y su interpretacion. *Rev. Interam. Psicol.* 5:27–37

Fernandez, M. E., Fernandez, G. 1974. Estudio preliminar a la estandarizacion y normas de los tests Otis Gamma y Dominos. See Aranda Lopez 1974, pp. 197–200

Fevreiski, J. 1982. Repaso primario y repaso secundario en una prueba de recuerdo libre. *Rev. Latinoam. Psicol.* 14(2):211–21

Figueroa, J., Bravo, P., Garcia, R. 1982a. La relacion de la imaginabilidad y la modalidad sensorial con tareas de memoria a corto plazo. *Tercer Congreso Mexicano de Psicologia, Resumenes de Sesiones Tematicas*, p. 76. Mexico: Soc. Mex. Psicol. A.C.

Figueroa, J., Carrasco, M. 1982b. La memoria de comparacion a alta velocidad como un proceso dependiente del tipo de material y de la escolaridad de los sujetos. *Tercer Congreso Mexicano de Psicologia, Resumenes de Sesiones Tematicas*, p. 75. Mexico: Soc. Mex. Psicol. A.C.

Figueroa, J., Carrasco, M., Sarmiento, C. 1982c. La funcion psicofisica de estimacion de longitud y su relacion con los procesos centrales de informacion. *Tercer Congreso Mexicano de Psicologia, Resumenes de Sesiones Tematicas*, p. 106. Mexico: Soc. Mex. Psicol. A.C.

Figueroa, J., Gonzalez, E. G. 1982d. Efectos de la cantidad de material sobre la memoria reconstructiva. *Rev. Latinoam. Psicol.* 14(1):55–62

Figueroa, J., Gonzalez, E. G., Solis, V. M. 1976. An approach to the problem of meaning: Semantic networks. *J. Psycholing. Res.* 5(2):107–15

Figueroa, J., Solis, B. M., Gonzalez, E. G. 1974. The possible influence of imagery upon retrieval and representation in L.T.M. *Acta Psychol.* 38:425–28

Gallegos, X. 1980. James M. Baldwin's visits to Mexico. In "Comments." *Am. Psychol.* 35:772–73

Garcia, B. E., Campos, M., Montero, M., Perez, A., Valderrama, P. 1982. *Curso de Practicas de Cuarto Nivel Social Multidimensional.* Mexico: Coord. Lab., Fac. Psicol., U.N.A.M.

Garza Garcia, F. 1953. La psicologia industrial en Mexico. In *Memoria del Congreso Cientifico Mexicano*, Vol. 15: *Ciencias de la Educacion, Psicologia-Filosofia*, ed. Univ. Nac. Auton. Mexico, pp. 536–44

Gomez, A., Lambarri, A., Olvera, L. Y., Dominguez, B. 1982. Evaluacion del clima institucional en el consejo tutelar para menores infractores del Distrito Federal. *Tercer Congreso Mexicano de Psicologia, Resumenes de las Sesiones Tematicas*, p. 90. Mexico: Soc. Mex. Psicol., A.C.

Gomez Perez-Mitre, G. 1981. Autoestima: Expectativas de exito o de fracaso en la realizacion de una tarea. *Rev. Asoc. Latinoam. Psicol. Soc.* 1(1):135–56

Gomez Robleda, C. 1959. Realizaciones de la Psicologia Industrial en Mexico. *Revista del Instituto Tecnico Administrativo del Trabajo*, pp. 7–31

Gonzalez Cipres, F. 1968. *Deficiencia Mental. Algunos Problemas que Plantea la Labor Post-Escolar con los Deficientes Mentales.* Tesis Profesional. Mexico: Fac. Psicol., U.N.A.M.

Guzman, J. J. C. 1981. *Estudio Poblacional de la Escuela de Psicologia, U.N.A.M. 1940–1978.* Thesis to obtain the degree of Licenciado en Psicologia. Mexico: Fac. Psicol. U.N.A.M.

Hernandez-Holtzman, E. 1984. *Relationship between social network support and psychological functioning of dual working parents in Mexican-American families. Diss. Abst.* In press

Hernandez-Holtzman, E., Holtzman, W. H. Jr. 1983. Adaptacion de una escala de actitudes hacia la mujer en Mexico. *Rev. Asoc. Latinoam. Psicol. Soc.* 1(2):In press

Hernandez Luna, J. 1948. *La Universidad de Justo Sierra.* Coleccion de Documentos Universitarios. Mexico: Sec. Educ. Publica

Holtzman, W. H. Jr. 1970. Los seminarios internacionales de psicologia en Texas: Un experimento de intercambio transcultural en psicologia. *Rev. Interam. Psicol.* 4(3–4):279–82

Holtzman, W. H. Jr. 1980. *Divergent thinking as a function of the degree of bilingualism of 5th grade Mexican-American and Anglo pupils.* PhD thesis. Univ. Texas, Austin

Holtzman, W. H., Diaz-Guerrero, R., Swartz, J. D. 1975. *Personality Development in Two Cultures.* Austin/London: Univ. Texas Press

Holtzman, W. H., Iscoe, I., Neal, J. W. 1964. Final report, Mexican Psychology Student Seminar, Jan. 5–25. Austin: Univ. Texas

Huerta-Ibarra, J. 1974. La sociedad Mexicana de psicologia y la psicologia industrial en Mexico. See Aranda Lopez 1974, pp. 281–83

Iscoe, I. 1972. Mental health in the Americas. *Interam. J. Psychol.* (Special issue) 6:1–2

La Ciudad. 1982. Monographic number. *Comunidad CONACYT* 8 (136–137):53–240

Lafarga, J. 1976a. ¿Quien es hoy el profesor de psicologia? (editorial). *Enseñanza Invest. Psicol.* 2(1):3–4

Lafarga, J. 1976b. Psicologia, ciencia o profesion (editorial). *Enseñanza Invest. Psicol.* 2(2):3–4

Lafarga, J. 1977a. Proliferacion de escuelas de psicologia en el pais (editorial). *Enseñanza Invest. Psicol.* 3(1):3–4

Lafarga, J. 1977b. Formacion del profesor de psicologia en la investigacion de las necesidades del pais. *Enseñanza Invest. Psicol.* 3(2):33–38

Lafarga, J. 1979. Programa de maestria en psicologia con especializacion en psicoterapia. *Enseñanza Invest. Psicol.* 5(1):502–9

Lara Tapia, H., Ramirez, L. 1975. Estudio clinico epidemiologico de padecimientos psiquiatricos dentro de un sistema de seguridad social. *Neurol. Neurocir. Psiquiatr.* 16(4):225–41

Lara Tapia, H., Velez, J. 1975. Alcoholismo y farmacodependencia en un sistema de seguridad social. Un estudio epidemiologico. *Salud Publica Mexico* 16(3):387–95

Lartigue, T. 1976. Entrenamiento para supervisores de trabajo de comunidad. *Enseñanza Invest. Psicol.* 2(1):15–18

Lichtszajn, J. L. 1979. *Correlatos Clinicos y Socioculturales de la Actitud hacia la Muerte en un Grupo de Adolescentes Mexicanos.* PhD thesis. Mexico: Fac. Psicol., U.N.A.M.

Lopez, M., Sierra, G. P., Castro, L. 1978. Comprension de lectura en Chino sin apoyo fonetico. *Interam. J. Psychol.* 12(2):189–92

Lopez Rodriguez, F. 1978. Consideraciones sobre las practicas basicas en psicologia. *Enseñanza Invest. Psicol.* 4(2):217–22

Loredo, O. 1982. Procedimiento de seleccion y ubicacion en actividades tecnologicas para alumnos del primer año de educacion secundaria S.E.P. *Tercer Congreso Mexicano de Psicologia, Resumenes de las Sesiones Tematicas,* p. 58. Mexico: Soc. Mexicana Psicol., A. C.

Loredo, O., Diaz-Guerrero, R. 1971. Estudio de la vocacion a traves de una prueba de intereses. *Rev. Latinoam. Psicol.* 3:211–22

Loredo, O., Diaz-Guerrero, R. 1972. Difference in vocational interests between Mexican male and female students in high schools and in the university. *Abst. Guide. 20th Int. Congr. Psychol.,* Tokyo, Japan, p. 702

Macotela, S., Espinosa, A. 1979. Un estudio explaratorio sobre la imagen del psicologo en la opinion publica. *2nd Congr. Mex. Psicol.* Mexico: Trillas

Maldonado, M. A., Mercado, S. J. 1974. La Ilusion de Müller-Lyer como un Fenomeno de Ajuste de la Constancia. See Aranda Lopez 1974, pp. 111–14

Meneses, E. 1976. Veinticinco años de enseñanza de la psicologia en la universidad Iberoamericana, 1950–1975. *Enseñanza Invest. Psicol.* 2(1):122–27

Mercado, D., Fernandez, G. 1974. Una nota sobre la formacion esquematica de conceptos. *Interam. J. Psychol.* 8(3–4):185–95

Mercado, D., Gonzalez, E., Fernandez, G. 1974a. Juicios de igualdad con histoformas al azar. *Proc. 25th Interam. Congr. Psychol., Bogota, Colombia,* pp. 282–83

Mercado, D., Gonzalez, E., Fernandez, G.

1974b. Sobre el libre recuerdo de Linguaformas. See Mercado et al 1974a, p. 283

Mercado, D., Ramirez, C., Martinez, L. 1979. Diagnostico academico-laboral del psicologo en el sector publico. See Macotela & Espinosa 1979

Mercado, S. 1982. Ruidos, ruidos, ruidos . . . *Comunidad CONACYT* 8 (136–137):114–19

Mercado, S. J., Diaz-Guerrero, R., Gardner, R. W. 1963. Cognitive control in children of Mexico and the United States. *J. Soc. Psychol.* 59(2):199–208

Mercado, S. J., Ribes, E., Barrera, F. 1967. Depth cues effects on the perception of visual illusions. *Rev. Interam. Psicol.* 1(2):137–42

Michaca, P. 1977. Consideraciones teoricas sobre el manejo de las sesiones de supervision con el modelo psicocomunidad. *Enseñanza Invest. Psicol.* 3(1):50–53

Morales, M. L. 1977. *Estudio Piloto Comparativo de la Transmision y Eficacia de la Informacion en Planificacion Familiar en un Grupo de Obreros.* Mexico: INCCAPAC (Mimeo)

Morgane, P. J. 1970. Raul Hernandez-Peon (1924–1968). *Physiol. Behav.* 5:379–88

Mouret Polo, E., Ribes Iñesta, E. 1977. Panoramica de la enseñanza de la psicologia en Mexico. *Enseñanza Invest. Psicol.* 3(2):6–20

Navarro, R. 1971. El MMPI aplicado a jovenes mexicanos: Influencias de sexo, edad y nivel de inteligencia. *Rev. Interam. Psicol.* 5:127–37

Navarro, R. 1973. Orientacion Vocacional, Primer Ingreso, Cambio de Carrera y Sexo en el MMPI. *Rev. Interam. Psicol.* 7(1–2):43–53

Navarro, R. 1979. Estandarizacion del MMPI y comparacion de estudiantes de primer ingreso a la U.I.A. segun las carreras solicitadas. *Enseñanza Invest. Psicol.* 5(2):626–40

Navarro, R., Chavez, P. 1976. El MMPI en diversos niveles de trabajadores al servicio del Estado. Primera parte: Los hombres. *Enseñanza Invest. Psicol.* 1(2):62–71

Navarro, R., Chavez, P., Rivera, M. E. 1976. El MMPI en diversos niveles de trabajadores al servicio del Estado. Segunda parte: Las mujeres. *Enseñanza Invest. Psicol.* 2(1):63–69

Nieto, J. 1979a. *Jornadas Conmemorativas del Centesimo Aniversario de la Fundacion por Wundt del Primer Laboratorio de Psicologia.* Mexico: E.N.E.P. Zaragoza, U.N.A.M.

Nieto, J. 1979b. Consideraciones sobre el analisis historico de la psicologia en Mexico. See Macotela & Espinosa 1979

Nieto-Cardoso, E. 1977. Efectos de un microlaboratorio de entrenamiento en relaciones interpersonales de ayuda sistematica sobre el nivel de discriminacion en la comunicacion. *Enseñanza Invest. Psicol.* 3(1):71–80

Nieto-Cardoso, E. 1979. Relaciones entre auto-revelacion, niveles de funcionamiento terapeutico y nivel de ansiedad manifiesta. *Enseñanza Invest. Psicol.* 5(1):468–89

Nieto-Cardoso, E. 1981. Experiencia de aprendizaje a traves de un mediador. *Enseñanza Invest. Psicol.* 7(2):217–21

Nuñez, R. 1962. *Problemas Psicosociales de la Profesion de la Psicologia Clinica en Mexico.* Mexico: Publ. realizada por el autor

Nuñez, R. 1968. *Aplicacion del Inventario Multifacico de la Personalidad (MMPI) a la Psicopatologia.* Mexico: El Manual Moderno, S.A.

Ortega, P., Lopez, M. 1953. La medicion psicologica en Mexico. See Garza Garcia 1953, pp. 323–31

Ortega, P., Urbina, J. 1982a. Efectos de la densidad social sobre la ejecucion de tareas y la percepcion de caracteristicas ambientales en escenarios laborales. *7th Conf. Internac. sobre Hombre Entorno, Barcelona, Spain*

Ortega, P., Urbina, J. 1982b. La organizacion ambiental de los centros de cuidado infantil y sus efectos sobre las interacciones sociales y el involucramiento en actividades academicas. See Ortega & Urbina 1982a.

Osgood, C. E., May, W. H., Miron, M. S. 1975. *Cross-Cultural Universals of Affective Meaning.* Urbana: Univ. Illinois Press

Otero, A. 1982. *Programa para Prescolares de Mexico.* Mexico: Sec. Educ. Publica (Mimeo)

Pick de Weiss, S. 1978. *A social psychological study of family planning in Mexico City.* PhD thesis. Univ. London, England

Pick de Weiss, S. 1980. *Estudio Social Psicologico de la Planificacion Familiar.* Mexico: Siglo XXI Editores

Pick de Weiss, S. 1982. Estado actual de la psicologia social. *Tercer Congreso Mexicano de Psicologia, Resumenes de Sesiones Tematicas,* p. 12. Mexico: Soc. Mex. Psicol., A.C.

I (Primera) Reunion sobre Investigacion y Enseñanza. 1982. Mexico: Inst. Mex. Psiquiatria

Reidl de Aguilar, L. 1981. Atraccion, semejanza e influencia personal. *Rev. Asoc. Latinoam. Psicol. Soc.* 1(1):93–108

Reyes, L., Gutierrez, R. E. 1982. Teoria de las expectativas y productividad. *Tercer Congreso Mexicano de Psicologia, Resumenes de Sesiones Tematicas,* p. 84. Mexico: Soc. Mex. Psicol. A.C.

Reyes Lagunes, I. 1982. *Actitudes de los maestros hacia la profesion magisterial y su contexto.* PhD thesis Mexico: Fac. Psicol., U.N.A.M.

Ribes, E. 1968. Psychology in Mexico. *Am. Psychol.* 23 (8):565–66

Ribes, E. 1972. *Tecnicas de Modificacion de Conducta. Su Aplicacion al Retardo en el Desarrollo.* Mexico: Trillas

Ribes, E. 1975. Some recent developments in psychology in Mexico. *Am. Psychol.* 30(7):774–76

Ribes, E. 1977. Un programa de formacion de profesores: Objectivos y algunos logros iniciales. *Enseñanza Invest. Psicol.* 3(2):39–44

Robles, O. 1952. Panorama de la psicologia en Mexico, pasado y presente. *Filos. Letras* 23(45–46):239–63

Rodriguez de Arizmendi, G. 1971–1972. L' enseignement universitaire de la psychologie au Mexique. *Bull. Psychol.* 25(1):38–44

Rodriguez de Arizmendi, G. 1980. Assumptions about sex role behaviors and their effects. *Abstract Guide, 2. Proc. 22nd Int. Congr. Psychol., Leipzig, GDR,* p. 473

Saldaña, M., Sierra, M., Valenzuela, M. L., Fernandez, G. 1974. De la enseñanza de la lectura I. -Global vs. Fonetico: ¿Adivinar vs. Deletrear? *Interam. J. Psychol.* 8(3–4):205–17

Sanchez Sosa, J. J. 1976. A methodological evaluation of contemporary research in complex academic responses in university teaching. *Rev. Mex. Anal. Conducta* 2:207–19

Sanchez Sosa, J. J. 1980. Experimental promotion of concept formation in university teaching. See Diaz-Guerrero 1980, pp. 218–26

Sanchez Sosa, J. J., Semb, G., Spencer, R. 1978. Using study guides to promote generalization performance in university instruction. *Rev. Mex. Anal. Conducta* 4:175–90

Sanchez de Almeida, M. E., Almeida, E. 1978. La comunidad de San Miguel Tzinacapan. *Am. Indig.* 38(3):607–30

Santoyo, C. 1982. Hacinamiento: Peligrosa ruptura con el medio ambiente. *Comunidad CONACYT* 8(136–137):127–29

Sociedad Mexicana de Analisis de la Conducta, eds. 1977. *Analisis de la Conducta, Investigacion y Aplicaciones.* Mexico: Trillas

Solis Quiroga, R. 1953. Los anormales mentales educables y la necesidad de maestros especialistas. See Garza Garcia 1953, pp. 332–41

Speller, P., ed. 1978. *Analisis de la Conducta, Trabajos de Investigacion en Latino America.* Mexico: Trillas

Urbina, J., Mercado, S., Colotla, V., Sanchez Bedolla, G., Aguilar, J. 1982. La investigacion en la Facultad de Psicologia de la U.N.A.M. Un analisis cuantitativo. *Tercer*

Congreso Mexicano de Psicologia, Resumenes de las Sesiones Tematicas, p. 37. Mexico: Soc. Mex. Psicol., A.C.

Urbina, J., Ortega, P. 1982. La psicologia ambiental. No lloremos mañana los errores de hoy. *Comunidad CONACYT* 8(136–137):130–34

Velasco Herandez, R. 1978. La enseñanza de la psicologia en Mexico. *Enseñanza Invest. Psicol.* 4(1):10–24

Villalpando Nava, J. M. 1953. La orientacion profesional en la vida de los pueblos cultos. See Garza Garcia 1953, pp. 342–78

Witzke, D. B., Castro, L., Dingman, H. F. 1969. Validation of a latent class analysis model for predicting mortality. *Interam. J. Psychol.* 3(1):31–36

Ann. Rev. Psychol. 1984. 35:113–38

CONCEPTS AND CONCEPT FORMATION

Douglas L. Medin

Department of Psychology, University of Illinois, Champaign, Illinois 61820

Edward E. Smith

Bolt Beranek and Newman Inc., 10 Moulton Street, Cambridge, Massachusetts 02238

CONTENTS

113

0066-4308/84/0201-0113$02.00

INTRODUCTION

In this chapter we review recent work on human concepts and concept formation. Our first task is to specify what we mean by *concept*. The term is a loaded one, as it serves several explanatory functions within psychology and related disciplines. The following four functions (after Rey 1983) seem particularly important:

1. *Simple categorization:* the means by which people decide whether or not something belongs to a simple class (e.g. deciding that a particular object is an instance of the concept *boy*).
2. *Complex categorization:* the means by which people decide whether or not something belongs to a complex class (e.g. deciding that a particular object is an instance of the concept *rich boy*).
3. *Linguistic meaning:* that part of the meaning of a term that explains relations of synonymy, antinomy, and semantic implication (e.g. that part of the meaning of "boy" that explains why it is roughly synonymous to "lad" and implies being male and young[1]).
4. *Components of cognitive states:* the critical components of beliefs, preferences, and other cognitive states; in this role, concepts are what provide a cognitive explanation of complex thought and behavior (e.g. the roles played by the concepts *rich, boys,* and *spoiled* in someone's belief that rich boys are spoiled).

Of these functions, simple categorization has been the major focus in the literature that explicitly concerns itself with concepts. We will emphasize this function in our review, and often take *concept* to mean a mental representation of a simple class (i.e. a class denoted by a single word). What holds for simple categorization, however, need not hold for other functions, so at various points we will deal explicitly with the other functions of concepts.

Moving on to more specific issues, we begin by summarizing three different views of concepts that emerged from research on simple categorization. The main body of this chapter will then examine questions raised by these previous analyses in light of newer research on concepts.

[1]We use quotes to indicate words, while reserving italics for the concepts that the words denote.

THREE VIEWS OF CONCEPTS

Background

Some of the central questions in categorization concern the structure of concepts. After several decades during which one particular view of concept structure held sway, recent times have witnessed the emergence (or reemergence) of alternative views along with an associated frenzy of research activity. There are several reviews of this work (Rosch 1978a,b, Herrnstein & deVilliers 1980, Mervis 1980, Millward 1980, Mervis & Rosch 1981, Epstein 1982), but for reasons both of familiarity and breadth, we will focus on our own published review of this literature, *Categories and Concepts* (Smith & Medin 1981).

Our 1981 review dealt mainly with object concepts, particularly natural kinds, e.g. *bird,* and artifacts, e.g. *hammer,* since such concepts have dominated categorization research. Our review was organized around three views of concepts, which we called the "classical," "probabilistic," and "exemplar" views. The classical view holds that all instances of a concept share common properties that are necessary and sufficient conditions for defining the concept. The probabilistic view denies that there are defining properties, and instead argues that concepts are represented in terms of properties that are only characteristic or probable of class members. Membership in a category can thus be graded rather than all-or-none, where the better members have more characteristic properties than the poorer ones. The exemplar view agrees with the claim that concepts need not contain defining properties, but further claims that categories may be represented by their individual exemplars, and that assignment of a new instance to a category is determined by whether the instance is sufficiently similar to one or more of the category's known exemplars.

The Classical View and its Problems

In *Categories and Concepts,* we detailed a number of criticisms of the classical view; here, we summarize the most important of them.

FAILURE TO SPECIFY DEFINING PROPERTIES   The severest problem for the classical view is that decades of analyses by linguists, philosophers, psychologists, and others have failed to turn up the defining properties of most object concepts.

UNCLEAR CASES   Since the classical view assumes that judgments about category membership are based on defining properties, category boundaries should be clear-cut. But people are often uncertain about category membership—e.g. is a rug *furniture?*—and may not answer consistently when asked to judge membership on different occasions (e.g. McCloskey & Glucksberg 1978).

TYPICALITY EFFECTS   Contrary to the classical view, not all members of a category have equal status. Exemplars judged to be typical of a concept (e.g. a robin for the concept *bird*) can be categorized faster and more accurately than exemplars judged less typical (e.g. an ostrich). Also, children learn typical exemplars of concepts before they learn atypical ones, and when retrieving concept members, people access typical instances before atypical ones.

FAMILY RESEMBLANCE AS A DETERMINANT OF TYPICALITY   In an attempt to understand the basis of typicality, Rosch & Mervis (1975) had subjects list properties of exemplars of a particular concept. Some exemplars had properties that occurred frequently in the concept while others had properties that occurred less frequently; the more frequent its properties the more typical an exemplar was rated. This measure of an exemplar in terms of the frequency of its properties is called *family resemblance,* and it is highly correlated with the speed with which the exemplar can be categorized as well as with other typicality effects.

USE OF NONNECESSARY PROPERTIES   Most of the properties people list for exemplars are not true of all exemplars, i.e. the properties are nonnecessary for concept membership. The fact that the distribution of these properties correlates with classification times (see above) strongly suggests that nonnecessary properties are being used to determine category membership.

NESTED CONCEPTS   The classical view assumes that a concept abstraction consists of the defining properties of its superordinate plus those defining properties that serve to distinguish it from other concepts at its own level. That is, a specific concept (e.g. *sparrow*) includes all the properties of its superordinate *(bird)*, which in turn includes all the properties of its superordinate *(animal)*. This means that the specific concept *(sparrow)* has more common properties and fewer distinctive ones with its immediate superordinate *(bird)* than with its distant one *(animal)*. It follows from many theories of similarity (e.g. Tversky 1977) that the specific concept should always be judged more similar to an immediate superordinate than to a distant one. This prediction fails often enough (e.g. *chicken, bird,* and *animal)* to be an embarrassment to the classical view (Smith et al 1974, McCloskey 1980, Roth & Mervis 1983).[2]

SUMMARY   None of the above criticisms is of and by itself decisive (see Smith & Medin 1981, Chapter 3), but the cumulative contortions needed to

---

[2]In this paragraph, we have talked in terms of whether a specific concept, e.g. *chicken,* is a subset of a more general one, while in other places we talk about whether a particular object, e.g. a chicken, belongs to a concept. Experiments reveal little difference between these two kinds of categorization situations.

address these criticisms reveal a picture not unlike Cinderella's stepsisters trying on the glass slipper—even if they could have gotten it on, certainly they would not have walked very gracefully. The upshot is that many investigators have turned to alternative views.

The Probabilistic View

The probabilistic view assumes that concepts are abstractions, or summary representations, but argues that for a property to be included in the summary it need have only a substantial probability of occurring in instances of the concept, i.e. it need only be characteristic of the concept, not defining. An object will then be categorized as an instance of some concept A if, for example, it possesses some criterial number of properties, or sum of weighted properties, included in the summary representation of A. Categorization is thus a matter of assessing similarity rather than of applying a definition.

ANSWERS TO PROBLEMS FOR THE CLASSICAL VIEW   The probabilistic view can answer the problems that plagued its predecessor. First, since the probabilistic view does not require defining properties, it is not embarrassed by their apparent absence. As for unclear cases, they may arise when an object either is close to the threshold level of similarity for membership in a particular concept, or when an object is close to the threshold for more than one concept (e.g. a tomato may be equally similar to both *fruit* and *vegetable*).

The probabilistic view is also tailored to address typicality effects. Items are typical of a concept to the extent that they contain properties that are characteristic of the concept; this idea makes typicality a disguised form of similarity. And the more similar an item to a concept, the faster and more reliably it can be judged to exceed some threshold level of similarity; hence the effects of typicality on categorization. As for the use of nonnecessary properties, such properties are built into probabilistic models. Finally, the view is consistent with similarity judgments for nested concepts. While usually a concept shares more properties with concepts one level removed than with more distant ones, nothing in principle prevents a reversal of this situation; e.g. *chicken* is judged less similar to *bird* than to *animal* because chickens possess several properties (walking, being found on farms) that tend to be characteristic of *animal* but not of *bird*. In sum, this loosened view of concepts fits the relevant phenomena better than does the classical view.

PROBLEMS FOR THE PROBABILISTIC VIEW   One general problem is that the probabilistic view may not adequately capture all of people's knowledge about concepts. In addition to knowing characteristic properties, people seem to know about the range of values a property of a concept might have (e.g. Walker 1975), as well as about relations among properties. For example, people know that birds are typically small and typically sing, and also that these properties are correlated such that large birds are unlikely to sing (Malt & Smith 1983). And there is evidence that people use knowledge about correlated attributes during categorization. A second general problem for the probabilistic view is that it may be too unconstrained, both with respect to what can be a possible property and what can be a possible category. Since similarity can be based on a *weighted* sum of properties, and since there are no constraints on the weights, this scheme may be too flexible.

The Exemplar View

The exemplar view assumes that, at least in part, a concept consists of separate descriptions of some of its exemplars. Some exemplar models allow for a more abstract representation as well (e.g. Medin & Schaffer 1978), but others (e.g. the average distance model evaluated by Reed 1972) are based on only exemplars. Exemplar models have in common the idea that categorization of an object relies on comparisons of that object to known exemplars of the category.

ANSWERS TO PROBLEMS FOR THE CLASSICAL VIEW   Since there is no reason why different exemplars need have the same properties, there is no reason to expect defining properties. Unclear cases can arise when an object is similar to exemplars of more than one category (e.g. a tomato is similar to exemplars of both *fruit* and *vegetable*), or when an object is not very similar to the exemplars of any category (e.g. a sea horse).

Typicality effects may arise because people are more likely to represent only typical members (e.g. Mervis 1980), or because more typical instances are more similar to other stored exemplars (this is just *family resemblance* at work). Being more similar to other stored exemplars of their own category, typical instances should readily retrieve exemplars from that category and hence be categorized quickly and accurately. Again, nonnecessary properties are built directly into the view. Finally, the exemplar view is consistent with similarity ratings for nested concepts; e.g. *chicken* might be rated more similar to *animal* than to *bird* because the particular exemplars associated with *chicken* may share more properties with the best exemplars of *animal* than with the best exemplars of *bird*. In sum, the exemplar view can handle the problems that plagued the classical view.

PROBLEMS WITH THE EXEMPLAR VIEW   Exemplar models appear to have some advantages over probabilistic ones in that exemplars can carry information concerning the range of values for a property as well as information about correlations among properties. With regard to range information, one could compute it when needed by sampling some exemplars that comprise the concept and determining their range. One could also use this kind of on-line computation to handle the effects of correlated attributes on categorization. (Alternatively, the effects of correlated attributes on categorization could be attributed to how the similarity between an object and exemplar is computed; see Medin & Schaffer 1978.) These successes, however, come at the cost of a total lack of constraints on what properties enter into concepts or even what constitutes a concept.

Questions Raised by the Preceding Analysis

The present state of affairs is less than satisfying. The classical view has its problems, which can be handled by the probabilistic and exemplar views, but, to return to our Cinderella analogy, if the slipper is too tight for the classical view, it may be too loose for the alternatives. The rest of this review is organized around questions growing out of this dilemma.

(a) Is there any role for the classical view? The facts about simple categorization fit the probabilistic and exemplar views better than they do the classical view. Most of these facts, however, concern object concepts. Further, what holds for simple categorization may not hold for other functions of concepts. The classical view may work better for other kinds of concepts and other kinds of functions.

(b) If concepts have the loose structure implied by the probabilistic and exemplar views, then what makes them psychologically cohesive? That is, how can we add constraints to what are called "prototype" views? (While the distinction between probabilistic and exemplar type concepts is important, sometimes all that matters is that the concept not contain defining properties; when this happens we refer to such concepts as "prototype" concepts.)

(c) What principles of processing regulate the categorization of prototype concepts? Thus far all we have claimed is that categorization with prototype concept amounts to a similarity computation.

(d) How are prototype concepts learned? While the knowledge in a concept is in part abstracted from experience with exemplars, little is known about the details of this process. In considering this question, we will emphasize concept learning in adults, as a proper treatment of the literature on concept acquisition in children would require a chapter in its own right. (For recent reviews, see Anglin 1977, Farah & Kosslyn 1982.)

(e) Are there different types of prototype concepts governed by different principles? Most research on categorization employs object concepts, but some recent work tries to extend the prototype approach to very different kinds of concepts.

(f) What are some of the newer directions in research on concepts? We will consider two new developments, research on complex concepts and challenges to the claim that categorization is nothing more than similarity.

POSSIBLE ROLES FOR THE CLASSICAL VIEW

The Classical View and the Distinction Between the Core and Identification Procedure

In Smith & Medin (1981) we borrowed a distinction from Miller & Johnson-Laird (1976) between the "core" and "identification procedure" of a concept. The core contains properties that reveal relations with other concepts, while the identification procedure contains properties that are used to categorize real-world objects. Consider the concept *boy;* its core might contain the properties of being human, male, and young, while its identification procedure might contain information about height, weight, and dress. The relevance of this distinction to the issue at hand is that while the identification procedure may have a prototype structure, the core may conform to the classic view.

We noted this possibility (Smith & Medin 1981, Chapter 3), but could find little evidence to support it. A recent paper by Armstrong et al (1983), however, provides some evidence. These authors investigated concepts that almost certainly have a classical core, specifically *even number, odd number, plane geometry figure,* and *female.* The intent of the authors was to show that even these concepts have identification procedures. As support for this, Armstrong et al demonstrated that subjects rated instances of these concepts as varying in typicality and categorized typical instances faster than atypical ones. For example, 22 was rated as more typical than 18 of *even number,* and 22 was also categorized faster. (See Bourne 1982 for similar results in a paradigm using artificial concepts). Armstrong et al interpret their typicality effects as reflecting only an identification procedure, which supports the idea that a prototype identification procedure can co-exist with a classical core.[3] Thus, many people's identification procedure for *even number* may focus only on the evenness of the last digit; since it is easier to establish that 2 is even than that 8 is, this would explain why subjects rated 22 as more typical than 18.

The Classical View as a Backup Procedure

An idea related to the above is that the classical core of a concept may be used to back up or justify categorizations based on an identification procedure. Again we considered but were unable to educe evidence bearing on this possibility earlier (Smith & Medin 1981, Chapter 3), but a recent paper provides some suggestive support for it. Landau (1982) used concepts that presumably have classical cores, namely female kin relations such as *grandmother.* She pre-

[3]In fairness to the spirit of the Armstrong et al paper, we should add that they argue that these and other observations raise serious problems with the general approach of analyzing concepts into features and the specific idea of using typicality effects to draw inferences concerning concept structure.

sented pictures to her subjects (children and adults) and had them perform two tasks: (*a*) categorize the picture as an instance or noninstance of some concept, e.g. *grandmother,* and (*b*) justify their decision. The categorization task should be based on an identification procedure and hence reflect characteristic properties, while the justification task should presumably reveal the core and hence reflect defining properties. To test these assumptions, Landau varied two aspects of the pictures. In those used with *grandmother,* for example, she always presented an adult woman but varied (*a*) her age, which is primarily characteristic of *grandmother,* and (*b*) whether or not there were young children present, which is presumably suggestive of a defining property of *grandmother* (being the mother of a parent). In line with her assumptions, Landau found that subjects of all ages relied more on the age of the adult woman when making categorical decisions than when justifying them, but more on the presence of young children when justifying decisions than when making the actual categorizations.

The Classical View and Other Types of Concepts

Although the classical view may not account for categorization with natural kinds and artifacts, it likely plays some role in categorization with other types of concepts. Clearly this seems to be true for various concepts drawn from geometry (e.g. *square*), other branches of mathematics (e.g. *even number*), kinship systems (e.g. *grandmother*), legal systems (e.g. *perjury*), sciences (e.g. *molecule* and *gene*), and other areas where there are definitions that are taught explicitly to students. Indeed, the studies of Armstrong et al (1983) and Landau (1982) reviewed above rest on the assumption that such "defined" concepts have a classical core. What is more controversial, however, is whether there are some types of "nondefined" concepts whose categorization behavior is governed by the classical view. We briefly consider two possibilities: ontological concepts and action concepts.

In Smith & Medin (1981), we gave special attention to ontological concepts, i.e. concepts that represent the basic categories of existence such as *thing, physical object, event, solid,* and *fluid.* Keil's (1979) work indicated that such concepts might conform to the classical view, at least in that they contain necessary properties. For example, his results in a sentence acceptability task indicated that ontological concepts are structured in a hierarchy—say, *thing* on top, branching to *physical object* and *event,* and the former branching to *solid* and *fluid*—and that similarity judgments conformed to the hierarchy, i.e. a concept was always judged more similar to its immediate than to a distant superordinate. These results have been challenged. Carey (1983) provides counterexamples to the claim that ontological concepts form a strict hierarchy, and Gerard & Mandler (1983) failed to replicate some of the sentence acceptability results that Keil used to generate the hierarchies. It is therefore unclear whether ontological concepts fit the classical view any better than do most object concepts.

Some have said that those interested in categorization think that concept is spelled "N, O, U, N" (G. A. Miller 1982, personal communication). Perhaps the action concepts denoted by verbs are more likely to conform to a classical-view account of categorization. As support for this possibility, we note that there are some psychologically motivated decompositions of verbs into meaning components where these components seem to function as defining conditions, e.g. Miller & Johnson-Laird 1976, Gentner 1981. However, we know of no adequate studies that directly address the question of whether categorization with simple action concepts conforms to the classical view.

The Classical View and Other Functions of Concepts

As mentioned earlier, in addition to categorization, concepts can serve the functions of fixing linguistic meaning and comprising cognitive states (e.g. beliefs and preferences). Recently, a number of researchers have argued that often it is the cores of concepts that are used in the latter two functions, and these cores may conform to the classical view.

With regard to linguistic meaning, Armstrong et al (1983) argue that it is the core of *grandmother* that allows one to infer that if someone is a *grandmother* then that someone is also a *female* and a *mother*. More generally, it seems that inclusion relations between concepts must be based on cores, not identification procedures. Suppose it were otherwise: then we might not be able to infer that a *grandmother* is a *mother* because such an inference could require that all the properties of *mother* be included in those of *grandmother,* yet the identification procedure for *mother* would include the property of being young-to-middle aged while that for *grandmother* would not.

Armstrong et al (1983) also argue that concept cores are often used to deduce one belief from another. This claim receives support from an experiment by Rips & Stubbs (1980). Subjects had to answer questions about kin relations (e.g. "Is Hank the cousin to Maude?") for families known to them. Rips and Stubbs were able to do a reasonable job of predicting the times to answer these questions by assuming that subjects considered only the core properties of these concepts, particularly the property denoted by "child of."

The Classical View as a Metatheory of Concepts[4]

The idea that object concepts do not have defining properties goes against many people's intuitions (see McNamara & Sternberg 1983). Though these intuitions frequently will yield to counterexamples, perhaps they should be considered as phenomena worthy of study. And what these intuitions suggest is that people

---

[4]The ideas in this paragraph grew partly out of a discussion with Dedre Gentner.

tend to approach the world as if it conformed to the classical view (even if it doesn't!). Thus, the classical view may serve as the layperson's metatheory of concepts (or the layperson's metaphysics). Assuming this is the case, how do people reconcile their belief in the classical view with their lack of defining properties for most object concepts? Perhaps by further assuming that the defining properties are hidden from ordinary observation but are available to experts, e.g. biologists, botanists, and so on. [This is related to Putnam's (1973) claim that meaning is distributed through the community, and we are suggesting that an awareness of this distribution of linguistic labor is part of the layperson's metatheory of concepts.]

Summary

There are reasons for maintaining the classical view. With "defined" concepts, a core that conforms to the classical view may be used as a backup or source of justification in categorization. It is possible that the classical view may play a comparable role with some nondefined concepts (e.g. action concepts). As for functions other than categorization, there are plausible arguments for thinking that the view has a role in accounting for linguistic meaning and reasoning, and speculative arguments for thinking the view may serve as a layperson's metatheory.

CATEGORY COHESIVENESS

Our experiences can be partitioned in a limitless variety of ways, and it is natural to ask why we have the concepts we have and not others. That is, what makes a concept sensible or a category cohesive?

Proposed Constraints from the Classical and Probabilistic Views

The classical view assumes that the defining properties provide the structure that holds a category together. But this may not be enough structure. For example, a category consisting of brown things bigger than a basketball and weighing between 10 and 240 kilograms satisfies a classical view definition but does not seem sensible or cohesive. Osherson (1978) and Keil (e.g. 1979) have worried about this problem and suggested that some of the needed constraints result from the hierarchical structuring of ontological concepts; but as we noted earlier, this hierarchical structuring is now a matter of debate (see also Krueger & Osherson 1980).

The probabilistic view is constrained primarily in that it implies that categories be partitionable on the basis of a summing of evidence, i.e. that the categories be separable on the basis of a weighted, additive combination of component information [this is called "linear separability" (Sebestyen 1962)].

One way of evaluating the importance of linear separability is to set up two categorization tasks that are similar in major respects except that in one the categories are linearly separable while in the other they are not. Using this strategy, in a series of four experiments Medin & Schwanenflugel (1981) found no evidence that linearly separable categories were easier to learn than categories that were not linearly separable.

The Basic Level

Another possible source of constraints on categories comes from research on the basic level of categorization. While any particular object, say a particular apple, can be assigned to a number of different concepts, e.g. *fruit, apple,* and *McIntosh apple,* one level seems to be the preferred or basic one for categorization as judged by speed of categorization, ease of learning, and a host of other criteria (e.g. Rosch et al 1976, Daehler et al 1979, Mervis & Crisafi 1982, Murphy & Smith 1982). To the extent we can determine what makes a concept basic, we may have determined what makes a category cohesive.

There is no shortage of ideas about determinants of basic levels. One is that the basic level is the most abstract level at which the instances of a concept have roughly the same shape (e.g. Rosch et al 1976). A related position (according to Hemenway & Tversky 1984) is that the basic level is the most abstract level at which the instances of a concept have roughly the same parts.[5] These ideas translate readily into possible reasons for why categories cohere, at least for object concepts. Another possible determinant of basic levels has the potential to constrain abstract concepts as well as concrete ones: namely, the basic level is that which maximizes the number of distinctive properties, where a distinctive property is common to most members of a concept but lacking to most members of contrasting concepts (see, e.g., Mervis & Rosch 1981, Murphy & Smith 1982). Whichever determinants turn out to be right, however, they cannot be the whole story about category cohesiveness, since nonbasic concepts like *fruit, plant,* and *thing* would lack the critical determinant yet constitute a coherent concept.

More Abstract Criteria of Category Cohesiveness

Rosch & Mervis (1975) suggested that the basic level maximizes "cue validity," i.e. the probability than an object is a member of a particular category given that it has a particular property. Murphy (1982), however, argued that the

---

[5]Another reason for thinking there is some link between parts and category cohesiveness comes from the work of Markman and her associates, (e.g. Markman & Callahan 1983). These authors have investigated "collection" concepts (e.g. *family, forest*), which are based on part-whole relations rather than class-inclusion ones (e.g. a son is part of a *family*), and have shown that young children find collections easier to understand than concepts based on class inclusion. Markman suggests that this difference may be due to part structures being more cohesive.

principle of maximizing cue validity will always pick out the most inclusive or abstract categories. That is, since cue validity is the probability of being in some category given some property, this probability will increase (or at worst not decrease) as the size of the category increases (e.g. the probability of being an *animal* given the property of flying is greater than the probability of *bird* given flying, since there must be more animals that fly than birds that fly).[6] The idea that cohesive categories maximize the probability of particular properties given the category fares no better. In this case, the most specific categories will always be picked out.

Medin (1982) has analyzed a variety of formal measures of category cohesiveness and pointed out problems with all of them. For example, one possible principle is to have concepts such that they minimize the similarity between contrasting categories; but minimizing between-category similarity will always lead one to sort a set of *n* objects into exactly two categories. Similarly, functions based on maximizing within-category similarity while minimizing between-category similarity lead to a variety of problems and counterintuitive expectations about when to accept new members into existent categories versus when to set up new categories.

At a less formal but still abstract level, Sternberg (1982) has tried to translate some of Goodman's (e.g. 1983) ideas about induction into possible constraints on natural concepts. Sternberg suggests that the apparent naturalness of a concept increases with the familiarity of the concept (where familiarity is related to Goodman's notion of entrenchment), and decreases with the number of transformations specified in the concept (e.g. *aging* specifies certain transformations).

Correlated Attributes

Rosch and Mervis have argued that natural categories are formed to take advantage of correlated attribute clusters (e.g. Rosch 1978a, Mervis & Rosch 1981). Certain attributes tend to co-occur—e.g. animals with feathers are likely to have wings and beaks, whereas animals with fur are unlikely to have wings and beaks—and cohesive categories may be those that follow the natural correlation of attributes. Medin (1983) has tried to extend this line of argument by noting that correlated attributes *within* a category provide further internal structure, e.g. birds with large wings tend to eat fish and live near the sea. There is now evidence that the members of natural categories do indeed have correlated attributes (Malt & Smith 1983), and that people are sensitive to such

---

[6]W. K. Estes (personal communication, 1983) has pointed out that this drawback to maximizing cue validity may be overcome by normalizing or subtracting out the prior probability of the class. Thus, the cue validity of flying for *bird* is now the (*a*) probability of *bird* given the property flying minus (*b*) the probability of *bird*. Now cue validity need no longer increase with the inclusiveness of the class.

correlated attributes when making categorization decisions (Medin et al 1982, Cohen & Younger 1983, Malt & Smith 1983). A major problem, however, with invoking correlated attributes as a constraint on concepts is that there are so many possible correlations that it is not clear how the correct ones are selected (see Keil 1981). Some auxiliary principles may be needed to provide further constraints on category cohesion.

Summary

The probabilistic and exemplar views provide few constraints on what can count as a natural concept or cohesive category. Research on the basic level of categorization—with its emphasis on shape, parts, and distinctive properties—may prove useful in formulating such constraints. Other approaches focus on more abstract constraints, such as cue validity, or on correlated attributes.

CATEGORIZATION PROCESSES WITH PROTOTYPE CONCEPTS

Recent work on prototype concepts has led to new problems and possibilities with respect to categorization models. We can give but a brief sample of this literature.

Categorization as Decision Making

Given that the distinction between categorization and decision making is rather fuzzy, there has been surprisingly little interplay between formal models in these two areas. There are some interesting points of contact. For example, categorization models that endorse linear separability correspond to linear decision models; this suggests that conjoint and functional measurement techniques developed in the domain of decision making can be brought to bear in categorization tasks. This point was illustrated by Wallsten & Budescu (1981), who asked clinical psychologists and graduate students to classify MMPI profiles. They used conjoint and functional measurement analysis from decision theory to show that although some of the less experienced judges processed the dimensions in an additive manner, the more experienced judges tended to use correlated dimensions in an interactive manner.

Another interesting relationship between categorization and decision making involves the analysis of optimal decision rules in psychophysical paradigms. Noreen (1981) showed that in certain forms of same-different judgment tasks, the optimal decision rule is to first categorize the inputs and then base the same-different judgment on whether or not the inputs were assigned to the same category.

Activation of Properties and Concepts

Many categorization models proceed as if the entire set of properties of a concept is invariably activated when the concept is mentioned. Barsalou (1982) argues instead that a concept has a subset of context-independent properties that are activated whenever the concept is accessed, but also a subset of context-dependent properties that are activated only when the relevant context is instantiated. For the concept *basketball,* for example, being round would be a context-independent property while being able to float would be a context-dependent property.

Context effects on property activation can alter standard typicality judgments. Roth & Shoben (1983) used a reading-time paradigm and measured the time needed to establish an anaphoric reference between an exemplar (e.g. chicken) and a concept (e.g. *bird*). The context was either neutral or biased; e.g. in "The bird walked across the barnyard," the context is biased to make chicken more typical of *bird* than is robin. Reading times were faster when the exemplar fit the bias, and the typicality rating for a usually atypical exemplar increased when it fit the bias.

This kind of bias or priming also occurs at the level of the entire concept in situations where several concepts might apply to the input; e.g. in the domain of person concepts where multiple concepts frequently apply to the same person or behavior. In a variety of paradigms it has been shown that the likelihood that a subject will use a particular concept to encode an input is increased by priming the concept in a context separate from that in which the input is presented (e.g. Higgins & King 1981, Wyer & Srull 1981).

Holistic Versus Component Processing

Although most categorization models assume that people are essentially making similarity judgments, often it is unclear whether these judgments constitute a holistic impression of overall similarity or a more analytic accumulation of matches and mismatches of components. One well-known determinant of holistic versus component similarity is whether the dimensions of the inputs are integral (e.g. hue and saturation of colors) or separable (e.g. size and shape of geometric forms), where integral dimensions lead to holistic similarity and separable dimensions to component similarity (e.g. Shepard 1964, Garner 1974). It now appears that whether similarity is computed holistically or componentially can also be a consequence of the processing strategy, (see, e.g., Pishkin & Bourne 1981). Indeed, it has been argued that for fixed inputs, there is a major developmental shift from treating the inputs in a holistic manner to treating them in a component-by-component manner (e.g. Burns et al 1978, L. B. Smith 1981, Kemler 1983, Ward 1983). This work indicates that categorization models must be flexible enough to permit either holistic or componential similarity computations, yet principled enough to specify why one type of similarity dominates in some circumstances and the other type dominates in other circumstances.

Summary

Some of the formal models developed in decision making might prove useful in categorization. Whatever their origin, categorization models are going to have to accommodate the facts that (*a*) some properties of a concept are activated only in certain contexts, and (*b*) similarity between an item and a concept can be computed either holistically or componentially.

ACQUISITION OF PROTOTYPE CONCEPTS

The literature at issue here focuses on the acquisition of prototype concepts that are usually artificial (rather than natural), that are learned by adults (rather than children), and that are based on experience only with exemplars (rather than on category-level information). Even with these restrictions, this literature is a burgeoning one, and we will have to be selective.

Variables Controlling Learning

Our knowledge of variables controlling learning is increasing. Some of the critical findings include these: basic-level concepts are easier to learn than their subordinates or superordinates (e.g. Murphy & Smith 1982); good examples of a concept are learned before poor ones (e.g. Rosch 1978a); transfer to new exemplars is facilitated by increases in the number of exemplars on which learning was originally based (e.g. Homa et al 1981, Omohundro 1981); and feedback is not always necessary for learning (e.g. Fried & Holyoak 1983).

Of the many variables that could be considered in detail, we will focus on one recent development: the role of unique properties, i.e. those properties unique to exemplars that allow them to be identified individually. While analyses of natural concepts assume that instances contain some unique properties, studies using artificial concepts usually employ instances with no unique properties (e.g. Medin & Schaffer 1978). A recent study of Medin et al (1983) suggests that when distinctive properties are present, abstraction is far from automatic. Medin et al used photographs of faces where the concepts were defined in terms of dimensions such as hair color and length, but where individual faces differed from each other along numerous other dimensions. In the first condition, subjects learned to assign photographs to one of two concepts; in a second condition, subjects learned not only the appropriate categorization but also a unique response for each photograph (the first name), which insured some attention to unique properties. In a subsequent transfer test, only subjects in the first condition showed substantial transfer to new faces that had the appropriate dimension values. These results imply that abstraction is not automatic, but rather governed by factors related to the presence or absence of unique properties (see Hartley & Homa 1981 for related work).

What is Learned?

Initial studies of learning prototype concepts were taken as evidence that people abstracted from exemplars the central tendency of a category. Although people might have some information about individual exemplars, the evidence suggested that exemplars were forgotten more rapidly than the central tendency, and that with increasing delays performance was increasingly based on the central tendency (e.g. Posner & Keel 1968, 1970).

These studies have sparked considerable interest. The major issue concerns whether the results taken as supporting extraction of a central tendency, or summary representation, can be derived from the assumption that people are representing only exemplars (e.g. Brooks 1978, Medin & Schaffer 1978, Nosofsky 1983). (This, of course, is the major issue that divides the probabilistic and exemplar views.) As support for the exemplar position, Medin & Schaffer (1978) controlled the distance of transfer items to the central tendencies of two categories and manipulated the similarity of transfer items to known exemplars. They found that learning and transfer were determined by similarity to known exemplars, not by distance from central tendencies. Hintzman & Ludlam (1980) demonstrated that the forgetting effects originally taken as supporting abstraction of a central tendency could be predicted from an exemplar model. The debate continues (see Homa et al 1981, for further criticism of exemplar models, and Medin, Busemeyer & Dewey 1983 for a reply).

In Smith & Medin (1981), we argued that models based on a mixture of exemplars and summary representations might be most successful in the long run. And there are, in fact, numerous mixture models around (e.g. Medin & Schaffer 1978, Elio & Anderson 1981, Homa et al 1981, Kellogg 1981). Given all this attention, it is surprising that there are so few theories or models for describing the *learning* process associated with mastering prototype concepts (for an exception, see Anderson et al 1979).

Analytic Versus Nonanalytic Strategies

People learning prototype concepts may use a variety of strategies ranging from hypothesis testing (Martin & Caramazza 1980, Kellogg 1981) to memorization of individual instances (e.g. Kossan 1981). While hypothesis testing is taken for granted as an efficient strategy, nonanalytic processes, such as memorizing the exemplars presented and classifying new ones on the basis of their similarity to memorized ones, are often thought of as antithetical to strategies. However, Brooks has made a convincing case for the benefits of nonanalytic processing (e.g. Brooks 1978, 1983, Vokey & Brooks 1983). (This, of course, fits well with the exemplar view of what is learned.) For example, Brooks (1983) shows that when the categorizer does not know the form of the rule that describes whether an item belongs in a concept, often the most efficient strategy is to respond on the basis of the similarity of the to-be-categorized item to known exemplars in memory. This holds true even for paradigms where the rules are well defined (i.e. the concepts have defining conditions) as long as the *form* of the rule is unknown.

Summary

Although knowledge of variables controlling learning is accumulating, what remains controversial is exactly what is learned. The use of nonanalytic strategies, which rest heavily on memorizing exemplars, favors the idea that part of what is learned is in the form of individual exemplars.

DIFFERENT TYPES OF PROTOTYPE CONCEPTS

Recently the prototype approach to categorization has been extended to domains other than object concepts. Some of these new domains are the following: abstract concepts such as *belief* (e.g. Hampton 1981); psychiatric diagnostic categories (Cantor et al 1980); the concept of *self* (Kihlstrom & Cantor 1983); concepts of psychological situations (Cantor et al 1982); emotion concepts (e.g. Fehr et al 1982); linguistic concepts (e.g. Lakoff 1982, Maratsos 1982); and concepts of environmental scenes (Tversky & Hemenway 1983). While the work in each of these domains seems promising, space limitations lead us to focus on just three new domains, namely goal-derived, person, and event concepts.

Goal-Derived Concepts

Barsalou (1981) argues that in the course of engaging in goal-directed behavior people often create specialized concepts. For example, a goal to lose weight can create the concept *foods not to eat on a diet*. Though these concepts are very complex, they still give rise to typicality effects. Thus, for the concept *foods not to eat on a diet,* people consider chocolate to be a better example than bread. Interestingly, the basis for these typicality effects is qualitatively different from that with simple object concepts. Recall that for the latter, family resemblance predicts typicality. Barsalou (1981) has shown that family resemblance does not predict typicality for goal-derived concepts. Rather the typicality of an item in a goal-derived concept is determined by: (*a*) its value or amount on the dimension(s) relevant to the concept (e.g. for *foods not to eat on a diet,* amount of calories is the relevant dimension, and chocolate clearly has a higher value than bread); and (*b*) the frequency with which that item has been used as an instance of the concept in the past (e.g. chocolate frequently arises as an instance of *foods not to eat on a diet).* Thus, comparable typicality effects in two domains do not imply common determinants of typicality.

Person Concepts

Cantor & Mischel (e.g. 1979) were among the first to investigate parallels between object concepts that have a prototype structure and person concepts such as *extrovert* and *cultured person*. They showed that the extent to which an "instance," i.e. a description of an individual, was judged typical of, say, *extrovert* increased with the number of properties that the individual shared with extroverts in general. This suggests that typicality effects with person concepts have the same basis—namely, family resemblance—as typicality effects with object concepts. Such parallels merely scratch the surface of recent work done on social categorization (see, e.g., Brown 1980, Hastie et al 1980, Cantor & Kihlstrom 1981, Higgins et al 1981, Srull 1981, Lingle et al 1983).

The similarities between person and object concepts are of considerable interest but so are their differences. One kind of difference is in taxonomic structure. Object concepts are tightly hierarchically structured, with concepts at the same level being mutually exclusive. Person concepts need not have a tight hierarchical structure as concepts at the same level can apply to the same person; e.g. somebody can be both an *extrovert* and *cultured person*. A second kind of difference concerns the consequences of categorization. Person categorizations, particularly stereotyping, can produce substantial affect in both the categorizer and the categorized, while object categorization usually leaves both parties cold. Also, person categorizations can be reactive. One's categorizaton of another influences the behaviors one unconsciously elicits from the other; e.g. having categorized someone as an extravert, we unconsciously act more friendly toward that person (e.g. Snyder 1981). A third kind of difference between person and object concepts concerns the properties involved. Presumably *extrovert* has properties like being outgoing and confident, which are more abstract and indeterminate than those of most object concepts.

However, categorization based on indeterminant properties is by no means the rule for person concepts. Brown (1980) points out that the most common means for classifying people are not concepts like *extrovert* but rather occupations (e.g. *butcher*), races (e.g. *black*), religions (e.g. *Jew*), and nationalities (e.g. *German*). Though these concepts are based on relatively easy-to-determine properties, somehow these concepts can mutate into stereotypes. What seems to be going on is this: (*a*) the properties needed to categorize someone as *black* are generally easier to determine that those needed to categorize an object; (*b*) but having classified someone as *black,* there are only weak links to nonperceptible properties, whereas usually there are strong links between object concept and nonperceptible properties. In short, deciding on class membership can be easier with people than with objects, but inferring the consequences of class membership is much easier with objects than with people.

Event Concepts: Scripts

Representations of sterotyped events, such as going to a restaurant, are called "scripts" (Schank & Abelson 1977). While usually thought of as components of story understanding, scripts can also be viewed as concepts (Abelson 1981). The properties of a script-as-concept would include the actions that comprise the event; e.g. some properties of the *restaurant* concept would include finding a table and getting a menu. A specific story based on a script can be construed as an instance of the concept, and to the extent its actions match those in the script (i.e. to the extent its properties match those in the concept), it will be judged typical of the script. In line with this view, Galambos & Rips (1982) found that when subjects had to make rapid decisions about whether a particular action was part of a script (e.g. determining that "getting a menu" is part of *restaurant*), the more important the action (as determined by prior ratings) the less time needed to make the decision. This result parallels a finding with object concepts, namely, the more salient a property the less time needed to decide it is part of the concept [e.g. Holyoak & Glass 1975; see Nottenburg & Shoben (1980) for a similar parallel between a script and an object concept.]

Recent work by Abbott et al (1984), however, suggests that rather than a script being akin to an object concept, it may be more like an entire hierarchy of object concepts. The contents of a script clearly seem to be hierarchically organized. At the top level is the general goal (e.g. eating at a restaurant), at the intermediate level are "scenes" which denote sets of actions (e.g. entering the restaurant, ordering, eating, and leaving), and at the lowest level are the actions themselves. Furthermore, Abbott et al found that the scenes appeared to be the basic level of description for events, which again fits with viewing a script as a hierarchy of concepts rather than as an individual concept.

Summary

The prototype approach to concepts is spreading to many domains and turning up interesting differences as well as communalities. While there are typicality effects with goal-derived concepts, their basis is *not* family resemblance. And though person concepts are like object concepts in several respects, they differ from object concepts with regard to taxonomic structure, the consequences of categorization, and the nature of the properties involved. As for event concepts, they are clearly related to concepts, but it is not yet clear whether they are more like concepts or taxonomies.

NEWER DIRECTIONS

Complex Categories

While research on concepts has been dominated by simple categorization, interest is growing in complex categorization, or how we decide on membership in classes that are composites of simple ones (e.g. *leather shoes, shirt with blue stripes*). For composites that have three or more simple concepts or constituents, there is a question about the order of combination. That is, when presented "shirt with blue stripes," in what order does one combine *shirt, blue,* and *stripes* in forming a new concept and using it to categorize a potential instance? One possibility is that the combination order is fixed, perhaps determined by syntactic considerations, e.g. first compose *blue stripes,* then combine this product with *shirt*). Contrary to this, Rips et al (1978) and Conrad & Rips (1981) found that subjects were able to vary the order in which they combined constituents, and that they favored those orders that made categorization easiest, i.e. first combining constituents that were easiest to check in the potential instance.

Other work has dealt with composites that usually have only two constituents, and has focused on the nature of categorization with composites. An important question has been: What is the relation between the typicality of an object in a composite and its typicalities in the constituents? For example, what is the relation between the typicality of a particular object in the composite *pet fish* and its typicalities in *pet* and *fish?* Zadeh's (1965) fuzzy-set theory claims that typicality in the composite is the minimum of the typicalities in the constituents, which means that something cannot be a better example of *pet fish* than it is of *pet* or *fish*. Osherson & Smith (1981), however, argue that there are many counterexamples to this—a guppie is a better example of *pet fish* than it is of either *pet* or *fish*. Mervis & Roth (1981) provide similar counterexamples in the domain of colors.

More recent studies provide extensive arguments against the use of fuzzy-set theory as an account of complex concepts (see Jones 1982, Osherson & Smith 1981, 1982 Smith & Osherson 1983, Roth & Mervis 1983; for rejoinders, see Lakoff 1982, Zadeh 1982). The problems with fuzzy-set theory are leading some to a more representational approach to the study of complex concepts. Rather than trying to relate typicality in a composite directly to typicalities in the constituents, Osherson et al (1984) propose explicit means for combining property sets of constituents into a property set for the composite, and then determine the typicality of an object to a composite by determining the object's similarity to the composite property set.

Is There More to Categorization than Similarity?

The prototype approach generally assumes that decisions about concept membership are based only on similarity (an item's similarity to a target concept as well as to contrasting concepts). This assumption is beginning to be challenged. For one thing, some recent models of categorization are based on probabilities, not similarities. In Fried & Holyoak (1983), for example, the critical information in each concept is captured by a probability distribution of exemplars over a feature space; the probability that a particular object will be judged to be an exemplar of a particular concept is determined, in part, by the frequency of known exemplars that have the features of the object. This approach may be particularly useful in elucidating the categorization of novel objects. Also, a model based on probabilities has a natural way of incorporating knowledge about the variability of properties.

A recent finding by Rips & Handte (1984) on property variability fits especially well with probabilities rather than similarities. We can best describe the finding by an example. Subjects were asked whether an object 5 inches in diameter was more likely to be a coin or a pizza. Though the object's size was roughly midway between large coins and small pizzas (as determined by prior norms), subjects tended to categorize it as a pizza. Presumably they did this because pizzas are more variable in size, and though the probability of a 5 inch pizza is very low, it is still higher than that of a 5 inch coin. As Rips & Handte (1984) point out, though, there may be more involved here than just brute knowledge about variability. We know that coins cannot be too large because of how they are made; i.e. we have some knowledge, or a "theory," about the nature of coins which supplies the information about size variability.

The idea of intuitive theories influencing categorization is a familiar one in conceptual development. Carey (1982), in particular, has emphasized the role that children's theories of biology play in their categorizations of animals and other objects. To cite one of her examples:

> . . . when subjects were asked to . . . rate similarity, a mechanical monkey that banged cymbals together, wore clothes, and screeched was judged more similar to people than was a worm by subjects of all ages . . . But when . . . taught a new property of people ("has a spleen," where a spleen was described as a green thing inside people), spleens were attributed to worms more than to the mechanical monkey, even by 4-year-olds . . . With respect to "spleenness," worms are more similar to people than are mechanical monkeys . . . The point is that the child's rudimentary biological knowledge [or theory] influences the structure of his concept *animal* (Carey 1982, pp. 385–86).

A theory-based approach is also showing up in other work on categorization. In the Fried & Holyoak (1983) model, which emphasizes probability distributions, people are assumed to approach each concept learning situation with some global assumptions, or rough theory, about the shape of the underlying distributions. To take an example based on sorting algorithms in computer science, Michalski's work (e.g. 1983) suggests that the algorithm that best captures people's categorizations is one that operates on *descriptions* of clusters (rather than matrices of similarities) and aims to maximize criteria having to do with what constitutes a good description. This is directly analogous to grouping entities in accordance with one's theory about them.

Summary

Recent studies indicate that fuzzy-set theory cannot account for many phenomena involving complex concepts. Another new direction challenges the idea that categorization is based solely on similarity; instead, newer work focuses on the role of probability and intuitive theories in making categorical decisions.

ACKNOWLEDGMENTS

We thank Dedre Gentner, Glenn Nakamura, Lance Rips, Brian Ross, and William Salter for their helpful comments. Preparation of this manuscript was supported by U.S. Public Health Service Grants MH32370 and MH37208 and by the National Institute of Education under Contract No. US-HEW-C-400–82–0030.

Literature Cited

Abbott, V., Black, J., Smith, E. E. 1984. The representation of scripts in memory. *J. Verb Learn. Verb. Behav.* In press

Abelson, R. P. 1981. Psychological status of the script concept. *Am. Psychol.* 36:715–29

Anderson, J. R., Kline, P. J., Beasley, C. M. 1979. A general learning theory and its application to schema abstraction. In *The Psychology of Learning and Motivation*, ed. G. H. Bower, 13:227–318. New York: Academic

Anglin, J. M. 1977. *Word, Object and Conceptual Development*. New York: Norton

Armstrong, S. L., Gleitman, L. R., Gleitman, H. 1983. What some concepts might not be. *Cognition* 13:263–308

Barsalou, L. W. 1981. *The determinants of graded structure in categories*. PhD thesis. Stanford Univ., Stanford, Calif.

Barsalou, L. W. 1982. Context-independent and context-dependent information in concepts. *Mem. Cognit.* 10:82–93

Bourne, L. E. Jr. 1982. Typicality effects in logically defined categories. *Mem. Cognit.* 10:3–9

Brooks, L. R. 1978. Nonanalytic concept formation and memory for instances. See Rosch & Lloyd 1978, pp. 169–215

Brooks, L. R. 1983. On the insufficiency of analysis. Unpublished manuscript, McMaster Univ., Hamilton, Ont., Canada

Brown, R. 1980. *Natural categories and basic objects in the domain of persons*. Katz-Newcombe lecture

Burns, B., Shepp, B. E., McDonough, D., Wiener-Ehrlich, W. K. 1978. The relation between stimulus analyzability and per-

ceived dimensional structure. See Anderson et al 1979, 12:77–115

Cantor, N., Kihlstrom, J. F., eds. 1981. *Personality, Cognition and Social Interaction*. Hillsdale, NJ: Erlbaum

Cantor, N., Mischel, W. 1979. Prototypes in person perception. *Adv. Exp. Soc. Psychol.* 12:3–52

Cantor, N., Mischel, W., Schwartz, J. C. 1982. A prototype analysis of psychological situations. *Cogn. Psychol.* 14:45–77

Cantor, N., Smith, E. E., French, R., Mezzich, J. 1980. Psychiatric diagnosis as prototype categorization. *Abnorm. Psychol.* 89:181–93

Carey, S. 1982. Semantic development: the state of the art. In *Language Acquisition: The State of the Art*, ed. E. Wanner, L. R. Gleitman, pp. 347–89. New York: Cambridge Univ. Press

Carey, S. 1983. Constraints on the meaning of natural kind terms. Unpublished manuscript, Mass. Inst. Technol., Cambridge, Mass.

Cohen, L. B., Younger, B. A. 1983. Perceptual categorization in the infant. In *New Trends in Conceptual Representation*, ed. E. Scholwick. In press

Conrad, F. G., Rips, L. J. 1981. Perceptual focus, text focus, and semantic composition. In *Language and Behavior*, ed. M. F. Miller, C. S. Masek, R. A. Hendrick. Chicago: Chicago Ling. Soc.

Daehler, M. W., Lonardo, R., Bukatkok, D. 1979. Matching and equivalence judgments in very young children. *Child Dev.* 50:170–79

Elio, R., Anderson, J. R. 1981. The effects of

category generalizations and instance similarity on schema abstraction. *J. Exp. Psychol: Hum. Learn. Mem.* 7:397–417

Epstein, R. 1982. A note on the mythological character of categorization research in psychology. *J. Mind Behav.* 3(2):161–69

Farah, M. J., Kosslyn, S. M. 1982. Concept development. *Child Dev. Behav.* 16:125–67

Fehr, B., Russell, J. A., Ward, L. M. 1982. Prototypicality of emotions: A reaction time study. *Bull. Psychon. Soc.* 20:253–54

Fried, L. S., Holyoak, K. J. 1983. Induction of category distribution: A framework for classification learning. *J. Exp. Psychol: Learn. Mem. Cognit.* In press

Galambos, J. A., Rips, L. J. 1982. Memory for routines. *J. Verb. Learn. Verb. Behav.* 21:260–81

Garner, W. R. 1974. *The Processing of Information and Structure.* New York: Wiley

Gentner, D. 1981. Verb semantic structures in memory for sentences: Evidence for componential representation. *Cognit. Psychol.* 13:56–83

Gerard, A. B., Mandler, J. M. 1983. Ontological knowledge and sentence anomaly. *J. Verb. Learn. Verb. Behav.* 22:105–20

Goodman, N. G. 1983. *Fact Fiction and Forecast.* Cambridge, Mass: Harvard Univ. Press. 4th ed.

Hampton, J. A. 1981. An investigation of the nature of abstract concepts. *Mem. Cognit.* 9:149–56

Hartley, J., Homa, D. 1981. Abstraction of stylistic concepts. *J. Exp. Psychol: Hum. Learn. Mem.* 7:33–46

Hastie, R., Ostrom, T. M., Ebbesen, E. B., Wyer, R. S., Hamilton, D. L., Carlston, D. E., eds. 1980. *Person Memory: The Cognitive Basis of Social Perception.* Hillsdale, NJ: Erlbaum

Hemenway, K., Tversky, B. 1984. Objects, parts, and categories. *J. Exp. Psychol: Gen.* In press

Herrnstein, R. J., deVilliers, P. A. 1980. Fish as a natural category for people and pigeons. See Anderson et al 1979, 14:59–95

Higgins, E. T., Herman, C. D., Zanna, M. P. 1981. *Social Cognition: The Ontario Symposium,* Vol. 1. Hillsdale, NJ: Erlbaum

Higgins, E. T., King, G. 1981. Accessibility of social constructs: Information processing consequences of individual and contextual variability. See Cantor & Kihlstrom 1981, pp. 69–122

Hintzman, D. L., Ludlam, G. 1980. Differential forgetting of prototypes and old instances: Simulation by an exemplar-based classification model. *Mem. Cognit.* 8:378–82

Holyoak, K. J., Glass, A. L. 1975. The role of contradictions and counterexamples in the

rejection of false sentences. *J. Verb. Learn. Verb. Behav.* 14:215–39

Homa, D., Sterling, S., Trepel, L. 1981. Limitations of exemplar-based generalization and the abstraction of categorical information. *J. Exp. Psychol: Hum. Learn. Mem.* 7:418–39

Jones, G. V. 1982. Stacks not fuzzy sets: An ordinal basis for prototype theory of concepts. *Cognition* 12:281–90

Keil, F. C. 1979. *Semantic and Conceptual Development: An Ontological Perspective.* Cambridge, Mass: Harvard Univ. Press

Keil, F. C. 1981. Children's thinking: What never develops? *Cognition* 10:159–66

Kellogg, R. T. 1981. Feature frequency in concept learning: What is counted? *Mem. Cognit.* 9:157–63

Kemler, D. G. 1983. Holistic and analytic modes in perceptual and cognitive development. In *Perception, Cognition, and Development: Interactional Analyses,* ed. T. Tighe, B. E. Shepp, pp. 77–102. Hillsdale, NJ: Erlbaum

Kihlstrom, J. F., Cantor, N. 1983. Mental representation of the self. *Adv. Exp. Soc. Psychol.* Vol. 16: In press

Kossan, N. E. 1981. Developmental differences in concept acquisition strategies. *Child Dev.* 52:290–98

Krueger, J., Osherson, D. N. 1980. On the psychology of structural simplicity. In *On the Nature of Thought,* ed. P. Jusczyk. Hillsdale, NJ: Erlbaum

Lakoff, G. 1982. Categories and cognitive models. Berkeley: *Cognit. Sci. Rep. No. 2*

Landau, B. 1982. Will the real grandmother please stand up? The psychological reality of dual meaning representations. *J. Psycholing. Res.* 11:47–62

Lingle, J. H., Altom, M. W., Medin, D. L. 1983. Of cabbages and kings: Assessing the extensibility of natural object concept models to social things. In *Handbook of Social Cognition,* ed. R. Wyer, T. Srull, J. Hartwick. Hillsdale, NJ: Erlbaum. In press

Malt, B. C., Smith, E. E. 1983. Correlated properties in natural categories. *J. Verb. Learn. Verb. Behav.* In press

Maratsos, M. 1982. The child's construction of grammatical categories. See Carey 1982, pp. 240–66

Markman, E. M., Callahan, M. A. 1983. An analysis of hierarchical classification. In *Advances in the Psychology of Human Intelligence,* ed. R. Sternberg, Vol. 2. Hillsdale, NJ:Erlbaum

Martin, R. C., Caramazza, A. 1980. Classification in well-defined and ill-defined categories: Evidence for common processing strategies. *J. Exp. Psychol: Gen.* 109:320–53

McCloskey, M. 1980. The stimulus familiarity

problem in semantic memory research. *J. Verb. Learn. Verb. Behav.* 19:485–502

McCloskey, M., Glucksberg, S. 1978. Natural categories: Well defined or fuzzy-sets? *Mem. Cognit.* 6:462–72

McNamara, T. P., Sternberg, R. J. 1983. Mental models of word meaning. Unpublished manuscript, Yale Univ.

Medin, D. L. 1983. Structural principles of categorization. In *Interaction: Perception, Development and Cognition,* ed. B. Shepp, T. Tighe, pp. 203–30. Hillsdale, NJ: Erlbaum

Medin, D. L. Altom, M. W., Edelson, S. M., Freko, D. 1982. Correlated symptoms and simulated medical classification. *J. Exp. Psychol: Learn. Mem. Cognit.* 8:37–50

Medin, D. L., Busemeyer, J. R., Dewey, T. D. 1983. Evaluation of exemplar-based generalizations and the abstraction of categorical information. Unpublished manuscript, Univ. Illinois

Medin, D. L., Dewey, G. I., Murphy, T. D. 1983. Relationships between item and category learning: Evidence that abstraction is not automatic. *J. Exp. Psychol: Learn. Mem. Cognit.* In press

Medin, D. L., Schaffer, M. M. 1978. Context theory of classification learning. *Psychol. Rev.* 85:207–38

Medin, D. L., Schwanenflugel, P. J. 1981. Linear separability in classification learning. *J. Exp. Psychol: Hum. Learn. Mem.* 7:355–68

Mervis, C. B. 1980. Category structure and the development of categorization. In *Theoretical Issues in Reading Comprehension,* ed. R. Spiro, B. C. Bruce, W. F. Brewer, pp. 279–307. Hillsdale, NJ: Erlbaum

Mervis, C. B., Crisafi, M. A. 1982. Order of acquisition of subordinate-, basic- and superordinate-level categories. *Child Dev.* 53: 258–66

Mervis, C. B., Rosch, E. 1981. Categorization of natural objects. *Ann. Rev. Psychol.* 32:89–115

Mervis, C. B., Roth, E. M. 1981. The internal structure of basic and non-basic color categories. *Language* 57:384–405

Michalski, R. S. 1983. A theory and methodology of inductive learning. *Artif. Intell. J.* In press

Miller, G. A., Johnson-Laird, P. N. 1976. *Language and Perception.* Cambridge, Mass: Harvard Univ. Press

Millward, R. B. 1980. Models of concept formation. In *Aptitude, Learning, and Instruction: Cognitive Processes Analysis,* ed. R. E. Snow, P. A. Frederico, W. E. Montague, pp. 245–75. Hillsdale, NJ: Erlbaum

Murphy, G. L. 1982. Cue validity and levels of categorization. *Psychol. Bull.* 91:174–77

Murphy, G. L., Smith, E. E. 1982. Basic-level superiority in picture categorization. *J. Verb. Learn. Verb. Behav.* 21:1–20

Noreen, D. L. 1981. Optimal decision rules for some common psychophysical paradigms. In *Mathematical Psychology and Psychophysiology,* SIAM-AMS Proc., ed. S. Grossberg, 13:237–79. Providence, RI: Am. Math. Soc.

Nosofsky, R. 1983. Choice, similarity and the context theory of classification. *J. Exp. Psychol: Learn. Mem. Cognit.* In press

Nottenburg, G., Shoben, E. J. 1980. Scripts as linear orders. *J. Exp. Soc. Psychol.* 16:329–47

Omohundro, J. 1981. Recognition vs. classification of ill-defined category exemplars. *Mem. Cognit.* 9:324–31

Osherson, D. N. 1978. Three conditions on conceptual naturalness. *Cognition* 6:263–89

Osherson, D. N., Smith, E. E. 1981. On the adequacy of prototype theory as a theory of concepts. *Cognition* 9:35–58

Osherson, D. N., Smith, E. E. 1982. Gradedness and conceptual combination. *Cognition* 12:299–318

Osherson, D. N., Smith, E. E., Rips, L. J., Albert, K. 1984. A theory of conceptual combination for prototype concepts. Unpublished manuscript, Mass. Inst. Technol

Pishkin, V., Bourne, L. E. Jr. 1981. Abstraction and the use of available information by schizophrenic and normal individuals. *J. Abnorm. Psychol.* 90(3):197–203

Posner, M. I., Keele, S. W. 1968. On the genesis of abstract ideas. *J. Exp. Psychol.* 77:353–63

Posner, M. I., Keele, S. W. 1970. Retention of abstract ideas. *J. Exp. Psychol.* 83:304–8

Putnam, H. 1973. Meaning and reference. *J. Philos.* 70:669–711

Reed, S. K. 1972. Pattern recognition and categorization. *Cogn. Psychol.* 3:382–407

Rey, G. 1984. Concepts and stereotypes: A critical discussion of categories and concepts. *Cognition.* In press

Rips, L. J., Handte, J. 1984. Classification without similarity. Unpublished manuscript, Univ. Chicago

Rips, L. J., Smith, E. E., Shoben, E. J. 1978. Semantic composition in sentence verification. *J. Verb. Learn. Verb. Behav.* 17:375–401

Rips, L. J., Stubbs, M. E. 1980. Genealogy and memory. *J. Verb. Learn. Verb. Behav.* 19:705–21

Rosch, E. 1978a. Principles of categorization. See Rosch & Lloyd 1978, pp. 28–49

Rosch, E., Lloyd, B. B., eds. 1978b. *Cognition and Categorization.* Hillsdale, NJ: Erlbaum

Rosch, E., Mervis, C. B. 1975. Family resemblances: Studies in the internal structure of categories. *Cogn. Psychol.* 7:573–605

138   MEDIN & SMITH

Rosch, E., Mervis, C. B., Gray, W., Johnson, D., Boyes-Braem, P. 1976. Basic objects in natural categories. *Cogn. Psychol.* 3:382–439

Roth, E. M., Mervis, C. B. 1983. Fuzzy-set theory and class inclusion relations. *J. Verb. Learn. Verb. Behav.* In press

Roth, E. M., Shoben, E. J. 1983. The effect of context on the structure of categories. *Cogn. Psychol.* In press

Schank, R. C., Abelson, R. P. 1977. *Scripts, Plans, Goals, and Understanding.* Hillsdale, NJ: Erlbaum

Sebestyen, G. S. 1962. *Decision-Making Processes in Pattern Recognition.* New York: Macmillan

Shepard, R. N. 1964. Attention and the metric structure of the stimulus space. *J. Math. Psychol.* 1:54–87

Smith, E. E., Medin, D. L. 1981. *Categories and Concepts.* Cambridge, Mass: Harvard Univ. Press

Smith, E. E., Osherson, D. N. 1983. Conceptual combination with prototype concepts. Unpublished manuscript, Bolt Beranek & Newman

Smith, E. E., Shoben, E. J., Rips, L. J. 1974. Structure and process in semantic memory: A featural model for semantic decisions. *Psychol. Rev.* 81:214–41

Smith, L. B. 1981. Importance of the overall similarity of objects for adults' and children's classifications. *J. Exp. Psychol: Hum. Percept. Perform.* 7:811–24

Snyder, M. 1981. On the self-perpetuating nature of social stereotypes. In *Cognitive Processes in Stereotyping and Intergroup Behavior*, ed. D. Hamilton, pp. 183–212. Hillsdale, NJ: Erlbaum

Srull, T. K. 1981. Person memory: Some tests of associative storage and retrieval models. *J. Exp. Psychol: Hum. Learn. Mem.* 7:440–63

Sternberg, R. J. 1982. Natural, unnatural, and supernatural concepts. *Cogn. Psychol.* 15:121–49

Tversky, A. 1977. Features of similarity. *Psychol. Rev.* 84:327–52

Tversky, B., Hemenway, K. 1983. Categories of environmental scenes. *Cogn. Psychol.* 15:121–49

Vokey, J. R., Brooks, L. R. 1983. Taming the clever unconscious: Analogic and abstractive strategies in artificial grammar learning. *Cognition.* In press

Walker, J. H. 1975. Real-world variability, reasonableness judgments, and memory representations for concepts. *J. Verb. Learn. Verb. Behav.* 14:241–52

Wallsten, T. S., Budescu, D. V. 1981. Additivity and nonadditivity in judging MMPI profiles. *J. Exp. Psychol: Hum. Percept. Perform.* 7:1096–1109

Ward, T. B. 1983. Response tempo and separable-integral responding: Evidence for an integral-to-separable processing sequence in visual perception. *J. Exp. Psychol: Hum. Percept. Perform.* 9:103–12

Wyer, R. S. Jr., Srull, T. K. 1981. Category accessibility: Some theoretical and empirical issues concerning the processing of social stimulus information. See Higgins et al 1981, pp. 161–98

Zadeh, L. 1965. Fuzzy sets. *Inf. Control* 8:338–53

Zadeh, L. A. 1982. A note on prototype theory and fuzzy sets. *Cognition* 12:291–97

Ann Rev. Psychol. 1984. 35:139–63

JUDGMENT AND DECISION:
Theory and Application

Gordon F. Pitz and Natalie J. Sachs

Department of Psychology, Southern Illinois University, Carbondale, Illinois 62901

CONTENTS

INTRODUCTION

Judgment and decision making are topics that for many years have stood apart from other areas of psychology. They are presumably facets of human information processing and part of the larger field of cognitive psychology. An informal survey of current textbooks suggests, however, that if the study of judgment and decision making is an important part of cognition, the fact is not widely recognized. Nevertheless, investigators studying these processes have recently shown an increased interest in their relationship with other cognitive mechanisms. The interaction between judgment and decision research and

139

0066-4308/84/0201-0139$02.00

other topics in psychology reflects important theoretical developments in the area.

A judgment or decision making (JDM) task is characterized either by *uncertainty* of information or outcome, or by a concern for a person's *preferences,* or both. Unlike other tasks, there may exist no criterion for determining whether a single choice or judgment is correct, since the response is based in part on personal opinions or preferences. It is possible, however, to impose a mathematical or logical structure on the task that defines the *consistency* of a set of responses. The prescriptions for consistent behavior are generally derived from formal probability theory and from Expected Utility (EU) theory,[1] a prescriptive model of choice founded on axioms proposed by von Neumann & Morgenstern (1947). Bayesian decision theory (e.g. Raiffa & Schlaifer 1961) is a prescriptive theory of choice based on a combination of probability theory and EU theory. The validity of these prescriptive models as descriptions of human behavior has for many years been a dominant theme in this area.

Numerous authors have demonstrated that judgments depart significantly from the prescriptions of formal decision theory (see Kahneman et al 1982). An earlier review of behavioral decision theory (Slovic et al 1977) was largely devoted to a description of these inconsistencies. To account for the findings, investigators have explored the information processing strategies, or heuristics, that people use when making judgments. The significance of these inconsistencies, and the status of judgmental heuristics, has been a matter of dispute. The inconsistencies may point to limitations of prescriptive models rather than to limitations of human judgment; heuristics may be adaptive mechanisms for coping with a complex, dynamic environment, not just efforts to overcome cognitive limitations (Hogarth 1981, 1982). Since theorists are also human, and hence liable to the same biases as their subjects, there may exist a "bias heuristic" that leads psychologists to see biases in all forms of judgment (Berkelely & Humphreys 1982). The last chapter in this area in the *Annual Review of Psychology* included a critical discussion of the adequacy of prescriptive models for evaluating judgment and decision making (Einhorn & Hogarth 1981). The debate is important and interesting; nevertheless, it should not distract attention from the cognitive mechanisms on which judgments are based. We are primarily concerned, therefore, with the degree to which prescriptive models clarify the JDM process itself.

One reason for the concern with prescriptive models is that they provide guidelines for aiding the decision process. The interaction between basic research and applied problem solving has been of continuing interest to investigators in this area (see, e.g., Humphreys et al 1983). Errors of judgment

---

[1]The following acronyms are used in this chapter: EU, expected utility; IIT, information integration theory; JDM, judgment or decision making; MAU, multiattribute utility; SJT, social judgment theory.

suggest ways in which performance might be improved, especially if one understands why the errors occurred. For this reason alone it is important to know if inconsistent judgments indicate human failures, biases in research methods, or the superiority of human judgment over prescriptive analyses.

THEORETICAL ORIENTATIONS

Historical Background

The current state of theory in judgment and decision making represents a blend of formal prescriptive approaches, other algebraic representations of JDM processes, and models based on hypothetical cognitive mechanisms. The influence of prescriptive decision theory has been strong, although it may in the past have served to keep the study of decision making separate from other topics in psychology. Basic concepts of decision theory have been used in other areas to account for behavior ranging from signal detection (Green & Swets 1966) to word recognition (Atkinson & Juola 1973). Prescriptive models apparently have been more successful in describing these simpler, automatic processes than in describing judgments that require thoughtful deliberation.

Within psychology, JDM theory has its origins in theories of perception, especially the probabilistic functionalism of Egon Brunswik (see Hammond 1966), and the methods of psychophysical measurement and scaling (Hammond et al 1980). Such traditions as associationist theory and information processing theory have until recently had little impact on JDM theory. While several authors have pointed out the relevance of theoretical developments in cognitive psychology for understanding decision behavior (Pitz 1977, Svenson 1979, Payne 1980), there is as yet little systematic formulation of any topic in JDM research based on associationist or information processing principles.

Apart from the EU tradition, the most important influences on research in judgment and decision processes have been the functional measurement methodology developed by N. H. Anderson (1970) and social judgment theory (Hammond et al 1975). These approaches share a concern with the information integration process and use algebraic models to show how judgments are related to stimulus information. In their origins these theories have little in common with other approaches to cognition. Recently, however, theorists using algebraic models have used the models to test hypotheses about the details of information processing (Lopes 1982b, Wallsten & Barton 1982, Wilkening & Anderson 1982).

Prescriptive Theories

Prescriptive decision theory provides a set of rules for combining beliefs (probabilities) and preferences (utilities) in order to select an option. The theoretical distinction between beliefs and preferences has been one of the most significant of decision theory's contributions to the study of behavior. In evaluating formal decision theory as a foundation for descriptive models, it is helpful to keep this distinction in mind. For example, it is possible in principle to validate a statement of belief but not a preference or value judgment. Because a prediction of future events can be verified, the probability theory component of formal decision theory has rather more prescriptive force than assumptions about the structure of a person's value system. The result is that the prescriptive role of EU theory remains controversial. Suppose, for example, that a person's stated preferences are inconsistent with the theory; should one try to convince him that the behavior is irrational, or seek a prescriptive model that is consistent with his stated preferences? The former solution is difficult, since there is no criterion other than personal judgment that can determine the validity of the prescriptive model (Einhorn & Hogarth 1981).

Two forms of criticism can be raised against prescriptive models: the general constraints may be unrealistic, or a specific model may be applied in a context for which it is not suitable. The particular axioms of EU theory have not been universally accepted. Recently the relevance of the more general principle of consistency has also been questioned. Hogarth (1982) points out that there are costs associated with consistency, that consistency is just one of several desirable properties associated with judgments. Inconsistency may itself have desirable properties, while forced consistency may interfere with a search for novel or creative solutions. Consistency, then, is just one attribute to be considered in choosing a problem solving strategy.

Apart from general concerns with EU theory, one might argue that it is often applied inappropriately. For example, Lopes (1981) discusses its limitations for prescriptive purposes when a person must make a single, isolated decision. Taking a different point of view, Hogarth (1981) makes a distinction between the natural, "continuous" environment, for which the usual prescriptive models are perhaps inappropriate, and the limited, "discrete" environment in which tests of prescriptive models are normally carried out. He suggests that the heuristics that lead to errors in the discrete environment may be quite adaptive in a continuous environment. An important point raised by Berkeley & Humphreys (1982) is that a judgment or decision problem involves multiple sources of uncertainty, some of the most important of which are not addressed by any prescriptive model.

Such criticisms suggest that a broader formulation of prescriptive theory is needed in which the distinction between description and prescription is made less important. One approach is to adopt a multidimensional definition of utility in which as many attributes are used as is necessary to describe the decision maker's preferences. Lopes (1981) suggests that additional attributes be incorporated into the analysis of a problem to provide a more realistic representation. Formal analyses that adopt a multiattribute perspective have been developed. Fishburn (1980) described an EU model that incorporates a separate utility for gambling, a concept that violates the spirit of the original theory, yet which may describe a person's preferences more accurately. Bell (1982) discussed the role of "regret" in the analysis of decision making. He assumes that the decision maker compares an obtained outcome with other outcomes that were not obtained, and that reduced monetary gain may be accepted in order to minimize this retrospective regret. Rohrbaugh et al (1980) provided evidence that the equity of the distribution of outcomes across people is an attribute that a decision maker might want to treat independently of total gain; a multiattribute extension of EU theory (Keeney & Winkler 1982) enables the theory to deal with concerns about equity.

The use of multiattribute utility (MAU) theory has greatly increased the scope of application of formal decision theory (see Keeney 1982). An analysis of a problem using MAU thoery still requires the construction of a logically coherent value structure, but it may be possible to resolve inconsistencies by adding more elements to the structure. MAU theory then becomes little more than a description of a decision maker's preferences, rather like the result of functional measurement or social judgment theory. This by no means reduces the practical value of the analysis, of course; more emphasis is placed on the clarification of a person's preferences and less on prescriptions for action. The use of the theory for explanatory purposes, however, demands that other constraints be imposed to provide parsimony of explanation.

The multiattribute application of prescriptive theory has had an important impact on psychological theory at a different level. It is widely recognized that JDM processes are not invariant across task environments (Payne 1982) and that a person might use any of a number of strategies to arrive at a judgment or decision. Beach & Mitchell (1978) and Russo & Dosher (1983) suggest that the choice of strategy depends on the cognitive effort that it requires (see also Smith et al 1982). There exists, therefore, a higher level process of cost-benefit analysis (Payne 1982) that might be used to select a strategy. The degree of effort used to reach a decision will be considered, along with the expected benefits of a more elaborate strategy. One problem with this approach is that it can lead to an infinite regress: since a cost-benefit analysis of possible strategies may itself require cognitive effort, how does a person decide to employ such a cost-benefit analysis? Is that decision also subject to a cost-benefit analysis? The problem of leaving a person paralyzed with indecision about his decision process can be solved by assuming that the analysis occurs automatically without deliberate control. As in the case of, say, word recognition, a prescriptive model may find its most suitable application in describing automatic, nondeliberate processes.

Schoemaker (1982), in a review of EU theory, concluded that the theory has been and continues to be productive. In spite of its limitations from both the prescriptive and descriptive perspective, "much of the research would not have resulted without the existence of EU theory in the first place. As such, the model has yielded deeper insights and more refined questions, both descriptively and normatively." The interaction of prescriptive and descriptive theory through multiattribute formulations of decision problems promises to increase further its prescriptive value (e.g. Kunreuther & Schoemaker 1981), as well as its descriptive power.

Algebraic Models of Judgment and Decision

The prescriptions of EU theory and its extensions can be presented in algebraic form. There are other algebraic models of judgment and decision that are not derived from normative considerations. The best known is N. H. Anderson's information integration theory (IIT: Anderson 1981), which uses algebraic formulations to describe judgments based on multiple sources of information. Hammond's social judgment theory (SJT: Hammond et al 1975), based on Brunswik's (1952) lens model, makes use of correlation and regression analysis to relate judgments to environmental variables. SJT generally uses external measurements of environmental cues; IIT provides a technique for establishing scales of psychological magnitude for external cues. Both theoretical approaches are concerned with the process by which information from different sources is combined. Theoretical methods for determining the integration rule are well established for IIT. Functional measurement (N. H. Anderson 1970) was designed to provide a simultaneous validation of the scale values and the algebraic model of the integration process, although Birnbaum (1982) has criticized some of the claims made for functional measurement in this respect.

Most algebraic models (including EU and MAU theory) rely on some version of a linear combination rule, at least as a first approximation. One advantage of a linear rule is that it serves as an excellent approximation to many nonlinear processes, which means that for prediction purposes a simple linear model is often sufficient (Dawes 1979). When one wants to know more about the process being modeled, however, a simple test of a linear model is rarely sufficient. Anderson's functional measurement methods provide a logic for testing a model of information integration. Birnbaum (1982) has extended the logic further, using the criterion of scale convergence to assess the adequacy of the algebraic model. He uses judgments of composites of stimulus features and judgments of differences between features to show that both can be accounted for by the same model.

The central concern in using algebraic models is to find an algebraic rule— e.g. adding, multiplying, or averaging—that can be used to describe judgments. At first the research consisted primarily of a catalog of tasks that give rise to each kind of integration process. Recently there has been progress toward a higher level of understanding that relates the integration rules to more general principles. For example, perhaps the most widely observed integration process is an averaging rule (see Shanteau & Nagy 1982 for a summary). Significant departures from an averaging rule can be observed, however, and Birnbaum (e.g. Birnbaum & Stegner 1981) has proposed a configural-weight averaging model to account for some of the failures of a simple averaging model. In these models the effect of a stimulus feature depends in part on its relation to other features. By including such contextual effects in the algebraic model, it becomes capable of describing a variety of cognitive operations.

In many respects, the most interesting findings in studies using algebraic models of information integration are the failures of the model. In a study of judgments based on MMPI profiles, Wallsten & Budescu (1981) found that failures of the additive model occurred more often with experts than with less expert subjects, presumably because of the experts' ability to use more complex rules. Hammond (1980) has proposed that an averaging process reflects an intuitive strategy that is more likely to be used when the task is complex and unfamiliar, a hypothesis that is supported by the Wallsten & Budescu results. Wallsten & Barton (1982) used an additive model to describe the processing of probabilistic information. While the model is of interest in its own right, violations of additivity do occur. The authors suggest that subjects use a two-stage judgment process; the first stage, suggestive of Hammond's intuitive processing, leads to a tentative judgment; the second incorporates a more complex, configural analysis.

Information Processing Orientations

The growing interest in cognitive mechanisms is the result of two sets of findings: the changes in judgments that occur as a function of changes in the way a task is presented (Payne 1982), and the observation that people use simplifying heuristics to deal with complex judgment tasks. These findings are interconnected; many demonstrations of task-dependent results, such as the effect of the "framing" of a task on judgments (Tversky & Kahneman 1981), show that the invariance demanded by prescriptive models is not present. What is significant for a cognitive psychologist is that the *context* in which a judgment is made affects that judgment. Many variables other than those to which a person is asked to respond can be shown to affect the judgment: the thematic background (Einhorn & Hogarth 1982b), the number of alternative choices given to or provided by a subject (Einhorn & Hogarth 1982b, Koriat et al 1980), the availability of irrelevant references (Gilovich 1981), and the kind of judgment required (Hershey & Schoemaker 1983). None of this is surprising, of course. The results emphasize how significant are factors that affect the salience of task features, and how important is the encoding of a problem and its representation prior to an attempted solution (Griggs & Newstead 1982). A review of findings in this area led Payne (1982) to conclude that an understanding of psychological mechanisms is emerging that relies on a "time-dependent" or process analysis of JDM tasks, and which involves a "contingent mixture" of several decision processes.

Studies of heuristics and task-dependent judgment processes generally adopt one of two perspectives that reflect different views of the automaticity of the processes. Some authors, notably Kahneman & Tversky (1982a), have drawn an analogy between judgmental heuristics and perceptual processes. They suggest that errors, biases, and context-dependent judgments are the result of cognitive mechanisms of which subjects are largely unaware (Tversky & Kahneman 1981). An alternative view is that strategies of judgment are under a person's deliberate control. This view is implied in studies that use process tracing techniques to examine strategies. Several studies have examined information search patterns to infer the underlying strategy (e.g. Herstein 1981, Montgomery & Adelbratt 1982, Shaklee & Fischhoff 1982). Subjects may be asked directly what decision rule they would use (Adelbratt & Montgomery 1980), or the decision rule may be inferred from verbal protocols (Crow et al 1980, Klein 1983). There has been some dispute concerning the suitability of verbal reports as a source of data (see Ericsson & Simon 1980). Kellogg (1982), in a study of concept learning, suggests that such reports are useful sources of information if the process is deliberate, but not if it occurs automatically. It is likely, therefore, that verbal protocols can provide useful information about deliberately selected judgment strategies but not about the more automatic, intuitive processes. Hammond (1980) makes much the same point.

Both automatic, perception-like heuristics and more deliberate information processing strategies are involved in most JDM tasks. So far neither has been the subject of a formal model or systematic body of research as have, say, EU theory or IIT. Process tracing studies have been successful in describing strategies, but generally not in predicting their use (Klein 1983). Theories of judgmental heuristics have often been ad hoc; Wallsten (1983) points out that much of the literature consists only of a catalog of biases. Such an approach is obviously limited in explanatory power unless it includes a statement of the principles that govern the use of each heuristic. A systematic theoretical presentation has not yet been developed, in part because it has proved difficult to specify the conditions under which a given finding will be observed. Consider one of the most widely used concepts in heuristic theory, representativeness. A dispute between Bar-Hillel & Fischhoff (1981) and Manis et al (1981) concerning the effect of base rates on inference illustrates the difficulty of making predictions based on the supposed representativeness of stimuli. A recent paper by Tversky & Kahneman (1982) does much to clarify the definition of representativeness, but it also implies that this is not a unitary concept.

Theories often proceed from loosely stated ideas to more formal model building. Loosely defined concepts abound in information processing accounts of JDM. Prescriptive and other algebraic models are readily given precise formulation, but formal models of encoding processes, judgmental heuristics, and decision strategies are rare. Apart from algebraic models, there are two other ways to formalize a theory: use complex information processing models to simulate the sequence of operations postulated by a theory (Simon 1979), or define elementary cognitive operations that can be used to predict performance in several tasks (Posner & McLeod 1982). Although initial steps in these directions have been taken, neither approach is well developed in the study of JDM. A positive development is the increasing integration of algebraic models and process models of cognitive mechanisms. Einhorn et al (1979) concluded that these are complementary approaches concerned with rather different aspects of the JDM task. That they are complementary is clear; that they must deal with different processes is less so. Lopes (1982b) has shown how process models might be integrated with algebraic models of the information integration task. Wallsten's research (Wallsten & Budescu 1981, Wallsten & Barton 1982) relies on algebraic models to test hypotheses about information acquisition processes. The stage seems to be set for the integration of theoretical orientations through the combined use of different methodologies.

JUDGMENT AND DECISION PROCESSES

If a general theory of judgment and decision making is to be found, it would be helpful to establish a compendium of basic cognitive mechanisms involved in JDM tasks. We organize this section of the review by assuming the existence of a sequential process that passes through separate stages. We recognize that it is a recursive activity; at each stage there may be subsidiary decisions to be made. When a problem is presented, salient features are identified, other information is retrieved from memory, and a meaningful organization of this information is created. The various sources of information are evaluated and integrated, and a judgment or choice is generated.

Sources of Information and Uncertainty

The description of a problem includes many features arranged in complex patterns. Before a person can respond he must encode the information and develop a representation for the problem. One way of describing the representation is as a "mental model" (Johnson-Laird 1981) that relates the problem to other knowledge. In building the mental model there are many issues left uncertain by the problem statement, uncertainties that must either be resolved or represented in the model in some way. These uncertainties include the unpredictability of future events, together with such less obvious unknown factors as one's likely feelings after a choice has been made (Berkeley & Humphreys 1982). The way in which these uncertainties are represented in the mental model has marked effect on the subsequent judgment. The nature of this effect is dependent in part on the way a problem statement is worded (Tversky & Kahneman 1981, Slovic et al 1982) and in part on the idiosyncratic perspective adopted by the decision maker; the result is not always easy to predict (Fischhoff 1983).

The perspective adopted by Berkeley & Humphreys (1982) suggests that judgments and decisions occur as responses to uncertainty; the initial statement of a problem leaves many questions unanswered, and a person's subsequent behavior is a reflection of efforts to remove or cope with the uncertainty. To resolve uncertainty, information is retrieved from memory and used to fill in missing details of the mental model. For example, while the hypotheses to be evaluated or the options to be considered are sometimes defined as part of the problem, in many cases they too are unknown and must be generated before a decision can be made. Mehle (1982) and Mehle et al (1981) suggest that people are unable or reluctant to search for more than a small number of plausible options.

Because recall is constructive rather than reproductive, the use of information is guided by the model itself in an interactive way. There are numerous sources of information that are likely to have different effects on construction of the model. Kahneman & Tversky (1982b) distinguish between external (environmentally determined) and internal (knowledge based) uncertainty, and between uncertainty based on event frequencies and uncertainty based on reasoned argument. The use of event frequencies is perhaps best understood and appears to be easiest for a person to deal with. Assuming that events are equally salient, information retrieved from memory can be used accurately to assess relative frequencies (Howell & Kerkar 1982), and tasks that demand the direct use of this information are performed more accurately than tasks that require frequencies to be translated into, say, probability judgments. The effect of other kinds of information is more complex. The more information is given directly or retrieved from memory, the less uncertainty the person feels, but there is often an unwarranted increase in confidence as additional information becomes available (Fischhoff & MacGregor 1982). If one draws attention to potentially conflicting information, it may be possible to reduce this overconfidence (Koriat et al 1980), but it is not always possible to direct attention exclusively to relevant information (Fischhoff & Bar-Hillel 1982).

No account of the JDM process is complete unless it speaks to the representation of the problem; the representation in turn depends on how prior experience is incorporated into the mental model created for the problem. In the study of deductive inference it is well known that the conclusions drawn from a set of premises are generally consistent with a person's experiences, but not necessarily with principles of deductive logic (Johnson-Laird & Wason 1977). If an abstract problem can be formulated in terms that are consistent with experience, the person responds appropriately (Cox & Griggs 1982). Thus, a critical variable in the successful application of an abstract principle is whether the wording of the problem leads to a representation that is consistent with the principle (Griggs & Newstead 1982). Kahneman & Tversky (1982a) draw similar conclusions concerning inductive inference: "human reasoning cannot be adequately described in terms of content-independent formal rules." A full understanding of the judgment process depends on how experience is organized. To obtain a complete specification of a person's knowledge is an overwhelming task, but there may be certain prototypical situations that are widely recognized (Cantor et al 1982); it may be possible to define general principles of judgment for these prototypes.

Bases for Inference

The use of existent information to derive further propositions about the problem is the basis for inference in a JDM task. The most frequent accounts of the inference process rely on the concept of "representativeness," a term that Tversky & Kahneman (1982) define as a relation between a hypothetical process and some event associated with the process. Use of the term for theoretical purposes is complicated by the fact that in different contexts it means different things. Sometimes it describes the relationship between a population (e.g. the population of undergraduate students at some college) and a sample selected from the population. In other situations representativeness is determined by the similarity of a hypothetical process (e.g. a possible disease) to observed outcomes (e.g. symptoms exhibited by a patient), or by the perception of a causal relationship between process and outcome.

For some problems the perception of representativeness is mediated by judgments of similarity, for example, the similarity of a personality description to a general stereotype. It has proved as difficult to define similarity satisfactorily as it is to define representativeness. One traditional approach is to use multidimensional geometric models in which the proximity of two items in space determines their perceived similarity. The difficulties with such models have been pointed out by Gati & Tversky (1982) and Tversky & Gati (1982). For example, by adding a common feature or extra constant dimension to two stimuli, the apparent similarity is increased; geometric models cannot account for such a result. Tversky and Gati propose instead a feature-based model in which similarity depends on a linear combination of common and distinctive features. For the most part their model applies to tasks that require direct perceptual judgments, using stimuli such as simple schematic figures. It is presumably easier to define relevant features for schematic figures than it is for complex decision problems. Nevertheless, these theoretical developments may be the first steps toward a general characterization of judgments based on perceived similarity.

A model of similarity judgments must consider not just single features or dimensions, but also the pattern of co-occurring features. For example, Bar-Hillel (1980) suggests that the judged likelihood of a sample is determined by the similarity of configural patterns in the sample (e.g. the configuration of test scores for a sample of students) to a prototypical sample. Studies of concept learning and categorization (e.g. Hayes-Roth & Hayes-Roth 1977) suggest that a person abstracts information about patterns of common events, so that the similarity of an event to a prototype depends on whether a pattern has occurred frequently for that prototype. There is much in common between judgments of category membership and judgments of representativeness. Like other judgments, covariation is evaluated in the context of a more general mental model. For example, Pitz et al (1981) suggested that frequency judgments in a complex environment are mediated by hypotheses about the structure of the problem; changes in judgment occur only if information disconfirms a current hypothesis. Perceptions of covariation are jointly dependent on observed information and prior assumptions about the problem setting; there is an interaction between the judged frequency of co-occurrence and knowledge of causal connections between the events (Adelman 1981, Jennings et al 1982). Thus, Abelson (1981) has argued that abstract generalizations of cause-effect relationships, or scripts, mediate the perception of covariation among events.

If perceived causality is an important determinant of how a person represents a problem and uses the information, it is necessary to know what determines the perception of causality. Einhorn & Hogarth (1982b) have conducted a detailed study based on the hypothesis that the perception of a causal relationship between two events is a function of several "cues to causality" that might be present. They assume that cues such as temporal order, contiguity in space, and similarity, combine additively to determine the strength of an impression of causality. A similar approach to defining indicators of causality was used by Schustack & Sternberg (1981), who used a regression analysis to determine the effect of various indicators.

It is unlikely that the outcome of these studies will be a simple definition of necessary and sufficient conditions for causality to be recognized. The perception of causality, like covariation, is a dynamic process. When people can select information relevant to a causal hypothesis, they seek mostly to confirm their current hypothesis rather than explore others (Shaklee & Fischhoff 1982). Einhorn & Hogarth (1982b) emphasize that judgments of causality depend on the context in which judgments take place; two events may be seen as causally connected in one context but not in another. In addition, an important determinant of perceived causation is the absence of other explanations for the phenomenon.

Inference can be regarded as filling in gaps in the representation of a problem. Building a mental model involves fitting known details of a problem to a network of abstract propositions in order to extrapolate beyond explicit information. Perceptions of causality are important in guiding this inference process. The process is apparently designed to make optimum use of a person's general knowledge; for example, when using categories to represent events there are certain "basic level" concepts: DOG is more basic than either POODLE or MAMMAL (Rosch 1978). The basic level category maximizes within-category similarity relative to between-category similarity, suggesting that there exists an optimal level of detail for descriptive and inferential tasks. Compare this result with one of the demonstrations of bias due to representativeness: an event such as "Bjorn Borg will lose the first set of a tennis match but win the match" is considered to be more probable than the more general event, "Bjorn Borg will lose the first set" (Tversky & Kahneman 1982). People do not recognize in this case that the probability of an event must decrease as the event is described in more detail. Presumably the added detail provided for the first event makes it more representative, i.e. more plausible given one's general knowledge, so it is judged more probable. While a person responding this way has clearly made an error, there is an important question not addressed: has the probability of the more general event been underestimated, the probability of the more detailed event been overestimated, or both? In other words, is there an optimum level of detail for making inferences, and does it correspond in some way to the optimum level of detail that applies to the use of categories? The answer to this question would have important practical as well as theoretical implications.

Conflict, Integration, and Tradeoff

Complex problems are characterized by conflict, either in the inferences to be drawn from the information or in the decision maker's preferences for outcomes. To resolve the conflict it is necessary either to eliminate all but a subset of mutually consistent features or to integrate the conflicting information to produce a composite judgment. Linear models of information integration, especially those that presume the existence of an averaging process, imply that integration occurs by averaging the values assigned to each feature according to their relative weight. The ubiquity of the averaging process is one of the most interesting findings to emerge from the information integration literature (Lopes 1982a, Shanteau & Nagy 1982).

In spite of the widespread use of averaging models, not much is known about the cognitive determinants of the weighting process. Weights are often considered to be a function of the salience of problem features (Shanteau & Ptacek 1983), but such an account partly begs the question and is to some extent misleading. Several procedures can be used for estimating weights, and different methods give rise to different estimates, perhaps because the methods are subject to different kinds of errors (Arnold & Feldman 1981, Barron 1981,

Murphy 1982). The most productive account of weights is that which shows relationships between estimated weights and other behaviors. Birnbaum & Stegner (1981), for example, demonstrated that estimates derived from a configural weight averaging model are predictive of a person's judgments in a different context. Estimates of IQ, based on information about the intelligence of a child's biological and adoptive parents, generated weight estimates that were related to a person's attitudes concerning the determination of IQ. Birnbaum & Mellers (1983) discuss a number of studies which together suggest that information is weighted according to the trustworthiness of its source.

An averaging process is a compensatory integration mechanism in which a judgment represents a tradeoff among conflicting evaluations. In most cases the averaging process is assumed to be automatic and not subject to deliberate control or verbal report. The concept of an autonomous compensatory tradeoff process appears in several explanations of judgment processes: Einhorn & Hogarth (1982a) refer to such a process in the evaluation of diagnostic evidence and in judgments of causality (Einhorn & Hogarth 1982b). Cost-benefit theories of strategy selection suggest that a tradeoff exists between cognitive effort and judgmental accuracy. The problem with theories that assume a tradeoff mechanism is that they are hard to distinguish from noncompensatory, feature selection processes. Simply demonstrating that judgments of, say, causal connections are related to several different cues does not show that the cues combine in a compensatory fashion. It has been possible to distinguish between compensatory and noncompensatory deliberate strategies by examining verbal protocols, eye movement data, or other extended sequences of behavior (see below); no analogous procedure has been developed for the detailed study of automatic judgment processes.

At the other extreme from automatic processes that implement a cost-benefit tradeoff are the very deliberate tradeoffs required in decision analyses based on MAU theory. Applications of MAU theory are based on the assumption that compensatory tradeoffs can be made explicit (see, e.g., Edwards & Newman 1982). It is further assumed that preferences can be described by a hierarchical structure in which the more global objectives are defined by more precise objectives or attributes at lower levels. While these analyses are extensions of prescriptive EU theory, they depend for their validity on their accuracy as descriptive statements of a person's preference structure. Detailed tests of these assumptions have not been carried out, although a study by Shapira (1981) casts doubt on the ability or willingness of decision makers to establish tradeoff functions consistently.

Behavioral Strategies in Judgment and Choice

Whatever information processing occurs as part of the JDM process, the only observable behavior is a response—usually a judgment or a choice. This has not been a serious limitation for theorists using algebraic models, who have generally ignored the sequence of unobservable events that precede the response. Information processing theorists, however, have taken as their major concern the strategies that people use in acquiring and using information. By examining verbal protocols (e.g. Klein 1983) or eye movement recordings (Russo & Dosher 1983), it has been possible to examine overt behavior that precedes the final judgment or choice. From the protocols one can trace the sequence of operations involved in information acquisition and make inferences about the way the information is used. In spite of the promise of this approach, it is not yet possible to define the conditions under which particular strategies will be used. Klein (1983) attempted to relate traditional assessments of utilities to subjects' decision rules; she was able to predict to some extent the attributes to which subjects would attend, but not the strategy they would use. Even the former result is subject to the usual caveats concerning correlational findings.

Most theories assume that evaluations of the information are translated into a response by procedures that are independent of the evaluation process. Functional measurement theory (N. H. Anderson, 1970) and Birnbaum's (1982) methods of scale free model testing are two methods for separating the judgment process from the evaluation process. Within an information processing framework the most common account of the response process relies on the concept of "anchoring and adjustment": an anchor point is selected that serves as a starting point for the response; it is then adjusted in a direction and by an amount determined by other features of the problem. The scope of application of such a process is very broad; it applies to any task in which a numerical response is required. Thus Einhorn & Hogarth (1982a) propose that anchoring and adjustment is a significant part of the inference process, Lopes & Ekberg (1980) show how the process might be used in evaluating the worth of risky gambles, and Lopes (1982b) uses a version of the process to explain how algebraic rules might be applied in an information integration task.

Some of the behavioral implications of judgment and decision strategies can be assessed by simulation studies. Using this approach it is possible to demonstrate the effect of any strategy that is defined explicitly for a given class of problems. Such an undertaking is a large one, because the results may depend on many problem parameters, but a first attempt has been reported by Kleinmuntz & Kleinmuntz (1981). The results can be helpful in providing a framework for describing observed decisions and for assessing the consequences of simplified heuristics from a prescriptive point of view. The latter concern is important because, as von Winterfeldt & Edwards (1982) demonstrate, large departures from the ideal strategy typically have little effect on the final payoff.

Development of Judgment and Decision Skills

There has been little integration of research on JDM processes with developmental theory (see Klayman 1982 for an exception). The neglect is unfortunate. Judgment processes are the consequence of many years of learning and maturation. Consider, for example, the assumption that preferences can be represented as a goal hierarchy and described by tradeoff functions among conflicting objectives. Very little is known about the organization of preferences from a developmental point of view, but a widely cited theory of moral development (Kohlberg 1979) suggests that values develop through separate moral stages. Is a hierarchical tree a suitable representation for values that represent different stages of moral development? Is it possible to establish tradeoffs between values at different stages? Rest (1979) claims that moral stages indicate different organization of thought processes. If this is so, the problems people have in establishing tradeoffs (e.g. Shapira 1981) may well be the result of an inability to integrate different forms of organization.

Judgment and decision skills must develop along with other abilities. For example, Brainerd (1981) shows that simple frequency estimation is a skill that parallels the development of working memory. There are numerous other skills involved in decision tasks: people do learn rules for making inferences, and heuristic strategies of judgment must be acquired in some way. Recently J. R. Anderson (1982) has proposed a general theory of cognitive skills acquisition that might throw light on the developmental issues; he suggests that skills are represented at first as declarative (verbalizable) knowledge and become automatic with extended practice. The autonomous stage is described by production systems that can be modified to reflect new learning; productions are generalized as a person learns new applications for a skill, and finer discriminations are added to make them more selective.

A theory such as Anderson's might account for many findings in JDM studies, and can also serve as a guide for the development of training procedures and decision aids. For example, the distinction between automatic and deliberate processes has been made at several points in this review; the distinction is based on the procedural, nonverbalizable nature of the former and the declarative, verbalizable nature of the latter. One would expect procedural and declarative judgment skills to be sensitive to different variables and be differentially modifiable. If judgmental heuristics, for example, are autonomous cognitive skills, their development and modification will be an important topic for research.

Many of the errors that result from the use of heuristics appear to represent inadequate refinement of principles that are normally quite adaptive; judgments by representativeness, for example, only lead to serious errors when a person ignores such other factors as base rates. Within Anderson's theory, autonomous skills are refined by learning successively finer discriminations in the use of productions, but the process is time consuming. To be most useful, therefore, efforts to debias judgments should focus on extended skills training; they may require far more extensive practice than is normally provided in studies of this sort. Decision aids should be designed from the perspective of a systems analysis, making optimum use of both human and mechanical skills in the analysis of complex problems (see Pitz 1983).

APPLICATIONS OF THEORY AND RESEARCH

The final test of an understanding of judgment and decision processes is to develop procedures for helping people make important decisions. Several investigators have described aids for application to a broad range of problems, including medical diagnosis and treatment (Wright & Ng 1981), program evaluation (Edwards & Newman 1982), managerial planning (Ballou & Mohan 1981), military strategy (Cohen & Brown 1980), and problems of personal choice (Sachs & Pitz 1981). The existence of biases and errors in unaided judgments is part of the motivation for aiding the judgment process; the assumption is that aided judgments are less subject to error. The aid is based on a prescriptive formulation that decomposes the problem into its separate elements and presumably helps the decision maker to overcome the limitations of unaided judgments. Thus the development of decision aids requires an understanding of the processes involved in performing the task, together with a suitable prescriptive theory that can serve as a normative formulation for the problem. We review several aspects of decision aids that are important in terms of both the theoretical and practical issues that arise.

Building a Structure for the Problem

Before an analysis of a problem can be implemented, it is necessary to define the elements of the problem and the structural interrelationships among them. Several authors have pointed out how critical the problem structure is to the decision aiding process. In a description of a career decision aid, for example, Wooler (1982) suggests that its most useful contribution may be in helping a person understand the interrelationships and conflicts among elements of the problem. To be successful, the structure must represent both the external features of the problem and the knowledge and values of the decision maker. If the structure is completely task-determined, it can be built into the decision aid prior to its use. Nevertheless, even if the structure can be predefined, it may still be more helpful to have the decision maker generate the structure (Sachs & Pitz 1981). It is important to know, therefore, how best to make explicit a person's knowledge about the problem.

The best approach to generating a problem structure is likely to be one based on a theoretical model of the structure of knowledge (Humphreys et al 1980). Pitz et al (1980b) discussed a number of methods for using a decision maker's description of problem elements to help the person recognize further details of the structure, based on assumptions about the organization of the underlying knowledge. Different methods may serve different purposes, depending on the way that the knowledge is to be used. Pearl et al (1981) found that a goal-directed approach proved best for encouraging a person to generate more options, while a decision tree structure was most successful in helping a person to recognize the best action.

Incorporating Judgments into the Aid

Decision aids require the decision maker to provide input in the form of judgments which are then integrated to provide feedback concerning appropriate courses of action. Following the tradition of EU theory, the required judgments are generally of two forms, predictions of uncertain future events and expressions of preference. The former usually take the form of probability statements, although some have suggested the use of concepts from fuzzy set theory for this purpose (Whaley 1981). Fuzzy sets are in principle more closely related to natural language and the organization of knowledge than is probability theory, although the applicability of fuzzy set theory to descriptions of language and knowledge has been questioned by Lakoff (1982).

Probability assessments require a person to make inferences about future events from whatever relevant information is available. The existence of biases in inferential judgment suggests that probabilistic inputs to a decision aid may often be in error. It is important, therefore, to determine under what conditions biases do occur and to measure their impact on the output of the decision aid. One approach has been to assess the *calibration* of probability judgments. An individual is said to be well calibrated if, in the long run, for all events assigned a given probability, the proportion of events that do occur is equal to the probability assigned (Lichtenstein et al 1982). In studies of calibration the dominant finding has been one of overconfidence: events occur in a proportion smaller than the assigned probability. There are important exceptions to this rule, however, that are apparently related to task characteristics. Accountants, for example, have been found to be underconfident (Tomassini et al 1982), while weather forecasters are well calibrated (see Lichtenstein et al 1982). People are also better calibrated when predicting future events than when answering general knowledge questions (Wright 1982, Wright & Wishuda 1982). This last result is significant for two reasons. First, it may provide a clue to the cognitive operations underlying estimates of uncertainty. Second, practical applications of decision aids are generally more concerned with predictions of future events than with assessing the accuracy of a person's general knowledge.

Two recent theoretical articles imply that studies of calibration are limited in their theoretical and practical usefulness. Kadane & Lichtenstein (1982) discuss the conditions under which, from a Bayesian point of view, one might expect a person to be calibrated. Their results imply that calibration depends more on the task—the events being predicted and relationships among them—than on characteristics of the probability assessor. Yates (1982) argues that other measures of performance in a probability assessment task are more appropriate for evaluating the performance of the assessor. It is likely, then, that calibration measures will be of limited value either for training users of decision aids or for understanding the cognitive mechanisms underlying uncertainty.

The coherence of probability assessments, i.e. the consistency of a set of judgments with the axioms of probability theory, is also a matter for concern when using decision aids. Here is an area in which training does seem to be effective. Wallsten et al (1983) demonstrated that consistency could be improved with practice. As noted earlier, Lopes (1982a) has shown that judgments can be made more consistent with prescriptive principles if one can identify the process by which the judgments are produced. Although not directly concerned with probability judgments, studies by Gaeth & Shanteau (1981, 1983) showing that expert judgments can be improved by training judges to ignore irrelevant information are potentially important for teaching people to use information more effectively.

A MAU model is usually employed to describe the decision maker's preferences. Preferences are assessed by means of single attribute utility functions, together with weights that determine the impact of each attribute on the aggregate utility. Some of the difficulties that arise in assessing utility functions have been discussed by Krzystofowicz & Duckstein (1980) and by Hershey et al (1982). Considerable attention has been paid to the problem of eliciting weights for MAU models. When using MAU theory for decision aiding purposes, the attribute weights should accurately describe the decision maker's preference structure. While it is not easy to evaluate assessment procedures on this basis, they can be compared in terms such as the reliability and consistency of the results, the acceptability of the procedure, and the results to the decision maker (see Shapira 1981, Stillwell et al 1981, Schoemaker & Waid 1982).

We noted earlier that multiattribute formulations of decision problems tend to blur the distinction between descriptive and prescriptive theory. The use of MAU theory for decision analysis leads to an emphasis on problem description rather than prescriptions for action. An important example can be found in the analysis of situations involving risk in societal or personal decision making. Risk has traditionally been defined in rather narrow terms. It is apparent that most definitions do not capture the significant features of, say, the problems of disposing of nuclear wastes or the use of novel surgical procedures. A multiattribute description of risk is more effective. Hohenemser et al (1983) addressed the problem by defining the term "hazard," a multiattribute description of threats to people and to what they value. They show that the description accounts well for people's judgments of risk. Slovic et al (1983), in their criticism of analyses of accidents that are based only on the number of fatalities, argue it is the perceived implications of accidents to which people respond; to understand their reactions demands an analysis of mental models that might be used as framework for understanding an accident.

Evaluation and Implementation of Decision Aids

Systematic research to evaluate decision aids is rare, in spite of the excellent review by Fischhoff (1980) of the need for such research. Fischhoff's parallel between decision aids and psychotherapy makes clear the difficulties of conducting an evaluation. There have been a few studies showing that decision analysis (like psychotherapy) can have a positive impact on the decision maker (Nezu & D'Zurilla 1981, Kanfer & Busemeyer 1982). Part of the problem in evaluating aids, however, is finding a suitable criterion for the evaluation. Rather than setting a single criterion, one might examine several benefits provided by a decision aid, including increased understanding of the complexities of the problem (Humphreys & McFadden 1980), as well as greater reliability and the absence of systematic error (Cornelius & Lyness 1980, Lyness & Cornelius 1982, Pitz 1980, Pitz et al 1980a). The designer and evaluator of decision aids might set limited but measurable goals for the aid and evaluate progress toward those goals. Following Fischhoff's analogy between decision analysis and psychotherapy further, one might note Winnicott's (1965) definition of the "good enough therapist"—one who is adequate for the purpose of helping a person work through conflicts. Rather than trying to define the "better decision," one might look for the "good-enough decision aid" that helps the decision maker achieve clarification of the problem.

If the emphasis for evaluative purposes is placed on clarification of the problem rather than on prescriptions for action, a critical concern is ensuring that an aid is used by those for whom it is designed. The problem of utilization has been raised by Wright & Ng (1981) and by McArthur (1980). Failure to use a decision aid can occur because the decision maker was not involved in its design (Adelman 1982) or because of a failure by the decision maker to accept assistance (Dickson 1981). Designing successful decision aids, therefore, requires the investigator to consider more than the cognitive mechanisms involved in the decision task; cognitive and affective variables related to the acceptability of the aid may be just as important.

In an important article, Tornatzky et al (1982) discuss the general problem of utilizing social science technology. Their comments are relevant in the present context. Among the causes of underutilization they list the nonproprietary nature of social science research, the disaggregation of support for the social sciences, and the isolation of the social sciences from political decision making. These are not concerns that can be addressed readily by an individual investigator, but they are issues that may increase in importance as the development of decision aids becomes more advanced.

CONCLUSION

We began by defining research in judgment or decision making as a part of cognitive psychology. We ended by pointing briefly to its role in the larger context of social science research, both theoretical and applied. As soon as one tries to use theoretical insights to solve significant social problems, the impossibility of disciplinary compartmentalization becomes apparent. Fortunately, narrowness of focus is not likely to limit further development; there are many theoretical and methodological tools available to an investigator in this area, and no shortage of critical discussions of these tools. There now exists the foundation of a technology for explicating both the processes involved in making important decisions and the preference structure that should guide those decisions. It may not be possible to define prescriptive rules for these preferences and the decisions; it is possible, however, to help the decision maker explore the implications of a set of judgments and recognize their relationship to more general cognitive and affective structures.

ACKNOWLEDGMENTS

We are grateful to the Center for Research on Judgment and Policy, University of Colorado, for the use of their library and their help in making material available. We would also like to thank the following people for their helpful comments and suggestions: Roger Garberg, Victoria Molfese, Robert Radtke, Sharon Riedel, and Ron Schmeck. We are especially grateful to Dan Lockhart for his help in reviewing and evaluating the literature.

Literature Cited

Abelson, R. P. 1981. Psychological status of the script concept. *Am. Psychol.* 36:715–29

Adelbratt, T., Montgomery, H. 1980. Attractiveness of decision rules. *Acta Psychol.* 45:177–85

Adelman, L. 1981. The influence of formal, substantive, and contextual task properties on the relative effectiveness of feedback in multiple-cue probability tasks. *Organ. Behav. Hum. Perform.* 27:423–42

Adelman, L. 1982. Involving users in the development of decision-analytic aids: The principal factor in successful implementation. *J. Oper. Res.* 33:333–42

Anderson, J. R. 1982. Acquisition of cognitive skill. *Psychol. Rev.* 89:369–406

Anderson, N. H. 1970. Functional measurement and psychophysical judgment. *Psychol. Rev.* 77:153–70

Anderson, N. H. 1981. *Foundations of Information Integration Theory.* New York: Academic

Arnold, H. J., Feldman, D. C. 1981. Social desirability response bias in self-report choice situations. *Acad. Manage. J.* 24:377–85

Atkinson, R. C., Juola, J. F. 1973. Factors influencing speed and accuracy of word recognition. In *Attention and Performance*, ed. S. Kornblum, Vol. 4. New York: Academic

Ballou, D. P., Mohan, L. 1981. A decision

model for evaluating transit pricing policies. *Transp. Res. Part A: General* 15:125–38

Bar-Hillel, M. 1980. What features make samples seem representative? *J. Exp. Psychol: Hum. Percept. Perform.* 6:578–89

Bar-Hillel, M., Fischhoff, B. 1981. When do base rates affect predictions? *J. Pers. Soc. Psychol.* 41:671–80

Barron, F. H. 1981. *Validation and error in multiplicative utility functions.* Sch. Bus., Univ. Kansas

Beach, L. R., Mitchell, T. R. 1978. A contingency model for the selection of decision strategies. *Acad. Manage. Rev.* 3:439–49

Bell, D. E. 1982. Regret in decision making under uncertainty. *Oper. Res.* 30:961–81

Berkeley, D., Humphreys, P. 1982. Structuring decision problems and the bias heuristic. *Acta Psychol.* 50:201–52

Birnbaum, M. H. 1982. Controversies in psychological measurement. In *Social Attitudes and Psychological Measurement*, pp. 401–85. Hillsdale, NJ: Erlbaum

Birnbaum, M. H., Mellers, B. A. 1983. Bayesian inference: Combining base rates with opinions of sources who vary in credibility. *Am. J. Psychol.* In press

Birnbaum, M. H., Stegner, S. E. 1981. Measuring the importance of cues in judgment for individuals: Subjective theories of IQ as a function of heredity and environment. *J. Exp. Soc. Psychol.* 17:159–82

Brainerd, C. J. 1981. Working memory and the developmental analysis of probability judgment. *Psychol. Rev.* 88:463–502

Brunswik, E. 1952. The conceptual framework of psychology. In *International Encyclopedia of Unified Science*. Chicago: Univ. Chicago Press

Cantor, N., Mischel, W., Schwartz, J. C. 1982. A prototype analysis of psychological situations. *Cogn. Psychol.* 14:45–77

Cohen, M. S., Brown, R. V. 1980. Decision support for attack submarine commanders. *Tech. Rep. 80–11,* Decis. Sci. Consortium

Cornelius, E. T. III, Lyness, K. S. 1980. A comparison of holistic and decomposed judgment strategies in job analyses by job incumbents. *J. Appl. Psychol.* 65:155–63

Cox, J. R., Griggs, R. A. 1982. The effects of experience on performance in Wason's selection task. *Mem. Cognit.* 10:496–502

Crow, L. E., Olshavsky, R. W., Summers, J. O. 1980. Industrial buyers' choice strategies: A protocol analysis. *J. Mark. Res.* 17:34–44

Dawes, R. M. 1979. The robust beauty of improper linear models in decision making. *Am. Psychol.* 34:571–82

Dickson, G. C. A. 1981. An empirical examination of the willingness of managers to use utility theory. *J. Manage. Stud.* 18:423–34

Edwards, W., Newman, J. R. 1982. *Multiattribute Evaluation.* Beverly Hills: Sage

Einhorn, H. J., Hogarth, R. M. 1981. Behavioral decision theory: Processes of judgment and choice. *Ann. Rev. Psychol.* 32:53–88

Einhorn, H. J., Hogarth, R. M. 1982a. *A theory of diagnostic inference: I. Imagination and the psychophysics of evidence.* Cent. Decis. Res., Grad. Sch. Bus., Univ. Chicago

Einhorn, H. J., Hogarth, R. M. 1982b. *A theory of diagnostic inference: II. Judging causality.* Cent. Decis. Res., Grad. Sch. Bus., Univ. Chicago

Einhorn, H. J., Kleinmuntz, D. N., Kleinmuntz, B. 1979. Linear regression and process-tracing models of judgment. *Psychol. Rev.* 86:465–85

Ericsson, K. A., Simon, H. A. 1980. Verbal reports as data. *Psychol. Rev.* 87:215–52

Fischhoff, B. 1980. Clinical decision analysis. *Oper. Res.* 28:28–43

Fischhoff, B. 1983. Predicting frames. *J. Exp. Psychol: Learn. Mem. Cognit.* 9:103–16

Fischhoff, B., Bar-Hillel, M. 1982. Focusing techniques as aids to probabilistic judgment. See Kahneman et al 1982.

Fischhoff, B., MacGregor, D. 1982. Subjective confidence in forecasts. *J. Forecasting* 1:155–72

Fishburn, P. C. 1980. A simple model for the utility of gambling. *Psychometrika* 45:435–48

Gaeth, G. J., Shanteau, J. 1981. Training expert decision makers to ignore irrelevant information: A comparison of lecture and interactive training procedures. *Tech. Rep. 81–1,* Appl. Psychol. Ser., Kansas State Univ., Manhattan

Gaeth, G. J., Shanteau, J. 1983. Training to reduce the use of irrelevant information in personnel selection. *Organ. Behav. Hum. Perform.* In press

Gati, I., Tversky, A. 1982. Representations of qualitative and quantitative dimensions. *J. Exp. Psychol: Hum. Percept. Perform.* 8:325–40

Gilovich, T. 1981. Seeing the past in the present: The effect of associations to familiar events on judgments and decisions. *J. Pers. Soc. Psychol.* 40:797–808

Green, D. M., Swets, J. A. 1966. *Signal Detection Theory and Psychophysics.* New York: Wiley

Griggs, R. A., Newstead, S. E. 1982. The role of problem structure in a deductive reasoning task. *J. Exp. Psychol: Learn. Mem. Cognit.* 8:297–307

Hammond, K. R. 1966. *The Psychology of Egon Brunswik.* New York: Holt, Rinehart & Winston

Hammond, K. R. 1980. *The integration of re-*

search in judgment and decision theory. Cent. Res. Judgment Policy, Univ. Colorado

Hammond, K. R., McClelland, G. H., Mumpower, J. 1980. Human Judgment and Decision Making: Theories, Methods, and Procedures. New York: Praeger

Hammond, K. R., Stewart, T. R., Brehmer, B., Steinman, D. 1975. Social judgment theory. In Human Judgment and Decision Processes, ed. M. Kaplan, S. Schwartz, pp. 271–312. New York: Academic

Hayes-Roth, B., Hayes-Roth, F. 1977. Concept learning and the recognition and classification of exemplars. J. Verb. Learn. Verb. Behav. 16:321–38

Hershey, J. C., Kunreuther, H. C., Schoemaker, P. J. H. 1982. Sources of bias in assessment procedures for utility functions. Manage. Sci. 28:936–54

Hershey, J. C., Schoemaker, P. J. H. 1983. Equivalence judgments that are not equivalent: Probability vs. certainty equivalence methods in utility measurement. Cent. Decis. Res., Grad. Sch. Bus., Univ. Chicago

Herstein, J. A. 1981. Keeping the voter's limits in mind: A cognitive process analysis of decision making in voting. J. Pers. Soc. Psychol. 40:843–61

Hogarth, R. M. 1981. Beyond discrete biases: Functional and dysfunctional aspects of judgmental heuristics. Psychol. Bull. 90:197–217

Hogarth, R. M. 1982. On the surprise and delight of inconsistent responses. In New Directions for Methodology of Social and Behavioral Science: The Framing of Questions and the Consistency of Response, ed. R. M. Hogarth, pp. 3–20. San Francisco: Jossey-Bass

Hohenemser, C., Kates, R. W., Slovic, P. 1983. The nature of technological hazard. Science 220:378–84

Howell, W. C., Kerkar, S. P. 1982. A test of task influences in uncertainty measurement. Organ. Behav. Hum. Perform. 30:365–90

Humphreys, P. C., McFadden, W. 1980. Experiences with MAUD: Aiding decision structuring through reordering versus automating the composition rule. Acta Psychol. 45:51–69

Humphreys, P. C., Svenson, O., Vari, A. 1983. Analysing and Aiding Decision Processes. Amsterdam: North Holland. In press

Humphreys, P. C., Wooler, S., Phillips, L. D. 1980. Structuring decisions: The role of structuring heuristics. Tech. Rep. 80–1, Decis. Anal. Unit, Brunel Univ., Uxbridge, England

Jennings, D. L., Amabile, M., Ross, L. 1982. Informal covariation assessment: Data-based versus theory-based judgments. See Kahneman et al 1982, pp. 211–30

Johnson-Laird, P. N. 1981. Mental models in cognitive science. In Perspectives on Cognitive Science, ed. D. A. Norman, pp. 147–91. Hillsdale NJ: Erlbaum

Johnson-Laird, P. N., Wason, P. C., eds. 1977. Thinking. Cambridge: Cambridge Univ. Press

Kadane, J. B., Lichtenstein, S. 1982. A subjectivist view of calibration. Tech. Rep. 82–6, Decis. Res., Eugene, Ore.

Kahneman, D., Slovic, P., Tversky, A. 1982. Judgment Under Uncertainty: Heuristics and Biases. Cambridge: Cambridge Univ. Press

Kahneman, D., Tversky, A. 1982a. On the study of statistical intuitions. See Kahneman et al 1982, pp. 493–508

Kahneman, D., Tversky, A 1982b. Variants of uncertainty. See Kahneman et al 1982, pp. 509–20

Kanfer, F. H., Busemeyer, J. R. 1982. The use of problem solving and decision making in behavior theory. Clin. Psychol. 2:239–66

Keeney, R. L. 1982. Decision analysis: State of the field. Oper. Res. 30:803–38

Keeney, R. L., Winkler, R. L. 1982. Von Neumann-Morgenstern utility and equity of public risks. Tech. Rep. 82–3, Woodward-Clyde Consultants, San Francisco

Kellogg, R. T. 1982. When can we introspect accurately about mental processes? Mem. Cognit. 10:141–44

Klayman, J. 1982. Decision making in children: An analysis of decision strategies and their adaptation to task characteristics. Cent. Decis. Res., Grad. Sch. Bus., Univ. Chicago

Klein, N. M. 1983. Utility and decision strategies: A second look at the rational decision maker. Organ. Behav. Hum. Perform. 31:1–25

Kleinmuntz, D. N., Kleinmuntz, B. 1981. Decision strategies in simulated environments. Behav. Sci. 26:294–305

Kohlberg, L. 1979. The Meaning and Measurement of Moral Development. Clark Lectures, Clark Univ.

Koriat, A., Lichtenstein, S., Fischhoff, B. 1980. Reasons for confidence. J. Exp. Psychol: Hum. Learn. Mem. 6:107–18

Krzysztofowicz, R., Duckstein, L. 1980. Assessment errors in multiattribute utility functions. Organ. Behav. Hum. Perform. 26:326–48

Kunreuther, H. C., Schoemaker, P. J. H. 1981. Decision analysis for complex systems. Knowledge: Creation, Diffusion, Utilization 2:389–412

Lakoff, G. 1982. Categories and cognitive models. Rep. No. 2, Cognit. Sci. Program, Univ. Calif., Berkeley

Lichtenstein, S., Fischhoff, B., Phillips, L. D. 1982. Calibration of probabilities: The state of the art to 1980. See Kahneman et al 1982, pp. 306–34

Lopes, L. L. 1981. Decision making in the short run. *J. Exp. Psychol: Hum. Learn. Mem.* 7:377–85

Lopes, L. L. 1982a. Procedural debiasing. *Tech. Rep. No. 15,* Wis. Hum. Inf. Process. Program, Madison

Lopes, L. L. 1982b. Toward a procedural theory of judgment. *Tech. Rep. No. 17,.* Wis. Hum. Inf. Process. Program, Madison

Lopes, L. L., Ekberg, P. H. S. 1980. Test of an ordering hypothesis in risky decision making. *Acta Psychol.* 45:161–67

Lyness, K. S., Cornelius, E. T. III. 1982. A comparison of holistic and decomposed judgment strategies in a performance rating simulation. *Organ. Behav. Hum. Perform.* 29:21–38

Manis, M., Avis, N. E., Cardoze, S. 1981. Reply to Bar-Hillel and Fischhoff. *J. Pers. Soc. Psychol.* 41:681–83

McArthur, D. S. 1980. Decision scientists, decision makers, and the gap. *Interfaces* 10:110–13

Mehle, T. 1982. Hypothesis generation in an automobile malfunction inference task. *Acta Psychol.* 52:87–106

Mehle, T., Gettys, C. F., Manning, C., Baca, S., Fisher, S., 1981. The availability explanation of excessive plausibility assessments. *Acta Psychol.* 49:127–40

Montgomery, H., Adelbratt, T. 1982. Gambling decisions and information about expected value. *Organ. Behav. Hum. Perform.* 29:39–57

Murphy, K. R. 1982. Assessing the discriminant validity of regression models and subjectively weighted models of judgments. *Multivar. Behav. Res.* 17:359–70

Nezu, A., D'Zurilla, T. J. 1981. Effects of problem definition and formulation on decision making in the social problem-solving process. *Behav. Ther.* 12:100–6

Payne, J. W. 1980. Information processing theory: Some concepts applied to decision research. In *Cognitive Processes in Choice and Decision Behavior,* ed. T. S. Wallsten, pp. 95–115. Hillsdale, NJ: Erlbaum

Payne, J. W. 1982. Contingent decision behavior. *Psychol. Bull.* 92:382–402

Pearl, J., Kim, J., Fiske, R. 1981. Goal-directed decision structuring systems. *Tech. Rep. CLA-ENG-81-21,* Cogn. Syst. Lab., Univ. Calif., Los Angeles

Pitz, G. F. 1977. Decision making and cognition. In *Decision Making and Change in Human Affairs,* ed. H. Jungermann, G. de Zeeuw. Dordrecht, Holland: Reidel

Pitz, G. F. 1980. Sensitivity of direct and derived judgments to probabilistic information. *J. Appl. Psychol.* 65:164–71

Pitz, G. F. 1983. Human engineering of decision aids. See Humphreys et al 1983

Pitz, G. F., Englert, J. A., Haxby, K., Leung, L. S. 1981. Learning conditional frequencies in a probability learning task. *Acta Psychol.* 47:229–43

Pitz, G. F., Heerboth, J., Sachs, N. J. 1980a. Assessing the utility of multiattribute utility assessments. *Organ. Behav. Hum. Perform.* 26:65–80

Pitz, G. F., Sachs, N. J., Heerboth, J. 1980b. Procedures for eliciting choices in the analysis of individual decisions. *Organ. Behav. Hum. Perform.* 26:396–408

Posner, M. I., McLeod, P. 1982. Information processing models—in search of elementary operations. *Ann. Rev. Psychol.* 33:477–514

Raiffa, H., Schlaifer, R. 1961. *Applied Statistical Decision Theory.* Div. Res., Harvard Bus. Sch., Boston, Mass.

Rest, J. R. 1979. *Development in Judging Moral Issues.* Minneapolis: Univ. Minn. Press

Rohrbaugh, J., McClelland, G., Quinn, R. 1980. Measuring the relative importance of utilitarian and egalitarian values: A study of individual differences about fair distribution. *J. Appl. Psychol.* 65:34–49

Rosch, E. 1978. Principles of categorization. In *Cognition and Categorization,* ed. E. Rosch, B. B. Lloyd, pp. 169–215. Hillsdale, NJ: Erlbaum

Russo, J. E., Dosher, B. A. 1983. Strategies for multiattribute binary choice. *J. Exp. Psychol: Learn. Mem. Cognit.* In press

Sachs, N. J., Pitz, G. F. 1981. Choosing the best method of contraception: Application of decision analysis to contraceptive counseling and selection. South. Ill. Univ., Carbondale

Schoemaker, P. J. H. 1982. The expected utility model: Its variants, purposes, evidence and limitations. *J. Econ. Lit.* 20:529–63

Schoemaker, P. J. H., Waid, C. C. 1982. An experimental comparison of different approaches to determining weights in additive utility models. *Manage. Sci.* 28:101–20

Schustack, M. W., Sternberg, R. J. 1981. Evaluation of evidence in causal inference. *J. Exp. Psychol: Gen.* 10:101–20

Shaklee, H., Fischhoff, B. 1982. Strategies of information search in causal analysis. *Mem. Cognit.* 10:520–30

Shanteau, J., Nagy, G. F. 1982. Information integration in person perception: Theory and application. In *Progress in Person Perception,* ed. M. Cook. London: Metheun

Shanteau, J. C., Ptacek, C. H. 1983. Role and implications of averaging processes in advertising. In *Advertising and Consumer Psychology,* ed. L. Percy, A. Woodside. New York: Lexington. In press

Shapira, Z. 1981. Making trade-offs between job attributes. *Organ. Behav. Hum. Perform.* 28:331–55

Simon, H. A. 1979. Information processing models of cognition. *Ann. Rev. Psychol.* 30:363–96

Slovic, P., Fischhoff, B., Lichtenstein, S. 1977. Behavioral decision theory. *Ann. Rev. Psychol.* 28:1–39

Slovic, P., Fischhoff, B., Lichtenstein, S. 1982. Response mode, framing, and information-processing effects in risk assessment. In *New Directions for Methodology of Social and Behavioral Science: Question Framing and Response Consistency,* ed. R. Hogarth, pp. 21–36. San Francisco: Jossey-Bass

Slovic, P., Lichtenstein, S., Fischhoff, B. 1983. Modeling the societal impact of multiple-fatality accidents. *Manage. Sci.* In press

Smith, J. F., Mitchell, T. R., Beach, L. R. 1982. A cost-benefit mechanism for selecting problem-solving strategies: Some extensions and empirical tests. *Organ. Behav. Hum. Perform.* 29:370–96

Stillwell, W. G., Seaver, D. A., Edwards, W. 1981. A comparison of weight approximation techniques in multiattribute utility decision making. *Organ. Behav. Hum. Perform.* 28:62–77

Svenson, O. 1979. Process descriptions of decision making. *Organ. Behav. Hum. Perform.* 23:86–112

Tomassini, L. A., Solomon, I., Romney, M. B., Krogstad, J. L. 1982. Calibration of auditors' probabilistic judgments: Some empirical evidence. *Organ. Behav. Hum. Perform.* 30:391–406

Tornatzky, L. G., Solomon, T., et al. 1982. Contributions of social science to innovation and productivity. *Am. Psychol.* 37:737–46

Tversky, A., Gati, I. 1982. Similarity, separability, and the triangle inequality. *Psychol. Rev.* 89:123–54

Tversky, A., Kahneman, D. 1981. The framing of decisions and the psychology of choice. *Science* 211:453–58

Tversky, A., Kahneman, D. 1982. Judgments of and by representativeness. See Kahneman et al 1982, pp. 84–98

von Neumann, J., Morgenstern, O. 1947. *Theory of Games and Economic Behavior.* Princeton, NJ: Princeton Univ. 2nd ed.

von Winterfeldt, D., Edwards, W. 1982. Costs and payoffs in perceptual research. *Psychol. Bull.* 91:609–22

Wallsten, T. S. 1983. The theoretical status of judgmental heuristics. In *Decision Making Under Uncertainty,* ed. R. W. Scholz, Amsterdam: North Holland. In press

Wallsten, T. S., Barton, C. 1982. Processing probabilistic multidimensional information for decisions. *J. Exp. Psychol: Learn. Mem. Cognit.* 8:361–84

Wallsten, T. S., Budescu, D. V. 1981. Additivity and nonadditivity in judging MMPI profiles. *J. Exp. Psychol: Hum. Percept. Perform.* 7:1096–1109

Wallsten, T. S., Forsyth, B. H., Budescu, D. V. 1983. Stability and coherence of health experts' upper and lower subjective probabilities about dose-response functions. *Organ. Hum. Perform.* 31:277–302

Whaley, C. P. 1981. Computer-augmented decision making. *Behav. Res. Methods Instrum.* 13:294–97

Wilkening, F., Anderson, N. H. 1982. Comparison of two rule-assessment methodologies for studying cognitive development and knowledge structure. *Psychol. Bull.* 92:215–37

Winnicott, D. W. 1965. *The Maturational Processes and the Facilitating Environment.* New York: Int. Univ.

Wooler, S. 1982. A decision aid for structuring and evaluating career options. *J. Oper. Res.* 33:343–51

Wright, G. 1982. Changes in the realism and distribution of probability assessments as a function of question type. *Acta Psychol.* 52:165–74

Wright, G., Ng, K. 1981. Three methods for aiding decision making. In *Clinical Psychology and Medicine: A Behavioral Perspective.* New York: Plenum

Wright, G., Wishuda, A. 1982. Distribution of probability assessments for almanac and future event questions. *Scand. J. Psychol.* 23:219–24

Yates, J. F. 1982. External correspondence: Decompositions of the mean probability score. *Organ. Behav. Hum. Perform.* 30:132–56

Ann. Rev. Psychol. 1984. 35:165–200
Copyright © 1984 by Annual Reviews Inc. All rights reserved

HORMONES AND SEXUAL BEHAVIOR

H. H. Feder

Institute of Animal Behavior, Rutgers University, Newark, New Jersey 07102

CONTENTS

INTRODUCTION

Hormones produced by the gonads influence a variety of behaviors in vertebrates. In this review, I focus attention on the relationships between gonadal
hormones and the expression of copulatory and precopulatory behaviors in
some commonly studied mammals maintained under laboratory conditions.
The review cannot be comprehensive even in this narrow context, and I have
further limited the scope of material to be covered by emphasizing biochemical
mechanisms that may be involved in hormonal influences on behavior. Gonadal hormones act on prenatal brain tissues destined to mediate sexual behaviors
(organizational action) and on adult brain tissues that mediate sexual behaviors
(activational action): the review is accordingly divided into two main sections.

165

Each section begins with a consideration of data obtained from laboratory studies with animals. In each section, this is followed by an examination of some implications of the research on animals for the study of hormone-behavior interactions in humans. An overview completes discussion of each section.

The first book to explore hormone-sexual behavior relationships systematically was by Beach (1948). Subsequently, several books have been devoted to this topic. Recent examples are those written or edited by Bermant & Davidson (1974), Montagna & Sadler (1974), Musaph & Money (1977), McGill et al (1978), Hutchison (1978), Leshner (1978), Beyer (1979), Adler (1981). A valuable survey of the historical origins of research on hormones and behavior was recently prepared by Beach (1981).

GONADAL STEROIDS OF THE FETAL AND NEONATAL PERIOD ORGANIZE CNS TISSUES DESTINED TO MEDIATE ADULT SEXUALLY DIMORPHIC BEHAVIORS

Studies with Animals

The concept that steroid hormones of gonadal origin act on fetal central nervous system (CNS) tissues to permanently alter the function of these tissues and the behaviors they will mediate can be traced back about 50 years. Dantchakoff (1938a,b) made the statistically unverified observation that female offspring born to guinea pigs treated with androgen preparations during pregnancy show elevated levels of masculine sexual behavioral responses in adulthood. For a variety of reasons discussed elsewhere (Feder 1981a), this important observation was not pursued further until a now classic paper by Phoenix et al (1959) appeared. These authors showed that treatment of pregnant guinea pigs with the androgen preparation testosterone propionate (TP) was associated with an increased frequency of display of male-like mounting behavior (in comparison with controls whose mothers were not given TP during gestation) in adulthood when the offspring were ovariectomized (ovx) and then given TP treatment. Thus, prenatal exposure to high levels of exogenous androgen permanently masculinized peripheral and/or CNS tissues involved in male-like mounting behavior. Furthermore, unlike control animals, prenatally androgenized female guinea pigs failed to show female sexual behaviors such as lordosis (a concave arching of the back that facilitates intromission) in response to treatment with the estrogen estradiol benzoate (EB) and progesterone (P) when the steroids were given in adulthood after ovx. Thus, in addition to masculinization, prenatal exposure to exogenous androgen apparently resulted in defeminization of peripheral and/or CNS tissues mediating reproductive behaviors in genotypic female rodents.

The next obvious question was whether removal of the testes (presumably a source of endogenous androgen) of developing animals would have converse permanent effects in genotypic males. That is, would castration of developing males demasculinize and feminize the substrates of copulatory behavior? This experiment was not technically feasible in guinea pigs because they have a long (68-day) gestation period and are fully sexually differentiated at birth, but it could be carried out in rats because they have a very short (22-day) gestation period and are not fully sexually differentiated at birth. Neonatal male rats (1–5 days old) were castrated; in adulthood they failed to display complete patterns of male sexual behavior after TP treatment and exhibited lordosis and other female sexual behaviors after EB+P treatment (Grady et al 1965). Controls castrated at 20 days of age or later showed normal male behavior after TP treatment and little or no female behavior after EB+P treatment in adulthood. These two publications from W. C. Young's research group (Phoenix et al 1959, Grady et al 1965) opened a new area of psychobiological investigation. Thousands of papers (e.g. see references in the book by Goy & McEwen 1980) were published on the topic of perinatal hormone manipulations and their effects on a variety of sexually dimorphic behaviors in adults of several species. (The term perinatal will be used here to denote prenatal and/or neonatal periods.) Young and co-workers termed the masculinizing and defeminizing effects of gonadal steroids on perinatal animals *organizational* effects (Young et al 1964). Subsequently it was shown that masculinization and defeminization are independent organizational processes (Goldfoot et al 1969). Although the term organizational is in some respects vague and ambiguous (Beach 1971), it appears to be the most useful term available for the set of concepts it attempts to embrace (Feder 1981a).

Work carried out since the 1960s has focused on five major questions about organizational actions of gonadal steroids: 1. At precisely which periods in their development are animals susceptible to organizational actions of steroids? 2. Which steroid hormones act to organize the substrates of sexually dimorphic behaviors? 3. Are CNS tissues "organized" by steroids? 4. What are the cellular mechanisms through which organizational effects of steroids on CNS exerted? 5. Are behaviors other than copulatory behaviors affected by steroid action during prenatal or early postnatal life? A summary of the results in each of these areas follows.

For rats, exogenous androgen defeminizes (decreased lordosis behavior in adulthood is usually used as an index of defeminization in rats) and masculinizes (increased intromission and ejaculatory motor patterns in adulthood are often used as indices of masculinization in rats) genotypic females particularly effectively in the first 1–3 days of postnatal life (Barraclough & Gorski 1962, Harris 1964, Harris & Levine 1965, Gerall & Ward 1966). However, even in short gestation species such as the rat there is evidence for prenatal defeminizing and masculinizing effects of testicular secretions or exogenous androgens

(Ward & Weisz 1980, Thomas et al 1982). There is also some evidence that fetal testicular secretions may masculinize adjacent female fetuses *in utero* in both rat (Clemens et al 1978) and mouse (vom Saal & Bronson 1978), but this has been disputed (Slob & van der Schoot 1982). In rodents with longer gestation periods, the defeminizing and masculinizing actions of steroids normally occur exclusively prenatally. For example, in guinea pigs, strong organizational actions of androgen occur at midgestation (Goy et al 1964) and are not evident after birth (Phoenix et al 1959). Clemens (1973) made the point that discrepancies in timing of organizational effects of steroids on CNS among rodent species shrink considerably if one uses the number of days since species-typical testicular differentiation rather than postcoital age as the index of developmental stage. With this measure, for example, defeminization by gonadal steroids begins at 4.5–5.0 days in rats, hamsters, and guinea pigs. Organizing actions of gonadal steroids have also been shown to occur prenatally in sheep (Short 1974) and rhesus macaques (Goy 1970, Goy & Resko 1972), and prenatally and postnatally in beagle dogs (Beach & Kuehn 1970).

It is important to note that the question of the period of sensitivity to organizing actions of gonadal steroids is complex. Although endogenous steroids may exert their actions at a rather circumscribed period of prenatal and/or postnatal development, large doses of exogenous steroids may exert masculinizing or defeminizing actions well after endogenously produced steroids would normally complete their organizational actions (Feder & Goy 1983). Furthermore, there is no single organizational process, but rather a multiplicity of processes related to neural activities whose later expression is influenced by steroids of the perinatal period. The substrates for various sexually dimorphic behavior patterns would be expected to develop at somewhat differing rates and to be maximally susceptible to steroid influences at various times during development. The notion of a single "critical period" for organizational effects of steroids on the CNS is therefore an oversimplification (Feder 1981a).

The question of which gonadal steroid acts as an "organizer" substance has received considerable attention. It is now clear that the prenatal testis secretes more androgen (particularly testosterone) than the prenatal ovary in a number of mammalian species studied (Erskine & Baum 1982). At first glance, this, along with the finding that exogenous TP masculinizes and defeminizes females of several species, suggested that testosterone is the factor responsible for masculinization and defeminization. This notion was soon challenged, because testosterone can be converted by aromatizing enzymes to estradiol, an estrogen. This aromatization process occurs in hypothalamic and limbic tissues of perinatal rats (Weisz & Gibbs 1974, Lieberburg & McEwen 1975). Furthermore, perinatal injection of EB masculinizes, and synthetic antiestrogens and aromatase inhibitors attenuate, the organizing actions of exogenous androgens or testicular secretions in rats and hamsters (McEwen et al 1977, 1979b, Goy & McEwen 1980). Androgens that cannot be aromatized (e.g. 5 α-dihydrotestosterone, DHT) are generally ineffective in causing masculinization or defeminization in female rats and hamsters (Goy & McEwen 1980). Furthermore, in a mutant strain of rats (Tfm) with complete androgen insensitivity, testicular secretion during perinatal life causes subsequent defeminization, suggesting that CNS sensitivity to estrogen but not androgen is required for defeminization in rats (Olsen 1979, Shapiro et al 1980). These data provide overwhelming evidence that androgens produced by the perinatal testis reach critical CNS tissues and are there transformed to estrogens in species such as rats and hamsters. Estrogen, particularly estradiol, therefore seems to be a major factor in the normal organizational process in male rats and hamsters.

Enthusiasm over the "aromatization hypothesis" has at times been too ardent. There are now increasing indications that at least some aspects of the organizational process depend on androgen itself instead of, or in addition to, the aromatized products of androgen metabolism. Thus, DHT given prenatally masculinizes copulatory behavioral capacity in female guinea pigs, ferrets, and rhesus macaques (Goldfoot & van der Werff ten Bosch 1975, Goy 1978, Baum et al 1982), and combinations of estrogen and DHT more effectively masculinize some strains of rats than estrogen or DHT given separately to perinatal animals (Booth 1977, van der Schoot 1980). Therefore, while there is compelling evidence for a major role of aromatized steroids in the defeminization of lordosis behavior in some rodent species, androgens per se may have a role in masculinization of CNS tissues (Baum 1979, Sheridan 1981). The relative contributions of estrogen or androgen to organizational processes may differ according to species, according to strain, and according to which aspect of the organizational process is being considered.

A key concept that emerges from studies with perinatal mammals is that the presence of testicular steroid secretion favors masculinization and defeminization of CNS tissues mediating reproduction, while the absence of testicular secretions favors demasculinization and feminization (Young et al 1964). The presence or absence of the ovary has, at most, only subtle effects on the organization process in mammals (Gerall et al 1973). Perinatal female mammals are protected against potential masculinizing and defeminizing effects of maternal steroids or their own ovarian steroids by a variety of mechanisms including α-fetoprotein that binds and inactivates estrogen in perinatal rats (Plapinger et al 1973), maternal progestins that act as antiestrogens (Dorfman 1967), and perhaps by rapid metabolism of estrogens (Freeman & Hobkirk 1976) and genetically determined refractoriness to organizing actions of estrogen in some species (R. W. Goy, personal communication).

A thorough discussion of the role of the testis and the ovary in the sexual differentiation of behavioral mechanisms in nonmammalian forms is provided by Adkins-Regan (1981). It is noteworthy that in nonmammalian vertebrates in which the female is heterogametic, such as birds, it is the presence or absence of the ovary rather than the testis that seems crucial in determining the direction of sexual differentiation of tissues mediating sexually dimorphic behavior.

Early experiments on the organizational effects of gonadal steroids strongly suggested, but did not directly demonstrate, that the CNS is a crucial site of action for the behavioral effects of perinatal hormones. It has since been shown that intracerebral implants of sex steroids exert organizational effects on reproductive behaviors (Christensen & Gorski 1978) even in the absence of apparent effects on peripheral structures. Additionally, perinatal treatments with nonaromatizable androgens cause masculinization of external genitalia unaccompanied by masculinization of behavioral capacity (Whalen & Luttge 1971), and perinatal treatments with estrogens fail to cause masculinization of the external genitalia yet result in masculinization and defeminization of behavioral capacity in rats and hamsters (Levine & Mullins 1964, Paup et al 1972). Thus, although hormones of the perinatal period act to cause sexual differentiation of the internal and external genitalia (Wilson et al 1981), hormonal effects on sexual differentiation (or organization) of CNS tissues are crucial for the behavioral consequences of perinatal hormone secretion or administration.

Direct evidence has accumulated to indicate that gonadal steroids present during perinatal life exert effects on the structure of specific, but widespread, areas of the CNS. For example, perinatal secretions of the rat testis influence cell nuclear volume in preoptic area (POA) and ventromedial nucleus (VMN) (Dörner & Staudt 1969) and also influence brain cell nuclear and nucleolar size in hypothalamus, hippocampus, neocortex, and reticular formation (Pfaff 1966). Perinatal gonadal steroids in rats also influence the ratio of synapses on dendritic shafts/spines in POA (Raisman & Field 1973), the ratio of axosomatic/axodendritic spine synapses in the arcuate nucleus (AN) (Matsumoto & Arai 1980), and the size of the sexually dimorphic nucleus of the POA (Jacobson & Gorski 1981). There is evidence from studies with adult spinal rats for a spinal cord site of action of perinatal gonadal steroids (Hart 1979), and a more recent study demonstrates the presence of a sexually dimorphic spinal nucleus that concentrates labeled androgens (Breedlove et al 1982). Studies with mammalian species other than rats are less numerous, but Greenough et al (1977) found sex differences in dorsomedial POA distribution of dendritic processes in hamsters, and Toran-Allerand (1980) found outgrowth of neuronal processes from POA and hypothalamic tissue from neonatal mice when these tissues were exposed to testosterone or estrogen in vitro. In *Macaca fascicularis,* Ayoub et al (1983) found that neurons of males had more dendritic bifurcations and a higher frequency of spines in the POA than prepubertal females. These data provide incontrovertible evidence that gonadal steroids exert permanent, widespread effects on the structure of the CNS, and that these changes occur in brain and spinal cord regions known to mediate expression of reproductive behaviors in adulthood (Bermant & Davidson 1974).

The mechanisms by which organizational actions of steroids are exerted on CNS tissues destined to regulate sexually dimorphic behaviors patterns are still unclear. In rats there is ample evidence that hypothalamic aromatase systems are present before birth (Reddy et al 1974) and enzyme activity involved in conversion of testosterone to DHT is evident by birth (Martini 1976). In rats and mice, intracellular receptors for androgen and estrogen are present before birth and increase toward the end of gestation and the early neonatal period (MacLusky et al 1979, Lieberburg et al 1980, Vito & Fox 1982). Estrogen receptors are occupied by estrogen in prenatal male rat brain (MacLusky et al 1979). These data suggest that steroids of the perinatal period effect their organizational actions by binding to cytoplasmic receptors, translocating these receptors to the nuclear compartment of particular CNS cells and then altering genomic expression of these cells by interacting with acceptor sites on chromatin and influencing protein synthesis (McEwen 1981, Pfaff & McEwen 1983). Alternative modes of CNS organizational activity by perinatal steroids have not been ruled out, but additional circumstantial evidence points to at least some role for receptor-mediated effects of perinatal steroids. Neonatal administration of TP to female rats is known to influence various aspects of nucleic acid metabolism and protein synthesis in brain (Gorski 1979). In some experiments, DNA synthesis inhibitors, RNA synthesis inhibitors, or protein synthesis inhibitors have been reported to attenuate the defeminizing effects of perinatal androgen administration, but these results are not always consistent or easily interpretable (Gorski 1979).

In recent review, McEwen (1982) speculates on several ways in which receptor-mediated effects of steroids could permanently influence neuronal growth and connectivity. One way perinatal steroids may act is by preventing nerve cell death in particular brain areas. This may account for the larger size of the sexually dimorphic nucleus of POA in male than in female rats (Jacobson & Gorski 1981). A potentially exciting approach to the problem of organizational actions of steroids on CNS anatomy and connectivity is suggested by the finding that POA fragments from perinatal male rats can be transplanted to perinatal females and the transplants can mediate changes in reproductive behavior in adulthood (Arendash & Gorski 1982).

In view of well-established, behaviorally relevant interactions between gonadal steroids and catecholamines (CA) in adults (Crowley & Zemlan 1981), another promising future area will undoubtedly involve exploration of whether perinatal steroids influence the development of adult patterns of CA transmission and whether CA transmission influences onset of steroid receptor synthesis in perinatal animals. It seems likely that organizational actions of steroids on the developing CNS are accompanied by, and functionally linked to, organizational actions of CA and other transmitter systems (Dörner 1980). This potentially rich area of research has obvious implications for the analysis of development of behaviors other than those strictly related to reproduction. The interesting observation has already been made that β-adrenergic transmission attenuates some physiological aspects of masculinization of the CNS, apparently by suppressing aromatization (Raum & Swerdloff 1981).

In addition to influencing organization of CNS tissues destined to mediate various aspects of adult copulatory behavior, gonadal secretions of the perinatal period influence neural substrates for several other sexually dimorphic behaviors. These include the precopulatory proceptive behaviors of female rats (hopping and darting, ear-quivering, and affiliative behavior) (Fadem & Barfield 1981), aggressive behavior in mice (Edwards 1969), territorial marking in gerbils (Turner 1975), and maternal behavior in rats (Ichikawa & Fujii 1982). Because these categories of behaviors are normally dependent for their expression in rodents on steroid hormones in adulthood, it has sometimes been implied that the sole mechanism involved in the organization process is permanent sensitization or desensitization of neural tissues to subsequent hormonal stimulation (Beach 1971). That this is not the case can be seen from the fact that several sexually dimorphic behavior patterns are influenced by perinatal gonadal hormones, but these behavior patterns do *not* normally require stimulation by hormones in prepubertal or adult life in order to be expressed. These patterns include social play in rhesus macaques and rats (Goy 1970, Meaney & Stewart 1981), micturition patterns in dogs (Martins & Valle 1948), and open-field and emergence behaviors in rats (Pfaff & Zigmond 1971). Thus, organization of CNS tissues by perinatal gonadal steroids has much more far-reaching consequences than alteration of sensitivity to steroids in adulthood. Recognition of this fact makes it easier to comprehend the widespread effects of perinatal steroids on CNS structure and function and draws us to the question of whether complex patterns of human behavior might be influenced by the presence or absence of fetal testicular secretions or by exogenous steroids administered during gestation.

Implications for Human Behavior

Studies of organizational effects of steroids in animals have focused almost exclusively on sexually dimorphic behavior patterns, particularly copulatory behavior in adulthood. It should be apparent that a particular motor pattern involved in copulation in one species may be highly (though rarely exclusively) sexually dimorphic while the same motor pattern may be less sexually dimorphic in another species. For example, male rats and Topeka guinea pigs rarely display lordosis in adulthood, but male hamsters (Beach 1971) and Strain 2 guinea pigs (Thornton et al 1982) may readily be induced to display this behavior. Furthermore, motor patterns used in copulation for some species are not the same as patterns used in other species. Thus, lordosis is a feminine copulatory behavior in rats, guinea pigs, and hamsters, but not rhesus macaques or humans. In fact, for humans there are no exclusively masculine or feminine motor patterns of copulation (Beach 1978). Therefore, no analysis of the sex differentiation of copulatory motor patterns by the agency of prenatal gonadal hormones is feasible. Some noncopulatory behaviors that are quantitatively sexually dimorphic in humans may be sensitive to organizing actions of prenatal gonadal steroids. Human females exposed to higher than normal levels of androgen during prenatal life (due to congenital adrenal hyperplasia or to administration of exogenous steroids with androgenic properties) have been reported to show increased energy expenditure in play, increased association with male playmates, identification as a "tomboy" by self and others, decreased role rehearsal for wife and mother roles, and increased participation in contact sports in childhood in comparison with females not exposed to high androgen levels during pregnancy (Ehrhardt & Meyer-Bahlburg 1981). These changes were not, however, considered as abnormal for females in this culture, and despite the apparent quantitative shift in a masculine direction, there is no evidence that these changes are attributable to organizational effects of gonadal steroids on human brain. Furthermore, Money & Mathews (1982) recently reported that 12/12 females exposed prenatally to androgenic progestins did not pursue sports as a major pastime when they reached adolescence or adulthood. Data on erotic experience were available for only 6 of these women. The youngest of them reported no erotic experience, and the remaining 5 reported exclusively heterosexual erotic experiences and imagery.

There is a disorder in genotypic males in which there is complete or partial insensitivity of tissues to androgens (testicular insensitivity or testicular feminization syndrome). In the complete form of the syndrome, the person is phenotypically female; childhood play behavior is also feminine in these individuals (Ehrhardt & Meyer-Bahlburg 1981). Clearly, one cannot definitively ascribe the feminine behavior displayed to lack of prenatal androgen stimulation, because these individuals are raised as females and have a female phenotype. Social and endocrine factors therefore cannot be disentangled in this syndrome. Studies of individuals exposed to synthetic progestins during gestation suggest that play behavior in males is not affected when reasonable control procedures are employed (Meyer-Bahlburg 1977), even though the progestins used might have been expected to exert antiandrogenic and/or antiestrogenic actions. Therefore, with the possible exception of certain transient, quantitative aspects of childhood play behavior, there is no evidence for an effect of prenatal steroids on human gender role. Even for these play behaviors of childhood there is no evidence that effects are attributable to sex-differentiating steroid actions on the brain.

It has been forcefully proposed that perinatal gonadal secretions influence human sexual orientation (Dörner 1980). The basis of this idea is said to rest on findings from laboratory experiments with rats. Dörner and co-workers found that male rats deprived of normal androgenization in the perinatal period showed an increased proportion of lordosis responses/mounting and ejaculatory responses compared to normally androgenized males when both groups were tested in adulthood. The conditions of testing in adulthood included administration of androgen to experimental subjects and simultaneous exposure of each subject to sexually active stimulus males and females. Conversely, neonatally androgenized females showed a decreased proportion of lordosis responses/mounting and ejaculatory responses when compared in adulthood to neonatally nonandrogenized females (Dörner 1980). These data suggested to Dörner that hypoandrogenization of perinatal males or hyperandrogenization of perinatal females results in a predominantly heterotypical pattern of copulatory behavior which he then proceeded to term "homosexual" behavior. Even if one were to take these poorly designed and loosely interpreted animal experiments at face value, the term "homosexuality" which Dörner uses for his rats has no obvious relation to what the term "homosexuality" denotes in humans. Yet Dörner equates the two terms and seems prepared to offer endocrine preventives for homosexuality in humans on the basis of this equation (Dörner 1980). This line of reasoning seems patently unjustified. As Beach (1978) points out, the word "homosexual" has been used in animal research in two different circumstances: (a) as a description of individuals that exhibit coital responses typical of their genetic sex, but do so in response to a like-sexed partner; (b) as a description of animals that exhibit coital patterns typical of the opposite sex. Dörner's description falls primarily in the second category, and flatly ignores the Kinsey et al (1948) stricture that this category cannot appropriately be compared with human homosexuality. In human heterosexual interactions males may play female roles and females play male roles. This is more properly termed "inversion" and inversion is not equivalent to human homosexuality. Dörner now uses the term "inversion" in his recent (1980) review, but he does not distinguish it from "homosexuality." If sexual orientation comprises erotic attraction, sexual fantasies, and sexual experiences with the same or opposite sex individual, it is obvious that no "animal model" of homosexuality has been generated by rat studies although such a "model" is claimed to exist by Dörner (1980).

What, in fact, is the direct evidence for an effect of prenatal gonadal steroids on the organization of human sexual orientation? In human females exposed to hyperandrogenization (due to congenital adrenal hyperplasia), no homosexuality was evident in women treated with adrenal corticoids from birth (Ehrhardt & Meyer-Bahlburg 1981). In 23 women from the USA treated with corticoids beginning in adulthood, none was exclusively or predominantly homosexual,

10 had bisexual fantasies, and 4 had bisexual experiences (Ehrhardt et al 1968). Of 18 USSR women similarly treated, none had any homosexual interest (Lev-Ran 1974). These data do not permit the conclusion that hyperandrogenization in human females during prenatal life inevitably leads to homosexuality. Data on prenatal hypoandrogenization of genotypic human males similarly run counter to the idea of a deterministic role for perinatal gonadal steroids in human sexual orientation. Perinatally hypoandrogenized genotypic males raised as males have a heterosexual orientation (Ehrhardt & Meyer-Bahlburg 1981). Genotypically male humans with androgen insensitivity syndrome who are raised as females are oriented to males as sexual partners, and some authors have pointed to this as evidence that prenatal hypoandrogenization results in homosexuality (Dörner 1980). A much more reasonable conclusion is that the sex of rearing has a more powerful role than sex genotype in guiding human sexual orientation.

There is some evidence from work with rats that prenatal stress causes decreased perinatal androgen secretion (Ward & Weisz, 1980 Dörner 1980) and behavioral demasculinization and feminization (Ward 1972) in adulthood. Dörner (1980), on the basis of some retrospective questionnaire studies and a review of the number of registered homosexuals in Germany, has proposed that stresses (including those associated with war) decrease fetal testicular androgen secretion and thereby increase the frequency of occurrence of male homosexuality. The reasoning is again more than daring, and takes no account of myriad factors that could contribute to the claimed effects even if these are taken at face value. Another argument sometimes put forward is that hypoandrogenization of males and hyperandrogenization of females perinatally affects sexual differentiation of neuroendocrine tissues mediating pituitary function, and pituitary secretion can be used as a marker of sexual differentiation of the brain (Dörner 1980). While this is merely dubious for many nonprimate species, it is certainly not a valid argument for primates such as rhesus macaques (Goodman & Knobil 1981). Furthermore, in human females with congenital adrenal hyperplasia there is a female pattern of gonadotropin release and ovarian cyclicity in adulthood (Money & Ehrhardt 1972), and in androgen-insensitive genotypic rat and human males there is a male pattern of gonadotropin release (Shapiro et al 1975, Van Look et al 1977, Aono et al 1978). The claim by Dörner (1980) that male human homosexuals have a female pattern of gonadotropin release and that this is a marker for feminization of brain tissue is therefore highly suspect. Furthermore, if the Dörner hypothesis were valid, one would predict that all homosexual women would be anovulatory, and all anovulatory women would be homosexual; there are no supporting data for these predictions. In point of fact, the elegant work of Knobil and associates (Goodman & Knobil 1981) suggests that in primates such as rhesus macaques, the aspect of pituitary function studied by Dörner is primarily mediated by steroid action on the anterior pituitary gland rather than on the brain. Therefore, patterns of gonadotropin release in homosexuals probably cannot be used as a marker of sexual differentiation or organization of brain tissues in humans. I have spent a fair amount of time discussing the ideas of Dörner with regard to sexual orientation in humans because he has embarked on a program in which he proposes to measure fetal androgen production by examination of amniotic fluids to prospectively relate the prenatal androgen levels to incidence of homosexuality, and perhaps eventually to exogenously "correct" improper fetal androgen levels to decrease incidence of homsexuality. Because the theoretical and data bases for this program are highly questionable, as discussed above, because amniocentesis is not always an entirely innocuous procedure, and because ethical issues are raised, there seems a need for the most open discussion possible.

A third aspect of human sexuality that might conceivably be influenced by prenatal gonadal hormones is gender identity. This facet of human sexuality has no analog in animal research (Ehrhardt & Meyer-Bahlburg 1981). There is a condition in humans in which an enzyme (5 α-reductase) deficiency results in significantly abnormally low conversion of testosterone to DHT, but not abnormally low synthesis of testosterone itself (Imperato-McGinley et al 1981a,b). In genotypic human males, this deficiency results in a labial-like scrotum, a clitoral-like phallus, and a urogenital sinus with a blind vaginal pouch. When these severe morphological effects occur, affected persons are likely to be raised as females. At puberty, testicular testosterone production increases and this is sufficient to cause phallic growth, deepening of the voice, and a muscular appearance typical of males. During the postpubertal period 16/18, affected Central American persons said to be raised unambiguously as females assumed a male gender identity and male gender role. These data have been used to support the idea that prenatal androgens have a role in organizing neural substrates underlying gender identity (Imperato-McGinley et al 1981a,b). However, this argument is flawed. Let us assume first that DHT is an organizing principle in prenatal human males. If so, the 5 α-reductase deficient males should not be able to assume a male gender identity (or gender role) in adulthood. Because a male gender identity is often assumed in these cases, DHT cannot be considered a potent prenatal organizing principle for gender identity. Next, let us assume that prenatal testosterone (or its aromatized metabolites) organizes neural substrates for human gender identity. In this case, one would expect that despite castration after birth (with subsequent estrogen treatment to develop female anatomical features) and despite continuing to be regarded as female by others, affected individuals should still assume a male gender identity in adolescence. This does not appear to occur (Wilson et al 1981). Therefore, no strictly deterministic role for prenatal DHT, testosterone, or estrogen in organization of neural substrates for gender identity is supported. Further difficulties with acceptance of this notion have been discussed by Wilson (1979). A more reasonable interpretation of these intriguing findings is that the pubertal anatomical virlization that takes place in 5α-reductase-deficient persons calls forth gender identity doubts that may gradually, and with some difficulty, best be resolved in some cases by assuming a male gender identity (Ehrhardt & Meyer-Bahlburg 1981, Meyer-Bahlburg 1982).

In addition to sex role, sexual orientation, and gender identity, a possible role of prenatal gonadal steroids in cognition and personality has been considered. There is no convincing evidence for effects of exogenous steroids administered prenatally on general intelligence or on sex-dimorphic cognitive abilities (Ehrhardt & Meyer-Bahlburg 1981). The question of whether sex-dimorphic cognitive abilities are partially attributable to endogenous prenatal gonadal steroids is unresolved. Interestingly, there appear to be sex differences in the shape and surface area of the splenium of the corpus callosum in fetal and adult humans (Baack et al 1982, DeLacoste-Utamsing & Holloway 1982). There are also indications in rhesus monkeys of sex differences in maturation tempo of cortical tissues involved in performance of object reversal tests (Goldman et al 1974), and work with rats suggests the existence of estrogen receptors in perinatal cerebral cortical tissue (MacLusky et al 1979, Sheridan 1979). Thus, the possibility of subtle organizational effects of gonadal steroids on cerebral cortical tissues mediating cognitive abilities cannot be dismissed completely at this time.

Reinisch & Karow (1977) reported that prenatal exposure to exogenous progestin alone (or in combination with low doses of estrogen) resulted in male and female subjects that were more independent, sensitive, and self-assured than controls or subjects exposed prenatally to higher doses of estrogen than progestin when responses to a personality questionnaire were evaluated. Reinisch (1981) also reported that males and females exposed to androgen-based synthetic progestins prenatally subsequently showed a higher potential for physical aggression than their sex-matched unexposed siblings. These data with exogenous steroids suggest that human brain tissue is sensitive to actions of steroids during prenatal life, but the question of whether prenatal endogenous steroids might be a contributory factor in personality development in both sexes remains open.

Organizational Effects of Hormones—Overview

The finding of organizational effects of steroid hormones on neural substrates for a variety of copulatory and noncopulatory behaviors in animals has led to attempts at extrapolation to humans. In general, these extrapolations have been unconvincing and may have received more attention than they merit. However, it seems likely that gonadal steroids exert the same actions in humans as in animals at the cellular level, and these cellular actions may affect development of neural tissues in such a way as to facilitate or inhibit neural impulse traffic mediating some adult behaviors. It would be reasonable to expect that such actions might subtly affect human behavioral predispositions. What seems unreasonable at this stage is to argue that prenatal gonadal steroids predetermine characteristics such as gender role behaviors, sexual orientation, or gender identity. In fact, it is erroneous to argue that predetermination by perinatal steroids of behavioral capacity occurs even in rodents. For example, social or testing factors can obscure or enhance the effects of perinatal steroids on copulatory responses in rodents (Brown-Grant 1975, Thornton et al 1982). It has even been suggested that in an inbred strain of guinea pigs, the effect of prenatal testosterone is not so much to determine whether lordosis will occur, but under what social or environmental conditions the response will be displayed (Thornton et al 1982). If these considerations are of importance in rodents, they must be vastly magnified in humans, presumably to the extent of "emancipating" humans from predeterministic effects of prenatal steroids on adult behavioral capacities. It appears that attempts to preventively "correct" human behavioral capacities by prenatal hormonal manipulations are ill justified. Rather, basic research into the ways in which environmentally altered neural impulse flow affects cellular actions of steroids and the ways in which steroid-sensitive cells alter neurotransmission may give valuable insights into one biological root of animal and human behavior. Such insights are unlikely to emerge from pharmacological manipulations of human fetuses initiated in the context of the hypothesis that steroids play a major, deterministic role in the development of human behaviors.

GONADAL STEROIDS ACTIVATE NEURAL TISSUES MEDIATING SEXUALLY DIMORPHIC BEHAVIORS IN ADULTS

Studies with Animals

PREPUBERTAL PERIOD   The permanent, perinatal organizing effects of steroids can be contrasted with *activational* effects of steroids on neural tissues mediating behavior at puberty and in adulthood. Activational effects of steroids on behavior are transient and are often exerted more or less concurrently with alterations in plasma steroid concentrations (Young et al 1964). Because gonadal steroid secretion in male and female nonprimate mammals is usually low after the perinatal organizational phase, steroid-dependent copulatory behaviors are not normally activated during the prepubertal period (Moltz 1975). However, successful attempts have been made to activate precocious copulatory behavior in prepubertal female rats with exogenous steroids. Normal onset of puberty in female rats occurs at about day 40, yet estrogen (or sequential treatment with estrogen and progestin) facilitates lordosis responses beginning at about day 20 in rats kept at room temperature (Södersten 1975) and at day 4–6 in rats kept at 34°C at the time of testing (C. Williams, cited in Feder 1981a). The latter result is particularly interesting because it implies that behavior-facilitating effects of estrogen can occur even before completion of the organizational phase in rats. In contrast to rats, female guinea pigs (usual onset of puberty 50–68 days) given estrogen-progestin combinations during the first week of postnatal life do not show steroid-dependent lordosis responses, and only gradually become more responsive to these steroids over the next 3–4 weeks (Goy et al 1967) despite the fact that estrogen and progestin receptors are present in hypothalamus in the first week of life (Ryer & Feder 1984a,b). An interesting finding is that lordosis responses occur within hours after birth in female and male guinea pigs and normally persist through the infantile period. However, these responses occur independently of estrogen and/or progestin, and appear to be stimulated by maternal contact and especially by maternal licking of the pup's anogenital region (Beach 1966). These steroid-independent lordosis responses are part of the infantile micturition and defecation pattern. Beach (1966) has hypothesized that as guinea pigs mature, spinal reflexes mediating infantile lordosis progressively fall under supraspinal inhibition; finally, after about four weeks, estrogen-progestin treatment becomes effective at alleviating the supraspinal inhibition in females (but not in males), and steroid-dependent lordosis occurs. Thus, the same behavioral pattern (lordosis) undergoes a transformation during development from a steroid-independent, sexually isomorphic behavior subserving excretion to a steroid-dependent, sexually dimorphic behavior subserving reproduction. The foregoing data suggest a more rapid transition in female rats than in guinea pigs from the perinatal organizational phase of steroid action to the phase of capability of responding to activational effects of steroids. However, both species are similar in that they do not absolutely require ovarian secretions during prenatal or prepubertal life in order to respond to estrogen-progestin treatment with display of lordosis behavior by the expected time of puberty (Young 1969, Södersten 1975).

In male rats, mounting, intromission, and ejaculation patterns usually begin to be displayed at about day 55, but treatment with testosterone preparations can induce precocious display of these male copulatory behaviors (Beach 1942). In contrast, although some preocity in mounting could be induced by exogenous androgens in prepubertal guinea pigs, there was no impressive induction of precocious intromission or ejaculation patterns (Gerall 1963). Thus, male and female guinea pigs are more refractory than rats to activational effects of steroids during the early prepubertal period. The basis of species (and perhaps strain) differences in rate of maturation of capability to respond to activational effects of steroids is not known. As for females, males do not require the action of gonadal steroids on CNS during the prepubertal (but postorganizational) period in order to develop the capacity to respond to exogenous steroids with display of copulatory behavior in adulthood (Grady et al 1965, Young 1969).

PUBERTY AND ADULTHOOD

Females   Intact female rats and guinea pigs reach puberty and display spontaneous, steroid-dependent lordosis in response to tactile cues several hours prior to their first ovulation, but the duration of estrous receptivity is shorter at this stage than at ensuing cyclic receptive periods in adulthood (Blandau & Money 1943, Young 1969). The reasons for the subtle increase in behavioral responsiveness after the first one or two estrous cycles are not clear. It is clear, however, that in rodents such as rats and guinea pigs, increases in ovarian secretion of estrogen (particularly estradiol) begin to occur about 40 hours before the onset of lordosis and associated proceptive behaviors, and a sudden surge of progesterone occurs almost simultaneously with the onset of these behaviors (Feder 1981b). These data from intact animals suggest that sequential secretion of estradiol and progesterone activates neural tissues mediating receptive and proceptive behaviors. When the ovaries are removed, these behaviors no longer occur, but if sequential treatment with estradiol and progesterone is instituted, the behaviors are restored (Young 1961); in some instances estradiol alone is sufficient for restoration of sexual receptivity, particularly in rats (Davidson et al 1968).

The question of specificity and of relative potencies of various steroids with respect to lordosis activation has been reviewed recently (Feder 1978). Work with rats and guinea pigs indicates that the optimal mode of systemic estradiol administration is pulsed injection of small quantities of the steroid rather than a single, larger injection (Clark & Roy 1983, Wilcox et al 1983). Related data suggest that early pulses sensitize the hypothalamus to later actions of estrogen (Parsons et al 1981), that early and late stages of estrogen action may be qualitatively different (Wilcox & Feder 1983), and that the minimum period required to complete estrogen-priming processes in rodents is about 16–24 hours (Lisk 1978). In contrast, facilitative actions of progesterone on lordosis behavior in estrogen-primed rodents require an hour or less (Lisk 1978). Initial research with rats given intracerebral implants of estradiol and progesterone showed that these hormones act directly on a number of brain areas (McEwen et al 1979b). Our work with guinea pigs given intracerebral implants of estradiol or progesterone preparations focused attention on the ventromedical nucleus (VMN) as the most sensitive site for lordosis-facilitating actions of these hormones (Morin & Feder 1974a,b). Reexamination of this question in rats with more refined intracerebral implantation techniques has confirmed that VMN is the brain area most critically involved in steroid-facilitated lordosis behavior (Davis et al 1982, Rubin & Barfield 1983).

The biochemical basis of sequential estrogen-progestin action on hypothalamic tissues mediating lordosis has been examined. Autoradiographic analyses indicate estrogen uptake not only in cell groups in midline hypothalamus, but also in medial POA, medial amygdala, and lateral septum in an evolutionarily conserved pattern similar across all classes of vertebrates (Stumpf & Sar 1978, Pfaff 1980). Cell fractionation studies of these areas have also demonstrated cytoplasmic and nuclear receptors that specifically bind estrogens with high affinity (McEwen et al 1979a, 1982). It is currently thought that, as in other estrogen target tissues such as uterus and oviduct, estrogen enters neural cells by passive diffusion. In particular target cells the estrogen binds to cytoplasmic receptor, and the estrogen-receptor complex is translocated to the nucleus where it interacts with chromatin components to stimulate mRNA and synthesis of particular proteins involved in facilitation of lordosis behavior (Feder et al 1979, Pfaff & McEwen 1983). There is now evidence that estrogen causes structural changes associated with protein synthesis detectable with electron microscopy in VMN neurons (Cohen & Pfaff 1981) and that axoplasmic transport from VMN to midbrain of estrogen-induced prolactin (or prolactin-like material) is involved in lordosis facilitation (Harlan et al 1983). The precise nature of estrogen-induced products is not known, but, in addition to the prolactin-like substance, they appear to fall into several categories, including factors that influence neurotransmitter synthesis (Wallis & Luttge 1980), factors that influence the density of muscarinic (Rainbow et al 1980), β-adrenergic (Wilkinson et al 1979) and serotonergic receptors (Biegon & McEwen 1982), and factors promoting synthesis of cytoplasmic receptor for progesterone (Pfaff & McEwen 1983). The stimulatory effect of estrogen on progestin receptor synthesis occurs in hypothalamus and preoptic area of rats and guinea pigs (but not in other brain areas such as amygdala and cerebral cortex) and probably sets the stage for the facilitative actions of progesterone on lordosis seen in estrogen-primed animals (MacLusky & McEwen 1978, Blaustein & Feder 1979). As progesterone levels in plasma increase in estrogen-primed animals (in the course of a normal estrous cycle or after progesterone injection), progesterone enters neurons by passive diffusion. In target cells, progesterone binds to progestin receptors, the progesterone-receptor complex is translocated to the nucleus, and presumably mRNA and protein synthesis involved in lordosis facilitation are altered (Blaustein & Feder 1980, Rainbow et al 1982a,b). It is noteworthy that male guinea pigs and male rats which do not normally display lordosis in response to estrogen-progestin treatment are less responsive to estrogen induction of progestin receptors than their female counterparts when hypothalamus (Blaustein et al 1980), and particularly VMN, is evaluated (Rainbow et al 1982c). However, it is not established whether the deficiency in estrogen-inducible progestin receptors in male hypothalamus adequately accounts for lack of lordosis behavior in males (Blaustein et al 1980).

In guinea pigs, and less strikingly in rats, the facilitation of lordosis by estrogen and progesterone is followed by a period of refractoriness to further hormonal stimulation of lordosis (Feder & Marrone 1977). Termination of receptivity and subsequent refractoriness may be caused by depletion of cytoplasmic progestin receptor in hypothalamus after receptor translocation (Blaustein 1982), by steroid-induced production of proteins inhibitory to lordosis (Parsons & McEwen 1981; but see Blaustein et al 1982 for a rejoinder), and/or by progesterone action on inhibitory extrahypothalamic (particularly midbrain) structures (Morin & Feder 1974c).

This picture of hypothalamic biochemical events correlating estrogen-progestin action with display of lordosis behavior does not by itself provide much insight into the question of how hormones activate expression of behavior. It seems likely that input to critical areas such as VMN is influenced by estrogen-induced changes in (a) hypothalamic and POA monoamine turnover (Barraclough & Wise 1982); (b) enzymes involved in neurotransmitter synthesis (Wallis & Luttge 1980); (c) receptor density for hypothalamic transmitters (Rainbow et al 1980), and possible changes in ratio between α-andβ-receptors in hypothalamus (Leung et al 1982). These changes may serve to enhance excitatory input to VMN and to suppress inhibitory input to the nucleus. For example, estrogen suppresses electrical activity of neurons in the rat POA, which has inhibitory actions on lordosis behavior (Pfaff & McEwen 1983). In a remarkable, sustained, systematic study of the lordosis response in rats (Pfaff 1980), it was concluded that another mechanism through which estrogen facilitates lordosis is excitation of VMN neurons with consequent enhancement of excitatory output from VMN to midbrain central gray, and relays to medullary reticular formation, reticulospinal tract, and ultimately, spinal ventral horn cells that innervate back muscles mediating assumption of the lordosis posture. Thus, one way in which estrogen probably influences lordosis behavior activation is by altering input to and output from VMN.

Environmental factors interact with hormonal factors to activate lordosis behavior: for example, in ovx rats, touch and pressure applied by an experimenter to the flanks, tailbase, and perineum summate to induce lordosis even in the absence of circulating estradiol. When estradiol is administered, the tactile pressure required to activate the lordosis response is decreased (Pfaff 1980).

The pathways by which hormones and environmental factors influence lordosis responses are summarized by Pfaff (1980). The issue of which neurotransmitters are involved in these pathways has received considerable attention since Meyerson's pioneering studies in the 1960s (Meyerson & Malmnäs 1978). Briefly, there appears to be evidence for a predominantly facilitative effect of noradrenergic transmission in guinea pigs with somewhat conflicting evidence on this point in rats (Nock & Feder 1979). Cholinergic transmission appears to facilitate lordosis in rats (Dohanich & Clemens 1981). In contrast, serotonin, dopamine, and GABA exert primarily inhibitory effects on lordosis (Crowley & Zemlan 1981, Pfaff & McEwen 1983). However, the intensity or direction of effect of these transmitters may also depend on the stage of priming with estrogen (Gorski & Yanase 1981) or progesterone (O'Connor & Feder 1983). In addition to the forementioned transmitters, the decapeptide luteinizing hormone-releasing hormone (LHRH) facilitates lordosis responding in appropriately estrogen-primed ovx rats (Moss & McCann 1975), but the physiological significance of this finding and its generalizability to other species remain open to investigation.

Although most animal research on hormonal influences over sexual behavior involves particular rodent species in which a sequence of estrogen followed by progesterone action normally facilitates lordosis, estrogen alone, progesterone action followed by estrogen secretion, or estrogen followed by appropriate tactile stimulation may normally facilitate female copulatory behavior in other nonprimate mammalian species (Feder 1981b). In general, intact nonprimate mammals show sexual receptivity for only a brief period during the estrous cycle, at around the time of spontaneous ovulation. Among primates, intact females of several species of Old World monkeys and apes can copulate throughout the menstrual cycle with little variation in frequency (e.g. stumptail macaques: Slob et al 1978; orangutans: Nadler 1982) or with higher frequency in the follicular phase than in the luteal phase of the cycle (e.g. macaques: Eaton & Resko 1974, Dixson 1977; baboons: Saayman 1970; chimpanzees: Young & Orbison 1944; talapoins: Scruton & Herbert 1970). In contrast, copulation is usually restricted to the periovulatory period in prosimians (van Horn & Eaton 1979), some New World monkeys (e.g. squirrel monkeys: Wilson 1977), and gorillas (Nadler 1982). These data illustrate an enormous variability in hormone-behavior interactions across primate species. Rhesus macaques have been particularly intensively studied to further characterize the role of gonadal hormones in sexual behavior, but it is obvious that free extrapolation to other primate species would be unwarranted. Intact rhesus macaques may not exhibit much cyclic variation in proceptive or receptive behaviors when tested in an opposite-sex pair situation, but in group testing situations, proceptivity increases in midcycle (Baum et al 1977). (Proceptive behaviors = behaviors that incite mounting by males, receptivity = acceptance of male mounting; see Beach 1976.) Ovariectomy of these macaques does not abolish copulatory activity, but copulation rates and interest in gaining access to males decline, partly as a function of partner preference (Keverne 1976, Michael 1980). Replacement therapy with estrogen alone increases proceptivity and perhaps receptivity; replacement therapy with estrogen-progestin-androgen combinations that mimic secretion of these steroids during a normal menstrual cycle restores cyclic variations in proceptive behavior (Michael

1980). Some investigators have claimed a significant role for adrenal androgens (perhaps acting on anterior hypothalamus) in rhesus macaque proceptive behavior (Baum et al 1977), but this is disputed (Johnson & Phoenix 1978, Michael 1980). Another area of current interest and dispute involves the question of whether significant effects on reproductive behavior result from facilitative actions of estrogen, and inhibitory actions of progestin, on attractiveness of female rhesus monkeys to males by effects of these steroids on production of vaginal pheromones (Keverne 1976).

This discussion of hormones and female copulatory behavior has centered on a few themes: (*a*) gonadal hormones facilitate or inhibit activation of behavior; (*b*) hormonal activational effects on behavior are exerted directly on CNS; and (*c*) hormone effects on CNS areas involved in sexual behavior are mediated by intracellular steroid receptors, particularly in VMN. To partially counterbalance the bias imposed by writing within the constraints of these ideas, it is necessary at least to mention three ways in which these themes can be broadened: (*a*) Behavioral and environmental factors exert influence over steroid hormone action. Two major mechanisms can be postulated. First, environmental stimuli (including behavior of conspecifics) cause changes in neurotransmission that result in release of hypothalamic peptides which release gonadotropins from the pituitary; the gonadotropins then act on ovarian tissue to regulate steroid secretion (Harris 1955, Komisaruk et al 1981). Second, environmentally provoked changes in neurotransmission may influence steroid action through alteration of steroid metabolism in target tissues (e.g. Verhoeven 1980) or alteration in steroid receptor density. For example, drug-induced decreases in α_1-receptor stimulation result in decreased levels of cytoplasmic progesterone receptor specifically in hypothalamus (Nock & Feder 1981, 1983). (*b*) In addition to effects of steroids on CNS tissue, steroids also act on peripheral tissues such as skin and vagina in ways that may influence behavioral interactions (Michael 1980, Pfaff 1980). (*c*) In addition to intracellular steroid receptor mechanisms in VMN, steroids also bind to intracellular receptors in many other loci outside of the hypothalamus (Stumpf & Sar 1979, Pfaff 1980), and several extrahypothalamic sites of steroid action influence female sexual behavior (these sites include POA, septum, midbrain, amygdala, and habenula: McEwen et al 1979a, Gorski & Yanase 1981, Tennent et al 1982). Steroids may also influence female reproductive behavior through rapid effects on nerve cell membranes (Pfaff & McEwen 1983).

Males   By comparison with biochemical research on hormone-behavior interactions in females, study of this topic in males has lagged. The major reason for this appears to lie with the fact that elements of male copulatory behavior persist for extended periods of time after castration (although androgen levels decline within hours of castration) and are not restored quickly by treatment with steroid hormones (although androgen levels increase within minutes after exogenous androgen). Thus, correlations between expression of male behavior and such biochemical parameters as plasma levels of gonadal steroids or occupation or translocation of steroid receptors in CNS tissues have been elusive (Davidson 1980). This contrasts, at least in some respects, with the situation in female rodents and other nonprimate mammals in which ovariectomy brings about almost immediate cessation of female copulatory behavior, and steroid replacement therapy results in resumption of copulatory behavior in a matter of hours (Young 1961).

Nevertheless, a great deal of reasearch on hormone-behavior interactions in males has been carried out. In rats approaching puberty, penile reflexes and male copulatory behaviors (including mounts, intromissions, and ejaculations) are shown as endogenous testosterone levels in plasma are rising, but before peak concentrations are reached at about 50 days of age (Sachs & Meisel 1979). In several species, including guinea pigs, there is evidence that social factors during prepubertal life influence later behavioral responsiveness to androgens (Young 1969). In squirrel monkeys, seasonal increases in androgen begin to occur at about 2.5–3.0 years. Males of this species continue for some time afterwards in a subadult state with respect to copulatory behavior because they remain peripheral from the main troop and subordinate to the adult male hierarchy (Coe et al 1981). In other nonhuman primates such as rhesus macaques, adult male copulatory behavior is androgen-dependent, yet it should be noted that elements of male sexual behavior such as erection, mounting, and thrusting are shown even in prepubertal life and at this time do not require androgen for their expression (Goy 1978).

Adults of various species have been castrated and given replacement therapy to determine which steroids are the most efficacious in restoring male copulatory behaviors (Feder 1978). The findings that: (a) brain tissue contains aromatase enzyme systems that convert androgen to estrogen, (b) estradiol can activate expression of male copulatory responses, and (c) DHT does not activate male sexual behavior in castrate rats, led to the proposition that androgen must be converted to estrogen for activation of male behaviors (McDonald et al 1970, Naftolin et al 1972, Parrott 1975). The data seemed most compelling for rats, but it soon became evident that synergistic actions of estradiol and DHT (an androgen that is not aromatized) are involved in facilitating male behavior in rats (Baum & Vreeburg 1973). Indeed, in several species, including guinea pigs and rhesus macaques, DHT by itself is highly effective in restoring male copulatory responses after castration (Alsum & Goy 1974, Phoenix 1974). Therefore, the "aromatization hypothesis" has limited applicability for activation, just as we saw earlier that it could not completely account for organizational processes.

Attempts to correlate levels of plasma androgens in intact adult males with levels of male copulatory activity have been generally unsuccessful (Harding & Feder 1976, Damassa et al 1977). At least two factors contribute to this problem. First, males may secrete far more androgen than they minimally require for display of normal levels of copulatory activity (Damassa et al 1977). Second, in at least some species (e.g. guinea pig) the character of the soma on which androgen acts sets a limit on behavioral responsiveness to androgen (Grunt & Young 1953).

Behaviorally relevant sites of action of androgen include peripheral tissues such as the penis (Beach & Westbrook 1968), the spinal cord (Hart 1978), and brain, especially the anterior hypothalamus-POA (Davidson 1966). The anterior hypothalamus-POA seems to be a particularly sensitive site of androgen action because implants of testosterone in this region activate male copulatory responses in the absence of significant leakage of androgen into the peripheral circulation (Davidson 1980). However, it has also been noted that these localized intracerebral implants of testosterone are consistently less effective in activating male behavior than systemic administration of testosterone preparations (Davidson 1980).

The mechanisms of androgen action on male copulatory behaviors may involve intracellular androgen receptors in anterior hypothalamus-POA and spinal cord (Stumpf & Sar 1979) and/or androgenic actions on membrane functions that rapidly alter neural firing (Kubli-Garfias et al 1982). An accelerometric technique has been used in rabbits to demonstrate that exogenous androgen given to castrated subjects increases the strength and frequency of pelvic thrusting (Beyer et al 1980). It is possible that arousal mechanisms involved in male copulatory behavior are mediated by anterior hypothalamus-POA while the mounting pattern itself is integrated at spinal and hindbrain levels (Hart 1978, Beyer et al 1980).

As in the case of females, there is a great deal of evidence supporting the notion that behavioral and environmental factors influence steroid secretion, in addition to the usually emphasized influences of steroids on behavioral patterns. Olfactory, tactile, and visual stimuli have all been implicated in alterations of androgen secretion in mammals (Feder 1983). Studies of monoamine neurotransmitter involvement in male copulatory behavior of rats generally suggest an inhibitory role for serotonin and a facilitative role for dopamine (Crowley & Zemlan 1981).

Implications for Human Behavior

Hormone-behavior interactions at puberty have received relatively little attention in humans (Hays 1978). At puberty, the second great increase in sexual dimorphism occurs, and this phase, just as the prenatal organizational phase, is marked by a divergence between gonadal activities in males and females. In males, increasing plasma androgens at about 12–16 years of age are correlated with onset of nocturnal emission, masturbation, dating, and first infatuation (Beach 1974). In male precocious puberty, accelerated onset of androgen secretion is sometimes accompanied by an earlier interest in sexuality and by erotic fantasies, but not all indices of erotic age develop parallel with hormonal age. Prepubertal castration generally, but not always, is followed by sexual apathy in adulthood, and there is anecdotal evidence to suggest that prepubertal castration has more severe effects in this respect than postpubertal castration (Money & Ehrhardt 1972). Thus, there is a general correlation between onset of sexual activity and onset of gonadal secretion in boys. The correlation, if there is one, is not as evident in girls. Precocious puberty in girls is not usually accompanied by erotic imagery (Money & Ehrhardt 1972).

In adult humans, ovariectomy is not necessarily, or even usually, associated with decreased sexual activity or interest (Dennerstein & Burrows 1982). Many studies have attempted to find whether cyclic variations in ovarian steroid secretion are correlated with changes in various aspects of female sexuality. These studies are often beset with numerous methodological problems including failure to (a) directly assay plasma hormones; (b) define and adequately measure libido, arousability, or quality of sexual response; (c) separate cyclic changes in sexuality from cyclic changes in feeling of well-being; (d) devise appropriately rigorous statistical tests; or (e) distinguish between female-initiated and male-initiated sexual activity (Kruse & Gottman 1982, Parlee 1982, Sanders & Bancroft 1982). This list of difficulties is by no means exhaustive, but illustrates the nature of some of the difficulties encountered. Not surprisingly, reports have variously suggested that the highest degree of sexuality in women occurs premenstrually, postmenstrually, during menstration, or at the periovulatory period (Sanders & Bancroft 1982). Most evidence seems to favor a perimenstrual rather than a periovulatory increase in sexual activity and interest (Sanders & Bancroft 1982), with decreased coital activity in the luteal phase and lowest frequency of intercourse during the menstrual period (Morris & Udry 1982, Williams & Williams 1982). These cyclic variations, when they do occur, are easily submerged by social, cultural, and psychological factors. It is apparent that ovarian secretions play, at most, a minor role in human female sexuality during the reproductive years and one that is not nearly as predictable as in some nonhuman mammals (Sanders & Bancroft 1982). Treatment of women with estrogen and/or progestin as replacement therapy or for contraception, accompanied by attempts to assess effects of the exogenous steroids on sexuality, has led to similar difficulties in interpretation of results. There is evidence for "erasure" of the luteal trough of coital activity (Morris & Udry 1982, Williams & Williams 1982) and increased frequency of coitus, especially during the pill-free week, in women using contraceptive pills (Sanders & Bancroft 1982). For women given estrogen replacement therapy with steroids, there is a suggestion that coital frequency, sexual interest, and frequency of orgasm are increased in menopausal women, but these effects may be due to estrogen action on vaginal tissue rather than CNS (Dennerstein & Burrows 1982). Overall, evidence tends to suggest subtle facilitative effects of estrogen, and inhibitory effects of progesterone on human female sexuality, but this generalization must be hedged with so many qualifications as to make its force negligible; certainly no deterministic role of steroids in human female sexual behavior is supported.

Older work had suggested that androgens increase libido in women, but these studies were unconvincing for a variety of reasons. More recent work suggests that androgens have no or negative associations with sexual aspects of interpersonal relationships, but a positive correlation with sexuality that is independent of a relationship (masturbation, response to erotic stimuli) (Sanders & Bancroft 1982). This intriguing idea merits further investigation. Similarly, some recent studies cited by Meyer-Bahlburg (1979) require replication. These studies suggest higher than normal androgen levels in a proportion of homosexual women. However, as Meyer-Bahlburg (1979) indicates, this is not interpretable as a deterministic role of androgens in human sexual preference, and as Sanders & Bancroft (1982) point out, increased androgen level may be a consequence rather than a cause of particular life-styles. Further evidence for environmental influences over ovarian secretion in women is reviewed by Cutler & García (1980).

In men, castration is often but not always associated with drastic decreases in sexual behavior (Pirke & Kockott 1982). Testosterone enanthate treatment of androgen-deficient men causes increased frequency of erections, and a dose-response relationship between androgen and frequency of erection can be detected within a particular range (Davidson et al 1982). As in the case of animals, a dose-response curve is demonstrable below androgen levels found among normal individuals, indicating that for at least some facets of sexual activity there is "redundancy" in androgen secretion in men (Davidson et al 1982). Davidson et al (1982) have suggested that androgen acts initially to increase libido perhaps through stimulation of genital sensations or other pleasurable awareness of sexual response. These authors and Bancroft (1978) have pointed out that reliable data on relationships between androgen level and libido are yet to be established, and that the question of whether aromatizable or nonaromatizable androgens are involved in human male sexuality is yet to be resolved. There are no convincing data to indicate that low androgen levels favor homosexual preferences (Meyer-Bahlburg 1977, Bancroft 1978), although several studies cited in these reviews have purported to demonstrate such a correlation. It is worth noting that no animal studies indicate alterations in sexual preference as a result of decreased androgen level in adulthood.

In contrast to many animal species including rats, guinea pigs, rabbits, bulls, and monkeys (Feder 1983), men do not show significant increases in plasma androgen after coitus (Davidson 1980). However, psychological factors such as stress and mood state may affect plasma androgen levels in men (Mazur & Lamb 1980, Feder 1983).

Activational Effects of Hormones—Overview

Activational effects of hormones on sexual behavior and motivation have been clearly demonstrated in nonhuman mammalian species, and are at least partly mediated by genomic effects of steroids in the CNS (Pfaff 1982, Pfaff & McEwen 1983). The steroids may act by exciting and/or inhibiting neural activity in specific brain areas (Beach 1966, Pfaff & McEwen 1983). Despite the strength of these observations, it is clear that external environmental and behavioral factors can compensate for the effects of steroids on sexual behavior even in nonprimates (Rosenblatt & Aronson 1958, Pfaff 1980), or can diminish or abolish such effects (Goldfoot & Goy 1970, Lisk 1978), thus negating the idea of an automatic relationship between steroid activity and expression of behavior.

There is even less evidence for a deterministic relationship between hormones and sexual behavior in some primate species. Factors such as partner preference (Michael 1980) or even size of the testing arena (Wallen 1982) have powerful influences over expression of sexual behavior in rhesus monkeys. The idea that reproductive hormones are crucial to female sexuality in women is not tenable, but it is premature to rule out entirely any role for hormones (Sanders & Bancroft 1982, Moss & Dudley 1982). Potentially more significant than a direct role of hormones on sexual behavior may be the effects of ovarian or exogenous steroids on mood state in women (Dalton 1982, Klaiber et al 1982). There is some evidence that estrogen may act as an antidepressive by enhancing adrenergic functioning in humans (Klaiber et al 1982), and there is some evidence from research on animals that responses to antidepressant drugs are altered by estrogen (Kendell et al 1982). Male sexual behavior in nonhuman primates is partially androgen-dependent (Phoenix, 1974). In addition, social factors may alter secretion of androgen, and plasma androgen level may show correlations with social rank (Eberhart et al 1980). Sexuality in men, as in other male mammals, is partially dependent on androgens (Davidson et al 1982), but the argument that this suggests a more evolutionarily stable relationship between androgens and male sexual behavior than between estrogens and female sexual behavior may need reexamination. For example, in some strains of male mice, replacement therapy with androgen after castration results in decreases of some aspects of male behavior (McGill 1978), and in bats copulatory behavior occurs after plasma androgen levels have undergone a seasonal decline (Feder 1983).

CONCLUSIONS, PROBLEMS, PROSPECTS

Gonadal steroids can be demonstrated to exert effects on the organization and activation of neural tissues mediating some reproductive behaviors. Under controlled laboratory conditions in certain species, these behavioral effects are so reliably elicitable that they can essentially be used as a bioassay for steroid actions on the nervous system at various stages of development. This has facilitated study of cellular actions of steroids in the CNS, and has targeted attention on particular brain areas (e.g. VMN in females, POA in males) for more detailed neuroanatomical and biochemical analysis. In this way, interdisciplinary study of behavior and cellular activity in the CNS is leading to exciting new areas in neurochemistry and genomic mechanisms. For this aspect of hormone-sexual behavior interactions, increasingly sophisticated biochemical analyses need not be accompanied by corresponding refinement in behavioral measurement techniques. The already-established connections between, for example, lordosis and estradiol + progesterone provide sufficient material for meaningful analysis of estrogen-progestin actions in brain.

These considerations are cause for some optimism, but there is a trend of thought that can easily distort the meaning of experimentally verifiable relationships between hormones and the expression of sexual behaviors. This trend of thought takes the view that correlations between hormones and sexual behavior shown in some animals under laboratory conditions imply a deterministic role of hormones on behavior. Similarly, evidence for VMN involvement in female behavior and POA involvement in male behavior are sometimes taken as evidence that these areas are "female and male behavior centers" (Dörner 1980). This approach ignores the fact that a major reason for replicability of hormone effects on sexual behavior is that testing for behavior is carried out under standardized laboratory conditions that purposely minimize the chances for modulation of hormonal effects by other internal and external factors. When this is done, what emerges is a seemingly deterministic role for hormones. Similarly, as actions of steroids on the VMN and POA have been identified, and as research efforts have intensified on these areas, one may be tempted to forget that steroids also influence many other parts of the CNS. Forgetfulness of this type can lead to simplistic proposals such as those for prevention of human male homosexuality by prenatal androgen treatment (Dörner 1980) and outrageous practices such as lesioning of VMN as a treatment for human male homosexuality (Müller et al 1974). To their great credit, a group of scientists has publicly objected to these proposals and practices (Schmidt & Schorsch 1981, Sigusch et al 1982). The general issue of physical predetermination of human behavioral traits is admirably discussed by Gould (1981).

It is probable that extrapolations from work on rodents can be made to humans with respect to cellular aspects of steroid action on brain; it should be obvious, however, that interspecies extrapolations cannot be made with respect to the ways in, and degrees to, which steroids will influence reproductive behaviors. The answer to the question of how hormones influence behavior will differ from species to species as a function of the sum of evolutionary factors, including social organization, that have acted to form and maintain the species (Beach 1974, 1977). With our present knowledge, attempts to predict the nature of hormone-behavior relationships in one species using another species as a "model" are doomed to failure for at least two reasons. First, there has been no clear delineation of the precise way in which the term "model" is being used, and little or no appreciation that the term is often used ambiguously or is misused (Black 1962). Second, some older essays at integrating hormone-behavior interactions into an evolutionary context emphasized rather than reduced our ignorance on this topic. For example, Beach's (1947) attempt to correlate increasing neocortical development in females of various species with increasing "emancipation" from hormonal influences over behavior does not stand up well to more detailed analysis (e.g. Nadler 1975). Degree of neocortical development by itself, therefore, appears to be too restrictive a part of evolutionary processes on which to base a more general theory (Beach 1974, 1977). It is here that students of comparative neuroendocrinology and of behavior can make their greatest impact on the further analysis of hormone-behavior interactions. Contributions can be expected to flow from comparative behavior studies (e.g. Dewsbury 1978), from endocrinological studies carried out under field rather than, or in addition to, laboratory conditions (e.g. Wingfield & Farner 1979), and from more precise observations and measurements of behavior patterns (e.g. Sachs & Barfield 1976, Pfaff 1980), moods, and personality. For the human, it is conceivable that effects of steroid hormones on behavior and mood may be even more widespread than for nonhuman species, partly *because* of some consequences associated with a high degree of neocortical development. Emergent properties of neocortical activity such as consciousness (Sperry 1981) may provide an even richer substrate for hormone-behavior interactions than is the case for nonhuman species. The challenge is to unravel physiological mechanisms associated with behavior patterns without feeling that single-minded research effort on one or another cellular process necessarily implies an equally exclusive, deterministic role of that cellular process in the behavior of an organism.

ACKNOWLEDGMENTS

This is Publication No. 389 of the Institute of Animal Behavior. Support from NIH Research Grant HD-04467 and NIMH Research Scientist Award MH-29006 is acknowledged. Dr. E. Roy offered helpful comments on portions of the manuscript, and Dr. S. Carter-Porges provided valuable reference materials. Drs. E. Banks and E. Donchin provided excellent facilities and support during my stay at the University of Illinois. This essay is dedicated to my parents, Rose and Sol Feder, with love and admiration.

Literature Cited

Adkins-Regan, E. 1981. Early organizational effects of hormones: an evolutionary perspective. See Adler 1981, pp. 159–228

Adler, N. T., ed. 1981. *Neuroendocrinology of Reproduction.* New York: Plenum

Alsum, P., Goy, R. W. 1974. Actions of esters of testosterone, dihydrotestosterone, or estradiol on sexual behavior in castrated male guinea pigs. *Horm. Behav.* 5:207–17

Aono, T., Miyake, A., Kinugasa, T., Kurachi, K., Matsumoto, K. 1978. Absence of positive feedback effect of oestrogen on LH release in patients with testicular feminization syndrome. *Acta Endocrinol.* 87:259–67

Arendash, G. W., Gorski, R. A. 1982. Enhancement of sexual behavior in female rats by neonatal transplantation of brain tissue from males. *Science* 217:1276–78

Ayoub, D. M., Greenough, W. T., Juraska, J. M. 1983. Sex differences in dendritic structure in the preoptic area of the juvenile macaque monkey brain. *Science* 219:197–98

Baack, J., De Lacoste-Utamsing, C., Woodward, D. J. 1982. Sexual dimorphism in human fetal corpora callosa. *Soc. Neurosci.* 8(1):213 (Abstr.)

Bancroft, J. 1978. The relationship between hormones and sexual behavior in humans. See Hutchison 1978, pp. 493–520

Barraclough, C. A., Gorski, R. A. 1962. Studies on mating behavior in the androgen-sterilized female rat in relation to the hypothalamic regulation of sexual behaviour. *J. Endocrinol.* 25:175–82

Barraclough, C. A., Wise, P. M. 1982. The role of catecholamines in the regulation of pituitary luteinizing hormone and follicle-stimulating hormone secretion. *Endocr. Rev.* 3:91–119

Baum, M. J. 1979. Differentiation of coital behavior in mammals: a comparative analysis. *Neurosci. Biobehav. Rev.* 3:265–84

Baum, M. J., Everitt, B. J., Herbert, J., Keverne, E. B. 1977. Hormonal basis of proceptivity and receptivity in female primates. *Arch. Sex. Behav.* 6:173–92

Baum, M. J., Gallagher, C. A., Martin, J. T., Damassa, D. A. 1982. Effects of testosterone, dihydrotestosterone, or estradiol administered neonatally on sexual behavior of female ferrets. *Endocrinology* 111:773–80

Baum, M. J., Vreeburg, J. T. M. 1973. Copulation in castrated male rats following combined treatment with estradiol and dihydrotestosterone. *Science* 182:283–85

Beach, F. A. 1942. Sexual behavior of prepuberal male and female rats treated with gonadal hormones. *J. Comp. Psychol.* 34:285–92

Beach, F. A. 1947. Evolutionary changes in the physiological control of mating behavior in mammals *Psychol. Rev.* 54:279–315

Beach, F. A. 1948. *Hormones and Behavior.* New York: Hoeber

Beach, F. A. 1966. Ontogeny of "coitus-related" reflexes in the female guinea pig. *Proc. Natl. Acad. Sci. USA* 56:526–33

Beach, F. A. 1971. Hormonal factors controlling the differentiation, development, and display of copulatory behavior in the ramstergig and related species. In *The Biopsychology of Development,* ed. E. Tobach, L. R. Aronson, E. Shaw, pp. 249–95. New York: Academic

Beach, F. A. 1974. Human sexuality and evolution. See Montagna & Sadler 1974, pp. 333–66

Beach, F. A. 1976. Sexual attractivity, proceptivity and receptivity in female mammals. *Horm. Behav.* 7:105–38

Beach, F. A. 1977. Cross-species comparisons and the human heritage. In *Human Sexuality in Four Perspectives,* ed. F. A. Beach, pp. 296–316. Baltimore: Johns Hopkins Univ. Press

Beach, F. A. 1978. Sociobiology and interspecific comparisons of behavior. In *Sociobiology and Human Nature,* ed. M. S. Gregory. A. Silvers, D. Sutch, pp. 116–35. San Francisco: Jossey-Bass

Beach, F. A. 1981. Historical origins of modern research on hormones and behavior. *Horm. Behav.* 15:325–76

Beach, F. A., Kuehn, R. E. 1970. Coital behavior in dogs X. Effects of androgenic stimulation during development on feminine mating responses in females and males. *Horm. Behav.* 1:347–67

Beach, G. A., Westbrook, W. H. 1968. Dissociation of androgen effects on sexual morphology and behavior in male rats. *Endocrinology* 83:395–98

Bermant, G., Davidson, J. M. 1974. *Biological Bases of Sexual Behavior.* New York: Harper & Row

Beyer, C., ed. 1979. *Endocrine Control of Sexual Behavior.* New York: Raven

Beyer, C., Valazquez, J., Larsson, K., Contreras, J. L. 1980. Androgen regulation of the motor copulatory pattern in the male New

Zealand white rabbit. *Horm. Behav.* 14:179–90

Biegon, A., McEwen, B. S. 1982. Modulation by estradiol of serotonin₁ receptors in brain. *J. Neurosci.* 2:199–205

Black, M. 1962. *Models and Metaphors. Studies in Language and Philosophy.* Ithaca: Cornell Univ. Press

Blandau, R. J., Money, W. L. 1943. The attainment of sexual maturity in the female albino rat as determined by the copulatory response. *Anat. Rec.* 86:197–215

Blaustein, J. D. 1982. Alteration of sensitivity to progesterone facilitation of lordosis in guinea pigs by modulation of hypothalamic progestin receptors. *Brain Res.* 243:287–300

Blaustein, J. D., Brown, T. J., Reading, D. S. 1982. Failure of protein synthesis inhibition to block progesterone desensitization of lordosis in female rats. *Physiol. Behav.* 29:475–81

Blaustein, J. D., Feder, H. H. 1979. Cytoplasmic progestin receptors in guinea pig brain: characteristics and relationship to the induction of sexual behavior. *Brain Res.* 169:481–97

Blaustein, J. D., Feder, H. H. 1980. Nuclear progestin receptors in guinea pig brain measured by an *in vitro* exchange assay after hormonal treatments that affect lordosis. *Endocrinology* 106:1061–69

Blaustein, J. D., Ryer, H. I., Feder, H. H. 1980. A sex difference in the progestin receptor system of guinea pig brain. *Neuroendocrinology* 31:403–9

Booth, J. E. 1977. Sexual behaviour of neonatally castrated rats injected during infancy with oestrogen and dihydrotestosterone. *J. Endocrinol.* 72:135–41

Breedlove, S. M., Jacobson, C. D., Gorski, R. A., Arnold, A. D. 1982. Masculinization of the female rat spinal cord following a single neonatal injection of testosterone propionate but not estradiol benzoate. *Brain Res.* 237:173–81

Brown-Grant, K. 1975. A re-examination of the lordosis response in female rats given high doses of testosterone propionate or estradiol benzoate in the neonatal period. *Horm. Behav.* 6:351–78

Christensen, L. W., Gorski, R. A. 1978. Independent masculinization of neuroendocrine systems by intracerebral implants of testosterone or estradiol in the neonatal female rat. *Brain Res.* 146:325–40

Clark, A. S., Roy, E. J. 1983. Behavioral and cellular responses to pulses of low doses of estradiol-17β. *Physiol. Behav.* In press

Clemens, L. G. 1973. Development and behavior. In *Comparative Psychology,* ed. D. A. Dewsbury, D. A. Rethlingshafer, pp. 238–68. New York: McGraw-Hill

Clemens, L. G., Gladue, B. A., Coniglio, L.

P. 1978. Prenatal endogenous androgenic influences on masculine sexual behavior and genital morphology in male and female rats. *Horm. Behav.* 10:40–53

Coe, C. L., Chen, J., Lowe, E. L., Davidson, J. M., Levine, S. 1981. Hormonal and behavioral changes at puberty in the squirrel monkey. *Horm. Behav.* 15:36–53

Cohen, R., Pfaff, D. W. 1981. Ultrastructure of neurons in the ventromedial nucleus of the hypothalamus in ovariectomized rats with or without estrogen treatment. *Cell Tissue Res.* 217:451–70

Crowley, W. R., Zemlan, F. P. 1981. The neurochemical control of mating behavior. See Adler 1981, pp. 451–84

Cutler, W. B., García, C. R. 1980. The psychoneuroendocrinology of the ovulatory cycle of woman: a review. *Psychoneuroendocrinology* 5:89–111

Dalton, K. 1982. Premenstrual tension: an overview. In *Behavior and the Menstrual Cycle,* ed. R. C. Friedman, pp. 217–42. New York: Dekker

Damassa, D. A., Smith, E. R., Davidson, J. M. 1977. The relationship between circulating testosterone levels and sexual behavior. *Horm. Behav.* 8:275–86

Dantchakoff, V. 1938a. Role des hormones dans la manifestation des instincts sexuels. *Compt. Rend.* 206:945–47

Dantchakoff, V. 1938b. Sur les effets de l'hormone male dans une jeune cobaye femelle traite depuis un stade embryonnaire (inversions sexuelles). *Compt. Rend. Soc. Biol.* 127:1255–58

Davidson, J. M. 1966. Activation of the male rat's sexual behavior by intracerebral implantation of androgen. *Endocrinology* 79:783–94

Davidson, J. M. 1980. Hormones and sexual behavior in the male. In *Neuroendocrinology,* ed. D. T. Krieger, J. C. Hughes, pp. 232–38. Sunderland, Mass: Sinauer

Davidson, J. M., Kwan, M., Greenleaf, W. J. 1982. Hormonal replacement and sexuality in men. In *Clinics in Endocrinology and Metabolism, Diseases of Sex and Sexuality,* ed. J. Bancroft, 11:599–624. Philadelphia: Saunders

Davidson, J. M., Rodgers, C. H., Smith, E. R., Bloch, G. J. 1968. Stimulation of female sex behavior in adrenalectomized rats with estrogen alone. *Endocrinology* 82:193–95

Davis, P. G., Krieger, M. S., Barfield, R. J., McEwen, B. S., Pfaff, D. W. 1982. The site of action of intrahypothalamic estrogen implants in feminine sexual behavior: an autoradiographic analysis. *Endocrinology* 111:1581–86

DeLacoste-Utamsing, C., Holloway, R. L. 1982. Sexual dimorphism in the human corpus callosum. *Science* 216:1431–32

Dennerstein, L., Burrows, G. D. 1982. Hormone replacement therapy and sexuality in women. See Davidson et al 1982, pp. 661–80

Dewsbury, D. A. 1978. The comparative method in studies of reproductive behaviors. See McGill et al 1978, pp. 83–114

Dixson, A. F. 1977. Observations on the displays, menstrual cycles and sexual behaviour of the "black ape" of Celebes (*Macaca nigra*). *J. Zool.* 182:63–84

Dohanich, G. P., Clemens, L. G. 1981. Brain areas implicated in cholinergic regulation of sexual behavior. *Horm. Behav.* 15:157–67

Dorfman, R. I. 1967. The antiestrogenic and antiandrogenic activities of progesterone in the defense of a normal fetus. *Anat. Rec.* 157:547–57

Dörner, G. 1980. Sexual differentiation of the brain. *Vitam. Horm.* 38:325–81

Dörner, G., Staudt, J. 1969. Structural changes in the hypothalamic ventromedial nucleus of the male rat, following neonatal castration and androgen treatment. *Neuroendocrinology* 4:278–81

Eaton, G. G., Resko, J. A. 1974. Ovarian hormones and sexual behavior of *Macaca nemestrina*. *J. Comp. Physiol. Psychol.* 86:919–24

Eberhart, J. A., Keverne, E. B., Meller, R. E. 1980. Social influences on plasma testosterone levels in male Talapoin monkeys. *Horm. Behav.* 14:247–66

Edwards, D. A. 1969. Early androgen stimulation and aggressive behavior in male and female mice. *Physiol. Behav.* 4:333–38

Ehrhardt, A. A., Evers, K., Money, J. 1968. Influence of androgen and some aspects of sexually dimorphic behavior in women with the late-treated adrenogenital syndrome. *Johns Hopkins Med. J.* 123:115–22

Ehrhardt, A. A., Meyer-Bahlburg, H. F. L. 1981. Effects of prenatal sex hormones on gender-related behavior. *Science* 211:1312–18

Erskine, M. S., Baum, M. J. 1982. Plasma concentrations of testosterone and dihydrotestosterone during perinatal development in male and female ferrets. *Endocrinology* 111:767–72

Fadem, B. H., Barfield, R. J. 1981. Neonatal hormonal influences on the development of proceptive and receptive feminine sexual behavior in rats. *Horm. Behav.* 15:282–88

Feder, H. H. 1978. Specificity of steroid hormone activation of sexual behavior in rodents. See Hutchison 1978, pp. 395–424

Feder, H. H. 1981a. Perinatal hormones and their role in the development of sexually dimorphic behaviors. See Adler 1981, pp. 127–58

Feder, H. H. 1981b. Estrous cyclicity in mammals. See Adler 1981, pp. 279–349

Feder, H. H. 1983. Peripheral plasma levels of gonadal steroids in adult male and adult, nonpregnant female mammals. In *Handbook of Behavioral Neurobiology*, Vol. 8, *Neurobiology of Reproduction*, ed. N. T. Adler. New York: Plenum. In press

Feder, H. H., Goy, R. W. 1983. Effects of neonatal estrogen treatment of female guinea pigs on mounting behavior in adulthood. *Horm. Behav.* In press

Feder, H. H., Landau, I. T., Walker, W. A. 1979. Anatomical and biochemical substrates of the actions of estrogens and antiestrogens on brain tissues that regulate female sex behavior of rodents. See Beyer 1979, pp. 317–40

Feder, H. H., Marrone, B. L. 1977. Progesterone: its role in the central nervous system as a facilitator and inhibitor of sexual behavior and gonadotropin release. *Ann. NY Acad. Sci.* 386:331–54

Freeman, D. J., Hobkirk, R. 1976. Metabolites of estradiol-17β in guinea pig uterus late in pregnancy. *Steroids* 28:613–19

Gerall, A. A. 1963. The effect of prenatal and postnatal injections of testosterone propionate on prepuberal male guinea pig sexual behavior. *J. Comp. Physiol. Psychol.* 56:92–95

Gerall, A. A., Dunlap, J. L., Hendricks, S. E. 1973. Effect of ovarian secretions on female behavioral potentiality in the rat. *J. Comp. Phsyiol. Psychol.* 82:449–65

Gerall, A. A., Ward, I. L. 1966. Effects of prenatal exogenous androgen on the sexual behavior of the female albino rat. *J. Comp. Physiol. Psychol.* 62:370–75

Goldfoot, D. A., Feder, H. H., Goy, R. W. 1969. Development of bisexuality in the male rat treated neonatally with androstenedione. *J. Comp. Physiol. Psychol.* 67:41–45

Goldfoot, D. A., Goy, R. W. 1970. Abbreviation of behavioral estrus by coital and vagino-cervical stimulation. *J. Comp. Physiol. Psychol.* 72:426–34

Goldfoot, D. A., van der Werff ten Bosch, J. J. 1975. Mounting behavior of female guinea pigs after prenatal and adult administration of the propionates of testosterone, dihydrotestosterone, and androstanediol. *Horm. Behav.* 6:139–48

Goldman, P. S., Crawford, H. T., Stokes, L. P., Galkin, T. W., Rosvold, H. E. 1974. Sex-dependent behavioral effects of cerebral cortical lesions in the developing rhesus monkey. *Science* 186:540–42

Goodman, R. L., Knobil, E. 1981. The sites of action of ovarian steroids in the regulation of LH secretion. *Neuroendocrinology* 32:57–63

Gorski, R. A. 1979. Nature of hormone action in the brain. In *Ontogeny of Receptors and*

Reproductive Hormone Action, ed. T. H. Hamilton, J. H. Clark, W. A. Sadler, pp. 371–92. New York: Raven

Gorski, R. A., Yanase, M. 1981. Estrogen facilitation of lordosis behavior in the female rat. In *Gonadal Steroids and Brain Function,* ed. W. Wuttke, R. Horowski, pp. 222–37. *Exp. Brain Res. Suppl. 3.* New York: Springer-Verlag

Gould, S. J. 1981. *The Mismeasure of Man.* New York: Norton

Goy, R. W. 1970. Experimental control of psychosexuality. In *A Discussion on the Determination of Sex,* ed. G. W. Harris, R. G. Edwards. *Philos. Trans. R. Soc. London, Ser. B.* 259:149–62

Goy, R. W. 1978. Development of play and mounting behavior in female rhesus monkeys virilized prenatally with esters of testosterone and dihydrotestosterone. In *Recent Advances in Primatology,* ed. D. J. Chivers, J. Herbert, 1:449–62. New York: Academic

Goy, R. W., Bridson, W. E., Young, W. C. 1964. Period of maximal susceptibility of the prenatal female guinea pig to masculinizing actions of testosterone propionate. *J. Comp. Physiol. Psychol.* 57:166–74

Goy, R. W., McEwen, B. S. 1980. *Sexual Differentiation of the Brain.* Cambridge, Mass: MIT Press

Goy, R. W., Phoenix, C. H., Meidinger, R. 1967. Postnatal development of sensitivity to estrogen and androgen in male, female, and pseudohermaphroditic guinea pigs. *Anat. Rec.* 157:87–96

Goy, R. W., Resko, J. A. 1972. Gonadal hormones and behavior of normal and pseudohermaphroditic nonhuman female primates. *Recent Prog. Horm. Res.* 28:707–33

Grady, K. L., Phoenix, C. H., Young, W. C. 1965. Role of the developing rat testis in differentiation of the neural tissues mediating mating behavior. *J. Comp. Physiol. Psychol.* 59:176–82

Greenough, W. T., Carter, C. S., Steerman, C., DeVoogd, T. 1977. Sex differences in dendritic patterns in hamster preoptic area. *Brain Res.* 126:63–72

Grunt, J. A., Young, W. C. 1953. Consistency of sexual behavior patterns in individual male guinea pigs following castration and androgen therapy. *J. Comp. Physiol. Psychol.* 46:138–44

Harding, C. F., Feder, H. H. 1976. Relation between individual differences in sexual behavior and plasma testosterone levels in the guinea pig. *Endocrinology* 98:1198–1205

Harlan, R. E., Shivers, B. D., Pfaff, D. W. 1983. Midbrain microinfusions of prolactin increase the estrogen-dependent behavior, lordosis. *Science* 219:1451–53

Harris, G. W. 1955. *Neural Control of the Pituitary Gland.* London: Arnold

Harris, G. W. 1964. Sex hormones, brain development and brain function. *Endocrinology* 75:627–48

Harris, G. W., Levine, S. 1965. Sexual differentiation of the brain and its experimental control. *J. Physiol.* 181:379–400

Hart, B. L. 1978. Hormones, spinal reflexes, and sexual behaviour. See Hutchison 1978, pp. 319–48

Hart, B. L. 1979. Sexual behavior and penile reflexes of neonatally castrated male rats treated in infancy with estrogen and dihydrotestosterone. *Horm. Behav.* 13:256–68

Hays, S. E. 1978. Strategies for psychoendocrine studies of puberty. *Psychoneuroendocrinology* 3:1–15

Hutchison, J. B., ed. 1978. *Biological Determinants of Sexual Behaviour.* New York: Wiley

Ichikawa, S., Fujii, Y. 1982. Effect of prenatal androgen treatment on maternal behavior in the female rat. *Horm. Behav.* 16:224–33

Imperato-McGinley, J., Peterson, R. E., Gautier, T. 1981a. Male pseudohermaphroditism secondary to 5α-reductase deficiency: a review. In *Fetal Endocrinology,* ed. M. J. Novy, J. A. Resko, pp. 359–82. New York: Academic

Imperato-McGinley, J., Peterson, R. E., Gautier, T., Sturla, E. 1981b. The impact of androgens on the evolution of male gender identity. In *Pediatric Andrology, Clinics in Andrology,* ed. S. J. Kogan, E. S. E. Hafez, 7:99–108. Boston: Nijhoff

Jacobson, C. D., Gorski, R. A. 1981. Neurogenesis of the sexually dimorphic nucleus of the preoptic area in the rat. *J. Comp. Neurol.* 196:519–29

Johnson, D. F., Phoenix, C. H. 1978. Sexual behavior and hormone levels during the menstrual cycles of rhesus monkeys. *Horm. Behav.* 11:160–74

Kendall, D. A., Stancel, G. M., Enna, S. J. 1982. The influence of sex hormones on antidepressant-induced alterations in neurotransmiter receptor binding. *J. Neurosci.* 2:354–60

Keverne, E. B. 1976. Sexual receptivity and attractiveness in the female rhesus monkey. *Adv. Study Behav.,* 7:155–96

Kinsey, A. C., Pomeroy, W. B., Martin, C. E. 1948. *Sexual Behavior in the Human Male.* Philadelphia: Saunders

Klaiber, E. L., Broverman, D. M., Vogel, W., Kennedy, J. A., Nadeau, C. J. L. 1982. Estrogens and central nervous system function: electroencephalography, cognition, and depression. See Dalton 1982, pp. 267–90

Komisaruk, B. R., Terasawa, E., Rodriguez-Sierra, J. F. 1981. How the brain mediates ovarian responses to environmental stimuli: neuroanatomy and neurophysiology. See Adler 1981, pp. 349–76

Kruse, J. A., Gottman, J. M. 1982. Time series methodology in the study of sexual hormonal and behavioral cycles. Arch. Sex. Behav. 11:405–15

Kubli-Garfias, C., Canchola, E., Arauz-Contreras, J., Feria-Velasco, A. 1982. Depressant effect of androgens on the cat brain electrical activity and its antagonism by ruthenium red. Neuroscience 7:2777–82

Leshner, A. I. 1978. An Introduction to Behavioral Endocrinology. New York: Oxford Univ. Press

Leung, P. C. K., Whitmoyer, D. I., Garland, K. E., Sawyer, C. H. 1982. β-Adrenergic suppression of progesterone-induced luteinizing hormone surge in ovariectomized, estrogen-primed rats. Proc. Soc. Exp. Biol. Med. 169:161–64

Levine, S., Mullins, R. F. Jr. 1964. Estrogen administered neonatally affects adult sexual behavior in male and female rats. Science 144:185–87

Lev-Ran, A. 1974. Sexuality and educational levels of women with the late-treated adrenogenital syndrome. Arch. Sex. Behav. 3: 27–32

Lieberburg, I., MacLusky, N. J., McEwen, B. S. 1980. Androgen receptors in the perinatal rat brain. Brain Res. 178:207–12

Lieberburg, I., McEwen, B. S. 1975. Estradiol-17β: a metabolite of testosterone recovered in cell nuclei from limbic areas of neonatal rat brains. Brain Res. 85:165–70

Lisk, R. D. 1978. The regulation of sexual "heat". See Hutchison 1978, pp. 425–66

MacLusky, N. J., Lieberburg, I., McEwen, B. S. 1979. The development of estrogen receptor systems in the rat brain: perinatal development. Brain Res. 178:129–42

MacLusky, N. J., McEwen, B. S. 1978. Oestrogen modulates progestin receptor concentrations in some rat brain regions but not in others. Nature 274:276–78

Martini, L. 1976. Androgen reduction by neuroendocrine tissues: physiological significance. In Subcellular Mechanisms in Reproductive Neuroendocrinology, ed. F. Naftolin, K. J. Ryan, J. Davies, pp. 327–55. Amsterdam: Elsevier

Martins, T., Valle, J. R. 1948. Hormonal regulation of the micturition behavior of the dog. J. Comp. Physiol. Psychol. 421:301–11

Matsumoto, A., Arai, Y. 1980. Sexual dimorphism in "wiring pattern" in the hypothalamic arcuate nucleus and its modification by neonatal hormonal environment. Brain Res. 190:238–42

Mazur, A., Lamb, T. A. 1980. Testosterone, status, and mood in human males. Horm. Behav. 14:236–46

McDonald, P., Beyer, C., Newton, F., Brien, B., Baker, R., et al. 1970. Failure of 5α – dihydrotestosterone to initiate sexual behaviour in the castrated male rat. Nature 227:964–65

McEwen, B. S. 1981. Neural gonadal steroid actions. Science 211:1303–11

McEwen, B. S. 1982. Sexual differentiation of the brain: gonadal hormone action and current concepts of neuronal differentiation. In Molecular Approaches to Neurobiology, ed. I. R. Brown, pp. 195–219. New York: Academic

McEwen, B. S., Biegon, A., Davis, P. G., Krey, L. C., Luine, V. N., et al. 1982. Steroid hormones: humoral signals which alter brain cell properties and functions. Recent Prog. Horm. Res. 38:41–92

McEwen, B. S., Davis, P. G., Parsons, B., Pfaff, D. W. 1979a. The brain as a target for steroid hormone action. Ann. Rev. Neurosci. 2:65–112

McEwen, B. S., Lieberburg, I., Chaptal, C., Davis, P. G., Krey, L. C., et al 1979b. Attenuating the defeminization of the neonatal rat brain: mechanisms of action of cyproterone acetate, 1,4,6-androstatriene-3, 17-dione and a synthetic progestin, R5020. Horm. Behav. 13:269–81

McEwen, B. S., Lieberburg, I., Chaptal, C., Krey, L. C. 1977. Aromatization: important for sexual differentiation of the neonatal rat brain. Horm. Behav. 9:249–63

McGill, T. E. 1978. Genetic factors influencing the action of hormones on sexual behavior. See Hutchison 1978, pp. 277–318

McGill, T. E., Dewsbury, D. A., Sachs, B. D., eds. 1978. Sex and Behavior. New York: Plenum

Meaney, M. J., Stewart, J. 1981. Neonatal androgens influence the social play of prepubescent rats. Horm. Behav. 15:197–213

Meyer-Bahlburg, H. F. L. 1977. Sex hormones and male homosexuality in comparative perspective. Arch. Sex. Behav. 6:297–325

Meyer-Bahlburg, H. F. L. 1979. Sex hormones and female homosexuality: a critical examination. Arch. Sex. Behav. 8:101–19

Meyer-Bahlburg, H. F. L. 1982. Hormones and psychosexual differentiation: implications for the management of intersexuality, homosexuality and transsexuality. See Davidson et al 1982, 11:681–701

Meyerson, B. J., Malmnäs, C.-O. 1978. Brain monoamines and sexual behaviour. See Hutchison 1978, pp. 521–54

Michael, R. P. 1980. Hormones and sexual behavior in the female. See Davidson 1980, pp 223–31

Moltz, H. 1975. The search for the determinants of puberty in the rat. In Hormonal

Correlates of Behavior, B. E. Eleftheriou, R. L. Sprott, 1:35–154. New York: Plenum

Money, J., Ehrhardt, A. A. 1972. Man & Woman, Boy & Girl. Baltimore: Johns Hopkins Univ. Press

Money, J., Mathews, D. 1982. Prenatal exposure to virilizing progestins: an adult followup study of twelve women. Arch. Sex. Behav. 11:73–74

Montagna, W., Sadler, W. A., eds. 1974. Reproductive Behavior. New York: Plenum

Morin, L. P., Feder, H. H. 1974a. Intracranial estradiol benzoate implants and lordosis behavior of ovariectomized guinea pigs. Brain Res. 70:95–102

Morin, L. P., Feder, H. H. 1974b. Hypothalamic progesterone implants and facilitation of lordosis behavior in estrogen-primed ovariectomized guinea pigs. Brain Res. 70:81–93

Morin, L. P., Feder, H. H. 1974c. Inhibition of lordosis behavior in ovariectomized guinea pigs by mesencephalic implants of progesterone. Brain Res. 70:71–80

Morris, N. M., Udry, J. R. 1982. Epidemiological patterns of sexual behavior in the menstrual cycle. See Dalton 1982, pp. 129–54

Moss, R. L., Dudley, C. A. 1982. Hypothalamic peptides and sexual behavior. See Dalton 1982, pp. 65–76

Moss, R. L., McCann, S. M. 1975. Action of luteinizing hormone-releasing factor (LRF) in the initiation of lordosis behavior in the estrone-primed ovariectomized female rat. Neuroendocrinology 17:309–18

Müller, D., Orthner, H., König, F., Bosse, K., Kloos, G. 1974. Einfluss von hypothalamusläsionen auf sexualverhalten und gonadotrope Funktion beim Menschen. Bericht über 23 Fälle. In Endocrinology of Sex, ed. G. Dörner. Leipzig: Barth

Musaph, H., Money, J., eds. 1977. Handbook of Sexology. Amsterdam: ASP Biol. Med. Press

Nadler, R. D. 1975. Sexual cyclicity in captive lowland gorillas. Science 189:813–14

Nadler, R. D. 1982. Laboratory research on sexual behavior and reproduction of gorillas and orangutans. Am. J. Primatol. 1:57–66 (Suppl.)

Naftolin, F., Ryan, K. J., Petro, Z. 1972. Aromatization of androstenedione by the anterior hypothalamus of adult male and female rats. Endocrinology 90:295–98

Nock, B., Feder, H. H. 1979. Noradrenergic transmission and female sexual behavior of guinea pigs. Brain Res. 166:369–80

Nock, B., Feder, H. H. 1981. Neurotransmitter modulation of steroid action in target cells that mediate reproduction and reproductive behavior. Neurosci. Biobehav. Rev. 5:437–47

Nock, B., Feder, H. H. 1983. α_1-Noradrenergic regulation of hypothalamic progestin receptors and guinea pig sexual behavior. Brain Res. Submitted for publication

O'Connor, L. H., Feder, H. H. 1983. Effects of serotonin agonists on lordosis, myoclonus and cytoplasmic progestin receptors. Horm. Behav. 17:183–96

Olsen, K. L. 1979. Androgen-insensitive rats are defeminized by their testes. Nature 279:238–39

Parlee, M. B. 1982. The psychology of the menstrual cycle: biological and physiological perspectives. See Dalton 1982, pp. 77–100

Parrott, R. F. 1975. Aromatizable and 5α-reduced androgens: differentiation between central and peripheral effects on male rat sexual behavior. Horm. Behav. 6:99–108

Parsons, B., McEwen, B. S. 1981. Sequential inhibition of sexual receptivity by progesterone is prevented by a protein synthesis inhibitor and is not causally related to decreased levels of hypothalamic progestin receptors in the female rat. J. Neurosci. 1:527–31

Parsons, B., Rainbow, T. C., Pfaff, D. W., McEwen, B. S. 1981. Oestradiol, sexual receptivity and cytosol progestin receptors in rat hypothalamus. Nature 292:58–59

Paup, D. C., Coniglio, L. P., Clemens, L. G. 1972. Masculinization of the female golden hamster by neonatal treatment with androgen or estrogen. Horm. Behav. 3:123–31

Pfaff, D. W. 1966. Morphological changes in the brains of adult male rats after neonatal castration. J. Endocrinol. 36:415–16

Pfaff, D. W. 1980. Estrogens and Brain Function: Neural Analysis of a Hormone-Controlled Mammalian Reproductive Behavior. New York: Springer-Verlag

Pfaff, D. W. 1982. Neurobiological mechanisms of sexual motivation. In the Physiological Mechanisms of Motivation, ed. D. W. Pfaff, pp. 287–318. New York: Springer-Verlag

Pfaff, D. W., McEwen, B. S. 1983. Actions of estrogens and progestins on nerve cells. Science 219:808–14

Pfaff, D. W., Zigmond, R. E. 1971. Neonatal androgen effects on sexual and non-sexual behavior of adult rats tested under various hormone regimes. Neuroendocrinology 7:129–45

Phoenix, C. H. 1974. Effects of dihydrotestosterone propionate on sexual behavior of castrated male rhesus monkeys. Physiol. Behav. 12:1045–55

Phoenix, C. H., Goy, R. W., Gerall, A. A., Young, W. C. 1959. Organizing action of prenatally administered testosterone propionate on the tissues mediating mating behavior in the female guinea pig. *Endocrinology* 65:369–82

Pirke, K. M., Kockott, G. 1982. Endocrinology of sexual dysfunction. See Davidson et al 1982, 11:625–38

Plapinger, L., McEwen, B. S., Clemens, L. E. 1973. Ontogeny of estradiol-binding sites in rat brain. II. Characteristics of a neonatal binding macromolecule. *Endocrinology* 93:1129–39

Rainbow, T. C., DeGroff, V., Luine, V. N., McEwen, B. S. 1980. Estradiol 17β increases the number of muscarinic receptors in hypothalamic nuclei. *Brain Res.* 198:239–43

Rainbow, T. C., McGinnis, M. Y., Davis, P. G., McEwen, B. S. 1982a. Application of anisomycin to the lateral ventromedial nucleus of the hypothalamus inhibits the activation of sexual behavior by estradiol and progesterone. *Brain Res.* 233:417–23

Rainbow, T. C., McGinnis, M. Y., Krey, L. C., McEwen, B. S. 1982b. Nuclear progestin receptors in rat brain and pituitary. *Neuroendocrinology* 34:426–32

Rainbow, T. C., Parsons, B., McEwen, B. S. 1982c. Sex differences in rat brain oestrogen and progestin receptors. *Nature* 300:648–49

Raisman, G., Field, P. M. 1973. Sexual dimorphism in the neuropil of the preoptic area of the rat and its dependence on neonatal androgen. *Brain Res.* 54:1–29

Raum, W. J., Swerdloff, R. F. 1981. The role of hypothalamic adrenergic receptors in preventing testosterone-induced androgenization in the female rat brain. *Endocrinology* 109:273–78

Reddy, V. V. R., Naftolin, F., Ryan, K. J. 1974. Conversion of androstenedione to estrone by neural tissues from fetal and neonatal rats. *Endocrinology* 94:117–21

Reinisch, J. M. 1981. Prenatal exposure to synthetic progestins increases potential for aggression in humans. *Science* 211:1171–73

Reinisch, J. M., Karow, W. G. 1977. Prenatal exposure to synthetic progestins and estrogens: effects on human development. *Arch. Sex. Behav.* 6:257–88

Rosenblatt, J. S., Aronson, L. R. 1958. The decline in sexual behavior in male cats after castration with special reference to the role of prior sexual experience. *Behaviour* 12:285–338

Rubin, B. S., Barfield, R. J. 1983. Progesterone in the ventromedial hypothalamus facilitates estrous behavior in ovariectomized, estrogen-primed rats. *Endocrinology.* 113:797–804

Ryer, H. I., Feder, H. H. 1984a. Development of steroid receptor systems in guinea pig brain. I. Cytoplasmic estrogen receptors. *Dev. Brain Res.* In press

Ryer, H. I., Feder, H. H. 1984b. Development of steroid receptor systems in guinea pig brain. II. Cytoplasmic progestin receptors. *Dev. Brain Res.* In press

Saayman, G. S. 1970. The menstrual cycle and sexual behaviour in a troop of free-ranging chacma baboons (*Papio ursinus*). *Folia Primatol.* 12:81–110

Sachs, B. D. Barfield, R. J. 1976. Functional analysis of masculine copulatory behavior in the rat. *Adv. Study Behav.* 7:92–154

Sachs, B. D., Meisel, R. L. 1979. Pubertal development of penile reflexes and copulation in male rats. *Psychoneuroendocrinology* 4:287–96

Sanders, D., Bancroft, J. 1982. Hormones and the sexuality of women—the menstrual cycle. See Davidson et al 1982, pp. 639–60

Schmidt, G., Schorsch, E. 1981. Psychosurgery of sexually deviant patients: review and analysis of new empirical findings. *Arch. Sex. Behav.* 10:301–23

Scruton, D. M., Herbert, J. 1970. The menstrual cycle and its effect upon behaviour in the talapoin monkey (*Miopithecus talapoin*). *J. Zool.* 162:419–36

Shapiro, B. H., Goldman, A. S., Gustafsson, J.-A. 1975. Masculine-like hypothalamic-pituitary axis in the androgen-insensitive genetically male rat pseudohermaphrodite. *Endocrinology* 97:487–92

Shapiro, B. H., Levine, D. C., Adler, N. T. 1980. The testicular feminized rat: a naturally occurring model of androgen independent brain masculinization. *Science* 209:418–20

Sheridan, P. J. 1979. Estrogen binding in the neonatal neocortex. *Brain Res.* 178:201–6

Sheridan, P. J. 1981. Unaromatized androgen is taken up by the neonatal rat brain: two receptor systems for androgen. *Dev. Neurosci.* 4:46–54

Short, R. V. 1974. Sexual differentiation of the brain of the sheep. In *Endocrinologie Sexuelle de la Période Périnatale*, ed. M. G. Forest, J. Bertrand, 32:121–42. Paris: INSERM

Sigusch, V., Schorsch, E., Dannecker, M., Schmidt, G. 1982. Official statement by the German Society for Sex Research (Deutsche Gesellschaft für Sexualforschung e.V.) on the research of Prof. Dr. Gunter Dörner on the subject of homosexuality. *Arch. Sex. Behav.* 11:455–49

Slob, A. K., Baum, M. J., Schenck, P. E. 1978. Effects of the menstrual cycle, social grouping and exogenous progesterone on heterosexual interaction in laboratory housed stumptail macaques (*Macaca arctoides*). *Physiol. Behav.* 21:915–21

Slob, A. K., van der Schoot, P. 1982. Testosterone induced mounting behavior in adult female rats born in litters of different female to male ratios. *Physiol. Behav.* 28:1007–10

Södersten, P. 1975. Receptive behavior in developing female rats. *Horm. Behav.* 6:307–17

Sperry, R. W. 1981. Changing priorities. *Ann. Rev. Neurosci.* 4:1–15

Stumpf, W. E., Sar, M. 1978. Anatomical distribution of estrogen, androgen, progestin, corticosteroid and thyroid hormone target sites in the brain of mammals: phylogeny and ontogeny. *Am. Zool.* 18:435–45

Stumpf, W. E., Sar, M. 1979. Steroid hormone target cells in the extrahypothalamic brain stem and cervical spinal cord: neuroendocrine significance. *J. Steroid Biochem.* 11:801–7

Tennent, B. J., Smith, E. R., Davidson, J. M. 1982. Effects of progesterone implants in the habenula and midbrain on proceptive and receptive behavior in the female rat. *Horm. Behav.* 16:352–63

Thomas, D. A., Barfield, R. J., Etgen, A. M. 1982. Influence of androgen on the development of sexual behavior in rats I. *Horm. Behav.* 16:443–54

Thornton, J. E., Cadwallader, J. V., Goy, R. W. 1982. *An unusual organizational effect of prenatal testosterone on lordosis in guinea pigs*. Presented at East Coast Conf. Reprod. Behav., 14th, East Lansing, Mich.

Toran-Allerand, C. D. 1980. Sex steroids and the development of the newborn mouse hypothalamus and preoptic area *in vitro:* II. Morphological correlates and hormonal specificity. *Brain Res.* 189:413–27

Turner, J. W. Jr. 1975. Influence of neonatal androgen on the display of territorial marking behavior in the gerbil. *Physiol. Behav.* 15:265–70

van der Schoot, P. 1980. Effects of dihydrotestosterone and oestradiol on sexual differentiation in male rats. *J. Endocrinol.* 84:397–407

Van Horn, R. N., Eaton, G. G. 1979. Reproductive physiology and behavior in prosimians. In *The Study of Prosimian Behavior,* ed. G. A. Doyle, R. D. Martin, pp. 79–122. New York: Academic

Van Look, P. F. A., Hunter, W. M., Corker, C. S., Baird, D. T. 1977. Failure of positive feedback in normal men and subjects with testicular feminization. *Clin. Endocrinol.* 7:353–66

Verhoeven, G. 1980. Steroids and neuroendocrine activities. Effects of neurotransmitters and follicle stimulating hormone on the aromatization of androgens and the production of adenosine 3'5'-monophosphate by cultured testicular cells. *J. Steroid Biochem.* 12:315–22

Vito, C. C., Fox, T. O. 1982. Androgen and estrogen receptors in embryonic and neonatal rat brain. *Dev. Brain Res.* 2:97–110

Vom Saal, F. S., Bronson, F. H. 1978. *In utero* proximity of female mouse fetuses to males: effect on reproductive performance during later life. *Biol. Reprod.* 19:842–53

Wallen, K. 1982. Influence of female hormonal state on rhesus sexual behavior varies with space for social interaction. *Science* 217:375–76

Wallis, C. J., Luttge, W. G. 1980. Influence of estrogen and progesterone on glutamic acid decarboxylase activity in discrete regions of rat brain. *J. Neurochem.* 34:609–13

Ward, I. L. 1972. Prenatal stress feminizes and demasculinizes the behavior of males. *Science* 175:82–84

Ward, I. L., Weisz, J. 1980. Maternal stress alters plasma testosterone in fetal males. *Science* 207:328–29

Weisz, J., Gibbs, C. 1974. Metabolites of testosterone in the brain of the newborn female rat after an injection of tritiated testosterone. *Neuroendocrinology* 14:72–86

Whalen, R. E., Luttge, W. G. 1971. Perinatal administration of dihydrotestosterone to female rats and the development of reproductive function. *Endocrinology* 89:1320–22

Wilcox, J. N., Barclay, S. R., Feder, H. H. 1983. Administration of estradiol-17β in pulses to female guinea pigs: self-priming effects of estrogen on brain tissues mediating lordosis. *Physiol. Behav.* Submitted for publication

Wilcox, J. N., Feder, H. H. 1983. Long-term priming with a low dosage of estradiol benzoate or an antiestrogen (Enclomiphene) increases nuclear progestin receptor levels in brain. *Brain Res.* 266:243–51

Wilkinson, M., Herdon, H., Pearce, M., Wilson, C. 1979. Radioligand binding studies on hypothalamic noradrenergic receptors during the estrous cycle or after steroid injection in ovariectomized rats. *Brain Res.* 168:652–55

Williams, G. D., Williams, A. M. 1982. Sexual behavior and the menstrual cycle. See Dalton 1982, pp. 155–76

Wilson, J. D. 1979. Sex hormones and sexual behavior. *N. Engl. J. Med.* 300:1269–70

Wilson, J. D., Griffin, J. E., George, F. W., Leshin, M. 1981. The role of gonadal steroids in sexual differentiation. *Recent Prog. Horm. Res.* 37:1–39

Wilson, M. I. 1977. Characterization of the oestrous cycle and mating season of squirrel monkeys from copulatory behaviour. *J. Reprod. Fertil.* 51:57–63

Wingfield, J. C., Farner, D. S. 1979. Some endocrine correlates of renesting after loss of clutch or brood in the white-crowned sparrow, *Zonotrichia leucophrys gambelii. Gen. Comp. Endocrinol.* 38:322–31

Young, W. C. 1961. The hormones and mating

behavior. In *Sex and Internal Secretions,* ed. W. C. Young, 2:1173–1239. Baltimore: Willimas & Wilkins. 3rd ed.

Young, W. C. 1969. Psychobiology of sexual behavior in the guinea pig. *Adv. Study Behav.* 2:1–110

Young, W. C., Goy, R. W., Phoenix, C. H. 1964. Hormones and sexual behavior. *Science* 143:212–18

Young, W. C., Orbison, W. D. 1944. Changes in selected features of behavior in pairs of oppositely-sexed chimpanzees during the menstrual cycle and after ovariectomy. *J. Comp. Psychol.* 37:107–43

Ann. Rev. Psychol. 1984. 35:201–26

SPATIAL VISION

Gerald Westheimer

Department of Physiology-Anatomy, University of California,
Berkeley, California 94720

CONTENTS

INTRODUCTION

Visual experiences have certain attributes that are, so to speak, given, i.e. that do not yield further scientific insights on deeper analysis. Brightness and color are examples of such attributes, but the most celebrated of them are time and space, subject to much discussion in philosophical circles.

The word "space" has different connotations depending on the context. For mathematicians, a space is a manifold of one or more dimensions in which elements obey certain relationships. These relationships are freely invented, subject only to the constraint that they must be internally consistent, i.e. that

201

0066-4308/84/0201-0201$02.00

they are not mutually contradictory. But the word space was borrowed by mathematicians from its "common sense" use; it should, therefore, not be assumed that the obvious point of departure for an inquiry into human spatial responses is the apparatus developed around the word by mathematicians, be it that unitary descriptions of phenomena issue from it.

The immediate beginning of the subject is the simple intuitive statement that two visual experiences differ in an attribute, which is not brightness nor color nor time, but characterized by some phrase as "here" and "there." The next step is a further analysis of the properties of this attribute. For example, visual experiences having their origin in, say, stars in the sky may have their attributes compared and conventions established about this comparison: right and left, up and down, nearer and farther. When this is done systematically, it is found that a normal human observer's visual experiences in this domain—i.e. not color, brightness, or time but place or position—has three dimensions. That is to say, a single object can be displaced up or down without changing the value of its right/left or nearer/farther attribute.

Most of science has been carried out within such a framework. For example, all of physics can be reduced to the observation of coincidence of pointers with suitably designed marks on scales. And indeed, the psychophysical study of spatial vision has flowered using an absolute minimum of definitional overhead.

Scope of This Review

The determination of brightness thresholds is the most traditional method of studying the visual sensitivity. Quite early in the history of this discipline, the study of brightness thresholds was extended to encompass spatial factors as well. Intensity discrimination was measured as a function of stimulus area as early as 1877 by Ricco. This facet of intensity discrimination remained of interest during the days of Hecht's theory and has again moved into prominence with the advent of contemporary sets of spatially distributed stimuli, notably sinusoidal gratings and sombrero functions.

It is, therefore, important to distinguish between the studies in which spatial factors of the stimuli are being varied in the cause of investigating brightness coding and those deliberately directed to investigating the spatial sense of the eye. Brightness or color cues are, of course, necessary to mark spatial differences of stimuli. But, as was pointed out at the beginning of this review, a spatial attribute of a visual experience is so basic or, if you will, primitive, that its investigation on its own terms can be accepted as a matter of course. In experimental formulations this translates into asking subjects to make distinctions that are specifically spatial in nature. The breakpoint between studies of visual sensitivity and of spatial vision is most conveniently set where the inquiry extends beyond the detection of spatial inhomogeneity of the visual field. When the experimental subject has merely to determine whether during a stimulus presentation the field remained uniform or whether it was spatially differentiated, this would not yet be counted as research into spatial vision, but if the distinction had to be made between specific spatial configurations, it would.

DISCRIMINATION VS DETECTION   In this spirit, the many and thorough investigations into thresholds for single and multiple sinusoidal grating stimuli are regarded as beyond the scope of this review. It should be noted, however, that attempts are being made to bridge the gap between these two classes of experiments. Thus Thomas et al (1982) looked for the difference in target contrast needed for the detection of a stimulus and the contrast required to make a truly spatial judgment, in this case to correctly identify the orientation of a pattern. In a similar vein, Olzak & Thomas (1981) investigated the relationship between frequency discrimination of gratings and their detection, and King-Smith & Kulikowski (1981) investigated the relationship between the detection of the presence of a stimulus in a given time interval and the discrimination—whether it consisted of one or two lines. Asking a very specific question ("Are the detectors labelled?") concerning the number of channels for small patches of sinusoidal gratings, Watson & Robson (1981) also approached the subject by simultaneously employing the detection and discrimination criteria.

Except where it was thought appropriate to provide some perspective, this review is restricted to journal articles published during 1980, 1981, and 1982. It follows recent reviews in the *Annual Review of Psychology,* one on "Spatial Vision" by De Valois & De Valois (1980) and one on "Early Visual Processing" by Julesz & Schumer (1981). Not covered is a large volume of current research reports regularly appearing in abstracts of society meetings: Society of Neuroscience (Abstracts, Volumes 6–8, 1980–82), Association for Research in Vision and Ophthalmology (Supplements to *Investigative Ophthalmology,* Volumes 19, 20, 22, 1980–82), Optical Society of America (*Journal of the Optical Society of America,* Volumes 70–72, 1980–82), Physiological Society (*Journal of Physiology,* Volumes 298–333, 1980–82). Abstracts of contributions to several conferences also appeared in this period: Visual Mechanisms in Primates and Lower Mammals (*Experimental Brain Research,* 1980, 41:A1–40), IBRO Workshop on Neurobiology (*IBRO News* 1982, 10:5–41), and Fifth European Conference on Visual Perception (*Perception* 1982, 11:A1–36).

THE NEURON DOCTRINE

While the tradition, going back to Helmholtz, continues of seeking substrates in anatomy and physiology for visual responses, the conceptual gap separating these two approaches is beginning to attract the attention of reviewers (Barlow

1981, Uttal 1981, Westheimer 1981). Followers of what is often called the neuron doctrine (Marr 1982) seek the embodiment of a subject's response categorizations in individual neurons. This view has gained immeasurable support from neurophysiology during the last quarter of a century, predominantly in the area under review here, namely spatial vision. Specifically, it has been found that the optimum light configurations needed to elicit the maximal spike discharge from nerve cells is not always a point of light, as might be thought if one came to the subject from a study of the anatomy of the retina, which shows a mosaic of small tightly-packed receptors, or if one started with textbook preconceptions from geometry, with their idealizations of a point and their subsequent axiomatic development of the whole edifice of geometry (e.g. Euclid, Hilbert). Instead, the cells, already in the retina and certainly in the visual cortex of the mammal, respond best to complex patterns of light stimuli, called receptive fields (after original observations by Sherrington concerning the convergence of sensory stimuli on motoneurons). Characterizations of receptive fields of neurons in the visual sensory pathways of experimental animals is now a most widely practiced experimental procedure and is uncovering a rich diversity of cell classes.

It is here that the field has shown its greatest activity in the last few years. But the origin of this development goes back at least 100 years. In laying the foundation of physiological optics in the 1850s and 1860s, Helmholtz was content to leave wide open the mechanism of processing punctate neural images issuing from retinal receptors. His physicalist biases made him recognize the vast gap between the retinal image and what he knew to be involved in the ultimate cognitive ability of the human observer. He was, therefore, content to draw a parallel between the processing mechanism for the simplest visual phenomena and those playing a role in, for example, the acquisition of language. Some of his contemporaries, however, were bolder. Both Mach and Hering postulated that some visual phenomena were mediated by the operation of strictly physiological apparatuses. Neural recording from retinal ganglion cells, and later from cortical cells, has demonstrated that individual nerve cells have response properties—i.e. stimulus profiles for maximal impulse generation—matching those that may be expected if the visual phenomena were indeed stamped out already at that level of processing. For example, Mach bands, Hermann grids, etc imply an interaction of neural signals of opposite polarity ("The directly stimulated part reacts by increased dissimilation and the surround by increased assimilation"—Hering 1874), precisely what is found in the receptive field organization of cat retinal ganglion cells ("The discharge pattern of the central region is the opposite of that found in the periphery or surround"—Kuffler 1953).

The match between predictions from the psychophysics of the 1860s and 1870s and the recordings of neurophysiologists of the 1950s and 1960s, which can be read as a vindication of the research strategy of vision researchers, deserves closer examination. It is afforded by a more detailed statement of how these results were achieved. Mach and Hering studied what may actually be regarded as a visual illusion, in their case the appearance of dark and light bands on the two sides of a gradient of light. To Mach this meant that he was dealing with the overshoot in the response of a second-order system to a ramp function—a straight-out system's theorists way of analyzing the situations and, indeed, Mach was a physicist by training, albeit the most imaginative of his generation. But he did not shirk the physiological interpretation that there is interaction between the excitation of neighboring retinal points, a view given explicit formulation by Hering a few years later. Kuffler, on the other hand, recorded impulses from cat ganglion cells and found that they responded in one manner (on-responses) when one region of the retina was stimulated (the center of the receptive field) and in an opposite manner (off-responses) when another region was stimulated (concentric annular surround) and that this antagonism was evident also on simultaneous stimulation of center and surround. The current view of the situation, well articulated by Ratliff (1965), is that the retinal light distribution is "filtered" through concentric center/surround "units" (presumably retinal ganglion cells) and that the central representation of a visual scene consists of the output of an array of such units.

SPATIAL FILTERING

More recently there have been attempts to express this situation in quasi-mathematical terms. The most successful of these was first enunciated by Otto Schade (1956), who regarded the representations to "correspond to the addition of a large-diameter point image of negative intensity to the normal positive point image," and identified these two components as "error curves." In other words, Schade postulated that the filtering involved the operation of taking the algebraic sum of two concentric gaussian distributions. This is now called a DOG (difference of two gaussian) function (Wilson & Bergen 1979) and is identical to the formulation used for cat ganglion cell receptive fields by Rodieck (1965). Thus the stage is set for the next scene: if one were to succeed in stimulating a single such unit and its overall role were prominent enough to lead to a change in the perceived visual world—left otherwise unchanged—would the subject report a point of light, or a bright point surrounded by halo darker than the background? When Brindley (1982) implanted small electrodes in the cortex of blind humans, the subjects reported phosphenes looking like small points or patches of light, sometimes elongated and occasionally multiple patches. Of course, the implanted electrodes were large with respect to the size of individual cortical units.

It must be recognized that the identification of spatial filtering operations, which takes place by virtue of the funneling of the retinal image through center/surround units, is only one step in all the processing to which the visual stimulus is subjected and insufficient for any tolerably complete description of visual space perception in intact observers. The optical transformation between the physical object space of the eye and the optical retinal image is another stage, preceding it, whose properties are fairly well understood (Westheimer 1972). The fundamental difference between the two stages is that the former is much more complex, quite nonlinear and, by virtue of the structural differentiation of the retina in the fovea and retinal periphery, not isotropic.

There have been insistent attempts at mathematical formulations for this transformation process. We can sketch one at this level. Suppose one wishes to identify as succinctly as possible the properties of a retinal ganglion cell in the transformation process of object space $\rightarrow$ central visual representation. It is necessary at the outset to specify the orientation of the fixation axis (i.e. where the fovea points) and that the eye must be kept still. Two coordinates suffice for the location of the center of the cell's receptive field—either the retinal meridian and the eccentricity along it, or the x, y coordinates of a horizontal/vertical cartesian grid centered on the fovea. If it is accepted that the receptive field components are circular, concentric, and have a gaussian profile, there is need for four more parameters, the height and standard deviation of each of the two gaussian curves. To the extent that it is true that the center and surround have Gaussian profiles that have fixed ratios of heights and/or variances, the number of parameters for a single cell may be reduced. Because of the change of the descriptor parameters with retinal location (measured in alert monkeys by Dow et al 1981) it is obviously impossible to use a single homogeneous mathematical formulation for the transfer of excitation from retinal location (itself obtained by convolution of the object stimulus space with the eye's point spread function) into that of the ensemble of ganglion cell axons leaving the retina—even assuming the most unrestricted conditions of linear signal processing and knowledge of the location of the individual receptive fields.

Inquiry into this kind of analysis is appropriate also for central representations of the visual scene. The lateral geniculate nucleus used to be thought of as a simple relay station, but this seems an inadequate view in the light of recent anatomical and electrophysiological findings. The first cortical projection, the striate areas 17, 18 and 19, have been a favorite locale for receptive field characterization ever since Hubel's (1982) and Wiesel's (1982) collaboration in the 1960s. Most receptive fields here seem elongated and furnished with inhibitory surrounds, but their sensitivity profiles can take a variety of shapes. A development of uncommon interest here is the relatively recent identification of purely monocular cells with small concentric receptive fields. The celebrated columnar organization for orientations of receptive fields and ocular dominance is now being shown to be interrupted by clusters of cells of a different class.

Nevertheless the interest runs high to produce a unitary description for the spatial transformation that the visual scene undergoes in the elaboration of the primary cortical representation. To the extent that it is possible, this is a definite advance over such a description at the retinal level because the additional changes are no doubt part of the total process of perception.

The most prominent difference between receptive fields at the retina and the cortex seems to be the fact that most of the latter are elongated. This requires that not only the x, y coordinates of the center of the receptive field be specified, but also the angular orientation of the major axis. Even if there is a clear excitatory center and inhibitory surround, this will demand at least the same number of additional parameters as those for retinal receptive fields. Their specialization (or specificity of trigger features, as many sensory physiologists would say) is bringing with it an increase in the information needed to give a full account of the stimulus acceptance properties of these cells. Global thinkers in biology like to regard some cells in the frog as "bug detectors," but the graphic immediacy of such description masks the difficulty of its translation into conventional geometrical terms. We have here in a nutshell the conceptual problems at the root of a successful apposition of the disciplines of perception and cognition on the one hand and artificial intelligence, machine recognition, and robotics on the other.

One shorthand way of dealing with this question is to assume that there is uniform distribution of cells of a given class. This is, of course, an unacceptable generalization if the whole visual field is considered, but it is not unreasonable for small patches just a few times larger than the receptive field diameters of the cells considered (Robson 1980). The situation is not too different from what was said above about the retina, only here one thinks mainly of linearly extended patterns such as lines, bars, and gratings.

The now conventional view is that the visual signals when they reach the cortex are routed through cells that are excited by light reaching the center of their elongated, oriented receptive fields and inhibited by light falling on adjoining regions. Although there are reports of cells with receptive fields with multiple peaks, these are rare. It has never been demonstrated conclusively that the typical cell's inhibitory surround is flanked by another excitatory region. Some cells show end-inhibition, i.e. reduction of their sensitivity if stimulation extends beyond the major region of excitability in their long direction. The general nature of these receptive fields makes it convenient to locate them in the first instance by using extended targets, such as lines of various orientations, that are swept through the visual field. This leads naturally into inquiries as to the range of orientations to which the cell are most responsive, i.e. their orientation tuning. Much effort has gone into such determinations, and the data show half-widths at half-height varying from 2 to 10 degrees, depending on the type of cell and the animal preparation. That is, for a given cell the stimulus orientation has to be changed by 2 to 10 degrees away from the optimum to reduce the cell's discharge rate to half. In this connection it is of interest to note that the orientation discrimination of the human observer for short foveal lines is less than one degree.

Another popular approach to mapping cortical receptive fields is by use of grating targets. This had its origin in the use of sinusoidal test patterns for electrical devices, which in a natural way was extended to optical (Duffieux 1946) and electro-optical devices (Schade 1956). The application to optical systems is particularly appropriate because optical imaging calculations use Fourier analysis implicitly, since the electromagnetic diffraction equations are Fourier transforms. This leads to the significant property that grating targets whose spatial intensity profile is sinusoidal will have optical images of a similar profile with changes merely in the modulation depth (gain) and phase. The widespread use of optical transfer curves, showing gain and phase changes for sinusoidal targets of a range of spatial frequencies, as quality indicators of optical and electro-optical devices, has been taken over into the optics of the eye and is most helpful there to insure matches between instrumentation and the optical capacity of the eye. Such an analysis included the resolving power of the eye as an optical system, but also extends to the way coarser targets are handled, something of value for optical aberrations and defocusing.

Sinusoidal grating targets have been found most useful in plotting receptive fields of cortical cells because they are oriented and cover an extended portion of the field. Moreover, a sinusoidal grating target within the right range of spatial frequencies will address the cell unusually well, because it simultaneously delivers appropriate stimuli—excitatory or inhibitory, i.e. more or less light respectively, than a uniform background—to the individual components of the cell's receptive field. The standard way of conducting these experiments is to obtain spatial frequency tuning curves in much the same way as one obtains orientation tuning curves, i.e. by measuring the firing response of cells to sinusoidal gratings of fixed contrast and orientation but with a range of spatial frequencies. While relatively easy to conduct, such experiments leave the specification of the cell's spatial response incomplete. In the language of systems theory, they measure only the power spectrum, while the full characterization needs amplitude and phase. This distinction is not trivial because it is not possible to reconstruct a cell's actual spatial properties from the power spectrum alone—it gives neither the actual location of the receptive area within the total extent of the visual field nor the particular shape of the excitatory/inhibitory profile. Identical tuning curves can be seen in cells of quite different receptive field shapes and positions. The recognition of this deficiency of the "Fourier" view of visual processing has led to a greater emphasis on the phase component of the grating stimuli, particularly to the relative phase when the stimulus consists of gratings of several spatial frequencies.

Recently there has been a move to seek reconciliation between the admittedly local processing exemplified by the restricted spatial extent of receptive fields and the extended spatial acceptance properties implied by a Fourier view of spatial visual processing. After all, in its strict interpretation, Fourier analysis is based on infinite sinusoidal components. The more limited the frequency band of a pattern the higher the number of oscillations. Couched in terms of spatial vision, the more narrowly tuned the spatial frequency band of an analyzing module (such as a cell) the more spatially extended its receptive field has to be and the more zones of opposite polarity it will exhibit. But almost universally, receptive fields show only one clear band of surround inhibition so their spacial frequency specificity cannot be regarded, measured by the standards of strict Fourier theory, as anything but rather feeble.

As quantum theory developed 50 years ago, the dilemma of a wave formulation of particles and the fact that they could also be localized was handled by a formulation involving gaussian wave-packets, i.e. sine and cosine waves of fixed frequency with a gaussian error curve as amplitude envelope. These are now called Gabor functions (1950). Besides having the obvious advantage of being spatially restricted, they also come in orthogonal pairs: the sine function crosses zero in the center of the field and matches a band-pass edge detector; the cosine function can be made to look like a Mexican-hat function by the right choice of spatial frequency and gaussian space constant. Gabor functions can be found to fit most receptive fields. But such a curve-fitting procedure skirts physiological questions of the presence, and if so, the interactions underlying secondary excitatory bands of receptive fields.

The widespread acceptance of Mexican-hat and Gabor functions as models of receptive fields of visual neurons and hence of the spatial filtering operations to which visual signals are being subjected has resolved the dominant question of spatial vision of the 1970s: the visual system does not perform a Fourier analysis of the optical image in the way Fourier analysis is understood by mathematicians and systems analysts. Processing is local, receptive fields have strictly identifiable positions, and features can be localized with excellent precision on the basis of information of limited spatial extent.

CHANNELS

A recent development is the emphasis of the concept of channels in spatial vision. While there have been only one or two attempts at more rigorous definitions of channels (Westheimer 1981, Regan 1982), the general idea is not too different from the separation of color signals into three compartments. In the wavelength domain this is accomplished by three cone pigments. Once a photon has been absorbed in a cone containing the red pigment, the signal generated there follows a certain path which is distinct and different from that generated in green or blue cones. This is not a radical view and seems easily compatible with Müller's law of specific nerve energies, but there is an important additional concept involved. There is no immediate problem in accepting qualitative differences between the effects of acoustic and visual stimulation: both the physical variables and the neural paths and their connectivity are different. In color vision, however, the stimulus separation occurs within a single physical variable, wavelength. Moreover, the acceptance curves along the wavelength axis of the three cone pigments *overlap,* so that a stimulus of a given wavelength will usually yield a signal in all three color channels, albeit of different magnitudes. Light of a wavelength that is called green generates activities in all three primary color channels.

The idea of spatial channels arose in connection with the modulation sensitivity measurements of the human observer by Campbell and Robson in 1968. These workers found that square and sine wave grating stimuli had characteristically different modulation thresholds, and they interpreted this to mean that the third harmonic, which marks the essential difference between a sine and a square wave grating, has its threshold determined by a mechanism different from that for the fundamental. This led Campbell and Robson to postulate that the modulation sensitivity curve represented the envelope of a number of narrower curves, much as the eye's photopic luminosity curve can in a beginning discourse be regarded as the envelope of the spectral sensitivity curves of the primary color channels. There are, in this view, a number of independent mechanisms, each tuned to a narrow band of spatial frequencies. Adaptation studies (Blakemore & Campbell 1970, and many subsequent studies) reveal an increase in threshold for sinusoidal patterns following lengthy exposures (of the order of minutes) to patterns of the same and adjacent spatial frequencies. There is as yet no unanimity of opinion of the tuning widths of the underlying mechanisms that such experiments allow one to postulate, but they seem to be less than one octave—a term borrowed from music and denoting a factor of two on the frequency scale.

It is a worthwhile exercise to establish what information a visual system with such characteristics can extract from the visual field. At the outset, the reciprocal relationship between the space domain (Where is the target? What is its light distribution?) and the spatial frequency domain (in which modulation sensitivity and tuning curves are specified) has to be recognized. Thus there are two complementary descriptions of visual targets and receptive fields of neurons in the visual pathways. In the conventional method one would specify the light distribution in the visual field. When the spatial frequency description first became popular, one was satisfied to specify what amounts to the power spectrum of the patterns. But it is not possible to reconstruct a visual target or a receptive field from the power spectrum. First of all, position information has been lost—all targets or receptive fields of the same pattern have the same power spectrum, regardless of where in the visual field they are situated. Secondly, patterns even in the same retinal position and with the same power spectrum can look quite different—they can, for example, be sensitive to edges (have odd symmetry) or to bars (have even symmetry). In order to encode all the information that is needed for a full reconstruction of the target pattern or the receptive field, both amplitude and phase responses across the spatial frequency spectrum have to be provided. Thus even if the visual system processed the visual scene through a series of channels of limited spatial frequency acceptance, the amplitude of the response in each channel would not be sufficient without the phase. In theory, this can be done also via the amplitude response in properly paired sine and cosine channels, i.e. channels with 90 degree phase differences but otherwise identical.

As full information encoders of the visual scene, simple spatial frequency channel models are, therefore, inadequate. Human observers, primates, and indeed many of the other mammals whose visual pathways are subjected to single-unit analysis are capable of many remarkable spatial judgments. It is perhaps too early to ask of models of spatial processing that they account for the majority of them, but it must always be expected that they at least leave room for them.

The essence of the channel concept in spatial vision transcends, however, the spatial frequency approach. Wilson, in a series of papers in the late 1970s used more localized patterns which probed the center/surround nature of visual processing and mapped out their sensitivity as a function of what he termed their "space constant," i.e. the second moment of their constituent gaussian functions. The pattern was modulated into a uniform background and the measurement was that of the minimum contrast required to bring it to visibility. In any retinal position, the threshold was least for an intermediate space constant and increased for both larger and smaller ones. Assuming that this maps the sensitivity of a single, spatially homogeneous population of detectors, one can derive their spatial sensitivity profiles, occasionally called their "line-spread function" (see Wilson 1978), leaning on the term traditionally used in the description of the optical impulse function. Here it would designate the pattern of (positive or negative) excitation in a theoretical row of detecting units for an object impulse function. The next step was to calculate the response of such an array of detectors for sinusoidal light patterns of different spatial frequencies and compare it with the measured modulation transfer function of the visual system in the same retinal location. The two do not match. There are deficits both at the higher and lower spatial frequencies.

In an elaborate scheme, Wilson & Bergen (1979) built a model to account for the responses in the full spatial frequency range for both transient and sustained stimulation. They postulated four populations of responders, differing in their temporal sensitivity and their spatial response profiles, and proceeded to demonstrate how this can satisfactorily account for the modulation sensitivity curve. It has subsequently been pointed out (Marr et al 1980) that the population of smallest detecting units is still too wide to account for the ordinary resolution limit of the eye.

Wilson's populations of detecting units are called channels. The salient point of this model is not whether there are exactly four such channels, but (a) that one is dealing with homogeneous populations, at least in any one retinal location, and (b) that these are of the same general type and merely differing in their space constants (and also in their temporal response characteristics). Many elaborations of this general channel scheme (e.g. Marr 1982, Sakitt & Barlow 1982) accept the assumptions, but others do not. Campbell et al (1981), for example, suggest that the modulation sensitivity for low spatial frequency sinusoidal patterns, which Wilson and Bergen fitted by a channel populated by long space constant DOG detectors, can be accounted for by postulating not Mexican hat but gradient detecting functions. This is an important departure from the Wilson channel model because there would no longer be just one general type of detector. This turn in thinking is also important because it returns consideration from the spatial frequency domain back into the space domain. Even so, Stromeyer et al (1982) found that low spatial frequency stimuli were subject to adaptation by low frequency spatial stimuli, and this implies the existence of a mechanism for their detection as such.

Evidence for a wide distribution of receptive field sizes in a given region of the monkey visual field can be seen in the study of De Valois, Albrecht & Thorell (1982). Work from that laboratory is always expressed in the spatial frequency domain, but it is relatively easy to recalculate this into terms of retinal distance. Significantly, however, these workers do not find any segregation of receptive fields into size bins; instead there seems to be a uniform distribution of sizes over a wide range.

Thus there seems to be a wide-ranging consensus that there is size coding—in addition to position coding—of visual signals at an early stage of analysis and that the size tag does not only affect contrast threshold but that it is available for use later on in the elaboration of visual percepts. There is, however, no strong evidence for a segregation of size signals into clearly distinguishable bins similar to what happens to wavelength in color vision.

BINOCULAR VISION

An immediate aspect of seeing an object binocularly is whether it appears single or double. There are two components here: the vergence component of oculomotor control, which allows changes in positioning of one eye relative to the other, and the facility of "fusion," where single vision is reported over a range of relative target positions on the two retinas. Fusion is a strictly subjective phenomenon and is determined by the subject's response of "single" or "double" while targets are placed on the two retinas in different relative positions; a meaningful experiment on this topic requires that vergence eye movements be factored out. As was first clearly pointed out by Panum in 1860, stereoscopic depth perception is quite separate from fusion; fusion of a target is not a precondition of stereoscopic depth discrimination. Measurement of Panum's fusional areas, i.e. the range of relative target positions for which singleness is reported, goes back a long time, but it has been extended recently to two additional variables. Schor & Tyler (1981) found that the size of fusional areas depends on the rate of disparity movement. Targets were oscillated sinusoidally in opposite directions in the two eyes in the absence of eye movements. At a frequency of 0.1 Hz, 20 minutes of arc disparity was tolerated without diplopia, but at 5 Hz only 2.5 minutes of arc. There is also a difference between horizontal and vertical; fusional areas are wider horizontally than vertically.

According to Burt & Julesz (1980), nearby objects modify the disparity limits for binocular fusion. They "warp" the fusional space, creating "forbidden zones" in which changes in disparity are too steep for fusion.

The sharpness of objects is also a factor in their being seen in diplopia. Kulikowski (1978) found that objects with sharply outlined contours and patterns with gradual luminance gradients have different ranges of disparity over which they are seen singly, or at least not as rival double images: the range of single vision is inversely related to spatial frequencies present in the patterns. Using sinusoidal gratings of different spatial frequencies in the two eyes, Levinson & Blake (1979) found that fusion breaks down when cycle width in one eye exceeds that in the other by about 20%.

Anomalous retinal correspondence is a much neglected subject. It occurs in entrenched, early-onset strabismics who show an apparent fusion of retinal images on widely disparate locations, together with diplopia when identical stimuli are presented to the two foveas which normally strictly correspond and hence should elicit single binocular vision. Nelson (1981) has worked up a connection between this syndrome and the mechanism of sensory fusion, suggesting that they obey similar principles. The significance of these ideas lies in the use of anomalous correspondence as a pointer to the role of plasticity in the development of normal correspondence.

Stereoscopy is an aspect of vision that has also been included in developmental studies in infants (see DEVELOPMENTAL STUDIES), in methodological studies (see METHODS USED FOR MEASUREMENTS), and in receptive field mapping of single cortical units in the cat and monkey visual cortex (see VISUAL PATHWAYS).

Insights continue to be gained by psychophysical research into the mode of interaction of the signals reaching the brain through the two eyes. Richards &

Foley (1981) studied the interaction of differing complex waveforms presented to each eye in yielding a three-dimensional slant perception. The interocular transfer of aftereffects is being subjected to greater scrutiny as more sophisticated experiments uncover just how subtly it may depend on the test conditions. An example of this situation is the transfer of adaptation to a set of tilted lines. Moulden (1980) found that binocular adaptation has more of a monocular tested aftereffect than monocular adaptation of the other eye. He used a single grating target. Wolfe & Held (1981), on the other hand, using a chevron type of pattern containing two grating orientations, found that there was more of a monocularly measured aftereffect when the other eye was adapted than when both eyes were adapted. However, when they repeated Moulden's experiment in the supine position, they obtained results similar to their own findings with the chevron targets (Wolfe & Held 1982), which are not as dependent on the perceived vertical (and the effect of gravity on it) as a single grating pattern.

In stereoblind subjects who have no interocular transfer of the tilt aftereffect there is nevertheless an interocular transfer of grating threshold elevation following monocular inspection of a high contrast grating (Anderson et al 1980).

New results on stereoscopic aspects of visual illusions have been obtained by Troscianko (1982), who studied the Herrman grid effect and concluded that his results strongly indicate a concentric peripheral perceptive field mechanism as being responsible for a large part of the illusion.

The random dot stereogram technique has been thoroughly reviewed by Julesz & Schumer (1981). It has recently been used by Adler & Grusser (1982) in their sigma-movement studies; this effect can also be demonstrated with stroboscopically illuminated random dot patterns containing monocularly invisible stripes. Rogers & Graham (1982) see similarities in the visual system's sensitivity to motion parallax information and to disparity when both are carried by random dot patterns. A newer view of the process of decoding random stereograms made of lines rather than squares was presented by Nishihara & Poggio (1982).

Detection of vertical disparity is apparently not a closed chapter. Extending his earlier work (Arditi et al 1981), which was subjected to criticism by Mayhew & Frisby (1982), Arditi (1982) concluded that the matching of oblique contours shown with vertical disparities occurs between points which are nearest in a fixed binocular coordinate map, not just by purely horizontal point matching. Mayhew & Longuet-Higgins (1982), however, basing their case on computational arguments involving the detection of the orientation of planes seen with asymmetric convergence, insist that vertical disparities can be utilized in practice and dismiss previous experimental rejections of this view as being incorrectly designed.

DEVELOPMENTAL STUDIES

Spatial capabilities are now regularly included in the studies of infant vision. Although the preferential viewing techniques are now routinely employed, some procedural details remain to be ironed out (Banks et al 1982, Teller et al 1982).

A possible role of optical factors in the improvement with age of visual acuity of infants was examined by Williams & Boothe (1981), using objective measures of the line-spread function of monkey babies. The optics are good at birth, but there is an improvement of contrast transmission at all spatial frequencies with age; adult levels are reached at 13 weeks, when visual acuity is still improving.

Studying the development of grating acuity with age with behavioral techniques in preterm human infants, Dobson et al (1980) came to the conclusion that visual acuity is more closely correlated with age from conception than from birth.

The preferential looking technique is yielding firm results as regards the emergence of stereopsis in infants (Fox et al 1980, Held et al 1980). Using random dots, Fox et al estimate the time of onset of stereopsis in human infants to be 3.5 to 6 months. Held et al saw the stereoacuity of 16 infants improve from a threshold greater than 1 degree to less than 1 arc minute between the ages of 10 and 20 weeks, most of the change occurring in a small fraction of this time span. For kittens, there is a rapid improvement during the fifth and sixth weeks (Timney 1981).

There have been suggestions that depth perception with uncrossed disparity (i.e. behind the fixation plane) is subserved by a mechanism separate from that with crossed disparity. There is, therefore, considerable interest in the findings of Birch et al (1982) that crossed stereoacuity in human infants develops earlier but at approximately the same rate as uncrossed stereoacuity.

All aspects of visual neural development have been reviewed extensively by Movshon & van Sluyters (1981).

AMBLYOPIA

The syndromes associated with disuse of one eye in binocular species are receiving a good deal attention by researchers. Of interest in this review are the several studies published in the last 3 years that illuminate the mechanisms by which human eyes might become amblyopic and that characterize in detail the deficits of amblyopic eyes.

There now appears to be a consensus that there is a difference between strabismic and anisometropic amblyopia, i.e. amblyopia associated with strabismus when the other eye is used exclusively for fixation or at least is strongly preferred, and the amblyopia in an eye that has a prominently different refractive state from the other. The threshold modulation sensitivity curves in the two kinds of amblyopia are not the same (Hess et al 1980, 1981). Contrast matching above threshold is also different in the two syndromes (Hess & Bradley 1980). Severe amblyopia subsequent to stimulus deprivaton early in life, such as may occur in a case of congenital uniocular cataract, is more like the anisometropic than the strabismic kind.

That the deficit in amblyopia is not secondary to unsteady fixation was demonstrated by Higgins et al (1982), who found no significant change in the modulation sensitivity curve with image stabilization. Abnormalities in the detection of temporal modulation in amblyopic eyes were investigated by Manny & Levi (1982) and by Wesson & Loop (1982). Reaction times are longer when measured through the amblyopic eye than the normal eye of the same observer (Hamasaki & Flynn 1981). Pattern movement detection at higher spatial frequencies is more impaired than is the detection threshold for such pattern (Rentschler et al 1981), yet there remains a substantial amount of interocular transfer of motion aftereffects (Keck & Price 1982).

In patients with permanent unilateral concomitant esotropia, where fixation occurs with only one eye, there is deep suppression in the nasal retina receiving the (diplopic) image of the fixation target. Long standing cases of this condition exhibit a reduced visual acuity in the near periphery of the nasal retina of the amblyopic eye compared to the temporal retina of the same eye (Sireteanu & Fronius 1981). This is not found in alternating esotropes, who have normal peripheral acuity throughout the visual field (Sireteanu 1982). Eyes suffering from strabismic amblyopia also do not exhibit the familiar "oblique" effect, i.e. a reduction in sensitivity and acuity for gratings along oblique meridians. Instead they have a "vertical effect," i.e. a lower resolution for vertical than horizontal gratings (Sireteanu & Singer 1980).

Amblyopes are now beginning to be probed with spatial tests more sophisticated than visual resolution and modulation sensitivity. Bedell & Flom (1981) had patients execute relative directionalization and spatial partitioning tasks with their amblyopic eyes and found consistent errors. This suggested to them that monocular space perception of strabismic amblyopic eyes is severely distorted and characterized by local expansions and contractions of horizontal spatial values. Edges—which they call "broad-band aperiodic stimuli"—were used by Levi et al (1981) to demonstrate that amblyopic eyes have a wider sensitivity profile than normal.

Amblyopic eyes are now also being tested for hyperacuity (Levi & Klein 1982a). Vernier acuity of ansisometropic amblyopes is similar to normals when scaled to the respective grating acuity limits, but strabismic amblyopes have poorer vernier acuity than might be expected even after such scaling, a phenomenon attributed to a "crowding effect" (Levi & Klein 1982b). An interesting concept, based on Barlow's (1981) theory of hyperacuity, is the possibility than the nondeprived eye of an amblyope may have supernormal vernier acuity. This might occur if vernier acuity depended on the number of available cortical cells and the wider ocular dominance columns devoted to the nondeprived eye gave the latter access to more cells. Preliminary findings pointing that way (Freeman & Bradley 1980) have not found confirmation (Johnson et al 1982, Levi & Klein 1982b).

Animal models of amblyopia are beginning to be helpful. Although amblyopia need not be featured in the rare cases of naturally occurring strabismus in monkeys (Kiorpes & Boothe 1981), it is possible to produce anisometropic amblyopia in macaques by atropinization of one eye during development (Booth et al 1982). Such eyes show loss of sensitivity at all spatial frequencies. Kittens raised with astigmatic visual deprivation showed diminished acuity through the affected eye (in all orientations!) but no optical changes in the eye, nor any resolution deficit or orientation bias of ganglion cell responses (Thibos & Levick 1982). In strabismic amblyopia of kittens there is also normal resolution of retinal ganglion cells according to Cleland et al (1982), who could not confirm earlier claims for abnormalities at that level (Chino et al 1980). These animal studies thus provide good evidence for a cortical site of amblyopia and have allowed Singer et al (1980) to postulate a central gating process which prevents signals from the deviated eye from consolidating cortical pathways ascending from layer IV to supragranular layers.

METHODS USED FOR MEASUREMENTS

Use of Moiré fringes for measuring visual acuity is desribed (Lotmar 1980). They can give gratings of easily variable pitch. It has been shown that there is an excellent correlation between subjectively measured checkerboard visual acuity and averaged pupil responses of seven cycles in which checkerboards were alternated with blank fields of the same average luminance (Slooter & van Norren 1980). The visual evoked response continues to be a useful measure of visual resolution. It was employed by Julesz et al (1980) to study human random-dot stereopsis and by Bonds (1982) to demonstrate that the cat has an "oblique effect." In the human, it was shown that a patient with unilateral optic nerve section of traumatic origin has no visual evoked potential nor any pattern evoked retinal response when the affected eye was stimulated even though its ERG was normal (Dawson et al 1982). Behavioral techniques for measuring visual spatial functions in experimental animals are now widely employed; the results are referred to throughout this review. In an ablation study involving the frontal eye fields and the superior colliculus, Collin & Cowey (1980) found the colliculus to be the more important structure for displacement detection in the rhesus monkey.

Methodological considerations enter into the classification of stereopsis into local and global (Dunlop et al 1980). It is possible to design simple line stereograms that test local stereopsis and contain no monocular cues (Westheimer & McKee 1980).

VISUAL PATHWAYS

A great deal of research activity is devoted to animal studies of the visual pathways, some of it of relevance for the understanding of human spatial vision. Detailed survey of the cat retina is uncovering interesting new facts. Kolb et al (1981) could identify 22 types of amacrine cells and 23 types of ganglion cells. Ganglion cell responses have an orientation basis: their responses to sinusoidal grating stimuli vary with orientation in the manner of a cosine function (Levick & Thibos 1982).

Spatial characterization of the receptive field of cortical neurons in the cat and the monkey continues to yield more detailed information. Inhibitory interaction effects are being emphasized both for spatial stimuli within individual receptive fields (Heggelund 1981) and between cells (Burr et al 1981). Responses to sinusoidal gratings, with their implication of spatial frequency coding, are now being compared with those of patterns emphasizing local changes, such as edges and bars (Albrecht et al 1980, Kulikowski & Bishop 1981, Kulikowski et al 1981, Pollen & Ronner 1982) and even within the spatial frequency framework there is more emphasis on tuning width (De Valois et al 1982) and phase relationships (Lee et al 1981, Pollen & Ronner 1981). Interesting anatomical studies allow some workers (Tootell et al 1981, Tolhurst & Thompson 1982) to come to grips with the concepts of spatial frequency columns in the cortex. The fine structure of orientation tuning is also being investigated (Berardi et al 1982; De Valois, Yund & Hepler 1982). A theoretical analysis was presented by Marcelja (1980).

New viewpoints about the binocularity of striate cortical cells are emerging. Hammond (1980) found ocular dominance to be time dependent, and Sillito et al 1980 demonstrated significant changes in ocular dominance of cells during bicuculline application, thus revealing GABA-mediated inhibition normally suppressing nondominant eye input. Kato et al 1982 also conclude that virtually all cells in the cat cortex are either binocularly discharged or strongly binocularly influenced. That this binocular influence can be disparity dependent is shown by the detailed study of Ferster (1981), whose findings have strong implications for the neural basis of depth perception. Even more relevant to the mechanisms of human stereopsis is the work of Poggio & Talbot (1981), who are able to delineate the disparity tuning of foveal cortical units in the alert monkey. Regan & Cynader (1982, Cynader & Regan 1982) are continuing to describe the property of neurons in the cat striate cortex signaling motion in depth.

Quite ingeneous mathematical modeling is now being applied to the formation of the particular columnar organization seen in the visual cortex (Swindale 1980, 1982, Bienenstock et al 1982).

FOVEA AND RETINAL PERIPHERY

The columnar organization of the visual cortex has been viewed as an expression of a modular arrangement of the visual system, with the modules being strung along, each performing a similar operation on an input from a different part of the visual field. Because the grain of the retina is manifestly different in the primate, going from the fovea to the periphery (with roughly circular symmetry), there is an interest in the structural and functional variations with retinal eccentricity. Dow et al (1981) performed a detailed investigation of the magnification factor and receptive field size of the striate cortex in the monkey.

There is need for caution in applying simple scales to the size of ocular dominance columns in arriving at magnification factors (Sakitt 1982). Imaginative formulations of how this spatial mapping could lead to such phenomena as size and other perceptual invariances (Schwartz 1980) do not, however, remain unchallenged (Cavanagh 1982).

Several psychophysical studies addressed themselves to the variation of thresholds for detection and resolution (Lie 1980), sine wave contrasts (Kroon et al 1980), and hyperacuity (Westheimer 1982) with eccentricity. The idea of single magnification factors which would allow all peripheral and foveal visual functions to be superimposed on each other does not, however, fit all measurements.

At eccentricities larger than 20 degrees, the oblique effect seems to be replaced by a meridional resolution effect: the resolution is systematically best for meridionally oriented gratings (Rovamo et al 1982).

SPATIAL JUDGMENTS

One of the most enduring research topics in human spatial perception is the judgment of line orientations, especially since it is often thought to have immediate affinity with the elongated receptive field characteristics of cells in the visual cortex. Scobey (1982) had subjects discriminate between a fixed number of possible line orientations and found that their performance in this task improved with line length up to about 12 minutes of arc in the fovea, 28 minutes in the 5 degree, and 45 minutes in the 10 degree periphery. The tilt aftereffect also used to investigate binocular interaction (see above) was shown to summate linearly with a simultaneous tilt illusion (Magnussen & Kurtenbach 1980). The influence of movement and eye fixation on it was investigated by Carney (1982), and it was embedded in a scheme involving inhibition, disinhibition, and summation of orientation detectors (Kurtenbach & Magnussen 1981).

In many ways the simplest spatial judgment is the detection of target displacement. Johnson & Scobey (1980, 1982, Scobey & Johnson 1981) have studied it as a function of stimulus luminance, line length, duration of movement—both unidirectional and oscillatory movement—and presence of a reference line. Hadani et al (1980) found that at 7″ to 14″ absolute displacement a random dot pattern could be detected, and when it occurred as a relative displacement, the value was as low as 2″ to 6″. When there was a reference circle 3 degrees in diameter and the interstimulus interval .9 seconds, the detection of the presence of a spatial offset of a spot had only a slightly lower threshold than the discrimination of direction of offset (Allick et al 1982). Using dark intervals ranging up to .8 seconds, Matin et al (1981) gauged the effects of eye movements and short-term memory on the discrimination of vernier offsets of sequentially flashed lines.

Hyperacuity

The topic of hyperacuity, i.e. spatial discriminations involving retinal distances much smaller than the diameter of receptors or the resolution limit, is generating further measurements and deeper theoretical probing (Fahle & Poggio 1981). Hirsch & Hylton (1982), approaching the subject both as spatial frequency discrimination and spatial interval discrimination tasks, are seeking fine structure consonant with spatial channel separations. Watt & Andrews (1982) identify the hyperacuity element in detection of contour curvature, and Hamerly & Springer (1981) identify it in the detection of edge raggedness and the discrimination of blur in edges and lines (Hamerly & Dvorak 1981).

Morgan & Watt (1982a,b) investigated further the mechanism of identifying the three-dimensional trajectory which a moving bar seems to follow when it is exposed intermittently both in time and space; they were able to show that simple eye movement explanations are insufficient. The more general question of sampling and spatial interpolation which such findings imply was addressed experimentally by Morgan & Watt (1982c) and Nyman & Laurinen (1982) and theoretically by Snyder (1982). A comprehensive review of the subject of hyperacuity was presented by Westheimer (1981).

SPATIAL COHERENCE OF PATTERNS

Attention is now being focused on more global questions of just how patterns emerge from ensembles of apparently random dots. van Meeteren & Barlow (1981), for example, are wondering about the statistical efficiency for detecting sinusoidal modulation of average dot density in random figures. Phenomenal coherence of noise patterns was investigated by Baker & Braddick (1982b) and, for stroboscopic movement, by Koenderink & van Doorn (1980). Nakayama (1981) found that differential motion of two fields of random dots can be detected with hyperacuity thresholds. Baker & Braddick (1982a), investigating the segregation of differentially moving areas of random dots, concluded that the correspondence problem is solved by short-range motion detection acting on each region separately.

Jenkins & Cole (1982) explored the visual processes for detecting a target in a complex background by size difference, and Adelson & Movshon (1982) investigated the phenomenal coherence of sinusoidal gratings of differing orientation, contrast, spatial frequency, and direction and speed of movement.

COMPUTATIONAL THEORIES

No review of vision research in the 1980s will be complete without reference to the impulse given it by the group around David Marr. Basing his approach strongly on what has been called "artificial intelligence," Marr emphasized the three levels of understanding visual information processing: hardware implementation, representation, and algorithm and computational theory. The latter, which concerns itself with the goal of the process and the logic of the strategy by which it is carried out, can, according to Marr, be considered apart from the next lower, that is, where the manner of representation of the input and output and the algorithms for the transformation are studied. Finally there is the level of the physical representation of the variables. As applied to spatial vision, the eye and neural structures obviously belong to the level of hardware implementation. The rules according to which neural signals are gated and compared—how, for example, an array of local retinal signals are made to interact to yield stereoacuity or how they are sorted out to see depth in a random dot stereogram—belong into the second realm, that of the algorithms for transforming signals. Marr, however, stresses the need for considering vision at a yet more overarching level, namely of the kind of problems that need to be solved by the visual process, i.e. the "what" rather than the "how."

In practice, the Marr approach starts with the identification of a problem, say, the fact that it is a three-dimensional pattern that has to be recognized. Knowledge of the hardware available—optical images, placement of the eyes—allows models to be created for the algorithms being utilized. This approach is bound to be fruitful, particularly since there is the danger of the whole field being overwhelmed by a plethora of research results of how single cells (even in the alert primate) respond to isolated stimuli. The high level of skill with which this approach is practiced by the leaders of this group (Ullman 1979, Marr 1982) has generated an enthusiasm for it which is creating a marked change in the atmosphere in which spatial vision research is carried out (see, for example, Crick et al 1981). Models constitute in essence a correlation between two ends of a process. There are, of course, qualitative differences between models; those being developed by the computational theorists in vision have never been surpassed in elegance, imagination, and sheer craftsmanship, and hence they will have a deservedly significant impact on the field.

The success of this kind of endeavor depends on how completely charted the knowledge at the two ends of the correlation process is. Compared to previous tries, even such cornerstone ones as Köhler's "Physische Gestalten" of the early 1920s, the efforts of Marr and his colleagues have the advantage that the knowledge of the "hardware" of the primate central visual information process has been advanced beyond recognition in the last three decades and has reached a stage when it can be profitably related to psychophysics in much the same way as was done a generation ago with rhodopsin, rod function, and scotopic vision.

The dialectic between conceptual frameworks and empirical data is central to modern science. The most outstanding figures in vision research in the past had incorporated both phases in their make-up: Young, Helmholtz, Hering, and Mach in the last century, Selig Hecht and William Rushton in more recent memory. As the accomplishments of the computational theorists grow and their influence on the design of experiments expands, one wonders whether vision research is about to go the way of physics and astronomy with their dichotomous tracks of theory and experiment.

Literature Cited

Adelson, E. H., Movshon, J. A. 1982. Phenomenal coherence of moving visual patterns. *Nature* 300:523–25

Adler, B., Grusser, O. J. 1982. Sigmamovement and optokinetic nystagmus elicited by stroboscopically illuminated stereopatterns. *Exp. Brain Res.* 47:353–64

Albrecht, D. G., De Valois, R. L., Thorell, L. G. 1980. Visual cortical neurons: are bars or gratings the optimal stimuli? *Science* 207:88–90

Allik, J., Dzhafarov, E., Rauk, M. 1982. Position discrimination may be better than detection. *Vision Res.* 22:11079–81

Anderson, P., Mitchell, D. E., Timney, B. 1980. Residual binocular interaction in stereoblind humans. *Vision Res.* 20:603–12

Arditi, A. 1982. The dependence of the induced effect on orientation and a hypothesis concerning disparity computation in general. *Vision Res.* 22:247–56

Arditi, A., Kaufman, L., Movshon, J. A. 1981. A simple explanation of the induced size effect. *Vision Res.* 21:755–64

Baker, C. L., Braddick, O. J. 1982a. Does segregation of differentially moving areas depend on relative or absolute displacement? *Vision Res.* 22:851–56

Baker, C. L., Braddick, O. J. 1982b. The basis of area and dot number effects in random dot motion perception. *Vision Res.* 22:1253–59

Banks, M. S., Stephens, B. R., Dannemiller, J. L. 1982. A failure to observe negative preference in infant acuity testing. *Vision Res.* 22:1025–31

Barlow, H. B. 1981. Critical limiting factors in the design of the eye and visual cortex. *Proc. R. Soc. London Ser. B* 212:1–34

Bedell, H. E., Flom, M. C. 1981. Spatial distortion in strabismic amblyopia. *Invest. Ophthalmol.* 20:262–68

Berardi, N., Bisti, S., Cattaneo, A., Fiorentini, A., Maffei, L. 1982. Correlation between the preferred orientation and spatial frequency of neurons in visual area 17 and 18 in the cat. *J. Physiol.* 323:603–18

Bienenstock, E. L., Cooper, L. N., Munro, P. W. 1982. Theory for the development of neuron selectivity: orientation specificity and binocular interaction in visual cortex. *J. Neurosci.* 2:32–48

Blakemore, C., Campbell, F. W. 1969. On the existence of neurons in the human visual system selectively sensitive to the orientation and size of retinal images. *J. Physiol.* 203:237–60

Birch, E. E., Gwiazda, J., Held, R. 1982. Stereoacuity development for crossed and uncrossed disparities in human infants. *Vision Res.* 22:507–14

Bonds, A. B. 1982. An "oblique effect" in the visual potential of the cat. *Exp. Brain Res.* 46:151–54

Boothe, R. G., Kiorpes, L., Hendrickson, A. 1982. Anisometropic amblyopia in *macaca nemestrina* monkeys produced by atropinization of one eye during development. *Invest. Ophthalmol.* 22:228–33

Brindley, G. S. 1982. Effects of electrical stimulation of the visual cortex. *Hum. Neurobiol.* 1:281–83

Burr, D., Morrone, C., Maffei, L. 1981. Intracortical inhibition prevents simple cells from responding to textured visual patterns. *Exp. Brain Res.* 43:455–58

Burt, P., Julesz, B. 1980. A disparity gradient limit for binocular fusion. *Science* 208:615–17

Campbell, F. W., Johnstone, J. R., Ross, J. 1981. An explanation of the visibility of low frequency gratings. *Vision Res.* 21:723–30

Campbell, F. W., Robson, J. G. 1968. Applications of Fourier analysis to the visibility of gratings. *J. Physiol.* 197:551–66

Carney, T. 1982. Directional specificity in tilt aftereffect induced with moving contours: a reexamination. *Vision Res.* 22:1273–75

Cavanagh, P. 1982. Functional size invariance is not provided by the cortical magnification factor. *Vision Res.* 22:1409–12

Chino, Y. M., Shansky, M. S., Hamasaki, D. I. 1980. Development of receptive field properties of retinal ganglion cells in kittens raised with convergent squint. *Exp. Brain Res.* 39:313–20

Cleland, B. G., Crewther, D. P. Crewther, S. G., Mitchell, D. E. 1982. Normality of spatial resolution of retinal ganglion cells in cats with strabismic amblyopia. *J. Physiol.* 326:235–49

Collin, N. G., Cowey, A. 1980. The effect of ablation of frontal eye fields and superior colliculi on visual stability and movement discrimination in rhesus monkey. *Exp. Brain Res.* 40:261–60

Crick, F. H. C., Marr, D., Poggio, T. 1981. An information-processing approach to understanding the visual cortex. In *The Organization of the Cerebral Cortex*, ed. F. Schmidt. Cambridge, Mass: MIT Press

Cynader, M., Regan, D. 1982. Neurons in cat visual cortex tuned to the direction of motion in depth: effect of positional disparity. *Vision Res.* 22:967–82

Dawson, W. W., Maida, T. M., Rubin, M. L. 1982. Human pattern-evoked retinal responses are altered by optic atrophy. *Invest. Ophthalmol.* 22:796–803

De Valois, R. L., Albrecht, D. G., Thorell, L. G. 1982. Spatial frequency selectivity of cells in macaque visual cortex. *Vision Res.* 22:545–59

De Valois, R. L., De Valois, K. K. 1980. Spatial vision. *Ann. Rev. Psychol.* 31:309–41

De Valois, R. L., Yund, E. W., Hepler, N. 1982. The orientation and direction selectivity of cells in macaque visual cortex. *Vision Res.* 22:531–44

Dobson, V., Mayer, D. L., Lee, C. P. 1980. Visual acuity screening in preterm infants. *Invest. Ophthalmol.* 19:1498–1505

Dow, B. M., Snyder, A. Z., Vautin, R. G., Bauer, R. 1981. Magnification factor and receptive field size in foveal striate cortex of the monkey. *Exp. Brain Res.* 44:213–29

Duffieux, P. M. 1946. L'integrale de Fourier et ses applications a l'optique. Rennes.

Dunlop, D. B., Neill, R. A., Dunlop, P. 1980. Measurement of dynamic stereoacuity and global stereopsis. *Aust. J. Ophthalmol.* 8:35

Fahle, M., Poggio, T. 1981. Visual hyperacuity: spatiotemporal interpolation in human vision. *Proc. R. Soc. London Ser. B* 213:451–77

Ferster, D. 1981. A comparison of binocular depth mechanisms in areas 17 and 18 of the cat visual cortex. *J. Physiol.* 311:623–55

Fox, R., Aslin, R. N., Shea, S. L., Dumais, S. T. 1980. Stereopsis in human infants. *Science* 207:323–24

Freeman, R. D., Bradley, A. 1980. Monocularly deprived humans: nondeprived eye has supernormal visual acuity. *J. Neurophysiol.* 43:1645–51

Gabor, D. 1950. Communication theory and physics. *Philos. Mag.* Ser. 7, 41:1161–85

Hadani, I., Gur, M., Meiri, A. Z., Fender, D. H. 1980. Hyperacuity in the detection of absolute and differential displacements of random dot patterns. *Vision Res.* 20:947–51

Hamasaki, D. I., Flynn, J. T. 1981. Amblyopic eyes have longer reaction times. *Invest. Ophthalmol.* 21:846–53

Hamerly, J. R., Dvorak, C. A. 1981. Detection and discrimination of blur in edges and lines. *J. Opt. Soc. Am.* 71:449–52

Hamerly, J. R., Springer, R. M. 1981. Raggedness of edges. *J. Opt. Soc. Am.* 71:285–88

Hammond, P. 1980. Non-stationarity of ocular dominance in cat striate cortex. *Exp. Brain Res.* 42:189–95

Heggelund, P. 1981. Receptive field organization of simple cells in cat striate cortex. *Exp. Brain Res.* 42:89–98

Held, R., Birch, E., Gwiazda, J. 1980. Stereoacuity of human infants. *Proc. Natl. Acad. Sci. USA* 77:5572–74

Hering, E. 1874. Zur Lehre vom Lichtsinne. V. Sitzber. *Akad. Wiss. Wien, Math. Naturwiss. Kl.* 69:Abth. III, 179–217

Hess, R., Bradley, A. 1980. Contrast perception above threshold is only minimally impaired in human amblyopia. *Nature* 287:463–64

Hess, R. F., Campbell, F. W., Zimmern, R. 1980. Differences in the neural basis of human amblyopia. *Vision Res.* 20:295–305

Hess, R. F., France, T. D., Tulunay-Keesey, U. 1981. Residual vision in humans who have been monocularly deprived of pattern stimulation in early life. *Exp. Brain Res.* 44:295–311

Higgins, K. E., Daugman, J. G., Mansfield, R. J. W. 1982. Amblyopic contrast sensitivity: insensitivity to unsteady fixation. *Invest. Ophthalmol.* 23:113–20

Hirsch, J., Hylton, R. 1982. Limits of spatial-frequency discrimination as evidence for neural interpolation. *J. Opt. Soc. Am.* 72:1367–74

Hubel, D. H. 1982. Exploration of the primary visual cortex. *Nature* 299:515–24

Jenkins, S. E., Cole, B. L. 1982. The effect of the density of background elements on the conspicuity of objects. *Vision Res.* 22:1241–52

Johnson, C. A., Post, R. B., Chalupa, L. M., Lee, T. J. 1982. Monocular deprivation in humans: a study of identical twins. *Invest. Ophthalmol.* 23:135–38

Johnson, C. A., Scobey, R. P. 1980. Foveal and peripheral displacement thresholds as a function of stimulus luminance, line length and duration of movement. *Vision Res.* 20:709–16

Johnson, C. A., Scobey, R. P. 1982. Effects of reference lines on displacement thresholds at various durations of movement. *Vision Res.* 22:819–21

Julesz, B., Kropfl, W., Petrig, B. 1980. Large evoked potentials to dynamic random-dot correlograms and stereograms. *Proc. Natl. Acad. Sci. USA* 77:2348–51

Julesz, B., Schumer, R. A. 1981. Early visual perception. *Ann. Rev. Psychol.* 32:575–627

Kato, H., Bishop, P. O., Orban, G. A. 1982. Binocular interaction on monocularly discharged lateral geniculate and striate neurons in the cat. *J. Neurophysiol.* 46:932–51

Keck, M. J., Price, R. L. 1982. Interocular transfer of the motion aftereffect in strabismus. *Vision Res.* 22:55–60

King-Smith, P. E., Kulikowski, J. J. 1981. The detection and recognition of two lines. *Vision Res.* 21:235–50

Kiorpes, L., Boothe, R. G. 1981. Naturally occurring strabismus in monkeys *(macaca nemestrina). Invest. Ophthalmol.* 20:257–62

Koenderink, J. J., van Doorn, A. J. 1980. Dual percept of movement and spatial periodicity in stroboscopically illuminated noise patterns. *J. Opt. Soc. Am.* 70:456–58

Kolb, H., Nelson, R., Mariani, A. 1981. Amacrine cells, bipolar cells and ganglion cells of the cat retina: a Golgi study. *Vision Res.* 21:1081–1114

Kroon, J. N., Rijsdijk, J. P., van der Wildt, G. J. 1980. Peripheral contrast sensitivity for sine wave gratings and single periods. *Vision Res.* 20:243–52

Kuffler, S. W. 1953. Discharge patterns and functional organization of mammalian retina. *J. Neurophysiol.* 16:37–68

Kulikowski, J. J. 1978. Limits of single vision in stereopsis depends on contour sharpness. *Nature* 275:126–27

Kulikowski, J. J., Bishop, P. O. 1981. Fourier analysis and spatial representation in the visual cortex. *Experientia* 37:160–62

Kulikowski, J. J., Bishop, P. O., Kato, H. 1981. Spatial arrangements of responses of cells in the cat visual cortex to light and dark bars and edges. *Exp. Brain Res.* 44:371–85

Kurtenbach, W., Magnussen, S. 1981. Inhibition, disinhibition summation among orientation detectors in human vision. *Exp. Brain Res.* 43:193–98

Lee, B. B., Elepfandt, A., Virsu, V. 1981. Phase of responses to sinusoidal gratings of simple cells in cat striate cortex. *J. Neurophysiol.* 45:818–28

Levi, D. M., Harweth, R. S., Pass, A. F., Venverloh, J. 1981. Edge sensitive mechanisms in humans with abnormal visual experience. *Exp. Brain Res.* 43:270–80

Levi, D. M., Klein, S. 1982a. Hyperacuity and amblyopia. *Nature* 298:268–70

Levi, D. M., Klein, S. 1982b. Differences in vernier discrimination for gratings between strabismic and anisometropic amblyopes. *Invest. Ophthalmol.* 23:398–407

Levick, W. R., Thibos, L. N. 1982. Analysis of orientation bias in cat retina. *J. Physiol.* 329:243–61

Levinson, E., Blake, R. 1979. Stereopsis by harmonic analysis. *Vision Res.* 19:73–78

Lie, I. 1980. Visual detection and resolution as a function of retinal locus. *Vision Res.* 20:967–74

Lotmar, W. 1980. Apparatus for the measurement of retinal visual acuity by moire fringes. *Invest. Ophthalmol.* 19:393–400

Magnussen, S., Kurtenbach, W. 1980. Linear summation of tilt illusion and tilt after-effect. *Vision Res.* 20:39–42

Manny, R. E., Levi, D. M. 1982. Psychophysical investigations of the temporal modulation sensitivity function in amblyopia: uniform field flicker. *Invest. Ophthalmol.* 22:515–24

Marcelja, S. 1980. Mathematical description of the responses of simple cortical cells. *J. Opt. Soc. Am.* 70:1297–1300

Marr, D. 1982. *Vision*. San Francisco: Freeman

Marr, D., Poggio, T., Hildreth, E. 1980. Smallest channel in early human vision. *J. Opt. Soc. Am.* 70:868–70

Matin, L., Pola, J., Matin, E., Picoult, E. 1981. Vernier discrimination with sequentially-flashed lines: roles of eye movements, retinal offsets and short-term memory. *Vision Res.* 21:647–56

Mayhew, J. E. W., Frisby, J. P. 1982. The induced effect: arguments against the theory of Arditi, Kaufman and Movshon (1981). *Vision Res.* 22:1225–28

Mayhew, J. E. W., Longuet-Higgins, H. C. 1982. A computational model of binocular depth perception. *Nature* 297:376–78

Morgan, M. J., Watt, R. J. 1982a. Hyperacuity for luminance phase angle in the human visual system. *Vision Res.* 22:863–66

Morgan, M. J., Watt, R. J. 1982b. Effect of motion sweep duration and number of stations upon interpolation in discontinuous motion. *Vision Res.* 22:1277–84

Morgan, M. J., Watt, R. J. 1982c. Mechanism of interpolation in human spatial vision. *Nature* 299:553–55

Moulden, B. 1980. After-effects and the integration of patterns of neural activity within a channel. *Philos. Trans. R. Soc. London Ser. B* 290:39–55

Movshon, J. A., van Sluyters, R. C. 1981. Visual neural development. *Ann. Rev. Psychol.* 32:477–522

Nakayama, K. 1981. Differential motion hyperacuity under conditions of common image motion. *Vision Res.* 21:1475–82

Nelson, J. I. 1981. A neurophysiological model for anomalous correspondence based on mechanisms of sensory fusion. *Doc. Ophthalmol.* 51:3–100

Nishihara, H. K., Poggio, T. 1982. Hidden cues in random-line stereograms. *Nature* 300:347–49

Nyman, G., Laurinen, P. 1982. Reconstruction of spatial information in the human visual system. *Nature* 297:324–25

Olzak, L. A., Thomas, J. P. 1981. Gratings: why frequency discrimination is sometimes better than detection. *J. Opt. Soc. Am.* 71:64–70

Poggio, G. F., Talbot, W. H. 1981. Mechanism of static and dynamic stereopsis in foveal cortex of the rhesus monkey. *J. Physiol.* 315:469–92

Pollen, D. S., Ronner, S. F. 1981. Phase relationships between adjacent simple cells in the cat visual cortex. *Science* 212:1409–11

Pollen, D. A., Ronner, S. F. 1982. Spatial computation performed by simple and complex cells in the visual cortex of the cat. *Vision. Res.* 22:101–18

Ratliff, F. 1965. *Mach Bands*. San Francisco: Holden-Day

Regan, D. 1982. Visual information channeling in normal and disordered vision. *Psychol. Rev.* 89:407–44

Regan, D., Cynader, M. 1982. Neurons in cat visual cortex tuned to the direction of motion in depth: effect of stimulus speed. *Invest. Ophthalmol.* 22:535–50

Rentschler, I., Hilz, R., Brettel, H. 1981. Amblyopic abnormality involves neural mechanisms concerned with movement processing. *Invest. Ophthalmol.* 20:695–700

Richards, W., Foley, J. M. 1981. Spatial bandwidth of channels for slant estimated from complex gratings, *J. Opt. Soc. Am.* 71:274–79

Robson, J. G. 1980. Neural images: the physiological basis of spatial vision. In *Visual Coding and Adaptibility*, ed. C. S. Harris. Hillsdale, NJ: Erlbaum

Rodieck, R. W. 1965. Quantitative analysis of cat retinal ganglion cell response to visual stimuli. *Vision Res.* 5:583–601

Rogers, B., Graham, M. 1982. Similarities between motion parallax and stereopsis in human depth perception. *Vision Res.* 22:261–70

Rovamo, J., Virsu, V., Laurinen, P., Hyvarinen, L. 1982. Resolution of gratings oriented along and across meridians in peripheral vision. *Invest. Ophthalmol.* 23:666–70

Sakitt, B., 1982. Why the cortical magnification factor in rhesus cannot be isotropic. *Vision Res.* 22:417–21

Sakitt, B., Barlow, H. B. 1982. A model for the economical encoding of the visual image in cerebral cortex. *Biol. Cybern.* 43:97–108

Schade, O. H. 1956. Optical and photoelectric analog of the eye. *J. Opt. Soc. Am.* 46:721–39

Schor, C. M., Tyler, C. W. 1981. Spatiotemporal properties of Panum's fusional areas. *Vision Res.* 21:683–92

Schwartz, E. 1980. Computational anatomy and functional architecture of striate cortex: a spatial mapping approach to perceptual coding. *Vision Res.* 20:645–70

Scobey, R. P. 1982. Human visual orientation discrimination. *J. Neurophysiol.* 48:18–26

Scobey, R. P., Johnson, C. A. 1981. Displacement thresholds for unidirectional and oscillatory movement. *Vision Res.* 21:1297–1302

Sillito, A. M., Kemp, J. A., Patel, H. 1980. Inhibitory interactions contributing to the ocular dominance of monocularly dominant cells in the normal cat striate cortex. *Exp. Brain Res.* 41:1–10

Singer, W., von Grunau, M., Rauschecker, J. 1980. Functional amblyopia in kittens with unilateral exotropia. *Exp. Brain Res.* 40:294–304

Sireteanu, R. 1982. Binocular vision in strabismic humans with alternating fixation. *Vision Res.* 22:889–96

Sireteanu, R., Fronius, M. 1981. Nasotemporal asymmetries in human amblyopia: consequence of long-term interocular suppression. *Vision Res.* 21:1055–63

Sireteanu, R., Singer, W. 1980. The "vertical effect" in human squint amblyopia. *Exp. Brain Res.* 40:354–57

Slooter, J., van Norren, D. 1980. Visual acuity measured with pupil responses to checkerboard stimuli. *Invest. Ophthalmol.* 19:105–8

Snyder, A. W. 1982. Hyperacuity and interpolation by the visual pathway. *Vision Res.* 22:1219–20

Stromeyer, C. F., Klein, S., Dawson, B. M., Spillmann, L. 1982. Low spatial frequency channels in human vision: adaptation and masking. *Vision Res.* 22:225–34

Swindale, N. V. 1980. A model for the formation of ocular dominance stripes. *Proc. R. Soc. London Ser. B* 208:243–64

Swindale, N. V. 1982. A model for the formation of orientation columns. *Proc. R. Soc London Ser. B* 215:211–30

Teller, D. Y., Mayer, D. L., Makous, W. L., Allen, J. L. 1982. Do preferential looking techniques underestimate infant visual acuity? *Vision Res.* 22:1017–24

Thibos, L. N., Levick, W. R. 1982. Astigmatic visual deprivation in cat: behavioral, optical and retinophysiological consequences. *Vision Res.* 22:43–53

Thomas, J. P., Gille, J., Barker, R. A. 1982. Simultaneous visual detection and identification: theory and data. *J. Opt. Soc. Am.* 72:1642–51

Timney, B. 1981. Development of binocular depth perception in kittens. *Invest. Ophthalmol.* 21:493–96

Tolhurst, D. J., Thompson, I. D. 1982. Organization of neurones preferring spatial frequency in cat striate cortex. *Exp. Brain Res.* 48:217–27

Tootell, R. B., Silverman, M. S., De Valois, R. L. 1981. Spatial frequency columns in primary visual cortex. *Science* 214:813–15

Troscianko, T. 1982. A stereoscopic presentation of the Hermann Grid. *Vision Res.* 22:485–90

Ullman, S. 1979. *The Interpretation of Visual Motion.* Cambridge, Mass: MIT Press

Uttal, W. R. 1981. *A Taxonomy of Visual Processes.* Hillsdale, NJ: Erlbaum

van Meeteren, A., Barlow, H. B. 1981. The statistical efficiency for detecting sinusoidal modulation of average dot density in random figures. *Vision Res.* 21:765–77

Watson, A. B., Robson, J. G. 1981. Discrimination at threshold: labelled detectors in human vision. *Vision Res.* 21:1115–22

Watt, R. J., Andrews, D. P. 1982. Contour curvature analysis: hyperacuities in the discrimination of detailed shape. *Vision Res.* 22:449–60

Wesson, M. D., Loop, M. S. 1982. Temporal contrast sensitivity in amblyopia. *Invest. Ophthalmol.* 22:98–102

Westheimer, G. 1972. Optical properties of vertebrate eyes. In *Handbook of Sensory Physiology,* ed. M. G. F. Fuortes, 7(2):449–82. Berlin: Springer

Westheimer, G. 1981. Visual hyperacuity. *Prog. Sens. Physiol.* 1:1–30

Westheimer, G. 1982. The spatial grain of the perifoveal visual field. *Vision Res.* 22:157–62

Westheimer, G., McKee, S. P. 1980. Stereogram design for testing local stereopsis. *Invest. Opthalmol.* 19:802–9

Wiesel, T. N. 1982. Postnatal development of the visual cortex and the influence of environment. *Nature* 299:583–91

Williams, R. A., Boothe, R. G. 1981. Development of optical quality in the infant monkey *(macaca nemestrina)* eye. *Invest. Ophthalmol.* 21:728–36

Wilson, H. R. 1978. Quantitative characterization of two types of line-spread function near the fovea. *Vision Res.* 18:971–81

Wilson, H. R., Bergen, J. R. 1979. A four mechanism model for threshold spatial vision. *Vision Res.* 19:19–32

Wolfe, J. M., Held, R. 1981. A purely binocular mechanism in human vision. *Vision Res.* 21:1755–59

Wolfe, J. M., Held, R. 1982. Gravity and the tilt aftereffect. *Vision Res.* 22:1075–78

Ann. Rev. Psychol. 1984. 35:227–56

PSYCHOPATHOLOGY OF CHILDHOOD

Thomas M. Achenbach

Department of Psychiatry, University of Vermont, Burlington, Vermont 05401

Craig S. Edelbrock

Western Psychiatric Institute and Clinic, University of Pittsburgh, Pittsburgh, Pennsylvania 15261

CONTENTS

Alan Ross and William Pelham (1981) opened the previous chapter on child psychopathology in the *Annual Review of Psychology* by stating that "most of the major questions regarding the etiology, nature, treatment, and prognosis of childhood psychological disorders remain unanswered" (p. 244). They cited several reasons why the major questions remain unanswered, but "Foremost among these are difficulties in classifying childhood disorders" (p. 244). Ross

227

0066-4308/84/0201-0227$02.00

and Pelham chose to illustrate research problems and needs by focusing on hyperactivity and early infantile autism. These were indeed apt examples for illustrating issues common to disorders that otherwise differ greatly in prevalence, severity, and age of diagnosis.

If we were to adopt Ross and Pelham's strategy of focusing on prototypical disorders, we would likewise choose autism and hyperactivity, or "attention deficit disorder with hyperactivity," as it is designated in the official nosology of the American Psychiatric Association (1980). Moreover, current knowledge of these disorders would not require much revision of Ross and Pelham's conclusions. Instead, research since their review has continued to cast doubt on previously favored explanations for these disorders, such as parental psychodynamics as an explanation for autism, and brain damage, food sensitivities, and neurotransmitter abnormalities as explanations for hyperactivity (see Achenbach 1982, 1984). We would now add childhood depression as a further illustration of the points made by Ross and Pelham. Like the other childhood disorders, "depressive illness" is being viewed as a distinct nosological entity for which a host of specific etiologies and treatments are proposed without a satisfactory operational definition of the disorder itself (see Achenbach 1982, 1984, Carlson & Cantwell 1982, Petti 1983).

Rather than choosing specific disorders to illustrate general problems of research on child psychopathology, however, we shall focus on certain general problems that hinder our understanding of specific disorders. The chief problem is what Ross and Pelham called the "foremost" difficulty, that of classifying childhood disorders. We shall break it down into two phases of what should be a continuous process: (a) assessment of the behavior of individual children; (b) the use of assessment data to identify important similarities and differences among groups of children. This is the problem of *taxonomy*, which, as we shall propose, can also be conceived in quantitative terms as *taxometry*.

Although we would still concur with Ross and Pelham that "most of the major questions remain unanswered," we feel that a shift in conceptions of assessment and taxonomy can rephrase the major questions in more readily answerable forms.

DEVELOPMENTAL PERSPECTIVES

Before considering assessment and taxonomy, it is important to point out that we will be concerned with psychopathology across the period of rapid development from birth to late adolescence. For convenience, we will use the term "childhood" in reference to the whole period, including infancy and adolescence. Although the differences between infants, toddlers, preschoolers, elementary school children, and adolescents are as great as their similarities, we will stress issues that are common to the entire period of rapid development.

The following factors make developmental perspectives especially pertinent to assessment and taxonomy during this period:

1. Unlike adults, who normally reach plateaus in many aspects of development, children continually experience major *changes* in the biological, cognitive, social, emotional, and educational spheres.
2. Whereas adult psychopathology is often marked by declines from attained levels of functioning or the emergence of pathognomonic behavior, child psychopathology more often involves *failure to develop* or *quantitative deviance* in behavior that most children show at some point in their development.
3. The judgment that a child needs professional help, the assessment data, and the negotiation of treatment all *depend on other people,* such as parents and teachers, to a much greater extent than is true for adults who receive mental health services.
4. To judge whether a child's behavior is indeed "pathological," we need to know the *likely outcome* of such behaviors in subsequent developmental periods.
5. To design appropriate interventions, we need to know how to *facilitate development* rather than merely to reduce discomfort, remove "symptoms," or restore a previous level of functioning.

The foregoing considerations dictate that we must view problem behavior in a relativistic fashion. Rather than being intrinsically pathological, many problem behaviors of childhood arouse concern because of the degree to which they deviate from the range of behavior normally expected for the child's age, sex, environmental settings such as school or home, previous behavior, and so on. Relativism is also necessitated by the variability of children's behavior from day to day, from situation to situation, and from one interaction partner to another. Furthermore, behavioral problems can be offset to varying degrees by competencies, such that a particular problem may seem more benign in a child who displays many socially valued characteristics than in a child who does not.

Some childhood behaviors are intrinsically pathognomonic or dangerous enough to warrant concern. Echolalia and lack of eye contact by a 5-year-old, chronic firesetting by an 8-year-old, or life-threatening anorexia in a 13-year-old, for example, would be unequivocal signs of trouble. Yet, even in the relatively small proportion of cases showing such blatant deviance, a comprehensive evaluation of the child requires a broad picture of other behavior that may not be so easy to categorize as "deviant" versus "normal." We therefore need to know a child's standing relative to peers in terms of other behavioral problems and competencies, as seen from a variety of perspectives. And in the many cases that lack blatantly pathognomonic or dangerous behaviors, the decision as to whether help is needed requires a composite picture of the child's behavioral strengths and deficiencies relative to expectations for the child's age.

In addressing research on assessment of behavior, we will emphasize approaches having a potential for quantification, for comparison with normative groups of peers, and for the coordination of multiple perspectives on children's functioning. We will then consider taxonomic and taxometric approaches to utilizing assessment data in grouping children according to important similarities and differences among them. Space limitations restrict us to illustrative examples of recent work rather than an exhaustive review.

ASSESSMENT OF BEHAVIOR

The Ideal of "Behavioral Assessment"

The renaissance of behavioral approaches during the 1960s and 1970s helped to promote the ideal of *behavioral assessment* as an alternative to "traditional assessment," meaning mainly psychodynamic, medically oriented, and trait approaches. In one of the first major books on behavioral assessment of childhood disorders, Mash & Terdal (1981) drew the following contrasts between behavioral assessment and traditional assessment:

1. On the assumption that environmental factors maintain behavior, behavioral assessment dispenses with the inferred constructs at the heart of traditional assessment.
2. Behavioral assessment regards behavior as situationally specific, whereas traditional assessment assumes consistency across situations.
3. Behavioral assessment regards stability and change in behavior as a function of stability and change in the environment, whereas traditional assessment infers internal causes.
4. Behavioral assessment views responses as samples of behavior, whereas traditional assessment interprets responses as clues to underlying attributes.
5. Behavioral assessment focuses on variables involved directly in treatment, whereas traditional assessment seeks to diagnose underlying conditions and evaluate their prognosis.
6. Behavioral assessment obtains observations of problem behavior in its natural environment, whereas traditional assessment is done in clinical settings.
7. Behavioral assessment is a continuous process integrated into treatment, whereas traditional assessment is a separate process that precedes treatment.

Consistent with these principles, published examples of behavioral assessment often report direct observations of target behaviors in their natural environments (e.g. Patterson 1980). Yet, surveys of behavioral clinicians show that they do not actually use these methods much in their practices (Swan &

MacDonald 1978, Wade et al 1979). Instead, they rely on "traditional" methods such as interviews and tests to a surprising degree. Furthermore, the hope that behavioral assessment would somehow avoid all the reliability and validity problems of traditional assessment has not been fulfilled. Reflecting on the history of behavioral assessment, Patterson (1981) writes:

> Within a short time, we found ourselves engaged with the traditional psychometric problems of interobserver agreement, validity, stability of behavior over time, bias, the effects of observer presence, and normative data. The old questions are still with us. If anything, they were more demanding and more difficult to answer (Patterson 1981, p. vii).

Even in *tour-de-force* observational studies that obtain reliable observations of complex behavioral interactions under natural conditions, the observed contingencies seem to account for little of the variance in children's problem behaviors (e.g. Patterson 1980).

SECOND THOUGHTS ON BEHAVIORAL ASSESSMENT   The ideal of behavioral assessment has undoubtedly fostered better documentation of behavior problems, highlighted specific contingencies affecting behavior, and underlined the need for continuity between assessment and intervention. Nevertheless, the failure to attain the ideal in practice has prompted some second thoughts on behavioral assessment. In his inaugural statement as editor of *Behavioral Assessment,* Donald Hartmann (1983), for example, cited the following issues raised by leaders in assessment and behavioral psychology:

> 1. Behavioral assessment should drop its defensive, insular and provincial status. It has much to learn from traditional assessment—including attention to normative data, reliability, and validity—and need not be besmirched nor sullied by close contact with other assessment approaches.
> 2. Behavioral assessment must be made relevant to treatment selection as well as treatment evaluation, to the prediction and understanding of socially significant behaviors such as violence, and to improving the conduct of our daily affairs.
> 3. There is some danger that people in the behavioral assessment field are too procedure-oriented, too concerned with concrete methods and data—with means rather than ends (Hartmann 1983, p. 2).

One response to the difficulty and limitations of idealized behavioral assessment has been to advocate *multimethod behavioral assessment* (Nay 1979). For assessment of children, the multiple methods include interviews, standardized tests, checklists and log books completed by parents, observations in clinical as well as natural settings, and simulation of problem situations. Once we acknowledge the need for multiple methods, however, we face not only all the "traditional" assessment problems of reliability, validity, representativeness, and generalizability, but another problem initially skirted by behavioral assessment: the problem of aggregating diverse and often contradictory data into a coherent picture of the child that enables us to draw upon previously accumulated knowledge in order to help the child.

Regardless of the assessment procedure, data must be aggregated across cases to detect covariation among reported characteristics, and data obtained on the individual child must be aggregated to compare perceptions of the child's functioning in different contexts. Studies of clinical judgment show that clinicians (like people in general) are very poor at (*a*) mentally detecting covariation of attributes across cases (Arkes 1981), and (*b*) mentally combining assessment data into judgments of individual cases (Wiggins 1981). In the following sections, we therefore survey approaches to obtaining data on children's behavior in forms amenable to systematic detection of covariation across cases and systematic combination of data on individual cases.

Reports and Ratings by Parents

Parents are usually the chief source of information about children's problem behavior. They are directly involved in most clinical referrals of children, they are asked to describe the referred child's behavior, and they play a primary role in determining what will be done about the behavior.

The customary clinical approach has been to obtain parents' reports of their concerns in a narrative fashion via interviews ranging widely over the child's behavior and developmental history, family dynamics, and parents' own problems. Interviews are, of course, essential for enabling clinicians and families to get acquainted and negotiate arrangements for services. However, the diversity of families, clinicians, and agendas limits the interview's potential for obtaining parents' reports of their children's behavior in forms amenable to detection of covariation across cases and to systematic aggregation of data on the individual case. The central importance of parents' reports of their children's behavior and the need to obtain such reports in a more standardized fashion have stimulated the development of numerous behavior checklists and inventories designed to be filled out by parents.

MULTIVARIATE ANALYSES OF BEHAVIORAL RATINGS   The most common approach has been to provide a list of behavior problems that parents either check as present versus absent or rate on multistep scales reflecting the frequency and/or intensity of each problem. Parents' responses are then factor analyzed or cluster analyzed to identify syndromes of problems that tend to occur together. The number and nature of the syndromes obtained may be affected by many variables. For example, large item pools generally yield more syndromes than small item pools, and rotated factor solutions divide high loading items into more syndromes than unrotated solutions (see Achenbach &

Edelbrock 1978). Furthermore, syndromes of extremely deviant behavior cannot be found in samples where the behaviors are too rare. This means that many clinically important syndromes may be missed in analyses of nonclinical samples. Similarly, analyses of mildly disturbed children may not detect syndromes characteristic of severely disturbed children, and vice versa. A corollary is that a sample of one sex or age group cannot yield syndromes peculiar to the other sex or other age groups. Conversely, analysis of a sample containing both sexes or different age groups may obscure syndromes that are present in only one sex or age group within the sample.

Perhaps the most fundamental difference in findings among studies of checklists filled out by parents has been in the number of syndromes identified. The precise number identified is a function of methodological factors such as those discussed above, selection of items to tap few or many types of disorders, and the researcher's criteria for the number and size of item loadings required to constitute a syndrome. Checklists containing relatively few items (e.g. Quay & Peterson 1975) and those targeted mainly on one type of disorder (e.g. Conners 1970) have generally yielded from about two to four global, broad-band syndromes, whereas longer, more differentiated checklists have generally yielded from about 8 to 15 more specific, narrow-band syndromes (e.g. Miller 1967, 1977, Achenbach 1978, Lessing et al 1981, Achenbach & Edelbrock 1983). However, Dreger (1981) reported 30 syndromes from a factor analysis of an exceptionally large pool of items (274), scored on an extremely heterogeneous sample and using very liberal criteria for retention of factors.

Differences in instruments, subject samples, and methods of analysis naturally cause considerable variation among the findings of different studies. Nevertheless, by excluding methodologically inadequate studies and focusing on general similarity of content among syndromes from different studies, two reviews discerned considerable consistency in certain syndromes across studies (Achenbach & Edelbrock 1978, Quay 1979).

Apparent disagreements between studies that identify a few broad-band syndromes and those that identify more numerous narrow-band syndromes have been explicated by second-order analyses of the narrow-band syndromes (Miller 1967, Achenbach 1978, Achenbach & Edelbrock 1979, 1983). These show that narrow-band syndromes of hyperactivity, aggression, and delinquent behavior covary to form a broad-band grouping of "undercontrolled" behavior. Conversely, narrow-band syndromes of anxiety, depression, somatic complaints, and obsessive-compulsive behavior covary to form a broad-band grouping of "overcontrolled" behavior. Although not all narrow-band syndromes group together to form a particular broad-band grouping, the second-order analyses show that most of the narrow- and broad-band syndromes can be seen as representing more and less differentiated levels of a hierarchy rather than being mutually contradictory.

Carrying hierarchical analyses a step further, Dreger (1981) performed not only a second-order analysis of the 30 first-order factors he found, but also a third-order analysis of his 9 second-order factors. (He rejected a fourth-order analysis of the four third-order factors in view of the low correlations among them.) As noted earlier, Dreger's identification of 30 first-order factors, rather than the smaller number usually reported, reflected an exceptionally large item pool and lenient criteria for retention of factors. In effect, Dreger's nine second-order factors represent a level of differentiation similar to that of most studies that identify narrow-band syndromes, whereas his four third-order factors represent a level of differentiation similar to that of most studies that identify a few broad-band syndromes.

In summary, the important point here is that no one level of differentiation or number of syndromes is intrinsically "correct." When viewed in light of hierarchical analyses, studies reporting a few broad-band factors are not intrinsically contradictory to studies reporting more numerous narrow-band factors. Different degrees of differentiation may be useful for different purposes. The global distinction between broad-band undercontrolled and overcontrolled behavior, for example, may be useful for general management purposes. Narrow-band hyperactive, delinquent, aggressive, depressed, obsessive-compulsive, somatic, and anxious syndromes, by contrast, may provide a better basis for detecting specific etiologies and prescribing specific treatments.

OTHER APPROACHES TO STRUCTURED PARENTAL REPORTS   The multivariate analyses of parents' ratings have empirically identified syndromes of behavior problems perceived by parents. Other efforts to obtain structured reports from parents have employed scales constructed on more of an a priori basis. The Minnesota Child Development Inventory (MCDI; Ireton & Thwing 1974), for example, was constructed by first assembling a large pool of items describing the developmental skills of preschool children. Items were retained that showed strong increases with age in the percentage of children reported to pass them. Rather than being grouped on the basis of empirical analyses, the items were then grouped into seven scales "that are commonly differentiated in the child development literature and in various developmental tests" (Ireton & Thwing 1974, p. 2). These scales are entitled Gross Motor, Fine Motor, Expressive Language, Comprehension-Conceptual, Situation Comprehension, Self Help, and Personal-Social. The items that show the strongest age discriminations are also scored on a General Development Scale. Responses by suburban Minneapolis mothers provided normative data for ages 6 months to 6 years.

Beside being constructed on an a priori basis, the MCDI scales differ from the empirically derived syndromes in focusing mainly on developmental accomplishments, such as motor skills, language, self-care, and socialization, rather than on problem behavior per se. Developmental accomplishments are an especially important aspect of assessment during the infant and toddler periods, and a lack of developmental progress is a common reason for seeking professional help during these years.

Another Minnesota effort, but aimed at psychopathology of the later years of childhood and adolescence, is the Personality Inventory for Children (PIC; Wirt et al 1977). Resembling the MMPI in many ways, the PIC contains 600 items to be scored *true* or *false*. Some of the items are descriptions of current behavior, whereas others pertain to the child's past history. Still others require the mother to describe or judge herself, the child's father, or the family situation. The items were initially written to cover 11 a priori content areas, but subsequent clinical judgment and empirical analyses eliminated some of the intended scales and added others. Normative data were obtained on Minneapolis school children during the early 1960s. Clinical groups in various settings have been used to establish cutoff points on the scale scores. A factor analysis geared to broad-band dimensions has identified general undercontrolled and overcontrolled dimensions resembling those found in analyses of behavior checklists (Lachar et al 1982).

Other efforts to obtain parents' reports in a structured format have focused on competencies that may be as important to children's adaptation as behavioral problems are. Although competencies have recently received considerable attention in the developmental literature, most of the research has been with nonclinical samples. However, after experimenting with various approaches to obtaining competency data from parents of children referred for mental health services, Achenbach (1978) obtained good discrimination between referred and nonreferred children by having parents rate the quality and quantity of their child's involvement in sports, nonsports recreational activities, organizations, jobs and chores, friendships, other social relations, and school. These items are included on the same questionnaire (the Child Behavior Checklist) as a set of behavior problems from which empirically derived behavior problem syndromes are scored. However, because of the intrinsic interdependence of some of the social competence items, they are grouped according to face similarity of content rather than empirically derived dimensions. The scores on these dimensions discriminate significantly between normal and clinical samples, and the total social competence score increases the power of the Child Behavior Checklist to discriminate between normal and clinical samples beyond the discrimination obtained with behavior problem scores alone (Achenbach & Edelbrock 1983).

Reports and Ratings by Teachers

Next to parents, teachers are the adults who have the most contact with children. They are in an exceptionally good position to observe children's social skills, peer relations, and responses to tasks requiring sustained attention, persistence, and organization. In addition, teachers' perceptions often help to determine what is done for disturbed children.

Numerous procedures have been developed for obtaining teachers' reports and ratings. These include *nomination procedures* designed to identify particular types of children (Bolstad & Johnson 1977, Green et al 1980); *brief screening instruments* (Rutter 1967, Cowen et al 1973); *ratings of social and prosocial behavior* (Roper & Hinde 1979, Weir & Duveen 1981); and *instruments scorable in terms of a priori scales* (Brown & Hammill 1978). We will, however, focus mainly on the derivation of behavior problem syndromes from teacher ratings through multivariate analyses of a broad range of behavior. Analyses limited to single diagnostic groups, such as psychotic children (e.g. Prior et al 1975) and retarded children (e.g. Lambert & Nicoll 1976) are excluded, as are measures of molecular classroom behaviors oriented toward psychoeducational evaluations (e.g. Spivack & Swift 1972).

PRESCHOOL CHILDREN   Kohn & Rosman (1972) factor analyzed their 58-item Symptom Checklist and 90-item Social Competence Scale completed by teachers of 407 children aged 3–6. Because scores on the first factor obtained from the Checklist correlated negatively with scores on the first factor from the Competence Scale, they were combined to form one bipolar scale labeled *Cooperation-Compliance vs Anger-Defiance*. On the same grounds, the second factors in each analysis were combined into a bipolar scale labeled *Interest-Participation vs Apathy-Withdrawal*. Scores on these scales have been found to be moderately stable in a longitudinal followup of preschoolers into 1st grade (Kohn & Rosman 1973a) and have identified emotionally disturbed children in general population samples (Kohn & Rosman 1973b).

Behar & Stringfield (1974) administered the 36-item Preschool Behavior Questionnaire (PBQ) to teachers of 496 children enrolled in regular preschools and 102 children attending preschools for the emotionally disturbed. Factor analysis of the combined sample revealed three syndromes which were labeled *Hostile-Aggressive, Anxious-Fearful,* and *Hyperactive-Distractible.* The first two resembled the two factors found by Kohn and Rosman for teachers' ratings of preschoolers and found in most analyses of parents' ratings.

OLDER CHILDREN   Most teacher rating scales have been designed for grade school children. In one of the first efforts to construct behavior problem scales empirically, Peterson (1961) factor analyzed teachers' responses to his 58-item Behavior Problem Checklist (BPC) for children in grades K-6. Separate factor analyses for each grade yielded the usual two broad-band dimensions: *Conduct Problem,* comprised of disruptive behaviors such as fighting and disobedience, and *Personality Problem,* comprised of items such as withdrawal, anxiety, and feelings of inferiority. These were replicated in samples of normal 7th and 8th graders (Quay & Quay 1965), emotionally disturbed children (Quay et al 1966), deaf students (Reivich & Rothrock 1972), and preadolescent delinquents (Quay 1966). A third factor, labeled "Immaturity" or "Inadequacy-Immaturity" has also been obtained in some analyses of the BPC (Quay & Quay 1965, Pimm et al 1967).

The 39-item Teacher Rating Scale (TRS) was developed by Conners (1969) mainly to evaluate drug therapy for hyperactive children, but versions of it have been used for more diverse purposes, such as determining the prevalence of learning and behavior problems (e.g. Trites 1979) and studying stability and change in behavior problems over time (e.g. Glow et al 1982). Conners' original factor analysis of data on children referred for drug therapy revealed five factors which were labeled *Aggressive-Conduct Disorder, Hyperactivity, Daydreaming-Inattentive, Anxious-Fearful,* and *Social-Cooperative.* TRS scores have been shown to be sensitive to drug effects and to discriminate significantly between normal and disturbed children (see Goyette et al 1978 for a review). A revised version of the TRS yielded somewhat different factors, including *Conduct Problem, Hyperactivity,* and *Inattentive-Passive* (Goyette et al 1978). A multitrait-multimethod analysis has supported the convergent and discriminant validity of the scales reflecting aggression, hyperactivity, and inattentiveness (Roberts et al 1981).

The Teacher's Report Form (TRF) of the Child Behavior Checklist includes items related to school performance and adaptive functioning, plus 118 behavior problems, most of which are identical to those on the Child Behavior Checklist designed for parents (Achenbach & Edelbrock 1983). Factor analysis of TRFs for 450 boys referred for mental health services revealed eight reliable factors, labeled *Anxious, Social Withdrawal, Unpopular, Self-Destructive, Obsessive-Compulsive, Inattentive, Nervous-Overactive,* and *Aggressive.* Second-order factor analysis revealed the usual two broad-band syndromes: An "Internalizing" or overcontrolled syndrome comprising the first two factors, and an "Externalizing" or undercontrolled syndrome comprising the last three factors. Factor-based scales have been normed on a sample of 300 randomly selected nonreferred boys attending regular grade school classes in several school systems. The factor-based scales are scored on the Teacher Version of the Child Behavior Profile, for which editions are also being developed for boys aged 12–16 and girls age 6–11 and 12–16.

Other teacher rating instruments scorable in terms of empirically derived behavior problem scales include the School Behavior Checklist (Miller 1972), which yields nine factor-based scales for 4- to 6-year-olds and six for 7- to 13-year-olds; The Teacher Referral Form (Clarfield 1974), which was developed to evaluate children referred to a school-based mental health program and has been factored into three dimensions designated as *Learning Problem,*

Acting-Out, and *Shy-Anxious;* and Walker's (1976) Checklist, which has yielded five factors designated as *Acting-Out, Withdrawal, Distractibility, Disturbed Peer Relations,* and *Immaturity.*

In summary, teachers' ratings yield broad-band undercontrolled versus over-controlled syndromes analogous to those found in most analyses of parents' ratings. Among studies yielding three or more narrow-band factors, there is good evidence for separate *Aggressive* and *Anxious* syndromes. There is also evidence for a syndrome comprising items such as poor peer relations, being unliked, being teased by others, and loneliness, which has been labeled *Asocial* (Trites et al 1982), Hostile-*Isolation* (Miller 1972), *Unpopular* (Edelbrock & Achenbach 1984), and *Disturbed Peer Relations* (Walker 1976). A factor reflecting withdrawl, shyness, and apathy has been obtained in two studies and has been labeled *Social Withdrawal* (Edelbrock & Achenbach 1984), and *Withdrawal* (Walker 1976). Lastly, two distinct syndromes have been identi-fied which pertain to different aspects of hyperactivity. One encompasses items such as restlessness, fidgets, can't sit still, and nervous movements; the second encompasses items such as short attention span, easily distracted, can't concen-trate, and daydreams (Conners 1969, Goyette et al 1978, Trites et al 1982, Edelbrock & Achenbach 1984). This contrasts with syndromes derived from parents' ratings where overactivity and inattentiveness tend to load on a single factor. It no doubt reflects the fact that teachers are in a better position to observe children's failure to attend to structured tasks. Conversely, the pre-sence of somatic complaints and delinquent behavior syndromes in parents' ratings but not in teacher's ratings no doubt reflects parents' greater opportuni-ties to observe these behaviors.

Reports and Ratings by Others

Most measures of children's behavior are based on reports by parents, teachers, trained observers, or the children themselves. A few instruments, however, have been developed to utilize reports and ratings by other informants. Lefko-witz & Tesiny (1980), for example, developed the Peer Nomination Inventory for Depression (PNID), which includes items reflecting *depression* (e.g. Who often cries?), *happiness* (e.g. Who often looks happy?), and *popularity* (e.g. Who would you like to sit next to?). Depression scores for children in grades 4 and 5 had low but significant correlations with the children's self-ratings of depression ($r = .23$) and with teachers' ratings of depression ($r = .41$). PNID depression scores were also negatively related to measures of happiness, popularity, and self-esteem, and positively related to number of times tardy and absent from school.

Other measures tap the perceptions of clinicians and child-care workers. Lessing and her colleagues, for example, have developed a version of the Institute for Juvenile Research (IJR) Checklist designed to be completed by clinicians following an interview with the child (Lessing et al 1981). Cluster analysis of clinicians' ratings of 115 items for children aged 5–17 revealed seven item clusters that have counterparts in the parent and teacher versions of the IJR Checklist. Another example is the Adolescent Symptom Checklist for delinquent youth, which includes 89 items reflecting personality and conduct problems (Kohn et al 1979). Factor analysis of child care workers' ratings revealed two dimensions, labeled *Apathy-Withdrawal* and *Anger-Defiance,* which are similar to the broad-band syndromes found in other measures.

Self-Report Measures

Early efforts to elicit self descriptions from children focused on "private" phenomena such as *self-esteem* (Coopersmith 1967), *fears* (Miller et al 1972), and *anxiety* (Castaneda et al 1956). Although there is renewed interest in these areas, self-report measures for children are being extended increasingly to more overt behavior. Unlike most of the research reviewed in the previous sections, research in this area has focused mainly on narrower categories of problems such as anxiety, self-control, depression, and social behavior.

ANXIETY   Developed more than 25 years ago (Castaneda et al 1956), the Children's Manifest Anxiety Scale (CMAS) has been the most widely used anxiety scale. Recently it has undergone psychometric refinements and restandardization (Reynolds & Richman 1979, Reynolds & Paget 1981). The revised CMAS has 28 anxiety items (e.g. I worry a lot), plus 9 lie scale items. It is scorable in terms of three factor-based scales labeled *Physiological, Worry-Oversensitivity,* and *Concentration.* The validity of the revised CMAS as a measure of chronic anxiety has been supported by a significant correlation of .85 with the Trait scale and a nonsignificant correlation of .24 with the State scale of Spielberger's (1973) State-Trait Anxiety Inventory for Children.

SELF-CONTROL   Children's self-control (ability to delay, plan ahead, tolerate frustration, and resist temptation) has often been assessed through reports and ratings by adults (e.g. Kendall & Wilcox 1979). Behavioral and performance measures, such as contrived tests of resistance to temptation, have also been employed (e.g. Fry 1977).

To tap children's perceptions of their own self-control, Humphrey (1982) developed the 11-item Children's Perceived Self-Control Scale, which parallels a 15-item self-control scale completed by teachers. Children respond to each item (e.g. It is hard to wait for something I want) by indicating "Usually Yes," or "Usually No." Factor analysis of responses by 763 4th and 5th graders revealed four factors which were labeled *Personal Self Control, Interpersonal Self-Control, Self-Evaluation,* and *Consequential Thinking.* However, with only 11 items in the entire scale, the "factors" had only from one to four items loading ≥.30. Individual children's ratings of their own self-control did not correlate significantly with classroom observations of self-control, but classroom mean scores for interpersonal self-control did correlate significantly with classroom mean scores on several observational variables. The general approach may thus be viable, but the measures need to be strengthened before they can be used to assess individual children.

CHILDHOOD DEPRESSION   Several self-report measures of childhood depression have been developed, most of which represent modifications of adult depression inventories (see Kazdin & Petti 1982 for a review). The Beck Depression Inventory (BDI; Beck 1967), originally designed for adults, has been administered to adolescents with little or no modification (Teri 1982) and has spawned a number of child versions. The Child Depression Inventory (CDI) is a 27-item self-report inventory for children modeled after the BDI (Kovacs & Beck 1977). It focuses on depressive symptoms such as sadness and sleep and appetite disturbance. The CDI yields a single depression score which has been shown to be moderately stable over a 1-month period (r = .72), and to discriminate significantly between children referred for mental health versus pediatric services (Kovacs 1981). The Short Children's Depression Inventory (Carlson & Cantwell 1979), also modeled after the BDI, is a 13-item self-report inventory which has discriminated significantly between children meeting diagnostic criteria for affective disorders versus other disorders. Lefkowitz & Tesiny (1980) and Weissman et al (1980) have adapted other adult depression inventories for use with children, while Birleson (1981) has developed a self-report depression inventory for children aged 7–13.

SOCIAL BEHAVIOR   Several measures have been developed for assessing children's social behavior and social skills. Two self-report measures are marked by their similarity in approach and age range. The first, the Children's Action Tendency scale (CATS; DeLuty 1979), measures children's assertiveness, submissiveness, and aggression. The CATS describes conflict situations (e.g. someone shoves you out of line) followed by three pairs of alternatives representing all combinations of assertive, submissive, and aggressive responses. Items and response alternatives were selected to represent common problem situations and probable courses of action for children aged 6–12. CATS scores have correlated significantly with teacher and peer ratings of children's behavior, and scores on the Aggressive and Assertive scales discriminate significantly between hyperactive/aggressive boys and normal controls.

The second measure, the Children's Assertive Behavior Scale (CABS; Michelson & Wood 1982), includes 27 multiple choice items for responses to common social situations such as giving and receiving compliments, handling complaints, and making requests. The CABS yields a total score for assertive behavior, plus separate passive and aggressive scores. CABS scores have correlated significantly with classroom observations and teachers' ratings of social behavior and social skill. The CABS has also been shown to be sensitive to the effects of a social skills training program for elementary school children (Michelson & Wood 1980).

Interviews

Parent interviews have long been the mainstay of child clinical assessment, but they cannot be counted on to provide either a comprehensive description of the child's behavior or a reliable basis for differentiating among disturbed children. Unstructured interviews are vulnerable to serious information variance in that different interviewers elicit different information from different interviewees and may seek the same information in different ways. Efforts have been made to reduce information variance by standardizing interview procedures. Although most structured interviews are designed for parents, there are parallel versions for directly interviewing the child. Unlike checklists and rating scales, structured interviews have not been used to derive syndromes and categories of psychopathology, but have been employed either to screen children for psychiatric disturbance or to formulate diagnoses.

EARLY EFFORTS   In one of the first efforts to assess the prevalence of problem behaviors among a representative sample of children, Lapouse & Monk (1958, 1964) interviewed mothers of 482 children aged 6–12 from randomly selected homes in Buffalo. The 1½ hour interview included 200 questions covering a broad range of clinically relevant child behaviors. Most items required a yes/no response, but some were designed to elicit information regarding the frequency or intensity of target behaviors. Re-interview of mothers indicated high test-retest reliability (90% agreement) for concrete, easily observable behaviors such as bedwetting, thumb sucking, and stuttering, but low to moderate reliability (52–87% agreement) for behaviors requiring more subjective judgments (e.g. fears and worries) or precise estimates of frequency (e.g. number of temper tantrums). Also, mother-child agreement for 8- to 12-year-olds was good for behaviors such as bedwetting, temper tantrums, and biting fingernails, but was poor for many other behaviors. Analysis of discrepancies between mother and child revealed the following pattern: mothers tended to report more overt behaviors that are particularly irksome to adults (e.g. bedwetting, restlessness, overactivity), whereas children tended to report more covert problems (e.g. fears and worries, nightmares). This general pattern has been replicated in other studies.

In another pioneering effort, Rutter & Graham (1968) developed "semistructured" child interviews in which the content areas and coding were specified, but the exact wording of questions was left to the interviewer (see also Graham

& Rutter 1968). These semistructured interviews were reliable enough for purposes of identifyng children with psychiatric disturbances, but not for precise diagnostic formulations. For separate interviews of the child conducted by different clinicians, for example, overall ratings of whether the child had *no psychiatric impairment, some impairment,* or *definite or marked impairment* correlated .84. However, inter-rater reliability was mediocre for items pertaining to attention and motor behavior (average r = .61) and social relations (average r = .64), and was low for items pertaining to anxiety and depression (average r = .30). Two conclusions from this early work have been borne out in recent studies. First, many interview procedures yield reliable information regarding global psychiatric functioning, but not regarding specific syndromes or behaviors. Second, reliability is generally lower for "internalizing" problems such as fears, anxiety, and depression than for more overt "externalizing" problems.

SCREENING PROCEDURES   The Behavior Screening Questionnaire (BSQ; Richman & Graham 1971) is designed to identify preschool aged children with psychiatric disorders. It includes 60 questions concerning the health, development, and behavior of the child. A behavior problem scale was constructed from the 12 items that discriminated best between clinically referred and nonreferred children. BSQ scores have been shown to discriminate significantly between clinically referred and nonreferred children (Richman & Graham 1971) and to correlate significantly with clinicians' ratings of psychiatric disorder, although both these findings may have been biased by the raters' knowledge of other data provided by the parent in the interview (Richman & Graham 1971, Earls et al 1982).

To develop a screening inventory for children aged 6–18, Langner et al (1976) began by administering structured interviews to 2034 parents in Manhattan. The Child Screening Inventory was constructed by factor analyzing a large item pool into seven factors. The five items with the highest loadings on each factor were used to form a 35-item screening scale that correlated .69 with total impairment ratings derived from the entire interview, .49 with clinical referral, and .33 with psychiatrists' ratings of psychiatric impairment based on direct interviews with the child. These low correlations led the authors to recommend their scale as a descriptive tool rather than as a screening method (Langner et al 1976).

STRUCTURED INTERVIEWS WITH CHILDREN   Two structured interviews have been developed that are not tied to a specific diagnostic system, although they yield data relevant to psychiatric diagnoses. The Child Assessment Schedule (CAS; Hodges et al 1982) includes 75 questions about school, family, and friends, and 53 items pertaining to insight, grooming, attention span, etc, which the clinician rates following the interview with the child. Scores are obtained for total pathology, 11 content areas, and 9 "symptom complexes." Independent ratings of 53 videotaped interviews yielded an inter-rater correlation of .90 for total pathology score, but consistent with earlier findings, reliabilities for content areas and symptom complexes have been lower (average r = .73 and .69, respectively). Total pathology score has discriminated significantly between inpatient, outpatient, and normal control groups, and has correlated .53 with total behavior problem score on the Child Behavior Checklist completed by mothers. In addition, scores on the CAS Overanxious scale correlated .57 with scores on Spielberger's (1973) State-Trait Anxiety Scale for Children, and scores on the CAS Depression scale correlated .53 with scores on the Child Depression Inventory (Kovacs & Beck 1977).

The Interview Schedule for Children (ISC; Kovacs 1983) is a structured symptom-oriented interview designed for children aged 8–17. One form is for initial evaluations, while a second is for follow-up assessments. The ISC focuses on signs and symptoms related to depression, but includes items related to other childhood disorders (e.g. Conduct Disorder, Attention Deficit Disorder). It also includes a mental status exam; behavioral observations of the child's speech, motor behavior, attention span, etc; and the clinician's impressions in five areas such as grooming and cooperation. Most items are rated on an 0–8 scale ranging from *none* to *severe*—a procedure that appears to yield very reliable assessments. Two clinicians' interview ratings of the severity of the current disorder yielded an intraclass correlation of .92. Parent and child interviews have shown high agreement on items pertaining to conduct disorder but lower agreement for affective, cognitive, and vegetative symptoms (Kovacs 1983).

DIAGNOSTIC INTERVIEWS   The evolution of more explicit diagnostic criteria (Feighner et al 1972, American Psychiatric Association 1980) stimulated the development of highly structured diagnostic interviews for both adults and children. The Kiddie-SADS (Puig-Antich & Chambers 1978) is a structured interview for children aged 6–17 modeled after the Schedule for Affective Disorders and Schizophrenia (SADS), a structured interview for adults developed by Spitzer & Endicott (1978). The K-SADS covers episodes of current psychopathology and is designed to yield DSM-III diagnoses. It features an elaborate skip structure, with screening questions or "probes" beginning each section. Responses to these probes determine whether the subsequent questions should be asked or whether the section can be skipped. An epidemiological version (K-SADS-E) is designed for ascertaining both past and current problems (Orvaschel et al 1982). The K-SADS is widely cited in child psychiatry, but validation rests mainly on its use in identifying children who meet DSM-III criteria for major affective disorders (Puig-Antich et al 1978).

The Diagnostic Interview for Children and Adolescents (DICA) is a highly structured diagnostic interview that specifies the order and specific wording of questions as well as the response coding. Questions cover the frequency and duration of a broad range of psychiatric symptoms pertaining to DSM diagnoses. Herjanic & Campbell (1977) found that the number of symptoms computed from the DICA discriminated significantly between children attending a pediatric clinic versus a psychiatric clinic. Behavior and school items discriminated best between these groups, whereas items related to neurotic and somatic symptoms yielded the poorest discrimination. Agreement between mother and child has averaged 80% for the 207 DICA items (Herjanic et al 1975), but, because many DICA items are of low prevalence, high agreement is expected by chance. The statistic kappa, which corrects for chance agreement, averaged .22 for DICA items pertaining to psychiatric symptoms (Herjanic & Reich 1982). Agreement on diagnoses is only slightly better (Reich et al 1982).

Lastly, NIMH has commissioned development of the Diagnostic Interview Schedule for Children (DISC), a highly structured diagnostic interview designed to yield DSM-III diagnoses (Costello et al 1982, unpublished). Parallel versions of the DISC have been developed for parents and children. They cover a broader range of diagnoses than previous interview schedules and are designed for use by lay interviewers. Scheduled for completion in 1984, the DISC project is comparing data from parents and children at two points in time, data obtained by lay interviewers and clinicians, and interview data with behavioral, cognitive, medical, and school measures.

In summary, most structured psychiatric interviews for children and adolescents yield global indices that are reliable enough for ascertaining general deviance, but few validly discriminate among specific syndromes or problems. Reliability is generally higher for the presence versus absence of overt behaviors than for more covert phenomena or precise estimates of frequency. Validation consists mainly of "face" validity and the ability to discriminate between psychiatrically referred and nonreferred samples.

Comparisons between interviews of parents and children have generally revealed low levels of agreement, but this is not an indictment of either informant. There are consistencies in the disagreements, with mothers generally reporting more overt behavior problems while their children reported more neurotic problems. Because it is probably not realistic to expect exact agreement between parent and child, it would be more profitable to determine who can provide the most useful information for particular purposes.

Direct Observations

PARENT-CHILD INTERACTION   A variety of observational methods have been developed for assessing maladaptive interactions between parent and child (see

Roberts & Forehand 1978). Early assessment efforts used narrative descriptions of parent-child interactions in playrooms, clinic waiting rooms, and homes. These "open" assessment procedures have been largely replaced by "closed" assessment procedures for recording observations in predetermined categories.

Time sampling procedures, in which prespecified events are recorded during a series of brief time intervals, provide forced-choice formats that require the observer to choose between alternative codes for each interval (Forehand & Scarboro 1975). More complex forced-choice coding procedures have been developed for simultaneously recording the behavior of parent and child. For example, Hawkins et al (1966) recorded parents' attention/inattention and children's objectionable/nonobjectionable behavior during each time sample. This permits the analysis of the temporal continuity of parent and child behaviors and provides a basis for determining how changes in the behavior of one subject affect the behavior of the other.

Efforts have been made to move beyond the within-interval co-occurrence of behaviors to the analysis of *sequences* of behaviors over time. The response-class matrix developed by Mash et al (1973), for example, is designed to record antecedent-response "chains" in parent-child interaction. Two matrices are used in which the child's behaviors are considered antecedents and the parents' are considered consequences, and vice versa. Two synchronized observers record behaviors, each using one matrix. Taken together, the two matrices permit the analysis of target behaviors of parent or child, their antecedents, and consequences. Interobserver agreement has ranged from 76% to 96% for individual matrix cells. The resulting data have been used to select target behaviors and to evaluate interventions aimed at modifying parent-child interaction (Mash & Terdal 1973).

Although the response-class matrix permits analysis of simple behavioral sequences, it still imposes the constraints of circumscribed time intervals and predetermined antecedent-response chains. *Sequential event recording* procedures eliminate both constraints. Multiple events can be recorded in the order in which they occur, and all possible combinations of antecedents and consequences can be analyzed. One of the most widely used sequential event recording systems is the Family Interaction Coding System (FICS) developed by Patterson et al (1969). The FICS includes 29 codes for verbal and nonverbal behaviors of parent and child. Observations in the home are coded to enable any behavior of the target subject to be analyzed with respect to consequent behaviors of any other family member. Although the FICS is designed to analyze event sequences, most research has focused on analysis of "Total Deviant Behavior," a summary index reflecting the average number of aversive or noxious behaviors per minute (Patterson 1977).

CHILDREN'S PROBLEM BEHAVIOR   Direct observation procedures have also been developed to tap a broad range of behavior problems. The Direct Observation Form (DOF) of the Child Behavior Checklist includes 96 behavior problem items and a measure of on-task behavior (Achenbach & Edelbrock 1983, Reed & Edelbrock 1983). The observer writes a narrative description of the child's behavior over a 10-minute period, noting the occurrence, duration, and intensity of problem behaviors. Following the observation period, the observer rates the 96 behavior problem items on 0–1–2–3 scales that reflect a combination of occurrence, duration, and severity. The sum of scores on all 96 items constitutes a total behavior problem score. At the end of each minute of observation, the observer also notes on-task behavior for a period of 5 seconds. If the child's behavior is mainly on-task during the 5-second interval, he/she receives one point. To obtain a representative sample of a child's behavior, scores are averaged across six 10-minute sessions.

Interobserver correlations in the .90s have been obtained for total behavior problem scores (Achenbach & Edelbrock 1983). DOF scores have also correlated significantly with teachers' ratings of problem behavior, school performance, and adaptive functioning, and have discriminated significantly between referred and nonreferred children (Edelbrock & Reed 1983, Reed & Edelbrock 1983).

Several other omnibus observation systems deserve mention. First, Werry & Quay (1969) developed a 14-item coding system for deviant behaviors (e.g. out of seat), attending behaviors (e.g. attending, daydreaming), and teacher contact (rated as either teacher- or child-initiated and either positive or negative). Behaviors are coded every 20 seconds for a total of 15 minutes. Several codes have discriminated between normal and conduct-disordered children, and on-task score is sensitive to drug effects (Werry & Quay 1969). Second, Strain & Ezzell (1978) developed an 11-category observational system focused on disruptive/inappropriate behavior which has been used to assess disturbed children in residential treatment. Behaviors are coded continuously in 10-second blocks to permit analysis of sequences over time. Third, Patterson et al (1972) developed a complex system for coding behaviors in school settings. At the start of each observational period, the observer records the current academic activity (e.g. reading, arithmetic), judges whether the children's activities are currently *structured* or *unstructured* by the teacher, and records whether *group* or *individual* work is involved. Nineteen codes are used to record behaviors of the child and the responses of the teacher and/or peers. Following 4 hours of videotape training, interobserver agreement of 85% was achieved. This system has been shown to be sensitive to several types of interventions aimed at modifying classroom behavior. Lastly, Wahler et al (1976) developed an observational scheme covering 6 social event categories and 19 child behaviors, which fits into Wahler's broader "ecological assessment" of child behavior.

Observational measures have also been developed to assess specific categories of problems. One example is a 14-item observational code for identifying hyperactive children (Abikoff et al 1980). A second is the Preschool Observation Scale of Anxiety developed by Glennon & Weisz (1978) as an alternative to self-report anxiety inventories for young children. It includes 30 behaviors (e.g. cry, expression of fear or worry) that are recorded every 30 seconds for a 10-minute period. The interobserver correlation was .78 for total score and averaged .80 for the 23 codes having sufficient frequency to permit correlational analysis. Total score has correlated significantly with parent and teacher ratings of separation anxiety and with parent ratings of general anxiety. Lastly, the Behavior Observation Scale for Autism (Freeman et al 1978) includes 67 behaviors rated for nine 3-minute intervals. Inter-rater correlations have exceeded .84 for all but 12 items. Scores have discriminated significantly between normal, autistic, and retarded children.

METHODOLOGICAL ISSUES IN THE ASSESSMENT OF BEHAVIOR PROBLEMS

To provide a broad sample of research on the assessment of children's problem behavior, we had to sacrifice the space required for detailed methodological critiques. However, we now offer some summary generalizations regarding methodological issues that span much of the work in this area. (For more detailed methodological critiques, see Achenbach & Edelbrock 1978, Mash & Terdal 1981, Cone & Foster 1982).

Test-Retest Reliability and Stability

For direct observational measures, test-retest reliabilities are affected by changes in the child's behavior, as well as by the observers and the rating system. Because the behavior of disturbed children often varies from one observational setting and session to another, low test-retest reliabilities do not necessarily constitute error. Instead, multiple observation sessions are needed to obtain representative samples of a child's behavior. When scores for total observed behavior problems have been averaged over several sessions, they show moderate short-term test-retest reliability [e.g. $r = .78$ for home observations over a one-week interval (Patterson 1980)], and longer-term stability [$r = .55$ for classroom and $r = .60$ for recess observations over a 6-month interval (Achenbach & Edelbrock 1983)].

For ratings that reflect an informant's knowledge and judgment of a child's behavior rather than direct observations, changes in the child's behavior are not likely to affect short-term test-retest reliability much. Ratings by parents and teachers have generally yielded short-term test-retest correlations in the .80s and .90s (e.g. Conners 1969, Clarfield 1974, Achenbach & Edelbrock 1983), while self-ratings and ratings by peers have yielded correlations in the .70s (e.g. Kovacs & Beck 1977, Lefkowitz & Tesiny 1980, Humphrey 1982). Correlations in the .70s and .80s have been found for parent and teacher ratings over periods of 1½ to 6 months, .49 to .68 for parent ratings over 1½ years, and .39 for parent ratings over 5 years (see Achenbach & Edelbrock 1978). Although there is little long-term stability data on peer and self-ratings, Achenbach & Edelbrock (1983) obtained a 6-month test-retest correlation of .69 for total behavior problem scores by clinically-referred adolescents on the Youth Self-Report Form of the Child Behavior Checklist. It should be noted that behavior problem scores often decline significantly as a function of treatment or age, but the substantial correlations over short- and long-term test-retest intervals indicate considerable stability in rank ordering of scores.

Agreement Between Raters

Although test-retest reliabilities are typically lower for direct observational ratings than ratings by informants, the pattern is reversed with respect to inter-rater agreement. This is because inter-rater agreement for direct observations reflects the same input to both raters, whereas different informants are not exposed to identical samples of the subjects' behavior. Different informants see children's behavior under different circumstances and they exert different impacts on the behavior. Their personal standards for judging children may also affect their ratings more than those of trained observers recording behaviors within precisely defined categories, time intervals, and settings.

Although agreement on the specific coding of behavior problems tends to be lower, interobserver correlations between total scores for directly observed behavior problems have often been in the .90s (e.g. Patterson 1980, Achenbach & Edelbrock 1983). Agreement between pairs of informants who see the subjects under generally similar circumstances, such as mothers and fathers, teachers in the same classroom, and residential staff caring for children at the same time, have yielded correlations from the .60s to the .80s (see Achenbach & Edelbrock 1978). However, informants who see the subjects in markedly different situations, such as parents versus teachers, teachers versus child care workers, teachers of the same children in different classes, and teachers versus psychological examiners, show less agreement, with correlations ranging from about .20 to .50 (see Achenbach & Edelbrock 1978).

Consistency Among Empirically Identified Syndromes

In their reviews of multivariate analyses of behavior checklists, Achenbach & Edelbrock (1978) and Quay (1979) concluded that there was considerable consistency in the identification of certain syndromes across numerous studies. Although Quay (personal communication) focused mainly on agreement in four broad-band syndromes, he has acknowledged that when syndromes are viewed in a hierarchical fashion, there is consistency among findings of several additional narrow-band syndromes.

Lessing et al (1981) have argued that differences among studies in the specific content of syndromes contradict the conclusions regarding consistency, but this may reflect a disagreement over whether "the glass is half full or half empty." Despite differences in the specific items analyzed, the consistency among 27 studies was sufficient to enable two other psychologists to independently classify 90% of 124 obtained factors into 4 broad-band and 14 narrow-band categories we had established (Achenbach & Edelbrock 1978).

Considering the diversity of item pools and other methodological differences, these findings do not mean that factors are directly interchangeable from one study to another. Nevertheless, the correlations found between different instruments suggest that there is sufficient covariation among children's behavior problems as perceived by various informants to warrant an empirically based taxonomy (Achenbach & Edelbrock 1983). Based on this conclusion, Achenbach, Conners, and Quay are now collaborating on a project to test 12 syndromes derived from surveys of previous research. The syndromes are being tested through confirmatory multivariate analyses of data obtained on items designed to tap each hypothesized syndrome in new clinical samples.

Validity

Most multivariate analyses of behavior ratings were prompted by the lack of well-established diagnostic categories for childhood disorders. This lack of diagnostic categories makes it difficult to select criteria against which to validate the findings. The most common solution has been to compare scores obtained by children who, on other grounds, were judged to be deviant versus normal. According to this criterion, many of the measures have discriminated well (e.g. Werry & Quay 1969, Miller 1977, Goyette et al 1978, Abikoff et al 1980, Achenbach & Edelbrock 1981, 1983, Edelbrock & Achenbach 1983, Edelbrock & Reed 1983). Some measures have also been shown to discriminate among children who were grouped by categories such as depressed, delinquent, hyperactive, and aggressive (e.g. Ross et al 1965, Cowen et al 1973, Wirt et al 1977, Carlson & Cantwell 1979). However, research on assessment procedures has greatly outweighed research on the taxonomic distinctions they should help to make. We turn now to taxonomic concepts that shape the criteria against which assessment is to be validated.

TAXONOMY AND TAXOMETRY

In the nineteenth century, organic disease models were instrumental in promoting the scientific study of psychopathology. It was expected that systematic descriptions of symptom syndromes would enable researchers to pinpoint organic etiologies specific to each syndrome. Drawing upon a mélange of syndromes proposed by various authors, Kraepelin (1883) originated a classification system whose categories have continued to mold psychiatric thought for a century.

In certain respects, the most recent edition of the American Psychiatric Association's (1980) *Diagnostic and Statistical Manual of Mental Disorders* ("DSM-III") conforms more closely to the ideals of Kraepelinian nosology than the two preceding editions had (American Psychiatric Association 1952, 1968). Whereas the preceding editions presented most disorders in terms of narrative descriptions and psychodynamic inferences, DSM-III provides explicit criteria for each disorder. DSM-III emphasizes the nosological model through repeated references to disorders as "illnesses" and decision rules whereby some diagnoses are considered secondary to others. Each criterion for each disorder must be judged as either present or absent. If the requisite criteria are judged to be present, then the subject is concluded to have the disorder. Each disorder is thus conceptualized as a categorical entity which is either present or absent.

The official psychiatric nosology is not the sole source of categorical concepts in taxonomic thinking about behavior disorders. Scales constructed on an a priori basis, for example, are predicated on categories such as delinquency, depression, or hyperactivity. Even where factor analysis is used to identify covariation among behaviors in a quantitative fashion, studies often end with the naming of factors plus speculative interpretations about a class of children who have the disorders represented by the factors. Where external validation is sought for multivariate findings, it is often in terms of agreement with diagnostic categories.

Taxometric Approaches

As we stressed at the beginning of the chapter, most childhood behavior problems arouse concern when they seem *quantitatively* deviant from expectations for the child's age, for particular environmental situations, etc. They are also variable from day to day, from one situation to another, and from one interaction partner to another, and they can be offset to varying degrees by competencies.

Both the intrinsic importance of quantitative variations in children's behavior and the value of quantitative methods for identifying covariation among behaviors argue for metrical approaches to taxonomic problems. The term *taxometrics* has previously been applied to the use of cluster analysis to form taxonomies. More recently, Paul Meehl has called taxometrics "the branch of applied mathematics that treats of problems of classification" (Meehl & Golden 1982, p. 127). Meehl has illustrated his own taxometric concepts largely through the use of psychometric procedures for identifying a class of adult schizophrenics. This may be quite appropriate for traditional adult diagnostic categories such as schizophrenia. However, it is the conceptual shift from a *nominal* to a *metrical* framework that may be most helpful at this stage of research on childhood behavior disorders. Such a shift can help link assessment and taxonomy and can sharpen research on taxonomic problems in the following ways:

1. *Operational definition of phenotypes.* Behavior disorders can be defined operationally through the multivariate derivation of behavioral syndromes.
2. *Quantification of phenotypes.* Individuals can be assessed in terms of the number and intensity of a syndrome's behaviors that they manifest, rather than being judged in a yes-or-no fashion as to whether they show the syndrome. Quantification of syndromes also facilitates measurement of change as a function of interventions or development.
3. *Normative-developmental context.* By obtaining distributions of scores on each syndrome for representative samples of children at each age level, we can view the standing of individual children in relation to norms for their age. Thus, rather than having to make a forced choice as to whether a child is "sick" or "well," we can determine the degree to which the child's reported behavior deviates from that reported for other children. However, we can also adopt cutoffs on the distribution of scores in order to discriminate among groups in a categorical fashion, if desired.
4. *Profiles of scores.* If syndromes are viewed in quantitative terms rather than as categorical constructs, then a profile format can be used for simultaneously displaying each child's standing across all syndromes relevant to his/her age group. This provides a comprehensive picture of the degree of deviance in all areas assessed, rather than representing multiple problems in terms of multiple categorical diagnoses or neglecting some problems because they are preempted by a particular diagnosis. Profiles can also include positive adaptive competencies on separate scales.
5. *Quantitative derivation of typologies.* Quantitative clustering algorithms can be used to group children according to similarities in their overall profile patterns. Once profile types have been identified, we can compute the degree to which an individual child's profile resembles each type, rather than having to assign children to types in a yes-or-no fashion (see Achenbach & Edelbrock 1983).
6. *Multiple perspectives on behavior.* A metrical approach highlights the fact that there is no absolute criterion for what a disorder "really" is, independent

of human observations and judgment. Reports by trained observers, parents, teachers, clinicians, and children themselves are all constrained by the informants' perspectives and the ways in which we assess these perspectives. Instead of viewing disagreements among informants as error, we should recognize that different assessment systems can validly convey different pictures of a child. The differing pictures obtained from observers, parents, teachers, clinicians, and children may each contain valuable guides to action. To test the value of data from each source, we need to make these pictures as clear as possible.

SUMMARY

We considered problems of assessment and taxonomy that have hindered the study of childhood disorders. Many instruments have been developed for assessing children's behavior as seen by parents, teachers, clinicians, trained observers, peers, and children themselves. Multivariate analyses of behavior problems show consistencies in the identification of a few broad-band patterns and more numerous narrow-band syndromes, despite differences in specific items comprising different instruments. Satisfactory reliability has been achieved in many instances, although the variability of children's problem behavior limits agreement among informants who see children under different conditions. Despite their disagreements, however, each informant's perspective may validly contribute to the comprehensive assessment of a child's needs. The quantitative, relativistic, and developmental aspects of children's behavior disorders argue for replacing categorical approaches to assessment and taxonomy with taxometric approaches that capitalize on quantitative methods for identifying and assessing children's behavioral problems and competencies.

Literature Cited

Abikoff, H., Gittelman, R., Klein, D. F. 1980. Classroom observation code for hyperactive children: A replication of validity. *J. Consult. Clin. Psychol.* 48:555–65

Achenbach, T. M. 1978. The Child Behavior Profile: I. Boys aged 6–11. *J. Consult. Clin. Psychol.* 46:478–88

Achenbach, T. M. 1982. *Developmental Psychopathology.* New York: Wiley. 2nd ed.

Achenbach, T. M. 1984. Developmental psychopathology. In *Developmental Psychology: An Advanced Textbook,* ed. M. E. Lamb, M. H. Bornstein. Hillsdale, NJ: Erlbaum

Achenbach, T. M., Edelbrock, C. S. 1978. The classification of child psychopathology: A review and analysis of empirical efforts. *Psychol. Bull.* 85:1275–1301

Achenbach, T. M., Edelbrock, C. S. 1979. The Child Behavior Profile: II. Boys aged 12–16

and girls aged 6–11 and 12–16. *J. Consult. Clin. Psychol.* 47:223–33

Achenbach, T. M., Edelbrock, C. S. 1981. Behavioral problems and competencies reported by parents of normal and disturbed children aged four through sixteen. *Monogr. Soc. Res. Child Dev.* 46:Serial No. 188

Achenbach, T. M., Edelbrock, C. S. 1983. *Manual for the Child Behavior Checklist and Revised Child Behavior Profile.* Burlington, VT: Dep. Psychiatry, Univ. Vermont

American Psychiatric Association. 1980. *Diagnostic and Statistical Manual of Mental Disorders.* Washington DC: Am. Psychiatric Assoc. 3rd ed.; 2nd ed. 1968; 1st ed. 1952

Arkes, H. R. 1981. Impediments to accurate clinical judgment and possible ways to minimize their impact. *J. Consult. Clin. Psychol.* 49:323–30

Beck, A. T. 1967. *Depression: Causes and Treatment*. Philadelphia: Univ. Pennsylvania Press

Behar, L. B., Stringfield, S. 1974. A behavior rating scale for the preschool child. *Dev. Psychol.* 10:601–10

Birleson, P. 1981. The validity of depressive disorder in childhood and the development of a self rating scale: A research report. *J. Child Psychol. Psychiatry* 22:73–88

Bolstad, O. D., Johnson, S. M. 1977. The relationship between teachers' assessment of students and the students' actual behavior in the classroom. *Child Dev.* 48:570–78

Brown, L. L., Hammill, D. D. 1978. *Behavior Rating Profile: An Ecological Approach to Behavioral Assessment*. Austin, Tex: Pro-Ed

Carlson, G. A., Cantwell, D. P. 1979. A survey of depressive symptoms in a child and adolescent psychiatric population. *J. Am. Acad. Child Psychiatry* 18:587–99

Carlson, G. A., Cantwell, D. P. 1982. Diagnosis of childhood depression: A comparison of the Weinberg and DSM-III criteria. *J. Am. Acad. Child Psychiatry* 21:247–50

Castaneda, A., McCandless, B., Palermo, D. S. 1956. The Children's Form of the Manifest Anxiety Scale. *Child Dev.* 27:317–26

Clarfield, S. P. 1974. The development of a teacher referral form for identifying early school maladaptation. *Am. J. Community Psychol.* 2:199–210

Cone, J. D., Foster, S. L. 1982. Direct observation in clinical psychology. In *Handbook of Research Methods in Clinical Psychology*. New York: Wiley

Conners, C. K. 1969. A teacher rating scale for use in drug studies with children. *Am. J. Psychiatry* 126:884–88

Conners, C. K. 1970. Symptom patterns in hyperkinetic, neurotic and normal children. *Child Dev.* 4:667–82

Coopersmith, S. 1967. *The Antecedents of Self-Esteem*. San Francisco: Freeman

Cowen, E. L., Dorr, D., Clarfield, S., Kreling, B., McWilliams, S. A., et al. 1973. The AML: A quick-screening device for early identification of school maladaptation. *Am. J. Community Psychol.* 1:12–35

DeLuty, R. H. 1979. Children's Action Tendency Scale: A self-report measure of aggressive, assertiveness, and submissiveness in children. *J. Consult. Clin. Psychol.* 47:1061–71

Dreger, R. M. 1981. First-, second-, and third-order factors from the children's behavioral classification project instrument and an attempt at rapprochement. *J. Abnorm. Psychol.* 90:242–60

Earls, F., Jacobs, G., Goldfein, D., Silbert, A., Beardslee, W., et al. 1982. Concurrent validation of a behavior problem scale to use with 3-year-olds. *J. Am. Acad. Child Psychiatry* 21:47–57

Edelbrock, C. S., Achenbach, T. M. 1984. The teacher version of the Child Behavior Profile: I. Boys aged 6–11. *J. Consult. Clin. Psychol.* In press

Edelbrock, C. S., Reed, M. L. 1983. Convergent and discriminant validity of the teacher version of the Child Behavior Profile. Submitted for publication

Feighner, J. P., Robins, E., Guzé, S. B., Woodruff, R. A., Winokur, G., Muñoz, R. 1972. Diagnostic criteria for use in psychiatric research. *Arch. Gen. Psychiatry* 26:57–63

Forehand, R., Scarboro, M. E. 1975. An analysis of children's oppositional behavior. *J. Abnorm. Child Psychol.* 3:27–31

Freeman, B. J., Ritvo, E. R., Guthrie, D., Schroth, P., Ball, J. 1978. The Behavior Observation Scale for Autism. *J. Am. Acad. Child Psychiatry* 17:576–88

Fry, P. S. 1977. Success, failure, and resistance to temptation. *Dev. Psychol.* 13:519–20

Glennon, B., Weisz, J. R. 1978. An observational approach to the assessment of anxiety in young children. *J. Consult. Clin. Psychol.* 46:1246–57

Glow, R. A., Glow, P. H., Rump, E. E. 1982. The stability of child behavior disorders: A one year test-retest study of Adelaide versions of the Conners teacher and parent rating scales. *J Abnorm. Child Psychol.* 10:33–60

Goyette, C. H., Conners, C. K., Ulrich, R. F. 1978. Normative data on revised Conners Parent and Teacher Rating Scales. *J. Abnorm. Child Psychol.* 6:221–36

Graham, P., Rutter, M. 1968. The reliability and validity of the psychiatric assessment of the child: II. Interview with the parent. *Br. J. Psychiatry* 114:581–92

Green, K. D., Beck, S. J., Forehand, R., Vosk, B. 1980. Validity of teacher nominations of child behavior problems. *J. Abnorm. Child Psychol.* 8:397–404

Hartmann, D. 1983. Editorial. *Behav. Assess.* 5:1–3

Hawkins, R. P., Peterson, R. F., Schweid, E., Bijou, S. W. 1966. Behavior therapy in the home: Amelioration of problem parent-child relations with the parent in the therapeutic role. *J. Exp. Child Psychol.* 4:99–107

Herjanic, B., Campbell, W. 1977. Differentiating psychiatrically disturbed children on the basis of a structured interview. *J. Abnorm. Child Psychol.* 5:127–34

Herjanic, B., Herjanic, M., Brown, F., Wheatt, T. 1975. Are children reliable reporters? *J. Abnorm. Child Psychol.* 3:41–48

Herjanic, B., Reich, W. 1982. Development of a structured psychiatric interview for children: Agreement between child and parent on individual symptoms. *J. Abnorm. Child Psychol.* 10:307–24

Hodges, K., McKnew, D., Cytryn, L., Stern, L., Kline, J. 1982. The Child Assessment Schedule (CAS) Diagnostic Interview: A report on reliability and validity. *J. Am. Acad. Child Psychiatry* 21:468–73

Humphrey, L. L. 1982. Children's and teachers' perspectives on children's self-control: The development of two rating scales. *J. Consult. Clin. Psychol.* 50:624–33

Ireton, H., Thwing, E. 1974. *The Minnesota Child Development Inventory.* Minneapolis: Behav. Sci. Syst.

Kazdin, A. E., Petti, T. A. 1982. Self-report and interview measures of childhood and adolescent depression. *J. Child Psychol. Psychiatry* 23:437–57

Kendall, P. C., Wilcox, L. E. 1979. Self-control in children: Development of a rating scale. *J. Consult. Clin. Psychol.* 47:1020–29

Kohn, M., Koretsky, M. B., Haft, M. S. 1979. An adolescent symptom checklist for juvenile delinquents. *J. Abnorm. Child Psychol.* 7:15–29

Kohn, M., Rosman, B. L. 1972. A social competence scale and symptom checklist for the preschool child: Factor dimensions, their cross-instrument generality, and longitudinal persistence. *Dev. Psychol.* 6:430–44

Kohn, M., Rosman, B. L. 1973a. Cross-situational and longitudinal stability of social-emotional functioning in young children. *Child Dev.* 44:721–27

Kohn, M., Rosman, B. L. 1973b. A two-factor model of emotional disturbance in the young child: Validity and screening efficiency. *J. Child Psychol. Psychiatry* 14:31–56

Kovacs, M. 1981. Rating scales to assess depression in school aged children. *Acta Paedopsychiatry* 46:305–15

Kovacs, M. 1983. The longitudinal study of child and adolescent psychopathology: I. The semi-structured psychiatric interview schedule for children (ISC). Submitted for publication

Kovacs, M., Beck, A. T. 1977. An empirical-clinical approach toward a definition of childhood depression. In *Depression in Childhood: Diagnosis, Treatment, and Conceptual Models,* ed. J. G. Schulterbrandt, A. Raskin. New York: Raven

Kraepelin, E. 1883. *Compendium der Psychiatrie.* Leipzig: Abel

Lachar, D., Gdowski, C. L., Snyder, D. K. 1982. Broad-band dimensions of psychopathology: Factor scales for the Personality Inventory for Children. *J. Consult. Clin. Psychol.* 50:634–42

Lambert, N. M., Nicoll, R. C. 1976. Dimensions of adaptive behavior of retarded and nonretarded public-school children. *Am. J. Ment. Defic.* 81:135–46

Langner, T. S., Gersten, J. C., McCarthy, E. D., Eisenberg, J. G., Greene, E. L., et al. 1976. A screening inventory for assessing psychiatric impairment in children 6 to 18. *J. Consult. Clin. Psychol.* 44:286–96

Lapouse, R., Monk, M. A. 1958. An epidemiologic study of behavior characteristics of children. *Am. J. Public Health* 48:1134–44

Lapouse, R., Monk, M. A. 1964. Behavior deviations in a representative sample of children: Variations by sex, age, race, social class and family size. *Am. J. Orthopsychiatry* 34:436–46

Lefkowitz, M. M., Tesiny, E. P. 1980. Assessment of childhood depression. *J. Consult. Clin. Psychol.* 48:43–50

Lessing, E. E., Williams, V., Revelle, W. 1981. Parallel forms of the IJR Behavior Checklist for parents, teachers, and clinicians. *J. Consult. Clin. Psychol.* 49:34–50

Mash, E. J., Terdal, L. G. 1973. Modification of mother-child interactions: Playing with children. *Ment. Retard.* 11:44–49

Mash, E. J., Terdal, L. G., eds. 1981. *Behavioral Assessment of Childhood Disorders.* New York: Guilford

Mash, E. J., Terdal, L., Anderson, K. 1973. The response-class matrix: A procedure for recording parent-child interactions. *J. Consult. Clin. Psychol.* 40:163–64

Meehl, P. E., Golden, R. R. 1982. Taxometric methods. In *Handbook of Research Methods in Clinical Psychology,* ed. P. C. Kendall, J. N. Butcher. New York: Wiley

Michelson, L., Wood, R. 1980. A group assertive training program for elementary school children. *Child Behav. Ther.* 2:1–9

Michelson, L., Wood, R. 1982. Development and psychometric properties of the Children's Assertive Behavior Scale. *J. Behav. Assess.* 4:3–13

Miller, L. C. 1967. Louisville Behavior Checklist for males 6–12 years of age. *Psychol. Rep.* 21:885–96

Miller, L. C. 1972. School Behavior Checklist: An inventory of deviant behavior for elementary school children. *J. Consult. Clin. Psychol.* 38:134–44

Miller, L. C. 1977. *Louisville Behavior Checklist Manual.* Los Angeles: West. Psychol. Serv.

Miller, L. C., Hampe, E., Barrett, C. L., Noble, H. 1972. Test-retest reliability of parent ratings of children's deviant behavior. *Psychol. Rep.* 31:249–50

Nay, W. R. 1979. *Multimethod Clinical Assessment.* New York: Gardner

Orvaschel, H., Puig-Antich, J., Chambers, W., Tabrizi, M. A., Johnson, R. 1982. Retrospective assessment of prepubertal major depression with the Kiddie-SADS-E. *J. Am. Acad. Child Psychiatry* 21:392–97

Patterson, G. R. 1977. Naturalistic observation in clinical assessment. *J. Abnorm. Child Psychol.* 5:309–22

Patterson, G. R. 1980. Mothers: The unacknowledged victims. *Monogr. Soc. Res. Child Dev.* 45:Serial No. 186

Patterson, G. R. 1981. Forward. See Mash & Terdal 1981, pp. vii–viii

Patterson, G. R., Cobb, J. A., Ray, R. S. 1972. Direct intervention in the classroom: A set of procedures for the aggressive child. In *Implementing Behavioral Programs for Schools and Clinics*, ed. F. Clark, D. Evans, L. Hamerlynck. Champaign, Ill: Research Press

Patterson, G. R., Ray, R. S., Shaw, D. A., Cobb, J. A. 1969. *Manual for Coding of Family Interactions*. Eugene: Oregon Res. Inst.

Peterson, D. R. 1961. Behavior problems of middle childhood. *J. Consult. Psychol.* 25:205–9

Petti, T. A. 1983. Depression and withdrawal in children. In *Handbook of Child Psychopathology*, ed. T. H. Ollendick, M. Hersen. New York: Plenum

Pimm, J. B., Quay, H. C., Werry, J. S. 1967. Dimensions of problem behavior in first grade children. *Psychol. Sch.* 4:155–57

Prior, M., Boulton, D., Gajzago, C., Perry, D. 1975. The classification of childhood psychoses by numerical taxonomy. *J. Child Psychol. Psychiatry* 16:321–30

Puig-Antich, J., Blau, S., Marx, N., Greenhill, L. I., Chambers, W. 1978. Pre-pubertal major depressive disorder: a pilot study. *J. Am. Acad. Child Psychiatry* 17:695–707

Puig-Antich, J., Chambers, W. 1978. *The Schedule for Affective Disorders and Schizophrenia for School-aged Children (Kiddie-SADS)*. New York: NY State Psychiatric Inst.

Quay, H. C. 1966. Personality patterns in preadolescent delinquent boys. *Educ. Psychol. Meas.* 26:99–110

Quay, H. C. 1979. Classification. In *Psychopathological Disorders of Childhood*, ed. H. C. Quay, J. S. Werry. New York: Wiley. 2nd ed.

Quay, H. C., Morse, W. C., Cutler, R. L. 1966. Personality patterns of pupils in special classes for the emotionally disturbed. *Except. Child.* 32:297–301

Quay, H. C., Peterson, D. R. 1975. *Manual for the Behavior Problem Checklist*. Coral Gables, Fla: Univ. Miami. Rev. ed.

Quay, H. C., Quay, L. C. 1965. Behavior problems in early adolescence. *Child Dev.* 36:215–20

Reed, M. L., Edelbrock, C. S. 1983. Reliability and validity of the Direct Observation

Form of the Child Behavior Checklist. *J. Abnorm. Child Psychol.* In press

Reich, W., Herjanic, B., Welner, Z., Gandhy, P. R. 1982. Development of a structured psychiatric interview for children: Agreement on diagnosis comparing child and parent interviews. *J. Abnorm. Child Psychol.* 10:325–36

Reivich, R. S., Rothrock, I. A. 1972. Behavior problems of deaf children and adolescents: A factor analytic study. *J. Speech Hear. Res.* 15:93–104

Reynolds, C. R., Paget, K. D. 1981. Factor analysis of the Revised Children's Manifest Anxiety Scale for Blacks, Whites, Males and Females with a national normative sample. *J. Consult. Clin. Psychol.* 44:352–59

Reynolds, C. R., Richman, B. O. 1979. Factor structure and construct validity of "What I Think and Feel": The Revised Children's Manifest Anxiety Scale. *J. Pers. Assess.* 43:281–83

Richman, N., Graham, P. 1971. A behavioral screening questionnaire for use with three-year-old children: Preliminary findings. *J. Child Psychol. Psychiatry* 12:5–33

Roberts, M. A., Milich, R., Loney, J., Caputo, J. 1981. A multitrait multimethod analysis of variance of teachers' ratings of aggression, hyperactivity, and inattention. *J. Abnorm. Child Psychol.* 9:371–80

Roberts, M. W., Forehand, R. 1978. The assessment of maladaptive parent-child interaction by direct observation: An analysis of methods. *J. Abnorm. Child Psychol.* 6:257–70

Roper, R., Hinde, R. A. 1979. A teacher's questionnaire for individual differences in social behavior. *J. Child Psychol. Psychiatry* 20:287–98

Ross, A. O., Lacey, H. M., Parton, D. A. 1965. The development of a behavior checklist for boys. *Child Dev.* 36:1013–27

Ross, A. O., Pelham, W. E. 1981. Child psychopathology. *Ann. Rev. Psychol.* 32:243–78

Rutter, M. 1967. A children's behaviour questionnaire for completion by teachers: Preliminary findings. *J. Child Psychol. Psychiatry* 8:1–11

Rutter, M., Graham, P. 1968. The reliability and validity of the psychiatric assessment of the child: I. Interview with the child. *Br. J. Psychiatry* 114:563–79

Spielberger, C. D. 1973. *Manual for the State-Trait Anxiety Inventory for Children*. Palo Alto: Consult. Psychol. Press

Spitzer, R. L., Endicott, J. 1978. *Schedule for Affective Disorders and Schizophrenia*. NIMH Clin. Res. Branch. Washington DC; GPO

Spivack, G., Swift, M. 1972. *Hahnemann High School Behavior Rating Scale (HHSB)*

Manual. Philadelphia: Hahnemann Med. Coll. Hosp.

Strain, P. S., Ezzell, D. 1978. The sequence and distribution of behavioral disordered adolescents' disruptive/inappropriate behaviors. *Behav. Modif.* 2:403–25

Swan, G. E., MacDonald, M. L. 1978. Behavior therapy in practice: A national survey of behavior therapists. *Behav. Ther.* 9:799–807

Teri, L. 1982. The use of the Beck Depression Inventory with adolescents. *J. Abnorm. Child Psychol.* 10:277–84

Trites, R. L. 1979. Prevalence of hyperactivity in Ottawa, Canada. In *Hyperactivity in Children: Etiology, Measurement and Treatment Implications*. Baltimore: Univ. Park Press

Trites, R. L., Blouin, A. G. A., Lapvade, K. 1982. Factor analysis of the Conners Teacher Rating Scale based on a large normative sample. *J. Consult. Clin. Psychol.* 50:615–23

Wade, T. C., Baker, T. B., Hartmann, D. P. 1979. Behavior therapists' self-reported views and practices. *Behav. Ther.* 2:3–6

Wahler, R., House, A., Stambaugh, E. 1976. *Ecological Assessment of Child Problem Behavior*. New York: Pergamon

Walker, H. M. 1976. *Walker Problem Behavior Identification Checklist*. Los Angeles; West. Psychol. Serv.

Weir, K., Duveen, G. 1981. Further development and validation of the prosocial behavior questionnaire for use by teachers. *J. Child Psychol. Psychiatry* 22:357–74

Weissman, M. M., Orvaschel, H., Padian, N. 1980. Children's symptom and social functioning self-report scales: comparisons of mothers' and children's reports. *J. Nerv. Ment. Dis.* 168:736–40

Werry, J. S., Quay, H. C. 1969. Observing the classroom behavior of elementary school children. *Except. Child.* 35:461–70

Wiggins, J. S. 1981. Clinical and statistical prediction: Where are we and where do we go from here? *Clin. Psychol. Rev.* 1:3–18

Wirt, R. D., Lachar, D., Klinedinst, J. K., Seat, P. D. 1977. *Multidimensional Description of Child Personality. A Manual for the Personality Inventory for Children*. Los Angeles: West. Psychol. Serv.

Ann. Rev. Psychol. 1984. 35:257–76
Copyright © 1984 by Annual Reviews Inc. All rights reserved

BIOLOGICAL MOTIVATION

Richard E. Whalen and Neal G. Simon

Department of Psychology, University of California, Riverside, California 92521

CONTENTS

INTRODUCTION

Traditionally, behaviorists have felt the need for some concept of motivation to explain the fact that organisms do not respond in an invariant manner to some defined stimulus. Organisms eat only when hungry, drink only when thirsty, mate only when horny, and fight or flee only when afraid. As an intervening variable between stimulus and response, motivation has been a handy concept. More importantly, when applied with some rigor, such concepts have led to novel experimentation and unexpected findings. A classic example in this regard was the prediction that if rats with lesions to the ventromedial nucleus of the hypothalamus become hyperphagic and obese, they must be hungrier than neurologically intact rats. If they are hungrier, they should be willing to work harder to obtain food. As Miller et al (1950) showed, this is not the case. The novel conclusion was that the lesion had interfered with a neural satiety mechanism.

A less powerful motivational concept is that of instinct (less powerful because the term "instinct" has been applied in so many ways—to describe

257

movement patterns, to suggest that a behavior is inherited and not learned, and to account for changes in response emission under constant stimulation). While attempts to eradicate the instinct concept have been numerous, the concept remains with us.

Most instinct theories include the inference that genes regulate behavior. And indeed, individual differences in genotype are related to individual differences in behavior. We feel, however, that behavior genetic analysis is used too seldom to understand motivated behavior. It can be a powerful tool, and we will illustrate its use in the study of aggressive behavior and its hormonal control.

One way that gene action may be expressed is through the regulation of neurotransmitter function. The investigation of the relationships between neurotransmitters and behavior has been an exciting area of study in recent years, but one fraught with difficulties. We will review studies on the neurochemistry of aggression to illustrate this point.

The most commonly studied drives are regulated by changing internal states, and some of this research will be reviewed. However, it is noteworthy that incentive motivation, now discussed in terms of "hedonic processes," is receiving renewed attention and some of this work will be described.

Within the past few years a new dimension has been added to the study of behavior: regulation by neural and peripheral peptides. We will note some of the recent work indicating that the peptide cholecystokinin may serve as a hunger satiety signal.

In our final section, we will consider how motivated states can fluctuate in systematic ways, namely in the form of biological rhythms. Chronopsychology is in its infancy, but doubtless will prove important in the future.

SOURCES OF INFORMATION

In earlier days, two mainline journals of the American Psychological Association, the *Psychological Bulletin* and the *Psychological Review,* were considered major outlets for reviews and theoretical pieces on the biology of motivated behavior. For example, in 1962, Teitelbaum & Epstein published their influential article, "The lateral hypothalamic syndrome: Recovery of feeding and drinking after lateral hypothalamic lesions" in *Psychological Review,* and in 1964 Goddard published his widely read "Functions of the amygdala" in the *Psychological Bulletin.* Articles of this type have almost completely disappeared from these two journals, but some still appear in other publications.

M. Wayner provided an alternative outlet, now called *Neuroscience and Biobehavioral Reviews* (N&BR), of which Volume 7 was published in 1983. During the past 2 years nearly every one of the quarterly issues has contained at least one article of interest to the student of the biology of motivation.

One important theme that has captured the editors of N&BR has been addiction, one of the most powerful of motivating states, but one that traditionally has not been considered by motivational theorists. Schuster & Johanson (1981) reviewed drug seeking and reported that several variables, including reinforcement conditions, deprivation states, genotype, and age, can influence the self-administration of drugs.

Animal models of addiction were difficult to generate until Falk in 1961 discovered that intermittent food reinforcement led to polydipsia. In 1972, Falk and co-workers demonstrated that these procedures could be used to induce rats to consume sufficiently large volumes of ethanol to become dependent. Schedule-induced polydipsia, now termed "adjunctive behavior," is considered by Colotla (1981) to be ". . . the best available model of alcoholism . . .".

Interestingly, schedule-induced polydipsia has presented some difficulties for the study of drugs other than alcohol ingestion because of taste factors. Singer, et al (1982) have found that it is possible to apply the principles of adjunctive behavior control to get rats to self-inject drugs. Using a fixed-interval of 60 sec for food delivery, and allowing the rat to lever press as the adjunctive behavior, they found that rats would self-inject, via a venous catheter, alcohol, heroin, methadone, and nicotine. The procedure was ineffective with haloperidol. With cocaine, the schedule was without effect, although restriction of the body weight to 80% of normal greatly facilitated cocaine injection. The authors make the important point that it is the interaction of environmental variables such as food restriction and reinforcement schedule with the pharmacological properties of the drugs that determines the success of drug self-administration.

Although there is still controversy about whether adjunctive behavior is fundamentally different from operant and respondent conditioning (Wetherington 1982) the procedure has nonetheless proved valuable for the study of addiction.

N&BR has also published in more traditional areas of ingestion. Rossi et al (1982) raised the controversy of the role of norepinephrine (NE) in feeding and provide data in support of a role for NE in feeding regulation. Houpt (1982) provides an extensive review of gastrointestinal factors in hunger and satiety, reminding us that, as phrased by Novin & Vander Weele (1977) ". . . there is more to regulation than the hypothalamus."

Also of interest to students of the biology of motivation are reviews on the neural sites that may be involved in the inhibition of defensive behavior, predatory killing, and social attack in rats (Albert & Walsh 1982), the changing responsiveness of aging rats to the action of estrogen on sexual behavior and body weight control (Dudley 1982), and the role of neurotransmitter activity on neural hormone-sensitive cells that control reproductive behavior (Nock & Feder 1981).

Finally, in the summer of 1981, N&BR published a series of articles by Katz and colleagues on a topic that should be of interest to students of motivation, namely, an animal model of depression. Katz reviewed animal models and human depressive disorders; Katz, Roth and Carroll developed a possible model which involved a comparison of the effects of acute stress on the open-field activity of rats which had or had not been subjected to prior chronic stress. In the control rats, acute stress increased activity; in the chronically stressed rats, acute stress failed to increase activity levels. Treatment with the antidepressant monoamine oxidase inhibitor pargyline reduced the inhibitory effect of chronic stress.

Roth & Katz demonstrated that the tricyclic antidepressant imipramine also restored the response to acute stress of chronically stressed rats, and Katz, Roth & Schmaltz showed a similar effect of tranylcypromine, an effect not duplicated by amphetamine. Katz & Hersh showed that the antidepressant amitriptyline was effective, but that the anticholinergic agent scopolamine was only marginally effective. Finally, Katz demonstrated that electroconvulsive shock would also dissipate the inhibitory effects of chronic stress. While one might argue that the suppression of open-field activity can at best provide a limited model of human depression, these studies deserve critical attention.

In addition to journal articles, one book has appeared which is a must for the serious student of biological motivation. The volume is "The Physiological Mechanisms of Motivation," edited by D. W. Pfaff (1982a). Part I, with chapters by Pfaff and by Epstein, is concerned with motivational concepts; Part II (Pfaffmann, Norgren & Grill, Smith, Grinker, Epstein) deals with hunger and thirst; Part III discusses thermal, maternal, and sexual motivation (Satinoff, Fahrbach & Pfaff, Pfaff); Part IV concerns approach and avoidance (Solomon, Halperin & Pfaff, Stellar, Miller, Mayer & Price). The articles are for the most part well written, thorough, and challenging.

One can argue that Epstein's comparison of instinct and motivation as explanations for complex behavior is basically futile. For example, he argues that instinct is simpler than motivation, is a heritable phenotype, is species-specific and occurs in small-brained, short-lived animals that live in isolation. Motivation, on the other hand, seems to be characterized by instrumental learning, is goal directed and occurs with affect. These defining attributes of instinct and motivation seem arbitrary and of little value in understanding the ontogeny and display of behavior. For example, what does "species-specific" mean? In one sense, all behaviors (or internal states) are species-specific, and in another sense, many behaviors often called species-specific might more accurately be termed sex-specific. Similarly, how small is "small brained"? Since all behaviors and motivational states are influenced by genotype and since genotypes are only expressed as a result of environmental influences (of which instrumental learning is only one), it would seem more productive to analyze the interaction of genotype and environment for an understanding of the expression of a behavioral phenotype.

It might be useful here to recall McGaugh's studies of the S1 and S3 derivatives of Tryon's rats that were selectively bred to be "maze-bright" or "maze-dull." In one of a series of studies of these animals, McGaugh and colleagues (1961, 1962) showed that under "standard" test conditions, that is, with a 30 sec interval between trials, on a Lashley III maze the descendents of the maze-bright animals made fewer errors in learning the maze than did the descendents of the maze-dull line. However, when the intertrial interval was increased to 300 sec, the "dull" rats made fewer errors than the "bright" rats. Clearly, the expression of these genotypes was a function of the environment and the categorization of "bright" and "dull" a misnomer. Similarly, those behaviors termed instinctive by Epstein might simply reflect low variability in the environment in which those behaviors are expressed relative to the environmental variability typical of the expression of "motives."

Pfaffmann reminds us of the importance of the quality of incentives in the regulation of motivation and of the difficulty of moving from behavioral phenomenology to an understanding of the physiology of behavior. Norgren and Grill echo this theme and describe fascinating studies of oral factors in the acceptance and rejection of gustatory stimuli and their control at different levels of the neuroaxis.

Grinker provides a valuable review of human obesity with an update on the role of adipose tissue, reminding us that the hypothesis that brown fat plays a role in obesity remains speculative. He also reminds us that the exciting studies of the late 1970s by Schachter emphasizing "externality and internality" in the regulation of food intake have in several instances not been confirmed and in other instances have been reinterpreted.

Epstein reviews the physiology of thirst, emphasizing the important distinction between thirst induced by cellular dehydration and that induced by reduced blood volume (hypovolemia). The lateral preoptic area is identified as the site of maximum concentration of osmoreceptors, with hypovolemic thirst being controlled at other sites. Indeed, Fitzsimons showed that hypovolemic thirst was reduced in nephrectomized animals, a finding that has led to extensive research on the role of angiotensin II in water regulation. As noted by Epstein, this has been a controversial area of research which was further complicated by the finding of an independent angiotensin system within the brain. While heat seems to be off this research area, the light is still only flickering at the end of the tunnel. According to Epstein, a neuropharmacology of thirst has yet to develop. Some evidence suggests that angiotensin-induced thirst may be mediated by dopamine, with some contribution by serotonin and possibly by histamine and acetylcholine.

Quite often investigators become so involved in examining the motivational system of their choice that they fail to seek possible insights provided by studies of other motivational systems. In an interesting chapter, Satinoff goes beyond this bias and directly compares her "system of choice," thermoregulation, with the neural control of sexual behavior. First, the neural regulation of thermoregulation is reviewed and the hierarchical organization of multiple "miniature thermoregulatory systems" at several levels of the neuraxis is noted. Stress on the existence of multiple thermostats is important because of the widely held view that "the" thermostat is located in the preoptic area.

Placing thermoregulation in an evolutionary context, Satinoff is able to clarify the reason for multiple thermostats—they evolved separately, initially serving other functions. Using this model, the similarities between thermal and sexual behaviors are then considered. As with thermoregulation, the preoptic area is important for sexual responding, particulary for the initiation of male copulation. This appears to require intact fibers from the medial preoptic area (POA) to the medial forebrain bundle. Lesions that interrupt fibers from the POA-anterior hypothalamus allow male rats to initiate copulation, but the patterning of their mounts, intromissions, and ejaculations is altered. Satinoff notes that the components of female sexual behavior are also separable, with the ventromedial hypothalamic area now playing a major role.

Satinoff likens temperature detectors to hormone receptors in that they are both widely distributed in the brain, an interesting analogy, even though the time constant for thermal sensors and hormone receptors are certainly quite different—following the onset of hormonal stimulation, several hours or even days pass before behavioral change is observed. Satinoff argues cogently that thermoregulatory processes evolved from systems originally serving other functions. Her suggestion of a parallelism with components of sexual response systems is much less compelling. All in all, however, Satinoff's analysis is quite intriguing.

Fahrbach and Pfaff discuss the neural and hormonal mechanisms in the regulation of maternal behavior. The focus is on maternal performance rather than maternal motivation because, as the authors point out, few studies have used the intervening variable approach (e.g. requiring the performance of an arbitrary response to gain access to pups or nest material) to study maternalism. Fahrbach and Pfaff provide evidence that while nest building, pup carrying and pup licking can occur in the absence of hormonal stimulation, both estrogen and progesterone, and their interaction can facilitate and inhibit maternal behavior. As with sexual behavior, the medial preoptic area appears to be a nodal point in the control of maternal behavior.

Pfaff reviews sexual motivation. He makes what appears to be a strained argument that lordosis, the concave arching of the back shown by females of many species when receptive, is a motivated behavior. This response, which involves both spinal and supraspinal components, still seems basically "reflex-ive." Had what Beach (1976) has termed "proceptive" behavior been discussed, a better argument for motivation might have been made. Nonetheless, Pfaff does make an interesting argument for reciprocal regulation of lordosis and pain. In this the probability of lordosis is related to sensitivity to somatosensory input.

Pfaff does consider sexual motivation, reviewing the classic work of Warner (1927) and Nissen (1929), using variants of the Columbia Obstruction Apparatus and the more recent work of Meyerson's laboratory (Meyerson and Lindstrom 1971, 1973), but these are studies of females approaching male incentives and not studies of females seeking an opportunity to display lordosis. Male behavior receives a similar treatment, i.e. a greater emphasis on sexual performance than on tests of sexual motivation.

Students might compare carefully the Satinoff and Pfaff analyses of thermoregulation and copulation. It is our belief that even though hormones control copulation and temperature stimuli control thermoregulation, not all aspects of either process are most fruitfully conceptualized in terms of "motivation."

Initiating Part IV of this valuable book, Solomon reviews his "opponent process" theory. There is little new here, but it is a worthwhile reminder of a different conceptual approach.

Also reviewing mainly older literature, Halperin and Pfaff "entertain a hypothesis that relates brain control of ICSS (intracranial self-stimulation) and autonomic function." Their "simplest hypothesis" is that neural loci that are positive for ICSS should "exert excitatory control over the parasympathetic nervous system." The evidence they present supports a positive correlation for sites in the forebrain; however, positive sites in the midbrain stimulate sympathetic arousal. A clever "out" is not yet at hand, but seems worth pursuing. The effects of vagotomy on hyperphagia and ICSS reviewed by these authors are particularly intriguing.

Two "senior citizens" in the motivation game, Eliot Stellar and Neal Miller, are still making their points. Stellar updates his well-known 1954 paper on the physiology of motivation with a consideration of hedonic processes. He is now highlighting the possible role of peptides such as cholecystokinin (CCK) in the regulation of "hunger."

Miller, who has been the master of the intervening variable model of motivation, reviews the model once again, but over 40% of his citations are to papers published in the past decade. In this review Miller emphasized the effects of stress in taking two philosophical positions, namely, (a) a theory is important because it stimulates experiments, and (b) a theory is not overthrown by facts, but is replaced by a better theory. In this piece Miller applies the intervening variable model effectively in the context of psychosomatic medicine.

In a final chapter, Mayer and Price analyze pain as a model of motivation. As they point out, scientists have concerned themselves more with the sensory aspects of pain than with its motivational properties, even though experimental psychologists regularly use pain as a motivator. This may reflect the fact that when we experience serious pain—from burns, mutilated muscles, broken bones, or cancer—we don't have the option that the rat usually has of pressing a lever or running to a safe compartment. When we run, we take our pain with us.

Advances have been made in pain research—spectacular advances. But it would appear that the advances reflect current concepts of endogenous opiates and opiate receptors and how these systems interact with pain stimuli (which are clearly different from intense pressure stimuli).

We know more about the neurology of pain, but still not an impressive amount. Mayer and Price specify three distinct components of pain—sensory-discriminative, affective-motivational, and cognitive-evaluative. The pathways of the sensory-discriminative component are becoming understood in terms of both afferent and efferent control, but we still know little of the neurology of the other components, although Mayer and Price feel that current evidence indicates a "divergence of neural processing of nocioceptive information" at the mesencephalic level, with sensory components running laterally and the affective components running medially, the sensory component showing specialization at the thalamic level.

One of the conceptually important points made by Mayer and Price from their own work is the existence of dual opioid and nonopioid pain systems. How these multiple systems relate to motivation can lead to fascinating speculation, and one might hope to a better understanding of the intense motivational states that result from opiate addiction.

GENES AND MOTIVATIONAL SYSTEMS

Individual differences (and species differences) in the performance of motivated responses are certainly regulated epigenetically, that is, by environmental control of gene expression. It is our belief that genetic analyses could prove to be powerful tools for dissecting the physiological mechanisms underlying motivated states. However, with the possible exception of studies of genetically obese animals (Castonguay et al 1982) to understand feeding and the use of selected lines to study alcohol consumption (Anderson & McClearn 1981), surprisingly few studies of feeding, drinking, mating, etc have been published in the past few years that have utilized the principles of behavioral genetics to understand biological motivation.

One behavior system that has received the attention of the genetically oriented is aggression. Sporadically since the 1940s, reports have appeared demonstrating that genotype is an important determinant of the display of aggression (Scott & Frederickson 1951, Lagerspetz et al 1968, Simon 1979). Also since the 1940s (Beeman 1947), studies have appeared showing that the expression of an "aggression positive genotype" depends upon testicular secretions in an important way. Since it is generally accepted that gonadal hormones exert their morphological and behavioral effects via an activation of the genome, it is possible that studies of the hormonal regulation of aggression in animals of different genotypes will prove valuable for understanding the biology of aggression.

Ten or more years ago the question would have been one of how the primary testicular secretion testosterone induces aggression. In the past 10 years, however, the question has become more complex as we learned that in some instances it is not testosterone that is the active agent, but rather one or more of its metabolites. Testosterone can be metabolized to dihydrotestosterone, a 5 α-reduction process, and it can be aromatized to estradiol in neural tissues (Naftolin et al 1975, Jouan & Samperez 1980). Thus it became possible to propose that aggression is controlled by testosterone itself, by dihydrotestosterone, by estradiol, or by some combination of these steroids. Indeed, each of these hypotheses has been advanced (Finney & Erpino 1976, Beatty 1979, Clark & Nowell 1979a,b, Simon & Gandelman 1978, Gandelman 1980, Simon et al 1980).

Over the past decade, progress was also being made in elucidating the intracellular events involved in the production of steroid-dependent effects. These investigations have led to the currently accepted model of steroid hormone action which holds that steroids, after entering target cells, initially bind to specific cytoplasmic receptor proteins. The hormone-receptor complex, after undergoing a temperature-dependent transformation, translocates to the cell nucleus where it binds to the chromatin and/or DNA and initiates RNA and subsequently protein synthesis.

Taken as a whole, it is apparent that a comprehensive model of the neuroendocrine regulation of aggression will require a consideration of the intracellular metabolism of hormones and various aspects of receptor binding in both cytoplasm and nucleus.

To date, efforts to establish the existence of a unitary neuroendocrine mechanism for aggression have not been successful. Of the various pathways through which testosterone could induce fighting behavior, the position that has attracted the most interest is the aromatization hypothesis, which holds that estradiol is the active behavior promoting agent (Beatty 1979, Bowden & Brain 1978, Brain & Bowden 1979, Clark & Nowell 1979a,b). Others, however, have presented evidence indicating a direct androgenic effect of testosterone (Simon & Gandelman 1978, Schecter et al 1981), and Finney & Erpino (1976) have argued that the induction of fighting can be traced to a synergy between the androgenic and estrogenic metabolities of testosterone. Despite obvious differences between these positions, each hypothesis has received some support. This suggests that there may be unrecognized complexities in the neuroendocrine mechanisms that regulate aggressive behavior.

A careful review of the studies that led to the various hypotheses about the hormonal control of aggression reveals that mice from a number of different strains were utilized. For example, support for the aromatization hypothesis comes primarily from observations of CF-1, CD-1, and TO male mice (Luttge 1972, Luttge & Hall 1973, Bowden & Brain 1978, Brain & Bowden 1979, Clark & Nowell 1979a,b), while evidence for direct androgenic activation of aggression is drawn primarily from Rockland-Swiss (R-S) mice (Simon & Gandelman 1978, Gandelman 1980, Schecter et al 1981). Finally, the hypothesis of a synergistic action of androgen and estrogen was based on studies of CD-1 mice. These observations suggest that there might be multiple mechanisms for the activation of aggression and that the functional pathway in any given animal is determined by genotype.

The concept of genotype specific androgen-sensitive and/or estrogen-sensitive regulatory systems for aggression in mice appears reasonable in light of the well-documented relationship between genotype, enzyme activity, receptor function, and steroid responsiveness in male mammals. Prominent examples include the Tfm (androgen-insensitive) mutation where an inability to respond to androgens is a product of a significantly reduced number of target tissue receptors (Bardin & Wright 1980) and deficiencies in 5 α-reductase activity which reduces the conversion of testosterone to dihydrotestosterone and results in pseudohermaphroditism (Pinsky 1981, Saenger 1981).

In contrast to studies of animal aggression and its possible regulation by hormones at the cellular level, most studies of human aggression and violence have attempted to establish a correlation between circulating levels of testosterone and either paper and pencil measures of hostility or the commission of violent crimes such as murder, rape, or injurious assault (Simon 1981). With few exceptions, a systematic relationship has not been found. This may reflect the fact that "normal" levels of testosterone vary widely in human males (4–11 ng/ml).

NEUROCHEMISTRY OF AGGRESSION

Attempts to define the neurobiological substrate of aggression have included assessments of drug effects on behavioral outputs. These investigations are directed primarily at elucidating the role of various neurotransmitters in the expression of the behavior.

In reviewing recent work on the pharmacological control of aggression it is important to recognize that fighting represents a complex sequence of non-reflexive species-typical behaviors (Banks 1962, Grant & MacKintosh 1963).

The presence of multiple components in agonistic behavior would suggest that its regulation involves several neurotransmitters, and the available evidence implicates the catecholamines, serotonin, and acetylcholine (Eichelman et al 1981, Miczek & Krsiak 1981, Valzelli 1981). While there are methodological differences among pharmacological studies of conspecific aggression, some trends are evident. The available data suggest that (a) higher levels of catecholamines are associated with higher levels of intermale aggression; (b) higher levels of serotonin are associated with lowered aggressiveness; and (c) cholinergic agonists facilitate offensive aggressive displays, while anticholinergic drugs decrease attack behavior (Eichelman et al 1981, Miczek & Krsiak 1981, Valzelli 1981). The last finding is the most consistent and has been reported for a number of species (Miczek & Krsiak 1979). Even this observation, however, should not be construed as evidence for a single neurochemical modulatory system for aggression since cholinergic transmission is influenced by dopaminergic and serotonergic pathways (Butcher et al 1976).

A more general concern in evaluating pharmacological studies of intermale aggression is that these systems are also under neuroendocrine control. The interaction of neurochemical and neuroendocrine mechanisms is undoubtedly critical in the physiological regulation of aggression. The importance of these interactions has been demonstrated recently by Nock & Feder (1981), using female mating behavior in the guinea pig as a model system. Their studies indicate that noradrenergic transmission influences the ability of estrogen to induce hypothalamic progestin receptors, thereby suggesting a mechanism through which neurotransmitters influence female reproductive behavior. The strength of these studies lies in the utility of lordotic behavior as a model. Because the neuroanatomical locus of the sites of estrogen and progesterone are reasonably well defined (Lisk 1978, Pfaff 1982c), the task of elucidating neurochemical influences on female sexual behavior is facilitated. These circumstances contrast sharply with our understanding of, for example, the neuroanatomy of intermale aggression and represents one reason why an analysis of the neurochemical processes involved in the regulation of aggression currently represents a formidable task.

The neuroendocrine regulation of aggression in mice appears to vary with genotype. It is likely then that the neurotransmitter modulation of aggression is also genotype specific. Indeed, both the number of dopamine receptors and the action of enzymes that mediate the production and degradation of neurotransmitters is under genetic control (Boehme & Ciaranello 1981, Ingram & Corfman 1980). These observations indicate that the development of a general model of the neurochemical modulation of intermale aggression may not be possible. As an example, Bernard and coworkers (1975) compared the behavior of BALB, ICR, and C57B1/6J male mice and found age-related changes in aggressiveness that were accompanied by genotype-specific changes in whole brain norepinephrine and dopamine levels. The neurochemical changes were not associated with consistent alterations in aggressiveness across the strains, however.

A further complicating factor in neurochemical studies of aggression involves the neuroanatomy of the behavior. Most of the neurochemical studies conducted thus far have measured whole brain levels of norepinephrine, dopamine, or serotonin (e.g. Bernard et al 1975, Kantak et al 1981a,b). This procedure could obscure important local changes in transmitters. In fact, Tizabi et al (1980) found differences in steady state levels of monoamines between aggressive and nonaggressive mice in olfactory tubercle, substantia nigra, and septum, but they did not detect group differences in 14 other neural loci.

While Albert (1983) has noted that the neuroanatomy of testosterone-dependent aggression is poorly understood in comparison to other aggressive behaviors, available evidence suggests that the septum and preoptic area are part of the neural substrate for intermale aggression (Owen et al 1974, Slotnick & McMullen 1972). These observations, when combined with the Tizabi et al findings, indicate that the measurement of neurochemical changes in more discrete tissue sections would be a better strategy for analyzing neurotransmitter effects associated with increased or decreased aggression.

An alternative approach to the study of neurotransmitter function and aggression has been employed recently by Kantak et al (1981a,b), who made use of the "second messenger" hypothesis of neurotransmitter function and have shown that cyclic nucleotides can reduce fighting. The "second messenger" hypothesis postulates that neurotransmitter actions are mediated by cyclic adenosine monophosphate (cAMP) and/or by cyclic guanosine monophosphate (cGMP) (Cooper et al 1982, Greengard 1978, Rodbell 1980). The types of receptors that have been linked to nucleotide effects include D_1 dopaminergic, B_1 and B_2 adrenergic (adenosine nucleotide mediation), and muscarinic cholinergic, and type 1 serotonergic receptors (guanine nucleotide mediation), although the existence of specific neurotransmitter-guanylate cyclase systems has been questioned (Bradham & Cheung 1982, Murad et al 1979, Sharma 1982).

Kantak and colleagues administered dibutryl cAMP and cGMP intraventricularly in mice. Both nucleotides produced a significant dose-dependent reduction in aggression toward a conspecific. The effective treatments did not alter general activity level, and changes in whole brain monoamine levels were not detected. These investigations appear to represent a potentially fruitful line of inquiry for examining the neurochemical modulation of intermale aggression. Moreover, since recent evidence suggests that nucleotides may also modulate steroid hormone binding (Fleming et al 1982), this type of investigation may provide a bridge for assessing neurotransmitter and neuroendocrine interactions in the regulation of aggression.

It is clear that much work is still needed to clarify the role of neurotransmitters in intermale aggression. Neuroanatomical studies appear to be an essential prerequisite; further studies of gene regulation of behavior, of hormone action, and of neurotransmitter function would be of great value and, although not detailed, the use of a wider variety of behavioral test paradigms would be helpful. Despite these difficulties, some progress has been made.

PEPTIDES AND BEHAVIOR

For many years DeWied and his colleagues (e.g. DeWied 1980) published very interesting and important research on the regulation of learning and the performance of learned responses by adrenal corticoids and the pituitary peptide ACTH (adrenocorticotropic hormone). This research did not seem to have much impact beyond the group that studied animal learning until two developments occurred: the identification of the neural peptides that control pituitary function and the discovery of the endogenous opioid peptides. These developments provided a broader context for DeWied's work and together led to a blossoming of research on the role of peptides in the regulation of brain function and behavior.

While it is beyond the scope of this paper to review developments in this field, we will comment on one area which is both of general interest and illustrates the complexity of the field, namely the role of cholecystokinin (CCK) in hunger satiation.

The cholecystokinins are a family of peptides initially identified as gut peptides. They are now known to be found widely in the nervous system (Dockray 1976, Goltermann 1982). Moreover, specific neural receptors for CCK have been identified (Saito et al 1980). The most commonly studied of the CCKs is the octopeptide CCK-8. The suppression of feeding by CCK has now been demonstrated in a number of species, rat, chick, sheep, hamsters, rhesus monkeys, and humans. Not surprisingly, species differences in sensitivity to CCK are large. Hamsters, for example, seem much less sensitive to CCK than are rats (Miceli & Malsbury 1983).

The potential clinical significance of CCK inhibition of eating in humans will doubtless spur research in this area. For example, Pi-Sunyen et al (1982) reported that in six of eight obese men, weighing on the average 209 pounds, CCK-8 substantially reduced meal size from 977 g to 852 g and reduced the duration of eating nearly 25%. These data suggest that CCK could be an effective anorectic agent. Whether CCK will prove to be useful in reducing obesity remains an open question. Metzger & Hansen (1983) found that rhesus monkeys fasted overnight and given CCK showed a dose-related cessation of an ongoing meal within 2 min, but total consumption was back to control levels within 3 hours. It should be noted, however, that Metzger and Hansen studied lean, not obese, monkeys. Since there is reason to believe that most, if not all, of CCK's effects are mediated by peripheral systems, including possibly the pancreas, it is possible that obese and lean individuals respond differently to CCK. In one pertinent study, Vander Weele (1982) reported that CCK inhibits feeding in a manner that is independent of insulin in both normal and diabetic rats.

There is evidence for involvement of both peripheral systems and the central nervous system in CCK's effects. The primary evidence for the involvement of peripheral systems comes from studies showing that vagotomy eliminates the satiety-inducing effects of CCK in rats (Smith et al 1981, Lorenz & Goldman 1982). Stellar (1982) argues that the demonstration that CCK application directly to the ventricular system inhibits feeding (Della-Fera & Baile 1979) indicates central nervous system involvement. This demonstration of CCK's effects in sheep may not have wide species generality. Lorenz & Goldman (1982), for example, reported that in rats CCK inhibition of feeding was minimal when the peptide was given by intraventricular injection. This may just represent another species difference in sensitivity to CCK, but this remains to be established.

Waldbillig & Bartness (1982) feel that oral-sensory factors are important in mediating CCK's effects, although their data could be more compelling. Stellar (1982), however, does present preliminary data suggesting sensory involvement. He finds that CCK inhibits the intake of saccharin, possibly a pure sensory effect, and he finds that CCK does not inhibit ingestion of a highly palatable mixture of glucose and saccharin. Since palatability has long been an important variable in controlling intake, particularly in neurally damaged rats, further attention in this direction is warranted.

The nature of CCK's regulation of behavior may be complex. For example, Stellar (1982) finds that CCK not only inhibits food intake, it also reduces the speed at which a rat will run in a simple maze to a food reward. Hsiao & Deupree (1983) find a parallel effect using a lever-pressing operant response. CCK treatment suppressed lever pressing for food as much as did food pretreatment. However, CCK did not inhibit lever pressing during extinction when food was no longer available, but food pretreatment did. Clearly, the technique used to assess CCK's satiety-promoting properties critically determines our view of the nature of these effects.

Nonetheless, evidence is accumulating that CCK's actions are not simply pharmacological. Hsiao & Wang (1983) have found that when CCK is continuously infused into rats there is a reduction in the number of meals, but there is no change in the circadian pattern of meal taking. In addition, Mansbach & Lorenz (1983) found that CCK elicits rest and synchronous sleep which is quite similar to that found in postprandial controls. Thus, CCK seems to be mimicking natural events.

There is a great deal of simple phenomenology of CCK action yet to be revealed. The great problem will be in establishing the mechanisms of that action and determining whether these actions are mediated by the CCK receptors that are found in cortex, olfactory bulb, caudate, hippocampus, and hypothalamus.

BIOLOGICAL RHYTHMS

It should be clear that most of the current research on the biology of what we usually consider motivated states is not research on motivation per se, but represents an attempt to understand the physiology of behavior. From that perspective, we feel that it is important for psychologists to consider another domain in which systematic fluctuations are the norm, namely, the world of chronobiology. Much of what has been published in this field has been done by investigators who identify as botanists, zoologists, or physiologists, even though rhythms in behavior have often been the subject of study. In recent years, behaviorists, psychologists and psychiatrists, have become involved in chronobiology, usually through studies of clearly cyclic events such as sleep, mating, and depression and manic-depressive illness. Until last year there was no easy way for the novice to gain an introduction to the field and to its specialized vocabulary. Moore-Ede, Sulzman & Fuller (1982) now bring us that introduction in their excellent book *"The Clocks That Time Us."*

Except when we suffer those effects of a rapid change in time zones known as "jet lag," we are usually unaware of the powerful regulation of our physiology and behavior by internal clocks. Indeed, it was not until 1962 that Aschoff and Wever demonstrated that the human activity-rest cycle reflected an endogenous circadian rhythm with a free-running period of about 25 hours. And it was only in 1972 that Moore and Eicher and, independently, Stephan and Zucker discovered that the suprachiasmatic nucleus of the anterior hypothalamus plays a crucial role in the regulation of rhythms.

Moore-Ede et al explain the fundamentals of time measurement and the concepts of entrained and free-running rhythms. They describe the characteristics of circadian clocks, including the criteria for entrainment. They note that the endogenous oscillators show a limited range to which they can be entrained. A zeitgeber (or time giver) such as a periodic change in lighting, which has too short or too long a period, will fail to entrain the oscillator. For example, the activity rhythm of mice can be entrained by the light-dark cycle, but only when the light cycle is at least 21 hours. When the light-dark period is reduced from 21 hours, activity "free-runs," that is, cycles of activity occur as determined by endogenous factors. Similarly, entrainment is lost if the light-dark cycle is extended beyond 28 hours.

In mammals, the light-dark cycle is an important time cue in both diurnal and nocturnal animals. Food availability can be an important cue and, in some species, temperature cycles can be used to entrain behavior. Social cues and systematic changes in sound patterns can also serve to entrain behavior. Curiously, cyclic availability of water does not appear to act to entrain animals to a 24-hour period. The differences between food and water systems should be of interest to students of ingestion.

It has become clear that multiple oscillators must exist if one is to account for the phenomena revealed by circadian studies. One such phenomenon is termed "splitting." Normally, activity occurs as a block during the diurnal cycle. Under some conditions, however, the block will split into two or more components, each of which may free-run with a different period.

Moore-Ede et al then provide a thorough discussion of the neural basis of circadian rhythms. While they emphasize research on the suprachiasmatic nucleus, the authors clearly remind the reader that the SCN is not "the" biological clock. Studies of humans show that there are at least two sets of coordinated cycles, one associated with the sleep-wake cycle and another set associated with the core body temperature. The locus of the non-SCN pacemakers is not yet known, so what is presented is an excellent discussion of the anatomy, histology, pathways, and function of the SCN system.

Understandably, the authors discuss the regulation of sleep-wake rhythms, but they also consider the control of feeding, drinking, thermoregulation, endocrine rhythms, and reproduction, topics also covered by the various authors in the Pfaff book. In the final two chapters, Moore-Ede et al consider human circadian rhythms and the medical implications of rhythms. They find coordinated rhythms of REM sleep, core body temperature, plasma cortisol and potassium excretion, and separate coordinated rhythms of slow wave sleep, skin temperature, plasma growth hormone, and calcium excretion. Under normal conditions these two sets of rhythms are coupled with the pacemaker that regulates the first set of rhythms, exerting a more powerful control over the pacemaker that regulates the second set than vice versa. Overall, Moore-Ede et al present a wide-ranging introduction to circadian rhythms. It is highly recommended to students of motivation.

CONCLUSIONS

The biological bases of motivation continue to attract the interest of behavioral scientists and progress is being made. Old issues, such as the proper definition of motivation and instinct, remain. This may be fruitless and may be the reason so many investigators now study what might be termed "motivated behaviors" rather than motivation per se. With some exceptions, attention is directed toward ingestion, mating, and flight rather than hunger, thirst, sex drive, or fear.

There are also changes in the way we view the locus of regulation of motivated behaviors. Twenty-five years ago we thought in terms of neural centers that organized response patterns. Today we recognize that the brain is attached to the rest of the body and that the peripheral nervous system, either directly or through the control of secretion, plays an important role in regulation. Studies showing that vagotomy prevents obesity induced by hypothalamic lesions and that vagotomy prevents the satiety-inducing effect of cholecystokinin are compelling in this regard. A renewed interest in sensory control and hedonics also indicates that we are viewing motivational processes in a broader perspective.

We now see an increased awareness, at least in some areas, that genotype is an important variable—rats are not cats, and even all mice are not created equal.

Recent years have seen a rapid growth of interest in the biochemistry of behavior. Twenty-five years ago drug manipulations were popular. Today we see sophisticated manipulations of individual neurotransmitter systems, and these manipulations are accompanied by biochemical analyses. And we are now seeing the manipulation and assay of peptide systems that were not even imagined 25 years ago. Progress indeed!

It appears to us that progress is being made at a reasonable pace in the behavioral, anatomical, and chemical approaches to understanding motivation. We would, however, urge that additional attention be given to genetic analyses and to a consideration of the roles played by biological clocks in the regulation of motivated behavior.

Literature Cited

Albert, D. J. 1983. *Neural mechanisms in the inhibitory modulation of aggression: comparisons across species.* Presented at Int. Soc. Res. Aggression, Victoria, British Columbia

Albert, D. J., Walsh, M. L. 1982. The inhibitory modulation of agonistic behavior in the rat brain: A review. *Neurosci. Biobehav. Rev.* 6:125–43

Anderson, S. M., McClearn, G. E. 1981. Ethanol consumption: selective breeding in mice. *Behav. Genet.* 11:291–303

Banks, E. M. 1962. A time and motion study of prefighting behavior in mice. *J. Genet. Psychol.* 101:165–83

Bardin, C. W., Wright, W. 1980. Androgen receptor deficiency: testicular feminization, its variants, and differential diagnosis. *Ann. Clin. Res.* 12:236–42

Beach, F. A. 1976. Sexual attractivity, proceptivity and receptivity in female mammals. *Horm. Behav.* 7:105–38

Beatty, W. W. 1979. Gonadal hormones and nonreproductive behaviors in rodents: Organizational and activational influences. *Horm. Behav.* 12:112–63

Beeman, E. A. 1947. The effect of male hormone on aggressive behavior in male mice. *Physiol. Zool.* 20:373–405

Bernard, B. K., Finkelstein, E. R., Everett, G. M. 1975. Alterations in mouse aggressive behavior and brain monoamine dynamics as a function of age. *Physiol. Behav.* 15:731–36

Boehme, R. E., Ciaranello, R. D. 1981. Strain differences in mouse brain dopamine receptors. In *Genetic Research Strategies for Psychobiology and Psychiatry,* ed. E. S. Gershon, S. Matthysse, X. O. Breakefield, R. Ciaranello, pp. 231–40. Pacific Grove: Boxwood

Bowden, N. J., Brain, P. F. 1978. Blockade of testosterone-maintained intermale fighting in albino laboratory mice by an aromatization inhibitor. *Physiol. Behav.* 20:543–46

Bradham, L. S., Cheung, W. Y. 1982. Nucleotide cyclases. *Prog. Nucleic Acid Res.* 27:189–231

Brain, P. F., Bowden, N. J. 1979. Sex steroid control of intermale fighting in mice. *Curr. Dev. Psychopharmacol.* 5:403–65

Butcher, S. H., Butcher, L. L., Cho, A. K. 1976. Modulation of neostriatal acetylcholine in the rat by dopamine and 5-hydroxytryptamine afferents. *Life Sci.* 18: 733–44

Castonguay, T. W., Upton, D. E., Leung, P. M. B., Stern, J. S. 1982. Meal patterns in the genetically obese Zucker rat: A reexamination. *Physiol. Behav.* 28:911–16

Clark, C. R., Nowell, N. W. 1979a. The effect of the non-steroidal antiandrogen flutamide on neural receptor binding of testosterone and intermale aggressive behavior in mice. *Psychoneuroendocrinology* 5:39–45

Clark, C. R., Nowell, N. W. 1979b. The effect of the antiestrogen CI-628 on androgen-induced aggressive behavior in castrated male mice. *Horm. Behav.* 12:205–10

Colotla, V. A. 1981. Adjunctive polydipsia as a model of alcoholism. *Neurosci. Biobehav. Rev.* 5:335–42

Cooper, J. R., Bloom, F. E., Roth, R. H. 1982. Cyclic nucleotides, prostoglandins, and histamine. In *The Biochemical Basis of Neuropharmacology*, pp. 335–58. New York: Oxford Univ. Press

Della-Fera, M. A., Baile, C. A. 1979. Cholecystokinin octapeptide: Continuous picomole injections into the cerebral ventricles of sheep suppress feeding. *Science* 206:471–73

DeWied, D. 1980. Hormonal influences on motivation, learning, memory and psychosis. In *Neuroendocrinology*, ed. D. T. Krieger, J. C. Hughes, pp. 194–204. Sunderland, Mass: Sinauer

Dockray, G. J. 1976. Immunochemical evidence of cholecystokinen-like peptides in brain. *Nature* 264:568–70

Dudley, S. D. 1982. Responsiveness to estradiol in central nervous system of aging female rats. *Neurosci. Biobehav. Rev.* 6:39–46

Eichelman, B., Elliott, G. R., Barchas, J. D. 1981. Biochemical, pharmacological, and genetic aspects of aggression. In *Biobehavioral Aspects of Aggression*, ed. D. A. Hamburg, pp. 51–84. New York: Liss

Epstein, A. N. 1982a. Instinct and motivation as explanations for complex behavior. See Pfaff 1982a, pp. 25–58

Epstein, A. N. 1982b. The physiology of thirst. See Pfaff 1982a, pp. 164–214

Fahrbach, S. E., Pfaff, D. W. 1982. Hormonal and neural mechanisms underlying maternal behavior in the rat. See Pfaff 1982a, pp. 253–86

Falk, J. L. 1961. Production of polydipsia in normal rats by an intermittent food schedule. *Science* 133:195–96

Falk, J. L., Samson, H. H., Winger, G. 1972. Behavioral maintenance of high concentrations of blood ethanol and physical dependence in the rat. *Science* 177:811–13

Finney, H. C., Erpino, M. J. 1976. Synergistic effect of estradiol benzoate and dihydrotestosterone on aggression in mice. *Horm. Behav.* 7:391–400

Fleming, H., Blumenthal, R., Gurpide, E. 1982. Effects of cyclic nucleotides on estradiol binding in human endometrium. *Endocrinology* 111:1671–77

Gandelman, R. 1980. Gonadal hormones and the induction of intraspecific fighting in mice. *Neurosci. Biobehav. Rev.* 4:133–40

Goddard, G. 1964. Functions of the amygdala. *Psychol. Bull.* 62:89–109

Goltermann, N. R. 1982. In vivo synthesis of cholecystokinin in the rat cerebral cortex: Identification of COOH-terminal peptides with labeled amino acids. *Peptides* 3:733–37

Grant, E. C., Mackintosh, J. H. 1963. A comparison of the social postures of some common laboratory rodents. *Behaviour* 21:246–59

Greengard, P. 1978. *Cyclic Nucleotides, Phosphorylated Proteins, and Neuronal Function.* New York: Raven

Grinker, J. A. 1982. Physiological and behavioral basis of human obesity. See Pfaff 1982a, pp. 145–63

Halperin, R., Pfaff, D. W. 1982. Brain-stimulated reward and control of autonomic function: Are they related? See Pfaff 1982a, pp. 337–76

Houpt, K. A. 1982. Gastrointestinal factors in hunger and satiety. *Neurosci. Biobehav. Rev.* 6:145–64

Hsiao, S., Deupree, D. 1983. Cholecyotokinin and bombesin effects on rewarded and nonrewarded operants. *Peptides* 4:1–3

Hsiao, S., Wang, C. H. 1983. Continuous infusion of cholecystokinin and meal pattern in the rat. *Peptides* 4:15–17

Ingram, D. K., Corfman, T. P. 1980. An overview of neurobiological comparisons in mouse strains. *Neurosci. Biobehav. Rev.* 4: 421–35

Jouan, P., Samperez, S. 1980. Metabolism of steroid hormones in the brain. In *The Endocrine Functions of the Brain*, ed. M. Motta, pp. 95–115. New York: Raven

Kantak, K. L., Hegstrand, L. R., Eichelman, B. 1981a. Influence of cyclic GMP on rodent aggressive behavior. *Life Sci.* 29:1379–85

Kantak, K. L., Hegstrand, L. R., Eichelman, B. 1981b. Aggression-altering effects of cyclic AMP. *Neuropharmacology* 20:79–82

Katz, R. J. 1981a. Animal models and human depressive disorders. *Neurosci. Biobehav. Rev.* 5:231–46

Katz, R. J. 1981b. Animal model of depression: Effects of electroconvulsive shock therapy. *Neurosci. Biobehav. Rev.* 5:273–78

Katz, R. J., Hersh, S. 1981. Amitriptyline and scopolamine in an animal model of depression. *Neurosci. Biobehav. Rev.* 5:265–72

Katz, R. J., Roth, K. A., Carroll, B. J. 1981a. Acute and chronic stress effects on open field activity in the rat: Implications for a model of depression. *Neurosci. Biobehav. Rev.* 5: 247–52

Katz, R. J., Roth, K. A., Schmaltz, K. 1981b. Amphetamine and tranylcypromine in an animal model of depression: Pharmacological specificity of the reversal effect. *Neurosci. Biobehav. Rev.* 5:259–64

Lagerspetz, K. Y. H., Tirri, R., Lagerspetz, K. M. J. 1968. Neurochemical and endocrinological studies of mice selectively bred for aggressiveness. *Scand. J. Psychol.* 9:157–60

Lisk, R. D. 1978. The regulation of sexual 'heat'. In *Biological Determinants of Sexual Behaviour*, ed. J. B. Hutchison, pp. 425–66. New York: Wiley

Lorenz, D. N., Goldman, S. A. 1982. Vagal mediation of the cholecystokinin satiety effect in rats. *Physiol. Behav.* 29:599–604

Luttge, W. G. 1972. Activation and inhibition of isolation induced intermale fighting behavior in castrate male CD-1 mice treated with steroidal hormones. *Horm. Behav.* 3:71–81

Luttge, W. G., Hall, N. R. 1973. Androgen-induced agonistic behavior in castrate Swiss-Webster mice: Comparison of four naturally occurring androgens. *Behav. Biol.* 8:725–32

Mansbach, R. S., Lorenz, D. N. 1983. Cholecystokinin (CCK-8) elicits prandial sleep in rats. *Physiol. Behav.* 30:179–83

Mayer, D. J., Price, D. D. 1982. A physiological and psychological analysis of pain: A potential model of motivation. See Pfaff 1982a, pp. 433–72

McGaugh, J. L., Jennings, R. D., Thomson, C. W. 1962. Effects of distribution of practice on the maze learning of descendents of the Tryon maze bright and maze dull strains. *Psychol. Rep.* 10:147–50

McGaugh, J. L., Westbrook, W., Burt, G. 1961. Strain differences in the facilitative effects of 5-7-diphenyl-1-3-diazadamantan-6-01 on maze learning. *J. Comp. Physiol. Psychol.* 54:502–5

Metzger, B. L., Hansen, B. C. 1983. Cholecystokinin effects on feeding glucose and pancreatic hormones in rhesus monkeys. *Physiol. Behav.* 30:509–18

Meyerson, B. J., Lindstrom, L. H. 1971. Sexual motivation in the estrogen treated ovariectomized rat. *Excerpta Medica*, pp. 731–37

Meyerson, B. J., Lindstrom, L. H. 1973. Sexual motivation in the female rat: A methodological study applied to the effect of estradiol benzoate. *Acta Physiol. Scand. Suppl.* 389:1–80

Miceli, M. C., Malsbury, C. W. 1983. Feeding and drinking responses in the golden hamster following treatment with cholecystokinin and angiotensin II. *Peptides* 4:103–6

Miczek, K. A., Krsiak, M. 1979. Drug effects on agonistic behavior. In *Advances in Behavioral Pharmacology*, ed. T. Thompson, P. B. Dews, pp. 87–162. New York: Academic

Miczek, K. A., Krsiak, M. 1981. Pharmacological analysis of attack and flight. In *Multidisciplinary Approaches to Aggression Research*, ed. P. E. Brain, D. Benton, pp. 341–54. New York: Elsevier/North Holland Biomed. Press

Miller, N. E. 1982. Motivation and psychological stress. See Pfaff 1982a, pp. 409–32

Miller, N. E., Bailey, C. J., Stevenson, J. A. F. 1950. Decreased "hunger" but increased food intake resulting from hypothalamic lesions. *Science* 112:256–59

Moore-Ede, M. C., Sulzman, F. M., Fuller, C. A. 1982. *The Clocks That Time Us*. Cambridge, Mass: Harvard Univ. Press

Murad, F., Arnold, W. P., Mittal, C. K., Braughler, J. M. 1979. Properties and regulation of guanylate cyclase and some proposed functions for cyclic GMP. *Adv. Cyclic Nucleotide Res.* pp. 176–97

Naftolin, F., Ryan, K. J., Davies, I. J., Reddy, V. V., Flores, F., et al. 1975. The formation of estrogens by central neuroendocrine tissues. *Recent Prog. Horm. Res.* 31:295–15

Nissen, H. W. 1929. Experiments on sex drive in rats. *Genet. Psychol. Monogr.* 5:451–548

Nock, B., Feder, H. H. 1981. Neurotransmitter modulation of steroid action in target cells that mediate reproduction and reproductive behavior. *Neurosci. Biobehav. Rev.* 5:437–48

Norgren, R., Grill, H. 1982. Brain-stem control of ingestive behavior. See Pfaff 1982a, pp. 99–132

Novin, D., Vander Weele, D. A. 1977. Visceral involvement in feeding: there is more to regulation than the hypothalamus. In *Progress in Psychobiology and Physiological Psychology*, ed. J. M. Sprague, A. N. Epstein, pp. 193–241. New York: Academic

Owen, K., Peters, P. J., Bronson, F. H. 1974. Effects of intracranial implants of testosterone propionate on intermale aggression in the castrate male mouse. *Horm. Behav.* 5:83–92

Pfaff, D. W., ed. 1982a. *The Physiological Mechanisms of Motivation*. New York: Springer-Verlag

Pfaff, D. W. 1982b. Motivational concepts: Definitions and distinctions. See Pfaff 1982a, pp. 3–24

Pfaff, D. W. 1982c. Neurobiological mechanisms of sexual motivation. See Pfaff 1982a, pp. 287–318

Pfaffmann, C. 1982. Taste: A model of incentive motivation. See Pfaff 1982a, pp. 61–98

Pinsky, L. 1981. Sexual differentiation. In Pediatric Endocrinology, ed. R. Collu et al, pp. 231–91. New York: Raven

Pi-Sunyen, X., Kissileff, H. R., Thornton, J., Smith, G. P. 1982. C-terminal octapeptide of cholecystokinin decreases food intake in obese men. Physiol. Behav. 29:627–30

Rodbell, M. 1980. The role of hormone receptors and GTP-regulatory proteins in membrane transduction. Nature 284:17–22

Rossi, J., Zolovick, A. J., Davies, R. F., Panksepp, J. 1982. The role of norepinephrine in feeding behavior. Neurosci. Biobehav. Rev. 6:195–204

Roth, K. A., Katz, R. J. 1981. Further studies on a novel animal model of depression: Therapeutic effects of a tricyclic antidepressant. Neurosci. Biobehav. Rev. 5:253–58

Saenger, P. 1981. Steroid 5 α-reductase deficiency. In Pediatric and Adolescent Endocrinology, ed. Z. Laron, P. Tikva, pp. 156–70. Basel: Karger

Saito, A., Sankaran, H., Goldfine, I. D., Williams, J. A. 1980. Cholecystokinin receptors in the brain: Characterization and distribution. Science 208:1155–56

Satinoff, E. 1982. Are there similarities between thermoregulation and sexual behavior? See Pfaff 1982a, pp. 217–52

Schecter, D., Howard, S. M., Gandelman, R. 1981. Dihydrotestosterone promotes fighting behavior of female mice. Horm. Behav. 15:233–37

Schuster, C. R., Johanson, C. E. 1981. An analysis of drug-seeking in animals. Neurosci. Biobehav. Rev. 5:315–23

Scott, J. P., Frederickson, E. 1951. The causes of fighting in mice and rats. Physiol. Zool. 24:273–309

Sharma, R. K. 1982. Cyclic nucleotide control of protein kinases. Prog. Nucleic Acid Res. 27:233–88

Simon, N. G. 1979. The genetics of intermale aggression in mice: Recent research and alternative strategies. Neurosci. Biobehav. Rev. 3:97–106

Simon, N. G. 1981. Hormones and human aggression: A comparative perspective. Int. J. Ment. Health 10:60–74

Simon, N. G., Gandelman, R. 1978. The estrogenic arousal of aggressive behavior in female mice. Horm. Behav. 10:118–27

Simon, N. G., Gandelman, R., Howard, S. M. 1980. MER-25 does not inhibit the activation of aggression by testosterone in adult Rockland-Swiss mice. Psychoneuroendocrinology 6:131–37

Singer, G., Oei, T. P. S., Wallace, M. 1982. Schedule-induced self-injection of drugs. Neurosci. Biobehav. Rev. 6:77–83

Slotnick, B. M., McMullen, M. F. 1972. Intraspecific fighting in Albino mice with septal forebrain lesions. Physiol. Behav. 8:333–37

Smith, G. P. 1982. Satiety and the problem of motivation. See Pfaff 1982a, pp. 33–44

Smith, G. P., Jerome, C., Cushin, B. J., Eterno, R., Simansky, K. J. 1981. Abdominal vagotomy blocks the satiety effect of cholecystokinin in the rat. Science 213:1036–37

Solomon, R. L. 1982. Approach vs. avoidance in motivation and emotion. See Pfaff 1982a, pp. 321–36

Stellar, E. 1982. Brain mechanisms in hedonic processes. See Pfaff 1982a, pp. 377–406

Teitelbaum, P., Epstein, A. N. 1962. The lateral hypothalamic syndrome: Recovery of feeding and drinking after lateral hypothalamic lesions. Psychol. Rev. 69:74–90

Tizabi, Y., Massari, J., Jacobowitz, D. M. 1980. Isolation induced aggression and catecholamine variations in discrete brain areas of the mouse. Brain Res. Bull. 5:81–86

Valzelli, L. 1981. Psychobiology of Aggression and Violence. New York: Raven

Vander Weele, D. A. 1982. CCK, endogenous insulin condition and satiety in free-fed rats. Physiol. Behav. 29:961–64

Waldbillig, R. J., Bartness, T. J. 1982. The suppression of sucrose intake by cholecystokinin is scaled according to the magnitude of the orosensory control over feeding. Physiol. Behav. 28:591–95

Warner, L. H. 1927. A study of sex behavior in the white rat by means of the obstruction method. Comp. Psychol. Monogr. 4:1–66

Wetherington, C. L. 1982. Is adjunctive behavior a third class of behavior? Neurosci. Biobehav. Rev. 6:329–50

Ann Rev. Psychol. 1984. 35:277–308
Copyright © 1984 by Annual Reviews Inc. All rights reserved

BRAIN FUNCTION: NEURAL ADAPTATIONS AND RECOVERY FROM INJURY

John F. Marshall

Department of Psychobiology, University of California, Irvine, California 92717

CONTENTS

INTRODUCTION

The behavioral consequences of damage to the nervous system typically change as the time following injury increases. The normalization of behavior with time, or recovery of function, has long fascinated psychologists, neuroscientists, and clinicians. Within the last decade, however, interest in this phenomenon has increased significantly because of advances in understanding how neurons can change their structure or function after CNS injury. Nowhere have these advances been more apparent than in the research on axonal sprouting. Because of this work in the neurosciences the view of the brain and spinal cord

277

as static organs has yielded to the overwhelming evidence that CNS neurons may undergo structural and/or biochemical changes according to use or specific experience, as a consequence of normal synapse replacement, or in response to injury.

As a subject for review, recovery of function was last considered in *Annual Review of Psychology* by Rosner (1970). Since then, much progress has been made in understanding the neural events that contribute to recovery from brain injury, and one goal of this review is to describe these advances. A second goal is to suggest approaches that seem particularly promising. I start by considering the theories that have influenced this field in the past. I then describe the forms of neural plasticity that are thought to mediate recovery of function, reviewing those systems for which neurobiological explanations of a recovery sequence have been suggested.

THEORIES OF RECOVERY OF FUNCTION

The recovery that humans and animals frequently show from the initial motor, sensory, or cognitive consequences of CNS injury represented a disturbing challenge to those neurologists and neuroscientists of the nineteenth and early twentieth centuries who adhered to the tenet that functions are strictly localized to particular brain structures. Flourens, who in 1824 described recovery from brain injury in experimental animals, concluded that behaviors could not be localized to specific cortical regions. However, during the latter half of the nineteenth and the first part of the twentieth centuries, the overwhelming evidence for localization of function in the brains of animals and humans silenced the critics (see Rosner 1974). Several theories were advanced that attempted to account for the existence of behavioral recovery within the framework of the localizationist doctrine. Four such theories will be stated and evaluated next.

Alternate Strategies

Humans and animals with CNS injury may develop strategies, or tricks, that allow them to circumvent their lost capacities. These alternative strategies permit the subject to achieve the same behavioral end using means that are very different from neurologically intact individuals. For example, many humans that suffer damage to the visual cortex show active eye movements that scan the visual field, thereby circumventing the scotomatous retinal regions (Teuber et al 1960). Also, monkeys with lesions of the dentate and interpositus cerebellar nuclei display a syndrome of limb ataxia followed by tremor from which they subsequently recover. These dyskinesias result from an inability to fixate the affected limb at the precise moment that a phasic movement is initiated (Goldberger & Growden 1973). During recovery the monkey avoids limb positions that are likely to result in these oscillatory dyskinesias, a compensation that depends upon somatosensory information from the affected limb.

Although some neurologists and psychologists have argued that most, if not all, instances of behavioral restoration can be attributed to these compensatory strategies rather than to a true recovery, this conclusion is difficult to reconcile with the growing number of model systems in which correlates between neuronal plasticity and behavioral recovery have been identified.

Redundancy

The recovery from a particular behavioral impairment after damage may depend upon uninjured neurons that normally contribute to that behavior. This redundancy can arise (a) as a result of a hierarchical representation of functions at different levels of the neuraxis (Hughlings Jackson, reprinted in 1958), or (b) because the neurons subserving a particular function (e.g. maze learning) can be distributed equally throughout all regions of a particular brain structure (e.g. cerebral cortex) (Lashley 1929).

More recent work suggests that considerable redundancy exists even within topographically organized sensory and motor systems (Frommer 1978). Monkeys with pyramidal tract injury show at least some recovery unless virtually all of the fibers have been injured (Lawrence & Kuypers 1968, Beck & Chambers 1970). Also, cats with damage to 98–99% of optic tract axons can perform a visual pattern discrimination (Galambos et al 1967). The number of spared fibers rather than their position within the damaged optic or pyramidal tracts, appears critical for the functional sparing.

However, the survival of redundant neurons does not offer a *sufficient* explanation for behavioral recovery because it does not specify what events occur within the surviving neurons during the postoperative period to mediate the recovery. For example, after damage to the optic nerve fibers, an impairment in acuity is evident with as little as 33% damage to the tract, and the rate of recovery from the acuity deficit is inversely related to the extent of fiber loss (Jacobson et al 1979). Also, although irreversible impairments in somatosensory localization occur in rats with damage to 95% or more of the nigrostriatal dopaminergic terminals (Marshall 1979), significant but brief impairments in this behavior result from destruction of only 25–30% of these terminals (Marshall et al 1980). The duration of the impairment is inversely proportional to the extent of damage to this population of dopaminergic cells (Marshall 1979).

That significant behavioral deficits do result from even small lesions within redundantly organized systems suggests that compensatory neural events within the surviving elements underlie the behavioral improvement. Thus, the spared neurons provide a substrate in which the dynamic events leading to behavioral improvement may occur.

Vicarious Functioning

According to the theory of vicarious functioning, brain regions that survive the injury have a latent ability to carry out the functions of the damaged system. In contrast to the redundancy explanation, this theory postulates that neurons not previously involved in a particular function may alter their properties to assume that function after injury. The results of several experiments employing brain lesions are consistent with the theory.

For example, after ablation of the visual cortex, cats show an initial impairment in discriminating patterns, but extensive postoperative training promotes relearning. The lateral suprasylvian gyrus is especially important to the residual pattern discrimination abilities, since its removal after recovery from the initial injury results in a pattern discrimination loss that is not reversed by retraining (Baumann & Spear 1977). Removal of the suprasylvian gyrus alone, however, has a negligible effect on pattern vision (Wood et al 1974).

Electrophysiological evidence can provide more direct evidence concerning vicarious functioning. The hypothesis predicts that the properties of neurons in regions presumed to take over the impaired behaviors should be altered by the lesion with a time course corresponding to the behavioral recovery. Because of the behavioral findings cited above, Spear & Baumann (1979) investigated whether after visual cortex damage the receptive field characteristics of lateral suprasylvian gyrus cells change to become like those of visual cortex neurons. For example, unlike lateral suprasylvian cells, visual cortex neurons are sensitive to the orientation of bars or slits in the receptive field. After visual cortex removal, however, the lateral suprasylvian neurons remain insensitive to orientation even in cats that have been successfully retrained to perform a pattern discrimination during several months postoperatively.

Thus, these experiments provide no evidence for vicarious functioning of spared visual structures. Presumably, the lateral suprasylvian gyrus provides the destriate cat with redundant information concerning visual form that allows discriminations to be achieved after extensive retraining.

Diaschisis

von Monakow (1914) proposed that behavioral functions are lost after brain injury for two reasons. First, the injury destroys neurons. Because these neurons are not replaced, he argued that the impairments resulting from their loss must be irreversible. Second, the destruction of nerve cells alters the excitability of neurons that normally receive axonal inputs from the damaged cells, a phenomenon termed diaschisis or neural shock. This transsynaptic effect of the injury, von Monakow argued, is reversible. As the excitability of the denervated neurons returns to normal, behavioral functions should be restored. Both the precise definition of the excitability changes and the mechanism by which injury induces diaschisis were not specified.

The clearest behavioral example of neural shock is the depression of spinal reflex activity that occurs after transection of the spinal cord (Sherrington 1906). Depending upon species, the period of areflexia lasts from minutes to days. More encephalized animals display a more prolonged areflexia, suggesting that the duration of the shock to spinal centers depends upon the volume of the descending supraspinal projections that are severed (Mountcastle 1974).

Electrophysiological changes suggestive of neural shock have been indentified in the spinal cord. Cord potentials that reflect spinal interneuronal response to dorsal root stimulation are acutely depressed after transection in dog and cat, paralleling the depression of spinal reflexes (Stewart et al 1940). Barnes et al (1962) recorded the membrane potentials of lumbar motoneurons after cooling the thoracic spinal cord in cats (which eliminated the crossed extensor reflex). Spinal cooling induces a prompt 2–8 mV hyperpolarization of motoneurons, and the resting potential returns to normal within 30 seconds of rewarming. Unfortunately, the effects of cooling on the response of motoneurons to afferent driving was not determined.

However, West et al (1976) obtained no evidence for diaschisis in the hippocampus. The hypothesis predicts that after denervating the granule cells of the dentate gyrus of their entorhinal afferents, their response to remaining inputs (i.e. commissural-associational) should diminish. However, the extracellular field potentials elicited by commissural stimulation were unchanged from control levels in rats 30 minutes to 11 days following removal of the ipsilateral entorhinal cortex.

Also, several investigations have provided evidence against diaschisis in the visual system. Even immediately after visual cortex injury, tectal and suprasylvian neurons display receptive field properties indicative of their continued responsiveness to retinal and thalamic visual inputs (Wickelgren & Sterling 1969, Rosenquist & Palmer 1971, Spear & Baumann 1979).

Therefore, it is clear that neural shock is not a general consequence of injury. The conditions under which it occurs are poorly understood, as is its relevance to functional restoration. Because the acute loss of spinal reflex activity after transection is such a powerful behavioral demonstration of neural shock, insights concerning the cellular events mediating the phenomenon could be provided by further electrophysiological investigations of the spinal interneurons and motor neurons of transected animals.

OVERVIEW OF NEURAL EVENTS MEDIATING RECOVERY

Although the preceding theories have provided a major organizational influence on research in this field, for three reasons they have not yielded answers as to how recovery from CNS injury occurs. First, these theories have often proved resistant to experimental test. Second, in cases where they have been tested (i.e. vicarious functioning and diaschisis), the results have been either strongly disconfirmatory or equivocal. Third, each theory seeks to provide a general account of recovery rather than explaining recovery from particular instances of CNS injury.

In contrast to the theories of recovery discussed in the previous section, more recent accounts of behavioral restoration emphasize the capacity of the CNS to undergo specific synaptic changes in response to injury. These forms of neural adaptation may lead to behavioral recovery by normalizing synaptic transmission within the injured nervous system. In the following two sections I consider these types of neuronal plasticity and review the evidence suggesting that they may contribute to specific instances of behavioral recovery after CNS injury.

The neurobiological explanations for recovery sequences fall into two general categories: morphological and neurochemical. The morphological accounts emphasize the ability of the injured CNS to form new synapses by, for example, axon sprouting. In contrast, neurochemical explanations stress the ability of existing synapses to modify their activity by, for example, increasing transmitter synthesis and release or by elevating the postsynaptic response to transmitter. This classification provides a conceptual framework for the organization of the remainder of this review.

Before considering these explanations in detail it is important to recognize that the successful analysis of the neuronal events mediating a recovery sequence depends critically upon the choice of an appropriate model system. Two criteria must be fulfilled. 1. The relationship between the CNS region under investigation and the behavior of interest must be thoroughly characterized. Damage to the brain region should result in a well-defined behavioral impairment followed by postoperative improvement. The time course and behavioral characteristics of the recovery should be thoroughly documented. Ideally, it should be possible to associate the behavioral abnormality with the injury of one or more identified populations of nerve cells within the damaged region. Fulfilling this criterion is a major hurdle because the behavioral consequences of selective injury to only a few cell populations in the CNS can be stated with confidence. 2. The varieties of neuronal plasticity that occur within these identified cells, their targets, or their afferents must either be known or amenable to study using available techniques. The extent of knowledge concerning the neurobiology of the system under investigation limits the hypotheses that can be explored.

MORPHOLOGICAL ADAPTATIONS AND RECOVERY

After its injury the nervous system may undergo structural alterations that permit lost functions to be restored. These morphological changes include regenerative and collateral axon sprouting, expansion of dendritic surface area

(Cotman et al 1981), and a replacement of lost neurons by cell division similar to that occurring in the olfactory epithelium (Graziadei & Graziadei 1978). The present review limits itself to the axonal growth responses, which have been investigated extensively.

Determinants of Axonal Growth

Peripheral nerves have a striking capacity to grow after injury (Edds 1953, Guth 1956). The sprouting can take two forms. In regenerative sprouting, the distal end of the severed axon degenerates and the proximal stump emits a growth cone that can enter the Schwann cell sheaths. Under optimal circumstances, these growing processes follow the denervated sheaths to the vacated tissue, at which point they form synaptic contacts. Collateral sprouting occurs when only part of the innervation to a tissue is removed. Uninjured axons extend collateral branches (or extend the surface area of their terminals) to increase the innervation of the partly denervated tissue.

REGENERATIVE GROWTH   Although CNS neurons do not ordinarily display the extensive regenerative growth typical of peripheral axons (Ramon y Cajal 1928; Bernstein & Bernstein 1973), several conditions favor central growth. One such condition is the positioning of a target tissue appropriate for reinnervation in the vicinity of the transected fibers. For example, when smooth muscle grafts that normally receive an adrenergic sympathetic innervation (e.g. iris or portal vein) are positioned along the course of brain catecholaminergic axon bundles, regenerating sprouts grow across the scar tissue at the graft-CNS interface and innervate the transplant (Björklund & Stenevi 1971, Björklund et al 1975a). Central transplants of embryonic brain tissue can also attract regenerative growth. When transplants of embryonic hippocampus are placed into a cavity along the severed fimbria of adult rats, fimbrial cholinergic axons from the host animal innervate the transplant during the subsequent 1–2 months (Kromer et al 1981a). After innervating the transplant, the growing cholinergic axons often continue to grow into the host hippocampus, their normal target tissue, and the pattern of reinnervation by these axons is similar to that of the normal cholinergic lamination (Kromer et al 1981b).

A second condition that influences the regenerative growth of CNS axons is the extent of glial scarring at the site of injury (Guth & Windle 1970). Whereas mechanical transection or electrolysis of brain tissue leads to the local formation of a dense scar, the monoamine neurotoxins, 6-hydroxydopamine (6-OHDA), 5,6-dihydroxytryptamine (5,6-DHT), and 5,7-dihydroxytryptamine (5,7-DHT) do not. When CNS monoamine-containing axons are damaged by the injection of these neurotoxins into the parenchyma or CSF, regenerative growth from injured axons can occur. Thus, after intraspinal injection of 6-OHDA, the number of fluorescent catecholamine axons in the spinal cord decreases dramatically, but the brainstem catecholamine cell bodies that give rise to the spinal projection survive (Nygren & Olson 1977). Fluorescent profiles reappear in the spinal cord within 3 days and extensively reinnervate the spinal cord during the next 1–2 months (Nygren et al 1971). After intraventricular injections of these neurotoxins, brain serotonergic and noradrenergic axons can also grow (Björklund et al 1973, 1975b, Wuttke et al 1977, Björklund & Lindvall 1979). Monoamine-containing axons that regenerate in the brain, like those in the spinal cord, preferentially reinnervate structures near to the origin of axonal sprouting (Björklund et al 1975b).

A third determinant of CNS axonal regeneration is the neuroglial environment through which the sprouting fibers grow (Guth & Windle 1970). Because Schwann cells provide a substrate for the growth of regenerating peripheral axons, their role in CNS regrowth has received recent attention. When a length of sciatic nerve forms a bridge between the cranial and caudal ends of the severed dog or rat spinal cord, axons of CNS origin grow through the peripheral nerve segment during the subsequent 1–3 months (Kao et al 1977, Richardson et al 1980, David & Aguayo 1981; see Figure 1). Many of the growing fibers become ensheathed by Schwann cells, and the sciatic nerve bridges can sustain growth for distances as great as 35 mm (David & Aguayo 1981).

COLLATERAL GROWTH   Although collateral sprouting in the mammalian CNS was first demonstrated by Liu & Chambers in 1958, only by the mid-1970s was this form of synaptic plasticity recognized as a common neural adaption to CNS injury (reviewed by Kerr 1975). The dentate gyrus of the rat hippocampus has proved to be an extremely useful system in which to study collateral sprouting. The apical dendrites of dentate granule cells extend through the width of the molecular layer and receive afferent projections from several sources in a precise laminar organization (reviewed by Cotman & Nadler 1978). In brief, the extensive projection from the ipsilateral entorhinal cortex (perforant path) terminates in the outer two-thirds of the molecular layer, as does a sparse projection from the contralateral entorhinal cortex. Axons from the ipsilateral and contralateral hippocampal pyramidal cells (i.e. associational and commissural fibers) terminate in the inner one-third of the molecular layer. The septohippocampal fibers project to narrow zones of the molecular layer: one in the inner molecular layer and a second in the outer layer.

Removal of one entorhinal cortex induces an extensive rearrangement of the remaining afferent fibers in the molecular layer. The cholinesterase-staining septal axon terminals to the outer molecular layer increase their distribution (Lynch et al 1972), the commissural-association afferent fibers move into the denervated outer molecular layer (Lynch et al 1973), and the projection of the contralateral entorhinal cortex to the denervated molecular layer increases (Steward et al 1974).

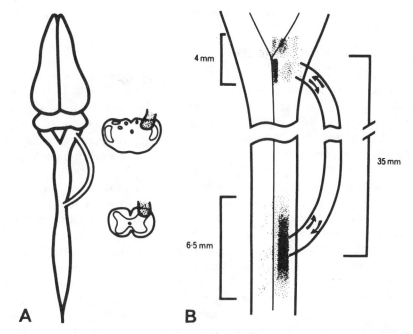

Figure 1 A. Diagram of the dorsal surface of the rat CNS, showing a peripheral nerve "bridge" linking the medulla and thoracic spinal cord. Cross sections depict the regions where the ends of the nerve graft were inserted. B. Approximate rostrocaudal position of 1472 labeled CNS neurons (dots) demonstrated in 7 grafted rats. In the brainstem the territory occupied by 450 of these cells extended along 4 mm, whereas 1022 labeled neurons were scattered along a 6.5 mm segment of the spinal cord. Reprinted from David & Aguayo (1981) *Science* 214:931–933, with permission of the American Association for the Advancement of Science.

Although collateral sprouting in the CNS is now a well-documented phenomenon, the stimulus responsible for its appearance is poorly understood. At the neuromuscular junction, muscle inactivity appears to be important in initiating sprouting because chronic electrical stimulation of a denervated muscle prevents the ingrowth of axon terminals from a foreign nerve positioned on its surface (Lømo & Slater 1978). Furthermore, a terminal sprouting from intact axons innervating the rodent soleus muscle occurs if the muscle activity is decreased by conduction block of its axonal input, prevention of ACh release at the neuromuscular junction, or acetylcholine receptor blockade (Brown & Ironton 1977, Brown et al 1977, Holland & Brown 1980). In the CNS, trophic factors transported down the axon may be important in regulating sprouting. When colchicine, a drug that blocks fast axoplasmic transport, is applied to the commissural fibers innervating the inner molecular layer of dentate gyrus, the density of commissural projection in this zone increases (Goldowitz & Cotman 1980). Because the colchicine treatment leads to little or no degeneration of the exposed axons, a role for axonally transported trophic factors in the regulation of synapse formation is suggested.

Axonal Growth and Recovery of Function

Explanations of functional recovery based upon axonal growth after nervous system injury are not new, especially for the peripheral nervous system. The discovery of collateral sprouting of somatosensory nerves (Weddell et al 1941) resulted from research inspired by the observation that skin sensitivity could return to normal after cutaneous nerve injury. Also, a collateral sprouting of motor nerves contributes to the recovery of muscle tension after damage to spinal ventral roots (reviewed by Edds 1953).

A similar relationship between synaptic remodeling and recovery has been observed in the sympathetic nervous system. The CNS control of the cat nictitating membrane is mediated by preganglionic axons exiting in the thoracic ventral roots and synapsing in the superior cervical ganglion. Several months after severing 90% of the preganglionic axons controlling one nictitating membrane, electrical stimulation of the remaining 10% of the fibers on that side evokes a membrane response equal to that resulting from stimulation of all the preganglionic axons on the intact side. This compensation is achieved in several stages. By 4–5 days postoperatively the decentralized membrane becomes supersensitive to norepinephrine, resulting in partial compensation. Within two weeks the intact preganglionic axons sprout collaterals in the partially denervated superior cervical ganglion, leading to a further normalization of the response to stimulation and a return of normal membrane sensitivity to norepinephrine (Murray & Thompson 1957). Functional studies suggest that the collateral sprouts are eventually replaced by regenerating terminals of the severed preganglionic axons (Guth & Bernstein 1961). These experiments demonstrate elegantly how postsynaptic supersensitivity, collateral sprouting and regenerative growth can interact sequentially to contribute to the recovery of function at peripheral synapses.

Determining the neural events mediating recovery from CNS injury is more difficult than for peripheral nerves. Nevertheless, during the last decade important advances have been made in understanding the neuronal events mediating recovery from CNS injury. Much of the success in this field has occurred in neonatal animals, in which the capacity for injury-induced growth is far greater than in adults.

RETINOTECTAL PROJECTION   The integrity of the retinal projection to the superior colliculus of the Syrian hamster is essential for its head-turning toward visual stimuli (Schneider 1969). In neonates in which the superficial layers of the superior colliculus have been removed, the ingrowing retinal fibers terminate exclusively in the deeper layers of this structure, rather than synapsing in their normal superficial postion. In those hamsters in which the terminations are distributed throughout the medio-lateral extent of the deeper layers, adult visual orientation is remarkably normal, indicating that the terminations in the inappropriate tectal layers are functional. In other hamsters in which the terminations are restricted to the lateral aspect of the deep layers, however, orientation occurs only toward stimuli in the lower visual field (corresponding to the retinotopic organization of this structure) (Schneider 1973).

In hamsters with unilateral removal of the superficial collicular layers soon after birth, axons from the contralateral retina not only synapse in the deeper layers of the injured tectum but also decussate across the tectal midline where they terminate in the medial aspect of the superficial layers of the intact superior colliculus. This anomalous crossed projection can be induced to grow throughout the entire superficial gray layer of the intact colliculus if the eye projecting to that colliculus (i.e. ipsilateral to the injured tectum) is also removed at birth. As adults such hamsters frequently show misdirected head orientation: stimuli presented to the intact eye may elicit head-turning toward the opposite visual field (Schneider 1973). When this anomalous crossed projection is transected in the adult hamster, the misdirected turning is nearly totally abolished (Schneider 1979).

PYRAMIDAL TRACT   Damage to the neonatal hamster brain can induce redirected axonal growth in pathways other than the retinotectal projection. After one pyramidal tract is interrupted between the fourth and eighth day of life, the severed axons grow out dorsolaterally in the brainstem to occupy an anomalous position. During the subsequent weeks, however, these redirected axons grow and form synaptic connections in the dorsal column nuclei of the brainstem and in the dorsal horn of the spinal cord. The positioning and ultrastructural appearance of these terminals appears remarkably normal, despite the anomalous course that the regenerating axons take to reach these sites. The ability of severed pyramidal tract fibers to regenerate into the spinal cord diminishes when they are injured after the eighth day of life and is absent in hamsters operated as adults (Kalil & Reh 1979, 1982).

This regeneration has important behavioral consequences for the manual dexterity of the hamsters. Normal adult hamsters shell sunflower seeds with their teeth, using the digits of the forepaws to grasp and rotate the seeds. Hamsters with interruption of one pyramidal tract in adulthood shell seeds clumsily. They use the affected paw to support the seed but lose the use of digits. As a result, the time required for them to shell seeds increases significantly, relative to neurologically intact adults.

In contrast, the hamsters given unilateral pyramidotomy at 4–8 days of age show good use of the affected forepaw in this behavior as adults, and the times required to shell seeds are nearly normal (Figure 2). When the infant-operate

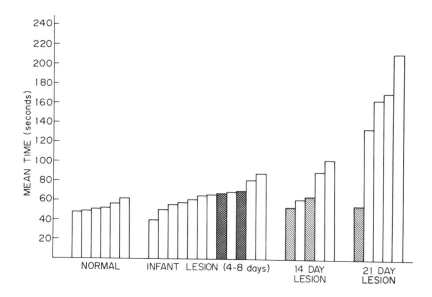

Figure 2   Histogram comparing the average time required for animals with pyramidal tract lesions at three postnatal ages to shell and eat sunflower seeds. Open bars represent scores of hamsters with unilateral lesions; cross-hatched bars represent scores of animals with bilateral lesions; bars with angled lines represent the scores of sham-operated animals. Reprinted from Reh & Kalil (1982) *Journal of Comparative Neurology* 211:276–83, with permission of Alan R. Liss, Inc.

animals undergo a second surgery as adults to sever the regenerated pyramidal axons, the impairments of manual usage are evident. These results indicate that integrity of the regenerated fibers is responsible for the sparing of manual function in the infant-operates (Reh & Kalil 1982).

HIPPOCAMPUS   In spite of the extensive work done on synaptic remodeling in the partially denervated hippocampus, the behavioral consequences of sprouting in this structure are poorly understood. The hippocampus appears to contribute to spatial tasks (O'Keefe & Nadel 1978). One measure of this ability is the learned alternation task, in which an animal must alternate between running down the left and right arms of a maze on successive trails to obtain food reward. Bilateral lesions of the entorhinal cortex, which denervates the dentate gyrus of each hemisphere of its major source of extrinsic afferents, leads to a long-lasting impairment in alternation behavior. Rats with such lesions are equally likely to enter the left and right arms of a maze regardless of their choice on the previous trial.

Each entorhinal cortex projects heavily to the ipsilateral dentate gyrus and sparsely to the contralateral dentate. After unilateral entorhinal cortex lesion, the projection of the contralateral entorhinal cortex to the ipsilateral dentate gyrus increases markedly between days 8 and 12 postoperatively (Steward et al

1974, 1976). The possible functional consequences of this sprouting of a homologous source of afferents to the dentate have been examined by Loesche & Steward (1977). Unilateral lesions of the entorhinal cortex produce a decrement in alternation performance that returns to preoperative levels during the first 12 days postoperatively. Furthermore, after recovery has occurred, a secondary lesion of the remaining entorhinal cortex or of its crossed projection to the dentate (via dorsal psalterium) reinstates the deficit (however, see Ramirez 1980, cited in Finger & Stein 1982, pp. 98–99).

Based on these observations, Loesche & Steward (1977) suggest that the sprouting of crossed entorhinal-dentate projections may underlie the recovery of the spatial task. However, approximately two-thirds of the recovery of alteration performance that these investigators observe occurs by postoperative day 7, prior to the reported onset of sprouting. One possibility not discussed by these authors is that the early improvement in alternation performance depends upon a supersensitivity of the partially denervated granule cells to the neurotransmitter released by the intact crossed projection (see section on Neurochemical Adaptations and Recovery). This mechanism would account both for the early onset of the recovery and its dependence upon the integrity of the crossed projection.

SPINAL CORD   An extensive research program has been undertaken by Goldberger & Murray (see review 1978) to investigate the role of axonal growth responses in the recovery of limb function after spinal cord injury. In this work they have compared the recovery of hindlimb movements with morphological adaptations that occur following either spinal hemisection or limb deafferentation.

Cats that have spinal hemisections (sparing the dorsal columns) at lower thoracic or upper lumbar levels show a considerable initial depression of the motor functions of the ipsilateral hindlimb. This motor depression affects reflexes intrinsic to that limb (tendon, cutaneous flexor), contralateral segmental reflexes (crossed extensor), descending reflexes (vestibular, ear scratch), limb tone, and the use of the limb in spontaneous movements such as locomotion. During the 2–3 weeks postoperatively the use of the ipsilateral hindlimb in locomotion recovers so that it appears normal. During this time the contralateral segmental and intrinsic reflexes also grow in strength. The marked increase in intrinsic reflexes appears to contribute to the restoration of locomotion because deafferentation of the affected hindlimb prevents the recovery of the hemisected cat. Murray & Goldberger (1974) found an increased termination of dorsal roots within the intermediate layers and the base of the dorsal horn at spinal levels caudal to the hemisection. Electrophysiological receptive field correlates of this expanded projection to the dorsal horn (Brenowitz & Pubols 1981) suggest that terminal expansion occurs within the first 3 weeks after the hemisection, a time course consistent with the interpretation that this collateral growth mediates the reflex and locomotor recovery.

Cats in which all of the lumbar dorsal roots supplying one hindlimb have been sectioned show an immediate flaccid paralysis of that limb. The limb is dragged passively during spontaneous locomotion, lacks tone, and cannot be driven to activity by the residual pathways (postural reflex systems arising in the trunk, contralateral segmental reflex pathways, or the descending projections). By 2 days postoperatively the reflex control of the limb by these residual pathways begins to recover, and during the second week the descending reflexes (vestibular placing, ear scratch) become hyperactive. Shortly thereafter the cat appears to use cues from its trunk to place the limb accurately during locomotion. The hyperactivity of the supraspinal reflexes suggested to Murray & Goldberger (1974) that the descending projections to the lumbar spinal cord might sprout following hindlimb deafferentation. In confirmation, cats that received upper lumbar transections 12 months after unilateal deafferentation showed a greater distribution of degeneration products in laminae IV through VIII of the ipsilateral lumbar cord.

NEUROCHEMICAL ADAPTATIONS AND RECOVERY

In addition to the morphological forms of plasticity described above, central synapses can respond to injury by modifying their rate of chemical transmission. Neurons spared from injury may contribute to a recovery of function by increasing their rate of transmitter synthesis and release or by decreasing the rate of inactivation of released transmitter. Also, neurons postsynaptic to the injured pathway may show an enhanced response to the transmitter released by surviving terminals (postsynaptic supersensitivity).

Within the CNS these adaptations are best documented for the central monoamine-containing neurons, where the regulation of transmitter synthesis, release, inactivation, and postsynaptic sensitivity have been studied extensively.

Determinants of Neurochemical Adaptations

SYNTHESIS AND RELEASE   After incomplete damage to a central catecholamine (CA)-containing projection, the surviving nerve terminals of that pathway typically show an enhanced rate of transmitter synthesis and release. After extensive but subtotal damage to nigrostriatal dopaminergic projection, for instance, the rate of incorporation of ^{3}H-tyrosine into ^{3}H-dopamine (DA) in the neostriatum is increased when expressed as a proportion of the endogenous DA remaining in this structure (Agid et al 1973). Similarly, the ratios of the dopamine metabolities, dihydroxyphenylacetic acid and homovanillic acid, to DA are enhanced, suggesting an increased rate of transmitter metabolism by the surviving terminals (Sharman et al 1967, Hefti et al 1980). Similar increases in the ratio of homovanillic acid to DA occur in patients with Parkinson's disease in which many of the nigral DA-containing neurons degenerate (Bernheimer & Hornykiewicz 1962). Also, after partial injury to the central noradrenergic axons that innervate the hippocampus or cerebellum, the activity of tyrosine hydroxylase (TH), the rate-limiting enzyme in CA biosynthesis, is increased within the remaining norepinephrine-containing terminals of these structures. At 1.5–5 days after the injury, TH activity is enhanced due to an allosteric modification of the TH molecule which increases its affinity for the reduced pteridine cofactor. By 3 weeks postoperatively this allosteric modification is no longer evident, but the surviving cerebellar and hippocampal noradrenergic nerve terminals contain a greater than normal number of TH molecules (Acheson & M. Zigmond 1981; Figure 3). After incomplete injury to a monoamine-containing projection, the elevated rate of transmitter synthesis and release is at least partly the result of an increased rate of action potentials ("impulse flow") in the surviving axons.

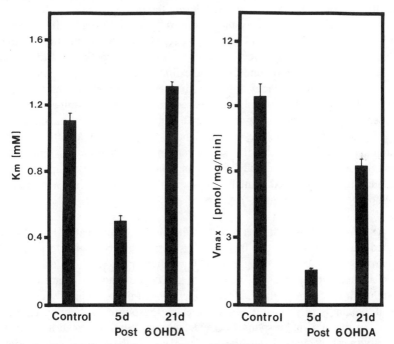

Figure 3   Kinetics of effect of pterin cofactor (6MPH$_4$) on tyrosine hydroxylase activity of hippocampus 5 or 21 days after intraventricular injection of 6-OHDA (250 μg) in rats. Tyrosine hydroxylase activity was measured in the presence of varying concentrations of 6MPH$_4$ in Tris/acetate buffer, pH 6.2. Values represent the mean ± SEM for 5 separate animals. Note that this analysis was carried out at the pH optimum for the enzyme in untreated control rats, thus minimizing the change in the K_m at 5 days postlesion. Adapted from Acheson & M. J. Zigmond (1981) *Journal of Neuroscience* 1:493–504.

INACTIVATION   After monoamines are released into the synaptic cleft, their principal route of inactivation is by reuptake into the nerve terminals (Iversen 1971). After monoamine-containing neurons have been axotomized, the nerve terminals distal to the injury cease releasing transmitter immediately. However, the high-affinity uptake sites that concentrate monoamines in the nerve terminals continue to function until the anterograde degeneration affects the integrity of the nerve terminal membrane (typically, at least 24 hours postoperatively). This lag between the time at which release ceases and uptake sites are lost can limit the rate of recovery from partial injury to monoaminergic pathways, as shown elegantly by R. Zigmond et al (1981).

The pineal gland is innervated by noradrenergic axons whose cell bodies reside in the left and right superior cervical ganglia (SCG). These noradrenergic neurons regulate the large circadian rhythm of pineal serotonin N-acetyltransferase (NATase) activity, since this rhythm is largely abolished by bilateal SCG removal (denervation) or by removal of the cervical sympathetic trunk innervating each SCG (decentralization). After unilateral pineal denervation the NATase rhythm is depressed during the initial 24-hour cycle, but its magnitude is fully restored by the second day postoperatively. In contrast, unilateral decentralization leads to a major decrease in NATase rhythmicity that is not reversed by 3 days. R. Zigmond et al (1981) hypothesized that after unilateral decentralization and during the first cycle following unilateral denervation, the uptake capacity of the inactive neurons persists, thereby limiting the effectiveness of norepinephrine released from the active terminals. During the second day after denervation, however, the degeneration of the terminals and attendant loss of uptake sites enhances the postsynaptic action of the norepinephrine released by the active terminals. In support of this view, administration of the norepinephrine uptake blocker desmethylimipramine to unilaterally decentralized animals led to a restoration of NATase activity (R. Zigmond et al 1981; Figure 4).

POSTSYNAPTIC SUPERSENSITIVITY   Cannon & Rosenblueth (1949) suggested that a loss of nervous input renders tissues supersensitive to naturally occurring substances and drugs. This "law of denervation" includes smooth, cardiac, and skeletal muscle, neurons of the central and peripheral nervous system, and the pineal gland. Because denervated tissues typically require a smaller quantity of agonist to elicit a threshold response (without necessarily changing the maximal response), Trendelenburg (1963) indicated that supersensitivity is best quantified by the horizontal shift of the dose-response curve.

Trendelenburg (1963) identified both pre- and postsynaptic components of denervation supersensitivity. Those mechanisms that change the concentration of the agonist at the postsynaptic membrane are presynaptic, and one of these has already been considered (R. Zigmond et al 1981). Those that alter the

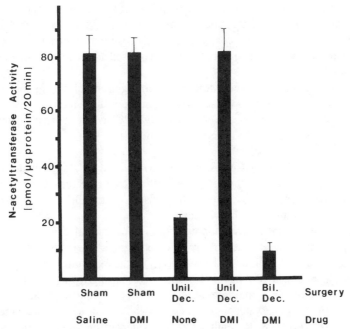

Figure 4   Effect of desmethylimipramine on pineal N-acetyltransferase activity in normal and decentralized animals. Rats were sham-operated (Sham), unilaterally decentralized (Unil. Dec.), or bilaterally decentralized (Bil. Dec.). The next day they were injected with saline or desmethylimipramine (DMI) or were untreated. All rats were killed 5–8 hours after the onset of darkness. Rats given DMI were injected i.p. with this drug 30 minutes before the onset of darkness (20 mg/kg) and again 5 hours after the onset of darkness (10 mg/kg). Two hours later they were killed and enzyme activity was measured. Adapted from R. Zigmond, Baldwin & Bowers (1981) *Proceedings of the National Academy of Sciences,* USA 78:3959–63.

response of the tissue to a particular concentration of agonist are postsynaptic and are the subject of the remainder of this section.

Research on postsynaptic supersensitivity has focused on three tissues: skeletal muscle, smooth muscle, and CNS structures. The sensitivity of muscles is typically quantified by measuring (*a*) the extent of contractile force in response to systemic or bath application of an agonist, or (*b*) the electrophysiological response of the muscle cell to iontophoretic application of the agonist. Within the CNS, iontophoresis, biochemical measures of cellular sensitivity (e.g. catecholamine-stimulated adenylate cyclase), and behavioral measures are used.

Denervation of skeletal muscle or CNS regions can also lead to marked changes in the density of membrane-binding sites for ligands of the endogenous transmitter. In skeletal muscle there is a quantitative relationship between sensitivity of the muscle fiber to ACh iontophoresis and its binding of $^{125}\text{I-}\alpha$-

bungarotoxin (Hartzell & Fambrough 1972). However, the postsynaptic super-sensitivity of smooth muscle appears unrelated to membrane receptor changes (Fleming 1976). Therefore, changes in membrane-binding sites may underlie some instances of supersensitivity but cannot be used uncritically as an index of tissue sensitivity.

Two issues have dominated research concerning the regulation of postsynaptic sensitivity. First, what is the stimulus (or stimuli) that act on the postsynaptic cell to regulate the extent of its sensitivity? Second, what postsynaptic cellular events mediate the change in sensitivity?

Stimuli regulating sensitivity   Although the sensitivity of denervated skeletal muscle may be controlled by several stimuli, recent research has focused on distinguishing between the roles of (*a*) muscle contractile activity, and (*b*) trophic factors transported by the nerve.

Many investigations have supported the importance of decreased muscle activity. Whereas denervation of the rat diaphragm or soleus muscles leads to an enhanced acetylcholine (ACh) sensitivity in the extrajunctional regions of the muscle within a few days, this spread of sensitivity can be limited if electrical stimulation is intermittently applied to the distal segment of the cut nerve or to the denervated muscle (Jones & Vrbová 1971, Drachman & Witzke 1972, Lømo & Rosenthal 1972). Evidence for axonally transported factors comes from experiments (e.g. Tiedt et al 1977, Warnick et al 1977) in which the application of substances that block axon transport (colchicine, vinblastine) to the motor nerve induces an increased ACh sensitivity of the muscle. Even under favorable conditions, however, colchicine or vinblastine application to the sciatic nerve produces an ACh supersensitivity in the soleus or extensor digitorum longus muscles only 10–20% of that observed following denervation (Warnick et al 1977), suggesting that the contribution of axonally transported trophic factors to the supersensitivity is likely to be small.

For smooth muscle and CNS neurons that normally are sensitive to catechol-amines, the level of aminergic receptor activation appears to be very important in controlling postsynaptic sensitivity. For example, the time course of de-velopment of postsynaptic supersensitivity in the nictitating membrane is similar when it is induced by denervation, decentralization, or chronic adminis-tration of the catecholamine-depleting drug reserpine (Fleming et al 1973). Also, the development of neostriatal supersensitivity to dopamine receptor stimulants is similar after intracerebral 6-OHDA injections that destroy the dopaminergic innervation to this structure or followng chronic administration of dopamine receptor blocking agents (Ungerstedt 1971, Feltz & de Champlain 1972, Mishra et al 1974, Iwatsubo & Clouet 1975, Yarbrough 1975, Yar-brough & Kostopoulos 1975, Burt et al 1977, Creese et al 1977). Chronic treatment with the dopamine precursor L-dopa prevents the supersensitivity otherwise resulting from dopamine insufficiency (Gudelsky et al 1975, Friedhoff et al 1977, Ezrin-Waters & Seeman 1978).

Finally, destroying the noradrenergic innervation of the neocortex results in increased cortical norepinephrine-stimulated adenylate cyclase and elevated binding of ligands for the β-adrenoceptor (Huang et al 1973, Kalisker et al 1973, Harden et al 1977, Skolnick et al 1978, Minneman et al 1979, U'Prichard et al 1980), similar to what is observed following chronic reserpine administration (French et al 1974, Baudry et al 1976, Palmer et al 1976, Sharma et al 1981).

Cellular events mediating supersensitivity   Innervated skeletal muscle shows a high degree of ACh sensitivity at the end plate and little or no ACh sensitivity of the surrounding membrane. In denervated muscle the sensitivity of the extrajunctional membrane to ACh can increase more than 1000-fold (Axelsson & Thesleff 1959, Miledi 1960). This extrajunctional ACh supersensitivity is explained by the dramatic increase in the number of nicotinic ACh receptors in the extrajunctional region of the muscle fiber. In the rat diaphragm, for example, denervation increases the density of extrajunctional receptors labeled by ^{125}I-α-bungarotoxin from fewer than 5 per μm^2 to 1695 per μm^2 (Hartzell & Fambrough 1972). The added receptors are synthesized de novo and inserted into the membrane (Fambrough 1979).

The cellular events underlying supersensitivity in smooth muscle appear to be quite different. The postsynaptic supersensitivity is relatively nonspecific: i.e. the supersensitivity to norepinephrine, ACh, histamine, K^+ and other transmitters and ions does not vary by more than one order of magnitude (Hudgins & Fleming 1966, Westfall 1970, Westfall et al 1972, Fleming et al 1973). No difference is found between the adrenergic receptor binding of normal and denervated smooth muscle (Page & Neufeld 1978, Seidel et al 1982). Thus, the cellular mechanism of the supersensitivity appears to occur after the receptor occupancy (Fleming et al 1973). Two candidates have been suggested: (*a*) a 7-10 mV depolarizing shift in the resting membrane potential resulting from a decreased activity of the membrane Na^+, K^+ electrogenic pump (Urquilla et al 1978, Gerthoffer et al 1979, Wong et al 1981); (*b*) a redistribution of intracellular calcium (Garrett & Carrier 1971, Carrier 1975, Westfall 1977).

Within the CNS, the finding that denervation or pharmacological blockade of DA, norepinephrine, serotonin, or muscarinic ACh receptors induces them to increase in number suggests that a receptor proliferation may contribute to the postsynaptic supersensitivity. However, events subsequent to receptor occupancy may also contribute to the supersensitivity of denervated CNS neurons.

Neurochemical Adaptations and Recovery of Function

Cannon & Rosenblueth (1949) and Stavraky (1961) suggested that a denervation-induced supersensitivity to transmitter may be one mechanism by which animals with nervous system injury recover from the functional consequences of that damage. This explanation requires that there be a source of transmitter remaining after the injury that is able to reach the denervated cells. In those model systems in which postsynaptic supersensitivity does appear to contribute to recovery of function, a small proportion of the original innervation of the target tissue remains intact, providing a source of neurotransmitter to drive the postsynaptic cells. The other forms of neurochemical plasticity described previously (enhanced synthesis and release of transmitter or decreased rate of inactivation) have been considered as possible mechanisms of recovery by relatively few investigators (Stricker & M. Zigmond 1976, R. Zigmond et al 1981).

SPINAL SEROTONERGIC INNERVATION   The activity at spinal serotonergic synapses importantly modulates certain nociceptive reflexes (e.g. heat-induced tail-flick). After intrathecal injections of 5,6-DHT that produce extensive but incomplete damage to the spinal serotonergic innervation, rats show an initial decline in the latency of the tail-flick, followed by complete recovery within two weeks. This recovery depends upon spinal serotonergic receptor activity because it is reversed by intrathecal administration of the serotonin receptor antagonist metergoline (Berge et al 1983).

Although the descending 5-HT-containing projections do reinnervate the lumbar spinal cord between the second and sixth month after their injury by 5,6-DHT (Nygren et al 1974), the spontaneous normalization of the nociceptive reflex latency begins within 3 days of the injury (Berge et al 1983). Within several days of interrupting the spinal serotonin innervation, the spinal cord becomes supersensitive to serotonin precursors or receptor stimulants (Nygren et al 1974, Barbeau & Bedard 1981). Because the time course of this supersensitivity closely matches that of the normalization of the nociceptive reflex, the reflex normalization may depend upon neurochemical adaptations occurring at the surviving serotonergic synapses rather than on the growth of serotonin-containing axons (Berge et al 1983).

MESOSTRIATAL DOPAMINERGIC PROJECTION   When the ascending dopamine-containing projections are interrupted, animals show impairments in ingestive behaviors, exploratory locomotion, and sensorimotor capacities (Ungerstedt 1974, Stricker & M. Zigmond 1976, Marshall & Teitelbaum 1977, Fink & Smith 1979). One behavioral impairment resulting from this brain damage that is particularly amenable to study is somatosensory inattention, or the failure to orient toward tactile stimuli applied to the body surface (Marshall et al 1971, 1974, Marshall 1979). In rats with unilateral injury this impairment is restricted to the contralateral body surface.

The somatosensory inattention results specifically from the interruption of mesostriatal dopaminergic projections, since (*a*) it can be produced by 6-OHDA injections that specifically destroy neostriatal dopaminergic terminals (Marshall et al 1980, Dunnett & Iversen 1982), and (*b*) the impairments are reversed by transplants of fetal nigral dopaminergic cells that reinnervate the lateral neostriatum (Dunnett et al 1981) or by intrastriatal injection of the DA receptor stimulant apomorphine (Marshall et al 1980).

Many rats with such brain injury show a remarkable recovery from their somatosensory inattention. When it occurs, the recovery has a characteristic spatiotemporal course. The animals begin to recover orientation to touch of the snout by 4 days postoperatively, and by 28 days the recovery concludes with a return of orientation to touch of the hindquarters (Marshall 1979, Kozlowski & Marshall 1981).

The recovery of somatosensory localization depends upon the survival and continued functioning of a small population (5–10%) of the dopaminergic terminals in the neostriatum. When the mesostriatal damage is so extensive as to deplete the DA content of this structure by more than 95%, recovery never occurs; those rats that do recover have less extensive striatal DA depletions (Marshall 1979, Kozlowski & Marshall 1981).

Metabolic correlates   To begin to understand the neural events responsible for this well-characterized recovery sequence, the ^{14}C-2-deoxyglucose (2DG) autoradiographic procedure (Sokoloff et al 1977) was used to visualize the metabolic activity of the neostriatum during recovery from the somatosensory impairments. Rats given unilateral mesostriatal 6-OHDA injections that have a marked impairment in contralateral somatosensory localization at 3 days postoperatively show significant hemispheric asymmetries of [14]C-2DG uptake at this time. The uptake of the glucose analog is depressed ipsilaterally to the lesion in forebrain structures that normally receive a dense dopaminergic innervation (i.e. the neostriatum and limbic forebrain structures—Schwartz 1978, Kozlowski & Marshall 1980), while its uptake is enhanced ipsilaterally in basal gangliar structures that receive neostriatal efferent fibers (i.e. globus pallidus, entopeduncular nucleus, and substantia nigra pars reticulata—Schwartz 1978, Kozlowski & Marshall 1980, Wooten & Collins 1981). Most of the lesion-induced asymmetries of [14]C-2DG incorporation are reversed by the intrastriatal injection of apomorphine (a procedure that also restores somatosensory localization), indicating that they result from decreased neostriatal dopaminergic receptor stimulation (Kozlowski & Marshall 1980).

This pattern of altered ^{14}C-2DG uptake is also seen at 6 weeks postoperatively in rats that have shown no recovery of somatosensory orientation. However, in animals that recover spontaneously during this time, the hemispheric asymmetries in the anterior neostriatum, globus pallidus, and substantia nigra pars reticulata are no longer evident at 6 weeks postoperatively. Moveover, the time course with which these basal gangliar asymmetries are reversed is quite similar to that of the behavioral recovery (Kozlowski & Marshall 1983; Figure 5).

Pre- and postsynaptic neurochemical changes   Whereas the behavioral recovery and restoration of basal gangliar metabolism could be mediated by any of several synaptic events, they are not likely to be caused by a regrowth or collateral sprouting of dopaminergic axons within this structure. Electron microscopic, fluorescence microscopic, and biochemical experiments have failed to find evidence for a postsynaptic normalization of DA terminal number after 6-OHDA injections along these axons (Hökfelt & Ungerstedt 1973, Neve et al 1982, Reis et al 1978).

Instead, the recovery of somatosensory localization appears to depend upon an increased functioning within the small population (5–10%) of surviving dopaminergic synapses. This recovery could be mediated by an elevated synthesis and release of DA by the residual dopaminergic terminals, an elevated response of the postsynaptic neurons to the available DA, or both (Stricker & M. Zigmond 1976). From this perspective, rats with greater than 95% destruction of this neuronal population fail to recover from their somatosensory impairments because these pre- and postsynaptic compensations are insufficient to restore the dopaminergic receptor activity of the neostriatum to a level compatible with this behavior.

The well-defined time course of the recovery of somatosensory localization leads to strong predictions regarding the temporal limits of any neural event hypothesized to mediate this behavioral restoration. To assess the contribution of postsynaptic events to this recovery sequence, Neve et al (1982) quantified the postoperative time course of development of postsynaptic supersensitivity to DA agonists and found that this time course corresponds closely to that of the behavioral recovery. In separate work, C. A. Altar & J. F. Marshall (unpublished results) determined the postoperative time course of development of elevated DA synthesis by measuring the accumulation of neostriatal dopa following dopa decarboxylase inhibition. The time course of the increase in DA synthesis matches that of the behavioral restoration poorly because it is maximal at the onset of the recovery (3 days postoperatively). These findings suggest that (*a*) the compensatory events critical for recovery occur postsynaptic to the surviving dopaminergic innervation, and (*b*) an increased DA synthesis does not limit the rate at which this recovery occurs.

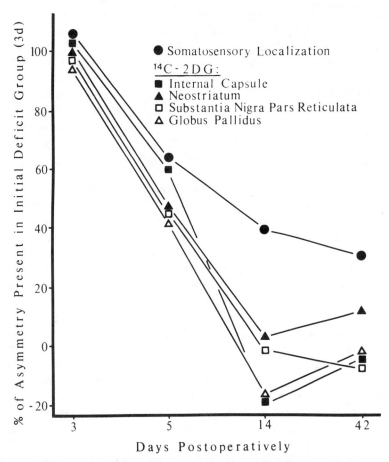

Figure 5   Time course for recovery of contralateral somatosensory localization compared to the time courses for the normalization of ^{14}C-2DG uptake in the anterior neostriatum, globus pallidus, ventral internal capsule, and substantia nigra pars reticulata of recovering rats. Values represent the asymmetries in each of these measures at 3, 5, 14, and 42 days postoperatively as a percent of the asymmetry at 3 days. Negative values represent a reversal of the direction of the asymmetry. The asymmetry in somatosensory localization is not fully reversed by 42 days because of residual impairments in orienting to touch of the most caudal points. Reprinted from Kozlowski & Marshall (1983) *Brain Research* 259:249–60, with permission from Elsevier Biomedical Press.

Dopamine receptor proliferation   What postsynaptic changes mediate this recovery? Neve et al (1982) used the in vivo binding of ^{3}H-spiroperidol to the neostriatum to label one class of dopamine receptors in this structure (D-2) that does not stimulate adenylate cyclase activity (Kebabian & Calne 1979, Seeman 1980). The binding of this ligand to the denervated neostriatum is significantly elevated by 4 days after extensive mesostriatal injury, and the denervation-induced elevation in binding continues to increase during the first month postoperatively. Also, using autoradiography to visualize the binding of ^{3}H-spiroperidol to rat forebrain sections in vitro, Neve et al (1983) observed a denervation-induced increase in ^{3}H-spiroperidol binding to D-2 sites in the neostriatum within the first week postoperatively (Figure 6).

These results are consistent with the hypothesis that an increased density of D-2 receptors on neostriatal cells mediates the observed postsynaptic supersensitivity and the recovery of somatosensory localization, but they do not eliminate the possibility that changes in neostriatal neurons subsequent to the binding of DA to its receptors may also contribute.

CONCLUSIONS AND FUTURE DIRECTIONS

During the past 15 years many investigators have been interested in providing neurobiological explanations for the recovery of function that follows specific types of CNS injury. Much of this research has focused on the behavioral consequences of injury-induced axon growth, and two approaches have yielded significant advances. First, the extensive axonal growth that can occur following brain injury in the neonatal animal may help determine the motor function of that animal as an adult. After neonatal pyramidotomy, this growth leads to a later sparing of forepaw dexterity (Reh & Kalil 1982), whereas the anomalous retinotectal connections that result from neonatal collicular injury can result in misdirected head-orientation toward visual cues as an adult (Schneider 1973). Second, the axonal outgrowth that occurs from fetal neurons transplanted into the brains of adult rats can result in the replacement of a severed pathway and concomitant improvements in motor functions (Dunnett et al 1981) or the performance of a spatial task (Low et al 1982).

These experiments emphasize the capacity of immature nerve cells for axonal growth and the formation of functional circuits. What can be said concerning the behavioral consequences of axonal growth in adult CNS neurons? The only system in which strong arguments can be made is the cat spinal cord. Sectioning of the dorsal roots innervating one hindlimb leads to an increased distribution of the axons descending to the ipsilateral lumbar spinal cord, a hyperactivity of descending reflex controls over the denervated limb, and an improvment in the use of that limb during locomotion (Goldberger & Murray 1978). The locomotor recovery of the denervated hindlimb indicates that hindlimb afferents and descending axons share control over the interneuron-motoneuron pool responsible for this coordinated behavior such that one source of inputs can substitute for the other. A major goal for future research in this field is to identify other systems in the adult CNS in which a collateral sprouting after injury can be shown to have behavioral consequences (facilitatory or deleterious) so that the interaction between multiple afferent sources can be studied further.

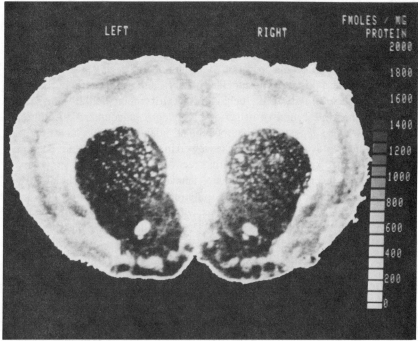

Figure 6 Computer-generated image of an autoradiograph of a rat brain section, depicting the quantity of ^{3}H-spiroperidol (in fmoles per mg tissue protein) bound to each region. This coronal section is from a rat sacrificed 7 days after a unilateral (left) 6-hydroxydopamine injection along the mesotelencephalic dopaminergic projection. The section was incubated in 1.1 nM ^{3}H-spiroperidol. The image has been "linerarized," so that the gray value of each pixel (0–255) is linearly related to the local concentration of ^{3}H-spiroperidol (see scale) Quantification reveals an 18.9% increase in specific binding to the denervated neostriatum.

Compared to these morphological approaches, less attention has been paid to the possibility that neurochemical adaptations at surviving synapses may mediate behavioral recovery. Although the hypothesis that neurochemical changes such as denervation supersensitivity may mediate recovery is not new (Cannon & Rosenblueth 1949), direct experimental support for this hypothesis is. Alternations in transmitter synthesis, release, and postsynaptic sensitivity mediate the recovery of ingestive behaviors and sensorimotor functions after injury to brain dopaminergic neurons (Stricker & M. Zigmond 1976, Marshall 1980), and the normalization of spinal nociceptive reflexes after injury to bulbospinal serotonergic projections suggests a similar conclusion (Berge et al 1983). For the recovery of somatosensory localization after nigrostriatal injury, a supersensitivity of the neostriatal neurons to dopamine appears to determine the rate at which this behavior is restored (Neve et al 1982), and a proliferation of dopamine receptors of the D-2 class may mediate this enhanced cellular sensitivity.

Neurochemical adaptations may underlie the recovery that occurs after damage to many CNS systems. For instance, the recovery of somatosensory localization after nigrostriatal injury has a time course that is characteristic for the recovery of other behaviors after other forms of brain injury. This similar time course may reflect the operation of a common underlying process (i.e. the development of a postsynaptic supersensitivity), and a contribution of a postsynaptic supersensitivity to the behavioral improvement should be suspected whenever this time course of behavioral recovery is encountered. Additional evidence which suggests that neurochemical adaptations may contribute to other instances of recovery has been reviewed in the section on "Redundancy." After damage to several fiber systems, recovery occurs only if some small population of the axons escape injury. I have argued that this relationship between the extent of damage to a population of neurons and recovery may suggest that neurochemical adaptations within the surviving axons or their postsynaptic cells subserve recovery. The dependence of recovery on the survival of a small population of axons within the injured projection is not expected if the recovery is mediated by the collateral sprouting of axons from another source into the denervated region.

Some investigators have argued that supersensitivity may alter only the central excitatory state of the denervated neurons, thereby mediating generalized aspects of recovery, but that the recovery of patterned motor responses must be mediated by the more selective process of axon sprouting (Goldberger 1974). This view of supersensitivity implies a lack of specificity of the partially denervated neurons to the neurohumoral agents reaching their surface. However, recent evidence suggest that the supersensitivity of denervated CNS neurons is mediated, at least in part, by a proliferation of receptors for the depleted neurotransmitter. This proliferation can be quite specific. Thus, after nigrostriatal injury the density of D-2 receptors in the neostriatum increases significantly, but the binding of ligands for the muscarinic or nicotinic cholinergic receptors, β-adrenoceptors, opiate, and γ-aminobutyric acid receptors does not increase in this structure (Kato et al 1978, McGeer et al 1979, Reisine et al 1979, Schallert et al 1980, Suga 1980). One important future direction is to determine the cellular processes responsible for the development of denervation supersensitivity in other populations of CNS neurons in order to determine whether this degree of specificity is commonplace. At present, however, there is no reason to suppose that the supersensitivity of denervated CNS neurons cannot be a transmitter-selective process responsible for the recovery of patterned responses in many systems.

ACKNOWLEDGMENTS

This review was written while the author was a fellow in Neuroscience of the Alfred P. Sloan Foundation. Some of the author's research described herein was supported by National Science Foundation.

Literature Cited

Acheson, A. L., Zigmond, M. J. 1981. Short and long term changes in tyrosine hydroxylase activity in rat brain after subtotal destruction of central noradrenergic neurons. *J. Neurosci.* 1:493–504

Agid, Y., Javoy, F., Glowinksi, J. 1973. Hyperactivity of remaining dopaminergic neurones after partial destruction of the nigro-striatal dopaminergic system in the rat. *Nature New Biol.* 245:150–51

Axelsson, J., Thesleff, S. 1959. A study of supersensitivity in denervated mammalian skeletal muscle. *J. Physiol.* 147:178–93

Barbeau, H., Bedard, P. 1981. Denervation supersensitivity to 5-hydroxytryptophan in rats following spinal transection and 5,7-dihydroxytryptamine injection. *Neuropharmacology* 20:611–16

Barnes, C. D., Joynt, R. F., Schottelius, B. A. 1962. Motoneuron resting potentials in spinal shock. *Am. J. Physiol.* 203:1113–16

Baudry, M., Martres, M.-P., Schwartz, J.-C. 1976. Modulation in the sensitivity of noradrenergic receptors in the CNS studied by the responsiveness of the cyclic AMP system. *Brain Res.* 116:111–24

Baumann, T. P., Spear, P. D. 1977. Role of the lateral suprasylvian visual area in behavioral recovery from effects of visual cortex damage in cats. *Brain Res.* 138:445–68

Beck, C. H., Chambers, W. W. 1970. Speed, accuracy and strength of forelimb movement after unilateral pyramidotomy in rhesus monkeys. *J. Comp. Physiol. Psychol.* 70:1–22

Berge, O.-G., Fasmer, O. B., Flatmark, T., Hole, K. 1983. Time course of changes in nociception after 5,6-dihydroxytryptamine lesions of descending 5-HT pathways. *Pharmacol. Biochem. Behav.* 18:637–43

Bernheimer, H., Hornykiewicz, O. 1962. Das Verhalten einiger Enzyme im Gehirn normaler und Parkinson-kranker Menschen. *Nauyn-Schmiedeberg's Arch. Exp. Pathol. Pharmakol.* 243:295–96

Bernstein, M. E., Bernstein, J. J. 1973. Regeneration of axons and synaptic complex formation rostral to the site of hemisection in the spinal cord of the monkey. *Int. J. Neurosci.* 5:15–26

Björklund, A., Baumgarten, H. G., Lachenmayer, L., Rosengren, E. 1975a. Recovery of brain noradrenaline after 5,7-dihydroxytryptamine-induced axonal lesions in the rat. *Cell Tissue Res.* 161:145–55

Björklund, A., Johansson, B., Stenevi, U., Svendgaard, N.-A. 1975b. Reestablishment of functional connections by regenerating central adrenergic and cholinergic axons. *Nature* 253:446–48

Björklund, A., Lindvall, O. 1979. Regeneration of normal terminal innervation patterns by central noradrenergic neurons after 5,7-dihydroxytryptamine-induced axotomy in the adult rat. *Brain Res.* 171:271–93

Björklund, A., Nobin, A., Stenevi, U. 1973. Regeneration of central serotonin neurons after axonal degeneration induced by 5,6-dihydroxytryptamine. *Brain Res.* 50:214–20

Björklund, A., Stenevi, U. 1971. Growth of central catecholamine neurones into smooth muscle grafts in the rat mesencephalon. *Brain Res.* 31:1–20

Brenowitz, G. L, Pubols, L. M. 1981. Increased receptive field size of dorsal horn neurons following chronic spinal cord hemisections in cats. *Brain Res.* 216:45–59

Brown, M. C., Goodwin, G. M., Ironton, R. 1977. Prevention of motor nerve sprouting in botulinum toxin poisoned mouse soleus muscles by direct stimulation of the muscle. *J. Physiol.* 267:42P–43P

Brown, M. C., Ironton, R. 1977. Motor neuron sprouting induced by prolonged tetrodotoxin block of nerve action potentials. *Nature* 265:495–61

Burt, D. R., Creese, I., Snyder, S. H. 1977. Antischizophrenic drugs: chronic treatment elevates dopamine receptor binding in brain. *Science* 196:326–28

Cannon, W. B., Rosenblueth, A. 1949. *The Supersensitivity of Denervated Structures: A Law of Denervation.* New York: Macmillan

Carrier, O. 1975. Role of calcium in postjunctional supersensitivity. *Fed. Proc.* 34:1975–80

Cotman, C. W., Nadler, J. V. 1978. Reactive synaptogenesis in the hippocampus. In *Neuronal Plasticity*, ed. C. W. Cotman, pp. 227–71. New York: Raven

Cotman, C. W., Nieto-Sampedro, M., Harris, E. W. 1981. Synapse replacement in the nervous system of adult vertebrates. *Physiol. Rev.* 61:684–784

Creese, I., Burt, D. R., Snyder, S. H. 1977. Dopamine receptor binding enhancement accompanies lesion-induced behavioral supersensitivity. *Science* 197:596–98

David, S., Aguayo, A. J. 1981. Axonal elongation into peripheral nervous system "bridges" after central nervous system injury in adult rats. *Science* 214:931–33

Drachman, D. B., Witzke, F. 1972. Trophic regulation of acetylcholine sensitivity of muscle. *Science* 176:514–16

Dunnett, S. B., Björklund, A., Stenevi, U., Iversen, S. D. 1981. Behavioural recovery following transplantation of substantia nigra in rats subjected to 6-OHDA lesions of the nigrostriatal pathway. II. Bilateral lesions. *Brain Res.* 229:209–17

Dunnett, S. B., Iversen, S. D. 1982. Sensorimotor impairments following localized kainic acid and 6-hydroxydopamine lesions of the neostriatum. *Brain Res.* 248:121–27

Edds, M. V. 1953. Collateral nerve regeneration. *Q. Rev. Biol.* 28:260–76

Ezrin-Waters, C., Seeman, P. 1978. L-dopa reversal of hyperdopaminergic behaviour. *Life Sci.* 22:1027–32

Fambrough, D. M. 1979. Control of acetylcholine receptors in skeletal muscle. *Physiol. Rev.* 59:165–227

Feltz, P., de Champlain, J. 1972. Enhanced sensitivity of caudate neurons to microiontophoretic injections of dopamine in 6-hydroxydopamine treated cats. *Brain Res.* 43:601–5

Finger, S., Stein, D. G. 1982. *Brain Damage and Recovery: Research and Clinical Perspectives.* New York: Academic

Fink, J. S., Smith, G. P. 1979. Decreased locomotor and investigatory exploration after denervation of catecholamine terminal fields in the forebrain of rats. *J. Comp. Physiol. Psychol.* 93:34–65

Fleming, W. W. 1976. Variable sensitivity of excitable cells: Possible mechanisms and biological significance. In *Reviews of Neuroscience,* ed. S. Ehrenpreis, I. J. Kopin, pp. 43–90. New York: Raven

Fleming, W. W., McPhillips, J. J., Westfall, D. P. 1973. Postjunctional supersensitivity and subsensitivity of excitable tissues to drugs. *Ergeb. Physiol. Biol. Chem. Exp. Pharmakol.* 68:56–119

Flourens, P. 1824. *Recherches Experimentales sur les Proprietes et les Fonctions du Systeme Nerveux dans les Animaux Vertebres.* Crevot: Paris

French, S. W., Palmer, D. S., Narod, M. E. 1974. Adrenergic subsensitivity and supersensitivity of the cerebral cortex after reserpine treatment. *Fed. Proc.* 34:297

Friedhoff, A. J., Bonnet, K., Rosengarten, H. 1977. Reversal of two manifestations of dopamine receptor supersensitivity by administration of L-Dopa. *Res. Commun. Chem. Pathol. Pharmacol.* 16:411–23

Frommer, G. P. 1978. Subtotal lesions: Implications for coding and recovery of function. In *Recovery from Brain Damage,* ed. S. Finger, pp. 217–80. New York: Plenum

Galambos, R., Norton, T. T., Frommer, G. P. 1967. Optic tract lesions sparing pattern vision in cats. *Exp. Neurol.* 18:8–25

Garrett, R. L, Carrier, O. Jr. 1971. Alteration of extracellular calcium dependence in vascular tissue by reserpine. *Eur. J. Pharmacol.* 13:306–11

Gerthoffer, W. T., Fedan, J. S., Westfall, D. P., Goto, K., Fleming, W. W. 1979. Involvement of the sodium-potassium pump in the mechanism of post-junctional supersensitivity of the vas deferens of the guinea pig. *J. Pharamacol. Exp. Ther.* 210:27–36

Goldberger, M. E. 1974. Recovery of movement after CNS lesions in monkeys. In *Plasticity and Recovery of Function in the Central Nervous System,* ed. D. G. Stein, J. J. Rosen, N., Butters, pp. 265–337. New York: Academic

Goldberger, M. E., Growden, J. H. 1973. Pattern of recovery following cerebellar deep nuclear lesions in monkeys. *Exp. Neurol.* 39:307–22

Goldberger, M. E., Murray, M. 1978. Recovery of movement and axonal sprouting may obey some of the same laws. See Cotman & Nadler 1978, pp. 73–96

Goldowitz, D., Cotman, C. W. 1980. Do neurotrophic interactions control synapse formation in the adult rat brain? *Brain Res.* 181:325–44

Graziadei, P. P. C., Graziadei, G. A. M. 1978. The olfactory system: A model for the study of neurogenesis and axon regeneration in mammals. See Cotman & Nadler 1978, pp. 131–53

Gudelsky, G. A., Thornburg, J. E., Moore, K. E. 1975. Blockade of α-methyltyrosine-induced supersensitivity to apomorphine by chronic administration of L-dopa. *Life Sci.* 16:1331–38

Guth, L. 1956. Regeneration in the mammalian peripheral nervous system. *Physiol. Rev.* 36:441–78

Guth, L., Bernstein, J. J. 1961. Selectivity in the re-establishment of synapses in the superior cervical sympathetic ganglion of the cat. *Exp. Neurol.* 4:59–69

Guth, L., Windle, W. F. 1970. The enigma of central nervous regeneration. *Exp. Neurol. Suppl.* 5:1–43

Harden, T. K., Wolfe, B. B., Sporn, J. R., Poulos, B. K., Molinoff, P. B. 1977. Effects of 6-hydroxydopamine on the development of the *beta* adrenergic receptor/adenylate cyclase system in rat cerebral cortex. *J. Pharmacol. Exp. Ther.* 203:132–43

Hartzell, H. C., Fambrough, D. M. 1972. Acetylcholine receptors. Distribution and extrajunctional density in rat diaphragm after denervation correlated with acetylcholine sensitivity. *J. Gen. Physiol.* 60:248–62

Hefti, F., Melamed, E., Wurtman, R. J. 1980. Partial lesions of the dopaminergic nigrostriatal system in rat brain: biochemical characterization. *Brain Res.* 195:123–37

Hökfelt, T., Ungerstedt, U. 1973. Specificity of 6-hydroxydopamine-induced degeneration of central monoamine neurones: an electron and flourescence microscopic study with special reference to intracerebral injection on the nigrostriatal dopamine system. *Brain Res.* 60:269–97

Holland, R. L, Brown, M. C. 1980. Postsynaptic transmission block can cause terminal sprouting of a motor nerve. *Science* 207: 649–51

Huang, M., Ho, A. K. S., Daly, J. W. 1973. Accumulation of adenosine cyclic 3'5'-monophosphate in rat cerebral cortical slices. Stimulatory effect of *alpha* and *beta* adrenergic agents after treatment with 6-hydroxydopamine, 2,3,5-trihydroxyphenyl-ethylamine, and dihydroxytryptamines. *Mol. Pharmacol.* 9:711–17

Hudgins, P. M., Fleming, W. W. 1966. A relatively nonspecific supersensitivity in aortic strips resulting from pretreatment with reserpine. *J. Pharmacol. Exp. Ther.* 153: 70–80

Iversen, L. L. 1971. Role of transmitter uptake mechanisms in synaptic neurotransmission. *Br. J. Pharmacol.* 41:571–91

Iwatsubo, K. Clouet, D. H. 1975. Dopamine-sensitive adenylate cyclase of the caudate nucleus of rats treated with morphine or haloperidol. *Biochem. Pharmacol.* 24: 1499–1503

Jackson, J. H. 1958. Evolution and dissolution of the nervous system. In *Selected Writings of John Hughlings Jackson*, ed. J. Taylor, 2:45–75. New York: Basic Books

Jacobson, S. G., Eames, R. A., McDonald, W. I. 1979. Optic nerve fiber lesions in adult cats: pattern of recovery of spatial vision. *Exp. Brain Res.* 36:491–508

Jones, R., Vrbová, G. 1971. Can denervation hypersensitivity be prevented? *J. Physiol.* 216:67P–68P

Kalil, K., Reh, T. 1979. Regrowth of severed axons in the neonatal central nervous system: Establishment of normal connections. *Science* 205:1158–61

Kalil, K., Reh, T. 1982. A light and electron microscopic study of regrowing pyramidal tract fibers. *J. Comp. Neurol.* 211:265–75

Kalisker, A., Rutledge, O., Perkins, J. P. 1973. Effect of nerve degeneration by 6-hydroxydopamine on catecholamine-stimulated adenosine 3',5'-monophosphate formation in rat cerebral cortex. *Mol. Pharmacol.* 9:619–29

Kao, C. C., Chang, L. W., Bloodworth, J. M. B. Jr. 1977. Axonal regeneration across transected mammalian spinal cords: An electron microscopic study of delayed microsurgical nerve grafting. *Exp. Neurol.* 54:591–615

Kato, G., Carson, S., Kemel, M. L., Glowinski, J., Giorguieff, M. F. 1978. Changes in striatal specific ³H-atrophine binding after unilateral 6-hydroxydopamine lesions of nigrostriatal dopaminergic neurones. *Life Sci.* 22:1607–14

Kebabian, J. W., Calne, D. B. 1979. Multiple receptors for dopamine. *Nature* 277:93–96

Kerr, F. W. L. 1975. Structural and functional

evidence of plasticity in the central nervous system. *Exp. Neurol.* 48:16–31

Kozlowski, M. R., Marshall, J. F. 1980. Plasticity of ¹⁴C-2-deoxy-D-glucose incorporation into neostriatum and related structures in response to dopamine neuron damage and apomorphine replacement. *Brain Res.* 197:167–83

Kozlowski, M. R., Marshall, J. F. 1981. Plasticity of neostriatal metabolic activity and recovery from nigrostriatal injury. *Exp. Neurol.* 74:318–23

Kozlowski, M. R., Marshall, J. F. 1983. Recovery of function and basal ganglia ¹⁴C-2-deoxyglucose uptake after nigrostriatal injury. *Brain Res.* 259:237–48

Kromer, L. F., Björklund, A., Stenevi, U. 1981a. Innervation of embryonic hippocampal implants by regenerating axons of cholinergic septal neurons in the adult rat. *Brain Res.* 210:153–71

Kromer, L. F., Björklund, A., Stenevi, U. 1981b. Regeneration of the septohippocampal pathways in adult rats is promoted by utilizing embryonic hippocampal implants as bridges. *Brain Res.* 210:173–200

Lashley, K. S. 1929. *Brain Mechanisms and Intelligence.* Chicago: Univ. Chicago Press

Lawrence. D. G., Kuypers, H. G. J. M. 1968. The functional organization of the motor system in the monkey. I. The effects of bilateral pyramidal lesions. *Brain* 91:1–14

Liu, C.-N., Chambers, W. W. 1958. Intraspinal sprouting of dorsal root axons. *Arch. Neurol. Psychol.* 79:46–61

Loesche, J., Steward, O. 1977. Behavioral correlates of denervation and reinnervation of the hippocampal formation of the rat: Recovery of alternation performance following unilateral entorhinal cortex lesions. *Brain Res. Bull.* 2:31–39

Lømo, T., Rosenthal, J. 1972. Control of ACh sensitivity by muscle activity in the rat. *J. Physiol.* 221:493–513

Lømo, T., Slater, C. R. 1978. Control of acetylcholine sensitivity and synapse formation by muscle activity. *J. Physiol.* 275:391–402

Low, W. C., Lewis, P. R., Bunch, S. T., Dunnett, S. B., Thomas, S. R., et al. 1982. Function recovery following neural transplantation of embryonic septal nuclei in adult rats with septohippocampal lesions. *Nature* 300:260–62

Lynch, G., Deadwyler, S., Cotman, C. 1973. Post lesion axonal growth produces permanent functional connections. *Science* 180: 1364–66

Lynch, G., Matthews, D. A., Mosko, S., Parks, T., Cotman, C. 1972. Induced acetylcholinesterase-rich layer in rat dentate gyrus following entorhinal lesions. *Brain Res.* 42:311–18

Marshall, J. F. 1979. Somatosensory inattention after dopamine-depleting intracerebral 6-OHDA injection: Spontaneous recovery and pharmacological control. *Brain Res.* 177:311–24

Marshall, J. F.,. Berrios, N., Sawyer, S. 1980. Neostriatal dopamine and sensory inattention. *J. Comp. Physiol. Psychol.* 94:833–46

Marshall, J. F., Richardson, J. S., Teitelbaum, P. 1974. Nigrostriatal bundle damage and the lateral hypothalamic syndrome. *J. Comp. Physiol. Psychol.* 87:808–30

Marshall, J. F., Teitelbaum, P. 1977. New considerations in the neuropsychology of motivated behavior. In *Handbook of Psychopharmacology,* ed. L. L. Iversen, S. D. Iversen, S. H. Snyder, 7:201–29. New York: Plenum

Marshall, J. F., Turner, B. H., Teitelbaum, P. 1971. Sensory neglect produced by lateral hypothalamic damage. *Science* 174:523–25

McGeer, P. L., McGeer, E. G., Innanen, V. T. 1979. Dendroaxonic transmission. I. Evidence from receptor binding of dopaminergic and cholinergic agents. *Brain Res.* 169:433–41

Miledi, R. 1960. The acetylcholine sensitivity of frog muscle fibres after complete or partial denervation. *J. Physiol.* 151:1–23

Minneman, K. P., Dibner, M. D., Wolfe, B. B., Molinoff, P. B. 1979. β_1- and β_2-adrenergic receptors in rat cerebral cortex are independently regulated. *Science* 204:866–68

Mishra, R. K., Gardner, E. L., Katzman, R., Makman, M. H. 1974. Enhancement of dopamine-stimulated adenylate cyclase activity in rat caudate after lesions in substantia nigra: Evidence for denervation supersensitivity. *Proc. Natl. Acad. Sci. USA* 71:3883–87

Mountcastle, V. B. 1974. Effects of spinal transection. In *Medical Physiology,* ed. V. B. Mountcastle, 1:662–67. St. Louis: Mosby

Murray, J. G., Thompson, J. W. 1957. The occurrence and function of collateral sprouting in the sympathetic nervous system of the cat. *J. Physiol.* 135:133–62

Murray, M., Goldberger, M. E. 1974. Restitution of function and collateral sprouting in the cat spinal cord: the partially hemisected animal. *J. Comp. Neurol.* 158:19–36

Neve, K. A., Altar, C. A., Wong, C. A., Marshall, J. F. 1983. ^{3}H-Spiroperidol binding to rat forebrain sections. 1. Quantitative analysis and determination of lesion effects. *Neurosci. Abstr.* In press

Neve, K. A., Kozlowski, M. R., Marshall, J. F. 1982. Plasticity of neostriatal dopamine receptors after nigrostriatal injury: Relationship to recovery of sensorimotor functions and behavioral supersensitivity. *Brain Res.* 244:33–44

Nygren, L.-G., Fuxe, K., Jonsson, G., Olson, L. 1974. Functional regeneration of 5-hydroxytryptamine nerve terminals in the rat spinal cord following 5,6-dihydroxytryptamine induced degeneration. *Brain Res.* 78:377–94

Nygren, L.-G., Olson, L. 1977. Intracisternal neurotoxins and monoamine neurons innervating the spinal cord: Acute and chronic effects on cell and axon counts and nerve terminal densities. *Histochemistry* 52:281–306

Nygren, L.-G., Olson, L., Seiger, Å. 1971. Regeneration of monoamine-containing axons in the developing and adult spinal cord of the rat following intraspinal 6-OH-dopamine injections or transections. *Histochemie* 28:1–15

O'Keefe, J., Nadel, L. 1978. *The Hippocampus as a Cognitive Map.* New York: Oxford Univ. Press

Page, E. D., Neufeld, A. H. 1978. Characterization of α and β-adrenergic receptors in membranes prepared from the rabbit iris before and after development of supersensitivity. *Biochem. Pharmacol.* 27:953–58

Palmer, D. S., French, S. W., Narod, M. E. 1976. Noradrenergic subsensitivity and supersensitivity of the cerebral cortex after reserpine treatment. *J. Pharmacol. Exp. Ther.* 196:167–71

Ramon y Cajal, S. 1928. *Degeneration and Regeneration of the Nervous System.* Transl. R. M. May. London: Oxford Univ. Press

Reh, T., Kalil, K. 1982. Functional role of regrowing pyramidal tract fibers. *J. Comp. Neurol.* 211:276–83

Reis, D. J., Gilad, G., Pickel, V. M., Joh, T. H. 1978. Reversible changes in the activities and amounts of tyrosine hydroxylase in dopamine neurons of the substantia nigra in response to axonal injury as studied by immunochemical and immunocytochemical methods. *Brain Res.* 144:325–42

Reisine, J. D., Nagy, J. I., Beaumont, K., Fibiger, H. C., Yamamura, H. I. 1979. The localization of receptor binding in substantia nigra and striatum of the rat. *Brain Res.* 177:241–52

Richardson, P. M., McGuinness, U. M., Aguayo, A. J. 1980. Axons from CNS neurones regenerate into PNS grafts. *Nature* 284:264–65

Rosenquist, A. C., Palmer, L. A. 1971. Visual receptive field properties of cells of the superior colliculus after cortical lesions in the cat. *Exp. Neurol.* 33:629–52

Rosner, B. S. 1970. Brain functions. *Ann. Rev. Psychol.* 21:555–94

Rosner, B. S. 1974. Recovery of function and localization of function in historical perspective. In *Plasticity and Recovery of Function in the Central Nervous System,* ed. D. G.

Stein, J. J. Rosen, N. Butters, pp. 1–29. New York: Academic

Schallert, T., Overstreet, D. H., Yamamura, H. I. 1980. Muscarinic receptor binding and behavioral effect of atropine following chronic catecholamine depletion or acetylcholinesterase inhibition in rats. *Pharmacol. Biochem. Behav.* 13:187–92

Schneider, G. E. 1969. Two visual systems. *Science* 163:895–902

Schneider, G. E., 1973. Early lesions of superior colliculus: Factors affecting the formation of abnormal retinal projections. *Brain Behav. Evol.* 8:73–109

Schneider, G. E. 1979. Is it really better to have your brain lesion early? A revision of the "Kennard principle." *Neuropsychologia* 17: 557–83

Schwartz, W. J. 1978. A role for the dopaminergic nigrostriatal bundle in the pathogenesis of altered brain glucose consumption after lateral hypothalamic lesions. Evidence using the ^{14}C-labeled deoxyglucose technique. *Brain Res.* 158:129–47

Seeman, P. 1980. Brain dopamine receptors. *Pharmacol. Rev.* 32:229–313

Seidel, E. R., Miller, T. A., Johnson, L. R. 1982. Distribution of [^{3}H] QNB binding in dog gastric smooth muscle pre- and postvagotomy. *Life Sci.* 31:749–56

Sharma, V. K., Harik, S. I., Busto, R., Banerjee, S. P. 1981. Effects of noradrenaline depletion on adrenergic and muscarinic cholinergic receptors in the cerebral cortex, hippocampus, and cerebellum. *Exp. Neurol.* 72:179–94

Sharman, D. F., Poirier, L. J., Murphy, G. F., Sourkes, T. L. 1967. Homovanillic acid and dihydroxyphenylacetic acid in the striatum of monkeys with brain lesions. *Can. J. Physiol. Pharmacol.* 45:57–62

Sherrington, C. S. 1906. *The Integrative Action of the Nervous System.* New Haven: Yale Univ. Press

Skolnick, P., Stalvey, L.P., Daly, J. W., Hoyler, E., Davis, J. N. 1978. Binding of α- and β-adrenergic ligands to cerebral cortical membranes: Effect of 6-hydroxydopamine treatment and relationship to the responsiveness of cyclic AMP-generating systems in two rat strains. *Eur. J. Pharmacol.* 47:201–10

Sokoloff, L., Reivich, M., Kennedy, C., Des Rosiers, M. H., Patlak, C. S., et al. 1977. The [^{14}C] deoxyglucose method for the measurement of local cerebral glucose utilization: Theory, procedure, and normal values in the conscious and anesthetized albino rat. *J. Neurochem.* 28:897–916

Spear, P. D., Baumann, T. P. 1979. Neurophysiological mechanisms of recovery from visual cortex damage in cats: Properties of lateral suprasylvian visual area neurons following behavioral recovery. *Exp. Brain Res.* 35:177–92

Stavraky, G. W. 1961. *Supersensitivity Following Lesions of the Nervous System.* Toronto: Univ. Toronto

Steward, O., Cotman, C. W., Lynch, G. S. 1974. Growth of a new fiber projection in the brain of adult rats: Re-innervation of the dentate gyrus by the contralateral entorhinal cortex following ipsilateral entorhinal lesions. *Exp. Brain Res.* 20:45–66

Steward, O., Cotman, C. W., Lynch, G. S. 1976. A quantitative autoradiographic and electrophysiological study of the reinnervation of the dentate gyrus by the contralateral entorhinal cortex following ipsilateral entorhinal lesions. *Brain Res.* 114:181–200

Stewart, W. B., Hughes, J., McCouch, G. P. 1940. Cord potentials in spinal shock: Single volleys. *J. Neurophysiol.* 3:139–45

Stricker, E. M., Zigmond, M. J. 1976. Recovery of function following damage to central catecholamine-containing neurons: A neurochemical model for the lateral hypothalamic syndrome. In *Progress in Physiological Psychology and Psychobiology,* ed. J. M. Sprague, A. N. Epstein, 6:121–88. New York: Academic

Suga, M. 1980. Effect of long-term L-DOPA administration on the dopaminergic and cholinergic (muscarinic) receptors of striatum in 6-hydroxydopamine lesioned rats. *Life Sci.* 27:877–82

Teuber, H.-L., Battersby, W. S. Bender, M. B. 1960. *Visual Field Defects after Penetrating Missile Wounds of the Brain.* Cambridge, Mass: Harvard Univ. Press

Tiedt, T. N., Wisler, P. L., Younkin, S. G. 1977. Neurotrophic regulation of resting membrane potential and acetylcholine sensitivity in rat extensor digitorum longus muscle. *Exp. Neurol.* 57:766–91

Trendelenburg, U. 1963. Supersensitivity and subsensitivity to sympathomimetic amines. *Pharmacol. Rev.* 15:225–76

Ungerstedt, U. 1971. Postsynaptic supersensitivity after 6-hydroxydopamine induced degeneration of the nigro-striatal dopamine system. *Acta Physiol. Scand. Suppl.* 367: 69–93

Ungerstedt, U. 1974. Brain dopamine neurons and behavior. In *The Neurosciences: Third Study Program,* ed. F. O. Schmitt, F. G. Worden, pp. 695–703. Cambridge: MIT Press

U'Prichard, D. C., Reisine, T. D., Yamamura, S., Mason, S. T., Fibiger, H. C., et al. 1980. Differential supersensitivity of β-receptor subtypes in rat cortex and cerebellum after central noradrenergic denervation. *Life Sci.* 26:355–64

Urquilla, P. R., Westfall, D. P., Goto, K., Fleming, W. W. 1978. The effects of ouabain and alterations in potassium concentration on the sensitivity to drugs and the membrane potential of the smooth muscle of the guinea-pig and rat vas deferens. *J. Pharmacol. Exp. Ther.* 207:247–355

von Monakow, C. 1914. *Die Lokalisation im Grosshirnrinde und der Abbau der Funktion durch Koricale Herde.* Wiesbaden: Bermann

Warnick, J. E., Albuquerque, E. X., Guth, L. 1977. The demonstration of neurotrophic function by application of colchicine or vinblastine to the peripheral nerve. *Exp. Neurol.* 57:622–36

Weddell, G., Guttmann, L, Gutmann, E. 1941. The local extension of nerve fibers into denervated areas of skin. *J. Neurol. Psychiatry* 4:206–25

West, J. R., Deadwyler, S. A., Cotman, C. W., Lynch, G. S. 1976. An experimental test of diaschisis. *Behav. Biol.* 18:419–25

Westfall, D. P. 1970. The effect of reserpine treatment and decentralization on the ion distribution in the vas deferens of the guinea pig. *Br. J. Pharmacol.* 39:110–20

Westfall, D. P. 1977. The effects of denervation, cocaine, 6-hydroxydopamine and reserpine on the characteristics of drug-induced contractions of the depolarized smooth muscle of the rat and guinea-pig vas deferens. *J. Pharmacol. Exp. Ther.* 201:267–75

Westfall, D. P., McClure, D. C., Fleming, W. W. 1972. The effects of denervation, decentralization and cocaine on the response of the smooth muscle of the guinea-pig vas deferens to various drugs. *J. Pharmacol. Exp. Ther.* 181:328–38

Wickelgren, B. G., Sterling, P. 1969. Influence of visual cortex on receptive fields in the superior colliculus of the cat. *J. Neurophysiol.* 32:16–23

Wong, S. K., Westfall, D. P., Fedan, J. S., Fleming, W. W. 1981. The involvement of the sodium-potassium pump in postjunctional supersensitivity of the guinea-pig vas deferens as assessed by [³H] ouabain binding. *J. Pharmacol. Exp. Ther.* 219:163–69

Wood, C. C., Spear, P. D., Braun, J. J. 1974. Effects of sequential lesions of suprasylvian gyri and visual cortex on pattern discrimination in the cat. *Brain Res.* 66:443–66

Wooten, G. F., Collins, R. C. 1981. Metabolic effects of unilateral lesion of the substantia nigra. *J. Neurosci.* 1:285–91

Wuttke, W., Björklund, A., Baumgarten, H. G., Lachenmayer, L., Fenske, M., et al. 1977. De- and regeneration of brain serotonin neurons following 5,7-dihydroxytryptamine treatment: Effects on serum LH, FSH and prolactin levels in male rats. *Brain Res.* 134:317–31

Yarbrough, G. G. 1975. Supersensitivity of caudate neurones after repeated administration of haloperidol. *Eur. J. Pharamcol.* 31:367–69

Yarbrough, G. G., Kostopoulos, G. K. 1975. Microiontophoretic studies on denervation supersensitivity in the CNS. *Fed. Proc.* 34:331

Zigmond, R. E., Baldwin, R. C., Bowers, C. W. 1981. Rapid recovery of function after partial denervation of the rat pineal gland suggests a novel mechanism for neural plasticity. *Proc. Natl. Acad. Sci. USA* 78:3959–63

Ann. Rev. Psychol. 1984 35:309–31
Copyright © 1984 by Annual Reviews Inc. All rights reserved

LIFE-SPAN DEVELOPMENT

Marjorie P. Honzik

Institute of Human Development, University of California, Berkeley, California 94720

CONTENTS

INTRODUCTION

The first review of life-span development in the *Annual Review of Psychology* appeared in 1980 (Baltes, Reese & Lipsitt). This second review covers the years 1980 through 1982, together with a few relevant earlier publications.

According to Baltes et al (1980), life-span developmental psychology is not a theory but an orientation to the study of behavior and development. The first assumption of this orientation is that development is a life-long process beginning at conception and ending in death. This view differs from that of developmental psychologists who have considered the age periods of somatic growth as their domain: infancy, childhood, and adolescence. The implicit assumption of this viewpont is that development ends with the end of growth or "maturity." In contrast, life-span developmental psychologists have been largely concerned with the adult years and aging. Currently, there is a noticeable trend for developmental psychologists to show more interest in the adult years (Eichorn et al 1981, Lefkowitz 1981, Young & Ferguson 1981, Kuhn 1982, Lamb & Sutton-Smith 1982, Lazar & Darlington 1982, Lerner 1982, Lipsitt 1982a,

309

Waterman 1982) and the life-span developmental psychologists to show some consideration for the issues of infancy and childhood (Baltes et al 1980, Baltes & Brim 1982, Lerner et al 1982).

In their review, Baltes et al (1980) state that it is "obvious that much of the work of the life-span developmental psychologists [in the 1970s] has been conceptual and methodological rather than empirical." In this review we will emphasize empirical findings published since the last review as well as theories and research of the entire life span. However, the coverage will necessarily be selective since there has been not only an explosion of interest and number of publications on aging during the past 5 years, but there has been an equally exciting upsurge of interest in the competencies of infants. Poon & Welford (1980) report an increase in psychological aging publications from about 250 per year in 1975 to more than 600 in 1980. The number of studies and publications about infants and young children has also been increasing at an astronomical rate.

At both ends of the life span there is concern with neurological impairments that may adversely affect normal functioning in both the infant and elderly adult. This fact indicates the need for an interdisciplinary approach in studies of life-span development. It will not be possible in this review to cover more than a few reports on the relation of and possible effects of certain neurological and somatic ills to development.

HISTORICAL BACKGROUND

Earliest studies of child development were baby biograhies often written by relatives of the infant (Darwin 1877, Shinn 1900). Child psychology, later called "developmental psychology," began as a science taught in colleges and universities in the late 1920s. I was a member of the first class offered in Child Psychology at the University of California in 1928–29. Harold E. Jones was the professor. There were no textbooks available. The first "Child Psychology" text was published by Jersild in 1933. However, Gesell (1928), Piaget (1923), Terman (1916), Vigotsky & Luria (1929), and others had all reported significant research findings by that time; and research in developmental psychology was underway in many centers in the U.S. with funds provided by the Laura Spelman Rockefeller Foundation. Acceleration in the empirical studies of the young child had begun. The Society for Research in Child Development (SRCD) had its first meeting in 1933. By 1981 more than 3000 eager individuals interested in child development crowded into the hotels of Boston for SRCD's biennial meeting.

Life-span developmental psychology had a different course with the first major works appearing in Europe in the last century. In this country, the life-span approach was slow to gain momentum until the 1960s and 70s (Baltes et al 1980). However, a few important treatises appeared earlier by investigators interested in the adult as well as the childhood years. G. Stanley Hall wrote a book on *Adolescence* in 1904 and one on *Senescence* in 1922. Other authors with a life-span approach include Sanford (1902), Hollingworth (1927), Buhler (1933), and Pressey et al (1939).

A number of factors have contributed to the current upsurge in interest. These include research on aging initiated at a number of universities and at the National Institute of Health; longitudinal studies of children continuing into the adult years (Kagan & Moss 1962, Block 1971); and the founding of the Gerontological Society (1946) and a Division of the American Psychological Association on Maturity and Old Age (later called Adult Development and Aging). Interest in life-span development has also been stimulated by a series of conferences at the University of West Virginia beginning in 1969 and still continuing. Conference papers are published and have yielded six volumes to date (Goulet & Baltes 1970, Baltes & Schaie 1973, Nesselroade & Reese 1973, Datan & Ginsberg 1975, Datan & Reese 1977, Turner & Reese 1980). Proceedings of the two most recent conferences covering "Non-normative Life Events" and "Historical and Generative Effects on Life Span Development" have yet to appear. A second yearly series entitled "Life Span Development and Behavior," edited by Baltes in 1978 and by Baltes & Brim in 1979, 1980, and 1982, provides reviews of research and theory.

The chapters in these two life-span series vary in quality, significance, and coverage of the life span. There are very few studies of infants and children and not many studies based on empirical findings. Baltes et al (1980) recognize this lack, concluding that there "can be no satisfactory life-span developmental psychology without a strong foundation in studies of infants and children." A second imperative mentioned was a need for "a stronger infusion of empirical research in the study of the life span." The *Life-Span Development and Behavior* series has begun to correct these lacks. The 1982 volume includes a number of important empirical studies, one of which is based on infants. Kopp & McCall (1982) explore the stability of mental test performance in normal babies, infants at risk, and handicapped infants. They note that data from many longitudinal studies reveal patterns of mental instability in early life for all but the most severely impaired infants. In this same volume an important paper by Pulkkinnen (1982) describes the continuity of self-control from childhood to adolescence in a Finnish longitudinal Study of Social Development. A third significant paper by Himmelweit & Turner (1982) reports that certain social and psychological antecedent conditions in adolescence (13–14 years) predict depression in a nonclinic sample of men aged 24–25 years. Predictive antecedents include poor family relations in childhood, introversion, and high educational and occupational achievement. Himmelweit concludes that depression is most likely to occur in men who have achieved their aspirations early in life.

Their goals reached, they have no need to strive. Macfarlane (1963) reports a somewhat similar finding in the Berkeley Guidance Study. Some of the young people who were early achievers, highly successful socially, or in athletics appeared less satisfied with their lives as adults than did individuals who encountered some problems as children and who were slower in achieving success.

Texts and handbooks with a life-span approach are appearing with increasing frequency (e.g. Ambron 1982, Rogers 1982). Among the most recent is a sizeable text by Lerner & Hultsch (1983) entitled *Human Development: A Life Span Perspective*. All texts and overviews of life-span development report empirical findings by age periods. Wolman's (1982) handbook by 75 authors describes human development from infancy to old age. The first section of this book is devoted to a discussion of research methods and theories. Succeeding sections cover research on infancy (eight chapters), childhood (seven chapters), adolescence (nine chapters), adulthood (ten chapters), and aging (seven chapters). This book gives a reasonably substantive overview of the current state of the field. Field et al (1982) edited a review of human development research with a large proportion of the chapters written by those actively engaged in research at the age period covered (e.g. the infancy chapters are by Fagan 1982, Lewis, 1982, Lipsitt 1982b, Papousek & Papousek 1982). Field's purpose in compiling this volume is to provide the researcher, teacher, and student with a current view of "the state of the art." Field writes in summary that "throughout each stage reviewed, [we are impressed] with the description of an increasingly sophisticated human being whether infant or aged." She concludes with the comment that "almost every contribution spoke of the importance of studying individuals and their differences across time for further enlightenment of the developmental process." In addition to the handbooks and overviews, a number of books covering specific age periods have appeared: *Handbook of Infant Development* (Osofsky 1979), *Handbook of Child Psychology* (Mussen 1983), *Handbook of Adolescent Psychology* (Adelson 1980), *Aging Research in the 1980s* (Poon 1980).

EMPIRICAL RESEARCH

The major questions asked in a life-span approach are the nature of the changes that take place during development and what determines these changes. The simplest method of studying change is a comparison of developmental status, or behaviors of groups of individuals, at successive ages. This method gives a rough approximation of change but may yield erroneous results because of either basic or experiential differences in the cohorts studied at the ages compared (Elder 1981). The classic series of investigations showing this phenomenon most clearly were the studies of the decline of intelligence in the later adult years by H. E. Jones & Conrad (1933). Eichorn et al (1981) and Schaie (1982a) discuss the differences in results obtained in studies of age changes in different cohorts versus repeated assessment of the same individuals.

Age Differences

No studies at the present time cover the entire life span, but there are many investigations of age differences for various behavioral domains and developmental periods. These will be covered by topic.

REACTION TIME AND MEMORY   Gottsdanker (1982) finds a reliable but slight increase in reaction time to a tone with age (18 to 93 years), indicating no deterioration of underlying neural mechanisms. Greater differences were found favoring the young when certain procedural changes were introduced. Faulty control processes rather than structural impairment in the elderly may be the basis for widespread behavioral slowing with age.

Immediate recall   In a free recall task of digits and word span, Parkinson et al (1982) note that 20-year-olds did significantly better than 71-year-olds. However, the older participants scored significantly higher on vocabulary and scored higher on the information test but not significantly so.

Acoustic and semantic recognition memory   Coyne and associates (1980) found that for subjects ranging in age from 8 to 75 years, there were no age differences in acoustic and semantic recognition memory. Neither errors nor latencies indicated any age differences in encoding patterns.

In a later study of the effect of aging on recognition memory, Bowles & Poon (1982) agree with Coyne et al in finding no significant age differences in accuracy on a recognition memory test. In this later study a young adult group (average age 22 years) was compared with an older group (average age of 74 years). Bowles et al note that although there was not a significant difference, the distribution of recognition scores was bimodal in the older group with an upper mode that did not differ from the younger group and a lower mode representing a decrement. In the older adults, recognition performance was related to verbal ability (WAIS vocabulary).

Metamemory   Bruce and associates (1982) compared the metamemory of three groups in their 20s, 60s, and 70s. The groups were similar in their ability to predict the number of words they could recall but differed in the number they actually did recall. Increased age was associated with overestimation.

Lachman et al (1979) also assessed the accuracy and efficiency of metamemory in three groups with average ages of 20, 50 and 69 years. All age groups showed comparable ability to achieve answers from memory. These authors suggested "caution among the elderly in suppressing available but low confidence answers."

Wechsler memory scores   In the Duke longitudinal study, Wechsler memory scores of the participants aged 60 to 94 years were significantly correlated with education. Correlations with age were not statistically significant. Nonverbal test scores decreased more with age than verbal test scores (McCarty et al 1982). In a second study of this population (Siegler et al 1982), significant declines with age in scores were found only for visual reproduction but not for logical memory or paired associate learning. A significant relationship was found between visual reproduction and distance from death.

Choice reaction time task   Salthouse & Somberg (1982) compared the relationship between time and accuracy in young (18 to 21 years) and old (60 to 84 years) adults on a choice reaction time task. Both groups showed equivalent rates of increasing accuracy, but members of the older group were slower in information integration but not in actual rate of information extraction.

Picture superiority: effect on recall   Winograd et al (1982) compared verbal and visual encoding using the picture superiority effect (the finding that pictures are remembered better than words). In the first experiment, younger subjects recalled more pictures than words while older subjects did not. In further experiments, the picture superiority effect was found in both groups. Denney & List (1979) report that older individuals, in the age range 30 to 80 years, had longer response latencies in a matching familiar figures test and made more errors than younger individuals.

The above-cited studies of age differences in reaction time and memory are all recent journal publications, many of which are mentioned in Salthouse's recent book (1982) on "Adult Cognition." This volume is well-organized and written with remarkable clarity. It is encouraging that such a lucid and comprehensive account could be written about this somewhat fragmented but significant area of adult development and aging. This book also discusses some of the important studies of the 1930s and 40s by Harold E. Jones (ten references) and Walter and Catherine Miles (four references). Unfortunately, the book does not include studies of infants and young children. Watson (1983) describes three basic types of infant memory: reactive, regenerative, and associative. He writes that there is much to be learned about the workings of memory in infancy and concludes that the empirical base of the present state of knowledge is precariously thin in contrast to that of the state of knowledge about adult memory.

In summary, within the age ranges investigated, studies of age changes in reaction time and memory do not give clear-cut answers to questions about the relationship of aging and memory. The problems are even more complex when the infant studies of memory are taken into consideration. It would appear that the time has come for much more intensive, qualitative studies of the memory of older persons. First, the subjects should be screened with extreme care for incipient health problems that would affect memory. It would also be desirable to interview each subject to determine his/her evaluation of his/her memory and experiences in remembering different materials. To what extent does the individual use his mental abilities? A longitudinal study would be desirable. And finally, the measurable effects of stimulation on the brains of older rats (Diamond & Connor 1981) should be kept in mind.

Spatial Representation and Behavior across the Life Span is the title of an important book by Liben et al (1981). All age periods are discussed as well as the physical, cognitive, and socioemotional differences that occur over the life span in an individual's reaction to and representation of spatial characteristics of his environment. Another consideration discussed is the individual's perceived control of his environment, which is especially salient at both ends of the life span.

One of the few reports of age changes during childhood published during the past several years is that of Achenbach & Edelbrock (1981), who compare the prevalence of behavior problems in large groups of normal and disturbed children aged 4 through 16 years. The problem incidence was remarkably higher in the sample of disturbed children. A tendency was noted for a decline in incidence with age and for parents of lower SES children to report more problems.

McCrae (1982) attempted to assess the influence of age on the use of coping mechanisms in a group aged 24 to 91 years. Findings are that older persons coped in much the same way as the younger persons but middle-aged and older individuals were consistently less inclined than younger ones to rely on hostile reactions and escapist fantasy regardless of the type of stress.

In a very different type of study of age differences, Reedy et al (1981) compared certain characteristics of happily married young (28 years), middle-aged (45 years), and older (65 years) couples and found that the older couples had high ratings for emotional security and loyalty but lower ratings of sexual intimacy than the younger couples. Men were found to have higher ratings for loyalty and women for emotional security.

Birren (1980) discusses progress in research on aging in the behavioral and social sciences and concludes that "the elite aged" appear to have some inner structure that enables them to be strong yet flexible, feeling yet controlled, living in the present yet planning for tomorrow, feeling less need to justify their past views and behavior, which brings them into the present with pride and strength.

Longitudinal Research

It is only when individuals are studied longitudinally that rank order stability or sameness (no change in what is being measured) can be assessed. Studies of age changes provide a rough measure of change with age, but it is not possible to evaluate factors related to these changes unless the *same* individuals are evaluated at successive ages. Longitudinal studies are demanding of both the persons studied and the investigators, but the yield in understanding developmental processes is great. A sizeable number of such studies that have been in progress for many years are increasingly yielding their findings for extended periods of the life span.

Three significant books appearing in the 1980s chart the course of development of groups of individuals studied longitudinally in different parts of the world. Werner & Smith (1982) describe the growth and development of children born on the island of Kauai from the time of conception to early adulthood. Eichorn and associates (1981) edited a volume entitled *Present and Past in Middle Life.* This book describes the participants of the Berkeley longitudinal samples at middle age. Precursors in adolescence are related to adult status. Young & Ferguson (1981) followed the growth of three groups of boys of Italian parentage growing up in Palermo, Rome, and Boston.

As though to herald the appearance of findings from these three long-term studies, Brim & Kagan (1980) compiled a comprehensive volume entitled *Constancy and Change in Human Development.* These authors state that the view emerging from this work is that humans have a capacity for change across the entire life span. Substantive chapters are included on maturational timing, the endocrine and central nervous systems, as well as physical health, cognitive development in childhood and adulthood, and personality.

The purpose of the Kauai Pregnancy Study was to determine the sources of strength and resiliency in a multiracial group of 690 children who grew up in poverty and were exposed to a series of stressful life events (Werner & Smith 1982). These children were followed from early in the pregnancy to age 20 years. Development from the prenatal period to age 10 years is described in *The Children of Kauai* (Werner et al 1971). Approximately 90% of these children were included in a follow-up at age 18 years (Werner & Smith 1977). The most recent book, *Vulnerable but Invincible* (Werner & Smith 1982), evaluates the significant discriminators between resilient children or youth and their peers with coping problems. In this cohort one of every five children developed serious behavior problems at some time during the first two decades. Werner and Smith found in the first decade of life that more boys than girls experienced serious defects or illness requiring medical care and more of the boys had learning problems. Trends were reversed in the second decade when the number of boys with serious learning problems dropped while the number of girls with serious problems increased. Control of aggression appeared a major problem for the boys and dependency for the girls. More of the high-risk girls than boys grew into resilient young adults. Werner et al list the key factors in the environment that appeared to contribute to resilience. Nearly all these factors relate to the caretaking of the infant and young child: cohesiveness of the family, the presence of a multigenerational network of kin and friends in addition to having four or fewer children in the family, alternate caretakers, workload of the mother, and attention given to the child. These families were poor by material standards, but a strong bond was forged between the infant and the primary caretaker. The *resilient* child was physically robust, had a high activity level, was socially responsive, and there had been little prolonged separation from the family. The authors conclude that the central component of effective coping with the multiplicity of inevitable life stresses appears to be a sense of coherence and a feeling of confidence.

Young & Ferguson's book (1981) describes a study of the development of 300 boys of similar Italian ancestry from puberty to manhood (in their 20s). These boys had in common four grandparents born in Palermo, but one-third of the group grew up in Rome, one-third in Boston, and one-third in Palermo. Thus the boys had roughly a similar genetic background but were reared in different cultural settings. The authors conclude that the phenomenon of human physical growth and mental growth showed only limited plasticity to environmental change of the kind provided by the "natural experiment" of migration from Southern Italy. There were similarities in the three groups in customs, traditional ways of rearing children, and patterns of family life. However, there were differences. The boys in Boston were heavier. More elevated blood pressure was found in the Rome sample. A child rearing difference was noted. The Italian parents were more indulgent with their sons in early childhood and exerted more control of them in adolescence. In contrast, the Italian-American families in Boston made earlier demands for self-help and control but in early adulthood encouraged the boys to make their own decisions.

What were the effects of the different environments? The young men in Rome had the highest scores on the Raven Progressive Matrices. They scored higher on measures of creative thinking and had more sophisticated aesthetic and social attitudes. The authors attribute part of this superiority to selective migration. The families in Rome had typically migrated because many of the fathers were minor civil servants. The Boston families had emigrated as impoverished peasants, but they had absorbed more democratic orientations to child rearing. The adolescent boys in Boston reflected these differences in their higher achievement motivation, and their vocational aspirations were more realistic. They were more open and self-confident and seemed to have a greater sense of mastery over their own destinies as compared with their peers in Italy. In contrast, the young men in Palermo manifested a sense of being locked in to their family's place in society.

Another major multidisciplinary study describes stability and change from adolescence to middle age in the three Berkeley longitudinal studies (Eichorn et al 1981). This book is based on the second adult follow-up of the subjects studied from birth to age 42 years (Berkeley Growth and Guidance studies) and from 10–11 years to 50 years (Oakland Growth Study). Age trends in health, IQ, and personality are described as are evidences of stability and change. One of the most important contributions of this book are the interrelationships between aspects of development. Personality is described by a 100-item Q set and six factor scores that take the four time periods into account (early and late adolescence and early and middle adulthood). Haan (1981) reports that the study participants showed marked gains in the factor "cognitively invested" between the ages of 14 and 47 years. There were also marked gains in self-confidence, and the women in the studies became markedly more nurturant in their adult years. The pervasive influence of personality is shown in its significant association with physical health, IQ, and occupational attainment. Self-control in early adolescence is related to both health status in the 1940s (Bayer et al 1980, 1981) and moderate consumption of alcohol (M. C. Jones 1981). Other chapters in this book discuss the historical period in which the study participants lived while growing up (Elder 1981), prediction of "psychological health" at age 40 from adolescent personality (Livson & Peskin 1981), social maturity in middle age and its developmental antecedents (Brooks 1981), longitudinal perspectives on marriage (Skolnick 1981), men's occupations (Clausen 1981), and women's careers (Stroud 1981). Skolnick concudes in her chapter on marriage that "marriages do change over time, more in a positive than a negative directon; and external life circumstances seemed to be an important influence on the observed changes in marital satisfaction."

Mussen et al (1980) report on the consistency of 21 ratings of cognitive and personality characteristics over four decades. The mothers of the members of the Berkeley longitudinal studies were rated at age 30 years on 21 cognitive and personality characteristics and again by different raters at age 70 years. All 5 of the cognitive variables and 10 of the 16 personality variables proved relatively stable over the 40-year period. The most stable personality variable was *talkativeness*. Others were *self-esteem, cheerfulness, excitability*, and *energy output*. Replication of these findings was obtained for a second group of mothers of the Control Group for the cognitive variables and for *talkativeness, cheerfulness*, and *excitability*. The Control Group was matched with the Guidance Group on socioeconomic variables at the time of the birth of the study members. It is our hypothesis that these phenotypic personality variables may have in part a genotypic basis. The reason for this hypothesis is not only the stability of these personality characteristics over a 40-year period in the mothers' sample but also the stability of the same characteristics from adolescence to middle age in their children, the study members (Block 1971, Haan &

Day 1976). These findings of stability of certain personality traits are relevant to the discussion of temperament in a later section of this review.

Precursors of Later Development

Skill in caring for infants in the perinatal period has led to the survival of many babies who are at risk. Prospective studies of the progress of these infants have been reported by a number of investigators in this country (Broman 1981b, Hunt 1981, 1983, Kopp & McCall 1982, Kopp 1983).

Mednick & Baert (1981) edited a large volume on *Prospective Longitudinal Research: An Empirical Basis for the Primary Prevention of Psychosocial Disorders*. Mednick and Baert first discuss the methods of prospective longitudinal research and describe a statistical model for the analysis of longitudinal data. A description of 63 longitudinal studies being carried on in Europe follows. Ten of these investigations are based on prospective birth cohorts; ten more began with school-age cohorts; there are studies of adult or community cohorts and of nonrepresentative populations such as twins, adopted children, or first cousins. There are 26 studies of infants with possible neonatal damage and epidemiological studies of deviant groups. These studies were undertaken in 16 different countries with 27 of the 63 taking place in Great Britain and Switzerland. Czechoslovakia is the only communist country listed where longitudinal studies of children at risk are being followed. Each of the 63 studies is described in some detail including methods used and findings. This volume is a gold mine of information and also suggests the possibility of continued study of the cohorts leading to life-span coverage.

In this country, Falkner (1978) describes the development of a pair of identical twins. The placental blood supply to twin *one* was good but twin *two's* supply was severely impaired. At birth twin *one* was normal in size and well nourished. Twin *two* was very small and emaciated. There was a marked catch-up in size and weight by twin *two* until age 13 years when growth slowed down and twin *two* was definitely shorter than his brother and had a smaller head circumference. This study points up both the resilience of human beings to marked deprivation and the fact that even with the same genetic background complete compensation for deprivation may not occur.

THE FAMILY   Werner & Smith (1982) emphasized the importance of the family support system in the resilience of the children in the Kauai longitudinal study. Confirmatory evidence of the long-range effects of the family is to be found in a number of investigations.

Broman (1981a), using data from the Collaborative Perinatal Project, describes the long-term development of children born to teenagers. She found that biological deficits were not associated with early childbearing but that environmental deficits were—even for those mothers who received at least some prenatal care. Another study by Broman (1981b) considered risk factors in relation to cognitive development at age 7 years. She concludes that although low achievers at age 7 years differed in several developmental areas from their academically successful controls, the largest and most consistent differences of etiological significance were in aspects of the family environment that were closely associated with opportunities for verbal-conceptual stimulation.

Broman has written an as yet unpublished overview of the Collaborative Perinatal Project which will appear in S. S. Mednick and M. Harway's "Longitudinal Research in the United States." This volume will complement the earlier one edited by Mednick & Baert (1981) based on the European studies of individuals at risk for psychosocial disorders.

Matějček et al (1980) followed a group of 220 children born in Prague of mothers who had repeatedly sought interruption of the pregnancy. This group was matched with a second group of children of accepted pregnancies. There were no differences between these groups at birth in weight or length or in their WISC scores at age 9 years, but performance in school was somewhat poorer among the unwanted children. Both the mothers and teachers rated the unwanted children as being more nervous, irritable, and explosive. The boys born of unwanted pregnancies were more endangered in the development of their personalities than the girls. The children were eveluted again at ages 14 to 16 years, at which time the unwanted children were doing significantly less well in school and were under-represented in the above average categories. The difference continued to be greater for the boys.

de Chateau (1980) describes a group of newborn infants in Sweden given extra contact with their mothers immediately after birth. These mothers had significantly more contact with their infants at ages three months and one year, and the babies smiled more and cried less than was true for the control group. The babies with extra contact also did better than the control group on the Gesell Test, but by three years no differences were found on the Denver Developmental Screening Test.

Grigoroiu-Serbanescu (1981) followed a group of 317 prematures and 78 full-term infants from birth to age 5 years. Emotional and intellectual deficits were found in premature boys born at a gestational age of 29 weeks. Up until age 3 years, the recovery period depended on the degree of prematurity. After 3 years no manifest effect of prematurity on development could be seen.

In a 4-year longitudinal study of 193 normal, healthy, primiparous children, Bee et al (1982) found that perinatal variables were weak predictors of 4-year IQ or language, but mother-infant interaction and general environmental quality were among the best predictors of IQ and language at ages 2, 3, and 4 years.

Roe et al (1982) report that 12 three-month-old first-born male infants who were differentially responsive to an interactive mother as opposed to an interactive stranger obtained higher verbal subscale scores at 12 years on the WISC-R and higher scores on the Peabody Picture Vocabulary Test. The rank order correlation of vocal interaction with the WISC-R performance scale was not significant.

In summary, the relevance of the family environment to an infant's psychosocial development is clear in the studies cited above. The interaction is usually with the mother, but other members of the family may be equally or more important as the child grows older. Kivnick (1982) has investigated the roles of grandparents in a child's life. Lamb & Sutton-Smith (1982) have edited a book on *Sibling Relationships: Their Nature and Significance Across the Lifespan*. Cicirelli's (1982) chapter on "Sibling Influence through the Life Span" presents a thoughtful overview of sibling interactions. He concludes that the evidence presently available indicates that topics such as sibling attachment and sibling influence in adulthood would be worthy of further study. Rosenberg's (1982) chapter on "Life Span Stability in Sibling Status" is based on data at four age periods (early and late adolescence, early and middle adulthood) from the Berkeley longitudinal samples. He concludes that boys have more impact on their sisters than the reverse; firstborns have more impact on secondborns than the reverse; boys with sisters are more verbally fluent, value intellectual matters more, and are less masculine than boys with brothers.

Biographical Studies and Life Satisfaction in Later Life

Howe (1982) writes persuasively that biographical sources of information should be drawn on to provide accounts of long-term progress of development in individual people. He adds that biographical information can demonstrate the effects of timing and sequencing of events in a person's life. He believes that there are two additional sources that might provide insights. The first concerns the sheer individuality of human development. Greater success might be achieved if greater emphasis was placed on the individual person as the unit of study. The second concern is the dimension of time—*what* events are experienced *when*. Himmelweit & Turner's (1982) study of depressed men who achieved great success at a very early age is relevant here. Howe quotes Freud's statement: "If a man has been his mother's undisputed darling, he retains throughout life the triumphant feeling, the confidence in success which not seldom brings actual success along with it" (Clark 1980). This statement can be contrasted with Dylan Thomas's remark: "There's only one thing that's worse than having an unhappy childhood and that's having a too-happy childhood" (Ferris 1977).

Sears (1977) reports that the high IQ men in Terman's group achieved high average success in their occupations but at age 60 placed greater importance on achieving satisfaction in their family life than in their work—and they believed they had found it.

Mussen et al (1982) find for the mothers of the participants in the Berkeley Guidance Study that ratings of life satisfaction at age 70 years are significantly predicted by two characteristics assessed at age 30 years: marital compatibility and satisfaction with husband's job. In contrast, characteristics of the fathers at age 30 which significantly predicted life satisfaction at 70 are his health, stamina, and energy level; an emotionally stable wife; job satisfaction; and marital compatibility.

Runyan (1982), in his book *Life Histories and Psychobiography*, analyzed some of the basic conceptual issues in the study of individual life histories. He illustrates his points with descriptions of episodes in the life course of a number of famous individuals (e.g. Freud, Lincoln, Van Gogh, and others). Runyan concludes that progress in the social sciences should be measured not only by elaborate experimental and statistical approaches, but also by more rigorous and insightful case studies.

Significant Developmental Areas

HEALTH   For most inhabitants of the United States at the present time, health hazards are few during childhood, adolescence, and early adulthood, but infants born at risk and aging adults may be beset by serious health problems. Hunt (1983) has summarized the environmental risks in fetal and neonatal life that may lead to neurological impairment which may in turn become biological determinants of later intelligence.

Factors leading to ill health in the elderly are many, including the sheer probability that something is likely to happen to one or another of the organ systems as the person grows older. Bayer et al (1980, 1981) described the health status of the study members in the three Berkeley longitudinal studies at ages 42 to 50 years. Two of the cohorts were followed from birth and the third from early adolescence. In the 40-year interview, more than 80% of the study members considered themselves to be in good health. In spite of these generally favorable assessments of their health, the 395 medical protocols record many and increasing numbers of complaints and illnesses. The most consistent source of malaise in women throughout the middle years is the reproductive system. In men, it is the digestive system. In both sexes, acute complaints diminish while chronic complaints increase. Women report more physical malfunctions but men evidence more degenerative disease. The females seem both more aware of debility and more resilient. A provocative finding in this study is that a calm, self-controlled, and responsible personality manifest as early as 11–13 years is related to adult health. The correlations are statistically significant for both males and females but are higher for the males.

Barrett et al (1982) report on the social and emotional development of Guatamalan children who were chronically malnourished. High levels of caloric supplementation from birth to 2 years predicted high levels of social involvement, with both happy and angry affect, and moderate activity level at school age. Low supplementation was associated with passivity, dependency, and anxious behavior.

In a study of rats fed 60% of the usual intake, the mean length of life was extended. Two-thirds of the rationed rats lived longer than the longest lived rat on full rations (Yu et al 1982). The authors did not report on the behaviors of the rats on reduced rations. It would be of interest to know if there is any resemblance in the behavior patterns of malnourished children and rats on reduced rations.

TEMPERAMENT   Thomas & Chess (1981) define temperament as the behavioral style of the individual. Although they believe the environment to be important, they are impressed by the individuality of the newborn infant with his unique behavioral repertoire that actively shapes his reaction to the environment. They also note that the parent-child relationship is not unidirectional but a mutually interactive process. Data from the NYLS (New York Longitudinal Study) yielded nine categories of temperament: activity level, rhythmicity (regularity), approach or withdrawal, adaptability, threshold of resonsiveness, intensity of reaction, quality of mood, distractibility, attention span. These authors write that their data suggest an appreciable but not exclusive genetic role, and they conclude that temperamental characteristics are an important, active factor for individuals in the production of their development. They add that data for this generalization are most abundant and detailed for the infancy and childhood periods.

Several other investigators have described major dimensions of temperament in their studies: (a) Lipsitt (1982a) considers two characteristics of the newborn, "perturbability" and "hedonic responsivity," as critical early life attributes. (b) Lerner et al (1982) have identified and developed a measure of the dimensions of temperament which are continuous in the behavioral repertoire from childhood to young adulthood. A factor analysis of data using this scale revealed a 5-factor model: activity level, attention span, adaptability, rhythmicity, and reactivity. (c) Wilson & Mathany (1983) have also constructed a laboratory assessment of temperament for their study of twins. The principal dimensions of their factor analysis were: positive emotional tone, sustained attention and receptiveness. They found significant continuity in the expression of temperament according to the parents and research staff. (d) Olweus (1980) studied familial and temperamental determinants of aggressive behavior in adolescent boys in Sweden. Four factors contributed in an additive way to the development of an aggressive reaction pattern. These were mother's negativism, mother's permissiveness for aggression, mother's and father's use of power assertion methods, and the boy's temperament. The first two factors had the greatest causal impact. (e) Personality characteristics mentioned above of the mothers of study members that were found to be highly consistent over a 40-year period in the Berkeley longitudinal studies probably have a temperamental basis (Mussen et al 1980). These include talkativeness, cheerfulness, excitability, and self-esteem. These same characteristics also proved to be highly stable in the study members from adolescence to middle age (Block in collaboration with Haan 1971, Haan & Day 1976).

The characteristics mentioned by the different investigators as dimensions of temperament vary markedly and yet there is overlap. Studies of parent-child resemblance in these behaviors may begin to clarify the extent to which they have a genetic or environmental basis.

INTELLIGENCE   Psychometric intelligence is one characteristic that has been systematically studied across the life span. Bayley's (1949) findings that infant test scores are not predictive of later IQ have been replicated using five different infant tests in longitudinal studies in London, Stockholm, and Brussels, as well as in the United States (Honzik 1983).

Recently a number of psychologists have reported alternate cognitive measures to be relatively more predictive of childhood IQ. Fagan & McGrath (1981) find that tests of visual recognition memory based on differential fixation observed at 4 to 7 months are predictive of vocabulary test scores at ages 4 to 7 years. Lewis & Brooks-Gunn (1981) noted that measures of visual attention at 3 months predicted later intellectual functioning at 2 years better than the 3-month mental test score. Lewis suggests that changes in cognitive functioning may be viewed as a transformation of skills from one age to another rather than as a continuum of the same skills. Sternberg (1981) states that novelty-seeking and novelty-finding, as well as the ability to learn and reason with novel kinds of concepts, are critical aspects of intelligence at all ages from infancy onward. He adds that "by necessity these skills must be measured in different ways at different times of life."

A finding from the Berkeley longitudinal studies that is of special interest is the fact of an IQ gain between 17–18 years and 36–48 years occurring in all three studies and for both men and women. In the two samples given a Wechsler at both age periods, the men showed greater gains in Performance than in Verbal IQs while the women's IQ gains were greater in Verbal IQ. Combining all three samples, the correlations between 17–18 years and 36–48 years was .83 for the men and .77 for the women. Correlational analyses of IQ change with possible determinants yielded very low relationships. However, when the characteristics of individuals showing the greatest gains and losses (top and bottom 11%) were compared, marked differences between the increasers and decreasers were found. Extreme decreasers had a disproportionate incidence of heavy alcohol consumption and of debilitative illness. In contrast, none of the increasers were heavy drinkers. Many of the increasers had traveled outside the United States, and they were more likely to be married to a spouse whose adult IQ was at least ten points higher than that of the study member at adolescence. In summary, the study members who showed the largest increases had had stimulating intellectual experiences during early adulthood. Seventy-five percent of the decreasers had had drinking problems; others were depressed and case history evidence suggested very little mental stimulation.

Baltes & Willis (1982) are investigating the plasticity of intellectual functioning in old age. The subjects of this study range in age from approximately 60 to 80 years with an average of 70. Practice is given the subjects on tests measuring both crystallized and fluid intelligence. Preliminary findings suggest "considerable plasticity in fluid intellectual performance in old age."

Schaie (1982b) reports on his 21-year exploration of psychometric intelligence in adulthood. He concludes that reliable age changes in psychometric abilities are not demonstrated before age 60 years but that a reliable decrement can be shown for all abilities by age 74 years. He stresses that there are vast individual differences in intellectual change across adulthood, leading to early decrement for some and maintenance of function into very advanced age for others. What accounts for intra-individual changes in intelligence test scores with age? Schaie states that a favorable environment and varied opportunities for environmental stimulation are important as is the maintenance of a flexible life-style.

SELF-CONCEPT, SELF-UNDERSTANDING, SELF-ESTEEM, SELF-CONTROL, AND ALTRUISM   Lewis (1979) conceptualizes the development of the self as having two major features. First, the infant has to differentiate itself from others. The second feature of self-development is the acquisition of categories of self.

Dusek & Flaherty (1982) undertook a 3-year longitudinal study of the self-concept during the adolescent years. The adolescents rated "my characteristic self" each year. Longitudinal analyses indicated that the self-concept developed in a continuous and stable way. The authors conclude that the self-concept does not evidence dramatic change, and they find no evidence to support the "storm and stress" view of adolescence. Similar results were obtained for the boys and girls in the study.

Damon & Hart (1982) trace the development of self-understanding from infancy through adolescence. These authors believe that William James contributed one of the most insightful and influential theoretical analyses of the self to be found in the psychological literature. James's discussion of self-understanding serves as a framework for the organization of the research in this review. For James, the self was divided into two main components, the "Me" and the "I." The "Me" is the sum total of all the person can call his, while the "I" is the self as "knower." Damon and Hart discuss relevant empirical research on self-understanding according to the two "selves," and they present a comprehensive model covering four developmental levels: infancy and childhood, late childhood, early and late adolescence.

McCarthy & Hoge (1982) analyzed the effects in longitudinal studies of adolescent self-esteem and found systematic increases in self-esteem in three different cohorts. The authors were able to rule out the possibility that subject attrition, effects of testing, or carelessness of the subjects had contributed to these results.

Peterson (1982) discusses altruism and the development of internal control. Peterson believes that in addition to control exerted by emotions and external contingencies, much of altruistic responding is determined by internalized rules. A model suggesting an individualized rule of altruism is proposed. This model provides an integration of many fragmented approaches to understanding prosocial behavior.

Carver & Scheier (1982) consider control theory a general approach to the understanding of self-regulating systems. This theory provides a model of self-regulation that they believe is useful in the analysis of human behavior.

THEORETICAL ORIENTATIONS

In a symposium chaired by Hoyer (1980) on conceptions of learning and the study of life-span development, Baltes & Lerner (1980) describe the "Roles of the operant model and its methods in the life-span approach to human development." Reese (1980) provides "A learning theory critique of the operant approach to life-span development." The thesis of Fitzgerald's (1980) paper is that "learning is a functionally invariant process, a process which is vital to the survival and development of the organism and the species." He believes that learning and development have a mutual basis in a dialectical perspective. Dusek & Meyer (1980) present a dialectic analysis of learning theory's contributions to understanding human development. They conceptualize development as more than a simple change in behavior; it reflects a structural change in the organism. This structural change, often indexed by qualitative stages, is development.

Hoyer (1980) writes that implicit in the operant model is the assumption that the causes of behavior lie not within the organism but are to be found external to the organism. In contrast with this stance, Gollin (1981) argues that the relationship between organisms and environments are not interactionist, as interaction implies that the organism and environment are separate entities that come together at an interface. Gollin believes that organism and environment constitute a single life process. Thus, according to this theory the ambient world is uniquely defined by each living creature . . . and living systems are organized systems with internal coherence and what we typically designate as environment is unique to each individual. This theory resembles Scarr & McCartney's (1983) theory of development in which experience is directed by genotypes. According to Scarr and McCartney, both genes and environments are constituents in the developmental system, but they have different roles. Genes determine much of human experience, but experiential opportunities are necessary for development to occur. Individual differences can arise from restrictions in environmental opportunities to experience what the genotype would find compatible.

Lerner & Busch-Rossnagel (1981) edited a book with the provocative title, *Individuals as Producers of their Development: A Life Span Perspective*. The concept that organisms act to create their environment has many ramifications that will be of interest to explore in the coming years.

Belsky & Tolan (1981) write that students of infancy have long recognized the active role the child plays in contributing to its own development.

SUMMARY

The great increase in interest in life-span development that began in the 1970s continues unabated in the 1980s. Most impressive is the large number of excellent, thought-provoking books appearing since the last review 3 years ago. In addition to earlier publications concerned with theory, methodology, and specific aspects of development, we now have books and papers describing multidisciplinary, empirical studies covering fairly long age spans: infancy to the early adult years, early adolescence to the 20s and to middle age, middle to old age. These long-term investigations are pioneering ventures that need replication and cross-validation but they do provide exciting hypotheses to be tested in future research.

This review has emphasized empirical findings. The studies of age changes in reaction time and aspects of memory are difficult to evaluate because so many factors have to be controlled. In-depth, longitudinal studies of healthy, older individuals over certain age periods might yield greater insights into the memory problems of the aged.

A number of important concepts have surfaced in recent investigations. The significance of *self-control* in adolescence was noted in both the Finnish and California long-term studies as predictive of health and drinking patterns in adulthood. The *resilience* of many children in coping with physical problems, poverty, and learning problems is reported. Resilience appears to result from a robust personality and supportive home environment. *Plasticity* in the early adult years is suggested by an increasing IQ that is related to stimulating environmental experiences.

A multidisciplinary approach to studies of life-span development would appear to be an imperative leading to more comprehensive investigations of development over the life span.

Literature Cited

Achenbach, T. M., Edelbrock, C. S. 1981. Behavioral problems and competencies reported by parents of normal and disturbed children aged four through sixteen. *Monogr. Soc. Res. Child Dev.* 46:Ser. 188. 82 pp.

Adelson, J., ed. 1980. *Handbook of Adolescent Psychology.* New York: Wiley

Ambron, S. R. 1982. *Life Span Development.* New York: Holt, Rinehart & Winston. 2nd ed.

Baltes, M. M., Lerner, R. M. 1980. Roles of the operant model and its methods in the life span approach to human development. *Hum. Dev.* 23:362–67

Baltes, P. B., ed. 1978. *Life-Span Development and Behavior,* Vol. 1. New York: Academic

Baltes, P. B., Brim, O. G. Jr., eds. 1979. *Life-Span Development and Behavior,* Vol. 2. New York: Academic

Baltes, P. B., Brim, O. G. Jr., eds. 1980. *Life-Span Development and Behavior,* Vol. 3. New York: Academic

Baltes, P. B., Brim, O. G. Jr., eds. 1982. *Life-Span Development and Behavior,* Vol. 4. New York: Academic

Baltes, P. B., Reese, H. W., Lipsitt, L. P. 1980. Life-span developmental psychology. *Ann. Rev. Psychol.* 31:65–110

Baltes, P. B., Schaie, K. W., eds. 1973. *Life-Span Developmental Psychology: Personality and Socialization.* New York: Academic

Baltes, P. B., Willis, S. L. 1982. Plasticity and enhancement of intellectual functioning in old age: Penn State's adult development and enrichment. In *Aging and Cognitive Processes,* ed. F. I. M. Craik, S. E. Trehub. In press

Barrett, D. E., Radke-Yarrow, M., Klein, R. E. 1982. Chronic malnutrition and child behavior: Effects of early caloric supplementation on social and emotional functioning at school age. *Dev. Psychol.* 18:541–56

Bayer, L. M., Whissell-Buechy, D., Honzik, M. P. 1980. Adolescent health and personality: Significance for adult health. *J. Adolesc. Health Care* 1:101–7

Bayer, L. M., Whissell-Buechy, D., Honzik, M. P. 1981. Health in the middle years. See Eichorn et al 1981, pp. 55–88

Bayley, N. 1949. Consistency and variability in the growth of intelligence from birth to eighteen years. *J. Genet. Psychol.* 75:165–69

Bee, H. L., Barnard, K. E., Eyres, S. J., Gray, C. A., Hammond, M. A., et al. 1982. Prediction of IQ and language skill from perinatal status, child performance, family characteristics, and mother-infant interaction. *Child Dev.* 53:1134–56

Belsky, J., Tolan, W. J. 1981. Infants as producers of their own development: An ecological analysis. See Lerner & Busch-Rossnagel 1981, pp. 87–116

Birren, J. E. 1980. Progress in research on aging in the behavioral and social sciences. *Hum. Dev.* 23:33–45

Block, J. in collaboration with Haan, N. 1971. *Lives Through Time.* Berkeley: Bancroft

Bowles, N. L., Poon, L. W. 1982. An analysis of the effect of aging on recognition memory. *J. Gerontol.* 37:212–19

Brim, O. G., Kagan, J., eds. 1980. *Constancy and Change in Human Development.* Cambridge: Harvard Univ. Press

Broman, S. H., 1981a. Longterm development of children born to teenagers. In *Teenage Parents and their Offspring,* ed. K. G. Scott, T. Field, E. Robertson. New York: Grune & Stratton

Broman, S. H. 1981b. Risk factors for deficits in early cognitive development. In *Measurement of Risks,* ed. G. G. Berg, H. D. Maille, pp. 131–38. New York: Plenum

Brooks, J. B. 1981. Social maturity in middle age and its developmental antecedents. See Eichorn et al 1981, pp. 243–65

Bruce, P. R., Coyne, A. C., Botwinick, J. 1982. Adult age differences in metamemory. *J. Gerontol.* 37:354–57

Buhler, A. 1933. *Der menschliche Lebenslauf als psychologisches Problem.* Leipzig: Hirzel

Carver, C. S., Scheier, M. F. 1982. A useful conceptual framework for personality-social, clinical, and health psychology. *Psychol. Bull.* 92:111–35

Cicirelli, V. G. 1982. Sibling influence throughout the lifespan. See Lamb & Sutton-Smith 1982, pp. 267–84

Clark, R. W. 1980. *Freud: The Man and the Cause.* London: Cape/Weidenfeld

Clausen, J. A. 1981. Men's occupational careers in the middle years. In Eichorn et al 1981, pp. 321–51

Coyne, A. C., Herman, J. F., Botwinick, J. 1980. Age differences in acoustic and semantic recognition memory. *Percept. Mot. Skills* 51:439–45

Damon, W., Hart, D. 1982. The development of self-understanding from infancy through adolescence. *Child Dev.* 53:841–64

Darwin, C. 1877. A biographical sketch of an infant. *Mind* 2:285–94

Datan, N., Ginsberg, L. H., eds. 1975. *Life-Span Developmental Psychology: Normative Life Crises.* New York: Academic

Datan, N., Reese, H. W., eds. 1977. *Life-Span Developmental Psychology: Dialectical Perspectives on Experimental Research.* New York: Academic

de Chateau, P. 1980. Early post-partum contact

and later attitudes. *Int. J. Behav. Dev.* 3:273–86

Denney, N. W., List, J. A. 1979. Adult age differences in performance on the matching familiar figures test. *Hum. Dev.* 22:137–44

Diamond, M. C., Connor, J. R. 1981. A search for the potential of the aging cortex. In *Brain-Neuro-Transmitters and Receptors in Aging and Age Related Disorders,* ed. S. J. Enna et al, 17:43–58. New York: Raven

Dusek, J. B., Flaherty, J. F. 1981. The development of the self-concept during the adolescent years. *Monogr. Soc. Res. Child Dev.* 46: Ser. 191. 67 pp.

Dusek, J. B., Meyer, W. J. 1980. A dialectic analysis of learning theory contributions to understanding human development. *Hum. Dev.* 23:382–88

Eichorn, D. H., Clausen, J. A., Haan, N., Honzik, M. P., Mussen, P. H., eds. 1981. *Present and Past in Middle Life.* New York: Academic

Eichorn, D. H., Hunt, J. V., Honzik, M. P. 1981. Experience, personality, and IQ: Adolescence to middle age. See Eichorn et al 1981, pp. 89–116

Elder, G. H. Jr. 1981. Social history and life experience. See Eichorn et al 1981, pp. 3–31

Fagan, J. F. 1982. Infant memory. See Field et al 1982, pp. 79–92

Fagan, J. F., McGrath, S. K. 1981. Infant recognition memory and later intelligence. *Intelligence* 5:121–30

Falkner, F. 1978. Implications for growth in human twins. In *Human Growth,* ed. F. Falkner, J. M. Tanner, pp. 397–413. New York: Plenum

Ferris, P. 1977. *Dylan Thomas.* London: Hodder & Stoughton

Field, T. M., Huston, A., Quay, H. C., Troll, L., Finley, G. E. 1982. *Review of Human Development.* New York: Wiley

Fitzgerald, J. M. 1980. Learning and development: Mutual bases in a dialectical perspective. *Hum. Dev.* 23:376–82

Gesell, A. 1928. *Infancy and Human Growth.* New York: Macmillan

Gollin, E. S., ed. 1981. *Developmental Plasticity: Behavioral and Biological Aspects of Variations in Development.* New York: Academic (Dev. Psychol. Ser.)

Gottsdanker, R. 1982. Age and simple reaction time. *J. Gerontol.* 37:342–48

Goulet, L. R., Baltes, P. B., eds. 1970. *Life-Span Developmental Psychology: Research and Theory.* New York: Academic

Grigoroiu-Serbanescu, M. 1981. Intellectual and emotional development in premature children from 1 to 5 years. *Int. J. Behav. Dev.* 4:183–99

Haan, N. 1981. Common dimensions of personality development: Early adolescence to middle life. See Eichorn et al 1981, pp. 117–51

Haan, N., Day, D. 1976. Change and sameness reconsidered. *Natl. J. Aging Hum. Dev.* 7:59–65

Hall, G. S. 1904. *Adolescence.* New York: Appleton

Hall, G. S. 1922. *Senescence: The Last Half of Life.* New York: Appleton

Himmelweit, H. T., Turner, C. F. 1982. Social and psychological antecedents of depression: A longitudinal study from adolescence to early adulthood of a nonclinical population. See Baltes & Brim 1982, 4:315–41

Hollingworth, H. L. 1927. *Mental Growth and Decline: A Survey of Developmental Psychology.* New York: Appleton

Honzik, M. P. 1983. Measuring abilities in infancy: Value and limitations. In *Origins of Intelligence,* ed. M. Lewis. New York: Plenum. 2nd ed.

Howe, N. J. A. 1982. Biographical evidence and the development of outstanding individuals. *Am. Psychol.* 37:1071–81

Hoyer, W. J. 1980. Conceptions of learning and the study of life span development: A symposium. *Hum. Dev.* 23:361–89

Hunt, J. V. 1981. Predicting intellectual disorders in childhood for preterm infants with birthweights below 1501 gm. In *Preterm Birth and Psychological Development,* ed. S. L. Friedman, M. Sigman, pp. 329–51. New York: Academic

Hunt, J. V. 1983. Environmental risks in fetal and neonatal life as biological determinants of infant intelligence. In *Origins of Intelligence.* New York: Plenum. 2nd ed.

Jersild, A. T. 1933. *Child Psychology.* Englewood Cliffs, NJ: Prentice-Hall

Jones, H. E., Conrad, H. S. 1933. The growth and decline of intelligence: A study of a homogeneous group between the ages of ten and sixty. *Genet. Psychol. Monogr.* 13:223–98

Jones, M. C. 1981. Midlife drinking patterns: Correlates and antecedents. See Eichorn et al 1981, pp. 223–42

Kagan, J., Moss, H. 1962. *Birth to Maturity.* New York: Wiley

Kivnick, H. Q. 1982. *The Meaning of Grandparenthood.* Michigan: UMI Research

Kopp, C. B. 1983. Risk factors in development. See Mussen 1983.

Kopp, C. B., McCall, R. B. 1982. Predicting later mental performance for normal, at-risk and handicapped infants. See Baltes & Brim 1982, 4:33–61

Kuhn, D. 1982. Child development: Life-span perspectives (Commentary). *Hum. Dev.* 25: 79–84

Lachman, J. L., Lachman, R., Thronesberry, C. 1979. Metamemory through the adult life span. *Dev. Psychol.* 15:543–51

Lamb, M. E., Sutton-Smith, B., eds. 1982. *Sibling Relationships: Their Nature and Significance Across the Lifespan*. Hillsdale, NJ: Erlbaum

Lazar, I., Darlington, R. 1982. Lasting effects of early education: A report from the consortium for longitudinal studies. *Monogr. Soc. Res. Child Dev.* 47: Ser. 195. 151 pp.

Lefkowitz, M. M. 1981. Smoking during pregnancy: Long-term effects on offspring. *Dev. Psychol.* 17:192–94

Lerner, R. M. 1982. Child development: Lifespan perspectives (Introduction). *Hum. Dev.* 25:38–41

Lerner, R. M., Busch-Rossnagel, N. A., eds. 1981. *Individuals as Producers of their Development: A Life Span Perspective*. New York: Academic

Lerner, R. M., Hultsch, D. F. 1983. *Human Development: A Life Span Perspective*. New York: McGraw-Hill

Lerner, R. M., Palermo, M., Spiro, A. III, Nesselroade, J. R. 1982. Assessing dimensions of temperamental individuality across the life span: The dimensions of temperament survey. *Child Dev.* 53:149–59

Lewis, M. 1979. The self as a developmental concept. *Hum. Dev.* 22:416–19

Lewis, M. 1982. The social network systems model: Toward a theory of social development. See Field et al 1982, pp. 180–214

Lewis, M., Brooks-Gunn, J. 1981. Visual attention at three months as a predictor of cognitive functioning at two years of age. *Intelligence* 5:131–40

Liben, L. S., Patterson, A. H., Newcombe, N., eds. 1981. *Spatial Representation and Behavior Across the Life Span*. New York: Academic (Dev. Psychol. Ser.)

Lipsitt, L. P. 1982a. Infancy and life-span development. *Hum. Dev.* 25:41–48

Lipsitt, L. P. 1982b. Infant learning. See Field et al 1982, pp. 62–78

Livson, N., Peskin, H. 1981. Psychological health at age 40: Prediction from adolescent personality. See Eichorn et al 1981, pp. 183–221

Macfarlane, J. W. 1963. From infancy to adulthood. *Child. Educ.* 39:336–42

Matějček, A., Dytrych, Z., Schüller, V. 1980. Follow-up study of children born from unwanted pregnancies. *Int. J. Behav. Dev.* 3:243–51

McCarthy, J. D., Hoge, D. R. 1982. Analysis of age effects in longitudinal studies of adolescent self-esteem. *Dev. Psychol.* 18:372–79

McCarty, S. M., Siegler, I. C., Logue, P. E. 1982. Cross-sectional and longitudinal patterns of three Wechsler Memory Scale Subtests. *J. Gerontol.* 37:169–75

McCrae, R. R. 1982. Age differences in the use of coping mechanisms. *J. Gerontol.* 37:454–60

Mednick, S. A., Baert, A. E. III. 1981. *Prospective Longitudinal Research: An Empirical Basis for the Prevention of Psychosocial Disorders*. Oxford: Oxford Univ. Press

Mussen, P. H., ed. 1983. *Handbook of Child Psychology*. New York: Wiley. 4th ed.

Mussen, P. H., Honzik, M. P., Eichorn, D. H. 1982. Early adult antecedents of life satisfaction at age 70. *J. Gerontol.* 37:316–22

Mussen, P. H., Eichorn, D. H., Honzik, M. P., Bieber, S. L., Meredith, W. M. 1980. Continuity and change in women's characteristics over four decades. *Int. J. Behav. Dev.* 3:333–47

Nesselroade, J. R., Reese, H. W., eds. 1973. *Life-Span Developmental Psychology: Methodological Issues*. New York: Academic

Olweus, D. 1980. Familial and temperamental determinants of aggressive behavior in adolescent boys: A causal analysis. *Dev. Psychol.* 16:644–60

Osofsky, J., ed. 1979. *Handbook of Infant Development*. New York: Wiley

Papousek, H., Papousek, M. 1982. Infant-adult social interactions: Their origins, dimensions and failures. See Field et al 1982, pp. 148–63

Parkinson, S. R., Lindholm, J. M., Inman, V. W. 1982. An analysis of age differences in immediate recall. *J. Gerontol.* 37:425–31

Peterson, L. 1982. Altruism and the development of internal control: An integrative model. *Merrill-Palmer Q.* 28;197–222

Piaget, J. 1923. *Le langage et la pensee chez l'enfant*. Neuchatel/Paris: Delachaux & Nestle

Poon, L. W., ed. 1980. *Aging Research in the 80s: Psychological Issues*. Washington DC: Am. Psychol. Assoc.

Poon, L. W., Welford, A. T. 1980. Prologue: A historical perspective. See Poon 1980, pp. xiii–xvii

Pressey, S. L., Janney, J. E., Kuhlan, R. G. 1939. *Life: A Psychological Survey*. New York: Harper

Pulkkinen, L. 1982. Self-control and continuity from childhood to late adolescence. See Baltes & Brim 1982, pp. 63–105

Reedy, M. M., Birren, J. E., Schaie, K. W. 1981. Age and sex differences in satisfying love relationships across the adult life span. *Hum. Dev.* 24:52–66

Reese, H. W. 1980. A learning theory critique of the operant approach to life span development. *Hum. Dev.* 23;368–76

Roe, K. V., McClure, A., Roe, A. 1982. Vocal interaction at 3 months and cognitive skills at 12 years. *Dev. Psychol.* 18:15–16

Rogers, D. 1982. *Life Span Development*. Monterey: Brooks/Cole

Rosenberg, B. G. 1982. Life span personality stability in sibling status. See Lamb & Sutton-Smith 1982, pp. 167–224

Runyan, W. McK. 1982. *Life Histories and Psychobiography*. New York: Oxford Univ. Press

Salthouse, T. A. 1982. *Adult Cognition: An Experimental Psychology of Human Aging*. New York: Springer-Verlag

Salthouse, T. A., Somberg, B. L. 1982. Time-accuracy relationships in young and old adults. *J. Gerontol.* 37:349–53

Sanford, E. C. 1902. Mental growth and decay. *Am. J. Psychol.* 13:426–29

Scarr, S., McCartney, K. 1983. How people make their own environments: A theory of genotype-environment effects. *Child. Dev.* 54:424–35

Schaie, K. W. 1982a. *Historical time and cohort effects*. Presented at West Virginia Conf. Life-Span Dev. Psychol.

Schaie, K. W. 1982b. The Seattle longitudinal study: A twenty-one year exploration of psychometric intelligence in adulthood. In *Longitudinal Studies of Adult Psychological Development*, ed. K. W. Schaie. New York: Guilford

Sears, R. R. 1977. Sources of life satisfactions of the Terman gifted men. *Am. Psychol.* 32:119–28

Shinn, M. W. 1900. *The Biography of a Baby*. Boston: Houghton Mifflin

Siegler, I. C., McCarty, S. M., Logue, P. E. 1982. Wechsler Memory Scale Scores, selective attrition and distance from death. *J. Gerontol.* 37:176–81

Skolnick, A. 1981. Married lives: Longitudinal perspectives on marriage. See Eichorn et al 1981, pp. 269–98

Sternberg, R. J. 1981. Novelty-seeking, novelty-finding, and the developmental continuity of intelligence. *Intelligence* 5:149–55

Stroud, J. G. 1981. Women's careers: Work, family, and personality. See Eichorn et al 1981, pp. 353–90

Terman, L. M. 1916. *The Measurement of Intelligence*. Boston: Houghton-Mifflin

Thomas, A., Chess, S. 1981. The role of temperament in the contributions of individuals to their development. See Lerner et al 1981, pp. 231–55

Turner, R. R., Reese, H. W., eds. 1980. *Life-Span Developmental Psychology: Intervention*. New York: Academic

Vigotsky, L. S., Luria, A. R. 1929. The function and fate of egocentric speech. Proc. Pap. 9th Int. Congr. Psychol., pp. 464–65

Waterman, A. S. 1982. Identity development from adolescence to adulthood: An extension of theory and a review of research. *Dev. Psychol.* 18:341–58

Watson, J. S. 1983. Memory in infancy. In *Encyclopedie de la Pleiade: La Psychologie*, ed. J. Piaget, J. P. Bronkart, P. Mounoud, Paris: Gallimard. In press

Werner, E. E., Bierman, J. M., French, F. E. 1971. *The Children of Kauai*. Honolulu: Univ. Hawaii Press

Werner, E. E., Smith, R. S. 1977. *Kauai's Children Come of Age*. Honolulu: Univ. Hawaii Press

Werner, E. E., Smith, R. S. 1982. *Vulnerable but Invincible: A Longitudinal Study of Resilient Children and Youth*. New York: McGraw-Hill

Wilson, R. S., Matheny, A. P. Jr. 1983. Assessment of temperament in infant twins. *Hum. Dev.* 19:172–83

Winograd, E., Smith, A. D., Simon, E. W. 1982. Aging and the picture superiority effect in recall. *J. Gerontol.* 37:70–75

Wolman, B. B., ed. 1982. *Handbook of Developmental Psychology*. Englewood Cliffs, NJ: Prentice-Hall

Young, H. B., Ferguson, L. R. 1981. *Puberty to Manhood in Italy and America*. New York: Academic

Yu, B. P., Masoro, E. J., Murata, I., Bertrand, H. A., Lynd, F. T. 1982. Life span study of SPF Fischer 344 male rats fed *ad libitum* on restricted diets: Longevity, growth, lean body mass and disease. *J. Gerontol.* 37:130–41

Ann. Rev. Psychol. 1984. 35:333–60

SOCIAL AND COMMUNITY INTERVENTIONS

Ira Iscoe and Lorwen C. Harris

Department of Psychology, University of Texas, Austin, Texas 78712

CONTENTS

333

0066-4308/84/0201-0333$02.00

INTRODUCTION

Social and community interventions (SCIs) are part of the fabric of American life. They range from federally funded, large-scale programs such as Welfare, Food Stamps, and Medicare, to block and neighborhood organizations dealing with problems and issues of local or national importance. The arena is usually at the community (local) level and the targets are groups, institutions, and organizations. The purpose is the betterment of the human condition with efforts directed mainly toward assisting the poor, the underprivileged, and the dependent to cope with problems and to improve or maintain a quality of life. Recently there is an increasing number of SCIs directed toward neighborhood and environmental concerns, of interest to middle class populations. Church and voluntary philanthropic groups (e.g. United Way) also initiate and maintain a variety of SCIs. Existing and potential roles for psychologists in SCI range from that of researcher, evaluator, and organizer through that of consultant, planner, and negotiator. The clients may include state and national agencies, schools, hospitals, community-based institutions, minority populations and special groups, among others.

The priorities of a nation in many ways are a reflection of the amount, type, and extent of its SCIs. Competition for resources is increasingly severe, and as community and neighborhood organizations note, "the military do not have to hold bake sales to buy a new airplane." Currently, we are in the midst of a period of pessimism, reassessment, and retrenchment. Programs and strategies for the improvement of the human condition are being questioned and many are being reduced, altered, or terminated. It is not as if SCIs have failed completely as much as they have not fulfilled their promise. An almost 40-year trend of government activity in SCIs is being reversed by the New Federalism. The election of 1980 overwhelmingly endorsed a platform of conservativism and the need to reappraise the degree of involvement of the federal government in SCIs. Other competing demands have arisen and alternatives, including greater involvement of the private sector, are being proposed. The failure of a multibillion dollar weapon system does not evoke the outcry generated when an SCI, of much lesser financial magnitude but of equal or greater complexity, fails to meet its goal.

Symbolic of the changing climate is the concept of block grants to the states. Carried out appropriately, block grants could very well constitute one of the more important SCIs in the latter half of this century. They offer the potential for program implementation, administration, and consumer input at the local level. Whether all problems of national scope and importance can be better addressed at the state level remains to be seen. It is unclear how the maintenance of minimal standards and the allocation of appropriate resources for target populations will be safeguarded. Funds alone do not determine successful SCIs. Some of the most innovative SCIs are the results of departures from a "more of the same" philosophy.

The literature does not yet fully reflect the stress and reappraisal that is taking place in the entire fabric of American culture. Huge budget deficits raise questions of how increasingly scarce monies should be allocated. What proportion can be diverted from a casualty-deficit model to one that emphasizes competence and resource building? Will the humanistic, compassionate approach be underemphasized in the torrent of computer printouts?

SCI Literature and Research

The literature is widely scattered in behavioral science and human service journals. A relatively small percentage appears in publications labeled psychological and less in refereed prestigious journals. The complexities of SCIs are reflected by an increasing number of edited volumes. There are also many top quality government publications, some incorporating the proceedings of research symposia and clarifying the "state of the art" in a particular area. The catalog and reports from state departments of community affairs, health, and human services are also good sources of information. Many SCI reports and studies may not be Library of Congress referenced but are being increasingly included in data banks. Well-designed scientifically respectable studies, until quite recently, have been the exception. It seems that the more important the problem to human beings and communities, the less the rigor of the research. The movement from the laboratory to the community is admittedly difficult, but once having established credibility and obtained the cooperation of the neighborhood group or agency, the way is to open to gathering gold mines of data. Advances in qualitative and quantitative analyses allow for the overcoming of some of the limitations previously inherent in community-based research.

Fragmentation of Services and the Redefinition of Professionalism

Mental illness, delinquency, criminal justice, aging, unmarried teenage pregnancy, abortion, single parents, poverty, and unemployment, among others, are treated as separate entities despite their obvious communalities and interrelationships. There is a need for a dialogue and a systems approach in which SCIs cut across different aspects of the same problem. Related to this is an increasing emphasis on regionalism, ethnocentrism, and single purpose groups. Yet another trend is neighborhood and citizen groups rallying around threats to the immediate environment such as contamination and pollution or the defense of open space.

The democraticization and wider dissemination of knowledge plus the inability of professionals to meet the increasing needs of consumers has resulted

in a blurring of boundaries and an emergence of new personnel. The paraprofessionals of yesteryear are now the new professionals. There has been a huge
increase in the number of nontraditionally trained personnel (and sometimes
untrained) in the human service fields (Riessman 1980). There is concomitantly
a decline in the number and degree of involvement of persons from the
traditional mental health and human service disciplines (Fink & Weinstein
1979). We turn now to topics covered in the present review.

A Framework for Considering SCIs

Our review covers the period December 1979 through December 1982 (with a
few exceptions) and continues the thrust of previous reviews by Cowen (1973),
Kelly, Snowden & Muñoz (1977), and Bloom (1980). Some 850 pieces of
literature have come to our attention. We hope to impart a "feel" for the current
status of SCIs, its problems, failures, and exciting future given a modicum of
support and increasing involvement of psychologists. Our presentation is
organized around the areas of: 1. social policy, research, and theory; 2.
community mental health, consultation, and advances in community psychology; 3. primary prevention and health promotion; 4. self-help, social networks, and social support; 5. deinstitutionalization; and 6. the underserved and
unserved populations. Each of the above certainly merits a separate review
chapter.

SCIs may be conceptualized as the interaction, between and within, of at
least these three variables: (a) source of funds (federal, state, or local, singly or
in combination; how much and for how long?); (b) personnel (professional,
nonprofessional, volunteers, consultants, etc; their role relationships); (c)
populations served and advocacy groups (how targeted and served; what
benefits derived?). This framework will be helpful to keep in mind and apply as
we proceed to discuss the topics of this review.

SOCIAL POLICY, RESEARCH, AND THEORY

Seidman (1983) has produced a handbook of social interventions which makes
a valuable contribution to theory, research, and practice of SCIs. There are
other evidences of growing maturity. Muñoz et al (1979) have rendered a
singular service to research-oriented interventions by addressing the processes
involved in bringing about change in nonlaboratory community settings.
Mechanic (1980) deals with major issues and questions that mental health
planners, practitioners, and researchers face in implementing programs in the
private and public sectors. Another mark of maturity is the important and oft
neglected question of ethics and responsibility. Bermant et al (1978) examine
the ethics of social interventions and point out the dilemmas in gaining consent
of target populations, assessing unforeseen negative consequences of SCIs, and

ascribing responsibility when social experiments fail. The implications for research are enormous.

Some major theoretical advances have appeared which directly relate to SCIs. Cowen (1980) clarifies the crucial parameters of primary prevention and opens the way for the development and testing of genuine primary prevention endeavors. Brickman et al (1982) present a social psychological framework for the assignment of responsibility and the planning of remediation in SCIs. Their framework, derived from attribution theory, clarifies the underlying assumptions of responsibility in traditional help-giving perspectives (e.g. the medical model) and sheds light on the assumptions underlying less well-defined perspectives (e.g. the compensatory model). Rappaport (1981) advances a theory of empowerment of individuals and communities and argues for the recognition of the paradoxical nature of community intervention. Once a particular type of SCI becomes institutionalized, efforts are then made to divert persons or groups away from its services. He recommends the study of how communities cope with various problems on a local level. The impending changes in sources and patterns of funding for SCIs may very well be a reflection of Rappaport's contentions (e.g. the movement to divert youth away from the juvenile justice system).

Failure to consider humanistic variables in SCIs is voiced by several writers. Taber (1980), in a review of 38 appropriate journals, concludes that the social sciences "have not studied and analyzed the helping situation to any significant degree" (p. 5). He also asserts that we have neglected to study the social environments in which persons are receiving help and care. Shore (1981) notes that in the human services there is a movement away from a compassionate approach toward a managerial, bureaucratic one. M. Levine (1979) goes further and states that

> the exclusive emphasis on hard-headed realities, to the exclusion of equally careful consideration of how we can guide and monitor the implementation of our ideals, has resulted in a betrayal of our ideals. As social scientists and evaluators, we need to learn how to be as sophisticated about theory, the philosophy, the operationalization, and the measurement of actions that meet our ideals as we are about fiscal matters, head counts, and other hard data (pp. 15–16).

The work of a number of researchers indicates increasing sensivitiy to the valid criticisms voiced above. Changes in patterns and utilization of mental health services between 1955 and 1975 have been carefully studied by Veroff et al (1981a), and in a companion volume, Veroff et al (1981b) present a rich and detailed picture of Americans' attitudes toward themselves, their work, their troubles, and the remedies they seek. Both of these volumes are abundant in data and possess enormous implications for the design, delivery, and evaluation of SCIs. The careful sampling and methodological rigor make these findings especially important.

On the community level, A. Levine (1982), working with the residents of Love Canal, provides an outstanding example of onsite scientific research. She details the problems of citizens struggling for the recognition of the legitimacy of their complaints in the face of bureaucratic obstacles, chicanery, and denial. Gibbs (1982) presents a resident's view of Love Canal and identifies many of the factors affecting a community's response to an environmental problem. As more and more "Love Canals," both nuclear and chemical, are discovered the importance of these two publications will be enhanced.

The need for more sophisticated research methodologies and evaluations in community settings is being increasingly recognized. For example, Dooley & Catalano (1980) report that changes in economic climate expose existing and *untreated behavior disorders* in contrast to the prevailing theory of provoking symptoms in previously normal persons. This finding has important ramifications for the nature and type of community interventions related to unemployment. Price & Polister (1980) present new paradigms for social research and practice with special emphasis on community and human service fields. Stahler & Tash (1982) deal with innovative approaches to the complex field of mental health evaluation.

On a social policy level, Albee (1982a) explores the politics of nature and nurture and emphasizes the need for sophistication on the part of psychologists. Zigler & Gordon (1981) discuss provisions of youth services in relation to social policy. Kiesler (1981, 1982) and Kiesler & Sibulkin (1982), in a series of ground-breaking papers, deal with the social policy implications of mental health research, the problems and issues in the identification of the mentally ill, and community implications of de jure vs de facto treatment approaches. In 1981, in recognition of changing political realities, APA set up an Institute of Policy Analysis and, beginning in 1982, the *American Psychologist* incorporated a continuing section called "Psychology in the Public Forum" which deals with policy-related issues. A rich variety of public interest and policy topics are presented on an almost monthly basis. The APA Congressional Fellows program and the Bush Foundation Fellowships in Child Development and Social Policy are examples of efforts to produce knowledgeable younger psychologists to add to an increasing cadre of psychologists in the public policy area. The link between research, theory, and social policy will undoubtedly be strengthened by these new developments.

COMMUNITY MENTAL HEALTH AND COMMUNITY PSYCHOLOGY: DEVELOPMENTS AND PROSPECTS

The Community Mental Health Centers (CMHCs) Act of 1965 laid the basis for SCIs in the area of mental health and mental illness. CMHCs were to deliver services to a wide variety of needy populations, in particular those formerly treated in state hospitals. Boards of citizens rather than professionals were to determine policy and exercise control of these centers. By the 1980s, CMHCs became the third largest component of the mental health service delivery system (Thompson et al 1982). Seven hundred and sixty CMHCs (composed of catchment areas of approximately 100,000 persons) are presently operational, serving an average of 54% of the population in each state and averaging approximately 3.1 million patient episodes yearly (Klerman 1981). These centers receive about 25% of state mental health dollars and are involved in approximately 75% of all psychiatric episodes (Andrulis & Mazade 1983). The Mental Health Systems Act of 1980 embodied changes which would have greatly improved the scope and quality of CMHCs as well as secured a continual financial support. Unfortunately, the Act was not funded and it is unclear how different funding sources will be combined to meet programs such as those involving the chronically mentally ill, children, the elderly, and ethnic minorities. It does seem likely that as financial support shrinks, we are going to see more conflict and competition among CMHC program sectors (e.g. preventive vs treatment services) as well as between CMHCs and other human service facilities (e.g. State Hospitals; Tarail 1980).

Changing Perspectives in Community Mental Health

An examination of the community mental health literature between 1979 and 1982 reveals the following major issues, that: (a) there is a movement toward marketing CMHC services more competitively to consumers in the private sector; (b) CMHCs are becoming more dependent on the need for third party payments (D'Augelli 1982a); (c) a marked exodus of mental health professionals is occurring as a result of an ideological split in what the priorities are in meeting the mental health needs of the community (Fink & Weinstein 1979); and (d) CMHCs are not meeting the needs of the chronically mentally ill (Rose 1979).

With the loosening of federal guidelines, each state has the opportunity to define community mental health in its own way. Some states may reinforce community-based programs which serve needy populations such as the chronically mentally ill while others may continue to support inpatient facilities. By examining the historical antecedents of the present mental health system, Levine (1981) and Sarason (1981) shed light on the overarching social and political processes which shape our current notions of community mental health. In addition, Schulberg & Killilea (1982), in an edited volume honoring Gerald Caplan, provide a valuable overview of the past, present, and future status of practically every aspect of community mental health as we know it today. Bloom's (1983) second edition of *Community Mental Health* adds to this knowledge, and we particularly note his timely contribution to the area of mental health education.

COMMUNITY PSYCHOLOGY'S MOVEMENT AWAY FROM COMMUNITY MENTAL HEALTH   At its origins in 1965, community psychology was closely identified with clinical and community mental health. The failure of community psychology to separate from these concerns was discussed by Novaco & Monahan (1980), McClure et al (1980), and Lounsbury et al (1980). We now note a decided turn toward environmental issues and activities involving target populations which have not previously been identified as mentally ill or in need of treatment. For example, there are now articles in the *American Journal of Community Psychology* on neighborhood groups and urban environments (Unger & Wandersman 1982), interventions promoting safety-belt use (Geller et al 1982), and the training of natural helpers in rural communities (D'Augelli & Ehrlich 1982). Additionally, a number of books and articles have emerged which reflect community psychologists' growing interest in and application of social psychological, cognitive, and behavioral theories. O'Neill (1981) approaches community psychology from a cognitive perspective, Jeger & Slotnick (1982) take a behavioral-ecological approach, and Glenwick & Jason (1980) present the first book on behavioral community psychology. O'Neill & Trickett (1982) combine the areas of social cognition and biological-ecology to analyze consultation from a systems perspective. Gibbs et al (1980), in a basic text, explore the contributions to community psychology from a number of fields primarily within psychology (e.g. labeling theory, learned helplessness, and environmental stress).

ECONOMICS AND MENTAL HEALTH SYSTEMS   The inclusion of economic research into the mental health field is heralded by McGuire & Weisbrod (1981). Mental health will be viewed increasingly as a commodity rather than a humanitarian endeavor. Cost benefit analysis and other economic terminology will be heard of more frequently. Broskowski et al (1981), in a very important edited volume, note the advantages of delivering health and mental health services in one setting. CMHCs could very well be combined with health centers which already have a long tradition of serving needy populations. Although there is a threat to the autonomy of mental health personnel, a more holistic approach to health (physical and mental) would be welcome.

MENTAL HEALTH ADMINISTRATION AND PERSONNEL   Mental health administration has come into its own as a discipline and must be recognized as a reality in SCIs. Austin & Hershey (1982) give a general survey of this area, and a source book for governing and advisory boards of CMHCs has appeared (Silverman 1981). The journal *Administration and Mental Health* (Saul Feldman, general editor) has been in existence for a decade and offers valuable information on management and leadership issues, particularly for CMHCs. In addition, the recommendations of a conference on ethical issues on mental health administration and an annotated bibliography were published by Bayer et al (1981).

In the personnel realm, PhD level psychologists and psychiatrists are having less and less to do with the severely mentally ill and comprise a decreasing percentage of CMHC staff (Berlin et al 1981). The so-called paraprofessionals have moved into what is called the "new" professional status and have taken over more and more aspects of care and treatment for the mentally ill. This trend is decried by some professionals who recommend a return to a medical model as opposed to a socioenvironmental model (Langsley 1980, Winslow 1982).

Community Mental Health and Prevention

Glasscote (1980) reviewed the programs of six selected CMHCs. In none of these centers was more than a small fraction of hours, less than 3%, devoted to prevention activities and there was no prevention policy per se. Primary prevention, as a CMHC service, lacks a clarification of goals. D'Augelli (1982b) contends that it has always been, and will remain, a controversial goal for consultation and education (C & E) in CMHCs until there is a delineation between C & E and primary prevention's goals and techniques. In the absence of funds for specialty activities, primary prevention is likely to gain only a modicum of CMHC financial support.

Nevertheless, there is a thrust toward advancing CMHCs activities to include a variety of community-related issues. Both Insel (1980) and Glasscote (1980) urge mental health professionals to broaden their community mental health goals to encompass unsound environmental conditions. Adler (1982) expands the concept of CMHCs beyond the role of microsystem toward a macrosystem analysis, in which problems involving the entire community are examined. Through an organizational competency model, Adler sees CMHCs promotive and preventive activities as being integrated into the fabric of the community. A recent example of this concept is seen in Berkowitz's (1982) work on implementing and evaluating small-scale social change programs such as anti-crime patrols, car pools, and community gardens in community settings. At the same time, prevention programs directed toward general community issues are less likely to be funded by the state as are C & E programs directed toward the support of chronic care and treatment issues (Ritter 1982).

To this end, Lamb & Zusman (1979, 1981) contend that mental health professionals should not be involved in primary prevention activities, claiming that their priorities should be to treat those presently suffering. They contend that prevention should be a function of social policy and social institutions. Bloom (1979, 1981), in response to Lamb & Zusman, clarifies prevention activities and makes a distinction between predisposing and precipitating factors. He urges a research shift from specific causes to general nonspecific causes of emotional problems. The assignment of responsibility and the implementation of appropriate preventive SCIs still await a national preventive policy.

CMHCs and Consultation (C & E)

As a mandated service of CMHCs, C & E was to be one of the main approaches for increasing the skill of caregivers such as teachers, nurses, physicians, and parents, as well as an avenue through which paraprofessional and indigenous nonprofessionals could enhance their skills, thereby increasing the pool of competent personnel available to deal with various mental health problems. This hope has not been realized and presently only about 5% of the total CMHC staff hours are devoted to C & E (Glasscote 1980). The 1982 meeting of the National Council of Community Mental Health Centers included much talk about the imminent demise of C & E. Under the proposed block grant funding, C & E will receive a lower priority (Stockdill 1982). Clearly, C & E is facing a crisis.

Beset with financial problems, CMHCs have had difficulties providing consultation services (at minimum reimbursement) to clients, especially schools and community agencies. Although they find the services useful, the funds to pay for them have not received appropriate budgetary support. The continued dominance of the medical model and the lack of federal guidelines have inhibited C & E's growth and progress (Ketterer 1981). The National Council of Community Mental Health Centers published a set of guidelines for C & E services which broadens the C & E domain to include community network development, interventions focused on social support linkages, self-help groups, and natural helpers, as well as policy-centered and environmental activities (Snow & Swift 1981). Unanswered is the question of who will pay? Those agencies which need consultation the most are least able to afford it.

C & E RESEARCH AND THEORY   A number of useful edited volumes and books have appeared in the area of C & E which merit full-scale review (Meyers et al 1979, Rogawski 1979, Curtis & Zins 1981, Ketterer 1981, Alpert 1982, Gallessich 1982, O'Neill & Trickett 1982). In general, these volumes emphasize the need for new and integrative conceptual frameworks as well as sophisticated evaluation research and planning of future C & E services. In recognition of the need for quality control and communications, NIMH established an experimental publication entitled *Consultation,* which deals with organizational development consultation within CMHCs and other human service agencies.

The training of consultants for work with organizations and communities continues to be a vexing problem, and little if any research has been carried out in this area. The appropriate mix of academic and field experiences has yet to be agreed upon. This situation may be somewhat remedied, however, by the publication of an edited volume devoted to training in consultation (Alpert & Meyers 1983). The authors approach training from an interdisciplinary perspective, focusing on topics such as professional identity, goals, evaluation of training techniques, and transfer of effects. This volume should function as a major reference in the area of C & E training.

Grady et al (1981), in an exhaustive review of the consultation literature between 1972 and 1979, conclude that mental health consultation is still not a primary research commitment, and our review since 1979 supports this contention. Outcome measures in consultation research have, for the most part, been chosen without concern for reliability, validity, and comparability to other studies. Also, the effects of consultation, as reflected in improved or changed behavior in the clients of consultees, have yet to be substantiated (Cowen 1980, Davis et al 1981). Mannino (1981) contends that mental health consultation as a field will continue to be cut back and "trimmed" during austere times until increased sophistication and rigor become more apparent.

On the positive side, Ketterer (1981) provides a typology of C & E techniques which is neutral enough to be applied to a variety of mental health goals such as prevention, remediation, etc. D'Augelli (1982b) conceptualizes the C & E service as "an intervention at a specific *level of analysis* pursuing a *goal or intent* using a *technique or strategy*" (p. 29). He also develops a typology for considering the diversity of mental health personnel (e.g. paraprofessionals, informal helpers, and gatekeepers) and their relationship to various C & E goals (e.g. protection, promotion, or prevention) and techniques (e.g. train non-professionals, organize local helpers, promote lobbying). These underlying conceptual models are greatly needed in the design, implementation, and evaluation of C & E activities. As D'Augelli (1982b) remarks: "The challenge of the future will be whether or not C & E can overcome its current marginality as a mental health specialty and become a viable force for the promotion of mental health in communities" (p. 5).

C & E services have the potential for strengthening mental health resources in various settings. Whether such services are continued, however, will depend on the ability of C & E practitioners to demonstrate their unique contribution to the mental health field. It would be a tremendous loss if the advances in theory and growing sophistication of the field were not put to use.

PRIMARY PREVENTION AND HEALTH PROMOTION

We attempt a brief "state of the art" description. The public health areas related to life-style problems (e.g. smoking, eating, and drinking) are focusing more on prevention. NIMH in 1982 established the Prevention Research Branch (PRB) with a National Office of Prevention Policy. Prevention Intervention

Centers are currently being funded, and it is anticipated that three or four regional centers will be started up nationally each year for the next 3 years. ADAMHA (Klerman 1981) addresses issues in prevention policy including funding and joint programming. In terms of total budget, prevention expenditures are miniscule indeed.

The Journal of Primary Prevention was founded in 1980 and its "Clearing House" section for primary prevention programs is especially valuable. The *Prevention in Human Service Series* (1981) is also evidence of mounting interest in prevention. Issues dealing with the preventive impact of television (Sprafkin et al 1982) and early intervention programs for infants (Moss et al 1982) are excellent contributions. Moreover, Felner & Jason's (1983) edited volume on preventive psychology, the recommendations of the Task Force on Prevention of the President's Committee on Mental Health and the seven volumes contaning the papers delivered at the Vermont Conferences on Primary Prevention of Psychopathology (G. W. Albee and J. M. Joffe, General Editors) singly and collectively have made significant contributions to the area of primary prevention. The *Wellness Resource Bulletin,* published by the California State Department of Mental Health (1981), and the monograph by Aronowitz (1982) on state prevention programs are welcome additions. New York and Michigan have developed prevention components in their state departments of mental health.

Prevention Research and Theory

Much of the verbiage, rhetoric, and methodological underbrush are being cleared away in primary prevention (Cowen 1980). In discussing policy guidelines for primary prevention, Cowen (1980), Iscoe (1980), and Bloom (1981) extend the base of prevention knowledge so that new research questions can be generated. Lorion (1983) offers a set of research principles for systematically analyzing preventive interventions, and Lorion & Lounsbury (1982) present conceptual and methodological guidelines for evaluating such programs. In addition, Cowen (1980) and D'Augelli (1982b) have contributed to the understanding of the differences between C & E and primary prevention. Albee (1982b) has presented a formula for determining the incidence of mental illness. Price et al (1980) make a distinct contribution to the area of prevention by discussing critical research concerns. This volume marks the first in a series of Sage annual reviews of mental health, and the field is well served. A "special number" of the *American Journal of Community Psychology* (Cowen 1982) is comprised of nine studies specifically selected to meet rigorous criteria of primary prevention research. A "compleat roadmap," offered by Cowen (1982), synthesizes each of the studies from the point of view of the target group, objectives, major methodologies, and variables affected.

To investors and investigators primary prevention activities and research must indeed appear as a "hi risk" endeavor. While the findings of Shure & Spivack (1981), Bloom et al (1982), Tableman et al (1982) suggest that primary prevention programs can have significant short-term effects, these interventions have not been subjected to long-term scrutiny. Evaluation of whether these effects are lasting or not necessitates complex costly longitudinal research. Therefore, support for evaluation of primary prevention programs is not a major policy priority.

SELF-HELP GROUPS, SOCIAL SUPPORT, AND SOCIAL NETWORK SYSTEMS

There are at least 500,000 self-help groups in the U.S. embracing a total membership of about 23,000,000 (Katz 1981). Gartner & Riessman (1980) have compiled a working guide of many of these groups, cross-referenced by problem and location. They range from those groups involving persons experiencing similar circumstances or misfortunes (e.g. single parents groups, Parents Without Partners, Alcoholics Anonymous) to those involving organizations of persons designed to deal with a national problem at the local level [e.g. Mothers Against Drunk Driving (MADD)]. Characteristic of self-help groups is that the initiators and members perceive existing social institutions or agencies as not meeting their needs (Knight et al 1980). Typically there is a shared belief system and, in some instances, the focus is on the social origins of problems rather than the individualistic, introspective origins espoused by clinicians. Additionally, nonprofessional involvement is a common factor in many self-help groups.

Self-help Groups: Sociopolitical Aspects and Professionalism

Self-help groups partially reflect a reaction to political and economic changes in the past two decades. There is an emphasis on closely tied small groups and the development of new strategies for dealing with human or environmental concerns against which a single individual feels powerless. In many ways self-help groups can be a source of community empowerment (Gartner & Riessman 1982). The joining of forces by like-minded people leads to a singleness of purpose which can effect policy changes at the local, state, or national levels. Taking a cross-cultural perspective, Weber & Cohen (1982) examine the unique ways in which ethnicity and beliefs structure and define self-help groups. In this same volume, Schensul & Schensul (1982) deal with the distinction between social advocacy and mutual assistance in relation to ethnicity, socialization, beliefs and group organization.

Voluntary grass roots involvement is a key to successful community action and the basis of citizen groups of all types. The fact that they exist and are increasing indicates continued need. Spiegel (1982) notes that groups are more likely to be found in areas where there are few professionals or the individual lacks access to professional services. Many self-help groups function as an information source or a psychological support. For example, Spiegel notes that "Ostomy Clubs" deal with an aspect of postsurgical care, working with patients and their families on important problems rarely dealt with by physicians. He outlines the main types of self-help groups and discusses self-help in relation to deviance theory, professionalism, and transition phases in life.

Warren (1981) notes that a majority (72%) of middle class Americans enter and leave helping pathways and resources at frequent intervals and present problems which are well over the capacity of any agency or group of professionals to deal with effectively. Cowen et al (1981) emphasize the growing importance of informal help-giving processes and how effective they are with different types of helper groups. Rodolfa & Hungerford (1982), expressing the concern of many mental health professionals, contend that the self-help approach encourages individuals to neglect mental health care and rely exclusively on the group where symptoms rather than the underlying problem are treated. A two-way referral (and possibly screening process) has yet to be developed. A genuine collaborative relationship between professionals and various self-help and social support groups would be a constructive step in meeting the diverse needs of individuals in the community. To this end, Jeger & Slotnick (1982) develop a "self-help-professional collaborative" perspective within an ecological context.

Research Issues in Self-help

Evaluating the effectiveness of self-help groups poses considerable challenge. Little is known about how members are recruited, the extent of their dependence on group support, how they evolve and change within the group, and on a macro level, the social forces which have given birth to such a movement (Knight et al 1980). Lieberman & Bond (1978) contend, and we agree, that it is still uncertain who is served, what problems are highlighted, and the process by which needs are met in self-help groups. To answer such questions one needs to examine systems level criteria as outcome measures as well as individual level criteria involving the lifestyles and values of the clients. This research entails a compilation of methodological techniques from a number of disciplinary perspectives such as sociology, anthropology, and psychology. Until a multidisciplinary perspective is implemented, the boundary and domain of self-help groups will remain unclear.

Developments in Social Network Analysis and Social Support

Wellman & Leighton (1979) advance the notion of networks in examining social linkages within communities. Subsequently a number of conceptual, methodological, and program advances in the area of social networks have appeared (Wellman 1980, *Connections* 1982). Gottlieb & Hall (1980) provide a model by which to conceptualize the referral pattern and utilization of individuals into social support networks. In addition, Gottlieb (1981) discusses the functions of social networks as positive additions to the professional sector and as support in times of crisis. Sarason & Lorentz (1979) address the complexities of resource exchange networks in a complex setting and furnish some cogent observations on the negative role of professionalism in our society.

Definitions of social support range from extensive, close interpersonal ties to those involving only key individuals or groups (Heller 1979). In a factor analysis of the social support construct, Heller & Swindle (1983) report four main elements: the structure and function of support networks, personal attributes of individuals that keep the network open, cognitive appraisal that discerns if support is available, and support-seeking behavior (usually generated from the cognitive appraisal component). Recent reviews of the buffering hypothesis of social support were conducted by Thoits (1982) and Heller & Swindle (1983). Wilcox (1981) found that quality of support rather than quantity was a significant factor in buffering stress. In addition, Porritt (1979) reports a relationship between the source and quality of social support in a crisis situation and favorableness of outcome.

Implications for Mental Health

Biegel & Naparstek (1982) give an overview of conceptual and research issues related to the role of social networks and social support systems in mental health. Greenblatt et al (1982), in a review of networks and mental health, found adaptative social networks to vary with the type of situation and the quality of relationships. These findings have important implications for the structuring of institutional environments for the mentally ill and for the chronically dependent. Holahan & Moos (1981) analyze the relationship between degree of social support and psychological distress, while Hatfield (1981) focuses on the role of families in mental illness. Hammer (1981) feels that social supports are not always positive and as such may misdirect planning and treatment for schizophrenics. She reports that while schizophrenic subjects seem to receive as much support as nonschizophrenics, they do not give support. The type of networks in which individuals and groups participate, how they are aided and under what circumstances, assumes tremendous importance and suggest new approaches to community-based interventions.

DEINSTITUTIONALIZATION: MORE APPARENT THAN REAL?

Deinstitutionalization (DE) helped to change the organizational structure of the mental health service delivery system and modified policies and practices in institutions. It also highlighted the importance of social support systems programs, family involvement, and alternative living situations to maintain the chronically mentally ill in the community. It has served to reemphasize the complexity of problems faced by the chronically mentally ill and severely questioned the sufficiency of the medical model. While state hospital census has markedly decreased, there is an increased concern about whether the deinstitutionalized are better off in terms of quality of life and health status. DE as a concept rests on a set of assumptions about the needs of the chronically mentally ill in relation to institutional vs community-based care and treatment. These assumptions are now becoming increasingly questioned (Goldman et al 1983). There is a high proportion of mentally disabled persons in institution-like community-based facilities. In addition, Weinstein (1982) points out that there have been only a few studies which have asked deinstitutionalized patients about their perceptions of the institution. He suggests that many ex-mental patients view the institution in more favorable terms than was previously supposed.

At least 60 major publications have appeared since 1979, ranging from anecdotal accounts (Sheehan 1982) to scholarly works documenting the impact of program and systems level interventions (Levine 1980, Talbott 1981, Krauss & Slavinsky 1982, Tessler & Goldman 1982). Some of these are focused on the planning of alternative care facilities (Rutman 1981) such as nursing homes (Vladeck 1980), and others are more concerned with specific research issues such as public attitudes toward the chronically mentally ill in the community (Rabkin et al 1980), the pioneering work of Gordon Paul on treatment modalities (Rhoades 1981) and cross-disciplinary perspectives (Lerman 1981). In addition, several journals have published special issues on DE. These journals include the *Journal of Social Issues* (1981), *Archives of General Psychiatry* (1980), *Milbank Memorial Fund Quarterly* (1979), and *Hospital & Community Psychiatry* (1982, 1983). Topics such as community support systems for chronic patients (Stein 1979), longitudinal follow-up of the Fairweather Lodge (Fairweather 1980), community residential treatment (Budson 1981), and the young adult chronic patient (Pepper & Ryglewicz 1982) have appeared in a series entitled *New Directions in Mental Health* (R. Lamb, editor).

Alternative Treatment and the Chronic Mental Patient

Except for a few well-conceptualized and supported programs, DE has not lived up to its humanitarian goals. Discharge from the institution, in many cases, has resulted in increased exposure to a hostile environment, lack of health care, and deterioration of living conditions (Gruenberg & Archer 1979, Rose 1979, Lamb 1981, G. E. Miller 1981). Fifteen years after DE was formally launched as an intervention policy, NIMH, responding to mounting criticism, began the Community Support Program (CSP). As a demonstration program, the CSP was to facilitate planning and coordination of program services for the chronically mentally ill. Highlights on the CSP federal initiative are covered in *A Network for Caring* (Turner & Stockdill 1982), and Tessler & Goldman (1982) present the evaluation results of various CSP programs. There are some encouraging signs. Rightly, the dissemination of these findings would be aided if they appeared in journals or as an NIMH report. Presently, CSP efforts are stifled by a limited federal funding, and it is still unknown whether, in the reduction of funding, the CSP philosophy will be taken up and acted upon by the states.

Braun et al (1981), in a critical review of outcome studies on DE, conclude that satisfactory DE appears to depend on the availability of appropriate programs for care in the community—a finding that applies to virtually all types of chronic conditions. While Test (1981) offers some laudable conditions regarding effective treatment of the chronic patient in a minimally restrictive environment, it is unrealistic to suppose such approaches can be implemented given the scarce resources presently available. The extensive work by Stein & Test (1980) involves issues of continuity of care and the provision of appropriate resources for the DE patient. They contend that in the long run high direct costs will reduce overall patient costs and will yield a richer quality of life. Promising alternative treatment, programs such as Horizon House in Philadelphia and Fountain House in New York City utilize a variety of resources, including inexpensive apartments, job training, psychiatric coverage, and numerous social and recreational activities. It is to be hoped that these promising programs will be able to articulate the factors that contribute to their success, thus permitting replication in other settings. Of particular concern is whether these programs meet the needs of long-term chronic patients who have limited education and manifest little or no job and social skills before hospitalization. There are, however, still a number of methodological difficulties in assessing quality of life variables and relating these in a causal fashion to the DE movement (Schulberg & Bromet 1981, Morrissey 1982, Tessler & Goldman 1982).

Apropos of quality, the literature suggests that approximately 50% of the deinstitutionalized live in settings that provide little or no supervision: private homes, single room occupancy hotels (SROs), boarding houses, or unsupervised cooperative apartments (Tessler et al 1982); are uneployed or, if working, hold low-paying service jobs; and, on the average, are hospitalized for approximately one month every 3 to 5 years (Estroff 1981).

An emerging population of young adult chronic patients has recently come to the attention of investigators (Schwartz & Goldfinger 1981, Lamb 1982, Sheets et al 1982). This group evidences a unique combination of problems involving violence, a lack of control, and management in community settings (Stelovich 1979), thus placing considerable challenges on service delivery systems (Bachrach 1982b, Lamb 1982, Pepper & Ryglewicz 1982). To date, little research has documented the plight of the young adult chronic patient and few programs have been developed to address their special needs (Spivack et al 1982). Further, little is known of patients who do not participate in community aftercare treatment programs.

Issues of Restriction and Freedom for the Chronically Dependent

The balance between the conflicting needs of the chronically mentally ill as patients and as citizens is still unresolved. There is a lack of conceptual clarity and definitional rigor regarding the area of restrictiveness (Bachrach 1980), and vagueness of the term "least restrictive alternative" has allowed a number of unwarranted assumptions to be made about the chronically mentally ill on the social, legal, and clinical levels. Also, faulty generalizations about service delivery to the chronically mentally ill have occurred (Miller 1982). Bachrach (1980) suggests that a number of levels of restrictive conditions (e.g. cross-classify patient according to degree of supervision and functional ability) be taken into account when planning community-based services for the chronic patient. The chronic patient is faced with the task of coordinating a variety of disjunct services within the community. Unable to perform such a task, many drop out of service care and join the ranks of the "not" served. There is little advocacy for the rights of the chronically mentally ill (Bachrach 1982a). Bloom & Asher (1982) give a well-rounded presentation of the main issues in patient rights and advocacy. In the same volume, Monahan (1982) makes a valuable distinction between positive and negative patient rights and contends that a macrosociological analysis of patient rights and patient advocacy should be among the highest research priorities in the field. Anchor Mental Health Association (1982), as an example of an innovative, inexpensive local SCI, has created a community guidebook for the former ex-mental patient which gives a list of all halfway houses, formal social support systems, rehabilitation centers, and agencies in the Washington, D.C. area.

The Role of Institutions in DE

Several authors speak to the changing roles of institutions in light of DE. Morrissey et al (1980), in a well-balanced and thorough presentation, describe the historical and evolutionary changes in treatment policies at Worcester State Hospital. They contend that the two-tiered system of care insures a continuance of state hospitals and perhaps the continuance of problems between institutional facilties and community-based services. Thus, continuity of care and patient monitoring systems could be difficult to sustain.

Shore & Shapiro (1979) note that DE has changed the type of patient population treated in institutions. They identify three types of patients: the "old long-stay," the "new long-stay," and the "short-stay." Each of these groups requires different treatment plans and different amounts of attention by staff. Dorwart (1980) found the patient population in a Massachusetts state hospital to be predominantly comprised of individuals with acute psychotic symptoms, labels of dangerousness, and needs for intensive care and social skills training. To care effectively for their unique problems, Ashbaugh & Bradley (1979) contend that facilities must be well-organized and adequately staffed. This implies resources which are presently unavailable to most insitutions. Consequently, institutions as well as community-based facilities are faced with similar problems in the care and treatment of the chronically mentally ill. In short, the myriad arrangement of services to this heterogeneous population demands a systems approach for solutions (Bachrach 1982a). Such a perspective is not addressed in the experimental or synthesized community support systems projects, nor is it apparent in institutional planning and residential care programs.

Research and Evaluation Issues

Research on DE and the fate of the DE patient is hampered by the frequent failure to recognize that there are degrees of institutionalization ranging from traditional restrictions of freedom and lack of treatment (the warehouse concept) to benign regimes which impose a minimum of restrictions and have a treatment program. Also, there has been a failure of middle class planners to comprehend fully the life-styles and priorities of the poor. The literature is lacking sound evaluations accounting for differential adjustment patterns (Talbott 1981) and, we note, has not substantially advanced beyond the descriptive level. This bottleneck in research activity appears to be due partly to a lack of standardized measures and comparable definitional terms. A host of evaluation studies have been published on various model programs and alternative treatment packages; however, an assessment of the totality of treatment effects has yet to be done. Additionally, little attention has been paid to impact evaluation research and a systems theory approach to examining DE (Bachrach & Lamb 1982).

The current status of DE is an example of failing to consider the framework presented at the beginning of this chapter. Until the contending forces of genuine humanistic motivation, political and economic realities, plus legitimate community concerns are equitably resolved, DE will remain a vexing and troublesome SCI. Any reappraisal should certainly include a consideration of the definitions and purposes of asylum and sanctuary.

UNDERSERVED AND UNSERVED POPULATIONS

Reasonably accurate estimation of what groups are unserved, underserved, or badly served is difficult and fraught with value judgments at all levels. Many individuals, young and old, singly and collectively, need some form of assistance; however, it is a formidable problem to ascertain genuine needs and assign priorities for this diverse group of individuals. For example, on all fronts (e.g. mental health, education, etc) the persons within the age range 10 to 14 years remain particularly underserved or badly served. If indeed 10% of the population at any one time are in need of mental health services, then only about one-third come to the attention of any sort of mental health treatment facility. The fate (good or bad) of the rest of this population is as yet undetermined.

Snowden (1982) has compiled a timely volume which addresses the complex issues facing the underserved (e.g. minorities, women, children, and the elderly). Gonzales et al (1983) provide a review of the current status of underserved and badly served groups and note that the impending takeover by the states of such programs as AFDC, Medicare, and Food Stamps is unlikely to result in an ideological advance. The Manpower Demonstration Research Corporation (MDRC) (1980) has designed, implemented, and evaluated a number of interventive projects addressing the needs of underserved populations. The national work support project, for example, demonstrated that welfare recipients (females on AFDC) could acquire and maintain employment after work skills training, counseling, and general supportive environments. Additionally, a significant proportion of the exaddict population obtained jobs with adequate earnings and were less likely subsequently to be involved in drug-related or other types of crime. It was, however, only marginally effective with exconvicts (nondrug-related offenses) and had little or no effect on adults who were early school dropouts. Auletta (1982) details the human aspects of the MDRC programs and coins the term "underclass" to cover some 9,000,000 Americans who have not assimilated the dominant American culture.

Rural Mental Health, Ethnic Minorities, and Women

In rural mental health a welcome handbook has appeared (Keller & Murray 1982). This volume addresses recent changes in rural life, the mental health of rural populations, and the critical factors that influence service delivery. There are generally few health/mental health resources in these areas and very few rural mental health training programs (Solomon 1980). At the same time, there is a high proportion of the elderly, migrant workers and persons in poor physical health, all needing such services. Certainly appropriate SCIs, meeting the unique needs of rural populations, deserve high priority.

A number of research developments have occurred for ethnic minority populations. Jones & Korchin (1982), in a sophisticated edited volume on minority mental health, examine change-oriented community interventions and organizational structures designed to empower particular ethnic groups such as

Japanese Americans, Chinese, Blacks, Hispanics, and Cubans. An exhaustive annotated bibliography of American Indian research is now available (Kelso & Attneave 1981), and the *Hispanic Journal of Behavioral Sciences*, first published in 1980, clearly marks a movement toward more rigorous experimental research on the Hispanic cultures. Barón (1981) has edited a volume rich in foundation work for Chicano psychology, and M. Ramirez (1983) advances the theoretical base by including a bicultural/bicognitive perspective. In terms of mental health service utilization, more clarity is being achieved (Acosta 1979). D. G. Ramirez (1982), in an extensive study on the underutilization of mental health services by Mexican Americans in Texas, suggests that the relative youth (median age 17 years) of the Mexican American population is a major factor in their underutilization of services. D. G. Ramirez predicts increased utilization of mental health services as the Hispanic population grows older. This parsimonious explanation is a welcome replacement for the rhetoric which has accumulated in the area of Mexican American underutilization of mental health facilities. Hopefully, similar findings will be obtained with other Hispanic populations.

Methodological problems in studying women in the midst of economic, social, and environmental changes have recently been addressed (Stewart & Platt 1982). Contrary to popular notions of service utilization, women are still underserved, especially when the problem runs counter to societal stereotypes (Gonzales et al 1983). For example, seldom are the needs of the female alcoholic taken into account by program designers and service providers (Russo & Sobel 1981). Clearly much remains to be done. The rapid increase in centers for battered women and counseling devoted to women's problems testify that the needs of this group are not being met within the existing context of community services. Paradoxically, the involvement of women's organizations in the fabric of American life has increased as well. Clearly, research in this area could expand our knowledge base by including information on the vast array of organized women's groups and more informal systems of mutual support for women.

Concern for the Elderly and Children

By the year 2000 one out of every six Americans will be over the age of 65. We are witnessing increased political activism of the elderly population at the local level (e.g. the Gray Panthers) and a rise in policy-related literature such as *Ageing and Society* (Johnson 1982). The American Psychological Associations' Boulder Conference in 1981 is a benchmark for psychology's involvement in older populations (Santos & VandenBos 1982). In addition, The White House Conference on Aging produced a series of volumes on national policy issues and proceedings (Armitage 1981). These hopeful developments should not obscure the myriad problems that need to be dealt with at national and community levels. The developing political "clout" of the elderly is an avenue for influencing policy.

Somewhat in contrast, Grubb & Lazerson (1982) carefully detail the lack of equitable distribution of resources and services for children in proportion to the entire population. Gabarino (1981) asserts that the utilization and dissemination of research-based knowledge about children has low priority in the activities of social scientists, policymakers and practitioners, while Garduque & Peters (1982) note the gap between information needs of child care program personnel and developmental research. Two out of three seriously disturbed children in the U.S. are not receiving the mental health services they need, and only 17% of CMHC funds are spent on children. Under the new mental health block grant program, not a cent is required to be spent on disturbed children (Children's Defense Fund 1982). The assault on children is all-pervasive. Reduction in support for nutrition, education, day care, safety, and AFDC typify the low priority to SCIs for children. If the priorities of a nation are mirrored in its SCIs, the welfare of children and youth are clearly not uppermost in the minds and intentions of policymakers.

Encouragingly, Zigler & Valentine (1979) detail the clear gains to children and families in the Head Start Program, and Lazar & Darlington (1982) present the highly significant combined results of 11 studies demonstrating the beneficial long-lasting effects of day care. Clearly some SCIs work. However, the failure to commit adequate resources for children is particularly disheartening when, for example, single-parent families (mostly mothers) today comprise the largest poverty group in America. We hope that the present reality will give way to more optimistic findings in the future.

Suggestions for Research Directions

Our review of the burgeoning and scattered literature in the "underserved" section strongly suggests the need for a more precise definition of the populations covered. For example, the comparison of Hispanics and Anglos without careful specification leads to understandably vague and nonreplicable findings. Generalities such as the underclass, the underserved, single parent families, rural mental health, the needs of women, although valuable for preliminary identification of groups or areas, must eventually undergo refinement if research is to be advanced in the area of SCIs. Such refinements, in our opinion, are best forthcoming through the development of an expanded psychology of individual differences.

CONCLUSIONS

Our review has touched on only a small portion of the programs and activities under the title of SCIs. The many diciplines and belief systems involved in SCIs raise the question of the optimum role for psychologists and psychology.

Although we note an encouraging increase in published research, we also note a clear need for more methodological and procedural sophistication to produce the knowledge required for the planning and execution of effective SCIs. This calls for a movement from the laboratory of the university to the laboratory of the community, using data often already in the possession of an agency, group, or neighborhood or by "piggy-backing" onto an ongoing SCI or one in the planning stage. This holds for more traditional as well as newer SCIs, the "hard" as well as the "soft" areas of psychology. The necessary cognitive reorientations for SCI research can be facilitated by open and continued dialogue between those who fund and administer programs and those who wish to research and evaluate them.

It is in the research and consultant areas that psychologists can make unique contributions. Existing fragmentations can be reduced, ambiguities clarified, and more unified concepts and paradigms can be advanced. Many of the conditions to which SCIs presently address themselves can be prevented or reduced were valid knowledge available about causality and the collaborative efforts of communities and investigators harnessed. We urge a social and research policy which encourages psychologists to adopt appropriate ecological and system approaches to unraveling the complex interactive phenomena to which SCIs address themselves. The potential contributions and benefits to psychology are enormous, the challenge formidable indeed.

ACKNOWLEDGMENTS

Our gratitude to Jerry B. Harvey, Brian Wilcox, Brian Rasmussen, and Jeffrey Anderson for helpful comments about the manuscript; to Shannon Minter and Terry Foster for locating library materials; to Karen Bordelon, Patricia Britton, and Nadea Gizelbach for compilation of the bibliography. A special note to Ms. Bertha Shanblum for putting up with all of us while typing many drafts of this manuscript.

Literature Cited

Acosta, F. X. 1979. Barriers between mental health services and Mexican Americans: An examination of a paradox. *Am. J. Community Psychol.* 7:503–20

Adler, P. T. 1982. An analysis of the concept of competence in individuals and social systems. *Community Ment. Health J.* 18:34–45

Albee, G. W. 1982a. The politics of nature and nurture. *Am. J. Community Psychol.* 10:1–36

Albee, G. W. 1982b. Preventing psychopathology and promoting human potential. *Am. Psychol.* 37:1043–50

Alpert, J. L., ed. 1982. *Psychological Consultation in Educational Settings*. San Francisco: Jossey-Bass

Alpert, J. L., Meyers, J. 1983. *Training in Consultation*. Springfield, Ill: Thomas

Anchor Mental Health Association. 1982. *Community Guidebook*. Washington DC

Andrulis, D. P., Mazade, N. A. 1983. American mental health policy: Changing directions in the 80s. *Hosp. Community Psychiatry* 34:601–6

Armitage, C. C., Chairman. 1981. *Final Report on the 1981 White House Conference on Aging*, Vols. 1–3. Washington DC: GPO

Aronowitz, E., ed. 1982. *Prevention Strategies for Mental Health*. New York: Prodist

Ashbaugh, J. W., Bradley, V. J. 1979. Linking deinstitutionalization of patients with hospital phase-down: The difference between success and failure. *Hosp. Community Psychiatry* 30:105–10

Auletta, K. 1982. *The Underclass.* New York: Random House

Austin, M. J., Hershey, W. E., eds. 1982. *Handbook on Mental Health Administration.* San Francisco: Jossey-Bass

Bachrach, L. L. 1980. Is the least restrictive environment always the best? Sociological and semantic implications. *Hosp. Community Psychiatry* 31:97–102

Bachrach, L. L. 1982a. Assessment of outcomes in community support systems: Results, problems, and limitations. *Schizophr. Bull.* 8:39–61

Bachrach, L. L. 1982b. Young adult chronic patients: An analytical review of the literature. *Hosp. Community Psychiatry* 33:189–97

Bachrach, L. L., Lamb, R. 1982. Conceptual issues in the evaluaton of the deinstitutionalization movement. See Stahler & Tash 1982

Barón, A. Jr., ed. 1981. *Explorations in Chicano Psychology.* New York: Praeger

Bayer, R., Feldman, S., Reich, W. 1981. *Ethical Issues in Mental Health Policy and Administration.* DHHS Publ. (ADM) 81–1116

Berkowitz, W. R. 1982. *Community Impact: Creating Grass Roots Change.* Cambridge, Mass: Schenkman

Berlin, R. M., Kales, J. D., Humphrey, F. J. II, Kales, A. 1981. The patient care crises in community mental health centers: A need for more psychiatric involvement. *Am. J. Psychiatry* 138:450–54

Bermant, G., Kelman, H. C., Warwick, D. P., eds. 1978. *The Ethics of Social Intervention.* Washington: Hemisphere

Biegel, D. E., Naparstek, A. J. 1982. *Community Support Systems and Mental Health.* New York: Springer

Bloom, B. L. 1979. Prevention of mental disorders: Recent advances in theory and practice. *Community Ment. Health J.* 15:179–91

Bloom, B. L. 1980. Social and community interventions. *Ann. Rev. Psychol.* 31:111–42

Bloom, B. L. 1981. The logic and urgency of primary prevention. *Hosp. Community Psychiatry* 32:839–43

Bloom, B. L. 1983. *Community Mental Health: A General Introduction.* Monterey: Brooks/Cole. 2nd ed.

Bloom, B. L., Asher, S. J., eds. 1982. *Psychiatric Patient Rights and Patient Advocacy.* New York: Human Sci. Press

Bloom, B. L., Hodges, W. F., Caldwell, R. A. 1982. A preventive program for the newly separated: Initial evaluation. *Am. J. Community Psychol.* 10:251–64

Braun, P., Kochansky, G., Shapiro, R., Greenberg, S., Gudeman, J., et al. 1981.

Overview: Deinstitutionalization of psychiatric patients, a critical review of outcome studies. *Am. J. Psychiatry* 138:736–49

Brickman, P., Rabinowitz, V. C., Karuza, J., Coates, D., Cohn, E., et al. 1982. Models of helping and coping. *Am. Psychol.* 37:368–84

Broskowski, A., Marks, E., Budman, S., eds. 1981. *Linking Health and Mental Health,* Vol. 2. Beverly Hills: Sage

Budson, R. D. 1981. *New Directions for Mental Health Services: Issues in Community Residential Care.* No. 11. San Francisco: Jossey-Bass

California Department of Mental Health: Mental Health Promotion Branch. 1981. *Wellness Resource Bulletin*

Children's Defense Fund. 1982. *Unclaimed Children, the Failure of Public Responsibility to Children and Adolescents in Need of Mental Health Services.* Washington DC: GPO

Connections: Bulletin of the International Network for Social Network Analysis. 1982. Vol. 5: Structural Analysis Programme, Univ. Toronto, Canada

Cowen, E. L. 1973. Social and community interventions. *Ann. Rev. Psychol.* 24:423–72

Cowen, E. L. 1980. The wooing of primary prevention. *Am. J. Community Psychol.* 8:258–84

Cowen, E. L. 1982. The special number: A compleat roadmap. *Am. J. Community Psychol.* 10:239–49

Cowen, E. L., issue ed. 1982. *Special issue: Research in Primary Prevention in Mental Health. Am. J. Community Psychol.* 10:239–67

Cowen, E. L., Gesten, E., Davidson, E., Wilson, A. 1981. Hairdressers as caregivers II: Relationships between helper characteristics and helping behaviors and feelings. *J. Prev.* 1:225–39

Curtis, M. J., Zins, J. E., eds. 1981. *The Theory and Practice of School Consultation.* Springfield, Ill: Thomas

D'Augelli, A. R. 1982a. A funny thing happened on the way to the community: Consultation and education in community mental health centers, or how I learned to stop worrying about prevention and love third-party payments. *J. Primary Prev.* 2:235–39

D'Augelli A. R. 1982b. Historical synthesis of consultation and education. See Ritter 1982, pp. 3–50

D'Augelli, A. R., Ehrlich, R. P. 1982. Evaluation of a community-based system for training natural helpers. II. Effects on informal helping activities. *Am. J. Community Psychol.* 10:447–56

Davis, D. Z., Osborne, G. E., Dahn, A. J.,

Conyne, R. K., Matice, K. L. 1981. Caveats in the consultation process. *Adm. Ment. Health* 2:137–48

Dooley, D., Catalano, R. 1980. Economic change as a cause of behavioral disorder. *Psychol. Bull.* 87:450–68

Dorwart, R. A. 1980. Deinstitutionalization: Who is left behind? *Hosp. Community Psychiatry* 31:336–38

Estroff, S. E. 1981. Psychiatric deinstitutionalization: A sociocultural analysis. *J. Soc. Issues* 37:116–31

Fairweather, G. W. 1980. *New Directions for Mental Health Services: The Fairweather Lodge: A Twenty-Five Year Retrospective.* No. 7. San Francisco: Jossey-Bass

Felner, R. D., Jason, L. A., eds. 1983. *Preventive Psychology: Theory, Research and Practice.* New York: Pergamon

Fink, P., Weinstein, S. 1979. Whatever happened to psychiatry? The deprofessionalization of community mental health centers. *Am. J. Psychiatry* 136:406–9

Gabarino, J. 1981. Knowledge in the service of children and youth. *Child. Youth Serv. Rev.* 3:269–75

Gallessich, J. 1982. *The Profession and Practice of Consultation.* San Francisco: Jossey-Bass

Garduque, L., Peters, D. 1982. Toward reapproachment in child care research: An optimistic view. *Child Care Q.* 2:12–21

Gartner, A., Riessman, F. 1980. *Help: A Working Guide to Self Help Groups.* New York: Viewpoint, Franklin Watts

Gartner, A., Riessman, F. 1982. Self-help and mental health. *Hosp. Community Psychol.* 33:631–35

Geller, E. S., Johnson, R. P., Pelton, S. L. 1982. Community-based interventions for encouraging safety belt use. *Am. J. Community Psychol.* 10:183–95

Gibbs, L. M. 1982. *Love Canal: My Story.* New York: Grove

Gibbs, M. S, Lachenmeyer, J. R., Sigal, J., eds. 1980. *Community Psychology.* New York: Gardner

Glasscote, R. M., Chief. 1980. *Preventing Mental Illness: Efforts and Attitudes.* Washington DC: Joint Inf. Serv. Am. Psychiatric Assoc.

Glenwick, D., Jason, L., eds. 1980. *Behavioral Community Psychology.* New York: Praeger

Goldman, H. H., Adams, N. H., Taube, C. A. 1983. Deinstitutionalization: The data demythologized. *Hosp. Community Psychiatry* 34:129–34

Gonzales, L. R., Hays, R. B., Bond, M. A., Kelly, J. G. 1983. Community mental health. In *The Clinical Psychology Handbook*, ed. M. Hersen, A. E. Kazdin, A. S. Bellack. New York: Pergamon

Gottlieb, B. H. 1981. *Social Networks and Social Support.* Beverly Hills: Sage

Gottlieb, B. H., Hall, A. 1980. Social networks and the utilization of preventive mental health services. See Price et al 1980, pp. 167–94

Grady, M. A., Gibson, J. S., Trickett, E. J. 1981. *Mental Health Consultation: Theory, Practice, and Research 1973–1978.* DHHS Publ. (ADM) 81–948

Greenblatt, M., Becerra, R. M., Serafetinides, E. A. 1982. Social networks and mental health: An overview. *Am. J. Psychiatry* 139:977–84

Grubb, W. N., Lazerson, M. 1982. *Broken Promises.* New York: Basic Books

Gruenberg, E. M., Archer, J. 1979. Abandonment of responsibility for the seriously mentally ill. *Milbank Mem. Fund Q./Health Soc.* 57:485–506

Hammer, M. 1981. Social supports, social networks, and schizophrenia. *Schizophr. Bull.* 7:45–56

Hatfield, A. B. 1981. Self-help groups for families of the mentally ill. *Soc. Work.* 26:408–13

Heller, K. 1979. The effects of social support: Prevention and treatment implications. In *Maximizing Treatment Gains; Transfer Enhancement in Psychotherapy*, ed. A. P. Goldstein, F. H. Kanfer, pp. 353–82. New York: Academic

Heller, K., Swindle, R. W. 1983. Social networks, perceived social support and coping with stress. In *Preventive Psychology: Theory, Research and Practice in Community Intervention*, ed. R. D. Felner, L. A. Jason, pp. 87–103, New York: Pergammon

Holahan, C. J., Moos, R. H. 1981. Social support and psychological distress: A longitudinal analysis. *J. Abnorm. Psychol.* 90: 365–70

Insel, P. M., ed. 1980. *Environmental Variables and the Prevention of Mental Illness.* Lexington, Mass: Lexington Books

Iscoe, I. 1980. Conceptual barriers to training for the primary prevention of psychopathology. In *Prevention Through Political Action and Social Change*, ed. J. M. Joffe, G. W. Albee. Hanover, NH: Univ. Press New England

Jeger, A. M., Slotnick, R. S., eds. 1982. *Community Mental Health and Behavioral-Ecology.* New York: Plenum

Johnson, M. L., ed. 1982. *Ageing and Society. J. Cent. Policy Ageing and Br. Soc. Gerontol.*, Vol. 2. Cambridge, Mass: Cambridge Univ. Press

Jones, E. E., Korchin, S. J. 1982. *Minority Mental Health.* New York: Praeger

Katz, A. H. 1981. Self-help and mutual aid: An emerging social movement. *Ann. Rev. Sociol.* 7:129–55

Keller, P. A., Murray, J. D. 1982. *Handbook of Rural Community Mental Health*. New York: Human Sci. Press

Kelly, J. G., Snowden, L. R., Muñoz, R. F. 1977. Social and community interventions. *Ann. Rev. Psychol.* 28:323–61

Kelso, D. R., Attneave, C. L., eds. 1981. *Bibliography of North American Indian Mental Health*. Conn: Greenwood

Ketterer, R. 1981. *Consultation and Education in Mental Health: Problems and Prospects,* Vol. 3, Sage Studies in Community Mental Health Ser. Beverly Hills: Sage

Kiesler, C. A. 1981. Barriers to effective knowledge use in national mental health policy. *Health Policy Q.* 1:201–15

Kiesler, C. A. 1982. Mental hospitals and alternative care. *Am. Psychol.* 37:349–60

Kiesler, C. A., Sibulkin, A. E. 1982. People, clinical episodes, and mental hospitalization: A multiple-source method of estimation. In *Advances in Applied Social Psychology,* ed. R. F. Kidd, M. J. Saks, 2:131–61. Hillsdale, NJ: Erlbaum

Klerman, G. 1981. *Report of the Administrator: Alcohol, Drug Abuse and Mental Health Administration, 1980.* DHHS Publ. 81–1165

Knight, B., Wollert, R., Levy, L., Frame, C., Padgett, V. 1980. Self-help groups: The members' perspectives. *Am. J. Community Psychol.* 8:53–65

Krauss, J. B., Slavinsky, A. T. 1982. *The Chronically Ill Psychiatric Patient and the Community.* Boston: Blackwell

Lamb, H. R. 1981. What did we really expect from deinstitutionalization? *Hosp. Community Psychiatry* 32:105–9

Lamb, H. R. 1982. Young adult chronic patients: The new drifters. *Hosp. Community Psychiatry* 33:465–68

Lamb, H. R., Zusman, J. 1979.. Primary prevention in perspective. *Am. J. Psychiatry* 136:12–17

Lamb, H. R. Zusman, J. 1981. A new look at primary prevention. *Hosp. Community Psychiatry* 32:839–43

Langsley, D. G. 1980. The community mental health center: Does it treat patients? *Hosp. Community Psychiatry* 31:815–19

Lazar, I., Darlington, R. B. 1982. Lasting effects of early education. *Monogr. Soc. Res. Child Dev.* 47:1–151

Lerman, P. 1981. *Deinstitutionalization: A Cross-Problem Analysis.* DHHS Publ. (ADM) 81–987

Levine, A. 1982. *Love Canal: Science, Politics, and People.* Lexington, Mass: Lexington Books

Levine, M. 1979. Congress (and evaluators) ought to pay more attention to history. *Am. J. Community Psychol.* 7:1–17

Levine, M. 1980. *From State Hospital to Psychiatric Center: The Implementation of Planned Organizational Change.* Lexington, Mass: Lexington Books

Levine, M. 1981. *The History and Politics of Community Mental Health.* New York: Oxford Univ. Press

Lieberman, M. A., Bond, G. R. 1978. Self-help groups: Problems of measuring outcome. *Small Group Behav.* 9:221–41

Lorion, R. P. 1983. Evaluating preventive interventions: Guidelines for the serious social change agent. See Felner & Jason 1983, pp. 251–68

Lorion, R. P., Lounsbury, J. W. 1982. Conceptual and methodological considerations in evaluating preventive interventions. See Stahler & Tash 1982, pp. 23–57

Lounsbury, J. W., Leader, D. S., Meares, E. P., Cook, M. P. 1980. An analytic review of research in community psychology. *Am. J. Community Psychol.* 8:415–41

Mannino, F. V. 1981. Empirical perspectives in mental health consultation. *J. Prev.* 1:147–55

Manpower Demonstration Research Corporation, N. Y. 1980. *Summary and Findings of the National Supported Work Demonstration.* Cambridge: Ballinger

McClure, L., Cannon, D., Allen, S., Belton, E., Connor, P., et al. 1980. Community psychology concepts and research base: Promise and product. *Am. Psychol.* 35: 1000–11

McGuire, T. G., Weisbrod, B. A. 1981. *Economics and Mental Health.* DHHS Publ. (ADM) 81–1114

Mechanic, D. 1980. *Mental Health and Social Policy.* New Jersey: Prentice Hall

Meyers, J., Parsons, R. C., Martin, R. 1979. *Mental Health Consultation in the Schools.* San Francisco: Jossey-Bass

Miller, G. E. 1981. Barriers to serving the chronically mentally ill. *Psychiatric Q.* 53:118–31

Miller, R. D. 1982. The least restrictive alternative: Hidden meanings and agendas. *Community Ment. Health J.* 18:46–54

Monahan, J. 1982. Three lingering issues in patient rights. See Bloom and Asher 1982, pp. 263–77

Morrissey, J. P. 1982. Deinstitutionalizing the mentally ill: Processes, outcomes, and new directions. In *Deviance and Mental Illness,* ed. W. R. Gove, Beverly Hills: Sage

Morrissey, J. P., Goldman, H. H., Klerman, L. V., et al, eds. 1980. *The Enduring Asylum: Cycles of Institutional Reform at Worcester State Hospital.* New York: Grune & Stratton

Moss, H. A., Hess, R., Swift, C., eds. 1982. *Prevention in Human Services. Early Intervention Programs for Infants,* Vol. 1. New York: Haworth

Munõz, R. F., Snowden, L. R., Kelly, J. G., eds. 1979. *Social Psychological Research in Community Settings*. San Francisco: Jossey-Bass

Murray, J. D., Keller, P. A., eds. 1982. *Innovations in Rural Mental Health*. New York: Human Sci. Press

Novaco, R. W., Monahan, J. 1980. Research in community psychology: An analysis of work published in the first 6 years of the *American Journal of Community Psychology*. *Am. J. Community Psychol.* 8:131–45

O'Neill, P. 1981. Cognitive community psychology. *Am. Psychol.* 36:457–69

O'Neill, P., Trickett, E. J. 1982. *Community Consultation*. San Francisco: Jossey-Bass

Pepper, B., Ryglewicz, H., eds. 1982. *New Directions for Mental Health Services: The Young Adult Chronic Patient*. No. 14. San Francisco: Jossey-Bass

Porritt, D. 1979. Social support in crisis: Quantity or quality. *Soc. Sci. Med.* 13A:715–21

Price, R. H., Ketterer, R., Bader, B., Monahan, J., eds. 1980. *Prevention in Mental Health: Research, Policy and Practice*. Beverly Hills: Sage

Price, R. H., Polister, P. E., eds. 1980. *Evaluation and Action in the Social Environment*. New York: Academic

Rabkin, J., Gelb, L., Lazar, J. B., eds. 1980. *Attitudes Toward the Mentally Ill: Research Prospectives*. Rep. NIMH workshop. Rockville, Md: NIMH

Ramirez, D. G. 1982. *An empirical assessment of the concept of Mexican Americans' underutilization of mental health services*. PhD thesis. Univ. Texas, Austin, DAI 43:3-B

Ramirez, M. 1983. *Psychology of the Americas: Mestizo Perspectives on Personality and Mental Health*. New York: Pergamon

Rappaport, J. 1981. In praise of paradox: A social policy of empowerment over prevention. *Am. J. Community Psychol.* 9:1–25

Rhoades, L. J. 1981. *Treating and Assessing the Chronically Mentally Ill: The Pioneering Research of Gordon L. Paul*. DHHS Publ. (ADM) 81–1100

Riessman, F. 1980. The role of the paraprofessional in the mental health crisis. *Paraprof. J.* 1:1–3

Ritter, D. R., ed. 1982. *Consultation, Education and Prevention in Community Mental Health*. Springfield: Thomas

Rodolfa, E., R., Hungerford, L. 1982. Self-help groups: A referral resource for professional therapists. *Prof. Psychol.* 13:334–53

Rogawski, A. S., ed. 1979. *New Directions for Mental Health Services: Mental Health Consultation and Community Setting*, No. 3. San Francisco: Jossey-Bass

Rose, S. M. 1979. Deciphering and deinstitutionalization: complexities in policy and program analysis. *Milbank Mem. Fund Q./ Health Soc.* 57:429–57

Russo, N. P., Sobel, S. D. 1981. Sex preference in the utilization of mental health facilities. *Prof. Psychol.* 12:7–19

Rutman, I. D., ed. 1981. *Planning for Deinstitutionalization*. *Hum. Serv. Monogr. Ser.* 28. DHEW Publ. (OS) 76–130

Santos, J. D., VandenBos, G. R., eds. 1982. *Psychology and the Older Adult: Challenges for Training in the 1980's*. Washington DC: Am. Psychol. Assoc.

Sarason, S. B. 1981. *Psychology Misdirected*. New York: Free Press

Sarason, S. B., Lorentz, E. 1979. *The Challenge of the Resource Exchange Network*. San Francisco: Jossey-Bass

Schensul, S. L., Schensul, J. J. 1982. Self-help groups and advocacy. See Weber & Cohen 1982, pp. 298–336

Schulberg, H. C., Bromet, E. 1981. Strategies for evaluating the outcome of community services for the chronically mentally ill. *Am. J. Psychiatry* 138:930–35

Schulberg, H. C., Killilea, M., eds. 1982. *The Modern Practice of Community Mental Health: A Volume in Honor of Gerald Caplan*. San Francisco: Jossey-Bass

Schwartz, S. R., Goldfinger, S. M. 1981. The new chronic patient: Clinical characteristics of an emerging group. *Hosp. Community Psychiatry* 32:470–74

Seidman, E., ed. 1983. *Handbook of Social Intervention*. Beverly Hills: Sage

Sheehan, S. 1982. *Is There No Place on Earth For Me?* Boston: Houghton Mifflin

Sheets, J. L., Prevost, J. A., Reihman, J. 1982. The young adult chronic patient: Three hypothesized subgroups. See Pepper & Ryglewicz 1982, pp. 15–24

Shore, M. F. 1981. Marking time in the land of plenty: Reflections on mental health in the United States. *Am. J Orthopsychiatry* 51:391–402

Shore, M. F., Shapiro, R. 1979. The effect of deinstitutionalization on the state hospital. *Hosp. Community Psychiatry* 30:605–8

Shure, M. B., Spivack, G. 1981. The problem solving approach to adjustment: a competency-building model of primary prevention. *Prev. Hum. Serv.* 1:87–103.

Silverman, W. H. 1981. *Community Mental Health: A Sourcebook for Professionals and Advisory Board Members*. New York: Praeger

Snow, D., Swift, C. 1981. *Recommended Policies and Procedures for Consultation and Education Services Within Community Mental Health Systems/Agencies*. Washington DC: Natl. Counc. Community Ment. Health Cent.

Snowden, L., ed. 1982. *Reaching the Under-*

served: Mental Health Needs of Neglected Populations. Beverly Hills: Sage

Solomon, G. 1980. Problems and Issues in Rural Community Mental Health: A Review. ERIC Doc. Reprod. No. 182101. Lubbock: Texas Tech

Spiegel, D. 1982. Self-help and mutual-support groups; A synthesis of the recent literature. See Biegel & Naparstek 1982, pp. 98–117

Spivack, G., Siegel, J., Sklaver, D., Deuschle, L., Garrett, L. 1982. The long-term patient in the community: Life style patterns and treatment implications. Hosp. Community Psychiatry 33:291–95

Sprafkin, J., Swift, C., Hess, R., eds. 1982. Prevention in Human Services: Rx Television: Enhancing the Preventive Impact of TV, Vol 2. New York: Haworth

Stahler, G. J., Tash, W. R., eds. 1982. Innovative Approaches to Mental Health Evaluation. New York: Academic

Stein, L. I., ed. 1979. New Directions for Mental Health Services: Community Support Systems for the Long-Term Patient, No. 2. San Francisco: Jossey-Bass

Stein, L. I., Test, M. A. 1980. Alternative to mental hospital treatment. Arch. Gen. Psychiatry 37:392–97

Stelovich, S. 1979. From the hospital to the prison: A step forward in deinstitutionalization? Hosp. Community Psychiatry 30:618–20

Stewart, A. J., Platt, M. B. 1982. Studying women in a changing world. J. Soc. Issues 38:1–16

Stockdill, J. W. 1982. ADM block grants: Political context, implementation philosophy, and issues related to consultation in mental health. Consultation 1:20–24

Taber, M. A. 1980. The Social Context of Helping: A Review of the Literature on Alternative Care for the Physically and Mentally Handicapped. NIMH Stud. Soc. Change. DHHS Publ. (ADM) 80–842

Tableman, B., Marciniak, D., Johnson, D., Rodgers, R. 1982. Stress management training for women on public assistance. Am. J. Community Psychol. 10:357–67

Talbott, J. A., ed. 1981. The Chronic Mentally Ill: Treatment, Programs and Systems. New York: Human Sci. Press

Tarail, M. 1980. Current and future issues in community mental health. Psychiatric Q. 52:27–38

Tessler, R. C., Bernstein, A. G., Rosen, B. M., Goldman, H. H. 1982. The chronically mentally ill in community support systems. Hosp. Community Psychiatry 33:208–11

Tessler, R. C., Goldman, H. H. 1982. The Chronically Mentally Ill: Assessing Community Support Programs. Cambridge: Ballinger

Test, M. A. 1981. Effective community treatment of the chronically mental ill: What is necessary? J. Soc. Issues 37:71–86

Thoits, P. A. 1982. Conceptual methodological and theorietical problems in studying social support as a buffer against life stress. J. Health Soc. Behav. 23:145–59

Thompson, J. W., Bass, R. D., Witkin, M. J. 1982. Fifty years of psychiatric services: 1940–1990. Hosp. Community Psychiatry 33:711–21

Turner, J. C., Stockdill, J. W. 1982. A Network for Caring: The Community Support Program of the National Institute of Mental Health. Proc. 4 natl. conf., 1978–79. DHHS Publ. (ADM) 81–1063

Unger, D. G., Wandersman, A. 1982. Neighboring in an urban environment. Am. J. Community Psychol. 10:493–509

Veroff, J., Douvan, E., Kulka, R. A. 1981a. The Inner American. New York: Basic Books

Veroff, J., Kulka, R., Douvan, E. 1981b. Mental Health In America: Patterns of Help-Seeking from 1957–1976. New York: Basic Books

Vladeck, B. C. 1980. Unloving Care; The Nursing Home Tragedy. New York: Basic Books

Warren, D. I. 1981. Helping Networks: How People Cope with Problems in the Urban Community. Notre Dame, Ind: Univ. Notre Dame Press

Weber, G. H., Cohen, L. M., eds. 1982. Beliefs and Self-Help. New York: Hum. Sci. Press

Weinstein, R. M. 1982. The mental hospital from the patient's point of view. In Deviance and Mental Illness, ed. W. R. Gove. Beverly Hills: Sage

Wellman, B. 1980. A Guide to Network Analysis. Univ. Toronto, Dep. Sociol.: Work. Pap. Ser.

Wellman, B., Leighton, B. 1979. Networks, neighborhood, and communities. Urban Affairs Q. 14:363–90

Wilcox, B. L. 1981. Social support, life stress, and psychological adjustment: A test of the buffering hypothesis. Am. J. Community Psychol. 9:371–85

Winslow, W. W. 1982. Changing trends in CMHCs: Keys to survival in the eighties. Hosp. Community Psychiatry 33:273–77

Zigler, E. F., Gordon, E. W., eds. 1981. Day Care: Scientific and Social Policy Issues. Boston: Auburn House

Zigler, E. F., Valentine, J., eds. 1979. Project Head Start: A Legacy of the War on Poverty. New York: Free Press

Ann. Rev. Psychol. 1984. 35:361–94

HUMAN LEARNING AND MEMORY

David L. Horton and Carol Bergfeld Mills

Department of Psychology, University of Maryland, College Park, Maryland 20742

CONTENTS

INTRODUCTION

We begin with a brief account of general trends in the field. In Jenkins' (1974) discussion of contextualist philosophy, he concludes that "What is remembered in a given situation depends on the physical and psychological context in which the event was experienced, the knowledge and skills that the subject brings to the context, the situation in which we ask for evidence for remembering, and

0066-4308/84/0201-0361$02.00

the relation of what the subject remembers to what the experimenter demands" (p. 793). If there is a single principle that best describes the current status of the cognitive psychology of human memory, it is that the contextualist thesis is alive and well at both the empirical and theoretical levels. In some instances contextual dependencies make it difficult to reconcile conflicting findings, while in others the consistency of results across different experimental contexts allows interpretations to be made with greater confidence. In fact, context effects are so pervasive that we chose to note that here and not in every subsequent section of this review.

Trends are also apparent in terms of those research problems that receive the greatest attention. There continues to be considerable interest in the encoding processes involved in the initial study of to-be-remembered events. Much of this work continues to be influenced by the levels-of-processing framework (Craik & Lockhart 1972) in one way or another. Most of the recent research continues to support the basic prediction of levels that semantic encoding leads to better memory performance than nonsemantic encoding. Despite this fact, the levels concept continues to have major definitional and empirical problems. Although the spirit of levels continues to be sound, other concepts such as elaboration of encoding, distinctiveness of encoding, or the effort expended in encoding appear to have greater potential for explaining memory performance.

Retrieval processes also have received considerable attention in recent years. The nature of the processes that underlie recognition memory is one major concern, as is the phenomenon of recognition failure of subsequently recallable events. Of course, a major concern in all of this work is the relationship between recall and recognition memory. During recent years there has been a convergence of both theoretical concepts and empirical findings in the study of both retrieval and encoding processes. Thus, while we have separate sections on encoding and retrieval, many papers are relevant to both.

Memory researchers continue to have their favorite experimental paradigms and related theoretical issues which contribute to our taxonomy of human memory. Auditory memory is popular with many researchers. Recent research in this area suggests that a reevaluation of influential views, including the precategorical acoustic store, may be in order. While the distinction between short-term and long-term memory continues to be maintained, most research in recent years has dealt with short-term memory and the specific characteristics of the memory trace. In the case of episodic and semantic memory, the main issue in recent years is whether these memory systems are functionally distinct or simply represent a convenient way of classifying our knowledge of human memory (Tulving 1972). Recent research with amnesic patients as well as normal subjects has enlivened this issue. The issue of different memory codes (verbal, imaginal) continues to dominate the study of memory for pictures, faces, and words. Many investigations in this area have attempted to specify whether the same variables influence memory for faces and pictures that influence memory for words and other verbal materials.

Research employing fairly complex verbal materials, such as sentences and stories, continues to be popular with many investigators. The issues here are what is retained, how the overall structure of the materials influence memory, and how the learner's prior knowledge affects what is remembered. The influence of the learner's prior knowledge in recall is evident in the work on schemata. While problems remain with schema theory, it has been widely employed as a psychological model in the study of complex verbal materials.

Because of page limitations this review is quite selective. We chose to focus almost exclusively on empirical research and those theoretical concepts and issues arising in that context. The literature reviewed mainly covers the period from 1979 through 1982. Again, because of page restrictions earlier work is cited very selectively even though many earlier papers deserve citation for historical precedence or importance. Book publications have not been reviewed because they focus mainly on empirical work from earlier years. We also have not reviewed work closely related to perception and the area of concepts because of reviews appearing in the 1983 (Kolers) or 1984 (Medin & Smith) volumes of the *Annual Review of Psychology*. The main criterion employed for including material in this chapter was the centrality of the work to human memory.

The topics reviewed under the headings of encoding and retrieval processes are treated somewhat more extensively than those in the remainder of the chapter. This reflects the centrality of encoding and retrieval to all of human memory and because recent work in these areas can be characterized as having a certain freshness of approach and style.

ENCODING PROCESSES

Automatic Encoding

The investigation of automatic aspects of encoding has been on the rise during the past 5 years. Much of the impetus for this work derives from two important papers: Shiffrin & Schneider (1977), Hasher & Zacks (1979). Automatic encoding, among other things, occurs without intention, it does not benefit from practice, and it does not interfere with other encoding activities. Hasher & Zacks (1979) distinquish between learned automatic encoding, which requires practice until the automatic stage is reached (word meaning), and unlearned automatic processing, which does not show developmental changes (event-frequency). There have been several recent reports showing automatic encoding of event-frequency (Hintzman et al 1982, Zacks et al 1982) and automatic encoding of word meaning (Shaffer & LaBerge 1979, Alba et al 1980, Lupker

& Katz 1981). The demonstrations of automatic encoding of word meaning have implications for findings discussed subsequently in this chapter.

Type of Processing

As any student of memory knows, the results of memory experiments often depend on the type of processing that subjects engage in during encoding. Differences in type of processing may be influenced by the organizational structure of input materials (Mandler 1968, Bower 1970a) as well as by the processing instructions given to the subjects (Hyde & Jenkins 1969). The former manipulation tends to emphasize similarities or relations among input events, while the latter manipulation tends to emphasize characteristics of individual input events. The relational emphasis is associated with the study of organizational processes in memory which was prominent in the 1960s and early 1970s. The emphasis on individual characteristics of events tends to be associated with the levels-of-processing approach advanced by Craik & Lockhart (1972). Hunt and his associates, in an important series of studies, have provided an integration of these two types of processing which appears to have considerable potential for explaining a variety of findings.

Einstein & Hunt (1980) provided subjects with lists of categorizable items during encoding, followed by both a free recall and a recognition memory test. During encoding the subjects were required to perform a semantic orienting task (taxonomic categorization or pleasantness rating), a nonsemantic orienting task (classify items by first letter or a rhyme rating), or two of the four orienting tasks. Each of the orienting tasks also occurred alone. In free recall the results indicated that either semantic task produced better recall than either nonsemantic task and that the effect of combining the two semantic tasks was superior to either task alone. However, the two types of processing have different effects on memory, as reflected in clustering indices and performance in recognition memory. To use Einstein & Hunt's terminology, *relational processing* (taxonomic categorization) produces much greater category clustering in recall than does *item-specific processing* (pleasantness rating). But in recognition memory, item-specific processing leads to more hits and fewer false alarms than relational processing. As the authors note, these results support the view that relational processing facilitates the formation of effective retrieval schemes whereas item-specific processing facilitates discrimination among items.

Hunt & Einstein (1981) have extended these findings by showing that item-specific processing leads to better recall of lists of highly related items than does relational processing. Presumably the relations among list items are apparent in this case, and even with item-specific instructions relational processing also occurs. With lists of relatively unrelated items, however, relational processing leads to better recall. Again, combining the two types of processing produces the best recall. In addition, recognition memory for either highly related or unrelated items is best following item-specific processing.

The concepts of relational and item-specific processing appear to be applicable to a number of recent findings. For example, Mayer & Cook (1981) report a study in which subjects either shadowed an input prose passage by sections or simply listened to it. If it is assumed that shadowing emphasizes item-specific processing while just listening encourages relational processing, their results appear quite reasonable. Shadowers are better at recognition of lexical items from the passage but poor at transfer of general principles to new situations. In recall, shadowers are better on minor details from the passage, but nonshadowers are better at recall of more conceptual (higher order) information.

Ritchey & Beal (1980) report differences in recall as a function of the degree of detail required in forming images corresponding to concrete nouns. Recall increases with greater detail of images, but only when the word list consists of unrelated items. In addition, with lists of related items considerable clustering is found in recall. The authors discuss these findings in terms of within-item and between-item elaboration at encoding which is essentially item-specific and relational processing. Thus, the integration of organizational factors (relational processing) and levels-of-processing manipulations (item-specific processing) appears to have considerable generality.

Levels of Processing

The levels- or depth-of-processing framework introduced by Craik & Lockhart (1972) continues to stimulate important research. This is particularly true for the extended levels concept which includes elaboration and distinctiveness of encoding. However, the levels concept continues to be plagued by the lack of an independent definition of depth and by continued demonstrations of context dependencies.

Craik (1979) states that "Two central postulates of the levels-of-processing view are first that deeper codes are more meaningful and second that such deeper codes are more durable" (p. 80). Research evidence, usually based on incidental learning comparing semantic (deep) and nonsemantic (shallow) orienting tasks, continues to be consistent with the levels view in both recall (Eysenck & Eysenck 1979, Tyler et al 1979) and recognition memory (DaPolito et al 1981, Jacoby & Dallas 1981). However, in a series of studies using the cuing paradigm, Nelson and his associates have reported contradictory results. For example, Nelson & McEvoy (1979) have shown that nonsemantic cues such as word endings (IME for DIME) presented at both study and test are just as effective as taxonomic cues (an American coin for DIME). In fact, with rapid presentation during encoding (1.5 sec) word ending cues are better than taxonomic cues, but with slower presentation (3.0 sec) the opposite result is found. These findings, showing equal effectiveness of nonsemantic and semantic cues as well as context dependency effects for presentation rate, are difficult to reconcile with the levels-of-processing view.

Hunt & Elliott (1980) have also demonstrated the importance of a nonsemantic feature, orthographic distinctiveness, in long-term memory. Distinctive
words have irregular orthographic patterns (e.g. phlegm) in contrast to orthographically common patterns (e.g. primate). They report that orthographic
distinctiveness only influences performance when distinctive words contrast
with common words. For example, the distinctiveness effect occurs with
orthographically mixed lists but not with unmixed lists. It does not occur when
all words are typed in capital letters or when words are presented auditorily.
The effect of orthographic distinctiveness is present in the incidental learning
paradigm following both semantic and nonsemantic orienting tasks. Thus,
nonsemantic information (orthographic distinctiveness) is retained in memory
even when the orienting task is semantic in nature.

Hunt & Elliott (1980) interpret their findings in terms of differential utility of
features rather than differential durability of information. Thus, their emphasis
on the utility of qualitatively different features contrasts with the transient trace
assumption of the levels-of-processing approach. Hunt & Elliott also argue that
the encoding of orthographically distinctive information is an automatic by-
product of the pattern recognition process and as such it is not consciously
available to the subject (see also Jacoby & Dallas 1981, Hunt & Mitchell 1982).
The general pattern emerging from these and related studies is that semantic
(deep) processing is usually, but not always, superior to nonsemantic (shallow)
processing. In addition, nonsemantic processing sometimes results in more
durable memory traces than the levels-of-processing view would predict. Both
of these findings seriously question the adequacy of the levels view.

Elaboration, Distinctiveness, and Effort

While these concepts, particularly elaboration and distinctiveness of encoding,
have frequently been discussed within the levels-of-processing framework, we
treat them separately here because there is no necessary relation between these
concepts and levels-of-processing. One problem with the concepts of elaboration and distinctiveness has been that they are often intuitively defined rather
than indexed independently. The concepts are defined in any given experiment,
but they are not defined in a way that generalizes across experiments. As a
result, the concepts of elaboration and distinctiveness often appear to be
interchangeable.

ELABORATION   Three studies have dealt with elaborations of sentences produced either by the experimenters or by the subjects themselves. Two of these
studies (Stevenson 1981, Bradshaw & Anderson 1982) showed that elaborations of target sentences reflecting cause or effect resulted in substantially
improved memory performance when compared to elaborations that were
neutral or unrelated to the target sentences. The third study (Stein & Bransford

1979) showed that elaborations only facilitate performance when they clarify the precise significance of a target word contained in each sentence presented for study. For example, if "The fat man read the sign" is elaborated as "The fat man read the sign warning of thin ice," recall of fat is facilitated. An interesting facet of this investigation is that subjects generating elaborations following prompts such as "What else might have happened here?" did not recall target concepts as well as subjects given prompts like "Why might this man be doing this?" (see example above). Thus, all three studies point to the importance for memory performance of using elaborations that reflect on the significance of what is to be remembered.

Fisher & Craik (1980) report an effect of elaboration at encoding in recognition of target concepts from input sentences. Their sentences varied in both complexity (length) and level of redintegration where redintegration was defined in terms of whether or not the sentences contained words which were strong associates of the target concepts. Both complexity and redintegration positively influenced performance. Fisher & Craik argue that their elaborations were effective because they permitted a reinstatement of the original encoding context (see also Fisher 1981). However, it should be noted that the high redintegrative elaborations employed by Fisher & Craik were very similar to those used by Stein & Bransford (1979). Thus, these studies indicate that reinstatement of the encoding context is important for retrieval, but that such a reinstatement is more likely when the elaborations have implications concerning the material to be remembered.

DISTINCTIVENESS   It is well established that in learning pairs of items, interactive imagery benefits memory more than does separation imagery (Bower 1970b). However, Winograd & Lynn (1979) have shown that the advantage of interactive imagery is markedly reduced when a uniquely distinctive imaginary context (e.g. different physical settings) is provided for each to-be-remembered word pair. When the same imaginary context is provided for all pairs the usual advantage for interactive imagery is found. The distinctive context facilitates performance in separation imagery but not in interactive imagery. In the case of separation imagery, the distinctive context appears to provide a way for the separate images to interact with the context. However, when the images are already interacting, the distinctive context is not facilitating (see also Rothkopf et al 1982).

The concept of distinctiveness at encoding appears to be important to the explanation of findings reported by Jacoby et al (1979). In a series of experiments, these investigators show that increasing the difficulty of semantic decisions that subjects are required to make at encoding is positively related to retention. Their view is that decision difficulty is related to distinctiveness of the memory trace and that it is distinctiveness, and not depth, that underlies improved retention. However, they also stress that distinctiveness is context sensitive. That is, concepts that are distinctive in one context because they share few features with other concepts in that context may not be distinctive in a different context. This relativity of distinctiveness and similarity in perceptual and conceptual contexts has also been emphasized by Tversky (1977), who has provided a basis for indexing distinctiveness.

EFFORT   The idea that the amount of effort expended during processing is an important factor in memory has also received support in recent years. Tyler et al (1979) define cognitive effort as the amount of the limited capacity available for processing that is required for a given task. In a series of experiments they demonstrated a beneficial effect of increased cognitive effort which was independent of a levels-of-processing effect. Their levels manipulation compared performance on a nonsemantic task (anagrams) with a semantic task (sentences) and their cognitive effort variable was task difficulty. They also showed that reaction time on a secondary tone-detection task was faster for easy tasks than for hard tasks, thus providing an independent index of cognitive effort.

Eysenck & Eysenck (1979) also address the effort issue, although these authors use the concept of *expended processing capacity*. Their procedure involved a variation of the divided attention methodology (Johnston et al 1972). The critical trials in their experiments allowed reaction-time (RT) measurements on both a main task and a secondary task (simple RT to an auditory or visual stimulus). By including other trials which involved only the secondary task, expended processing capacity could be indexed in terms of increases in RT on the secondary task on trials involving both tasks. Thus, expended processing capacity could be measured independently of the time required to perform the main task which consisted of either semantic or nonsemantic orienting conditions. In general, they found that semantic processing requires more expended processing capacity and leads to better memory performance than nonsemantic processing. Greater elaboration at encoding also takes longer to perform and requires more expended processing capacity but only leads to better memory performance following semantic processing.

The most significant aspect of this investigation, however, was the measurement of expended processing capacity and its relation to the primary findings. In these experiments expended processing capacity can be seen as providing an independent measure of depth-of-processing, or elaborative processing (at least with semantic tasks), or possibly some other factor. It certainly was the case in these experiments that the amount of expended processing capacity was more closely related to performance than was the total amount of time spent performing the main task.

RETRIEVAL PROCESSES
Recognition Memory

MODELS OF RECOGNITION   The nature of the recognition process continues to be a topic of interest and importance to human memory. Mandler (1980) has provided an extensive review of recent literature concerning the judgment of prior occurrence of an event. In line with earlier suggestions (Atkinson & Juola 1974), he proposes a dual-process model of recognition which is based on familiarity and retrieval. Familiarity is the result of intraevent integration of the sensory and perceptual elements, with events becoming more familiar the more often these combinations of elements are encountered. Retrieval is the result of interevent integration. The retrieval processes involved in recognition are presumably the same as those involved in recall.

Familiarity and retrieval are seen as independent processes operating in parallel at the time of event presentation. However, retrieval processes are generally slower so that the initial factor in recognition of prior occurrence of an event is familiarity. The familiarity factor is seen as independent of the general context in which familiarity is incremented (Atkinson et al 1974), so long as the event being incremented consists of the same combination of sensory-perceptual elements. Changes in presentation modality from study to test (Jacoby & Dallas 1981), or even in the voice of the speaker (Geiselman & Bjork 1980), may reduce or eliminate the effect of prior study.

Jacoby & Dallas (1981) propose a very similar model of recognition memory based on a series of experiments showing that performance in recognition memory and perceptual recognition is differentially influenced by several factors. Their findings indicate that recognition memory is influenced by both task difficulty and semantic vs nonsemantic processing whereas perceptual recognition is not. However, variables such as the number and spacing of repetitions and word frequency have parallel effects in both tasks.

Jacoby & Dallas (1981) propose that two factors, relative perceptual fluency (familiarity) and retrieval of study context, are involved in recognition memory. However, perceptual recognition is only influenced by relative perceptual fluency. In both tasks physical (graphemic) information appears to be the basis for relative perceptual fluency. In recognition memory someone can become aware that he or she is remembering because of relative perceptual fluency. Therefore, factors such as word frequency or repetitions will have parallel effects on both tasks. However, recognition memory can also be the result of retrieval of study context following elaborate or distinctive encoding.

The empirical evidence reviewed by Mandler (1980) and reported by Jacoby & Dallas (1981) provides substantial support for their dual-process accounts. Carroll & Kirsner (1982) also report support for the importance of relative perceptual fluency in a comparison of a lexical decision task and a recognition memory task. Their conclusion was that relative perceptual fluency (familiarity) was the main factor in lexical decision performance. Other research is consistent with the importance of interevent elaboration in recognition memory (McGee 1980, Donaldson 1981).

Both Mandler (1980) and Jacoby & Dallas (1981) see dual-process views of recognition memory as accounting for memory performance in amnesic patients (Warrington & Weiskrantz 1974). Amnesic patients are comparable to normal subjects in word fragment completion (e.g. completing table from t_b_e), while they perform much poorer than normals on recognition memory for the same words. In Jacoby & Dallas (1981) the parallel effect is that prior study has as large an influence on perceptual recognition of words when recognition memory for these words is poor as when it is nearly perfect. Perceptual recognition performance is attributable to relative perceptual fluency (familiarity), and presumably this factor accounts for amnesic performance in word fragment completion. The poor recognition memory of amnesics is then due to their inability to retrieve the study context during the recognition test or to an inability to encode the study context in the first place.

Jacoby & Witherspoon (1982) report a study comparing the memory performance of amnesics and normal subjects. The issue they raise is whether the dissociation of memory performance and awareness of remembering shown by amnesics is characteristic of certain aspects of normal memory as well. To test this possibility they biased a less frequent spelling of a list of homophones by initially asking a series of questions. For example, reed (read) was biased by asking a question like "can you name a musical instrument that employs a reed?" The subjects were then given a spelling test on the homophones. The questions and the spelling test both involved auditory presentation. Following the spelling test a recognition memory test was administered.

The biasing effect was clearly evident in the spelling test, with amnesics showing the bias even more strongly than normals. In recognition memory the amnesics were much poorer than normals. Recognition performance also was conditionalized on the particular spelling biased by the questions. This procedure indicated that the conditionalized probability was no different than the unconditionalized probability for either group of subjects. Thus, both groups showed a dissociation between the bias reflected in the spelling task and awareness of remembering as reflected in recognition memory.

WORD FREQUENCY EFFECT   Prior exposure to low frequency words leads them to be recognized better than high frequency words even though high frequency words are recalled better. This is known as the word frequency effect. Mandler (1980) suggests that the advantage of low frequency words in recognition is due to a greater incremental integration resulting from prior exposure. That is, the effect is not traceable to base familiarity but to the relative increase in familiarity for low frequency words being greater than that for high frequency words. Mandler et al (1982) provide empirical support for this view and also show that nonwords are not better recognized than high frequency words. They suggest that nonwords, which have no prior base familiarity, do not activate the incremental rule.

SIMILARITY RELATIONS   The similarity between old and new test items is an important factor in recognition as everyone knows. However, Tulving (1981) has shown that under certain conditions performance in a forced-choice recognition task is better when targets and distractors are similar than when they are dissimilar. The stimuli employed in his experiments were pictures of complex scenes that were divided in two halves. One half of each picture was presented at study. In the forced-choice recognition test the two halves of the same picture were discriminated better than two dissimilar halves when the distractor in the dissimilar pair was the other half of a different picture presented during study. On the basis of these findings, Tulving (1981) suggests two forms of similarity relations for recognition memory. Perceptual similarity referring to target-distractor similarity and ecphoric similarity referring to the similarity between the recognition test distractor and a previously established memory trace. Thus, ecphoric similarity can be a more critical factor in discrimination than perceptual similarity.

Recognition Failure

The phenomenon of failure to recognize previously presented items which are subsequently produced in cued recall continues to provoke controversy at both the empirical and theoretical level. Bowyer & Humphreys (1979) and Humphreys & Bowyer (1980) have challenged the Flexser & Tulving (1978) mathematical account of recognition failure on the grounds that priming effects in cued recall, resulting from the prior recognition test, are not considered and at least under some circumstances priming effects may be substantial. However, priming effects have recently been incorporated into this account (Flexser & Tulving 1982) which is based fundamentally on the assumption that the recognition and recall cues for a given pair tap independent information.

A major issue in the phenomenon of recognition failure is the concern about its generality across materials. Obviously, if recognition performance is quite good, the incidence of recognition failure will be low or nonexistent. However, Gardiner & Tulving (1980) argue that it is not the absolute level of recognition failure that is important, but rather the extent of recognition failure given the overall level of recognition. An empirical function describing this relationship has been reported previously (Tulving & Wiseman 1975).

Gardiner & Tulving (1980) report two experiments using item pairs that are normally difficult to associate. The stimuli were either pairs of abstract words (Honor-Anxiety) or one was a two-digit number and the to-be-recalled word was highly familiar (47-Wet). With typical instructions, they report substantial deviations from the Tulving-Wiseman function, but with highly elaborative instructions designed to relate the members of each pair, these deviations were markedly reduced. If the pairs are not encoded together (shallow processing), performance in cued recall would tend to be poor and hence the degree of recognition failure of recallable items would be low, irrespective of performance on the recognition task. The authors offer a levels-of-processing interpretation of their findings and go on to argue that the findings cannot be explained plausibly by alternative theories. Begg (1979) also has reported a closer fit to the Tulving-Wiseman function with instructions to meaningfully relate word pairs and substantial deviations from this function with rote repetition instructions. Thus, Begg's results also support a levels interpretation, but they are also consistent with interpretations based on elaboration, distinctiveness, or expended effort at the time of encoding as well.

Recall and Recognition

The role of retrieval processes is often seen as basic when comparing recall and recognition, particularly in the context of recognition failure. Mandler (1980) says that recognition of the target item following prior study of a cue-target pair is dependent on a familiarity judgment and on retrieval of the pair given the target item. In contrast, cued recall depends on retrieval of the pair given only the cue. As noted previously, the Flexser & Tulving (1978, 1982) account also assumes independent retrieval information in recall and recognition, although their account stresses retrieval of specific features rather than the whole item. Support for the general view of independent retrieval information is reported by Fisher (1979) in a study comparing recall and recognition as a function of cue-target relations. He found that cue-to-target associative strength only affected cued recall and that target-to-cue strength only affected recognition. Interestingly, a levels-of-processing manipulation had no differential effect, thus supporting the emphasis on retrieval processes when comparing recall and recognition.

The role of retrieval processes is also central to an evaluation of generation-recognition theory. This theory assumes that recall begins by implicitly generating potential target items and then recognizing those items that were previously studied. The theory thus assumes that recall and recognition involve very similar processes, although the decision criteria employed during the recognition phase of the two tasks may be different (Kintsch 1978). Differences in decision criteria can be invoked to explain the phenomenon of recognition failure, although such an account is far from satisfying. The theory has difficulty with results such as those noted above (Fisher 1979). In addition, when subjects are instructed to employ generation-recognition as a recall strategy, their performance suggests that it is not particularly effective (Nelson & McEvoy 1979). Rabinowitz et al (1979) suggest that generation-recognition is at best an auxiliary retrieval strategy. Watkins & Gardiner (1979) have reviewed the successes and failures of generation-recognition theory and conclude, quite reasonably, that while it remains a useful model for integrating some facts about recall and recognition, it fails as a theory to account for the weight of empirical findings.

Tulving (1982) has proposed a rather general model of retrieval, focusing on recall and recognition, which he terms the Synergistic Ecphory Model of Retrieval. While he acknowledges that the model makes no specific predictions, it does provide a framework for integrating a wide variety of basic empirical facts about recall and recognition. As such it may provide as useful a framework for studying retrieval processes as the levels-of-processing framework has for studying encoding processes.

The basic elements of the model can only be sketched here. Retrieval begins when information available in the retrieval environment (instructions, cues) and information in the memory trace interact through a process of "ecphory" to jointly produce what Tulving calls *ecphoric information*. The information in the memory trace need not be what was originally encoded but may appear in recoded form. Ecphoric information in turn gives rise to *recollective experience,* or what the individual is aware of remembering. Up to this point in the model, recall and recognition are the same. They begin to differ when recollective experience and ecphoric information jointly, through the process of conversion, are translated into memory performance. In recall, conversion requires a description of some aspect of the target event, such as its name, while recognition requires identification of the target event as "old" based on similarity with the originally experienced event. An interesting implication of the model concerns the previously noted memory performance of amnesics. When the retention task requires awareness of remembering, these patients, who apparently lack recollective experience, should and do show poor memory performance. Further details of the description of this model are beyond the scope of this review, and only time will tell us about its utility.

Context Effects in Cued Recall

The principle of encoding specificity (Tulving & Thomson 1973) emphasizes the importance of reinstating the encoding context at the time of retrieval. Throughout this review strong support for this principle is in evidence. Even such a seemingly minor factor as having subjects image printed words being spoken in the same voice that produced them previously can have a facilitating effect on recognition memory (Geiselman & Bjork 1980).

Roediger & Adelson (1980) have provided a somewhat different demonstration of encoding specificity. They first presented subjects with word pairs consisting of homographic targets and context cues that biased one of the target meanings. In cued recall, extralist cues that were congruous in meaning with the encoded pairs produced better recall than extralist incongruous cues. However, observing this effect depended on scoring recall of either the context cue or the target as correct or requesting recall of both words when extralist cues were presented.

Nelson and his associates have provided a significant body of evidence concerning context effects in cued recall. A major factor in this research is the size of the category activated by a particular cue or target. Category size is normatively defined as the number of associates or the number of rhymes given to a cue or target event, and the norms also provide an index of cue-target strength. Targets are always words, while cues are either words or word endings (IME for DIME). For experimental purposes, category size is typically defined as being small or large, and category size of cues and targets is investigated separately.

When cues (endings or associates) are presented only at test, associative and ending category size are independent and equally effective, with small categories producing better recall than large categories. This observation holds for variations in category size of either cues (Nelson & McEvoy 1979) or targets (Nelson & Friedrich 1980). However, ending category size does not affect recall when only associative cues are provided at test. In addition, when associative cues are present at study, and a mixture of word endings and associative cues are provided at test, associative category size of either cues or targets is not a factor in cued recall. In this case only word ending category size and cue-target strength influence recall.

These results appear to be interpretable in terms of two factors: the size of the search category activated at recall and cue-target strength. Small categories are more effectively searched than large categories, and when associative cues are present at both study and test, homogeneously small search categories result. The associative category size effects are consistent with encoding specificity if it is assumed that the extralist cues provided at test (no cues at study) are more likely to have been previously encoded if they are part of a small category than a large category (Nelson 1981).

The effects of ending category size are more difficult to understand. For example, unless rhymes or word endings are presented at either study or test, ending category size of targets does not affect recall. This suggests that the nonsemantic information contained in word endings must be primed for it to affect recall. But if nonsemantic cues (rhyme or word ending) are only provided at test, it is difficult to see why ending category size should influence recall unless the nonsemantic cues somehow provide access to the semantic information encoded at study (Nelson 1981). In any event, these findings clearly demonstrate the extreme complexity of context effects in cued recall.

TAXONOMY OF MEMORY

Iconic Memory

Much of the research dealing with iconic memory has been reviewed by Kolers (1983) and hence will not be treated in this review. However, in a significant paper, Coltheart (1980) persuasively argues that most of this work pertains to visible or neural persistence and not to iconic memory as traditionally conceived. He also suggests that iconic memory is postcategorical, occurring after a rapid automatic process of stimulus identification which does not require buffer storage. In other words, Coltheart (1980) proposes an automatic lexical access to semantic memory which provides no information about episodic properties of the visual stimulus. In view of the previously cited evidence concerning automatic encoding of word meaning, this suggestion deserves careful consideration.

Auditory Memory

According to most conceptualizations, auditory memory is assumed to store relatively literal copies of auditory information for brief periods of time. This information is then processed further or it is forgotten. Recent research has focused on clarifying the characteristics of auditory memory. A common reference point in this work has been the Crowder & Morton notion of the precategorical acoustic store (PAS). Most of this research has been concerned with either the suffix effect or the modality effect.

SUFFIX EFFECT   A substantial amount of research has concerned the stimulus suffix effect in immediate recall of vocally presented lists of words. The suffix effect is defined by reduced recall, particularly in the last part of the list, when an extra word (suffix) is presented after the final item and subjects are told to ignore the extra word. In the comparison or control condition, the extra item is either omitted or it is a nonvocal item such as a tone.

Crowder & Morton (1969) have interpreted the suffix effect as an indication that auditory memory can be masked by subsequent vocally presented items. They suggested that reduced recall of the last few list items is the primary indication of auditory memory masking. However, recent studies have suggested that reduced recall of only the last item should be taken as an index of masking in auditory memory (Baddeley & Hull 1979, Balota & Engle 1981). It has been suggested that the duration of auditory memory is about 2 seconds since a delay in presentation of the suffix of about 2 seconds or more does not affect recall. However, recent investigations suggest that auditory memory may have a much longer duration. M. Watkins & Todres (1980) showed that when subjects were engaged in an arithmetic task between the end of the list and suffix presentation, the suffix effect occurred with delays as long as 20 seconds (also see O. Watkins & M. Watkins 1980).

Crowder (1982a) has suggested that the suffix effect is produced at the sensory level through a process of lateral inhibition. Other investigators (Ayres et al 1979, O. Watkins & M. Watkins 1982) have suggested that more cognitive processes are involved. One reason for this suggestion is that the size of the suffix effect is determined by how an ambiguous suffix is categorized, and not only by its physical properties (Ayres et al 1979).

Other investigators have been concerned with when the information in auditory memory is used to aid recall. O. Watkins & M. Watkins (1980) have suggested that this information is used directly at the time of recall. M. Watkins & Todres (1980), however, have suggested that information in auditory memory is used during the delay to build up a more permanent memory for list items. Thus, the exact way in which auditory memory operates in suffix experiments has not been resolved.

While the suffix effect has been used to support the existence of an auditory memory, several studies call that interpretation into question. Suffix effects have been reported with mouthed but not articulated suffixes, which were produced either by the experimenter (Spoehr & Corin 1978) or by the subject (Nairne & Crowder 1982). The suffix effect also is obtained with auditory suffixes when the lists are lip-read (Campbell & Dodd 1980). In addition, an American Sign Language (ASL) sign suffixed to a list of other signs produces a suffix effect for congenitally deaf signers (Shand & Klima 1981). Taken together these studies have shown that the suffix effect can be obtained with nonauditory stimuli (either the suffix, the recall list, or both) and hence cannot be explained by auditory memory in all cases.

Shand & Klima (1981) have suggested that the suffix effect is based on the input mode that functions as the channel for primary linguistic input (native language). For their subjects this channel was visually presented signs. Alternatively, Crowder (1982b) has suggested that the findings for lip-read and sign stimuli may be explained in terms of movement perception. However, a more explicit interpretation of these findings is that the suffix effect reflects an articulatory-motor encoding of the stimuli. For vocally or lip-read stimuli the motor system for speech is involved, while for sign stimuli motor movements of the hands and arms are encoded.

MODALITY EFFECT   The modality effect is reflected in superior recall of the recency items in auditory presentation relative to visual presentation. The PAS account of the modality effect is that following auditory presentation, information from auditory memory is available for a longer time to aid recall than is the case for visual information following visual presentation. Engle et al (1980) provide at least indirect support for the auditory memory basis of the modality effect in a series of studies in which subjects were differentially informed about when the recency portion of the list begins. They showed that giving subjects prior knowledge of when the recency portion of the list begins does not alter the modality effect. Gathercole et al (1982) found that the use of phonologically similar words reduced the modality effect, as would be expected if the effect resulted from auditory memory.

Research on the modality effect suggests that auditory memory may persist for at least 20 seconds (O. Watkins & M. Watkins 1980), which is consistent with the evidence from studies of the suffix effect but not with the PAS account. In addition, Gardiner & Gregg (1979) have obtained the modality effect in experiments where subjects engaged in extensive oral distractor activity before and after presentation of each list item. This observation shows that the modality effect is not dependent on auditory memory, which is consistent with the findings noted above showing that the suffix effect does not depend on the use of auditory stimuli. Thus, the research on auditory memory leaves many questions unanswered. It appears, however, that some of the assumptions made concerning auditory memory, and the PAS in particular, should be reevaluated.

Short-Term and Long-Term Memory

The distinction between short-term memory (STM) and long-term memory (LTM) has provided a useful way of organizing many aspects of human memory whether or not one is referring to different memory stores, memory processes, or research paradigms. For example, Geiselman et al (1982) report experiments in which physiological and verbal report measures were recorded during learning as indicators of type of rehearsal, recall from STM, recall from LTM, and processing intensity. One of their main findings was that the STM recall measures and the LTM recall measures were negatively correlated, suggesting that a single process model of memory is not reasonable. Further statistical analyses indicated that a dual-process model provides an acceptable representation of the data.

According to two-store models of memory, the recency effect in free recall is due to recall from STM. However, long-term recency effects occur in experimental situations where STM would not be useful, such as delayed free recall of items whose presentations were separated by distractor activity (Glenberg et al 1980). Whether or not this long-term recency effect is caused by the same factors that produce the usual recency effect in immediate free recall cannot be determined at this time.

Most recent research in this area has been concerned with characteristics of STM and not with the single vs dual store issue. Recent models of STM have used attributes as the unit of discussion rather than the unitary stimulus item (Drewnowski 1980, Lee & Estes 1981). For example, Drewnowski (1980) proposed that attributes concerning information about ordinal position, auditory traces, and interitem relationships are encoded and stored in STM. These stored attibutes are then consulted as cues during recall based on an ordered priority.

Recent research using STM or immediate memory paradigms also suggests that a stimulus item is represented in STM as sets of attributes rather than as a unitary encoded representation. The category (letter or digit) of the stimulus may be one of the attributes stored in STM (Estes 1980). The relative location of an item in a sequence may be another attribute which is stored. Memory for relative location of an item may be represented by an uncertainty gradient centered around its correct location in a series (Estes 1980). In addition, STM for relative location may be hierarchically represented with the relative location of items within segments of a trial as well as the relative position of the segments being encoded (Lee & Estes 1981).

Other research has shown that acoustic attributes of the stimulus affect STM for items, as evidenced by intrusion and confusion errors. For monosyllabic items, the forgotten items tend to be replaced by acoustically similar ones (Conrad 1964). Drewnowski & Murdock (1980) have shown that for disyllabic words which are presented either visually or auditorily, acoustic confusions are made on the basis of the syllabic stress pattern, the identities of the initial and terminal phonemes, and the identity of the stressed vowel. This study suggests that both phonemic and nonphonemic attributes of the stimulus items are encoded even when the items are presented visually. Thus, the research concerning attributes appears to suggest that items are not remembered in an all-or-none manner, but rather that some or all of the attributes of the items are represented in STM.

In addition to the research concerning attributes, other STM experiments also support the notion that acoustic or articulatory factors are encoded in STM. Salamé & Baddeley (1982) have shown that unattended speech causes a clear decrement in the immediate recall of visually presented digits. The degree of decrement is a function of the phonological similarity of the irrelevant speech to the digits. These results seem to suggest that there is some type of interference between the encoded representation of the visual items (subvocal rehearsal) and the irrelevant speech which is to be ignored. Schiano & Watkins (1981) have shown that even STM for readily nameable pictures seems to be mediated by a speech-like code. In their study, phonological similarity, length of names, and irrelevant vocalization influenced picture span and word span in similar ways.

There is strong evidence then that acoustic or articulatory codes are used in a number of STM paradigms. This even appears to be true in some experimental paradigms for deaf subjects whose native and presumably primary language is visual-gestural in nature (Hanson 1982). Hanson found that for both sign and printed word presentation deaf subjects used a speech-based encoding in STM as evidenced by a reduction in ordered recall of acoustically similar items compared to acoustically dissimilar items. Hanson also found evidence that deaf subjects encoded signs in STM in terms of their formational attributes. This latter finding is consistent with results from other studies using deaf subjects and either signs (Poizner et al 1981, Shand 1982) or printed words (Shand 1982). Thus, the type of encoding that occurs in STM appears to depend on the prior linguistic experience of the learner, the modality of presentation, and the particular paradigm employed.

Episodic and Semantic Memory

Tulving (1972) proposed a distinction between episodic and semantic memory as a potentially useful way of classifying knowledge concerning memory. According to Tulving, episodic memory is autobiographical in nature and stores information about events in terms of the time and place of occurrence. Semantic memory stores more general information about language and our knowledge of the world. While most writers appear to accept this distinction as a useful one, in recent years researchers have been investigating the question of whether or not episodic and semantic memory represent functionally distinct systems. A common approach in attempting to answer this question is to determine whether the laws governing episodic memory are comparable to those for semantic memory. An alternative approach is to examine the extent to which episodic memory influences semantic memory and vice versa.

Some studies employing these approaches have reported evidence in favor of the episodic-semantic distinction (Shoben et al 1978, Herrmann & Harwood 1980) while others report evidence against it (McKoon & Ratcliff 1979, Anderson & Ross 1980, McClosky & Santee 1981). A primary difficulty that arises in attempting to evaluate these and related findings is that it is not all that apparent what task is an episodic task or a semantic task, or what kind of information is episodic and what kind is semantic. In other words, it is difficult to rule out a possible role for semantic memory in what appears to be an episodic task and vice versa.

Hannigan et al (1980) stress that both episodic and semantic memory may affect performance on almost any cognitive act. They also report two experiments that nicely make this point. In these experiments subjects were presented with a long list of unrelated sentences. Some subjects were provided with a framework for relating these sentences while others were not. The test involved presenting sentences masked by white noise which the subjects were asked to repeat aloud. Subjects not provided with a framework performed better on previously presented sentences than baseline subjects who were not exposed to the study sentences. This finding reveals an episodic memory effect. Subjects provided with a framework perform better than all other subjects on previously presented sentences as well as on new sentences appropriate to the framework, which reveals the effect of semantic memory. The performance of subjects in the framework condition on new-appropriate sentences is of particular importance here because it involves a conjunction of episodic information from the study sentences and semantic information from the framework based on general knowledge of the world.

While Hannigan et al (1980) support a role for both episodic and semantic memory on the same task, evidence for an apparent dissociation of episodic and semantic memory has been provided by Kihlstrom (1980). In one experiment subjects learned a list of unrelated words while under hypnosis. Following list learning they were given the posthypnotic suggestion that they would not remember learning the list until a particular signal was given. The most hypnotizable subjects showed very poor episodic memory for the word list although they performed well on a semantic memory task in which stimuli that elicited the list words as primary associates were presented in a word association task. Even after this priming experience episodic memory remained poor. However, after the signal was given to remove the posthypnotic amnesia, their recall was essentially perfect.

The findings reported by Kihlstrom (1980) are highly similar to those obtained with amnesic patients when episodic and semantic tasks are compared. As noted previously, priming effects from prior study are equally strong in amnesics and normals when awareness of remembering is not required (word fragment completion), but normals are superior when such awareness is required (recognition memory). According to Stern (1981), context-encoding deficit theories are best equipped to explain these and related findings concerning the memory of amnesic patients. However, these findings also support the episodic-semantic distinction, since episodic memory is defined as context sensitive while semantic memory is not.

Perhaps one of the main reasons for considering a functional distinction between episodic and semantic memory is that it appears to fit the growing body of research on the memory performance of amnesic patients. In the case of nonverbal tasks, Cohen & Squire (1980) report that amnesics acquire and retain a mirror-reading skill as well as normals. Similar results have been reported for solutions to the Tower-of-Hanoi problem (Cohen & Corkin 1982). In both of these cases the amnesic patients show good performance over long intervals of time and little or no episodic memory for the tasks employed.

There are parallels between the performance of these amnesic patients and recent studies with normal humans. Using verbal tasks with normal subjects, Tulving et al (1982) report that priming effects in word fragment completion do not decline over a 7-day retention interval. Similarly, Jacoby & Dallas (1981) have shown that priming effects in perceptual recognition of words do not decline over 24 hours. In both of these investigations recognition memory (episodic) declines over the retention interval. Finally, Jacoby & Witherspoon (1982), in the spelling experiment noted previously, report that both amnesics and normals show dissociation of memory performance and awareness of remembering.

With the exception of recognition memory, the verbal tasks used in the studies just cited do not require an awareness of remembering, which appears to be critical for amnesics to show good memory performance. The verbal tasks used in these studies are typically regarded as semantic memory tasks, although Tulving et al (1982) suggest that word fragment completion may involve a memory system that is independent of either episodic or semantic memory. This interpretation is difficult to accept in view of the parallels noted between performance on word fragment completion and perceptual recognition in which semantic access is clearly required. In addition, the previously cited evidence for automatic encoding of word meaning suggests that semantic memory may be involved in word fragment completion. Perhaps semantic access in word fragment completion is mediated by the orthography, but semantic access may not activate the corresponding name code. If this is the case, a change in modality from presentation to test would reduce or eliminate priming in perceptual recognition, as Jacoby & Dallas (1981) report. Whatever the situation actually is, studies of the sort mentioned here appear to add an important dimension to our taxonomy of human memory.

Picture, Face, and Word Memory

ALTERNATIVE MEMORY CODES   One of the recurrent findings in studies which compare memory for pictures and words is that pictures are remembered better than words. The predominant theoretical explanation for this picture superiority effect has been Paivio's dual-coding theory. According to this view, pictures are more likely to be dually coded (stored in both a verbal and image memory system) than words and hence are remembered better. Recently, dual-coding theory has been expanded to include more than one verbal system (Paivio & Desrochers 1980) in order to account for the way the verbal systems and an image system might interact in bilinguals. Paivio & Lambert (1981) found evidence supporting this bilingual version of dual-coding theory in an incidental memory task in which recall increased from unilingual encoding to bilingual encoding to both a verbal and image encoding.

There are a large number of reports which are generally supportive of the notion of dual coding. For example, te Linde (1982) found that for comparisons of object size, RT for picture-picture pairs was faster than for word-word pairs. However, that was not the case for judgments of associative relatedness. These results are more consistent with a dual-coding view than with a single-coding view, because in a single-coding model the same pattern of results should be obtained for both tasks.

Other recent studies, however, have failed to support the notion of dual coding. For example, Intraub (1979) found no systematic relationship between how rapidly a picture could be named and its retention for each of five presentation rates. If the retention of pictures is enhanced by implicit naming, as suggested by dual-coding theory, a relationship would have been expected at some of the presentation rates used. Other studies have suggested that the name code is not necessarily activated for picture stimuli (Babbitt 1982). This finding appears to be inconsistent with the dual-coding explanation of the picture superiority effect which assumes that implicit naming of pictures is what accounts for superior picture memory.

An alternative model, the sensory semantic model of picture and word encoding (Nelson 1979), has also been proposed to explain the picture superiority effect. According to this model, the picture superiority effect occurs because pictures have a more distinctive sensory code than do words. In addition, pictures are more likely to undergo semantic processing than words, and from a levels-of-processing viewpoint, semantic processing should lead to better recall. The assumption that semantic processing is more likely for pictures has been supported by a number of recent experiments using different experimental paradigms (Durso & Johnson 1980, Smith & Magee 1980). These studies have shown that pictures activate semantic codes more readily than name codes, while words activate name codes more readily than semantic codes. See Smith & Magee (1980) for a review of this literature.

In addition to the research on the picture superiority effect, other research suggests that pictures and words are handled differently in memory. Deffenbacher et al (1981) found evidence for three distinct classes of stimuli in memory: (a) common objects and their names, (b) landscapes and complex scenes, and (c) faces. Woodhead & Baddeley (1981), however, found evidence for only two classes of stimuli: (a) verbal materials (words) and (b) visual materials (faces and paintings).

The converging evidence is that pictures, words, and perhaps faces are treated differently in memory. However, the theoretical issue concerning whether there are different stores for the different types of stimuli or whether there are just different processing functions in one memory system is far from settled. Nor is it clear that experimental studies will provide the evidence needed to resolve this issue since the same outcomes can follow from either point of view (Anderson 1978).

PRIMING   There have been numerous studies of picture-word priming. There is a facilitating effect of prior picture or word presentation on recognition latency of the same concept presented as either a picture or a word (Guenther et al 1980, Carr et al 1982). These studies have shown that for both pictures and words priming effects occur both within and across type of stimuli, suggesting a common memorial representation for pictures and words. However, there does not appear to be a complete overlap of memorial representation for pictures and words since priming effects are generally larger within stimulus type than across stimulus type (Guenther et al 1980). The greatest priming effects have usually been obtained when pictures are both the prime and the target, which suggests that picture stimuli may be more similar to the memory representation of concepts than are word stimuli (Carr et al 1982).

REHEARSAL   A number of recent studies dealt with whether or not rehearsal is as effective in improving memory for pictures and faces as is the case for verbal materials. In general, the results of these studies are consistent with the notion that memory for pictures can be improved by rehearsal, although there are exceptions to this finding (Bird & Cook 1979). Picture recognition and recall improves as the interval between pictures increases, presumably allowing more time for rehearsal (Intraub 1979). Other findings indicate that recognition is better following instructed or cued rehearsal for faces, scenes, random shapes, and simple line drawings (Graefe & Watkins 1980). Furthermore, only the items that are cued to be rehearsed benefit, indicating that the rehearsal process is under the subject's control (Graefe & Watkins 1980). Watkins & Graefe (1981) showed that rehearsal improves recognition memory even when the picture being rehearsed is not the last one presented. However, as the number of pictures between picture presentation and the rehearsal cue increases, the effectiveness of the cue decreases.

Several studies have been concerned with the effects of different types of supplementary verbal or written tasks on picture and face memory. Naming a picture of a common object (Warren & Horn 1982), writing a detail of a scene (Loftus & Kallman 1979), or writing a description of a scene (Bartlett et al 1980) at presentation has been shown to aid later recognition of the same picture. Whether providing a name or description facilitates the descrimination of the original pictures from visually similar pictures seems to depend upon the exact experimental procedures used (Bartlett et al 1980, Warren & Horn 1982). Thus, performing different tasks during encoding can facilitate encoding and retrieval of pictorial stimuli as is the case for verbal stimuli.

FACE RECOGNITION   Several recent studies on face recognition have investigated what effect context at the time of initial presentation has on later recognition. Kerr & Winograd (1982) found that subjects were more likely to recognize a face when context information concerning personality characteristics, profession, etc has been received about a person than when such information has not been provided. In a similar experiment, however, Baddeley &

Woodhead (1982) found no such facilitating effect. Klatzky et al (1982) have shown that faces can be meaningfully related to occupational categories (accountant, farmer), and when a congruent occupational label is presented at the time of study, later recognition that the face had previously been seen was enhanced. However, forced-choice recognition requiring fine discrimination was not enhanced. In addition, all of these studies show that reinstatement of the encoding context at recognition facilitates face recognition. This finding is consistent with the notion of encoding specificity. Thus, in at least some experimental paradigms, contextual information improves the later recognition of faces.

State Dependent Memory

Eich (1980) has provided an extensive review of the literature concerning pharmacological state dependent memory. He concludes that state dependent memory is not differentially influenced by type of drug given, dosage (within reasonable limits), nature of the material to be remembered, or levels-of-processing of the material. He also points out that state dependency is not observed when explicit retrieval cues are provided as in cued recall or recognition memory tests. Rather, it is when "implicit" retrieval cues traceable to the reinstated pharmacological context are the only cues provided that state dependent memory is observed. A similar conclusion is offered by Baddeley (1982) for state dependency of environmental context.

Bower (1981) reports on experiments demonstrating a mood state dependent memory across a variety of materials ranging from recall of word lists to recall of childhood experiences. He also reports a mood congruity effect during learning with material congruous with the learners' affective state being remembered best. Leight & Ellis (1981) have also reported mood state dependent memory. In their studies, one mood state (depression) was also shown to lead to poorer recall of learned material and poorer performance on a subsequent transfer task whether or not the same mood state was induced prior to transfer. They suggest that the poorer transfer observed is caused by the strategies employed when learning the initial task in a depressed state.

MEMORY FOR SENTENCES AND STORIES AND THE ROLE OF SCHEMATA

Many psychologists are studying complex verbal materials such as sentences and stories rather than the more traditional individual items. The results of some of these studies could have been predicted by your grandparents, but the results of other studies are less intuitive. In any case, the empirical findings provide the basis needed to develop more specific and refined memory models for these materials.

Sentences and Stories

A study by Sachs (1967) indicated that once the meaning of an auditorily presented sentence is comprehended, the gist of the sentence is retained but the exact wording is forgotten. A recent study with deaf subjects and ASL sentence stimuli (Hanson & Bellugi 1982) also supports this conclusion. In this study, at delayed testing, paraphrases were not as well discriminated from originally presented sentences as were changes in semantic content. Thus, it appears that the gist of either signed or spoken sentences constitutes the primary information retained.

Both the sign study above and recent studies with English sentences indicate that more than just the gist is retained. Hanson & Bellugi (1982) found that with delayed testing, changes in sign order and lexical changes which preserved meaning were detected better than would be expected by chance. Yekovich & Thorndyke (1981) found that information concerning the gist as well as the exact wording is retained. They showed that sentence paraphrases could be discriminated from sentences previously read in a story even after a one-hour delay. Furthermore, this effect varied inversely as a function of the importance or centrality of the sentence to the story. In other words, the more important a sentence was, the less well subjects retrieved the exact wording of the sentence. Christiaanson (1980) found that after one week, sentence wording was retained at an above chance level; however, the wording was not remembered as well as information about sentence gist or paragraph theme.

The gist of simple English sentences and of propositions in complex sentences tend to be recalled in an all-or-none manner. Goetz et al (1981) have interpreted this finding as support for a Gestalt view of sentence memory in which propositions are well-formed wholes and are remembered as such. Anderson (1976), however, has suggested that an associative view, in which the memory representation of a sentence consists of a set of independently linked concepts, can adequately account for the all-or-none recall of sentence gist.

Recent research with sentence materials has shown that sentences tend to be recalled better when they have an integrated structure than when they do not. Goetz et al (1981) showed that sentences were easier to recall when they were judged to characterize ordinary situations in which actors and objects "go together," than when the sentences described unlikely situations. Yekovich & Manelis (1980) found that when the same concepts were repeated across propositions (integrated structure), immediate recall and delayed cued recall were better than when the same concepts were not repeated (nonintegrated structure).

Similar results have been reported with a series of conceptually related sentences. That is, recall is better when sentences are integrated into a coherent whole than when they are not. Black & Bern (1981) have shown that when the events described in two adjacent sentences of a narrative story are causally related, they are easier to recall than when not causally related. Black et al (1979) found that narratives with a consistent point of view were remembered better, read faster, and rated as more comprehensible than those with a change in point of view. Other studies (Morris et al 1979, Owens et al 1979) have shown that presenting relevant information prior to a story can provide a coherent framework in which to interpret the prose. Whether this prior information provides a motive for the story character (Owen et al 1979) or allows for elaboration (Morris et al 1979), it can result in improved recall of the story. However, Morris et al (1979) showed that recall improved only when the prior information was consistent with the learner's general knowledge of the world. These studies then show that interrelationships between sentences in stories, as well as their relationship to the reader's knowledge, affect retention.

It does appear that not all sentences in a story are interrelated, however, Stories seem to have constituent structures made up of episodes such as subgoals. These episodes appear to be "chunks" in the memory representation of stories. Black & Bower (1979) have shown that recall of an episode is affected by the length of the episode but not by the length of other episodes in the story. Specifically, adding actions to a given episode increases the recallability of the important information in that episode but not in the other episodes. Hence memory for different episodes appears to be independent.

The evidence reviewed here indicates that gist is recalled better than surface details of sentences and stories even though details are remembered. Recall of sentences and stories is better when they are well integrated or more coherent. In addition, encoding of stories is by "chunks" or episodes, with the episodes being relatively independent of each other. Thus, memory for sentences and stories, like memory for individual items, emphasizes the importance of organizational or relational processing of meaning.

The Role of Schemata

Some of the results discussed above concerning coherence are consistent with the notion of schemata which has become a prominent theoretical construct in the area of story memory. Schemata are generally considered to be structural clusters of knowledge concerning particular concepts. One type of memory schema which has been discussed widely in the area of story memory is scripts. Scripts are the cognitive structures concerning events or routines such as eating at a restaurant. Research concerning the effect of schemata and scripts on memory for stories has revealed a number of interesting findings.

Bower et al (1979) showed that subjects tended to fill gaps in a script-based story with unstated actions implied by the script. They also found that when an action was displaced in a script-based story, the displaced action regressed toward its appropriate location in recall. Owens et al (1979) have also shown transformations occur in story recall, particularly with delayed testing. They report that the transformations made the story more consistent with the subjects' schema for the story.

Graesser and his associates have conducted a number of studies which support the schema-pointer-plus-tag model in story recall. This model assumes that the memory representation for a script-based story consists of a generic schema plus memory tags for atypical events. Smith & Graesser (1981) suggest that the generic schema becomes progressively more important in guiding retrieval over time. They report that recall of atypical events is initially better than recall of typical events. However, after one week, recall is better for the typical events.

If schemata are used to aid retrieval of stories, then one might expect that higher level schema information would be retained better than lower level, less important information. Some studies support this notion (e.g. Yekovich & Thorndyke 1981), but a recent study by Christiaanson (1980) does not. He found that forgetting rates for paragraph theme (higher level) and sentence gist (lower level) were parallel over time.

Spiro (1980) tested the idea that story memory is primarily a reconstructive process based on schemata—that is, a process of inferring the past rather than reproducing it. Consistent with this idea, he found that the recall of stories is affected by information presented at a later time. Accommodative recall errors are produced to make the story more consistent with the subsequently presented information. Furthermore, the amount of accommodation increases over time. For delayed recall tests, subjects were more confident about having read the information in the story when it was an accommodative error than when it was correctly presented information.

Research on memory for scripts per se (rather than on script-based stories) has shown that subjects generally agree on the nature of the activities that occur in a script, as well as the order of the activities. Subjects also agree on which activities are more central to the script and on the constituent structure of the script (Bower et al 1979, Galambos & Rips 1982). In addition, more central events can be verified faster as events which belong to the script than can more peripheral events (Galambos & Rips 1982). These results suggest that memory for scripted activities is hierarchically organized.

It has also been suggested that schemata play a role in memory for pictures (Friedman 1979, Goodman 1980). For example, Goodman (1980) found that items with high relevance to the theme of a picture are poorly recognized but well recalled. This finding is consistent with the idea that schemata are used in the retrieval of pictorial information.

Research concerning memory differences of novice and expert learners, and concerning the way new information is integrated with prior knowledge, can also be interpreted in terms of schemata. In general, these areas of research demonstrate how prior knowledge influences what is remembered as well as how much is remembered. Chiesi et al (1979) have shown that when recalling baseball event sequences, individuals high in baseball knowledge are superior to individuals low in baseball knowledge. Presumably this occurs because high knowledgeable individuals can more easily map the new information onto their existing knowledge structure, which is structurally more complex than that of low knowledgeable individuals.

Schustack & Anderson (1979) have shown that providing subjects with a good analogy between new information and prior knowledge can improve memory for the newly studied material as well as increase false recognition of statements consistent with prior knowledge. Clifton & Slowiaczek (1981) have shown, however, that there are limits to when new information is integrated with old information. For example, they found that when new information is presented about famous people in biography format, the information is integrated with old information about the people; however, it is not when the information is presented in list format.

Schemata provide a plausible, descriptive framework for discussing a number of empirical findings. However, there are unresolved issues concerning schema theory, particularly its explanatory power (Thorndyke & Yekovich 1980). Schema theory can explain nearly any set of findings which constitutes both a strength and a weakness of the theory. Perhaps, as empirical findings accumulate, more specific and testable versions of schema theory will be developed.

CONCLUDING REMARKS

During the past decade or so, considerable progress has been made in the cognitive psychology of human learning and memory. In the domain of encoding processes the recent integration of organizational (relational) processing and levels-of-processing (item-specific) constitutes an important development which appears to have implications and applications across a wide range of materials and situations. Admittedly, the value of this integration cannot be fully assessed until the concepts of levels-of-processing or elaboration and distinctiveness of encoding are more adequately defined than they are at present.

In the domain of retrieval processes there is a growing consensus that the retrieval information provided in recognition is independent of the information provided in recall. This view is consistent with the apparent generality of the phenomenon of recognition failure of recallable words and with recent models of recognition memory. In addition, research in this area strongly implicates the importance of including perceptual processes in the study of learning and memory—a development which has been too long in coming.

Current models of recognition memory focus on two basic processes: relative perceptual fluency (familiarity) and retrieval. Although the nature of retrieval processes requires further clarification, these models also provide a basis for understanding the memory performance of both amnesics and normals in tasks that require an awareness of remembering (recognition memory) and tasks that do not require such an awareness (word fragment completion).

The memory performance of amnesics can also be understood in terms of episodic and semantic memory if the two systems are seen as being functionally distinct, or at least partially so. However, disentangling episodic and semantic memory at the empirical level has proved to be difficult.

Psychologists continue to study memory for a wide variety of materials such as pictures, faces, words, and ASL signs. This work has implications for our taxonomy of memory. Research on pictures, faces, and words suggests that there may be two or even three memory codes for these kinds of materials. Research on memory for ASL signs has implications for auditory memory, since it has been shown that the suffix effect is not always dependent on the presence of an auditory code.

A substantial body of literature now exists concerning memory for relatively natural verbal material such as sentences and stories. Much of this work reveals parallels with research dealing with memory for lists of words. The facilitating effects in memory of integrated sentence structure and coherent stories generally are consistent with the facilitating effects of relational processing of individual words. Also, the effects of integrated or coherent structure in sentences and stories is in accord with evidence from studies of elaborative encoding, showing that elaborations are only effective when they have implications for the material to be remembered. In addition, research with story materials has revealed an influence of general knowledge on memory, which has been widely interpreted in terms of schema theory.

At the beginning of this chapter we commented on the pervasiveness of contextual factors in memory research. One such factor concerns the principle of encoding specificity which emphasizes the importance for memory of reinstating the encoding context at the time of retrieval. Strong support for this principle can be found throughout the sections on encoding and retrieval processes and in other areas as well, such as face recognition and state dependent memory.

In the area of memory for pictures, faces, and words, contextual effects are found, with different empirical findings being associated with different experimental paradigms or subject tasks. A similar situation exists in the study of auditory memory. This is not to imply that research in these areas is unique in terms of context effects. However, in many cases such contextual dependencies make it difficult to reconcile discrepant findings.

What are the trends for future research in human learning and memory?

Believing, as we do, that the recent past is the best predictor of what will follow, we expect that those research areas mentioned in this section will receive the most attention. Encoding and retrieval processes will continue to be studied intensively because of their centrality to memory. It also seems likely that perceptual processes will receive greater attention in memory research. Other research areas that will continue to be popular include auditory memory, memory for pictures, words and faces, and memory for sentences and stories. The latter area is likely to be quite popular because of its implications for text processing and the development of story grammars.

ACKNOWLEDGMENTS

We would like to acknowledge the assistance of Gerry Gingrich and Jeff Schwartz for their work on the literature search. Special thanks are given to Nancy Anderson and Sigfrid Soli for their comments on an earlier draft as well as other assistance they provided.

Literature Cited

Alba, J. W., Chromiak, W., Hasher, L., Attig, M. S. 1980. Automatic encoding of category size information. *J. Exp. Psychol: Hum. Learn. Mem.* 6:370–78

Anderson, J. R. 1976. *Language, Memory, and Thought.* Hillsdale, NJ: Erlbaum

Anderson, J. R. 1978. Arguments concerning representations for mental imagery. *Psychol. Rev.* 85:249–77

Anderson, J. R., Ross, B. H. 1980. Evidence against a semantic-episodic distinction. *J. Exp. Psychol: Hum. Learn. Mem.* 6:441–66

Atkinson, R. C., Herrmann, D. J., Wescourt, K. T. 1974. Search processes in recognition memory. In *Theories in Cognitive Psychology: The Loyola Symposium*, ed. R. L. Solso. Hillsdale, NJ: Erlbaum

Atkinson, R. C., Juola, J. F. 1974. Search and decision processes in recognition memory. In *Contemporary Developments in Mathematical Psychology: Learning, Memory, and Thinking*, Vol. 1, ed. D. H. Krantz, R. C. Atkinson, R. D. Luce, P. Suppes. San Francisco: Freeman

Ayres, T. J., Jonides, J., Reitman, J. S., Egan, J. C., Howard, D. A. 1979. Differing suffix effects for the same physical suffix. *J. Exp. Psychol: Hum. Learn. Mem.* 5:315–21

Babbitt, B. C. 1982. Effect of task demands on dual coding of pictorial stimuli. *J. Exp. Psychol: Learn. Mem. Cognit.* 8:73–80

Baddeley, A. D. 1982. Domains of recollection. *Psychol. Rev.* 89:708–29

Baddeley, A. D., Hull, A. 1979. Prefix and suffix effects: Do they have a common basis? *J. Verb. Learn. Verb. Behav.* 18:129–40

Baddeley, A. D., Woodhead, M. 1982. Depth of processing, context, and face recognition. *Can. J. Psychol.* 36:148–64

Balota, D. A., Engle, R. W. 1981. Structural and strategic factors in the stimulus suffix effect. *J. Verb. Learn. Verb. Behav.* 20:346–57

Bartlett, J. C., Till, R. E., Levy, J. C. 1980. Retrieval characteristics of complex pictures: Effects of verbal encoding. *J. Verb. Learn. Verb. Behav.* 19:430–49

Begg, I. 1979. Trace loss and the recognition failure of unrecalled words. *Mem. Cognit.* 7:113–23

Bird, J. E., Cook, M. 1979. Effects of stimulus duration and ISI on accuracy and transference errors in pictorial recognition. *Mem. Cognit.* 7:469–75

Black, J. B., Bern, H. 1981. Causal coherence and memory for events in narratives. *J. Verb. Learn. Verb. Behav.* 20:267–75

Black, J. B., Bower, G. H. 1979. Episodes as chunks in narrative memory. *J. Verb. Learn. Verb. Behav.* 18:309–18

Black, J. B., Turner, T. J., Bower, G. H. 1979. Point of view in narrative comprehension, memory, and production. *J. Verb. Learn. Verb. Behav.* 18:187–98

Bower, G. H. 1970a. Organizational factors in memory. *Cognit. Psychol.* 1:18–46

Bower, G. H. 1970b. Imagery as a relational organizer in associative learning. *J. Verb. Learn. Verb. Behav.* 9:529–33

Bower, G. H. 1981. Mood and memory. *Am. Psychol.* 36:129–48

Bower, G. H., Black, J. B., Turner, T. J. 1979.

Scripts in memory for text. *Cognit. Psychol.* 11:177–220

Bowyer, P. A., Humphreys, M. S. 1979. Effect of a recognition test on a subsequent cued-recall test. *J. Exp. Psychol: Hum. Learn. Mem.* 5:348–59

Bradshaw, G. L., Anderson, J. R. 1982. Elaborative encoding as an explanation of levels of processing. *J. Verb. Learn. Verb. Behav.* 21:165–74

Campbell, R., Dodd, B. 1980. Hearing by eye. *Q. J. Exp. Psychol.* 32:85–99

Carr, T. H., McCauley, C., Sperber, R. D., Parmelee, C. M. 1982. Words, pictures, and priming: On semantic activation, conscious identification, and the automaticity of information processing. *J. Exp. Psychol: Hum. Percept. Perform.* 8:757–77

Carroll, M., Kirsner, K. 1982. Context and repetition effects in lexical decision and recognition memory. *J. Verb. Learn. Verb. Behav.* 21:55–69

Chiesi, H. L., Spilich, G. J., Voss, J. F. 1979. Acquisition of domain-related information in relation to high and low domain knowledge. *J. Verb. Learn. Verb. Behav.* 18:257–73

Christiaanson, R. E. 1980. Prose memory: Forgetting rates for memory codes. *J. Exp. Psychol: Hum. Learn. Mem.* 6:611–19

Clifton, C. Jr., Slowiaczek, M. L. 1981. Integrating new information with old knowledge. *Mem. Cognit.* 9:142–48

Cohen, N. J., Corkin, S. 1982. *Learning to solve the Tower of Hanoi puzzle in anmesia.* Presented at Ann. Meet. Psychon. Soc., 23d, Minneapolis

Cohen, N. J., Squire, L. R. 1980. Preserved learning and retention of pattern-analyzing skill in amnesia: Dissociation of knowing how and knowing that. *Science* 210:207–10

Coltheart, M. 1980. Iconic memory and visible persistence. *Percept. Psychophys.* 27:183–228

Conrad, R. 1964. Acoustic confusions in immediate memory. *Br. J. Psychol.* 55:75–84

Craik, F. I. M. 1979. Human memory. *Ann. Rev. Psychol.* 30:63–102

Craik, F. I. M., Lockhart, R. S. 1972. Levels of processing: A framework for memory research. *J. Verb. Learn. Verb. Behav.* 11:671–84

Crowder, R. G. 1982a. Disinhibition of masking in auditory sensory memory. *Mem. Cognit.* 10:424–33

Crowder, R. G. 1982b. The demise of short-term memory. *Acta Psychol.* 50:291–323

Crowder, R. G., Morton, J. 1969. Precategorical acoustic storage (PAS). *Percept. Psychophys.* 5:365–73

DaPolito, F. J., Hale, C., Shew, R. L. 1981. Processing level and recognition: A search method for inducing alternative encodings of unrelated words. *Mem. Cognit.* 9:17–22

Deffenbacher, K. A., Carr, T. H., Leu, J. R. 1981. Memory for words, pictures, and faces: retroactive interference, forgetting, and reminiscence. *J. Exp. Psychol: Hum. Learn. Mem.* 7:299–305

Donaldson, W. 1981. Context and repetition effects in recognition memory. *Mem. Cognit.* 9:308–16

Drewnowski, A. 1980. Attributes and priorities in short-term recall: A new model of memory span. *J. Exp. Psychol: Gen.* 109:208–50

Drewnowski, A., Murdock, B. B. Jr. 1980. The role of auditory features in memory span for words. *J. Exp. Psychol: Hum. Learn. Mem.* 6:588–98

Durso, F. T., Johnson, M. K. 1980. The effects of orienting tasks on recognition, recall, and modality confusion of pictures and words. *J. Verb. Learn. Verb. Behav.* 19:416–29

Eich, J. E. 1980. The cue-dependent nature of state-dependent retrieval. *Mem. Cognit.* 8:157–73

Einstein, G. O., Hunt, R. R. 1980. Levels of processing and organization: Additive effects of individual-item and relational processing. *J. Exp. Psychol: Hum. Learn. Mem.* 6:588–98

Engle, R. W., Clark, D. D., Cathcart, J. S. 1980. The modality effect: Is it a result of different strategies? *J. Verb. Learn. Verb. Behav.* 19:226–39

Estes, W. K. 1980. Is human memory obsolete? *Am. Sci.* 68:62–69

Eysenck, M. W., Eysenck, M. C. 1979. Processing depth, elaboration of encoding, memory stores, and expended processing capacity. *J. Exp. Psychol: Hum. Learn. Mem.* 5:472–84

Fisher, R. P. 1979. Retrieval operations in cued recall and recognition. *Mem. Cognit.* 7:224–31

Fisher, R. P. 1981. Interaction between encoding distinctiveness and test conditions. *J. Exp. Psychol: Hum. Learn. Mem.* 7:306–10

Fisher, R. P., Craik, F. I. M. 1980. The effects of elaboration on recognition memory. *Mem. Cognit.* 8:400–4

Flexser, A. J., Tulving, E. 1978. Retrieval independence in recognition and recall. *Psychol. Rev.* 85:153–71

Flexser, A. J., Tulving, E. 1982. Priming and recognition failure. *J. Verb. Learn. Verb. Behav.* 21:237–48

Friedman, A. 1979. Framing pictures: The role of knowledge in automatized encoding and memory for gist. *J. Exp. Psychol: Gen.* 108:316–55

Galambos, J. A., Rips, L. J. 1982. Memory for routines. *J. Verb. Learn. Verb. Behav.* 21:260–81

Gardiner, J. M., Gregg, V. H. 1979. When auditory memory is not overwritten. *J. Verb. Learn. Verb. Behav.* 18:705–19

Gardiner, J. M., Tulving E. 1980. Exceptions to recognition failure of recallable words. *J. Verb. Learn. Verb. Behav.* 19:194–209

Gathercole, S. E., Gardiner, J. M., Gregg, V. H. 1982. Modality and phonological similarity effects in serial recall: Does one's own voice play a role? *Mem. Cognit.* 10:176–80

Geiselman, R. E., Bjork, R. A. 1980. Primary versus secondary rehearsal in imagined voices: Differential effects on recognition. *Cognit. Psychol.* 12:188–205

Geiselman, R. E., Woodward, J. A., Beatty, J. 1982. Individual differences in verbal memory performance: A test of alternative information-processing models. *J. Exp. Psychol: Gen.* 111:109–34

Glenberg, A. M., Bradley, M. M., Stevenson, J. A., Kraus, T. A., Tkachuk, M. J., et al. 1980. A two-process account of long-term serial position effects. *J. Exp. Psychol: Hum. Learn. Mem.* 6:355–69

Goetz, E. T., Anderson, R. C., Schallert, D. L. 1981. The representation of sentences in memory. *J. Verb. Learn. Verb. Behav.* 20:369–85

Goodman, G. S. 1980. Picture memory: How the action schema affects retention. *Cognit. Psychol.* 12:473–95

Graefe, T. M., Watkins, M. J. 1980. Picture rehearsal: An effect of selectively attending to pictures no longer in view. *J. Exp. Psychol: Hum. Learn. Mem.* 6:156–62

Guenther, R. K., Klatzky, R. L., Putnam, W. 1980. Commonalities and differences in semantic decisions about pictures and words. *J. Verb. Learn. Verb. Behav.* 19:54–74

Hannigan, M. L., Shelton, T. S., Franks, J. J., Bransford, J. D. 1980. The effects of episodic and semantic memory on the identification of sentences masked by white noise. *Mem. Cognit.* 8:278–84

Hanson, V. L. 1982. Short-term recall by deaf signers of American Sign Language: Implications of encoding strategy for order recall. *J. Exp. Psychol: Learn. Mem. Cognit.* 8:572–83

Hanson, V. L., Bellugi, U. 1982. On the role of sign order and morphological structure in memory for American Sign Language sentences. *J. Verb. Learn. Verb. Behav.* 21: 621–33

Hasher, L., Zacks, R. T. 1979. Automatic and effortful processes in memory. *J. Exp. Psychol: Gen.* 108:356–88

Herrmann, D. J., Harwood, J. R. 1980. More evidence for the existence of separate semantic and episodic stores in long-term memory. *J. Exp. Psychol: Hum. Learn. Mem.* 6:467–78

Hintzman, D. L., Nozawa, G., Irmscher, M. 1982. Frequency as a nonpropositional attribute of memory. *J. Verb. Learn. Verb. Behav.* 21:127–41

Humphreys, M. S., Bowyer, P. A. 1980. Sequential testing effects and the relationship between recognition and recognition failure. *Mem. Cognit.* 8:271–77

Hunt, R. R., Einstein, G. O. 1981. Relational and item-specific information in memory. *J. Verb. Learn. Verb. Behav.* 20: 497–514

Hunt, R. R., Elliott, J. M. 1980. The role of nonsemantic information in memory: Orthographic distinctiveness effects on retention. *J. Exp. Psychol: Gen.* 109:49–74

Hunt, R. R., Mitchell, D. B. 1982. Independent effects of semantic and nonsemantic distinctiveness. *J. Exp. Psychol: Learn. Mem. Cognit.* 8:81–87

Hyde, T. S., Jenkins, J. J. 1969. Differential effects of incidental tasks on the organization of recall of a list of highly associated words. *J. Exp. Psychol.* 82:472–81

Intraub, H. 1979. The role of implicit naming in pictorial encoding. *J. Exp. Psychol: Hum. Learn. Mem.* 5:78–87

Jacoby, L. L., Craik, F. I. M., Begg, I. 1979. Effects of decision difficulty on recognition and recall. *J. Verb. Learn. Verb. Behav.* 18:585–600

Jacoby, L. L., Dallas, M. 1981. On the relationship between autobiographical memory and perceptual learning. *J. Exp. Psychol: Gen.* 110:306–40

Jacoby, L. L., Witherspoon, D. 1982. Remembering without awareness. *Can. J. Psychol.* 36:300–24

Jenkins, J. J. 1974. Remember that old theory of memory? Well, forget it! *Am. Psychol.* 29:785–95

Johnston, W. A., Griffith, D., Wagstaff, R. R. 1972. Speed, accuracy, and ease of recall. *J. Verb. Learn. Verb. Behav.* 11:512–20

Kerr, N. H., Winograd, E. 1982. Effects of contextual elaboration on face recognition. *Mem. Cognit.* 10:603–9

Kihlstrom, J. F. 1980. Posthypnotic amnesia for recently learned material: Interactions with "episodic" and "semantic" memory. *Cognit. Psychol.* 12:227–51

Kintsch, W. 1978. More on recognition failure of recallable words: Implications for generation-recognition models. *Psychol. Rev.* 85:470–73

Klatzky, R. L., Martin, G. L., Kane, R. A. 1982. Semantic interpretation effects on memory for faces. *Mem. Cognit.* 10:195–206

Kolers, P. A. 1983. Perception and representation. *Ann. Rev. Psychol.* 34:129–66

Lee, C. L., Estes, W. K. 1981. Item and order information in short-term memory: Evidence for multilevel perturbation processes. *J. Exp. Psychol: Hum. Learn. Mem.* 7:149–69

Leight, K. A., Ellis, H. C. 1981. Emotional mood states, strategies, and state-dependency in memory. *J. Verb. Learn. Verb. Behav.* 20:251–75

Loftus, G. R., Kallman, H. J. 1979. Encoding and use of detail information in picture recognition. *J. Exp. Psychol: Hum. Learn. Mem.* 5:197–211

Lupker, S. J., Katz, A. N. 1981. Input, decision, and response factors in picture-word interference. *J. Exp. Psychol: Hum. Learn. Mem.* 7:269–82

Mandler, G. 1968. Association and organization: Facts, fancies, and theories. In *Verbal Behavior and General Behavior Theory*, ed. T. R. Dixon, D. L. Horton. Englewood Cliffs, NJ: Prentice-Hall

Mandler, G. 1980. Recognizing: The judgment of previous occurrence. *Psychol. Rev.* 87:252–71

Mandler, G., Goodman, G. O., Wilkes-Gibbs, D. L. 1982. The word-frequency paradox in recognition. *Mem. Cognit.* 10:33–42

Mayer, R. E., Cook, L. K. 1981. Effects of shadowing on prose comprehension and problem solving. *Mem. Cognit.* 9:101–9

McCloskey, M., Santee, J. 1981. Are semantic memory and episodic memory distinct systems? *J. Exp. Psychol: Hum. Learn. Mem.* 7:66–71

McGee, R. 1980. Imagery and recognition memory: The effects of relational organization. *Mem. Cognit.* 8:394–99

McKoon, G., Ratcliff, R. 1979. Priming in episodic and semantic memory. *J. Verb. Learn. Verb. Behav.* 18:463–80

Medin, D. L., Smith, E. E. 1984. Concepts and concept formation. *Ann. Rev. Psychol.* 35:113–38

Morris, C. D., Stein, B. S., Bransford, J. D. 1979. Prerequisites for the utilization of knowledge in recall of prose passages. *J. Exp. Psychol: Hum. Learn. Mem.* 5:253–61

Nairne, J. S., Crowder, R. G. 1982. On the locus of the stimulus suffix effect. *Mem. Cognit.* 10:350–57

Nelson, D. L. 1979. Remembering pictures and words: Appearance, significance, and name. In *Levels of Processing in Human Memory*, ed. L. S. Cermak, F. I. M. Craik. Hillsdale, NJ: Earlbaum

Nelson, D. L. 1981. Many are recalled but few are chosen: The influence of context on the effects of category size. *Psychol. Learn. Motiv.* 15:129–62

Nelson, D. L., Friedrich, M. A. 1980. Encoding and cuing sounds and senses. *J. Exp. Psychol: Hum. Learn. Mem.* 6:717–31

Nelson, D. L., McEvoy, C. L. 1979. Encoding context and set size. *J. Exp. Psychol: Hum. Learn. Mem.* 5:292–314

Owens, J., Bower, G. H., Black, J. B. 1979. The "soap opera" effect in story recall. *Mem. Cognit.* 7:185–91

Paivio, A., Desrochers, A. 1980. A dual-coding approach to bilingual memory. *Can. J. Psychol.* 34:388–99

Paivio, A., Lambert, W. 1981. Dual coding and bilingual memory. *J. Verb. Learn. Verb. Behav.* 20:532–39

Poizner, H., Bellugi, U., Tweney, R. D. 1981. Processing of formational semantic, and iconic information in American Sign Language. *J. Exp. Psychol: Hum. Percept. Perform.* 7:1146–59

Rabinowitz, J. C., Mandler, G., Barsalou, L. W. 1979. Generation-recognition as an auxiliary retrieval strategy. *J. Verb. Learn. Verb. Behav.* 18:57–72

Ritchey, G. H., Beal, C. R. 1980. Image detail and recall: Evidence for within-item elaboration. *J. Exp. Psychol: Hum. Learn. Mem.* 6:66–76

Roediger, H. L. III, Adelson, B. 1980. Semantic specificity in cued recall. *Mem. Cognit.* 8:65–74

Rothkopf, E. Z., Fisher, D. G., Billington, M. J. 1982. Effects of spatial context during acquisition on the recall of attributive information. *J. Exp. Psychol: Learn. Mem. Cognit.* 8:126–38

Sachs, J. S. 1967. Recognition memory for syntactic and semantic aspects of connected discourse. *Percept. Psychophys.* 2:437–42

Salamé, P., Baddeley, A. 1982. Disruption of short-term memory by unattended speech: Implications for the structure of working memory. *J. Verb. Learn. Verb. Behav.* 21:150–64

Schiano, D. J., Watkins, M. J. 1981. Speech-like coding of pictures in short-term memory. *Mem. Cognit.* 9:110–14

Schustack, M. W., Anderson, J. R. 1979. Effects of analogy to prior knowledge on memory for new information. *J. Verb. Learn. Verb. Behav.* 18:565–83

Shaffer, W. O., LaBerge, D. 1979. Automatic semantic processing of unattended words. *J. Verb. Learn. Verb. Behav.* 18:413–26

Shand, M. A. 1982. Sign-based short-term coding of American Sign Language signs and printed English words by congenitally deaf signers. *Cognit. Psychol.* 14:1–12

Shand, M. A., Klima, E. S. 1981. Nonauditory suffix effects in congenitally deaf signers of American Sign Language. *J. Exp. Psychol: Hum. Learn. Mem.* 7:464–74

Shiffrin, R. M., Schneider, W. 1977. Controlled and automatic human information processing: II. Perceptual learning, automatic attending, and a general theory. *Psychol. Rev.* 84:127–90

Shoben, E. J., Wescourt, K. T., Smith, E. E. 1978. Sentence verification, sentence recognition, and the semantic-episodic distinction. *J. Exp. Psychol: Hum. Learn. Mem.* 4:304–17

Smith, D. A., Graesser, A. C. 1981. Memory

for actions in scripted activities as a function of typicality, retention interval, and retrieval task. *Mem. Cognit.* 9:550-59

Smith, M. C., Magee, L. E. 1980. Tracing the time course of picture-word processing. *J. Exp. Psychol: Gen.* 109:373–92

Spiro, R. J. 1980. Accommodative reconstruction in prose recall. *J. Verb. Learn. Verb. Behav.* 19:84–95

Spoehr, K. T., Corin, W. J. 1978. The stimulus suffix effect as a memory phenomenon. *Mem. Cognit.* 6:583–89

Stein, B. S., Bransford, J. D. 1979. Constraints on effective elaboration: Effects of precision and subject generation. *J. Verb. Learn. Verb. Behav.* 18:769–77

Stern, L. D. 1981. A review of theories of human amnesia. *Mem. Cognit.* 9:247–62

Stevenson, R. J. 1981. Depth of comprehension, effective elaboration, and memory for sentences. *Mem. Cognit.* 9:169–76

te Linde, J. 1982. Picture-word differences in decision latency: A test of common-coding assumptions. *J. Exp. Psychol: Learn. Mem. Cognit.* 8:584–98

Thorndyke, P. W., Yekovich, F. R. 1980. A critique of schema-based theories of human story memory. *Poetics* 9:23–49

Tulving, E. 1972. Episodic and semantic memory. In *Organization of Memory*, ed. E. Tulving, W. Donaldson. New York: Academic

Tulving, E. 1981. Similarity relations in recognition. *J. Verb. Learn. Verb. Behav.* 20:479–96

Tulving, E. 1982. Synergistic ecphory in recall and recognition. *Can. J. Psychol.* 36:130–47

Tulving, E., Schacter, D. L., Stark, H. A. 1982. Priming effects in word-fragment completion are independent of recognition memory. *J. Exp. Psychol: Learn. Mem. Cognit.* 8:336–42

Tulving, E., Thomson, D. M. 1973. Encoding specificity and retrieval processes in episodic memory. *Psychol. Rev.* 80:352–73

Tulving, E., Wiseman, S. 1975. Relation between recognition and recognition failure of recallable words. *Bull. Psychon. Soc.* 6:79–82

Tversky, A. 1977. Features of similarity. *Psychol. Rev.* 84:327–52

Tyler, S. W., Hertel, P. T., McCallum, M. C., Ellis, H. C. 1979. Cognitive effort and memory. *J. Exp. Psychol: Hum. Learn. Mem.* 5:607–17

Warren, L. R., Horn, J. W. 1982. What does naming a picture do? Effects of prior picture naming on recognition of identical and same-name alternative. *Mem. Cognit.* 10:167–75

Warrington, E. K., Weiskrantz, L. 1974. The effect of prior learning on subsequent retention in amnesic patients. *Neuropsychologia* 12:419–28

Watkins, M. J., Gardiner, J. M. 1979. An appreciation of generate-recognize theory of recall. *J. Verb. Learn. Verb. Behav.* 18:687–704

Watkins, M. J., Graefe, T. M. 1981. Delayed rehearsal of pictures. *J. Verb. Learn. Verb. Behav.* 20:276–88

Watkins, M. J., Todres, A. K. 1980. Suffix effects manifest and concealed: Further evidence for a 20-second echo. *J. Verb. Learn. Verb. Behav.* 19:46–53

Watkins, O. C., Watkins, M. J. 1980. The modality effect and echoic persistence. *J. Exp. Psychol: Gen.* 109:251–78

Watkins, O. C., Watkins, M. J. 1982. Lateral inhibition and echoic memory: Some comments on Crowder's (1978) theory. *Mem. Cognit.* 10:279–86

Winograd, E., Lynn, D. S. 1979. Role of contextual imagery in associative recall. *Mem. Cognit.* 7:29–34

Woodhead, M. M., Baddeley, A. D. 1981. Individual differences and memory for faces, pictures and words. *Mem. Cognit.* 9:368–70

Yekovich, F. R., Manelis, L. 1980. Accessing integrated and nonintegrated propositional structures in memory. *Mem. Cognit.* 8:133–40

Yekovich, F. R., Thorndyke, P. W. 1981. An evaluation of alternative functional models of narrative schemata. *J. Verb. Learn. Verb. Behav.* 20:454–69

Zacks, R. T., Hasher, L., Sanft, H. 1982. Automatic encoding of event frequency: Further findings. *J. Exp. Psychol: Learn. Mem. Cognit.* 8:106–16

Ann. Rev. Psychol. 1984. 35:395–426

ATTITUDES AND ATTITUDE CHANGE

Joel Cooper and Robert T. Croyle

Department of Psychology, Princeton University, Princeton, New Jersey 08544[1]

CONTENTS

INTRODUCTION

Perhaps no area of research in social psychology has been as active as the formation and change of attitudes (McGuire 1969). Nonetheless, research interest in attitudes has had its peaks and valleys. In the early 1970s, research in attitudes seemed to reach one of those valleys, only to begin to climb out again by the end of the decade (see review by Eagly & Himmelfarb 1978). In the last review of attitudes published in this series, Cialdini, Petty & Cacioppo (1981) predicted that the revival of interest in attitude change seemed destined to

---

[1]Robert T. Croyle is now at Williams College, Williamstown, Massachusetts 01267

0066-4308/84/0201-0395$02.00

remain steady in the years ahead. Our review of the major journals and volumes of the past 3 years suggests that this prophecy has indeed been supported.

In our review, we have selected what we believe to be the major trends in attitude change research. By focusing on major lines of research, we recognize that there may be several studies on other facets of attitudes and attitude change that we cannot present. However, focusing on these trends will serve as a guide for organizing the vast literature and as an indication of what are likely to be future concerns of research.

Three major lines of research are evident: attitude-behavior consistency, persuasion, and cognitive dissonance. It is our view that the major focus of theoretical attention has been the question of the consistency of attitudes and behaviors. Interest in attitude-behavior consistency is not new, as evidenced by the often-cited study by La Piere (1934). Cialdini et al (1981) noted that the pessimism or skepticism that used to attach to the question of consistency gave way to marked optimism by the late 1970s. Nonetheless, the work remained focused on advances in methodology and measurement and less on substantive theory. While the 1980s have seen no less emphasis on methodological concerns, the development of theory has made great gains. Perhaps spurred on by symposia devoted to this topic (e.g. Zanna et al 1982), theoretical models have appeared to address the mediation of consistency between attitudes and behaviors.

Persuasion research continues to be dominated by the cognitive response perspective. Indeed, the current literature is practically devoid of any mention of affect, emotion, or arousal. We suspect that the preeminence of cognitive models will soon be challenged by a renewed interest in motivational constructs. Such a shift in emphasis is suggested by a flurry of new research which underlines the role of personal involvement in a message recipient's response to a persuasion attempt.

A third major trend in the literature has been the continued resurgence of research in cognitive dissonance. Cialdini et al (1981) took note of the advance of this trend when they observed, "Consistency is back" (p. 358). They particularly cited a revival of interest in balance theory and dissonance theory. The literature of the past few years has seen a shift in the balance theory research from attitudes to person perception (e.g. Crockett 1982). Therefore, our review will focus on the theoretical and applied emphases of research in dissonance.

Finally, we note two areas of ongoing research that reaffirm the interplay among cognitive, psychophysiological, and social psychology. The first area integrates concerns of cognitive and social psychology, employing attitude as an independent variable while examining consequences for social information processing. The second area, social psychophysiology, relates bodily responses to attitude measurement and attitude change. The theoretical potential of both domains of research remains uncertain.

THE ATTITUDE-BEHAVIOR RELATIONSHIP

Three questions have persistently challenged investigators interested in the relationships between attitudes and behavior: (*a*) Do attitudes predict and/or cause behavior? (*b*) What mediates the attitude-behavior relationships? (*c*) How can psychologists best predict behavior from attitudes? Although some controversy remains regarding the best answer to the first two questions, the research so stimulated continues to provide concrete suggestions for answering the third.

Two Perspectives

Throughout most of the history of social psychology, the study of attitudes was, in large part, motivated by the assumption that individuals tend to act in accordance with them. This assumption seemed so trite that two of the provocative and influential attitude theories of the 1960s and 1970s focused instead on the reverse process, i.e. the role of experienced behavior in determining attitudes (Festinger 1957, Bem 1972). The numerous research efforts in the persuasion domain have been predicated on the same assumption of causal (or at least empirical) linkages between attitudes and behavior.

Investigators holding the assumption that individuals generally behave in accordance with their attitudes were put on the defensive, however, with the publication of reviews such as Wicker's (1969) that suggested a weak relationship between measured attitudes and subsequent behavior. Generally, researchers have met this challenge in one of two ways. One group (e.g. Ajzen & Fishbein 1977) sees the problem as largely a methodological one. They argue that an assessment of behavioral *intentions* will lead to the most accurate behavioral predictions. However, if attitudes and behavior of comparable levels of specificity are measured, they argue, even attitudes will be found to be excellent predictors of behavior. Such an approach assumes, a priori, that people behave in accordance with their attitudes. If such relationships have not been demonstrated empirically, the methods of assessment are at fault.

A second group concedes that, taken alone, attitudes are often inadequate predictors of behaviors. Unless mediational variables and processes are taken in account, they argue, the psychologist is bound to oversimplify the complex roles of experience, perception, cognition, context, and goals (e.g. Fazio & Zanna 1981, Abelson 1982). Because such a view assumes that the nature and impact of attitudes varies both within and between individuals and situations, it becomes crucial to take these individual differences into account. As indicated in the discussion below, both the methodological and the mediational perspectives have continued to generate a great deal of thoughtful and productive research on the attitude-behavior relation.

A METHODOLOGICAL PERSPECTIVE   Ajzen (1982) has provided a concise restatement of the methodological perspective on the attitude-behavior controversy. Low attitude-behavior correlations, according to Ajzen, are due more to sloppy psychometrics than to complex mediational factors. He argues that a strong relationship between attitudes and behavior exists, and outlines evidence that supports his contention. Much of this evidence has been summarized in the last two reviews of attitude research in this series (Eagly & Himmelfarb 1978, Cialdini et al 1981). Since the current purpose is to update these previous reviews, we will present only a brief summary of the latest studies embracing the methodological perspective. Readers interested in a more detailed description of the theoretical models underlying this approach are referred to published volumes and articles by Fishbein & Ajzen (1975, Ajzen & Fishbein 1977, 1980).

Measurement correspondence   The last review of attitude research in this series (Cialdini et al 1981) noted that the most influential statement on attitude-behavior relations during the time span reviewed (1977–1979) had been Ajzen & Fishbein's 1977 paper in the *Psychological Bulletin*. The present review found additional support for viewing that work as a significant and impactful one.

The empirical lesson of Ajzen and Fishbein was summarized cogently by Bagozzi (1981): "A general attitude will predict a multiple-act criterion better than a single-act criterion, whereas a specific attitude will predict a single-act criterion better than a multiple-act criterion" (p. 608). Therefore, an investigator is likely to find higher correlations between measures of attitude and behavior when they correspond in their level of specificity (see Fishbein & Ajzen 1974 for a description of supportive research).

Sjöberg (1982) provided further support for the importance of measurement correspondence in a study using high school students. Self-reported attitudes and behavior relevant to aid to developing countries were assessed. As predicted, a global attitude measure was more predictive of the multiple-act criterion than of single acts. In the case of single acts, a subject's perception of an act as socially desirable seemed to enhance its predictability, although this simply may have been due to a tendency to justify reported behavior.

The intentions model   A second product of the methodological perspective that has continued to stimulate research and controversy is Fishbein & Ajzen's (1975) model of intentions. An intention, according to Fishbein and Ajzen, is a function of two components: a person's attitude toward performing a specific behavior, and a subjective view of the social norms regarding that behavior. According to what is now referred to as the "theory of reasoned action" (Ajzen & Fishbein 1980), attitudes toward behavior are better predictors of intentions and actual behavior than attitudes toward objects or issues. The measurement of intentions, it is argued, permits the nearly perfect predictability of the corresponding behavior. These investigators report a great deal of data to support their two-component model of intentions, and others have also found high correlations between intentions and subsequent behaviors (e.g. Davidson & Jaccard 1979).

Bagozzi (1981), using a single-act criterion, employed a causal modeling methodology to explore attitude-intention-behavior relations. A critical premise of Fishbein & Ajzen's model is that attitudes influence behavior only through their impact on intentions. Bagozzi's longitudinal study of blood donation provided support for this notion. Attitudes toward blood donation influenced blood donation behavior only through their effect on donation intentions. The significance of this study is due in part to the methods employed by the investigator. Unlike many of the methodologically oriented studies of attitude-behavior relations, Bagozzi's study employed objective behavioral measures of blood donation.

Saltzer (1981) reported data that were less supportive of the intentions model. In a study of weight loss intentions and behaviors, Saltzer measured weight locus of control (Saltzer 1978) and values on health and appearance. Although intentions were found to correlate significantly with behavior (defined as weight loss), this relationship was mediated by the two individual difference factors. Subjects with high values for the behavioral outcome and the external locus of control apparently performed behaviors that were unrelated to behavioral intentions. In defense of the intentions model, it could be argued that actual weight loss is only an indirect indicant of weight-loss *behavior* such as dieting, exercise, etc. Saltzer's analysis must assume that factors outside of the personal control of subjects (e.g. physiological) did not account for a significant attenuation of intention-behavior correlations. Nevertheless, this was not the only study that appeared to yield data inconsistent with Fishbein and Ajzen's model. Bentler and Speckart found not once (1979) but twice (1981) that the strength of the intention-behavior relationship depends on the behavior domain. For one domain (exercise) it was found that attitudes were better predictors of behavior than intentions. Similar data were obtained by Manstead et al (1983) in their examination of mothers' infant-feeding intentions and behavior. Attitudes were found to increase significantly the predictive capabilities of a regression model, even after intentions were taken into account. These studies suggest that further research is needed to resolve inconsistencies within the intention-behavior literature.

A second focus of intentions model critics has been the two components of behavioral intention—attitude and subjective norm. Miniard & Cohen (1981) argue that Fishbein & Ajzen's distinction between normative compliance and value-motivated behavior is a muddled one, since these factors inherently overlap. In an experiment conducted to test their hypothesis, they found that independent variables designed to affect one component also affected the other. In a published rebuttal, Fishbein & Ajzen (1981) managed to interpret the results of the Miniard & Cohen study as further support for their model. While conceding that some factors may influence both components, Fishbein and Ajzen argue that sufficient evidence exists to support their original distinction. Furthermore, they properly point out that Miniard & Cohen appear to have tested their own conceptions of social and personal influence rather than Fishbein and Ajzen's conceptions of social norms and attitudes.

Finally, two studies attempted to test the two-component intention model in applied contexts. While McCarty (1981) found experimental evidence that generally supports the model, Kantola et al (1982) found that age accounted for variance in intention that was unexplained by social norms and attitudes.

THE MEDIATIONAL PERSPECTIVE   Although few would disagree that the methodological perspective has significantly advanced our understanding of how attitudes can be used to predict behaviors, some investigators have questioned that perspective's contributions to any real understanding of the psychological processes underlying the attitude-behavior relation. This point of view is exemplified by Abelson's (1982) reaction to Ajzen and Fishbein's (1977) recommendations regarding measurement correspondence: "Ajzen and Fishbein's advice leaves us travelling a road paved with psychometric intentions, which does not necessarily take us near to understanding the dynamics of attitudes and behaviors" (p.132)

The differences between the methodological and mediational perspectives are reflected as well in the research methods employed. Research performed within the mediational perspective continues to rely more on the laboratory experiment than on field surveys, with the manipulation of independent variables receiving more attention than the sophisticated analysis of multiple dependent measures. The most widely cited review within the mediational framework has been that of Fazio and Zanna (1981). Those authors summarized research which indicated that attitudes based on direct experience with the attitude object are typically more predictive of behaviors than attitudes not so based. This work was extended by Sherman et al (1982) in a rebuttal of Fishbein & Ajzen's (1980) explanation of direct experience effects. Fishbein & Ajzen argued that attitudes based on direct experience are better predictors of later behavior simply because of their greater stability over time. According to their analysis, experience should not strengthen the attitude-intention relationship on initial assessment. In a study of smoking intentions in adolescents, however, Sherman et al found that direct smoking experience increased the predictability of intentions from the attitude component. Sherman et al suggest that attitudes based on experience are more accessible and therefore are more likely to guide behavior.

Borgida & Campbell (1982) examined a situation in which behavioral experience (problems with finding campus parking space) was inconsistent with the implications of a global attitude (environmental concern). They found that the impact of a manipulation of the cognitive accessibility and relevance of the global attitude depended on the amount of personal experience a subject had with the specific attitude-issue. Attitude-behavior consistency was increased by magnifying the cognitive accessibility of global attitude relevance only among subjects with minimal behavioral experience.

The demonstrated importance of more "psychological" variables such as behavioral experience has led many social psychologists to search for nonattitudinal characteristics that strengthen or attenuate the attitude-behavior relation. Recent work has focused on both personality and situation factors.

Mediating personality factors   One personality factor that has been explored in the context of the attitude-behavior relationship is self-monitoring tendency (Snyder 1979). Individuals who are high self-monitors tend to be sensitive to, and thus influenced by, situational cues. Low self-monitors, however, tend to rely on their inner states and dispositions when making behavioral decisions. In the case of attitude-behavior correspondence, low self-monitors have shown higher correspondence between attitudes and later behavior than high self-monitors (e.g. Snyder & Swann 1976), and low self-monitors express attitudes that are more predictable from prior behavior than are attitudes expressed by high self-monitors (Snyder & Tanke 1976).

Snyder (1981) has argued that low self-monitoring leads to greater behavioral consistency and a preference for social situations that will permit and/or encourage the expression of stable attitudes. Snyder & Kendzierski (1982a) recently supplied data to support the hypothesis of situational preference. They found that low self-monitors preferred a social situation only when it allowed the open expression of attitudes—in this case, attitudes toward affirmative action. Zanna et al (1980) provided further support for the importance of self-monitoring and behavioral consistency in a study of religious attitudes and behaviors. They found that attitude-behavior consistency was strongest among low self-monitors who had reported low variablity across attitude-relevant behaviors. This suggests that individual differences in the perception of attitude-relevant experience are due, in part, to differences in self-monitoring tendencies. In an improvement on the retrospective self-report measures used in the above study, Olson & Zanna (1980) had subjects keep daily behavioral diaries for three weeks. In addition, objective observations of behavor were obtained when subjects returned to the laboratory. The data obtained by Olson & Zanna and again by Coreless & Zanna (1980) replicated the Zanna et al findings. The highest attitude-behavior correlation was obtained from those low self-monitors who reported relatively low variability of attitude-relevant behaviors.

Person-situation processes   Since social behavior is typically conceptualized as being a function of the interaction of person and situation variables, it is not surprising that the attitude-behavior relation has been explored with the same framework. But what are the actual cognitive processes that account for these interactions? As social psychologists have grown more cognitive in their orientation, the study of cognitive mediators in the attitude-behavior domain has increased significantly.

One example relevant to the previous discussion of self-monitoring is an investigation by Snyder & Kendzierski (1982b). In their study, Snyder & Kendzierski tested the impact of contextual factors intended to increase either the availability or the behavioral relevance of attitudes. Whereas making attitudes more salient (by encouraging subjects to ruminate about them) led to more consistent behavior only for low self-monitors, increasing relevance (by emphasizing consequences of the behavior relevant to the attitude issue) increased attitude-behavior correspondence among both high and low self-monitors. Thus, the impact of contextual variables on an individual's likelihood to behave in accordance with prior attitudes depends on that individual's dispositional tendency to be sensitive to those contextual cues. The authors argue that situational cues will increase correspondence to the extent that they induce a "believing-means-doing" approach to selecting appropriate behaviors.

Ajzen and Fishbein's theory of reasoned action (1980) was invoked by Ajzen et al (1982) to explain the locus of the effect of self-monitoring dispositions on the attitude-behavior relation. They found little difference between high and low self-monitors in the strength of the attitude-intention relationship. Differences between these two groups were quite apparent, however, when the strengths of the intention-behavior correlations were examined. Low self-monitors were more likely to perform their intentions. Ajzen et al saw this evidence as contradicting Snyder's (1982) contention that high and low self-monitors differ in their perception of the relevance of attitudes to actions. Rather, the evidence was interpreted as supporting Snyder's (1974) original notion regarding high self-monitors: despite the presence (and recognition of) a prior attitude, the behavior of high self-monitors will tend to be shaped by situational cues.

In a provocative review of the attitude-behavior issue, Abelson (1982) proposed three modes of attitude-behavior consistency as mediated by situational context. Under *individuating* conditions, individuals are induced to focus greater attention on their personal attitudes, dispositions, and behavioral history (see Wicklund 1982). Social circumstances which call for or encourage a great deal of personal deliberation are likely to be individuating. Attitude-behavior correspondence is achieved because the individual's reflective posture brings attitude-relevant material into consciousness, thus increasing the probability that behavior will be guided by the application of such material. Discrepencies can occur, however, when only attitude measurement or behavioral choice take place in individuating circumstances. Contexts in which behavioral sequences are *scripted* (Abelson 1981) raise different issues relevant to the attitude-behavior relation. Scripts are defined as "conceptual representations of stereotyped event sequences" (1981, p. 715). Scripted behavior, according to Abelson, is usually automatic, since it is driven by experience and prior expectations of normative behavior. Scripts allow behavior to flow without constant interruption by unexpected behaviors, effortful decision-making, and reevaluation. Abelson sees the scripted context as one that obscures individual differences, since the constraints on behavior that the situation requires may result in behavioral homogeneity, despite the presence of unexpressed attitudinal variation. *Deindividuating* circumstances turn the individual's attention toward more general symbolic attitudes (see Sears et al 1979) that define an ingroup's identity. If symbolic attitudes have been measured, then attitude-behavior correlations will be high. Otherwise, individual behavior is likely to be interpreted as highly irrational and attitude-discrepent.

A process model   Fazio et al (1983) have proposed a process model of the attitude-behavior relation. The focus of the model reflects the rapid growth of interest in social cognition among social psychologists (Cantor & Kihlstrom 1981, Higgins et al 1981). Fazio et al conceive attitudes as performing a functional role as an organizer of objects in the environment. For attitudes to play a role in the behavioral selection process, they must first be accessed from memory. Because social perception is assumed to be colored only by accessed attitudes, the determination of how and when particular attitudes are brought into play is an important first step toward an understanding of how and when attitudes will guide behavior. Fazio and his colleagues have examined experimentally several of the factors assumed to impinge upon attitude accessibility. Fazio et al (1982), for example, found that attitudes based on personal experience were more accessible, as indicated by shorter latencies on a reaction time task. Fazio et al (1983) found that prior exposure to an attitude object led subjects to evaluate a new stimulus in a manner consistent with the attitude. Apparently the "priming" of an attitude by incidental exposure to the attitude object can lead to behaviors that are attitude-consistent. This suggests that explicit references to an individual's attitude are not necessary for triggering an immediate heightening of attitude-behavior correspondence, as long as that attitude is based on direct personal experience.

New Directions

It is clear that our understanding of the attitude-behavior problem has advanced significantly in the past 10 years. Zanna & Fazio (1982) have characterized this area of research as having already moved through two stages of development. They characterize the first stage as one where concerns with "Is" questions, such as "Is there an effect?" were predominant. Can attitudes be used to predict behavior? This question has been answered in the affirmative (largely, we feel, through the work of Fishbein and Ajzen and their colleagues). Psychologists have since moved on to "When" questions. Here we see the divergence of the psychometric and mediational points of view. The differences we have outlined above are not trivial. Nevertheless, they may be reconciled as investigators address what Zanna & Fazio refer to as third generation "How" questions. These mediational process questions will be the most difficult to answer, and the methods and talents of both camps will be required to address them adequately.

One encouraging sign is the growing collaboration between those interested in attitude-behavior consistency issues and those interested in personality-behavior consistency issues. Ironically, the early stages of attempted integration seem to have been stimulated more by common frustration and failure than by common accomplishments (e.g. Abelson 1972). Nevertheless, our review of the attitude-behavior literaure indicates that a fruitful synthesis may be emerging. Fazio & Zanna sounded an optimistic call to arms in their influential chapter in the 1981 volume of the *Advances* series. Deliberate attempts to bring experts from the fields of attitudes and personality together have occurred. *Consistency in Social Behavior* (edited by Zanna, Higgins & Herman 1982), which consists of contributions presented at the second Ontario symposium, is a landmark in this respect and sets a precedent worthy of being repeated.

COGNITIVE DISSONANCE

Cognitive dissonance theory passed its first quarter century during the period covered by this review. It is certainly testimony to the theory's tendency to provoke debate and discussion that research continues to accumulate in this area. While the rate of research cannot equal the tremendous outpouring that the 1960s witnessed, dissonance theory remains one of the more active foci of research. Extrapolating from Frey's (1982) count, we estimate that the literature has now nearly 1000 entries pertaining to dissonance.

Dissonance theory is not exclusively a theory of attitudes. Since attitudes are cognitive elements that are usually least resistant to change, research in dissonance theory has often focused on attitude change. Most, but not all, of the research we will review continues this tradition. Some influential work during this period concentrates on other aspects of the dissonance process. We shall review these as well.

Recent research and writing about dissonance has fallen into several not mutually exclusive categories. Much of the work has explored conceptual bases of the dissonance phenomenon and has concentrated on revisions and modifications of the theory (e.g. Schlenker 1982, Steele & Liu 1983, Fazio and Cooper 1983). Other work has concentrated on the practical implications of dissonance theory with an attempt to apply the theoretical framework to other areas (e.g. Steele et al 1981). Meanwhile, a high volume of research activity has focused on areas of dissonance theory that have been relatively overlooked in the 1960s and 1970s. Notable here is the work of Frey and his colleagues in the selective exposure field. We shall examine each of these broad categories in turn.

Toward Fuller Understanding of the Theory

VALUE REAFFIRMATION   One of the exciting trends in recent research in dissonance is a new set of ideas about the mechanisms that underlie the dissonance process. Steele & Liu (1983) argue that the self-justificatory attitude change that follows counterattitudinal advocacy is based not upon inconsistency among cognitions but upon an ego-based need for a positive and efficacious self-image. A person who writes an essay opposed to building handicapped facilities may well feel that his or her ego identity of being a good and caring person is threatened. This is precisely the situation established in a study by Steele & Liu (1981). The authors argued that if dissonance is aroused because of such a threat, then giving subjects an expectation that they would be able to help handicapped students after the experiment was over should reduce the dissonance. Their results supported this hypothesis.

In a subsequent study, Steele & Liu (1983) took their approach one step further. They argue that dissonance can be reduced by any action that affirms one of the actor's important values. In contrast to their original statement, Steele & Liu argued that the reaffirmed value did not have to be related to the dissonant act at all. In three experiments, they manipulated dissonance arousal by counterattitudinal essay writing and then had subjects respond to a value questionnaire that enabled them to reaffirm important, self-relevant values. Subjects given the opportunity to reaffirm their values did not show the need for dissonance reducing attitude change.

The ramifications of the self-affirmation approach still need to be explored. Questions relating to potential alternative interpretations such as distraction deserve to be addressed, and whether there are meaningful similarities between the self-affirmation view and Aronson's (1969) view of cognitive dissonance as discrepancy with expectations based on self-esteem have to be analyzed. Steele & Liu's approach however, is a provocative view that is bound to generate yet another flurry of research activity in dissonance theory.

THE SEARCH FOR AROUSAL   Festinger (1957) initially likened dissonance to a drive and offered several analogies to the way dissonance functioned. Hunger and thirst were the major analogues, and so it was thought that dissonance was a "drive-like state." Curiously, a close examination of Festinger's original work finds no explicit statement that dissonance is a drive nor that it has arousal properties (cf Fazio & Cooper 1983). Indeed, several investigators working within the dissonance tradition (Higgins et al 1979) have questioned whether dissonance is arousing at all.

Nonetheless, the search for the elusive arousing properties of dissonance continued during the period under review. The literature was reviewed extensively by Fazio & Cooper (1983). They pointed out that it is important to identify arousal in the dissonance process in order to help differentiate dissonance from alternative processes that do not posit arousal. Fazio and Cooper's review concluded that there was now substantial evidence from several research paradigms (see Cotton's 1981 review of the misattribution paradigm) that dissonance does evoke arousal.

What kind of arousal does dissonance evoke? One of the newer pieces of evidence (Croyle & Cooper 1983) indicates that there is physiological activity associated with dissonance. Croyle & Cooper had subjects write an essay that was contrary to their attitudes. The essays were written under either high choice or low choice conditions. Compared with subjects in other conditons, high choice counterattitudinal essay writers displayed a significantly greater number of spontaneous skin conductance responses, a reliable indicant of heightened physiological arousal (see Masling et al 1981). The research appears to support what Festinger had implied—that there is an arousal consequent to engaging in attitude discrepant behavior.

FROM IMPRESSION MANAGEMENT TO IDENTITY THEORY: AN ALTERNATIVE APPROACH   For the past several years, Tedeschi and his colleagues (e.g. Tedeschi et al 1971) have proposed an approach known as impression management. The supposition behind this approach is that people try persistently to manage the impressions that other people have of them. Attitude change following counterattitudinal advocacy is conceived of as nothing more than an attempt to manipulate one's impression in the eyes of a high status experimenter and to absolve oneself from the embarrassment of appearing inconsistent. Research by Tedeschi and his colleagues has continued during this period. (Tedeschi 1981, Riess et al 1981, Malkis et al 1982). Much of the research has taken the form of the "critical test" between impression management and dissonance in the forced compliance paradigm. Critical tests have often proved elusive in social psychology, and they continue to be elusive in the impression mangement-dissonance debate. There seems little question that people are concerned about the impressions they present to people (Jones & Pittman 1982). But is the management of impressions the *only* or even major concern that people have when they are faced with inconsistency? Research done during this period has not shed greater light on this question, leaving in force Cialdini et al's conclusion after their survey of the impression management-dissonance literature. They concluded that they could "not agree with the claim that self-presentational influences are the sole mediators of the compliance effects" (1981, p. 382). Perhaps a better question for future research is how much of the variance is accounted for by the arousal of dissonance and how much is accounted for by the manipulation and management of impressions.

A major development in the self-presentational view of the consequences of inconsistency is Schlenker's (1980, 1982) identity-analytic model. Schlenker's approach offers a view so compatable with the basic tenets of recent work in dissonance that it may best be viewed not as an opposing theory but rather as an intriguing expansion of dissonance theory. Schlenker basically accepts the model of dissonance that indicates that people change their attitudes when they accept responsibility for the aversive consequences of their behavior (Cooper 1971, Collins & Hoyt 1972). However, he proposes, as mediating mechanisms, concepts similar to those suggested by Scott & Lyman's (1968) sociological perspective. The identity-analytic model holds that people change their attitudes in an attempt to avoid being held responsible for reprehensible behavior. They accomplish this by means of a variety of excuses called accounts and explanations. Similarly, people attempt to gain credit for positive outcomes of behavior by claiming credit where credit was not due.

Identity analysis claims to place dissonance findings in a broader context. For example, the identity approach asserts an explanation not only of dissonance theory's inverse incentive effects, but also incorporates the occasional direct effect of incentive magnitude on attitude change when dissonance is not applicable (Schlenker et al 1980, Schlenker & Goldman 1982). Schlenker et al (1980) conducted three experiments in which they used identity-analytic theory to predict the conditions under which a direct effect of incentive magnitude on attitude change would occur after subjects wrote counterattitudinal essays. The results supported Schlenker et al's prediction. However, the study failed to produce the predicted inverse effects of incentive on attitude change. This failure leaves the empirical support for the identity-analytic view somewhat ambiguous.

The identity-analytic approach offers a theoretical point of view much more compatible with various versions of dissonance theory than does impression management. One important distinction between identity theory and impression management is that the former does not take the position that attitude change is simply feigned public behavior. For example, Schlenker states, "it may be premature to conclude that the appearance of attitude change is merely a public illusion" (Schlenker 1982 p. 236).

Finally, impression management itself has undergone some major revisions during the last few years. As we pointed out above, the search for the discovery of arousal processes was undertaken, in part, to differentiate dissonance from a variety of competing theories. Researchers have used indications of arousal as an argument that cast doubt upon such explanations as self-perception (e.g. Bond 1981) and impression management (Worchel & Cooper 1983). However, a revised version of impression management theory has appeared (Tedeschi & Rosenfeld 1981). Although presenting a morally upright image is still seen as a person's major goal, Tedeschi & Rosenfeld (1981) also write, "As a consequence (of the self-presentational goal), subjects feel uncomfortable, embarrassed and/or socially anxious" (p. 155). The revised impression management theory, then, also accommodates the concept of arousal. As a consequence, impression management may have lost some of the sharp points of contrast with dissonance theory and may have moved toward becoming a translation of dissonance terminology into the language of self-evaluation and self-presentation.

Dissonance Applied to Social Concerns

Steele et al (1981) suggested that the arousal that accompanies inconsistency can lead to behaviors that do not necessarily restore the inconsistency but rather lead to a reduction of the unpleasant arousal. Drinking alcohol, they reasoned, may be one such behavior. Based upon evidence that alcohol leads to a postive emotional experience (McCollam et al 1980), Steele et al predicted and found that subjects who wrote counterattitudinal essays and who have the opportunity to drink alcohol after writing their essay, will do so. Steele et al (1981) reasoned that the pleasantness engendered by alcohol consumption obviates the need for cognitive changes and, instead, directly alleviates the unpleasant arousal. Consistent with this logic, Steele et al found no attitude change among subjects who had the opportunity to drink alcohol *prior* to the post-measure.

Cooper (1980) and Cooper & Axsom (1982) applied the logic of dissonance theory to an analysis of psychotherapy. They argued that psychotherapy can be viewed as an example of the effort justification paradigm in cognitive dissonance research. In psychotherapy, people choose to engage in a high degree of an unpleasant or effortful experience in order to reach a goal. When that situation is set up in the laboratory, research has consistently demonstrated that the effort leads to more positive attitudes toward the goal object (Aronson & Mills 1959, Seta & Seta 1982). The dissonance created by the effortful experiences that occur within psychotherapy may cause attitudes toward the goal to become more positive and therefore lead to the desired therapeutic outcome. One of Cooper's (1980) experiments dealt with subjects who were phobic about snakes. It was reasoned that the effort in psychotherapy would lead to greater liking for, or a greater ability to approach, snakes. Indeed, it was found that subjects who engaged in highly effortful tasks under conditions of high choice were able to show significant improvement in their willingness to approach snakes.

In subsequent studies, Cooper (1980) found that people who were fearful of being assertive could be helped by effort justification-based psychotherapeutic procedures. Cooper & Axsom (1982) showed that obese subjects lost a significant amount of weight after being placed in a highly difficult series of perceptual discrimination tasks. They also found that weight loss in the high dissonance conditions increased significantly over a six month period following the conclusion of the therapy. Similarly, Mendonca (1980) had children in a weight loss program either choose (high dissonance) or be assigned to (low dissonance) an effortful treatment for the purpose of losing weight. Mendonca found that the treatment engaged in with high choice was considerably more effective in producing weight loss than the very same treatment under low choice conditions.

Alternative Modes of Dissonance Reduction

Several studies have examined the effects of cognitive dissonance when attitude change was not a viable possibility. Cooper & Mackie (1983) used the concept of a membership group to render attitudes quite resistant to change. Students who were members of organized political groups were asked to make counterattitudinal speeches against the election of their party's candidate for President of the United States. Since the major purpose of the group to which the subjects belonged was to elect a party member, changing one's attitude in the direction of the communication would contradict the central purpose of the group. Since dissonance is experienced as unpleasant arousal and since attitudes had been rendered highly resistant to change by the group context, it was predicted that the unpleasant arousal would be misattributed to members of the outgroup. The results showed that group members who make such counterattitudinal statements came to express very negative feelings about members of the opposing political party.

Scheier & Carver (1980) also established a situation that rendered attitudes difficult to change. In a series of studies, they had subjects write an essay arguing against greater student control of university curricula. Subjects wrote the essay either in front of a mirror or in front of a TV camera. The mirror was a manipulation of private self-awareness—"an awareness of the more covert and personal aspects of the self" (Scheier & Carver 1980, p. 394; cf Buss 1980, Carver & Scheier 1981, Froming & Carver 1981). Included in the personal aspect of self are one's privately held attitudes and values. The TV camera, on the other hand, manipulated public self-awareness—an awareness of the overtly displayed or social aspects of the self. Included here would be public behavior such as the essay that the subjects wrote. Scheier & Carver found that attitudes about student control of the curriculum changed when the TV camera was focused on them. The camera's manipulation of public self-awareness forced subjects to focus their attention on their behavior. As Festinger (1957) originally pointed out, it is usually difficult for subjects to deny their behavior, thus leaving the attitude as the least resistant element to change. On the other hand, people whose essays were written in front of the mirror were focusing on private elements of the self, presumably including their initial attitudes on the student control question. These subjects reduced their dissonance arousal not by any change of attitude but rather by distorting their behavior. Subjects in the high choice-mirror condition asserted that they had not written a strong essay against student control of the curriculum. A judge, blind to the condition of the subjects, rated the actual essays that were written. Unlike the subjects' perceptions, the judge found no difference in the strength of the essays written by subjects in any of the conditions. Apparently, the private self focus of attention rendered attitudes more resistant to change, therefore leading to dissonance reduction via a distortion of behavior.

A study by White (1980) also examined alternative modes of dissonance reduction. White's major focus was whether counterattitudinal behavior provoked as much dissonance when it was also engaged in by many other people (high consensus) as when it was engaged in only by the subject (low consensus). White found dissonance reducing attitude change in the low consensus conditions. He also found attitude change in one of three high consensus conditions—i.e. when the reason for the consensus was attributed explicitly to the personal dispositon of the other participants. But when any other high consensus information was used, subjects did not show any change of attitudes as a function of their discrepant behavior. White interprets this finding as an alternate mode of dissonance arousal on the part of subjects. When subjects in the high consensus conditions experienced dissonance, they searched for consonant cognitions to reduce their unpleasant tension state. Finding reason to attribute their behavior to the environment, they did not have to accept the responsibility for their behavior. This study, which modifies and partially contradicts an earlier study by Cooper et al (1972), can also be seen as consistent with an attributional, rather than a dissonance, approach to counterattitudinal advocacy.

The role of consensus in counterattitudinal advocacy was further investigated by Stroebe & Diehl (1981). They induced subjects in a group situation to choose to write a counterattitudinal statement. Other group members either complied with the same request or refused to comply. Consistent with White's finding, Stroebe & Diehl found that social support from others in the group reduced attitude change. On the other hand, the lack of social support from other group members exacerbated the dissonance and led to even greater attitude change. When subjects wrote counterattitudinal essays under conditions of low choice, however, the effect of social support was reversed: greater support led to greater change, while the lack of support minimized attitude change. Stroebe & Diehl interpret this finding as the effect of social reinforcement. When the conditions for dissonance are not met, then social support acts as a reinforcer that produces attitude change (cf Linder et al 1967).

Selective Exposure

Selective exposure is a proposition derived from the earliest theorizing about dissonance. It asserts that people seek information that supports a decision between choice alternatives and avoid information inconsistent with the choice. Since Freedman & Sears' (1965) review of selective exposure studies concluded that the research had failed to provide much support for the hypothesis, research output has been but a trickle (e.g. Lowin 1967, Kleinhesselink & Edwards 1975, Frey & Wicklund 1978)—until recently. In the past few years, investigations by Frey and his associates has quickened the pace of selective exposure research. The research has tended to present a mosaic of independent variables that increase, decrease, or modify the degree to which selective exposure follows a dissonance-producing decision.

Frey (1981a) showed that the closer two alternatives were in attractiveness, the greater was the tendency to prefer supportive information to contradictory information. Subjects made a choice between two books that were to be presented as a gift. They were then asked to rate their desire to read information that supported or refuted their decision. When the books involved in the choice were both highly attractive, dissonance should be higher (Brehm & Cohen 1959). Thus, it was interesting that Frey found a greater tendency to read the supportive as opposed to the contradictory as the magnitude of dissonance increased. This was true, however, only if the decision was irreversible. If subjects thought they might be able to change their decision in the future, then there was a greater tendency to prefer the choice-inconsistent information. Frey interprets his data to suggest that there is a competing tendency to want to change a decision if dissonance gets too great. Reversible decisions accentuate this tendency and highlight the utility of choice-inconsistent information.

Frey (1982) showed the existence of competing tendencies even more clearly. In this study, subjects had to chose which of two game strategies to use whereby they might win or lose money. Frey argued that if a strategy a subject selects causes him to lose money, greater dissonance will be created. Frey predicted that selective exposure would increase as the subjects' profits turned to moderate losses. Large losses, however, would invoke the competing tendency to change the decision. Frey argues, "it is more tolerable (less dissonance arousing) to change the decision than to retain the original commitment" (Frey 1982, p. 1176). After subjects learned that they had either won, lost a moderate amount, or lost a large amount of money, Frey asked subjects to rate the attractiveness of information that supported or opposed their choice of a game strategy. As predicted, Frey found a curvilinear effect. The difference in the rated desirability between the decision-consonant and decision-discrepant information was small in the low dissonance condition, increased significantly in the moderate dissonance condition, and decreased again in the high dissonance condition. Frey suggests that the previous inconsistencies in the literature of selective exposure might be due to experimenters inducing only two levels of dissonance in an experiment. If the effect is truly curvilinear, then the selection of different magnitudes of dissonance in different studies would render the studies noncomparable. It is an intriguing suggestion that future research will need to clarify.

Other variables have also been examined in relation to selective exposure. Schwartz et al (1980) examined the role played by wanting to appear fair and impartial in the selection of supporting versus contradictory information. They concluded that dissonance, rather than the appearance of impartiality, was a better predictor of the selective exposure effect. In a subsequent study, Frey (1981b) examined the conditions under which subjects desire supporting over discrepant information. He found that if the source of the supporting information is competent, then subjects want to see that information. If the source of the supporting information is not competent, then the subjects desire the opposing information regardless of the competence of its source. Frey interprets these data to mean that the most useful information is supportive information. It provides the consonant cognitions that are important in reducing the magnitude of dissonance. However, information by an incompetent communicator is not useful. At that point, Frey believes that subjects turn to the opposing information, hoping that they can refute it and thereby reduce their lingering dissonance.

Clearly, the past few years have witnessed a change in selective exposure research. Rather than asking the question of whether selective exposure exists, Frey and his colleagues have turned our attention to a consideration of when and under what circumstances selective exposure is likely to occur. The next step to be hoped for in this area would be to emphasize a more cumulative progression of research findings rather than the mosaic that has characterized the area thus far.

In summary, though dissonance research may no longer hold the forefront of attention in social psychology, research has been active and debate has been lively. Major trends have included the application of dissonance to other areas of concern and further elaboration of the theoretical underpinnings of the phenomenon. Significant in the latter regard has been the change of competing theories (e.g. Schlenker's work on self-identity 1980, 1982) into a position where they are more compatible with dissonance and can help to drive dissonance researchers into new areas of investigation.

PERSUASION

No domain of attitude research has more relevance to modern political culture than the study of persuasion. While sociologists have long been concerned with the study of charisma and the dynamics of social movements, the mass of accumulated data on the persuasion process is largely a product of experimental social psychology. The pervasive fascination with persuasion phenomena was stimulated by the rise of fascist dictatorships in the 1930s and the emergence of the modern mass media. But it was the work of Carl Hovland and his colleagues (e.g. Hovland et al 1949, 1953) that provided the empirical catalyst for most of the work that has emerged since. Whether the worth of the product has matched the amount of effort invested has been a matter of much debate. In a previous review of persuasion research in this series, Eagly & Himmelfarb (1978) observed that "ambiguities and unknowns still abound" (p. 544), after noting previously that "after several decades of research, there are few simple and direct empirical generalizations that can be made concering how to change attitudes" (Himmelfarb & Eagly 1974, p. 594). This problem has been particularly acute in analyses of the impact of persuasive communications, we would argue, because so much of this research has been purely descriptive and has *not* been driven by well-formulated theory. Nevertheless, we found positive evidence that theory-construction concerns are growing (e.g. Jaccard 1981, Petty & Cacioppo 1981, Eagly 1983). We can only hope that the next such review will provide additional evidence of a continued trend toward more rigorous theories of the persuasion process.

Cognitive Response Analyses

With the continued growth of the information processing perspective, investigations of cognitive responses continue to proliferate. The cognitive response approach to the study of persuasion has been summarized by Petty et al (1981):

> The approach postulates that attitude change processes can best be understood by taking into account the thoughts that arise in the persuasion situation. To the extent that the persuasion situation elicits thoughts that are favorable, attitude change in the direction advocated should be facilitated; but if negative thoughts are elicited, attitude change should be inhibited (p. 29).

Although the quotation above includes a general hypothesis, there is no one cognitive response theory, just as there is no one theory of attribution. Rather, investigators in this area share interests and some assumptions regarding the persuasion process. The locus of this interest reflects waning concern with purely contextual variables and a growing interest in the manipulation and measurement of cognitive processes. The development of valid measures of cognitive responses has been, and will continue to be, a source of some controversy (e.g. Miller & Colman 1981). Nevertheless, the successful construction of theories in this area will depend to a large degree on whether the validity of such measurement can be firmly established. Some progress has been made (see e.g. Cacioppo et al 1981), and the current cognitive response measure of preference is the written thought-listing technique (e.g. Petty & Cacioppo 1977). In this procedure subjects are given a specified period of time to list all of the thoughts that occurred to them either before, during, or after exposure to a persuasive communication. These responses are then categorized by the subjects themselves or by blind judges along one or more dimensions relevant to the purposes of the investigation (e.g. favorable vs unfavorable thoughts regarding the communication). The thought-listing technique has been used as a primary outcome measure, a mediational process measure, and as a manipulation check. As indicated below, investigations that employ the thought-listing technique as a tool to assess the frequency and character of cognitive responses have continued to proliferate.

COGNITIVE EFFORT AND ABILITY   According to the cognitive response approach, an individual's motivation to process a message will affect information processing, and the nature of these effects will often be manifested in responses on a thought-listing task. Greater cognitive effort, according to Petty & Cacioppo (1979), will result when conditions such as high issue involvement motivate an individual to pay close attention to the content and quality of a persuasive message. This will typically lead to a greater number of message-relevant thoughts. By examining factors that influence the amount of cognitive effort invested in the analysis of a persuasive communication, one can specify the conditions under which the quality of arguments in a message will be an important determinant of persuasion.

In one such study, Petty et al (1980) found a "social loafing" effect (Latané et al 1979) on cognitive effort. Subjects who were asked to rate student editorials reported more cognitive effort if they believed that they were the only person assigned to evaluate a particular essay. When subjects believed that they were one of ten evaluators, less cognitive effort was reported. The finding replicates the standard social loafing effect: individuals withdraw effort on a task when they are members of a group in which responsibility for performing that task is diffused. The implications of this effect for persuasion phenomena, however, were revealed in the cognitive response measures. A manipulation of the quality of the essays had more impact on the thoughts generated by the individual evaluators than on the thoughts listed by the group evaluators.

Individual raters reported more favorable thoughts and a more favorable evaluation of the high quality essay than did group evaluators. When exposed to an essay containing very weak arguments, individual evaluators reported a higher number of negative thoughts and a lower evaluation of the communication than did subjects who believed they were one of ten evaluators.

A similar logic was applied by Harkins & Petty (1981a) to an examination of multiple source effects. They found that subjects were more persuaded and reported a greater number of positive message-relevant thoughts when three strong arguments were presented by three communicators instead of one. A multiple message source also led to an increase in (negative) thoughts and minimized persuasion when poor arguments were employed. Harkins & Petty (1981b) replicated these effects and found that, in the case of multiple arguments, distraction could eliminate the persuasive advantage of the multiple source. Their data indicated that this attenuation was due to the distracting task having interfered with the subject's ability to produce positive thoughts, particularly since memory (i.e. comprehension) of the arguments themselves was not affected (see also Lammers & Becker 1980). These data support Harkins & Petty's cognitive response explanation of the multiple source effect. Petty et al (1981b) found that distraction-like effects can occur when rhetorical questions are included in a personally relevant communication. When personal relevance (and thus involvement and motivation) is low, the inclusion of rhetoricals led to an increase in what would otherwise be minimal message-relevant thought and persuasion. When involvement and motivation were already high, however, the inclusion of rhetoricals lessened thought about, and the impact of, arguments contained in a persuasive communication. In general, these studies provide further evidence that persuasion is more dependent on argument quality when contextual factors allow or encourage respondents to put forth a greater amount of message-processing effort.

CENTRAL VS PERIPHERAL ROUTES   In a general review of the persuasion literature, Petty & Cacioppo (1981) proposed that persuasion can occur in one of two ways. The *central route* to persuasion, according to their Elaboration Likelihood Model, is through a respondent's active processing of the message itself. This central route has been the focus of most research on cognitive responses. Petty & Cacioppo argue that persuasion via the central route occurs when the individual is motivated to think about the attitude issue, as is the case when the issue has a high degree of personal relevance. Since greater cognitive effort and elaboration occurs under these conditions (according to their model), the quality of the arguments contained in the message are of the utmost importance in determining whether or not persuasion will occur. Factors that inhibit message-relevant thought production (such as distraction) will attenuate persuasion via the central route.

Peripheral route persuasion is said to occur when cognitive elaboration of the message is minimal and nonmessage factors account for obtained attitude change. Source characteristics (see Hass 1981, Eagly 1983 for reviews), for example, have been found to play an important yet complex role in persuasion. Petty & Cacioppo suggest that persuasion via the peripheral route (e.g. as a result of high source credibility) occurs when a respondent's motivation or ability to process message content is low.

In an experimental demonstration of these two routes to persuasion, Petty et al (1981a) examined the interactive effects of personal involvement, argument quality, and source expertise on a communications' impact on undergraduates' attitudes toward comprehensive exams. As predicted, attitudes were significantly influenced by high quality arguments (the central route) only when personal relevance was high. When relevance was low, however, source expertise (the peripheral route) was the most important determinant of persuasion (see also Petty & Cacioppo 1983a). A similar interaction of involvement, argument quality and source characteristics was found by Petty et al (1983) in a study of advertising effectiveness. Together, these findings provide strong support for Petty & Cacioppo's notion that level of involvement is an important determinant of the route to persuasion. It remains to be seen, however, whether argument quality remains an important determinant of persuasion under conditions of *very* high involvement. Nevertheless, the empirical differentiation of the conditons under which the two forms of persuasion occur will complement what is already a significant contribution to the persuasion literature.

Effects of Source Characteristics

The analysis of source effects has long been a popular domain of persuasion research. While the "source" of a persuasive communication need not be a particular individual (as in the case of a newspaper or an organization), recent research has tended to focus on characteristics of individual communicators. As indicated by McGuire's review of attitude change (1969), investigators have been concerned with three general categories of source characteristics: credibility (expertise or trustworthiness), attractiveness, and power. Our review reveals that work on the first two categories of source characteristics continues while investigations which explicitly manipulate power variables have all but disappeared from the leading journals.

CREDIBILITY

An attribution analysis   While source credibility traditionally has been construed as an objective stimulus characteristic, one contemporary model views credibility as the product of a subjective inference made by the message recipient. Eagly and her associates (see Eagly et al 1981 for a review) have applied attribution theory (e.g. Kelley 1967, Jones & McGillis 1976; see also Harvey & Weary, this volume), to the inferences made by message recipients regarding the *causes* of a communicator's advocacy of a particular position. These causal inferences are seen as crucial determinants of recipients' judgments of the communicator's credibility. As suggested by an attributional perspective, a listener may attribute a communicator's behavior to either dispositional or situational factors. The direction of these attributions depends on the kind of information a recipient has about situational constraints on the communicator's behavior as well as given or inferred information about the communicator's true attitudes and motives. Eagly et al (1978), for example, found that persuasion was less likely to occur when a communicator's advocacy of a particular position on the attitude issue could be attributed to audience pressures (implying a *reporting bias*) or to a strong prior commitment to the position (implying a *knowledge bias*). When the advocated position contradicted the expectancy formed by such information, however, persuasion occurred. Wood & Eagly (1981) recently followed up this research by conducting a structural analysis of recipients' attributions, message comprehension, and subsequent attitude change in response to a persuasive communication. The experiment included a manipulation of the discrepancy between the advocated position and the subjects' prior attitudes as well as a manipulation of position expectancy confirmation. In a stage model yielded by the analysis, persuasion was again found to be magnified when the position advocated disconfirmed subject's expectancies about the communicator's position. This occurred under both levels of recipient-communicator position discrepancy. The analysis indicated that persuasion occurred when a communicator's disconfirmation of subjects' expectancies led subjects to attribute the presenter's advocacy of the position to the weight of supporting evidence and thus to view the communicator as unbiased. Ironically, while message comprehension generally led to greater opinion change, subjects who viewed the source of the disconfirming communication as unbiased displayed less message comprehension. Consistent with the cognitive response literature (cf Petty et al 1981a), comprehension was apparently unnecessary for attitude change when the target relied on salient source characteristics which suggested that the source was high in credibility (see also Chaiken 1980).

Cialdini et al (1981) have criticized the attributional analysis for its limited applicability. They argued that recipients often have little information about a communicator's dispositions or the constraints on the communicator's behavior. Though we would concede that this may often be the case in the experimental laboratory, there is substantial evidence that perceivers require only minimal information to form expectations and/or make attributional inferences (Asch 1946, Taylor & Fiske 1978, Darley & Fazio 1980, Wilder & Cooper 1981). Furthermore, an attributional analysis suggests the examination of conditions in which individuals are reluctant to make specific inferences about a communicator's behavior (see Snyder & Wicklund 1981). Further experimental evidence will be required to confirm the validity of the attributional model of persuasion proposed by Wood & Eagly. Nevertheless, the attribution approach has great potential for clarifying our understanding of the role played by recipient expectancies and communicator characteristics in the persuasion process.

Expertise vs trustworthiness   Research investigations of the effects of source credibility typically have manipulated either the expertise of the communicator on the message-relevant topic or the sincerity or trustworthiness of the communicator. As noted in two recent reviews (Hass 1981, Eagly 1983), the accumulated literature on communicator credibility has firmly established the expert communicator as being more persuasive than a communicator who lacks expertise. Maddux & Rogers (1980), for example, recently replicated this effect and found that it persisted over a two week period. The results reported in the literature are less consistent, according to the reviews cited, in the case of trustworthiness. Nevertheless, there is now a strong consensus that either form of credibility is likely to be a more important component of the persuasion equation when the recipient is *not* highly motivated to process the communication (e.g. Petty et al 1981a).

ATTRACTIVENESS   Since Chaiken (1983) has provided an up-to-date review of research on the effects of physical attractiveness on the effectiveness of persuasion, we will only note some of the recent findings.

Chaiken & Eagly (1983) conducted an investigation into the effects of likability on persuasion as a function of communication modality. The authors hypothesized that communicator likability would be an important determinant of persuasion only when the mode of communication made the communicator salient. As predicted, they found that likability was a significant determinant of persuasion in the videotape and audiotape modalities but not in the written modality. Subjects exposed to the videotaped and audiotaped communications also reported more communicator-oriented thoughts than subjects given written messages. Chaiken (1980, 1983) suggests that a communicator's physical attractiveness or likability may often provide a simple decision cue when the recipient prefers to make an effortless response to the persuasion attempt.

OTHER ADVANCES

Effects of Attitudes on Information Processing

While the majority of research discussed thus far employed attitude as the critical dependent variable, a smaller collection of studies examined the effects of attitudes on cognitive processes. Traditionally, research on the cognitive effects of attitudes has focused on the differential learning of attitude-consistent and -inconsistent information (e.g. Jones & Aneshansel 1956). The burgeoning of interest in social cognition appears to have reawakened interest in this area. Most of this recent work has tested memory for attitude-relevant stimuli after a judgement task. Judd & Kulik (1980), for example, found better recall for attitude statements that had elicited either extreme agreement or extreme disagreement on a judgment task. Lingle & Ostrom (1981) argued that attitudes act as thematic frameworks for the interpretation of new stimulus information. In support of their formulation, they summarized evidence which indicated that attitudes toward a person can be important determinants of the organization and later recall of trait descriptors of that person. Other work found attitudinal effects on recall of personal histories (Ross et al 1981), the behavioral histories of others (Clark & Woll 1981), and a biased communication (Weldon & Malpass 1981). This literature continues to provide evidence suggesting a complex relationship between prior attitude and the perception, encoding, and recall of subsequent information. At this point, the attainment of a firm understanding of these processes in the near future appears unlikely.

Psychophysiology

Although psychophysiological approaches in attitude research have been on the scene for some time (e.g. Rankin & Campbell 1955), an early review of the area (Shapiro & Crider 1969) noted a paucity of experimental investigations. This lack of interest was encouraged by pessimistic commentaries which appeared at that time. Mueller (1970), for example, likened strongly held attitudes to emotions and suggested that the psychophysiological measurement of attitudes would continue to be plagued by problems inherent to the emotion concept. In his influential review of the attitude literature, McGuire (1969) appeared to have sounded the final death knell when he concluded that "psychophysiological measures usually promise, at best, a measure of *intensity* of attitude, without any indication of its direction" (p. 143).

Within the past few years, however, a significant resurgence of interest in social psychophysiology has occurred (e.g. Cacioppo & Petty 1983). This general interest has led to renewed attempts to examine attitudes and attitude changes with psychophysiological instruments. In the case of attitude measurement, one source of inspiration has been the influential work of Izard (e.g. 1979), Ekman (e.g. Ekman et al 1972), and others on the measurement of human emotion. Their work suggests that an analysis of facial patterns might be successfully used to measure the *direction* of an attitude. Cacioppo & Petty (1979), for example, have measured the facial muscle activity of subjects exposed to a persuasive communication. Their psychophysiological data corroborated their cognitive response data, providing further support for the potential of physiological measures for directional attitude assessment.

As suggested by Petty & Cacioppo (1983b) in their review of the psychophysiology/attitude literature, the greatest potential in this area may lie in the domain of attitude change processes. Recent work indicates that bodily response data can provide a unique form of support for theoretical constructs within models of attitude change (e.g. Cacioppo & Sandman 1981; Croyle & Cooper 1983). Such research also suggests the formulation of attitude change theories that incorporate explicitly the physiological mediators and manifestations of the change process. Petty & Cacioppo's (1983b) biosocial model of attitude change is an early prototype of such a theory and one that is likely to encourage more psychophysiologists to extend their interests into the social psychological domain. As Crider (1983) has suggested, the fruitful development of social psychophysiology will depend, in large part, on the continuing ability of social psychologists to place theoretical flesh on the bones of psychophysiological data.

CONCLUSION

Research during the last several years has shown us that the concepts of attitude and attitude change have continued to be a central topic in social psychology. Berscheid (1982), for example, still refers to the attitude as "the construct of choice" among social psychologists. Our view of the literature suggests that even within the venerable areas of attitude change research, subtle changes have crept in.

Most pronounced is the infusion of greater theoretical insights into the areas we have reviewed. The question of consistency between attitudes and behaviors has resisted theory for several decades. Advances in understanding attitude structure and attitude measurement were achieved, but theory lagged far behind. We now see a number of theories beginning to take hold to explain why and when attitudes predict behaviors. By contrast, empirical tests of consistency models have always been theory driven. The work published within the last few years is no exception as different ways of viewing the process continued to emerge. We see the changes in the self-presentational perspective during the review period as particularly encouraging. We may have moved a step closer to integrating conditions under which inconsistency leads to attitude change because of an uncomfortable tension state and when it leads to attitude change as a function of self-presentation. Movement toward conceptual coherence has also characterized the work in persuasion. Major conceptual models have been added to the original groundbreaking work of Hovland and his colleagues. Another interesting development has been the movement of these models toward one another and toward a more comprehensive view of persuasion processes (e.g. Petty & Cacioppo 1981, Chaiken 1983, Eagly 1983).

The impact of cognitive approaches in the study of attitude change has been almost as pervasive in the last decade as it has been in the fields of social judgment, person perception, and interpersonal influence (Wicklund & Frey 1981). Concepts such as schemas, priming, category accessibility and cognitive biases that came to the social judgment literature from the information processing perspective of cognitive psychology have all left their mark on the study of attitude change. Even the traditional, affect-laden dependent measure of attitude change research—the rating scale—has had to share center stage with such measures as reaction time and thought listing.

In his address to the American Psychological Association, Zajonc (1980) proposed a two-process system of evaluation—a fast, crude system of affect and a slower, more detailed system of cognition. The apparent call for more emphasis on the affective component of evaluation led Abelson et al (1982) to remark, "Suddenly it (has become) fashionable to write about emotion" (p. 619). Changes sometimes are slow in coming, however. Even the renewed emphasis on affect has been subsumed by the information processing perspective, leading to only minimal accommodation of strictly cognitive models. As Wicklund & Frey (1981) noted, "there is a strong tendency to cast human beings as *mere* cognitive organisms, and to rule out altogether human drive, motivations and tensions as explanatory devices" (p. 142).

It may be that we are beginning to see a swing of the pendulum once again. Critics of the cognitive emphasis on attitude change point out that attitudes have rarely been studied effectively as cognitions (Zajonc 1980). Kiesler (1982) observed that the vast literature on attitude change has consistently come back to the more powerful role that affect plays on cognition than cognition plays on affect. Further, Kiesler bemoans the lack of concordance between the major issues in attitude change and the available concepts of social cognition. "One particular villain in this drama," he asserts, "is that of schema," which he refers to as a concept that is "vague around the edges" (p. 115).

Abelson et al (1982) provide a strong case for the role of affect in political attitudes. Their empirical research on attitudes toward political candidates suggested that affective reports were qualitatively different even from bipolar semantic judgments. They also found that in the evaluation of candidates for political office, affect scores added significantly to the amount of variance explained by trait judgments, behavioral descriptions, or party affiliations.

The view of affect expressed by Abelson et al is more akin to the kind of affect that characterized earlier work on attitude change. Affect, in this view, reflects motivation. People are seen as motivated to adopt attitudes, change existing attitudes, or act in ways consistent with their attitudes as a function of motivational constructs.

The work in attitude change has never been purely cognitive nor has it been purely motivational. Perhaps that is one reason that it has lasted so long and resisted the shift in experimental zeitgeists. Our review suggests that the emphasis of research in attitude change over the last several years has been on the cognitive side of center. But significant calls are being heard for a return to the other side. We suspect that the pendulum pulled by cognition has come near the apex of its arc and that the next few years will see a greater pull exerted by motivational forces.

ACKNOWLEDGEMENTS

The authors would like to thank John Darley, Debra Godfrey, Ned Jones, Diane Mackie, Jeanne Smith, and Abe Tesser for helpful comments on a draft of this chapter.

Literature Cited

Abelson, R. P. 1972. Are attitudes necessary? In *Attitudes, Conflict and Social Change*, ed. B. T. King, E. McGinnies, pp. 19–32. New York: Academic. 234 pp.

Abelson, R. P. 1981. The psychological status of the script concept. *Am. Psychol.* 26:715–29

Abelson, R. P. 1982. Three modes of attitude-behavior consistency. See Zanna et al 1982

Abelson, R. P., Kinder, D. R., Peters, M. D., Fiske, S. T. 1982. Affective and semantic components in political person perception. *J. Pers. Soc. Psychol.* 42:619–30

Ajzen, I. 1982. On behaving in accordance with one's attitudes. See Zanna et al 1982.

Ajzen, I., Fishbein, M. 1977. Attitude-behavior relations: A theoretical analysis and review of empirical research. *Psychol. Bull.* 84:888–918

Ajzen, I., Fishbein, M. 1980. *Understanding Attitudes and Predicting Social Behavior*. Englewood Cliffs, N.J.: Prentice-Hall. 278 pp.

Ajzen, I., Timko, C., White, J. B. 1982. Self-monitoring and the attitude-behavior relation. *J. Pers. Soc. Psychol.* 42:426–35

Aronson, E. 1969. The theory of cognitive dissonance: A current perspective. *Adv. Exp. Soc. Psychol.* 4:1–34

Aronson, E., Mills, J. 1959. The effects of severity of initiation on liking for a group. *J. Abnorm. Soc. Psychol.* 59:177–81

Asch, S. 1946. Forming impressions of personality. *J. Abnorm. Soc. Psychol.* 410:258–90

Bagozzi, R. P. 1981. Attitudes, intentions, and behavior: A test of some key hypotheses. *J. Pers. Soc. Psychol.* 41:607–27

Bem, D. J. 1972. Self-perception theory. *Adv. Exp. Soc. Psychol.* 6:1–62

Bentler, P. M., Speckart, G. 1979. Models of attitude-behavior relations. *Psychol. Rev.* 86:452–64

Bentler, P. M., Speckart, G. 1981. Attitudes "cause" behaviors: A structural equation analysis. *J. Pers. Soc. Psychol.* 40:226–38

Berscheid, E. 1982. Attraction and emotion in interpersonal relations. In *Affect and Cognition: The Seventeenth Annual Carnegie Symposium on Cognition*, ed. M. S. Clark, S. T. Fiske, pp. 37–54. Hillsdale, NJ: Erlbaum. 357 pp.

Bond, C. F. 1981. Dissonance and the pill: An interpersonal simulation. *Pers. Soc. Psychol. Bull.* 7:398–403

Borgida, E., Campbell, B. 1982. Belief relevance and attitude-behavior consistency: The moderating role of personal experience. *J. Pers. Soc. Psychol.* 42:239–47

Brehm, J. W., Cohen, A. R. 1959. Reevaluation of choice alternatives as a function of their number and qualitative similarity. *J. Abnorm. Soc. Psychol.* 58:373–78

Buss, A. H. 1980. *Self-Consciousness and Social Anxiety*. San Francisco: Freeman. 270 pp.

Cacioppo, J. T., Harkins, S. G., Petty, R. E. 1981. The nature of attitudes and cognitive responses and their relationship to behavior. See Petty et al 1981, pp. 31–54

Cacioppo, J. T., Petty, R. E. 1979. Attitudes and cognitive response; An electrophysiological approach. *J. Pers. Soc. Psychol.* 37:2181–99

Cacioppo, J. T., Petty, R. E., eds. 1983. *Social Psychophysiology: A Sourcebook*. New York: Guilford.

Cacioppo, J. T., Sandman, C. A. 1981. Psychophysiological functioning, cognitive responding, and attitudes. See Petty et al 1981, pp. 81–103

Cantor, N., Kihlstrom, J. F., eds. 1981. *Personality, Cognition, and Social Interaction.* Hillsdale, NJ: Erlbaum, 362 pp.

Carver, C. S., Scheier, M. F. 1981. *Attention and Self-Regulation: A Control-Theory Approach to Human Behavior.* New York: Springer-Verlag. 403 pp.

Chaiken, S. 1980. Heuristic versus systematic information processing and the use of source versus message cues in persuasion. *J. Pers. Soc. Psychol.* 39:752–66

Chaiken, S. 1983. Physical appearance variables and social influence. In *Physical Appearance, Stigma and Social Behavior: The Ontario Symposium,* Vol. 3, ed. C. P. Herman, E. T. Higgins, M. P. Zanna. Hillsdale, NJ: Erlbaum. In press

Chaiken, S., Eagly, A. H. 1983. Communication modality as a determinant of persuasion: The role of communicator salience. *J. Pers. Soc. Psychol.* 45:241–56

Cialdini, R. B., Petty, R. E., Cacioppo, J. T. 1981. Attitude and attitude change. *Ann. Rev. Psychol.* 32:357–404

Clark, L. F., Woll, S. B. 1981. Stereotype biases: A reconstructive analysis of their role in reconstructive memory. *J. Pers. Soc. Psychol.* 41:1064–72

Collins, B. E., Hoyt, M. F. 1972. Personal responsibility for consequences: An integration and extension of the "forced compliance" literature. *J. Exp. Soc. Psychol.* 8:558–93

Cooper, J. 1971. Personal responsibility and dissonance: The role of foreseen consequences. *J. Pers. Soc. Psychol.* 18:354–63

Cooper, J. 1980. Reducing fears and increasing assertiveness: The role of dissonance reduction. *J. Exp. Soc. Psychol.* 16:199–213

Cooper, J., Axsom, D. 1982. Effort justification in psychotherapy. In *Integrations of Clinical and Social Psychology,* ed. G. Weary, H. L. Mirels, pp. 214–30. New York: Oxford Univ. Press. 318 pp.

Cooper, J., Jones, E. E., Tuller, S. M. 1972. Attribution, dissonance, and the illusion of uniqueness. *J. Exp. Soc. Psychol.* 8:45–57

Cooper, J., Mackie, D. 1983. Cognitive dissonance in an intergroup context. *J. Pers. Soc. Psychol.* 44:536–44

Coreless, P., Zanna, M. P. 1980. Attitude-behavior consistency: Self-monitoring and behavioral variability aid in predicting real behavior. Unpublished manuscript. Data reported in Zanna & Olson chapter, Zanna et al 1982

Cotton, J. L. 1981. A review of research on Schachter's theory of emotion and misattribution of arousal. *Eur. J. Soc. Psychol.* 11:365–97

Crider, A. 1983. The promise of psychophysiology. See Cacioppo & Petty 1983

Crockett, W. H. 1982. Balance, agreement and positivity in the cognition of small group structures. *Adv. Exp. Soc. Psychol.* 15:1–57

Croyle, R. T., Cooper, J. 1983. Dissonance arousal: Physiological evidence. *J. Pers. Soc. Psychol.* In press

Darley, J. M., Fazio, R. H. 1980. Expectancy confirmation processes arising in the social interaction sequence. *Am. Psychol.* 35:867–81

Davidson, A. R., Jaccard, J. 1979. Variables that moderate the attitude-behavior relation: Results of a longitudinal survey. *J. Pers. Soc. Psychol.* 37:1364–76

Eagly, A. H. 1983. *Who says so? The processing of communicator cues in persuasion.* Presented at East. Psychol. Assoc., 54th, Philadelphia

Eagly, A. H., Chaiken, S., Wood, W. 1981. An attributional analysis of persuasion. In *New Directions in Attribution Research,* ed. J. H. Harvey, W. J. Ickes, R. F. Kidd, 3:37–62. Hillsdale, NJ: Erlbaum, 540 pp.

Eagly, A. H., Himmelfarb, S. 1978. Attitudes and opinions. *Ann. Rev. Psychol.* 29:517–54

Eagly, A. H., Wood, W., Chaiken, S. 1978. Causal inferences about communicators and their effect on opinion change. *J. Pers. Soc. Psychol.* 36:424–35

Ekman, P., Friesen, W. V., Ellsworth, P. 1972. *Emotion in the Human Face.* New York: Pergamon. 191 pp.

Fazio, R. H., Chen, J., McDonel, E. C., Sherman, S. J. 1982. Attitude accessibility, attitude-behavior consistency, and the strength of the object-evaluation association. *J. Exp. Soc. Psychol.* 18:339–57

Fazio, R. H., Cooper, J. 1983. Arousal in the dissonance process. See Cacioppo & Petty 1983

Fazio, R. H., Powell, M. C., Herr, P. M. 1983. Toward a process model of the attitude-behavior relation: Accessing one's attitude upon mere observation of the attitude object. *J. Pers. Soc. Psychol.* 44:724–35

Fazio, R. H., Zanna, M. P. 1981. Direct experience and attitude-behavior consistency. *Adv. Exp. Soc. Psychol.* 14:161–202

Festinger, L. 1957. *A Theory of Cognitive Dissonance.* Stanford, Calif: Stanford Univ. Press. 291 pp.

Fishbein, M., Ajzen, I. 1974. Attitudes toward objects as predictors of single and multiple behavioral criteria. *Psychol. Rev.* 81:59–74

Fishbein, M., Ajzen, I. 1975. *Belief, Attitude, Intention and Behavior: An Introduction to Theory and Research.* Reading, Mass: Addison-Wesley, 578 pp.

Fishbein, M., Ajzen, I. 1981. On construct validity: A critique of Miniard and Cohen's paper. *J. Exp. Soc. Psychol.* 17:340–50

Freedman, J. L., Sears, D. O. 1965. Selective exposure. *Adv. Exp. Soc. Psychol.* 2:58–97

Frey, D. 1981a. Reversible and irreversible

decisions: Preference for consonant information as a function of attractiveness of decision alternatives. *Pers. Soc. Psychol. Bull.* 7:621–26

Frey, D. 1981b. Postdecisional preference for decision relevant information as a function of the competence of its source and the degree of familiarity with this information. *J. Exp. Soc. Psychol.* 17:51–67

Frey, D. 1982. Different levels of cognitive dissonance, information seeking, and information avoidance. *J. Pers. Soc. Psychol.* 43:1175–83

Frey, D., Wicklund, R. A. 1978. A clarification of selective exposure: The impact of choice. *J. Exp. Soc. Psychol.* 14:132–39

Froming, W. J., Carver, C. S. 1981. Divergent influences of private and public self-consciousness in a compliance paradigm. *J. Res. Pers.* 15:159–71

Harkins, S. G., Petty, R. E. 1981a. The effects of source magnification of cognitive effort on attitudes: An information processing view. *J. Pers. Soc. Psychol.* 40:401–13

Harkins, S. G., Petty, R. E. 1981b. The multiple source effect in persuasion: The effects of distraction. *Pers. Soc. Psychol. Bull.* 7:627–35

Hass, R. G. 1981. Effects of source characteristics on cognitive responses in persuasion. See Petty et al 1981, pp. 141–72

Higgins, E. T., Herman, C. P., Zanna, M. P., eds. 1981. *Social Cognition: The Ontario Symposium*, Vol. 1. Hillsdale, NJ: Erlbaum. 437 pp.

Higgins, E. T., Rhodewalt, F., Zanna, M. P. 1979. Dissonance motivation: Its nature, persistence and reinstatement. *J. Exp. Soc. Psychol.* 15:16–34

Himmelfarb, S., Eagly, A. H., eds. 1974. *Readings in Attitude Change.* New York: Wiley, 665 pp.

Hovland, C. I., Janis, I. L., Kelley, H. H. 1953. *Communication and Persuasion: Psychological Studies of Opinion Change.* New Haven: Yale Univ. Press. 315 pp.

Hovland, C. I., Lumsdaine, A. A., Sheffield, F. D. 1949. *Experiments on Mass Communication.* Princeton, NJ: Princeton Univ. Press

Izard, C. E. 1979. Emotions as motivations: An evolutionary-developmental perspective. *Nebr. Symp. Motiv.* 26:163–200

Jaccard, J. 1981. Toward theories of persuasion and belief change. *J. Pers. Soc. Psychol.* 40:260–69

Jones, E. E., Aneshansel, J. 1956. The learning and utilization of contravaluant material. *J. Abnorm. Soc. Psychol.* 53:27–33

Jones, E. E., McGillis, D. 1976. Correspondent inferences and the attribution cube: A comparative reappraisal. In *New Directions in Attribution Research*, ed. J. H. Harvey,

W. J. Ickes, R. F. Kidd, 1:389–420. Hillsdale, NJ. Erlbaum. 467 pp.

Jones, E. E., Pittman, T. S. 1982. Toward a general theory of strategic self presentation. In *Psychological Perspectives on the Self*, ed. J. Suls, pp. 231–62. Hillsdale, NJ: Erlbaum. 272 pp.

Judd, C. M., Kulik, J. A. 1980. Schematic effects of social attitudes on information processing and recall. *J. Pers. Soc. Psychol.* 38:569–78

Kantola, S. G., Syme, G. J., Campbell, N. A. 1982. The role of individual differences and external variables in a test of the sufficiency of Fishbein's model to explain behavioral intentions to conserve water. *J. Appl. Soc. Psychol.* 12:70–83

Kelley, H. H. 1967. Attribution theory in social psychology. *Nebr. Symp. Motiv.* 15:192–238

Kiesler, C. A. 1982. Comments. See Berscheid 1982, pp. 111–16

Kleinhesselink, R. R., Edwards, R. E. 1975. Seeking and avoiding belief-discrepant information as a function of its perceived refutability. *J. Pers. Soc. Psychol.* 31:787–90

Lammers, H. B., Becker, L. A. 1980. Distraction effects on the perceived extremity of a communication and on cognitive responses. *Pers. Soc. Psychol. Bull.* 6:261–66

LaPiere, R. 1934. Attitudes versus actions. *Soc. Forces* 13:230–37

Latané, B., Williams, K., Harkins, S. 1979. Many hands make light the work: The causes and consequences of social loafing. *J. Pers. Soc. Psychol.* 5:189–202

Linder, D. E., Cooper, J., Jones, E. E. 1967. Decision freedom as a determinant of the role of incentive magnitude in attitude change. *J. Pers. Soc. Psychol.* 6:245–54

Lingle, J. H., Ostrom, T. M. 1981. Principles of memory and cognition in attitude formation. See Petty et al 1981, pp. 399–420

Lowin, A. 1967. Further evidence for an approach-avoidance interpretation of selective exposure. *J. Exp. Soc. Psychol.* 5:265–71

Maddux, J. E., Rogers, R. W. 1980. Effects of source expertness, physical attractiveness, and supporting arguments on persuasion: A case of brains over beauty. *J. Pers. Soc. Psychol.* 39:235–44

Malkis, F. S., Kalle, R. J., Tedeschi, J. T. 1982. Attitudinal politics in the forced compliance situation. *J. Soc. Psychol.* 117:79–91

Manstead, A. S. R., Profitt, C., Smart, J. L. 1983. Predicting and understanding mothers' infant-feeding intentions and behavior: Testing the theory of reasoned action. *J. Pers. Soc. Psychol.* 44:657–71

Masling, J., Price, J., Goldband, S., Katkin, E. S. 1981. Oral imagery and autonomic arousal in social isolation. *J. Pers. Soc. Psychol.* 40:395–400

McCarty, D. 1981. Changing contraceptive usage intentions: a test of the Fishbein model of intention. *J. Appl. Soc. Psychol.* 11:192–211

McCollam, J. B., Burish, T. G., Maisto, S. A., Sobell, M. B. 1980. Alcohol's effects on physiological arousal and self-reported affect and sensations. *J. Abnorm. Psychol.* 89:224–33

McGuire, W. J. 1969. The nature of attitudes and attitude change. In *The Handbook of Social Psychology*, ed. G. Lindzey, E. Aronson, 3:136–314. Reading, Mass: Addison-Wesley, 978 pp. 2nd ed.

Mendonca, P. 1980. The effects of choice and client characteristics in the behavioral treatment of overweight children. Unpublished manuscript

Miller, N., Coleman, D. E. 1981. Methodological issues in analyzing the cognitive mediation of persuasion. See Petty et al 1981, pp. 105–25

Miniard, P. W., Cohen, J. B. 1981. An examination of the Fishbein-Ajzen behavioral-intentions model's concepts and measures. *J. Exp. Soc. Psychol.* 17:309–39

Mueller, D. J. 1970. Physiological techniques of attitude measurement. In *Attitude Measurement*, ed. G. G. Summers. Chicago: Rand McNally

Olson, J. M., Zanna, M. P. 1980. Individual differences in attitude-behavior consistency: Replication and extension. Unpublished manuscript. Data reported in Zanna & Olson chapter, Zanna et al 1982

Petty, R. E., Cacioppo, J. T. 1977. Forewarning, cognitive responding, and resistance to persuasion. *J. Pers. Soc. Psychol.* 35:645–55

Petty, R. E., Cacioppo, J. T. 1979. Issue involvement can increase or decrease persuasion by enhancing message-relevant cognitive responses. *J. Pers. Soc. Psychol.* 37:1915–26

Petty, R. E., Cacioppo, J. T. 1981. *Attitudes and Persuasion: Classic and Contemporary Approaches*. Dubuque, Iowa: Brown. 314 pp.

Petty, R. E., Cacioppo, J. T. 1983a. The effects of involvement on responses to argument quantity and quality: Central and peripheral routes to persuasion. *J. Pers. Soc. Psychol.* In press

Petty, R. E., Cacioppo, J. T. 1983b. The role of bodily responses in attitude measurement and change. See Cacioppo & Petty 1983

Petty, R. E., Cacioppo, J. T., Goldman, R. 1981a. Personal involvement as a determinant of argument based persuasion. *J. Pers. Soc. Psychol.* 41:847–55

Petty, R. E., Cacioppo, J. T., Heesacker, M. 1981b. The use of rhetorical questions in persuasion: A cognitive response analysis. *J. Pers. Soc. Psychol.* 40:432–40

Petty, R. E., Cacioppo, J. T., Schumann, D. 1983. Central and peripheral routes to advertising effectiveness: The moderating role of involvement. *J. Consum. Res.* In press

Petty, R. E., Harkins, S. G., Williams, K. D. 1980. The effects of group diffusion of cognitive effort on attitudes: An information processing view. *J. Pers. Soc. Psychol.* 38:81–92

Petty, R. E., Ostrom, T. M., Brock, T. C. 1981. Historical foundations of the cognitive response approach to attitudes and persuasion. In *Cognitive Responses in Persuasion*, ed. R. E. Petty, T. M. Ostrom, T. C. Brock. Hillsdale, NJ: Erlbaum. 476 pp.

Rankin, R. E., Campbell, D. T. 1955. Galvanic skin responses to Negro and white experimenters. *J. Abnorm. Soc. Psychol.* 51: 30–33

Riess, M., Kalle, R. J., Tedeschi, J. T. 1981. Bogus pipeline attitude assessment, impression management, and misattribution in induced compliance settings. *J. Soc. Psychol.* 115:247–58

Ross, M., McFarland, C., Fletcher, G. J. O. 1981. The effect of attitude on the recall of personal histories. *J. Pers. Soc. Psychol.* 40:627–34

Saltzer, E. B. 1978. Locus of control and the intention to lose weight. *Health Educ. Monogr.* 6:118–28

Saltzer, E. B. 1981. Cognitive moderators of the relationship between behavioral intention and behavior. *J. Pers. Soc. Psychol.* 41: 260–71

Scheier, M. F., Carver, C. S. 1980. Private and public self-attention, resistance to change, and dissonance reduction. *J. Pers. Soc. Psychol.* 39:390–405

Schlenker, B. R. 1980. *Impression Management: The Self-Concept, Social Identity, and Interpersonal Relations*. Monterey, Calif: Brooks/Cole. 344 pp.

Schlenker, B. R. 1982. Translating actions into attitudes: An identity-analytic approach to the explanation of social conduct. *Adv. Exp. Soc. Psychol.* 15:193–247

Schlenker, B. R., Forsyth, D. R., Leary, M. R., Miller, R. S. 1980. Self-presentational analysis of the effects of incentives on attitude change following counterattitudinal behavior. *J. Pers. Soc. Psychol.* 39: 533–77

Schlenker, B. R., Goldman, H. J. 1982. Attitude change as a self-presentation tactic following attitude-consistent behavior: Effects of choice and role. *Soc. Psychol. Q.* 45:92–99

Schwartz, N., Frey, D., Kumpf, M. 1980. Interactive effects of writing and reading a persuasive essay on attitude change and selective exposure. *J. Exp. Soc. Psychol.* 16:1–17

Scott, M. B., Lyman, S. M. 1968. Accounts. *Am. Sociol. Rev.* 33:46–62

Sears, D. O., Hensler, C. P., Speer, L. K. 1979. Opposition to busing: Self-interest or symbolic politics? *Am. Polit. Sci. Rev.* 73:369–84

Seta, J. J., Seta, C. E. 1982. Personal equity: An intrapersonal comparator system analysis of reward value. *J. Pers. Soc. Psychol.* 43:222–35

Shapiro, D., Crider, A. 1969. Psychophysiological approaches in social psychology. In *The Handbook of Social Psychology*, ed. G. Lindzey, E. Aronson, 3:1–49. Reading, Mass: Addison-Wesley. 978 pp. 2nd ed.

Sherman, S. J., Presson, C. C., Chassin, L., Bensenberg, M., Corty, E., Olshavsky, R. W. 1982. Smoking intentions in adolescents: Direct experience and predictability. *Pers. Soc. Psychol. Bull.* 8:376–83

Sjöberg, L. 1982. Attitude-behaviour correlation, social desirability and perceived diagnostic value. *Br. J. Soc. Psychol.* 21:283–92

Snyder, M. 1974. The self-monitoring of expressive behavior. *J. Pers. Soc. Psychol.* 30:526–37

Snyder, M. 1979. Self-monitoring processes. *Adv. Exp. Soc. Psychol.* 12:85–128

Snyder, M. 1981. On the influence of individuals on situations. See Cantor & Kihlstrom 1981, pp. 309–29

Snyder, M. 1982. When believing means doing: Creating links between attitudes and behavior. See Zanna et al 1982, pp. 105–30

Snyder, M., Kendzierski, D. 1982a. Choosing social situations: Investigating the origins of correspondence between attitudes and behavior. *J. Pers.* 50:280–95

Snyder, M., Kendzierski, D. 1982b. Acting on one's attitudes; Procedures for linking attitude and behavior. *J. Exp. Soc. Psychol.* 18:165–83

Snyder, M., Swann, W. B. 1976. When actions reflect attitudes; The politics of impression management. *J. Per. Soc. Psychol.* 34:1034–42

Snyder, M., Tanke, E. D. 1976. Behavior and attitude: Some people are more consistent than others. *J. Pers.* 44:510–17

Snyder, M. L., Wicklund, R. A. 1981. Attribute ambiguity. See Eagly et al 1981, pp. 197–221

Steele, C. M., Liu, T. J. 1981. Making the dissonant act unreflective of self: Dissonance avoidance and the expectancy of a value-affirming response. *Pers. Soc. Psychol. Bull.* 7:393–97

Steele, C. M., Liu, T. J. 1983. Dissonance processes as self-affirmation. *J. Pers. Soc. Psychol.* 45:5–19

Steele, C. M., Southwick, L. L., Critchlow, B. 1981. Dissonance and alcohol: Drinking your troubles away. *J. Pers. Soc. Psychol.* 41:831–46

Stroebe, W., Diehl, M. 1981. Conformity and counterattitudinal behavior: The effect of social support on attitude change. *J. Pers. Soc. Psychol.* 41:876–99

Taylor, S. E., Fiske, S. T. 1978. Salience, attention and attribution: Top of the head phenomena. *Adv. Exp. Soc. Psychol.* 11:249–88

Tedeschi, J. T., ed. 1981. *Impression Management Theory and Social Psychological Research.* New York: Academic. 369 pp.

Tedeschi, J. T., Rosenfeld, P. 1981. Impression management theory in the forced compliance situation. See Tedeschi 1981

Tedeschi, J. T., Schlenker, B. R., Bonoma, T. V. 1971. Cognitive dissonance: Private ratiocination or public spectacle? *Am. Psychol.* 26:685–95

Weldon, D. E., Malpass, R. S. 1981. Effects of attitudinal, cognitive and situational variables on recall of biased communications. *J. Pers. Soc. Psychol.* 40:39–52

White, G. L. 1980. Consensus and justification effects on attitude following counterattitudinal behavior. *Soc. Psychol. Q.* 43:321–27

Wicker, A. W., 1969. Attitudes versus action: The relationship of verbal and overt behavioral responses to attitude objects. *J. Soc. Issues* 25:41–78

Wicklund, R. A. 1982. Self-focused attention and the validity of self-reports. See Zanna et al 1982, pp. 149–72

Wicklund, R. A., Frey, D. 1981. Cognitive consistency: Motivational vs. non-motivational perspectives. In *Social Cognition: Perspectives on Everyday Understanding*, ed. J. P. Forgas, pp. 141–63. London: Academic. 219 pp.

Wilder, D. A., Cooper, W. E. 1981. Categorization into groups: Consequences for social perception and attribution. See Eagly et al 1981, pp. 247–77

Wood, W., Eagly, A. M. 1981. Stages in the analysis of persuasive messages: The role of causal attributions and message comprehension. *J. Pers. Soc. Psychol.* 40:246–59

Worchel, S., Cooper, J. 1983. *Understanding Social Psychology.* Homewood, Ill: Dorsey. 593 pp.

Zajonc, R. B. 1980. Feeling and thinking: Preferences need no inferences. *Am. Psychol.* 35:151–75

Zanna, M. P., Fazio, R. H. 1982. The attitude-behavior relation. Moving toward a third generation of research. See Zanna et al 1982, pp. 283–301

Zanna, M. P., Higgins, E. T., Herman, C. P., eds. 1982. *Consistency in Social Behavior: The Ontario Symposium*, Vol. 2. Hillsdale, NJ: Erlbaum. 314 pp.

Zanna, M. P., Olson, J. M., Fazio, R. H. 1980. Attitude-behavior consistency: An individual difference perspective. *J. Pers. Soc. Psychol.* 38:432–40

Ann. Rev. Psychol. 1984. 35:427–59

CURRENT ISSUES IN ATTRIBUTION THEORY AND RESEARCH

John H. Harvey

Department of Psychology, Texas Tech University, Lubbock, Texas 79409

Gifford Weary

Department of Psychology, Ohio State University, Columbus, Ohio 43210

CONTENTS

It now has been over 40 years since Fritz Heider began to deliver talks on the psychology of interpersonal relations at the University of Graz, Austria, over 25 years since the appearance of Heider's (1958) classic book on that topic, and approaching two decades since Jones & Davis (1965) and Kelley (1967) gave the attribution area definition and momentum with their influential analyses

427

0066-4308/84/0201-0427$02.00

based to a great extent on Heider's earlier writing. Thus, the area of attribution research and theory, lodged primarily in social psychology, is reaching midlife in its development. As with any entity reaching middle age, one may now ask of attribution, how successful has the course of development been? How healthy is the field? Are its "golden years" apt to be rich and fulfilling? While we will not provide full answers to such questions in this paper, we will examine recent directions of attribution work that provide an index of progress, vitality, and hints about future directions and prosperity.

In its simplest form, attribution work is concerned with attempts to understand the factors involved in perceived causation. Also, the foci of attribution conceptions have included a variety of perceptions, including the perception of responsibility and freedom. What is an attribution? We endorse a broad answer to this question. Such an answer is provided by Heider (1976), who said, "Attribution is part of our cognition of the environment. Whenever you cognize your environment you will find attribution occurring" (p. 18). Why do people make attributions? Frequently it is assumed that the basic reason people make attributions is to achieve a greater degree of understanding of, and hence control over, their environment.

Focus of Review

In this review, we have assumed the task of reviewing a sample of attribution work that has been published during the period of approximately 1978 to 1983. Our review will start from the date that represents approximately the last year covered in Kelley & Michela's (1980) review of the area. Their coverage, though selective, provided a broad review of attribution work from early studies in the late 1950s and 1960s until around 1978 to 1979. The reader interested in a more comprehensive survey of the breadth of work in the area may choose to examine a host of edited books (e.g. Jones et al 1972, Harvey et al 1976, 1978a, 1981a, Frieze et al 1979, Antaki 1981, Jaspars et al 1983, Hewstone 1983) and even a few textbooks (e.g. Shaver 1975, Harvey & Smith 1977, Harvey & Weary 1981).

Kelley & Michela's (1980) review of attribution work involved a characterization of the general model of the attribution field as shown in Figure 1. In our review, we also will show that much of the recent work in the attribution area can be seen as falling into the causes of or basic processes underlying attributions and the consequences of attribution categories. We will not, however, use the term "attribution theory" to refer to analyses concerned with the effect of various factors on perceived causation and the term "attributional theories" to refer to analyses focusing on the consequences of attributions. We agree with Kelley and Michela's suggestion that in both types of theories, causal attributions are assumed to play a central role in the phenomena in question. Our own preference is to consider what might be called generic attribution theory

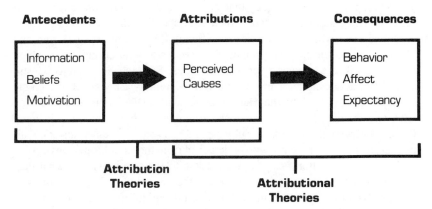

Figure 1   General model of the attribution field (from Kelley & Michela 1980).

composed of a variety of different theoretical strands and approaches) as potentially applying to all segments of the general model proposed by Kelley and Michela.

A final basic assumption to mention before beginning this review is our view that there is no monolithic theory of attribution. While there have been ambitious attempts at comprehensive analysis and integration (e.g. Kruglanski 1980), the most influential broad statements continue to be those provided by Heider (1958) and Jones and Kelley and their colleagues (e.g. Jones & Davis 1965, Kelley 1967, 1972a,b). In addition, Bem's (1967, 1972) theory of self-perception and Schachter's (1964) theory of emotion have become part of the general set of major attribution approaches, although neither theory was advanced initially as an attributional analysis. As we will suggest later, the 1970s and early 1980s represent a period of "mini-theory" work in the attribution area. Recent theoretical statements often involve qualifications of earlier, more general conceptions [e.g. qualifications to Jones & Nisbett's (1972) influential statement of the actor-observer hypothesis such as those provided by Monson & Snyder (1977), Watson (1982), and Farr & Anderson (1983)].

We begin the present review with an examination of work concerned with the measurement of attributions.

MEASUREMENT OF ATTRIBUTION

A set of basic questions that has been pursued with some vigor in attribution work in recent years include: how do we measure attributions in a manner so as to preserve their naturalistic character, and how natural are the attributions subjects are induced to make in laboratory settings?

Studies by Harvey et al (1980) and by Wong & Weiner (1981) are relevant to the development of techniques that better capture naturalistic attributional activity. These studies were concerned with showing that people ask "why" questions even when they are not specifically directed to do so. Wong and Weiner's procedure involved subjects' responses to a questionnaire in which they were asked to imagine various outcomes. Subsequently, subjects were asked, "What questions, if any, would you most likely ask yourself (given the situation imagined)?" In the Harvey et al work (1980), subjects observed relatively dramatic social interactions being enacted by actors on videotape. Before observing the videotape, subjects had received different kinds of cognitive sets (e.g. to be empathic with or detached from the stimulus persons). After viewing the interaction, subjects were asked to indicate in writing what they saw on the videotape and what they felt as they watched it. This measure was referred to by Harvey et al as an "unsolicited attribution" measure. Presumably, in this conception, subjects would naturally report various types of attribution, as well as particular magnitudes of attribution, in the course of describing the dramatic event and how they felt about it.

The findings by Wong and Weiner and Harvey et al showed that the independent variables under study significantly influenced the free response, relatively unsolicited attributional activity. A major difficulty with these studies, however, is that the attributions have to be coded for number and type of attributions made. While interrater reliability in the coding procedure was high in these studies, the coding procedures may or may not be generalizable to other studies in which naturalistic attribution is being investigated. Also, some attributional constructions will be inherently more difficult to code (e.g. compound thoughts: "he was angry so he hit her after she spilled the beans") than will others (e.g. simple declarative sentences: "she is immature").

Elig & Frieze (1979) provided evidence that questions the relative value of free response attribution measures that involve an explicit focus on making attributions. In their work, causal attributions for a manipulated success-failure event were collected from college students on five different measuring instruments. It was found that relative to structured measures (e.g. rating scales), open-ended response measures (e.g. "Why do you think you succeeded or failed on the task?") showed relatively poor reliability and interest validity. A somewhat similar conclusion was reached by F.D. Miller et al (1981) in work involving a quite different procedure than that employed by Elig and Frieze.

Another set of studies bearing on measurement issues derives from archival searches. If amenable to coding, there is a plethora of natural attribution on display in the written records of humans. Research by Lau & Russell (1980) and Felson & Ribner (1981) reveals that coders may be able to find and make discriminations readily about attributions in written records. Lau and Russell, for instance, coded newspaper accounts of baseball and football games for attributional content. Their data showed that players, coaches, and sports writers tended to make internal attributions for success and external attributions for failure.

Other recent contributions to the measurement of attributions literature have included: (*a*) the development of a causal dimension scale for achievement situations (Russell 1982); (*b*) a demonstration of the importance of the response format in structured attribution probes for discovering dispositional or situational response biases (Goldberg 1981); and (*c*) an argument that un-equivocal conclusions are possible only if dispositional and situational attributions are measured on separate scales (S. Solomon 1978; but see E. R. Smith & Miller 1982 for an opposing argument).

NATURE OF ATTRIBUTION

During the last 5 years, considerable debate has occurred regarding the nature of attributions. A number of diverse topics may be included such as: the extent to which attributions are accurate or inaccurate, whether they are represented in statements of reasons as well as statements of causes, whether or not they are part of the attributor's awareness, and how they may be represented in the relatively elaborate accounts people give for the significant events in their lives. Also, some analysis and research has continued on the development of attributional structure and processing attributional content.

Fundamental Attribution Error

The so-called fundamental attribution error has become a focus of exchange. L. Ross (1977) argued that "the tendency of attributors to underestimate the impact of situational factors and to overestimate the role of dispositional factors in controlling behavior" was the fundamental attribution error. Attributors' inclination to overattribute to dispositional factors has long been recognized as a prominent attributional tendency (Heider 1958, Jones 1979). In their well-known statement of the actor-observer hypothesis, Jones & Nisbett (1972) contended that as an actuarial proposition, attributors tend to emphasize personal causes for behavior at the expense of potent situational factors. Evidence accumulating over the years has supported this proposition (e.g. Quattrone 1982). However, whether or not this tendency represents an error has been called into question (Hamilton 1980, Harvey et al 1981b, Funder 1982). The issues raised in this controversy include: (*a*) what questions research subjects think they are answering in studies purporting to show the working of the fundamental attribution error (Hamilton 1980); (*b*) what criteria to use in establishing the accuracy of attribution (Harvey et al 1981b); (*c*) whether under certain conditions overattribution to situational factors also may represent incorrect judgment (Harvey et al 1981b); and (*d*) the idea that an important difference between situational and dispositional attributions is level of analysis;

that is, situational attributions describe environmental circumstances associated with behavior, while dispositional attributions are intended to describe how a given action fits into the larger pattern of the actor's behavior over time (Funder 1982). At this time, this controversy about error may be as much a matter of semantics as it is a topic for empirical resolution (Harvey & McGlynn 1982, Reeder 1982). Less controversial is the simple view that overattribution to dispositional factors represents a potent social judgment *bias* (A. W. Kruglanski and I Ajzen, unpublished, 1979).

Causes and Reasons, Endogenous and Exogenous Behavior

Two useful distinctions developed in attributional analyses are: (*a*) Buss's (1978) argument that "causes" represent the necessary and sufficient conditions for a behavior and that "reasons" represent the purposes or goals of a behavior; and (*b*) Kruglanski's (1975, 1979) distinction between explanations of behavior as "endogenous" (the behavior as an end in itself) versus "exogenous" (the behavior as a means to a further end). These theorists at least imply strongly that people are aware of such distinctions in their attributional activities, but there is little evidence one way or another on this possibility. Further, Buss's (1978) assertion that observers can explain behavior either by citing causes or giving the actor's reasons, whereas actors can only give reasons, has been challenged (Harvey & Tucker 1979, Locke & Pennington 1982). Available evidence indicates that actors and observers both are adroit at making what might be seen as distinctive causal versus reason statements.

Awareness of Attributional Activity

Nisbett & Wilson (1977) and Wilson & Nisbett (1978) have provided arguments and evidence which they claim show that people have no direct access to the cognitive processes that presumably determine behavior. This thesis has been challenged as it applies to attribution (Sabini & Silver 1981) and more generally as it relates to people's awareness of their cognitive functioning (Smith & Miller 1978, Ericsson & Simon 1980). Major issues in this debate include the difficulty of establishing what is essentially a null hypothesis (i.e. that people have little or no access), research subjects' typical motivation to have and display access, and what kinds of evidence would be necessary to make a strong case about degree of accessibility.

BASIC PROCESSES

Instigators

CONTROL MOTIVATION   A prominent assumption in attribution work is that people spontaneously engage in attributional activities. The previously mentioned broad definition of attribution espoused by Heider (1976) that links attribution with cognizing the environment implies such a spontaneity. But what factors make more probable explicit attribution-type inquiries on the part of the attributor? In an often-cited early probe, Berscheid et al (1976) hypothesized and found evidence to support the idea that the perceiver's outcome dependency on a target person may be such an instigator. They reasoned that the greater the target person's ability to control the perceiver's rewards and punishments, the more important it is for the perceiver to understand the target person's behavior and hence the greater the motivation to engage in causal analysis.

The idea that desire for control is a key motivating force behind attributional activity is pervasive in the literature, but most of the evidence on this question is indirect. Pittman & Pittman (1980) found evidence consistent with the hypothesis that attributions are instigated by control motivation and that attributional activity increases following an experience with lack of control. In their procedure, subjects received one of three levels of helplessness training (none, low, or high) and then read an essay under three sets of attribution instructions (the writer prepared it for pay, did not prepare it for pay, no information about the writer). The attribution variation had greater impact on attributions about the internal-external influences on the writer when the subject was in either low or high helplessness conditions; subjects who had had no experience with helplessness did not show differences as a function of the attribution manipulation.

EXPECTANCY DISCONFIRMATION   In other research on instigators, Wong & Weiner (1981) and Pyszczynski & Greenberg (1981) found that expectancy disconfirmation promotes attributional search. This finding is consistent with an hypothesis formulated by Kelley (1972b) that the more extreme the effect to be attributed, the more likely the attributor is to assume that it entails multiple necessary causes. In another study that relates to Kelley's (1967) statement of how different types of information affect attribution, it was found that attributional activity is facilitated by the priming of an attributor's accessibility to consensus, consistency, and distinctiveness information (Ferguson & Wells 1980).

DIRECT ATTRIBUTIONAL QUESTIONS   Enzle & Schopflocher (1978) demonstrated that direct attributional questions may instigate attributional processes that do not occur in the absence of such questions. Subjects received help from a confederate that either occurred in the presence of facilitating instructions or appeared to be spontaneous. One-half of the subjects were asked to evaluate the confederate's prosocial dispositional qualities; the other half were not. All subjects later rated the confederate's attractiveness. According to the discounting principle (Kelley 1972a), subjects who were helped in the absence of facilitating instructions should have viewed the favor as more initially moti-vated and thus should have evaluated the confederate more positively than subjects who were helped after facilitating instructions had been given. This effect occurred, however, only for those subjects who had previously been asked to make attributions regarding the confederate's prosocial disposition. Subjects who were not asked to make such attributions apparently did not do so spontaneously; they did not differ in their ratings of the attractiveness of the confederate.

Perceptual Processes

The theoretical bases of the variables of salience of information, imagery, and temporal perspective may be found in the writings of Jones & Davis (1965), Kelley (1967), and Jones & McGillis (1976). These writings emphasized the role of beliefs, sets, and the integration of different types and amounts of information in the causal attribution process.

SALIENCE   A prominent prediction in attribution research is that the salience of stimuli influences the attribution of causality, and there is some evidence that supports this prediction (Taylor & Fiske 1975). Salience often is used synony-mously with availability and vividness to suggest that some factor is literally prominent in the perceiver's field of view. The salience manipulation may be carried out through a written presentation (Pryor & Kriss 1977) or via videotape and interaction formats (Taylor & Fiske 1975). A variety of theoretical posi-tions has been advanced to explain why salient factors may draw causal attributions. One view is that attributions are often perceptually based with subjects perceiving dynamic events directly (Lowe & Kassin 1980). Relatedly, salience effects have been depicted as "top-of-the-head" phenomena because of their basic perceptual nature; hence, salient factors may be relatively easy to recall. Another position is that salience effects occur directly at the encoding stage of information processing (Taylor & Thompson 1982). A more elaborate view is that salience and informational factors exert influence on the attributor across a series of stages of encoding, processing, and recall. Smith & Miller (1979) endorse this position and suggest that attributional processing as a function of salience can take place at the time of the encoding and storage of information, as well as at the time of this retrieval from memory. Also, McArthur & Ginsburg (1981) obtained evidence suggesting that salience effects on attribution are not due simply to increased duration of attention to salient stimuli. Such evidence would argue against an interpretation of salience effects based simply upon recall (see also Fiske et al 1982).

IMAGERY AND PERSPECTIVE   A closely related line of work has focused on the role of the attributor's imagery and perspective in influencing attributions.

In particular, does the construction of mental images account for the effects of empathy sets on attribution? Inducing an observer to be empathic with an actor's perspective in a situation has been found to lead to convergence in attributions between actor and observer (Regan & Totten 1975). In addition to the imagery explanation for this effect, it may be argued that differential visual perspective leads to differential storage of information, and that this information underlies subsequent attributions. Fiske et al (1979) provide data and argue that the imagery explanation of empathy effects on attribution is untenable. These authors suggest that imagery and empathy may be separated as phenomena and their effects on attribution, recall, and other measures may be tested differentially.

COMMENT   It is likely that research on perceptual factors in attributional phenomena will continue with zest in coming years. Such a prediction is based on the active interplay among this area of research, social cognition work, and research on basic cognitive processes in experimental psychology.

Cognitive Processes

Kelley (1967) theorized that people often make causal attributions as if they were analyzing data patterns by means of an analysis of variance. According to this conception, attributors mainly use three types of information to verify whether they have correctly linked causes and effects. These types of information are the distinctiveness, consistency, and consensus associated with the possible causes. Covariation, in Kelley's conception, is the process by which an individual attributes effects to those causal factors with which they covary, rather than to those from which they are relatively independent.

CONSENSUS   Throughout the 1970s, the role and impact of consensus information in attributional phenomena have been debated in the literature. The debate stems largely from Nisbett & Borgida's (1975) finding that consensus has no effect on attribution. Subsequent research (Wells & Harvey 1977) showed consensus effects under a stronger manipulation of consensus information and when it was stressed that information about the persons comprising the consensus sample were randomly selected. However, more recent work by Major (1980) revealed the weakness of consensus information relative to distinctiveness and consistency information in a situation in which subjects could ask for different types of information to explain why an event occurred. Also, Hansen & Donoghue (1977) provided evidence that attributions are more affected by knowledge of one's own behavior (self-based consensus) than by others' behavior (sample-based consensus). This finding, however, was disputed by Kulik & Taylor (1980), who found that both types of consensus affect trait attributions.

As research in the late 1970s and early 1980s suggests, the consensus-attribution controversy appears to be virtually resolved by the delineation of several conditions when consensus is and is not influential. For example, M. R. Solomon et al (1981) provided evidence that type of consensus and its mode of presentation represent orthogonal dimensions that affect the impact of consensus on attributions. In a useful review, Kassin (1979) suggested that consensus effects depend upon such mediating factors as: the strength of magnitude of the base rate information, the salience of the information and the ease with which it may be applied, the perceived representativeness (and hence generalizability of the base rate sample), and the causal relevance of the base rate. Kassin also distinguishes between implicit and explicit consensus. Implicit consensus refers to subjective—often normative—expectancies for behavior in a situation, while explicit consensus refers to the actual behavior of individuals in a sample. Kassin contends that the type of consensus and/or the discrepancy between types may be crucial to whether or not such information affects attribution. Another useful review of the current state of affairs with consensus effects is provided by Borgida & Brekke (1981).

DISTINCTIVENESS AND CONSISTENCY   Although not as vigorously pursued, the attributional criteria of distinctiveness and consistency also have been investigated in recent years. For example, Enzle et al (1980) showed that one set of observers' evaluations of a target person reflected typical distinctiveness findings, with high distinctiveness yielding less extreme evaluations than low distinctiveness for both positive and negative acts. However, for observers more involved in an interaction with an actor, stronger positive qualities were attributed to the actor when positive rather than negative acts occurred regardless of distinctiveness information.

DISCOUNTING   According to Kelley (1972a), the discounting principle in attribution refers to the attributor's giving less weight to a particular cause in producing an effect if other plausible causes are also present. Discounting effects have been examined in recent years by Kruglanski et al (1978), Kassin et al (1980), and Hull & West (1982). In the latter study, Hull and West provided evidence and argued for a major qualification of the discounting idea. They suggested that attributional discounting is more adequately represented by a model based on the proportion of total variance associated with the alternative effects of a given effect than by Kelley's notion that emphasizes the number of those effects. Hull and West found, for example, that a single high-valenced alternative effect was associated with greater discounting than two lesser-valenced effects.

CAUSAL SCHEMATA   Kelley's great influence on the study of basic attributional processes is further illustrated by the continued interest in causal schemata. Kelley (1972b) posited that a causal schema is a conception of the manner in which two or more causal factors interact in relation to a particular kind of effect. Theoretically, a schema allows the attributor to operate more quickly in making inferences than is the case when a full-blown ANOVA-type operation is required. Types of schemata specified in Kelley's analysis include an attributor's tendency to invoke multiple sufficient causes, multiple necessary causes, and a schema for compensatory causes.

Reeder & Brewer (1979) provided a useful extension of the schemata reasoning. They argued that different schemata are stimulated by different types of dispositions. They suggested that observers make certain systematic assumptions about the range of behavior that is implied by a given disposition. These assumptions are called implicational schemata. For example, a skillful disposition appears to imply that the actor has the ability to perform both skillful and unskillful overt behavior. On the other hand, an unskillful disposition implies that the actor has the capability to perform unskillful but not skillful overt behavior. Evidence congenial to this argument is presented by Reeder & Fulks (1980). They found that when observers witnessed an overt portrayal of the actor's ability, dispositional inferences of ability based on the actor's skillful behavior were less affected by situational demands than were inferences based on unskillful behavior. These findings suggest that dispositional inferences depend on the complex interaction of implicational schemata and the situational demands in a given situation. They also suggest that situational attributions may be a function only of situational demands.

An analysis by Fiedler (1982) critically analyzes the causal schemata construct and related research. Fiedler argues that to date studies have not been designed to test observable schema properties and that the available research lacks essential features of natural causal problems. Further, Fiedler contends that although an important aspect of natural causal tasks is the encoding of unstructured empirical information, the stimulus material in most schema research has been prestructured to such a degree that the task left to judge is simply reporting semantic relations. Although Fiedler's analysis should prove helpful in refining the causal schemata construct, it is too early to say what influence the analysis will have on empirical research. In many ways, his request for both greater rigor in analysis and greater naturalism in stimulus material could be applied to any area of contemporary cognitive-social psychology.

Related to the concept of causal schemata are the notions of attributional accounts and perceived causal structure. Accounts are relatively elaborate analyses of why and how events occurred. For example, Weiss (1975) and Harvey et al (1983) have examined written and oral accounts given by persons experiencing conflict in close relationships or whose relationships have recently ended. Account-making pertaining to a variety of social situations also has been investigated and/or theorized about by several other workers (Scott & Lyman 1968, Sabini & Silver 1981).

Promising work on a dimensional analysis of perceived causal structure is offered by Kelley (1983). He suggests that focal events are interpreted—understood, explained, and evaluated—in terms of their location within a perceived causal structure. Kelley theorizes that such a structure has direction (past to future), extent (proximal-distal), patterning (simple-complex), components of varying stability-instability, both actual and potential features, and various types of causes (e.g. those associated with persons vs those associated with environment). In this analysis of perceived causal structure, Kelley concurs with other theorists (e.g. Weary et al 1980) in emphasizing the need to study attribution in social contexts and as it often occurs as part of interpersonal communication.

An interesting line of work that relates to schemata and structure ideas is Hansen's (1980) depiction of the process of commonsense attribution. He argues that: (a) attributors come to the attributional setting with at least three causal explanations in mind (that behavior is facilitated by forces in the person, the entity, or the circumstance under which the person is interacting with the entity); (b) one of these hypotheses is tentatively advanced when an event is observed (this hypothesis is seen as a crude attribution); (c) the tentative hypothesis guides the search for causal information; and (d) this search follows a principle of *cognitive economy*. While Hansen provided some data in support of this analysis, the theoretical ideas are rich and deserving of further inquiry.

MEMORY   In recent years, the relationship between attribution and memory has become a topic for considerable investigation. Memory sometimes has been considered to be a possible mediator of the relationship between attribution and some dependent variable (e.g. Fiske et al 1979, Harvey et al 1980). Other work has examined the effect of causal information on memory (e.g. Sherman & Titus 1982, Wells 1982). Of particular interest in this latter line of work is the possible role of attribution in reconstructive memory (Bartlett 1932, Yarkin et al 1981). In a provocative illustration of this role, Wells (1982) asked subjects in one study to observe a scenario in which an actor's behavior was associated with high or low distinctiveness across situations and high or low consensus with others' actions. Subjects either made attributions for the actor's behavior immediately following their observation of the scenario or not at all. One week later, subjects were asked to recall consensus and distinctiveness for the actor's original behavior. Subjects who made attributions were significantly more accurate in their recall than were no-attribution subjects. Wells suggested that making an attribution may allow for a reconstructive memory for the original event, but not enhance direct access to the original event information.

Another interesting line of work on attribution-memory links has been carried out by Moore et al (1979), who identified a "dispositional shift" in memory for causation. These investigators found that when asked to explain an action in which they had just engaged, subjects interpreted it in terms of situational demands [consistent with Jones & Nisbett's (1972) actor-observer hypothesis]. But when asked to explain the identical behavior several weeks later, these same subjects interpreted it in terms of their own dispositional characteristics. Hence, the properties of self-dispositions, not immediately present, appeared and took on causal significance over time—the "dispositional shift." Peterson (1980b) replicated this effect by a content analysis of attributions extracted from the autobiographies of 77 famous psychologists. Attributions about early actions were more dispositional than were attributions about recent actions.

COMMENT   Given the extensive literature that now exists, it seems likely that in the future, less research attention may be given to questions about basic criteria for covariation analysis. However, the rules by which discounting occurs, the types and functions of various causal schemata, attributional accounts, and structure, and the relationship between attribution and memory, promise to provide fodder for research and theory for many years to come.

Motivational Processes

In recent years, there has been renewed interest among personality and social psychologists in the relations between affect and cognition (Zajonc 1980, Lazarus 1982). Within the attribution domain, this interest has taken the form of lively debate on the role, if any, of motivation in the causal inference process. Contemporary attribution theorists and researchers have, for the most part, been preoccupied with examination of the informational rules people use to infer causal relations among events. However, over 25 years ago Heider (1958) argued that "attributions and cognitions are influenced by the mere subjective forces of needs and wishes as well as by the more objective evidence presented in the raw material" (pp. 120–21). In this section, we will examine research that focuses on the influence of three such "subjective forces": self-esteem, self-presentation, and control motivations.

SELF-ESTEEM   One of the more robust findings in social psychology is the tendency for individuals to accept more causal responsibility for their positive outcomes than for their negative outcomes (Greenwald 1980). The operation of self-serving, or ego-defensive, biases has generally been used to explain these results. That is, by taking credit for good acts and denying blame for bad outcomes, an individual presumably is able to enhance or protect his or her self-esteem.

Miller & Ross (1975) questioned this motivational interpretation, suggesting that the results of many of the studies often cited as support for self-serving attributional biases could readily be "interpreted in information-processing terms" (p. 224). Specifically, these authors contended that the observed tendency for individuals to accept greater responsibility for positive than for negative outcomes may occur for any or all of several reasons: (*a*) individuals intend and expect success more than failure and are more likely to make self-ascriptions for expected than unexpected outcomes; (*b*) perceived covariation between response and outcome may be more apparent for individuals experiencing a pattern of increasing success than for individuals experiencing constant failure; and (*c*) people erroneously base their judgments of the contingency between response and outcome on the occurrence of the desired outcome than on any actual degree of contingency.

Miller & Ross (1975) concluded that motivated distortions in the causal inference process had not been demonstrated. Kelley & Michela (1980) have argued, however, that more recent, methodologically improved studies of self-serving attributions are difficult to reinterpret in nonmotivational terms and consequently provide a fairly strong case for motivational effects (see reviews by Snyder et al 1978, Weary Bradley 1978, Zuckerman 1979). Indeed, since Kelley & Michela's (1980) review, a number of studies have investigated explicitly the presumed motivational mediators of self-serving attributional biases (e.g. Stephan & Gollwitzer 1981, McFarland & Ross 1982).

Weary (Weary Bradley 1978, Weary 1980) proposed that positive and negative affective states produced by success and failure experiences, respectively, mediate individuals' causal attributions for their behavioral outcomes. Specifically, she argued that self-enhancing attributions (i.e. high self-attributions) for success are mediated by and serve to maintain relatively high levels of positive affect, and self-protective attributions (i.e. low self-attributions following failure) are mediated by and function to alleviate high levels of negative affect (i.e. that self-protective attributions serve a threat-reducing purpose).

Gollwitzer et al (1982) designed a study to test the notion that outcome-related affect determines asymmetrical attributions for success and failure. In their study, Gollwitzer et al used a technique based on excitation transfer theory (Zillman 1982) that permitted affect to be manipulated directly. Zillman has suggested that the excitatory activity of emotions (positive and negative) is largely nonspecific and redundant. Therefore, residues of excitation from arousing tasks (e.g. physical exercise) can combine with and intensify subsequent affective states arising from a totally independent source. Gollwitzer et al reasoned that outcome-related affect and self-serving biases would be exaggerated if performance feedback were given under conditions in which residues of excitation from prior stimulation combine with the excitatory reaction to performance feedback.

In their study, Gollwitzer et al had college students engage in physical exercise after working on a social perceptivity task. The students then were given success or failure feedback on the test either 1, 5, or 9 minutes after exercising. The results of this study indicated that self-serving attributional biases were exaggerated under conditions permitting the transfer of excitation from an irrelevant source. When students were highly aroused but could associate their arousal to the physical exercise (1-minute condition) or when their arousal produced by the exercise had dissipated (9-minute condition), their attributions for their outcomes on the social perceptiveness test were less self-serving than when residual arousal could be transferred to outcome-related affect (5-minute condition). It is difficult to see how these results could be explained in nonmotivational terms since the information processing interpretations of asymmetrical attributions for success and failure (Miller & Ross 1975, Tetlock & Levi 1982) assign no role to affect and arousal.

Other recent work on self-serving attributional biases has taken two general forms. First, researchers have attempted to establish boundary conditions for the positive-negative outcome attributional differences. For example, research on sex differences in attributions for one's own success or failure indicates that males exhibit the typical self-serving bias when the task is described as stereotypically masculine while females show the usual positive-negative outcome bias when the task is described as stereotypically feminine (Mirels 1980, Rosenfield & Stephan 1978). Individuals also exhibit the bias when their performance outcomes and attributions are private (Greenberg et al 1982). Second, the generalizability of laboratory-based studies demonstrating self-serving attributional biases to real-world settings has been a focus of research efforts. Investigators have found evidence of self-esteem biases in coaches' and players' attributions for their wins and losses (Carver et al 1980, Lau & Russell 1980, Peterson 1980a) and in successful and unsuccessful medical school applicants' attributions for their admission decisions (Smith & Manard 1980).

SELF-PRESENTATION   Within the last several years, attribution theorists and researchers have begun to recognize the possibility that individuals may express causal judgments that are designed to gain approval from or otherwise control the responses of others. For example, in their investigation of attributional conflict in young couples, Orvis et al (1976) have suggested that communicated attributions may be used to defend or justify one's behavior or to call into question the behavior of one's partner. In a similar vein, Weary (Weary Bradley 1978, Weary 1979) has contended that individuals may as-

cribe causality for positive and negative outcomes associated with their behaviors in such a way that would avoid embarrassment and/or gain public
approval.

In their review, Kelley & Michela (1980) noted that the self-presentational
interpretations offered by Orvis et al (1976) and Weary (1979) were post hoc
and therefore ambiguous. Since then, however, there have been a number of
studies that have examined directly the notion that self-presentational concerns
may influence the causal inference process. In testing for the operation of
self-presentational motivations, investigators generally have employed two
procedures: first, they have compared subjects' attributions under two conditions that are identical except that one is relatively public and the other is
relatively private (e.g. Greenberg et al 1982, Weary 1980, Weary et al 1982),
and second, they have used the bogus-pipeline (a bogus lie-detector apparatus)
technique (Jones & Sigall 1971) as a strategy for reducing distortion and
dissimulation in verbal responses (e.g. Arkin et al 1980, Riess et al 1981). If
public awareness or potential discovery of misrepresentation affects attributors' communicated causal judgments, it presumably is because of a desire to
create a favorable impression on others.

In one study, for example, Arkin et al (1980) tested the notion based on a
self-presentation formulation that individuals would become more modest
about their abilities and attributes when others are not likely to be persuaded by
or to challenge publicly a too positive interpretation of events. They found that
participants accepted more credit for success than for failure when they did not
expect their behavior to be evaluated by a group of experts. However, there was
a reversal of this typical self-serving attributional bias among participants who
were high in social anxiety and who expected their behavior to come under
expert scrutiny. In a second experiment, this tendency for high social-anxiety
participants to accept more credit for failure than for success was replicated.
Moreover, it was found that both high- and low-social anxiety participants
portrayed the causes of their performance outcomes in a more modest fashion
when they responded via the bogus-pipeline.

Arkin et al's (1980) results, then, support the premise that self-presentation
motivations may bias causal attributions. They also shed some light on factors
such as individual differences in social anxiety that may influence the choice of
self-presentational strategy (e.g. modesty or self-enhancement). Other factors
may include a variety of social contextual factors prominently including the
prestige of the audience. Indeed, research suggests that public evaluation of a
person's performance by a committee of prestigious individuals leads to a
moderation or reversal of self-serving attributional tendencies (e.g. Arkin et al
1980, Greenberg et al 1982), while observation of a person's performance by
peers leads to an exaggeration of self-serving causal attributions (Weary 1980).
A taxonomy of variables that may determine the precise influence of self-

presentation motivations on attributors' causal judgments has been presented by Weary & Arkin (1981).

Despite the emphasis on the possible purposes that strategically communicated attributions may serve, little actually is known about the reactions of observers to individuals' causal judgments for their own or others' behavioral outcomes. This gap in the literature is particularly surprising since the topic of actor-observer differences in attributions has stimulated considerable interest among theorists and researchers (see Jones & Nisbett 1972, Monson & Snyder 1977).

Several recent studies, however, have examined individuals' reactions to another's strategic causal claims regarding his or her outcomes. An example of such work is a study reported by Tetlock (1980). This study simulated an experiment by Ross et al (1974) in which teachers were led to believe that they had been successful or unsuccessful in teaching a lesson to a student. Ross et al found that teachers tended to take responsibility for failure but attributed success to the student. In this study, Tetlock provided subjects with written descriptions of the Ross et al procedures and included information indicating that a particular teacher had either succeeded or failed and had made either self-serving attributions (i.e. the teacher had taken credit for success or had denied responsibility for failure) or counterdefensive attributions. Tetlock reasoned that society generally expects teachers to take responsibility for pupil failure but to reward pupil success. Teachers in the Ross et al study, then, may have strategically selected attributions that were in accord with normative requirements of the teacher role in an attempt to create a positive public image. In accord with this reasoning, Tetlock found that his subjects evaluated the teacher who made counterdefensive attributions more positively than the teacher who made defensive attributions.

Tetlock's (1980) study demonstrated that what actors say about the causes of their own outcomes affects observers' evaluations of them. It is important to note, however, that this study as well as the other investigations of audience reactions to attributors' ascriptions of causal responsibility (Forsyth et al 1981, Tetlock 1981) only begin to examine the mechanisms underlying individuals' reactions to others' expressions of their causal judgments. After all, observers in these studies were unacquainted with and had minimal information (e.g. consistency, distinctiveness, and consensus) about the actors. Moreover, these studies do not address the mechanisms involved in observers' reactions to causal explanations for an event when there are few, if any, cues as to the social value or desirability of such judgments. It is surely the case that there are many everyday situations where individuals' expressions of their causal judgments for events have little or no presentational value. Since such expressed causal judgments may evoke important reactions from others, it is important to understand the nature and basis of these reactions.

Considerable progress has been made in recognizing and understanding the role of self-presentation motives in attributional activities. Future directions for research may very well include examination of factors that determine the choice of a specific attributional self-presentation strategy and the effects of these strategies on attributors' self-concepts.

CONTROL   Classic approaches to attribution processes have taken as a major assumption the notion that perceivers attempt to specify the single cause of their own and others' behavior. As we have noted, one motive for such attributional activity is a desire to achieve greater control over the social world. A recent program of research, however, suggests that under some conditions the perceiver may want to locate multiple causes for an event rather than a specific cause. M. L. Snyder & Wicklund (1981) have argued that individuals have a desire to view themselves as possessing a range of behaviors. Since attributions of some dispositions may have control-reducing implications, attributors may behave in such a way that the result of any "search" for causality would be ambiguous. For example, if a student is uncertain of how well he may perform on the GRE exam, he may stay up very late the night before the exam. Should he then perform poorly, the cause of his performance would not be clear. His performance outcome could be attributed to his state of exhaustion, to his lack of ability (an attribution that would imply constraint on the range of his future performance outcomes), or to both of these factors.

In a test of the attribute ambiguity notion, T. W. Smith et al (1982) asked students who were high and low in trait anxiety to take an intelligence test that was known to be either affected or unaffected by anxiety. These authors reasoned that highly test-anxious students would be more likely than low test-anxious students to use their symptoms to create ambiguity about the causes of their negative outcomes and, consequently, would be more likely to report anxiety when anxiety was presented as a viable explanation for poor performance on the intelligence test. Smith et al's (1982) results supported these predictions. Moreover, when highly test-anxious subjects could not create ambiguity about the cause of their potentially negative outcomes via self-reports of anxiety, they did so by reporting less expenditure of effort on the test. While these results are consistent with the notion that individuals will under certain conditions create causal ambiguity to preserve their behavioral control, they also are consistent with interpretations in terms of self-esteem protection (Berglas & Jones 1978, T. W. Smith et al 1982) and self-presentation motivations (Kolditz & Arkin 1982).

COMMENT   Proponents of motivational processes have emphasized consistently the interaction of motivation and cognition. Moreover, the bulk of evidence seems to argue strongly in favor of it. Specification of the precise nature of the motivation-cognition interaction, however, must await greater theoretical development of the cognitive and motivational formulations.

CONSEQUENCES

Social Interaction

Since the inception of attribution work, the relationship between attribution and social interaction has been a topic of interest (Kelley 1972a). Such interest could be expected because attribution theorists typically assume, either explicitly or implicitly, that attributions directly influence behavior or mediate the relationship between other factors and behavior. In the general conception of attribution, therefore, the attributor is not "lost in thought" as has sometimes been contended by critics of attribution theory. Rather, in this conception the attributor either is influenced to take action via the attribution process or acquires the potential to act because of this process. Kelley (1973) articulated this general position as follows, "Causal attributions play an important role in providing the impetus to action and decisions among alternative courses of action" (p. 127).

Despite the stature of assumptions about the relationship between attribution and social interaction, there has been little research aimed at direct examination of the relationship. Indirectly, evidence about this relationship in the 1950s and 1960s is illustrated by the classic "warm-cold" study by Kelley (1950) and by studies examining how various types of stigma affect interaction (Farina et al 1966, Kleck et al 1966). In the study by Kelley, some college students were presented with information that a visiting instructor would be "rather warm"; whereas other students were informed that the visiting instructor would be "rather cold." Subsequently, observation of the interaction between the students and the instructor revealed more approach behavior (e.g. question-asking) by students in the warm condition than by students in the cold condition. Also, adjective ratings collected after the interaction showed that students formed relatively positive impressions of the instructor in the warm condition and relatively negative impressions of the instructor in the cold condition. These interaction patterns and ratings emerged even though the instructor performed in virtually the same fashion in both conditions.

Kelley's study shows a relationship between social perception and social interaction. It may be inferred that various kinds of attributions made by the students about the instructor mediated the course of interaction as it unfolded (e.g. warm condition subjects may have imputed to the instructor a relatively accepting, noncritical orientation toward students—hence the asking of questions). However, no direct evidence of this possibility exists.

In the research by Kleck et al (1966), subjects engaged in a brief interaction with a person who was physically handicapped (in a wheelchair), or they encountered a person who showed no sign of physical handicap. It was found that subjects terminated the interaction significantly more quickly when they were interacting with the handicapped person than when they were interacting with the nonhandicapped person.

In the work by Farina et al, subjects were given a task to work on with a person whom they were led to believe was mentally ill or with a person about whom no such information was presented. These investigators found that subjects talked less and initiated less conversation and expressed opinions less representative of their beliefs when they worked on the task with the supposedly mentally ill person than did subjects who worked on the task with the person who was not labeled mentally ill. As with the "warm-cold" study, these investigations of the effects of stigma variables on social interaction may be interpreted to suggest that subjects' attributions about their interaction partners play at least a catalytic role in regulating the course of interaction.

These studies in the 1950s and 1960s set the stage for more detailed work on the relationship between social perception and social interaction in the 1970s and early 1980s. In one major line of work, Snyder and colleagues (e.g. Snyder & Swann 1978, Snyder & Gangestad 1981, Skrypnek & Snyder 1982) have investigated how people who are induced to hold certain hypotheses about others test those hypotheses through interaction with the target others. This research has shown that hypothesis-testing strategies may channel and constrain social interaction in ways that actually cause the target person to provide some degree of behavioral confirmation for the perceiver's hypothesis. It is readily possible to view these hypotheses as beliefs or attributions about the character or some other aspects of the target others. An assumption, sometimes implicit in this research, is that the perceiver's testing of hypotheses serves to make the target other more predictable (e.g. "he's a chauvinistic male") and thus to enhance a sense of personal control in interacting with the other.

In a related line of work, Zanna and his associates (e.g. Zanna & Pack 1975, von Baeyer et al 1981) have shown that stereotyped attributions about men and women may channel social interaction in ways that cause individuals to provide behavioral confirmation for these stereotypes. For example, von Baeyer et al found that when female job applicants knew they would be interviewed by a male who held traditional views of women, they dressed more traditionally and provided more traditional answers during the interview than did subjects who believed the interviewer held nontraditional views of women. Questions that still require attention in this interesting program of work include, when do people resist acting upon the basis of stereotyped sets? Do people sometimes test such sets before taking action?

Studies by Yarkin et al (1981) and Town & Harvey (1981) comprise a final strand of research in recent years concerning the attribution-social interaction relationship. These investigators attempted to assess directly the role of attributions in mediating the relationship between information about a person and social interaction with the person. In the process, they also examined the relationship between attributions about and behavior toward a stimulus person. In Yarkin et al, as an illustration, subjects received a set about the mental health of a stimulus person and then saw a brief videotape in which the stimulus person was conversing about general matters with another person; then they either made attributions about the stimulus person in the unsolicited attribution paradigm previously discussed or engaged in a distraction task; and finally they interacted with the person. Measures of approach behavior were developed from indices such as observed duration of eye contact and the rated positivity of the conversation.

Data from both Yarkin et al (1981) and Town & Harvey (1981) showed that relatively positive sets about others' mental health or sexual orientation were associated with positive attributions and approach behavior. The major role of attributions as a mediator was shown by the more pronounced behavioral responses in attribution versus distraction conditions. Also, attribution was highly positively correlated with behavior in both studies. These investigators argued that the data were interpretable in terms of a perceived control explanation. All subjects had knowledge that they would interact with the stimulus person prior to the attribution activity. Presumably, the attribution activity may have provided subjects with an opportunity to gain a greater sense of control regarding the course of the future interaction. Hence, more pronounced behavioral responses in line with the set would be expected from these subjects. The import of expected future interaction in this sequence has been demonstrated further by Yarkin (1983) and as a generally necessary condition for the production of meaningful attributions by Monson et al (1982).

The evidence from Yarkin et al and Town and Harvey provides a more detailed examination of set-attribution-behavior linkages than had been reported previously. Nevertheless, since subjects interacted with an experimental accomplice in this research, the work did not begin to show how causal loops, or reciprocal thought-interaction patterns, might unfold in such sequences [see Darley & Fazio (1980) for a related discussion], nor of the self-presentation strategies that might be involved on the part of the participants in such sequences (see Jones & Pittman 1982).

COMMENT   It seems likely that work on attribution and social interaction will continue and be seen as crucial for the field for many years. Indeed, people do not get "lost in thought." Rather, their thoughts and actions are woven together in intricate patterns.

Affective Consequences of Achievement-Related Attributions

In our discussion of motivational influences in the causal inference process, we examined research suggesting that outcome-related affect mediates self-serving attributions. Attribution theorists and researchers in the achievement motivation area have focused on affect not as an antecedent of causal attributions but as a consequence of causal attributions for success and failure. Weiner and his colleagues (Weiner et al 1978, 1979) have presented the most systematic consideration of the affective consequences of achievement-related attributions. They have proposed and provided some evidence consistent with the notion that there are outcome-related and attribution-related affects. More specifically, general positive and negative affects are thought to be associated with success and failure, respectively, regardless of the cause of the performance outcome. Affects relevant to self-esteem are dependent upon the attributions made for performance. For example, ability attributions following success presumably give rise to feelings of pride and competence, while ability attributions following failure may result in feelings of incompetence.

A study by McFarland & Ross (1982) examined the impact of outcome and attribution on affect in an achievement context. In this study, college students were led to believe that they had succeeded or failed on a social accuracy test. After receiving the performance feedback, the students were induced to attribute their test outcome either to their ability or to task difficulty. The results of a factor analysis performed on affective reactions revealed three factors: a negative affect, a positive affect, and a self-esteem factor. Subsequent analyses indicated that the nature of the attribution determined all three types of affective reactions. Success led to greater positive affect, less negative affect, and greater feelings of self-esteem than failure only when students attributed the performance to ability. While secondary analyses revealed some evidence supportive of the proposed outcome-dependent affects, in general the results of McFarland & Ross's (1982) study suggest that in achievement settings affect is determined primarily by attributions.

Research on the affective consequences of achievement-related attributions is in its infancy and is likely to be an active area of future work. There are many questions that remain. For example, whether and what affects are linked specifically to outcomes and whether these outcome-dependent affects coexist with or are transformed into attribution-related affects will need to be determined by theoretical and empirical work. A perhaps more fundamental question that will be important to address is the process by which attributions produce the affective consequences they do.

Arousal Effects

Schachter's (1964) well-known theory of emotion posits that both perceptible physiological arousal and labeling of this arousal in accord with situational or cognitive factors are necessary for the subjective experience of emotional stress. An attributional analysis of Schachter's theory suggests that diffuse physiological arousal motivates the individual to make causal attributions about the source of his or her autonomic arousal and that these causal attributions in turn provide the individual with cognitive labels (e.g. euphoria or fear) for the arousal state (Valins & Nisbett 1972). According to this analysis, then, physiological arousal attributed to an emotionally relevant source should result in emotional behavior, while arousal attributed to a nonemotional source should not result in emotional behavior.

This attributional analysis of Schachter's (1964) emotion theory has stimulated a considerable amount of research. For example, some research has attempted to demonstrate motivational biases in the choice of causal attributions for arousal (e.g. Gibbons & Wright 1981). Other work in this area has been concerned with showing that undesirable emotional behaviors may be reduced by inducing individuals to misattribute their heightened autonomic arousal to nonemotional sources. Storms & Nisbett (1970), for example, provided evidence suggesting that insomniacs who were led to attribute part of their arousal at bedtime to a drug (actually a placebo) experienced less emotionality and, consequently, got to sleep sooner (the so-called reverse placebo effect). Such misattribution effects, however, have been difficult to replicate. Sometimes null effects and sometimes standard placebo effects (changes in the recipient's condition in accord with the placebo's alleged impact) have been obtained.

Ross & Olson (1981) have presented an expectancy-attribution model of the effects of placebos in an attempt to resolve the inconsistencies in the literature. The model distinguishes primary assessments, which measure the direct effects of the expectancies associated with the placebo, from secondary assessments, which measure the recipient's inferences about underlying dispositions that are not believed to be directly affected by the placebo (inductive effects). Also, placebos whose presumed impact will counteract the recipient's symptoms (counteractive expectancies) are distinguished from placebos whose presumed effects will parallel the recipient's symptoms (parallel expectancies). According to the model, standard placebo effects are expected on primary assessments of counteractive expectancies placebos. Reverse inductive effects (altered inferences about an underlying disposition in the direction opposite to the placebo's alleged impact) are likely on secondary assessments of parallel expectancies placebos. Consider, for instance, what happens when recipients of *parallel expectancies placebos* attempt to gauge the severity of their underlying condition from examination of their symptoms. The expectancy-attribution model predicts that if individuals exaggerate the effect the placebo had on their symptoms (i.e. they believe their symptoms are caused by the placebo), then they are likely to underestimate the degree to which symptoms are caused by their underlying condition. Consequently, they may believe that their underlying condition is *less* severe than they would have believed it to be had the placebo not been administered (reverse inductive effects).

Research on Ross & Olson's (1981) expectancy-attribution model of placebo effects is, of course, necessary. In particular, evidence regarding the attributions that presumably mediate placebo effects is critical. However, the model is theoretically compelling and promises to bring order to an important but chaotic literature.

Symptoms of Depression and Loneliness

Recently, theorists and researchers have applied attribution formulations to the clinical symptoms of depression (Miller & Norman 1979, Abramson & Martin 1981) and to a related problem, loneliness (Peplau & Perlman 1981). One prominent attributional theory of depression (Abramson et al 1978), for example, proposes that individuals who characteristically make internal, stable, and global attributions for their negative outcomes are prone to depression. According to this reformulated learned helplessness theory, internal attributions following failure are thought to produce the lowered self-esteem and attributions to stable and global factors are thought to lead to the chronic and general motivational and performance deficits characteristic of the depressive syndrome. A similar pathogenic attributional style has been identified for loneliness. Specifically, Peplau et al (1979) have contended that internal and stable attributions for failure are associated with loneliness.

There is at least some support for a depressive attributional style. In one study, Seligman et al (1979) developed an attributional style questionnaire in which college students were asked to imagine themselves in situations receiving positive and negative outcomes and to describe the major cause of the outcome. The students then were asked to rate that cause on the dimensions of internality, stability, and globality. Seligman et al found that depressed students explained negative outcomes in terms of internal, stable, and global factors to a greater degree than nondepressed students. Depressed students' attributions for positive outcomes were more external and unstable. In another study, Rapps et al (1982) found that depressed patients were more likely to attribute bad outcomes to internal, stable, and global causes than were nondepressed schizophrenic and nondepressed medical patients. These results, then, support the notion of a depressive attributional style that is not a general characteristic of psychopathology.

Janoff-Bulman (1979) has argued that only one type of internal attribution should be associated with depression and that the attributional dimensions of stability and globality are important in determining subsequent helplessness and depression because of their contribution to a fourth dimension—controllability. Specifically, she has distinguished between two types of internal attributions for negative outcomes: blame directed at one's character (e.g. ability) and blame directed at one's behavior (e.g. effort). Since character is fixed and less controllable than behavior, attributions to characterological factors should lead to helplessness and depression. Attributions to behavior for negative outcomes should have no such effects.

In a test of Janoff-Bulman's proposal, Anderson et al (1983) devised a questionnaire to tap subjects' attributional style. This questionnaire consisted of 20 hypothetical situations, half of which described successful and half of which described unsuccessful outcomes. In addition, half of the outcomes were interpersonal and half were not. Subjects were required to imagine themselves in each situation and select among six empirically derived categories (strategy, ability, effort, trait, and other external circumstances) the best explanation for the outcome. It was predicted that both lonely and depressed students would ascribe failure to characterological defects in themselves. Further, the prototypes for the lonely and depressed person (Horowitz et al 1982) suggest that this attributional style should hold mainly for interpersonal failures. The results of this study were consistent with these predictions. Moreover, loneliness showed a higher correlation with the attributional style, a finding that was anticipated since the prototype of a lonely person is more singularly interpersonal than the prototype of a depressed person.

It appears that characterological attributions may be associated with depression (and loneliness). The reformulated learned helplessness model is very specific about the nature of this association. The model posits that the depressive attributional style *predisposes* individuals to depression. The available evidence suggests, however, that attributions may not play a causal role in producing depressive symptoms. In a recent study, Peterson et al (1981) found that the depressive symptoms of college students correlated with characterological self-blame. In contrast, behavioral self-blame correlated with a lack of depressive symptoms. However, characterological blame did not precede the onset of depressive symptoms 6 or 12 weeks later. The authors concluded that attributions to characterological deficits may be a major concomitant of depression, but not a cause. A similar conclusion has been drawn by Lewinsohn et al (1981) regarding other depression-related cognitions.

By modifying individuals' characteristic attributional style, can corresponding changes in motivation and performance be produced? C. A. Anderson (1983) addressed this question by preselecting subjects who tend to attribute their failures either to unchangeable character defects (lack of ability or interfering personality traits) or to changeable behavioral mistakes (lack of effort or use of wrong strategy). Subjects then were led to attribute potential failure at an interpersonal persuasion task either to their character or to their behavior or because they were given no attribution manipulation. Subsequently, subjects engaged in a telephone blood drive task, trying to persuade other students to donate blood. Anderson reported that subjects who made behavioral attributions, whether by preselection or by experimental manipulation, expected more success, expected more improvement with practice, displayed higher levels of motivation, and performed better at the task than did subjects who made characterological attributions.

Research on attributional models of depression and loneliness has answered many questions. Future work will need to examine a number of additional issues, including how attributional styles develop, how malleable such styles are in more naturalistic, everyday settings of importance, and under what conditions a characterological attributional style contributes to depression and loneliness.

Close Relationships

Attribution has proved to be a useful concept in analyses and research on close relationships. One of the earliest studies on the topic was conducted by Orvis et al (1976). Findings deriving from this research suggested that intact couples often use attributions as a means of communicating praise, blame, hurt, and other feelings. Harvey et al (1978b) also found evidence indicating that separated and divorced persons often use attributions to exonerate self and blame others for the outcome of their marriage.

More recent work by Ross & Sicoly (1979) and Thompson & Kelley (1981) provides further evidence about egocentric bias in ongoing close relationships. These studies show that when partners in a relationship judge the extent of their contribution to an activity that is not potentially blameworthy, each one tends to claim more responsibility for the event than the other is willing to attribute to them. A study by Fincham & O'Leary (1983) provided data showing that distressed and nondistressed couples make different attributions for spouse behavior. As compared to nondistressed couples, distressed couples were more likely to preceive the causes of negative spouse actions as affecting various areas of their marriage, whereas causes of positive acts were seen as specific to the action portrayed (often as beyond the control of their mate). Two other promising lines of work pertain to the communication of reasons for rejecting relationship advances (Folkes 1982) and how attribution styles are related to sex, personality variables, and relationship events (Ickes 1983).

In theoretical work, Kelley (1979) identified attribution to stable dispositions as a central process in the development and maintenance of personal relationships. Thompson & Kelley (1981) showed evidence for a pronounced dispositional attributional focus in ongoing personal relationships. Newman (1981) reviewed work on attribution and close relationships and concluded that a category of attribution that emphasizes interpersonal communication (e.g. that other is to blame for certain events) may be more central to relationships than is dispositional or situational attribution.

COMMENT   The import of relationship phenomena in contemporary work in the social sciences assures that attribution research on relationship issues will continue to prosper. Research and theory in the area continue to show the integral role of attribution in the events that unfold at the beginning, during, and at the termination of personal relationships.

CONCLUSIONS

Kelley & Michela (1980) concluded that the problems of the attribution field are those of psychology in general—too few researchers spread too thinly over too many problems. Kelley and Michela suggested that each question had received far less attention in terms of number of paradigms and replications than its answer requires and that available theories are piecemeal and greatly in need of synthesis. In the mid-1980s, Kelley and Michela's general conclusions still are tenable. As should be clear from this review and recent general theoretical commentaries (e.g. Harré 1981, Harris & Harvey 1981, Harvey & Harris 1983), the field is alive with controversy and issues. On the one hand, this controversy reflects the lack of consensus about certain key concepts and about the most defensible theoretical interpretations for phenomena. It also reflects the fact that in certain domains of attribution work, the relevant evidence and the appropriate paradigms and procedures are in question. On the other hand, the controversy that has swirled about in the attribution literature may reflect the vitality and appeal of the topic and its constituent set of phenomena.

At the beginning of this review, we asked how successful the course of development has been for attribution theory and research. We would answer one of our initial questions about the status of attribution in its midlife by suggesting that it is still a highly fertile area of work. As should be evident, attributional analyses and ideas are becoming pervasive over a wide spectrum of contemporary psychology, including strands of work in clinical/counseling, cognitive, developmental psychology, and the major segment in social psychology. Our review of work in the latter field perforce has been selective, and by no means does it begin to exhaust discussion of the diverse phenomena with which attributional processes have been associated over the last 5 years. Additionally, attribution has been linked to: (a) attitude change and persuasion (Wood & Eagly 1981); (b) pity, guilt, and anger (Weiner et al 1982); (c) commitment (Mayer et al 1980); (d) helping behavior (Meyer & Mulherin 1980, Weiner 1980); (e) liking for other (Wachtler & Counselman 1981); (f) equity behavior (Greenberg 1980); (g) frustration, blame, and aggression (Kulik & Brown 1979). In part this breadth supports Heider's broad conception of attribution as a quest for meaning that may occur spontaneously and continuously in our daily lives.

As for the future, many steps are necessary for the continued development of the attribution area. Work is needed on such topics as how cognitive and motivational systems interact to influence attribution, how attribution unfolds in dyads, close relationships, groups, and other complex social systems, how to understand and measure naturalistic attributions such as those presented in accounts and archival records, and how to conceive and study cognitive-attributional structures.

At a more general level, an old refrain is that the area badly needs greater theoretical integration. Ostrom (1981) made such a point and also argued that enough research has accumulated on attribution for its workers to begin to identify its place in the constellation of knowledge about social processes. We agree with both points. But we view the recent integration of attributional concepts with other major theoretical positions (e.g. symbolic interaction, Stryker & Gottlieb 1981; learned helplessness and depression, Abramson & Martin 1981) as representing a step toward identification of attribution's place in the wider scope of work on social processes.

These needed developments notwithstanding, the concept of attribution is a rich one and likely to remain viable in psychology for many years to come. Kelley's (1978) vision of this viability still seems true:

> It [attribution theory and research] came out of phenomena that psychologists have looked at and tried to interpret. I just can't imagine that the phenomena that are hooked into that kind of cognition will change or be modified. They'll never go away. We'll always have to have that kind of explanation (p. 384).

ACKNOWLEDGMENTS

We are indebted to Patti Watson for help in preparing this manuscript and to William Swann for comments on an earlier draft.

Literature Cited

Abramson, L. Y., Martin, D. J. 1981. Depression and the causal inference process. See Harvey et al 1981a, pp. 117–68

Abramson, L. Y., Seligman, M. E. P., Teasdale, J. D. 1978. Learned helplessness in humans: Critique and reformulation. *J. Abnorm. Psychol.* 87:49–74

Anderson, C. A. 1983. Motivational and performance deficits in interpersonal settings: The effect of attributional style. *J. Pers. Soc. Psychol.* In press

Anderson, C. A., Horowitz, L. M., deSales French, R. 1983. Attributional style of lonely and depressed people. *J. Pers. Soc. Psychol.* 45:127–36

Antaki, C., ed. 1981. *The Psychology of Ordinary Explanations of Social Behaviour.* London: Academic

Arkin, R. M., Appelman, A. J., Burger, J. M. 1980. Social anxiety, self-presentation, and the self-serving bias in causal attributions. *J. Pers. Soc. Psychol.* 38:23–35

Bartlett, F. C. 1932. *Remembering.* London: Cambridge Univ. Press

Bem, D. J. 1967. Self-perception: An alternative interpretation of cognitive dissonance phenomena. *Psychol. Rev.* 74:183–200

Bem, D. J. 1972. Self-perception theory. *Adv. Exp. Soc. Psychol.* 6:1–62

Berglas, S., Jones, E. E. 1978. Drug choice as an internalization strategy in response to noncontingent success. *J. Pers. Soc. Psychol.* 36:405–17

Berscheid, E., Graziano, W., Monson, T., Dermer, M. 1976. Outcome dependency:

Attention, attribution, and attraction. *J. Pers. Soc. Psychol.* 34:978–89

Borgida, E., Brekke, N. 1981. The base rate fallacy in attribution and prediction. See Harvey et al 1981a, pp. 63–95

Buss, A. R. 1978. Causes and reasons in attribution theory: A conceptual critique. *J. Pers. Soc. Psychol.* 36:1311–21

Carver, C. S., DeGregorio, E., Gillis, R. 1980. Field-study evidence of an ego-defensive bias in attribution among two categories of observers. *Pers. Soc. Psychol. Bull.* 6:44–50

Darley, J. M., Fazio, R. H. 1980. Expectancy confirmation processes arising in the social interaction sequence. *Am. Psychol.* 35:867–81

Elig, T. W., Frieze, I. H. 1979. Measuring causal attributions for success and failure. *J. Pers. Soc. Psychol.* 37:621–34

Enzle, M. E., Harvey, M. D., Wright, E. F. 1980. Personalism and distinctiveness. *J. Pers. Soc. Psychol.* 39:542–52

Enzle, M. E., Schopflocher, D. 1978. Instigation of attribution processes by attributional questions. *Pers. Soc. Psychol. Bull.* 4:595–98

Ericsson, K. A., Simon, H. A. 1980. Verbal reports as data. *Psychol. Rev.* 87:215–51

Farina, A., Allen, J., Saul, G. 1966. The role of the stigmatized person in affecting social relationships. *J. Pers.* 71:421–28

Farr, R. M., Anderson, A. 1983. Beyond actor/observer differences in perspective: Extensions and applications. See Hewstone 1983

Felson, R. B., Ribner, S. A. 1981. An attributional approach to accounts and sanctions for criminal violence. *Soc. Psychol. Q.* 44:137–42

Ferguson, T. J., Wells, G. L. 1980. Priming of mediators in causal attribution. *J. Pers. Soc. Psychol.* 38:461–70

Fiedler, K. 1982. Causal schemata: Review and criticism of research on a popular construct. *J. Pers. Soc. Psychol.* 42:1001–13

Fincham, F., O'Leary, K. D. 1983. Causal inferences for spouse behavior in maritally distressed and non-distressed couples. *J. Soc. Clin. Psychol.* 1:42–57

Fiske, S. T., Kenny, D. A., Taylor, S. E. 1982. Structural models for the mediation of salience effects on attribution. *J. Exp. Soc. Psychol.* 18:105–27

Fiske, S. T., Taylor, S. E., Etcoff, N. L., Laufer, J. K. 1979. Imaging, empathy, and causal attribution. *J. Exp. Soc. Psychol.* 15:356–77

Folkes, V. S. 1982. Communicating the reasons for social rejection. *J. Exp. Soc. Psychol.* 18:235–52

Forsyth, D. R., Berger, R. E., Mitchell, T. 1981. The effects of self-serving vs. other-serving claims of responsibility on attraction

and attribution in groups. *Soc. Psychol. Q.* 44:59–64

Frieze, I. H., Bar-Tal, D., Carroll, J. S., eds. 1979. *New Approaches to Social Problems: Applications of Attribution Theory.* San Francisco: Jossey-Bass

Funder, D. C. 1982. On the accuracy of dispositional vs. situational attributions. *Soc. Cognit.* 1:205–22

Gibbons, F. X., Wright, R. A. 1981. Motivational biases in causal attributions of arousal. *J. Pers. Soc. Psychol.* 40:588–600

Goldberg, L. R. 1981. Unconfounding situational attributions from uncertain, neutral, and ambiguous ones: A psychometric analysis of descriptions of oneself and various types of others. *J. Pers. Soc. Psychol.* 41:517–52

Gollwitzer, P. M., Earle, W. B., Stephan, W. G. 1982. Affect as a determinant of egotism: Residual excitation and performance attributions. *J. Pers. Soc. Psychol.* 43:702–9

Greenberg, J. 1980. Attentional focus and locus of performance causality as determinants of equity behavior. *J. Pers. Soc. Psychol.* 38:579–85

Greenberg, J., Pyszczynski, T., Solomon, S. 1982. The self-serving attributional bias: Beyond self-presentation. *J. Exp. Soc. Psychol.* 18:56–67

Greenwald, A. G. 1980. The totalitarian ego: Fabrication and revision of personal history. *Am. Psychol.* 35:603–18

Hamilton, V. L. 1980. Intuitive psychologist or intuitive lawyer: Alternative models of the attribution process. *J. Pers. Soc. Psychol.* 39:767–72

Hansen, R. D. 1980. Commonsense attribution. *J. Pers. Soc. Psychol.* 39:996–1009

Hansen, R. D., Donoghue, J. M. 1977. The power of consensus: Information derived from one's own and others' behavior. *J. Pers. Soc. Psychol.* 35:294–302

Harré, R. 1981. Expressive aspects of descriptions of others. See Antaki 1981, pp. 139–56

Harris, B., Harvey, J. H. 1981. Attribution theory: From phenomenal causality to the intuitive scientist and beyond. See Antaki 1981, pp. 57–95

Harvey, J. H., Harris, B. 1983. Commentary on extensions and applications of attribution theory. See Hewstone 1983

Harvey, J. H., Ickes, W., Kidd, R. F., eds. 1976. *New Directions in Attribution Research,* Vol. 1. Hillsdale, NJ: Erlbaum

Harvey, J. H., Ickes, W., Kidd, R. F., eds. 1978a. *New Directions in Attribution Research,* Vol. 2. Hillsdale, NJ: Erlbaum

Harvey, J. H., Ickes, W., Kidd, R. F., eds. 1981a. *New Directions in Attribution Research,* Vol. 3 Hillsdale, NJ: Erlbaum

Harvey J. H., McGlynn, R. P. 1982. Matching words to phenomena: The case of the fundamental attribution error. *J. Pers. Soc. Psychol.* 43:345–46

Harvey, J. H., Smith, W. P. 1977. *Social Psychology: An Attributional Approach.* St. Louis: Mosby

Harvey, J. H., Town, J. P. Yarkin, K. L. 1981b. How fundamental is "The fundamental attribution error"? *J. Pers. Soc. Psychol.* 40:346–49

Harvey, J. H., Tucker, J. A. 1979. On problems with the cause-reason distinction in attribution theory. *J. Pers. Soc. Psychol.* 37:1441–46

Harvey, J. H., Weary, G. 1981. *Perspectives on Attributional Processes.* Dubuque, Ia: Brown

Harvey, J. H., Weber, A. L., Galvin, K. S., Huszti, H., Garnick, N. 1983. Attribution and the termination of close relationships: A special focus on the account. In *Personal Relationships,* ed. R. Gilmour, S. Duck. Hillsdale, NJ: Erlbaum. In press

Harvey, J. H., Wells, G. L., Alvarez, M. D. 1978b. Attribution in the context of conflict and separation in close relationships. See Harvey et al 1978a, pp. 235–59

Harvey, J. H., Yarkin, K. L., Lightner, J. M., Town, J. P. 1980. Unsolicited attribution and recall of interpersonal events. *J. Pers. Soc. Psychol.* 38:551–68

Heider, F. 1958. *The Psychology of Interpersonal Relations.* New York: Wiley

Heider, F. 1976. A conversation with Fritz Heider. See Harvey et al 1976, pp. 3–18

Hewstone, M., ed. 1983. *Attribution Theory: Extensions and Applications:* Oxford: Blackwell. In press

Horowitz, L. M., deSales French, R., Anderson, C. A. 1982. The prototype of a lonely person. See Peplau & Perlman 1982, pp. 183–205

Hull, J. G., West, S. G. 1982. The discounting principle in attribution. *Pers. Soc. Psychol. Bull.* 8:208–13

Ickes, W. 1983. Attributional styles and the self-concept. In *Attributional Processes and Clinical Psychology,* ed. L. Y. Abramson. New York: Guilford. In press

Janoff-Bulman, R. 1979. Characterological versus behavioral self-blame: Inquiries into depression and rape. *J. Pers. Soc. Psychol.* 37:1795–1809

Jaspars, J., Fincham, F., Hewstone, M., eds. 1983. *Attribution Theory and Research: Conceptual, Developmental and Social Dimensions.* London: Academic

Jones, E. E. 1979. The rocky road from acts to dispositions. *Am. Psychol.* 34:104–17

Jones, E. E., Davis, K. E. 1965. From acts to dispositions: The attributions process in person perception. *Adv. Exp. Soc. Psychol.* 2:219–66

Jones, E. E., Kanouse, D. E., Kelley, H. H.,

Nisbett, R. E., Valins, S., et al, eds. 1972. *Attribution: Perceiving the Causes of Behavior.* Morristown, NJ: General Learning Press

Jones, E. E., McGillis, D. 1976. Correspondent inferences and the attribution cube: A comparative reappraisal. See Harvey et al 1976, pp. 389–420

Jones, E. E., Nisbett, R. E. 1972. The actor and the observer: Divergent perceptions of the causes of behavior. See Jones et al 1972, pp. 79–94

Jones E. E., Pittman, T. S. 1982. Toward a general theory of strategic self-presentation. In *Psychological Perspectives on the Self,* ed. J. Suls, pp. 231–62. Hillsdale, NJ: Erlbaum

Jones, E. E., Sigall, H. 1971. The bogus pipeline: A new paradigm for measuring affect and attitude. *Psychol. Bull.* 76:349–64

Kassin, S. M. 1979. Consensus information, prediction, and causal attribution: A review of the literature and issues. *J. Pers. Soc. Psychol.* 37:1966–81

Kassin, S. M., Lowe, C. A., Gibbons, F. X. 1980. Children's use of the discounting principle: A perceptual approach. *J. Pers. Soc. Psychol.* 39:719–28

Kelley, H. H. 1950. The warm-cold variable in the first impressions of persons. *J. Pers.* 18:431–39

Kelley, H. H. 1967. Attribution theory in social psychology. *Nebr. Symp. Motiv.* 15:192–238

Kelley, H. H. 1972a. Attribution in social interaction. See Jones et al 1972, pp. 1–26.

Kelley, H. H. 1972b. Causal schemata and the attribution process. See Jones et al 1972, pp. 151–74

Kelley, H. H. 1973. The process of causal attribution. *Am. Psychol.* 28:107–28

Kelley, H. H. 1978. A conversation with Edward E. Jones and Harold H. Kelley. See Harvey et al 1978a, pp. 371–88

Kelley, H. H. 1979. *Personal Relationships: Their Structures and Processes.* Hillsdale, NJ: Erlbaum

Kelley, H. H. 1983. Epilogue: Perceived causal structures. See Jaspars et al 1983, pp. 388–415

Kelley, H. H., Michela, J. L. 1980. Attribution theory and research. *Ann. Rev. Psychol.* 31:457–501

Kleck, B., Ono, H., Hastorf, A. H. 1966. The effects of physical space upon face to face interaction. *Hum. Relat.* 19:425–36

Kolditz, T. A., Arkin, R. M. 1982. An impression management interpretation of the self-handicapping strategy. *J. Pers. Soc. Psychol.* 43:492–502

Kruglanski, A. W. 1975. The endogenous-exogenous partition in attribution theory. *Psychol. Rev.* 82:387–406

Kruglanski, A. W. 1979. Causal explanation, teleological explanation: On radical particularism in attribution theory. *J. Pers. Soc. Psychol.* 37:1447–57

Kruglanski, A. W. 1980. Lay epistemo-logic process and contents. *Psychol. Rev.* 87:70–87

Kruglanski, A. W., Schwartz, J. M., Maider, S. A., Hamel, I. A. 1978. Covariation, discounting, and augmentation: Toward a clarification of attributional principles. *J. Pers.* 46:176–89

Kulik, J. A., Brown, B. 1979. Frustration, attribution of blame, and aggression. *J. Exp. Soc. Psychol.* 15:183–94

Kulik, J. A., Taylor, S. E. 1980. Effects of sample-based versus self-based consensus information. *J. Pers. Soc. Psychol.* 38:871–78

Lau, R. R., Russell, D. 1980. Attributions in the sports pages. *J. Pers. Soc. Psychol.* 39:29–38

Lazarus, R. S. 1982. Thoughts on the relations between emotion and cognition. *Am. Psychol.* 37:1019–24

Lewinsohn, P. M., Steinmetz, J. L., Larson, D. W., Franklin, J. 1981. Depression-related cognitions: Antecedent or consequence? *J. Abnorm. Psychol.* 90:213–19

Locke, D., Pennington, D. 1982. Reasons and other causes: Their role in the attribution process. *J. Pers. Soc. Psychol.* 42:212–23

Lowe, C. A., Kassin, S. M. 1980. A perceptual view of attribution: Theoretical and methodological implications. *Pers. Soc. Psychol. Bull.* 6:532–42

Major, B. 1980. Information acquisition and attribution processes. *J. Pers. Soc. Psychol.* 39:1010–23

Mayer, F. S., Duval, S., Duval, V. H. 1980. An attributional analysis of commitment. *J. Pers. Soc. Psychol.* 39:1072–80

McArthur, L. Z., Ginsburg, E. 1981. Causal attributions to salient stimuli: An investigation of visual fixation mediators. *Pers. Soc. Psychol. Bull.* 7:547–53

McFarland, C., Ross, M. 1982. Impact of causal attributions on affective reactions to success and failure. *J. Pers. Soc. Psychol.* 43:937–46

Meyer, J. P., Mulherin, A. 1980. From attribution to helping: An analysis of the mediating effects of affect and expectancy. *J. Pers. Soc. Psychol.* 39:201–10

Miller, D. T., Ross, M. 1975. Self-serving biases in the attribution of causality: Fact or fiction? *Psychol. Bull.* 82:213–25

Miller, F. D., Smith, E. R., Uleman, J. 1981. Measurement and interpretation of situational and dispositional attributions. *J. Exp. Soc. Psychol.* 17:80–95

Miller, I. W., Norman, W. H. 1979. Learned helplessness in humans: A review and

attribution theory model. *Psychol. Bull.* 86:93–118

Mirels, H. L. 1980. The avowal of responsibility for good and bad outcomes: The effects of generalized self-serving biases. *Pers. Soc. Psychol. Bull.* 6:299–306

Monson, T. C., Keel, R., Stephens, D., Genung, V. 1982. Trait attributions: Relative validity, covariation with behavior, and prospect of future interaction. *J. Pers. Soc. Psychol.* 42:1014–24

Monson, T. C., Snyder, M. 1977. Actors, observers, and the attribution process: Toward a reconceptualization. *J. Exp. Soc. Psychol.* 13:89–111

Moore, B. S., Sherrod, D. R., Liv, T. J., Underwood, B. 1979. The dispositional shift in attribution over time. *J. Exp. Soc. Psychol.* 15:553–69

Newman, H. 1981. Communication within ongoing intimate relationships: An attributional perspective. *Pers. Soc. Psychol. Bull.* 59–70

Nisbett, R. E., Borgida, E. 1975. Attribution and the psychology of prediction. *J. Pers. Soc. Psychol.* 32:932–43

Nisbett, R. E., Wilson, T. D. 1977. Telling more than we know: Verbal reports on mental processes. *Psychol. Rev.* 84:231–59

Orvis, B. R., Kelley, H. H., Butter, D. 1976. Attributional conflict in young couples. See Harvey et al 1976, pp. 353–86

Ostrom, T. M. 1981. Attribution theory: Whence and whither. See Harvey et al 1981a, pp. 405–24

Peplau, L. A., Perlman, D. 1981. *Loneliness: A Sourcebook of Current Theory, Research, and Therapy.* New York: Wiley-Interscience

Peplau, L. A., Russell, D., Heim, M. 1979. An attributional analysis of loneliness. See Frieze et al 1979, pp. 53–78

Peterson, C. 1980a. Attribution in the sports pages: An archival investigation of the covariation hypothesis. *Soc. Psychol. Q.* 43:136–41

Peterson, C. 1980b. Memory and the "dispositional shift." *Soc. Psychol. Q.* 43:372–80

Peterson, C., Schwartz, S. M., Seligman, M. E. P. 1981. Self-blame and depressive symptoms. *J. Pers. Soc. Psychol.* 41:253–59

Pittman, T. S., Pittman, N. L. 1980. Deprivation of control and the attribution process. *J. Pers. Soc. Psychol.* 39:377–89

Pryor, J. B., Kriss, M. 1977. The cognitive dynamics of salience in the attribution process. *J. Pers. Soc. Psychol.* 35:49–55

Pyszczynski, T. A., Greenberg, J. 1981. Role of disconfirmed expectancies in the instigation of attributional processing. *J. Pers. Soc. Psychol.* 40:31–38

Quattrone, G. A. 1982. Overattribution and unit formation: When behavior engulfs the person. *J. Pers. Soc. Psychol.* 42:593–607

Rapps, C. S., Peterson, C., Reinhard, K. E., Abramson, L. Y., Seligman, M. E. P. 1982. Attributional style among depressed patients. *J. Abnorm. Psychol.* 91:102–8

Reeder, G. D. 1982. Let's give the fundamental attribution error another chance. *J. Pers. Soc. Psychol.* 43:341–44

Reeder, G. D., Brewer, M. B. 1979. A schematic model of dispositional attribution in interpersonal perception. *Psychol. Rev.* 86:61–79

Reeder, G. D., Fulks, J. F. 1980. When actions speak louder than words: Implicational schemata and the attribution of ability. *J. Exp. Soc. Psychol.* 16:33–46

Regan, D. R., Totten, J. 1975. Empathy and attribution: Turning observers into actors. *J. Pers. Soc. Psychol.* 32:850–56

Riess, M., Rosenfeld, P., Melburg, V., Tedeschi, J. T. 1981. Self-serving attributions: Biased private perceptions and distorted public descriptions. *J. Pers. Soc. Psychol.* 41:224–31

Rosenfield, D., Stephan, W. G. 1978. Sex differences in attributions for sex-typed tasks. *J. Pers.* 46:244–59

Ross, L. 1977. The intuitive psychologist and his shortcomings: Distortions in the attribution process. *Adv. Exp. Soc. Psychol.* 10:174–220

Ross, L., Bierbrauer, G., Pally, S. 1974. Attribution of educational outcomes by professional and nonprofessional instructors. *J. Pers. Soc. Psychol.* 29:609–18

Ross, M., Olson, J. M. 1981. An expectancy-attribution model of the effects of placebos. *Psychol. Rev.* 88:408–37

Ross, M., Sicoly, F. 1979. Egocentric biases in availability and attribution. *J. Pers. Soc. Psychol.* 37:322–36

Russell, D. 1982. The causal dimension scale: A measure of how individuals perceive causes. *J. Pers. Soc. Psychol.* 42:1137–45

Sabini, J., Silver, M. 1981. Introspection and causal accounts. *J. Pers. Soc. Psychol.* 40:171–79

Schachter, S. 1964. The interaction of cognitive and physiological determinants of emotional state. *Adv. Exp. Soc. Psychol.* 1:49–80

Scott, M. B., Lyman, S. 1968. Accounts. *Am. Sociol. Rev.* 33:46–62

Seligman, M. E. P., Abramson, L. Y., Semmel, A., Von Baeyer, C. 1979. Depressive attributional style. *J. Abnorm. Psychol.* 88:242–47

Shaver, K. G. 1975. *An Introduction to Attribution Processes.* Cambridge, Mass: Winthrop

Sherman, R. C., Titus, W. 1982. Covariation information and cognitive processing: Effects of causal implications on memory. *J. Pers. Soc. Psychol.* 42:989–1000

Skrypnek, B. J., Snyder, M. 1982. On the self-perpetuating nature of stereotypes about women and men. *J. Exp. Soc. Psychol.* 18:277–91

Smith, E. R., Manard, B. B. 1980. Causal attributions and medical school admissions. *Pers. Soc. Psychol. Bull.* 6:644–50

Smith E. R., Miller, F. D. 1978. Limits on perception of cognitive processes: A reply to Nisbett and Wilson. *Psychol. Rev.* 85:355–62

Smith, E. R., Miller, F. D. 1979. Salience and the cognitive mediation of attribution. *J. Pers. Soc. Psychol.* 37:2240–52

Smith, E. R., Miller, F. D. 1982. Latent-variable models of attributional measurement. *Pers. Soc. Psychol. Bull.* 8:221–25

Smith, T. W., Snyder, C. R. Handelsman, M. M. 1982. On the self-serving function of an academic wooden leg: Test anxiety as a self-handicapping strategy. *J. Pers. Soc. Psychol.* 42:314–21

Snyder, M., Gangestad, S. 1981. Hypothesis-testing processes. See Harvey et al 1981a, pp. 171–96

Snyder, M., Swann, W. B. Jr. 1978. Hypothesis-testing processes in social interaction. *J. Pers. Soc. Psychol.* 36:1202–12

Snyder, M. L., Stephan, W. G., Rosenfield, D. 1978. Attributional egotism. See Harvey et al 1978, pp. 91–117

Snyder, M. L., Wicklund, R. A. 1981. Attribute ambiguity. See Harvey et al 1981a, pp. 197–221

Solomon, M. R., Drenan, S., Insko, C. A. 1981. Popular induction: When is consensus informative? *J. Pers.* 49:212–24

Solomon, S. 1978. Measuring dispositional and situational attributions. *Pers. Soc. Psychol. Bull.* 4:589–93

Stephan, W. G., Gollwitzer, P. M. 1981. Affect as a mediator of attributional egotism. *J. Exp. Soc. Psychol.* 17:442–58

Storms, M., Nisbett, R. E. 1970. Insomnia and the attribution process. *J. Pers. Soc. Psychol.* 16:319–28

Stryker, S., Gottlieb, A. 1981. Attribution theory and symbolic interactionism: A comparison. See Harvey et al 1981a, pp. 425–58

Taylor, S. E., Fiske, S. T. 1975. Point of view and perceptions of causality. *J. Pers. Soc. Psychol.* 32:439–45

Taylor, S. E., Thompson, S. C. 1982. Stalking the elusive "vividness" effect. *Psychol. Rev.* 89:155–81

Tetlock, P. E. 1980. Explaining teacher explanations of pupil performance: A self-presentation interpretation. *Soc. Psychol. Q.* 43:283–90

Tetlock, P. E. 1981. The influence of self-presentation goals on attributional reports. *Soc. Psychol. Q.* 44:300–11

Tetlock, P. E., Levi, A. 1982. Attribution bias:

On the inconclusiveness of the Cognition-Motivation Debate. *J. Exp. Soc. Psychol.* 18:68–88

Thompson, S. C., Kelley, H. H. 1981. Judgments of responsibility for activities in close relationships. *J. Pers. Soc. Psychol.* 41:469–77

Town, J. P., Harvey, J. H. 1981. Self-disclosure, attribution, and social interaction. *Soc. Psychol. Q.* 44:291–300

Valins, S., Nisbett, R. E. 1972. Attribution processes in the development and treatment of emotional disorders. See Jones et al 1972, pp. 137–50

Von Baeyer, C. L., Sherk, D. L., Zanna, M. P. 1981. Impression management in the job interview: When the female applicant meets the male "chauvinist" interviewer. *Pers. Soc. Psychol. Bull.* 7:45–51

Wachtler, J., Counselman, E. 1981. When increasing liking for a communicator decreases opinion change: An attribution analysis of attractiveness. *J. Exp. Soc. Psychol.* 17:386–95

Watson, D. 1982. The actor and the observer: How are their perceptions of causality divergent? *Psychol. Bull.* 92:682–700

Weary Bradley, G. 1978. Self-serving biases in the attribution process: A reexamination of the fact or fiction question. *J. Pers. Soc. Psychol.* 36:56–71

Weary, G. 1979. Self-serving attributional biases: Perceptual or response distortions. *J. Pers. Soc. Psychol.* 37:1418–20

Weary, G. 1980. Examination of affect and egotism as mediators of bias in causal attributions. *J. Pers. Soc. Psychol.* 38:348–57

Weary, G., Arkin, R. M. 1981. Attributional self-presentation. See Harvey et al 1981a, pp. 223–46

Weary G., Harvey, J. H., Schwieger P., Olson, C. T., Perloff, R., et al. 1982. Self-presentation and the moderation of self-serving attributional biases. *Soc. Cognit.* 1:140–59

Weary, G., Swanson, H., Harvey, J. H., Yarkin, K. L. 1980. A molar approach to social knowing. *Pers. Soc. Psychol. Bull.* 6:574–81

Weiner, B. 1980. A cognitive (attribution)-emotion-action model of motivated behavior: An analysis of judgments of helpgiving. *J. Pers. Soc. Psychol.* 39:186–200

Weiner, B., Graham, S., Chandler, C. 1982. Pity, anger, and guilt: An attributional analysis. *Pers. Soc. Psychol. Bull.* 8:226–32

Weiner, B., Russell, D., Lerman, D. 1978. Affective consequences of causal ascriptions. See Harvey et al 1978, pp. 59–90

Weiner, B., Russell, D., Lerman, D. 1979. The cognition-emotion process in achievement-related contexts. *J. Pers. Soc. Psychol.* 37:1211–20

Weiss, R. S. 1975. *Marital Separation.* New York: Basic Books

Wells, G. L. 1982. Attribution and reconstructive memory. *J. Exp. Soc. Psychol.* 18:447–63

Wells, G. L., Harvey, J. H. 1977. Do people use consensus information in making causal attributions? *J. Pers. Soc. Psychol.* 35:279–93

Wilson, T. D., Nisbett, R. E. 1978. The accuracy of verbal reports about the effects of stimuli on evaluations and behavior. *Soc. Psychol.* 41:118–31

Wong, P. T. P., Weiner, B. 1981. When people ask "why" questions, and the heuristics of attributional search. *J. Pers. Soc. Psychol.* 40:650–63

Wood, W., Eagly, A. H. 1981. Stages in the analysis of persuasive messages: The role of causal attributions and message comprehension. *J. Pers. Soc. Psychol.* 40:246–59

Yarkin, K. L. 1983. Anticipated interaction, attribution, and social interaction. *Soc. Psychol. Q.* In press

Yarkin, K. L., Harvey, J. H., Bloxom, B. M. 1981. Cognitive sets, attribution, and social interaction. *J. Pers. Soc. Psychol.* 41:243–52

Yarkin, K. L., Town, J. P., Harvey, J. G. 1981. The role of cognitive sets in interpreting and remembering interpersonal events. In *Cognition, Social Behavior, and the Environment,* ed. J. H. Harvey, pp. 289–308. Hillsdale, NJ: Erlbaum

Zajonc, R. B. 1980. Feeling and thinking: Preferences need no inferences. *Am. Psychol.* 35:151–75

Zanna, M. P., Pack, S. J. 1975. On the self-fulfilling nature of apparent sex differences in behavior. *J. Exp. Soc. Psychol.* 11:583–91

Zillman, D. 1982. Transfer of excitation in emotional behavior. In *Social Psychophysiology,* ed. J. T. Caccioppo, R. E. Petty, pp. 88–112. New York: Guilford

Zuckerman, M. 1979. Attribution of success and failure revisited, or: The motivational bias is alive and well in attribution theory. *J. Pers.* 47:245–87

Ann. Rev. Psychol. 1984. 35:461–518

PSYCHOLOGICAL ISSUES IN PERSONNEL DECISIONS

Sheldon Zedeck

Department of Psychology, University of California, Berkeley, California 94720

Wayne F. Cascio

Graduate School of Business, University of Colorado, Denver, Colorado 80204

CONTENTS

0066-4308/84/0201-0461$02.00

". . . to be efficient it was necessary to be able to learn from the past, which meant having a fairly accurate idea of what happened in the past."

1984, George Orwell, 1949, p. 163.

INTRODUCTION

Previous chapters in the *Annual Review of Psychology* on this subject have been titled "Personnel Selection," with occasional inclusion of the terms "Classification and Placement." We have adopted a new title for several reasons, mainly because the field encompasses more than selection, classification, and placement. Personnel selection has evolved into a decision theoretic discipline focusing on assessment, evaluation, judgment, prediction, forecasting, utility, and practicality. Within this framework, and during the 1981–82 years covered by this review, the field has been driven by statistical and methodological approaches such as meta analyses; statistical techniques for clustering and distinguishing jobs; policy capturing of decisions and assessments; applications of item response theory for test development and job evaluation; and estimations of utility of selection systems and performance. The title change also was dictated by the literature. While previous reviewers in this series (e.g. Owens & Jewell 1969, Bray & Moses 1972) have recognized the potential value of an integrative classification/placement system, there is very little research in this area within an employment setting.

Personnel/human resource issues are parts of an open system. Of necessity, this review will treat topics in a fragmented fashion; yet, consideration of selection issues is nonpragmatic and theoretically bankrupt unless consideration is given to issues such as organizational design, motivation, career pathing, training and the like—topics for which there have been and currently are other chapters in the *Annual Review of Psychology*. For example, training and selection are part of a continuum. The greater the emphasis on selection for those who possess specific skills, the less the need for training for those skills; the interaction between these two areas cannot be ignored.

The field also is moving toward an integration with other psychological disciplines such as social, cognitive, and personality psychologies. Personnel researchers are working with social cognition models of performance appraisal and interviewer decision making; person perception, information processing heuristics, and personality theories are used to explain findings. These are all positive incorporations as we strive to develop a theory of personnel decisions.

Since the field of personnel has broadened, it has become difficult for reviewers to identify the appropriate subject matter. We have included that which is the core of personnel—job analysis, performance measurement, performance predictors, validity concepts, methodological/statistical issues, classification and placement, and equal employment opportunity (EEO) and legal concerns. To reflect broadening of the field, human resource planning, utility (cost/benefit) analyses, and job evaluation are included. Because of space constraints, our review of all of these topics is generally confined to that which was published in refereed journals or has undergone some independent review process; as a result, many relevant papers, manuscripts, and technical reports have been omitted. In sum, we have not covered the complete field or all of that which is relevant to specific topics; the references cited should be viewed as samples of that which is being studied as we attempt to learn about psychological issues in personnel decisions.

HUMAN RESOURCE PLANNING

Human resource planning (HRP) can be defined broadly as an effort to *anticipate* future business and environmental demands on an organization and to meet the personnel requirements dictated by those conditions (Cascio 1982a). Dyer (1982) has noted a variety of HRP applications. For example, HRP can be strategic (long-term and general) or operational (short-term and specific), organization-wide or restricted to selected units or employee groups, and carried out on a recurring basis (e.g. annually) or only sporadically (e.g. when launching a new product line). Almost all authors agree that if HRP is to be genuinely effective, it must be linked with strategic business planning (the process of setting organizational objectives and deciding on action programs to achieve the objectives) (Smith 1982a,b, Tichy et al 1982). Evidence indicates that such a linkage does not take place (Rowland & Summers 1981).

There is no shortage of conceptual models of the HRP process (Alpander & Botter 1981, Buller & Maki 1981, Dyer 1982, Sistrunk & Smith 1982), though evaluative work is sorely lacking. Much of the HRP literature is still prescriptive and exhortatory (Gehrman 1981, 1982, Muczyk 1981, Russ 1982a,b), though a number of case studies are beginning to appear (Buller & Maki 1981, Pinfield 1981, Dyer et al 1982). A review of available HRP models by Dyer (1982) seems to suggest that the integrated process involves three interrelated phases: 1. setting HRP objectives; 2. planning personnel programs; and 3. evaluation and control. To date, however, integrated HRP is more of an ideal than a reality (Russ 1982a,b). Thus after an in-depth field study of HRP at Corning Glass Works, Dyer et al (1982) concluded that while the internal staffing process was improved as a result of HRP, and to a lesser extent, recruiting, career planning and development, and EEO, HRP had no observable effect on education and training, compensation, communications, or on the relationships among these.

Most attention has been focused on human resource supply and demand forecasting (Frantzreb 1981, Scarborough & Zimmerer 1982). Despite its assumed popularity for forecasting supply, research into the accuracy and applicability of Markov analysis is not extensive. Results so far are mixed. Both Buller & Maki (1981) and Hooper & Catalanello (1981) found that the model provided accurate, useful information that was accepted by decision makers, but Dyer et al (1982) reported that Markov analysis failed in two other attempts. Clearly, research is needed to identify the variables that dictate the success or failure of Markov analysis as an HRP forecasting technique. An extension of Markov analysis, computer simulation, allows a decision maker to generate possible alternative personnel flows that might fit personnel availabilities with established staffing needs. Such simulation is especially popular in affirmative action planning, where affirmative action goals are analogous to established staffing levels. Ledvinka et al (1982) used this approach to assess the long-range impact of alternative "fair selection" standards on minority employment. One potential drawback of simulation is that typically the costs associated with alternative strategies are not considered explicitly. This need not be the case, for Davis & Pinto (1975) developed a cost model for evaluating alternative staffing strategies that also incorporates utility considerations. Although the model needs further development (at present a dichotomous criterion is assumed), it does represent a useful start in an area that has been underemphasized to date.

Demand forecasting research is scarce and nonrigorous. While statistical techniques dominate the research literature, judgmental techniques predominate in practice. We know almost nothing about the decision-making models that managers use, the extent to which they make use (or will make use) of decision aids (e.g. statistical forecasts), or the accuracy of their forecasts (Dyer 1982). But even if the forecasts are inaccurate, the raison d'etre for making them is unmistakable: it is better to be roughly right than precisely wrong. Research on the accuracy of alternative decision-making strategies in personnel selection (particularly with respect to assessment center predictions) suggests that subjective judgment simply should be one input to a statistical forecasting model (Borman 1982). This is a needed research issue in HRP. Many different types of data are and can be used for demand forecasting, but for affirmative action forecasting, the 1980 Census/EEO Special File will be the principal source of data throughout the 1980s (EEO Today 1982).

In addition to forecasting demand, researchers are also developing forecasts of terminations (Pinfield 1981) and retirements (Morrow 1982), and doing management succession planning (Bucknall 1981, Reypert 1981). The latter is the one activity found by Rowland & Summers (1981) to be both pervasive and well accepted in the six firms they studied. In fact, succession planning was considered by many to be the sum and substance of HRP, and it was the only activity that had a proved record of success in integrating HRP with strategic business planning. In short, there were large differences between the literature's prescriptions for HRP and the views and practices of the companies studied. Human resource forecasting had been tried and discarded at several firms, and while five of the six firms had a human resources information system, computer-assisted position-person matching or candidate searching was seldom used. What can be done? We agree with Dyer (1982) that research is needed to test the usefulness of the various HRP methods and techniques, both statistical and judgmental, with special emphasis on external as well as internal validity. Political issues involved in getting various methods and techniques adopted should be addressed, as well as various change strategies that might help to overcome problems at the implementation stage. It is our view that HRP is still a high potential area, but careful attention to critical research issues and less prescriptive exhortation are needed if real progress is to be made.

JOB ANALYSIS

Methodology

A plethora of new job analytical procedures has not recently emerged, a fact that is encouraging since many of the previously developed methodologies were accepted uncritically, and they were used according to the individual taste of the personnel researcher. Research on previously developed methods, their validity, accuracy, and usefulness was and still is needed. One technique that had not received previous attention is Threshold Traits Analysis (TTA), a trait-oriented approach used to determine the relevance, level, and practicality of each of 33 traits for acceptable job performance (Lopez et al 1981).

Needed research on the impact of personal and organizational factors on job analytical techniques was conducted for two frequently used procedures, the Position Analysis Questionnaire (PAQ; McCormick et al 1972) and Functional Job Analysis (FJA; Fine & Wiley 1971). Rousseau (1982) found that job codes that indicated dealing with "data" and "people" were correlated with perceptions of task characteristics such as autonomy, variety, and task significance; dealing with "things" contributed little to job perceptions. Arvey et al (1982) found that job analysts' PAQ assessments were not affected by job incumbents' expressions of interest in the job though the amount of content provided by the incumbent influenced PAQ descriptions.

The use of job analysis data for purposes other than job descriptions per se was illustrated by Olson et al's (1981) use of FJA to develop job-related performance standards, and Ramos's (1982) use of task statements to develop a strategy for predicting candidate effectiveness in an assessment center and as an entry level manager, and a form on which a candidate rates him/herself on interest and ability to perform. Finally, Lyness & Moses (1981) used task statements to develop a career planning form for managers.

The questions of who and how many job analysts should be used have been raised. Ash et al (1982) found that a small number of "subject matter experts" provide results similar to those obtained from large numbers of job incumbents; success is due to experience and training in the procedure. In contrast, Jones et al (1982) found that meaningful PAQ analyses can be achieved when the analysts are graduate students who rely on existing narrative descriptions, but who have not performed the jobs or observed or interviewed job incumbents.

Comparative research on methods was performed by Sistrunk et al (1982), who compared seven job analytic procedures in terms of the degree to which they fulfilled 11 organizational purposes and the degree to which they achieved 11 concerns for practicality. Not surprisingly, procedures were perceived as differentially effective and practical for various human resource purposes. In addition, there was a strong preference that a combination of methods be used.

Task Similarities/Differences

Key concerns in the job analysis literature are whether particular methods are sensitive enough to identify similarities and differences among jobs. The adequacy of the job analytic procedure for accomplishing these goals appears to be based on the statistical technique or algorithm used to study the questions. Hamer & Cunningham (1981) have shown that correlational measures yield better representations of jobs than distance measures, while Zimmerman et al (1982) found that a hierarchical clustering procedure and a centroid method were superior to a density search technique for clustering purposes. Arvey et al (1981) and Lee & Mendoza (1981) found that though the ANOVA model is robust and appropriate for detecting job differences, the efficiency (power and control for Type I error) of the test is a function of whether underlying assumptions are met. In sum, it appears that our focus on sophisticated analytical techniques may not be a panacea. Whether jobs are similar/dissimilar may depend on how similarity is statistically defined; sometimes one may conclude that a brain surgeon is like a belly dancer (after all, both jobs involve fine motor movements). Results also may depend on whether the investigator is looking for differences or for similarities. Unfortunately, there is no research that addresses this issue of job analytic "set."

Task Differences as Moderators of Validity

Validity generalization research (reviewed in a subsequent section) has important implications for job analysis. Schmidt et al's (1981b) meta analysis of 3368 validity coefficients representing 698 independent samples indicated that the mean observed and estimated true validities of 8 test constructs were similar across 5 clerical job families, both for overall job proficiency and for training criteria. A second result from the same study found small but unimportant differences in the validities of 10 tests (Army Classification Battery) for 35 different jobs; the criterion was success in training. Pearlman (1982) examined 15 job groupings formed by one random grouping and four systematic grouping methods and found no support for a conclusion of between-group validity differences for any of the 15 job family systems, and only minor differences in effectiveness of the systematic grouping methods. The overall conclusion to be drawn is that task differences between job families within an occupational area have little or no effect on test validities. Furthermore, differences in test validity among different jobs are small. These results suggest (Pearlman 1982, Schmidt et al 1981b) that broad content types of job analyses are appropriate and therefore fine, detailed task analyses are unnecessary when the focus is on validation. Additional support for this conclusion stems from Sackett et al's (1981) finding that a global, paired comparison analysis of eight supervisory jobs yielded the same job grouping as did a more elaborate task-oriented analysis of 237 statements.

Global job analytical procedures, however, do not provide sufficient information for other personnel purposes such as performance appraisal feedback systems, development of career ladders, and the like. Osburn et al (1981) found that when experienced interviewers rated applicants on dimensions keyed to important job behaviors, rather than on generalized dimensions, they were better able to discriminate accurately between the more qualified and the less qualified.

Taxonomies

Although little research has been done on the formation of job attribute profiles (Sparrow et al 1982), classifications are necessary for drawing generalizations across events and for efficient communication among researchers. Classifications facilitate the description of structure and relationships of the constituent objects to each other and to similar objects, and they simplify these relationships in such a way that general statements can be made about classes of objects (Fleishman 1982). For a comprehensive review of task and attribute taxonomies, see Peterson & Bownas (1982). However, formation of job attribute profiles (Sparrow et al 1982) is the task of the future.

In sum, the job analysis literature has moved from endless searches for *the* job analytic method to a concern with process issues (e.g. factors affecting job analysis results, affects of job analysis results on other personnel issues) and toward a greater understanding of tasks and attributes. Such concerns will facilitate the integration of personnel with job redesign, motivation, and vocational psychology. Research is needed, however, on the influence of analysts' perceptions and environmental cues on job analysis results.

PERFORMANCE MEASUREMENT

For years, researchers have addressed the "criterion problem" and its implications for all aspects of industrial/organizational psychology. Attempts to resolve the problem have focused on a search for *the* performance measurement method. As methods proliferated, comparative research focused on identifying methods that were better or worse at minimizing response biases such as halo, leniency, central tendency, and the like. Presently there is an effort to determine whether "halo" is error, truth, or illusory, and to understand the rating process.

Performance appraisal's popularity is evidenced by the number of books (e.g. Carroll & Schneier 1982, DeVries et al 1981, Latham & Wexley 1981), edited series (Alluisi & Fleishman 1982, Dunnette & Fleishman 1982, Howell

& Fleishman 1982), special journal issue (*Public Personnel Management Journal*, 1982, Volume 11, No. 4), and conferences (e.g. Landy et al 1983; Johns Hopkins University symposium, November 1982, "Performance Assessment: The State of the Art") devoted to the topic within the 2 year review period, each with a different theme.

Performance Appraisal Methods

No new methods have emerged recently, but behaviorally anchored rating scales (BARS) and their derivatives continue to attract attention such that a shortcut method for their development has been suggested (Green et al 1981). Yet another review of BARS (Kingstrom & Bass 1981) indicated the all-too-familiar conclusion: BARS are no better or worse than alternatives, though the authors claim there is insufficient evidence to warrant a firm and final conclusion. Bernardin & Smith (1981) suggested that the original BARS formulation (intended to affect and be part of a rating process that includes observation, inference, scaling, recording, and a summary rating product) has been misunderstood and ignored.

Behavioral observation scales (BOS), based on critical incident technology, may be the fad of the future. Claims regarding its value and appropriateness (see Latham & Wexley 1981) need to be researched. The assumption that BOS differs from typical judgmental scales because it only requires frequency ratings and simple observations was not supported (Murphy et al 1982b). Another criticism of BOS is that there is not constant level of satisfactoriness across behaviors in the typical BOS (Kane & Bernardin 1982). A frequency of 80% may be "good" for some behaviors but "poor" for others.

An interesting modification of the mixed standard scale (MSS) was suggested by Rosinger et al (1982). Their MSS triads were developed to describe proficiency levels of specific job tasks instead of the more usual triads of traits.

Research also has focused on general formats. Lee et al (1981) found high convergent validity, strong discriminant validity, and no method bias for a summated rating procedure and a global dimension form. Schriesheim & Gattiker (1982) concluded that there were no real reliability and validity differences between a trait-oriented and a behaviorally based rating format.

The rater becomes the method when peer ratings and self-assessments are used to obtain appraisal data. Peer ratings have been found to have high interjudge agreement (Siegel 1982), high accuracy, and low influence by halo (Imada 1982). Love (1981) compared nominations, rankings, and ratings by peers and found comparable reliability and validity but also equivalent negative reactions from the rater group. A meta analysis by Mabe & West (1982) indicated that accuracy of self-evaluation is fostered by intelligence, high achievement status, and an internal locus of control.

Effects of Training on Performance Appraisal Results

Training is often the presumed salvation of any method; it is commonly accepted that training raters will result in "better" performance appraisal results. Bernardin & Buckley (1981) concluded that training has been effective for inducing the rater to focus on rating "behavior" and to emphasize distributions, but it has had less impact on validity or accuracy of the ratings. They suggested that more attention needs to be given to modeling, to a focus on standardization, and to an emphasis on observational skills, particularly, diary keeping. The practicality of diary keeping in the work world is of obvious concern. Studies that examined the effects of training found no effect on discriminability (Zedeck & Cascio 1982), but a positive effect for accuracy (Fay & Latham 1982).

Criteria for Evaluating Methods

Performance appraisal systems are considered effective if they are relevant, sensitive, reliable, acceptable, and practical (Cascio 1982b). From a psychometric perspective, performance appraisals are judged in terms of the degree to which they minimize response biases and yield accurate assessments. The issue of halo has been examined from both a conceptual and statistical frame of reference. Cooper (1981a) identified six sources of halo, five of which are examples of illusory halo that can be attributed to raters' use of a representativeness heuristic, schemas, attributions, and other social cognitive factors; the sixth source is correlated true scores. True halo probably exists because a job is a relatively homogeneous cluster of work tasks (Cooper 1981b).

The halo measure is problematic. Landy et al (1980) suggested a statistical control for halo by partialling out an overall rating, but this approach has been criticized in terms of the definition of halo and the unit of analysis (Murphy 1982), the method of factor analysis (Harvey 1982, Hulin 1982), and the assumption of causality between dimension and overall ratings (Harvey 1982). A theme common to these criticisms was the unknown amount of true halo. In response, Landy et al (1982b) suggested that the expected value of dimension intercorrelations be assessed by taking the mean of a distribution of observed intercorrelations gathered on a constant set of rating scales and dividing the observed/expected difference by the standard error of this difference.

"True" scores are important when an accuracy index is used. Murphy et al (1982a) compared Cronbach's (1955) four types of accuracy and concluded that accuracy in observing or evaluating performance is not a generalized ability, but rather that different types of accuracy are relatively independent.

"Truth" often has been assessed as the mean rating provided by "subject matter experts" for behavioral statements. We are particularly concerned with this operationalization. Many of the expert raters are often a sample from the population that is asked to complete the rating or are external observers to the situation. We question how viewers of tapes (the stimuli often used in such studies) can be presumed to be experts when they have not performed the job or even have been trained in its tasks. Also, our overall review of accuracy studies indicated that mean expert ratings are the only data reported when, in fact, the variance of such ratings deserves serious attention. Sample sizes of expert raters are often small, and without analyzing the means relative to the variances it is difficult to interpret the adequacy of the items and their "truths" as they are ordered on a dimension.

In essence, we have developed procedures and conducted comparative studies of appraisal methods using indices as criteria that are unclear, ambiguous, and in part, wrong. In addition to the problems of operationalization, results also may be confounded by differences among studies in samples, organizations, types of raters, number of responses provided by the rater per dimension, small samples of raters, studies with one ratee, and anchor point problems and differences (Kingstrom & Bass 1981). It is no wonder that the typical conclusion regarding the value of a method is that "it is no better or worse." But do the methods or results of comparative analyses impact the ratee, rater, or organization? Perhaps rather than focusing on psychometric characteristics, an index of utility that indicates the impact of a product of performance appraisal, such as feedback (Landy et al 1982a), would be a useful guide for judging performance appraisal methods.

Performance Feedback

Cederblom (1982), Wexley (1982), and Ivancevich (1982) have discussed the requirements for a good performance appraisal feedback interview. These include participation, support, goal setting, focused discussions, minimal criticism, and a splitting of administrative and developmental feedback. Ivancevich (1982) found that training managers on how to give feedback and on the goal-setting procedure resulted in positive perceptions of the process; Ilgen et al (1981b) found supervisor-subordinate similarities in perceptions of feedback, though there were level differences such as overestimation of one's own performance by subordinates. Stone & Stone (1982) found that consistent feedback from multiple agents was most beneficial. In addition to affecting perceptions, the feedback interview affects performance (DeNisi et al 1982, Ivancevich & McMahon 1982).

Ashford & Cummings (1981) identified tolerance of ambiguity, role ambiguity, level of job involvement, and leader behaviors as variables that influence one's seeking of feedback. Parsons et al (1981) developed an individual differences measure for feedback preference that focuses on propensities for seeking internal and external feedback as well as the ability to self-assess. There is also some evidence that type of performance appraisal device (e.g. BARS) may affect results of feedback (Hom et al 1982).

Promotions

Promotions are an aspect of performance receiving some theoretical attention. Anderson et al (1981) proposed a promotion model that incorporates nine specific propositions. Stumpf & London (1981a) developed a conceptual scheme for managerial promotion that leads to 16 testable propositions. An archival analysis by Campion et al (1981) found that those who refuse promotions tend to be older, female, and less educated. They suggested that refusal is a strategy for handling stress.

Performance Theory

Though a good portion of the reviewed material deals with methodological issues, we question whether such research is leading to any resolution or productive outcome. A more encouraging body of literature considers the theoretical basis of performance and appraisal process issues such as information processing and social cognition influences.

Blumberg & Pringle (1982) have reconceptualized the standard view that performance = motivation × ability. In their model, performance is the product of *capacity, willingness,* and *opportunity* to perform. A more elaborate approach can be found in the reintroduction of Wherry's 1952 work, involving a series of mathematical equations designed to describe the rating process, and 46 theorems and corollaries that provide a testable set of hypotheses (Wherry & Bartlett 1982).

INFORMATION PROCESSING   Hobson et al (1981) clearly described the policy-capturing technique as it was applied to faculty evaluation. Their results generally are consistent with the information processing literature that finds that three dimensions of performance are capable of explaining an overall effectiveness rating; that self-insight and mathematical representations of dimension utilization differ, and that there is an overestimate of number of performance dimensions used. A study by Stumpf & London (1981b) found similar results but, in addition, found that configural models provided increased explanatory power. Another policy-capturing study showed how strategies for combining and utilizing data on performance dimensions varied as a function of the purpose of the rating (Zedeck & Cascio 1982). The purpose result has implications for much of the methodological literature discussed above. Since few studies identify for the rater the purpose for which the ratings are being collected, purpose confounds the results and could explain the underwhelming results of method assessments and comparisons.

A laboratory study by Lyness & Cornelius (1982) compared holistic and dimension-based strategies for forming overall evaluations. Their results indicated that an algorithm yielded better agreement than clinical composition, though some of the conclusions depended on how the criteria were operationalized. This last result has implications for much research. Multiple criteria are valuable research qualities, but we need to specify on an a priori basis just what construct is being operationalized rather than seek criterion fulfillment for its own sake.

SOCIAL COGNITION THEORIES   Attribution theory is the major social cognition theory (i.e. emphasis on cognitive structures and processes underlying social judgment and social behavior) applied to performance appraisals. According to the theory, behavior is not simply judged by its objective components, but behavior is interpreted by the observer (the rater). This leads to causal attributions for a stimulus person's (ratee's) behavior. For example, Hargett (1981) examined the causal attributions made by observers regarding a prospective employee's performance (successful and unsuccessful actors). Results showed that the amount and type of internality (control) attributed to the performer varies as a function of whether performance is successful or unsuccessful.

Considerable research using an attribution model has been conducted by T. R. Mitchell and his colleagues, particularly as the theory is applied to poor performers (Ilgen et al 1981a, Mitchell & Kalb 1981, 1982, Wood & Mitchell 1981). These studies have found that experienced supervisors more readily use environmental explanations of poor performance than inexperienced ones; that outcome knowledge results in more internal attributions than when outcome is not known; and that impression management on the part of a subordinate influences the attributions made by a manager. Pence et al (1982) found that causal explanations of poor performance have an impact on recommendations for corrective action.

Another aspect of social cognition is the formation of a schema, the cognitive representation of knowledge concerning some stimulus, a framework for encoding and integrating new information, and a basis for evaluating experience. A thorough discussion of schemas is provided by Dorfman (1982). Both Cooper (1981a) and Feldman (1981) have presented models that provide a number of hypotheses to be tested regarding categorization and schema formation. Their models focus on recognition, organization, storage, judgment, recall, integration, encoding, decay, and other such cognitive processes.

In sum, rating processes per se, as well as determinants of the ratings, have been proposed. Much current research, however, involves simulated, hypothetical stimuli—"paper people." The studies are appropriate for capturing or explaining a decision such as an overall performance rating, but the procedure does not necessarily capture the precise means by which the judgment is formed; perhaps only introspection will do this! This is a serious limitation of policy capturing, and we encourage researchers to devise procedures and strategies for pursuing the important question of how information is processed. Also, too many of the studies use student raters who are role playing. Finally, limited information is given to the untrained rater, and performance often is viewed as stable (Wendelken & Inn 1981). Much field research is needed to determine the extent to which the processes do in fact model ratings, and their generalizability across situations, methods, tasks, and criteria.

Factors Affected By and Affecting Performance and Appraisals

The literature is rife with studies that examine the influence of specific variables on appraisals as well as how appraisals impact these same variables. Examples are: factors such as the social contextual variables of group leadership skills and likeability (T. R. Mitchell & Liden 1982); leadership style (Kipnis et al 1981); situational control of performance variability (Peters et al 1982). Also, organizational differences in the manner in which employee performance is assessed (Zammuto et al 1982), have been studied. There is an increased concern for the performance of groups as opposed to individuals (B. M. Bass 1982, Tziner & Vardi 1982). Other investigation has dealt with personality and motivational variables such as perceived locus of control (Spector 1982); trust in the appraisal process and its influence on ratings (Bernardin et al 1981, Bernardin & Cardy 1982) and perceptions of the process (Barr et al 1981); perceptions of others' performance (Smircich & Chesser 1981), and of the appraisal process (Dipboye & dePontbriand 1981); prior commitment to ratee (Bazerman et al 1982); cognitive complexity (Bernardin & Cardy 1981, Lahey & Saal 1981, Sauser & Pond 1981, Bernardin et al 1982); and congruence between environmental control and one's ability to use that control (Bazerman 1982). In addition, sex, race, and age have been studied (Cleveland & Landy 1981, Mobley 1981, 1982a, Wexley & Pulakos 1982). Finally, the influence of appraisals on retirement decisions (Rosen et al 1981, Zedeck 1981) and the impact of prior patterns of performance (DeNisi & Stevens 1981) have been examined.

We hope that future research on such factors will be derived from coherent theoretical frameworks, that it will be based on field research, and that there will be reports of replications (cognitive complexity research is an exception rather than the rule regarding replication). Studies for studies' sake will not advance the field.

Turnover/Absenteeism: Objective Criterion Measures

The above review focused on subjective performance appraisals, but there is also a considerable amount of literature that uses more objective criteria— turnover and absenteeism (as well as an initial interest in lateness (Adler & Golan 1981). The subjective–objective distinction is not a clear one. Muckler (1982) indicated that all criterion measures involve some subjectivity. There is subjectivity in selecting particular indices of turnover/absenteeism, how and from whom the data are collected, and in interpretations and implications drawn.

TURNOVER MODELS   Mobley and his associates (1982b) have proposed one of the more frequently researched models of turnover. Mitchel's (1981) test of it with managers found strong support (cross-validated) for the links between turnover intentions and tenure. Michaels & Spector (1982) also found support for the model, particularly for stronger relationships between most of the adjacent as opposed to the distant variables. Mobley (1982c) has posed several questions of his own theory, some of which can be asked of any theory: 1. Where is the process? Research needs to emphasize change, time, multiple actions, and operations. 2. What are the consequences of turnover and the processes related to the consequences? We need to study the utility of turnover. 3. What is the role of performance in the turnover process? Are leavers better performers. 4. What are the conceptual and empirical relationships among turnover and other so-called "withdrawal" actions?

A causal analysis of a turnover model proposed by Price (Price & Mueller 1981) yielded low but supportive relationships; in particular, that intentions to stay, promotional opportunity, and occupational socialization had the greatest impact on turnover. Arnold & Feldman (1982), Wunder et al (1982), and Hom & Hulin (1981) also tested and reported support for their hypothesized models and relationships. All of the models appear to incorporate the same categories of variables with differences appearing in the causal order. Other studies have investigated the relationship of turnover to such processes as job scope (Mowday & Spencer 1981), rewards and costs of alternatives (Farrell & Rusbult 1981), role of leadership (Graen et al 1982), trait anxiety and felt stress (Parasuraman 1982), role of performance level (Spencer & Steers 1981), career development (Krau 1981), and potential aptitude and career advancement differences (Dreher 1982).

Given the proliferation of models, research will obviously continue until the "best fit" is determined. Like performance appraisal, individual studies of turnover need to be integrated into a broader conceptual scheme. Other areas of interest that models ought to take into account are a concern for employees who intend to quit but do not, and the consequences (Bowen 1982), as well as an assessment of attributions made by "stayers" toward "leavers" (Mowday 1981). Progress may be limited, however, until a definition of turnover includes more than leaving/staying or voluntary/involuntary leaving.

TURNOVER DEFINITIONS   Dalton and his associates have generated a turnover taxonomy that focuses on costs and benefits (Dalton & Todor 1982, Dalton et al 1981, 1982). Voluntary turnover can be separated into functional (i.e. positive for the organization) and dysfunctional (i.e. leaver is someone the organization would like to retain). Furthermore, there is unavoidable turnover that is not subject to organizational control versus controllable turnover resulting from an organizational intervention such as skills training (Krackhardt et al 1981). We need to consider the impact of specific classes of leavers on organizational properties and characteristics (Martin et al 1981). Consideration of these factors results in a more accurate portrayal of the problem, and from a research interpretation perspective, could yield different percentages of leavers from the organization than that which has been reported and analyzed. Reanalysis within the framework of the proposed taxonomy could alter the results of some of the studies that have examined antecedents and consequences of turnover.

ABSENTEEISM   Models of absenteeism are similar to those of turnover in that they include personal, organizational, and situational categories of variables that impact attendance. Yet absenteeism and turnover are only moderately related (Stumpf & Dawley 1981). A model developed by Steers & Rhodes (1978) found little support in a study by Watson (1981); 13 variables explained 12% of a time-lost measure of absenteeism. However, the inclusion of past absenteeism into an equation that contained factors such as job satisfaction and involvement yielded a significant increase in predictability of subsequent absenteeism (Breaugh 1981a). A meta analysis of a few studies showed that the absenteeism–attitude relationship generalizes across situations (Terborg et al 1982). Absenteeism operationalization and definition, too, have a number of problems, as well as statistical ones such as skewness (Hammer & Landau 1981).

Summary

Given the work on methods, taxonomies, processes, models, and theories, we seem to be on the threshold of developing a human resource performance system. However, this system needs to take into account training for skills acquisition, changes in performance, and utility. We need to understand better the cognitive structure of the performer as well as the processes involved in the transformation of a novice into an expert (Glaser 1981).

PERFORMANCE PREDICTORS

Employment testing has been highlighted in the last 2 years in special reports and journal issues promulgated by professional groups. The National Research Council's Committee on Ability Testing produced a two-part multidisciplinary view of testing (Wigdor & Garner 1982a,b), and the *American Psychologist* published a special issue on testing, edited by Glaser & Bond (1981). Such interest has also gone abroad. A special issue of the *International Review of Applied Psychology* (Poortinga 1982) contained a series of papers dealing with test use in Western Europe.

The current state of the art can be summarized by Boehm's (1982a) review of criterion-related validity studies published in the *Journal of Applied Psychology* and *Personnel Psychology* between 1960 and 1979. She concluded that there has been (*a*) an absolute and relative decline in the volume of reported validation research, (*b*) an increase in average sample size, (*c*) a decline in proportion of studies using supervisory ratings as criteria, (*d*) a deemphasis on studies using aptitude tests as predictors, (*e*) greater use of predictive research designs, and (*f*) a *constant* absolute validity coefficient equal to .22. Reilly & Chao's (1982) review of alternatives to conventional testing found promise for biodata and peer evaluations, but no new devices appear on the horizon.

The above reviews were based on published and unpublished papers, but one may question the adequacy and comprehensiveness of some of the research reports. Friedman & Williams (1982) reported that there are gaps in the data and disparities in the methods of data presentation. We urge that, at the very least, reports contain *basic* descriptive statistics; i.e. sample sizes, means, variances, and complete zero order correlation matrices (predictors and criteria). Such data availability will facilitate meta analytic studies. Consideration also should be given to revival of a validity information exchange source.

Background Information as Predictors

BIOGRAPHICAL INFORMATION   A biographical questionnaire developed by Owens & Schoenfeldt (1979) was found by Eberhardt & Muchinsky (1982a) and Neiner & Owens (1982) to have a reasonably stable factor structure over time, and it was predictive of another biodata form. Eberhardt & Muchinsky (1982b) also found that factor analytically derived clusters based on responses to the questionnaire are a determinant, in part, of a person's modal vocational type. However, T. W. Mitchell & Klimoski (1982) found that an empirically weighted form that they developed was slightly more valid than one based on factor analysis.

The role of seniority as a performance predictor has been studied and reviewed by Gordon and associates (Gordon & Fitzgibbons 1982, Gordon & Johnson 1982). While past performance tends to be related to output in a new position, seniority by itself or in combination with past performance did not improve prediction. However, the degree of interjob similarity between a past and new job was a valid predictor.

Studies of seniority need clear operationalizations of seniority, as well as designs that allow statistical control over a number of time-related threats to internal validity (e.g. age/seniority covariation, organization level, salary). In view of the widespread speculation regarding the impact of seniority on job satisfaction and on job performance, and in view of its use as a basis for personnel decisions, additional research on its validity and overall impact on performance is needed.

BEHAVIORAL CONSISTENCY MODELS   Behavioral consistency models (past behavior is the best predictor of future behavior) require self-reports of prior achievements, accomplishments, and experiences pertinent to the job in question and its dimensions. A study by Hough (1981) demonstrated good interrater agreement in the use of benchmarks for scoring the "accomplishment record" as well as significant adjusted correlations between "record" scores and five performance indices. A form developed by Grove (1981) also indicated good interrater reliabilities in scoring experiences. The value of these models is that they tap a component of an individual's background that is not measured by typical biodata inventories or by performance tests (see Arvey & McGowen 1982 for an overview).

The means by which training and experience data are collected and scored was examined by Ash & Levine (1982). They found that a task-based inventory yielded the best interrater agreement though validities were low for all methods. Regarding behavioral consistency, its practical usefulness was questioned because a large proportion of applicants refused to complete the forms. From the perspective of the applicant, Oliphant & Alexander (1982) found that ambiguity in responses about background distorts the evaluation process, though in an inconsistent manner.

Interviewing

In spite of the fact that there is no new research to show that the interview is reliable and valid, a considerable amount of research is devoted to process questions, often independent of the validity/reliability questions. The literature suggests that decisions are a function of stereotypes, attributions, background characteristics, format characteristics, and the like, but there is little evidence to show that any level of the variables studied is associated with any level of decision that is valid. Arvey & Campion (1982) indicated the interview still is used despite its psychometric problems and its susceptibility to bias and distortion because: (*a*) it is "really" valid, particularly for certain dimensions, but typical psychometric models cannot detect it; (*b*) practical considerations make it popular, particularly when there is not a large number of applicants; (*c*) it does other things well, such as selling the job and company; and (*d*) interviewers maintain great faith and confidence in their judgments. Regarding this last comment, perhaps if we treated the interviewer as the "test" (rather than aggregating all interviewers into a pool and considering them as parallel forms) and then analyzed individual interviewer reliability and validity, results would be more positive.

PROCESS   Webster's (1982) book focuses on decision making in the interview with particular attention to decision making models and social cognition theories. Herriot (1981) hypothesized that the interview is a rule-governed social interaction in which attributions to personal characteristics are made, and decisions arrived at, in part, due to attributions of dispositional traits to applicants. Dipboye (1982) proposed that self-fulfilling prophecy is the process that mediates the effects of expectancies on outcomes of the interview.

Research on process questions has found support for stereotyping as a function of interviewer sex (Giles & Feild 1982), but no support that interviewers consistently seek to confirm impressions (Sackett 1982b). Interviewer accountability and responsibility produce descriptions of a target person that more reliably reflect the target's characteristics (Rozelle & Baxter 1981). Studies on sex of interviewer (Elliott 1981), interviewer racial attitudes (Mullins 1982), and interviewee physical attractiveness (Beehr & Gilmore 1982) yielded minimal support for the influence of such variables.

FORMAT   Janz (1982a) found that a patterned behavior description interview that focused on critical incidents yielded more reliable and valid assessments of teaching assistant ratings than did an interview that focused on establishing rapport and control. Cann et al (1981) found that forcing an interviewer to attend to specific items did not reduce attractiveness and sex discrimination in hiring decision recommendations.

INTERVIEW USE   The interview does not necessarily have a positive impact. Herriot & Rothwell (1981) found that strength of a candidate's intention to accept generally decreased as a consequence of the interview, particularly if the interviewee's expectations of what would occur in the interview failed to be met. A realistic job preview (RJP) has been proposed as a means by which to reduce turnover and to provide more accurate information about expectations and job content. Popovich & Wanous (1982) suggested that the RJP process is a technique for attitude change and can be explained in terms of group dynamics, attribution theory, cognitive consistency, and communications models. Results for RJPs, however, are not impressive. Dugoni & Ilgen (1981) found no support for effectiveness of RJP when comparing an experimental to a control group. Reilly et al (1981) studied the role of RJP for telephone service representatives and found it to be ineffective, but its effectiveness may be a function of the type of role being previewed.

Source of RJP information may be relevant. Zaharia & Baumeister (1981) found no difference in survival rates of those exposed to a booklet or videotape job portrayal, whereas Breaugh (1981b) and Quaglieri (1982) found better information was provided from self-initiated walk-ins and friends than from newspaper ads.

SUMMARY   As with the performance appraisal literature, much interviewing research is based on simulated laboratory experiments with students role-playing interviewers and interviewees or being asked to evaluate hypothetical "paper people." While such strategies certainly have heuristic value for generating hypotheses subsequently to be tested in the field or in laboratory manipulations of processes observed in the field, current interviewing research is stagnant. We need to capture more realistic stimulus situations and interviewer responses as well as to develop new dependent variables for the process research (Arvey & Campion 1982). We need to determine whether any of the process variables affect valid decisions and ultimately demonstrate utility. Furthermore, there need to be greater efforts made to merge research with application in this area, for there are few guidelines concerning the improvement of interview effectiveness based on research findings.

Assessment Centers

Thornton & Byham's (1982) comprehensive book traces the historical development of the assessment center procedure, critiques published and unpublished research, and integrates methodology and results into human judgment processes and theories. In spite of its apparent validity and utility, some researchers have begun to study the assessment *process* and to question its validity foundation. Sackett (1982a) provided an overview of some of these issues.

PROCESS ISSUES   The main process questions pertain to the factors that influence the consensus assessment rating, the role individual exercises play in that decision, and dimension ratings. Jones (1981) found that across four exercises the interrater agreements before discussion ranged from .65 to .73 and after judgment ranged from .67 to .86. An examination of archival data by Sackett & Wilson (1982) revealed that no discussion among assessors was needed for 78% of the ratings and that use of the frequency with which an assessor changed his/her rating as an index indicated differential influence among assessors. In addition, a simple mechanical rule predicted consensus for 95% of all ratings made. Consequently, Sackett & Wilson (1982) suggested that the consensus process can be replaced with a mechanical one. Regarding this last issue, Borman (1982) found that unit weighting of exercises yielded higher validities than consensus ratings. On the other hand, based on a correlation of .70 between a mechanical formation of the overall rating and the consensus formation, Gilbert (1981) concluded there is no basis for determining which is better.

Our sense of the issue is that a mechanical process can represent what occurred in the discussion, but we do not know enough about the process to suggest replacing consensus discussions. Even if we did, it is not clear whether it would be advantageous to do so from a "fidelity in the process" point of view. In assessment center research of decision formation, as in other areas reviewed (performance appraisal and interviewing), mechanical models are means by which to represent behavior efficiently and statistically, but they may not in fact represent *how* that decision was made. Assessment center research may well profit from an examination of that done in group dynamics.

Regarding the role of exercises in dimension ratings, Borman's (1982) study had pairs of assessors who observed the assessee in only one exercise, and consequently there was no contamination across exercises. He found that the median interrater correlation between assessors on each dimension for each of six exercises was high. Factor analyses of ratings on dimensions in individual exercises yielded a strong general factor that suggested that assessors were making global judgments of candidates' performance, a result supported by Turnage & Muchinsky (1982). Finally, he reported differential contribution of exercises to consensus judgment and concluded that levels of validity for predictors depend on the nature of criteria. Sackett & Dreher (1982) found near zero correlations among across-exercise ratings of individual dimensions, but good agreement among the dimensional ratings made in each exercise (a result also found by Turnage & Muchinsky 1982).

In sum, it appears that dimensions are differentially affected by different exercises and that the overall decision can be modeled mechanically. Our reluctance in removing the consensus process at this time is based on the fact that none of the reported research used an on-the-job performance criterion against which to validate the ratings. Clearly, there are impacts on decisions, but how do these impacts affect job performance criteria?

VALIDITY: CONTENT OR CONSTRUCT?   Boehm (1981) and Haymaker & Grant (1982) have argued for the validity of assessment centers on the basis of content validity. Sackett & Dreher (1982) noted that assessment centers have been defended on the basis of construct validity, a view with which they are in disagreement. The "type" of validity was debated between Sackett and Dreher versus Norton (Dreher & Sackett 1981, Norton 1981, Sackett & Dreher 1981). Sackett and Dreher argued that content validity concerns itself with current proficiency and therefore is not appropriate for predicting future behavioral tendencies (e.g. first level supervisory skills), and in addition, requires a high degree of congruence between the test environment and the actual work environment. Norton rebutted, in part, that the assessment center should be viewed as a process and a sample of the *whole* of the manager's job and that specific exercises need not be the focus. Moreover, global judgments are *summaries* of an assessor's careful review of a large body of specific observations.

The above discussion reflects the underlying operational notion of an assessment center—it is dimension driven. The developmental sequence is to conduct a job analysis, construct exercises, and then develop a dimension × exercise grid to show which exercises measure what dimensions (Boehm 1982b). We suggest that the dimensions be given a secondary role and that assessment centers be driven by tasks and behaviors that are representative of the position for which one is interested in selecting or developing managers. This is not to suggest that dimensional considerations be ignored or eliminated. The overall rating in assessment centers is often cast in terms of "potential" or "likelihood" of success, but it can be viewed as an evaluation of success in the whole exercise process. Over time, these ratings have been demonstrated to be valid (Thornton & Byham 1982). Dimension and exercise ratings and discussions may serve as a cognitive means for the assessor to structure observations. No two situations on the job are alike, and no two exercises purporting to measure the same dimensions need yield the same rating. This complex, multifaceted situation contributes to the richness of the center. The assessment center can be an organizational intervention. If the global rating works, don't fix the process, but continue to research the process to get a better understanding of it. Focusing on tasks and behaviors may facilitate our understanding of what an evaluation reflects about *absolute* behavioral performance; this is more important than concentrating on dimension scores that describe *relative* performance on perhaps poorly specified dimensions. More research is needed on the use of performance in specific exercises as a means by which to *place* and *develop* potential managers. We need to understand the effect, if any, of feedback to the candidates *and* management. Finally, the value of assessor training and its generalizability to management development needs to be studied.

ASSESSEE CHARACTERISTICS   A relatively new research area focuses on the identification of individual characteristics such as intelligence (Dulewicz & Fletcher 1982) and prior supervisory experience (Vosburgh 1982) that have been found to be predictive of success in assessment centers. Perhaps the Supervisory Profile Record form developed by Erwin (1981) or that developed by Ramos (1982) can be used to prescreen candidates into assessment.

Summary

Our review of performance predictors suggests that not much new, except for behavioral consistency models, has been attempted. Surprisingly little is being done with work samples (Robertson & Kandola 1982) or with physical ability measures (Arnold et al 1982). We need to develop new assessment tools; we may need to consider different uses of tests such as self-screening devices. Also, we need to examine the role of theory in test development (Wigdor & Garner 1982a). Testing has been quantitative and pragmatic so far; we have used sophisticated data analytic strategies and examined all types of relationships, but do we have a better understanding of what we are measuring? Theories of intelligence, creativity, information processing, and the like need to be integrated into our test development programs.

METHODOLOGICAL/STATISTICAL CONSIDERATIONS

As previously indicated, the field pertaining to personnel decisions has become more sophisticated in terms of its measurement procedures, models, and analyses. At one extreme, meta analyses are being conducted to determine *generalities* of obtained relationships; at the other extreme, measurement models are focusing on *individualized* assessments of traits and abilities.

Item Response Theory

Perhaps the most significant trend in test methodology research is a shift in emphasis from classical test theory to item response theory (IRT), tailored testing, or latent trait models (Ghiselli et al 1981). As Hambleton & van der Linden (1982) reported in their introduction to a special issue of *Applied Psychological Measurement* (1982, Volume 6, Number 4) devoted to IRT, it is being used to develop tests, to equate scores from nonparallel tests, to investigate item bias, and to address many other measurement problems. IRT is an express train that we should be boarding. Classical test theory results in true scores of ability that are dependent on the specific test and sample; it requires estimates of item and test parameters based on the parallel test concept. IRT, on the other hand, starts with a model of the trait of interest and moves to an assessment of the fit of the model to item responses. The focus is on the item and probabilities of responses. Moreover, the true score in IRT is not indexed to the test, but rather it is a latent parameter; IRT offers descriptors of items that do not depend upon the particular selection of standard test items.

Sequential testing, a form of IRT, was demonstrated by Weitzman (1982) to be an effective and accurate means by which to make selection decisions. Other research has focused on types of models (e.g. Yen 1981) and the accuracy of simultaneous estimation of item and person parameters (e.g. Hulin et al 1982). Future studies should illustrate the use of IRT in real selection decisions (see Ironson et al 1982), assessments of performance, and analysis of responses to surveys, job analysis inventories, and the like.

Formula Corrections

Corrections for range restriction and for unreliability (Winne & Belfry 1982) are becoming more important, particularly as we undertake meta analyses of observed relationships. Research has demonstrated that corrections for range restriction are robust in the face of assumption violations (Gross 1982) and alternative correction sequences (Lee et al 1982), though yielding possibly conservative estimates of the true relationships (Linn et al 1981a). The best strategy is to report both corrected and uncorrected results.

Corrections are also important when considering alternative selection devices to the one used for selection. Hsu (1982) demonstrated that an alternative that has a higher validity in a group of selected applicants has, in fact, a lower validity in the entire applicant pool.

Test Fairness

Linn (1982a, Linn & Dunbar 1982), Cole (1981), and the reports edited by Wigdor & Garner (1982a,b) have repeated the conclusion that there is little prediction bias for tests and groups studied. Nevertheless, research continues to focus on the strategies and statistical tests for assessing whether there is differential prediction for subgroups. Stricker (1982) compared item difficulty, item characteristic curves, and partial correlation as means by which to assess item differentiation of subgroups and concluded that the last procedure was most useful. Drasgow (1982) presented equations that can be used to investigate the likelihood of detecting bias for tests with different numbers of items, reliabilities, and validities, while Schmidt & Hunter (1982) pointed out the situations in which pooled intercepts and ANCOVA are appropriate in studies of bias.

Validity Generalization

Discussion and debate have been generated on the methods, results, and implications of the meta analyses performed by Schmidt, Hunter, and their associates. The results of their work have lead to a conclusion of validity generalization that, in part, states: ". . . cognitive ability tests of the kind generally used in personnel selection are valid predictors of successful performance for all jobs in all settings" (Schmidt & Hunter 1981, p. 1128). Consequently, the doctrine of situational specificity for test validities can be rejected.

Meta analytical methods for cumulating research findings across studies are presented by Hunter et al (1982a); the particular method as well as a summary of validity generalization findings can be found in Hunter & Schmidt (1982) and Schmidt & Hunter (1981). In brief, results indicate that test-job performance validity variability (75% or greater) is due to statistical, measurement, and other artifacts that are unrelated to the true relationship between the test and job performance. By correcting for measurement errors, range restriction, and sampling error, Schmidt, Hunter, and colleagues have found that for most *cognitive* test-job combinations examined the remaining validity variance is near zero or zero.

RECENT RESULTS   Within the last 2 years, additional support has been obtained for validity generalization. Schmidt et al (1981a) found strong support for a mechanical and chemical comprehension test, with less support for arithmetic reasoning and general intelligence tests. The previously cited Schmidt et al (1981b) and Pearlman (1982) studies support the position that task differences have minimal effect on cognitive test validities and differences in cognitive test validity among different jobs are small. Perhaps the most impressive support comes from a consortium study in which the *same* tests (cognitive and noncognitive) and criteria were used in 70 companies and 6 different power plant operator jobs, covering over 3000 operators (Dunnette et al 1982). This type of study is in contrast to previous research on validity generalization that cumulated findings across studies (i.e. combining different measures of the same predictor and criterion types.) Meta analysis of the operator plant data indicated that validities of all predictor composites generalized across companies, race, and sex groups. In addition, whereas the Schmidt and Hunter studies have used an overall criterion, Dunnette and associates found generalizability for dimensional criteria such as emotional stability and competence in plant operations.

Some degree of validity generalization also has been found in the academic environment. Linn et al (1981b) analyzed 726 validity studies of the Law School Admissions Test and found that 70% of variance in observed validities could be accounted for by the artifacts; however, Linn et al concluded that there was some situational validity as a function of the law school and the time period in which the validity studies were conducted.

Using a dollar criterion and a noncognitive biodata test instrument for 12 companies and over 12,000 life insurance sales agents, Brown (1981) found that 62% of observed variation was accounted for by the artifacts; the remainder may have been due to company differences. Consequently, though support was found for validity generalization, this study cannot totally reject situational specificity.

DEBATE   Several statistical models have been proposed for estimating the extent of variance due to artifacts. The models range from a "bare bones" one in which only sampling error is of concern to ones in which several adjustments are made independently or simultaneously. Schmidt, Hunter, and Pearlman (Hunter et al 1982b, Schmidt et al 1982a) have debated Callender, Osburn, and associates (Callender & Osburn 1981, 1982, Callender et al 1982) on the estimation procedures and models. Linn & Dunbar (1982), who provide an excellent review of nine analytical procedures, effectively sum up the debate: "All of the evidence leads to the conclusion that for practical purposes the difference between the . . . procedures are quite small" (p. 25). If anything, all procedures overestimate the variance of true validities, creating a slight bias that works *against* a conclusion of validity generalization.

IMPLICATIONS   The obvious practical implication of the validity generalization results is that selection procedure development can become less costly and time consuming. Furthermore, Baker & Terpstra (1982) suggested that organizations may increase their use of tests without necessarily validating them. One can even go so far as to suggest that practitioners and researchers will only need to analyze jobs or situations of concern, and on the basis of these analyses, consult tables of generalized validities from the numerous previous studies using various predictors in similar circumstances (Schoenfeldt 1982). Compilation and subsequent use of such tables represents a reliance on a data base that is generally much greater than one obtained in an individual study.

ISSUES IN GENERALIZING VALIDITY GENERALIZATION   Perhaps the two major impacts of the work by Schmidt, Hunter, and associates have been: (*a*) the application of meta analytical techniques to personnel selection; such analyses in all areas of industrial/organizational psychology will be fruitful as we strive to increase our theoretical understanding of personnel issues [see Reilly et al (1981), Terborg et al (1982) and Mabe & West (1982) for meta analyses of RJPs, absenteeism, and peer evaluation, respectively]; (*b*) the specific finding that *cognitive* ability tests have nonzero validities; one explanation for the latter result is that cognitive tests perhaps have a common general factor such as intelligence (Tenopyr 1981). But stating that tests have nonzero validities still leaves room for additional research on the impact of the situation on both validity and performance. It seems that at present an inferential leap needs to be made from concluding that validities are more generalizable than presumed and the position that there is no such thing as situational specificity (Linn & Dunbar 1982). More needs to be understood about validity generalization. For example:

1. Before situational specificity is to be rejected totally, we ought to know what defines the situation. In most of the validity generalization studies, situations are different validity studies. Situations, tasks, and jobs have been used as moderator variables. What are the constructs that cause the variability in these moderators? Perhaps the more interesting theoretical question is: What are the common denominators to the situations to suggest that validities are similar? It must be more than the tasks involved in the jobs, because work as a computer programmer for the federal government is not the same as a computer

programmer for a large corporation or local privately owned and operated business (or is it?). This is where research on taxonomies becomes relevant. The cognitive component of programming may be the same from situation to situation, but this is only one aspect of the job. Perhaps the commonality among situations is the factor that is related to the commonality among tests, and this commonality is unrelated to "true" performance.

2. The "criterion problem." In general, *overall* training or job performance criteria have been used. Where a number of dimensions have been available, composites are formed to represent overall job performance (see Schmidt et al 1981a). It is feasible that the composite measure does not reflect the raters' overall composition strategy. Thus, basic theoretical research interest should be to determine whether a test's validities are equivalent across dimensions that reflect the job as well as the overall measure; the Dunnette et al (1982) study is an initial start.

3. On a conceptual level, the statement that any cognitive test is a valid predictor of performance on any job suggests that Person A, who scores highly on Test 1, is likely to perform above average on Jobs X, Y, Z, etc. Does this mean that Person A will perform successfully as an accountant (Job X)? electrician (Job Y)? and Brain Surgeon (Job Z)? For a test-job performance validity to be relatively constant from situation to situation, Person A's test performance and job performance needs to be relatively constant. Job performance is a function of motivation, interests, and ability as well as situational variables such as reward systems, leadership style, group dynamics, and the like. Hence, a pure test of the influence of situational specificity may require a repeated measures design in which the same individual performs the same job in different situations or different jobs in the same/different situation (only possible in the laboratory!).

4. A lack of a difference in correlation coefficients may not preclude the possibility of situational differences either in slopes or in intercepts (Linn & Dunbar 1982); we may need to examine directly interactions between situational variables and validities (Cotton & Cook 1982).

5. Every test entails its own true score, even when it is known that a group of tests measures the same ability or achievement variable (Hambleton & van der Linden 1982). This condition has resulted in a pursuit of IRT as the modern measurement theory, a notion that individualizes tests and scores. Does the assumption of latent traits that can be assessed by different sets or combinations of items provide clues and/or support for the validity generalization results? Discussion of the relationship between IRT and validity generalization is needed.

6. The previously cited practical implications of a table of generalized validities is of particular concern. Concentration on situational specificity may have frozen the field into isolated attempts to validate particular tests. Validity

generalization moves us toward greater construct validation; the Bayesian emphasis within meta analytical techniques is a positive and advantageous use of integrating new data into our data base. However, if we rely exclusively on tables to implement selection systems, will the field again freeze and discourage attempts to develop new and better predictors? At best, individual validities may reach .4 or .5 while composites may reach .6; i.e. at most, 36% of criterion variance is accountable—more can be explained. In addition, there are situations for which content valid tests (e.g. performance tests) may be more useful than cognitive ability tests. We hope that the validity generalization result does not inhibit the search for better prediction.

Cross-Validation

The issue of cross-validation has always been a thorn in the side of personnel researchers. Textbooks state it must be done, published research shows it is a rarity. A recent symposium chaired by Grant (1982) may again bring the topic to the forefront, particularly since computers should facilitate analyses called for by some of the more interesting cross-validation strategies. For example, Drehmer & Morris (1981) have written a program for a most appealing cross-validation strategy in which equations are developed on N-1 subjects and the unbiased regression estimates are used to predict the criterion value of the single holdout. N-1 prediction equations are derived each time with a different single holdout and on as large a sample as is feasible.

Rather than using ordinary least squares (OLS) multiple regression, ridge regression has been found to produce better cross-validated results (Cattin 1981, Faden & Bobko 1982, Hornick 1982). Ridge regression weights have a lower mean square error than do the unbiased parameter estimates obtained with OLS. On the other hand, according to Schmitt (1982), shrinkage formulas are more appropriate than empirical cross-validation. His analysis was particularly supportive of the Cattin (1980) formula.

Cutoff Scores

One procedure for setting cutoff scores for a particular test is to have judges examine item content and subsequently estimate the probable score of a hypothetical examinee responding at the level of minimum acceptable performance. This strategy can be implemented by procedures developed by Angoff, Ebel, or Nedelsky (Saunders et al 1981), but comparative results indicate inconsistent conclusions (Harasym 1981, van der Linden 1982). Of special interest is van der Linden's (1982) use of an IRT procedure to compare cutoff methods. Procedures using utility concepts and Bayesian decision theory have also been suggested (Chuang et al 1981, Mellenbergh & van der Linden 1981).

VALIDITY CONCEPTS AND ISSUES

Although the recent past has generated conceptual discussions on content and construct validity, the last 2 years have been devoid of exciting or different viewpoints on validity. Perhaps we may be getting away from discussions of "types" of validity and recognizing that the nature of validity varies to greater or lesser degree as a function of the specific question being considered. However, most of what appeared in 1981–82 concerned the means by which to determine the several aspects of validity.

Criterion-Related Validity

Most textbooks dealing with validity have suggested that concurrent validation is not a substitute for predictive validity. Yet a review by Barrett et al (1981) concluded that predictive and concurrent validation yield the same results. They argued that the typical concerns for concurrent validity's representativeness of applicant population, restriction of range, and impact of training and experience are trivial. Guion & Cranny (1982) responded by pointing out distinctions between and within longitudinal, predictive, follow-up designs and cross-sectional, concurrent, and present-employee designs. Also, lack of data for informed estimates of appropriate population parameters suggests that the designs are not equivalent and interchangeable.

Construct Validity

Messick (1981) has continued to argue cogently for the usefulness of construct validity, particularly for developing intuitive systems of meaning for observed relationships. Emphasis on construct validity will not only lead to a better understanding of our measures, but also it will contribute to validity generalization and theoretical formulation of personnel decisions. We need to examine construct validity by means other than the usual multitrait-multimethod paradigms. We need to consider as well latent trait models (Schoenfeldt 1982), confirmatory factor analysis (Rezmovic & Rezmovic 1981), and fidelity coefficients (Drasgow & Miller 1982) that can be used to determine the relationship between predictor scores based on measurement operations and the underlying construct.

Another area that might foster our understanding and implementation of construct validity is generalizability theory. Even though generalizability theory is an extension of the concept of reliability, it clarifies both content and construct validity (Cronbach et al 1972). Recent contributions by Kane (1982), Conger (1981), and P. L. Smith (1981) show how generalizability theory is a useful means by which to estimate variance components for different effects.

Content Validity

One of the criticisms of content validity is that it is a judgment call without a quantifiable index. Hamilton (1981) argued for and showed how the J-coefficient derived from Primoff's (1975) job element method can provide evidence for content validity; it is a form of synthetic validity that can establish the link between tests and job elements. Trattner (1982), too, linked the J-coefficient to synthetic validity, though he claimed that construct validity as described in the Uniform Guidelines on Employee Selection Procedures (UN-GESP 1978) is, in effect, synthetic validity. Perhaps confusion would be clarified if we adopted the position that the *procedures* for criterion-related and content validities are reflections of construct validity.

CLASSIFICATION AND PLACEMENT

Though classification and placement systems are ideals for which we strive, little published research dealing with a work setting has appeared, except for a discussion on utility estimates (Hunter & Schmidt 1982). Published research has been either in a college (Eberhardt & Muchinsky 1982b, Mumford et al 1982) or in a military setting (Tubiana & Ben-Shakhar 1982). These examples focused on biodata, education level, test scores, and motivational factors as inputs into a classification system. Gottfredson (1982) took a different approach and suggested that classification can be accomplished by studying regularities in the movements of workers among jobs rather than worker characteristics per se.

Speculation on why classification has been ignored include: (*a*) its procedures and designs are too complex; (*b*) organizations are unwilling to hire without a specific opening for a specific job; (*c*) hiring a "generalist" prolongs a return on the organization's investment; and (*d*) individuals are unwilling to go into organizations that do not have specific jobs in mind. Without continuing the "call for more research on classification," we suggest that concern for career paths may foster such research. Perhaps the results of validity generalization may have more impact. That is, since cognitive ability tests have been demonstrated to be valid predictors for any job, organizations may feel more comfortable moving members around into and out of various positions.

UTILITY ANALYSIS

An unfortunate myth that has developed among many business decision makers is that employee selection methods and other behavioral science-based organizational interventions have had little impact on workforce productivity, in part because statistical indices of utility have had little impact on decision makers.

Like it or not, the language of business is dollars, not correlation coefficients, indicies of forecasting efficiency, r^2, or improved performance in terms of standard deviations.

Regression-based, decision-theoretic utility models have been available for years (see Cascio 1982c, Landy et al 1982a for reviews), but they were not applied much in practice, principally because of the difficulty of estimating a crucial parameter, the standard deviation of job performance in dollars (SD_e). It was thought that cost accounting procedures were necessary to estimate SD_e, but Schmidt et al (1979) developed a global estimation procedure as an alternative. Support for the major assumption of and the accuracy of that procedure has been obtained by Bobko & Karren (1982). Nevertheless, the procedure may also have its drawbacks. In a reanalysis of the Schmidt et al (1979) data, Janz (1982b) found that although a small standard error of the mean was reported, the actual within-sample distribution of estimates was large and also skewed. Variance of this sort is difficult to ascribe to idiosyncratic differences, and should be the focus of future tests of the method. However, understanding the components of supervisors' estimates may be more important from a theoretical than a practical perspective. This procedure does have the advantage of providing information about the degree of agreement among supervisors in terms of the distribution of value estimates for 15th, 50th, and 85th percentile employees, but further empirical work is needed to determine the minimal or optimal number of supervisors to use in making the estimates.

Three other approaches to estimating SD_e are now available, and all need further critical evaluation, preferably in a comparative framework. Janz (1982b) described and tested a method in which persons familiar with a job were asked to judge how often workers in the top, middle, and bottom thirds of the distribution on each behaviorally based job dimension exhibited effective and ineffective job behaviors (each dollar valued) associated with that dimension. The judgments are then summed within a dimension and combined to estimate SD_e. Although this method has promise, its major shortcoming seems to be in developing market values for outcomes in jobs other than short-cycle, production-oriented ones. Two other methods, CREPID (Cascio 1982c) and the method used by Arnold et al (1982), base estimates of SD_e on salary. Schmidt et al (1982b) estimated that SD_e for a given job falls between 40%–70% of annual salary. In a study of 602 Bell System first level managers located in three states and representing five different job classes, CREPID ratings varied from 40% to 50% of actual annual salaries (W. F. Cascio, unpublished report, 1982). While such results are encouraging, Cronbach (personal communication, 1982) has pointed out that whatever the SD of judged contribution, it is essentially scaled to be proportional to average salary. If job evaluation is adequate, CREPID may be justified in most jobs. On the other hand, supply and demand (as well as seniority) play a part in determining salary, and therefore the shape of the salary distribution within a job may not match that of the CREPID ratings for the same workers. If real progress is to be made, therefore, comparative studies of these various approaches to SD_e estimation are necessary in a context where meaningful accounting figures can also be brought to bear.

Schmidt et al (1982b) have shown that the formula for selection utility can be generalized to apply to any personnel program designed to increase job performance among those "treated" using the program (e.g. training programs). The key parameter necessary to do this is d_t, the true difference in job performance between the average trained and untrained employee in SD units. This parameter is directly analogous to the true validity coefficient in selection. Clearly experimental or quasi-experimental evaluations of "before" versus "after" intervention performance in the estimation of d_t are subject to the same threats to internal validity as are all other program evaluation efforts. On the other hand, the cumulated results of all available studies in a given area may provide more realistic estimates of d_t. Thus Landy et al (1982a) reported a conservative estimate of the "validity" of performance evaluation and feedback of .30. This value was then transformed to d_t and put into the general utility equation to yield a one-year payoff of $5.3 million. Similar cumulative reviews and subsequent utility analyses can make a valuable contribution to our knowledge of the potential impact of behavioral science interventions. Now that intervention evaluation research can be expressed in terms of dollars (and that traditional t, F, or correlation indicies can be converted to d_t), decision makers can more readily assess the merits of intervention programs. But the real question remains: will more evaluations of organizational interventions be done? Hopefully future *Annual Review* chapters can answer that question affirmatively.

Boudreau (1983a) has noted that the utility models proposed to date are deficient in that they do not recognize the economic effects of variable costs, corporate taxes, and discount rates. Since these are basic to organizational decision making, and therefore basic to the definition and interpretation of personnel program utility, they must be considered. Doing so could reduce existing utility estimates by 60% or more, but they arguably would be more accurate. A utility formula incorporating these economic factors is proposed. In another sense, however, existing utility estimates may understate the true total value of personnel programs, for they only express the utility of adding one treated cohort to the existing stock of employees. Yet personnel programs are typically not applied to only one group of employees. Often they are continued and reapplied to new groups of employees moving into and out of the workforce. Boudreau (1983b) has algebraically modified the general utility equation to take account of these "additive cohort effects." Using the Landy et al (1982a) data, their one-year estimate was cut in half, but it was expanded substantially when the impact of additional employee flows was taken into account. Consideration of the above economic effects and the effect of employee flows are important if the purpose of utility analysis is to determine absolute gain. The additional effort required to do the analysis is justifiable in that case. However, if the purpose of the analysis is simply to help decision makers choose one alternative program in preference to others, relative gains are most important, and the simpler utility model is appropriate. Indeed relative gains are likely to be most important in nearly all contexts, since it is extremely unlikely that the actual dollar savings indicated by the utility figures can ever be validated in practice. Because even slight variations in all parameters can lead to large changes in estimated dollar gains, it is probably safer to speak in terms of relative rather than absolute gains to be realized.

So far, theoretical developments in this area have outpaced practical applications. One theoretical question that should receive greater empirical attention in different organizational contexts is the relationships among the utilities of selection, training, and other organizational interventions. As Schmidt et al (1982b) and Landy et al (1982a) have noted, they may be interactive or additive, depending on such parameters as the selection ratio, selection validity, and SD_e. To be sure, these questions need to be addressed in the context of an overall personnel decision system.

LEGAL ISSUES IN PERSONNEL DECISIONS

Civil rights laws and agencies charged with enforcing those laws clearly have stimulated the development of personnel research and more enlightened personnel policies and practices in many organizations. Yet given the growing volume of case law in this area, it is apparent that the laws and federal agency interpretive guidelines for compliance are still subject to divergent interpretations. Thus professional practices will continue to evolve as additional research and judicial rulings accumulate. In the following sections we consider what has been learned from recent case law relevant to personnel decisions.

Job Analysis

Thompson & Thompson (1982) reviewed 26 federal court cases to determine the criteria used by the courts in their assessment of job analyses used to develop and validate selection tests. To withstand legal challenge, it was suggested that job analysis should focus on tasks, be in written form, include multiple data sources and large samples, and that relative degrees of entry-level competencies be specified. While this is certainly the case when a content-oriented validation strategy is used, such information might be essential to a thorough job analysis even if other descriptors were to be used for other functions. These might include criterion development, job family development, or inferences regarding constructs. Note, however, that these case-law-based suggestions for task-oriented job analysis are inconsistent with recent suggestions for global job analyses (see earlier Job Analysis section).

Selection

The UGESP (Equal Employment Opportunity Commission 1978) note that validity only becomes a relevant concern when adverse impact against a particular subgroup is demonstrated. However, suppose the "bottom line" of new hires for a job indicates no adverse impact, but a component of the selection procedure clearly does? Such was the issue in *Connecticut v. Teal* (1982). The Supreme Court ruled that a good "bottom line" does not preclude a prima facie case nor does it provide a defense to a prima facie case. According to the court, Congress never intended to give an employer license to discriminate against some employees on the basis of race or sex merely because other members of the employee's group are treated favorably. Title VII protects the individual employee rather than the minority group as a whole.

In a review of legal interpretations of tests, testing practices, and psychometric concepts, Bersoff (1981) noted that such scrutiny has alerted everyone to the pervasiveness of bias, even as a result of innocent and apparently benign practices; it has engendered more professional accountability; and it has accelerated the search for improved and alternative assessment techniques. On the other hand, the courts apparently still regard content, construct, and criterion-related validity as distinct forms of validation and not as subsets within the unifying and common framework of construct validity.

The Employment Interview

Litigation involving the employment interview has involved two types of issues: 1. do particular types of questions convey an impression of an underlying discriminatory attitude or intent; and 2. do interviewers' decisions demonstrate an adverse impact on protected groups? Stereotyping and differential behavior emitted during the interview could potentially contribute to disparate treatment across groups, yet little has been done to examine stereotyping or any other processes or variables (situational or personal) that might contribute to differential evaluations (Arvey & Campion 1982).

Experience Requirements

Arvey & McGowen (1982) reviewed 45 cases dealing with experience requirements and noted that judicial rulings seem more fragmented and arbitrary than in other areas (e.g. testing). This may be due to a lack of clear-cut statistical evidence on which to make decisions, but still there are discernible trends in the litigation to date: 1. experience requirements are typically upheld when there are greater economic and human risks involved with failure to perform adequately (e.g. airplane pilots) or for higher level jobs that are more complex, but they are typically not upheld when they perpetuate a racial imbalance or past discrimination or when applied differentially; and 2. courts review experience requirements for evidence of business necessity.

Reverse Racial Preferences

It is generally accepted by legal scholars that racial classifications are not presumptively unconstitutional, but they do require a close relation to a compelling government purpose. In the *Fullilove v. Klutznick* (1980) case, a test of the constitutionality of the funding quota (10%) for minority-owned businesses on government construction projects as required in the Public Works Employment Act of 1977, five distinct forms of analysis were used by the justices, thus suggesting a lack of a consistent method for testing the constitutionality of Congressionally enacted minority preferences. "Practically speaking, what the Court has accomplished in the three major 'reverse discrimination' decisions it has issued—*Bakke, Steelworkers v. Weber, and Fullilove*—is to legitimize certain discrete types of racial preferences, but to accomplish this in so muddled a fashion as to preserve its freedom of action when it considers related cases in years ahead" (Phillips 1981, pp. 211, 212).

Performance Appraisal

It is apparent from the litigation in this area that appraisal systems are considered "tests" if in any way they serve as bases for personnel decisions. In view of the *Teal* decision, it appears that appraisal systems must be validated whether or not they produce adverse impact. In independent reviews of performance appraisal cases, Cascio & Bernardin (1981) and Feild & Holley (1982) found similar results. Unsuccessful defendants' appraisal systems tended to be those of industrial organizations, raters were not given specific instructions on how to complete the appraisal, the appraisal system was trait- rather than behavior-oriented, the system was developed without the benefit of a job analysis, and the results of appraisals were not reviewed with each employee. There is both good news and bad news in these results. The good news is that the pattern of the results is consistent with current performance appraisal research. The bad news is that the lag between scientific knowledge and practical application seems so broad. At the very least, appraisal systems should be developed and applied in accordance with requirements specified in the UGESP (Equal Employment Opportunity Commission 1978), for the guidelines generally were cited by the courts as the principal basis for their rulings against the defendant.

A slightly different perspective on appraisal systems stems from their use in promotion decisions. Kleiman & Durham (1981) reviewed 23 Title VII cases in this area and offered the following suggestions (nonredundant but additive to those noted above). First, to assess possible adverse impact, an organization should keep accurate records of who is eligible for and interested in the promoted position. Eligibility and interest are important since the courts have used five different methods to gauge adverse impact. Second, appraisal systems and raters need to be validated. To use a lower level appraisal as a basis for promotion, be prepared to demonstrate high overlap between the requirements of the two positions. Continue to develop evidence to demonstrate the construct validity of the appraisal system.

Seniority

Of the major legal issues adjudicated relevant to seniority, perhaps the most important is the legality of seniority systems which, though neutral on their face, perpetuate employment disadvantages of minorities. A 1982 Supreme Court decision, *American Tobacco Company v. Patterson,* extended a previous ruling such that seniority systems initiated after the 1964 Civil Rights Act are legal as long as they were not designed intentionally to discriminate unfairly. Thus the legality of seniority systems will not be judged in terms of adverse impact on women or minorities, and it will be more difficult to challenge them as biased.

Sexual Harassment

Psychologists and other professionals can contribute to the understanding and control of sexual harassment in several ways, principally through research and subsequent guidance. At present there is not even a reliable account of how extensive sexual harassment is (Faley 1982). Existing survey data are unreliable because of inadequate definitions, "loaded" questions, poor sampling strategies, and low response rates. Multiple data sources, including less reactive measures (Webb et al 1981), are sorely needed in order to lend more credibility to such research. Perhaps a more important research need is an understanding of what sexual harassment is and how it affects employment. For example, we need a better specification of the hypothetical linkages that will cast this subject into a testable theoretical framework. Little is known about the antecedents of harassment or the precise relationship between harassment and other organizational variables (e.g. job performance, turnover, morale) (Faley 1982). Finally, information about the effects of harassment on productivity would make explicit to employers the monetary cost of ignoring the problem.

EQUAL EMPLOYMENT OPPORTUNITY

Every public opinion poll based on representative national samples drawn between 1950 and the present shows that a majority of Americans, black and white, support equal opportunity and reject differential treatment based on race, regardless of its alleged purposes or results (Lerner 1981). There is agreement on the ends to be achieved, but there is disagreement about the means to be used. EEO has been, and is still, an emotionally charged issue. To be sure, all of us have the right to decide these questions for ourselves, according to the dictates of our own consciences. Yet as social scientists we also have the obligation to examine the data carefully and objectively before doing so. One portion of those data are summarized below.

Adverse Impact

The triggering mechanism for the investigation of possible unlawful discrimination is adverse impact, a selection rate for any race, sex, or ethnic group which is less than 4/5ths (80%) of the rate of the group with the highest rate . . . but . . . greater differences in selection rate may not constitute adverse impact when the differences are based on small numbers (UGESP; Equal Employment Opportunity Commission 1978, Section 4D). The determination of adverse impact is not a trivial problem, especially when the numbers are small, since statistical power will generally also be small. Thus the equivocality in the UGESP permits compliance agencies to use other than statistical evidence when such evidence is equivocal. As we noted earlier, at least five different procedures have been used to determine adverse impact. In an effort to resolve this confusion, statistically and psychometrically acceptable standards for determining adverse impact have been proposed (Cronbach & Schaeffer 1981, Ironson et al 1982, Wing 1981, 1982). Thus Kriska & Milligan (1982) suggested using logit analysis when race and sex are used to predict the dependent variable of employment status (hired/not hired). Ironson et al (1982) have shown that tests of adverse impact are confounded with psychometric properties of the test. Adverse impact depends on true ability differences, test characteristic curves, and the cutting score used. Consequently, IRT should be used as a basis for assessing adverse impact.

The existence of adverse impact signals possible unfairness in selection or promotion. Although a number of fairness models exist, none enjoys unconditional acceptance either in the profession or in the courts. In short, disagreement over the appropriate means for implementing fairness and EEO has not been resolved in the almost 20 years since passage of Title VII. It may never be, since fairness is really a question of utilities (Cascio 1982d).

Alternative Selection Procedures

When adverse impact on a selection measure is shown, the UGESP urge employers to seek alternative selection measures that are equally valid but produce less adverse impact. Reilly & Chao (1982) examined the validity, fairness, and feasibility of operational use of eight alternatives to standardized tests. Only biodata and peer evaluations were found to have validities substantially equal to those of standardized tests. There was no evidence that any alternatives met the criterion of having equal validity with less adverse impact. Similar results were reported by Tenopyr (1981) and by Hough et al (1981). Despite this compelling scientific evidence that equally valid alternative assessment procedures will not be found, employers will probably continue the "cosmic search" for alternatives. Legal and regulatory pressure to do so is unlikely to abate despite the scientific facts involved (Tenopyr 1981).

Testing

Testing is again in the public's eye. Much of the criticism has involved charges of bias and overemphasis in policy making (Gould 1981, Strenio 1981). After reviewing the massive literature on this question, Cole (1981) concluded that questions of bias are fundamentally questions of validity. Yet whether or not tests are biased, their use is only a small part of the complex social policy issues facing the courts, the legislatures, and the citizenry at large. These policy issues require decisions about values that must be made whether or not tests are involved.

Proponents of tests claim that tests are unbiased because they accurately reflect ability. Critics argue that standardized tests are inappropriate because minority groups have lacked equal opportunity and therefore their abilities are not accurately assessed. These differences of opinion between proponents and critics of testing are nowhere better illustrated than in Nader's raid on the testing industry (Kaplan 1982, Linn 1982b), and in the consent decree surrounding the use of the PACE test to select college graduates for federal government jobs (Olian & Wilcox 1982). In the consent decree involving PACE, the impetus was adverse impact against Hispanics and blacks. Critics claimed that the validity evidence presented for the test was insufficient. On the other hand, the written test may not have been the catalyst for adverse impact against the Hispanics, for Ramos (1981) has shown that tests given in Spanish are more likely to improve scores on nonverbal than on written tests. In view of the accumulated evidence regarding the validity of alternatives to tests, it seems that both parties will lose. Virtually all alternatives to written tests are more costly, and applicants may well be evaluated on less valid instruments. In one instance, for example, a valid manual dexterity test that produced no adverse impact was not used in preference to interview judgments of manual dexterity. The interview judgments yielded an average validity of 0.05 and produced adverse impact (Guion & Imada 1981). At first glance it may appear that the goals of productivity improvement and social progress resulting from the use of tests are inconsistent. They need not be. Careful attention to the intrinsic quality of tests, plus proper interpretation of test scores, can contribute to both of these goals.

Unfair Discrimination

During the period of this review, members of three groups were the subjects of research on unfair discrimination: blacks, women, and the handicapped. In addition, the EEO implications of robotics were considered. Wendelken & Inn (1981) argued that the results of many studies of the impact of nonperformance factors (e.g. rater and ratee gender and race) on performance appraisals may be attributable to a research design that bears little resemblance to the appraisal process in real organizational contexts.

In an actual organizational context they found that all of these sources of variance accounted for no more than 4% of the total variance in performance ratings. This is encouraging, though future research should expand the range and complexity of the assessment exercises to simulate more completely actual job duties. In a laboratory study, Taylor & Ilgen (1981) found bias against females in initial placement decisions. On the bright side, though, the experience of working with and observing competent females reduced such bias. Two directions for research are suggested by these findings. First, field replications are needed. Second, and more important, are investigations of the impact that highly visible, well-established, successful women have on the motivation and career opportunities of other females within the organizational structure. A related study (Chacko 1982) found that women who perceived that they were selected because of their sex had less organizational commitment, less satisfaction with their work, with supervision, and with their co-workers, and they experienced more role conflict and role ambiguity than women who felt that sex was not an important factor in their selection.

In a review of the literature on the handicapped in the work force, Freedman & Keller (1981) found that case studies of demonstration projects that lack standardized and objective measures of variables and outcomes predominate. Many studies use a one-time cross-sectional design of after-only measures without control or comparison groups. Typically those responsible for the design, implementation, and success of the demonstration project are also those who evaluate its effectiveness. If valid inferences are to be drawn concerning policies that affect the handicapped, careful evaluation research, based on sound experimental design, is essential. Decision makers in many industries face a tough and wrenching policy choice in the coming years: to what extent, if at all, will the workforce be staffed by robots instead of humans? On most job-related criteria, the robot wins hands down (Whaley 1982). Research should be conducted now to assess the organizational impact of robotics (e.g.

on structure, span of control, job descriptions, job qualifications of the human workers).

Privacy

Little is known about the parameters of "invasion of privacy" perceptions, although evidence is beginning to accumulate (Noel 1981, Tolchinsky et al 1981, Woodman et al 1982). However, the attitudes of employees toward "invasion of privacy" may not be as important as the effects of perceived invasion of privacy on behavior. Future studies should investigate such behavioral responses, as well as the impact of privacy in the broader organizational context. That is, does perceived invasion of privacy also affect organizational factors such as productivity, job satisfaction, and organizational commitment? With the continued proliferation of both intra- and extra-organizational data banks, this kind of research is likely to find immediate application.

JOB EVALUATION

Job evaluation has received scant research attention from psychologists over the past 35 years. With the exception of one application of social judgment and latent trait theories to the process (Guion 1982), almost no research has been done on the reliability or validity of job evaluation systems. Despite such limitations, job evaluation does serve the administrative function of linking internal and external labor markets. No other procedure yet devised performs this function better.

Rekindled interest in job evaluation can be traced to the comparable worth issue. Comparable worth means that jobs that require comparable (not equal, but comparable) skills, effort, and responsibility should earn comparable wages. This is a compensation issue since it involves pay, and it is a discrimination issue since it deals with differences in levels of pay between men and women. The "earnings gap" between males and females has been documented carefully (D. Kully, unpublished report 1981), but it is important to stress that actual pay rates to individuals typically reflect not only the jobs they hold, but also their job-related qualifications, past job performance, and length of experience. Hence attribution of differences in pay only to a single source (e.g. gender) controlling for differences in job responsibility (Sigelman et al 1982) may be erroneous.

Advocates of comparable worth make two underlying assumptions: (a) the worth of each job can be measured independently of the market, and (b) the worth of dissimilar jobs can be compared and resulting differences in pay rates may be attributed to unlawful discrimination (Nelson et al 1980). These are questionable assumptions; support for them rests squarely on the careful implementation of job evaluation as a vehicle for determining the relative worth of jobs. As in other judgmental processes, bias is an ever-present threat.

In *County of Washington v. Gunther* (1981), the Supreme Court concluded that job evaluation could be used in a discriminatory fashion in establishing pay differentials. The National Academy of Science's study of job evaluation (Treiman & Hartmann 1981) reached a similar conclusion and identified two sources of potential bias. First, systematic sex-based errors (downgrading predominately female jobs and/or inflating predominately male jobs) could contaminate the job evaluation process. Cascio & O'Reilly (1981) found modest support for such bias in a laboratory investigation, but Arvey et al (1982), working in a job analysis context, did not.

A second source of possible bias is systematic error in the criteria typically used to validate job evaluation results—external market rates. This practice may confound the compensation issues of external and internal equity. If the National Academy of Science's conclusion is true that sex-based discrimination in external wage distributions is likely (Treiman & Hartmann 1981), then the use of external wage rates as criteria in validating job evaluation results will perpetuate sex discrimination in setting internal wage rates.

A construct validity paradigm appears to be a logical solution to the problem of validating any job evaluation technique. Convergence among alternative job evaluation measures of the same value or worth constructs and discrimination among measures of different value or worth constructs would be sought. Construct validity, however, is a technique that requires a theory or model upon which to base convergent and discriminant validity judgments. Compensation theory has not yet reached that stage. So until normative theories of job worth are developed, it will remain difficult to establish the construct validity of job evaluation as a measure of job worth (Wallace & Fay 1981).

Using mathematical simulation, Schwab & Wichern (1983) investigated the consequences of systematic sex-related bias in the evaluation and/or analysis of jobs and in the wage distribution used as the criterion in validation. Assuming true scores and no discrimination (all jobs paid according to their compensable factor scores), systematic error in the criterion was found to have the generally detrimental effects assumed. However, the widely accepted conclusion that pro-male sex bias in the job evaluation process *necessarily* increases wage differentials to the disadvantage of female jobs was not supported. The impact on total wages depends on the relationships among several interrelated variables. In addition, published recommendations made to establish sex-free wage rates, in some cases, would not do so. To identify random and systematic errors in the predictor variable(s), Schwab & Wichern (1983) applied a reverse regression procedure suggested by Roberts (1980). However, additional simulation research is necessary before we can assess the value of this proce-

dure with any degree of confidence. Future research also should use a multimethod approach to study the job evaluation process for possible systematic
errors; the general design employed in sex effects studies of performance
appraisal and selection could easily be extended to job evaluation (Schwab &
Wichern 1983). In fact, a major threat to the external validity of studies using
"paper people" would be less of an issue in job evaluation research since the
unit of analysis in such research is often a written job description.

Studies by Page et al (1982) and Gomez-Mejia et al (1982) comparing the
relative accuracy and practical utility of seven different job evaluation
approaches suggest that there is no "best" method of job evaluation. The results
of 657 job evaluations indicated that traditional and hybrid systems (regression
analysis incorporated within the framework of a traditional point-factor
method) are at least as accurate, reliable, and objective in predicting grade level
as are statistical policy-capturing methods. One issue that has been ignored
almost totally in the literature is the relative *acceptability* of alternative
methods. Gomez-Mejia et al (1982) assessed ten aspects of acceptability and
found that the hybrid system consistently was judged superior to other methods
across all ten dimensions.

SUMMARY

One of the purposes of a chapter in the *Annual Review of Psychology* is to
interpret the progress and direction of research in the field reviewed. We have
presented our interpretation of the field as it has been documented by mainly
published research during the 1981–82 years. In order to put the field into a
broader perspective, we developed a capsule summary of six previous *Annual
Review* chapters on personnel psychology (Guion 1967, Owens & Jewell 1969,
Bray & Moses 1972, Ash & Kroeker 1975, Dunnette & Borman 1979, Tenopyr
& Oeltjen 1982). Because of space limitations, the capsule summary is printed
in tabular form.

The summary begins with Guion's review (1967) since his coverage period
coincides with perhaps the most significant stimulant for the field, passage of
the 1964 Civil Rights Act and its Title VII, which evolved into federal
regulation, guidelines, and legal challenges to tests and selection issues. The
summary is built around the broad topical areas covered in our review. Within
these broad topics and for each of the six prior reviews, we have indicated,
where possible: (*a*) a select list of specific *topics*, items, and issues covered; (*b*)
themes and *conclusions* drawn by the reviewers; (*c*) *trends* emerging at the
time; and (*d*) *predictions* of where the area was going and what its research
needs were. These categorizations are admittedly fuzzy and forced, but we
hope that the reader's interpretation of our content analysis will provide some
insight into the past.

Table 1 Capsule summary of previous *Annual Reviews* on personnel issues

TOPIC	GUION (1/64–4/66)	OWENS & JEWELL (5/66–12/67)	BRAY & MOSES (1968–70)	ASH & KROEKER (1971–73)	DUNNETTE & BORMAN (1974–77)	TENOPYR & OELTJEN (1978–80)
Human Resource Planning		Topic: Recruitment Conclusion: It has been ignored Trend: Awareness of personnel selection as a systems function will increase	Theme: Selection procedures are part of a system that depends on job training and other factors Conclusion: We are missing a unified system that integrates manpower planning, selection, training, and development. Little effort to associate selection systems within overall manpower requirements Prediction: Aptitudes, motivations, training, organizational reward systems, quality of supervision, etc will be emphasized in selection systems considerations	Theme: Increased attention to systems approaches to selection and manpower problems Prediction: Little from literature will be translated into useful practices in near future	Theme: Planning, explicit decision making, and continuous monitoring of the HR system are the best ways to ensure EEO Trend: Present idealized, computer-assisted, interactive personnel selection and classification system; modeling internal labor markets to accomplish AA goals	Theme: Human resource planning is viewed as emerging field that has little input from industrial/organizational psychology; however, a well-developed HR system can provide valuable inputs to personnel psychologists
Job Analysis				Conclusion: A major area for exploration and theorizing	Predictions: 1. Increased knowledge about jobs and inferred attributes should be useful in improving matches between people and jobs (classification); 2. job data banks should facilitate idealized counseling and job placement system	Topics: Procedures for job analysis such as CODAP, PAQ; interpretation of results Conclusion: No consensus on the proper methods for assessing job similarities and for grouping jobs
Performance Measurement	Topics: The "criterion problem;" criteria dimensionality; rating formats—BARS can be expected to be used in the future	Topics: Multitrait-multimethod analysis; criteria dimensionality Themes: 1. Much of criterion research has been devoted to managerial performance; 2. concern for behavioral taxonomy for describing human tasks Prediction: Rating procedures of increasing sophistication and complexity will be utilized for management positions	Topics: The "criterion problem"; dimensionality of criteria; BARS; factors influencing performance of raters (a process issue) Themes: 1. Continued discredit of supervisory ratings; 2. unwillingness to use turnover and/or absenteeism in place of task performance as criterion; 3. few studies using job proficiency measures as criteria	Conclusion: Criterion is weak link in validation Theme: Status quo of the field Prediction: Major developments in the field are unlikely in the next half century	Topics: Errors in performance ratings; format comparisons; rater training; BARS; criteria dimensionality and validity; accuracy; individual differences correlates of performance ratings Theme: Process as opposed to outcomes Prediction: Increased emphasis of personality and person perception literature on ratings	Topics: Supervisory ratings (still most common criterion); peer and self assessment; rater training Trend: Lack of studies with objective performance criteria or with absenteeism and/or turnover as criteria in selection procedures

Table 1 *(continued)*

TOPIC	GUION (1/64–4/66)	OWENS & JEWELL (5/66–12/67)	BRAY & MOSES (1968–70)	ASH & KROEKER (1971–73)	DUNNETTE & BORMAN (1974–77)	TENOPYR & OELT-JEN (1978–80)
Performance Predictors	Topics: Selection studies for specific groups; predictors such as personality measures, personal history data, interview; clinical vs actuarial prediction Theme: Concern for wholeness and integrity of applicants as opposed to mechanistic, elementalistic view of human behavior Trends: More research and reports on mathematical models of clinical prediction Prediction: If process studies of interview decision making result in guides to making rational decisions, this line of research may prove to be most important selection research in decades	Topics: Maximum and typical performance measures; situation-specific studies; noncognitive measures; assessment centers (cautious about it) Trends: 1. Biodata are beginning to show true potential; 2. increased involvement with facilitating college recruitment due to interest in high-level personnel Predictions: 1. If criteria are judgmental, such as in management jobs, then there will be more use of judgmental predictors such as the assessment center; 2. selection interview will be subjected to intensive and extensive study regarding its reliability and validity; new interviewing methods will emerge	Topics: Aptitude tests; culture fair tests (fad is over); nonverbal tests Themes: Growth of interest in assessment center, biodata methods, and interview	Topics: Testing in public and private sectors; for females, professionals, education profession; assessment centers; reference checks; detection of proneness to theft Conclusions: 1. Continued strong use of assessment center; 2. too optimistic to conclude that significant advances have been made in interview process; 3. little published research on biodata despite great promise	Topics: Interview process, biodata, assessment centers; job samples Conclusions: 1. Little doubt that biodata can be used effectively to predict success in a variety of jobs; 2. favorable reports on assessment centers Needs: 1. Research should continue on the interview process; 2. need to know more on the technology related to job sample development	Topics: Alternatives to testing and selection procedures; interview process; experience and education; biodata; trainability; physical and perceptual tests; assessment centers Themes: 1. "Paper people" studies; 2. concern with what happens and not with what should happen in interview; 3. lack of published validation studies Needs: 1. Research on aging and handicapped; 2. theory of decision making in interview; catalogue of variables affecting interview; 3. validity generalization study of assessment center
Validity Concepts	Themes: 1. Growing awareness of distinction between description and prediction; 2. greater emphasis on predictive as opposed to concurrent validity	Trends: 1. Toward more sophisticated designs—moderator designs; 2. move away from concurrent to predictive validation Conclusion: The analytical search for enhanced differential validities is clearly a promising move in the right direction	Themes: 1. Convergent-discriminant validation; 2. expectancy tables as opposed to correlational statistics for validity reporting Trends: 1. Models emphasizing behavioral consistency and samples rather than signs; 2. focus on actual behavior at both predictor and criterion end	Topics: Synthetic validity; J–coefficient Conclusions: 1. Literature on a relevant methodology for demonstrating content validity is practically nonexistent; 2. the J–coefficient is one of most creative innovations but limited in use because of almost total absence of publication; 3. convergent-discriminant studies underrepresented	Conclusion: Compartmentalization of validity into content, construct, and criterion-related validities is oversimplification; too much emphasis on what type of validity to support as opposed to why one wants to use test	Conclusion: All validities are essentially construct validity Trend: More arguments for upgrading status of concurrent validity Needs: Research and development to prescribe the mechanics of establishing content or construct validity

Table 1 *(continued)*

TOPIC	GUION (1/64–4/66)	OWENS & JEWELL (5/66–12/67)	BRAY & MOSES (1968–70)	ASH & KROEKER (1971–73)	DUNNETTE & BORMAN (1974–77)	TENOPYR & OELT-JEN (1978–80)
Classification and Placement		Topics: Classification research section Theme: Emphasis on classification model in order to fit a maximum manpower utilization philosophy	Trend: Growing interest in developmental and placement strategies rather than selection per se		Prediction: Interactive personnel selection and classification system	
Methodological/Statistical Considerations	Topics: Response sets; answer sheet variations; factor scores as predictors; moderator designs Conclusions: 1. Disenchantment with traditional correlation; questioned homoscedasticity and linearity assumptions; 2. limited impact of decision theory because of complexity and near impossibility of translating designs to employment office; 3. validities will differ for different people Trends: Mathematical decision theory	Topics: Test bias; item selection and test length; cross-validation; statistical vs actuarial prediction Trends: Increased sensitivity to impact of experience, sets, and testing on test questionnaires	Topics: Moderator variables; multitrait analysis; test fairness, differential validity Themes: 1. Renewed interest in methodology for methodology's sake; 2. growing awareness of simulation techniques Conclusion: No firm conclusion on test fairness though most studies showing no differential validity need better criteria	Trend: 1. Increased application of multivariate statistical techniques to selection methodology; 2. slight activity in math modeling of decision strategies Conclusion: Given limited amount of hard data that are consistent, separate validation for ethnic subgroups should be undertaken Prediction: Development of selection procedures on industry-wide basis	Topics: Validity estimates and shrinkage, cross-validation Conclusions: 1. Differential validity is the exception rather than the rule; 2. better development of predictors and criteria is needed; 3. studies on nonlinear prediction have cooled Predictions: More emphasis on validity generalization	Topics: Shrinkage formulas and cross-validation; power; tailored testing Themes: 1. Little research on cutting scores; 2. little new development on selection fairness models Conclusions: 1. Differential validity is a pseudoproblem; 2. while there is validity generalization there is insufficient evidence to reject situational effects Needs: 1. A theory or taxonomy of situations; 2. study of effect of specific criteria on validity generalization
Utility	Conclusions: Not much impact of decision theory models on actual selection procedures Predicton: Decision theory is more sophisticated and more realistic than traditional validation model; its use will surely increase	Topic: Correlational decision theory vs functional utility	Topic: Measures of predictor efficiency Need: An inclusive utility view that encompasses training costs, turnover, proficiency, productivity as a function of total employment process Prediction: General utility considerations will come into play	Theme: A problem of considerable interest	Topic: Standard deviation of performance measured in dollars Predictions: Invocation of utility concepts will result in overcoming incompatibility between institutional (pure selection) and individual (classification) decision making	Need: The study of productivity relative to personnel selection should receive more attention

Table 1 *(continued)*

TOPIC	GUION (1/64–4/66)	OWENS & JEWELL (5/66–12/67)	BRAY & MOSES (1968–70)	ASH & KROEKER (1971–73)	DUNNETTE & BORMAN (1974–77)	TENOPYR & OELTJEN (1978–80)
EEO/Legal Issues	Topic: Civil Rights Act of 1964 and its full implications for personnel selection are unclear; invasion of privacy is an ethical concern	Topics: Invasion of privacy; negative feelings toward testing Trend: More consideration for rights, needs, and prior opportunities of applicants	Topics: Citation of cases Theme: Increased questioning of appropriateness of correlational validation model and its assumptions and components	Theme: Law, regulation, social and economic pressures have been shaping personnel practices in advance of, and sometimes in spite of the specific results of psychometric research on test technology Topics: Guidelines, standards; invasion of privacy Predictions: Those unwilling or unable to validate will give up testing	Topic: Selection research is a matter of legal concern since the Civil Rights Act of 1964	Topic: Comparison of Uniform Guidelines and Division 14 Principles
Job Evaluation						Theme: More input by industrial/organizational psychology into process

To us however, it appears that as a field we are still beating some areas into the ground (e.g. the interview); we are looking for new methodologies for old questions (e.g. indices of halo); we are jumping onto new hobby horses (e.g. BOS); we may even be going around in circles (e.g. return to emphasis on global supervisory ratings as criteria); and we are forever predicting and calling for the ideal human resources model, one that involves a classification base, in spite of the fact that there appears to be no one willing to do research on it in an employment setting (as evidenced by published literature). These pessimistic notes are in part countered by trends that may be viewed as positive. That is, we are attempting to find generalities in the field (e.g. validity generalization, construct validity, job similarities, taxonomies). At the same time, emphasis on details and processes is a positive step to further our understanding. We do not see a contradiction between the movement toward generalization and the emphasis on specific processes. Hopefully, the two will move our field from an applied, reactive orientation to external influences to one that has a theoretical formulation incorporating resources, tasks, environments, and systems.

The field's orientation toward research was an obvious theme throughout our review. Methods and strategies are more elegant and sophisticated than in the past, but such credits are diminished if they are applied to trivial issues or restricted samples. The external validity of research is a major concern. Much of the research is simulated, hypothetical, contrived, and based on students who are serving as subjects to fulfill a course requirement. Intentions rather than actual behaviors are too frequently the sole criterion. There is an increasing body of literature that suggests that cost/benefit analysis, accountability, and responsibility for decisions influence behavior (Payne 1982, Tetlock 1983). Responses in the hypothetical may not mirror responses in reality. We also need to consider and study more interesting questions within theoretical frameworks. We strongly suggest that the book by Campbell et al (1982) be reviewed for the series of questions that they found need studying.

Studies of the effects of subject characteristics (e.g. low or high on a variable, sex, age, etc) need to be undertaken because there is a theoretical basis for such expected differences. We need to focus meaningfully on the individual person and individual study and generate data that can be cumulated. In so doing, we need to incorporate that which we have shown can be derived from social, cognitive, and personality psychologies, but we also need to incorporate developmental psychology. Too much research is piecemeal, fragmented, and focused on minute aspects of a broader issue. We need to focus more on macro analyses that will identify critical variables. Then we must be concerned with implementation (Hakel et al 1982).

We indicated that processes are being studied in almost all domains of personnel research, but processes need to reflect time, change, and interactions. More longitudinal field research is needed that incorporates multiple measures and multiple measurements.

At several points in the chapter, we indicated specific research needs and questions to be asked. Our final "crystal ball gazing" suggests that we should also look to the following: 1. Within human resource planning and utility, more econometric models and issues should be studied by psychologists attempting to integrate human and economic factors into a system (e.g. role of pensions, no mandatory retirement. 2. Job analysis research should give secondary attention to methods and instead concentrate on examining the "truth" of responses. Results that indicate that all tasks are important, frequent, and difficult to perform simply are not convincing. Research should begin to examine response biases, perceptions, and response sets in relationship to job analysis results. 3. Performance measurement research will most likely continue to emphasize methods and attribution theory; indeed, the latter could replace cognitive dissonance theory as the pervasive explainer of all behavior. Hopefully, researchers will soon begin to focus on more objective indicators of criteria that have utility. 4. Performance predictors and assessment centers generally have been confined to rank and file or entry supervisory positions; there is a glaring omission in the literature on prediction/selection of performance for high level managers and executives. Perhaps the models and research strategies we have developed to date are not suitable for research with top managers. While idiographic approaches (case studies) may be a solution, there is a dire need for innovation in this area.

Finally, as we indicated earlier, our review was based on a topical approach. It is our hope and anticipation that future reviews will be able to depart from this strategy and will instead focus on issues or theories that illustrate the integrated nature of the field. This should come about as we engage in more research on models and processes and as we integrate data bases from diverse studies.

ACKNOWLEDGMENTS

The first author wrote his portion of this chapter while on sabbatical at AT&T's Human Resources Department. Special appreciation is offered to Drs. Richard J. Campbell and Joseph L. Moses, who provided opportunity, atmosphere, and support for this and other endeavors. We would like to thank Drs. Campbell, Moses, and Ken Pearlman for their constructive comments on portions of an earlier draft of this chapter.

Literature Cited

Adler, S., Golan, J. 1981. Lateness as a withdrawal behavior. *J. Appl. Psychol.* 66:544–54

Alluisi, E. A., Fleishman, E. A., eds. 1982. *Stress and Performance Effectiveness*, Vol. 3. Hillsdale, NJ: Erlbaum. 267 pp.

Alpander, G. C., Botter, C. H. 1981. An integrated model of strategic human resource planning and utilization. *Hum. Resour. Plan.* 4:189–208

American Tobacco Company v. Patterson. 1982. 102 Supreme Court Rep. 1534

Anderson, J. C., Milkovich, G. T., Tsui, A. 1981. A model of intra-organizational mobility. *Acad. Manage. Rev.* 6:529–38

Arnold, H. J., Feldman, D. C. 1982. A multivariate analysis of the determinants of job turnover. *J. Appl. Psychol.* 67:350–60

Arnold, J. D., Rauschenberger, J. M., Soubel, W. G., Guion, R. M. 1982. Validation and utility of a strength test for selecting steelworkers. *J. Appl. Psychol.* 67:588–604

Arvey, R. D., Campion, J. E. 1982. The employment interview: A summary and review of recent research. *Personnel Psychol.* 35:281–322

Arvey, R. D., Davis, G. A., McGowen, S. L., Dipboye, R. L. 1982. Potential sources of bias in job analytic processes. *Acad. Manage. J.* 25:618–29

Arvey, R. D., Maxwell, S. E., Gutenberg, R. L., Camp, C. 1981. Detecting job differences: A monte carlo study. *Personnel Psychol.* 34:709–30

Arvey, R. D., McGowen, S. L. 1982. *The use of experience requirements in selecting employees.* Presented at Ann. Meet. Am. Psychol. Assoc., 90th, Washington, DC

Ash, P., Kroeker, L. P. 1975. Personnel selection, classification, and placement. *Ann. Rev. Psychol.* 26:481–507

Ash, R. A., Levine, E. L. 1982. *Job applicant training and work experience evaluation: An empirical investigation.* Presented at Ann. Meet. Am. Psychol. Assoc., 90th, Washington, DC

Ash, R. A., Levine, E. L., Higbee, R. H., Sistrunk, F. 1982. *Comparison of task ratings from subject matter experts versus job incumbents.* Presented at Ann. Meet. Southeast. Psychol. Assoc., New Orleans

Ashford, S. J., Cummings, L. L. 1981. Strategies for knowing: When and from where do individuals seek feedback. *Proc. Acad. Manage.* 41:161–65

Availability of 1980 census data for affirmative action planning. 1982. *EEO Today* 9:86–91

Baker, D. D., Terpstra, D. E. 1982. Employee selection: Must every job test be validated? *Personnel J.* 61:602–5

Barr, S. H., Brief, A. P., Fulk, J. L. 1981. Correlates of perceived fairness and accuracy of performance. *Proc. Acad. Manage.* 41:156–60

Barrett, G. V., Phillips, J. S., Alexander, R. A. 1981. Concurrent and predictive validity designs: A critical reanalysis. *J. Appl. Psychol.* 66:1–6

Bass, B. 1982. Individual capability, team performance, and team productivity. See Dunnette & Fleishman 1982, pp. 179–232

Bazerman, M. H. 1982. Impact of personal control on performance: Is added control always beneficial? *J. Appl. Psychol.* 67:472–79

Bazerman, M. H., Beekun, R. I., Schoorman, F. D. 1982. Performance evaluation in a dynamic context: A laboratory study of the impact of a prior commitment to the ratee. *J. Appl. Psychol.* 67:873–76

Beehr, T. A., Gilmore, D. C. 1982. Applicant attractiveness as a perceived job-related variable in selection of management trainees. *Acad. Manage. J.* 25:607–17

Bernardin, H. J., Buckley, M. R. 1981. Strategies in rater training. *Acad. Manage. Rev.* 6:205–12

Bernardin, H. J., Cardy, R. L. 1981. Cognitive complexity in performance appraisal: It makes no nevermind. *Proc. Acad. Manage.* 41:306–10

Bernardin, H. J., Cardy, R. L. 1982. Appraisal accuracy: The ability and motivation to remember the past. *Public Personnel Manage. J.* 11:352–57

Bernardin, H. J., Cardy, R. L., Carlyle, J. J. 1982. Cognitive complexity and appraisal effectiveness: Back to the drawing board? *J. Appl. Psychol.* 67:151–60

Bernardin, H. J., Orban, J. A., Carlyle, J. J. 1981. Performance rating as a function of trust in appraisal and rater individual differences. *Proc. Acad. Manage.* 41:311–15

Bernardin, H. J., Smith, P. C. 1981. A clarification of some issues regarding the development and use of behaviorally anchored rating scales (BARS). *J. Appl. Psychol.* 66:458–63

Bersoff, D. N. 1981. Testing and the law. *Am. Psychol.* 36:1047–56

Blumberg, M., Pringle, C. D. 1982. The missing opportunity in organizational research: Some implications for a theory of work performance. *Acad. Manage. Rev.* 7:560–69

Bobko, P., Karren, R. 1982. The estimation of standard deviations in utility analyses. *Proc. Acad. Manage.* 42:272–76

Boehm, V. R. 1981. An assessment center practitioner's guide to the Division 14 Principles. *J. Assess. Cent. Technol.* 4(3):9–14

Boehm, V. R. 1982a. Are we validating more but publishing less? (The impact of governmental regulations on published validation research—An exploratory investigation). *Personnel Psychol.* 35:175–87

Boehm, V. R. 1982b. Assessment centers and management development. In *Personnel Management*, ed. K. M. Rowland, G. R. Ferris, pp. 327–62. Boston: Allyn & Bacon, 620 pp.

Borman, W. C. 1982. Validity of behavioral assessment for predicting military recruiter performance. *J. Appl. Psychol.* 67:3–9

Boudreau, J. W. 1983a. Utility analysis revisited: Economic considerations in estimating dollar-valued payoffs. *Personnel Psychol.* In press

Boudreau, J. W. 1983b. Effects of employee flows on utility analysis of human resource productivity programs. *J. Appl. Psychol.* 68:396–406

Bowen, D. E. 1982. Some unintended consequences of intention to quit. *Acad. Manage. Rev.* 7:205–11

Bray, D. W., Moses J. L. 1972. Personnel selection. *Ann. Rev. Psychol.* 23:545–76

Breaugh, J. A. 1981a. Predicting absenteeism from prior absenteeism and work attitudes. *J. Appl. Psychol.* 66:555–60

Breaugh, J. A. 1981b. Relationships between recruiting sources and employee performance, absenteeism, and work attitudes. *Acad. Manage. J.* 24:142–47

Brown, S. H. 1981. Validity generalization and situational moderation in the life insurance industry. *J. Appl. Psychol.* 66:664–70

Bucknall, W. L. 1981. Executive continuity planning: An idea whose time has come. *Manage. Rev.* 70:21–28

Buller, P. F., Maki, W. R. 1981. A case history of a manpower planning model. *Hum. Resour. Plann.* 4:129–38

Callender, J. C., Osburn, H. G. 1981. Testing the constancy of validity with computer-generated sampling distributions of the multiplicative model variance estimate: Results for petroleum industry validation research. *J. Appl. Psychol.* 66:274–81

Callender, J. C., Osburn, H. G. 1982. Another view of progress in validity generalization: Reply to Schmidt, Hunter & Pearlman. *J. Appl. Psychol.* 67:846–52

Callender, J. C., Osburn, H. G., Greener, J. M., Ashworth, S. 1982. Multiplicative validity generalization model: Accuracy of estimates as a function of sample size and mean, variance, and shape of the distribution of true validities. *J. Appl. Psychol.* 67:859–67

Campbell, J. P., Daft, R. L., Hulin, C. L. 1982. *What to Study: Generating and Developing Research Questions.* Beverly Hills: Sage. 168 pp.

Campion, M. A., Lord, R. G., Pursell, E. D. 1981. Individual and organizational correlates of promotion refusal. *J. Vocat. Behav.* 19:42–49

Cann, A., Siegfried, W. D., Pearce, L. 1981. Forced attention to specific applicant qualifications: Impact on physical attractiveness and sex of applicant biases. *Personnel Psychol.* 34:65–75

Carroll, S. J., Schneier, C. E. 1982. *Performance Appraisal and Review Systems: The Identification, Measurement, and Development of Performance in Organizations.* Glenview, Ill: Scott, Foresman. 284 pp.

Cascio, W. F. 1982a. *Applied Psychology in Personnel Management.* Reston, Va: Reston. 432 pp. 2nd ed.

Cascio, W. F. 1982b. Scientific, legal, and operational imperatives of workable performance appraisal systems. *Public Personnel Manage. J.* 11:367–75

Cascio, W. F. 1982c. *Costing Human Resources: The Financial Impact of Behavior in Organizations.* Boston: Kent. 244 pp.

Cascio, W. F. 1982d. *Fair personnel decision*

making. Presented at Measurement of Equal Employment Opportunity Symp., Ann. Meet. ORSA/TIMS, San Diego

Cascio, W. F., Bernardin, H. J. 1981. Implications of performance appraisal litigation for personnel decisions. *Personnel Psychol.* 34:211–26

Cascio, W. F., O'Reilly, C. A. 1981. *Comparable worth and job evaluation: The biasing effects of subfactors and contextual cues.* Presented at Ann. Meet. Am. Psychol. Assoc., 89th, Los Angeles

Cattin, P. 1980. Note on the estimation of the squared cross-validated multiple correlation of a regression model. *Psychol. Bull.* 87:63–65

Cattin, P. 1981. The predictive power of ridge regression: Some quasi-simulation results. *J. Appl. Psychol.* 66:282–90

Cederblom, D. 1982. The performance appraisal interview: A review, implications, and suggestions. *Acad. Manage. Rev.* 7:219–27

Chacko, T. I. 1982. Women and equal employment opportunity: Some unintended effects. *J. Appl. Psychol.* 67:119–23

Chuang, D. T., Chen, J. J., Novick, M. R. 1981. Theory and practice for the use of cut-scores for personnel decisions. *J. Educ. Stat.* 6:129–52

Cleveland, J. N., Landy, F. J. 1981. The influence of rater and ratee age on two performance judgments. *Personnel Psychol.* 34:19–29

Cole, N. S. 1981. Bias in testing. *Am. Psychol.* 36:1067–77

Conger, A. J. 1981. A comparison of multiattribute generalizability strategies. *Educ. Psychol. Meas.* 41:121–30

Connecticut v. Teal. 1982. *US Law Week* 50:4716–22

Cooper, W. H. 1981a. Ubiquitous halo. *Psychol. Bull.* 90:218–44

Cooper, W. H. 1981b. Conceptual similarity as a source of illusory halo in job performance ratings. *J. Appl. Psychol.* 66:302–7

Cotton, J. L., Cook, M. S. 1982. Meta-analysis and the effects of various reward systems: Some different conclusions from Johnson et al. *Psychol. Bull.* 92:176–83

County of Washington v. Gunther. 1981. 101 Supreme Court Rep. 2242

Cronbach, L. J. 1955. Processes affecting scores on "understanding of others" and "assumed similarity." *Psychol. Bull.* 52:177–93

Cronbach, L. J., Gleser, G. C., Nanda, H., Rajaratnam, N. 1972. *The Dependability of Behavioral Measurements: Theory of Generalizability for Scores and Profiles.* New York: Wiley. 410 pp.

Cronbach, L. J., Schaeffer, G. A. 1981. *Extensions of personnel selection theory to aspects*

of minority hiring. Stanford Univ: Inst. Res. Educ. Fin. Gov., Proj. Rep. 81–A2

Dalton, D. R., Krackhardt, D. M., Porter, L. W. 1981. Functional turnover. *J. Appl. Psychol.* 66:716–21

Dalton, D. R., Todor, W. D. 1982. Turnover: A lucrative hard dollar phenomenon. *Acad. Manage. Rev.* 7:212–18

Dalton, D. R., Todor, W. D., Krackhardt, D. M. 1982. Turnover overstated: The functional taxonomy. *Acad. Manage. Rev.* 7:117–23

Davis, T. C., Pinto, P. R. 1975. A cost model for evaluating alternative manpower input strategies. *Hum. Factors* 17:42–51

DeNisi, A. S., Randolph, W. A., Blencoe, A. G. 1982. Level and source of feedback as determinants of feedback effectiveness. *Proc. Acad. Manage.* 42:175–79

DeNisi, A. S., Stevens, G. E. 1981. Profiles of performance, performance evaluations, and personnel decisions. *Acad. Manage. J.* 24:592–602

DeVries, D. L., Morrison, A. M., Shullman, S. L., Gerlach, M. L. 1981. *Performance Appraisal on the Line.* New York: Wiley. 160 pp.

Dipboye, R. L. 1982. Self-fulfilling prophecies in the selection-recruitment interview. *Acad. Manage. Rev.* 7:579–86

Dipboye, R. L., dePontbriand, R. 1981. Correlates of employee reactions to performance appraisals and appraisal systems. *J. Appl. Psychol.* 66:248–51

Dorfman, P. W. 1982. *Schema and network representations of knowledge: Implications for performance appraisal.* Presented at Ann. Meet. Am. Psychol. Assoc. 90th, Washington, DC

Drasgow, F. 1982. Biased test items and differential validity. *Psychol. Bull.* 92:526–31

Drasgow, F., Miller, H. E. 1982. Psychometric and substantive issues in scale construction and validation. *J. Appl. Psychol.* 67:268–79

Dreher, G. F. 1982. The role of performance in the turnover process. *Acad. Manage. J.* 25:137–47

Dreher, G. F., Sackett, P. R. 1981. Some problems with applying content validity evidence to assessment center procedures. *Acad. Manage. Rev.* 6:551–60

Drehmer, D. E., Morris, G. W. 1981. Cross-validation with small samples: An algorithm for computing Gollob's estimator. *Educ. Psychol. Meas.* 41:195–200

Dugoni, B. L., Ilgen, D. R. 1981. Realistic job previews and the adjustment of new employees. *Acad. Manage. J.* 24:579–91

Dulewicz, V., Fletcher, C. 1982. The relationship between previous experience, intelligence and background characteristics of participants and their performance in an assessment centre. *J. Occup. Psychol.* 55:197–207

Dunnette, M. D., Borman, W. C. 1979. Personnel selection and classification systems. *Ann. Rev. Psychol.* 30:477–525

Dunnette, M. D., Fleishman, E. A., eds. 1982. *Human Capability Assessment,* Vol. 1. Hillsdale, NJ: Erlbaum. 296 pp.

Dunnette, M. D., Rosse, R. L., Houston, J. S., Hough, L. M., Toquam, J., et al. 1982. *Development and Validation of an Industry-wide Electric Power Plant Operator Selection System.* Minneapolis: Personnel Decisions Res. Inst. 266 pp.

Dyer, L. 1982. Human resource planning. See Boehm 1982b, pp. 52–77.

Dyer, L., Shafer, R. A., Regan, P. J. 1982. Human resource planning at Corning Glass Works: A field study. *Hum. Resour. Plann.* 5:115–84

Eberhardt, B. J., Muchinsky, P. M. 1982a. An empirical investigation of the factor stability of Owens' biographical questionnaire. *J. Appl. Psychol.* 67:138–45

Eberhardt, B. J., Muchinsky, P. M. 1982b. Biodata determinants of vocational typology: An integration of two paradigms. *J. Appl. Psychol.* 67:714–27

Elliott, A. G. P. 1981. Sex and decision making in the selection interview: A real-life study. *J. Occup. Psychol.* 54:265–73

Equal Employment Opportunity Commission, U.S. Civil Service Commission, Department of Justice, Department of Labor, 1978. Uniform guidelines on employee selection procedures. *Fed. Regist.* 43:38290–39315

Erwin, F. W. 1981. *The Supervisory Profile Record Technical Report I: Research studies I-V,* Washington, DC: RBH, 85 pp.

Faden, V., Bobko, P. 1982. Validity shrinkage in ridge regression: A simulation study. *Educ. Psychol. Meas.* 42:73–85

Faley, R. H. 1982. Sexual harassment: Critical review of legal cases with general principles and preventive measures. *Personnel Psychol.* 35:583–600

Farrell, D., Rusbult, C. E. 1981. Exchange variables as predictors of job satisfaction, job commitment, and turnover: The impact of rewards, costs, alternative and investments. *Organ. Behav. Hum. Perform.* 28:78–95

Fay, C. H., Latham, G. P. 1982. Effects of training and rating scales on rating errors. *Personnel Psychol.* 35:105–16

Feild, H. S., Holley, W. H. 1982. The relationship of performance appraisal system characteristics to verdicts in selected employment discrimination cases. *Acad. Manage. J.* 25:392–406

Feldman, J. M. 1981. Beyond attribution theory: Cognitive processes in performance appraisal. *J. Appl. Psychol.* 66:127–48

Fine, S., Wiley, W. 1971. *An Introduction to*

Functional Job Analysis: Methods for Manpower Analysis. Kalamazoo, Mich: Upjohn Inst. Employment Res.

Fleishman, E. A. 1982. Systems for describing human tasks. *Am. Psychol.* 37:821–34

Frantzreb, R. B. 1981. Human resource planning: Forecasting manpower needs. *Personnel J.* 60:850–57

Freedman, S. M., Keller, R. T. 1981. The handicapped in the workforce. *Acad. Manage. Rev.* 6:449–58

Friedman, T., Williams, E. B. 1982. Current use of tests for employment. See Wigdor & Garner 1982b, pp. 99–169

Fullilove v. Klutznik. 1980. *US Law Week* 48:4979–5008

Gehrman, D. B. 1981. Objective-based human resources planning. *Personnel J.* 60:942–46

Gehrman, D. B. 1982. Objective-based human resource planning. *Personnel Adm.* 27:71–75

Ghiselli, E. E., Campbell, J. P., Zedeck, S. 1981. *Measurement Theory for the Behavioral Sciences.* San Francisco: Freeman, 494 pp.

Gilbert, P. J. 1981. An investigation of clinical and mechanical combination of assessment center data. *J. Assess. Cent. Technol.* 4(2):1–10

Giles, W. F., Feild, H. S. 1982. Accuracy of interviewers' perceptions of the importance of intrinsic and extrinsic job characteristics to male and female applicants. *Acad. Manage. J.* 25:148–57

Glaser, R. 1981. The future of testing: A research agenda for cognitive psychology and psychometrics. *Am. Psychol.* 36:923–36

Glaser, R., Bond, L. 1981. Testing: Concepts, policy, practice, and research. *Am. Psychol.* 36:997–1000

Gomez-Mejia, L. R., Page, R. C., Tornow, W. W. 1982. A comparison of the practical utility of traditional, statistical, and hybrid job evaluation approaches. *Acad. Manage. J.* 25:790–809

Gordon, M. E., Fitzgibbons, W. J. 1982. Empirical test of the validity of seniority as a factor in staffing decisions. *J. Appl. Psychol.* 67:311–19

Gordon, M. E., Johnson, W. A. 1982. Seniority: A review of its legal and scientific standing. *Personnel Psychol.* 35:255–80

Gottfredson, G. D. 1982. An assessment of a mobility-based occupational classification for placement and counseling. *J. Vocat. Behav.* 21:71–98

Gould, S. J. 1981. *The Mismeasure of Man.* New York: Norton. 352 pp.

Graen, G. B., Liden, R. C., Hoel, W. 1982. Role of leadership in the employee withdrawal process. *J. Appl. Psychol.* 67:868–72

Grant, D. L. 1982. *The many faces of cross-validation: Background and purpose.* Pre-

sented at Ann. Meet. Am. Psychol. Assoc.,
90th, Washington, DC
Green, S. B., Sauser, W. I. Jr., Fagg, J. N.,
Champion, C. H. 1981. Shortcut methods
for deriving behaviorally anchored rating
scales. *Educ. Psychol. Meas.* 41:761–75
Gross, A. L. 1982. Relaxing the assumptions
underlying corrections for restriction of
range. *Educ. Psychol. Meas.* 42:795–801
Grove, D. A. 1981. A behavioral consistency
approach to decision making in employment
selection. *Personnel Psychol.* 34:55–64
Guion, R. M. 1967. Personnel selection. *Ann.
Rev. Psychol.* 18:191–216
Guion, R. M. 1982. *Social judgment and latent
trait theories applied to job analysis.* Presented at Ann. Meet. Am. Psychol. Assoc.,
90th, Washington, DC
Guion, R. M., Cranny, C. J. 1982. A note on
concurrent and predictive validity designs: A
critical reanalysis. *J. Appl. Psychol.* 67:239–
44
Guion, R. M., Imada, A. S. 1981. Eyeball
measurement of dexterity: Tests as alternatives to interviews. *Personnel Psychol.*
34:31–36
Hakel, M. D., Sorcher, M., Beer, M., Moses,
J. L. 1982. *Making it Happen: Designing
Research with Implementation in Mind.* Beverly Hills: Sage. 152 pp.
Hambleton, R. K., van der Linden, W. J. 1982.
Advances in item response theory and ap-
plications: An introduction. *Appl. Psychol.
Meas.* 6:373–78
Hamer, R. M., Cunningham, J. W. 1981.
Cluster analyzing profile data confounded
with interrater differences: A comparison of
profile association measures. *Appl. Psychol.
Meas.* 5:63–72
Hamilton, J. W. 1981. Options for small sam-
ple sizes in validation: A case for the J-
coefficient. *Personnel Psychol.* 34:805–16
Hammer, T. H., Landau, J. 1981.
Methodological issues in the use of absence
data. *J. Appl. Psychol.* 66:574–81
Harasym, P. H. 1981. A comparison of the
Nedelsky and modified Angoff standard-
setting procedure on evaluation outcome.
Educ. Psychol. Meas. 41:725–34
Hargett, N. T. 1981. Potential behavioral con-
sequences of attributions of locus of control.
J. Appl. Psychol. 66:63–68
Harvey, R. J. 1982. The future of partial cor-
relation as a means to reduce halo in perfor-
mance ratings. *J. Appl. Psychol.* 67:171–76
Haymaker, J. C., Grant, D. L. 1982. Develop-
ment of a model for content validation of
assessment centers. *J. Assess. Cent. Technol.* 5(2):1–7
Herriot, P. 1981. Towards an attributional
theory of the selection interview. *J. Occup.
Psychol.* 54:165–73
Herriot, P., Rothwell, C. 1981. Organizational

choice and decision theory: Effects of employers' literature and selection interview. *J.
Occup. Psychol.* 54:17–31
Hobson, C. J., Mendel, R. M., Gibson, F. W.
1981. Clarifying performance appraisal
criteria. *Organ. Behav. Hum. Perform.*
28:164–88
Hom, P. W., DeNisi, A. S., Kinicki, A. J.,
Bannister, B. D. 1982. Effectiveness of performance feedback from behaviorally
anchored rating scales. *J. Appl. Psychol.*
67:568–76
Hom, P. W., Hulin, C. L. 1981. A competitive
test of the prediction of reenlistment by
several models. *J. Appl. Psychol.* 66:23–29
Hooper, J. A., Catalanello, R. F. 1981. Markov analysis applied to forecasting technical
personnel. *Hum. Resour. Plann.* 4:41–45
Hornick, C. W. 1982. *Monte carlo comparison
of six methods of multiple liner regression.*
Presented at Meet. Am. Psychol. Assoc.,
90th, Washington DC
Hough, L. M. 1981. *The Development and
Evaluation of the "Accomplishment Record"
Method: An Alternative Selection Proce-
dure.* Minneapolis: Personnel Decisions
Res. Inst. 38 pp.
Hough, L. M., Dunnette, M. D., Keyes, M. A.
1981. *Evaluation of Three "Alternative"
Selection Strategies.* Minneapolis: Personnel
Decisions Res. Inst.
Howell, W. C., Fleishman, E. A., eds. 1982.
*Information Processing and Decision Mak-
ing,* Vol. 2. Hillsdale, NJ: Erlbaum. 193 pp.
Hsu, L. M. 1982. Estimation of the relative
validity of employee selection tests from in-
formation commonly available in the presence of direct and indirect range restriction.
J. Appl. Psychol. 67:509–11
Hulin, C. L. 1982. Some reflections on general
performance dimensions and halo rating
error. *J. Appl. Psychol.* 67:165–70
Hulin, C. L., Lissak, R. I., Drasgow, F. 1982.
Recovery of the two- and three-parameter
logistic item characteristic curves: A monte
carlo study. *Appl. Psychol. Meas.* 6:249–60
Hunter, J. E., Schmidt, F. L. 1982. Fitting
people to jobs: The impact of personnel
selection on national productivity. See Dun-
nette & Fleishman 1982, pp. 233–84
Hunter, J. E., Schmidt, F. L., Jackson, G. B.
1982a. *Meta-analysis: Cumulating Research
Findings Across Studies.* Beverly Hills:
Sage. 176 pp.
Hunter, J. E., Schmidt, F. L., Pearlman, K.
1982b. History and accuracy of validity
generalization equations: A response to the
Callender and Osburn reply. *J. Appl.
Psychol.* 67:853–58
Ilgen, D. R., Mitchell, T. R., Frederickson, J.
W. 1981a. Poor performers: Supervisors'
and subordinates' responses. *Organ. Behav.
Hum. Perform.* 27:386–410

Ilgen, D. R., Peterson, R. B., Martin, B. A., Boeschen, D. A. 1981b. Supervisor and subordinate reactions to performance appraisal sessions. *Organ. Behav. Hum. Perform.* 28:311–30

Imada, A. S. 1982. Social interaction, observation, and stereotypes as determinants of differentiation in peer ratings. *Organ. Behav. Hum. Perform.* 29:397–415

Ironson, G. H., Guion, R. M., Ostrander, M. 1982. Adverse impact from a psychometric perspective. *J. Appl. Psychol.* 67:419–32

Ivancevich, J. M. 1982. Subordinates' reactions to performance appraisal interviews: A test of feedback and goal-setting techniques. *J. Appl. Psychol.* 67:581–87

Ivancevich, J. M., McMahon, J. T. 1982. The effects of goal setting, external feedback, and self-generated feedback on outcome variables: A field experiment. *Acad. Manage. J.* 25:359–72

Janz, T. 1982a. Initial comparisons of patterned behavior description interviews versus unstructured interviews. *J. Appl. Psychol.* 67:577–80

Janz, T. 1982b. *Preliminary comparisons of direct v. behavioral estimates of the standard deviation of performance in dollars.* Presented at Ann. Conv. Acad. Manage., 42nd, New York

Jones, A. 1981. Inter-rater reliability in the assessment of group exercises at a UK assessment centre. *J. Occup. Psychol.* 54:79–86

Jones, A. P., Main, D. S., Butler, M. C., Johnson, L. A. 1982. Narrative job descriptions as potential sources of job analysis ratings. *Personnel Psychol.* 35:813–28

Kane, J. S., Bernardin, H. J. 1982. Behavioral observation scales and the evaluation of performance appraisal effectiveness. *J. Appl. Psychol.* 35:635–41

Kane, M. T. 1982. A sampling model for validity. *Appl. Psychol. Meas.* 6:125–60

Kaplan, R. M. 1982. Nader's raid on the testing industry: Is it in the best interest of the consumer? *Am. Psychol.* 37:15–23

Kingstrom, P. O., Bass, A. R. 1981. A critical analysis of studies comparing behaviorally anchored ratings scales (BARS) and other rating formats. *Personnel Psychol.* 34:263–89

Kipnis, D., Schmidt, S., Price, K., Stitt, C. 1981. Why do I like thee: Is it your performance or my orders? *J. Appl. Psychol.* 66:324–28

Kleiman, L. S., Durham, R. L. 1981. Performance appraisal, promotion, and the courts: A critical review. *Personnel Psychol.* 34:103–21

Krackhardt, D., McKenna, J., Porter, L. W., Steers, R. M. 1981. Supervisory behavior and employee turnover: A field experiment. *Acad. Manage. J.* 24:249–59

Krau, E. 1981. Turnover analysis and prediction from a career developmental point of view. *Personnel Psychol.* 34:771–90

Kriska, S. D., Milligan, G. W. 1982. Multiple regression analysis for categorical data with an illustrative application in personnel selection. *Psychol. Bull.* 92:193–202

Lahey, M. A., Saal, F. E. 1981. Evidence incompatible with a cognitive compatibility theory of rating behavior. *J. Appl. Psychol.* 66:706–15

Landy, F. J., Farr, J. L., Jacobs, R. R. 1982a. Utility concepts in performance measurement. *Organ. Behav. Hum. Perform.* 30:15–40

Landy, F. J., Vance, R. J., Barnes-Farrell, J. L. 1982b. Statistical control of halo: A response. *J. Appl. Psychol.* 67:177–80

Landy, F. J., Vance, R. J., Barnes-Farrell, J. L., Steele, J. W. 1980. Statistical control of halo error performance ratings. *J. Appl. Psychol.* 65:501–6

Landy, F. J., Zedeck, S., Cleveland, J. 1983. *Performance Measurement and Theory.* Hillsdale, NJ: Erlbaum. 416 pp.

Latham, G. P., Wexley, K. N. 1981. *Increasing Productivity Through Performance Appraisal.* Reading, Mass: Addison-Wesley. 262 pp.

Ledvinka, J., Markos, V. H., Ladd, R. T. 1982. Long-range impact of "fair selection" standards on minority employment. *J. Appl. Psychol.* 67:18–36

Lee, J. A., Mendoza, J. L. 1981. A comparison of techniques which test for job differences. *Personnel Psychol.* 34:731–48

Lee, R., Malone, M., Greco, S. 1981. Multi-trait-multimethod-multirater analysis of performance ratings for law enforcement personnel. *J. Appl. Psychol.* 66:625–32

Lee, R., Miller, K. J., Graham, W. K. 1982. Corrections for restriction of range and attenuation in criterion-related validation studies. *J. Appl. Psychol.* 67:637–39

Lerner, B. 1981. Equal opportunity versus equal results: Monsters, rightful causes, and perverse effects. *New Dir. Test. Meas.* 9:1–13

Linn, R. 1982a. Ability testing: Individual differences, prediction, and differential prediction. See Wigdor & Garner 1982b, pp. 335–88

Linn, R. L. 1982b. Admissions testing on trial. *Am. Psychol.* 37:279–91

Linn, R. L., Dunbar, S. B. 1982. *Validity generalization and predictive bias.* Presented at Johns Hopkins Natl. Symp. Educ. Res., "Performance assessment: The state of the art," 4th, Washington DC

Linn, R. L., Harnisch, D. L., Dunbar, S. B. 1981a. Corrections for range restriction: An empirical investigation of conditions resulting in conservative corrections. *J. Appl. Psychol.* 66:655–63

Linn, R. L., Harnisch, D. L., Dunbar, S. B. 1981b. Validity generalization and situational specificity: An analysis of the predictions of first-year grades in law school. *Appl. Psychol. Meas.* 5:281–89

Lopez, F. M., Kesselman, G. A., Lopez, F. E. 1981. An empirical test of a trait-oriented job analysis technique. *Personnel Psychol.* 34:479–502

Love, K. G. 1981. Comparison of peer assessment methods: Reliability, validity, friendship bias, and user reactions. *J. Appl. Psychol.* 66:451–57

Lyness, K. S., Cornelius, E. T. III. 1982. A comparison of holistic and decomposed judgment strategies in a performance rating simulation. *Organ. Behav. Hum. Perform.* 29:21–38

Lyness, K. S., Moses, J. L. 1981. *Career planning as an Advanced Management Potential Assessment Program.* Presented at Ann. Meet. Am. Psychol. Assoc., 89th, Los Angeles

Mabe, P. A. III, West, S. G. 1982. Validity of self-evaluation of ability: A review and meta analysis. *J. Appl. Psychol.* 67:280–96

Martin, T. N., Price, J. L., Mueller, C. W. 1981. Job performance and turnover. *J. Appl. Psychol.* 66:116–18

McCormick, E. J., Jeanneret, P. R., Mecham, R. C. 1972. A study of job characteristics and job dimensions as based on the Position Analysis Questionnaire (PAQ). *J. Appl. Psychol.* 56:347–68

Mellenbergh, G. J., van der Linden, W. J. 1981. The linear utility model for optimal selection. *Psychometrika* 46:283–93

Messick, S. 1981. Constructs and their vicissitudes in educational and psychological measurement. *Psychol. Bull.* 89:575–88

Michaels, C. E., Spector, P. E. 1982. Causes of employee turnover: A test of the Mobley, Griffeth, Hand, and Megline model. *J. Appl. Psychol.* 67:53–59

Mitchel, J. O. 1981. The effect of intentions, tenure, personal, and organizational variables on managerial turnover. *Acad. Manage. J.* 24: 742–51

Mitchell, T. R., Kalb, L. S. 1981. Effects of outcome knowledge and outcome valence on supervisors' evaluations. *J. Appl. Psychol.* 66:604–12

Mitchell, T. R., Kalb, L. S. 1982. Effects of job experience on supervisor attributions for a subordinate's poor performance. *J. Appl. Psychol.* 67:181–88

Mitchell, T. R., Liden, R. C. 1982. The effects of the social context on performance evaluations. *Organ. Behav. Hum. Perform.* 29: 241–56

Mitchell, T. W., Klimoski, R. J. 1982. Is it rational to be empirical? *J. Appl. Psychol.* 67:411–18

Mobley, W. H. 1981. Effects of rater and ratee race and sex on performance appraisals. *Proc. Acad. Manage.* 41:286–90

Mobley, W. H. 1982a. Supervisor and employee race and sex effects on performance appraisals: A field study of adverse impact and generalizability. *Acad. Manage. J.* 25:598–606

Mobley, W. H. 1982b. *Employee Turnover: Causes, Consequences, and Control.* Reading, Mass: Addison-Wesley. 212 pp.

Mobley, W. H. 1982c. Some unanswered questions in turnover and withdrawal research. *Acad. Manage. Rev.* 7:111–16

Morrow, P. C. 1982. Human resource planning and the older worker: Developing a retirement intentions model. *J. Occup. Behav.* 3:253–61

Mowday, R. T. 1981. Viewing turnover from the perspective of those who remain: The relationship of job attitudes to attributions of the causes of turnover. *J. Appl. Psychol.* 66:120–23

Mowday, R. T., Spencer, D. G. 1981. The influence of task and personality characteristics on employee turnover and absenteeism incidents. *Acad. Manage. J.* 24:634–42

Muckler, F. A. 1982. Evaluating productivity. See Dunnette & Fleishman 1982, pp. 13–47

Muczyk, J. P. 1981. Comprehensive manpower planning. *Manage. Plann.* 30:36–41

Mullins, T. W. 1982. Interviewer decisions as a function of applicant race, applicant quality and interviewer prejudice. *Personnel Psychol.* 35:163–74

Mumford, M. D., Jackson, K. E., Owens, W. A. 1982. *The durability of a classification of persons.* Presented at Meet. Int. Congr. Appl. Psychol., 20th, Edinburgh

Murphy, K. R. 1982. Difficulties in the statistical control of halo. *J. Appl. Psychol.* 67:161–64

Murphy, K. R., Garcia, M., Kerkar, S., Martin, C., Balzer, W. K. 1982a. Relationship between observational accuracy and accuracy in evaluating performance. *J. Appl. Psychol.* 67:320–25

Murphy, K. R., Martin, C., Garcia, M. 1982b. Do behavioral observation scales measure observation? *J. Appl. Psychol.* 67:562–67

Neiner, A. G., Owens, W. A. 1982. Relationships between two sets of biodata with 7 years separation. *J. Appl. Psychol.* 67:146–50

Nelson, B., Opton, E., Wilson, T. 1980. Wage discrimination and Title VII in the 1980's: The case against comparable worth. *Employee Relat. Law J.* 6:380–404

Noel, A. 1981. Privacy: A sign of our times. *Personnel Adm.* 26:59–62

Norton, S. D. 1981. The assessment center process and content validity: A reply to Dreher and Sackett. *Acad. Manage. Rev.* 6:561–66

Olian, J. D., Wilcox, J. C. 1982. The controversy over PACE: An examination of the evidence and implications of the Luevano consent decree for employment testing. *Personnel Psychol.* 35:659–76

Oliphant, V. N., Alexander, E. R. III. 1982. Reactions to resumes as a function of resume determinateness, applicant characteristics, and sex of raters. *Personnel Psychol.* 35:829–42

Olson, H. C., Fine, S. A., Myers, D. C., Jennings, M. C. 1981. The us of functional job analysis in establishing performance standards for heavy equipment operators. *Personnel Psychol.* 34:351–64

Osburn, H. G., Timmreck, C., Bigby, D. 1981. Effect of dimensional relevance on accuracy of simulated hiring decisions by employment interviewers. *J. Appl. Psychol.* 66:159–65

Owens, W. A., Jewell, D. O. 1969. Personnel selection. *Ann. Rev. Psychol.* 20:419–46

Owens, W. A., Schoenfeldt, L. F. 1979. Toward a classification of persons. *J. Appl. Psychol.* 64:569–607

Page, R. C., Gomez-Mejia, L. R., Tornow, W. W. 1982. *Compensation applications of the Management Position Description Questionnaire.* Presented at Ann. Meet. Am. Psychol. Assoc., 90th, Washington DC

Parasuraman, S. 1982. Predicting turnover intentions and turnover behavior: A multivariate analysis. *J. Vocat. Behav.* 21:111–21

Parsons, C. K., Herold, D. M., Turlington, B. 1981. Individual differences in performance feedback preferences. *Proc. Acad. Manage.* 41:166–70

Payne, J. W. 1982. Contingent decision behavior. *Psychol. Bull.* 92:382–402

Pearlman, K. 1982. *The Bayesian approach to validity generalization: A systematic examination of the robustness of procedures and conclusions.* Presented at Ann. Meet. Am. Psychol. Assoc., 90th, Washington DC

Pence, E. C., Pendleton, W. C., Dobbins, G. H., Sgro, J. 1982. Effects of causal explanations and sex variables on recommendations for corrective actions following employee failure. *Organ. Behav. Hum. Perform.* 29:227–40

Peters, L. H., Fisher, C. D., O'Connor, E. J. 1982. The moderating effect of situational control of performance variance on the relationship between individual differences and performance. *Personnel Psychol.* 35:609–21

Peterson, N. G., Bownas, D. A. 1982. Skill, task structure, and performance acquisition. See Dunnette & Fleishman 1982, pp. 49–105

Phillips, M. J. 1981. Reverse racial preferences under the Equal Protection clause: Round II. *Am. Bus. Law J.* 19:197–214

Pinfield, L. T. 1981. A case study of the application of a terminations forecast model. *Hum. Resour. Plann.* 4:18–32

Poortinga, Y. H. 1982. Introduction. *Int. Rev. Appl. Psychol.* 31:1–5

Popovich, P., Wanous, J. P. 1982. The realistic job preview as a persuasive communication. *Acad. Manage. Rev.* 7:570–78

Price, J. L., Mueller, C. W. 1981. A causal model of turnover for nurses. *Acad. Manage J.* 24:543–65

Primoff, E. S. 1975. *How to Prepare and Conduct Job Element Examinations.* Washington DC: GPO

Quaglieri, P. L. 1982. A note on variations in recruiting information obtained through different sources. *J. Occup. Psychol.* 55:53–55

Ramos, R. A. 1981. Employment battery performance of Hispanic applicants as a function of English or Spanish test instructions. *J. Appl. Psychol.* 66:291–95

Ramos, R. A. 1982. *The use of job analysis data for career identification and development.* Presented at Ann. Meet. Acad. Manage., 42nd, New York

Reilly, R. R., Brown, B., Blood, M. R., Malatesta, C. Z. 1981. The effects of realistic previews: A study and discussion of the literature. *Personnel Psychol.* 34:823–34

Reilly, R. R., Chao, G. T. 1982. Validity and fairness of some alternative employee selection procedures. *Personnel Psychol.* 35:1–62

Reypert, L. J. 1981. Succession planning in the Ministry of Transportation and Communications, Province of Ontario. *Hum. Resour. Plann.* 4:151–56

Rezmovic, E. L., Rezmovic, V. 1981. A confirmatory factor analysis approach to construct validation. *Educ. Psychol. Meas.* 41:61–72

Roberts, H. V. 1980. Statistical biases in the measurement of employment discrimination. In *Comparable Worth: Issues and Alternatives.* ed. E. R. Livernash, 7: 173–95. Washington DC: Equal Employment Advisory Council

Robertson, I. T., Kandola, R. S. 1982. Work sample tests: Validity, adverse impact and applicant reaction. *J. Occup. Psychol.* 55:171–83

Rosen, B., Jerdee, T. H., Lunn, R. O. 1981. Effects of performance appraisal format, age, and performance level on retirement decisions. *J. Appl. Psychol.* 66:515–19

Rosinger, G., Myers, L. B., Levy, G. W., Loar, M., Mohrman, S. A., et al. 1982. Development of a behaviorally based performance appraisal system. *Personnel Psychol.* 35:75–88

Rousseau, D. M. 1982. Job perceptions when working with data, people, and things. *J. Occup. Psychol.* 55:43–52

Rowland, K. M., Summers, S. L. 1981. Human resource planning: A second look. *Personnel Adm.* 26:73–80

Rozelle, R. M., Baxter, J. C. 1981. Influence of role pressures on the perceiver: Judgments of videotapes interviews varying judge accountability and responsibility. *J. Appl. Psychol.* 66:437–41

Russ, C. F. 1982a. Manpower planning systems: Part I. *Personnel J.* 61:40–45

Russ, C. F. 1982b. Manpower planning systems: Part II. *Personnel J.* 61:119–23

Sackett, P. R. 1982a. A critical look at some common beliefs about assessment centers. *Public Personnel Manage. J.* 11:140–47

Sackett, P. R. 1982b. The interviewer as hypothesis tester: The effects of impressions of an applicant on interviewer questioning strategy. *Personnel Psychol.* 35:789–804

Sackett, P. R., Cornelius, E. T. III, Carron, T. J. 1981. A comparison of global judgment vs. task oriented approaches to job classification. *Personnel Psychol.* 34:791–804

Sackett, P. R., Dreher, G. F. 1981. Some misconceptions about content-oriented validation: A rejoinder to Norton. *Acad. Manage. Rev.* 6:567–68

Sackett, P. R., Dreher, G. F. 1982. Constructs and assessment center dimensions: Some troubling empirical findings. *J. Appl. Psychol.* 67:401–10

Sackett, P. R., Wilson, M. A. 1982. Factors affecting the consensus judgment process in managerial assessment centers. *J. Appl. Psychol.* 67:10–17

Saunders, J. C., Ryan, J. P., Huynh, H. 1981. A comparison of two approaches to setting passing scores based on the Nedelsky procedure. *Appl. Psychol. Meas.* 5:209–17

Sauser, W. I. Jr., Pond, S. B. III. 1981. Effects of rater training and participation on cognitive complexity: An exploration of Schneier's cognitive reinterpretation. *Personnel Psychol.* 34:563–577

Scarborough, N., Zimmerer, T. W. 1982. Human resources forecasting: Why and where to begin. *Personnel Admin.* 27:55–61

Schmidt, F. L., Hunter, J. E. 1981. Employment testing: Old theories and new research findings. *Am. Psychol.* 36:1128–37

Schmidt, F. L., Hunter, J. E. 1981. Two pitfalls in assessing fairness of selection tests using the regression model. *Personnel Psychol.* 35:601–7

Schmidt, F. L., Hunter, J. E., Caplan, J. R. 1981a. Validity generalization results for two groups in the petroleum industry. *J. Appl. Psychol.* 66:261–73

Schmidt, F. L., Hunter, J. E., McKenzie, R. C., Muldrow, T. W. 1979. Impact of valid selection procedures on workforce productivity. *J. Appl. Psychol.* 64:609–26

Schmidt, F. L., Hunter, J. E., Pearlman, K. 1981b. Task differences as moderators of aptitude test validity in selection: A red herring. *J. Appl. Psychol.* 66:166–85

Schmidt, F. L., Hunter, J. E., Pearlman, K. 1982a. Progress in validity generalization: Comments on Callender and Osburn and further developments. *J. Appl. Psychol.* 67:835–45

Schmidt, F. L., Hunter, J. E., Pearlman, K. 1982b. Assessing the economic impact of personnel programs on workforce productivity. *Personnel Psychol.* 35:333–47

Schmitt, N. 1982. *Formula estimation of cross-validated multiple correlation.* Presented at Ann. Meet. Am. Psychol. Assoc., 90th, Washington DC

Schoenfeldt, L. F. 1982. *The status of test validation research.* Presented at Buros-Nebraska Symp. Testing, Lincoln, Neb.

Schriesheim, C. A., Gattiker, U. E. 1982. A study of the abstract desirability of behavior-based versus train-oriented performance appraisal ratings. *Proc. Acad. Manage.* 42:307–11

Schwab, D. P., Wichern, D. W. 1983. Systematic bias in job evaluation and market wages: Implications for the comparable worth debate. *J. Appl. Psychol.* In press

Siegel, L. 1982. Paired comparison evaluations of managerial effectiveness by peers and supervisors. *Personnel Psychol.* 35:843–52

Sigelman, L., Milward, H. B., Shepard, J. M. 1982. The salary differential between male and female administrators: Equal pay for equal work? *Acad. Manage. J.* 25:664–71

Sistrunk, F., Levine, E. L., Ash, R. A. 1982. *Multimethodological Job Analysis for Criminal Justice Organizations.* Tampa, Fla: Center for Evaluation Research, Univ. South Florida. 202 pp.

Sistrunk, F., Smith, P. L. 1982. *A Classification System for Human Resources Methods.* Tampa, Fla: Center for Evaluation Research, Univ. South Florida

Smircich, L., Chesser, R. J. 1981. Superiors' and subordinates' perceptions of performance: Beyond disagreement. *Acad. Manage. J.* 24:198–205

Smith, E. C. 1982a. Strategic business planning and human resources: Part I. *Personnel J.* 61:606–10

Smith, E. C. 1982b. Strategic business planning and human resources: Part II. *Personnel J.* 61:680–82

Smith, P. L. 1981. Gaining accuracy in generalizability theory: Using multiple designs. *J. Educ. Meas.* 18:147–54

Sparrow, J., Patrick, J., Spurgeon, P., Barwell, F. 1982. The use of job component analysis and related aptitudes in personnel selection. *J. Occup. Psychol.* 55:157–64

Spector, P. E. 1982. Behavior in organizations as a function of employee's locus of control. *Psychol. Bull.* 91:482–97

Spencer, D. G., Steers, R. M. 1981. Performance as a moderator of the job satisfaction-turnover relationship. *J. Appl. Psychol.* 66:511–14

Steers, R. M., Rhodes, S. R. 1978. Major influences on employee attendance: A process model. *J. Appl. Psychol.* 63:391–407

Stone, E. F., Stone, D. L. 1982. The effects of multiple sources of performance feedback on perceptions of task competence and feedback accuracy. *Proc. Acad. Manage.* 42:170–74

Strenio, A. J. Jr. 1981. *The Testing Trap.* New York: Rawson, Wade. 328 pp.

Stricker, L. J. 1982. Identifying test items that perform differentially in population subgroups: A partial correlation index. *Appl. Psychol. Meas.* 6:261–73

Stumpf, S. A., Dawley, P. K. 1981. Predicting voluntary and involuntary turnover using absenteeism and performance indices. *Acad. Manage. J.* 24:148-63

Stumpf, S. A., London, M. 1981a. Management promotions: Individual and organizational factors influencing the decision process. *Acad. Manage. Rev.* 6:539–49

Stumpf, S. A., London, M. 1981b. Capturing rater policies in evaluating candidates for promotion. *Acad. Manage. J.* 24:752–66

Taylor, M. S., Ilgen, D. R. 1981. Sex discrimination against women in initial placement decisions: A laboratory investigation. *Acad. Manage. J.* 24:859–65

Tenopyr, M. L. 1981. The realities of employment testing. *Am. Psychol.* 36:1120–27

Tenopyr, M. L., Oeltjen, P. D. 1982. Personnel selection and classification. *Ann. Rev. Psychol.* 33:581–618

Terborg, J. R., Lee, T. W., Smith, F. J., Davis, G. A., Turbin, M. S. 1982. Extension of the Schmidt and Hunter validity generalization procedure to the prediction of absenteeism behavior from knowledge of job satisfaction and organizational commitment. *J. Appl. Psychol.* 67:440–49

Tetlock, P. E. 1983. Accountability and complexity of thought. *J. Pers. Soc. Psychol.* 45:74–83

Thompson, D. E., Thompson, T. A. 1982. Court standards for job analysis in test validation. *Personnel Psychol.* 35:865–74

Thornton, G. C. III, Byham, W. C. 1982. *Assessment Centers and Managerial Performance.* New York: Academic. 458 pp.

Tichy, N. M., Fombrum, C. J., Devanna, M. A. 1982. Strategic human resource management. *Sloan Manage. Rev.* 23:47–61

Tolchinsky, P. D., McCuddy, M. K., Adams, J., Ganster, D. C., Woodman, R. W., et al.

1981. Employee perceptions of invasion of privacy: A field simulation experiment. *J. Appl. Psychol.* 66:308–13

Trattner, M. H. 1982. Synthetic validity and its application to the Uniform Guidelines validation requirements. *Personnel Psychol.* 35:383–97

Treiman, D. J., Hartmann, H. J., eds. 1981. *Women, Work, and Wages: Equal Pay for Jobs of Equal Value.* Washington DC: Natl. Acad. Press

Tubiana, J. H., Ben-Shakhar, G. 1982. An objective group questionnaire as a substitute for a personal interview in the prediction of success in military training in Israel. *Personnel Psychol.* 35:349–57

Turnage, J. J., Muchinsky, P. M. 1982. Trans-situational variability in human performance within assessment centers. *Organ. Behav. Hum. Perform.* 30:174–200

Tziner, A., Vardi, Y. 1982. Effects of command style and group cohesiveness on the performance effectiveness of self-selected tank crews. *J. Appl. Psychol.* 67:769–75

van der Linden, W. J. 1982. A latent trait method for determining intrajudge inconsistent in the Angoff and Nedelsky techniques of standard setting. *J. Educ. Meas.* 19:295–308

Vosburgh, R. M. 1982. Supervisory experience, reading ability, demographic variables and assessment center performance. *J. Assess. Cent. Technol.* 5(3):1–5

Wallace, M. J., Fay, C. H. 1981. Job evaluation and comparable worth: Compensation theory bases for molding job worth. *Proc. Acad. Manage.* 41:296–300

Watson, C. J. 1981. An evaluation of some aspects of the Steers and Rhodes model of employee attendance. *J. Appl. Psychol.* 66:385–89

Webb, E. G., Campbell, D. T., Schwartz, R. D., Sechrest, L., Grove, J. B. 1981. *Nonreactive Measures in the Social Sciences.* Boston: Houghton Mifflin. 394 pp.

Webster, E. C. 1982. *The Employment Interview: A Social Judgment Process.* Ontario, Canada: S.I.P. Publ. 144 pp.

Weitzman, R. A. 1982. Sequential testing for selection. *Appl. Psychol. Meas.* 6:337–51

Wendelken, D. J., Inn, A. 1981. Nonperformance influences on performance evaluations: A laboratory phenomenon? *J. Appl. Psychol.* 66:149–58

Wexley, K. N. 1982. *The performance appraisal interview.* Presented at Johns Hopkins Univ. Natl. Symp. Educ. Res., 4th, "Performance assessment: The state of the art," Washington DC

Wexley, K. N., Pulakos, E. D. 1982. Sex effects on performance ratings in manager-subordinate dyads: A field study. *J. Appl. Psychol.* 67:433–39

Whaley, G. L. 1982. The impact of robotics technology upon human resource management. *Personnel Adm.* 27:61–71

Wherry, R. J. Sr., Bartlett, C. J. 1982. The control of bias in ratings: A theory of rating. *Personnel Psychol.* 35:521–51

Wigdor, A. K., Garner, W. R., eds. 1982a. *Ability Testing: Use, Consequences, and Controversies. Part I: Report of the Committee.* Washington DC: Natl. Acad. Press. 242 pp.

Wigdor, A. K., Garner, W. R., eds. 1982b. *Ability Testing: Use, Consequences, and Controversies. Part II: Documentation Section.* Washington DC: Natl. Acad. Press. 414 pp.

Wing, H. 1981. Estimation of the adverse impact of a police promotion examination. *Personnel Psychol.* 34:503–10

Wing, H. 1982. Statistical hazards in the determination of adverse impact with small samples. *Personnel Psychol.* 35:153–62

Winne, P. H., Belfry, M. J. 1982. Interpretive problems when correcting for attenuation. *J. Educ. Meas.* 19:125–34

Wood, R. E., Mitchell, T. R. 1981. Manager behavior in a social context: The impact of impression management on attributions and disciplinary actions. *Organ. Behav. Hum. Perform.* 28:356–78

Woodman, R. W., Ganster, D. C., Adams, J., McCuddy, M. K., Tolchinsky, P. D., et al. 1982. A survey of employee perceptions of information privacy in organizations. *Acad. Manage. J.* 25:647–63

Wunder, R. S., Dougherty, T. W., Welsh, M. A. 1982. A causal model of role stress and employee turnover. *Proc. Acad. Manage.* 42:297–301

Yen, W. M. 1981. Using simulation results to choose a latent trait model. *Appl. Psychol. Meas.* 5:245–62

Zaharia, E. S., Baumeister, A. A. 1981. Job preview effects during the critical initial employment period. *J. Appl. Psychol.* 66:19–22

Zammuto, R. F., London, M., Rowland, K. M. 1982. Organization and rater differences in performance appraisals. *Personnel Psychol.* 35:643–58

Zedeck, S. 1981. Behaviorally based performance appraisals. *Aging and Work* 4:89–100

Zedeck, S., Cascio, W. F. 1982. Performance appraisal decisions as a function of rater training and purpose of the appraisal. *J. Appl. Psychol.* 67:752–58

Zimmerman, R., Jacobs, R., Farr, J. 1982. A comparison of the accuracy of four methods for clustering jobs. *Appl. Psychol. Meas.* 6:353–66

Ann. Rev. Psychol. 1984. 35:519–51

PERSONNEL TRAINING

Kenneth N. Wexley

Department of Management and Department of Psychology, Michigan State University, East Lansing, Michigan 48824

CONTENTS

This is the third review of the training literature to appear in the *Annual Review of Psychology*. The first two reviews by J. P. Campbell (1971) and I. L. Goldstein (1980) serve this reviewer as models of comprehensiveness, coherence, and scientific rigor. Hopefully, this chapter will approach the high standards which my colleagues have established. This review attempts to be both descriptive and prescriptive regarding training research since Goldstein's 1980 chapter. Continued fads, new concepts, emerging trends, likely developments, and research needs are given special emphasis. Although only 4 years have elapsed since the last review, much research has taken place in the training area. Training is here defined as a planned effort by an organization to facilitate the learning of job-related behavior on the part of its employees. The term

0066-4308/84/0201-0519$02.00

"behavior" is used in the broad sense to include any knowledge and skills acquired by an employee through practice (Wexley & Latham 1981).

Although training has traditionally been treated as an important area of applied psychology (e.g. Münsterberg 1913, Planty et al 1948), this topic takes on particular importance at the present time. Unfortunately, many workers in the United States are being left to fend for themselves when new technology or shifts in the economy have affected or eliminated their jobs. New technology is steadily increasing the need for retraining. Although no one has yet been laid off because of robotics, a 1981 study at Carnegie-Mellon University identified four million factory jobs that robots may perform by the year 2000 (Carnegie Mellon report 1982). Office automation may have an even greater impact because of continually evolving electronic equipment. It has been estimated that employers will have to retrain office workers five to eight times during their careers in the near future. Even when today's recession finally ends, America's blue-collar workers and the industries they serve will continue to have problems. From now on, traditional manufacturing industries such as steel, autos, and rubber will provide a smaller share of the nation's jobs. In these and other blue-collar industries, more than one million jobs have disappeared since 1978, and these are jobs that will never come back (Karmin & Sheler 1982). Instead, employment is growing in the high-technology, service, and information sectors. Feeling most of the brunt are the mechanics, assemblers, welders, painters, semiskilled and unskilled laborers who work in the factories of the northern industrial belt.

The push for training and retraining workers is now just beginning. Unions in dwindling industries are starting to win contract provisions requiring their organizations to retrain displaced workers (e.g. the United Auto Workers with General Motors and Ford). Legislation is currently pending in Congress that includes funds for retraining unemployed workers. The educational system is slowly trying to solve this problem through increased offerings of vocational and technical courses. Manufacturers of robots, computers, electronic office equipment, and other new technology are also functioning as a training source. In short, our society is rapidly changing, thereby requiring employed and displaced workers to continually acquire new knowledge and skills.

FORMAT OF THE REVIEW

In order to review the training literature comprehensively, computer searches from the Educational Resources Information Center and The National Technical Information Service data bases were undertaken. In addition, about 2000 members of the Society For Industrial and Organization Psychology were contacted, as well as certain members of the Personnel/Human Resources division of the Academy of Management who are known to be interested in personnel training. All these individuals were asked to send the reviewer any articles, technical reports, or refereed convention papers pertaining to the area of personnel training. Out of the vast number of references reviewed, approximately 150 are cited in this chapter. In deciding upon articles to cite, the reviewer chose primarily empirical research and conceptual works which fit into the five main topical areas of this chapter: Needs Assessment, Maximizing Trainees' Learning, Training Methods, Evaluating Training Programs, and Special Concerns. Originally, the reviewer intended to have an additional section called Management Development. Unfortunately, so little research has been conducted on this topic that the section had to be eliminated.

NEEDS ASSESSMENT

Needs assessment provides input in answering three important questions: *Where* within the organization can and should training be placed, *what* should be the content of training in terms of what an employee must learn to perform the job effectively, and *who* within the organization needs training and of what kind in terms of skills and knowledge. For almost 25 years, writers in the training area have adopted McGehee & Thayer's (1961) three-fold approach (i.e. organization, task or operations, and person analyses) for answering these questions about training requirements (Bass & Vaughan 1966, I. L. Goldstein 1974, 1980, Hinrichs 1976, Moore & Dutton 1978, Morano 1973, Wexley & Latham 1981). Since this is still the most comprehensive and sophisticated framework for considering an organization's training needs, the material reviewed will be considered by type of analysis.

Organization Analysis

This reviewer is appalled at the paucity of research on organization analysis. In Goldstein's (1980) review, merely a handful of research studies could be reported. They dealt with only one topic, namely, training programs judged to be failures because of organizational constraints such as supervisory and employee resistance (Anastasio & Morgan 1972, Salinger 1973). To make matters worse, no additional empirical research studies can be reported here. Clearly, training researchers have either intentionally or unintentionally chosen to ignore the influence of organizational variables on the training function. Apparently this restricted conception appears to be what "organization analysis" has come to mean to applied psychologists. However, if one uses McGehee & Thayer's original conception of organization analysis, it is clear that research is needed to develop a better understanding of how inefficient organizational units should be pinpointed and, when they are, how to determine whether training is the optimum solution to the performance problem. Most training analysts have defined inefficient operations as a discrepancy between desired performance (i.e. stated objectives) and actual performance (Mager & Pipe 1970, Odiorne 1970, Warren 1969). Unfortunately, relatively little is known about which of the numerous organization analysis variables enumerated by Moore & Dutton (1978) should be measured. Even if the analyst could know which variables to measure (e.g. efficiency indices, skills inventories, organizational climate indices), there is currently no systematic methodology to ascertain accurately why a particular unit is not meeting its stated objectives. The problem could be traced to such nontraining factors as low wages, inefficient work procedures, and/or defective raw materials rather than poor employee skills, knowledge, and/or abilities. Two potentially useful approaches for diagnosing the causes of organizational problems are the Nadler-Tushman (1977) Congruence Model and Weisbord's (1978) Six-Box Model.

Research is also needed to comprehend how the outside environment in which an organization operates affects the organization which, in turn, affects training needs. For example, the environment can affect the way the organization's managers design jobs, supervise their employees, and make decisions. The technological environment may also influence the structural nature of the organization itself. Lastly, research should be conducted to better understand in what ways specific organizational climate variables facilitate and impede various training interventions.

Task Analysis

Methodological sophistication in task analysis has continued to increase in recent years. For example, Goldstein (1980) reported that " . . . no procedures exist that empirically establish the content validity of a training program based upon a match of relevant tasks on the job and in the training program" (p. 234). Fortunately, Ford & Wroten (1982) have applied Lawshe's (1975) content validity ratio approach for evaluating the job relatedness of a training program for entry level patrol officers. "Subject matter experts" (i.e. patrol officers, sergeants, police personnel from similar sized communities outside the target city) independently rated the importance of knowledges, skills, abilities, and other personal characteristics (KSAOs) in the training content domain for job performance. The degree of consensus among the experts was quantified by calculating a content validity ratio (CVR) for each KSAO statement and tested for statistical significance. An overall summary of the content validity of the training program was then generated by taking the mean of all the CVR values. This summary statistic is called the Content Validity Index (CVI). By using Lawshe's CVR method, Ford & Wroten have taken an important step forward in measuring the content validity of training programs. One of the main concerns this reviewer and Goldstein (1982) share about this approach is that it neglects those KSAs judged as important for the job but not emphasized in training and those KSAs emphasized in training but judged as not being important for the job.

Ford and Wroten also show how a training curriculum can be redesigned, if needed, using the CVR and CVI values. Specifically, they demonstrate how a training curriculum can be divided into major categories and how the appropriate KSAO CVRs can be averaged to calculate a CVI for each category. The CVI for each category can then be linked to the amount of training class time devoted to the category. This comparison allows for the identification of training "hits" and "misses." Hits refer to those content areas (i.e. KSAOs) where the emphasis received in training time is justified or confirmed. Training misses can be separated into two types: deficiencies and excesses. Deficiencies are content areas whose high training needs suggest more emphasis is required than is currently received in training. Excesses, on the other hand, are areas receiving an undeserved amount of emphasis, relative to their need to be trained.

Recent work in task analysis should provide more sophisticated procedures for determining quantitatively what tasks are performed, what needs to be learned to perform these tasks, what ways these tasks should be performed, what should be taught in training, and what should be learned on the job. I. L. Goldstein et al (1981) and Macey & Prien (1981) differentiate task analysis methods on the basis of the *domain* of job content investigated and the specific operations that the researcher performs with respect to the *descriptors* of these domains. Specifically, they distinguish between three job content domains: task (activities or processes in which workers engage to produce an identifiable output), element (knowledge, skills, and abilities or other characteristics required to perform tasks), and performance (the interaction of the task and element domain; the description of observable worker activity). The reader should note that the task and element plus performance domains correspond to what McGehee & Thayer referred to as "task" and "person" analyses. By "descriptor" is meant an evaluative statement of the task; knowledge, skill, or ability; or examples of job behavior. With respect to tasks, subject matter experts may provide judgments as to the frequency of performance, relative importance, the opportunity to acquire task proficiency, and the relative difficulty to acquire task proficiency. Similarly, experts may be asked to provide judgments as to the relative importance of knowledge, skills, or abilities for full job performance, the opportunity to acquire these on the job, and their difficulty to learn for full job performance. With respect to the performance domain, specific performance appraisal instrumentation can be developed to assess individuals in terms of required task proficiency or in terms of the degree of possession of important job elements. Based on the researchers' preliminary findings, it appears that subject matter experts (SMEs) are capable of making reliable (i.e. interrater) judgments about the task content of jobs and the elements required for effective job performance. What still needs to be researched is the choice of using task versus element statements as stimuli for the individual assessment activity (see section on Person Analysis).

Goldstein et al (1981) also propose that when designing training curricula, one can develop composite indices that reflect the different judgments provided by the SMEs for the task and element statements. These composite indices should be developed to reflect the logic that the tasks considered most important in the development of training content are those given the highest priority in the job and those that are difficult to acquire proficiency in. Similarly, the content to be included in the training curriculum can be identified with reference to composite indices identifying the elements important for full performance and for which there is a minimum opportunity to learn on the job. Based on their review of job analysis techniques currently used in nuclear power plant operations, Olson et al (1980) generated criteria to be met in order to insure that job analysis data readily translate into effective training programs: coverage (do the task descriptions meet the objectives of the organization both in terms of its goals and the requirements of the engineering components?); linkage between behaviors and results (are task actions/behaviors clearly linked to task outcomes/results?); convertibility of task data to skills, knowledge, and abilities; and consideration of holistic functioning (does the job analysis approach insure "seeing" whole performance, particularly the incumbent's interface with other personnel in the installation?). Although Goldstein et al's approach is clearly a bright spot in task analysis, it neglects the behavior-results linkages. Sometimes several behaviors (tasks) need to be linked to achieve a result. It seems to this reviewer that this linkage should not be left to inference, particularly when there is a precise set of sequenced behaviors required to produce a precise result.

As Goldstein (1980) notes, the steps from task analysis to the design of training programs remain one of the most elusive aspects of training in work organizations. The steps are particularly problematic for supervisory, managerial, sales, and other occupations where the behaviors required for effective performance are uniquely contingent on varied situations (Macey 1982). Fortunately, there have been a few recent developments in this area worth noting. Macey (1982) recommended the use of critical incident data for designing behaviorally based instructional programs. Group meetings are held with SMEs to provide examples of effective and ineffective performance such as in the development of behaviorally based rating scales (Latham & Wexley 1981). These incidents are collected with reference to a previously generated task taxonomy to insure that the entire performance domain is represented as completely as possible. The critical incidents are placed into common categories. Each category reflects common KSAs. Summary descriptions of the common situations or circumstances within each category are then prepared, together with the corresponding effective behaviors relevant to the situation. Lastly, SMEs provide judgments as to the effectiveness of each behavior in the corresponding relevant situations. This information may then be used in several ways for the direct development of instructional content. For instance, the development of specific "modules" in behavioral modeling training programs requires the definition of relevant situations and behavioral guidelines to follow in these situations (A. P. Goldstein & Sorcher 1974). The results of these task analysis procedures are also relevant for determining the key learning points necessary for observing, practicing (role playing), and reproducing the appropriate behaviors on the job. Finally, appropriate training sequences should reflect the complexity of the situations as well as the logical sequencing of the effective behaviors within each situation. Macey suggests that various judgments used to represent complexity (e.g. difficulty to learn to perform tasks; difficulty to acquire knowledge, skills, and abilities) directly suggest which situations and behaviors should be presented in what order.

Chiles et al (1981) designed a shipboard training program for main propulsion operators. Structured interviews and questionnaires from managers and operators were used to collect data designed to identify the difference between actual and desired performance of main propulsion personnel and to assess deficiencies in the various support and administrative systems. Cross & Rogers (1980) evaluated the content of current training programs in map interpretation and land navigation for marine corps infantrymen by comparing program content with job duties. Specifically, the job responsibilities of a variety of infantry personnel under a variety of operating conditions were examined by studying field and technical manuals. The listing of job responsibilities was then used to compile a list of tasks, the accomplishment of which depended on the ability to use maps and map supplements for navigation or tactical decisions. Instructors at corps schools were interviewed to determine the extent to which each of these tasks were covered during training.

Person Analysis

Yukl (1981, 1982) proposed a new approach to person analysis for managerial jobs which focuses on observable behavior rather than abstract skills. It uses a typology of managerial behavior consisting of 23 behaviors measured by the Managerial Behavior Survey (MBS) (Yukl & Kanuk 1979, Yukl & Van Fleet 1982). Respondents (e.g. subordinates, peers, superiors) who have had ample opportunity to observe a manager's behavior are asked to describe this behavior using the MBS. The same respondents are then asked to fill out a parallel questionnaire on which they indicate what level of behavior is optimal for managerial effectiveness in the particular position. The discrepancy between "actual" and "ideal" behavior is computed. When a discrepancy occurs, it is usually a matter of actual behavior being less than ideal behavior. This kind of discrepancy may simply indicate that a manager is unaware of how important the behavior is, or it may indicate a need for additional training in how to do the behavior effectively. In a similar vein, Klimoski (1982) used self assessments as well as assessments by managers' subordinates and peers as sources of training need information in a personalized development program for managers in a city government agency. Subordinates rated their manager's job behavior on 20 of Yukl's leadership categories; peers rated the manager in terms of 27 dimensions derived from the assessment center literature (e.g. Finkle 1976). In this author's view, this survey-based approach to person analysis fits nicely with the mechanics of developing a personalized training program for each manager. It sounds strikingly similar to survey feedback (French & Bell 1978) and performance appraisal feedback approaches that use behaviorally based rating scales (Wexley 1982).

An important research question is "whom should we survey?" Many of the newer needs assessment approaches ask employees to diagnose their own training needs. Dreilinger & Robinson (1982) use employees' perceptions of their own and others technical/professional, managerial, and organizational practices. Mealiea & Duffy (1980) present a model which examines the measured difference (in terms of distance and shape) between two profiles: the skill profile most likely to produce success on the next highest job in the employee's career path (i.e. ideal skills profile) and the profile which reflects the employee's present potential to be successful in the next highest job (actual skills profile). The actual skills profile is obtained from superiors and subordinates as well as by means of self-evaluation. A review of 55 studies in which self-evaluations of ability were compared with measures of performance showed a low mean validity coefficient (mean $r = .29$) with high variability (SD $= .25$) (Mabe & West 1982).

General conclusions about the validity of self-evaluation of ability are not easily made because of the large standard deviation of the correlations. Studies examining the notion that self-evaluation of ability tends to be prone to errors of overestimation of ability also yielded inconsistent results. Mabe and West conducted a meta-analysis (Hunter et al 1982) of measurement conditions which revealed that self-evaluation validity is maximized when employees expect that the self-evaluation will be compared with criterion measures (Weary & Arkin 1982), have previous experience with self-evaluation (Levine et al 1977), are guaranteed anonymity of the self-evaluation (Gordon & Petty 1971), and are asked to make relative as opposed to absolute judgments (Raven & Fishbein 1965). Further, self-evaluations of performance (past and future) tend to be more valid than ability evaluations. Future research should be aimed at better understanding the development of valid self-evaluation skills, the person variables (e.g. internal locus of control) associated with accurate evaluations, and the interaction of person variables and measurement conditions.

Recent research has applied regression as a prediction technique to prescribe instructional strategies for individual trainees. McCombs (1979) reported modest savings in training time when regression models were used to select students for alternative training modules within the Air Force Inventory Management course. Savage et al (1982) used motor and information processing tests to develop empirical prediction models for assigning students to one of two training conditions based upon predicted training time for each type of training. Using multiple linear regression models and predicted training times resulted in a 47% savings in training time compared to random assignment and a 53% savings compared to mismatched assignment.

MAXIMIZING TRAINEES' LEARNING

Trainability

Trainability refers to a person's ability to acquire the skills, knowledge, or behavior necessary to perform a job at a given level and to achieve these outcomes in a given time (Robertson & Downs 1979). It is a multiplicative result of an individual's ability and motivation levels (Maier 1973). The prediction of trainability has continued to occupy researchers' attention since Campbell's (1971) review. Recently, Gill (1982) found that gain in decision making performance as a result of a 15-minute training program was moderated by trainees' intelligence levels. Specifically, he found a curvilinear (i.e. inverted-U) relationship between intelligence level and gain in quality of decision making using an in-basket exercise. Williams et al (1982) found that success in early combat training was predicted best by scores on a test of general intelligence and a measure of physical fitness (2-mile run time) for over 800 individuals in entry-level infantry training. Siegel (1983) showed that current methods for classifying enlisted navy personnel could be improved by using a new testing concept called "miniature training and evaluation testing." This concept involves training a person on a sample of the tasks he will be expected to perform in the navy and testing him on his ability to perform these tasks. The concept holds that a recruit who demonstrates that he can learn to perform a sample of the tasks of a navy rating will be able to learn and to perform satisfactorily all of the tasks of the rating, given appropriate on-the-job training. Siegel found that a battery of 11 training-evaluation situations which were derived from a job analysis of typical entry level tasks for seamen, foremen, and airmen was able to add substantially to the predictive power over that obtained with the Armed Services Vocational Aptitude Battery alone.

It should be noted that it is possible to have strong correlations between selection techniques and training performance and still have a poor training program. To prevent this situation, both the work sample and the training program must be carefully based upon a task analysis. Similarly, Zink (1982) demonstrated that a sampling of a trainee's ability level can be used as a valid predictor of subsequent success in training. Rather than using miniature training, he showed that time spent early in a self-paced training course for Bell

System service representatives could be used to terminate training for students whose total training time was predicted to be excessively long. Specifically, time spent early in training was highly predictive of total time taken to complete the course. A standard was set that is predicted to identify correctly neary 70% of those who would exceed the maximum allowable time for course completion, with a "false alarm" rate of only 5%.

Childs et al (1981) examined the relationship of pilot experience to the acquisition of instrument flight skills. The research was conducted in response to suggestions to reduce the 200-hour experience requirement for an instrument rating because during the experience requirement there is a high probability that the pilot will encounter weather conditions beyond the individual's capabilities. Seventy-nine aeronautical university students were assigned to one of three experimental training groups in which a full program of private, instrument, and commercial pilot training was administered. Prior to taking their instrument checkrides, the group had 113, 138, and 171 mean hours of flight time, respectively. Inflight performance was assessed objectively and subjectively. No statistically significant differences were found among tracks in instrument flying skill. These results suggested that a reduction in the 200-hour experience requirement should be considered. The study clearly illustrates the importance of checking the necessity of various personal requirements. Tubiana & Ben-Shakhar (1982) developed and validated an objective group questionnaire for predicting success in Israeli military training. The questionnaire focused on personality and motivational factors (i.e. activeness, sociability, responsibility, independence, promptness, motivation to serve in a combat unit) and, when combined with other predictors (e.g. level of intelligence, education, language score), correlated .46 with training success.

It is interesting to note that all of the aforementioned studies, with the exception of the last, focused on measuring "can do" (ability) factors while neglecting "will do" (motivational) factors. More importantly, researchers must begin studying trainability from an interactionist (i.e. person × situation) perspective. While this author finds it interesting to review studies that examine ability and motivation factors separately, it is unlikely that substantial predictability will ever be achieved unless we begin considering all factors (i.e. Ability, Motivation, Situational) simultaneously. The specific factors can be determined by conducting a facet design focusing on personal characteristics, social-interpersonal characteristics, physical-technological characteristics, and time (Terborg 1981).

Arrangement of the Training Environment

A number of publications have focused on the environmental arrangements that the trainer can control to facilitate learning such as amount of practice, task sequencing, overlearning, feedback, and adapting instruction to individual differences. Some of the best research in this area comes from the emerging field of Instructional Psychology, where there has been an interest in the conditions (e.g. instructional procedures, techniques, and materials) for transformation from the initial state of the learner to the acquisition of competence (Glaser 1982). Unlike the previous section which considered *internal* conditions necessary for learning to occur, this section will consider conditions *external* to the learner.

Hagman (1980) examined the effects of training task repetition on retention and transfer of maintenance skill. Fuel and electrical repairmen performed from zero to four repetitions on testing charging system electrical output. Their retention was tested immediately and 14 days after training; transfer to a different charging system was tested immediately after the delayed retention test. Retention was found to improve with three repetitions, with no added benefit resulting from a fourth. Transfer was better after task repetition (1–4 repetition groups) than after familiarization alone (0 repetition group). More than merely showing that trainees should be given the opportunity to practice what is being taught, this research suggests that there is an optimum number of task repetitions needed and this number will vary depending on training conditions.

Task sequencing has been studied for both cognitive and psychomotor skills. The sequencing of cognitive skills has been based on a hierarchical approach to cognitive skills acquisition (Gagné & Briggs 1974). The resulting theory is a structured learning hierarchy in which subordinate cognitive skills are prerequisite to the acquisition of superordinate skills. The validity of this approach has been demonstrated using transfer of training techniques (Gagné et al 1962). The concept of a learning hierarchy for psychomotor skill acquisition remains to be developed and tested. Several researchers have proposed task taxonomies (Melton 1964, McCormick et al 1972), but perhaps the most operationally defined taxonomy of psychomotor performance has been investigated by Fleishman (1975). Salvendy & Boydstun (1980) recently investigated the viability of a hierarchical model of psychomotor performance using two of Fleishman's factors: Control Precision and Rate Control. Their results are inconclusive regarding the concept of a hierarchical structure for the acquisition of psychomotor skills. Further research is therefore necessary to establish the viability of this concept. If a hierarchical model could be established, this would aid in the development of efficient acquisition procedures for those jobs involving psychomotor skills. Schendel & Hagman (1982) were also interested in the efficient training of psychomotor skills—disassembly/assembly of the M60 machine gun. They showed that overtraining was superior to refresher training in combating forgetting. That is, those soldiers trained to criterion who then received 100% initial overtraining exhibited better retention than soldiers given the same amount of additional training midway through the retention interval. These findings suggest that overtraining may be a potent way of increasing effectiveness when sustaining psychomotor skills over a fixed retention interval.

A few interesting studies in the performance feedback area are worth noting. Komaki et al (1980), obviously responding to the continuing debate regarding the relative effectiveness of feedback versus goal setting (Locke 1980), concluded that safety training was not sufficient to substantially improve and maintain performance even though desired practices were objectively defined and examples were tailored to specific job situations. It was not until feedback was provided that performance significantly improved. Knight & Salvendy (1981) and Matsui et al (1982) examined the moderating effects of task and person variables on feedback effectiveness, respectively. Knight & Salvendy studied the effects of feedback on two levels of pacing constraint. In one condition (most like standard self- or internal-pacing) subjects simply scheduled their own work rate. In the other condition (most like standard machine- or external-pacing) there was much more constraint placed upon a subject's freedom to devise a work schedule. Their results suggest that providing feedback may only be beneficial under conditions in which the operator can actually make use of it. That is, in the self-paced condition, subjects were able to use the feedback to their advantage and did so with three consequences: performance was improved, subjects utilized available work time more efficiently, and sinus arrhythmia (as assessed by the standard deviation of inter-heartbeat intervals) was reduced. This research suggests that feedback might be used as a means of reducing cognitive load, and thus work-induced physiological stress, in self-paced tasks (Manenica 1977, Knight et al 1980). Matsui et al (1982) showed that achievement need moderated the feedback-performance relationship. They found a significant 2 (high vs low achievement need) × 2 (prefeedback part vs postfeedback part) interaction on number of clerical problems attempted. Hunt (1982) examined the effects of self-assessment (SA) responding on acquisition rate in paired-associates learning. Trainees were required to indicate the degree of sureness in the correctness of their answers by pressing one of several buttons (representing different levels of sureness) either immediately before or after each answer. Even though learning was expedited by as much as 25% by SA responding after the answer, Hunt's findings are difficult to interpret since pressing a single button labeled *Record* enhanced learning as much as did SA responding. Additional research is needed to further understand the extent to which cognitive self-assessment versus some simple motor activity (e.g. pressing a Record button) facilitates learning. Moreover, continuing attention should be given to studying the processes underlying these phenomena. The research so far has been much too atheoretical.

Another issue that urgently needs empirical investigation is the influence of trainer behavior on trainee learning. The only study worthy of citation on this topic was conducted by Eden & Shani (1982). They demonstrated the applicability of the Pygmalion effect, so often shown for children in the classroom, in a 15-week combat command course with adult trainees. Trainees of whom instructors had been induced to expect better performance scored significantly higher on objective achievement tests, exhibited more positive attitudes, and perceived more positive leader behavior.

Most training research studies employ a main effect model which may fail to discern differential effects across trainees. Despite Goldstein's (1980) call for more systematical empirical research which matches individual differences among learners to various instructional strategies, only a handful of aptitude-treatment interaction research studies have been conducted to this author's knowledge (e.g. Hall & Freda 1982, McCombs 1979). Nevertheless, two theoretical papers deserve discussion. Weinstein et al (1980d) have developed the Learning Activities Questionnaire (LAQ) to identify the types of learning strategies (i.e. rote, physical, imagery, elaboration, grouping) used by individuals in a variety of academic and training tasks (i.e. free recall, paired-associate, reading comprehension). Validation of the LAQ to date has involved administering it to individuals at five different educational levels, ranging from graduate students to persons who have not completed high school. The findings with these diverse groups suggest the need to tailor training programs to take into account differences in learning strategies among trainees, and the need for programs designed to modify or enhance the learning strategies of trainees and students, particularly at lower educational levels. In fact, in a series of studies, Weinstein and her associates (1980b,c,e) have found that the acquisition of new cognitive learning strategies with student subjects requires practice, feedback, the ordering of training materials from easy to difficult, as well as training in the processes used to create the strategies. Unfortunately, when the Cognitive Learning Strategies Training Program was administered to army enlisted personnel, no significant differences were found between training and a control group or a posttest-only group (Weinstein et al 1980a). Clearly, a number of modifications in both the program and the posttest used to evaluate it are needed.

Mezoff (1982) provides a conceptual framework for a matching model approach to human relations training research. Based upon an extensive review of the literature on cognitive styles (especially field independence/field dependence), he hypothesizes how persons of different cognitive styles will be differentially responsive to structured (e.g. role plays, simulation games) and unstructured (e.g. T-group) human relations training. If future research corroborates Mezoff's propositions, trainers could use knowledge about participant cognitive style to modify the design or focus on their training. With large-scale training programs, they could group participants by cognitive style and provide each group with a more individualized training treatment.

Lastly, the Learning Style Inventory (Kolb 1981) measures a person's self-description of how he or she learns compared with similar self-descriptions of a normative sample. The inventory measures an individual's relative emphasis on four learning modes and four abilities. Kolb and his associates (Kolb et al 1979) see the inventory as a starting point for understanding a trainee's approach to learning that should be supported by other data about how the trainee learns. Knowing a trainee's current learning style could be useful in modifying the training content to fit the individual. Unfortunately, the Learning Style Inventory has come under severe attack by Freedman & Stumpf (1980) and Stumpf & Freedman (1981) regarding its low test-retest reliability and its weak construct validity. Hopefully, additional research will be conducted on improving this instrument and assessing its utility.

Transfer of Learning

Considering the importance of positive transfer for effective training in organizations, it is distressing that so little theorizing and applied research has been done. One exception is a continuing program of research by Baumgartel and his associates (Baumgartel et al 1978) on the nature of those factors which facilitate the adoption of new concepts and practices following management development programs. Their findings indicate that people in favorable organizational climates (e.g. freedom to set personal performance goals, risk taking encouraged, growth-oriented) are most likely to apply new knowledge; people with innovative personalities (e.g. high need achievement, high activity level) are more likely to adopt new practices; climate has its greatest effect on persons with innovative dispositions; and this effect is most striking for persons at lower levels in the organizational structure. Other articles by Leifer & Newstrom (1980) and Michalak (1981) contend that positive transfer is maximized by a number of factors including continued interest and involvement by superiors, awareness of the obstacles to transfer, strategies for overcoming these obstacles, and reinforcement for maintenance of behavior change.

Finally, Marx (1982) describes a cognitive-behavioral model that offers an integrated approach to the maintenance of behavior. It is based on the relapse prevention (RP) model by Marlatt & Gordon (1980), which consists of a set of self-control strategies designed to maintain abstinence from addictive behaviors such as smoking, alcoholism, and drugs. Although originally developed with addictive behaviors, the RP model appears to have implications for the maintenance of managerial training. It involves making managers aware of the relapse process itself, asking them to pinpoint situations that are likely to sabotage their attempts to maintain new behavior, and teaching them a variety of coping responses such as time management skills and a delegative leadership style. The opportunities for research on RP are enormous. An important empirical question that needs answering is whether a model designed to explain the long-term maintenance of addictive behaviors can be used for nonaddictive behaviors learned in personnel training.

TRAINING METHODS

Behavioral Role Modeling

Since the publication of Goldstein & Sorcher's (1974) book, behavior modeling has received attention in the training literature (Decker et al 1982, Manz & Sims 1982). Behavior modeling incorporates the concepts of social learning theory (Bandura 1977): modeling, role playing, social reinforcement, and positive transfer of learning. Studies have appeared in the literature showing that behavior modeling can be an effective training device in both industrial (Kraut 1976, Latham & Saari 1979) and nonindustrial (Decker 1979) contexts. Nevertheless, Hakel (1976), McGehee & Tullar (1978), Goldstein (1980) and others have suggested that additional research is needed concerning the appropriate development and use of this technique. Fortunately, some noteworthy progress has been made in this area during the past few years.

According to Bandura, attentional processes, retentional processes, motor reproduction, and motivational processes contribute to the learning of modeling behavior and the reproduction of responses. Goldstein & Sorcher (1974) included all of the processes in their description of behavior modeling, except for two retentional processes: symbolic coding and symbolic rehearsal. Decker (1980) used learning points to induce symbolic coding and instructions to induce symbolic rehearsal in a behavior modeling training procedure designed to teach college students assertiveness skills. In addition, he examined the effectiveness of learning point source (student vs experimenter generation of codes) and type (rule-oriented vs description of the model's behavior). He found, among other things, that symbolic rehearsal instructions (with or without coding) enhanced reproduction of modeled events and generalization of observational learning to novel contexts; presentation of descriptive learning points (a description of the model's key behaviors) enhanced reproduction but not generalization; and rule-oriented learning points (principles underlying the model's performance) generated by the trainee enhanced generalization significantly more than learning points provided by the experimenter, regardless of type. These laboratory results were replicated in a field study which showed that formalized attempts to stimulate symbolic coding and rehearsal facilities generalizational of observational learning to novel contexts compared with retention processes performed by first-line supervisors not given training in symbolic coding and rehearsal (Decker 1982). In another field study, Russell (1982) examined the trainer's role in modeling by substituting managers for professional trainers in some training classes to determine if the use of managerial models could improve training effectiveness. No significant differences were found between professional trainers and company managers in terms of trainees' reactions, learning, behavior, and work performance. Russell also found that trainee self-esteem was uncorrelated with any of these dependent variables. These results are particularly interesting in light of the fact that low self-esteem has been shown to cause increased imitation in laboratory studies involving children and students (de Charms & Rosenbaum 1960) and in subordinate-supervisor relationships (Weiss 1978).

On a more applied level, Porras & Anderson (1981) found that a modeling-based training program for first-level supervisors in a major forest products company improved organizational productivity and efficiency as measured by total monthly production per direct labor worker hour, average daily plant production, and recovery rate (an index reflecting the degree to which a log is effectively converted to an end product). Improved supervisory interpersonal behavior also had some effect on plant labor relations as indicated by reduced grievance, absentee, and turnover rates. Sorcher & Spence (1982) improved race relations between white supervisors and black employees in South Africa. Most of the training modules were designed to give supervisors and subordinates reciprocal training to facilitate their responses to one another. Structured interviews indicated dramatic improvements in inter-race relations 20 weeks after training. Evans et al (1981) used social modeling films to reduce smoking behavior by providing detailed techniques for coping with social influences (peers, parents, media) on desire to smoke. Analyses of these data revealed that the experimental group subjects smoked less frequently and intended to smoke less frequently than did the control group subjects, and that knowledge generated by the films was significantly related to smoking intention and behaviors. This reviewer has received numerous studies from consulting firms suggesting that their behavior-modeling approach improves managerial skills and organizational productivity. Although these studies en masse suggest that behavior-modeling programs can impact behavior and bottom-line improvements, many of the studies involved are merely case study and pretest-posttest (no control group) designs. Lastly, Graen et al (1982) found that managers who received six 2-hour sessions of leader-member exchange training were able to establish better reciprocal relationships (i.e. help and support) with their subordinates. The training, extending over a 6-week period, included lectures, group discussions, and role modeling.

Computer-Based Instruction

Despite the increasing use of computers in our society, surprisingly little research is currently being conducted on computer-based instruction. Nevertheless, a few noteworthy exceptions can be reported. Dossett & Hulvershorn

(1984) reported two studies of peer training via computer-assisted instruction (CAI) using Air Force personnel in a one-week experimental electronics training program. Their first study compared a peer-trained CAI group (i.e. students paired on relative levels of ability) to both an individually trained CAI group and a conventionally trained (i.e. classroom) group. The results indicated no differences in achievement levels across groups, but mean training times of both CAI groups were significantly less than that of the conventionally trained group. Further, the mean peer-trained CAI training time was significantly lower than that of the individually trained CAI group, thereby suggesting the feasibility of training two students simultaneously at a single CAI terminal. The second study investigated optimum pairing strategies in the peer-training mode. Trainees were grouped on the basis of their prior training performance into homogeneous, moderately heterogeneous, and very heterogeneous ability pairs. Although pairing strategies did not affect achievement scores, some strategies were consistently superior in reducing training times. According to Dossett & Hulvershorn, the importance of CAI peer training in both military and civilian technical training programs is the low student-instructor contact time (less than 2% of total training time in their study) required. This low contact suggests that instructors can provide greater individual student help when required, and that more training can be conducted with smaller staffs. Additional research should be conducted to determine if more than two students can be adequately trained at a computer terminal and what would be the optimum composition of these peer groups.

Hall & Freda (1982) examined the training effectiveness and efficiency of individual instruction (i.e. self-paced or computer-managed courses) relative to conventional instruction on over 5000 graduates of 19 Naval technical schools. They, too, found that individualized instruction and conventional group-paced instruction were equally effective. Moreover, individualized instruction benefited higher ability students during training more than it did lower ability students. Relative to the lower ability students, higher ability naval personnel mastered more course content (i.e. had higher end-of-course grades) and completed training in less time. No definitive evidence was obtained concerning which method of instruction most benefited lower ability personnel. Conventional instruction did not benefit one ability level of students over another during training. When course content was classified into generic training tasks, individual instruction was found to be more effective than conventional instruction in courses that taught primarily procedure tasks; conventional instruction was more effective than individual instruction in courses that taught primarily rule or principle tasks. Most importantly, no one method of instruction was found to be universally more effective in training all of the different types of tasks to different ability level students. This research suggests that a combination of methods used within a given course for conveying different instructional contents would most likely be more effective than the use of a single method for an entire course (i.e. aptitude-treatment interaction).

In another navy research study, K. A. Johnson et al (1982) showed that individualized, computer-managed training courses for maintenance technicians were superior to conventional instruction in terms of trainees' written and performance tests. The technicians' supervisors in the fleet indicated that both types of students had been adequately trained and that there were no substantial differences in their performance on the job despite the fact that students in the computer-managed courses had somewhat lower aptitude scores. The cost of developing the computer-based training materials for each of three types of maintenance technicians was fairly high, but was offset quite rapidly by the reductions in training time of 11%, 45%, and 62% for plane captain, power plant, and structures/hydraulics technical positions.

Finally, the main use of computer-based equipment simulators has been in flight training. Recent efforts have focused on simulation of flight crew members' interaction with flight instruments and controls (Houston 1979), map interpretation and terrain analysis methods for low-altitude flying (Qualy et al 1982), and flight motion (i.e. maneuver and disturbance) cues (Caro 1979).

At this point it seems clear that computer-based instruction requires less time than more conventional methods to teach the same amount of material, and that there are usually no significant differences in achievement scores between trainees taught by the two methods. Additional research replicating these findings seems misguided. Instead, future research of the type conducted by Dossett & Hulvershorn (1984) and Hall & Freda (1982) on improving the efficiency of computer-based instruction would be more productive.

Simulations

Campbell (1971) and Goldstein (1980) noted the lack of empirical studies investigating simulation methods such as case study, role playing, leaderless group discussions, and business games. Unfortunately, this reviewer must share their dismay. Despite the frequent use of these simulation techniques in management development and sales training programs (L'Herisson 1981, Neider 1981), rigorous research in this area is sorely needed. Although simulations generally incorporate active participation and practice opportunities on the part of trainees, there is little empirical evidence that they can change attitudes and behaviors that transfer to the work situation. For instance, Argyris (1980) argues that the case method rarely relates managers' behavior in the classroom to their behavior back home, or points out the discrepancies between their espoused theory and their actual managerial actions. On the positive side, Ivancevich & Smith (1981) successfully used role playing to improve sales managers' goal setting interview skills that carried over to their jobs three months after training. Reverse-role playing involves practice pertaining to complementary tasks which are not performed by the trainee in the operational environment, but by someone else. Using a video air-to-air combat game and male undergraduates, Laughery (1982) found that reverse-role trained subjects showed more aggressiveness (i.e. were more likely to be moving and pointing toward the opponent; were more likely to be attempting to meet the opponent) than subjects who received standard training procedures. Kurecka et al (1982) improved the performance of female undergraduates in assigned role leaderless group discussions when they were given behavioral examples of good performance in the dimensions by which they were to be assessed, actual practice, and feedback. Finally, Stein (1982) described a business game called Looking Glass, Inc., a 6-hour real-time organizational simulation in which participants manage a fictitious company. The design of Looking Glass has resulted in high content validity, which has been verified through two studies (McCall & Lombardo 1979, Stein 1980). It is currently being used as a diagnostic assessment center for identifying training and development needs and as a tool for diagnosing team interaction as a part of team-building programs. The reviewer hopes that more research is conducted on Looking Glass, Inc. as well as other simulation exercises within the next few years to determine whether they are able, in fact, to do what so many trainers have merely *assumed* they can.

Behavior Modification and Behavioral Self-Management

One comprehensive review of the training literature from 1963 to 1976 concluded that there is no evidence from reported research of the effectiveness of behavior modification in industrial training (McGehee & Tullar 1978). A later review by Andrasik (1979) revealed about 20 applications of behavior modification in business settings, but these fared poorly when evaluated with respect to the reviewer's criteria of measurement reliability, systematic intervention, and postintervention follow-up. Despite the large number of studies on operant techniques in work settings since Nord's (1969) claim that this is a "neglected area," many of the studies suffer from weak research designs. However, two recent bright spots can be cited. Komaki and her associates (Komaki et al 1978, 1980) have demonstrated that behavior modification can be used successfully to increase safety performance. Luthans et al (1981) found a significant change in the frequency of salespersons' retailing behavior after contingent reinforcement was introduced. The improvement in behavior was almost immediate and was maintained over time. In fact, the behavior did not return to baseline frequencies following the removal of the reinforcement intervention.

For over a decade now, researchers have been studying the effects of various schedules of reinforcement in complex work situations. Most of these studies used a repeated measures design wherein each subject worked for awhile under each of the schedules. Changing from one schedule to another, particularly when several schedules are used, would seem quite artificial to individuals in training contexts. Further, the demand characteristics produced by such changes may cause a number of unknown effects. Recent research by Pritchard et al (1980) improves on previous studies by using a between-groups design wherein each subject has experience with only one schedule. Moreover, it employs a partial schedule that has not often been used in previous operant work but occurs frequently in training contexts. In this schedule, the trainee does not know how many responses must be made before a reinforcer is given, and when the reinforcer is given, the trainee does not know how large it will be. Examples would include trainer recognition, peer approval, and changes in training conditions. Using task material consisting of self-paced programmed texts dealing with basic electricity and electronics, Pritchard et al examined three schedules of reinforcement: straight hourly pay, fixed ratio (FR), and variable ratio (VR). The two contingent schedules were found to be superior to the hourly schedule in terms of trainee's effort and performance. When performance data were examined, no differences emerged between the two contingent schedules. However, when trainee effort was investigated, FR was superior to VR. The measurement of *both* performance and effort is another asset of the present study over previous research in this area. In addition to improving effort and performance, partial schedules are perceived more by emloyees as including job environment variables such as recognition and feedback than is the case when reinforcement is provided on a continuous schedule (Saari & Latham 1982).

Behavioral self-management has recently appeared in the training literature (Luthans & Davis 1979, Manz & Sims 1982). Involving both stimulus management and consequence management, this training method involves teaching trainees to manipulate stimuli and rewards to help themselves change in ways they want to. In this reviewer's opinion, behavioral self-management is a fruitful area for future research. Up until now, its support has been primarily anecdotal and wishful thinking.

EVALUATING TRAINING PROGRAMS

Program evaluation is probably best defined as " . . . a set of procedures designed to systematically collect valid descriptive and judgmental information with regard to the ways in which a planned change effort has altered (or has failed to alter) organizational processes" (Snyder et al 1980, p. 433). Reports of human resources training programs in both the private and public sectors agree that attempts at evaluation in current practice remain quite poor (e.g. Owen & Croll 1974). Even in those cases when evaluation is attempted, it usually involves a pre-experimental design together with merely reaction and/or learning measures (A. P. Goldstein 1981, Wexley & Latham 1981). Despite these gloomy facts, there are several reasons to have guarded optimism about the future of program evaluation in organizations. In this section, we will discuss three of these reasons: overcoming resistance to evaluative research, accurate measurement of change, and use of utility concepts.

Snyder et al (1980) present a model for the systematic evaluation of human resource development programs which suggests several interesting ways to combat the tendency of organizations and their members to react negatively to evaluation as a concept. For instance, they suggest that active attempts must be made to avoid either/or approaches (i.e. a program is either valuable or valueless) and instill among organizational members a "spirit of inquiry" (Schein 1978) or "scientific attitude" (Bennis 1966). Staw (1977) has also recommended that organizations should evaluate programs, not people; reduce the tie between evaluation outcomes and resource allocation; and establish teams of politically neutral in-house evaluation consultants. Although these ideas make sense to this author, one needs considerably more detail on how they should be implemented as well as evidence that they can be implemented effectively.

Only 14 years ago, Cronbach & Furby (1970) asked "how we should measure change—or should we?" They concluded that the measurement of change was a complex and problematic undertaking. Recent work suggests that, particularly with regard to self-report data, the measurement of change is far more difficult than even they realized (Terborg et al 1980). It is now apparent that Cronbach & Furby's solutions to measuring change are inappropriate with Pre- and Post-self-report data since such data involve three potential types of change: alpha, beta, and gamma (Golembiewski et al 1976, Howard et al 1979a). If the effects of training programs are to be examined unambiguously, it is important to ascertain which types of change have occurred. Thus, recent articles by Zmud & Armenakis (1978), Lindell & Drexell (1979), Golembiewski & Billingsley (1980), Terborg et al (1980), and Schmitt (1982) have suggested methods for measuring these types of changes at the individual and/or group level. Golembiewski & Billingsley recommend factor analyzing pretest responses, posttest responses, and then comparing the resulting factor structures. Zmud & Armenakis recommend collecting Pre- and post ratings on both actual and ideal scores. Lindell & Drexell argue that if more psychometrically sound (i.e. multiple items and behavioral anchors) scales were used, problems associated with beta and/or gamma change would be less prevalent. Terborg et al suggest measuring change at the individual- and group-level using Pre, Post, and Then ratings that can then be examined using profile analysis. Specifically, they suggest using a "Then" measure after an intervention, in addition to the usual Pre- and Post- measures. Respondents are asked how they now perceive themselves to have been just before the training was conducted. In an impressive series of studies, Howard and his associates (e.g. Howard et al 1979a) have shown that the Then/Post measurement approach is more similar to objective ratings of change in behavior and performance than are results obtained from traditional Pre/Post self-report methods. Since Then and Post ratings are obtained in close temporal proximity, it is more likely that both ratings will be made from the same perspective, and therefore are free of response-shift bias (i.e. beta change). Schmitt recommends using a confirmatory factor analysis approach which allows for a determination of the extent of difference in the pattern of factor loadings, the scale units of measurement, and the uniqueness.

Training programs typically have been evaluated using conventional statistics that are difficult for managers to use in decision making. Recently, Schmidt et al (1982) and Landy et al (1982) have illustrated how the linear regression-based decision-theoretic equations used previously to estimate the dollar impact of valid selection procedures can be applied in evaluating training programs designed to improve job performance. Equations have been derived for evaluating the *dollar value* of a single intervention compared to a control group, an intervention readministered periodically (e.g. yearly), and a comparison among two (or more) different training interventions. Schmidt et al (1982) point out that because of the paucity of well-designed training evaluation studies in the literature, researchers unfortunately will be forced to conduct their own studies to obtain an estimate of d_t (i.e. the observed gain in performance in standard score units). However, when several studies have been conducted, d_t can be estimated by the cumulated results of all available studies. The calculation of the d_t parameter is directly analogous to estimates of true validity in validity generalization research (Pearlman et al 1980, Schmidt et al 1980). This author agrees with Schmidt et al's call for more research which quantitatively integrates findings across studies to produce stable and accurate estimates of effect sizes (d_t values) for various kinds of training interventions. Such effect size estimates are crucial to the application of the utility equations. This type of research will enable us to someday provide managers with accurate estimates of *dollar gains* in productivity of alternative training strategies. It will also make it easier for training specialists to "sell" managers on their personnel function. Finally, it can guide training specialists in adjusting their interventions so as to make them more attractive from a cost/benefit viewpoint.

SPECIAL CONCERNS

Rater Training

Several authors have called for rater training programs to improve performance appraisal ratings (e.g. DeCotiis & Petit 1978, Latham & Wexley 1981). Borman (1979) discussed three categories of criteria for assessing rater training programs: rating behavior (e.g. leniency error, halo, central tendency); interrater reliabiity and convergent/discriminant validity; and accuracy (i.e. the degree to which ratings are relevant to or correlated with true criterion scores). As for the first criterion, several studies have demonstrated that training can successfully reduce common rating errors (Spool 1978). However, mixed results have been found regarding interrater reliability (Bernardin & Walter 1977, Buckley & Bernardin 1980). Recent rater accuracy research has raised questions regarding the prevailing assumption that error and accuracy co-vary negatively (Bernardin & Buckley 1981). Specifically, this research suggests not only that rater accuracy is largely unaffected by training, but that there may even be a weak positive correlation between certain errors and accuracy (Cooper 1981). Bernardin & Pence (1980) presented evidence which suggets that rater training programs such as those used by Bernardin (1978) and Borman (1975) to reduce psychometric errors may merely foster a response set (e.g. "don't rate an individual high or low on all factors") in raters that results in lower levels of accuracy.

Future research is needed to discover ways to reduce errors and increase reliability, validity, and accuracy. Borman (1979) has recommended standardizing the observation of behavior by developing in raters a common frame of reference for spotting effective and ineffective behaviors. Bernardin & Walter (1977) showed that student raters who were trained to record critical incidents of instructors' behavior in a personal diary had significantly less leniency and halo and greater interrater reliability than did a group of untrained students. A common frame of reference for observing and rating can be trained by using the workshop approach developed by Wexley et al (1973) and used by Latham et al (1975). This workshop gives participants practice in rating persons shown on videotape. It also gives them an opportunity to compare their ratings with other trainees, to discuss the reasons for differences in their ratings, to find out what the correct ratings should be, and to discover the bases for their idiosyncratic rating tendencies. Pursell et al (1980) showed that this workshop approach significantly increased criterion-related validity coefficients by decreasing rating error in supervisory ratings. Fay & Latham (1982) found that this approach reduced rating errors regardless of whether BOS, BARS, or trait scales were used.

Goldstein (1980) pointed out that there was virtually no understanding of the differences, if any, between training raters to perform ratings for research only versus actual administrative purposes. Recent research by Zedeck & Cascio (1982) suggests that training raters for some purposes may lead to more accurate evaluations than training for others. Specifically, their results indicated that trained raters are more conservative (i.e. lower standard deviations) when considering ratees for merit raises versus recommending development or retaining a probationary employee. This research is extremely interesting because it examines the joint effect of an organizational contextual variable and rater training on appraisal decisions. Finally, more research other than that by Bernardin & Pence (1980) is needed which compares the effectiveness of rater error training (RET) and rater accuracy training (RAT). Recently, Pulakos (1983) compared a 1 1/2 hour version of Latham et al's method (1975) with a 1 1/2 hour RAT program using undergraduate students as subjects. The RAT program, based theoretically on Feldman's (1981) rating process model, stressed the multidimensionality of most jobs and the need to pay close attention to employee performance in terms of these dimensions. After discussing the general definitions of each dimension and the behavioral anchors that corresponded to different effectiveness levels, subjects practiced using the rating scales by rating the same two videotaped managers that were used in RET. After the RAT group rated each of these tapes, they discussed their ratings and received feedback on their accuracy. RAT had the effect of increasing accuracy and decreasing leniency error in subjects' ratings of Borman's (1977) videotapes, while RET decreased halo but had no effect on leniency. Ratings were made on seven dimensions of the manager's job. Interestingly, the significant Dimension × Training interactions suggest that the effectiveness of training strategies cannot be considered independent of the rating format and/or the rating task itself. Although the combination of RET and RAT proved to be somewhat *less* accurate than RAT alone, further research is needed to verify these findings, particularly in field settings.

Career Planning and Development

Career planning and development have become buzzwords among human resource specialists. Many organizations feel compelled to implement some sort of career development program simply to "keep up with the Joneses." In fact, this endeavor is probably one of those fads that J. P. Campbell (1971) warned us about! Much of the literature in this area tends to be evangelistic, obvious, and nonempirical. Nevertheless, there are a few bright spots worth noting.

Research by Schein (1978) and Super (1982) indicates that certain motivational, attitudinal, and value syndromes influence people's vocational decisions throughout their careers. Following this line of research, Miner & Crane (1981) have shown that individuals who have a stronger "motivation to manage" are more likely to manifest this motivation in career plans directed at managerial work. Besides supporting Miner's managerial role motivation theory (1965), this research suggests that the measurement of managerial motivation should be incorporated in career planning programs. Stumpf & Colarelli (1981) have studied the effects of career education programs on exploration strategies which, in turn, have differential effects on various career outcomes. Ramos (1982) developed the Individual Interest Inventory which allows nonmanagement people to rate their own interest and ability to perform core activities of first-level managers in the Bell System. Respondents then self-score their ratings so that they can be compared to the actual responses of first-level managers from various job families and/or positions who completed a similar instrument. Hopefully, by evaluating their interest in performing first-level work activities, individuals who are ill suited for management work would self-select themselves out of the promotional process. The developmental possibilities of this instrument will have to await future research. Lyness & Moses (1981) have incorporated various career planning activities into an assessment center used to evaluate middle level managers' potential to effectively perform upper management positions. Integrating career planning with ongoing staffing procedures makes sense to this reviewer because the assessment center provides a rigorous evaluation of an individual's strengths and weaknesses. Despite its intuitive appeal, this approach to career development also requires rigorous evaluation. Lastly, Super (1980) has broadened the definition of "career" to include the total combination and sequence of roles played by a person during the course of a lifetime (e.g. worker, spouse, parent). Super's Life-Career Rainbow portrays nine major life-career roles graphically. This model has been used as a counseling aid to help adults analyze their own careers and to project themselves into the future, both as they have been developing and as they might, with planning, develop.

Cross-Cultural Training

In light of the rise in popularity of multinational corporations and their demand for people who can operate effectively abroad, the need for training procedures to ensure better performance overseas is growing steadily. A recent survey of 105 American companies operating abroad revealed that only 32% of them had formal training programs of some sort to prepare individuals for overseas work. The remaining 68% reported having no training programs whatsoever. One of the main reasons given for omitting training programs was a doubting of their effectiveness (Tung 1981). This lack of training may partially account for the high failure rate (approximately 30%) among Americans abroad (Hays 1971).

Despite this need for effective cross-cultural training, this reviewer could find no research being conducted on this topic since Goldstein's 1980 chapter. Clearly, research is urgently needed to ascertain the types of training procedures (e.g. culture assimilator, sensitivity training, field experiences) that are more appropriate to use depending upon the type of culture, job, and person. This should entail the joint efforts of psychologists with sociologists, cultural anthropologists, and political scientists.

Other special issues that deserve investigation include stress management training (Shea 1981), physical skills training (Gebhardt et al 1979), appraisal feedback and goal setting training (Ivancevich 1982, Ivancevich & Smith

1981), training designed to reduce professional obsolescence (Kaufman 1982), antisexist training (Dunnette & Motowidlo 1981), female performance training (White et al 1981), training of the older (i.e. 40–70) worker (D. F. Johnson & White 1980), training of hard-to-employ (Bhagat 1979) as well as mentally and physically handicapped (A. P. Goldstein 1981) employees, creative problem solving (Basadur et al 1982), negotiation skills (Bazerman & Neale 1982), and conflict management skills (Wall et al 1981).

CONCLUDING COMMENTS

In looking back over this review of the training literature since 1980, there are clearly some peaks and some valleys. For clarity, some of these are listed below with the hope that these deficiencies can be partially alleviated by the time of the next *Annual Review* chapter on personnel training:

1. Research is needed in the area of Organizational Analysis to develop a better understanding of how inefficient organizational units should be pinpointed, to determine whether training is the optimum solution to performance problems, to comprehend how the outside environment in which an organization operates affects its training needs, and to understand better how specific organizational climate variables facilitate and disrupt various training interventions.

2. Recent work in Task Analysis provides more sophisticated procedures for determining quantitatively what tasks are performed, what needs to be learned to perform these tasks, what ways these tasks should be performed, what should be taught in training and what should be learned on the job. Despite these improvements in Task Analysis methodology, more research is needed on linking Task Analysis results with actual training program design.

3. Behavioral surveys completed by multiple sources appear to be an excellent new approach to Person Analysis. Nevertheless, additional research is needed on developing methods to diagnose whether individual performance deficiencies are caused by inability or motivational and/or environmental causes.

4. It is important to perform additional research on the influence of the trainer's behavior on trainee learning.

5. More studies need to be conducted on matching individual differences among trainee's (i.e. aptitudes) to various instructional strategies (i.e. treatments).

6. Too little research has been conducted on facilitating positive transfer of learning from the training situation to the job situation. It is recommended that the effects of having trainees set specific goals at the conclusion of formal training and having these goals monitored by trainers be investigated.

7. Excellent progress has been made in evaluation methodology. More needs to be done now in actually implementing these new techniques.

8. Considerably more research is urgently needed in the area of management development. Many of the simulation methods such as case study, role playing, and business games need immediate attention. Several theoretical approaches such as Double Loop Learning (Argyris 1976), Managerial Role Theory (Mintzberg 1975), Grid Seminars (Blake & Mouton 1978), and the Vroom-Yetton Model (Vroom 1976) require additional evaluative research.

9. Additional research is needed in the area of cross-cultural training.

10. Considering the rapid changes in our society, more research is clearly needed in the effective retraining of layed-off employees as well as career planning and development.

ACKNOWLEDGMENTS

I wish to acknowledge the help of Ray Noe and Rick Malacrea in preparing this review. These two psychology doctoral students did all of the preliminary work for this chapter in a highly professional manner. Special thanks also to I. L. (Irv) Goldstein, a friend and respected colleague, for his valuable insights on this manuscript. Claire Rammel and Pamela Cook Stoecker, Management Department secretaries, are to be commended for helping me to meet my deadlines in their usual patient and friendly manner. Finally, my wife and sons deserve more than these mere words for putting up with me during these busy times.

Literature Cited

Anastasio, E. J., Morgan, J. S. 1972. Factors inhibiting the use of computers in instruction. *Educ. Test. Serv.* NSF GJ 27427

Andrasik, F. 1979. Organizational behavior modification in business settings: A methodological and content review. *J. Organ. Behav. Manage.* 2:85–102

Argyris, C. 1976. Theories of action that inhibit individual learning. *Am. Psychol.* 31:638–54

Argyris, C. 1980. Some limitations of the case method: Experiences in a management development program. *Acad. Manage. Rev.* 5:291–98

Bandura, A. 1977. *Social Learning Theory.* Englewood Cliffs, NJ: Prentice-Hall

Basadur, M., Graen, G. B., Green, S. G. 1982. Training in creative problem solving effects on ideation and problem finding and solving in an industrial research organization. *Organ. Behav. Hum. Perform.* 30:41–70

Bass, B. M., Vaughan, J. A. 1966. *Training in Industry: The Management of Learning.* Belmont, Calif: Brooks/Cole

Baumgartel, H., Sullivan, G. J., Dunn, L. E. 1978. How organizational climate and personality affect the pay-off from advanced management training sessions. *Kans. Bus. Rev.* 5:1–10

Bazerman, M. H., Neale, M. A. 1982. Improving negotiation effectiveness under final offer arbitration: The role of selection and training. *J. Appl. Psychol.* 67:543–48

Bennis, W. G. 1966. *Changing Organizations.* New York: McGraw-Hill

Bernardin, H. J. 1978. Effects of rater training on leniency and halo errors in student ratings of instructors. *J. Appl. Psychol.* 63:301–8

Bernardin, H. J., Buckley, M. R. 1981. Strategies in rater training. *Acad. Manage. Rev.* 6:205–12

Bernardin, H. J., Pence, E. C. 1980. Effects of rater training: Creating new response sets and decreasing accuracy. *J. Appl. Psychol.* 65:60–66

Bernardin, H. J., Walter, C. S. 1977. Effects of rater training and diary-keeping on psychometric error in ratings. *J. Appl. Psychol.* 62:64–69

Bhagat, R. S. 1979. Black-white ethnic differences in identification with the work ethic: Some implications for organizational integration. *Acad. Manage. Rev.* 4:381–91

Blake, R. R., Mouton, J. S. 1978. *The New Managerial Grid.* Houston, Tex: Gulf Publ.

Borman, W. C. 1975. Effects of instructions to avoid error on reliability and validity of performance evaluation ratings. *J. Appl. Psychol.* 60:556–60

Borman, W. C. 1977. Consistency of rating accuracy and rating errors in the judgment of human performance. *Organ. Behave. Hum. Perform.* 20:233–52

Borman, W. C. 1979. Format and training effects on rating accuracy and rating errors. *J. Appl. Psychol.* 64:410–21

Buckley, M. R., Bernardin, H. J. 1980. *An assessment of the components of a rater training program.* Presented at Ann. Meet. Southeast. Psychol. Assoc., Washington DC

Campbell, J. P. 1971. Personnel training and development. *Ann. Rev. Psychol.* 22:565–602

Carnegie-Mellon Report. 1982. Retraining displaced workers: Too little too late, *Business Week,* July 19, pp. 178, 181, 183, 185

Caro, P. W. 1979. The relationship between flight simulator motion and training requirements. *Hum. Factors* 21:493–501

Childs, J. M., Prophet, W. W., Spears, W. D. 1981. *The effects of pilot experience on acquiring instrument flight skills: Phase I.* US Dep. Transp. Fed. Aviat. Adm., Washington DC

Chiles, C. R., Abrams, M. L., Flaningam, M. R., Vorce, R. V. 1981. Tailoring shipboard training to fleet performance needs: II. Propulsion engineering problem analysis. *NPRDC Tech. Rep. TR* 81–23, San Diego, Calif.

Cooper, W. H. 1981. Ubiquitous halo. *Psychol. Bull.* 90:218–44

Cronbach, L. J., Furby, L. 1970. How should we measure "change"—or should we? *Psychol. Bull.* 74:68–80

Cross, K. D., Rogers, S. P. 1980. Marine corps infantry training requirements for map interpretation and land navigation. *NPRDC Tech. Rep. SR 80–17* San Diego, Calif.

de Charms, R., Rosenbaum, M. E. 1960. Status variables and matching behavior. *J. Pers.* 28:492–502

Decker, P. J. 1979. Modesty and caution in reviewing behavior modeling: A reply to McGehee and Tullar. *Personnel Psychol.* 32:399–400

Decker, P. J. 1980. Effects of symbolic coding and rehearsal in behavior-modeling training. *J. Appl. Psychol.* 65:627–34

Decker, P. J. 1982. The enhancement of behavior modeling training of supervisory skills by the inclusion of retentional processes. *Personnel Psychol.* 35:323–32

Decker, P. J., Sullivan, E., Moore, R. 1982. Using behavioral modeling for supervisory development in health care settings. *Cross Ref. Hum. Manage.* 12(6):1–4

DeCotiis, T., Petit, A. 1978. The performance appraisal process: A model and some testable propositions. *Acad. Manage. Rev.* 3:635–46

Dossett, D. L., Hulvershorn, P. 1984. Increasing technical training efficiency: Peer training via computer-assisted instruction. *J. Appl. Psychol.* In press

Dreilinger, C., Robinson, B. 1982. *The organizational, managerial, and technical/professional needs assessment: An innovative approach to accurately assessing strengths, deficiencies, causes, and solutions.* Graduate School, USDA, Washington DC

Dunnette, M. D., Motowidlo, S. J. 1981. *Estimating benefits and costs of anti-sexist training programs in organizations,* Symp. women in the workforce. Virginia Polytech. Inst. & State Univ., Blacksburg

Eden, D., Shani, A. B. 1982. Pygmalion goes to boot camp: Expectancy, leadership, and trainee performance. *J. Appl. Psychol.* 67:194–99

Evans, R. I., Rozelle, R. M., Maxwell, S. E., Rains, B. E., Dill, C. A. 1981. Social modeling films to deter smoking in adolescents: Results of a three-year field investigation. *J. Appl. Psychol.* 66:399–414

Fay, C. H., Latham, G. P. 1982. Effects of training and rating scales on rating errors. *Personnel Psychol.* 35:105–16

Feldman, J. M. 1981. Beyond attribution theory: Cognitive processes in performance appraisal. *J. Appl. Psychol.* 66:127–48

Finkle, R. B. 1976. Managerial assessment centers. In *Handbook of Industrial and Organizational Psychology,* ed. M. D. Dunnette, pp. 861–88. Chicago: Rand McNally

Fleishman, E. A. 1975. Toward a taxonomy of human performance. *Am. Psychol.* 8:-1127–49

Ford, J. K., Wroten, S. P. 1982. *A content validity ratio approach to determine training needs.* Presented at Ann. Meet. Am. Psychol. Assoc., 90th, Washington DC

Freedman, R., Stumpf, S. 1980. Learning style inventory: Less than meets the eye. *Acad. Manage. Rev.* 5:445–47

French, W. L., Bell, C. H. Jr. 1978. *Organization Development: Behavioral Science Interventions for Organization Improvement.* Englewood Cliffs, NJ: Prentice-Hall

Gagné, R. M., Briggs, L. I. 1974. *Principles of Instructional Design.* New York: Holt, Rinehart & Winston

Gagné, R. M., Mayor, J. R., Paradise, N. E. 1962. Factors in acquiring knowledge of a mathematical task. *Psychol. Monogr.* 76:Whole No. 526

Gebhardt, D. L., Hogan, J., Fleishman, E. A. 1979. Development of a self-administered physical training program for AT&T pole climbing jobs. *ARRO Tech. Rep.* Washington DC

Gill, R. W. T. 1982. A trainability concept for management potential and an empirical study of its relationship with intelligence for two managerial skills. *J. Occup. Psychol.* 55:139–47

Glaser, R. 1982. Instructional psychology: Past, present, and future. *Am. Psychol.* 37:292–305

Goldstein, A. P. 1981. *Psychological Skill Training: The Structured Learning Technique.* New York: Pergamon

Goldstein, A. P., Sorcher, M. 1974. *Changing Supervisory Behavior.* New York: Pergamon

Goldstein, I. L. 1974. *Training: Program Development and Evaluation.* Monterey, Calif: Brooks/Cole

Goldstein, I. L. 1980. Training in work organizations. *Ann. Rev. Psychol.* 31:229–72

Goldstein, I. L. 1982. *Needs assessment and content validity.* Presented at Ann. Meet. Am. Psychol. Assoc., 90th, Washington DC

Goldstein, I. L., Macey, W. H., Prien, E. P. 1981. Needs assessment approaches for training development. In *Making Organizations Humane and Productive*, ed. H. Meltzer, W. R. Nord. New York: Wiley

Golembiewski, R. T., Billingsley, K. R. 1980. Measuring change in OD panel designs: A response to my critics. *Acad. Manage. Rev.* 5:97–103

Golembiewski, R. T., Billingsley, K. R., Yeager, S. 1976. Measuring change and persistence in human affairs: Types of change generated by OD designs. *J. Appl. Behav. Sci.* 12:133–57

Gordon, M. E., Petty, M. M. 1971. A note on the effectiveness of research conditions in reducing the magnitude of dissimulation on a self-report criterion. *Personnel Psychol.* 24:53–61

Graen, G., Novak, M. A., Sommerkamp, P. 1982. The effects of leader-member exchange and job design on productivity and satisfaction: Testing a dual attachment model. *Organ. Behav. Hum. Perform.* 24:109–31

Hagman, J. D. 1980. Effects of training task repetition on retention and transfer of maintenance skill. *ARI Res. Rep. 1271*, Alexandria, Va.

Hakel, M. D. 1976. Some questions and comments about applied learning. *Personnel Psychol.* 29:361–69

Hall, E. R., Freda, J. S. 1982. A comparison of individualized and conventional instruction in navy technical training. *Train. Anal. Eval. Group Tech. Rep. 117.* Orlando, Fla.

Hays, R. D. 1971. Ascribed behavioral determinants of success-failure among US expatriate managers. *J. Int. Bus. Stud.* 2:40–46

Hinrichs, J. R. 1976. Personnel training. See Finkel 1976, pp. 829–60

Houston, R. C. 1979. *Development in training technology.* Symp. Hum. Factors Civil Aviat., The Hague, Netherlands

Howard, G. S., Ralph, K. M., Gulanick, N. A., Maxwell, S. E., Nance, D. W., Gerber, S. R. 1979a. Internal invalidity in pretest-posttest self-report evaluations and a reevaluation of retrospective pretests. *Appl. Psychol. Meas.* 3:1–23

Howard, G. S., Schmeck, R. R., Bray, J. H. 1979b. Internal invalidity in studies employing self-report instruments: A suggested remedy. *J. Educ. Meas.* 16:129–36

Hunt, D. P. 1982. Effects on human self-assessment responding on learning. *J. Appl. Psychol.* 67:75–82

Hunter, J. E., Schmidt, F. L., Jackson, G. 1982. *Advanced Meta-analysis: Quantitative Methods For Cumulating Research Findings Across Studies.* San Francisco: Sage

Ivancevich, J. M. 1982. Subordinates' reactions to performance appraisal interviews: A test of feedback and goal-setting. *J. Appl. Psychol.* 67:581–87

Ivancevich, J. M., Smith, S. V. 1981. Goal setting interview skills training: Simulated and on-the-job analyses. *J. Appl. Psychol.* 66:697–705

Johnson, D. F., White, C. B. 1980. Effects on training on computerized test performance in the elderly. *J. Appl. Psychol.* 65:357–58

Johnson, K. A., Graham, L. L., Carson, S. B. 1982. An evaluation of individualized, job-specific maintenance training. *NPRDC Tech. Rep. 82–53.* San Diego, Calif.

Karmin, M. W., Sheler, J. L. 1982. Jobs: A million that will never come back. *U.S. News & World Report*, Sept. 13, 1982, pp. 53–56

Kaufman, H. G. 1982. Continuing professional development at midcareer. *College-Industry Educ. Conf. Proc.*, pp. 88–97. San Diego, Calif.

Klimoski, R. J. 1982. *Needs assessment for management development.* Presented at Ann. Meet. Am. Psychol. Assoc., 90th, Washington DC

Kolb, D. A. 1981. Experiential learning theory and the learning style inventory: A reply to Freedman and Stumpf. *Acad. Manage. Rev.* 6:289–96

Kolb, D., Rubin, I., McIntyre, J. 1979. *Organizational psychology: An experiential approach.* Englewood Cliffs, NJ: Prentice-Hall

Komaki, J., Barwick, K. D., Scott, L. R. 1978. A behavioral approach to occupational safety: Pinpointing and reinforcing safe performance in a food manufacturing plant. *J. Appl. Psychol.* 63:434–45

Komaki, J., Heinzmann, A. T., Lawson, L. 1980. Effects of training and feedback: Component analysis of a behavioral safety program. *J. Appl. Psychol.* 65:261–70

Knight, J. L., Geddes, L. A., Salvendy, G. 1980. Continuous unobtrusive performance and physiological monitoring of industrial workers. *Ergonomics* 23:501–6

Knight, J. L., Salvendy, G. 1981. Effects of task feedback and stringency of external pacing on mental load and work performance. *Ergonomics* 24:757–64

Kraut, A. I. 1976. Developing managerial skills via modeling techniques: Some positive research findings—A symposium. *Personnel Psychol.* 29:325–28

Kurecka, P. M., Austin, J. M. Jr., Johnson, W., Mendoza, J. L. 1982. Full and Errant coaching effects on assigned role leaderless group discussion performance. *Personnel Psychol.* 35:805–12

Landy, F. J., Farr, J. L., Jacobs, R. R. 1982. Utility concepts in performance measurement. *Organ. Behav. Human. Perform.* 30:15–40

Latham, G. P., Saari, L. M. 1979. The application of social learning theory to training supervisors through behavioral modeling. *J. Appl. Psychol.* 64:239–46

Latham, G. P., Wexley, K. N. 1981. *Increasing Productivity Through Performance Appraisal.* Reading, Mass: Addison-Wesley

Latham, G. P., Wexley, K. N., Pursell, E. D. 1975. Training managers to minimize rating errors on the observation of behavior. *J. Appl. Psychol.* 60:550–55

Laughery, K. R. 1982. *Quarterbacks as cornerbacks or American fighter pilots in migs: A study of reverse role training.* Presented at Hum. Factors Soc. Meet., Seattle, Wash.

Lawshe, C. H. 1975. A quantitative approach to content validity. *Personnel Psychol.* 28:563–75

Leifer, M. S., Newstrom, J. W. 1980. Solving the transfer of training problems. *Train. Dev. J.* 34:42–46

Levine, E. L., Flory, A., Ash, R. A. 1977. Self-assessment in personnel selection. *J. Appl. Psychol.* 62:428–35

L'Herisson, L. 1981. Teaching the sales force to fail. *Train. Dev. J.* 35(11):78–82

Lindell, M. K., Drexell, J. A. 1979. Issues in using survey methods for measuring organizational change. *Acad. Manage. Rev.* 4:13–19

Locke, E. A. 1980. Latham vs. Komaki: A tale of two paradigms. *J. Appl. Psychol.* 65:16–23

Luthans, F., Davis, T. R. V. 1979. Behavioral self-management—The missing link in managerial effectiveness. *Organ. Dyn.* 7:42–60

Luthans, F., Paul, R., Baker, D. 1981. An experimental analysis of the impact of contingent reinforcement on salespersons' performance behavior. *J. Appl. Psychol.* 66:-314–23

Lyness, K. S., Moses, J. L. 1981. *Career Planning in an Advanced Management Potential Assessment Program.* Basking Ridge, NJ: AT&T

Mabe, P. A. III, West, S. G. 1982. Validity of self-evaluation of ability: A review and meta-analysis. *J. Appl. Psychol.* 67:280–96

Macey, W. H. 1982. *Linking training needs assessment to training program design.* Presented at Ann. Meet. Am. Psychol. Assoc., 90th, Washington DC

Macey, W. H., Prien, E. P. 1981. *Needs assessment: Program and individual development.* Presented at Ann. Meet. Am. Psychol. Assoc., 89th, Los Angeles, Calif.

Mager, R. F., Pipe, P. 1970. *Analyzing Performance Problems.* Belmont, Calif: Fearon

Maier, N. R. F. 1973. *Psychology in Industrial Organizations.* Boston: Houghton Mifflin

Manenica, I. 1977. Comparison of some physiological indices during paced and unpaced work. *Int. J. Prod. Res.* 15:261–75

Manz, C. C., Sims, H. P. Jr. 1981. Vicarious learning: The influence of modeling on organizational behavior. *Acad. Manage. Rev.* 6:105–13

Manz, C. C., Sims, H. P. Jr. 1982. Self-management as a substitute for leadership: A social learning theory perspective. *Acad. Manage. Rev.* 5:361–67

Marlatt, G. A., Gordon, J. R. 1980. Determinants of relapse: Implications for the maintenance of behavior change. In *Behavioral Medicine: Changing Health Life Styles,* ed. P. O. Davidson, S. M. Davidson, pp. 410–52. New York: Brunner/Mazel

Marx, R. D. 1982. Relapse prevention for managerial training: A model for maintenance of behavior change. *Acad. Manage. Rev.* 7:-433–41

Matsui, T., Okada, A., Kakuyama, T. 1982. Influence of achievement need on goal setting, performance, and feedback effectiveness. *J. Appl. Psychol.* 67:645–48

McCall, M. W. Jr., Lombardo, M. M. 1979. Looking Glass, Inc. The first three years. *Cent. Creat. Leadership Tech. Rep. 13,* Greensboro, NC

McCombs, B. L. 1979. *Identifying individualization parameters, strategies and models that are acceptable and feasible: Methodological considerations.* Presented at Ann. Meet. Am. Educ. Res. Assoc., San Francisco

McCormick, E. J., Jeanneret, P. R., Mecham, R. C. 1972. A study of job characteristics and job dimensions as based on the position analysis questionnaire (PAQ). *J. Appl. Psychol.* 56:347–68

McGehee, W., Thayer, P. W. 1961. *Training in Business and Industry.* New York: Wiley

McGehee, W., Tullar, W. L. 1978. A note on evaluating behavior modification and behavior modeling as industrial training techniques. *Personnel Psychol.* 31:477–84

Mealiea, L. W., Duffy, J. F. 1980. An integrated model for training and development: How to build on what you already have. *Public Personnel Manage, J.* 9:1–8

Melton, A. W. 1964. The taxonomy of human learning: Overview. In *Categories of Human Learning,* ed. A. Melton. New York: Academic

Mezoff, B. 1982. Cognitive style and interpersonal behavior: A review with implications for human relations training. *Group Organ. Stud.* Amherst, Mass: Sage

Michalak, D. F. 1981. The neglected half of training. *Train. Dev. J.* 35:22–28

Miner, J. B. 1965. *Studies in Management Education.* Atlanta: Organ. Meas. Syst. Press

Miner, J. B., Crane, D. P. 1981. Motivation to management and the manifestation of a managerial orientation in career planning. *Acad. Manage. J.* 24:626–33

Mintzberg, H. 1975. The manager's job: Folklore and fact. *Harvard Bus. Rev.* 53(4):49–51

Moore, M. L., Dutton, P. 1978. Training needs analysis: Review and critique. *Acad. Manage. Rev.* 3:532–45

Morano, R. 1973. Determining organizational training needs. *Personnel Psychol.* 26:479–87

Münsterberg, H. 1913. *Psychology and Industrial Efficiency.* Boston: Houghton Mifflin

Nadler, D. A., Tushman, M. L. 1977. A diagnostic model for organization behavior. In *Perspectives on Behavior in Organizations,* ed. J. R. Hackman, E. E. Lawler, L. W. Porter, pp. 85–100. New York: McGraw-Hill

Nord, W. 1969. Beyond the teaching machine: The neglected area of operant conditioning in the theory and practice of management. *Organ. Behav. Hum. Perform.* 4:375–407

Neider, L. L. 1981. Training effectiveness: Changing attitudes. *Train. Dev. J.* 35(12):24–28

Odiorne, G. S. 1970. *Training by Objectives: An Economic Approach to Management.* New York: Macmillian

Olson, H. C., Fine, S. A., Ogden, G. D., Levine, J. M. 1980. Planning study on the use of job and task analysis for determining training requirements in nuclear power operations. *ARRO Tech. Rep. 3058-FR,* Washington DC

Owen, W. B., Croll, P. R. 1974. *Productivity enhancement efforts in the federal government: A report of survey results, program report evaluation, and implications for research.* Personnel Res. Rep. No. 74–1, Washington DC: US Civil Serv. Comm., Personnel Res. Dev. Cent.

Pearlman, K., Schmidt, F. L., Hunter, J. E. 1980. Validity generalization results for tests used to predict job proficiency and training success in clerical occupations. *J. Appl. Psychol.* 65:373–406

Planty, E. G., McCord, W. S., Efferson, C. A. 1948. *Training Employees and Managers.* New York: Ronald

Porras, J. I., Anderson, B. 1981. Improving managerial effectiveness through modeling-based training. *Organ. Dyn.* 9(4):60–77

Pritchard, R. D., Hollenback, J., DeLeo, P. J. 1980. The effects of continuous and partial schedules of reinforcement on effort, performance, and satisfaction. *Organ. Behav. Hum. Perform.* 25:336–53

Pulakos, E. D. 1983. *A comparison of two rater training programs: Error training versus accuracy training.* MA thesis. Mich. State Univ., East Lansing

Pursell, E. D., Dossett, D. L., Latham, G. P. 1980. Obtaining valid predictors by minimizing rating errors in the criterion. *Personnel Psychol.* 33:91–96

Qualy, J., Jahns, D. W., Gilmour, J. D., Paulson, D. 1982. Navigation training methods for low-altitude flight. *NPRDC Tech. Rep. 82–43,* San Diego, Calif.

Ramos, R. A. 1982. *The use of job analysis data for career identification and development.* Presented at Ann. Meet. Acad. Manage. Assoc., 42nd, New York

Raven, B. H., Fishbein, M. 1965. Social referents and self-evaluation in examinations. *J. Soc. Psychol.* 65:89–99

Robertson, I., Downs, S. 1979. Learning and the prediction of performance: Development of trainability testing in the United Kingdom. *J. Appl. Psychol.* 64:42–50

Russell, J. S. 1982. *A study of variables which can increase the effectiveness of behavior modeling training for supervisors and middle managers.* PhD thesis. Mich. State Univ., East Lansing

Saari, L. M., Latham, G. P. 1982. Employee reactions to continuous and variable ratio reinforcement schedules involving monetary incentive. *J. Appl. Psychol.* 67:506–8

Salinger, R. D. 1973. Disincentives to effective employee training and development. Washington DC: *US Civil Serv. Comm. Bur. Train.* 142 pp.

Salvendy, G., Boydstun, L. E. 1980. A conceptual approach to development and validation of hierarchical acquisition in psychomotor performance. *Jpn. Psychol. Res.* 22:-64–71

Savage, R. E., Williges, B. H., Williges, R. C. 1982. Empirical prediction models for training group assignment. *Hum. Factors* 24:417–26

Schein, E. H. 1978. *Career Dynamics: Matching Individual and Organizational Needs.* Reading, Mass: Addison-Wesley

Schendel, J. D., Hagman, J. D. 1982. On sustaining procedural skills over a prolonged retention interval. *J. Appl. Psychol.* 67:-605–10

Schmidt, F. L., Gast-Rosenberg, I., Hunter, J. E. 1980. Validity generalization results for computer programmers. *J. Appl. Psychol.* 65:635–42

Schmidt, F. L., Hunter, J. E., Pearlman, K. 1982. Assessing the economic impact of personnel programs on workforce productivity. *Personnel Psychol.* 35:333–47

Schmitt, N. 1982. The use of analysis of covariance structures to assess beta and gamma change. *Multivar. Behav. Res.* 17:343–58

Shea, G. F. 1981. Profiting from wellness training. *Train. Dev. J.* 35(10):32–37

Siegel, A. I. 1983. The miniature job training and evaluation approach: Additional findings. *Personnel Psychol.* 36:41–56

Snyder, R. A., Raben, C. S., Farr, J. L. 1980. A model for the systematic evaluation of human resource development programs. *Acad. Manage. Rev.* 5:431–44

Sorcher, M., Spence, R. 1982. The interface project: Behavior modeling as social technology in South Africa. *Personnel Psychol.* 35:557–81

Spool, M. 1978. Training programs for observers of behavior: A review. *Personnel Psychol.* 31:853–88

Staw, B. M. 1977. The experimenting organization: Problems and prospects. In *Psychological Foundations of Organizational Behavior,* ed. B. M. Staw. Santa Monica, Calif: Goodyear

Stein, R. T. 1980. A job analysis of Looking Glass, Inc.: A study of content validity. *Cent. Creat. Leadership,* Greensboro, NC

Stein, R. T. 1982. Using real-time simulations to evaluate managerial skills. *J. Assess. Cent. Tech.* 5(2):9–15

Stumpf, S. A., Colarelli, S. M. 1981. *The effects of career education on exploratory behavior and job search outcomes.* Acad. Manage. Conv. Proc., 81st, pp. 76–80, San Diego, Calif.

Stumpf, S. A., Freedman, R. D. 1981. The learning style inventory: Still less than meets the eye. *Acad. Manage. Rev.* 6:297–99

Super, D. E. 1980. A life-span, life-space approach to career development. *J. Vocat. Behav.* 16:282–98

Super, D. E. 1982. *Self concepts in career development: Theory and findings after thirty years.* Presented at Int. Congr. Appl. Psychol., 20th, Edinburgh

Terborg, J. R. 1981. Interactional psychology and research on behavior in organizations. *Acad. Manage. Rev.* 6:569–76

Terborg, J. R., Howard, G. S., Maxwell, S. E. 1980. Evaluating planned organizational change: A method for assessing alpha, beta, and gamma change. *Acad. Manage. Rev.* 5:109–21

Tubiana, J. H., Ben-Shakhar, G. 1982. An objective group questionnaire as a substitute for a personal interview in the prediction of success in military training in Israel. *Personnel Psychol.* 35:349–57

Tung, R. L. 1981. Selection and training of personnel for overseas assignments. *Columbia J. World Bus.* 16(1):68–78

Vroom, V. H. 1976. Can leaders learn to lead? *Organ. Dyn.* 4:17–28

Wall, S. J., Awal, D., Stumpf, S. A. 1981. *Conflict management: The situation, behaviors, and outcome effectiveness.* Presented at Ann. Meet. South. Manage. Assoc., 19th, Atlanta, Ga.

Warren, M. 1969. *Training For Results.* Menlo Park, Calif: Addison-Wesley

Weary, G., Arkin, R. M. 1982. Attributional self-presentation. In *New Directions in Attributional Research,* ed. J. H. Harvey, W. J. Ickes, R. F. Kidd. Hillsdale, NJ: Erlbaum

Weinstein, C. E., Rood, M. M., Roper, C., Underwood, V. L., Wicker, F. W. 1980a. Field test of a revised form of the cognitive learning strategies training program with Army enlisted personnel. *ARI Res. Rep. 462,* Alexandria, Va.

Weinstein, C. E., Underwood, V. L., Rood, M. M., Conlon, C. M. T., Wild, M., Kennedy, T. J. 1980b. The effects of selected instructional variables on the acquisition of cognitive learning strategies. *ARI Res. Rep. 463,* Alexandria, Va.

Weinstein, C. E., Washington, T. P., Wicker, F. W., Duty, D. C., Underwood, V. L. 1980c. The effects of material and task variations on a brief cognitive learning strategies program. *ARI Res. Rep. 461,* Alexandria, Va.

Weinstein, C. E., Wicker, F. W., Cubberly, W. E., Roney, L. K., Underwood, V. L. 1980d. Design and development of the learning activities questionnaire. *ARI Res. Rep. 459,* Alexandria, Va.

Weinstein, C. E., Wicker, F. W., Cubberly, W. E., Underwood, V. L., Roney, L. K. 1980e. Training versus instructions in the acquisition of cognitive learning strategies. *ARI Res. Rep. 460.* Alexandria, Va

Weisbord, M. R. 1978. *Organizational Diagnosis: A Workbook of Theory and Practice.* Reading, Mass: Addison-Wesley

Weiss, H. M. 1978. Social learning of work values in organizations. *J. Appl. Psychol.* 63:711–18

Wexley, K. N. 1982. *The performance appraisal interview.* Presented at Johns Hopkins Natl. Symp. Educ. Res., Washington DC

Wexley, K. N., Latham, G. P. 1981. *Developing and Training Human Resources in Organizations.* Glenview, Ill: Scott, Foresman

Wexley, K. N., Sanders, R. E., Yukl, G. A. 1973. Training interviewers to eliminate contrast effects in employment interview. *J. Appl. Psychol.* 57:233–36

White, M. C., Crino, M. D., DeSanctis, G. L. 1981. A critical review of female performance training and organizational initiatives designed to aid women in the work-role environment. *Personnel Psychol.* 34:227–48

Williams, B. B., Sauser, W. I. Jr., Kemery, E. R. 1982. *Intelligence and physical fitness as predictors of success in early infantry training.* Presented at Ann. Meet. Southeast. Am. Psychol. Assoc., New Orleans

Yukl, G. 1981. *Leadership in Organizations.* Englewood Cliffs, NJ: Prentice-Hall

Yukl, G. 1982. *A behavioral approach to needs assessment for managers.* Presented at Ann. Meet. Acad. Manage. Assoc., 42nd, New York

Yukl, G., Kanuk, L. 1979. Leadership behavior and effectiveness of beauty salon managers. *Personnel Psychol.* 32:663–75

Yukl, G., Van Fleet, D. D. 1982. Cross-situational, multi-method research on military leader effectiveness. *Organ. Behav. Hum. Perform.* 30:87–108

Zedeck, S., Cascio, W. F. 1982. Performance appraisal decisions as a function of rater training and purpose of the appraisal. *J. Appl. Psychol.* 67:752–58

Zink, D. L. 1982. *Standards for time taken in self-paced training.* Presented at Ann. Meet. Hum. Factors Soc., Seattle

Zmud, R. W., Armenakis, A. A. 1978. Understanding the measurement of change. *Acad. Manage. Rev.* 3:661–69

Ann. Rev. Psychol. 1984. 35:553–77

CHILD PSYCHOLOGY

Robert B. Cairns and Jaan Valsiner

Department of Psychology, University of North Carolina, Chapel Hill,
North Carolina 27514

CONTENTS

INTRODUCTION

This chapter covers the 3 years of activity in child psychology since the last
general review was prepared (Masters 1981). By tradition, child psychology
has been broadly defined. Accordingly, the most recent *Handbook of Child
Psychology* (Mussen 1983) encompasses social and personality development,
cognitive development, language development, life-span psychology, adolescent psychology, infancy, comparative-developmental psychology, and developmental aspects of ethology and evolutionary psychology. In the first 26
volumes of the *Annual Review of Psychology,* the field was covered each year
in a single chapter. More recently, its subareas have been reviewed separately

553

0066-4308/84/0201-0553$02.00

or in combination, and an inclusive chapter has become unnecessary. Nonetheless, it is useful at periodic intervals to "zoom out" in order to gain perspective on those activities and advances that are common to the several areas of development. This selective review was prepared with such an integrative function in mind. We begin with some overview comments on the history and current institutional status of child psychology. We then sample some of the advances of theory, substance, and method, and we close with some observations on the present state of the area.

HISTORICAL ROOTS AND CONTEMPORARY INSTITUTIONS

In the past triennium, over 6000 published journal articles, reviews, books, monographs, and book chapters have been concerned with developmental issues. This literature provokes two initial albeit superficial impressions; namely, (*a*) child psychology is a booming enterprise, and (*b*) a good deal of the work is business as usual. In this context, "as usual" means that investigators have tended to continue in previously defined theoretical and research trajectories. But there were notable exceptions, due in large measure to realignments within the area and the merger of orientations and methods. For example, there have been at least four different attempts to effect a social development/ cognitive development synthesis. Similarly, the past 3 years have seen new attempts to integrate evolutionary and developmental concerns and to synthesize applied and "pure science" approaches.

But even these mergers and conceptual realignments are hardly fresh; rather, they appear to be a return to an earlier, integrated view of development. This observation itself points to one of the major themes of the past 3 years; namely, a heightened awareness among developmental psychologists of the history of their field, its pioneers, and its discoveries (Reinert 1979, Oppenheim 1982, Borstelmann 1983, Bronfenbrenner & Crouter 1983, Lerner 1983). In 1980–1983, there were two major historical landmarks to commemorate. One widely publicized event was the 50th anniversary of the founding of the Society for Research in Child Development. The 1983 biennial meeting of the Society became the occasion for a retrospective look at its founders and at the events that brought the interdisciplinary organization into being. A second anniversary was curiously given no special celebration. The year 1982 was the centennial of the publication of William Preyer's *Die Seele des Kindes* (1882), the volume widely viewed as being the first significant scientific study in childhood development. [Competitors for the honor include D. Tiedemann's (1787) baby biography of one century earlier; C. R. Darwin's (1877) belated account of his son's first years; and Perez's (1878) study of childhood.]

The historical emphasis has gone beyond anniversaries. It has also been responsible for a critical reassessment of the area and the roles it can play in behavioral science. According to one significant revisionistic view, the primary antecedents for developmental psychology are different from general experimental psychology. The roots of developmental study are to be found in the embryological traditions of K. E. von Baer and W. Preyer and the evolutionary biology of C. R. Darwin and E. Haeckel (e.g. Oppenheim 1982). Hence its original domain was the clarification of behavioral origins, changes, and directionality as expressed over the lifetime of an individual organism. These features of developmental study may be contrasted on virtually every point with the background and goals historically identified in general experimental psychology (see Hearst 1979). Despite some significant commonalities, these orientations to behavioral phenomena differ in the time-frame of investigation, units of analysis, and concern with individual integration as opposed to variable manipulation. The failure to recognize these distinctions has been responsible for tensions between developmental and nondevelopmental approaches that persist to the present.

Not all of the history lessons have been revisionistic; some have been simply enlightening. The resurrection of J. M. Baldwin's genetic epistemology can be included in the latter category (Broughton & Freeman-Moir 1982). It is now generally recognized that Baldwin's (1895) view of cognitive development and genetic epistemology was exceedingly similar to the one later proposed by J. Piaget (Wozniak 1982). How, then, do the two views differ? According to Kohlberg (1982), "In the end, the fundamental distinction between Baldwin's moral psychology and Piaget's is that Piaget's psychology has no self" (p. 311). On this score, Baldwin himself claimed that his theory was appropriately seen as the "self-thought theory of social organization" (Baldwin 1897).

Developmentalists in 1980–1983 were also in the business of making history. The major publication event for the area as a whole was the preparation and publication of the fourth edition of the *Handbook of Child Psychology*. [Actually, it is the sixth of the line because the present work is the direct descendant of Murchison's first two *Handbooks* (1931, 1933).] The current version is twice as large as its immediate predecessor. It shows other signs of the times, including inflation in cost ($5.00 in 1933 vs $200.00 in 1983) and in authorship (1 editor, 24 chapters, and 24 authors in 1933 vs 7 editors, 41 chapters, and 83 authors in 1983). The task of preparing the early handbooks was shared by some of its most prominent contributors (including K. Lewin, C. Bühler, M. C. Jones, M. Mead, A. Gesell, and J. Piaget). That tradition continues to the present.[1] What the *Handbook of Child Psychology* (1983) does not cover, the *Handbook of Developmental Psychology* (Wolman 1982) does. These encyclopedic works provide the field with a comprehensive coverage of

---

[1]Because distribution of the new *Handbook of Child Psychology* has been delayed beyond the deadline for this chapter, we cannot review the contents of the most recent version. Preliminary chapters in circulation indicate that it will serve, like its predecessors, as the principal reference work for the area for the rest of the decade.

its current theories and findings. As in the past, the formidable task of integrating this mass of material is left to the readers.

There were other publication landmarks as well. Baldwin's classic *Theories of Child Development* has been revised and expanded (1980). Patterson (1982) completed a valuable analysis of interpersonal processes observed in coercive family systems. Beyond the continuation of the series on child and developmental psychology (e.g. *Minnesota Symposia on Child Development, Advances in Child Development and Behavior*), and related monograph series (e.g. *Advances in Life-Span Developmental Psychology*), journals were founded and series initiated. One major new series covers developmental psychology as a whole (*Advances in Developmental Psychology*, Lamb & Brown 1981) and one focuses on the intersect between pure and applied developmental work (*Advances in Applied Developmental Psychology*, Morrison, Lord & Keating 1983). One of the more welcome periodical additions is a new theoretical journal of developmental psychology, the *Developmental Review*. So far it has lived up to its promise to be "an international and interdisciplinary journal [which] publishes original articles that bear on conceptual issues in psychological development" (Whitehurst 1981).

On the international front, perhaps the most impressive institutional trend has been the explosive growth of developmental research in Europe and beyond (e.g. Hartup 1982). The International Society for the Study of Behavioral Development approximately doubled in size during this triennium, to approximately 600 members in 1983. Beyond numbers, non-American developmentalists have now taken the lead in formulating and completing new longitudinal studies (e.g. Olweus 1980, Magnusson & Dunér 1981, Rutter 1981, Pulkkinen 1982). Happily, the oldest continuing longitudinal study in America—L. Terman's sample of gifted children—is still ongoing, thanks to the efforts of R. R. Sears (1983).

COGNITIVE DEVELOPMENT

We sample now some topics that have been subsumed by the term *cognitive development*. We focus on issues of theory, investigations of memory development, and some areas of communication.

Some Issues of Theory

The cognitive revolution, now entering its third decade, seems ripe for a counter-revolution. All along there has been the problem that the two main components of the cognitive movement—the nondevelopmental emphases of experimental psychology and the nonexperimental propensities of cognitive-developmental theory—were not all that congenial. The theoretical shortcomings of stage theorizing have been long recognized (e.g. Flavell 1963, Kessen

1965), and they have surfaced again in this triennium (e.g. Brainerd 1981, Keil 1981, Flavell 1982). All this suggests that it is not enough simply to label stages; there must be inquiry into the precise skills, strategies, and capabilities required to solve particular kinds of problems. Then there is the enduring problem of how transitions are made between stages and what are the mechanisms of transition.

In one of the more important theoretical contributions to appear during this interval, Fischer (1980) proposes an integration of Piagetian and experimental/learning assumption that attempts to come to grips with developmental changes in skill characteristics and how they are acquired. This effort is significant because it attempts to deal with the basic discontinuity between analyses of learning and information processing on the one hand, and global Piagetian and Wernerian developmental concepts on the other. More important, Fischer's (1980) model is a serious attempt to integrate cognitive, social, motor, and linguistic domains.

But there are other alternatives. For instance, Keil (1981) uses the concept of prior constraints to account for differences in performances at the various age/developmental stages. What kind of constraints? Presumably they are to be found in the nature of the task or "cognitive domain" as well as in the minds of human beings. Keil (1981) argues for the universality of certain cognitive constraints across childhood to adulthood. He focuses on adult-child similarities, not differences. For empirical support he can cite recent demonstrations of infant and childhood competence (e.g. Chi 1981). In sum, Keil (1981) seems to have proposed a nondevelopmental account of cognitive development.

Then there are revisions of positions that may be appropriately seen as within the Piagetian framework, such as Feldman's (1980) *Beyond Universals in Cognitive Development* and Broughton's (1981) essay in *Human Development*. How does one "go beyond" universals? By attending to the stages or levels involved in the perfection of skills and performance in specific areas not subsumed by the Piagetian framework. These would include, according to Feldman (1981), "numerous pursuits that human beings engage in, ranging from the acquisition of culturally critical skills such as reading or arithmetic to relatively idiosyncratic activities that only come from extensive preparation in a discipline" (p. 85). An example of the latter would be open-heart surgery. All this is to say that Feldman is betting on the possibility that there are stages or levels of acquisition that are relatively specific to domains but which, in aggregate, conform to some highly general principles.

But what is the difference between a level, stage, phase, and interval? In a brief but useful discussion of these terms, von Glaserfeld & Kelley (1982) offer some semantic distinctions among the concepts. They argue that the term *level* has no inherent time component—it refers to a spatial orientation. The other three terms imply a temporal component. Accordingly, *period* is a stretch of time; *phase* also refers to an interval of time, but one in which there is some form of repetition or recurrence (such as phases of the moon). The term *stage* would be reserved by these authors for intervals of time in which there are qualitative differences from other intervals and that together imply "some form of progression towards an expected end state" (p. 154). Beyond semantics, the critical problem remains with the specification of stage and the definition of transition rules. Flavell (1982) observes that multiple test conditions, contexts, and prior experience can affect test performance, hence the apparent "stage" at which a child functions.

Of the theoretical trends distinguishable in cognitive developmental theories of this period, perhaps the most important is the reassessment of the developmental-contextual concepts of Vigotsky (1939) and their modern dialetical versions (e.g. Broughton 1981, Youniss 1983). Of the expositions of this model for cognitive psychology, Rogoff (1982) provides us with one more relevant to basic cognitive research. Drawing from the framework of dialectical psychology, Rogoff (1982) argues that cognitive development cannot be divorced from the personal/social/ecological context in which it occurs (Mandler et al 1980, Posner 1982, Rogoff & Waddell 1982). This generalization holds not only for the developmental process itself, but for the laboratory assessment devices that are employed. On this score, the usual laboratory procedures for cross-national and cross-personal comparisons themselves are inadequate. Why? Because they are divorced from the context of the experience of the individual and they provide only the illusion of comparability. This point of view has strong implications for theory; it has equally important directions for research design and statistical analyses. To the extent that one seriously adopts the idea that the configuration is more important than the elements taken alone, a contextual analysis of individual performance is no longer an option; it is required. The argument is not unlike that offered by Lewin (1933) in his initial *Handbook* chapters. At this juncture, it seems as fresh as it did 50 years ago. If Rogoff is correct, the problem lies with the research designs and statistics as much as with theoretical conceptualization and interpretation.

We cannot close these comments on theory in cognitive development without a note on metacognition, or one's awareness of one's own cognitions. One of its offspring concepts, metamemory, has been carefully evaluated and roundly criticized by Cavanaugh & Perlmutter (1982). These authors conclude that metamemory has been loosely employed and does not seem to have added a great deal to our understanding of cognitive processes. Paris & Lindauer (1982), no less critical, observe that the term implies a self to think about thinking. If nothing else, the term draws attention to the role of conscious (and unconscious) processes involved in performing cognitive operations (Wellman 1983). In addition, it invites comparable analyses in other domains than memory. So far, children's reflections have been assessed in studies of emotion

(Harris et al 1981), compositional aspects of stories (Yussen et al 1980), visual perception (Flavell et al 1981), appearance-reality distinctions (Flavell et al 1983), act-rule relations (Weston & Turiel 1980), and beliefs (Wimmer & Perner 1983). In these studies, it seems clear that children's reflections/reports about their thought processes often fail to correspond to nonsubjective measures of these processes. To bring attention to the self-report/observation discrepancies is a step forward. What is needed at this juncture is a direct confrontation of the reasons for the discrepancies, and for the consistencies. In an insightful consideration of the problem, Schneider (1984) observes that the relations between performance of the child's awareness of memory strategies changes as a function of age and competence. This raises the critical issue of developmental integration and whether different weights are assigned to component processes over time. On this score it seems safe to assume that the roles of self-conscious controls in guiding social and cognitive action are *not* the same at different stages of ontogeny, nor the same for all tasks.

The Development of Memory

Judging from the number of publications concerned with the problem, there is still much to be learned about how children remember and forget. What seems clear at this juncture is that very young children can recover previous experiences if the experimental setting is appropriate and meaningful (e.g. Daehler & O'Connor 1980, Mast et al 1980, Rovee-Collier & Sullivan 1980, Perlmutter et al 1981). Even infants respond to "hints" or "reactivation" (Sullivan 1982). It is also clear that young children perform considerably less well than do older children and adults, all things equal. The interesting outcomes occur when things are *not* equal. Accordingly, children can outperform adults when there is a differential in background, knowledge, and experience in the child's favor. For instance, 10-year-old chess "experts" outperformed adult "novices" in memorizing chess pieces and places on a chess board. But the same children did less well on memorizing 10 digits than the adults did (Chi 1981). Whether this is a demonstration of the effects of the "knowledge base" that children have available or a demonstration of the effects of motivation, personal meaning, and/or relevance remains to be determined.

The analysis of memory strategies and memory organization continues to be a major concern. Of the experimental studies on the matter, some of the more informative concern the performance of children in everyday settings where memory has social and adaptive significance. How do children, for instance, remember their classmates' names? According to an innovative analysis of the problem by Bjorklund & Zeman (1982), children's cognitive constructions of their classrooms are organized according to seating placements or other functional groups (e.g. reading placement). Chi (1981) also found a spatial hierarchical structure in classmate recall, where 22 children were divided into four sections with 5-6 children in each section. But spatial location is not the only means for organization. If children are asked to recall by social clusters (i.e. peer networks or cliques), they are adept at recalling the various members of the class in terms of social affiliations. The more general point is that the adaptive significance of the information-to-be-recalled seems to play a major role in the bases for organization and memory. All this supports the validity of Rogoff's (1982) point that there is a close correspondence between the social-physical context of cognitive activity and its apparent form and efficiency. In a related analysis of the comparative adaptiveness of memory development, Wagner & Paris (1981) came to similar general conclusions.

The problem of what develops in memory development remains to be resolved. Is there a bigger memory storage bin or more efficient cognitive processing (Guttentag 1981)? Are more appropriate strategies spontaneously employed (Corsale & Ornstein 1980), or are there higher levels of motivation and greater levels of attention? Or is it some optimal combination of these changes that is adapted to the task (Klicpera 1983)? The search for the critical events in memory development continues. One difficulty is that research has implicated each of the above possibilities, but it is unclear how they are melded together in the performance of the task. Now that it has been established that performance on memory tasks is multidetermined, the question can be raised on the weights that should be assigned to the several components. At this juncture, it appears that the weights themselves vary as a function of the age-developmental status of the child and the level of specific task mastery and knowledge. Naus & Ornstein (1983) provide an insightful review of the current state of the area.

Motivation and Control

The cognitive underpinnings for the development of achievement motivation have been studied extensively by German psychologists following the lead of Heckhausen (1980). Trudewind (1982) has developed a conceptual system that can be used to understand the field-relatedness of the development of motivation. This renewed theoretic interest in the motivational underpinnings of achievement has had a strong impact on European studies of academic performance (e.g. Langfeldt 1983, Ries et al 1983). In addition, the metamotivational issues of children's perception of convariation in actor-action attributes have been investigated (Krug et al 1982). Studies of children's development of control over their environment (Gunnar 1980) and their perception of the controllability of environmental events (Weisz 1981, Weisz & Stipek 1982) perhaps signal a new, systematic attack on a very old and important issue. Developmental studies of self-attributions of freedom and perceived control are, of course, closely related to recent social psychological analyses of causal attribution.

Language, Reading, and Communication

Clark & Hecht (1983) recently prepared a review of language research, and here we only mention a relationship to other trends within the field. As Miller (1980) indicates in the Festschrift for Jerome Bruner, *The Social Foundations of Language and Thought* (Olson 1980), there is a special folly in carving up the various areas of cognitive, developmental, and social psychology. The development of language depends on all three. Accordingly, it is difficult to imagine how productive social development research can be conducted without attention to linguistic communications and their properties. The reverse holds as well; namely, one can hardly divorce language development from the social/communicative context in which it occurs.

Acquiring the capability to read—fluently, meaningfully, fluidly—is a magnificent achievement, almost on par with the acquisition of language itself. One of the primary ways to disentangle the complex processes involved is to study persons who fail at the task. Recent attempts to account for reading disabilities have raised questions about the adequacy of information-processing deficit hypotheses. The problem for the deficit hypothesis stems from the failure of laboratory-based procedures to identify specific solutions in terms of one or more elementary cognitive processes. As Morrison & Manis (1982) point out, the "elementary cognitive deficit" proposal for reading disabilities has not been supported by current empirical evidence. Moreover, they conclude that on a logical level, "process-oriented theories cannot account adequately for the specificity of the disorder" (p. 84). A similar conclusion was reached by Vellutino (1979) on the inadequacy of the perceptual deficit proposal. Why, then, do some otherwise normal children have such serious problems learning to read? Morrison & Manis (1982) favor alternatives that focus on the failure of the poor reader to acquire key skills necessary for reading, as opposed to a basic process deficit. Among other things, poor readers may fail to acquire the rules that govern the relationship between English orthography and the speech sounds of the language.

But is it only the English language that presents a problem for readers? The claim that Chinese and Japanese populations fail to show the high incidence of reading problems observed in English-speaking countries stimulated a most informative set of cross-national comparisons by H. W. Stevenson and his colleagues. In a contrast of Chinese, Japanese, and American children, Stevenson et al (1982) report roughly the same proportion of children in all three countries experience reading difficulties. Beyond having clarified the empirical question, Stevenson et al (1982) nicely illustrate the gains to be made by escaping from the constraints of the culture in which one's original discovery is embedded.

So why the failure to read? Klicpera (1983) reminds us that poor readers are not a homogeneous group. They differ among themselves on key performance features, including word recognition, coding and decoding processes, and memory strategies. Hence a single causation seems unlikely but not impossible. It has been shown, in addition, that reading problems run in families (Decker & DeFries 1981). Until a precise genetic analysis of twins, nontwin sibs, and other kin is completed, the role of genetic variance will remain unclear. Paris and his colleagues (Paris et al 1983) suggest that the child's intentions, attributions, and ability to abstract meaning are key factors in discriminating good readers from poor ones.

Then there are the profound communicative disorders subsumed by the rubric "autism." The concept of *infantile autism* has undergone considerable change since it was introduced by L. Kanner in the early 1940s. Nowadays, infants are not the only persons who qualify. In their informative volume, *Autism in Adolescents and Adults,* Schopler & Mesibov (1983) discuss autism as a developmental disability rather than an emotional disorder resulting from parental psychopathology. Multiple problems confronting autistic adolescents and their families have been identified, and Schopler & Mesibov (1983) provide a useful guide to how these problems might be treated. No magic here, nor are there any startling shortcuts to normalcy. Treatment programs that work in day-to-day dealings with autistic adolescents are carefully described, and that is good enough. The implicit theoretical message is that changes may be introduced in key social and cognitive adaptations at adolescence and beyond, even among persons classified as autistic.

SOCIAL AND PERSONALITY DEVELOPMENT

This triennium has seen accelerated activity in the study of social processes and personality development. The work has been along six complementary lines that transcend both the topics studied and the age-developmental stages investigated. Overall, attention has focused on: 1. the integration of social processes with those of cognition on the one hand and affect on the other; 2. the role of development in social interactions; 3. individual difference continuity and change, and how differences might be predicted over the life span; 4. the universality of social processes across societies and across species; 5. the relations between the lifetime development of social phenomena in individuals and its evolution in the species; and 6. the methodological issue of how to study social interactions and integrate the information from other levels of analysis. Some comments on each of the issues are in order.

Integration with Cognition and Affect

There seems to be no doubt nowadays about the desirability for a synthesis of the separate areas of development. The problem has been to figure out the best way to achieve the integration.

The synthesis of social and cognitive developmental concepts is a case in point. There appear to be at least four different routes toward the synthesis, depending on what brand of cognitive or social process one begins with and which aspect is considered to be primary. First, for some writers the synthesis begins with Piaget's cognitive-developmental stages and looks for parallels in social development (e.g. Rubin & Daniels-Beirness 1983). Second, for others the synthesis could begin with social learning theory and consider cognitive variables as modulating or extending learning influences (Mischel 1973, Bandura 1977, Butler & Meichenbaum 1980, Dodge 1980, Casey & Burton 1982, Dodge & Frame 1982). Here, learning processes would be the basis for the integration. Third, the synthesis could take social attributions as its point of departure and look for parallel processes in children. This cognitive-social psychology of childhood would extend social attribution theory to behavior of children (e.g. Flavell & Ross 1981). Finally, the original social-cognitive synthesis of J. M. Baldwin could be revived. This would involve the resurrection of developmental symbolic interactionism and the related views of G. H. Mead and H. S. Sullivan (e.g. Lewis & Brooks-Gunn 1979, Selman 1980, Youniss 1980, Damon & Hart 1981).

A reasonable argument can be offered in support of each of the positions. But one of the recurring problems has been the failure to explicitly recognize the difference in orientations and to consider each to be equivalent and representative of the "social/cognitive" theory. There are *theories* of social-cognitive development—not *a* theory—and it remains to be seen which version will become dominant. Beyond this, certain problems remain for the synthesis as a whole. One is the stubborn gulf between some types of cognition—especially self-cognitions and self-concepts—and the social behaviors of individuals. Similarly, the relative independence of cognitive competence from social competence requires more careful attention than it has been given. All this is to say that the activity directed toward a social-cognitive synthesis has been well expended, but the work seems only to have begun.

The social and affective synthesis appears to be even less developed. Here, the difficulty seems to be the residual problem of measuring and analyzing affective states of both a positive and a negative sort. Two recent methodological advances seem especially promising. The procedure of using parents as collaborators in the assessment of intense emotional states in children represents an intelligent analysis of the problem and a promising way to use the cognitive skills of adults in analyzing what they view as the effective stimulus for behavior (Zahn-Waxler & Radke-Yarrow 1979). From a different approach, Masters and his colleagues (e.g. Barden et al 1981) have employed a useful technique for emotional induction. Barden et al (1981) find that just thinking about an emotion will make it so. Hence, recalling an incident involving happiness, anger, or sadness seems to be an effective and nonhazardous procedure for bringing about emotional states. Further, under prescribed conditions, social behaviors are supported by the emotion induced (Barnett et al 1982). In the long run, it appears that the theoretical synthesis of affect and social behavior must go hand in hand with advances in methodological innovation.

Toward a Developmental View of Social Interactions

Just as there is general agreement about the desirability for a synthesis of social, cognitive, and affective domains, so there is a consensus that a developmental orientation is probably required for the synthesis to be successful. But precisely what is meant by a "developmental orientation"? For a good many writers, including some within the area, the term has continued to have a projective quality. It is for this reason that the masterful contributions of Magnusson (1983) and Levine (1982) on the concept of development should prove to be especially helpful. A developmental orientation is one that is concerned with the *integration* of ontogenetic processes that are involved in the establishment, maintenance, and change of behavioral and cognitive patterns. This usage is consistent with that outlined earlier by Kessen (1965), Kuo (1967), Schneirla (1966), and Gottlieb (1976). Two operational consequences of this perspective are that research should be (*a*) longitudinal and (*b*) organismic, or integrated across psychobiological, cognitive, social, and contextual domains.

Is such research feasible? Judging from the number of relevant studies completed with humans, the question is still open. With animals, it is another matter. Depending on the species and on the problem, it is practical to aspire to such an integrated developmental analysis. On some counts, the results have been spectacularly successful. Reviews of such research efforts may be found in developmental accounts of perception (Aslin et al 1981, Gollin 1981) and behavioral development (Immelmann et al 1981).

In addition, some longitudinal studies (both short-term and long-term) successfully demonstrate the developmental perspective. The developmental-genetic analyses completed at Minnesota (Scarr & Weinberg 1983) and Colorado (Plomin & De Fries 1983) illustrate the importance of tracking biophysical-genetic effects beyond infancy. In the Scarr & Weinberg (1983) study, some of the stronger effects attributable to genetic factors occurred in late adolescence, not early childhood. Despite the lip service given to the need for developmental analyses, one finds few attempts to formulate a theoretical model that would integrate the organismic influences on human social development (but see Magnusson 1983 for a notable exception).

One relevant theoretical contribution that requires careful attention is contained in the model proposed by Block (1982). In a closely reasoned proposal, Block (1982) offers an analysis of Werner's orthogenetic principle on the one hand, and Piaget's concepts of assimilation and accommodation on the other. One aim of Block's analysis is to develop a model that does not overlook emotional states and their role in establishing and maintaining relatively durable personality dispositions. These dispositions, Block (1982) argues, become consolidated relatively early in the course of individual development.

Continuity and Early Experience Effects

Consistent with the ascendance of the concept of development, there has been renewed concern with the correlated issues of individual difference continuity and the enduring effects of early and later experiences. Probably the most important single volume on individual difference continuity and change was the edited volume, *Constancy and Change in Human Development* (Kagan & Brim 1980). The chapters cover virtually all areas of continuity, including personality and social development. The outcome is that the predictability is not as great as has been implicitly assumed with child development research, but not so modest as had been expected in situational models (Moss & Susman 1980).

Consider, for instance, the problem of whether or not one can predict from infancy the quality of the child's social adaptation. The predictor variables could be properties of a relationship, emotionality of the individual, or characteristics of the current and predicted social and nonsocial context. The problem has come to a head in the discrepant results that have been reported on the immediate effects and aftermath of social attachment patterns. The early claims of high levels of predictability have now been modified (Waters 1983) or disputed (Thompson et al 1982). Beyond theoretical debates, the problem seems to be a failure to replicate longitudinal predictions in independent samples. It may be the case that the explanation for the failure is one of different social-class status, as has been proposed. But that is simply one alternative, and it hardly accounts for the failure to obtain comparable results in within-national and cross-national comparisons (see Thomspon et al 1983, Waters 1983; see also Emde & Harmon 1982).

Rather than focus on why behavior *fails* to be predictable over time, it might be equally as valuable to attend to those events, contexts, and personal factors that make it predictable. This has been the strategy of Pulkkinen (1982) in her longitudinal study of children from 7 years through early adulthood. She finds that she can identify a "style of life" that emerges by adolescence and captures commonalities over time. Similarly, Kahn & Antonnucci (1980) refer to the social "convoys" which carry individuals in particular trajectories of experience and behavior over time.

Significant attempts have been made to identify the events and characteristics that bring about continuity and discontinuity (e.g. Bakeman & Brown 1980). The attitude is helpful if low levels of prediction are not seen as failures of the constructs or of the science. Within a developmental framework, continuity is partly a product of ontogenetic influences and cannot be understood without information over time (Sackett et al 1981).

The early experience debate has hardly simmered down. As argued in the chapters of Simmel's (1980) volume, *Early Experiences and Early Behavior,* it seems hardly profitable to make a boxscore of studies which demonstrate the effects of early experience and those which do not. Both effects can be demonstrated. But Henderson (1980) has found some order in the summary. He observes that the best evidence for the enduring effects of early experience in rodents comes from studies of biophysical events, whereby early experience influences the structures or functions of organ systems. On the other hand, purely psychological effects (due to learning mediation or memory) appear to be much less stable. Therein may lie one of the more profitable directions in further work in humans; namely, to disentangle the mediators and identify what kinds of early experience are likely to endure, and why (see also Clarke & Clarke 1981).

Cross-Cultural and Cross-Specific Comparisons

The internationalization and interdisciplinary emphases of the field have begun to have a significant scientific impact. Virtually all of the phenomena of social development in children that have been studied in North America can be studied elsewhere in societies that are organized differently from those found in the United States and Canada (see Triandis & Heron 1981, Wagner & Stevenson 1982). Moreover, the comparative generalizations implicit in sociobiology, ethology, and comparative-developmental psychology may be put to direct empirical assessment.

Cross-national work provides a direct opportunity to extend or restrict the implications of research with children in the U.S. At least some of the findings appear to be restrictive. For example, Grossman et al (1981) find that a minority of the babies studied in Bielefeld, West Germany, fit the "attached secure" depiction. This outcome contrasts with the findings in Baltimore, Minneapolis, and Berkeley. What are the implications of these differences in the behavior of the infants (and/or their mothers)? It may mean that the Germanic parents are more likely to support early infantile independence, that there is a cultural difference in security, or that the contextual/cultural differences in assessment are likely to produce differences in attachment outcomes. Similarly, Frankel & Roer-Bornstein (1982) find that the mothers in two Israeli communities differ markedly in infant care, and that these differences reflect background cultural differences in the communities. The investigations of Berland (1982) and Lancy (1983) demonstrate how interpersonal and cultural "amplifiers" can promote variations in cognitive development. For developmental psychology to become a science of human development—as opposed to a description of American development—more such cross-national and cross-cultural investigations are imperative.

Equally important are systematic comparative studies of nonhuman social development. Significant comparative contributions have been made to clarify the matters of individual difference continuity (e.g. Stevenson-Hinde et al 1980, Sackett et al 1981, Suomi 1983), early experience effects (e.g. Henderson 1980), and the relationships between biological control and developmental experience. These comparative studies continue to be filtered into the mainstream of child development research and theory, but in ways that are sometimes mysterious and at other times misleading. The task remains to specify systematically the state of affairs in studies of particular nonhuman species with as much clarity as in studies of human beings. The tendency in the recent period has been to use the nonhuman findings to illustrate or demonstrate, not to understand functional similarities and differences.

Development and Evolution

The study of social development continues to serve as a meeting ground for the analysis of the relation between evolutionary and developmental influences. This issue remains in the background of the nature-nurture debate and in the attempts to identify genetic determinants of emotional and social dispositions. So far, it appears that genetic factors will continue to be implicated in one form or another (Plomin & De Fries 1983). The study of developmental-genetic interactions has scarcely begun, however. Investigations of emotional disposition are good candidates for such analyses (Goldsmith 1983). But there is an important lesson in recent studies; namely, it may be the case that infancy is not the best place to look for the expression of genetic differences (Scarr & Weinberg 1983). This outcome would occur if the genetic effects were upon rates of development or the timing of the expression of events sooner (or later) in development (Cairns et al 1983). On this score, Drickamer (1981) has shown that in mice the rate of maturation is itself heritable.

Interactional Analyses

Doubtless the most important volume on social interactions in the triennium is Patterson's (1982) *Coercive Family Process*. Patterson summarizes much of his 20-year program on aggressive children and their families. Beyond his pioneering work in observing interactions, a unique feature of Patterson's work has been his ability to marry the techniques of behavioral analysis with the sociological concepts of social process and social organization. Working with a younger population (2- to 4-year-old twin boys and their families), Lytton (1980) has also attacked the problem of coordinating the outcomes of behavioral observations in natural settings, laboratory observations, and interview reports. He finds, not surprisingly, that the results do not always agree. The more general problem is that the use of multilevel analyses in the study of interactions frequently yields patterns of findings that are discordant.

On this score, sociometric measures appear to provide stable information similar to that obtained in observations (Puttallaz & Gottman 1981, Newcomb & Brady 1982, Coie & Dodge 1983). The discrepancies arise, however, in the failure of self-reports to fit in a direct fashion with observational and rating information. It seems likely that further progress on the study of interactions requires a clarification of the expected relations among assessment procedures. All this is to suggest that a systematic appraisal of the different kinds of information available in observations, interviews, ratings, and psychological tests is in order.

Various integration schemes have been proposed. Von Cranach's (1982) "action analysis" provides an emphasis on the directive role of consciousness and volition. Goodman (1981) has employed a promising procedure for analyzing the integration of verbal and motor behavior. To make progress in interpreting behavioral sequences, it is useful (and perhaps necessary) to translate second-by-second analyses into meaningful units of episodic interchange. These units have been called episodes or themes. Baltes (1982) has nicely illustrated how such a thematic analysis can be employed to clarify the caretaker-patient relationship in nursing homes. She concludes that the caretaking contingencies seem designed to keep the old persons dependent, not to encourage autonomy and independence. Apparently the strategy is unhappily effective.

To sum up this brief overview of social development, we must remark that the compartmentalization of "social development" as a separable area has now become outdated. With the integration of information over the life span—from embryonic states and infancy to adolescence and adulthood and senescence—the issues can hardly be limited to children. Nor can the understanding of social phenomena be divorced from the integrated cognitive and biological changes that occur in development.

DEVELOPMENT OF PERCEPTION AND ACTION

Detailed coverage of the areas of perceptual and motor development is provided in the second volume of the *Handbook* (Haith & Campos 1983) and in a number of edited volumes (e.g. Aslin et al 1981, Connolly & Prechtl 1981, Gollin 1981, Kelso & Clark 1982, Stratton 1982) and monographs (e.g. Haith 1980). It is in this domain of child development that the concepts of organismic development have their most concrete meanings and their most direct application to research design and interpretation. Hence, we could reasonably expect research on the development of perception and movement patterns to provide guides for areas of study where psychobiological foundations are less accessible. There are, however, strong temptations to become increasingly reductionistic in perceptual and motor analyses. One of the significant lessons that ethology teaches is that such basic processes are appropriately viewed in terms of the evolutionary adaptations and ontogenetic accommodations required of the child.

Those research programs which have attempted to place the changes in perceptual and motor development into the context of the child's adaptational circumstances are therefore of special interest. The research stimulated by the problem of intermodal transfer and association is a case in point. In everyday adaptations, perceptual events necessarily occur within a configural context. Variations in surrounding stimuli, prior cross-modal association, and differences in internal state presumably play a significant role in how information is processed. Such factors also should help determine how the information is interpreted and what kinds of action patterns are generated. Direct attacks on this problem of information integration have recently been generated in several laboratories (e.g. Lawson 1980, Lawson & Turkewitz 1980, Ruff 1980, Bahrick et al 1981, Lewkowicz & Turkewitz 1981, Rose et al 1981, Spelke 1981, von Hofsten 1982, Walker 1982). Collectively, this work demonstrates, in ingenious research procedures with infants, that the effective stimulus is multiply determined. The "transfer" of perceptual influence may be mediated by central arousal factors, experiences and "affordances," and the expectancies of the child. It would seem that such demonstrations should have a significant impact on how perceptual phenomena are analyzed, whether in infants or in adults.

The study of adaptive movement patterns presents special problems of quantification and analysis. It is perhaps for this reason that our understanding of motor development in humans is relatively less advanced than that of sensation and perception. In any event, Thelen (1981) has recently produced a set of papers on the ontogenetic transition from infantile kicking movements to toddler stepping movements. Using precise videorecording and microanalysis of the patterns and muscular systems involved, Thelen has demonstrated the continuity between the patterns and offered an elegantly simple explanation for the change in form.

Does the right hand know what the left hand is doing in infants—and does it care? Beyond the issue of cross-modal communication, there is a very old question of why right handedness dominates and why it dominates only incompletely. Harris (1980) provides a valuable overview addressed to the explanations for lateral dominance that have been proposed over the past 200 years. It turns out that virtually all of the "modern" concepts on laterality of function have been foreshadowed—sometimes stated with admirable clarity—

by developmentalists at one time or another over the past century. A side benefit of Harris's (1980) work is that he illustrates how the historical context may influence both developmental theory and research.

Finally, it is useful to learn that some experimental studies of vision in nonhuman infants do not generalize to children. The newborn infant suffering from neonatal jaundice is often placed in fluorescent blue light for continuous periods as part of a standard treatment practice. To protect the infant from retinal damage, patches are placed over both eyes during the treatment. But a wealth of evidence indicates that in infant cats and rabbits, abnormal visual experience leads to marked anomalies. Happily, such a result is not obtained with human infants who have been temporarily blinded. Assessments on standard visual tests at 5 years of age indicate no areas of difference between treated and nontreated children (Hoyt 1980). Why no difference? Hoyt (1980) notes that the visual occlusion was relatively brief and that the patching was not always continuous. It may also be the case that there is greater plasticity and recovery in the visual system than has been emphasized in prior experimental reports (see also Gollin 1981).

CONCLUDING COMMENTS

Comprehensive reviews of virtually every area of developmental thought and work have recently appeared, thanks in large measure to the contributors and editors of the new handbooks. Progress has been recorded on virtually every front, yet there remains a fragmentation of the area as a whole. In closing, we offer some observations on the state of the field and some issues that it now faces.

In the 3-year period covered in this review, we have often found key developmental concepts floating in the air, something like smog. It has become common for writers in child behavior to claim their contributions to be "developmental," "ecological," and/or "transactional." And it has become almost as common for reviewers or discussants to claim that the contributions are none of the above. All this suggests that some powerful ideas on development are at risk of becoming denuded of meaning. The concepts often have been employed with only a vague specification of their implications for research or their methodological properties. [The evisceration of significant ideas is not unprecedented. Over the past 40 years in child psychology, a number of concepts— including social reinforcement, dependency, modeling, authoritarianism— have enjoyed a period of wide and indiscriminate usage, then were critically evaluated and discarded. Such cyles make it difficult to achieve real progress on the problems to which the concepts refer, or even to recognize when progress has occurred.]

Each generation of child psychologists—from that of William Preyer and

James Mark Baldwin to Arnold Gesell and Jean Piaget to the present—seems to have had to discover the methodological and theoretical consequences of developmental concepts. On this score, one of the most bedeviling issues in ontogenetic study is the problem of integration; specifically, how endogenous and exogenous contributions are integrated in the self over time to enhance individual accommodation. The matter is especially treacherous because the conditions of this integration change over time and over the nature of the response system to be explained. Therein lie substantive problems on the nature of sensitive periods in development, the presumed importance of early (or later) experiences, and the age-relativity of metacognition.

How to unravel the age-related integration processes? One of the more important methodological insights which has regained support over this period is that developmental analyses must include a focus on the behaving individual, not merely the variable of interest. Such a "top-down" analysis would begin with the child-as-a-unit in which the dynamic influences of properties of the self, the social matrix, and the physical reality are integrated (cf Rogoff 1982, von Cranach 1982, Magnusson 1983). The effects of particular experiences or variables must be understood in terms of the special properties of the individual child. A developmental view implies that such person-oriented research should be longitudinal, or at least concerned with the elucidation of longitudinal integrative processes. It points as well to the need to go beyond correlational matrices in longitudinal analyses. More generally, it suggests the logical incompatibility of relying exclusively upon multivariate statistical models where variables are the sole focus of concern. On the other hand, the task of clarifying developmental integration seems unlikely to be wedded to a single method or form of analysis. It will be through the convergence of information—where individual-focus analyses are combined with variable-focus analyses—that enduring gains may be won.

Any continuing omissions or oversights that are likely to prove troublesome? A few. Biobehavioral events—the backbone of studies of developmental accommodations in nonhumans—continue to be given short shrift in human studies. The most conspicuous changes in human accommodations over time involve morphological, neurological, and physiological modifications which go hand-in-hand with behavior. It hardly seems reasonable to expect that much progress will be made in understanding an integration process if some of its key elements are omitted. This includes information about age- and sex-related differences in maturation rate and how these may be determined by genetic and ontogenetic influences.

On another level of concern, attitudes about "appropriate" research designs are firmly rooted in the dogma of the area and are perpetuated by the priority of parametric statistical analyses. In this regard, virtually no space was given in 1980 by the primary child development journals to reports of individual children. The long-term trend is startling. Over 50 years ago (1930), data on individual children were reported in about one-fourth of the tabular presentations in articles published in *Child Development* and the *Journal of Genetic Psychology*. The comparable figures in 1980 were near or at zero.[2] This editorial trend runs directly counter to current theoretical insights on the nature of development. The failure to appreciate the logical linkages between theoretical issues, research designs, and statistical analyses is likely to lead to continuing tension in the area.

Then there are the positive signs for the future. Thanks in large measure to the rebirth of European developmental research, it is no longer necessary to pay only lip service to the possibility of cross-national and comparative investigation. As indicated in this review, some of the most important longitudinal work is being conducted simultaneously in North America and abroad. For all the problems they present, developmental concepts have begun to have a significant impact on how researchers conceptualize and analyze empirical studies and interpret the outcomes. Our overview suggests that the dividends have begun to appear in virtually every area of psychological functioning, from social and cognitive development to the study of motor and communicative abilities. One of the concrete gains is the rediscovery of the role of affective characteristics in development and their necessary integration in cognitive and social functioning.

Finally, some progress may be claimed toward the formulation of a coherent theory of behavior development. Over the past 50 years, Piaget's constructivist theory provided an invaluable approximation toward such an inclusive model. But now its shortcomings in dealing with internal contradictions and the dynamics of developmental change severely limit its continued usefulness. Probably the most promising sign for the immediate future is that some of the brightest talents in the field have been recruited to the task. Progress on this matter should help reduce fragmentation within the field and clarify its relationship to other areas of behavioral science.

ACKNOWLEDGMENTS

This paper was facilitated by support from a grant from NICHD (R01–HD 14648–03). We thank Beverley D. Cairns for bibliographic assistance.

---

[2]The exact figures for the two journals are as follows: In 1930, some 22.8% of the tables published in *Child Development* contained information about individual subjects, and the percentage for the *Journal of Genetic Psychology* was 30.5%. Fifty years later, in 1980, the comparable figures were 0.5% for *Child Development* and 0.0% for the *Journal of Genetic Psychology*.

Literature Cited

Aslin, R. N., Alberts, J. R., Peterson, M. R., eds. 1981. *Development of Perception*. New York: Academic. Vol. 1, 463 pp.; Vol. 2, 387 pp.

Bahrick, L. E., Walker, A. S., Neisser, U. 1981. Selective looking by infants. *Cognit. Psychol.* 13:377–90

Bakeman, R., Brown, J. V. 1980. Early interaction: Consequences for social and mental development at three years. *Child Dev.* 51:437–47

Baldwin, A. 1980. *Theories of Child Development*. New York: Wiley. 582 pp. 2nd ed.

Baldwin, J. M. 1895. *Mental Development in the Child and the Race*. New York: Macmillan. 496 pp.

Baldwin, J. M. 1897. *Social and Ethical Interpretations of Mental Development: A Study in Social Psychology*. New York: Macmillan. 606 pp.

Baltes, M. 1982. Environmental factors in dependency among nursing home residents: A social ecology analysis. In *Basic Processes in Helping Relationships*, ed. T. A. Wills, pp. 405–25. New York: Am. Health Found. 528 pp.

Bandura, A. 1977. *Social Learning Theory*. Englewood Cliffs, NJ: Prentice-Hall. 247 pp.

Barden, R. C., Garber, J., Duncan, S. W., Masters, J. C. 1981. Cumulative effects of induced affective states in children: Accentuation, innoculation, and remediation. *J. Pers. Soc. Psychol.* 40:750–60

Barnett, M. A., Howard, J. A., Melton, E. M., Dino, G. A. 1982. Effect of inducing sadness about self or other on helping behavior in high- and low-empathic children. *Child Dev.* 53:920–23

Berland, J. C. 1982. *No Five Fingers Are Alike: Cognitive Amplifiers in Social Contexts*. Cambridge, Mass: Harvard Press. 246 pp.

Bjorklund, D. F., Zeman, B. R. 1982. Children's organization and metamemory awareness in their recall of familiar information. *Child Dev.* 53:799–810

Block, J. 1982. Assimilation, accommodation, and the dynamics of personality development. *Child Dev.* 53:281–95

Borstelmann, L. 1983. Children before psychology: Ideas about children from antiquity to the late 1800s. In *Handbook of Child Psychology: History, Theory, and Methods*, ed. W. Kessen, 2:1–41. New York: Wiley. 590 pp. 4th ed.

Brainerd, C. J. 1981. Stages II: A review of *Beyond Universals in Cognitive Development*. *Dev. Rev.* 1:63–81

Bronfenbrenner, U., Crouter, A. D. 1983. The evolution of environmental models in developmental research. In *Handbook of Child Psychology: History, Theory, and Methods*, ed. W. Kessen, 1:357–414. New York: Wiley. 590 pp. 4th ed.

Broughton, J. M. 1981. Piaget's structural developmental psychology: V, Ideology-critique and the possibility of a critical developmental theory. *Hum. Dev.* 24:382–411

Broughton, J. M., Freeman-Moir, D. J., eds. 1982. *The Cognitive Developmental Psychology of James Mark Baldwin: Current Theory and Research in Genetic Epistemology*. Norwood, NJ: Ablex. 460 pp.

Butler, L., Meichenbaum, D. 1980. The assessment of interpersonal problem-solving skills. In *Assessment Strategies for Cognitive Behavioral Interventions*, ed. P. C. Kendall, S. D. Hollon, pp. 197–225. New York: Academic. 425 pp.

Cairns, R. B., MacCombie, D. J., Hood, K. E. 1983. A developmental-genetic analysis of aggressive behavior in mice: I, Behavioral outcomes. *J. Comp. Psychol.* 97:69–89

Casey, W. M., Burton, R. V. 1982. Training children to be consistently honest through verbal self-instructions. *Child Dev.* 53:911–19

Cavanaugh, J., Perlmutter, M. 1982. Metamemory: A critical examination. *Child Dev.* 53:11–28

Chi, M. T. H.. 1981. Knowledge development and memory performance. In *Intelligence and Learning*, ed. M. Friedman, J. P. Das, N. O'Connor, pp. 221–30. New York: Plenum. 605 pp.

Clark, E., Hecht, B. F. 1983. Comprehension, production, and language acquisition. *Ann. Rev. Psychol.* 34:325–50

Clarke, A. D. B., Clarke, A. M. 1981. "Sleeper effects" in development: Fact or artifact. *Dev. Rev.* 1:344–60

Coie, J., Dodge, K. A. 1983. Continuities and changes in children's social status: A five-year longitudinal study. *Merrill-Palmer Q.* 29:261–82

Connolly, K. J., Prechtl, H. F. R., eds. 1981. *Maturation and Development: Biological and Psychological Perspectives*. London: Heinemann. 326 pp.

Corsale, K., Ornstein, P. A. 1980. Developmental changes in children's use of semantic information in recall. *J. Exp. Child Psychol.* 30:231–45

Daehler, M. W., O'Connor, M. P. 1980. Recognition memory for objects in very young children: The effect of shape and label similarity on preference for novel stimuli. *J. Exp. Child Psychol.* 29:306–21

Damon, W., Hart, D. 1982. The development of self-understanding from infancy through adolescence. *Child Dev.* 53:841–64

Darwin, C. R. 1877. Biographical sketch of an infant. *Mind* 2:285–94

Decker, S. N., DeFries, J. C. 1981. Cognitive ability profiles in familes of reading-disabled children. *Dev. Med. Child Neurol.* 23:217–27

Dodge, K. A. 1980. Social cognition and children's aggressive behavior. *Child Dev.* 51:162–70

Dodge, K. A., Frame, C. L. 1982. Social cognitive biases and deficits in aggressive boys. *Child Dev.* 53:620–35

Drickamer, L. C. 1981. Selection for age of sexual maturation in mice and the consequences for population regulation. *Behav. Neural Biol.* 31:82–89

Emde, R. M., Harmon, R. J. 1982. *The Development of Attachment and Affiliative Systems*. New York: Plenum. 200 pp.

Feldman, D. H. 1980. *Beyond Universals in Cognitive Development*. Norwood, NJ: Ablex. 204 pp.

Feldman, D. H. 1981. The role of theory in cognitive developmental research: A reply to Brainerd. *Dev. Rev.* 1:82–89

Fischer, K. W. 1980. A theory of cognitive development: The control and construction of hierarchies of skills. *Psychol. Rev.* 87:477–531

Flavell, J. H. 1963. *The Developmental Psychology of Jean Piaget*. Princeton, NJ: Van Nostrand. 472 pp.

Flavell, J. H. 1982. On cognitive development. *Child Dev.* 53:1–10

Flavell, J. H., Everett, B. A., Croft, K., Flavell, E. R. 1981. Young children's knowledge about visual perception: Further evidence for the level 1-level 2 distinction. *Dev. Psychol.* 17:99–103

Flavell, J. H., Flavell, E. R., Green, F. L. 1983. Development of the appearance-reality distinction. *Cognit. Psychol.* 15:95–120

Flavell, J. H., Ross, L., eds. 1981. *Social Cognitive Development: Frontiers and Possible Futures*. Cambridge: Cambridge Univ. Press. 322 pp.

Frankel, D. G., Roer-Bornstein, D. 1982. Traditional and modern contributions to changing infant-rearing ideologies of two ethnic communities. *Monogr. Soc. Res. Child Dev.* 47(4), Serial No. 196

Goldsmith, H. H. 1983. Genetic influences on personality from infancy to adulthood. *Child Dev.* 54:331–55

Gollin, E. S., ed. 1981. *Developmental Plasticity: Behavioral and Biological Aspects of Variation in Development*. New York: Academic. 288 pp.

Goodman, S. H. 1981. The integration of verbal and motor behavior. *Child Dev.* 52:280–89

Gottlieb, G. 1976. Conceptions of prenatal development. *Psychol. Rev.* 83:215–34

Grossman, K. E., Grossman, K., Huber, F., Wartner, U. 1981. German children's behavior towards their mother at 12 months and their fathers at 18 months in Ainsworth's Strange Situation. *Int. J. Behav. Dev.* 4:157–81

Gunnar, M. 1980. Control, warning signals, and distress in infancy. *Dev. Psychol.* 16:281–89

Guttentag, R. 1981. The role of word shape as a recognition cue in children's automatic word processing. *Child Dev.* 52:363–66

Haith, M. M. 1980. *Rules that Babies Look by: The Organization of Newborn Visual Activity*. Hillsdale, NJ: Erlbaum. 146 pp.

Haith, M., Campos, J., eds. 1983. *Handbook of Child Psychology*, Vol. 2: *Infancy and Developmental Psychobiology*. New York: Wiley. 1250 pp. 4th ed.

Harris, L. J. 1980. Left-handedness: Early theories, facts, and fancies. In *Neuropsychology of Left-Handedness*, ed. J. T. Herron, pp. 3–78. New York: Academic. 357 pp.

Harris, P. L., Olthof, T., Terwogt, M. M. 1981. Children's knowledge of emotion. *J. Child Psychol. Psychiatry* 22:247–61

Hartup, W. W., ed. 1982. *Review of Child Development Research*, Vol. 6. Chicago: Univ. Chicago Press. 780 pp.

Hearst, E., ed. 1979. *The First Century of Experimental Psychology*. Hillsdale, NJ: Erlbaum. 693 pp.

Heckhausen, H. 1980. *Motivation und Handeln*. Berlin: Springer-Verlag. 785 pp.

Henderson, N. D. 1980. Effects of early experience upon the behavior of animals: The second twenty-five years of research. See Simmel 1980, pp. 39–77

Hoyt, C. S. 1980. The long-term visual effects of short-term binocular occlusion of at-risk neonates. *Arch. Ophthalmol.* 98:1967–70

Immelmann, K., Barlow, G., Petrinovich, L., Main, M., eds. 1981. *Behavioral Development: The Bielefeld Interdisciplinary Project*. New York: Cambridge Univ. Press. 754 pp.

Kagan, J., Brim, O. G. Jr., eds. 1980. *Constancy and Change in Human Development*. Cambridge: Harvard Univ. Press. 754 pp.

Kahn, R. L., Antonucci, T. C. 1980. Convoys over the life course: Attachment, roles, and social support. In *Life-Span Development and Behavior*, ed. P. B. Baltes, O. G. Brim Jr. 3:254–86. New York: Academic. 412 pp.

Keil, F. C. 1981. Constraints on knowledge and cognitive development. *Psychol. Rev.* 88:197–227

Kelso, J. A. S., Clark, J. E., eds. 1982. *The*

Development of Movement and Coordination. Chichester: Wiley. 382 pp.

Kessen, W. 1965. *The Child.* New York: Wiley. 301 pp.

Klicpera, C. 1983. Kodierungsprozesse und Gedachtnisstrategien von legasthenen Schulern. Z. *Entwicklungspsychol. Pädagog. Psychol.* 15:42–65

Kohlberg, L. 1982. Moral development. See Broughton & Freeman-Moir 1982, pp. 277–325

Krug, S., Gurack, E., Krüger, M. 1982. Entwicklung anschauungsgestützter Konzepte für Fähigkeit und Anstrengung im Vorschulalter. Z. *Entwicklungspsychol. Pädagog. Psychol.* 14:1017

Kuo, Z-Y. 1967. *The Dynamics of Behavioral Development.* New York: Random House. 240 pp.

Lamb, M. E., Brown, A. L., eds. 1981. *Advances in Developmental Psychology,* Vol. 1. Hillsdale, NJ: Erlbaum. 256 pp.

Lancy, D. F. 1983. *Cross-Cultural Studies in Cognition and Mathematics.* New York: Academic. 248 pp.

Langfeldt, H. 1983. Schulbezogene Motivation, Schulleistung und Schullaufbahn. Z. *Entwicklungspsychol. Pädagog. Psychol.* 15:157–67

Lawson, K. R. 1980. Spatial and temporal congruity and auditory-visual integration in infants. *Dev. Psychol.* 16:185–92

Lawson, K. R., Turkewitz, G. 1980. Intersensory function in newborns: Effect of sound on visual preferences. *Child Dev.* 51:1295–98

Lerner, R. M., ed. 1983. *Developmental Psychology: Historical and Philosophical Perspectives.* Hillsdale, NJ: Erlbaum. 274 pp.

Levine, S. 1982. Psychobiology and the concept of development. *Minn. Symp. Child Psychol.* 15:28–53

Lewin, K. 1933. Environmental forces in child behavior and development. In *A Handbook of Child Psychology,* ed. C. Murchison, pp. 590–625. Worcester, Mass: Clark Univ. Press. 956 pp. 2nd ed.

Lewis, M., Brooks-Gunn, J. 1979. *Social Cognition and the Acquisition of Self.* New York: Plenum. 316 pp.

Lewkowicz, D. J., Turkewitz, G. 1981. Intersensory interaction in newborns: Modification of visual preferences following exposure to sound. *Child Dev.* 52:827–32

Lytton, H. 1980. *Parent-Child Interaction: The Socialization Process Observed in Twin and Singleton Families.* New York: Plenum. 364 pp.

Magnusson, D. 1983. *Implications of an Interactional paradigm for research on human development.* Invited address, 7th Bi-ennial Meet. Int. Soc. Study Behav. Dev., Munich

Magnusson, D., Dunér, A. 1981. Individual development and environment: A longitudinal study in Sweden. In *Prospective Longitudinal Research,* ed. S. E. Mednick, A. E. Baert, pp. 111–22. Oxford: Univ. Press. 382 pp.

Mandler, J. M., Scribner, S., Cole, M., De Forest, M. 1980. Cross-cultural invariance in story recall. *Child Dev.* 51:19–26

Mast, V. K., Fagan, J. F., Rovee-Collier, C. K., Sullivan, M. 1980. Immediate and long-term memory for reinforcement context: The development of learned expectancies in early infancy. *Child Dev.* 51:700–7

Masters, J. C. 1981. Developmental psychology. *Ann. Rev. Psychol.* 32:117–51

Miller, G. A. 1980. Foreword. See Olson 1980, pp. vii–viii

Mischel, W. 1973. Toward a cognitive social learning reconceptualization of personality. *Psychol. Rev.* 80:252–83

Morrison, F. J., Lord, C., Keating, D. P. 1983. Applied developmental psychology. In *Applied Developmental Psychology,* Vol. 1, ed. F. J. Morrison, C. Lord, D. P. Keating. New York: Academic. In press

Morrison, F. J., Manis, F. R. 1982. Cognitive processes and reading disability: A critique and proposal. In *Progress in Cognitive Developmental Research,* ed. C. J. Brainerd, M. I. Pressley, 2:59–93. New York: Springer-Verlag. 289 pp.

Moss, H. A., Susman, E. J. 1980. Longitudinal study of personality development. See Kagan & Brim 1980, pp. 530–95

Murchison, C., ed. 1931. *A Handbook of Child Psychology.* Worcester, Mass: Clark Univ. Press. 711 pp.

Murchison, C., ed. 1933. *A Handbook of Child Psychology.* Worcester, Mass: Clark Univ. Press. 956 pp. 2nd ed.

Mussen, P. H., ed. 1983. *Handbook of Child Psychology,* 4 vols. New York: Wiley. 4th ed.

Naus, M. J., Ornstein, P. A. 1983. Development of memory strategies: Analysis, questions, and issues. *Contrib. Hum. Dev.* 9:1–30

Newcomb, A. F., Brady, J. E. 1982. Mutuality in boys' friendship relations. *Child Dev.* 53:392–95

Olson, D. R., ed. 1980. *The Social Foundations of Language and Thought.* New York: Norton. 386 pp.

Olweus, D. 1980. Familial and temperamental determinants of aggressive behavior in adolescent boys: A causal analysis. *Dev. Psychol.* 16:644–60

Oppenheim, R. W. 1982. Preformation and epigenesis in the origins of the nervous system and behavior: Issues, concepts, and their history. In *Perspectives in Ethology: Ontogeny,* ed. P. P. G. Bateson, P. H. Klopfer, 5:1–100. New York: Plenum. 659 pp.

Paris, S. G., Lindauer, B. K. 1982. The development of cognitive skills during childhood. In *Handbook of Developmental Psychology,* ed. B. J. Wolman, pp. 333–49. Englewood Cliffs, NJ: Prentice-Hall. 960 pp.

Paris, S. G., Lipson, M. Y., Wixon, K. K. 1983. Becoming a strategic reader. *Contemp. Educ. Psychol.* 8: In press

Patterson, G. R. 1982. *Coercive Family Process.* Eugene: Castalia Press. 368 pp.

Perez, B. 1885. *The First Three Years of Childhood.* Chicago: Marquis (orig. publ. in French, 1878). 292 pp.

Perlmutter, M., Hazen, N., Mitchell, D. B., Grady, J. G., Cavanaugh, J. C., Flook, J. P. 1981. Picture cues and exhaustive search facilitate very young children's memory for location. *Dev. Psychol.* 17:104–10

Plomin, R., De Fries, J. C. 1983. The Colorado adoption project. *Child Dev.* 54:290–97

Posner, J. K. 1982. The development of mathematical knowledge in two West African societies. *Child Dev.* 53:200–8

Preyer, W. 1888–1889. *The Mind of the Child.* New York: Appleton (orig. publ. in German, 1882). 2 vols.

Pulkkinen, L. 1982. Self-control and continuity from childhood to late adolescence. In *Life-Span Development and Behavior,* ed. P. B. Baltes, O. G. Brim Jr., 4:64–105. New York: Academic. 362 pp.

Puttallaz, M., Gottman, J. M. 1981. An interactional model of children's entry into peer groups. *Child Dev.* 52:986–94

Reinert, G. 1979. Prolegomena to a history of life-span developmental psychology. In *Life-Span Development and Behavior,* ed. P. B. Baltes, O. G. Brim Jr., 2:205–54. New York: Academic. 348 pp.

Ries, G., Hahn, M., Barkowski, D. 1983. Die Entwicklung schulleistungsbezogener Ursachenerklärugen im Längsschnittvergleich des 2. und 4. Schuljahres. *Z. Entwicklungspsychol. Pädagog. Psychol.* 15:149–56

Rogoff, B. 1982. Integrating context and cognitive development. In *Advances in Developmental Psychology,* ed. M. E. Lamb, A. L. Brown, 2:125–70. Hillsdale, NJ: Erlbaum. 213 pp.

Rogoff, B., Waddell, K. J. 1982. Memory for information organized in a scene by children from two cultures. *Child Dev.* 53:1224–28

Rose, S. A., Gottfried, A. W., Bridger, W. H. 1981. Cross-modal transfer in 6-month-old infants. *Dev. Psychol.* 17:661–69

Rovee-Collier, C. K., Sullivan, M. 1980.

Organization of infant memory. *J. Exp. Psychol.: Hum. Learn. Mem.* 6:798–807

Rubin, K. H ., Daniels-Beirness, T. 1983. Concurrent and predictive correlates of sociometric status in kindergarten and grade one children. *Merrill-Palmer Q.* 29:337–52

Ruff, H. 1980. The development of perception and recognition of objects. *Child Dev.* 51:981–92

Rutter, M. 1981. Isle of Wight and inner London studies. In *Prospective Longitudinal Studies Research: An Empirical Basis for the Primary Prevention of Psychosocial Disorders,* ed. S. E. Mednick, A. E. Baert, pp. 122–37. Oxford: Oxford Univ. Press. 383 pp.

Sackett, G. P., Sameroff, A. J., Cairns, R. B., Suomi, S. F. 1981. Continuity in behavioral development: Theoretical and empirical issues. See Immelmann et al 1981, pp. 23–57

Scarr, S., Weinberg, R. A. 1983. The Minnesota adoption studies: Genetic differences and malleability. *Child Dev.* 54:260–67

Schneider, W. 1984. Developmental trends in the metamemory-memory behavior relationship. In *Metacognition, Cognition, and Human Performance,* ed. D. L. Forrest-Pressley, G. E. Mackinnon, T. G. Waller. New York: Academic. In press

Schneirla, T. C. 1966. Behavioral development and comparative psychology. *Q. Rev. Biol.* 51:283–302

Schopler, E., Mesibov, G. B., eds. 1983. *Autism in Adolescents and Adults.* New York: Plenum. 438 pp.

Sears, R. R. 1983. The Terman life-cycle study of children of high ability: 1922–1982. *Newsl. Soc. Res. Child Dev.,* Summer, p. 5

Selman, R. 1980. *The Growth of Interpersonal Understanding.* New York: Academic. 343 pp.

Simmel, E. C. 1980. *Early Experiences and Early Behavior: Implications for Social Development.* New York: Academic. 217 pp.

Spelke, E. S. 1981. The infant's acquistion of knowledge of bimodally specified events. *J. Exp. Child Psychol.* 31:279–99

Stevenson, H. W., Stigler, J. W., Lucker, G. W., Lee, S-Y., Hsu, C-C., Kitamura, S. 1982. Reading disabilities: The case of Chinese, Japanese, and English. *Child Dev.* 53:1164–81

Stevenson-Hinde, J., Stilwell-Barnes, R., Zunz, M. 1980. Individual differences in young rhesus monkeys: Consistency and change. *Primates* 21:498–509

Stratton, P., ed. 1982. *Psychobiology of the Human Newborn.* Chichester: Wiley. 470 pp.

Sullivan, M. W. 1982. Reactivation: Priming forgotten memories in human infants. *Child Dev.* 53:516–23

Suomi, S. J. 1983. Social development in rhesus monkeys: Consideration of individual differences. In *The Behaviour of Human Infants*, ed. A. Oliverio, M. Zappella, pp. 71–83. New York: Plenum. 295 pp.

Thelen, E. 1981. Rhythmical behavior in infancy: An ethological perspective. *Dev. Psychol.* 17:237–57

Thompson, R. A., Lamb, M. E., Estes, D. 1982. Stability of infant-mother attachment and its relationship to changing life circumstances in an unselected middle-class sample. *Child Dev.* 53:144–48

Thompson, R. A., Lamb, M. E., Estes, D. 1983. Harmonizing discordant notes: A reply. *Child Dev.* 54:521–24

Tiedemann, D. 1787/1927. Beobachtungen über die Entwickelung der Seelenfähigkeiten bei Kindern. *J. Genet. Psychol.* 34:205–30 (orig. publ. 1787)

Triandis, H. C., Heron, A., eds. 1981. *Handbook of Cross-Cultural Psychology*, Vol. 4: *Developmental Psychology*. Boston: Allyn & Bacon. 492 pp.

Trudewind, C. 1982. The development of achievement motivation and individual differences: Ecological determinants. See Hartup 1982, pp. 669–703

Vellutino, F. R. 1979. *Dyslexia: Theory and Research*. Cambridge: MIT Press. 427 pp.

Vigotsky, L. S. 1939. Thought and speech. *Psychiatry* 2:29–54

von Cranach, M. 1982. The psychological study of goal-directed action: Basic issues. In *The Analysis of Action: Recent Theoretical and Empirical Advances*, ed. M. von Cranach, R. Harré, pp. 35–79. Cambridge: Cambridge Univ. Press. 400 pp.

von Glasersfeld, E., Kelley, M. F. 1982. On the concepts of period, phase, stage, and level. *Hum. Dev.* 25:152–60

von Hofsten, C. 1982. Eye-hand coordination in the newborn. *Dev. Psychol.* 18:450–61

Wagner, D. A., Paris, S. G. 1981. Problems and prospects in comparative studies of memory. *Human Dev.* 24:412–24

Wagner, D. A., Stevenson, H. W., eds. 1982.

Cultural Perspectives on Child Development. San Francisco: Freeman. 315 pp.

Walker, A. S. 1982. Intermodal perception of expressive behaviors by human infants. *J. Exp. Child Psychol.* 33:514–35

Waters, E. 1983. The stability of individual differences in infant attachment: Comments on the Thompson, Lamb & Estes contribution. *Child Dev.* 54:516–20

Weisz, J. R. 1981. Illusory contingency in children at the state fair. *Dev. Psychol.* 17:481–89

Weisz, J., Stipek, D. 1982. Competence contingency and the development of perceived control. *Human Dev.* 25:250–81

Wellman, H. M. 1983. Metamemory revisited. *Contrib. Hum. Dev.* 9:31–51

Weston, D. R., Turiel, E. 1980. Act-rule relations: Children's concepts of social rules. *Dev. Psychol.* 16:417–24

Whitehurst, G. J. 1981. Information for authors. *Dev. Rev.* 1:i

Wimmer, H., Perner, J. 1983. Beliefs about beliefs: Representation and constraining function of wrong beliefs in young children's understanding of deception. *Cognition* 13:103–28

Wolman, B. B., ed. 1982. *Handbook of Developmental Psychology*. Englewood Cliffs, NJ: Prentice-Hall. 960 pp.

Wozniak, R. 1982. Metaphysics and science, reason and reality: The intellectual origins of genetic epistemology. See Broughton & Freeman-Moir 1982, pp. 13–45

Youniss, J. 1980. *Parents and Peers in Social Development*. Chicago: Univ. Chicago Press. 301 pp.

Youniss, J. 1983. Beyond ideology to the universals of development. *Contrib. Hum. Dev.* 8:31–52

Yussen, S. R., Matthews, S. R. II, Buss, R. R., Kane, P. T. 1980. Developmental change in judging important and critical elements of stories. *Dev. Psychol.* 16:213–19

Zahn-Waxler, C., Radke-Yarrow, M. 1979. Child rearing and children's prosocial initiations toward victims of distress. *Child Dev.* 50:319–30

Ann. Rev. Psychol. 1984. 35:579-604

COUNSELING PSYCHOLOGY

Fred H. Borgen

Department of Psychology, Iowa State University, Ames, Iowa 50011

CONTENTS

INTRODUCTION

Traditionally, counseling psychologists have been a rather tranquil bunch. Unconditional positive regard has been their approach to their clients and the world. Often they have considered themselves value-free and apolitical. Hence, the last decade has seen a crisis of identity as the marketplace and Capitol Hill have pressed a new world view on them and other professional psychologists. At the same time, counseling psychology has been reaching for a new posture in its science. Lively ferment and controversy are visible in the prime research journal, the *Journal of Counseling Psychology,* with an active and open contest of ideas encouraged by editor Charles Gelso (1982). *The*

0066-4308/84/0201-0579$02.00

Counseling Psychologist, since its inception in 1969, has also promoted dialogue. Its format of treatise, with numerous responses, has been fertile ground for stimulating thought and progress on theories, interventions, professional issues, and research. My perspective is that this stirring and searching is a sign of vigorous health. There is sufficient strength in the discipline to permit self-reflection—even publicly. These issues are not unique to this subdiscipline. The adequacy of the knowledge base and our sense of direction are central questions Koch (1981) and Bevan (1982) pose for all psychologists.

An author of a chapter in the *Annual Review of Psychology* quickly realizes that such a review cannot begin to be comprehensive. Fortunately, the editors focus the task with instructions to select a few topics and to focus on trends and future directions. Thus, several important areas have been omitted or given less coverage than they deserve. Excellent coverage of key areas neglected here can be found in the handbooks by Walsh and Osipow (1983a,b) and Brown & Lent (1984). The most recent *Annual Review of Psychology* chapter by Holland et al (1981) focused on career interventions, so vocational coverage is sharply limited. Emphasis is given to the field's two primary journals: *The Journal of Counseling Psychology* and *The Counseling Psychologist*. Coverage is for 1978–82, but later years are weighted more heavily to spotlight leading edges of the field and to facilitate readers' access to the topics discussed.

Previously it has been difficult to point to one source that reflected the scope and vigor that counseling psychology has attained. Now suddenly the maturation of the field is evident in the appearance of two handbooks that are exemplary presentations of counseling psychology. The broadest of these is Brown & Lent's (1984) *Handbook of Counseling Psychology*, containing some 20 chapters covering established and emerging activities in vocational psychology as well as chapters on newer developments in training and supervision, prevention and community interventions, and counseling with women and with racial/ethnic minorities. This becomes the definitive statement on the breadth and vigor currently represented in counseling psychology. The area's largest and most mature body of literature is covered in Walsh & Osipow's (1983a,b) two-volume *Handbook of Vocational Psychology*. Together these handbooks provide unprecedented coverage of the recent literature of counseling psychology. Their scholarly reviews give new impact to the empirical studies they summarize and integrate. In addition, these handbooks are packed with sufficient research agendas to keep a generation of investigators busy.

TRENDS AND EMERGING TRENDS

Following is one observer's view of some thematic impacts currently affecting research and thinking in counseling psychology. The emphasis is on selected theoretical positions and research topics that have momentum affecting the field and likely to have continuing impact in the period ahead. Although Corsini (1981) lists nearly 250 varieties of therapy, the theoretical perspectives covered here are limited to three vigorous but mainstream positions.

Cognitive-Behavioral Psychology

Mahoney's 1977 observation of a cognitive-behavioral revolution has been confirmed by the subsequent activity level of both clinicians and scholars. D. Smith's (1982) survey suggests this may be the most popular orientation of clinicians, aside from eclecticism. Integral to this trend is the resurgence of consciousness in psychology (Hilgard 1980). Bandura (1977, 1982) has been the intellectual lodestar of this movement. Influential work abounds: Meichenbaum (1977), Mahoney & Arnkoff (1978), Kendall & Hollon (1979), Rush (1982). The model underlies Stone and Bruch's exemplary research programs in counseling psychology. Betz & Hackett (1981) have developed Bandura's self-efficacy notions to the topic of women's and men's career development. Important books have been written by Stone (1980) and Merluzzi et al (1981).

Cognitive-behavioral empiricism has brought an individual differences focus back to factorial experimental designs. Stein & Stone (1978) used conceptual level in an "aptitude by treatment" design and stimulated similar promising work. Their study was identified by citation frequency (Heesacker et al 1982) as an "emerging classic" in counseling psychology. Bruch and associates have used conceptual complexity as an individual difference variable in similar designs and produced a rigorous group of studies that also integrate insights from social and personality psychology (e.g. Bruch 1981a,b, Bruch et al 1981, 1982).

Social Psychological Models

Few research topics covered in the *Journal of Counseling Psychology* have attained the critical mass to yield an integrative and evaluative review, but a prominent exception is the work stimulated by Strong (1968) on viewing counseling as a social influence process. At least 60 studies (mainly laboratory analogues) followed, which were reviewed by Corrigan et al (1980) and Heppner & Dixon (1981). The pace of this work has continued unabated with expansion of tests of the model in more real-world settings. Strong & Claiborn's recent (1982) book promises to keep this topic, with some potent new twists, in the forefront of counseling research.

Strong & Claiborn's (1982) *Change Through Interaction* marks a watershed in scholarship on the social influence model. One might have expected a fairly pedestrian synopsis of the social influence literature. That it certainly is not, although it covers the literature well. What is most impressive about their book is the boldness of their theoretical and clinical integration. One would be hard pressed to find a more exciting or important book in counseling psychology.

The excitement of Strong & Claiborn (1982) flows from the creative synthesis of otherwise disparate though potent ideas: the therapist as healer, the social influence model, and the family systems concepts of causation and therapeutic change. All three of these perspectives are rather novel in their impacts on traditional psychology; thus the excitement. The book is important because of its breadth of conceptual integration and its promise to generate research. The latter is assured because of the active research programs already being pursued by Strong and Claiborn.

Strong and Claiborn acknowledge their bold and broad statement may be wrong, especially on particulars. But it provokes many propositions that can be tested empirically—by clinicians and researchers alike. It is also a bold synthesis of new "spectacles" (cf Highlen & Hill 1984) to view the core issue of therapeutic change.

I suspect the boundaries between Strong and Claiborn and the recent eclecticism literature are fertile. Highlen & Hill (1984), if extended, come close to exploiting these possibilities. Curiously, one does not find "eclecticism" in the Strong and Claiborn index; yet theirs is the most comprehensive and most researched eclectic statement that exists. This is because they focus on generic processes underlying therapeutic change. They are distinctly atheoretical in that they interpret the "efficacy" of all theoretical systems within their viewpoint! Theirs is a science of myth in the sense that Frank (1961, 1973) introduced. The volume shows the generality of central concerns of counseling psychology when focus is placed on the change process.

In their potent final chapter, Strong & Claiborn (1982) see the stage set for a revolution from the intrapsychic to the interactional. Already their laboratories are busy with some surprising new topics in the interactional framework: paradox (Beck & Strong 1982, Feldman et al 1982, Lopez & Wambach 1982, Wright & Strong 1982); and resistance (Kerr et al 1983).

Analytic Models

While the analytic perspective has the longest historical influence on counseling psychology, it has never been in a dominating position, although its influence on clinicians has always been greater than is evident in our mainstream research journals. Currently, the level of research interest is high at some leading universities. A comprehensive summary of that empiricism is provided by Luborsky & Spence (1978). Bordin has long been the foremost exponent of the psychoanalytic position in counseling psychology, and his work continues (1979, 1981). Variations of the analytic influence can be seen in a Gestalt orientation (Greenberg & Webster 1982) and Kohut's psychology of the self (Patton et al 1982). In counseling psychology the University of Maryland has emerged as the leading producer of research from the analytic perspective, focusing on time-limited counseling, which was reviewed by

Johnson & Gelso (1980), studied by McKitrick & Gelso (1978) and Peabody & Gelso (1982), and most recently presented in a significant book-length treatment by Gelso & Johnson (1983).

Human Decision Making

One of the newest trends with major promise for the counseling setting is human decision making. This is a confluence from information processing and cognitive models (Horan 1979), modeling of decision making under uncertainty (Kahneman et al 1982), problem solving (Dixon et al 1979, Heppner 1978, Heppner & Petersen 1982, Heppner et al 1982, Kirschenbaum & Perri 1982), and social-personality perspectives (Janis & Mann 1977, Janis 1982). An excellent interdisciplinary survey is provided by Mitchell & Krumboltz (1984). Ivey also exemplifies the potency of this approach in his integration of "the interview as a decision-making process" (1980, Chapter 2). Ivey (Personal communication, January 1983) is incorporating more of this viewpoint in the revision of his widely used text (1980). The promise of this topic derives from the centrality of decision making in counseling and the progress being made in laboratory approaches.

Eclecticism, Prescription, and Nonspecific Effects

Many signs point to the trend of general acceptance of eclecticism by many counseling and clinical psychologists. The earliest empirical sign was the Garfield & Kurtz (1977) survey of clinical psychologists; 55% labeled themselves eclectic. The latest empirical confirmation is D. Smith's (1982) survey of counseling and clinical psychologists where 41% reported an eclectic orientation. (Smith included more categories than did Garfield and Kurtz: cognitive-behavioral, family systems, other.) Several influential writers now present eclecticism as the centerpiece of their therapy, both conceptually and practically. Wachtel (1977, 1982) has shown the most ambitious grasp in his efforts to unite the psychodynamic and behavioral approaches. Several eclectic statements (Garfield 1980, 1981, Goldfried 1980, 1982, Ivey 1980, Highlen & Hill 1984) are based on recent empirical studies showing equal outcome for therapists from different theoretical orientations (Luborsky et al 1975, Sloane et al 1975, Smith & Glass 1977). Two major texts in counseling psychology (Ivey 1980, Brammer & Shostrum 1982) take an eclectic position but choose not to call it that. Ivey calls his approach metatheoretical, and Brammer and Shostrum call theirs a creative synthesis. They seem reluctant to endorse a term that was once pejorative to earlier generations of psychologists (cf D. Smith 1982).

Hill's (1983) counseling rating system is presented in a pantheoretical context. Brown & Hosford (1981) argue for the widening of the behavioral counseling model, stating the "future of counseling resides not so much in continuing theoretical identifications, but rather in *an ongoing dialogue among empirically oriented researchers, writers, and practitioners*" (p. 12). While the winds of eclecticism are strong, opposition is apparent (Messer & Winokur 1980, Messer 1983, Wolpe 1981, 1982). Earlier, Lazarus (1967) was influential in proposing a *technical* eclecticism (combining intervention techniques), but his recent dissent (Fay & Lazarus 1982) on the psychoanalytic position exemplifies the large barriers many see in theoretically reconciling the disparate conceptual assumptions of different systems. For many (e.g. Garfield 1980, Ivey 1980) there is explicit recognition that an eclectic stance means differential treatment. Despite some notable efforts (Goldstein & Stein 1976, Beutler 1979), the empirical base for prescriptive treatment currently is weak, so the full-blown application of eclecticism currently must be an art.

As sketched above, the topics eclecticism and prescriptive treatment are closely related (cf Dimond et al 1978). Interestingly, Hosford et al (1984), rooted in a behavioral orientation, give an intensive analysis of prescriptive treatment but do not link it with eclecticism. In my view the linkage fits the analysis of variance metaphor. Recent studies show no main effects for therapists from different theoretical orientations. Then if we are to improve service delivery, we need to attend to the disordinal interactions and optimally match treatments with problems, that is, provide differential or prescriptive treatment.

The breadth of viewpoints on therapy is evident by contrasting the Highlen and Hill and Hosford et al chapters in the Brown & Lent (1984) handbook. Hosford et al state that truly prescriptive counseling will have arrived when variance due to specific treatments will surpass that due to individual and therapist variables. However, Highlen and Hill focus attention on therapist, client, and relationship variables. Since each viewpoint makes different bets on an unknown empirical reality, each deserves Godspeed in pursuing its goals. These disparate viewpoints also illustrate why the eclectic position can be controversial. For some it is a mandate to focus on common components in therapy, which threatens to draw research emphases away from demonstration of efficacy of specific therapies.

The current zeitgeist, for scholars and clinicians alike, nurtures the eclectic view. The empirical studies cited have suggested the lack of difference among theoretical positions—at least when they are translated into therapist practices (Glass & Kliegl 1983). Nonspecific effects are given unprecedented credence (Kazdin & Wilcoxon 1976, Strupp & Hadley 1979). Frank's (1961, 1973) statement of the generality of therapist influence is cited with increasing frequency. Bergin & Lambert (1979, p. 54) state: "it now seems clear that placebo factors are real therapeutic factors to be understood and utilized." The necessity of a quality therapeutic relationship is now widely acknowledged within all therapeutic schools. New viewpoints from social psychology on the counseling process are atheoretical (Strong & Claiborn 1982, Wills 1982).

Finally, emerging biological evidence on neuropsychological concomitants of hope, expectation, and placebo effects suggest basic mechanisms that may underlie nonspecific effects (Miller 1983).

Shifting Questions

In counseling and psychotherapy in the 1970s, the big research questions had a macrofocus on outcome. Moving from the most general to the more specific, the big questions were:

1. Do counseling and psychotherapy work?
2. Do different theoretical approaches differ in their efficacy?
3. Which approaches work best with which kinds of problems?

Questions 1 and 2 are now considered unsophisticated because of their excessively general flavor. Nonetheless, these questions have had high salience because of their immediate clinical and policy implications—at least in the short run. In addressing these questions, meta-analysis (see below) has recently been especially prominent. Question 3 is the most difficult to answer, and there are mixed views about the productivity of research to develop prescriptive treatments. Hosford et al (1984) present the case for prescription, but Bergin & Lambert (1979, p. 55) are not so hopeful: "While prescription is the ideal held to by leading researchers, there is growing disillusionment with it."

A continuing interest in outcome is evident, but with a greater interest in looking at it more specifically (Orlinsky & Howard 1978, Frank 1979, Gelso 1979, Lambert et al 1983) and with greater measurement and interpretive sophistication (Yeaton & Sechrest 1981, Sechrest 1982). Important work is also being done with generalization of outcome (Kazdin 1982b, Galassi & Galassi 1984). Concurrently there is a new sophistication in vocational psychology about examining outcome (criterion) issues (Oliver 1979, Lunneborg 1982, Osipow 1982, Spokane & Oliver 1983).

Several leaders now agree that sufficient attention has been given to Questions 1 and 2 and that it is time to renew our efforts answering more basic and specific questions (Bergin & Lambert 1979, Gelso 1979, 1982, Kiesler 1979b, Hill 1982, Garfield 1983, Highlen & Hill 1984). These questions might be phrased as:

What are the causes of problems seen in therapy?
What is the nature of therapeutic change?
What are the effective ingredients in therapeutic change?

These old questions (e.g. Rogers 1957, Strupp 1973) are being attacked with new energy and with the potential benefits of new thinking and methodologies (e.g. Hill 1978, 1982, Kiesler 1982, Rice & Greenberg 1983). These questions redirect attention to process, namely what is going on in the therapeutic encounter.

These trends, to eclecticism and to the dyadic interaction, narrow the historic gaps that created outcome researchers and process researchers. There are few inherent polarities between process and outcome. Increasingly, the terms describe not qualitatively different phenomena but semantic and conceptual emphases. Research is moving beyond global questions of outcome and focusing on specific ingredients of the change process. As we understand those specifics better, enhancement of outcome will fall into place (cf Hill 1982, Hill et al 1983, Highlen & Hill 1984). Counseling psychologists are well positioned to probe this frontier of therapy research. Their work of the past decade has rarely centered on global outcome, but rather has taken the counseling interaction as focal point. Broadly within this process tradition are three contrasting research programs initiated by Strong, Pepinsky, and Hill. Despite their differences, they speak to the common ingredients of therapeutic change. Strong's social influence model thus far has had greatest impact, as discussed throughout this chapter.

Probing the counseling interaction at the most basic level, Pepinsky, Meara, Patton and associates examine the structure of language usage, positing that counseling moves toward "concerted action" (Patton et al 1977, Meara et al 1979, Meara et al 1981). Wycoff et al (1982), studying empathic responding to anger, illustrate the flexibility of this computer-based approach to analyzing counseling interactions.

Hill (1978) introduced a meticulous system for rating counselor verbal response categories. Hill et al (1979b) studied differences among Rogers, Perls, and Ellis; Hill et al (1983) intensively studied a single case. This is the most ambitious and sophisticated approach to process thus far, poised to address the ultimate question "what is it that happens in counseling that is helpful to people?" Hill (1982, 1983) shows fine scholarship about past efforts in this rocky (and mushy!) terrain. Her system shows high rater reliabilities in the hands of her research team and early indications of its portability to other settings (Edwards et al 1982). Thus far the system has been tested on type but not quality of response. The latter is a large challenge, given prior struggles with empathy and other "core conditions" (Gladstein 1977, Lambert et al 1978). Hill has made a special contribution to the research enterprise by chronicling her research odyssey (1982, 1983).

The research approaches of Strong, Pepinsky, and Hill are robust and productive. Combinations of these approaches, while difficult, may be particularly rich.

Supervision and Skill Training

While supervision of beginning counselors has long been an inherent part of practice and graduate training, it has only recently been the subject of a serious body of research. Important reviews of this fledgling but promising literature are provided by Lambert (1980) and Russell et al (1984). The Hess (1980) volume presents a comprehensive treatment of supervision with theoretical and clinical perspectives. Promising conceptual models of supervision have appeared, especially from the developmental perspective (Loganbill et al 1982).

The current status of supervision research and thinking is captured by Russell et al's (1984) chapter conclusion:

> We are strongly encouraged by the renewed interest in the topic of supervision. The growth of developmental models of supervision, the expansion of empirical research (especially as it pertains to factorial designs), and the continued development of graduate-level courses in supervision all suggest a surge in activity relevant to supervision. While the area continues to be plagued by methodological and conceptual shortcomings, there is a clear sense of movement and growth.

Russell et al usefully classify the literature by design features and evaluate each study in terms of internal and external validity. They identify factorial designs—crossing supervisee, supervisor, and method—as the most promising. Their summation of the 18 studies of this kind, most since 1977, is particularly valuable. They state that future progress depends on more formal specification of theory, extending study to counseling skills beyond the neophyte's, and attending to internal and external validity of designs. The latter is a useful agenda in analysis of variance design terms. The nascent stage of this area also gives room for progress through naturalistic, correlational, and descriptive designs. For example, Hill et al (1981), in a valuable study that is much too rare, described growth in counseling skills for a cohort of counseling graduate students.

Counseling psychologists have made unique contributions in creating modules for focused training of counseling and interviewing skills at the prepracticum level. Lambert (1980), Hess (1980), and Russell et al (1984) provide overviews of the modules of Ivey, Kagan, Danish, and others. Cormier & Cormier's (1979) text is a good example of behaviorally focused training. Ivey has been particularly active with extensions of microcounseling (e.g. Ivey & Authier 1978, Ivey 1983).

Breadth of Application

Counseling psychology has been an active forum for pioneering scholarship and applications serving human diversity. Counseling women has been an active area of development. Division 17's Ad Hoc Committee on Women developed principles for counseling with women (Hill et al 1979a); subsequently these principles have been endorsed by Division 17 and other APA divisions (Schmidt & Meara 1984). Women's career development has been actively studied and conceptualized. Major conceptual statements are provided by Fitzgerald & Crites (1980) and Gottfredson (1981). Major recent reviews cover the vocational psychology of women (Fitzgerald & Betz 1983, Osipow 1983). Counseling psychologists have played an active part in the rapidly expanding vision of the possibilities for therapy with women (Hill et al 1979a, Gilbert 1980, Brodsky & Hare-Mustin 1980a,b, Richardson 1981, Richardson & Johnson 1984).

Improving the counseling provided for ethnic and racial minorities continues to be an important task. A valuable step is Sue et al's (1982) delineation of competencies for cross-cultural counseling. Recent work is evident in reviews of vocational counseling (E. J. Smith 1983) and counseling in general (Pedersen et al 1981, Casas 1984). These reviews indicate that steady progress has been made in the past decade but that there is a large continuing agenda for adequately addressing counseling issues with racial and ethnic minorities.

Vigor in Vocational Psychology

The limited space allocated to vocational psychology in this review does not reflect the vitality of this subfield. A high level of activity continues with sufficient maturity and focus to permit the preceding "counseling" chapter in the *Annual Review of Psychology* to be devoted to career interventions (Holland et al 1981). Diversity and vigor are evident in a two-volume handbook (Walsh & Osipow 1983a,b). The Brown & Lent (1984) handbook opens with a major section on vocational psychology. Fretz (1981) and Gottfredson (1981) have written monographs on career behavior. Osipow (1983) has prepared a third edition of his widely used text on *Theories of Career Development*. Erlbaum publishers is launching a forthcoming series on *Advances in Vocational Psychology*.

Unlike other areas of counseling, vocational psychology is not beset with self-doubt. It has a major paradigm with linkages to the past (Super 1983, Zytowski & Borgen 1983, Lofquist & Dawis 1984). This is the person-job matching model originated by Parsons in 1909 at the founding of the field and embedded in the trait model. To be sure, there are competing models such as the developmental, but they have found a comfortable co-existence. Likewise the trait model has not always well served new needs such as counseling with women and minorities. But such venerable tools as the Strong Vocational Interest Blank have undergone radical updating to meet needs such as sex-fair counseling (Campbell & Hansen 1981, Borgen & Bernard 1982).

Vocational psychology is distinctive because of the number of active contributors whose research careers span 30, 40, and more years (Kuder 1977, Holland et al 1981, Crites 1983, Super 1983). They seem to have found some meaty problems that continue to have empirical payoff. The subfield has a sizable cadre of now middle-aged psychologists with long and continuing active research careers. In my view, this stability and cumulativeness of the field can be traced to its robust phenomena. One can read E. K. Strong's (1943) classic on interest measurement and see its influence 40 years later in current vocational psychology (cf Walsh & Osipow 1983a,b). Vocational phenomena are sufficiently robust that they are tractable with traditional research methods and permit construct validation (Crites 1983). While examining how more counseling psychologists can be trained as productive researchers, Magoon & Holland (1984) observe that the success rate for vocational research is greater than for therapy studies. Vocational psychology has deep roots that continue to nourish its current life.

CONTROVERSY, CONFLICT, AND CHANGE

The level of self-analysis of counseling psychology is remarkable. Predominant stimuli for reflection on research have been articles and theme issues of *The Counseling Psychologist,* especially research pieces by Gelso in 1979 and Hill in 1982 (and others in Gelso & Johnson 1982). Another stimulus piece was Goldman's article in 1976. Equally active has been appraisal of the professional status of counseling psychology, with theme issues of *The Counseling Psychologist* on "Professional Identity" (Fretz 1977), "Counseling Psychology in the Year 2000 A.D." (Whiteley 1980b), and "Counseling Psychology: The Next Decade" (Kagan 1982). These theme issues have also been developed as books (Whiteley 1980a, 1983, Whiteley & Fretz 1980). Counseling psychology will progress with continuing dialogue and debate. Conflict is healthy in a growing science (cf Haase et al 1982a).

Developing a Profession

Fretz & Mills' (1980) book reflects the growing professionalism of counseling psychology in the prior decade. Charting core issues of credentialing for the specialty, it is a prime sourcebook on the rapid changes emanating from state licensing boards, accrediting agencies, and other national groups. Fretz and Mills show how advocacy for the profession underlies past changes and ongoing issues.

The Schmidt & Meara (1984) chapter nicely complements the Fretz & Mills (1980) book in giving the most comprehensive account to date of professional issues in counseling psychology. The chapter is unusually thorough in sketching the active professional changes of the past 3 years, yet it is anchored by interwoven historical accounts of professional psychology. These writings reflect the growing professionalism of counseling psychology, once sheltered by a naive idealism but now moving more actively, through the acute push of external events, to a growing political awareness and activism. Schmidt & Meara (1984) trace the recent professional tumult occurring on many fronts: credentialing, third party reimbursement, specialty guidelines, standards for service providers, counseling awareness of individual differences (especially gender and race).

While the pace of such recent events appears intense, Pepinsky (1983) perceptively traces how similar forces have shaped definitional issues in counseling psychology from its beginnings (see also Whiteley 1980a). Pepinsky sees a healthy organization aging into its late 30s, with its career development evolving through resolution of a series of identity crises.

Scientist-Practitioner Model: Search for Integration

In the 1970s, professional psychology showed a growing ambivalence about the vitality of the scientist-practitioner model. A special issue edited by Barlow (1981) centers on the topic. It is the recurring theme of the issues of *The Counseling Psychologist* on research (Gelso 1979, Gelso & Johnson 1982). The consensus of these observers comes close to Bergin & Lambert's (1979, p. 55) appraisal: "It is especially important to foster a kind of research that melds clinical and scientific interests. Too often we have been trying to fuse two types of functioning that cannot be alloyed, namely pure research and pure practice." There is increasing recognition that a single person cannot achieve excellence in each domain, but there is value in fostering environments with a mix of people with different combinations of skills (Kiesler 1979b).

The Next Decade Project, squarely facing many of these issues (Harmon 1982), endorsed the scientist-practitioner model but called for a renewal in its implementation. Acknowledging the general weaknesses of our scientific underpinnings, Harmon's committee suggested actions "to reaffirm the primacy of the 'scientist' in the counseling psychologist role" (p. 32). The committee stressed the importance of setting priorities for significant research problems. Finally, the study group "affirm[ed] the importance of identifying research methods which answer important questions in counseling psychology rather than the inverse—finding questions which fit certain methods" (p. 36).

A continuing goal of many thoughtful writers is to get the scientist-practitioner model to work—to merge the world views of scientist and clinician. It seems that our many anguished analyses and exhortations of research are really directed to this deeper issue of "How can the scientist and the practitioner co-exist with the same world views, goals, and epistemologies?" To read Goldman's (1976, 1982) critique of "scientistic" research,[1] one would have to conclude that the integrated model has not worked at all. He asks pungently, "has research ever informed our practice or our theory?" Barlow (1981, p. 147) echoes that sentiment for clinical psychology: "At present, clinical research has little or no influence on clinical practice. This state of affairs should be particularly distressing to a discipline whose goal over the last

---

[1]I use "scientistic" to convey a sense of a distorted science obsessed more with rules than substance.

30 years has been to produce professionals who would integrate the methods of science with clinical practice to produce new knowledge."

Hill's (1982) thoughtful analysis of our counseling research is not much more sanguine about past successes in merging science and practice (see pp. 9–10). Her extensive discussion of research is a significant step in merging the scientist and practitioner world views (see also Hill 1983, Hill et al 1983, Highlen & Hill 1984). She is attempting to reform research tradition to move it closer to the clinician's perspective. Her work reflects the evolution of the liberalized notions about research methods that are evident in Gelso's (1979) research treatise and the responses to it. Hill's position is that we are just beginning with counseling research.

Currently there is a healthy unrest with business as usual with counseling research. Energetic programs are starting afresh with excellent conceptualizations and methodological sophistication. What is disturbing at times is their lack of visible linkage to the lessons of efforts of the 1950s. For example, the Volsky et al (1965) study represented state-of-the-art work by some of "the best and the brightest" in counseling psychology. While it is easy with hindsight to find flaws (e.g. use of "uniformity myths"), there may not be a better example in counseling psychology of sophisticated measurement of counseling constructs. Perhaps there is a natural tendency to forget this "tarnished classic" that failed to show substantial results for counseling. Can we not learn from some of the field's "failures?" Our current efforts are products of this lineage, and can be seen as building upon it rather than starting over.

Life was simpler when the Boulder conference enunciated the scientist-practitioner model for professional psychology. In many ways the science and practice had more natural affinities. A predominant clinical activity was assessment and the trait model was unchallenged. Goldman was writing an influential text (1971) showing us how to link testing and counseling. Today most observers agree that the science-practice linkage has not been achieved with elegance in any area of professional psychology. (Vocational counseling comes close to being an exception here.) Many would agree with Fiske (1983, p. 66) that "the practice of clinical psychology is still largely an art." Barlow (1981) believes the failures of the model are responsible for the retreat of practitioners to "trial-and-error eclecticism."

Grounds for optimism are the number of researchers still guided by the scientist-practitioner ideal. Earlier, Kiesler (1966) contributed notably to the science-practice bridge by directing our research attention to what Gelso (1979) calls the "who, what, when, where" questions. Significantly, Kiesler (1979b, 1981) now presents the most optimistic defense of this unique model among mental health professions. He says (1979b, p. 46) that

> it's time for us . . . to quit apologizing for our . . . model and to get on, as we are, with increasingly creative efforts to implement the model. The unfortunate historic fact is that we

started to throw out the model at the very time in our development when we were acquiring new perspectives and learnings that could permit us to apply the model in truly meaningful ways . . . We are doing creative and exciting things with our programs . . . are more and more attaining our goal.

The topics that follow can be interpreted variously as continuing activities in that quest to join science and practice. A continuing theme in these often controversial developments is how empiricism can be molded to fit the complexities of the clinician's experience. That creates a tension, since the usual mode of science is to simplify.

Liberalizing Bases for Inference

When issues of the science-practice fit are translated into research, a prominent polarity is rigor versus relevance (Goldman 1976, Cohen 1979, Gelso 1979, Krumboltz & Mitchell 1979, Nelson 1981, Ross 1981). Many new methods represent an attempt to achieve a more palatable blend of both rigor and relevance. The past tilt has been to rigor, and thus psychology has tended to settle into one "right" approach to research. Wachtel (1980, p. 400) observes, "the typical model of psychological research and of research training tends to be far too monolithic." As editor of the *Journal of Counseling Psychology,* Gelso is committed to methodological diversity. He says (1982, p. 6):

There is a nascent sense that methods other than the traditional experimental and correlational designs will be useful or even necessary if we are to advance knowledge significantly. Furthermore, controversy exists with respect to a variety of methodological issues . . . Probably the strongest view I have as editor of JCP is that counseling psychology will be most positively affected if the journal is methodologically open.

ANALOGUE STUDIES   The prospect for progress from laboratory analogues is probably the most controversial methods issue in counseling psychology (cf Strong 1971, Gelso 1979, Hill 1982). Yet analogues have been pervasive in our literature and have, in fact, produced the largest body of studies—the social influence literature (Strong 1978, Strong & Claiborn 1982). Reviewers (Corrigan et al 1980, Heppner & Dixon 1981) have questioned the generalizability of these findings from brief analogues. A recent trend has been to test the social influence model with closer counseling simulations (Strong et al 1979, Feldman et al 1982, Lopez & Wambach 1982, Kerr et al 1983) and in actual counseling (LaCrosse 1980, Zamostny et al 1981, Heppner & Handley 1981, Heppner & Heesacker 1982, 1983). Heppner & Heesacker's (1983) study illustrates the inevitable trade-offs (Gelso 1979), where rival hypotheses intrude in interpretations of the less controlled studies of actual counseling.

SINGLE CASE DESIGNS   Interest in capturing the therapeutic encounter through single case designs is at an all-time high (Resnikoff 1978, Gelso 1979,

Hill 1982, Kazdin 1982a). This is a remarkable transformation for a discipline that bet so strongly in the past on the classic nomothetic method. Hill et al's (1983) case study is the most dramatic example of this transformation of thinking about routes to knowledge. The field's readiness for change is evident in editor Gelso's running the Hill et al case study as the lead article, while in 1979 he argued that single case studies could only be done with a discrete behavioral intervention.

STATISTICAL ANALYSES   Leary & Altmaier (1980) and Biskin (1980) have urged the use of multivariate analysis of variance in dealing with our typically correlated sets of dependent variables. Related commentaries have been provided by Strahan (1982) and Larrabee (1982). More general concerns with power and substantive significance have been expressed by Atkinson et al (1982) and Haase et al (1982a). The exchange between Patton & Wampold (1982) and Haase et al (1982b), more charged than typical of the *Journal of Counseling Psychology,* is a healthy and exciting level of dialogue and illustrates pivotal issues of scientific style.

META-ANALYSIS   In Fiske's (1983) apt phrase, meta-analysis has created a revolution in therapy outcome research. It is hard to identify anything previous that has stirred such high-powered debate and examination of therapy research. The result has been one of those fertile controversies in which bystanders may learn more than protagonists. As Fiske notes (1983, p. 66), "The controversy is healthy because it highlights the issues." We need more such productive controversies.

The intense interest in meta-analysis is partly due to its early application to psychotherapy (Smith & Glass 1977, Smith et al 1980). The ensuing debate engaged both therapy researchers and methodologists. The debate continues (e.g. Mintz 1983), but the approach is particularly fertile for reanalyses, which have tended to support the Smith and Glass work (Shapiro & Shapiro 1982). Glass & Kliegl (1983) emphasize that their approach is directed to integrating the published literature, not directly addressing either the clinical phenomena or the theories of the therapists studied. The technique is being widely applied in a variety of subject areas (Glass et al 1981, Bassoff & Glass 1982). Counseling psychology is ready for applications; a good place to start is the sizable social influence literature.

Philosophical Underpinnings

Epistemology is in disarray in much of psychology. The resulting malaise over method is evident in anguished and thoughtful appraisals of the "slow progress of soft psychology" (Meehl 1978, Cook 1982, Glass & Kliegl 1983, Rorer & Widiger 1983). The key lament (in my partly clinical interpretation) is that the vision for psychology of the 1950s, as exemplified in such advances as construct validation and the building of nomological nets (Cronbach & Meehl 1955), has not been achieved. The problem is put succinctly by Glass & Kliegl (1983, p. 38) as "the naive beliefs of logical empiricists that understanding of psychotherapeutic processes can be communicated in the operationist shorthand that defines the contemporary culture of research journals."

The painful irony is that the bulk of our research follows an obsolete philosophy of science (Mahoney 1976, Rychlak 1977, Weimer 1977, 1980, Meehl 1978, Thoresen 1979, Rorer & Widiger 1983). Our energy is misinvested with narrow operationism wedded to ever more skilled applications of Fisherian designs that do not fit our subject matter (Meehl 1978). "It is a regrettable egocentric failing of many scientists that they are unable to reflect self-consciously on the historical choices that have bequeathed to them their particular 'science,' but instead believe that logic demands they pursue their inquiries precisely as they are pursuing them" (Glass & Kliegl 1983, p. 35). Thoresen (1979) has been the most eloquent and forward-looking expert on "hardening of the categories" among counseling psychologists. Hoping to remove our conceptual blinders, he presents a different view with a sketch of an alternative philosophic base. For those ready to rethink the way we do science, other good sources are Meehl (1978), Rorer & Widiger (1983), and Howard (1983). Also, under development by George Howard for the *Journal of Counseling Psychology* is a special subsection on philosophy of science and counseling research.

Glass & Kliegl (1983) draw from Meehl's (1978) penetrating analysis of the "slow progress of soft psychology" in reflecting on their reasons for pursuing meta-analysis. While specifically directed to outcome, Glass & Kliegl's "worst features" of past research also characterize process research and pinpoint why our young science has not been cumulative or achieved a construct-level meaning that is satisfying to either scientist or clinician. Their supreme importance in encapsulating a tough and realistic appraisal of our field merits their quotation. Glass & Kliegl (1983, p. 28) say:

> The methodology of outcome research reflected the worst features of positivist operationism: trivial quantification of outcomes (Behavioral Avoidance Tests and fear thermometers) devoid of technological importance; reliance on statistical hypothesis testing as *the* scientific method; disregard of the search for "function forms" (Meehl 1978, p. 825) of practical and theoretical significance; belief on the part of psychotherapy researchers that they were engaged in the construction of grand theory about human behavior [instead of mapping a few "context-dependent stochastologicals" (Meehl 1978, pp. 812–13)]; and the tendency of researchers to ignore gross inconsistencies in findings from one laboratory to the next and to fail to draw the proper implications of such inconsistency for their field and its methodology.

Mentoring methodology is a growth industry, especially among psychologists. It is responsible for classics by Cronbach & Meehl (1955), Cronbach

(1957), Campbell & Fiske (1959) and emerging classics (Smith & Glass 1977, Meehl 1978, Smith et al 1980). Yet to read certain writers on method and epistemology, one might conclude that psychologists' approach to knowing is the most dismal of all scientists (cf Rorer & Widiger 1983). Another view is that psychologists have been among the most clever and insightful of all scientists in examining the bases for their knowledge and extending their conceptual and methodological tools. How well are these classics of the 1950s and 1960s being used now to build our knowledge base? What are we to make of the fact that Cronbach & Meehl (1955) are not cited once in the 1982 volume of the *Journal of Counseling Psychology?* I fear it means not that the ideas are so embedded that citation is not needed, but rather that the field is not achieving the kind of construct validation and building of nomological nets envisioned in the Cronbach and Meehl blueprint. Psychology has a decent game plan; we need to do the demanding work of executing it.

Donald Campbell's work represents a hopeful approach to "knowing." A festschrift by his students (Brewer et al 1981) attests to the wide generativity of his approach and is an excellent source on his many constructive influences on the way we do science. Campbell gives us what might be termed an eclectic epistemology, saying that through multiple determination (cf Cole et al 1981) and triangulation (cf Neimeyer & Resnikoff 1982) we can bring multiple methods to bear on a question. This is also the essence of construct validity and the multitrait-multimethod matrix. The beauty of this approach is that it becomes a resolution for some of the methods dialectics so prominent in our field. Thus our task becomes not that of rallying behind single case vs group designs, process vs outcome research, or analogue vs real-world studies, but in *triangulating* the knowledge we can gain from these disparate sources. Wimsatt (1981) introduces a valuable chapter on this topic by quoting Levins (1966, p. 423): "Our truth is the intersection of independent lies." One's visceral reaction to that statement may index one's readiness for "methodological pluralism" (Howard 1983).

Our young science is ripe for research integration. Much of our work has been technically well executed but only weakly linked to other work, especially in other laboratories. The result is that Krumboltz et al (1979) could review the counseling literature as "nuggets of knowledge," a phrase painfully akin to Meehl's (1978, pp. 812–13) "context-dependent stochastologicals." Such knowledge has some immediate value for clinicians, but our quest for a science will be better served by nomological nets and construct validity. It is a long way from nuggets to nomologicals.

There is a healthy area of counseling research that is not vitiated by problems of linking research operations and hypothetical constructs. This is the work done in counseling settings with direct measures with face and practical validity. Enhancement of service delivery is of prime import; theory testing has only a minor role. An example is the study of premature termination (Betz & Shullman 1979, Epperson 1981, 1983, Krauskopf et al 1981, Rodolfa et al 1983). Such empiricism has direct counseling implications by showing, for example, that clients fail to return because counselors misperceived their problems (Epperson et al 1983). Other useful research assesses potential users' perceptions of counseling (Carney et al 1979, Carney & Savitz 1980, Tinsley et al 1980, 1982). Tinsley's work, while intrinsically practical, is also notable for the quality of its construct development. Program evaluation (Oetting 1982) is another route to such direct payoff studies of our counseling centers. Such studies successfully meld our science and practice ideals.

Models of Causation

A revolutionary rethinking of the nature of causation has jumped from clinicia to academia. It is the centerpiece of Strong & Claiborn's (1982) *Change Through Interaction*, which posits a systems view of human problems and corollary innovations for therapeutic change. The nonlinear causal model has the potential to be the most important current event affecting research on counseling and psychotherapy. Already research effects are evident in new topics investigated by Strong and Claiborn and their associates (cited earlier).

What is now known as the systems view took root in the Palo Alto school of family therapy led by seminal thinkers Gregory Bateson and Don Jackson (Watzlawick et al 1974). These novel concepts were inspired clinically, pragmatically, and conceptually—not by university-based research. Eventually this idea that "problems" could only be understood contextually within family structures became central to the burgeoning field of family therapy. Their success there, and the related unorthodox treatment methods of Milton Erickson (Haley 1973), profoundly affected clinicians in the 1970s. An example of impact is that Cummings' (1979) APA presidential address presented his clinical use of paradox: telling substance abusers that he would not see them until they had stopped using their drugs.

This new view is quite a leap from the linear causal models that underlie our notions of stimulus-response, intrapsychic events, and independent and dependent variables. Implications for interventions do not follow a psychodynamic, and especially a Rogerian mode. At the pulse-points in counseling psychology, writers are beginning to incorporate contextual and systems notions in their research agenda. Strong & Claiborn (1982) present the most developed and most radical view. Context is central to Hill's (1982, 1983) and Highlen & Hill's (1984) renewed approach to process research. They eschew a traditional approach to study atomistic variables without regard to the larger tapestry of the dyadic interaction. While still a major change, the Highlen and Hill agenda is less visibly radical than Strong and Claiborn's because Highlen and Hill focus more on therapeutic *change* and less on a systems interpretation of *causation*. The contextual position is also central to Rice & Greenberg's (1983) book.

Discontent is now visible (Wachtel 1980) with old concepts, dogma, and method. To that extent we have the matrix for an analogue of a Kuhnian revolution. What we critically lack, however, is the paradigm only awaiting adoption to continue doing normal science. We do *not* have the methods to address adequately this new thinking about systems, contexts, and dyadic processes. Traditional input-output designs, even when enhanced with partials, multivariates, and three-way interactions, fail to capture expanding concepts of causation and change (Hill 1982). Moving in the right direction are statistical methods that address ongoing dyadic processes (Lichtenberg & Hummel 1976, Benjamin 1979, Gottman 1981, Holloway & Wolleat 1981, Margolin & Wampold 1981, Notarius et al 1981, Allison & Liker 1982, Greenberg & Webster 1982, Holloway 1982, Mendoza & Graziano 1982, Wampold & Margolin 1982). Single case designs also provide heuristics for these problems (Kazdin 1982a, Hill et al 1983). Kiesler (1979a, 1982, Anchin & Kiesler 1982) is at the leading edge of promising research approaches to reciprocal/circular causation in human interactions. The three dominant counseling process approaches—Strong's, Hill's, and Pepinsky's—will advance if methods catch up to their conceptions.

A FINAL WORD

It has now been over 30 years since the first chapter on counseling psychology in the *Annual Review of Psychology* (Zytowski & Rosen 1982). Likewise, the *Journal of Counseling Psychology* is 30 years old. Scientific progress has not followed a smooth and cumulative course, but the discipline teems with vitality and resolve. There is visible excitement about new concepts and methods to understand better the therapeutic essence. The one ingredient that will bring all of this together for progress is integration in its diverse forms.

ACKNOWLEDGMENTS

I am grateful to numerous colleagues who generously shared their work and their thinking with me, and to Connie Bailey, Dianne Borgen, Bob Seegmiller, and Pam Seegmiller, who assisted with final preparation of the manuscript. The Psychology Department, University of Minnesota, provided me with a productive working environment while I was an Honorary Fellow there during 1982–83.

Literature Cited

Allison, P. D., Liker, J. K. 1982. Analyzing sequential categorical data on dyadic interaction: A comment on Gottman. *Psychol. Bull.* 91:393–403

Anchin, J. C., Kiesler, D. J. 1982. *Handbook of Interpersonal Psychotherapy*. New York: Pergamon. 346 pp.

Atkinson, D. R., Furlong, M. J., Wampold, B. E. 1982. Statistical significance, reviewer evaluations, and the scientific process: Is there a (statistically) significant relationship? *J. Couns. Psychol.* 29:189–94

Bandura, A. 1977. Self-efficacy: Toward a unifying theory of behavioral change. *Psychol. Rev.* 84:191–215

Bandura, A. 1982. Self-efficacy mechanism in human agency. *Am. Psychol.* 37:122–47

Barlow, D. H. 1981. On the relation of clinical research to clinical practice: Current issues, new directions. *J. Consult. Clin. Psychol.* 49:147–55

Bassoff, E. S., Glass, G. V. 1982. The relationship between sex roles and mental health: A meta-analysis of twenty-six studies. *Couns. Psychol.* 10(4):105–12

Beck, J. T., Strong, S. R. 1982. Stimulating therapeutic change with interpretations: A comparison of positive and negative connotation. *J. Couns. Psychol.* 29:551–59

Benjamin, L. S. 1979. Use of structural analysis of social behavior (SASB) and Markov Chains to study dyadic interactions. *J. Abnorm. Psychol.* 88:303–19

Bergin, A. E., Lambert, M. J. 1979. Counseling the researcher. *Couns. Psychol.* 8(3):53–56

Betz, N. E., Hackett, G. 1981. The relationship of career-related self-efficacy expectations to perceived career options of college women and men. *J. Couns. Psychol.* 28:399–410

Betz, N. E., Shullman, S. L. 1979. Factors related to client return rate following intake. *J. Couns. Psychol.* 26:542–45

Beutler, L. E. 1979. Toward specific psychological therapies for specific conditions. *J. Consult. Clin. Psychol.* 47:882–97

Bevan, W. 1982. A sermon of sorts in three plus parts. *Am. Psychol.* 37:1303–22

Biskin, B. H. 1980. Multivariate analysis in experimental counseling research. *Couns. Psychol.* 8(4):69–72

Bordin, E. S. 1979. The generalizability of the psychoanalytic concept of the working alliance. *Psychother. Theory. Res. Pract.* 16:252–60

Bordin, E. S. 1981. A psychodynamic view of counseling psychology. *Couns. Psychol.* 9(1):62–69

Borgen, F. H., Bernard, C. B. 1982. Review of

Strong-Campbell Interest Inventory. *Meas. Eval. Guid.* 14:208–12

Brammer, L. M., Shostrum, E. L. 1982. *Therapeutic Psychology: Fundamentals of Counseling and Psychotherapy*. Englewood Cliffs, NJ: Prentice-Hall. 466 pp. 4th ed.

Brewer, M. B., Collins, B. E., eds. 1981. *Scientific Inquiry and the Social Sciences*. San Francisco: Jossey-Bass. 523 pp.

Brodsky, A. M., Hare-Mustin, R., eds. 1980a. *Women and Psychotherapy: An Assessment of Research and Practice*. New York: Guilford. 428 pp.

Brodsky, A. M., Hare-Mustin, R. 1980b. Psychotherapy and women: Priorities for research. See Brodsky & Hare-Mustin 1980a, pp. 385–409

Brown, S. D., Hosford, R. E. 1981. The future of behavioral counseling: Recommendations for a continued empiricism. *Behav. Couns. Q.* 1:9–28

Brown, S. D., Lent, R. W. 1984. *Handbook of Counseling Psychology*. New York: Wiley. In press

Bruch, M. A. 1981a. A task analysis of assertive behavior revisited: Replication and extension. *Behav. Ther.* 12:217–30

Bruch, M. A. 1981b. Relationship of test-taking strategies to test anxiety and performance: Toward a task analysis of examination behavior. *Cogn. Ther. Res.* 5:41–56

Bruch, M. A., Heisler, B. D., Conroy, C. G. 1981. Effects of conceptual complexity on assertive behavior. *J. Couns. Psychol.* 28:377–85

Bruch, M. A., Juster, H. R., Heisler, B. D. 1982. Conceptual complexity as a mediator of thought content and negative affect: Implications for cognitive restructuring interventions. *J. Couns. Psychol.* 29:343–53

Campbell, D. P., Hansen, J. C. 1981. *Manual for the SVIB-SCII*. Stanford, Calif: Stanford Univ. Press. 143 pp. 3rd ed.

Campbell, D. T., Fiske, D. W. 1959. Convergent and discriminant validation by the multitrait-multimethod matrix. *Psychol. Bull.* 56:81–105

Carney, C. G., Savitz, C. J. 1980. Student and faculty perceptions of student needs and the services of a university counseling center: Differences that make a difference. *J. Couns. Psychol.* 27:597–604

Carney, C. G., Savitz, C. J., Weiskott, G. N. 1979. Students' evaluations of a university counseling center and their intentions to use its programs. *J. Couns. Psychol.* 26:242–49

Casas, J. M. 1984. Policy, training and research in counseling psychology: The racial/ethnic minority perspective. See Brown & Lent 1984

Cohen, L. H. 1979. Clinical psychologists' judgments of the scientific merit and clinical relevance of psychotherapy outcome research. *J. Consult. Clin. Psychol.* 47:421–23

Cole, D. A., Howard, G. S., Maxwell, S. E. 1981. The effects of mono- versus multiple-operationalization in construct validation efforts. *J. Consult. Clin. Psychol.* 49:395–405

Cook, T. D. 1982. The social judgment in scientific evidence. Review of Brenner's *Social Method and Social Life. Contemp. Psychol.* 27:436–37

Cormier, W. H., Cormier, L. S. 1979. *Interviewing Strategies for Helpers: A Guide to Assessment, Treatment, and Evaluation.* Monterey, Calif: Brooks/Cole. 557 pp.

Corrigan, J. D., Dell, D. M., Lewis, K. N., Schmidt, L. D. 1980. Counseling as a social influence process: A review. *J. Couns. Psychol.* 27:395–441

Corsini, R. J., ed. 1981. *Handbook of Innovative Psychotherapies.* New York: Wiley. 997 pp.

Crites, J. O. 1983. Research methods in vocational psychology. See Walsh & Osipow 1983a

Cronbach, L. J. 1957. The two disciplines of scientific psychology. *Am. Psychol.* 12:671–84

Cronbach, L. J., Meehl, P. E. 1955. Construct validity in psychological tests. *Psychol. Bull.* 52:281–302

Cummings, N. A. 1979. Turning bread into stones: Our modern antimiracle. *Am. Psychol.* 34:1119–29

Dimond, R. E., Havens, R. A., Jones, A. C. 1978. A conceptual framework for the practice of prescriptive eclecticism in psychotherapy. *Am. Psychol.* 33:239–48

Dixon, D. N., Heppner, P. P., Petersen, C. H., Ronning, R. R. 1979. Problem solving workshop training. *J. Couns. Psychol.* 26:133–39

Edwards, H. P., Boulet, D. B., Mahrer, A. R., Chagnon, G. J., Mook, B. 1982. Carl Rogers during initial interviews: A moderate and consistent therapist. *J. Couns. Psychol.* 29:14–18

Epperson, D. L. 1981. Counselor gender and early premature terminations from counseling: A replication and extension. *J. Couns. Psychol.* 28:349–56

Epperson, D. L., Bushway, D. J., Warman, R. E. 1983. Client self-terminations after one counseling session: Failure of counselors to recognize client's problem definitions. *J. Couns. Psychol.* 30:307–15

Fay, A., Lazarus, A. A. 1982. Psychoanalytic resistance and behavioral nonresponsiveness: A dialectical impasse. See Wachtel 1982, pp. 219–31

Feldman, D. A., Strong, S. R., Danser, D. B. 1982. A comparison of paradoxical and nonparadoxical interpretations and directives. *J. Couns. Psychol.* 29:572–79

Fiske, D. W. 1983. The meta-analytic revolution in outcome research. *J. Consult. Clin. Psychol.* 51:65–70

Fitzgerald, L. F., Betz, N. E. 1983. Issues in the vocational psychology of women. See Walsh & Osipow 1983a

Fitzgerald, L. F., Crites, J. O. 1980. Toward a career psychology of women: What do we know? What do we need to know? *J. Couns. Psychol.* 27:44–62

Frank, J. D. 1961. *Persuasion and Healing.* Baltimore: Johns Hopkins Press. 282 pp. 1st ed.

Frank, J. D. 1973. *Persuasion and Healing.* Baltimore: Johns Hopkins Press. 378 pp. 2nd ed.

Frank, J. D. 1979. The present status of outcome studies. *J. Consult. Clin. Psychol.* 47:310–16

Fretz, B. R., guest ed. 1977. Professional identity. *Couns. Psychol.* 7(2):9–94

Fretz, B. R. 1981. Evaluating the effectiveness of career interventions. *J. Couns. Psychol. Monogr.* 28:77–90

Fretz, B. R., Mills, D. H. 1980. *Licensing and Certification of Psychologists and Counselors.* San Francisco: Jossey-Bass. 194 pp.

Galassi, J. P., Galassi, M. D. 1984. Promoting generalization and maintenance of counseling outcomes: How do we do it? How do we study it? See Brown & Lent 1984

Garfield, S. L. 1980. *Psychotherapy: An Eclectic Approach.* New York: Wiley. 315 pp.

Garfield, S. L. 1981. Psychotherapy: A 40-year appraisal. *Am. Psychol.* 36:174–83

Garfield, S. L. 1983. Effectiveness of psychotherapy: The perennial controversy. *Prof. Psychol. Res. Pract.* 14:35–43

Garfield, S. L., Bergin, A. E., eds. 1978. *Handbook of Psychotherapy and Behavior Change.* New York: Wiley. 1024 pp. 2nd ed.

Garfield, S. L., Kurtz, R. 1977. Clinical psychologists in the 1970s. *Am. Psychol.* 31:1–9

Gelso, C. J. 1979. Research in counseling: Methodological and professional issues. *Couns. Psychol.* 8(3):7–36

Gelso, C. J. 1982. Editorial. *J. Couns. Psychol.* 29:3–7

Gelso, C. J., Johnson, D. H., guest eds. 1982. Research in counseling psychology II. *Couns. Psychol.* 10(4):5–93

Gelso, C. J., Johnson, D. H. 1983. *Explorations in Time-limited Counseling and*

Psychotherapy. New York: Teachers Coll. Press. 265 pp.

Gilbert, L. A. 1980. Feminist therapy. See Brodsky & Hare-Mustin 1980, pp. 245–65

Gladstein, G. A. 1977. Empathy and counseling outcome: An empirical and conceptual review. *Couns. Psychol.* 6(4):70–79

Glass, G. V., Kliegl, R. M. 1983. An apology for research integration in the study of psychotherapy. *J. Consult. Clin. Psychol.* 51:28–41

Glass, G. V., McGaw, B., Smith, M. L. 1981. *Meta-analysis in Social Research.* Beverly Hills, Calif: Sage. 279 pp.

Goldfried, M. R. 1980. Toward the delineation of therapeutic change principles. *Am. Psychol.* 35:991–99

Goldfried, M. R. 1982. *Converging Themes in Psychotherapy: Trends in Psychodynamic, Humanistic and Behavioral Practice.* New York: Springer-Verlag. 404 pp.

Goldman, L. 1971. *Using Tests in Counseling.* Englewood Cliffs, NJ: Prentice-Hall. 483 pp.

Goldman, L. 1976. A revolution in counseling research. *J. Couns. Psychol.* 23:543–52

Goldman, L. 1982. Defining non-traditional research. *Couns. Psychol.* 10(4):87–89

Goldstein, A. P., Stein, N. 1976. *Prescriptive Psychotherapies.* New York: Pergamon

Gottfredson, L. S. 1981. Circumscription and compromise: A developmental theory of occupational aspiration. *J. Couns. Psychol. Monogr.* 28:545–79

Gottman, J. M. 1981. *Time-Series Analysis: A Comprehensive Introduction for Social Scientists.* Cambridge, England: Cambridge Univ. Press. 416 pp.

Greenberg, L. S., Webster, M. C. 1982. Resolving decisional conflict by Gestalt two-chair dialogue: Relating process to outcome. *J. Couns. Psychol.* 29:468–77

Haase, R. F., Biggs, D. A., Strohmer, D. C. 1982a. That's not my dog: A reply to Patton and Wampold. *J. Couns. Psychol.* 29:611–17

Haase, R. F., Waechter, D. M., Solomon, G. S. 1982b. How significant is a significant difference? Average effect size of research in counseling psychology. *J. Couns. Psychol.* 29:58–65

Haley, J. 1973. *Uncommon Therapy.* New York: Norton. 313 pp.

Harmon, L. 1982. Scientific affairs—the next decade. *Couns. Psychol.* 10(2):31–37

Heesacker, M., Heppner, P. P., Rogers, M. E. 1982. Classics and emerging classics in counseling psychology. *J. Couns. Psychol.* 29:400–5

Heppner, P. P. 1978. A review of the problem-solving literature and its relationship to the counseling process. *J. Couns. Psychol.* 25:366–75

Heppner, P. P., Dixon, D. N. 1981. A review of the interpersonal influence process in counseling. *Pers. Guid. J.* 59:542–50

Heppner, P. P., Handley, P. G. 1981. A study of the interpersonal influence process in supervision. *J. Couns. Psychol.* 28:437–44

Heppner, P. P., Heesacker, M. 1982. Interpersonal influences process in real-life counseling. *J. Couns. Psychol.* 29:215–23

Heppner, P. P., Heesacker, M. 1983. Perceived counselor characteristics, client expectations, and client satisfaction with counseling. *J. Couns. Psychol.* 30:31–39

Heppner, P. P., Hibel, J., Neal, G. W., Weinstein, C. L., Rabinowitz, F. E. 1982. Personal problem solving: A descriptive study of individual differences. *J. Couns. Psychol.* 29:580–90

Heppner, P. P., Petersen, C. H. 1982. The development and implications of a personal problem-solving inventory. *J. Couns. Psychol.* 29:66–75

Hess, A. K., ed. 1980. *Psychotherapy Supervision: Theory, Research and Practice.* New York: Wiley. 570 pp.

Highlen, P. S., Hill, C. E. 1984. Factors affecting client change in counseling: current status and theoretical speculations. See Brown & Lent 1984

Hilgard, E. R. 1980. Consciousness in contemporary psychology. *Ann. Rev. Psychol.* 31:1–26

Hill, C. E. 1978. Development of a counselor verbal response category system. *J. Couns. Psychol.* 25:461–68

Hill, C. E. 1982. Counseling process research: Philosophical and methodological dilemmas. *Couns. Psychol.* 10(4):7–19

Hill, C. E. 1983. An overview of the Hill counselor and client Verbal Response Modes Category Systems. In *Psychotherapeutic Process: A Research Handbook,* ed. L. Greenberg, W. Pinsof. New York: Guilford. In press

Hill, C. E., Birk, J. M., Blimline, C. A., Leonard, M. M., Hoffman, M. A., Tanney, M. F., guest eds. 1979a. Counseling women III. *Couns. Psychol.* 8(1):2–63

Hill, C. E., Carter, J. A., O'Farrell, M. K. 1983. A case study of the process and outcome of time-limited counseling. *J. Couns. Psychol.* 30:3–18

Hill, C. E., Charles, D., Reed, K. G. 1981. A longitudinal analysis of changes in counseling skills during doctoral training in counseling psychology. *J. Couns. Psychol.* 28:428–36

Hill, C. E., Thames, T. B., Rardin, D. K. 1979b. Comparison of Rogers, Perls, and Ellis on the Hill Counselor Verbal Response Category System. *J. Couns. Psychol.* 26:198–203

Holland, J. L., Magoon, T. M., Spokane, A.

R. 1981. Counseling psychology: Career interventions, research and theory. *Ann. Rev. Psychol.* 32:279–305

Holloway, E. L. 1982. Interactional structure of the supervision interview. *J. Couns. Psychol.* 29:309–17

Holloway, E. L., Wolleat, P. L. 1981. Style differences of beginning supervisors: An interactional analysis. *J. Couns. Psychol.* 28:373–76

Horan, J. J. 1979. *Counseling for Effective Decision Making: A Cognitive-Behavioral Perspective.* North Scituate, Mass: Duxbury

Hosford, R. E., Burnett, G. F., Mills, M. E. 1984. Toward prescription in counseling: Research status and future possibilities. See Brown & Lent 1984

Howard, G. S. 1983. Toward methodological pluralism. *J. Couns. Psychol.* 30:19–21

Ivey, A. E. 1980. *Counseling and Psychotherapy.* Englewood Cliffs, NJ: Prentice-Hall. 498 pp.

Ivey, A. E. 1983. *Intentional Interviewing and Counseling.* Monterey, Calif: Brooks/Cole. 324 pp.

Ivey, A. E., Authier, J. 1978. *Microcounseling: Innovations in Interviewing, Counseling, Psychotherapy, and Psychoeducation.* Springfield, Ill: Thomas. 584 pp.

Janis, I. L., ed. 1982. *Counseling on Personal Decisions.* New Haven: Yale Univ. Press. 409 pp.

Janis, I. L., Mann, L. 1977. *Decision-Making: A Psychological Analysis of Conflict, Choice, and Commitment.* New York: Free Press. 488 pp.

Johnson, D. H., Gelso, C. J. 1980. The effectiveness of time limits in counseling and psychotherapy: A critical review. *Couns. Psychol.* 9(1):70–83

Kagan, N., guest ed. 1982. Counseling psychology: The next decade. *Couns. Psychol.* 10(2):4–44

Kahneman, D., Slovic, P., Tversky, A., eds. 1982. *Judgment under Uncertainty: Heuristics and Biases.* New York: Cambridge Univ. Press. 556 pp.

Kazdin, A. E. 1982a. *Single-case Research Designs.* New York: Oxford Univ. Press. 381 pp.

Kazdin, A. E. 1982b. Symptom substitution, generalization, and response covariation: Implications for psychotherapy outcome. *Psychol. Bull.* 91:349–65

Kazdin, A. E., Wilcoxon, L. A. 1976. Systematic desensitization and nonspecific treatment effects: A methodological evaluation. *Psychol. Bull.* 83:729–58

Kendall, P. C., Hollon, S. D., eds. 1979. *Cognitive-Behavioral Interventions: Theory, Research, and Procedures.* New York: Academic. 481 pp.

Kerr, B. A., Olson, D. H., Claiborn, C. D.,

Bauers-Gruenler, S. J., Paolo, A. M. 1983. Overcoming opposition and resistance: Differential functions of expertness and attractiveness in career counseling. *J. Couns. Psychol.* 30:323–31

Kiesler, D. J. 1966. Some myths of psychotherapy research and the search for a paradigm. *Psychol. Bull.* 65:110–36

Kiesler, D. J. 1979a. An interpersonal communication analysis of relationship in psychotherapy. *Psychiatry* 42:299–311

Kiesler, D. J. 1979b. Commentary on Gelso's "Research in Counseling: Methodological and Professional Issues." *Couns. Psychol.* 8(3):44–47

Kiesler, D. J. 1981. Empirical clinical psychology: Myth or reality? *J. Consult. Clin. Psychol.* 49:212–15

Kiesler, D. J. 1982. The comeback trail for process analysis. *Couns. Psychol.* 10(4):21–22

Kirschenbaum, D. S., Perri, M. G. 1982. Improving academic competence in adults: A review of recent research. *J. Couns. Psychol.* 29:76–94

Koch, S. 1981. The nature and limits of psychological knowledge: Lessons of a century qua "science." *Am. Psychol.* 36:257–69

Krauskopf, C. J., Baumgardner, A., Mandracchia, S. 1981. Return rate following intake revisited. *J. Couns. Psychol.* 28:519–21

Krumboltz, J. D., Becker-Haven, J. F., Burnett, K. F. 1979. Counseling psychology. *Ann. Rev. Psychol.* 30:555–602

Krumboltz, J. D., Mitchell, L. K. 1979. Relevant rigorous research. *Couns. Psychol.* 8(3):50–52

Kuder, G. F. 1977. *Activity Interests and Occupational Choice.* Chicago: Sci. Res. Assoc. 326 pp.

LaCrosse, M. B. 1980. Perceived counselor social influence and counseling outcomes: Validity of the Counselor Rating Form. *J. Couns. Psychol.* 27:320–27

Lambert, M. J. 1980. Research and the supervisory process. See Hess 1980, pp. 423–50

Lambert, M. J., Christensen, E. R., DeJulio, S. S. 1983. *The Assessment of Psychotherapy Outcome: A Handbook.* New York: Wiley. 667 pp.

Lambert, M. J., DeJulio, S. S., Stein, D. M. 1978. Therapist interpersonal skills: Process, outcome, methodological considerations, and recommendations for future research. *Psychol. Bull.* 85:467–89

Larrabee, M. J. 1982. Reexamination of a plea for multivariate analyses. *J. Couns. Psychol.* 29:180–88

Lazarus, A. A. 1967. In support of technical eclecticism. *Psychol. Rep.* 21:415–16

Leary, M. R., Altmaier, E. M. 1980. Type I error in counseling research: A plea for multivariate analyses. *J. Couns. Psychol.* 27: 611–15

Levins, R. 1966. The strategy of model building in population biology. *Am. Sci.* 54:421–31

Lichtenberg, J. W., Hummel, T. J. 1976. Counseling as a stochastic process: Fitting a Markov chain model to initial counseling interviews. *J. Couns. Psychol.* 23: 310–15

Lofquist, L. H., Dawis, R. V. 1984. Research on work adjustment and satisfaction: Implications for career counseling. See Brown & Lent 1984

Loganbill, C., Hardy, E., Delworth, U. 1982. Supervision: A conceptual model. *Couns. Psychol.* 10(1):3–42

Lopez, F. G., Wambach, C. A. 1982. Effects of paradoxical and self-control directives in counseling. *J. Couns. Psychol.* 29:115–24

Luborsky, L., Singer, B. 1975. Comparative studies of psychotherapies: Is it true that "Everyone has won and all must have prizes"? *Arch. Gen. Psychiatry* 32:995–1008

Luborsky, L., Spence, D. P. 1978. Quantitative research on psychoanalytic therapy. See Garfield & Bergin 1978, pp. 331–68

Lunneborg, P. W. 1982. Underlining the criterion problem. *Couns. Psychol.* 10(4):35–36

Magoon, T. M., Holland, J. L. 1984. Research training and supervision. See Brown and Lent 1984

Mahoney, M. J. 1976. *Scientist as Subject: The Psychological Imperative.* Cambridge, Mass: Ballinger. 249 pp.

Mahoney, M. J. 1977. Reflections on the cognitive-learning trend in psychotherapy. *Am. Psychol.* 32:5–13

Mahoney, M. J., Arnkoff, D. 1978. Cognitive and self-control therapies. See Garfield & Bergin 1978, pp. 689–722

Margolin, G., Wampold, B. E. 1981. Sequential analysis of conflict and accord in distressed and nondistressed marital partners. *J. Consult. Clin. Psychol.* 49:554–67

McKitrick, D. S., Gelso, C. J. 1978. Initial client expectancies in time-limited counseling. *J. Couns. Psychol.* 25:246–49

Meara, N. M., Pepinsky, H. B., Shannon, J. W., Murray, W. A. 1981. Semantic communication and expectations for counseling across three theoretical orientations. *J. Couns. Psychol.* 28:110–18

Meara, N. M., Shannon, J. W., Pepinsky, H. B. 1979. Comparison of the stylistic complexity of the language of counselor and client across three theoretical orientations. *J. Couns. Psychol.* 26:181–89

Meehl, P. E. 1978. Theoretical risks and tabular asterisks: Sir Karl, Sir Ronald, and the slow progress of soft psychology. *J. Consult. Clin. Psychol.* 46:806–34

Meichenbaum, D. 1977. *Cognitive-Behavior Modification.* New York: Plenum. 305 pp.

Mendoza, J. L., Graziano, W. G. 1982. The statistical analysis of dyadic social behavior: A multivariate approach. *Psychol. Bull.* 92:532–40

Merluzzi, T. V., Glass, C. R., Genest, M., eds. 1981. *Cognitive Assessment.* New York: Guilford. 548 pp.

Messer, S. B. 1983. Resistance to integration. Review of Wachtel's *Resistance: Psychoanalytic and Behavioral Approaches. Contemp. Psychol.* 28:111–12

Messer, S. B., Winokur, M. 1980. Some limits to the integration of psychoanalytic and behavior therapy. *Am. Psychol.* 35: 818–27

Miller, N. E. 1983. Behavioral medicine: Symbiosis between laboratory and clinic. *Ann. Rev. Psychol.* 34:1–31

Mintz, J. 1983. Integrating research evidence: A commentary on meta-analysis. *J. Consult. Clin. Psychol.* 51:71–75

Mitchell, L. K., Krumboltz, J. D. 1984. Research on human decision-making: Implications for career decision-making and counseling. See Brown & Lent 1984

Neimeyer, G., Resnikoff, A. 1982. Qualitative strategies in counseling research. *Couns. Psychol.* 10(4):75–85

Nelson, R. O. 1981. Realistic dependent measures for clinical use. *J. Consult. Clin. Psychol.* 49:168–82

Notarius, C. I., Krokoff, L. J., Markman, H. J. 1981. Analysis of observational data. In *Assessing Marriage: New Behavioral Approaches,* ed. E. E. Filsinger, R. A. Lewis, pp. 197–216. Beverly Hills, Calif: Sage. 300 pp.

Oetting, E. R. 1982. Program evaluation, scientific inquiry, and counseling psychology. *Couns. Psychol.* 10(4):61–70

Oliver, L. 1979. Outcome measurement in career counseling research. *J. Couns. Psychol.* 26:217–26

Orlinsky, D. E., Howard, K. I. 1978. The relation of process to outcome in psychotherapy. See Garfield & Bergin 1978, pp. 283–329

Osipow, S. H. 1982. Research in career counseling: An analysis of issues and problems. *Couns. Psychol.* 10(4):27–34

Osipow, S. H. 1983. *Theories of Career Development.* Englewood Cliffs, NJ: Prentice-Hall. 339 pp. 3rd ed.

Parsons, F. 1909. *Choosing a Vocation.* Boston: Houghton-Mifflin. 110 pp.

Patton, M. J., Connor, G. E., Scott, K. J. 1982. Kohut's psychology of the self: Theory and measures of counseling outcome. *J. Couns. Psychol.* 29:268–82

Patton, M. J., Fuhriman, A. J., Bieber, M. R. 1977. A model and a metalanguage for research on psychological counseling. *J. Couns. Psychol.* 24:25–34

Patton, M. J., Wampold, B. E. 1982. Troubles in modeling the counselor's model. *J. Couns. Psychol.* 29:607–10

Peabody, S. A., Gelso, C. J. 1982. Countertransference and empathy: The complex relationship between two divergent concepts in counseling. *J. Couns. Psychol.* 29:240–45

Pedersen, P. B., Draguns, J. G., Lonner, W. J., Trimble, J. E., eds. 1981. *Counseling across Cultures.* Honolulu: Univ. Press. Hawaii. 380 pp.

Pepinsky, H. B. 1983. Perspectives on the aging of a persistent counseling psychology. See Whiteley 1983

Resnikoff, A. 1978. Scientific Affairs Committee Report, 1975–1977: A discussion on methodology. *Couns. Psychol.* 7(4):67–71

Rice, L., Greenberg, L. S. 1983. *Patterns of Change: Intensive Analysis of Psychotherapy Process.* New York: Guilford. In press

Richardson, M. S. 1981. Occupational and family roles: A neglected intersection. *Couns. Psychol.* 9(4):13–23

Richardson, M. S., Johnson, M. 1984. Counseling women. See Brown & Lent 1984

Rodolfa, E. R., Rapaport, R., Lee, V. E. 1983. Variables related to premature terminations in a university counseling service. *J. Couns. Psychol.* 30:87–90

Rogers, C. R. 1957. The necessary and sufficient conditions of therapeutic personality change. *J. Consult. Psychol.* 21:95–103

Rorer, L. G., Widiger, T. A. 1983. Personality structure and assessment. *Ann. Rev. Psychol.* 34:431–63

Ross, A. O. 1981. Of rigor and relevance. *Prof. Psychol.* 12:318–27

Rush, A. J., ed. 1982. *Short-term Psychotherapies for Depression: Behavioral, Interpersonal, Cognitive, and Psychodynamic Approaches.* New York: Guilford. 351 pp.

Russell, R. K., Crimmings, A. M., Lent, R. W. 1984. Counseling supervision: Theory and research. See Brown & Lent 1984

Rychlak, J. F. 1977. *The Psychology of Rigorous Humanism.* New York: Wiley. 547 pp.

Schmidt, L. D., Meara, N. M. 1984. Current ethical, professional and legal issues in counseling psychology. See Brown & Lent 1984

Sechrest, L. 1982. Program evaluation: The independent and dependent variables. *Couns. Psychol.* 10(4):73–74

Shapiro, D. A., Shapiro, D. 1982. Meta-analysis of comparative therapy outcome studies: A replication and refinement. *Psychol. Bull.* 92:581–604

Sloane, R. B., Staples, F. R., Cristol, A. H., Yorkston, N. J., Whipple, K. 1975. *Psychotherapy versus Behavior Therapy.*

Cambridge, Mass: Harvard Univ. Press. 264 pp.

Smith, D. 1982. Trends in counseling and psychotherapy. *Am. Psychol.* 37:802–9

Smith, E. J. 1983. Issues in racial minorities' career behavior. See Walsh & Osipow 1983a

Smith, M. L., Glass, G. V. 1977. Meta-analysis of psychotherapy outcome studies. *Am. Psychol.* 32:752–60

Smith, M. L., Glass, G. V., Miller, T. I. 1980. *The Benefits of Psychotherapy.* Baltimore: Johns Hopkins Univ. Press. 269 pp.

Spokane, A. R., Oliver, L. W. 1983. The outcomes of vocational intervention. See Walsh & Osipow 1983b

Stein, M. L., Stone, G. L. 1978. Effects of conceptual level and structure on initial interview behavior. *J. Couns. Psychol.* 25:96–102

Stone, G. L. 1980. *A Cognitive-Behavioral Approach to Counseling Psychology.* New York: Praeger. 194 pp.

Strahan, R. F. 1982. Multivariate analysis and the problem of Type I error. *J. Couns. Psychol.* 29:175–79

Strong, E. K. Jr. 1943. *Vocational Interests of Men and Women.* Stanford, Calif: Stanford Univ. Press

Strong, S. R. 1968. Counseling: An interpersonal influence process. *J. Couns. Psychol.* 15:215–24

Strong, S. R. 1971. Experimental laboratory research in counseling. *J. Couns. Psychol.* 18:106–10

Strong, S. R. 1978. Social psychological approach to psychotherapy research. See Garfield & Bergin 1978, pp. 101–35

Strong, S. R., Claiborn, C. D. 1982. *Change Through Interaction: Social Psychological Processes of Counseling and Psychotherapy.* New York: Wiley. 259 pp.

Strong, S. R., Wambach, C. A., Lopez, F. G., Cooper, R. K. 1979. Motivational and equipping functions of interpretation in counseling. *J. Couns. Psychol.* 26:98–107

Strupp, H. H. 1973. On the basic ingredients of psychotherapy. *J. Consult. Clin. Psychol.* 41:1–8

Strupp, H. H., Hadley, S. W. 1979. Specific versus nonspecific factors in psychotherapy: A controlled study of outcome. *Arch. Gen. Psychiatry* 36:1125–36

Sue, D. W., Bernier, J. E., Durran, A., Feinberg, L., Pedersen, P., et al. 1982. Position paper: Cross-cultural counseling competencies. *Couns. Psychol.* 10(2):45–52

Super, D. E. 1983. The history and development of vocational psychology: A personal perspective. See Walsh & Osipow 1983a

Thoresen, C. E. 1979. Counseling research: What I can't help thinking. *Couns. Psychol.* 8(3):56–61

Tinsley, H. E. A., de St. Aubin, T. M., Brown,

M. T. 1982. College students' help-seeking preferences. *J. Couns. Psychol.* 29:523–33

Tinsley, H. E. A., Workman, K. R., Kass, R. A. 1980. Factor analysis of the domain of client expectancies about counseling. *J. Couns. Psychol.* 27:561–70

Volsky, T. Jr., Magoon, T. M., Norman, W. T., Hoyt, D. P. 1965. *The Outcomes of Counseling and Psychotherapy.* Minneapolis: Univ. Minn. Press. 209 pp.

Wachtel, P. L. 1977. *Psychoanalysis and Behavior Therapy: Toward an Integration.* New York: Basic Books. 315 pp.

Wachtel, P. L. 1980. Investigation and its discontents. *Am. Psychol.* 35:399–408

Wachtel, P. L., ed. 1982. *Resistance: Psychodynamic and Behavioral Approaches.* New York: Plenum. 267 pp.

Walsh, W. B., Osipow, S. H., eds. 1983a. *Handbook of Vocational Psychology, Volume I: Foundations.* Hillsdale, NJ: Erlbaum.

Walsh, W. B., Osipow, S. H., eds. 1983b. *Handbook of Vocational Psychology, Volume II: Applications.* Hillsdale, NJ: Erlbaum.

Wampold, B. E., Margolin, G. 1982. Nonparametric strategies to test the independence of behavioral states in sequential data. *Psychol. Bull.* 92:755–65

Watzlawick, P., Weakland, J., Fisch, R. 1974. *Change: Principles of Problem Formation and Problem Resolution.* New York: Norton. 172 pp.

Weimer, W. B. 1977. *Notes on Methodology.* Hillsdale, NJ: Erlbaum. 257 pp.

Weimer, W. B. 1980. Psychotherapy and philosophy of science: Examples of a two-way street in search of traffic. In *Psychotherapy Process*, ed. M. J. Mahoney, pp. 369–93. New York: Plenum. 403 pp.

Whiteley, J. M., ed. 1980a. *The History of Counseling Psychology.* Monterey, Calif: Brooks/Cole. 209 pp.

Whiteley, J. M., ed. 1980b. Counseling psychology in the year 2000 A. D. *Couns. Psychol.* 8(4):2–60

Whiteley, J. M., ed. 1983. *The Coming Decade in Counseling Psychology.* Monterey, Calif: Brooks/Cole. In press

Whiteley, J. M., Fretz, B. R., eds. 1980. *The Present and Future of Counseling Psychology.* Monterey, Calif: Brooks/Cole. 235 pp.

Wills, T. A., ed. 1982. *Basic Processes in Helping Relationships.* New York: Academic. 520 pp.

Wimsatt, W. C. 1981. Robustness, reliability, and overdetermination. See Brewer & Collins 1981, pp. 124–63

Wolpe, J. 1981. Behavior therapy versus psychoanalysis: Therapeutic and social implications. *Am. Psychol.* 36:159–64

Wolpe, J. 1982. Missing the point: A reply to Wogan and Norcross. *Am. Psychol.* 37:1286–87

Wright, R. M., Strong, S. R. 1982. Stimulating therapeutic change with directives: An exploratory study. *J. Couns. Psychol.* 29:199–202

Wycoff, J. P., Davis, K. L., Hector, M. A., Meara, N. M. 1982. A language analysis of empathic responding to client anger. *J. Couns. Psychol.* 29:462–67

Yeaton, W. H., Sechrest, L. 1981. Critical dimensions in choice and maintenance of successful treatments: Strength, integrity, and effectiveness. *J. Consult. Clin. Psychol.* 49:156–67

Zamostny, K. P., Corrigan, J. D., Eggert, M. A. 1981. Replication and extension of social influence processes in counseling: A field study. *J. Couns. Psychol.* 28:481–89

Zytowski, D. G., Borgen, F. H. 1983. Assessment. See Walsh & Osipow 1983b

Zytowski, D. G., Rosen, D. A. 1982. The grand tour: 30 years of counseling psychology in the *Annual Review of Psychology. Couns. Psychol.* 10(1):69–81

Ann. Rev. Psychol. 1984. 35:605–25
Copyright © 1984 by Annual Reviews Inc. All rights reserved

SPORT PSYCHOLOGY

Margaret A. Browne

502B Strawberry Plains Road, Williamsburg, Virginia 23185

Michael J. Mahoney

Department of Psychology, Penn State University, University Park, Pennsylvania 16802

CONTENTS

INTRODUCTION

Sport psychology is the application of psychological principles to sport and physical activity at all levels of skill development. As such, it has tended to mirror the interests of psychology in both its focus and methods. While it has

605

0066-4308/84/0201-0605$02.00

enjoyed a longer history in Europe, especially Eastern Europe, sport psychology is a fledgling of academic and applied interest in the United States where it is 15–20 years old. While much of the prior work has been research related, it has more recently surged into practical pursuits of maximizing performance and applied clinical issues.

This expansion, while met with enthusiasm from sport participants, has brought new confusions to the field. In the past, most of the work was done in departments of physical education and sport sciences; now with enlarged boundaries, there are (the not unusual) territorial disputes and role confusions. This is compounded by the absence of an umbrella organization to act as arbiter, to assume responsibility for credentialing practitioners, for monitoring the services provided to the consumer.

Members of the American Psychological Association (APA) formed an interest group at the 1982 APA convention. The Sports Medicine Division of the United States Olympic Committee initiated a registry in 1982 for the purpose of referrals in the areas of education, research, and clinical sport psychology. The American College of Sports Medicine requires members to be in good standing of their own professional organizations, but otherwise imposes no additional code of conduct upon its members from various fields related to health, physical education, sports medicine, and exercise science. The North American Society for Psychology of Sport and Physical Activity (NASPSPA), founded in 1966, has no professional membership requirements so it can regulate neither those who call themselves sport psychologists nor what they do, though they have recently (1982) recommended that NASPSPA members follow the APA guidelines for testing, research, and clinical intervention.

Thus raised and nurtured in infancy by the single parent called Sport Sciences, with a modicum of child support from the (largely unrecognized) parent called Psychology, this exciting toddler named Sport Psychology is now attracting considerable professional and public attention.

HISTORY

Sport psychology has its roots in motor learning and motor performance. Before 1920, there were sporadic investigations by a few persons, none collaborating. The thrust of the research pertained to the influence of psychological variables on motor performance. The first known publication in the United States was on the role of audience effects on competitive bicycling (Tripplett 1898). In 1918 Coleman Griffith, a psychologist at the University of Illinois, compared the reaction times of football players with those of basketball players. These were mere seeds of what would follow. During this time, separate research was similarly ongoing in other countries—notably the Soviet Union, Germany, and Japan.

Between the years 1920–1940, research in sport psychology became a specialized interest for some. It was Coleman Griffith (1893–1966) who, as Father of Sport Psychology in this country, organized and directed the first sport psychology laboratory. His studies focused on learning, psychomotor skills, and personality variables. He developed a test for mental alertness of athletes and a theory on the role of motivation in sport, based on the experiences of football coaches. He initiated the first course in the psychology of sport in the United States, and supervised the first doctoral dissertations in this area in the 1930s. He published two books; a third was not completed (Kroll & Lewis 1970, Geron 1982b).

As sport psychology began to be considered a scientific field in Europe during the 1920s and 1930s, it became connected to institutes and laboratories of physical education and sports. World War II interrupted most of this work, though there is some indication that it continued in Germany, the USSR, and Hungary.

Between the end of World War II and 1965, interest spread to many countries with a rapid and intense advance of knowledge. In the Eastern European countries, it was rather centralized, organized, and unified. Stimulated by government institutions, organized under chairs of research departments, it was dominated by Soviet sport psychology which served as the model for some other Eastern European countries by dissemination of reading material, visiting lecturers, and trainees being sent to study in the Soviet Union.

Quite a different approach characterized the Western European countries and the United States, where a different philosophy about sport prevailed—with its relative lack of governmental financial support. Here the direction of research was separate within each country, and there was little communication among countries. It was of interest primarily to experts in physical education departments who were concerned with psychomotorics and motor development.

The year 1965 is considered a landmark year because of the first International Congress of Sport Psychology. Held in Rome under the chairmanship of Ferruccio Antonelli, there were 500 participants, 230 scientific contributions, and the International Society of Sport Psychology was founded with Antonelli elected president (Geron 1982a). The creation of an international society stimulated international contacts and provided for an important network of information exchange among different countries. Since that time, publications, congresses, and mutual exchange of information has flourished. The *International Journal of Sport Psychology*, the first of many to follow, began publication in 1970.

Though its content areas began with a behavioral emphasis, sport psychology is now looking at dynamic and interactional variables, with a major interest in mediating variables—the athlete's perceptions and cognitions.

Methodological advances have resulted in new instruments which are specialized to sport rather than borrowed from other disciplines: attitude scales, self-report measures, psychophysiological techniques to study somatic changes. There are still validity and reliability problems with many of these instruments, but these will likely diminish with further sophistication of the field.

Teaching continues within sport science departments, though there have been a few countries (e.g. Italy, Switzerland, Japan) which have separate lectures on sport psychology in psychology departments. There are some departments of psychology within physical education schools; and some physical education institutes and universities (e.g. USSR, Czechoslovakia, Canada, Brazil) offer graduate studies for masters and doctoral levels with specialization in sport psychology and motor learning (Salmela 1981).

Current trends over the world include interest in: (*a*) taking sport psychology out of the laboratory into the playing fields; (*b*) the typology of the successful athlete; (*c*) psychic preparation of the athlete; (*d*) psychology of children involved in sport; and (*e*) leisure and rehabilitative sport and exercise.

Although the United States has lagged behind many other countries in its involvement in these areas, it is now jumping on the bandwagon. Though there have been a few individuals who have made strong and continued efforts, sport psychology is just beginning to be accepted outside the walls of sport sciences as a scientific discipline and as an extension of academic psychology.

Because of space limitations, the rest of this brief review will focus on current sport psychology in the United States.

PERSONALITY OF THE ATHLETE

In trying to find out if athletes differed from nonathletes, a good deal of research has looked at physiological, personality, and perceptual style variables.

Genetics

The work in genetics has direct application to understanding the athlete's personality and his or her potential for athletic development. Research pertinent to this includes (*a*) morphology, (*b*) physiology, and (*c*) temperament.

MORPHOLOGY   Height, bone length, somatotype, and location of the center of gravity are examples of morphological variables relevant to the prediction of how well one might fare in a particular sport. For example, it would be unusual for a seven-foot tall person to excel in the highly coordinated and balanced movements of gymnastics, though this person might do exceptionally well on a basketball team. Morphological investigation is especially popular where emphasis is put on high levels of competition, where the training of athletes is guided by prediction of competitive outcomes.

PHYSIOLOGY   The physiology of an athlete is important because it limits the response to physical training. Besides the overlearning of skills such that they become "automatic," one goal of training is to increase endurance. That is, the body is trained in ways specific to the sport skills involved to expend less energy doing the same amount of work. There is good evidence that the limits of this physiological capacity to become more efficient with training is determined by genetics. Muscle fiber type (fast-twitch versus slow-twitch percentage) and the maximal amount of oxygen consumed per minute per body weight (called max $\dot{V}O_2$) are prime examples. Both are more than 90% determined by heredity for both males and females (Fox & Mathews 1981).

TEMPERAMENT   The literature on temperament (Thomas et al 1970, Yahraes 1977) has been reconceptualized in terms of comfortable arousal levels. These are determined, in part, by the functioning of the reticular activating system, biogenic amines (neurotransmitters which help to regulate the central nervous system), enzymes which regulate the biogenic amines and their degradation (e.g. monoamine oxidase), and hormones (e.g. testosterone; Zuckerman et al 1980). Extraverts are now considered "sensation-seekers" (Eysenck 1967, Klausner 1968, Reykowski 1982). They need more (externally generated) stimulation to attain comfortable arousal levels than do so-called introverts. Thus, extraverts are more socially inclined, more adventurous, take higher risks, and in general are more involved in sports—at least in those where there is a high level of incoming stimulation. Although the sport psychology literature on personality has yet to scratch beneath the surface of this multifaceted, integrative area of research, the extensive interest in extraversion can lead easily into this domain. It is mentioned here because of its genetic component, and because it cannot be ignored in future personality research of the athlete.

States, Traits, and Interactions

The late 1960s and the 1970s were characterized by sport psychologists trying to determine whether or not athletes were different in personality from nonathletes, and if athletes of different sports and different ability levels were different from each other. There was hope that this between-groups approach would yield predictions: who would (and would not) clutch under the pressure of competition; who would be a good team member; which player was a good investment; who would earn Olympic medals?

Although some trends emerged which accounted for part (20–45%) of the variance in the differences between groups (Morgan 1980), this era was severely criticized from within the field by the mid-70s (Martens 1975, Mahoney 1979, Morgan 1980). The criticisms revolved around unsound methodology which included biased subject selection, disregard for response distortion (of the frequently used Catellian 16 PF), an atheoretical, shotgun approach to the selection of tests used, the alleged abuse of tests, and the lack of training in personality research of most sport psychologist researchers with one-shot studies, no replications, and premature interpretations and conclusions.

A few hints garnered from this research were interesting, though they held no great surprises. Some of the dimensions on which athletes differed from their nonathletic counterparts included: somatotype, sensation-seeking/extraversion, and augmenting-reducing perceptual styles. There were fairly consistent differences between both male and female athletes and nonathletes (Balazs 1980, Kane 1980). And there was a trend for athletes from different sport groups to differ from those in other sport groups, though the differences were not as great as the athlete-nonathlete differences (e.g. Schurr et al 1977). Within a sport, there is still some question about differences between those who excel and those who do not, but certain consistencies appear to prevail: in general, the successful athlete will score higher than the less successful one on personality attributes of assertion, dominance, aggression, reservation, self-sufficiency, and need for achievement; and he/she will score lower on dimensions of high emotionality, anxiety, depression, schizoid features, fatigue, and confusion (e.g. Williams 1980). The data on intelligence is inconsistent. The research on need for achievement in women, and on androgeny (Kaplan & Bean 1976, Oglesby 1978, Bem 1981) is currently popular and seems to be eroding some of the social stigma associated with female athletic pursuits.

Perceptual Style

Research has also looked at athletes' perceptual styles. Coming as part of the shift in research designs which focused upon individual instead of group differences, this area has its roots also in pain perception. A relationship between a person's tolerance for pain and his or her selection of a particular sport was noted (Ryan & Kovacic 1966). Those in contact sports possessed greater pain tolerance than those in noncontact sports; and persons in noncontact sports appeared to have greater pain tolerance than nonathletes. Following the work of Petrie (1960, 1967) on augmenters and reducers of the intensity of perception of stimulation, it was found that the athlete-reducer subjects were more extraverted, more mesomorphic, more tolerant of pain, and judged time to pass more slowly than did athlete-augmenter subjects (Ryan & Foster 1967).

This dovetails nicely with the sensation-seeking literature, as the reducers, extraverts, and sensation-seekers require a higher level of pain (or other types of stimulation) than do others to reach the same internal level of (noxious) arousal. This may be helpful in shedding light on the problem with lack of adherence to rehabilitative exercise programs. That the reducers (sensation-seekers) share characteristics of type A personality profiles (e.g. Friedman & Rosenman 1974, Glass 1977) is food for future thought.

Sport Specificity

Besides finding that persons of different traits gravitated toward different sports—team versus individual, contact versus noncontact, endurance versus explosive—researchers realized the need to investigate the individual athlete within the context of his or her specific sport. It was shown that different sports and different positions within the same sport (with different degrees of predictability, of stimulation, of fine or gross motor skills, of eye-hand coordination), demand varying levels of arousal for optimal performance (e.g. Oxendine 1970). An ice hockey goalie, for example, needs to respond to many things in a manner that is different from a member of the forward line. Both people will likely reflect different personality styles from persons who run marathons. Research thus proceeded along the lines of a sport-specific, interactional (person × sport situation) approach (Martens 1977), and then on to a closer examination of the athlete.

Anxiety

Because excessive or uncontrolled anxiety is disruptive to both mental focus (attention, concentration) and the execution of motor skills in an automatic, flowing manner, much research has looked at this personality dimension. Whether anxiety is a "state" or a "trait" has been deemed important because of the corresponding differences in the potential for reducing it during competition. However, measuring anxiety levels without taking into account the optimal arousal level required for that person and task has so far contributed little to the athlete's advantage. There are some suggestive data on the importance of *how* an athlete experiences the anxiety and the use of skills in channeling the arousal into performance (e.g. Mahoney & Avener 1977, Mahoney et al 1983). Although it was argued extensively, most sport psychologists seem now to acknowledge that anxiety can be both a state and a trait, as well as an interactional variable (e.g. Epstein 1979). Controversy has paled in light of new interest in assisting the athlete to deal with anxiety at whatever its level.

In summary, the personality research in sport psychology got off to a poor start: it jumped out from the starting block on the wrong foot, so to speak. It offended many, was abusive, tried to make predictions it could not validate, and was perceived as invasive and threatening to the athlete.

Current research in the area, however, though still in need of methodological refinement, is less frantic, plucks from psychology those things which are of greater pragmatic value to the athlete, coach, and team, and is meanwhile developing more refined sport-specific instruments and techniques. No longer do univariate concepts dominate; rather, the current effort is comprised of person-situation interactions and an appreciation for both physiological and psychological predispositions of the participant.

More needs to be done with motivation (e.g. Singer 1977, Butt 1980); fear of success and failure (e.g. Ogilvie 1968); levels of aspiration, locus of control, and causal attributions (e.g. Iso-Ahola 1977, Mutrie et al 1983); sense of mastery (e.g. Bandura 1977, Abramson et al 1978); and familial-social contexts—the cultural templates which affect attitudes, values, and behaviors concerning sport (e.g. Sherif 1976). Longitudinal studies are in urgent demand as one of the few ways to sort out the effects of the heretofore correlational research. The field is wide open for exploration in other areas as well: injury and burnout, for examples (e.g. Bramwell et al 1980).

PEAK PERFORMANCE

The phenomenon of peak performance or "flow" in sport (Csikszentmihalyi 1975, Kauss 1980) is of such positive force that it compels athletes to strive to experience it again. It is not unlike Maslow's (1968) peak experience considered as part of the self-actualizing person's repertoire. Once a person can perform the basic sport skills automatically, peak performances are reachable and repeatable. Besides being a powerful intrinsic motivator (Deci 1975) for the athlete, peak performance has commanded a prime position in sport psychology.

Performance is at its best during these flow episodes in which athletes often report feeling as if they were in a trance. They report experiencing (a) dissociation and intense concentration, often being unaware of their surroundings during these times; (b) feeling neither fatigue nor pain, the body performing on its own; (c) perceptual changes which include time-slowing and object enlargement; and (d) feeling unusual power and control (Gallwey 1974, Jerome 1980, Unestähl 1983a). Although they can recall the kinesthetic feeling of this state, it is difficult to recall particular events which occur during peak performance; and it appears to be a form of consciousness different from usual.

An interesting aspect of flow is that one cannot force it to happen (as one cannot force oneself to fall asleep). It happens by itself. While in it, if a person reflects upon it, it goes away. Instead of a state which is achieved by greater voluntary effort, it requires the alternate route of "letting it happen"; an achievement rather unfamiliar to persons in our culture.

Sport psychologists are gaining some understanding of the variables which contribute to peak performance, and are working to help athletes develop more voluntary control of such variables. Although much of this work is at the international level of competition, the same type of work is progressing at many skill levels, and it comprises the bulk of the applied services of sport psychologists (e.g. Orlick 1980, Railo & Uneståhl 1980).

It is difficult to measure and/or evaluate its specific effects yet, but athletes in such training show gains in competitive performance measures and also appear to gain more from their physical training (Suinn 1980a; L.-E. Uneståhl, personal communication). As with any new skill, however, often there is a period of disruption and performance decrement prior to new and higher performance levels. This may result in discouragement in the less experienced athlete/coach, and it has resulted in premature termination of such training programs.

Arousal Level

An ubiquitous problem in athletics is coping with the pressure of competition which usually results in anxiety and heightened arousal levels. Overarousal can result in being out of the zone of optimal arousal level required for peak performance. It results in mental distraction, a loss of both focused attention and concentration on relevant task cues (e.g. Easterbrook 1959, Gallwey 1974). It also results in muscle tension which then inhibits or interferes with muscle contraction (which occurs only with antagonist muscle relaxation) essential for maximal performance.

Although debate has arisen over the best model for understanding the effects of different levels of arousal on performance—one based on the Yerkes-Dodson inverted-U (1908) or the updated drive theory model (e.g. Malmo 1959)—most sport psychologists conceptualize the performance-arousal level relationship within the inverted-U frame of reference. If a person is either underaroused (sleepy, lethargic, unmotivated) or overaroused (hyped-up, nervous, distractible), performance will suffer in comparison to when the person functions within his or her optimal range of arousal. This problem is reflected in athletes' statements of doing "terrific" in practice but then "blowing it" during competition. Although this happens at all skill levels, the more highly skilled athlete—with more automatic skill execution—can handle higher arousal levels than can the less skilled athlete.

Because many athletes are highly experienced but uninformed about this area, sport psychologists are training them to monitor and regulate their levels of arousal, especially overarousal. Underarousal is usually considered a problem with motivation and is dealt with accordingly.

CATEGORIES OF OVERAROUSAL   When one is overaroused, the autonomic nervous system (ANS) gets into the act. This physiological state which prepares the body for fight or flight is not usually conducive to maximal athletic performance (except for those tasks which require a burst of adrenalized energy like weightlifting and sprinting). Sweaty palms, nausea, diarrhea, feeling unable to breathe, muscle tremors, muscle tension, heavy legs, yawning, and fatigue are some of the somatic signs of ANS involvement.

Cognitive signs include confusion, inability to attend to important cues, narrowing of peripheral vision, loss of concentration, negative self-statements, fear of failure, and loss of self-confidence.

Recent work indicates that different persons exhibit overarousal in different ways: some with somatic symptoms, others with cognitive symptoms, and some with both (Schwartz et al 1978). These systems are considered separate but interactive with each other, as well as with the more global system of overt behavior (e.g. avoiding the competition). Viewed as multidimensional, then, competitive anxiety must be assessed in a way which profiles the system(s) affected by the stress.

ASSESSMENT   Though they have tried to identify those persons with high precompetitive anxiety (those more likely to choke during competition), the self-report measures used by sport psychologists have, for the most part, not kept pace with knowledge of the multidimensional nature of performance anxiety (Landers 1980a,b, 1982). Three of the most widely used self-report assessment instruments are: the Test of Attention and Interpersonal Style (TAIS) (Nideffer 1976a,b); the Sport Competition Anxiety Test (SCAT) (Martens 1977); and the State-Trait Anxiety Test (STAI) (Spielberger et al 1970). Clinical tests such as thought-sampling, a modified Thematic Apperception Test (TAT) (Murray 1943), hypnosis, and dream analysis can also be useful in uncovering contributions to and predictions of overarousal (e.g. Fenz & Epstein 1962, Mahoney & Avener 1977, Unestähl 1983b). Since most sport psychologists are not trained in these testing procedures, they do not use them most of the time.

Self-Regulation Training

There is a clear need, then, for athletes to regulate their arousal levels in order to maximize their performance capabilities. It has been demonstrated that the more successful athletes are able to reduce their arousal levels just prior to competition and are able to redirect their attentional focus (Fenz & Epstein 1969, Landers 1980b, Mahoney & Avener 1977). Even though many sport psychologists subscribe to an holistic (psychosomatic/somatopsychic) view of man (e.g. Harris 1973), self-regulation training for athletes is often conceptually divided into two segments of physical relaxation and mental training.

PHYSICAL RELAXATION   First, the athlete is helped to gain more control over tension in the major muscle groups, with the eventual goal of relaxation of specific muscle groups on autosuggestion of a key word or phrase. There are many avenues to this goal: progressive relaxation, meditation, breathing exercises, and hypnosis/autohypnosis (Borkovec & O'Brien 1977, Mahoney 1979, Pressman 1980). As with any other skill, an appropriate induction with realistic expectations and goals and regular daily practice are important. Initial training sessions with tape-recorded instructions are employed with teams (often immediately following practice) before moving onto abbreviated and more individualized conditioning cues for relaxation, dissociation, and detachment training. The use of tapes has the advantage of being available for extra sessions and requires less dependence upon the sport psychologist. Although the sport psychologist selects the technique now, it is likely that with more comprehensive training in these areas, the individual athlete's personal biases and preferred style will also determine the selection.

MENTAL TRAINING   Mental practice is then begun in this relaxed muscle state, later to be transferred to the sport situation. Imagery is used for both general relaxation and for mental rehearsal (e.g. Singer 1974). Since it is thought that mental imagery of a motor task results in the respective muscles being activated (Shaw 1940, Brown 1980), mental practice is really mental-plus-muscle practice. Because athletes say many negative things to themselves which, in turn, produce negative images and negative affect during performance, part of mental practice is self-instructional training. Maladaptive statements are replaced with pre-established positive ones which incorporate realistic goals set by the athlete alone or in collaboration with others (Meichenbaum 1977, McClements & Botterill 1980).

Mental training also includes the cognitive reappraisal of beliefs and irrational thoughts. It reframes competitive outcomes (winning) in terms of meeting prescribed goals and doing one's personal best. This cognitive restructuring provides a sense of control and positive expectations regardless of the particular variables of the competition. As such, it creates less disruptive anxiety and less erosion of self-confidence.

Techniques used in mental practice include guided imagery, internal (kinesthetic) and external (TV camera view of self) imagery, rehearsal, use of models, work on attention and concentration, elimination of self-imposed limitations from irrational attitudes and beliefs, systematic desensitization, hypnosis and autohypnosis, combinations of the above (e.g. Mahoney 1979, Lane 1980), and specific ritualized countdowns before competition (e.g. Rushall 1979, Smith 1980).

The best results appear when mental practice is used regularly in conjunction with, but not instead of, physical skills practice (Scott & Pelliccioni 1982,

Weinberg 1982). As with any other skill, it takes time and practice to achieve success, and individuals will vary in their readiness and the length of time it takes them to reach a degree of proficiency.

In brief, then, sport psychologists currently use many of the cognitive-behavioral techniques of clinical psychology (Mahoney 1974, Beck 1976, Lazarus 1977, Guidano & Liotti 1983). Although difficult to evaluate quantitatively, they seem to have been welcomed by athletes and coaches alike. In the near future, there will probably be an expansion in the diversity of both assessment and self-regulatory procedures.

SOCIAL PSYCHOLOGY OF THE TEAM

In contrast to the abundance of research about the individual athlete, there is a paucity of information about the sport team. Social forces in a team are complex, and the study of a team is met with inconveniences and other difficulties. Consequently, research has relied mainly upon extrapolation of information from small group research in business and general social psychology. This has provided useful leads, but the area is ripe for exploration. (Cartwright & Zander 1968, Carron 1980, Loy et al 1980).

Structure

One advantage of studying the sport team, as opposed to other small groups, is that its structure, its organizational hierarchy, and its roles are clearly defined by the rules of the sport. There is a designated authority, the coach, and peer leaders emerge.

The characteristics which contribute to a person's becoming a peer leader have generated some research. There are certain positions (e.g. pitcher in baseball, quarterback in football) which seem to have a higher proportion of peer leaders, and there has been speculation that their centrality and greater accessibility contribute to leadership roles (Zander 1971, Cratty 1981). However, the correlational research cannot eliminate the chicken-and-egg problem, That is, there may be a self-selection process by which persons either with leadership ability and inclinations and/or with greater skill level choose the more central positions (e.g. pitcher and quarterback).

The leadership styles of coaches have also been examined for their relative effectiveness, but the data are fraught with confusion. At times it seems best for the coach to act in an authoritarian manner (e.g. under conditions of team stress), but the more general trend is to have the coach act less authoritarian overall, to talk with the players as individuals, and to set personal goals with them and with the whole team (Rosenbaum & Rosenbaum 1971, Carron & Bennett 1977, Sage 1980, Rotella 1981).

Our current self-actualizing society emphasizes the importance of both the individual and the team. What used to be a locker room slogan "There is no I in T-E-A-M" is being replaced with something like "The TEAM and I."

Process

It is well known that the team is greater than the sum of its players. Attempts to predict a winning team based only on the composite of individual team members fail. The intangible stuff called "cohesion" or "team spirit" which can elevate (or deflate) a team's performance has invited the curiosity of sport psychologists (e.g. Carron et al 1977). Some investigators have tried to define the components of cohesion. It appears to include the following: (*a*) both Team and I; (*b*) mutual communication between coach and player and between player and player; (*c*) fairness from the coach in what is required of members; (*d*) shared goal-setting, with agreement about and internalization of team goals; (*e*) relative homogeneity of skill level, of aspiration levels, of value systems; and (*f*) the ability of some athletes to subordinate their strengths for the overall good of the team (e.g. Carron & Chelladurai 1979, Murray 1981a).

Other variables which contribute to team cohesion seem to include defense against external threats (e.g. another team), which enhances the in-group feeling, and positive achievement of goals (Lott & Lott 1965, Peterson & Martens 1972, Carron 1982a). Continuity and stability of membership are still being researched in terms of their effects (e.g. Zander 1976). With male sport teams, a general finding is that task agreement is more productive than affiliative agreement or lack of interpersonal tension (e.g. Loy et al 1978). This remains open for study in female teams where one might predict that affiliation needs also may be important.

Audience Effects

Audiences can greatly increase arousal levels of players with a differential effect on athletes of differing skill levels (e.g. Wankel 1975). It is difficult to separate social facilitation/coaction effects (Zajonc 1965, Martens & Landers 1969) from audience effects, since both things happen at once in a game situation. Research on the audience has defined the audience as either real people watching an athlete perform, or as imaginary, carried in the mind of the athlete while practicing in isolation. The critical variables contributing to the audience effect, however, seem to include the presence of significant others who can evaluate the performance of the athlete (Cottrell et al 1968, Martens 1976). Some teams now practice in the presence of invited audiences or taped audience noises, especially hostile ones, to help them learn to regulate their arousal levels under such conditions.

Much remains to be learned about the social psychology of teams, and it will likely be pursued in an interactional framework: (person) $\times$ (task) $\times$ (team). There could be intriguing work on the process of group or team formation—

stages of forming, storming, norming, and performing (Tuckman 1965), as well as an added stage of post-season mourning (M. A. Browne, book in preparation). Other topics which interest sport psychologists include competition, aggression, interpersonal tension among members of a team, team aspirations, and causal attributions for success and failure (Volkamer 1971, Sherif 1976, Carron 1982b).

EFFECTS OF SPORT

Although most of the work in sport psychology has studied the athlete—what he or she brings to sport, motivation variables, how to maximize performance—there is also interest in the converse: the effect of sport on the participant. Some early questions asked if participation in sport contributed to the positive psychological development of the participant (e.g. Stevenson 1975). That line of investigation resulted in some negative answers (Ogilvie & Tutko 1971, Murray 1981b) and remains to be pursued in longitudinal studies. More recent work in this area overlaps with health psychology and behavioral medicine, as it explores the application of exercise, physical fitness, and sport programs to children's development, to leisure-time and recreational pastimes, and to contributing to both the prevention and rehabilitation of illness.

Psychological Effects

Psychological benefits (not unique to sport) can be provided by successful participation in sport activity at any skill level (Folkins & Sine 1981, Sonstroem 1982). Of interest to sport psychologists have been: (a) the enhancement of body awareness, image, and its contribution to one's self-concept; (b) the regulating of arousal levels and sympathetic reactions to stress, as well as the transfer of training beyond the exercise/sport arena; (c) the provision for a "time out" from daily routines; (d) the enhancement of self-identity by the feeling of belonging to a group with shared values, interests, and activities; and (e) the rise in self-esteem from the process of setting goals, achieving those goals, and the consequent sense of competence and mastery which can be measured tangibly by both participant and observer (e.g. Bahrke & Morgan 1978, Cantor et al 1978). Self-confidence gained from such success experiences may have transfer value to other situations, but the parameters of this transfer still need to be experimentally defined.

Though this research has been plagued by methodological problems (e.g. lack of random subject assignment to groups, lack of adequate control groups, dependent variables subject to response bias, and overgeneralization of results), it has consistently revealed positive effects, with greater increases in psychological benefits for those subjects who were lower in pretest measures of fitness and self-esteem (deVries 1968, Hilyer & Mitchell 1979). More studies are needed to examine the persistence of positive changes and when they occur.

Above are some of the results from success in exercise and sport. On the other hand, the attrition rate of involuntary exercise programs (e.g. for weight reduction) needs to be addressed (e.g. Dishman 1982). Because the dropping-out process may leave the person with feelings of failure and lowered self-regard, it is important to avoid it by matching people with specific programs in which they are likely to continue. The research to date in sport psychology has depended upon self-selection of subjects which then biases the results. To begin to answer the important question of why some people abhor physical exertion remains to be explored.

Physiological Effects

Sport psychologists have asked why people enjoy sport. Some have viewed it as a form of play (e.g. Sutton-Smith 1974). Others have viewed it as a way to interrupt unpleasant affect by the activation of competing cortical circuits (e.g. Schwartz et al 1978). Recent focus centers more on aerobic activities which have both cardiorespiratory training effects and postexercise tranquilizing effects. Persons frequently become "addicted" to such exercise and sport activity (Glasser 1976), and reasons for this have included the play element, and physiological explanations concerning endorphins (e.g. Colt et al 1981, Bolles & Fanselow 1982, Moore 1982), elevation in plasma levels of neuro-transmitters (e.g. norepinephrine) (e.g. Ransford 1982), deep body tempera-ture increases which lead to greater cortical synchrony (deVries 1981) and other biological effects of such training.

The aerobic exercise/sport activities are those which use large muscle groups in rhythmic and continuous activity which raise heart rates in healthy adults to 60–90% of maximum (swimming, jogging-running, bicycling, skating, cross-country skiing, ballet, rowing, skipping rope are examples). Such endurance activities have their physiological training effect when done at least three times a week for 15–60 minutes continuously or noncontinuously, with intensity and duration inversely related. Cardiorespiratory systems become more efficient, at all ages, at doing more work with the same amount of effort (Cooper 1978, American College of Sports Medicine 1980).

The relaxation effects after such bouts of exercise include a reduction in resting muscle action potential and consequent subjective tension relief (de-Vries 1968, Morgan 1979, Mihevic 1982), followed by the promotion of delta sleep (Folkins et al 1972, Browman 1980, Horne 1981). Because these phys-iological effects are intertwined with the psychological effects noted earlier, it is difficult to separate them as responsible for any change in a person's affective state or self-concept. More research is needed which will include measures of each subject's cardiorespiratory fitness, both pre- and post-test, and the relative experimental workload required of each person before causal relations between physical fitness and psychological variables can be ascertained.

Clinical Applications

As more psychologists move into the field of sport psychology, there will probably be greater emphasis on clinical applications of exercise and sport.

DEPRESSION   Because becoming more physically fit is associated with elevations in mood states and "relief from depression" in some people, some sport psychologists have compared exercise therapy (jogging programs) with group psychotherapy (Brown et al 1978, Greist et al 1979), though not without serious research design problems. With very few exceptions (Kostrubala 1976, Lion 1978, Blue 1979), "depression" has been operationally defined as mild dysphoria in normal persons who are motivated for self-improvement and who voluntarily adhere to the several-week long exercise programs (Ledwidge 1980, Folkins & Sine 1981, Hesso & Sorensen 1982). Here, too, psychological versus physiological effects are not yet parcelled out (Buffone 1981). However, the positive results of such studies are impressively consistent in the mood-elevating properties of exercise, and there is currently a rush of doctoral dissertations in this area. It might be fruitful to look more carefully at the individual differences within the exercise groups as well as the between-group comparisons.

Other related areas of future interest likely will include cardiac rehabilitation (e.g. Hage 1982, Rejeski 1982), alcoholism, and other instances where exercise is recommended frequently as part of a treatment regime. Examples include diabetes, headaches, spastic colon, asthma, and Rayaud's disease (e.g. Gary & Guthrie 1972, Atkinson 1977, Marley 1977, Pinkerton et al 1982). The potential applications to geriatric populations is enormous.

CHILDREN   There is interest in the psychological impact of sport participation on children, the stress from competition, and developmental effects of sport on normal children and youth (Martens et al 1981, Magill et al 1982, Passer 1982a,b, Passer & Scanlan 1980). There is opportunity for sport psychologists to become involved in children's issues which concern less healthy states as well: obese or anorexic children, hyperactive ones, children with mood disorders, diabetes, type A personality proclivities, and mental retardation. All such pursuits can, in turn, begin the greatly needed collection of longitudinal data.

FUTURE OF SPORT PSYCHOLOGY

In the United States, sport psychology got off to a slow start but is now beginning to surge. It is catching fire with considerable interest being generated from applied areas of research and the direct delivery of services. Although many areas of research have had their surfaces scratched, much remains to be explored. This includes both the effects which are specific to exercise and sport activity and those which abound in sport but are not necessarily restricted to the effects of physical activity.

The time has arrived for sport psychology in this country to follow the lead of other countries where it is recognized as an interdisciplinary specialty which draws from both the sport sciences and psychology. This would involve training in sport, research, clinical issues, and consultation. Such pursuits would need to be shared by both sport sciences and psychology departments.

Unresolved questions remain: should a sport psychologist be (or have been) a competitive athlete? Should he/she be a trained clinician? An efficacious way to dissolve the mutual distrust and territory disputes between the two fields of inquiry seems to require an organization of sport psychologists which would be responsible for educating, credentialling, supervising, and monitoring the delivery of services to the public.

It is an exciting time in American sport psychology: time to collaborate, to gain credibility, to push forward.

ACKNOWLEDGMENTS

This paper was prepared while Dr. Browne was at Penn State University for a year of interdisciplinary study. She is grateful to both Dr. David J. Brown, Director of the Center for Psychological Services, and Dr. Dorothy V. Harris of the Department of Health, Physical Education, and Recreation for making this possible.

Literature Cited

Abramson, L. Y., Seligman, M. E. P., Teasdale, J. D. 1978. Learned helplessness in humans: Critique and reformulation. *J. Abnorm. Psychol.* 37:49–74

American College of Sports Medicine. 1980. *Guidelines for Graded Exercise Testing and Exercise Prescription.* Philadelphia: Lea & Febiger. 2nd ed.

Atkinson, R. 1977. Physical fitness and headache. *Headache* 17:189–91

Bahrke, M. S., Morgan, W. P. 1978. Anxiety reduction following exercise and meditation. *Cogn. Ther. Res.* 2:323–34

Balazs, E. K. 1980. Psycho-social study of outstanding female athletes. *Res. Q.* 46:267–73

Bandura, A. 1977. Self-efficacy: Toward a unifying theory of behavioral change. *Psychol. Rev.* 84:191–215

Beck, A. T. 1976. *Cognitive Therapy and the Emotional Disorders.* New York: International Universities

Bem, S. L. 1981. *Bem Sex-Role Inventory, professional manual.* Palo Alto, Calif: Consult. Psychol. Press. 37 pp.

Blue, F. R. 1979. Aerobic running as a treatment for moderate depression. *Percept. Mot. Skills* 48:228

Bolles, R. C., Fanselow, M. S. 1982. Endorphins and behavior. *Ann. Rev. Psychol.* 33:87–101

Borkovec, T. D., O'Brien, G. T. 1977. Regulation of autonomic perception and its manipulation to the maintenance and reduction of fear. *J. Abnorm. Psychol.* 86:163–71

Bramwell, S. T., Masuda, M., Wagner, N. N., Holmes, T. H. 1980. Psychosocial factors in athletic injuries: Development and application of the social and athletic readjustment rating scale (SARRS). See Suinn 1980b, pp. 119–23

Browman, C. P. 1980. Sleep following sustained exercise. *Psychophysiology* 17:577–80

Brown, B. B. 1980. *Supermind: The Ultimate Energy.* New York: Harper & Row

Brown, R. S., Ramirez, D. E., Taub, J. M. 1978. The prescription of exercise for depression. *Physician Sportsmed.* 6:35–45

Buffone, G. W. 1981. *Psychological changes associated with cognitive behavior therapy* and an aerobic running program in the treatment of depression. Presented at Ann. Meet. Assoc. Adv. Behav. Ther., Toronto

Bunker, L. K., Rotella, R. J., eds. 1981. *Psychological Considerations in Maximizing Sport Performance.* Charlottesville: Univ. Virginia Press

Butt, D. S. 1980. What can psychology offer to the athlete and the coach? See Suinn 1980b, pp. 78–85

Cantor, J. R., Zillman, D., Day, K. D. 1978. Relationships between cardio-respiratory fitness and physiological responses to films. *Percept. Mot. Skills* 46:1123–30

Carron, A. V. 1980. *Social Psychology of Sport.* Ontario: Univ. Ontario Press

Carron, A. V. 1982a. Cohesiveness in sport groups: Interpretations and considerations. *J. Sport Psychol.* 4:123–38

Carron, A. V. 1982b. Processes of group interaction in sport teams. *Quest* 33:245–70

Carron, A. V., Ball, J. R., Chelladurai, P. 1977. Motivation for participation, success in performance and their relationship to individual and group satisfaction. *Percept. Mot. Skills* 45:835–41

Carron, A. V., Bennett, B. B. 1977. Compatibility in the coach-athlete dyad. *Res. Q.* 48:671–79

Carron, A. V., Chelladurai, P. 1979. Cohesiveness as a factor in sport performance. Cited in Carron 1980, pp. 175–257, passim

Cartwright, D., Zander, A. 1968. *Group Dynamics: Research and Theory.* New York: Harper & Row. 3rd ed.

Colt, E. W. D., Wardlaw, S. L., Frantz, A. G. 1981. The effect of running on plasma B-endorphin. *Life Sci.* 28:1637–40

Cooper, K. H. 1978. *The Aerobics Way.* New York: Bantam

Cottrell, N. B., Wack, D. L., Sekerak, G. J., Rittle, R. H. 1968. Social facilitation of dominant responses by the presence of an audience and the mere presence of others. *J. Pers. Soc. Psychol.* 9:245–50

Cratty, B. 1981. *Social Psychology in Athletics.* Englewood Cliffs, NJ: Prentice-Hall

Csikszentmihalyi, M. 1975. *Beyond Boredom and Anxiety.* San Francisco: Jossey-Bass

Deci, E. L. 1975. *Intrinsic Motivation.* New York: Plenum

deVries, H. A. 1968. Immediate and long-term effects of exercise upon resting muscle action potential level. *J. Sports Med. Phys. Fitness* 8:1–11

deVries, H. A. 1981. Tranquilizer effect of exercise: A critical review. *Physician Sportsmed.* 9:47–55

Dishman, R. K. 1982. Compliance/adherence in health-related exercise. *Health Psychol.* 1:237–67

Easterbrook, J. A. 1959. The effect of emotion on cue utilization and the organization of behavior. *Psychol. Rev.* 66:183–201

Epstein, S. 1979. The stability of behavior: I. On predicting most of the people much of the time. *J. Pers. Soc. Psychol.* 37:1097–1126

Eysenck, H. J. 1967. *The Biological Basis of Personality.* Springfield, Ill: Thomas

Fenz, W. D., Epstein, S. 1962. Measurement of approach-avoidance conflict along a stimulus dimension by a Thematic Apperception Test. *J. Pers.* 30:613–32

Fenz, W. D., Epstein, S. 1969. Stress in the air. *Psychol. Today* Sept:27

Folkins, C. H., Lynch, S., Gardner, M. M. 1972. Psychological fitness as a function of physical fitness. *Arch. Phys. Med. Rehabil.* 53:503–8

Folkins, C. H., Sine, W. E. 1981. Physical fitness training and mental health. *Am. Psychol.* 36:373–89

Fox, E. L., Mathews, D. K. 1981. *The Physiological Basis of Physical Education and Athletics.* Philadelphia: Saunders. 3rd ed.

Friedman, M., Rosenman, R. H. 1974. *Type A Behavior and Your Heart.* New York: Knopf

Gallwey, W. T. 1974. *The Inner Game of Tennis.* New York: Random House

Gary, V., Guthrie, D. 1972. The effect of jogging on physical fitness and self-concept in hospitalized alcoholics. *Q. J. Stud. Alcohol* 33:1073–78

Geron, E. 1982a. History and recent position of sport psychology. See Geron 1982b, pp. 25–42

Geron, E., ed. 1982b. *Handbook of Sport Psychology, Vol. 1. Introduction to Sport Psychology.* Tel Aviv: Wingate Inst.

Glass, D. C. 1977. *Behavior Patterns, Stress and Coronary Disease.* Hillsdale, NJ: Erlbaum

Glasser, W. 1976. *Positive Addiction.* New York: Harper & Row

Greist, J. H., Klein, M. H., Eischens, R. R., Faris, J. W., Gurman, A. S., et al. 1979. Running as treatment for depression. *Comp. Psychiatry* 20:41–54

Guidano, V. F., Liotti, G. 1983. *Cognitive Processes and Emotional Disorders: A Structural Approach to Psychotherapy.* New York: Guilford

Hage, P. 1982. Diet and exercise programs for coronary heart disease: Better late than never. *Physician Sportsmed.* 10:121–26

Harris, D. V. 1973. *Involvement in Sport: A Somatopsychic Rationale for Physical Activity.* Philadelphia: Lea & Febiger

Hesso, R., Sorensen, M. 1982. Physical activity in the treatment of mental disorders. *Scand. J. Soc. Med. Suppl.* 29:259–64

Hilyer, J. C., Mitchell, W. 1979. Effect of systematic physical fitness training combined with counseling on the self-concept of college students. *J. Couns. Psychol.* 26: 427–36

Horne, J. A. 1981. The effects of exercise upon sleep—a critical review. *Biol. Psychol.* 12:4

Iso-Ahola, S. 1977. Effects of self-enhancement and consistency on causal and trait attributions following success and failure in motor performance. *Res. Q.* 48:717–26

Jerome, J. 1980. *The Sweet Spot In Time.* New York: Summit

Kane, J. E. 1980. Personality research: The current controversy and implications for sport studies. See Straub 1980, pp. 340–52

Kaplan, A. G., Bean, J. P. 1976. *Beyond Sex-Role Stereotypes.* Boston: Little, Brown

Kauss, D. R. 1980. *Peak Performance: Mental Game Plans for Maximizing Your Athletic Potential.* Englewood Cliffs, NJ: Prentice-Hall

Klausner, S. Z., ed. 1968. *Why Man Takes Chances.* Garden City, NJ: Doubleday

Klavora, P., Daniel, J., eds. 1980. *Coach, Athlete, and the Sport Psychologist.* Toronto: Univ. Toronto Press

Kostrubala, T. 1976. *The Joy of Running.* Philadelphia:Lippincott

Kroll, W., Lewis, G. 1970. America's first sport psychologist. *Quest* 13:1–4

Landers, D. M., ed. 1976. *Social Problems in Athletics.* Urbana: Univ. Illinois Press

Landers, D. M. 1980a. The arousal-performance relationship revisited. *Res. Q. Exer. Sport* 51:77–90

Landers, D. M. 1980b. Motivation and performance: The role of arousal and attentional factors. See Straub 1980, pp. 91–103

Landers, D. M. 1982. Arousal, attention, and skilled performance: Further considerations. *Quest* 33:271–83

Lane, J. F. 1980. Improving athletic performance through visuo-motor behavior rehearsal. See Suinn 1980b, pp. 316–20

Lazarus, A. 1977. *In the Mind's Eye: The Power of Imagery Therapy to Give You Control Over Your Life.* New York: Rawson

Ledwidge, B. 1980. Run for your mind: Aerobic exercise as a means of alleviating anxiety and depression. *Can. J. Behav. Sci./Rev. Can. Sci. Comp.* 12:126–40

Lion, L. S. 1978. Psychological effects of jogging: A preliminary study. *Percept. Mot. Skills* 47:1215–18

Lott, A. J., Lott, B. E. 1965. Group cohesiveness as interpersonal attraction: A review of relationships with antecedent and consequent variables. *Psychol. Bull.* 64:259–302

Loy, J. W., Kenyon, G. S., McPherson, B. D. 1980. The emergence and development of the sociology of sport as an academic specialty. *Res. Q. Exer. Sport* 51:91–109

Loy, J. W., McPherson, B., Kenyon, G. 1978. *Sport and Social Systems.* Don Mills, Ontario: Addison-Wesley

Magill, R. A., Ash, M. J., Smoll, F. L. 1982. *Children in Sport.* Champaign, Ill: Human Kinetics. 2nd ed.

Mahoney, M. J. 1974. *Cognition and Behavior Modification.* Cambridge, Mass: Ballinger

Mahoney, M. J. 1979. Cognitive skills and athletic performance. In *Cognitive-Behavioral Interventions: Theory, Research, and Procedures,* ed. P. C. Kendall, S. D. Hollon, pp. 423–43. New York: Academic

Mahoney, M. J., Avener, J., Avener, M. 1983. Psychological factors in competitive gymnastics. See Uneståhl 1983b, pp. 54–66

Mahoney, M. J., Avener, M. 1977. Psychology of the elite athlete: An exploratory study. *Cogn. Ther. Res.* 1:135–41

Malmo, R. B. 1959. Activation: A neuropsychological dimension. *Psychol. Rev.* 66:367–86

Marley, W. P. 1977. Asthma and exercise: A review. *Am. Correct. Ther. J.* 31:95–102

Martens, R. 1975. The paradigmatic crisis in American sport personology. *Sportwissenschaft* 5:9–24. Cited in Morgan 1980, pp. 50–76

Martens, R. 1976. Competition: In need of a theory. See Landers 1976, pp. 9–17

Martens, R. 1977. *Sport Competition Anxiety Test.* Champaign, Ill: Human Kinetics

Martens, R., Christina, R. W., Harvey, J. S. Jr., Sharkey, B. J. 1981. *Coaching Young Athletes.* Champaign, Ill: Human Kinetics

Martens, R., Landers, D. M. 1969. Coaction effects on a muscular endurance task. *Res. Q.* 40:733–37

Maslow, A. H. 1968. *Toward a Psychology of Being.* Princeton, NJ: Van Nostrand-Reinhold. 2nd ed.

McClements, J. D., Botterill, C. B. 1980. Goal-setting in shaping of future performance of athletes. See Klavora & Daniel 1980, pp. 199–210

Meichenbaum, D. 1977. *Cognitive-Behavior Modification: An Integrative Approach.* New York: Plenum

Mihevic, P. M. 1982. Anxiety, depression, and exercise. *Quest* 33:140–53

Moore, M. 1982. Endorphins and exercise. *Physician Sportsmed.* 10:111–19

Morgan, W. P. 1979. Anxiety reduction following acute physical activity. *Psychiatr. Ann.* 9:141–47

Morgan, W. P. 1980. The trait psychology controversy. *Res. Q. Exer. Sport* 51:50–76

Murray, H. A. 1943. *Thematic Apperception Test Manual.* Cambridge: Harvard Univ.

Murray, M. 1981a. Cooperation and cohesiveness: Setting a winning personal environment. See Bunker & Rotella 1981, pp. 13–17

Murray, M. 1981b. The self-esteem of winners and losers. See Bunker & Rotella 1981, pp. 169–73

Mutrie, N., Brooks, D. R., Mark, M. M., Harris, D. V. 1983. *Causal attributions of winners and losers in competitive squash and racquetball tournaments.* Presented at Ann. Meet. NASPSPA, E. Lansing, Mich.

Nideffer, R. M. 1976a. Test of attentional and interpersonal style. *J. Pers. Soc. Psychol.* 34:394–404

Nideffer, R. M. 1976b. *The Inner Athlete: Mind Plus Muscle for Winning.* New York: Crowell

Ogilvie, B. C. 1968. The unconscious fear of success. *Quest* 10:35–39

Ogilvie, B. C., Tutko, T. A. 1971. Sport: If you want to build character, try something else. *Psychol. Today* Oct. 5:60–63

Oglesby, C. A. 1978. *Women and Sport.* Philadelphia: Lea & Febiger

Orlick, T. 1980. *In Pursuit of Excellence.* Champaign, Ill: Human Kinetics

Oxendine, J. B. 1970. Emotional arousal and motor performance. *Quest* 13:23–32

Passer, M. W. 1982a. Children in sport: Participation motives and psychological stress. *Quest* 33:231–44

Passer, M. W. 1982b. *Participation motives of young athletes as a function of competitive trait anxiety, self-esteem, ability, and age.* Presented at Ann. Meet. NASPSPA, College Park, Md.

Passer, M. W., Scanlan, T. K. 1980. The impact of game outcome on the postcompetition affect and performance evaluations of young athletes. In *Psychology of Motor Behavior and Sport-1979,* ed. C. H. Nadeau, W. R. Halliwell, K. M. Newell, G. C. Roberts, pp. 100–11. Champaign, Ill: Human Kinetics

Peterson, J. A., Martens, R. 1972. Success and residential affiliation as determinants of team cohesiveness. *Res. Q.* 43:62–76

Petrie, A. 1960. Some psychological aspects of pain and the relief of suffering. *Ann. NY Acad. Sci.* 86:13–27

Petrie, A. 1967. *Individuality in Pain and Suffering.* Chicago: Univ. Chicago Press

Pinkerton, S. S., Hughes, H., Wenrich, W. W. 1982. *Behavioral Medicine: Clinical Applications.* New York: Wiley

Pressman, M. D. 1980. Psychological techniques for the advancement of sports potential. See Suinn 1980b, pp. 291–96

Railo, W. S., Unestahl, L.-E. 1980. The Scandinavian practice of sport psychology. See Klavora & Daniel 1980, pp. 248–71

Ransford, C. P. 1982. A role for amines in the antidepressant effect of exercise: A review. *Med. Sci. Sports Exer.* 14:1–10

Rejeski, W. J. 1982. Rehabilitation and prevention of coronary heart disease: An overview of the type A behavior pattern. *Quest* 33:154–65

Reykowski, J. 1982. Social motivation. *Ann. Rev. Psychol.* 33:123–54

Rosenbaum, L. L., Rosenbaum, W. B. 1971. Morale and productivity consequences of group leadership style, stress, and type of task. *J. Appl. Psychol.* 55:343–88

Rotella, R. J. 1981. The successful coach: A leader who communicates. See Bunker & Rotella 1981, pp. 2–12

Rushall, B. 1979. *Psyching in Sport: The Psychological Preparation for Serious Competition in Sport.* London: Pelham

Ryan, E. D., Foster, R. 1967. Athletic participation and perceptual augmentation and reduction. *J. Pers. Soc. Psychol.* 6:472–76

Ryan, E. D., Kovacic, C. R. 1966. Pain tolerance and athletic participation. *Percept. Mot. Skills* 22:383–90

Sage, G. H. 1980. Sociology of physical educator/coaches: Personal attributes controversy. *Res. Q. Exer. Sport* 51:110–21

Salmela, J. H. 1981. *The World Sport Psychology Sourcebook.* Ithaca, NY: Mouvement Publ.

Schurr, K. T., Ashley, M. A., Joy, K. L. 1977. A multivariate analysis of male athlete characteristics: Sport type and success. *Multivar. Exp. Clin. Res.* 3:53–68

Schwartz, G. E., Davidson, R. J., Goleman, D. J. 1978. Patterning of cognitive and somatic processes in the self-regulation of anxiety: Effects of meditation versus exercise. *Psychosom. Med.* 40:321–28

Scott, M. D., Pelliccioni, L. Jr. 1982. *Don't Choke: How Athletes Can Become Winners.* Englewood Cliffs, NJ: Prentice-Hall

Shaw, W. A. 1940. The relation of muscular action potentials to imaginal weight lifting. *Arch. Psychol.* 237:50

Sherif, C. W. 1976. The social context of competition. See Landers 1976, pp. 18–36

Singer, J. L. 1974. *Imagery and Daydream Methods in Psychotherapy and Behavior Modification.* New York: Academic

Singer, R. N. 1977. Motivation in sport. *Int. J. Sport Psychol* 8:1–22

Smith, R. E. 1980. A cognitive-affective approach to stress management training for athletes. In *Psychology of Motor Behavior and Sport-1980,* ed. G. C. Roberts, D. M. Landers, pp. 54–72. Champaign, Ill: Human Kinetics

Sonstroem, R. J. 1982. Exercise and self-esteem: Recommendations for expository research. *Quest* 33:124–39

Spielberger, C. D., Gorsuch, R. L., Luchene, R. E. 1970. *Manual for the State-Trait Anxiety Inventory.* Palo Alto, Calif: Consult. Psychol. Press

Stevenson, C. L. 1975. Socialization effects of participation in sport: A critical review of the research. *Res. Q.* 46:287–301

Straub, W. F., ed. 1980. *Sport Psychology: An Analysis of Athlete Behavior.* Ithaca, NY: Mouvement Publ. 2nd ed.

Suinn, R. M. 1980a. Psychology and sports performance: Principles and applications. See Suinn 1980b, pp. 26–36

Suinn, R. M., ed. 1980b. *Psychology in Sports: Methods and Applications.* Minneapolis: Burgess

Sutton-Smith, B. 1974. Towards an anthropology of play. Assoc. Anthropol. Study Play. *Newsletter* 1:2, pp. 8–15

Thomas, A., Chess, S., Birch, H. G. 1970. The origin of personality. *Sci. Am.* 223: 102–9

Tripplett, N. 1898. Dynamogenic factors in pacemaking and competition. Cited in Geron 1982b, p. 26

Tuckman, B. W. 1965. Developmental sequence in small groups. *Psychol. Bull.* 63: 384–99

Uneståhl L.-E. 1983a. Mental gymnastics. See Uneståhl 1983b, pp. 13–24

Uneståhl, L.-E., ed. 1983b. *The Mental Aspects of Gymnastics.* Orebro, Sweden: Veje

Volkamer, M. 1971. Zur aggressivitat in konkurrenz-orientierten sozialem systemen. Cited in Cratty 1981, p. 179

Wankel, L. M. 1975. The effects of social reinforcement and audience presence upon the motor performance of boys with different levels of initial ability. *J. Mot. Behav.* 7:207–16

Weinberg, R. S. 1982. The relationship between mental preparation strategies and motor performance: A review and critique. *Quest* 33:195–213

Williams, J. M. 1980. Personality characteristics of the successful female athlete. See Straub 1980, pp. 249–55

Yahraes, H. 1977. *Styles in Temperament and their Effect on Behavior.* DHEW No. (ADM) 77–462. Washington DC: GPO

Yerkes, R. M., Dodson, J. D. 1908. The relation of strength of stimulus to rapidity of habit-formation. *J. Comp. Neurol. Psychol.* 18:459–82

Zajonc, R. B. 1965. Social facilitation. *Science* 149:269–74

Zander, A. 1971. *Motives and Goals in Groups.* New York: Academic

Zander, A. 1976. The psychology of removing group members and recruiting new ones. *Hum. Relat.* 10:969–87

Zuckerman, M., Buchsbaum, M. S., Murphy, D. L. 1980. Sensation seeking and its biological correlates. *Psychol. Bull.* 88:187–214

Ann. Rev. Psychol. 1984. 35:627–66

ORGANIZATIONAL BEHAVIOR: A Review and Reformulation of the Field's Outcome Variables

Barry M. Staw

School of Business Administration and Institute of Industrial Relations, University of California, Berkeley, California 94720

CONTENTS

627

0066-4308/84/0201-0627$02.00

INTRODUCTION

Organizational behavior is an interdisciplinary field that examines the behavior of individuals within organizational settings as well as the structure and behavior of organizations themselves. Macro organizational behavior (sometimes called organization theory) has roots in sociology, political science, and economics, and deals with questions of organizational structure, design, and action within social/economic contexts. Micro organizational behavior is rooted in psychology and deals with individual attitudes and behavior and how they are influenced by and influence organizational systems.

With both micro and macro branches, the field of "OB" often functions as two separate subdisciplines. Macro researchers are frequently sociologists who identify with the Organizations and Occupations section of the American Sociological Association, while micro researchers most commonly align themselves with the Industrial and Organizational Psychology division of the American Psychological Association. There are, however, some integrating mechanisms which draw these camps together. The Academy of Management serves both branches of the field and brings micro and macro researchers together in a single forum. And, more importantly, both sides of the field are commonly housed within a single department or subarea within American business schools. To date, this integration has resulted in some common language as well as a recognition of the joint contribution of the two perspectives, but most research is still distinctly psychological or sociological in its approach to variables and levels of analysis.

Organizational Behavior as an Applied Field

At present, the two sides of organizational behavior are moving at cross directions regarding the issue of basic versus applied research. At the macro level, the legacy has been one of descriptive empirical research (e.g. relating organizational size to differentiation) with very little concern for application. The macro orientation is now shifting with a surge of interest in questions such as organizational design, strategy, and policy formulation. At the micro level, the history has been one of extremely applied research, exploring determinants of very few outcome variables and compiling findings in an almost atheoretical way. The development of models at the micro level has been slow but the trend is now clearly toward more theoretical work.

Although there are conflicts between the directions of micro and macro research, one might characterize the field's overall orientation by the notion of fundamental research on applied organizational issues. The main concern in the field appears to be upon important outcome variables, issues of concern to organizations and their participants. But, at the same time, there is increasing appreciation and some movement toward the development of fundamental theory, hypotheses that are neither simple collections of correlates nor direct applications of models from the parent disciplines.

Organizational Behavior as an Outcome-Oriented Field

The most popular way of summarizing the field has usually been some mixture of organizational practices (e.g. job design and pay systems), organizational processes (e.g. leadership and control), broad theoretical perspectives (e.g. reinforcement and expectancy theory), or outcomes (e.g. job satisfaction and productivity). Both Mitchell (1979) and Cummings (1982) touched on all three dimensions in their prior reviews for the *Annual Review of Psychology*. Mitchell concentrated on personality and individual differences, job attitudes, motivation, and leadership, while Cummings covered task design, feedback, structure, technology and control. The present review, like those of Mitchell's and Cummings', will concentrate on the psychological or micro side of the field. However, this review will be organized strictly by outcome variable, concentrating on issues directly related to organizational and individual welfare.

I have followed an outcome orientation for this review because it will highlight many of the shortcomings as well as opportunities for the field. To date, much of the research in industrial/organizational psychology has been devoted to questions of interest to personnel specialists, while micro OB has attempted to address issues related to managing human resources in organizations. The formulation of research has perhaps been broader in micro OB than I/O psychology, since the clients of OB have included general managers who are charged with running the entire organization rather than only those staff specifically engaged in personnel functions. Yet, both micro OB and I/O psychology can be criticized for taking an overly narrow focus. One criticism is that research questions are often biased to serve managerial rather than individual or societal interests (Braverman 1974). A second concern is that the field may not have even served managerial interests well, since research has taken a short-term problem focus rather than having formulated new forms of organization that do not currently exist (cf Argyris 1976). Finally, it could be argued that a descriptive science of organizations has been slow to develop because outcomes have been emphasized rather than more fundamental organizational processes.

While I am sympathetic to many of the criticisms of the field's outcome orientation (Staw 1980a), I will not in this review argue for a wholesale substitution of processes for outcomes. In my view, it is probably not the outcome approach per se that should be held responsible for the lack of progress in micro OB, but the way outcome research has been conducted. To date, the outcomes of interest to researchers in the field have been extremely limited, and even the ways these few outcomes have been conceptualized have been restricted. Thus, in addition to describing recent research on the most prevalent outcome variables, this review will try to push the field a bit toward a reformulation of these traditional variables as well as an expansion of the list of outcomes relevant for future research.

The first and most extensive part of this review will concentrate on four of the most heavily researched outcomes, variables that still account for a very large proportion of the field's research: job satisfaction, absenteeism, turnover, and performance. For each variable, a summary will be provided of the major theoretical approaches and prevailing research trends. An exhaustive review of all recent empirical research will not be provided, since this would require a separate and lengthy paper on each of the subtopics. Instead, the review will emphasize the prevalent research assumptions and outline the possibility for new formulations. A principal goal of this section of the chapter will be to show how research on these four traditional variables can be revitalized by taking on a different point of view (e.g. employee as opposed to management) or some alternative theoretical perspective.

The second part of the chapter will consider briefly three additional dependent variables. A great deal of research has recently addressed job stress, one of the few variables now researched from the employee's point of view. Relatively unresearched, but still important, is the recent work on individual dissent and whistleblowing. Finally, of increasing future importance to organizations is the issue of creativity and innovation. Recent research and trends will be briefly summarized on each of these three subtopics, as they represent only a sampling of research that can be performed on newer outcome variables. The chapter will conclude with some general discussion of theory development and research in organizational behavior.

JOB SATISFACTION

Job satisfaction has probably attracted more research than any other dependent variable in the field. Because of its ease of measurement, as well as the continued dependence of the field on attitudinal surveys, satisfaction measures have played some role in a very large proportion of organizational research studies. At last count (Locke 1976) over 3000 studies contained some documentation or examination of job satisfaction.

While job satisfaction measures continue to be abundant in research (almost to the extent of being "throw-away" variables), a much smaller stream of studies have specifically addressed the issue. Research on job satisfaction per se probably peaked in the 1960s and then declined when the presumed link between satisfaction and productivity was called into question (e.g. Schwab & Cummings 1970). However, satisfaction research has shown some resurgence of late as attitudes have been more specifically linked to absenteeism and turnover, once again providing an economic rationale for their study (Mirvis & Lawler 1977). Satisfaction research has also been aided by recent concerns over the quality of working life (e.g. Campbell et al 1976), the impact of work on mental health (Kahn 1980), and the relationship between work and family life (e.g. Kabanoff 1980).

Measurement and Meaning of Job Satisfaction

There is now wide acceptance of three job satisfaction measures: the Job Description Index (Smith et al 1969), the Minnesota Satisfaction Questionnaire (Weiss et al 1967), and the Michigan measure of facet satisfaction (Quinn & Staines 1979). Each of these is a simple additive measure of various aspects of the job, including supervision, working conditions, and the task itself. Very much out of favor are measurement devices which incorporate a particular theory of satisfaction such as need theory (Porter & Lawler 1968) or a weighted average in which some job factors are disproportionately emphasized over others (Herzberg et al 1959). Single items to measure overall or global job satisfaction are still in wide usage.

While much effort has historically been placed on developing reliable measures of satisfaction, little work has focused on the construct of satisfaction itself. With the exception of Locke's (1976) recent analysis of satisfaction as the fulfillment of individual values, there has been little debate about the meaning of satisfaction. The field's current usage of satisfaction is as a theory-free affective variable, yet the measurement of satisfaction probably involves additional conceptual baggage that leads one implicitly to discrepancy theories and models of social comparison. Dictionary definitions of the term usually note fulfillment or gratification, and it is not yet known what other connotations and cognitive schemata may be tapped by the term. Related but distinctly different terms such as job liking, vocational pleasure, or positive feelings may have different meanings, perhaps closer to general work affect. Thus, if we desire a relatively theory-free measure of job attitudes, measures such as Scott's (1967) semantic differential or Kunin's (1955) faces scale may be more appropriate than current indicators.

Correlates of Job Satisfaction

Over the last 30 years, most of the research on job satisfaction has been a rather atheoretical listing of variables that are statistically associated with work attitudes. Large-scale surveys as well as countless studies with more limited samples have examined the relationship between various working conditions, pay, supervision, promotion, and job features with satisfaction. As one might expect, data show that satisfaction covaries with level of pay, degree of promotional opportunities, the consideration of supervisors, recognition, pleasant working conditions, and the use of skills and abilities (see Locke 1976 for a review).

The first problem with much of the correlational work on job satisfaction is that the determinants of satisfaction are usually measured by perceptions rather than more objective measures of the job situation. The spillover from job satisfaction to perceptions of the job environment on questionnaires make cause-effect inferences almost impossible (Staw 1977). This is especially problematic when questions about job features are asked in a value-laden way (e.g. "the pay is good," or "the job is challenging"). The fact that there are so few disconfirmations of common sense should, by itself, cue us to this problem. Seldom do respondents note on questionnaires that the job is satisfying because it is easy, does not involve responsibility for others, or allows the separation between work and family life. Thus, more research needs to be done on the design of questionnaires that are neutrally toned as well as greater reliance on the objective measurement of job environments.

In general, advances in understanding the causes of job satisfaction have not come from large-scale surveys which have noted many statistical correlates of satisfaction, but instead from more theory-driven data collections. Contributions to job satisfaction have arrived more from theories and research on job design, equity, leadership, and participation, than from the research specifically charged with job satisfaction. I will consider the research work in only two of these subareas as examples of recent advances.

Job Design

Research on job design is currently the most active forum for work on job attitudes. Although job design theories are often intended to be predictors of work effort and quality, relationships with job attitudes are more consistently found than associations with archival measures of performance. Job design research has also stimulated more fundamental debate over the formulation of job attitudes than behavior, with consideration being placed on the social construction of reality as well as more objective work conditions.

The dominant job design theory over the last 5 years has been Hackman & Oldham's (1976, 1980) Job Characteristics Model. This formulation has posited that five job characteristics (skill variety, task identity, task significance, autonomy, and feedback) contribute to internal work motivation and positive job attitudes. The Hackman and Oldham model is based on a need-fulfillment theory of motivation (e.g. Maslow 1954) and is derived from a long tradition of concern with intrinsic aspects of the job (e.g. Herzberg et al 1959). It is essentially a refinement of the earlier models by Turner & Lawrence (1965) and

Hackman & Lawler (1971), although there are greater efforts in the current work to present a unified theory of job design.

Being the dominant job design model, Hackman and Oldham's work has attracted a large share of criticism and has stimulated most of the new competing work on job attitudes. In terms of methodological problems, Roberts & Glick (1981) and Aldag et al (1981) have presented excellent summaries. The reliability of measurement, lack of discriminant validity with other attitudinal measures, reliance on perceptual rather than objective measures of jobs, and positive or negative halo among job characteristics all loom as potential problems. Even more fundamental is the fact that most of the supporting evidence for the Hackman and Oldham model comes from cross-sectional surveys where cause-effect inferences are difficult. Field experiments have provided very weak support for the theory, even though its implications for job redesign are rather direct (Oldham & Hackman 1980 have recently offered some explanations of this problem). Thus, while research on the Hackman and Oldham model has consistently supported the relationship between certain perceptions of work and job attitudes, we still do not know whether changes in objective job characteristics will change job attitudes and behavior as predicted by the theory.

In a theoretical critique, Salancik & Pfeffer (1977) have assailed the Job Characteristics Model as being a derivative of need satisfaction theory and subject at least indirectly to all of the vagaries and difficulties in testing models of human needs (e.g. Wahba & Bridwell 1976). In addition, Salancik & Pfeffer (1978) have offered a social information processing approach to explain job satisfaction. Rather than satisfaction being determined by intrinsic characteristics of tasks, it is, they contend, more a product of self-inference and social influence. Many experiments have shown, for example, that salient external rewards can decrease job satisfaction, though this literature is itself controversial (see Deci & Ryan 1980 and Sandelands et al 1983 for reviews). Self-inference of task attitudes has also been shown to be influenced by simple questionnaire manipulations of the frequency of behavior directed toward or against a particular task or activity (Salancik & Conway 1975). Neither of these streams of research, however, has had as much impact on job design and job attitudes as have several recent experiments on social influence in a work setting.

As posited by Salancik and Pfeffer, tasks can be ambiguous activities potentially interpreted in both positive and negative ways. Thus, the simple labeling of tasks by others has been found to affect task attitudes in several laboratory studies. In one study subjects were told that a task was either liked or disliked by people with previous experience with it (O'Reilly & Caldwell 1979), and in two other studies a confederate who worked along with the subject noted positive or negative features of the activity (White & Mitchell 1979, Weiss & Shaw 1979). In each of these studies, positive labeling led to greater satisfaction than negative labeling.

Recently, in an effort to extend these findings to a field setting, Griffin (1983) experimentally manipulated both objective job conditions and social cues. Factory foremen were trained to provide cues about the job to their subordinates, and the effect of these cues as well as changes in more objective job characteristics were assessed. Results showed that perceptions of task characteristics (e.g. task variety, autonomous, feedback, and identity) as well as overall satisfaction with the job were affected by *both* objective job changes and social cues provided by the foremen.

At the present time, there is a conceptual stalemate between objective and subjective approaches to job design. Advocates of objective conditions being the determinants of job attitudes have relied on perceptual measures, no doubt capitalizing on subjective inference and halo in testing their models. Advocates of subjective conditions being the determinants of job attitudes have tended to hold job conditions constant or avoid the extremes of either boring or highly involving tasks. Thus, testing how much variance each approach explains may depend more on parameters of the tests themselves than upon the veracity of either of the models. Like the arguments of personality vs environment, a conclusive winner is not likely to be found. Future research, therefore, may be more productive in addressing boundary questions such as when objective changes will and will *not* be expected to change attitudes and when manipulations of social cues are likely to be major or minor events. Also useful will be studies to test the interaction of subjective and objective influences. Social influences and positive halo may be necessary factors for successful implementation of job redesign, and objective changes may be necessary to make credible many manipulations of the social reality surrounding jobs.

Comparison Theories

A second major group of studies concerned with job attitudes has taken the form of individual and social comparison theories. Comparison theories, like the social-information processing approach, have posited that satisfaction is not simply an additive function of the objective outcomes received by the individual. Comparison theories emphasize the choice of information sources about one's outcomes and the comparison between self and others. The major sources of research for this approach are work on adaptation level (Appley 1971), social comparison (Suls & Miller 1977), equity (Walster et al 1978) and relative deprivation (Martin 1981), not all of which has been carried forward or advanced in the organizational context.

At present, if one were to point to a dominant comparison model of satisfaction, it would probably be Lawler's (1973) formulation which incorporates both social and self comparisons. This model notes that satisfaction is a function of the discrepancy between the level of outcomes desired and the perceived level of outcomes that actually do exist. Prior experience with various job outcomes as well as social comparisons are hypothesized to affect the desired or expected level of outcomes, while the evaluation of pay, working conditions, and other job features are considered to be determinants of actual outcomes received. Because the Lawler model is so global, little research has gone into testing this particular formulation. Its components have been addressed, however, through a number of subtheories of social and self comparison.

In terms of intraindividual comparison of outcomes, the clearest study has been a laboratory experiment by Ilgen (1971). By manipulating the level of performance over several trials, Ilgen created different levels of expectations. He then changed the performance level so as to violate the level of expectations in a positive or negative direction. The results showed that satisfaction with one's performance was as much a function of prior expectations as the aggregate level of feedback. Little work has followed this study in examining rising expectations in organizational settings or the impact of personal variables (e.g. age, seniority, education) on levels of expected outcomes. However, a recent laboratory study (Austin et al 1980) compared the relative impact of intrapersonal and interpersonal comparisons on satisfaction. Both processes were found to be significant determinants of attitude and of approximately equal magnitude. Given these results, it is unfortunate that almost all our attention in comparison theories has involved social as opposed to self comparison.

EQUITY THEORY   In terms of social comparison models, equity theory has long dominated thinking in the area, though empirical research on equity has decreased drastically since the mid 1970s. For the conditions of underpayment, the hypotheses originally posed by Adams are now widely accepted, namely that underpaid workers will be dissatisfied, redress their inequity through lower effort, rationalize their underpayment through cognitive distortions, change social comparisons, or leave the field (Goodman & Friedman 1971). Adams' hypotheses for the condition of overpayment were the most controversial to the field, and they remain that way. Few researchers accept the notion that overpayment will lead to feelings of guilt and to subsequent behavior that may reduce the guilt such as increasing work performance.

As was the case over 10 years ago, two weaknesses plague equity theory. One is the ambiguity of the social comparison process, since the choice of a social comparison appears to be far from a deterministic process (Goodman 1977, Martin 1981). While equity experiments make salient a particular comparison other or limit the situation so that no information is available except as provided by the experimentor (e.g. "others have been paid $10.00), natural situations abound in ambiguity. To whom one compares himself may be a fluid enterprise, and the consequence as well as a cause of satisfaction. So far, the most thorough empirical investigation of social comparisons in an organizational setting has been a study by Goodman (1974) in which self, other (individuals, both inside and outside the organization), and system (the structure and administration of the pay system) referents were examined. In a series of recent studies, Martin (1981) also found deprivation to arise when individuals make comparisons across status groupings (i.e. secretaries comparing their outcomes with managers). Thus, although most theories of social comparison incorporate some notion of relevance or similarity for the determination of comparisons (Goodman 1977), the choice of referents may be subject to both social influence and conflict. Within the individual there may be a dynamic conflict between individual needs for accurate information versus the need for self-rationalization. External to the individual, there may also be conflicting social influences, such as when unions point to others who are substantially better off, while management notes how much things have improved.

The second major problem with equity theory has been its lack of specificity about the ways individuals can resolve inequity. Adams (1965) did not offer much help when he stated that inequity is resolved in a manner that is least costly to the individual. However, some real progress might be made by merging the theories of relative deprivation and equity, with Crosby's (1976) recent theoretical integration of deprivation research serving as a point of departure.

A MERGER OF EQUITY AND DEPRIVATION THEORIES   As Crosby noted, deprivation occurs when a person sees someone who possesses some outcome x, wants x, and feels entitled to x. To this point, the notions of underpayment inequity and relative deprivation are quite parallel, since they each posit a comparison other and some basis of calculating a just or equitable reward. The departure between the two theories occurs with predictions about how relative deprivation is resolved or channeled into action. An intro-punitive as opposed to extra-punitive orientation, or felt responsibility for not having x, might serve as major channeling devices. When blame is internally placed, reactions might be internally directed such as rationalization (e.g. distortion of outcomes) to increase the perception of outcomes received or concrete actions (e.g. self-improvement) to increase future outcomes. When blame is externally placed, deprivation may be reduced by more externally directed actions such as efforts to obtain greater outcomes from the system (e.g. politicking, theft, decreased quality) as well as efforts to change the system itself (e.g. lobbying, strikes, grievances). Another dimension that may also affect channeling is the feasibility of obtaining x. When outcomes are feasible and responsibility is internally directed, self-improvement can be hypothesized, whereas rationalization may be more likely to occur when outcomes are not feasible. When blame is externally directed, the feasibility of obtaining outcomes may determine whether acts that are destructive to the system (e.g. industrial sabotage) are used rather than efforts for constructive change.

To date, most of the evidence for the channeling of deprivation comes from political and sociological research. Crosby has, however, conducted a laboratory simulation and a cross-sectional survey which have provided some preliminary tests of these ideas (Bernstein & Crosby 1980, Crosby 1984). Unfortunately, little of this type of research has yet appeared in the organizational literature, although it would seem to present a major means of revitalizing work on equity and job satisfaction. According to this line of thinking, the major question is not whether underpayment or deprivation can cause dissatisfaction, but how this dissatisfaction will be channeled in terms of individual and organizational behavior. Dissatisfaction, therefore, would not be conceived as a uniformly negative outcome, but also as a possible means for individual and organizational improvement.

THE FUTURE OF GUILT AND OVERPAYMENT   While underpayment situations clearly comprise the most practical problem area for comparison theories, much of the early research and controversy centered on overpayment situations. Initial research showing that overpayment can lead to increased quality or quantity of work (e.g. Adams & Rosenbaum 1962) was criticized on many methodological fronts (e.g. Valenzi & Andrews 1971), and the field has basically given up on the belief that guilt can be harnessed into productive work. Yet the recent Austin et al (1980) study did show self-reports of guilt in overpayment conditions, and a few studies have shown that recipients of overpayments may be more helpful to others (Gibbons & Wicklund 1982) or lobby on others' behalf (Notz et al 1971, Staw et al 1974). These results suggest that overpayment may be disconcerting, if not dissatisfying, and that some means of restoring equity may be sought (see also Walster et al for a useful integration of the altruism and equity literatures). Future research might therefore assess guilt reactions by examining situations where there are strong social bonds and the expectation of future participation. When individuals care about the reactions of others and anticipate a long-term relationship, inequitably large rewards may need to be redressed. When social groups are less involving or transitory, overreward may simply be perceived as a message that one is superior on some dimension, or that social comparisons should be shifted to the group that receives greater reward.

Alternative Directions

While job design and comparison theories have served as the major means of examining job satisfaction, almost no work has looked at the individual's mood as a determinant of job-related cognitions. This is unfortunate because we know from psychological research that mood can affect the input and recall of information (Zajonc 1980, Bower 1981). The implication of a significant mood effect is that job satisfaction may be subject to any influence (both on or off the job) that can alter the affective state of the individual (see Caldwell et al 1983 for an initial study). Thus, working conditions and physical surroundings may be important for their effect on individual mood, which in turn could affect the perception and/or evaluation of various task characteristics.

A second change in satisfaction research would be to focus upon individual differences rather than contextual features in determining satisfaction (cf Epstein 1979). At the extreme, one might even think of job satisfaction itself as an individual characteristic, and study the persistence of job attitudes over time. The tendency to be happy or unhappy may vary little over time and context, since positive or negative features of employment can be deduced from most any job. Some preliminary research has shown job satisfaction to be relatively unaffected by changes in job status and pay and to be highly consistent over time (Staw & Ross 1983). Stable individual differences in job satisfaction may thus explain why it is so difficult to change job attitudes through job enlargement as well as other logically desirable treatments (cf Oldham & Hackman 1982).

A third redirection for satisfaction research, one already pointed to in the work on deprivation, is to recognize some of the functions of dissatisfaction. Dissatisfaction with one's performance may, for example, be the impetus for self-improvement. Dissatisfaction with the organization may also be the spark that alters the institution. Too often dissatisfaction is treated from the status quo position, as if changes by the individual are unnecessary or that lobbying, grievances, and protests are inevitably dysfunctional for the system. If research validates any of these predictions, dissatisfaction may in fact be a theoretical variable that is richer than we have given it credit for.

ABSENTEEISM

Like job satisfaction, absenteeism has long been a target of study by organizational psychologists. Behind the concern with absenteeism is the practical cost of the number of work days lost by the labor force, the cost of temporary replacement, and the overstaffing prompted by absenteeism. Steers & Rhodes (1978) recently estimated that the costs of absenteeism may run as high as $26.4 billion per year when estimated days lost are multiplied by approximate wage rates.

Current Models

Research on absenteeism has followed very simple theoretical lines. Historically, absenteeism has been considered as a form of withdrawal from work and a rather direct behavioral consequence of one's job attitude (Johns & Nicholson 1982). In general, satisfaction and other attitudinal variables are found to be negatively associated with absenteeism, but the magnitude of the correlations is rarely so large as to preclude other influences (Locke 1976). Therefore, efforts have also been placed into documenting personal, situational, and environmental variables which might help explain additional variance in this dependent variable. As one might expect, personal characteristics such as age, sex, family size, and health all relate to absenteeism. Likewise, situational factors such as incentive systems for job attendance, ease of transportation, flexible working hours, and external labor market conditions also appear capable of explaining some variance in this dependent variable.

Probably the most accepted theoretical model of absenteeism is the recent formulation by Steers & Rhodes (1978). They consider attendance as a variable which is determined by both motivational and ability factors. Motivation to attend, they contend, is influenced by job satisfaction as well as a host of external pressures such as fear of losing one's job, work group norms, and incentive systems. But motivation alone will not determine job attendance since one's ability to attend is often constrained by health, family responsibilities, transportation problems, and other involuntary factors. Using the Steers and Rhodes model, one can understand why satisfaction is often such a poor predictor of absenteeism. First, as an indicator of attraction toward the work role, satisfaction is only one of many reasons to attend. And, even if satisfaction is high, attendance may be constrained by other situational influences.

A slightly different approach to absenteeism is to consider whether one attends work or not to be a product of individual decision making with costs as well as benefits resulting from job attendance. A good example of this approach is a study by Morgan & Herman (1976). As those authors have noted, non-work activities often take precedence over work, and this may be especially true when the costs associated with absenteeism (e.g. paid "sick leave") are minimal. Likewise, if work is a major source of involvement for the individual or the penalties for nonattendance great, absenteeism will be minimal.

Other examples of the decision-making approach would be studies which show absenteeism to be strategically related to personal concerns. Rousseau (1978), for instance, found that the scope of one's nonwork activities was a better predictor of absenteeism than job scope, one of the typical correlates of job satisfaction. Chadwick-Jones et al (1973) found that women's absence peaked at times when household demands were greatest, and Nicholson & Goodge (1976) found absenteeism to cluster around holiday periods (see Johns & Nicholson 1982 for a more detailed review). But probably the best empirical study of individual decision making about absenteeism comes from a field experiment by Smith (1977). In a study of salaried employees working for Sears, Smith examined the relationship between job satisfaction and attendance at a very unusual time. After an extraordinary snowstorm that crippled the transportation system in Chicago, there was an extremely high correlation between job attitudes and attendance, while employees at a control location (New York headquarters) showed nonsignificant but positive correlations. These results were particularly interesting for two reasons. First, they show that it is possible to explain a significant portion of absenteeism behavior with job attitudes. Second, these results highlight the difference between situations in which attendance is largely voluntary (e.g. when a legitimate excuse for absence is provided) and contexts in which behavior is constrained by potential sanctions.

Theoretical Trends

As noted, current theoretical trends on absenteeism are best characterized by the work of Steers & Rhodes (1978) and Morgan & Herman (1976). Starting with a large listing of personal and situational correlates to absenteeism, Steers and Rhodes have placed the literature into an aggregate model that has intuitive appeal. In contrast to this aggregate model, Morgan and Herman's expectancy approach would posit a more microscopic explanation in which individuals' perceptions of cost/benefit would affect the number of future absences. Even more microscopic would be Johns & Nicholson's (1982) recent suggestion that we treat each instance of absence as unique, because aggregation of absences over time may reduce our understanding of the event.

Two logical extensions of current approaches to absenteeism would be to more strongly emphasize either individual or situational characteristics. Some research already shows that a small portion of the working population accounts for a disproportionally large number of absences (Yolles et al 1975, Garrison & Michinsky 1977). Therefore, further studies of this "problem" group, either in terms of their nonwork environment, personal values, or causal reasoning, could be useful. Likewise, because rates of absenteeism can vary widely across companies, plants, and work groups, research might well examine norms about absenteeism and how absenteeism might be associated with other dimensions of the organizational culture (Johns & Nicholson 1982).

More Divergent Approaches

While most research has attempted to find new determinants of absenteeism or to reorder these determinants into a causal model that will explain substantial variance in the behavior, very little attention has been given to the construct itself. Johns & Nicholson's (1982) recent paper is a notable exception since it discusses the phenomenological meaning of absence, its possible use as an upward control mechanism, and the relation between absence from work and attendance to various nonwork activities. These research avenues hold potential because they seek an understanding of absenteeism from the individual worker's perspective as opposed to the usual viewpoint of management.

Another way to reconceptualize the absenteeism construct is to view it as an event with positive as well as negative consequences. As Staw & Oldham (1978) have noted, absenteeism can have two sides: a *technical dysfunction* from not being present to do the work that is expected, and also a *maintenance function* in which one's capacity to perform is increased. Most research only acknowledges the dysfunctional aspects of absenteeism, with the emphasis being placed on the number of days lost to work. Although it is well known that work outcomes can deteriorate under some personal or situational conditions, we rarely acknowledge the possible *costs* of attendance rather than absenteeism. One exception appears to be the legal limitation to the number of hours pilots can fly, air-traffic controllers can work, or bus drivers can drive. In these potentially hazardous occupations we readily acknowledge the possible costs to the public from fatigue or excess stress. For nurses and doctors we acknowledge the costs of overwork, but norms against such conduct are not often developed into rules or sanctions.

Staw & Oldham (1978) argued that jobs that are particularly dissatisfying or where there is a poor fit with individual characteristics require higher levels of absenteeism. They found a positive correlation between absenteeism and performance under dissatisfying conditions, but a negative correlation under more satisfying circumstances. Thus, it is possible that the positive contribution of absenteeism (e.g. a mental health break) can more than outweigh the costs of taking time off when a job is particularly frustrating or dissatisfying.

In a practical sense, one could argue that the term "absenteeism" should never be used when nonattendance has positive value. When executives spend time away from the office to visit prospective clients, organize long-range plans, or even to "decompress" from a strenuous travel schedule, these activities are not labeled as absenteeism because of their (assumed) productive purpose. Therefore, greater research needs to be directed toward identifying the productive use of time away from work by lower and middle level personnel as well as executives. The use of flexible working hours and the four-day work week have shown some potential in reducing absenteeism (e.g. Golembiewksi & Proehl 1978, Ronen 1981, Narayanan & Nath 1982), but they have not yet been studied with the goal of specifying the optimal work week for different occupations. Nor have efforts to make lower and middle-level employees responsible for their own output (either through goal-setting or job design) been related to the workers' management of their own work attendance. Ideally, when work goals are emphasized, absenteeism should disappear as a managerial concern. Finally, as factory work is replaced by administrative and service tasks, and as computerization becomes widespread in these roles, the location of work may become more flexible. Already many staff functions can be performed at home on a computer terminal, and some firms encourage home as opposed to office work. However, as Becker (1981) has noted, the blending of work and family life may be a mixed blessing, because physical separation may be needed for psychological rather than technological purposes. This is a major question for future research and one that can draw on new developments in the social ecology literature.

TURNOVER

Like the study of absenteeism, research on turnover has largely been stimulated by the desire to reduce the costs associated with personnel leaving industrial and governmental organizations. Turnover has therefore been viewed as an important organizational problem, one which is worthy of both theoretical explanation and predictive models.

Current Approaches

Historically, research on turnover has long utilized models of rational individual decision making. Starting with March & Simon (1958), turnover has been conceived as a conscious process where one evaluates present and future alternatives in deciding to stay or leave the organization. Mobley's (1977) more recent model of turnover, probably the most widely accepted at the present time, is a direct descendent of the March and Simon decision approach. Mobley's model posits that job and working conditions affect job satisfaction which in turn leads to thoughts of quitting, to evaluation of the utility of searching behavior, job search, evaluation of alternatives, comparison of alternatives vs the present job, intention to quit or stay, and finally to turnover or retention behavior. Although it would be unlikely for any single individual to go through all of these decision steps, Mobley's elaboration of turnover as a rational decision process has served as a useful guideline for research (e.g. Miller et al 1979).

Empirical studies have shown that satisfaction is generally correlated with turnover, but as in the case of absenteeism, the magnitude of the relationship is not large. Satisfaction, as one would expect, is more strongly related to other attitudes or behavioral intentions than actual turnover (e.g. Mobley et al 1978), while intentions to quit are more strongly related to turnover (Arnold & Feldman 1982). Just as March and Simon noted over 25 years ago, dissatisfaction may provide the impetus to look for another job, but such plans may be blocked if economic conditions are poor, pension plans nontransferable, and one's skills unsaleable (see Price 1977, Steers & Mowday 1981, Mobley 1982 for recent reviews).

Theoretical Trends

Although there has been a recent upsurge of theoretical interest in turnover, the research can be criticized for being fairly narrow conceptually. In one grouping, one can place many studies which have treated turnover in a rather atheoretical manner, considering turnover simply as one of many possible dependent measures in the assessment of a new work procedure such as job redesign (e.g. Macy & Mirvis 1983) or a participative pay plan (Jenkins & Lawler 1981). Probably the only research on an organizational procedure with a theoretically developed link to turnover has been the study of realistic job previews (Wanous 1973, 1981). In a second grouping, one could place research on the process of turnover. The process research has taken an extremely rational decision making stance, examining the relation between intentions and actions or otherwise testing the cognitive links in the Mobley turnover model (e.g. Arnold & Feldman 1982, Miller et al 1978). These process studies have been criticized for examining theoretically unexciting relationships (Graen & Ginsburgh 1977), and it does appear that they have retread old ground from the expectancy and attitude-behavior literatures. Therefore, a possibility for improvement would be to incorporate recent ideas on attitude-behavior relationships (Fazio & Zanna 1981), but so far work linking job satisfaction, intention to stay, and turnover has not gone beyond commonsense theorizing.

One major advance in turnover research has been the recent work on organizational commitment. A program of research by Mowday et al (1982) has identified organizational commitment as being a prime determinant of turnover and as a more important predictor than job satisfaction. By commitment, Mowday et al mean a syndrome of variables such as belief in the organization's goals, willingness to work on the organization's behalf, and intention to stay in the organization. Conceptually, why this syndrome of variables are interrelated and how they can determine turnover remain unanswered questions. Also, because intentions to stay are included in the measurement of commitment, relationships with turnover may be overstated. Still, the empirical results showing the usefulness of commitment as a predictor of turnover are a welcome addition to the literature. In the future, alternative measures of commitment such as psychological investment in a job or side bets might be productively combined with the Mowday et al measures to predict turnover. Pension plans, number of children in school, home ownership, and friendship patterns are just a few of the economic and psychological bonds that may tie an individual to a job. The effects of these "behavioral" commitments on turnover have recently been documented in a longitudinal field study by Rusbult & Farrell (1983).

Some New Ideas

There have been three recent departures from traditional turnover research. In a very thorough yet innovative essay, Steers & Mowday (1981) discussed the importance of understanding the consequences of turnover decisions on the individuals making the decision to leave as well as other employees who are observers to the departure. For example, deciding to remain in an organization, though not satisfied, may constitute a dissonance-arousing decision and trigger increases in subsequent satisfaction. Likewise, leaving an organization when one is reasonably satisfied may cause one to justify the decision after departure. Equally interesting are the consequences of turnover on those who stay in the organization. As Steers and Mowday note, those who remain may become dissatisfied simply by watching others leave for other organizations. Such demoralization may be conditioned, however, by the attributions stayers make about the reasons for leaving (see Mowday 1981 for a recent test of these ideas).

An alternative approach to studying the consequences of turnover was suggested by Staw (1980). He noted that turnover has usually been considered a negative outcome variable or cost to be minimized by organizations (e.g. Gustafson 1982). The costs of turnover such as recruitment, training, and possible disruption of operations are all very real, but they are not the only consequences of turnover. Perhaps too little attention has been paid to possible benefits of turnover such as hiring someone with greater skill, increased mobility of others in the organization, and possible innovation (Dalton & Todor 1979, Dalton et al 1981). Interestingly, sociologists have long been interested in executive succession as a possible source of organizational improvement (e.g. Gamson & Scotch 1964, Brown 1982), but this literature has had little effect on traditional models of turnover. The reason for this disparity may be that organizational psychologists tend to develop models of concern to person-nel managers—the occupational group charged with reducing the costs of turnover rather than documenting its benefits.

Some obvious benefits of turnover come when the relation between skill and tenure has an inverted U shape, such as on sports teams in which performance peaks at an intermediate range of experience. Recently Katz (1982) has shown that research groups may also start to lose their productivity after they have remained together for many years. Future research needs to address the issue of whether turnover has an optional level below which it should not be reduced. Although we know from U.S. Labor Department data (see Staw 1981) that slow-growing industries have the lowest rates of turnover, cause and effect is impossible to establish with these data. Ideally, there should be research to discover the level of turnover appropriate for organizations in environments with various rates of change or innovation. There should also be work on the optimal level of turnover for various types of jobs within organizations, since each job (e.g. research scientist vs accountant) may have its own performance curve. Finally, it may be possible to reap the positive benefits of turnover by job rotation and reassignment rather than having to displace people from the organization. These are important but as yet unanswered questions on the consequences of turnover.

Even though there is almost no empirical research on the consequences of turnover, Pfeffer (1983) has already moved this literature an additional theoretical step. He notes that turnover rates may be less important to organizations than tenure distributions. Turnover rates do not reflect whether newcomers continually leave an organization or whether departure occurs throughout the ranks. Turnover as well as hiring patterns may create an evenly distributed organization or one with a bimodal distribution, and he argues that a bimodal distribution can create the potential for organizational conflict (see McCain et al 1984 for an early empirical study). With a bimodal distribution, conflicts of interest can develop between two distinct factions that consume organizational resources, and there may be a reduction in the coordination necessary for organizational effectiveness. Though sports teams seemingly adjust their rosters to maintain a desired mix of talent (e.g. rookies and veterans) and universities often attempt to maintain a flat distribution of faculty ranks, organizational psychologists have not yet addressed these demographic concerns.

MOTIVATION AND PERFORMANCE

Since its inception, the micro side of organizational behavior has considered individual performance as its primary dependent variable. While most studies do not focus directly on performance per se, nearly every research write-up attempts to draw some implications for management or for current organizational practices. These implications are usually couched in performance terms, since the major audience and/or sponsors of research have been managers of business and governmental organizations.

Because studies of most individual and organizational processes try to draw implications for performance, it is difficult to formulate any boundaries around performance research. I will therefore, rather arbitrarily, consider theories of work motivation as most directly relevant to performance, since they are primarily devoted to predicting changes in performance, with measures of motivation sometimes even being used as proxies for individual performance. I will also consider two techniques for increasing performance, reinforcement and goal-setting, since they have attracted a great deal of attention and appear capable of producing reliable changes in individual behavior.

Current State of Work Motivation Theory

As recently as a decade ago, researchers in the work motivation area could be placed rather neatly into one of three theoretical camps. Reinforcement theorists (e.g. Hamner 1974) were primarily concerned with behavior modification, demonstrating the power of extrinsic rewards in changing behavior, and arguing that motivation is basically a noncognitive form of learning in which one's actions are shaped by the scheduling of rewards and punishments. Contesting this radical form of behaviorism were need theorists who argued that knowledge of the need state of an individual is essential to behavioral prediction, because much of human motivation comes from inner drives which augment as well as define the value of external pleasures and pain (e.g. Porter 1961, Locke 1976). Largely allied with the need theorists were expectancy researchers (e.g. Vroom 1964, Lawler 1973) who posited that individuals seek to maximize valued outcomes, with those outcomes being determined by the reward system of the organization as well as the person's capability in achieving high performance.

In recent years, need theory has come under increasing attack on both methodological and theoretical grounds. Reliable scales of individual needs have been difficult to develop, and the leading model of human needs, Maslow's (1954) hierarchy theory, failed to be validated in several empirical tests (Wahba & Bridwell 1976). Aside from Alderfer's (1972) revision of Maslow's theory, direct interest in individual needs has therefore diminished. Still, need theory has continued to play a strong *indirect* role in several models of organizational behavior, having been folded into job design theory through needs for competence and personal achievement (Hackman & Oldham 1980) and integrated into expectancy theory through the use of valued outcomes (Lawler 1973).

Besides the deemphasis on explicit models of needs, motivation theory has recently witnessed a rapprochement between the reinforcement and expectancy perspectives. Debates between radical reinforcement and cognitive views of motivation have generally ebbed, with some notable exceptions (e.g. Karmel 1980, Locke 1980, Komaki 1981). In large part, expectancy theorists now acknowledge how previous reinforcement schedules can affect perceptions about future events—whether one's efforts will lead to accomplishment and whether accomplishment will lead to reward. Also, reinforcement theorists have started to acknowledge the cognitive side of learning with notions like personal efficacy (Bandura 1977), as well as renewed interest in behavior modeling and vicarious learning. The result of this accommodation can be seen in several hybrid motivation models such as those of Staw (1977), Naylor et al (1980), and Feldman & Arnold (1983). These models are amalgams of expectancy, reinforcement, and need theories, yet they are primarily expectancy-based, integrating past learning and needs into a hedonism of the future.

While expectancy formulations have probably assumed a dominant role among motivation models, their assumptions are themselves contested on empirical and conceptual grounds (e.g. Connolly 1977). One group of dissenters is composed of attribution researchers who have posited that intrinsic and extrinsic outcomes may not be additive in their effect on motivation. Starting with Deci (1971) and Lepper et al (1973), a whole body of research has developed over the question of whether extrinsic rewards can decrease intrinsic motivation (Deci & Ryan 1980 and Sandelands et al 1983). Although many social psychological studies have demonstrated the interaction of intrinsic and extrinsic rewards, this subarea of research has yet had little substantive influence on models of motivation in organizational behavior. One reason for this lack of influence is that most field studies have failed to demonstrate a negative relationship between pay and intrinsic interest (see Boal & Cummings 1981). Within industry, pay may be the only real feedback one has on performance, thus constituting a source of personal achievement rather than external control (Rosenfield et al 1980). And since payment is expected for industrial tasks, monetary rewards may not constitute the kind of unusual external control shown to alter the self-perception of motivation within laboratory studies (Staw et al 1980). Unfortunately, little work has yet focused on the effect of pay upon *voluntary* activities—those organizational actions that are truly motivated by an intrinsic rather than extrinsic source. Likely candidates for research would therefore be the conversion of voluntary to paid work and the use of external controls on activities which are normally voluntary such as participation in social events, expressions of loyalty, or work beyond the call of duty.

A second group of dissenters to expectancy theory has been forming around the information processing perspective, and this group may be more likely to reshape our notions of motivation than theorists concerned with intrinsic motivation. Because expectancy theory is basically a model of individual decision making, it is subject to all the limitations of human cognition. As shown by the recent work of Langer (1978) and Taylor & Fiske (1978), many of our daily activities are either noncognitive or governed by the most crude analyses of the situation. In addition, when behavior *is* based on conscious decision making, such decisions may be subject to numerous cognitive heuristics and biases (Nisbett & Ross 1980). Thus, rather than positing a thorough analysis of gains and losses as described by expectancy theory, there is now more interest in specifying the crude schemas, scripts, and prototypes that are used by individuals in social decisions.

It could be argued that if theories of work motivation continue to be based on individual perceptions of behavior leading to outcomes, both the number of linkages and types of outcomes considered by individuals should constitute valid empirical questions. In situations where consequences are potentially large and where individuals are accountable for their actions, there may well be the careful screening of alternatives and assessment of rewards that expectancy theory now assumes (cf McAllister et al 1979, Tetlock 1984). However, in more routine situations, attention and cognition may be more limited. Empirical research should therefore focus upon those scripts and limited action plans that are actually used by organizational actors in various contexts, as opposed to conducting simple tests of normative models of motivation. Research should also focus upon ways in which positive work behavior can become the scripted alternative, so that good performance will not call for either salient rewards or external exhortations.

Two Motivational Techniques

The two motivational techniques that have produced the most reliable changes in performance are behavior modification and goal setting. These two techniques are derived from extremely different theoretical positions, but in practice their operationalizations have often overlapped (Locke 1980). Behavior modification techniques, although derived from noncognitive reinforcement theory, frequently involve the setting of behavioral goals and instruction about desirable future behavior, in addition to the scheduling of positive outcomes such as verbal praise or bonus pay (e.g. Hamner & Hamner 1976, Komaki et al 1978, 1980). Behavior modification experiments often result in dramatic improvements in performance, significant in practical as well as statistical terms.

Goal-setting techniques derive from a distinctly cognitive approach in which individuals are assumed to formulate behavioral plans or strategies as a way to achieve personal values (Locke et al 1981). The principal addition of goal setting to a cognitive theory of motivation is the assumption that goals or intentions are an intermediate regulator of human action. A large body of research has shown that setting a specific goal leads to greater performance than general instructions to "do your best." There also appears to be a positive relationship between task difficulty and performance, although few studies have tested goal setting in a context where a difficult goal may create opposition or lack of acceptance. Participation in goal setting has not been found to be an important determinant of performance, but again, few studies have investigated the role of participation in gaining acceptance of unpopular performance goals. Finally, as Locke et al (1981) have noted, little is known about the exact mechanism by which goal setting works—by directing attention, mobilizing energy expenditure, prolonging effort, or developing task-relevant strategies. Even with these uncertainties, however, goal setting appears to be one of the most robust tools currently available for improving performance in organizations.

Specifying "Correct" Behavior

Because goal setting and behavior modification techniques have been so successful in changing behavior, the "correctness" of such behavioral changes has sometimes been highlighted as a potential problem for organizations. While many early debates centered on ethical questions of manipulation, more recent attention has focused on the unintended consequences of motivation techniques. Kerr (1975), for example, has outlined many cases in which behaviors are modified in ways that are disfunctional for the organizational system. Platt

(1973) has also outlined many individual and social traps in which short-term individual gains do not aggregate into longer-term, collective welfare. These questions are extremely important for conceptualizing the criteria of performance and how they are affected by behavioral changes, yet they remain virtually unexplored issues.

In most studies researchers have taken the organization's criteria of evaluation as accurately reflecting system performance. Often the construct of performance is relatively clear, as when physical or mechanical tasks must be completed with certain quality and quantity specifications. However, when tasks are ambiguous or involve the absorption of uncertainty (such as on administrative or managerial roles), the specification of "correct" behavior is more problematic. Naylor et al's (1980) recent theory of performance is explicit in its acceptance of managerially defined behavior as being task relevant, while most models of performance have made this an implicit assumption. My view is that a major emphasis of performance research should go into investigating how specific individual indicators of performance combine to create collective welfare or dysfunctions (Staw 1982). The performance of organizations is frequently found wanting, not for lack of motivation, but for performance of the wrong behaviors.

Although Naylor et al's recent model of performance does not address the relationship of individual to collective performance, it does make several advances in formulating the motivation construct. These authors note that increasing performance is seldom accomplished by raising the amount of energy expended by individuals, since total energy expenditure is probably rather constant over time. Instead, they argue that performance is raised by increasing one's attention to task-relevant activities as opposed to personal, family, or task-irrelevant concerns. By using this formulation, work motivation questions evolve from investigations of effort expenditure to issues of work involvement and the trade-offs between work and family life (Kabanoff 1980). This is a direction that should spur useful philosophical debate as well as empirical research.

Another issue that is provoked by the recent Naylor et al treatise is how individuals can better direct their energies on the job. In previous research, strategies for task accomplishment have not been addressed except by the implicit assumption that aptitude and ability are somehow fixed by individual differences. How individuals form performance strategies and how they can be improved are important questions that should not be assumed away as individual differences. To date, motivation has focused almost solely on the effort component of motivation and avoided the question of direction (see Terborg & Miller 1978 and Katerberg & Blau 1983 for notable exceptions). Logically, both the amplitude and direction of behavior can be governed by individual choice, subject of course to both external constraints and individual differences. The Naylor et al formulation has helped open this issue, one that could revitalize performance research.

Outcome Curves and the Multiple Purposes of Reward Schemes

Most research using a reinforcement perspective concentrates on the contingency between behavior and outcome. Likewise, research using an expectancy perspective has focused on the subjective probability that an action will be followed by a positive or negative outcome. Therefore, using either of these viewpoints, the contingency of outcomes could be stated by a curve relating behavior to outcomes (Lawler 1981). Unfortunately, little research has actually investigated the effects of various outcome curves, except for the simple linear positive relationship between performance and reward.

Numerous outcome curves are probably in existence within industry. In firms where company survival is dependent on key personnel, especially large raises may be given to high performers, thus creating a discontinuity at the high end of the curve. In other firms trying to rid themselves of poor performers, a discontinuity at the low end of the outcome curve could be present. Finally, in order to emphasize cooperation among employees, some firms may flatten the slope of the outcome curve, whereas other firms may heighten the slope in efforts to motivate most employees. Little is known about the prevalence of different outcome curves, how they relate to other organizational characteristics, and what their effects are likely to be on employee performance, turnover, or attitudes. Some preliminary ideas can be found in Staw (1983) and Naylor et al (1980), but empirical research has not appeared on these questions.

An Alternative Direction

Recently, one of the most severe challenges to conventional theories of work motivation has come, not from motivation theorists, but from organizational sociologists doing cross-cultural work (e.g. Cole 1979, Ouchi 1981). In comparing American and Japanese organizations, differences frequently have been cited in socialization, mobility, and production practices, and the popular press has often held out Japanese practices as the model to emulate. While there are many questions about the applicability of motivational practices across cultures (e.g. Schein 1981), these comparisons have highlighted what could be a fundamental omission in our motivation theories.

In organizational behavior nearly all models of motivation have been designed as direct forms of hedonism. Regardless of whether the driving force is thought to be prior reinforcement, need fulfillment, or expectancies of future gain, the individual is assumed to be a rational maximizer of personal utility. In line with these theories, our recommendations for practitioners usually attempt to link more closely personal welfare to performance, using contingent rewards, goal setting, or job enrichment (e.g. Latham et al 1981). In stark contrast, the Japanese model of motivation stresses attachment to the organization and achievement of organizational goals. Greater stress is placed upon cooperation, extending extra effort on behalf of the organization, loyalty and service to the long-term interests of the organization. Although there are many differences between the two approaches, a persistent theme dividing them is the relative emphasis upon collective versus individual motivation. Whereas Western models of motivation emphasize individual gain and self-interest, the Japanese system relies more heavily on motivation for collective welfare and appears to be more altruistically based.

Ouchi (1981) has outlined a syndrome of variables associated with Japanese management, but his descriptions have not specified which set of variables and by what theoretical mechanisms these variables operate on performance. A more explicit theoretical framework has been posited by Lawler (1982) which specifies how individual and organizational welfare can be linked through organizational practices such as participation, job redesign, and profit sharing. To Lawler, collectively oriented behavior is motivating if it contributes to organizational performance which, in turn, is linked to intrinsic or extrinsic rewards received by the individual, as follows:

Collective Motivation = Prob $(P_i \rightarrow P_o) \times$ Prob $(P_o \rightarrow O_i)$

where
P_i = Performance of the individual
P_o = Performance of the organization
O_i = Outcomes for the individual.

In essence, Lawler's model reduces collective motivation to a question of individual welfare, relying on an expectancy formulation. It can be argued, however, that the model does not fully capture the collectively oriented form of motivation. Although there is no empirical research on the model, this formulation logically would be a weak predictor of cooperative acts, since one person can rarely affect the performance of an entire organization, and even if he or she could, the relationship between organizational performance and individual outcomes would be at best tenuous.

An alternative and perhaps more fruitful approach to collective motivation is to view cooperation as prosocial behavior (Puffer 1983, Staw 1984). Rather than building more elaborate hedonistic models to explain behaviors such as cooperation, service, and loyalty, they might be more parsimoniously described as altruistic acts toward the organization. Many individuals (especially managers and staff employees) are asked to perform or to make decisions on behalf of the organization in ways which are irrelevant (and sometimes even damaging) to their personal welfare, yet these prosocial behaviors are commonly performed. Therefore, recent research on altruism (e.g. Wispe 1978, Rushton & Sorrentino 1981) might best be integrated into a model of collective motivation, as follows:

Collective Motivation $=$ ID $\times$ Prob $(P_i \rightarrow O_o)$

where
ID $=$ Identification with the organization
P_i $=$ Performance of the individual
O_o $=$ Outcomes for the organization.

The altruistic model of collective motivation represents the situation in which employees identify with the organization and act in ways to improve its welfare. The model does not require the explicit linking of individual and organizational outcomes, but relies on an empathetic relationship between the person and collectivity. Although not specified directly, this equation is consistent with Ouchi's emphasis on long-term employment and strong socialization, since they may be two mechanisms by which organizational identification is built. The model is also consistent with many of the assumptions in Mowday et al's (1982) recent work on commitment, although they have mainly attempted to predict turnover rather than prosocial behaviors within organizations.

At present, while collectively oriented behavior is frequently lauded as vital to organizational effectiveness, almost no research or theory has squarely addressed the issue. There needs to be research on the two models presented here as well as competing formulations of this potentially important side of motivation.

OTHER DEPENDENT VARIABLES

Although research on traditional variables such as job satisfaction, absenteeism, turnover, and performance can be faulted for being rather narrow, it is, as I have noted, possible to reformulate many of these older research topics into more vital questions. The investigation of organizational outcomes should not stop with these four dependent variables, however. Other variables may be of interest to individual participants in an organization and the general public as well as management. Though the list of additional outcome variables is potentially large, only three will be considered in this review. Job stress and dissent will be considered primarily because of their importance to individual employees, while creativity and innovation will be addressed as a contributor to organizational welfare.

Job Stress

Within the last 5 years there has been a burgeoning of research interest in job stress and an effort to specify its determinants. This rise of interest has paralleled the increase in stress research within social, cognitive, and clinical psychology. It has also resulted from a greater appreciation of the impact of work experiences on the mental and physical health of individuals, as opposed to the usual emphasis on the contributions of individuals to the organization (Katz & Kahn 1978, Kahn 1980).

Physical aspects of the work environment can be a common source of stress and result in an impairment of performance, accidents, and sheer personal discomfort. Physical factors such as noise, excess heat or cold, poor lighting, motion, and pollution have all been documented as potential stressors in the work environment which can adversely affect individual behavior (Poulton 1978, Ivancevich & Matteson 1980).

At the more psychological level the research becomes more confusing. Tasks which are monotonous or unchallenging have been identified as stressful (Gardell 1976), but so have jobs with substantial overload (Margolis et al 1974) as well as jobs with high degrees of role conflict and ambiguity (Kahn et al 1964). Likewise, jobs with little influence or participation have been associated with stress (French & Caplan 1972), whereas jobs with substantial responsibility for other people are found to be contributors to ulcers and hypertension (Cooper & Payne 1978). Finally, transitions in one's life have often been identified as major sources of stress (Holmes & Rahe 1967), but a well-documented study recently found job relocation not to be a stressful experience for most people (Brett 1982).

Some tentative conclusions might be drawn from this contradictory sample of research findings. First, it appears that almost any dissatisfying or negatively labeled work attribute can be associated statistically with stress, especially when work attributes as well as stress are both measured by a single questionnaire. Thus, greater confidence must be placed in studies which measure job characteristics and symptoms of stress in an objective manner (e.g. Caplan 1971) than in studies which rely on self-reports of both working conditions and stress. If we have learned anything from the information processing perspective (Salancik & Pfeffer 1978), it is that working conditions and individuals' reactions to them may be reported in ways that are consistent and make as much sense to the respondent as the researcher. A second conclusion that can be drawn from stress research is that the antecedents of stress and how they affect health outcomes are likely to be complex and moderated processes rather than a set of simple, direct relationships. Recent research (e.g. Seers et al 1983) showing the importance of social support of peers, supervisors, and subordinates on the effects of stress is one example. Another is Karasek's (1979; Karasek et al 1981) work showing reports of stress (and coronary heart disease) to be a joint function of high job demands and low decision latitude. A third conclusion is that we should expect the potential stressors of the work setting to impact individuals differently. Kobasa (1979; Kobasa, Maddi & Kahn 1982) has identified individuals who are hardy or resistent to stress, while Lazarus (1981; Lazarus & Folkman 1982) has concentrated on how individuals differ in their coping strategies.

Because of the many contradictions and complexities in individual reactions to stress, research in this area is still at a preliminary stage. Sources of stress, aside from the most physical of working conditions (e.g. noise, heat, crowding), are often difficult to understand and to reduce in an objective way. Those features which make jobs interesting, important, and meaningful, for exmaple appear to be quite similar to those which induce stress. It would therefore seem that the study of coping strategies (both physical and psychological) will hold the greatest promise for future research. Understanding how people can manage the stresses inherent in jobs will probably prove to be more important than changing the job itself. This may be especially true as the managerial component of jobs increase, with the resolution of conflict and ambiguity becoming the most essential parts of organizational work roles.

Dissent and Whistleblowing

Unlike the study of job stress, research on dissent and whistleblowing has not yet been integrated into a unified stream of research or even a recognized concern for the field. This is not to say that either the public or employees of organizations find the topic unimportant. Newspaper articles and television have made the public increasingly aware of the possibility of illegal or morally questionable practices by both public and private organizations. Individual employees have likewise become increasingly aware of their employment rights and grievance procedures (Aram & Salipante 1981) as well as their responsibility to dissent from certain policies or practices of organizations (Graham 1983).

Although organizational dissent is potentially an extremely wide topic, ranging from interpersonal role negotiations (Graen 1976) to system-wide upheavals (Zald & Berger 1978), much of the recent interest has centered on whistelblowing. From the individual's point of view, whistleblowing may sometimes be the only viable way to contest the organization's demands, providing an important source of individual freedom. From the organization's point of view, whistleblowing can be extremely threatening if negative information is brought to the outside media. However, when whistleblowing occurs within a single organization (e.g. divulging ills to a larger branch of government or corporate headquarters), it can be viewed as an extraordinarily loyal act. Federal legislation now protects whistleblowers, although reprisals to individuals by their supervisors and employing subunits still appear to be very common.

Recent work on whistleblowing has been primarily descriptive and philosophical. Discussions of the history of whistleblowing and its relation to business ethics can be found in Weinstein (1979) and Westin (1981). A recent case study of whistleblowing at BART (Bay Area Rapid Transit System) showed the decision to take grievances to the public depended on the perception of mutual support among dissenting employees as well as the view that management would resist change (Perrucci et al 1980). A recent survey of people who filed employment discrimination charges investigated a number of determinants of retaliation against whistleblowers (Parmerlee et al 1982). Parmerlee et al found that organizations were more likely to retaliate against whistleblowers who were highly valued by the organization, perhaps because of their potential threat to organizational interests, but retaliation was also concentrated on those who were vulnerable to counterattack—those who lacked public support for their charges. Finally, a large-scale survey of over 8000 government workers found that while 45% of all employees have witnessed gross mismanagement of funds or illegal practices, 70% have not reported these acts to supervisors or other governmental authorities. The perception of inaction by the government rather than a fear of reprisal was cited by most respondents as the source of their silence (Office of Merit Systems Review and Studies, 1981).

Although whistleblowing has attracted recent attention, it could be viewed as only the last recourse an employee has in dissenting from organizational policies and practices. If, for example, we consider individual freedom as an important organizational outcome, various forms of participation and governance can be viewed as ends in themselves. Along these lines, Strauss (1982) recently reviewed forms of worker participation, not as simple determinants of worker satisfaction or productivity (e.g. Locke & Schweiger 1979), but as means of serving norms of democracy and ways of developing a social consensus for decisions. Further work on the role of dissent and freedom in organizational governance should therefore be encouraged. Of course, there should also be future research on the relationship between dissent and outcomes received by the organization. Dissent might, for example, actually improve organizational performance by contributing to the thoroughness of decision making, if the recent research on minority influence (Nemeth 1979, Nemeth & Wachtler 1983) can be generalized to organizational settings. Internal dissent might also provide the capability for organizations to adapt to changing environmental conditions (Weick 1979a), although no empirical research has yet been conducted on this issue.

Creativity and Innovation

While research on job stress and dissent addresses important individual concerns with employment by organizations, work on creativity and innovation may in the future become increasingly important from the organization's point of view. As a greater percentage of work becomes highly skilled and professionalized, the criteria of performance will likely become more ambiguous and subject to change. Therefore, questions of productivity may become translated into inquiries about working smarter rather than harder. These tendencies will probably be compounded in situations where markets are rapidly changing or competition is fierce, such that innovation in these environments may become the organization's most important outcome variable.

At the individual level, there is a long stream of research on creativity, much of which is devoted to measurement issues and the relationship between creativity, intelligence, and various personality indices (see Barron & Harrington 1981 for a review). There is less work on the effect of external conditions such as supervision, job demands, and resources on creative behavior, but the literature is still substantial (e.g. Tushman 1977, Kohn & Schooler 1978, Basadur et al 1982). Unfortunately, most organizational research concentrates on the management of scientists and engineers (e.g. Allen 1977, Allen et al 1980) rather than upon ways to bring innovation into the production and general administration of the organization. Measures of originality and creative role making (Graen 1976) would therefore be useful additions to the measurement of individual performance in organizations, since determinants of efficient role behavior (e.g. quantity and quality) may be far different from the creative aspects of a role. The communality and possible trade-offs of these two sides of performance need to be addressed.

At the group level, there has been work on group composition and tenure upon the creative productivity of R&D groups (Katz 1982), structural dimensions of groups and group tasks which may impede the introduction of new ideas (Katz & Tushman 1979), and procedures for increasing group creativity (Maier 1970). Recent research on the effect of minority influence on the origination of new ideas (Nemeth & Wachtler 1983) and the effect of institutionalization upon conformity (Zucker 1977, 1981) are also noteworthy developments. However, little research has yet related group creativity to collective adaptation to new environmental conditions.

At the organizational level, literature ranges from population ecology research on the effect of environments on the life and death of organizations (Hannan & Freeman 1977, Aldrich & Mueller 1982, Freeman 1982) to the structural dimensions of organizations associated with innovativeness (Hedberg et al 1976, Galbraith 1977, Tushman 1977). Seldom are group or individual perspectives integrated into questions of organizational innovation or adaptation to new environments. One exception may be the recent theoretical work on organizational crises which merges individual reactions to threatening events with organizational responses to change (e.g. Billings et al 1980, Meyer 1982). A second exception may be the study of the escalation of commitment, in which rigidities in individual decision making are posited to account for (but not yet empirically linked to) organizational failures in adapting to changing environmental conditions (Tegar 1980, Staw 1982).

What is sorely needed at the present time are empirical studies which bridge the gap between research on individual and group creativity and organizational innovation. One step that has already been taken is the drawing of theoretical analogies in learning and flexibility in behavior across multiple levels of analysis (e.g. Duncan & Weiss 1979, Staw et al 1981). However, the more significant and difficult work that needs to be undertaken is the examination of how individual, group, and organizational factors interact to make an organization creative.

CONCLUSIONS

This review has concentrated on the four most traditional dependent variables, emphasizing where research has been and where it could potentially go in each of these major subareas. Since research has been rather stable (even stagnant) on each of these organizational outcomes, I have emphasized ways to transform these variables into more interesting (or at least newer) theoretical questions. In my view, work on job satisfaction may be transformed into the study of affective mood and disposition as well as an inquiry into the functions of dissatisfaction. From absenteeism research one can derive a more detailed study of physical presence in organizations. From turnover research, there is already a trend toward examining the consequences of turnover and organizational demography. And, from work on motivation and performance there are emergent efforts to specify the type of behavior needed in organizations as well as nonhedonistic predictors of performance. Thus, from the narrow range of variables encompassing much of current micro organizational behavior, it is possible to move toward a more fundamental stream of work within each of the traditional outcome variables. It is also possible to expand the list of outcomes beyond short-term managerial concerns, as shown by the more recent work on stress, dissent, and innovation.

Outcome vs Process in Organizational Research

While this review has strictly followed on outcome approach to organizational research, it could be argued that processes are more important or fundamental. If understanding organizational functioning is the goal, then perhaps problems should not be defined by the management of firms, their employees, or even the general public. Research on organizations should, by this argument, follow theoretically derived questions rather than study either traditional outcome variables (e.g. job performance) or established organizational functions (e.g. pay systems, selection, and training).

Theoretical analyses of organizational processes have appeared in greater numbers in recent years. Pfeffer (1982) has, for example, reviewed most of the major theoretical approaches to both individual and organizational behavior. And, in terms of specific theoretical processes, conceptual reviews have been published on topics such as socialization (Van Maanen & Schein 1979), information processing (O'Reilly 1983), decision making (Bass 1983), symbolism (Pfeffer 1981), justification (Staw 1980), time (McGrath & Rotchford 1983), and power (Pfeffer 1981, Porter et al 1981). At present, one of the "hottest" areas of research concerns the notion of organizational culture—whether it exists, how to measure it, its relation to organizational practices, and its possible contribution to organizational effectiveness (e.g. Deal & Kennedy 1982, Martin 1982, Louis 1983, Pondy et al 1983).

While theory-driven research is a necessary ingredient to our understanding of organizations, organizational researchers have had difficulty in sustaining interest in models that do not explain at least some variance in outcomes. Research on causal attribution, leadership, and group decision making are just a few of the areas that have declined because of this problem, and studies of organizational culture may be a future casualty [e.g. Martin et al (1983) found measures of culture to be unrelated to corporate performance]. Therefore, it may be advisable to bring multiple theories to bear on recognizably important problems rather than to frame organizational research around the testing of broad theoretical models. With the outcome approach, fundamental research would consist of middle-range theories that are capable of predicting specific outcomes, with processes and models organized around the type of outcome being examined. This approach would differ substantially from the usual practice of studying organizational processes across organizational outcomes or the testing of more general theoretical frameworks. It would also differ from the common practice of predicting outcomes by the atheoretical listing of correlates derived from empirical research.

From Method to Interdisciplinary Theory

As I noted at the outset of this review, the micro side of organizational behavior historically has not been strong on theory. Organizational psychologists have been more concerned with research methodology, perhaps because of the emphasis upon measurement issues in personnel selection and evaluation. As an example of this methodological bent, the I/O Psychology division of the American Psychological Association, when confronted recently with the task of improving the field's research, formulated the problem as one of deficiency in methodology rather than theory construction. An advisory group was formed and an excellent series of books have now been produced on innovations in methodology (Campbell et al 1982, Hakel et al 1982, Hunter et al 1982, James et al 1982, McGrath et al 1982, Van Maanen et al 1982).

It is now time to provide equal consideration to theory formulation. Of particular concern might be ways to integrate micro and macro organizational research on specific organizational problems or outcomes. Rather than arguing whether psychological or sociological constructs in general explain greater variance, there needs to be greater thinking and research on how to bring the sides of the field together in explaining specific outcomes. One means of interdisciplinary research would be to dissect sociological constructs or to specify their intermediate mechanisms in psychological terms (e.g. Collins 1981). At present, sociologists find this threatening since it seemingly denies the macro level of analysis (e.g. Mayhew 1980, 1981). Actually, it should be no more threatening or less useful than the common practice of aggregating individual perceptions and attitudes into more global variables such as organizational climate or culture.

A second and perhaps more fruitful means of interdisciplinary research are studies that cross levels of analysis. The best developed of such research ventures are studies of the effect of organizational structure on individual attitudes and behavior (see Berger & Cummings 1979 for a review). Another example might be research on the effect of individual leadership style or the succession of leaders upon organizational effectiveness (e.g. Chandler 1969). To date, however, most of our efforts have been theoretical attempts to draw analogies between individual and organizational behavior or to speculate on the interplay between individual and organizational variables. For example, Hall & Fukami (1979) have discussed the relation between organizational design and individual learning; Weick (1979a) frequently has drawn analogies from individual cognition to organizational action; and Staw et al (1981) have reviewed the evidence or parallels between individual, group, and organizational reactions to threat. A summary of this literature as well as a thoughtful analysis of the problems and the possibilities for research to cross levels of analysis can be found in Rousseau (1983).

In my view, probably the best current candidate for progress in integrating micro and macro research is the examination of organizational innovation. Adaptation and flexibility are often mentioned as some of the most important criteria of organizational effectiveness (Steers 1977), and there is now widespread recognition of the problems of organizational growth as well as survival. A multilevel theory, which extends across the boundaries of psychological and sociological research, would therefore provide a valuable model for understanding how we can develop fundamental (and interdisciplinary) theory on organizational outcomes. Although multilevel research is fraught with methodological and conceptual difficulties (Roberts et al 1978), it is, I would argue, where the future of the field lies.

ACKNOWLEDGMENTS

This work was supported by a Faculty Research Grant and by the Institute of Industrial Relations at the University of California, Berkeley. Pamela McKechnie provided valuable help in gathering materials for this review, while both Josef Chytry and Pat Murphy worked tirelessly in typing various versions of the manuscript.

Literature Cited

Adams, J. S. 1965. Inequity in social exchange. *Adv. Exp. Soc. Psychol.* 2:267–99

Adams, J. S., Rosenbaum, W. B. 1962. The relationship of worker productivity to cognitive dissonance about wage inequities. *J. Appl. Psychol.* 46:161–64

Aldag, R. J., Barr, S. H., Brief, A. P. 1981. Measurement of perceived task characteristics. *Psychol. Bull.* 90:415–31

Alderfer, C. P. 1972. *Human Needs in Organizational Settings.* Free press

Aldrich, H., Mueller, S. 1982. The evolution of organizational forms: Technology, coordination, and control. In *Research in Organizational Behavior,* Vol. 4, ed. B. M. Staw, L. L. Cummings. Greenwich, Conn.: JAI Press

Allen, T. 1977. *Managing the Flow of Technology.* Cambridge, Mass: MIT Press

Allen, T., Lee, D., Tushman, M. 1980. R&D performance as a function of internal communication, project management, and the nature of work. *IEEE Trans. Eng. Manage.* 27:2–12

Appley, M. H., ed. 1971. *Adaptation-Level Theory: A Symposium.* New York: Academic

Aram, J. D., Salipante, P. E. 1981. An evaluation of organizational due process in the resolution of employee conflict. *Acad. Manage. Rev.* 6:197–206

Argyris, C. 1976. Problems and new directions for industrial psychology. In *Handbook of Industrial and Organizational Psychology,* ed. M. Dunnette. Chicago: Rand-McNally

Arnold, H., Feldman, D. 1982. A multivariate analysis of the determinants of job turnover. *J. Appl. Psychol.* 67:350–60

Austin, W., McGinn, N., Susmilch, C. 1980. Internal standards revisited: Effects of social comparisons and expectancies of judgements of fairness and satisfaction, *J. Exp. Soc. Psychol.* 16:426–41

Bandura, A. 1977. Self-efficacy: Toward a unifying theory of behavioral change. *Psychol. Rev.* 84:191–215

Barron, F., Harrington, D. M. 1981. Creativity, intelligence, and personality. *Ann. Rev. Psychol.* 32:439–76

Basadur, M., Graen, G., Green, S. 1982. Training in creative problem solving: Effects on education and problem finding and solving in an industrial research organization. *Organ. Behav. Hum. Perform.* 30:41–70

Bass, B. M. 1983. *Organizational Decision Making.* Homewood, Ill: Irwin

Becker, F. D. 1981. *Workspace: Creating Environments in Organizations.* New York: Praeger

Berger, C. J., Cummings, L. L. 1979. Organizational structure, attitudes, and behaviors. In *Research in Organizational Behavior,* Vol. 1, ed. B. M. Staw. Greenwich, Conn.: JAI Press

Bernstein, M., Crosby, F. 1980. An empirical examination of relative deprivation theory. *J. Exp. Soc. Psychol.* 16:442–56

Billings, R. S., Milburn, T. W., Schaalman, M. L. 1980. A model of crisis perception: A theoretical and empirical analysis. *Adm. Sci. Q.* 25:300–16

Boal, K. B., Cummings, L. L. 1981. Cognitive evaluation theory: An experimental test of processes and outcomes. *Organ. Behav. Hum. Perform.* 28:289–310

Bower, G. H. 1981. Mood and memory. *Am. Psychol.* 36:129–48

Braverman, H. 1974. *Labor and Monopoly Capital: The Degradation of Work in the Twentieth Century.* New York: Monthly Rev. Press

Brett, J. M. 1982. Job transfer and well-being. *J. Appl. Psychol.* 67:450–63

Brown, M. C. 1982. Administrative succession and organizational performance: The succession effect. *Adm. Sci. Q.* 27:1–16

Caldwell, D. F., O'Reilly, C. A., Staw, B. M. 1983. The effects of moods on task perception. Sch. Bus. Adm., Univ. Santa Clara. Unpublished manuscript

Campbell, A., Converse, P. E., Rogers, W. L. 1976. *The Quality of American Life: Perceptions, Evaluations, and Satisfaction.* New York: Sage

Campbell, J. P., Daft, R. L., Hulin, C. L. 1982. *What to Study: Generating and Developing Research Questions.* Beverly Hills, Calif.: Sage

Caplan, R. D. 1971. *Organizational stress and individual strain: A socio-psychological study of risk factors in coronary heart disease among administrators, engineers, and scientists.* PhD thesis, Univ. Michigan, Ann Arbor; *Diss. Abstr. Int.* 1972, 32:6706b–6707b; Univ. Microfilms, 72–14822

Chadwick-Jones, J. K., Brown, C. A., Nicholson, N. 1973. A-type and B-type absence: Empirical trends for women employees. *Occup. Psychol.* 47:75–86

Chandler, A. D. 1969. *Strategy and Structure: Chapters in the History of Industrial Enterprise.* Cambridge, Mass.: MIT Press

Cole, R. E. 1979. *Work, Mobility and Participation.* Berkeley: Univ. Calif. Press

Collins, R. 1981. On the microfoundations of macrosociology. *Am. J. Sociol.* 86:984–1014

Connolly, T. 1977. Information processing and decision making in organizations. In *New Directions in Organizational Behav-*

ior, ed. B. M. Staw, G. Salancik. New York: Wiley

Cooper, C., Payne, R. 1978. *Stress at Work*. London: Wiley

Crosby, F. 1976. A model of egotistical relative deprivation. *Psychol. Rev.* 83:85–113

Crosby, F. 1984. Relative deprivation in organizational settings. In *Research in Organizational Behavior*, Vol. 6, ed. B. M. Staw, L. L. Cummings. Greenwich, Conn: JAI Press. In press

Cummings, L. L. 1982. Organizational behavior. *Ann. Rev. Psychol.* 33:541–79

Dalton, D. R., Krackhardt, D. M., Porter, L. W. 1981. Functional turnover: An empirical assessment. *J. Appl. Psychol.* 66:716–21

Dalton, D. R., Todor, W. D. 1979. Turnover turned over: An expanded and positive perspective. *Acad. Manage. Rev.* 4:225–35

Deal, T. E., Kennedy, A. A. 1982. *Corporate Cultures*. Reading, Mass.: Addison-Wesley

Deci, E. L. 1971. The effects of externally mediated rewards and controls on intrinsic motivation. *J. Pers. Soc. Psychol.* 18:105–15

Deci, E. L., Ryan, R. 1980. The empirical exploration of intrinsic motivational processes. *Adv. Exp. Soc. Psychol.*, pp. 39–80

Duncan, R., Weiss, A. 1979. Organizational design and adult learning. See Berger & Cummings 1979

Epstein, S. 1979. The stability of behavior: 1. On predicting most of the people much of the time. *J. Pers. Soc. Psychol.* 37:1097–1126

Fazio, R. H., Zanna, M. P. 1981. Direct experience and attitude-behavior consistency. *Adv. Exp. Soc. Psychol.* 14:161–202

Feldman, D. C., Arnold, H. J. 1983. *Managing Individual and Group Behavior in Organizations*. New York: McGraw-Hill

Freeman, J. 1982. Organizational life cycles and natural selection processes. See Aldrich & Mueller 1982

French, J. R. P., Caplan, R. D. 1972. Organizational stress and individual strain. In *The Failure of Success*, ed. A. J. Morrow. New York: AMACOM

Galbraith, J. 1977. *Organizational Design*. Reading, Mass: Addison-Wesley

Gamson, W. A., Scotch, N. 1964. Scapegoating in baseball. *Am. J. Sociol.* 70:69–76

Gardell, B. 1976. Arbetsinnehall och livskvalitet. Prisma, Stockholm (cited in D. Katz & R. Kahn 1978)

Garrison, K. R., Michinsky, P. M. 1977. Evaluating the concept of absentee-proneness with two measures of absence. *Personnel Psychol.* 30:389–93

Gibbons, F. X., Wicklund, R. A. 1982. Self-focused attention and helping behavior. *J. Pers. Soc. Psychol.* 43:462–74

Golembiewski, R. T., Proehl, C. W. 1978. A survey of the empirical literature on flexible work hours: Characteristics and consequences of a major innovation. *Acad. Manage. Rev.* 3:837–53

Goodman, P. S. 1974. An examination of referents used in the evaluation of pay. *Organ. Behav. Hum. Perform.* 12:170–95

Goodman, P. S. 1977. Social comparison processes in organizations. See Connolly 1977

Goodman, P. S., Friedman, A. 1971. An examination of Adams' theory of inequity. *Adm. Sci. Q.* 16:271–88

Graen, G. B. 1976. Role-making processes within complex organizations. See Argyris 1976

Graen, G. B., Ginsburgh, S. 1977. Job resignation as a function of role orientation and leader acceptance: A longitudinal investigation of organization assimilation. *Organ. Behav. Hum. Perform.* 19:1–17

Graham, J. W. 1983. Principled organizational dissent. Dep. Organ. Behav., Grad. Sch. Manage., Northwestern Univ., Evanston, Ill. Unpublished paper

Griffin, R. W. 1983. Objective and social sources of information in task redesign: A field experiment. *Adm. Sci. Q.* 28:184–200

Gustafson, H. W. 1982. Force-loss cost analysis. Appendix of W. Mobley, *Employee Turnover: Causes, Consequences, and Control*. Reading, Mass: Addison-Wesley

Hackman, J. R., Lawler, E. E. III. 1971. Employee reactions to job characteristics. *J. Appl. Psychol. Monogr.* 55:259–86

Hackman, J. R., Oldham, G. R. 1976. Motivation through the design of work: Test of a theory. *Organ. Behav. Hum. Perform.* 16:250–79

Hackman, J. R., Oldham, G. R. 1980. *Work Redesign*. Reading, Mass: Addison-Wesley

Hakel, M. D., Sorcher, M., Beer, M., Moses, J. L. 1982. *Making it Happen: Designing Research with Implementation in Mind*. Beverly Hills, Calif: Sage

Hall, D. T., Fukami, C. V. 1979. Organizational design and adult learning. See Berger & Cummings 1979

Hamner, W. C. 1974. Reinforcement theory and contingency management in organizational settings. In *Organizational Behavior and Management: A Contingency Approach*, ed. H. L. Tosi, W. C. Hamner. Chicago: St. Clair Press

Hamner, W. C., Hamner, E. P. 1976. Behavior modification on the bottom line. *Organ. Dyn.* 4:3–21

Hannan, M. T., Freeman, J. 1977. The population ecology of organizations. *Am. J. Sociol.* 82:929–64

Hedberg, B. L. T., Nystrom, P. C., Starbuck, W. H. 1976. Camping on seesaws: Prescriptions for a self-designing organization. *Adm. Sci. Q.* 21:41–65

Herzberg, F., Mausner, B., Snyderman, B.

1959. *The Motivation To Work*. New York: Wiley

Holmes, T. H., Rahe, R. H. 1967. The social readjustment rating scale. *J. Psychosom. Res.* 11:213–18

Hunter, J. E., Schmidt, F. L., Jackson, G. B. 1982. *Meta-analysis: Cumulating Research Findings Across Studies*. Beverly Hills, Calif: Sage

Ilgen, D. R. 1971. Satisfaction with performance as a function of the initial level of expected performance and the deviation from expectations. *Organ. Behav. Hum. Perform.* 6:345–61

Ivancevich, J. M., Matteson, M. T. 1980. *Stress and Work*. Glenview, Ill: Scott, Foresman

James, L. R., Mulaik, S., Brett, J. M. 1982. *Causal Analysis: Assumptions, Models, and Data*. Beverly Hills, Calif: Sage

Jenkins, G. D., Lawler, E. E. III. 1981. Impact of employee participation in pay plan development. *Organ. Behav. Hum. Perform.* 28:111–28

Johns, G., Nicholson, N. 1982. The meaning of absence: New strategies for theory and research. See Aldrich & Mueller 1982

Kabanoff, B. 1980. Work and nonwork: A review of models, methods, and findings. *Psychol. Bull.* 88:60–77

Kahn, R. L. 1980. *Work and Health*. New York: Wiley-Interscience

Kahn, R. L., Wolfe, D. M., Quinn, R. P., Snock, J. D., Rosenthal, R. A. 1964. *Organizational Stress: Studies in Role Conflict and Ambiguity*. New York: Wiley

Karasek, R. A. 1979. Job demands, job decision latitude, and mental strain: Implications for job redesign. *Adm. Sci. Q.* 29:285–307

Karasek, R. A., Baker, D., Marxer, F., Ahlbom, A., Theorell, T. 1981. Job decision latitude, job demands, and cardiovascular disease: A prospective study of Swedish men. *Am. J. Public Health* 71:694–705

Karmel, B. 1980. *Point and Counterpoint in Organizational Behavior*. Hinsdale, Ill: Dryden

Katerberg, R., Blau, G. J. 1983. An examination of level and direction of effort and job performance. *Acad. Manage. J.* 26:249–57

Katz, D., Kahn, R. L. 1978. *The Social Psychology of Organizations*. New York: Wiley 2nd ed.

Katz, R. 1982. The effects of group longevity on project communication and performance. *Adm. Sci. Q.* 27:81–104

Katz, R., Tushman, M. 1979. Communication patterns, project performance, and task characteristics: An empirical evaluation and integration in an R&D setting. *Organ. Behav. Hum. Perform.* 23:139–62

Kerr, S. 1975. On the folly of rewarding A,

while hoping for B. *Acad. Manage. J.* 18:769–83

Kobasa, S. C. 1979. Stressful life events, personality, and health: An inquiry into hardiness. *J. Pers. Soc. Psychol.* 37:1–11

Kobasa, S. C., Maddi, S. R., Kahn, S. 1982. Hardiness and health: A prospective study. *J. Pers. Soc. Psychol.* 42:168–77

Kohn, M. L., Schooler, C. 1978. The reciprocal effects of the substantive complexity of work and intellectual flexibility: A longitudinal assessment. *Am. J. Sociol.* 84:25–53

Komaki, J. 1981. A behavioral view of paradigm debates: Let the data speak. *J. Appl. Psychol.* 66:111–12

Komaki, J., Barwick, K. D., Scott, L. R. 1978. A behavioral approach to occupational safety: Pinpointing and reinforcing safe performance in a food manufacturing plant. *J. Appl. Psychol.* 63:434–45

Komaki, J., Heinzmann, A. T., Lawson, L. 1980. Effect of training and feedback: Component analysis of a behavioral safety program. *J. Appl. Psychol.* 65:261–70

Kunin, T. 1955. The construction of a new type of attitude measures. *Personnel Psychol.* 8:65–78

Langer, E. J. 1978. Rethinking the role of thought in social interaction. In *New Directions in Attribution Research*, ed. J. Harvey, W. Ickes, R. Kidd, 2:35–58. Hillsdale, NJ: Erlbaum

Latham, G. P., Cummings, L. L., Mitchell, T. R. 1981. Behavioral strategies to improve productivity. *Organ. Dyn.*, Winter, pp. 5–23

Lawler, E. E. III. 1973. *Motivation in Work Organizations*. Monterey, Calif: Brooks/Cole

Lawler, E. E. III. 1981. *Pay and Organization Development*. Reading, Mass: Addison-Wesley

Lawler, E. E. III. 1982. Increasing worker involvement to enhance organizational effectiveness. In *Change in Organizations*, ed. P. S. Goodman. San Francisco: Jossey-Bass

Lazarus, R. S. 1981. The stress and coping paradigm. In *Models for Clinical Psychological Pathology*, ed. C. Eisdorfer, D. Cohen, A. Kleinman, P. Maxim, pp. 177–214. New York: Spectrum

Lazarus, R. S., Folkman, S. 1982. Coping and adaptation. In *The Handbook of Behavioral Medicine*, ed. W. D. Gentry. New York: Guilford

Lepper, M. R., Greene, D., Nisbett, R. E. 1973. Undermining children's intrinsic interest with extrinsic rewards: A test of the "overjustification" hypothesis. *J. Pers. Soc. Psychol.* 42:51–65

Locke, E. A. 1976. The nature and causes of job satisfaction. See Argyris 1976

Locke, E. A. 1980. Latham versus Komaki: A

tale of two paradigms. *J. Appl. Psychol.* 65:16–23

Locke, E. A., Schweiger, D. M. 1979. Participation in decision-making: One more look. See Berger & Cummings 1979

Locke, E. A., Shaw, K. N., Saari, L. M., Latham, G. P. 1981. Goal setting and task performance: 1969–1980. *Psychol. Bull.* 90:125–52

Louis, M. 1983. Prerequisites for fruitful research on organizational culture. Sloan Sch. Manage. MIT, Boston. Unpublished manuscript

Macy, B. A., Mirvis, P. H. 1983. Assessing rates and costs of individual work behaviors. In *Assessing Organizational Change*, ed. S. Seashore, E. Lawler, P. Mirvis, C. Cammann. New York: Wiley-Interscience

Maier, N. R. F., ed. 1970. *Problem Solving and Creativity in Individuals and Groups.* Belmont, Calif: Brooks/Cole

March, J., Simon, H. A. 1958. *Organizations.* New York: Wiley

Margolis, B. L., Kroes, W. M., Quinn, R. P. 1974. Job stress: An unlisted occupational hazard. *J. Occup. Med.* 16:659–61

Martin, J. 1981. Relative deprivation: A theory of distributive justice in an era of shrinking resources. In *Research in Organizational Behavior*, Vol. 3, ed. L. L. Cummings, B. M. Staw. Greenwich, Conn: JAI Press

Martin, J. 1982. Stories and scripts in organizational settings. In *Cognitive Social Psychology*, ed. A. Hastorf, A. Isen. New York: Elsevier-North Holland

Martin, J., Anterasian, C., Siehl, C. 1983. Values, strategies, and financial performance in the Fortune 500. Grad. Sch. Bus., Stanford Univ., Stanford, Calif. Unpublished manuscript

Maslow, A. H. 1954. *Motivation and Personality.* New York: Harper

Mayhew, B. H. 1980. Structuralism versus individualism: Part I. Shadowboxing in the dark. *Soc. Forces* 59:335–75

Mayhew, B. H. 1981. Structuralism versus individualism: Part II. Ideological and other obfuscations. *Soc. Forces* 59:627–48

McAllister, D. W., Mitchell, T. R., Beach, L. R. 1979. The contingency model for the selection of decision strategies: An empirical test of the effects of significance, accountability, and reversibility. *Organ. Behav. Hum. Perform.* 24:228–44

McCain, B. R., O'Reilly, C. A., Pfeffer, J. 1984. The effects of departmental demography on turnover: The case of a university. *Acad. Manage. J.* In press

McGrath, J. E., Martin, J., Kulka, R. A. 1982. *Judgement Calls in Research.* Beverly Hills, Calif: Sage

McGrath, J. E., Rotchford, N. L. 1983. Time and organizational behavior. In *Research in*

Organizational Behavior, Vol. 5, ed. L. L. Cummings, B. M. Staw. Greenwich, Conn: JAI Press

Meyer, A. D. 1982. Adapting to environmental jolts. *Adm. Sci. Q.* 27:515–37

Miller, H., Katerberg, R., Hulin, C. 1979. Evaluation of the Mobley, Home, and Hollingsworth model of employee turnover. *J. Appl. Psychol.* 64:509–17

Mirvis, P. H., Lawler, E. E. III. 1977. Measuring the financial impact of employee attitudes. *J. Appl. Psychol.* 62:1–8

Mitchell, T. R. 1979. Organizational behavior. *Ann. Rev. Psychol.* 30:243–81

Mobley, W. H. 1977. Intermediate linkages in the relationship between job satisfaction and employee turnover. *J. Appl. Psychol.* 62: 237–40

Mobley, W. H. 1982. *Employee Turnover: Causes, Consequences, and Control.* Reading, Mass: Addison-Wesley

Mobley, W. H., Horner, S., Hollingsworth, A. 1978. An evaluation of the precursors of hospital employee turnover. *J. Appl. Psychol.* 63:408–14

Morgan, L. G., Herman, J. B. 1976. Perceived consequences of absenteeism. *J. Appl. Psychol.* 61:738–42

Mowday, R. T. 1981. Viewing turnover from the perspective of those who remain: The relationship of job attitudes to attributions of the causes of turnover. *J. Appl. Psychol.* 66:120–23

Mowday, R. T., Porter, L. W., Steers, R. M. 1982. *Employee—Organization linkages.* New York: Academic

Narayanan, V. K., Nath, R. 1982. A field test of some attitudinal and behavioral consequences of flextime. *J. Appl. Psychol.* 67:214–18

Naylor, C., Pritchard, R. D., Ilgen, D. R. 1980. *A Theory of Behavior in Organizations.* New York: Academic

Nemeth, C. J. 1979. The role of an active minority in intergroup relations. In *The Psychology of Intergroup Relations*, ed. W. Austin, S. Worchel, pp. 225–36. Belmont, Calif: Brooks/Cole

Nemeth, C. J., Wachtler, J. 1983. Creative problem solving as a result of majority vs. minority influence. *Eur. J. Soc. Psychol.* 13:45–55

Nicholson, N., Goodge, P. M. 1976. The influence of social, organizational, and biographical factors on female absence. *J. Manage. Stud.* 13:234–54

Nisbett, R. E., Ross, L. 1980. *Human Inference: Strategies and Shortcomings of Social Judgement.* Englewood Cliffs, NJ: Prentice-Hall

Notz, W. W., Staw, B. M., Cook, T. D. 1971. Attitude toward troop withdrawal from Indochina as a function of draft number: Dissonance or self-interest? *J. Pers. Soc. Psychol.* 20:118–26

Office of Merit Systems Review and Studies. 1981. *Whistleblowing and the Federal Employee.* Washington DC: GPO

Oldham, G. R., Hackman, J. R. 1980. Work design in the organizational context. In *Research in Organizational Behavior,* Vol. 2, ed. B. M. Staw, L. L. Cummings. Greenwich, Conn: JAI Press

O'Reilly, C. A. 1983. The use of information in organizational decision making: A model and some propositions. See McGrath & Rotchford 1983

O'Reilly, C. A., Caldwell, D. 1979. Informational influence as a determinant of perceived task characteristics and job satisfaction. *J. Appl. Psychol.* 64:157–65

Ouchi, W. G. 1981. *Theory Z: How American Business can meet the Japanese Challenge.* Reading, Mass: Addison-Wesley

Parmerlee, M. A., Near, J. P., Jensen, T. C. 1982. Correlates of whistle-blower's perceptions of organizational retaliation. *Adm. Sci. Q.* 27:17–34

Perrucci, R., Anderson, R. M., Schendel, D. E., Trachtman, L. E. 1980. Whistleblowing: Professionals' resistance to organizational authority. *Soc. Problems* 28:149–64

Pfeffer, J. 1981. Management as symbolic action: The creation and maintenance of organizational paradigms. See Martin 1981

Pfeffer, J. 1982. *Organizations and Organizational Theory.* Boston: Pitman

Pfeffer, J. 1983. Organizational demography. See McGrath & Rotchford 1983

Platt, J. Social traps. 1973. *Am. Psychol.* 28:641–51

Pondy, L., Frost, P., Morgan, G., Dandridge, T., eds. 1983. *Organizational Symbolism.* Greenwich, Conn: JAI Press

Porter, L. W. 1961. A study of perceived need satisfaction in bottom and middle management jobs. *J. Appl. Psychol.* 45:1–10

Porter, L. W., Allen, R. W., Angle, H. L. 1981. The politics of upward influence in organizations. See Martin 1981

Porter, L. W., Lawler, E. E. 1968. *Managerial Attitudes and Performance.* Homewood, Ill: Dorsey

Poulton, E. C. 1978. Blue collar stressors. In *Stress at Work,* ed. C. Cooper, R. Payne. New York: Wiley

Price, J. 1977. *The Study of Turnover.* Ames: Iowa State Univ. Press

Puffer, S. M. 1983. The effects of an altruistic motive on extra-role behavior in organizations. Sch. Bus. Adm., Univ. Calif., Berkeley. Unpublished manuscript

Quinn, R. P., Staines, G. L. 1979. *The 1977 Quality of Employment Survey.* Ann Arbor, Mich: Inst. Soc. Res.

Roberts, K. H., Glick, W. 1981. The job char-

acteristics approach to task design: A critical review. *J. Appl. Psychol.* 66:193–217

Roberts, K. H., Hulin, C. L., Rousseau, D. M. 1978. *Developing an Interdisciplinary Science of Organizations.* San Francisco: Jossey-Bass

Ronen, S. 1981. *Flexible Working Hours: An Innovation in the Quality of Work Life.* New York: McGraw-Hill

Rosenfield, D., Folger, R., Adelman, H. 1980. When rewards reflect competence: A qualification of the overjustification effect. *J. Pers. Soc. Psychol.* 39:368–76

Rousseau, D. M. 1978. Relationship of work to nonwork. *J. Appl. Psychol.* 63:513–17

Rousseau, D. M. 1984. Issues of level in organizational research: Multi-level and cross-level perspectives. In *Research in Organizational Behavior,* Vol. 7, ed. L. L. Cummings, B. M. Staw. Greenwich, Conn: JAI Press. In press

Rusbult, C. E., Farrell, D. 1983. A longitudinal test of the investment model: The impact on job satisfaction job commitment, and turnover of variations in rewards, costs, alternatives, and investments. *J. Appl. Psychol.* 68:429–38

Rushton, J. P., Sorrentino, R. M., eds. 1981. *Altruism and Helping Behavior.* Hillsdale, NJ: Erlbaum

Salancik, G. R., Conway, M. 1975. Attitude inferences from salient and relevant cognitive content about behavior. *J. Pers. Soc. Psychol.* 32:829–40

Salancik, G. R., Pfeffer, J. 1977. An examination of need satisfaction models of job attitudes. *Adm. Sci. Q.* 22:427–56

Salancik, G. R., Pfeffer, J. 1978. A social information processing approach to job attitudes and task design. *Adm. Sci. Q.* 23:224–53

Sandelands, L., Ashford, S. J., Dutton, J. E. 1983. Reconceptualizing the overjustification effect: A template matching approach. *Motivation and Emotion.* In press

Schein, E. H. 1981. Does Japanese management style have a message for American managers? *Sloan Manage. Rev.* Fall, pp. 55–68

Schwab, D. P., Cummings, L. L. 1970. Theories of performance and satisfaction: A review. *Ind. Relat.* 9:408–30

Scott, W. E. Jr. 1967. The development of semantic differential scales as measures of "morale." *Personnel Psychol.* 20:179–98

Seers, A., McGee, G. W., Serey, T. T., Graen, G. B. 1983. The interaction of job stress and social support: A strong inference investigation. *Acad. Manage. J.* 26:273–84

Smith, F. J. 1977. Work attitudes as predictors of attendance on a specific day. *J. Appl. Psychol.* 62:16–19

Smith, P. C., Kendall, L. M., Hulin, C. L.

1969. *The Measurement of Satisfaction in Work and Retirement.* Chicago: Rand McNally

Staw, B. M. 1977. Motivation in organizations: Toward synthesis and redirection. See Connolly 1977

Staw, B. M. 1980a. On dropping the "I" from *I/O psychology*. Presented at Am. Psychol. Assoc. Meet.

Staw, B. M. 1980b. The consequences of turnover. *J. Occup. Behav.* 1:253–73

Staw, B. M. 1982. Counterforces to change: Escalation and commitment as sources of administrative inflexibility. In *Change in Organizations,* ed. P. S. Goodman. San Francisco: Jossey-Bass

Staw, B. M. 1983. Motivation research versus the art of faculty management. *Rev. Higher Educ.* In press

Staw, B. M., Calder, B. J., Hess, R. 1980. Intrinsic motivation and norms about payment. *J. Pers.* 48:1–14

Staw, B. M., Notz, W. W., Cook, T. D. 1974. Vulnerability to the draft and attitudes toward troop withdrawal from Indochina: Replication and refinement. *Psychol. Rep.* 34:407–17

Staw, B. M., Oldham, G. R. 1978. Reconsidering our dependent variables: A critique and empirical study. *Acad. Manage. J.* 21:539–59

Staw, B. M., Ross, J. 1983. Job attitude as a stable individual characteristic. Sch. Bus. Adm., Univ. Calif., Berkeley. Unpublished manuscript

Staw, B. M., Sandelands, L. E., Dutton, J. E. 1981. Threat-rigidity effects in organizational behavior: A multilevel analysis. *Adm. Sci. Q.* 26:501–24

Steers, R. M. 1977. *Organizational Effectiveness: A Behavioral View.* Santa Monica, Calif: Goodyear

Steers, R. M., Mowday, R. T. 1981. Employee turnover and postdecision accommodation processes. See Martin 1981

Steers, R. M., Rhodes, S. R. 1978. Major influences on employee attendance: A process model. *J. Appl. Psychol.* 63:391–407

Strauss, G. 1982. Worker participation in management: An international perspective. See Aldrich & Mueller 1982

Suls, J. M., Miller, R. L., eds. 1977. *Social Comparison Processes.* New York: Wiley

Taylor, S. E., Fiske, S. T. 1978. Salience, attention, and attribution: Top of the head phenomena. *Adv. Exp. Soc. Psychol.,* pp. 249–88

Tegar, A. I. 1980. *Too Much Invested To Quit.* New York: Pergamon

Terborg, J. R., Miller, H. E. 1978. Motivation, behavior, and performance: A closer examination of goal setting and monetary incentives. *J. Appl. Psychol.* 63:29–39

Tetlock, P. E. 1984. Accountability: The neglected social context of judgment and choice. In *Research in Organizational Behavior,* ed. L. L. Cummings, B. M. Staw, Vol. 7. Greenwich, Conn: JAI Press. In press

Turner, A. N., Lawrence, P. R. 1965. *Industrial jobs and the worker: An investigation of response to task attributes.* Cambridge, Mass: Harvard Univ. Press

Tushman, M. 1977. Communication across organizational boundaries: Special boundary roles in the innovation process. *Adm. Sci. Q.* 22:587–605

Valenzi, E. R., Andrews, I. R. 1971. Effect of hourly overpay and underpay inequity when tested with a new induction procedure. *J. Appl. Psychol.* 55:22–27

Van Maanen, J., Dabbs, J., Faulkner, R. 1982. *Varieties of Qualitative Research.* Beverly Hills, Calif: Sage

Van Maanen, J., Schein, E. H. 1979. Toward a theory of organizational socialization. See Berger & Cummings 1979

Vroom, V. H. 1964. *Work and Motivation.* New York: Wiley

Wahba, M. A., Bridwell, L. G. 1976. Maslow reconsidered: A review of research on the need hierarchy theory. *Organ. Behav. Hum. Perform.* 15:212–40

Walster, E., Walster, G. W., Berscheid, E. 1978. *Equity: Theory and Research.* Boston: Allyn & Bacon

Wanous, J. P. 1973. Effects of a realistic job preview on job acceptance, job attitudes, and job survival. *J. Appl. Psychol.* 58:327–32

Wanous, J. P. 1981. *Organizational Entry.* Reading, Mass: Addison-Wesley

Weick, K. E. 1979a. *The Social Psychology of Organizing.* Reading, Mass: Addison-Wesley 2nd ed.

Weick, K. E. 1979b. Cognitive processes in organizations. See Berger & Cummings 1979

Weinstein, D. 1979. *Bureaucratic Opposition.* New York: Pergamon

Weiss, D. J., Dawis, R. V., England, G. W., Lofquist, L. H. 1967. Manual for the Minnesota Satisfaction Questionnaire. *Minnesota Studies in Vocational Rehabilitation,* Vol. 22. Minneapolis: Univ. Minn.

Weiss, H. M., Shaw, J. B. 1979. Social influences on judgements about tasks. *Organ. Behav. Hum. Perform.* 24:126–40

Westin, A., ed. 1981. *Whistleblowing: Loyalty and Dissent in the Corporation.* New York: McGraw-Hill

White, S. E., Mitchell, T. R. 1979. Job enrichment versus social cues: A comparison and competitive test. *J. Appl. Psychol.* 64:1–9

Wispe, L., ed. 1978. *Altruism, Sympathy, and Helping*. New York: Academic

Yolles, S. F., Carone, P. A., Krinsky, L. W. 1975. *Absenteeism in Industry*. Springfield, Ill: Thomas

Zajonc, R. B. 1980. Feeling and thinking: Preferences need no inferences. *Am. Psychol.* 35:151–75

Zald, M. N., Berger, M. A. 1978. Social movements in organizations: Coup d'etat, insurgency, and mass movements. *Am. J. Sociol.* 4:823–61

Zucker, L. 1977. The role of institutionalization in cultural persistence. *Am. Sociol. Rev.* 42:726–43

Zucker, L. 1981. Organizations as institutions. In *Perspectives in Organizational Sociology: Theory and Research*, ed. S. Bacharach. Greenwich, Conn: JAI Press

Ann. Rev. Psychology. 1984. 35:667–701

PERSONALITY ASSESSMENT

Richard I. Lanyon

Department of Psychology, Arizona State University, Tempe, Arizona 85287

CONTENTS

INTRODUCTION

Previous chapters in the *Annual Review of Psychology* in the personality assessment domain have tended to cover specific topics such as theory and methodology, inventories, or projective tests. The present chapter attempts to

0066-4308/84/0201-0667$02.00

provide a more comprehensive review, recognizing three potential audiences in personality assessment: (*a*) the conceptualizers, who develop theory and methodology; (*b*) the builders, who construct assessment devices; and (*c*) the users, in either research or clinical settings. This review covers the 3-year period 1980–1982, and includes journal articles, books, and commercially published tests. The DSM-III is excluded because it was covered last year (Eysenck et al 1983). Also excluded are papers that have focused solely on applied questions, such as the personality characteristics of ideal therapists, or papers that have used a personality assessment device solely in pursuit of particular hypotheses.

Recent reviewers of personality assessment have taken a wide range of positions on the health and future of the field, from the assertion that just about everything in personality assessment should be thrown out (Rorer & Widiger 1983) to the posture that just about everything should be left as it is (Korchin & Schuldberg 1981). *Annual Review* authors over the past 15 years have been somewhat reluctant to offer specific predictions about future trends, and there is little consistency in the predictions that have been made. Nevertheless, some rather definite changes are taking place. (*a*) There is increased interest in personality theory from the trait or structural viewpoint, and particularly in renewing the search for the optimal formulation of normal personality structure. (*b*) The content areas toward which test construction is oriented are tending to be more closely related to normal personality than to traditional concepts of psychopathology. (*c*) There is a greater interest in the direct assessment and prediction of concrete practical criteria which tend not to directly involve "personality" (e.g. alcoholism, marital satisfaction). (*d*) The improved test construction methodology which has been developed in the last 15 years is now more often being incorporated into practical use. (*e*) There is a proliferation of computer-based interpretation services.

Books

Books and tests of a general nature are reviewed next. Kleinmuntz's (1982) *Personality and Psychological Assessment* is a revision and condensation of an earlier book, now written at a more introductory level and covering assessment beyond the personality domain. While the text is not comprehensive, there is a particularly well written section on quantitative issues as applied to psychological assessment. Lanyon & Goodstein's (1982) expanded second edition of their textbook *Personality Assessment* contains new sections on behavioral assessment, automated interpretation, children, and law-related settings. Readers should not be misled by the title of the Kellerman & Burry (1981) *Handbook of Psychodiagnostic Testing*, which is neither a handbook nor about testing, but describes the preparation of the classical psychoanalytically oriented diagnostic report. Most users will see it as dated and of limited value.

Two books have been published on general psychological assessment. One is Anastasi's (1982) fifth edition of her well-established *Psychological Testing,* approximately one fifth of which is devoted to personality testing. Both objective and projective tests are covered in encyclopedic detail in a carefully balanced presentation at an introductory level. The other, by Kaplan & Saccuzzo (1982), contains relatively little on mainstream personality tests, but has up-to-date coverage of alternative procedures such as behavioral and psychophysiological assessment.

Woody's (1980) massive two-volume *Encyclopedia of Clinical Assessment* contains 91 chapters said to be "on the major categories of clinical assessment." However, a number of important categories are not represented, and the quality of the contributions varies widely. Two other edited books are the fifth volume of McReynolds' (1981) *Advances in Psychological Assessment,* and the first volume of *Advances in Personality Assessment* by Spielberger & Butcher (1982). Both collections have been evaluated positively (Grisso 1982, Sundberg 1982), and the relevant chapters are reviewed below in the context of their specific topic.

Finally, personality assessment has been presented in eight introductory personality texts published during 1980–1982, some beyond the first edition. Coverage ranges from nothing at all up to four chapters, and tends to give major attention and equal space to the MMPI and the Rorschach. Also frequently mentioned are the TAT, CPI, 16PF, and sentence completion, and some texts include behavioral assessment and psychometrics. Taken together, these presentations indicate that (*a*) psychologists differ greatly in their view of the importance of personality assessment within the context of personality; (*b*) there continues to be ambivalence about personality assessment as a mainstream enterprise in academic psychology; and (*c*) personality assessment is still viewed primarily in terms of "schools" and "camps" and not on the basis of empirical knowledge.

THEORETICAL

In the last few years there has been an increase in both the amount and the vigor of theorizing about personality, as well as an increasingly positive attitude toward the utility of this endeavor. Most theoreticians would now agree on the following: (*a*) it is useful to talk about stable personality characteristics; (*b*) it is meaningful to seek the optimal framework in which to conceptualize them; (*c*) accounting for behavior involves three sources of data: personality characteristics, situational characteristics, and their interactions. For a detailed review of theoretical aspects of personality that have implications for personality assessment, the reader is referred to a special topic issue of the *Journal of Personality* (West 1983).

Three shifts in theoretical focus can be identified over the past decade or two that have major implications for personality assessment. First, there is expanded interest in the study of normal personality from a structural viewpoint. Reasons for this interest could include the infusion of social psychologists into the area of personality (Kenrick & Dantchik 1983), the challenge and stimulation offered by social learning theorists of personality (e.g. Mischel & Peake 1982), the increased methodological sophistication afforded by the use of more directly behavioral procedures (e.g. Buss & Craik 1983), and the applicability to personality of basic work in cognition and social cognition (e.g. Cantor & Kihlstrom 1981).

The second shift has occurred over a period of years and is conceptual, having to do with how psychological disorder is viewed. In the traditional psychodynamic view, the major underlying cause of most psychological disorders was one's basic personality characteristics. Thus, comprehensive personality assessment was an important enterprise and gave rise to the popularity of the major general purpose instruments such as the Rorschach, TAT, and MMPI. Now that many psychological problems are approached directly and alleviated without a comprehensive study of personality, there is increased activity in the development of instruments that are disorder specific, such as the Beck Depression Inventory. Inevitably, instruments that are developed for specific purposes will prove more accurate than a general purpose instrument that may be pressed into service for the same task. The stage may thus be set for a gradual decline in use of comprehensive instruments except in situations in which broad-based assessments are desired.

The third shift in focus is the continuing influence of behavioral psychology and social learning theory on personality. This influence is seen in a number of ways. (a) There are active efforts to develop conceptual schema for the quantitative assessment of situations or environments (e.g. Wicker 1981). The assessment of life stress (e.g. Dohrenwend et al 1982) is relevant here. (b) The influence is also clear in many contemporary definitions of personality concepts and criterion measures (see West 1983). (c) The influence is seen in the recognition of the importance of using multiple methods in collecting assessment data in order to increase the accuracy of prediction. (d) There is a rapidly increasing variety of assessment methods that are themselves directly behavioral, as exemplified in several major edited texts (Barlow 1981, Hersen & Bellack 1981, Mash & Terdal 1981). Accompanying this literature are attempts to build bridges between behavioral assessment and more indirect procedures, such as Burns's (1980) "social behaviorism psychometrics" and alliances with cognitive psychology (Kendall & Hollon 1981, Merluzzi et al 1981).

These shifts in focus appear to have had two significant effects on the field of personality assessment. The first has been to divide the field into two parts: one involving the theoretical study of personality structure with emphasis on normal persons and on theory and underlying concepts; and the other involving the practical assessment of psychological problems, with emphasis on useful categories and predictive accuracy. An interesting new trend is the coming together of these two parts to give rise to the study of nonpathological characteristics that relate to psychological well-being, a topic which is discussed below. Second, more and more contemporary assessment procedures bypass any involvement with "personality" as a mediating construct, and therefore they should not, strictly speaking, be considered to belong within the field of personality assessment. What will happen to this term remains to be seen.

Structural Models

Dimensional factorial models of personality structure have always been popular with personality assessment researchers because they can be readily translated into practical assessment devices. In view of the amount of current theoretical interest in such models, we should soon be witnessing the development of a number of new tests for normal personality.

Goldberg (1981a,b, 1982) has engaged in a long-term project to develop a compelling taxonomic structure for the personality descriptive terms in natural language, including Dutch and German as well as English (John et al 1983). The ultimate goal is to discover as much as possible about the nature of the processes involved in description of oneself and others. This work began with approximately 27,000 terms related to personality, which was systematically reduced to 2,797. A number of different procedures were then employed to generate preliminary taxonomies of these terms. Goldberg's work is notable for its depth and completeness, as well as for the development of different methodologies that will be useful for other workers. While Goldberg has offered no final answer to the question of how many dimensions or in what order, he tends to favor the five-factor structure which has shown some consistency in the literature: surgency, agreeableness, conscientiousness, emotional stability, and culture. He believes, however, that a complete structure must be more complex.

Wiggins (1980, 1982, Wiggins et al 1981) has also worked extensively in this area, from the viewpoint that the circular or circumplex model has particular advantages and is perhaps the most appropriate integrative conceptual approach to personality structure. He has presented a variety of methodological tools for the study of circumplexity in personality data, and has also recommended this conceptualization for abnormal behavior. Wiggins views no one particular circumplex as final, but offers a particular 16-trait model as a starting point for further empirical work.

Hogan (1982) integrated recent models of personality structure in the context of relevant theory and research from diverse fields, and proposed a six-factor circumplex structure of personality as optimal (surgency, likability, sociability, conformity, adjustment, and intellectence). His as yet unpublished inventory, the HPI, was designed to assess these characteristics. Because each HPI scale consists of several (4–10) homogeneous item composites, there is the potential for both broad screening and finer grained analysis of personality characteristics.

A more complicated circumplex model for interpersonal traits was developed by Conte & Plutchik (1981). They were concerned only about the angular placement of personality trait terms on the circumference of their model and proposed no particular dimensions as more primary than any others. Their model was reported to be close to that of Wiggins, although developed by a different method. Finally, based on the argument that Osgood's three semantic differential dimensions reveal fundamental dimensions of emotional reaction, Mehrabian & O'Reilly (1980) have proposed eight temperament types based on combinations of these three presumed factors of emotion.

Definition and Measurement

A number of papers have to do with theoretical matters related to the definition of personality characteristics. While this work is beyond the scope of the present chapter, its methodological implications for improved measurement should be noted. For example, Buss & Craik (1980) have emphasized the concept of prototypically similar acts (Rosch & Mervis 1975); that is, acts which fit most centrally the essence of the characteristic of interest. Thus, Buss and Craik showed that prototypically dominant acts correlated more highly with their dominance criteria than did more peripheral acts within the dominance domain. Also of note is their direct behavioral approach of defining "dispositions" in terms of the frequency of relevant behaviors (Buss & Craik 1983).

Another significant concept is aggregation, referring to the procedure of averaging over many measurements. Epstein (1983), although not the originator of these ideas, published a careful review and integration of literature demonstrating the effect of aggregation across situations and occasions (for both predictors and criteria) in reducing unreliability and therefore increasing the strength of the obtained relationships.

Dispositions and Situations

The literature on the relative importance of dispositions versus situations in determining behavior might be ordered on a dimension anchored on one end by Mischel & Peake (1982), who continue to argue that situations are the primary determinants of behavior (or at least that dispositions are not). Lord's (1982) work, addressing the task of classifying situations, also belongs near this end. Toward the middle are studies of the impact of situations on behavior (Prescott et al 1981), and studies in the tradition of Bem and Allen arguing that some people are more consistent than others (e.g. Kenrick & Stringfield 1980, Underwood & Moore 1981, Kenrick & Braver 1982). The "dispositions" end of the dimension is represented by the studies of personality structure cited above, whose current emphasis is on the development of methodologically sounder measures. It is clear that theorists still differ substantially on the dispositions/situations question, although on a practical level, workers will probably continue to give situations less than their due weight simply because procedures for measuring them are not as readily available.

METHODOLOGY

This section reviews methodological work that is central to the field as a whole. Work related to specific areas is discussed in the context of those areas.

Reliability and Validity

As described above, much of the current work (e.g., prototypicality, aggregation) is heavily geared toward improving reliability of measurement and therefore validity (West 1983). There is conflicting evidence on the degree of temporal reliability of different instruments. Schuerger et al (1982) reviewed test-retest reliability coefficients of various personality and related instruments and found declines over time in all of them. However, the declines were less with older people, with homogeneous scales, and with measures of normal personality as compared to psychopathology. Some of these findings were contradicted by Costa et al (1980) using their own data. Here, older persons did not show higher test-retest coefficients than younger persons, and a normal characteristic did not show a higher coefficient than a pathological one.

In what might be termed an aggregation study over criterion situations, Cole et al (1981) compared single vs multiple operationalization of criterion variables in a study of heterosexual social skill and heterosexual anxiety. Four criterion measures and two different aggregation approaches were employed. As expected, validities based on multiple criteria were significantly higher than those based on unitary criteria, supporting the position of Epstein (1983) and others that much of the existing clinical validation literature might be underestimating actual predictor-criterion relationships. Similarly, Moskowitz & Schwarz (1982) studied the assessment of dependency and dominance in 56 preschool children, observing them over multiple periods per day for eight weeks and averaging to obtain single dominance and dependency scores. Criterion data involved multiple informants and multiple rating scales, also averaged to produce single scores. Validity coefficients clearly increased according to the number of observers and the number of weeks included in the observation.

An obvious antecedent to the welcome emphasis on multiple predictors and multiple criteria is the multitrait-multimethod approach of Campbell & Fiske (1959), and this approach is becoming more widely used (e.g. Beck & Beck 1980, Haynes et al 1981, Boals et al 1982, Bray 1982). Bray's extended study of the assessment center procedure is particularly noteworthy for its careful attention to multiple predictors and criteria. It should be emphasized that this method refers not to a shotgun approach involving many variables but to systematic representation of the domain to be assessed so that the predictors (or criteria) fully cover their domains from theoretical and/or rational viewpoints.

In an interesting approach to validity, Rezmovic & Rezmovic (1980) compared the factor structure of the Personality Research Form with the factor structure of peer ratings over 12 of Murray's needs. Because an invariant factor pattern common to the two methods could not be found, they concluded that the underlying structures of the two methods were not the same. Since these results contradicted those of an earlier similar study, however, more work is needed on such procedures.

The question of the validity of subtle versus obvious items continues to be debated. The notion that subtle items make a small but unique contribution to valid variance (Gynther et al 1979) has been eroded by the literature since that time. Studies by Burkhart et al (1980), Hovanitz & Gynther (1980), Holden & Jackson (1981), and Wrobel & Lachar (1982) involving the MMPI and the PRF have shown only one case in which subtle items contributed anything unique.

An excellent general discussion of validity in test development has been published by the APA Division of Industrial/Organizational Psychology (1980). This work could profitably be read by anybody undertaking the development of assessment procedures. Also of note is Jackson's (1980) general paper on the practical use of construct validity. Messick (1980) argued that construct validity provides the most important foundation for relevance and for predictiveness of any test, and warned that social consequences as well as validity must be considered in the appropriateness of test use.

Self-ratings and Others' Ratings

There is an overdue interest in the meaning of self-ratings and the question of what status they should be accorded. Beck & Beck (1980) employed four methods of assessing Murray's needs, and a convergent validity matrix showed that self-ratings were the most central. Kaufman & Murphy (1981) gathered data on six normal personality tests plus self- and others' ratings, and found satisfactory correlations between the test scores and self-ratings but not with others' ratings. The reliability of their others' ratings was questionable, however. Funder (1980) found substantial agreement between self- and others' descriptions on the California Q-Sort. In an extensive review paper, Shrauger & Osberg (1981) compared the relative accuracy of self-predictions with judgments by others in personality and related assessment areas. Self-assessments were at least as predictive as other assessment methods.

Gibbons (1983) reviewed the literature on internal focus of attention, a variable which appears to be related to accurate self-assessment. Johnson (1981) argued that objective self-report measures of personality are better regarded as ways to instruct others about how one is to be regarded (i.e. as self-presentations) than as sources of factual information about the self (i.e. as self-disclosures). However, his predictor-criterion relationships were modest, suggesting that important sources of variance were not identified.

It is tempting to conclude that simple self-ratings are no more biased or inaccurate than other data sources, such as scores on standardized tests or others' ratings. However, there is a lack of research in practical settings, where the potential for various kinds of biases is high, and on abnormal rather than normal personality characteristics.

Response Distortions

There is less literature on this topic than in previous years. Some traditional research still continues, examining whether scales are confounded with social desirability (e.g. Rock 1981) or with acquiescence (e.g. Ramanaiah & Martin 1980). Such research would seem to be superfluous in view of agreement that difficulties engendered by possible response distortion factors should be re-solved at the level of test construction rather than discovered afterwards. In a more useful study, Paulhus (1981) described his principal factor deletion technique, a procedure for controlling the effects of social desirability at the test construction stage.

On the topic of faking, Snyter & Allik (1981) reported that the Personal Orientation Dimensions was somewhat resistant to faking in a favorable direction by college students, while Thornton & Gierasch (1980) found that their empirically designed instrument for selecting management trainees could easily be faked by those motivated to do so. Grow et al (1980) studied a variety of MMPI faking indices with undergraduate subjects and concluded that linear combinations of F and K were the most accurate in detecting faking both good and bad.

COMMON PERSONALITY TESTS

In order to survey the current status of the most common personality tests (inventories and projectives), various counts and comparisons were made. Of the top 15 adult-oriented instruments in terms of publication during 1980–1982, the MMPI accounted for nearly half of the articles. The Rorschach was second, accounting for somewhat less than one quarter. Together these two instruments accounted for two-thirds of the literature involving the top 15 tests.

Comparing these figures with the tabulations in the *Eighth Mental Measurements Yearbook* (Buros 1978), it is evident that both instruments have increased their lead over other tests in their class (objective and projective).

It is tempting to conclude that researchers are increasingly going with the two "biggies." However, such a conclusion would ignore a more important trend, namely, the increasing tendency toward using specific instruments for particular purposes. These factors would suggest a somewhat diminished research use of "other" common personality tests, and this is consistent with the subjective impression gained from studying the literature. There is relatively little innovative or large-scale work, and in particular, no major efforts to increase the existing fund of empirical validity knowledge on any systematic basis.

It is also noteworthy that the literature relating to inventories and projectives continues to represent two somewhat different worlds. Thus, projective test studies tend to appear in the *Journal of Personality Assessment* and not in APA journals, while inventory studies are more evenly distributed. Perhaps related, the literature on projectives continues to be less scientifically sophisticated than the literature on inventories.

MMPI

Two books appeared on the MMPI during 1980–1982. Greene's (1980) introductory text contains sufficient material to give the reader an informed basis for using the MMPI, but with the following cautions. It does not distinguish between empirical and armchair interpretive information; base rates are ignored, leading to a lack of distinction between "normal" and "abnormal" interpretations; and there is a tendency toward overinterpretation. The other book, edited by Dahlstrom & Dahlstrom (1980), is an update of the 1956 *Basic Readings*. It contains reports of the original work in constructing the basic scales plus notable contributions of such authors as Meehl, Taylor, Edwards, Barron, Black, Jackson and Messick, Wiggins, and Byrne. Overall, the editors have shown good judgment in selecting among the thousands of available papers.

A number of articles have added to the extensive literature on the validity of the MMPI in psychiatric settings—the basic use of this test. Johnson et al (1980) undertook four different analyses of VA males to demonstrate that the MMPI predicted membership in narrow band categories more accurately than broad band. The 14 narrow band categories were the DSM-II diagnoses provided by the Spitzer & Endicott (1969) DIAGNO II program, while the five broad band categories represented groupings of these diagnoses. Miller et al (1982) demonstrated that the Golden-Meehl MMPI indicators for the detection of membership in the schizoid taxon were inadequate.

Studies on the utility of high-point code types were more negative than would have been expected on the basis of previous literature. Holland et al

(1981b) showed that scores on individual scales conveyed more information about differences among four major diagnostic groups than did two-point code types. Kelley & King (1980) showed substantial differences among the different two-point subgroupings of the 2–7–8 three-point code type and also between the sexes, but did not determine which of the codes led to the most accurate descriptions.

The substantial volume of literature on short forms of the MMPI indicates the popularity of this approach. A review of the 13 available short forms (Stevens & Reilly 1980) concluded that there has been little attempt to seek independent empirical support for these forms, which therefore remain only an area of future promise. Literature published since their review can be summarized as follows. Several studies have developed improved conversion tables in an attempt to enhance the correspondence between a short form, mostly the MMPI-168, and the full MMPI (e.g. Ward 1980, Moreland 1982). Related are studies which have proposed developing specific or local norms (Bennett & Cimbolic 1980, Bennett & Schubert 1981, Overall & Eiland 1982). Studies which have compared a short form with the full MMPI have shown inadequate correspondence (Noce & Whitmyre 1981, Svanum et al 1981, Griffin & Danahy 1982). One study on high-point code types from the Mini-Mult simply assumed correspondence and found limited utility of the code types in predicting DSM-III schizophrenia (Winters et al 1981).

There are criticisms and rebuttals regarding the merits of short forms (Butcher et al 1980, Newmark et al 1980, Edinger 1981, Greene 1982). Remarkably, no studies have compared the accuracy of a short form and the full form in practical use against an external criterion. The appropriate conclusion to be drawn on short forms (e.g. Edinger 1981) is that each is best considered a different test from the full MMPI, and norms and correlates must therefore be determined anew for each form.

The remainder of the MMPI literature is discussed below, in the context of specific topic areas. As would be expected, those instruments that have been built properly and specifically for particular uses tend to deliver higher validities than a multipurpose instrument such as the MMPI.

Other Inventories

As stated above, the volume of literature on other inventories has not kept pace with the MMPI. Much of this literature is internally oriented, evaluating characteristics of the tests themselves rather than their relationship to external criteria. This internal literature often does not contribute to the practical utility of the test, but is at times presented as though it does.

EYSENCK'S TESTS   The Eysenck Personality Inventory and its relatives, the Junior EPI and the Eysenck Personality Questionnaire, have a significant literature on internal aspects such as intercorrelations and factor structure (Oswald & Velicer 1980, Goh et al 1982), social desirability (Dunnett et al 1981), and test-retest reliability (Gabrys 1980). What external validity data exist mostly involve correlations with other inventory scales such as authoritarianism (Ray & Bozek 1981) and the Interpersonal Style Inventory (Forbes & Braunstein 1981). Thus, the practical usefulness of this family of tests remains to be demonstrated.

16PF   A book by Krug (1981) presents an objective code system for interpreting the 16PF. A total of 81 code types based on four second-order scores were identified by categorizing the profiles of more than 17,000 cases, and a fairly detailed descriptive narrative accompanies each code type. However, because of the complete absence of empirical data supporting these interpretive paragraphs, the book should be avoided unless one wishes to do validation studies on it.

Studies on internal characteristics of the 16PF include a test-retest reliability study (Baird 1981) reporting significantly lower reliabilities than reported by the test's authors, a clustering study employing a Q-type factor-analytic procedure which identified four modal profiles (Burger & Kabacoff 1982), and a large scale investigation of internal psychometric properties (Saville & Blinkhorn 1981). Studies on external validity include an unsuccessful attempt to discriminate among psychiatric groups (Howe & Helmes 1980) and a Hebrew translation study which investigated the relationship of all scales to six criteria of success for female military officers (Fox et al 1981). Despite the high degree of usage of the 16PF, the current literature does nothing to change the conclusions of previous reviewers that "it is impossible to recommend the 16PF in an unqualified manner for any use" (Walsh 1978).

CALIFORNIA PSYCHOLOGICAL INVENTORY   There was relatively little activity with the CPI, which has previously been reviewed in reasonably positive terms. Studies have contributed information about its relationship to age (Martin et al 1981) and to social desirability (Ellis & Leitner 1980), and have investigated factor structure and type patterns (Kelso & Taylor 1980, Levin & Karni 1981, Lorr & Burger 1981). External validity studies have been of a minor nature, involving its relationship to polygraph performance (Thurber 1981) and the prediction of hypnotizability (McKnight 1980).

PERSONALITY RESEARCH FORM   Several studies have addressed empirical validity. In two papers, Bridgewater (1981, 1982) utilized PRF and nontest criterion data from ski instructors to contribute to the construct validity of the PRF. Correlations with Adjective Check List scales were reported by Bessmer & Ramanaiah (1981). A second-order analysis by Rezmovic & Rezmovic

(1980) showed that the factor structure of PRF responses and that of peer ratings on the same 12 needs was not comparable.

MILLON CLINICAL MULTIAXIAL INVENTORY   A second edition of the *Manual* for the MCMI appeared in 1982 (Millon 1982) but contains no additional research beyond the first edition. Since the MCMI is used mainly by computer interpretation (including an automated DSM-III diagnosis), an urgent research need is to confirm the validity of the interpretation program. Green (1982) compared clinicians' ratings of the adequacy of the MCMI report and two different MMPI automated reports, but because no independent criteria were employed, the conclusion that the MCMI program was valid cannot be taken seriously.

PROJECTIVE TECHNIQUES: GENERAL

In former years entire chapters in the *Annual Review of Psychology* have been devoted to projectives. Their conclusions may be summarized as follows: (*a*) insufficient validity exists for comfortable practical application; (*b*) psychologists often use projectives primarily as a source of ideas, and will presumably continue to do so; and (*c*) it was hoped that Exner's (1974) work with the Rorschach would stimulate greater interest and research activity.

Several general books appeared on projectives. Rabin's (1981) edited introductory book, *Assessment with Projective Techniques,* is a condensation and revision of his 1968 work. While several chapters have been updated, the book remains subjective in nature. *A Human Science Model for Personality Assessment with Projective Techniques* (Dana 1982) was described by one reviewer as "full of new information and excellent documentation" (Klopfer 1982). The present reviewer, however, found little new; rather, traditional clinical beliefs are uncritically restated with no data base. *The Interpretation of Projective Test Data* by Wagner & Wagner (1981) also offers nothing data-based, but describes the authors' proposal for making diagnostic interpretations within their own unique theory of personality.

In the only study to be located on assumptions underlying projectives, Brody & Carter (1982) showed that children attributed more negative and intense responses to others than to the self. However, there was no independent confirmation that any of these attributions were descriptive of the respondents.

Rorschach

Two books were published on the Rorschach. One was Levitt's (1980) brief *Primer on the Rorschach Technique,* an introductory manual which summarizes traditional procedures of administration, scoring, and interpretation. A major work is the third volume of Exner's monumental project designed to put the Rorschach on a sound empirical footing. Volume 3 is devoted to children and adolescents (Exner & Weiner 1982). The most useful content is the extensive normative data for the formal scoring categories, also presented, in part, in Volume 2. As with previous volumes, the authors have continued to rely almost exclusively on case presentations as a substitute for external validity data. It is disappointing that these volumes, regarded by many as the best and most promising work on the Rorschach, still do not tackle this most urgent topic of external validity, the one which continues to deny the Rorschach the status of scientific respectability.

General articles on the Rorschach have included an introductory overview of the Exner system (Wiener-Levy & Exner 1981) and sympathetic promises that the Rorschach will have a long and healthy future (Exner 1980, Howes 1981). Two more useful papers are Amos's (1980) objective flow-chart for scoring certain Rorschach determinants, and a factor analysis of 24 formal scores by Shaffer et al (1981). The latter study is noteworthy for its sample size (more than 1000), its care in partialing out protocol length, and its examination of both group and individual Rorschachs. Its simplified formulas for deriving scores on six major factors representing traditional categories such as human movement provide stable indices of such concepts for use in future validity studies.

In the area of content, Reznikoff et al (1982) published a careful review of the reliability of inkblot content scales, and concluded that the reliabilities of Rorschach scales were generally inadequate. Reliabilities of Holtzman content scales were better and were recommended for research but not clinical use. Aron (1982) added to the construct validity of Elizur's content scoring system for anxiety, while Rose & Bitter (1980) proposed a content scoring system for destructive aggression as a means of assessing physical assaultiveness.

In regard to formal scoring categories, Lazar & Schwartz (1982) questioned traditional beliefs about the contamination response, while Kinder et al (1982) showed differences between the Exner and Beck systems for scoring form quality. Smith (1981) showed that the number and complexity of whole responses in children were related to the Piagetian stages of cognitive development, but failed to take into consideration either total number of responses or intelligence. Tamkin (1980, Kunce & Tamkin 1981) attempted to validate traditional hypotheses about the meaning of Rorschach color and human movement against the MMPI, with marginal results.

On the topic of more complex formal scores, Russ's (1980, 1981, 1982) studies on Holt's (1977) measure of primary process integration are noteworthy. This index was found to be related to academic achievement independent of intelligence, and the effect was still present one year later. It was also related to flexibility in problem solving for boys but not for girls. Ritzler et al (1980b) showed a relationship between psychosis and ego functioning as assessed by a complex object concept scoring system. Hathaway (1982) showed a high correlation between the Rorschach Prognostic Rating Scale and intelligence. The Affective Ratio was shown to be a function of age (Loucks et al 1980), while Stevens (1981) found some weak support for the utility of the Barrier score. Wiener-Levy & Exner (1981) reported a relationship between task persistence and a complex variable based on Experience Type.

The major contribution to methodology was a sophisticated, carefully reasoned model for approaching the question of construct validation (Widiger & Schilling 1980). Morley (1982) proposed a method for adjusting Rorschach protocols for overall length, yielding a system of MMPI-like T-scores. Albert et al (1980) showed that experts were unable to distinguish between faked and actual psychotic protocols, while Alheidt (1980) showed that formal scores in many categories were significantly related to reading ability in second grade children. Hopwood et al (1981) presented a program for printing out a scoring summary.

As with past Rorschach literature, validity has not been addressed systematically. Some individual studies have shown specific validities, most notably, studies of psychoanalytic concepts as assessed by Rorschach indices. However, because these indices are based on custom-built coding procedures that could in principle be scored from any focused verbal production, the findings are not exclusively a product of the Rorschach.

Has Exner's work proven to be a stimulating force? A count showed that fully 30 percent of articles examined utilized it in some manner. Thus, it is clearly having an impact, although its utility remains to be demonstrated.

Other Projectives

APPERCEPTION TESTS   Pollack & Gilligan (1982) published an interesting study on the TAT, confirming predictions that violent themes in women's stories would occur more often than in men's for situations of achievement, and for men's stories in situations of affiliation. This study adds to the construct validity of story-telling procedures for the assessment of needs. In an article employing data from the longitudinal Grant Study of Adult Development, McAdams & Vaillant (1982) found that intimacy motivation at age 30, as defined by a complex scoring procedure, was significantly associated with better adjustment 17 years later. The apparent omission of nonsignificant findings from the report weakens its impact, however. Shill (1981) utilized the TAT to show gender identity differences between college males from father-present and father-absent homes, and Squyres & Craddick (1982) reported on the reliability of their TAT time orientation scoring system.

In a study with the Children's Apperception Test, Passman & Lautmann (1982) found that young children responded more when a parent (but not a security blanket) was present, while older children did not. Some very abbreviated normative information on themes elicited by the 16 cards of the Senior Apperception Technique was reported by Stock & Kantner (1980).

Two new sets of cards have been offered. Ritzler et al (1980a) described their SM-TAT cards, which are said to be more contemporary, positively toned, and active than Murray's original set. The second is the Roberts Apperception Test for Children (McArthur & Roberts 1982), the product of an extensive psychometric development project. These cards are accompanied by a structured scoring system for 13 content scales and three validity scales, plus global validity data and children's norms for four different age ranges. While much more work on the RATC is required, it is a welcome addition to the very small group of projectives which have some degree of formal psychometric basis.

HUMAN FIGURE DRAWINGS   There is a particularly large discrepancy between the popularity of projective drawings and level of demonstrated validity, and recent publications have not altered this situation. Two well-known books by Hammer (1958) and Machover (1949) were reprinted in 1980, their sixth and eleventh printings respectively. Both remain unchanged despite the empirical literature. Delatte & Hendrickson (1982) found little direct evidence of a relationship between self-esteem and size of drawing, while Rierdan & Koff (1981) questioned whether the inability of some children to designate the sex of their drawing had any meaning. In a potentially useful study, Sturner et al (1980) reported that a stressful situation induced an increase in "emotional indicators" in children.

HOLTZMAN INKBLOT TECHNIQUE   Rosegrant (1982) contributed to the construct validity of Holt's system for scoring primary process manifestations, while Sison et al (1981) showed correlations between HIT variables and three of the Mosher Guilt Scales. Hayslip (1982) provided normative factor-analytic data for elderly noninstitutionalized persons, and Hartung & Skorka (1980) showed HIT differences between normals and psychedelic drug users.

SENTENCE COMPLETION   In contrast to the mediocre validities shown in most other literature on projectives, the results of a diverse group of studies based on Loevinger's assessment of ego development level are more positive. These studies offer construct validity for the Loevinger Sentence Completion Tests of Ego Development (Loevinger et al 1970), and have been reviewed in detail by Loevinger in the 1983 volume of the *Annual Review of Psychology*. In two other studies on sentence completion, Turnbow & Dana (1981) found that instructions for "speed" and "feelings" made no difference, while Fuller et al (1982) were able to discriminate normal and delinquent adolescent males with the maladjustment score of the Rotter Incomplete Sentences Blank.

PSYCHOLOGICAL WELL-BEING

This is a global category encompassing a number of new and interesting developments in assessing normal fluctuations in psychological states, independent of psychopathology but linked to the vicissitudes of daily living. Included are such dimensions as happiness and sadness, loneliness, self-esteem, strain, competence, and self-concept. Other possible names for this area would be positive mental health, personal effectiveness, and problems in living. It also includes certain traditional concepts such as depression, but addressed within a normal rather than a psychopathological perspective. Much of the psychometric work in this area is sound, and adequate attention has often been given to careful definition of conceptual areas and to the creation, development, and refinement of stimulus items based squarely within the domain of interest. For review purposes, the more general literature is considered first.

In a central study, Bryant & Veroff (1982) undertook an analysis of the domain of psychological well-being. A large and stable data base generated three factors: unhappiness vs happiness, strain vs freedom from strain, and personal inadequacy vs efficacy. The widespread use of the Tennessee Self-Concept Scale reflects the high degree of interest in this topic; however, the current literature is sparse and uninformative (e.g. Kernaleguen & Conrad 1980, Hinrichsen et al 1981). Stanwyck & Garrison (1982) showed that the TSCS is susceptible to faking.

Several measures for assessing loneliness were reported. Loucks (1980) showed the expected correlations between the Bradley Loneliness Scale and several other self-report instruments. Jones et al (1982) studied the relationship of the 20-item UCLA Loneliness Scale to social skill deficits, while Russell et al (1980) revised the UCLA scale to include an equal number of positively worded items. Unfortunately, no information was given on the development of these items. Jones & Russell (1982) introduced a related concept, shyness, and reported a 22-item scale to assess it, but again gave no information regarding item development. There is a wide literature on social deficits and their assessment, mainly within a direct behavioral model (e.g. Kolko et al 1981, McFall 1982), which is beyond the scope of this chapter.

The Maslach Burnout Inventory (Maslach & Jackson 1981) is a commercially published test with three factor-based scales assessing emotional exhaustion, depersonalization, and lack of personal accomplishment. The 22 items are each rated for strength and frequency on Likert type scales. No data are given on the source of the original 47 items, and most of the current validity data involve correlations with other self-reports.

Several new measures are oriented toward positive attributes. Getter & Nowinski (1981) described their Interpersonal Problem Solving Assessment

Technique, a free responding test involving six classes of problematic interpersonal situations. Responses are scored in one of five structured categories. A 22-item physical self-efficacy scale was presented by Ryckman et al (1982), together with correlations with other self-report measures. Filsinger (1981) described his "liking people" scale, involving 30 content-based Likert items.

Feelings

This category might also be called mood, affect, or emotion. Russell (1980) reported the development of a circumplex model of affective dimensions, analogous to circumplex models of personality. Several different subject samples and procedures were used to support an a priori model involving two basic dimensions: pleasure-misery and arousal-sleepiness. The model was shown to represent both cognitive structure for affect and actual structure of affective experience.

Two papers studied self-report anger measures. Biaggio (1980) factor-analyzed subscale scores on anger inventories and delineated five factors, of which the dominant one involved willingness to experience and express anger. Based on behavioral criterion data, Biaggio et al (1981) concluded that the Anger Self-Report Subscales (Zelin et al 1972) tended to show the best validities.

Lehrer & Woolfolk (1982) studied self-reported anxiety, hoping to demonstrate that somatic, cognitive, and behavioral aspects were orthogonal factors. Marginal support was found; the cognitive factor was the most central one. Kozak & Miller (1982) questioned the adequacy of this popular three-systems view of anxiety, and argued for the importance of retaining the concept of fear as a hypothetical construct, an unobservable functional state to be inferred from observables.

Validity studies continued on the Beck Depression Inventory (e.g. Reynolds & Gould 1981, Strober et al 1981), affirming its utility as a screening instrument for global depression. Berndt et al (1980) described their much more elaborate instrument, the Multiscore Depression Inventory, with ten subscales. The extensive care involved in its development suggests potential for satisfactory validity. A strength was the use of Jackson's (1970) sequential strategy for item selection; a weakness was the use of college students in most aspects of construction. Post & Lobitz (1980) examined the utility of a regression formula approach to diagnosing depression from the MMPI, and Lomranz et al (1981) reported a Hebrew version of the Depression Adjective Check Lists.

The Mood Survey (Underwood & Froming 1980) is a carefully developed instrument which approaches happy vs sad mood as a stable personality characteristic. It involves two major intercorrelated factors: level and reactivity. Stipek et al (1981) developed a children's measure of optimism, defined as generalized tendency to expect positive or negative outcomes.

Marriage and Family

There has been considerable activity in this area (see Snyder 1982 for a review), including the commercial publication of two multiscale instruments. In a creative and ambitious effort, Hudson (1982) developed the Clinical Measurement Package, a series of nine 25-item scales to be used either together or separately. Although certain of the development procedures were extensive, some very elementary aspects are lacking, such as norms (and even scale means) and specific information on construction of the scales. More satisfactory psychometrically is Snyder's (1981) Marital Satisfaction Inventory. Snyder employed primarily rational procedures to develop 11 scales (9 if children are not involved). Five of the scales correlate highly and include most of the total variance. Reliabilities and norms appear satisfactory. Snyder et al (1981) provided further empirical validity, while Snyder & Regts (1982) derived and validated two new factor scales, labeled disaffection and disharmony. The MSI appears to be an adequately constructed instrument with mounting empirical evidence of utility.

A number of studies, for the most part methodologically adequate, addressed other marital assessment procedures. Haynes et al (1981) developed joint and separate interview schedules which showed satisfactory validities in a multimethod criterion study. Lowman's (1980) Inventory of Family Feelings, which assesses the strength of positive affect of each family member in relationship to all other members, was also well developed and is potentially useful. In a careful multimethod study, Boals et al (1982) compared interview, self-report, and analogue data modes, and found modest superiority for the interview. Studies by Koren et al (1980) and Jacobson et al (1980) are also noteworthy because of their multimethod assessment procedures. Two studies were more directly behavioral. Robinson & Eyberg (1981) described their Dyadic Parent-Child Interaction Coding System, a comprehensive observational system for conduct problem families, and Wieder & Weiss (1980) demonstrated the validity and generalizability of the Marital Interaction Coding system.

Health Psychology

Assessment technology is growing in this rapidly developing field. Much of the literature is too specific to be reviewed here; however, three aspects can be noted: the Millon Behavioral Health Inventory, use of the MMPI, and the Type A Personality pattern. The *Manual* for the third edition of the MBHI (Millon et al 1982b) continues to reflect the inadequacies of earlier editions. In particular, the continued absence of independently published validity data is serious enough to recommend against its use.

The MMPI is the one traditional instrument that is actively used in health-related settings, most commonly to examine psychological correlates of particular disorders such as chronic hemodialysis (Osberg et al 1982). Other studies have attempted to discriminate groups such as cancer prone and not prone (Dattore et al 1980), organic and functional impotence (Marshall et al 1980, Staples et al 1980), to predict future onset of chronic disease (Gillum et al 1980); and to predict vocational rehabilitative potential in renal dialysis patients (Freeman et al 1980) and success in a pain program (Strassberg et al 1981). Prokop et al (1980) reported stable MMPI subtypes among chronic pain patients. In general, the utility of the MMPI is questionable or modest in these studies, and significant differences tend to be small. Exceptions are the pain studies, in which meaningful discriminations were reported, and the prediction of cancer, in which any significant findings in adequately designed studies must be viewed as meaningful.

Another exception to the rule of modest findings in health-related assessments is the Type A behavior pattern related to coronary disease. Type A behavior proneness is defined in various ways, the most popular being the Jenkins Activity Survey (Jenkins et al 1979). Matthews et al (1982) compared the Jenkins with the Structured Interview, while other studies have contributed to the construct validity of Type A as a personality characteristic (e.g. Gastorf 1980, Blumenthal et al 1981, Smith & Brehm 1981). Matthews (1982) reviewed the merits of the various assessment procedures, showing considerable independence among them, and also documented the psychological findings on Type A to date.

CHILDREN

The assessment of children was once a soft-headed enterprise which most scientifically and empirically oriented psychologists tried to avoid. Fortunately, this is no longer the case, and in the past decade there has been a substantial amount of empirical activity in the development of assessment procedures. Most instruments are designed to be completed by observers, usually a parent. Most of the current literature involves structured, objective procedures; the projective literature has been reviewed above.

The Personality Inventory for Children (see Wirt & Lachar 1981 for a general overview) was initiated in the 1970s, and work continues on its validity. Lachar et al (1982) developed four broad-band factor-based scales, with evidence for adequate reliability and validity. Most noteworthy is Lachar's revised format for the PIC, an ingenious procedure in which, as more items are answered, more scales can be scored. Thus, completion of the first 131 items covers the Lie scale plus the four factor scales; 280 items cover short forms of the regular scales, 420 items cover the full-length scales, and all 600 items cover the 17 additional scales. The 1982 *Manual Supplement* (Lachar 1982) provides all of this information in exhaustive psychometric detail, together with item selection procedures for the short-form scales, reliabilities, validities, and actuarial interpretation data.

The Child Behavior Profile is another carefully developed multiscale inventory for children, though as yet unavailable commercially. Edelbrock & Achenbach (1980) utilized hierarchical cluster analysis to identify reliable profile patterns that characterize clinically referred boys and girls aged 6–11 and 12–16. Data on at least 500 children in each category were employed, and the measure of profile similarity incorporated both pattern and elevation. Six or seven patterns were reported for each group, together with empirical correlates.

Several other observer rating instruments were introduced. In an extensive article, Lessing et al (1981) described the preliminary development of the IJR Behavior Checklist. A strength is the separate but parallel development of three forms (for parents, teachers, and clinicians) in such a way as to maximize the comparability of data across informants without sacrificing the different evaluators' frames of references. Nine syndromes are comparable across forms, while others are unique. Norms and external validity data are needed. Less well constructed was the Brief Behavior Rating Scale for use in school settings in identifying socially maladjusted, emotionally handicapped, and neurologically impaired children (Kahn & Ribner 1982). Preliminary development of a more directly behavioral instrument for research observation of children during play therapy was reported by Howe & Silvern (1981). Four a priori dimensions are assessed by 31 different behaviors. The high degree of standardization and the training required to use this procedure is both a desirable feature and a constraint on its widespread use.

A new multiscale instrument is the self-report Millon Adolescent Personality Inventory (Millon et al 1982a), which can be used only through a computer scoring and interpretation service. In developing the 20 scales of this test, more than 1000 initial items were reduced to 150 by a combination of psychometric procedures. Because validity data are essentially lacking, publication at this time is premature.

There has been significant interest in defining and assessing early childhood temperament. Most work has been based on the nine categories of the New York Longitudinal Study (NYLS) Parent Questionnaire (Thomas & Chess 1977). A major review by Hubert et al (1982) concluded that (a) there is no agreed upon definition of temperament, (b) there is no psychometrically satisfactory measure, and (c) there are some consistencies in categories across instruments. In subsequent work, Lerner et al (1982) described the careful development of their factor-based five-dimensional Dimensions of Temperament Survey. Construction involved nearly 1400 subjects in three different age groups through early adulthood, and more than 400 initial items which were ultimately reduced to 34. Stable norms and external validity data are lacking, however. In methodological contributions, Black et al (1981) showed that mothers and fathers were consistent as raters on the NYLS Questionnaire, while Billman & McDevitt (1980) showed convergences between parents' and teachers' ratings on two different instruments. However, Lyon & Plomin (1981) found only moderate agreement between parents' ratings on the EASI Temperament Survey (Buss & Plomin 1975).

In papers on psychological well-being (as defined above), instruments for assessing Type A behavior proneness have been reported for children (Wolf et al 1982b) and for adolescents (Siegel et al 1981). Lefkowitz & Tesiny (1980) employed a peer nomination technique with nearly 1000 children in their empirical development of an instrument to assess symptoms of depression, and reported extensive construct validity. Another carefully developed instrument is the Preschool and Primary Self-Concept scale of Stager & Young (1982), in which children rate the concept "me" on adjective scales (e.g. good-bad). Wolf et al (1982a) conducted a factor-analytic study of the Piers-Harris Children's Self-Concept Scale over a large biracial, rural group, and found substantial support for the factor-based data listed in the *Manual* for this broader sample.

MISCELLANEOUS

Race and Culture

Most studies on race and culture have involved black/white comparisons on the MMPI, and the evidence for biases with black populations continues to be equivocal and controversial. Pritchard & Rosenblatt (1980a,b) concluded that no methodologically sound studies exist to show racial bias in the MMPI, while Gynther (1981, Gynther & Green 1980) asserted that there are indeed striking item and scale score differences which lead to inappropriate interpretations of greater maladjustment for blacks. However, when Bertelson et al (1982) carefully matched 231 black and 231 white psychiatric patients on a large number of demographic variables, no significant differences emerged. Patterson et al (1981) also found few meaningful MMPI differences between blacks and whites, particularly when demographic factors were controlled. Differences appeared on the Family Environment Scale, however. McGill (1980) found no MMPI differences between black and white welfare recipients, and Newmark et al (1981) found no bias in MMPI-based diagnosis of schizophrenia. In an MMPI study of American Indians, Pollack & Shore (1980) found that different diagnostic groups had similar mean profiles, suggesting that culture significantly influenced responses on this test.

In work on other tests, Cross & Burger (1982) showed black/white differences on the CPI, while Reynolds & Paget (1981) found an invariant factor structure for the Children's Manifest Anxiety Scale on both race and sex. Gonzalez & Lanyon (1982) described a Spanish version of the Psychological Screening Inventory, with evidence of external validity and psychometric equivalence to the English version.

Substance Abuse

Most assessment research on this topic is on alcoholism and once again involves the MMPI. In line with global trends, there is now a gradual movement away from the MMPI in favor of instruments that are specific to a disorder and thus tend to fall outside the scope of this chapter. The MMPI research involving alcoholic "patterns" shows relatively limited utility for this instrument (e.g. Patalano 1980, Sutker et al 1980, Conley 1981, Eshbaugh et al 1982). Attempts to support specific alcoholism scales and items also showed limited success, even for traditional indices such as the MacAndrew scale (Clopton 1982, Conley & Kammeier 1980, Graham & Schwartz 1981, Merenda & Sparadeo 1981, Zager & Megargee 1981). Robinowitz et al (1980) likewise found evidence against the addiction-prone personality hypothesis for black heroin users.

Forensic Assessment

Much of this literature addresses violent behavior. Monahan's (1981) book, a review of research and methodology with recommendations for clinical practice, is a major contribution, particularly his focus on the need to specify the circumstances under which useful predictions might be possible. The direct prediction of violence from linear composites of MMPI scales showed mixed success (Holland et al 1981a, Jones et al 1981). Other studies have attempted to predict violence from the Rorschach (Rose & Bitter 1980) and from a video measure of interpersonal distance (Gilmour & Walkey 1981).

Roesch & Golding (1980) published a scholarly review of research and assessment approaches to competency to stand trial, together with suggestions for increased sophistication in this area. The Carlson Psychological Survey (Carlson 1982) is a brief five-scale assessment device specifically designed for offenders. Although the development of 18 profile types is a creative contribution, the *Manual* gives essentially no information on the development either of the scales or the types. Two studies showed specific patterns of defensiveness in insanity assessments on the MMPI (Audubon & Kirwin 1982) and the Rorschach (Seamons et al 1981). Also noteworthy is Ziskin's (1981) two-volume revision of his compendium for lawyers of all that is negative about psychological and psychiatric assessment.

Automated Interpretation

Commercially available automated test interpretation systems are growing exponentially. When Meehl (1956) developed a careful methodological basis for this area, he did not foresee how many inadequate systems would be thrown together and aggressively marketed using his work as a ticket to respectability. Almost any combination of procedures is available on-line or off-line, programs can be leased or bought outright, and sets of canned statements can be purchased for home assembly (e.g. Vincent 1980a,b). With the advent of the affordable computer, the trend is toward fully self-contained operations.

The overwhelming problem is lack of demonstrated validity for the printed interpretations. Phone calls to several of the companies were met with self-serving statements or papers that did not directly address validity, but did address any question to which some positive answer could be given. One company wrote simply that "the tests have been validated by the authors and publishers." Another junior staff member agreed fully with the criticisms but felt he had no control over company policy.

The most popularly automated test by far is the MMPI. However, there are interpretive systems for many common inventories, a number of less common ones, and the Rorschach. The available literature is of three kinds: (a) glossy promotional literature, sometimes masquerading as scientific data, and usually accompanied by sample reports; (b) studies of customer and user satisfaction, which has never been much of a problem (e.g. Katz & Dalby 1981, Harris et al 1981), and (c) an occasional paper giving actual information about the development or validation of an automated system (e.g. Gdowski et al 1980, Lachar 1982). There is the real danger that the few satisfactory services will be squeezed out by the many unsatisfactory ones, since the consumer professionals are generally unable to discriminate among them and are predisposed to believe whatever is printed. Particularly distressing is that the lack of demonstrated program validity has now become the norm, and there appear to be no checks against the further development of this untenable situation. Perhaps the time has now come when federal regulations for this industry are necessary for consumer protection.

Other

Other worthwhile work is briefly identified. There is a growing and generally positive literature on sex-role (masculine/feminine) characteristics (e.g. Bernard 1981, Major et al 1981, Orlofsky 1981, Wiggins & Holzmuller 1981), including the formal publication of the *Bem Sex-Role Inventory* (Bem 1981). The literature on internal vs external locus of control shows no signs of abating (e.g. Hill & Bale 1980, Strickland & Haley 1980, Walters & Klein 1981), particularly on the Rotter I-E scale. Correlates tend to be moderate rather than robust, and widespread rather than confined to specific content areas. A book on assessment of the elderly (Kane & Kane 1981) deserves mention; also noteworthy is Altemeyer's (1981) book-length account of his careful and sophisticated work in developing and validating the construct of right-wing authoritarianism as defined by his RWA scale.

Zuckerman et al (1980) published an excellent review of the literature on the sensation-seeking dimension, Hocevar (1981) reviewed the measurement of creativity, and Briggs et al (1980) reported three dimensions underlying the

Self-Monitoring Scale. Widiger (1982) drew negative conclusions after reviewing the literature on the utility of the "borderline" category of personality, and he also questioned the utility of "cognitive style" as a concept (Widiger et al 1980).

INTEGRATION

Writing on personality structure and assessment 4 years ago in the *Annual Review of Psychology*, Jackson & Paunonen (1980) were cautiously optimistic in their hope that the state of the field would continue to improve. This hope has been borne out in many aspects of personality assessment, outweighing those aspects for which the report card is negative.

1. There is a continuation of the recent interest and vigor in theorizing about normal personality from a structural viewpoint. Much of this work has a strong methodological emphasis, leading to an array of new practical possibilities for increasing the elegance, sophistication, and accuracy of measurement procedures. In view of these proposed structures and methods, it may perhaps be expected that improved assessment devices for the domain of normal personality structure will start to appear in the next few years.

2. The influence of the behavioral (social learning) approaches is strong and pervasive in theory, method, and practice, while adherents to the "behavioral assessment" movement are expressing the need for closer ties with traditional psychometric methods. Thus, there are signs that these two areas are beginning to influence each other significantly, although no marriage should be expected.

3. It is pleasing to note that assessment procedures are becoming more specific to the task of interest, and that the routine employment of multipurpose instruments for specific practical assessment questions seems to be diminishing. Exceptions are the MMPI, which is now firmly established as the most widely utilized personality assessment device in the literature, and (to a lesser extent) the Rorschach, which continues to have its faithful stream of adherents. Specific assessment devices, if constructed appropriately, must inevitably outperform general instruments on the specific task. A disadvantage is that the generality of findings based on highly focused instruments is obviously limited, and if generalization is desired, multiple measures should be employed.

4. There is increasing interest in exploring psychological well-being. Interest in this area, involving such concepts as happiness, loneliness, marital satisfaction, coronary disease proneness, etc reflects a number of influences such as the rise of community psychology with its emphasis on primary prevention and positive mental health approaches to human welfare.

5. Greatly increased psychometric attention is being paid to the personality assessment of children, a field in which such work is long overdue. Further useful developments are predicted here as empirical validities are accumulated

for the newer instruments, although the extreme heterogeneity of "children" as a category, due in major part to age variability, will slow the rate of this accumulation.

6. Little that is encouraging can be said about projective techniques, the literature on which continues to reflect a lack of interest in the generally accepted standards of empirical validation. Exceptions are the several complex, content-oriented scoring systems for theoretical concepts; these, however, have no impact on the major use to which projectives are put; namely, practical assessment tasks.

7. The proliferation of unvalidated computer programs for automated assessment is truly alarming, the more so because most users are not equipped to make intelligent choices, and there appear to be no natural checks and balances on these developments. Thus, imposed controls are urgently needed.

8. The experience of preparing this chapter has given an appreciation of how very widely scattered and inaccessible much of the useful material is. It is unlikely that any given user of an assessment device will employ it with maximal effectiveness, or even that the device chosen will be the optimal one in that particular situation. Badly needed are up-to-date indexes, bibliographies, and guidebooks to the empirical literature (e.g. Chun et al 1975). Also needed are more large-scale comprehensive validity studies in the vein of the early MMPI code books. We must squarely face the necessary and urgent task of systematically validating tests and organizing the empirical literature for proper application. We must also recognize that without such systematization, even the most elegantly developed assessment procedure is largely wasted effort.

ACKNOWLEDGMENTS

The author is grateful to his colleagues, Paul Karoly, Douglas T. Kenrick, and Stephen G. West, for their many informal contributions during the preparation of this chapter, and also for reading and commenting on the manuscript draft.

Literature Cited

Albert, S., Fox, H. M., Kahn, M. W. 1980. Faking psychosis on the Rorschach: Can expert judges detect malingering? *J. Pers. Assess.* 44:115–19

Alheidt, P. 1980. The effect of reading ability on Rorschach performance. *J. Pers. Assess.* 44:3–10

Altemeyer, R. A. 1981. *Right-wing Authoritarianism.* Winnipeg: Univ. Manitoba Press. 352 pp.

American Psychological Association, Division of Industrial/Organizational Psychology. 1980. *Principles for the Validation and Use of Personnel Selection Procedures.* Berkeley, Calif: Am. Psychol. Assoc. 28 pp.

Amos, S. P. 1980. A test-operate-test-exit model for Rorschach scoring. *J. Pers. Assess.* 44:234–36

Anastasi, A. 1982. *Psychological Testing.* New York: Macmillan. 784 pp. 5th ed.

Aron, L. 1982. Stressful life events and Rorschach content. *J. Pers. Assess.* 46:582–85

Audubon, J. J., Kirwin, B. R. 1982. Defensiveness in the criminally insane. *J. Pers. Assess.* 46:304–11

Baird, J. S. Jr. 1981. Reliability of the 16PF Questionnaire for security guard applicants. *J. Pers. Assess.* 45:545–46

Barlow, D. H., ed. 1981. *Behavioral Assessment of Adult Disorders.* New York: Guilford. 500 pp.

Beck, M. D., Beck, C. K. 1980. Multitrait-multimethod validation of four personality measures with a high-school sample. *Educ. Psychol. Meas.* 40:1005–11

Bem, S. L. 1981. *Bem Sex-Role Inventory, professional manual.* Palo Alto, Calif: Consult. Psychol. Press. 37 pp.

Bennett, F. W., Cimbolic, P. 1980. Use of local norms to improve high-point code-type concordance of two short forms of the MMPI. *J. Pers. Assess.* 44:639–43

Bennett, F. W., Schubert, D. S. P. 1981. Use of local norms to improve configural reproducibility of an MMPI short form. *J. Pers. Assess.* 45:40–43

Bernard, L. C. 1981. The multidimensional aspects of masculinity-femininity. *J. Pers. Soc. Psychol.* 41:797–802

Berndt, D. J., Petzel, T. P., Berndt, S. M. 1980. Development and initial evaluation of a Multiscore Depression Inventory. *J. Pers. Assess.* 44:396–403

Bertelson, A. D., Marks, P. A., May, G. D. 1982. MMPI and race: A controlled study. *J. Consult. Clin. Psychol.* 50:316–18

Bessmer, M. A., Ramanaiah, N. V. 1981. Convergent and discriminant validity of selected need scales from the Adjective Check List and Personality Research Form. *Psychol. Rep.* 49:311–16

Biaggio, M. K. 1980. Assessment of anger arousal. *J. Pers. Assess.* 44:289–98

Biaggio, M. K., Supplee, K., Curtis, N. 1981. Reliability and validity of four anger scales. *J. Pers. Assess.* 45:639–48

Billman, J., McDevitt, S. C. 1980. Convergence of parent and observer ratings of temperament with observations of peer interaction in nursery school. *Child Dev.* 51:395–400

Black, F. W., Gasparrini, B., Nelson, R. 1981. Parental assessment of temperament in handicapped children. *J. Pers. Assess.* 45:155–58

Blumenthal, J. A., McKee, D. C., Williams, R. B., Haney, T. 1981. Assessment of conceptual tempo in the Type A (coronary prone) behavior pattern. *J. Pers. Assess.* 45:44–51

Boals, G. F., Peterson, D. R., Farmer, L., Mann, D. F., Robinson, D. L. 1982. The reliability, validity, and utility of three data modes in assessing marital relationships. *J. Pers. Assess.* 46:85–95

Bray, D. W. 1982. The assessment center and the study of lives. *Am. Psychol.* 37:180–89

Bridgewater, C. A. 1981. Construct validity of the Personality Research Form: Further evidence. *Educ. Psychol. Meas.* 41:533–35

Bridgewater, C. A. 1982. Personality characteristics of ski instructors and predicting teacher effectiveness using the PRF. *J. Pers. Assess.* 46:164–68

Briggs, S. R., Cheek, J. M., Buss, A. H. 1980.

An analysis of the Self-Monitoring Scale. *J. Pers. Soc. Psychol.* 38:679–86

Brody, L. R., Carter, A. S. 1982. Children's emotional attributions to self versus other: An exploration of an assumption underlying projective techniques. *J. Consult. Clin. Psychol.* 50:665–71

Bryant, F. B., Veroff, J. 1982. The structure of psychological well-being: a socio-historical analysis. *J. Pers. Soc. Psychol.* 43:653–73

Burger, G. K. Kabacoff, R. I. 1982. Personality types as measured by the 16 PF. *J. Pers. Assess.* 46:175–80

Burkhart, B. R., Gynther, M. D., Fromuth, M. E. 1980. The relative predictive validity of subtle vs. obvious items on the MMPI Depression scale. *J. Clin. Psychol.* 36:748–51

Burns, G. L. 1980. Indirect measurement and behavioral assessment: A case for social behaviorism psychometrics. *Behav. Assess.* 2:197–206

Buros, O. K., ed. 1978. *The Eighth Mental Measurements Yearbook,* Vols. 1, 2. Highland Park, NJ: Gryphon. 1115 pp., 1067 pp.

Buss, A. H., Plomin, R. 1975. *A Temperament Theory of Personality Development.* New York: Wiley

Buss, D. M., Craik, K. H. 1980. The frequency concept of disposition: Dominance and prototypically dominant acts. *J. Pers.* 48:379–92

Buss, D. M., Craik, K. H. 1983. The act frequency approach to personality. *Psychol. Rev.* 90:105–26

Butcher, J. N., Kendall, P. C., Hoffman, N. 1980. MMPI short forms: Caution. *J. Consult. Clin. Psychol.* 48:275–78

Campbell, D. T., Fiske, D. W. 1959. Convergent and discriminant validation by the multitrait-multimethod approach. *Psychol. Bull.* 56:81–105

Cantor, N., Kihlstrom, S. F., eds. 1981. *Personality, Cognition, and Social Interaction.* Hillsdale, NJ: Erlbaum

Carlson, K. A. 1982. *Carlson Psychological Survey: Manual.* Port Huron, Mich: Res. Psychol. Press. 29 pp.

Chun, K., Cobb, S., French, J. R. P. Jr. 1975. *Measures for Psychological Assessment.* Ann Arbor, Mich: Inst. Soc. Res., Univ. Mich.

Clopton, J. R. 1982. MMPI scale development methodology reconsidered. *J. Pers. Assess.* 46:143–46

Cole, D. A., Howard, G. S., Maxwell, S. E. 1981. Effects of mono versus multiple-operationalization in construct validation efforts. *J. Consult. Clin. Psychol.* 49:395–405

Conley, J. J. 1981. An MMPI typology of male alcoholics: Admission, discharge and outcome comparisons. *J. Pers. Assess.* 45:33–39

Conley, J. J., Kammeier, M. S. 1980. MMPI item responses of alcoholics in treatment: Comparisons with normals and psychiatric patients. *J. Consult. Clin. Psychol.* 48:668–69

Conte, H. R., Plutchik, R. 1981. A circumplex model for interpersonal personality traits. *J. Pers. Soc. Psychol.* 40:701–11

Costa, P. R. Jr., McCrae, R. R., Arenberg, D. 1980. Enduring dispositions in adult males. *J. Pers. Soc. Psychol.* 38:793–800

Cross, D. T., Burger, G. 1982. Ethnicity as a variable in responses to California Psychological Inventory items. *J. Pers. Assess.* 46:153–58

Dahlstrom, W. G., Dahlstrom, L. 1980. *Basic Readings on the MMPI.* Minneapolis: Univ. Minn. Press. 430 pp.

Dana, R. H. 1982. *A Human Science Model for Personality Assessment with Projective Techniques.* Springfield, Ill: Thomas

Dattore, P. J., Shontz, F. C., Coyne, L. 1980. Premorbid personality differentiation of cancer and noncancer groups: A test of the hypothesis of cancer proneness. *J. Consult. Clin. Psychol.* 48:388–94

Delatte, J. G., Hendrickson, N. J. 1982. Human figure drawing size as a measure of self-esteem. *J. Pers. Assess.* 46:603–6

Dohrenwend, B. S., Krasnoff, L., Askenasy, A. R., Dohrenwend, B. P. 1982. The Psychiatric Epidemiology Research Interview Life Events Scale. In *Handbook of Stress: Theoretical and Clinical Aspects,* ed. L. Goldberger, S. Breznitz, pp. 332–63. New York: Free Press. 804 pp.

Dunnett, S., Loun, S., Barber, P. J. 1981. Social desirability in the Eysenck Personality Inventory. *Br. J. Psychol.* 72:19–26

Edelbrock, C., Achenbach, T. M. 1980. A typology of Child Behavior Profile patterns: Distribution and correlates for disturbed children. *J. Abnorm. Child Psychol.* 8:441–70

Edinger, J. D. 1981. MMPI short forms: A clinical perspective. *Psychol. Rep.* 48:627–31

Ellis, R. A., Leitner, D. W. 1980. Social desirability as a variable affecting responses on the California Psychological Inventory. *Psychol. Rep.* 47:1223–26

Epstein, S. 1983. Aggregation and beyond: Some basic issues on the prediction of behavior. *J. Pers.* In press

Eshbaugh, D. M., Dick, K. V., Tosi, D. J. 1982. Typological analysis of MMPI personality patterns of drug dependent females. *J. Pers. Assess.* 46:488–94

Exner, J. E. Jr. 1974. *The Rorschach: A Comprehensive System.* New York: Wiley. 488 pp.

Exner, J. E. Jr. 1980. But it's only an inkblot. *J. Pers. Assess.* 44:562–77

Exner, J. E., Weiner, I. B. 1982. *The Ror-schach: A Comprehensive System.* Volume 3: *Assessment of Children and Adolescents.* New York: Wiley. 449 pp.

Eysenck H. J., Wakefield, J. A., Friedman, A. F. 1983. Diagnosis and clinical assessment: The DSM III. *Ann. Rev. Psychol.* 34:167–93

Filsinger, E. E. 1981. A measure of interpersonal orientation: the Liking People Scale. *J. Pers. Assess.* 43:295–300

Forbes, A. H., Braunstein, S. 1981. Relationships between the Eysenck Personality and Interpersonal Style Inventories. *Pers. Individ. Differ.* 2:167–68

Fox, S., Haboucha, S., Dinur, Y. 1981. The predictive validity of the Sixteen Personality Factors Questionnaire relative to three independent criterion measures of military performance. *Educ. Psychol. Meas.* 41:515–21

Freeman, C. W., Calsyn, D. A, Sherrard, D. J., Paige, A. B. 1980. Psychological assessment of renal dialysis patients using standard psychometric techniques. *J. Consult. Clin. Psychol.* 48:537–39

Fuller, G. B., Parmelee, W. M., Carroll, J. L. 1982. Performance of delinquent and nondelinquent high school boys on the Rotter Incomplete Sentence Blank. *J. Pers. Assess.* 46:506–10

Funder, D. C. 1980. On seeing ourselves as others see us: Self-other agreement and discrepancy in personality ratings. *J. Pers.* 48:473–93

Gabrys, J. B. 1980. Stability of scores on the Junior Eysenck Personality Inventory in an outpatient population. *Percept. Mot. Skills* 51:743–46

Gastorf, J. W. 1980. Time urgency of the Type A behavior pattern. *J. Consult. Clin. Psychol.* 48:299

Gdowski, C. L., Lachar, D., Butkus, M. 1980. A methodological consideration in the construction of actuarial interpretation systems. *J. Pers. Assess.* 44:427–32

Getter, H., Nowinski, J. K. 1981. A free response test of interpersonal effectiveness. *J. Pers. Assess.* 45:301–8

Gibbons, F. X. 1983. Self-attention and self-report: The "veridicality" hypothesis. *J. Pers.* In press

Gillum, R., Leon, G. R., Kamp, J., Becerra-Aldama, J. 1980. Prediction of cardiovascular and other disease onset and mortality from 30-year longitudinal MMPI data. *J. Consult Clin. Psychol.* 48:405–6

Gilmour, D. R., Walkey, F. H. 1981. Identifying violent offenders using a video measure of interpersonal distance. *J. Consult. Clin. Psychol.* 49:287–91

Goh, D. S., King, D. W., King, L. A. 1982. Psychometric evaluation of the Eysenck Personality Questionnaire. *Educ. Psychol. Meas.* 42:297–309

Goldberg, L. R. 1981a. Developing a taxonomy of trait-descriptive terms. In *New Directions for Methodology of Social and Behavioral Science Problems with Language Imprecision*, No. 9, ed. D. Fiske, pp. 43–65. San Francisco: Jossey-Bass

Goldberg, L. R. 1981b. Language and individual differences: The search for universals in personality lexicons. In *Review of Personality and Social Psychology*, ed. L. Wheeler, 2:141–65. Beverly Hills, Calif: Sage

Goldberg, L. R. 1982. From ace to zombie: Some explorations in the language of personality. See Spielberger & Butcher 1982, pp. 203–34

Gonzalez, J. R., Lanyon, R. I. 1982. A Spanish Psychological Screening Inventory: Norms and validity for Costa Rican Adolescents. *J. Cross-Cult. Psychol.* 13:71–85

Graham, J. R., Schwartz, M. F. 1981. Methodological issues and the construct validity of the MacAndrew Alcoholism Scale: A response to the rebuttal and constructive comments of Merenda and Sparadeo. *J. Consult. Clin. Psychol.* 49:971–73

Green, C. J. 1982. The diagnostic accuracy and utility of MMPI and MCMI computer interpretive reports. *J. Pers. Assess.* 46:359–65

Greene, R. L. 1980. *The MMPI: An Interpretive Manual.* New York: Grune & Stratton. 306 pp.

Greene, R. L. 1982. Some reflections on "MMPI short forms: A literature review". *J. Pers. Assess.* 46:486–87

Griffin, P. T., Danahy, S. 1982. Short form MMPIs in medical consultation: Accuracy of the Hs-Hy Dyad compared to the standard form. *J. Clin. Psychol.* 38:134–36

Grisso, T. 1982. Review of *Advances in Psychological Assessment*, Vol. 5., ed. P. McReynolds. *J. Pers. Assess.* 46:325–27

Grow, R., McVaugh, W., Eno, T. D. 1980. Faking and the MMPI. *J. Clin. Psychol.* 36:910–17

Gynther, M. D. 1981. Is the MMPI an appropriate assessment device for blacks? *J. Black Psychol.* 7:67–75

Gynther, M. D., Burkhart, B. R., Hovanitz, C. 1979. Do face-valid items have more predictive validity than subtle items? The case of the MMPI *Pd* scale. *J. Consult. Clin. Psychol.* 47:295–300

Gynther, M. D., Green, S. B. 1980. Accuracy may make a difference, but does a difference make for accuracy? A response to Pritchard and Rosenblatt. *J. Consult. Clin. Psychol.* 48:268–72

Hammer, E. F., ed. 1980. *The Clinical Application of Projective Drawings.* Springfield, Ill: Thomas. 663 pp. 6th printing.

Harris, W. G., Niedner, D., Feldman, C., Fink, A., Johnson, J. H. 1981. An on-line interpretive Rorschach approach: Using Ex-

ner's Comprehensive System. *Behav. Res. Methods Instrum.* 15:588–91

Hartung, J., Skorka, D. 1980. The HIT clinical profile of psychedelic drug users. *J. Pers. Assess.* 44:237–45

Hathaway, A. P. 1982. Intelligence and nonintelligence factors contributing to scores on the Rorschach Prognostic Rating Scale. *J. Pers. Assess.* 46:8–11

Haynes, S. N., Jensen, B. J., Wise, E., Sherman, J. 1981. The marital intake interview: A multimethod criterion validity assessment. *J. Consult. Clin. Psychol.* 49:379–87

Hayslip, B. Jr. 1982. The Holtzman Inkblot Technique and aging: Norms and factor structure. *J. Pers. Assess.* 46:248–56

Hersen, M., Bellack, A. S., eds. 1981. *Behavioral Assessment: A Practical Handbook.* New York: Pergamon. 603 pp. 2nd ed.

Hill, D. J., Bale, R. M. 1980. Development of the Mental Health Locus of Control and Mental Health Locus of Origin Scales. *J. Pers. Assess.* 44:148–56

Hinrichsen, J. J., Follansbee, D. J., Ganellen, R. 1981. Sex-role-related differences in self-control and mental health. *J. Pers. Assess.* 45:584–92

Hocevar, D. 1981. Measurement of creativity: review and critique. *J. Pers. Assess.* 46:450–64

Hogan, R. 1982. A socioanalytic theory of personality. In *1982 Nebraska Symposium on Motivation*, ed. M. M. Page, pp. 55–89. Lincoln: Univ. Nebr. Press. 276 pp.

Holden, R. R., Jackson, D. N. 1981. Subtlety, information, and faking effects in personality assessment. *J. Clin. Psychol.* 37:379–86

Holland, T. R., Beckett, G. E., Levi, M. 1981a. Intelligence, personality, and criminal violence: A multivariate analysis. *J. Consult. Clin. Psychol.* 49:106–11

Holland, T. R., Levi, M., Watson, C. G. 1981b. MMPI basic scales vs. two-point codes in the discrimination of psychopathological groups. *J. Clin. Psychol.* 37:394–96

Holt, R. R. 1977. A method for assessing primary process manifestations and their control in Rorschach responses. In *Rorschach Psychology*, ed. M. Rickers-Ovsiankina, pp. 375–420. New York: Krieger. 653 pp. 2nd ed.

Hopwood, J. H., Wei, K. H., Yellin, A. M. 1981. A computerized method for generating the Rorschach's structural summary from the sequence of scores. *J. Pers. Assess.* 45:116–17

Hovanitz, C. A., Gynther, M. D. 1980. The prediction of impulsive behavior: Comparative validities of obvious vs. subtle MMPI hypomania (*Ma*) items. *J. Clin. Psychol.* 36:422–27

Howe, M. G., Helmes, E. 1980. Validation of

the 16 PF in a psychiatric setting. *J. Clin. Psychol.* 36:927–31

Howe, P. A., Silvern, L. E. 1981. Behavioral observation of children during play therapy: Preliminary development of a research instrument. *J. Pers. Assess.* 45:168–82

Howes, R. J. 1981. The Rorschach: Does it have a future? *J. Pers. Assess.* 45:339–51

Hubert, N. C., Wachs, T. D., Peters-Martin, P., Gandour, M. J. 1982. The study of early temperament: Measurement and conceptual issues. *Child Dev.* 53:591–600

Hudson, W. W. 1982. *The Clinical Measurement Package: A Field Manual.* Homewood, Ill: Dorsey. 159 pp.

Jackson, D. N. 1970. A sequential system for personality scale development. In *Current Topics in Clinical and Community Psychology,* ed. C. D. Spielberger, 2:61–96. New York: Academic. 217 pp.

Jackson, D. N. 1980. Construct validity and personality assessment. In *Construct Validity in Psychological Measurement,* ed. A. Maslow, H. Wing, pp. 81–91. Princeton, NJ: Educ. Test. Serv

Jackson, D. N., Paunonen, S. V. 1980. Personality structure and assessment. *Ann. Rev. Psychol.* 31:503–51

Jacobson, N. S., Waldron, H., Moore, D. 1980. Toward a behavioral profile of marital distress. *J. Consult. Clin. Psychol.* 48:696–703

Jenkins, C. D., Zyzanski, S. J., Rosenman, R. H. 1979. *Manual for the Jenkins Activity Survey.* New York: Psychol. Corp.

John, O. P., Goldberg, L. R., Angleitner, A. 1983. Better than the alphabet: Taxonomies of personality-descriptive terms in English, Dutch, and German. In *Personality Psychology in Europe,* ed. H. Bonarius, G. van Heck, N. Smit. London: Erlbaum. In press

Johnson, J. A. 1981. The "self-disclosure" and "self-presentation: views of item response dynamics and personality scale validity. *J. Pers. Soc. Psychol.* 40:761–69

Johnson, J. H., Klingler, D. E., Giannetti, R. A. 1980. Band width in diagnostic classification using the MMPI as a predictor. *J. Consult. Clin. Psychol.* 48:340–49

Jones, T., Beidleman, W. B., Fowler, R. D. 1981. Differentiating violent and nonviolent prison inmates by use of selected MMPI scales. *J. Clin. Psychol.* 37:673–78

Jones, W. H., Hobbs, S. A., Hockenbury, D. 1982. Loneliness and social skill deficits. *J. Pers. Soc. Psychol.* 42:682–89

Jones, W. H., Russell, D. 1982. The Social Reticence Scale: An objective instrument to measure shyness. *J. Pers. Assess.* 6:629–31

Kahn, P., Ribner, S. 1982. A brief behavior rating scale for children in a school setting. *Psychol. Sch.* 19:113–16

Kane, R. A., Kane, R. L. 1981. *Assessing the Elderly: A Practical Guide to Measurement.* Lexington, Mass: Lexington Books. 301 pp.

Kaplan, R. M., Saccuzzo, D. T. 1982. *Psychological Testing: Principles, Application, and Issues.* Monterey, Calif: Brooks/Cole. 575 pp.

Katz, L., Dalby, J. T. 1981. Computer-assisted and traditional psychological assessment of elementary-school-aged children. *Contemp. Educ. Psychol.* 6:314–22

Kaufman, L., Murphy, N. C. 1981. Validation through self and other ratings on dimensions of six nonstressful multiscale personality instruments. *J. Pers. Assess.* 45:86–89

Kellerman, H., Burry, A. 1981. *Handbook of Psychodiagnostic Testing.* New York: Grune & Stratton. 222 pp.

Kelley, C. K., King, G. D. 1980. Two- and three-point classification of MMPI profiles in which scales 2, 7, and 8 are the highest elevations. *J. Pers. Assess.* 44:25–33

Kelso, G. I., Taylor, K. F. 1980. Psychologists as judges: A consensual validation of a personality typology. *Aust. Psychol.* 32:135–39

Kendall, P. C., Hollon, S. D., eds. 1981. *Assessment Strategies for Cognitive-Behavioral Interventions.* New York: Academic

Kenrick, D. T., Braver, S. L. 1982. Personality: idiographic and nomothetic. A rejoiner. *Psychol. Rev.* 89:182–86

Kenrick, D. T., Dantchik, A. 1983. Interactionism, idiographics, and the social psychological invasion of personality. *J. Pers.* In press

Kenrick, D. T., Stringfield, D. O. 1980. Personality traits and the eye of the beholder: crossing some traditional philosophical boundaries in the search for consistency in all of the people. *Psychol. Rev.* 87:88–104

Kernaleguen, A., Conrad, G. 1980. Analysis of five measures of self-concept. *Percept. Mot. Skills.* 51:855–61

Kinder, B., Brubaker, R., Ingram, R., Reading, E. 1982. Rorschach form quality: A comparison of the Exner and Beck systems. *J. Pers. Assess.* 46:131–38

Kleinmuntz, B. 1982. *Personality and Psychological Assessment.* New York: St. Martin's Press. 446 pp.

Klopfer, W. G. 1982. Review of *A Human Science Model for Personality Assessment with Projective Techniques,* by R. H. Dana. *J. Pers. Assess.* 46:658–59

Kolko, D. J., Dorsett, P. G., Milan, M. A. 1981. A total-assessment approach to the evaluation of social skills training: The effectiveness of an anger control program for adolescent psychiatric patients. *Behav. Assess.* 3:383–402

Korchin, S. J., Schuldberg, D. 1981. The future of clinical assessment. *Am. Psychol.* 36:1147–58

Koren, P., Carlton, K., Shaw, D. 1980. Marital conflict: Relations among behaviors, outcomes, and distress. *J. Consult. Clin. Psychol.* 48:460–68

Kozak, M. J., Miller, G. A. 1982. Hypothetical constructs versus intervening variables: A reappraisal of the three-systems model of anxiety assessment. *Behav. Assess.* 4:347–58

Krug, S. E. 1981. *Interpreting 16PF Profile Patterns*. Champaign, Ill: Inst. Pers. and Ability Test. 191 pp.

Kunce, J. T., Tamkin, A. S. 1981. Rorschach movement and color responses and MMPI social extraversion and thinking introversion personality types. *J. Pers. Assess.* 45:5–10

Lachar, D. 1982. *Personality Inventory for Children (PIC): Revised Format Manual Supplement*. Los Angeles: West. Psychol. Serv. 105 pp.

Lachar, D., Gdowski, C. L., Snyder, D. K. 1982. Broad-based dimensions of psychopathology: Factor scales for the Personality Inventory for Children. *J. Consult. Clin. Psychol.* 50:634–42

Lanyon, R. I., Goodstein, L. D. 1982. *Personality Assessment*. New York: Wiley. 311 pp. 2nd ed.

Lazar, Z. L., Schwartz, F. 1982. The contaminated Rorschach response: Formal features. *J. Clin. Psychol.* 38:415–19

Lefkowitz, M. M., Tesiny, E. P. 1980. Assessment of childhood depression. *J. Consult. Clin. Psychol.* 48:43–50

Lehrer, P. M., Woolfolk, R. L. 1982. Self-report assessment of anxiety: Somatic, cognitive, and behavioral modalities. *Behav. Assess.* 4:167–77

Lerner, R. M., Palermo, M., Spiro, A., Nesselroade, J. R. 1982. Assessing the dimensions of temperamental individuality across the life span: The dimensions of temperament survey. *Child Dev.* 53:149–59

Lessing, E. E., Williams, V., Revelle, W. 1981. Parallel forms of the IJR Behavior Checklist for parents, teachers, and clinicians. *J. Consult. Clin. Psychol.* 49:34–50

Levin, J., Karni, E. S. 1981. A note on the interpretation of the factor pattern of the California Psychological Inventory *J. Pers. Assess.* 45:430–32

Levitt, E. E. 1980. *Primer on the Rorschach Technique*. Springfield, Ill: Thomas. 103 pp.

Loevinger, J., Wessler, R., Redmore, C. 1970. *Measuring Ego Development*, Vols. 1, 2. San Francisco: Jossey-Bass

Lomranz, J., Lubin, B., Eyal, N., Medini, G. 1981. A Hebrew version of the Depression Adjective Check Lists. *J. Pers. Assess.* 45:380–84

Lord, C. G. 1982. Predicting behavioral consistency from an individual's perception of situational similarities. *J. Pers. Soc. Psychol.* 42:1076–88

Lorr, M., Burger, G. K. 1981. Personality types in data from California Psychological Inventory as defined by cluster analysis. *Psychol. Rep.* 48:115–18

Loucks, S. 1980. Loneliness, affect, and self-concept: Construct validity of the Bradley Loneliness Scale. *J. Pers. Assess.* 44:142–47

Loucks, S., Burstein, A. G., Boros, T., Kregor, E. 1980. The affective ratio in Rorschach's test as a function of age. *J. Pers. Assess.* 44:590–91

Lowman, J. 1980. Measurement of family affective structure. *J. Pers. Assess.* 44:130–41

Lyon, M. E., Plomin, R. 1981. The measurement of temperament using parental ratings. *J. Child Psychol. Psychiatry* 22:47–53

Machover, K. 1980. *Personality Projection in the Drawing of the Human Figure*. Springfield, Ill: Thomas. 11th printing

Major, B., Carnevale, P. J. D., Deaux, K. 1981. A different perspective on androgyny: Evaluations of masculine and feminine personality characteristics. *J. Pers. Soc. Psychol.* 41:988–1001

Marshall, P., Surridge, D., Delva, N. 1980. Differentiation of organic and psychogenic impotence on the basis of MMPI decision rules. *J. Consult. Clin. Psychol.* 48:407–8

Martin, J. D., Blair, G. E., Dannenmaier, W. D., Jones, P. C., Asako, M. 1981. Relationship of scores on the California Psychological Inventory to age. *Psychol. Rep.* 49:151–54

Mash, E. J., Terdal, L. G., eds. 1981. *Behavioral Assessment of Childhood Disorders*. New York: Guilford. 749 pp.

Maslach, C., Jackson, S. E. 1981. *Maslach Burnout Inventory: Manual*. Palo Alto, Calif: Consult. Psychol. Press. 19 pp.

Matthews, K. A. 1982. Psychological perspectives on the Type A behavior pattern. *Psychol. Bull.* 91:293–323

Matthews, K. A., Krantz, D. S., Dembroski, T. M., MacDougall, J. M. 1982. Unique and common variance in Structured Interview and Jenkins Activity Survey measures of the Type A behavior pattern. *J. Pers. Soc. Psychol.* 42:303–13

McAdams, D. P., Vaillant, G. E. 1982. Intimacy motivation and psychosocial adjustment: A longitudinal study. *J. Pers. Assess.* 46:586–93

McArthur, D. S., Roberts, G. E. 1982. *Roberts Apperception Test for Children: Manual*. Los Angeles: West. Psychol. Serv. 118 pp.

McFall, R. M. 1982. A review and reformulation of the concept of social skills. *Behav. Assess.* 4:1–37

McGill, J. C. 1980. MMPI score differences among anglo, black, and Mexican-American welfare recipients. *J. Clin. Psychol.* 36:147–51

McKnight, R. T. 1980. Prediction of hypnotizability from personality variables of the California Psychological Inventory: A multiple regression analysis. *Psychol. Rep.* 47:1319–22

McReynolds, R., ed. 1981. *Advances in Psychological Assessment,* Vol. 5. San Francisco: Jossey-Bass. 564 pp.

Meehl, P. E. 1956. Wanted—A good cookbook. *Am. Psychol.* 11:263–72

Mehrabian, A., O'Reilly, E. 1980. Analysis of personality measures in terms of basic dimensions of temperament. *J. Pers. Soc. Psychol.* 38:492–503

Merenda, P. F., Sparadeo, F. 1981. Rebuttal to and constructive comments on "construct validity" of the MacAndrew Alcoholism Scale". *J. Consult. Clin. Psychol.* 49:968–70

Merluzzi, T. V., Glass, C. R., Genest, M., eds. 1981. *Cognitive Assessment.* New York: Guilford. 532 pp.

Messick, S. 1980. Test validity and the ethics of assessment. *Am. Psychol.* 35:1012–27

Miller, H. R., Streiner, D. L., Kahgee, S. L. 1982. Use of the Golden-Meehl indicators in the detection of Schizoid-Taxon membership. *J. Abnorm. Psychol.* 91:55–60

Millon, T. 1982. *Millon Clinical Multiaxial Inventory: Manual.* Minneapolis: Natl Computer Systems. 73 pp. 2nd ed.

Millon, T., Green, C. J., Meagher, R. B. Jr. 1982a. *Millon Adolescent Personality Inventory: Manual.* Minneapolis: National Computer Systems 60 pp.

Millon, T., Green, C. J., Meagher, R. B. Jr. 1982b. *Millon Behavioral Health Inventory: Manual.* Minneapolis: National Computer Syst. 40 pp. 3rd ed.

Mischel, W., Peake, P. K. 1982. Beyond *déja vu* in the search for cross-situational consistency. *Psychol. Rev.* 89:730–55

Monahan, J. 1981. *The Clinical Prediction of Violent Behavior.* Rockville, MD: Natl. Inst. Mental Health. 134 pp.

Moreland, K. L. 1982. A comparison of methods of scoring the MMPI-168. *J. Consult. Clin. Psychol.* 50:451

Morley, L. C. 1982. An adjustment for protocol length in Rorschach scoring. *J. Pers. Assess.* 46:338–40

Moskowitz, D. S., Schwarz, J. C. 1982. Validity comparison of behavior counts and ratings by knowledgeable informants. *J. Pers. Soc. Psychol.* 42:518–28

Newmark, C. S., Gentry, L., Warren, N., Finch, A. J. 1981. Racial bias in an MMPI index of schizophrenia. *Br. J. Clin. Psychol.* 20:215–16

Newmark, C. S., Woody, G. G., Ziff, D. R., Finch, A. J. Jr. 1980. MMPI short forms: A different perspective. *J. Consult. Clin. Psychol.* 48:279–83

Noce, S. F., Whitmyre, J. W. 1981. Comparison of MMPI and Mini-Mult with both psychiatric inpatients and screening nursing students. *J. Pers. Assess.* 45:147–50

Orlofsky, J. L. 1981. Relationship between sex role attitudes and personality traits and the Sex Role Behavior Scale-1: A new measure of masculine and feminine role behaviors and interests. *J. Pers. Soc. Psychol.* 40:927–40

Osberg, J. W. III, Meares, G. J., McKee, D. C., Burnett, G. B. 1982. The MMPI as a measure of the emotional correlates of chronic hemodialysis: A review. *J. Pers. Assess.* 46:268–78

Oswald, W. T., Velicer, W. F. 1980. Item format and the structure of the Eysenck Personality Inventory: A replication. *J. Pers. Assess.* 44:283–88

Overall, J. E., Eiland, D. C. 1982. MMPI-168 norms and profile sheets for bright young college graduates. *J. Clin. Psychol.* 38:109–14

Passman, R. H., Lautmann, L. A. 1982. Fathers', mothers', and security blankets' effects on the responsiveness of young children during projective testing. *J. Consult. Clin. Psychol.* 50:310–12

Patalano, F. 1980. MMPI two-point code-type frequencies of drug abusers in a therapeutic community. *Psychol. Rep.* 46:1019–22

Patterson, E. T., Charles, H. L., Woodward, W. A., Roberts, W. R., Penk, W. E. 1981. Differences in measures of personality and family environment among black and white alcoholics. *J. Consult. Clin. Psychol.* 49:1–9

Paulhus, D. L. 1981. Control of social desirability in personality inventories: Principal-factor deletion. *J. Res. Pers.* 15:383–88

Pollack, D., Shore, J. H. 1980. Validity of the MMPI with native Americans. *Am. J. Psychiatry* 137:946–50

Pollack, S., Gilligan, C. 1982. Images of violence in Thematic Apperception Test stories. *J. Pers. Soc. Psychol.* 42:159–67

Post, R. D., Lobitz, W. C. 1980. The utility of Mezzich's MMPI regression formula as a diagnostic criterion in depression research. *J. Consult. Clin. Psychol.* 48:673–74

Prescott, S., Csikszentmihalyi, M., Graef, R. 1981. Environmental effects on cognitive and affective states: The experiential time sampling approach. *Soc. Behav. Pers.* 9:23–32

Pritchard, D. A., Rosenblatt, A. 1980a. Racial bias in the MMPI: A methodological review. *J. Consult. Clin. Psychol.* 48:263–67

Pritchard, D. A, Rosenblatt, A. 1980b. Reply

to Gynther and Green. *J. Consult. Clin. Psychol.* 48:273–74

Prokop, C. K., Bradley, L. A., Margolis, R., Gentry, W. D. 1980. Multivariate analysis of the MMPI profiles of patients with multiple pain complaints. *J. Pers. Assess.* 44:246–52

Rabin, A. I., ed. 1981. *Assessment with Projective Techniques.* New York: Springer. 342 pp.

Ramanaiah, N. V., Martin, H. J. 1980. On the two-dimensional nature of the Marlowe-Crowne Social Desirability Scale. *J. Pers. Assess.* 44:507–14

Ray, J. J., Bozek, R. S. 1981. Authoritarianism and Eysenck's *P* scale. *J. Soc. Psychol.* 113:231–34

Reynolds, C. R., Paget, K. D. 1981. Factor analysis of the Revised Children's Manifest Anxiety Scale for blacks, whites, males, and females with a national normative sample. *J. Consult. Clin. Psychol.* 49:352–59

Reynolds, W. M., Gould, J. W. 1981. A psychometric investigation of the standard and short form Beck Depression Inventory. *J. Consult. Clin. Psychol.* 49:306–7

Rezmovic, E. L., Rezmovic, V. 1980. Empirical validation of psychological constructs: A secondary analysis. *Psychol. Bull.* 87:66–71

Reznikoff, M., Aronow, E., Rauchway, A. 1982. The reliability of inkblot content scales. See Spielberger & Butcher 1982, 1:83–113

Rierdan, J., Koff, E. 1981. Sexual ambiguity in children's human figure drawings. *J. Pers. Assess.* 45:256–57

Ritzler, B. A., Sharkey, K. J., Chudy, J. F. 1980a. A comprehensive projective alternative to the TAT. *J. Pers. Assess.* 44:358–62

Ritzler, B. A., Zambianco, D., Harder, D., Kaskey, M. 1980b. Psychotic patterns and the concept of the object on the Rorschach test. *J. Abnorm. Psychol.* 89:46–55

Robinowitz, R., Woodward, W. A., Penk, W. E. 1980. MMPI comparison of black heroin users volunteering or not volunteering for treatment. *J. Consult. Clin. Psychol.* 48:540–42

Robinson, E. A., Eyberg, S. M. 1981. The Dyadic Parent-Child Interaction Coding System: Standardization and validation. *J. Consult. Clin. Psychol.* 49:245–50

Rock, D. L. 1981. The confounding of two self-report assertion measures with the tendency to give socially desirable responses in self-description. *J. Consult. Clin. Psychol.* 49:743–44

Roesch, D., Golding, S. L. 1980. *Competency to Stand Trial.* Champaign, Ill: Univ. Ill. Press. 268 pp.

Rorer, L. G., Widiger, T. A. 1983. Personality structure and assessment. *Ann. Rev. Psychol.* 34:431–63

Rosch, E., Mervis, C. B. 1975. Family resemblances: Studies in the internal structure of categories. *Cogn. Psychol.* 7:573–605

Rose, D., Bitter, E. J. 1980. The Palo Alto Destructive Content Scale as a predictor of physical assaultiveness in men. *J. Pers. Assess.* 44:228–33

Rosegrant, J. 1982. Primary process patterning in college students' inkblot responses. *J. Pers. Assess.* 46:578–81

Russ, S. W. 1980. Primary process integration on the Rorschach and achievement in children. *J. Pers. Assess.* 44:338–44

Russ, S. W. 1981. Primary process integration on the Rorschach and achievement in children: A follow-up study. *J. Pers. Assess.* 45:473–84

Russ, S. W. 1982. Sex differences in primary process thinking and flexibility in problem-solving in children. *J. Pers. Assess.* 46:569–77

Russell, D., Peplau, L. A., Cutrona, C. E. 1980. The revised UCLA Loneliness Scale: Concurrent and discriminant validity evidence. *J. Pers. Soc. Psychol.* 39:472–80

Russell, J. A. 1980. A circumplex model of affect. *J. Pers. Soc. Psychol.* 39:1161–78

Ryckman, R. M., Robbins, M. A., Thornton, B., Cantrell, P. 1982. Development and validation of a physical self-efficacy scale. *J. Pers. Soc. Psychol.* 42:891–900

Saville, P., Blinkhorn, S. 1981. Reliability, homogeneity, and the construct validity of Cattell's 16 PF. *Pers. Individ. Diff.* 2:325–33

Schuerger, J. M., Tait, E., Tavernelli, M. 1982. Temporal stability of personality by questionnaire. *J. Pers. Soc. Psychol.* 43:176–82

Seamons, D. T., Howell, R. J., Carlisle, A. L., Roe, A. V. 1981. Rorschach simulation of mental illness and normality by psychotic and nonpsychotic legal offenders. *J. Pers. Assess.* 45:130–35

Shaffer, J. W., Duszynski, K. R., Thomas, C. B. 1981. Orthogonal dimensions of individual and group forms of the Rorschach. *J. Pers. Assess.* 45:230–39

Shill, M. 1981. TAT measures of gender identity (castration anxiety) in father-absent males. *J. Pers. Assess.* 45:136–46

Shrauger, J. S., Osberg, T. M. 1981. The relative accuracy of self-predictions and judgments by others in psychological assessment. *Psychol. Bull.* 90:322–51

Siegel, J. M., Matthews, K. A., Leitch, C. J. 1981. Validation of the Type A interview assessment of adolescents: A multidimensional approach. *Psychosom. Med.* 43:311–21

Sison, G. F., Fehr, L. A., Muhoberac, B. P. 1981. A projective analysis of guilt: The

Holtzman Inkblot Technique. *J. Pers. Assess.* 45:23–26

Smith, N. M. 1981. The relationship between the Rorschach whole response and level of cognitive functioning. *J. Pers. Assess.* 45:13–19

Smith, T. W., Brehm, S. S. 1981. Person perception and the Type A coronary-prone behavior pattern. *J. Pers. Soc. Psychol.* 40:1137–49

Snyder, D. K. 1981. *Marital Satisfaction Inventory: Manual.* Los Angeles: West. Psychol. Serv. 59 pp.

Snyder, D. K. 1982. Advances in marital assessment: behavioral, communications, and psychometric approaches. See Spielberger & Butcher 1982, 1:169–201

Snyder, D. K., Regts, J. M. 1982. Factor scales for assessing marital disharmony and disaffection. *J. Consult. Clin. Psychol.* 50: 736–43

Snyder, D. K., Wills, R. M., Keiser, T. W. 1981. Empirical validation of the Marital Satisfaction Inventory: An actuarial approach. *J. Consult. Clin. Psychol.* 49: 262–68

Snyter, C. M., Allik, J. P. 1981. The fakability of the Personal Orientation Dimensions: Evidence for a lie profile. *J. Pers. Assess.* 45:533–38

Spielberger, C. D., Butcher, J. N. 1982. *Advances in Personality Assessment,* Vol. 1. Hillsdale, NJ: Erlbaum. 249 pp.

Spitzer, R. L., Endicott, J. 1969. DIAGNO II: Further developments in a computer program for psychiatric diagnosis. *Am. J. Psychiatry* 125:12–21 (Suppl.)

Squyres, E. M., Craddick, R. A. 1982. A measure of time perspective with the TAT and some issues of reliability. *J. Pers. Assess.* 46:257–59

Stager, S., Young, R. D. 1982. A self-concept measure for preschool and early primary grade children. *J. Pers. Assess.* 46:536–43

Stanwyck, D. J., Garrison, W. M. 1982. Detection of faking on the Tennessee Self-Concept Scale. *J. Pers. Assess.* 46:426–31

Staples, R. B., Ficher, I. V., Shapiro, M., Martin, K., Gonick, P. 1980. A reevaluation of MMPI discriminators of biogenic and psychogenic impotence. *J. Consult. Clin. Psychol.* 48:543–45

Stevens, E. D. 1981. Barrier score and the values ascribed to selected individuals by high school students. *J. Pers. Assess.* 46:352–58

Stevens, M. R., Reilly, R. R. 1980. MMPI short forms: A literature review. *J. Pers. Assess.* 44:368–76

Stipek, D. J., Lamb, M. E., Zigler, E. F. 1981. OPTI: A measure of children's optimism. *Educ. Psychol. Meas.* 41:131–43

Stock, N. A., Kantner, J. E. 1980. Themes elicited by the Senior Apperception Test in institutionalized older adults. *J. Pers. Assess.* 44:600–2

Strassberg, D. S., Reimherr, F., Ward, M., Russell, S., Cole, A. 1981. The MMPI and chronic pain. *J. Consult. Clin. Psychol.* 49:220–26

Strickland, B. R., Haley, W. E. 1980. Sex differences on the Rotter I-E scale. *J. Pers. Soc. Psychol.* 39:930–39

Strober, M., Green, J., Carlson, G. 1981. Utility of the Beck Depression Inventory with psychiatrically hospitalized adolescents. *J. Consult. Clin. Psychol.* 49:482–83

Sturner, R. A., Rothbaum, F., Visintainer, M., Wolfer, J. 1980. The effects of stress on children's figure drawings. *J. Clin. Psychol.* 36:324–31

Sundberg, N. 1982. Review of *Advances in Personality Assessment,* Vol. 1, ed. C. D. Spielberger, J. N. Butcher. *J. Pers. Assess.* 46:555–56

Sutker, P. B., Brantley, P. J., Allain, A. N. 1980. MMPI response patterns and alcohol consumption in DUI offenders. *J. Consult. Clin. Psychol.* 48:350–55

Svanum, S., Lantz, J. B., Lauer, J. B., Wampler, R. S., Madura, J. A. 1981. Correspondence of the MMPI and the MMPI-168 with intestinal bypass surgery patients. *J. Clin. Psychol.* 37:137–41

Tamkin, A. S. 1980. Rorschach experience balance, introversion, and sex. *Psychol. Rep.* 46:843–48

Thomas, A., Chess, S. 1977. *Temperament and Development.* New York: Brunner Mazel

Thornton, G. C. III, Gierasch, P. F. III. 1980. Fakability of an empirically derived selection instrument. *J. Pers. Assess.* 44:48–51

Thurber, S. 1981. CPI variables in relation to the polygraph performance of police officer candidates. *J. Soc. Psychol.* 113:145–46

Turnbow, K., Dana, R. H. 1981. The effects of stem length and directions on sentence completion test responses. *J. Pers. Assess.* 45:27–32

Underwood, B., Froming, W. J. 1980. The Mood Survey: A personality measure of happy and sad moods. *J. Pers. Assess.* 44:404–14

Underwood, B., Moore, B. S. 1981. Sources of behavioral consistency. *J. Pers. Soc. Psychol.* 40:780–85

Vincent, K. R. 1980a. *Semi-automated Full Battery.* Houston: Psychometric Press. 88 pp.

Vincent, K. R. 1980b. *MMPI: Semi-automated Interpretive Statements.* Houston: Psychometric Press. 72 pp.

Wagner, E. E., Wagner, C. E. 1981. *The Interpretation of Projective Test Data.* Springfield, Ill: Thomas

Walsh, J. A. 1978. Review of the 16PF Test. In *The Eighth Mental Measurements Yearbook*, ed. O. K. Buros, 1:1081–83. Highland Park, NJ: Gryphon. 2 vols: 1115 pp., 1067 pp.

Walters, L. H., Klein, A. E. 1981. Measures of anomie and locus-of-control for adolescents: Evidence of factorial validity. *Educ. Psychol. Meas.* 41:1203–13

Ward, L. C. 1980. Conversion equations for modified scoring of the MMPI-168. *J. Pers. Assess.* 44:644–46

West, S. G., ed. 1983. Personality and predictions: nomothetic and idiographic approaches. *J. Pers.*, Special issue. In press

Wicker, A. W. 1981. Nature and assessment of behavior settings: Recent contributions from the ecological perspective. See Mc Reynolds 1981, 5:22–61

Widiger, T. A. 1982. Psychological tests and the borderline diagnosis. *J. Pers. Assess.* 46:227–38

Widiger, T. A., Knudson, R. M., Rorer, L. G. 1980. Convergent and discriminant validity of measures of cognitive styles and abilities. *J. Pers. Soc. Psychol.* 39:116–29

Widiger, T. A., Schilling, K. M. 1980. Toward a construct validation of the Rorschach. *J. Pers. Assess.* 44:450–59

Wieder, G. B., Weiss, R. L. 1980. Generalizability theory and the coding of marital interactions. *J. Consult. Clin. Psychol.* 48:469–77

Wiener-Levy, D., Exner, J. E. Jr. 1981. The Rorschach EA-ep variable as related to persistence in a task frustration situation under feedback conditions. *J. Pers. Assess.* 45:118–24

Wiggins, J. S. 1980. Circumplex models of interpersonal behavior. In *Review of Personality and Social Psychology*, ed. L. Wheeler, 1:265–94. Beverly Hills, Calif: Sage

Wiggins, J. S. 1982. Circumplex modes of interpersonal behavior in clinical psychology. In *Handbook of Research Methods in Clinical Psychology*, ed. P. C. Kendall, J. H. Butcher, pp. 183–221. New York: Wiley

Wiggins, J. S., Holzmuller, A. 1981. Further evidence on androgyny and interpersonal flexibility. *J. Res. Pers.* 15:67–80

Wiggins, J. S., Steiger, J. H., Gaelich, L. 1981. Evaluating circumplexity in personality data. *Multivar. Behav. Res.* 16:263–86

Winters, K. C., Weintraub, S., Neale, J. M. 1981. Validity of MMPI codetypes in identifying DSM-III schizophrenics, unipolars, and bipolars. *J. Consult. Clin. Psychol.* 49:486–87

Wirt, R. D., Lachar, D. 1981. The Personality Inventory for Children: Development and clinical applications. See McReynolds 1981, 5:353–92

Wolf, T. M., Sklov, M. C., Hunter, S. D., Webber, L. S., Berenson, G. S. 1982a. Factor-analytic study of the Piers-Harris Children's Self-concept scale. *J. Pers. Assess.* 46:511–13

Wolf, T. M., Sklov, M. C., Wenzl, P. A., Hunter, C. M., Berenson, G. S. 1982b. Validation of a measure of Type A behavior pattern in children: Bogalusa heart study. *Child Dev.* 53:126–53

Woody, R. H., ed. 1980. *Encyclopedia of Clinical Assessment*, Vols. 1, 2. San Francisco: Jossey-Bass. 574 pp., 606 pp.

Wrobel, T. A., Lachar, D. 1982. Validity of the Wiener subtle and obvious scales for the MMPI: Another example of the importance of inventory-item content. *J. Consult. Clin. Psychol.* 50:469–70

Zager, L. D., Megargee, E. I. 1981. Seven MMPI alcohol and drug abuse scales: An empirical investigation of their interrelationships, convergent and discriminant validity, and degree of racial bias. *J. Pers. Soc. Psychol.* 40:532–44

Zelin, M. L., Adler, G., Myerson, P. G. 1972. Anger self-report: An objective questionnaire for the measurement of aggression. *J. Consult. Clin. Psychol.* 39:340

Ziskin, J. 1981. *Coping with Psychiatric and Psychological Testimony*, Vols. 1, 2. Venice, Calif: Law and Psychology Press. 466 pp., 506 pp. 2nd ed.

Zuckerman, M., Buchsbaum, M. S., Murphy, D. L. 1980. Sensation seeking and its biological correlates. *Psychol. Bull.* 88:187–214

AUTHOR INDEX

A

Abelson, R. P., 150, 397, 400, 402-4, 421
Abikoff, H., 247, 249
Abrams, M. L., 525
Abramson, L. Y., 450, 454, 612
ACHENBACH, T. M., 227-56; 228, 232, 233, 235, 237, 238, 246-49, 251, 315, 687
Acheson, A. L., 291
Acosta, F. X., 353
Adam, N., 23
Adams, J., 500
Adams, J. S., 636, 637
Adams, N. H., 348
Adams, R. D., 15
Adelbratt, T., 146
Adelman, H., 647
Adelman, L., 150, 158
Adelson, B., 374
Adelson, E. H., 221
Adelson, J., 312
Adkins-Regan, E., 170
Adler, B., 214
Adler, G., 684
Adler, N. T., 166, 169
Adler, P. T., 341
Adler, S., 474
Agid, Y., 290
Aguayo, A. J., 284, 285
Aguilar, J., 104
Ahlbom, A., 653
Aiello, B., 28
Ajzen, I., 397-400, 402
Alba, J. W., 363
Albee, G. W., 338, 344
Albert, D. J., 259, 268
Albert, K., 133
Albert, S., 681
Alberts, J. R., 564, 568
Albrecht, D. G., 212, 218
Albuquerque, E. X., 294
Alcaraz, V. M., 89
Aldag, R. J., 633
Alderfer, C. P., 646
Aldrich, H., 656
Alexander, E. R. III, 478
Alexander, R. A., 489
Alheidt, P., 681
Allain, A. N., 689
Allan, L. G., 5-7, 9-13
Allen, D. A., 20
Allen, J., 445
Allen, J. L., 215
Allen, R. W., 658
Allen, S., 340

Allen, T., 656
Allik, J., 220
Allik, J. P., 675
Allison, P. D., 597
Allport, D. A., 7
Alluisi, E. A., 468
Almeida, E., 97, 103, 104
Alpander, G. C., 464
Alpert, J. L., 342, 343
Alsum, P., 185
Altar, C. A., 300
Altemeyer, R. A., 690
Altmaier, E. M., 593
Altom, M. W., 126, 131
Alvarado Tenorio, R., 87
Alvarez, B. M., 90
Alvarez, G., 97, 98
Alvarez, M. D., 452
Amabile, M., 150
Ambron, S. R., 312
American Psychiatric Association, 228, 243, 250
American Psychological Association, 98
Amos, S. P., 680
Anastasi, A., 669
Anastasio, E. J., 521
Anchin, J. C., 597
Anderson, A., 429
Anderson, B., 534
Anderson, C. A., 451
Anderson, J. C., 472
Anderson, J. R., 129, 154, 366, 379, 382, 385, 388
Anderson, K., 245
Anderson, N. H., 141, 144, 153
Anderson, P., 214
Anderson, R. C., 385
Anderson, R. M., 655
Anderson, S. M., 264
Andrasik, F., 537
Andrews, D. P., 220
Andrews, G., 41
Andrews, I. R., 637
Andrulis, D. P., 339
Aneshansel, J., 419
Angle, H. L., 658
Angleitner, A., 671
Anglin, J. M., 119
Antaki, C., 428
Anterasian, C., 658
Antes, J. R., 17
Antonucci, T. C., 565
Aono, T., 175
Appelbaum, S. A., 91
Appelman, A. J., 442
Appley, M. H., 634

Arabie, P., 69, 76
Arai, Y., 170
Aram, J. D., 654
Aranda Lopez, J., 91
Arauz-Contreras, J., 186
Archer, J., 348
Archer, R. L., 102
Ardila, R., 85
Arditi, A., 214
Arenberg, D., 673
Arendash, G. W., 171
Argyris, C., 536, 545, 629
Arias Galicia, F., 101
Arkes, H. R., 232
Arkin, R., 48
Arkin, R. M., 442-44, 526
Armenakis, A. A., 539
Armitage, C. C., 353
Armstrong, S. L., 120-22
Arnkoff, D., 581
Arnold, A. D., 170
Arnold, H. J., 151, 475, 642, 643, 646
Arnold, J. D., 483, 491
Arnold, W. P., 268
Aron, L., 680
Aronow, E., 680
Aronowitz, E., 344
Aronson, E., 405, 408
Aronson, L. R., 189
Arvey, R. D., 466, 467, 478, 480, 494, 501
Asako, M., 678
Asch, S., 417
Ash, M. J., 620
Ash, P., 502
Ash, R. A., 466, 478, 526
Ashbaugh, J. W., 351
Asher, S. J., 350
Ashford, S. J., 471, 633, 646
Ashley, M. A., 610
Ashworth, S., 485
Askenasy, A. R., 670
Aslin, R. N., 215, 564, 568
Atkinson, D. R., 593
Atkinson, R., 620
Atkinson, R. C., 141, 369
Attig, M. S., 363
Attneave, C. L., 353
Audubon, J. J., 689
Auletta, K., 352
Austin, J. M. Jr., 537
Austin, M. J., 340
Austin, W., 635, 637
Authier, J., 587
Avant, L. L., 17
Avener, J., 611

703

Warren, M., 522
Warren, N., 688
Warrington, E. K., 370
Wartner, U., 566
Warwick, D. P., 336
Washington, T. P., 531
Wason, P. C., 148
Waterman, A. S., 310
Waters, E., 565
Watkins, M. J., 373, 376-78, 383
Watkins, O. C., 376, 377
Watson, A. B., 203
Watson, C. G., 676
Watson, C. J., 476
Watson, D., 429
Watson, J. S., 314
Watt, R. J., 220
Watzlawick, P., 596
Weakland, J., 596
WEARY, G., 427-59; 428, 438, 440-43, 526
Weary Bradley, G., 440, 441
Weaver, W. B., 15, 22
Webb, E. G., 496
Webber, L. S., 688
Weber, A. L., 437
Weber, G. H., 345
Webster, E. C., 479
Webster, M. C., 582, 597
Weddell, G., 286
Weeks, D. G., 63, 68
Wei, K. H., 681
Weick, K. E., 643, 655, 659
Weimer, W. B., 594
Weinberg, R. A., 564, 567
Weinberg, R. S., 616
Weiner, B., 429, 433, 448, 453
Weiner, I. B., 680
Weinstein, C. E., 531
Weinstein, C. L., 583
Weinstein, D., 654
Weinstein, R. M., 348
Weinstein, S., 336, 339
Weintraub, S., 677
Weir, K., 236
Weisbord, M. R., 522
Weisbrod, B. A., 340
Weiskott, G. N., 596
Weiskrantz, L., 370
Weiss, A., 657
Weiss, D. J., 631
Weiss, H. M., 534, 634
Weiss, R. L., 685
Weiss, R. S., 437
Weissman, M. M., 240
Weisz, J., 168, 175
Weisz, J. R., 247, 560
Weitzman, R. A., 483
Weldon, D. E., 419
Welford, A. T., 310
Wellman, B., 346

Wellman, H. M., 558
Wells, G. L., 433, 435, 438, 452
Welner, Z., 244
Welsh, M. A., 475
Wendelken, D. J., 474, 499
Wendrich, W. W., 620
Wenzl, P. A., 688
Werner, E. E., 316, 319
Werry, J. S., 237, 246, 249
Wescourt, K. T., 369, 379
Wessler, R., 682
Wesson, M. D., 216
West, J. R., 281
West, S. G., 436, 469, 486, 526, 558, 669, 670, 673
Westbrook, W., 261
Westbrook, W. H., 186
Westfall, D. P., 294, 295
WESTHEIMER, G., 201-26; 5, 204, 206, 209, 218-20
Westin, A., 654
Weston, D. R., 559
Wetherington, C. L., 259
WEXLEY, K. N., 519-51; 468, 469, 471, 474, 520, 521, 524, 526, 539-42
WHALEN, R. E., 257-76; 170
Whaley, C. P., 156
Whaley, G. L., 499
Wheatt, T., 244
Wherry, R. S. Sr., 472
Whipple, K., 583
Whissell-Buechy, D., 318, 322
White, C. B., 544
White, G. L., 410
White, J. B., 402
White, K. R., 39, 44, 45, 50
White, M. C., 544
White, S. E., 634
Whitehurst, G. J., 556
Whiteley, J. M., 589, 590
Whitmoyer, D. I., 182
Whitmyre, J. W., 677
Wichern, D. W., 501, 502
Wickelgren, B. G., 281
Wicker, A. W., 397, 670
Wicker, F. W., 531
Wicklund, R. A., 403, 411, 418, 421, 444, 637
Widiger, T. A., 593-95, 681, 691
Wieder, G. B., 685
Wiener-Ehrlich, W. K., 127
Wiener-Levy, D., 680, 681
Wiesel, T. N., 206
Wigdor, A. K., 476, 483, 484
Wiggins, J. S., 232, 671, 690
Wilcox, B. L., 347
Wilcox, J. C., 498
Wilcox, J. N., 180
Wilcox, L. E., 239

Wilcoxon, L. A., 584
Wild, M., 531
Wilder, D. A., 417
Wiley, W., 466
Wilkening, F., 141
Wilkes-Gibbs, D. L., 371
Wilkinson, M., 181
Willette, M. V., 22
Williams, A. M., 187
Williams, B. B., 527
Williams, E. B., 477
Williams, G. D., 187
Williams, J. A., 269
Williams, J. M., 610
Williams, K. D., 414
Williams, R. A., 215
Williams, R. B., 686
Williams, V., 233, 239, 249, 687
Williges, B. H., 527
Williges, R. C., 527
Willis, S. L., 325
Wills, R. M., 685
Wills, T. A., 584
Wilson, A., 346
Wilson, C., 181
Wilson, H. R., 205, 211
Wilson, J. D., 170, 176, 177
Wilson, M. A., 480
Wilson, M. I., 183
Wilson, R. S., 323
Wilson, T., 500
Wilson, T. D., 432
Wimmer, H., 559
Wimsatt, W. C., 595
Windle, W. F., 283, 284
Wing, H., 497
Winger, G., 259
Wingfield, J. C., 191
Winkler, R. L., 143
Winne, P. H., 484
Winnicott, D. W., 158
Winograd, E., 314, 367, 383
Winokur, G., 243
Winokur, M., 584
Winsberg, S., 64, 69, 73, 75
Winslow, W. W., 341
Winters, K. C., 677
Wirt, R. D., 235, 249, 686
Wise, E., 674, 685
Wise, P. M., 182
Wiseman, S., 371
Wish, M., 69
Wishuda, A., 156
Wisler, P. L., 294
Wispe, L., 651
Witherspoon, D., 370, 381
Witkin, H. V., 25
Witkin, M. J., 339
Witzke, D. B., 96
Witzke, F., 294

SUBJECT INDEX

CUMULATIVE INDEXES

CONTRIBUTING AUTHORS, VOLUMES 31–35

CHAPTER TITLES, VOLUMES 31–35